Mexico City Metro

CW00521126

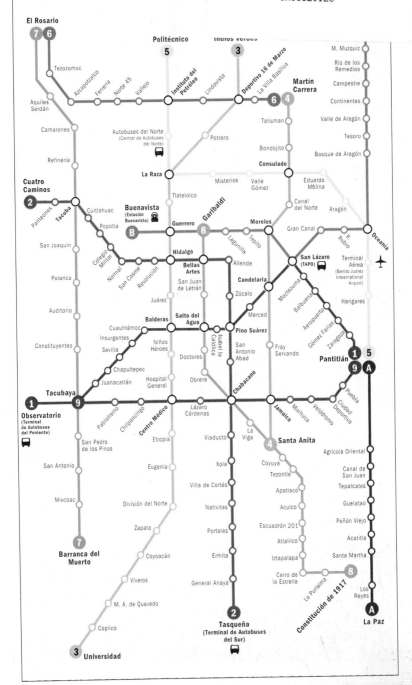

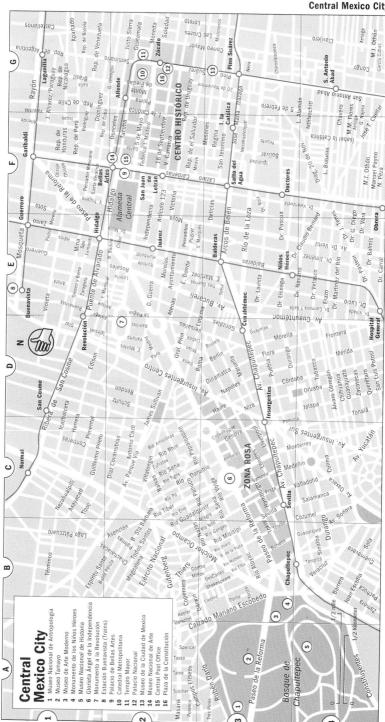

Central Mexico City

Central Mexico City

1 Museo Nacional de Antopología
2 Museo Tamayo
3 Museo de Arte Moderno
4 Monumento de los Niños Héroes
5 Museo Nacional de Historia
6 Glorieta Ángel de la Independencia
7 Monumento a la Revolución
8 Estación Buenavista (Trains)
9 Palacio de Bellas Artes
10 Catedral Metropolitana
11 Templo Mayor
12 Palacio Nacional
14 Museo de la Ciudad de Mexico
15 Museo Nacional de Arte
16 Central Post Office
16 Plaza de la Constitución

CENTRO HISTÓRICO

ZONA ROSA

◪ Let's Go writers travel on your budget.

"Guides that penetrate the veneer of the holiday brochures and mine the grit of real life."
—*The Economist*

"The writers seem to have experienced every rooster-packed bus and lunar-surfaced mattress about which they write."
—*The New York Times*

"All the dirt, dirt cheap."
—*People*

◪ Great for independent travelers.

"The guides are aimed not only at young budget travelers but at the independent traveler; a sort of streetwise cookbook for traveling alone."
—*The New York Times*

"Flush with candor and irreverence, chock full of budget travel advice."
—*The Des Moines Register*

"An indispensible resource, *Let's Go*'s practical information can be used by every traveler."
—*The Chattanooga Free Press*

◪ Let's Go is completely revised each year.

"Only *Let's Go* has the zeal to annually update every title on its list."
—*The Boston Globe*

"Unbeatable: good sightseeing advice; up-to-date info on restaurants, hotels, and inns; a commitment to money-saving travel; and a wry style that brightens nearly every page."
—*The Washington Post*

◪ All the important information you need.

"*Let's Go* authors provide a comedic element while still providing concise information and thorough coverage of the country. Anything you need to know about budget traveling is detailed in this book."
—*The Chicago Sun-Times*

"Value-packed, unbeatable, accurate, and comprehensive."
—*Los Angeles Times*

Let's Go Publications

Let's Go: Alaska & the Pacific Northwest 2000
Let's Go: Australia 2000
Let's Go: Austria & Switzerland 2000
Let's Go: Britain & Ireland 2000
Let's Go: California 2000
Let's Go: Central America 2000
Let's Go: China 2000 **New Title!**
Let's Go: Eastern Europe 2000
Let's Go: Europe 2000
Let's Go: France 2000
Let's Go: Germany 2000
Let's Go: Greece 2000
Let's Go: India & Nepal 2000
Let's Go: Ireland 2000
Let's Go: Israel 2000 **New Title!**
Let's Go: Italy 2000
Let's Go: Mexico 2000
Let's Go: Middle East 2000 **New Title!**
Let's Go: New York City 2000
Let's Go: New Zealand 2000
Let's Go: Paris 2000
Let's Go: Perú & Ecuador 2000 **New Title!**
Let's Go: Rome 2000
Let's Go: South Africa 2000
Let's Go: Southeast Asia 2000
Let's Go: Spain & Portugal 2000
Let's Go: Turkey 2000
Let's Go: USA 2000
Let's Go: Washington, D.C. 2000

Let's Go *Map Guides*

Amsterdam	New Orleans
Berlin	New York City
Boston	Paris
Chicago	Prague
Florence	Rome
London	San Francisco
Los Angeles	Seattle
Madrid	Washington, D.C.

Coming Soon: Sydney and Hong Kong

Let's Go

2000

MEXICO

Arthur Koski-Karell
Editor

Frances Tilney
Associate Editor

Peter Overland
Associate Editor

Researcher-Writers:
Erik Beach
Carla Blackmar
John Connolly
Ruthie Flores
Javier Mixco
Ellen Schneider

Macmillan

HELPING LET'S GO

If you want to share your discoveries, suggestions, or corrections, please drop us a line. We read every piece of correspondence, whether a postcard, a 10-page email, or a coconut. Please note that mail received after May 2000 may be too late for the 2001 book, but will be kept for future editions. **Address mail to:**

> **Let's Go: Mexico**
> **67 Mount Auburn Street**
> **Cambridge, MA 02138**
> **USA**

Visit Let's Go at **http://www.letsgo.com,** or send email to:

> **feedback@letsgo.com**
> **Subject: "Let's Go: Mexico"**

In addition to the invaluable travel advice our readers share with us, many are kind enough to offer their services as researchers or editors. Unfortunately, our charter enables us to employ only currently enrolled Harvard students.

Published in Great Britain 2000 by Macmillan, an imprint of Macmillan Publishers Ltd., 25 Eccleston Place, London, SW1W 9NF, Basingstoke and Oxford
Associated companies throughout the world
www.macmillan.co.uk

Maps by David Lindroth copyright © 2000, 1999, 1998, 1997, 1996, 1995, 1994, 1993, 1992, 1991, 1990, 1989, 1988 by St. Martin's Press

Published in the United States of America by St. Martin's Press

ISBN: 0 333 77982 7

First edition
10 9 8 7 6 5 4 3 2 1

Let's Go: Mexico is written by Let's Go Publications, 67 Mount Auburn Street, Cambridge, MA 02138, USA.

Let's Go® and the thumb logo are trademarks of Let's Go, Inc.
Printed in the USA on recycled paper with biodegradable soy ink.

ABOUT LET'S GO

FORTY YEARS OF WISDOM

As a new millennium arrives, *Let's Go: Europe*, now in its 40th edition and translated into seven languages, reigns as the world's bestselling international travel guide. For four decades, travelers criss-crossing the Continent have relied on *Let's Go* for inside information on the hippest backstreet cafes, the most pristine secluded beaches, and the best routes from border to border. In the last 20 years, our rugged researchers have stretched the frontiers of backpacking and expanded our coverage into Asia, Africa, Australia, and the Americas. We're celebrating our 40th birthday with the release of *Let's Go: China*, blazing the traveler's trail from the Forbidden City to the Tibetan frontier; *Let's Go: Perú & Ecuador*, spanning the lands of the ancient Inca Empire; *Let's Go: Middle East*, with coverage from Istanbul to the Persian Gulf; and the maiden edition of *Let's Go: Israel.*

It all started in 1960 when a handful of well-traveled students at Harvard University handed out a 20-page mimeographed pamphlet offering a collection of their tips on budget travel to passengers on student charter flights to Europe. The following year, in response to the instant popularity of the first volume, students traveling to Europe researched the first full-fledged edition of *Let's Go: Europe*, a pocket-sized book featuring honest, practical advice, witty writing, and a decidedly youthful slant on the world. Throughout the 60s and 70s, our guides reflected the times. In 1969 we taught travelers how to get from Paris to Prague on "no dollars a day" by singing in the street. In the 80s and 90s, we looked beyond Europe and North America and set off to all corners of the earth. Meanwhile, we focused in on the world's most exciting urban areas to produce in-depth, fold-out map guides. Our new guides bring the total number of titles to 48, each infused with the spirit of adventure and voice of opinion that travelers around the world have come to count on. But some things never change: our guides are still researched, written, and produced entirely by students who know first-hand how to see the world on the cheap.

HOW WE DO IT

Each guide is completely revised and thoroughly updated every year by a well-traveled set of over 250 students. Every spring, we recruit over 180 researchers and 70 editors to overhaul every book. After several months of training, researcher-writers hit the road for seven weeks of exploration, from Anchorage to Adelaide, Estonia to El Salvador, Iceland to Indonesia. Hired for their rare combination of budget travel sense, writing ability, stamina, and courage, these adventurous travelers know that train strikes, stolen luggage, food poisoning, and marriage proposals are all part of a day's work. Back at our offices, editors work from spring to fall, massaging copy written on Himalayan bus rides into witty, informative prose. A student staff of typesetters, cartographers, publicists, and managers keeps our lively team together. In September, the collected efforts of the summer are delivered to our printer, which turns them into books in record time, so that you have the most up-to-date information available for your vacation. Even as you read this, work on next year's editions is well underway.

WHY WE DO IT

We don't think of budget travel as the last recourse of the destitute; we believe that it's the only way to travel. Living cheaply and simply brings you closer to the people and places you've been saving up to visit. Our books will ease your anxieties and answer your questions about the basics—so you can get off the beaten track and explore. Once you learn the ropes, we encourage you to put *Let's Go* down now and then to strike out on your own. You know as well as we that the best discoveries are often those you make yourself. When you find something worth sharing, please drop us a line. We're Let's Go Publications, 67 Mount Auburn St., Cambridge, MA 02138, USA (email: feedback@letsgo.com). For more info, visit our website, http://www.letsgo.com.

LET'S GO PICKS

BEST RUINS
Chichén Itzá, especially during the equinox (p. 608); **Las Pozas,** for 20th-century psychedelic madness (p. 297); **Palenque,** for the inscriptions and the dense jungle (p. 559); **Teotihuacán,** for sheer size and stunning views (p. 131); and **Yaxchilán,** where howler monkeys outnumber people (p. 564).

BEST PLACES TO CHILL
Isla Holbox, where all you need is a hammock (p. 627); **La Paz,** to eat ice cream with an ocean view (p. 175); and **Zipolite,** where time passes slowly and people are naked (p. 486).

BEST PLACES TO LIVE THE HIGH LIFE
Puerto Vallarta, where the rich frolic in lusty pleasure (p. 391); and **Mexico City,** where you can mingle with Mexico's beautiful people (p. 78).

BEST BAREFOOT CARMELITE CONVENT
Desierto de los Leones, self-flagellation just an hour out of Mexico City (p. 334).

BEST PLACES TO PARTY
Cabo San Lucas, if you graduated high school and just don't care (p. 184); **Guanajuato,** for its young bar/cafe scene (p. 302); **Cuernavaca,** for ritzy nightlife and salsa (p. 337); **Veracruz,** for outdoor marimba and sweaty dance clubs (p. 508); and **Mexico City,** duh (p. 78).

MOST OVERRATED PLACES TO PARTY
Tijuana (p. 140) and **Cancún** (p. 621).

BEST BEACHES
We can't pick—Mexico's got thousands of kilometers of them. Some offbeat suggestions: **Bahía de Navidad** for picture-perfect coast and no tourists (p. 400); **Zihuatanejo,** close to great nightlife, but still removed and untouched (p. 448); **Bahía de la Concepción,** for a piece of paradise pie on the Sea of Cortés (p. 170); **Isla Mujeres,** for better-than-Cancún beaches and less-than-Cancún hustle (p. 629).

BEST GAY NIGHTLIFE
Mexico City, bigger, brasher, and better than anywhere else in the country (p. 124); **Monterrey,** for its new and thriving scene (p. 266); and **Puerto Vallarta,** for cruises and all-night beach parties (p. 391).

BEST WATERFALLS
Misol-Ha and **Agua Azul,** site of 500 jungle falls (p. 563); and **Cascada de Texolo,** for the dramatic and beautiful setting of many movies (p. 500).

BEST MUSEUMS
Museo Nacional de Anthropología, one of the world's finest museums and Mexico's largest (p. 113); **Museo de Frido Kahlo,** shows the immense talent and conflict of the daughter of Mexico (p. 118); and Xalapa's **Museo de Anthropología,** has a multi-tiered insight into the oldest Mesoamerican civilization (p. 498).

BEST PLACES TO SLEEP
Margarita's Casa de Huéspedes, truly *the* mecca of backpackers in the middle of the Copper Canyons (p. 230); **Na-Bolom,** in San Cristóbal de las Casas is a living monument to the Lacandón Maya (p. 546); and on any hammock under a **palapa** on the beach of Puerto Escondido (p. 488)..

HOW TO USE THIS BOOK

Budget travel does not necessarily imply sleeping in hovels and living solely on soggy tacos. Yes, *Let's Go: Mexico 2000* is a budget guide, but it is not a ghetto guide. Our six diligent researchers hauled themselves all over Mexico during the summer of 1999 with one goal: to find the cheapest and the best. Night after night, our writers scoured the cities and towns of Mexico searching for enticing cuisine, bouncy beds, mysterious cafes, swinging nightclubs, and the best way to conserve those precious pesos. For travelers less-than-proficient in Spanish, fear not: sights are explained thoroughly; an **orientation** begins every section, and the **Glossary** and **Phrasebook** in the **Appendix** contain the most essential aids in travel-talk.

If you're unsure of the nuances of skulking past border officials, packing for a trek down the coast, or surviving alone as a single woman, the **Essentials** chapter at the beginning of the book includes every bit of instruction needed to live Mexico to the fullest. If you don't mind tackling the mini-thesis in the beginning of the book describing centuries of history from Mesoamerican to modern-day, you will be fully prepared to launch yourself into this land of sparkling sand, towering ruins, crumbling churches, and, most of all, overwhelming freedom.

Let's Go is not shy. Every area has a candid **introduction** followed by listings of **accommodations, food, sights,** and **entertainment.** We have an opinion about your destination and arrange the sleeping, eating, and dancing in the order of must-see to skip-it-if-you-must. If a club or hostel is absolutely unbeatable, a perky little thumb will be thrust to the left of the 🔲 listing. Each section is rife with **practical information** explaining everything from the hangout of the police in the plaza to the latest cybercafe offering Internet datesites.

To further inflict our opinion, each chapter has **highlights of the region,** a box full of hints toward getting the best deals and seeing the greatest locations. Superlatives continue to abound throughout Mexico, but for a dose of some serious "best of" convictions, look no further than the **Let's Go Picks** at the beginning of the book. Our researchers compiled their personal favorites into a mega-list of attractions ranging from best museum and biggest waves, to best ruin and most romantic makeout spot.

However, even though *Let's Go: Mexico* is filled to the brim with suggestions and opinions, don't be afraid to put the book down or use it to swat at mosquitoes. The only way we found some of these superb budget locales was by leaving the pavement and following the cow path. Once on the road less traveled, *Let's Go* might not be so much of a necessity. Mexico is a place to discover without the constant harangue of a guidebook; eccentricities lurk around every corner.

But if all you see around the corner is another taco stand, don't worry. We have scattered the bizarre, the macabre, the intriguing, and the delightful throughout the pages of this venerable tome. Grossly overweight monkeys, cheese-making Mennonites, Trotsky's bullet-ridden apartment, fried grasshoppers covered in chocolate and chile, musical stalactites, and flesh-eating cosmic tigers await. But don't just rediscover our idiosyncrasies—find your own and follow the mantra of Yogi Berra: "When you come to a fork in the road, take it."

CONTENTS

MAPS

COLOR INSERTS

RESEARCHER-WRITERS

Erik Beach *Northwest and Central Mexico*

Talk about mellow. Fearing the worst after a week of silence, Erik finally called the U.S. from a lone LADATEL in the midst of the Copper Canyons. "I'm fine," he said. "That train just takes a long time." Constantly upbeat and always relaxed, Erik vigorously plowed some of the roughest terrain in Mexico and sent back fabulously witty copy to boot. Always running into new experiences, and somewhat oblivious to the armies of spiders lurking around the next budget corner, Erik transformed a once-barren region into a haven of bizarre allusions and rants about the evils of TV. His retro-hippie attitude was much appreciated, but above all, his iconoclastic prose took the cake.

Carla Blackmar *Central and Southern Pacific, Central Mexico, Veracruz, Chiapas*

With her red, curly hair and zealous determination, Carla obviously stuck out in Mexico. She stuck out in our minds because of her unfailing courage and unbelievable copy. Occasionally we cursed her: every single region was metamorphized by her immaculate hand over pages and pages complete with Willie Wonka references and allusions to *A Room With a View* and *Apocalypse Now*. She maintained her composure through a Puebla earthquake, an unfortunate fall down a hole, and, much to our astonishment, an interview with the *Associated Press*. Throughout it all, she managed to transform the Southern Pacific Coast into the next great American novel.

John Connolly *Baja California, Northwest Mexico*

John never lost touch. Whether it was with the grim reality of a cheap, pseudo-Nissan *sans* steering wheel or the equally stark lives of his editors thousands of miles away, John kept a bemused SoCal smile through it all. His matter-of-fact copy never failed to amuse; from his accounts of the "Crazies" of Los Cabos, Coco, the one-legged man and Orr, the hairy Deadhead dying to trade journal accounts to reach a deeper truth, John maintained a dry wit that certainly reduced his editors to tears (of mirth). Winner of the Most Naked Postcards award, John exemplified the quirky, laid-back nature of the region he traveled in.

Ruthie Flores *Yucatán and Chiapas*

Having to bear the wistful ramblings of her editor, Ruthie set out and made this fascinating route her own. Throughout the Yucatán and Chiapas, Ruthie eagerly delved into archaic and contemporary cultural nuances of this particularly complicated and colorful region. From the sand-swept streets of Progreso to the swirling masses of Tapachula, she meticulously related the anecdotes of multitudinous townspeople. Her copy was positively euphoric and she was always proud of the people and places she encountered.

Javier Mixco *Northeast Mexico and Mexico City*

Getting calls from Javier was always a treat, as his super-*tranquilo* demeanor was an instant stress-reliever for the office staff. His clear, concise copy made the work pass more easily as well. While he faced the highlights and hazards of the border and Mexico City with equal aplomb, Javier really found his element in and about the quiet deserts. His trip can be neatly summed up by his experience in Real de Catorce. With feet planted in stirrups and brim askew, Javier took the reins of his mount and set off at an easy gait toward the sunset and *Let's Go* Northeast Mexico history.

Ellen Schneider *Central Pacific Coast and Central Mexico*

Ellen had an uncanny knack for sweet-talking bouncers, waiters, and bartenders and Mexico was eager to show her a party-'til-dawn mentality. She blew through every nightclub with the spirit of no other and enthusiastically sent back glossy photos of beachside resorts (meanwhile lamenting that most budget hotels did not come with the Olympic-size pool). Luckily enough, her tan blossomed during her beach route and despite an initial "bubbly feeling" from the *comida corrida*, Ellen persevered. Without her, Puerto Vallarta would never be the same.

ACKNOWLEDGMENTS

These books don't just put themselves together, you know. They are assembled by machine.

WE THANK: Professor and Mrs. Vogt for their infinite wisdom; Kaya for his insanely brilliant editing; Christian because he's our favorite; TP, the Salsa Pod and the music police; Peter and Lisa for laughing at us and counselling us; Elena for doing everything; Shay's; and Marvin Gaye, Al Green, Stan Getz, Wide Awake in America, and Barry White. Oh yeah.

ART: This book goes out to my AEs, who despite my efforts produced the finest guide to Mexico, bar none. Also the guys at Frost St. and the boys back home—Al and Aaron, Fats, Dr. Dulle and DirkyV. AEG—I've wanted to put those initials in a book for a while. Freddy for the graybox; Lisa, Peter R. and Meeks for the support group. *La familia:* Stonewall Danny, Willie, Ana Karina, Natalie, Vicki—you're all nuts, and Mom and Dad, cause you still love me. Thanks, security guard with key to observatory. Y por supuesto, Frances, para todo.

FRANCES: Arturo, para todo: caminando para café, los huevos y los frijoles, los gritos, y México. Mostraremos a Stonewall-Danny la vida aquí. Peter and Lisa, I wish I was always going to be across the hall from SEAS. Coops and Kerry—I just want to write your names down. M & P: I know you worried, but thanks for trusting me to get it done. Oink: not your wish to be immortalized in another book, but you were sweetly swine-ish when I was a smelly hen. C.T.A.L. for putting up with it all, and especially, with me.

PETER: My gratitude goes to all my zany chaps and chapettes at the Pudding and H.G.C., thanks for the laughs. To my fellow editors Art, Frances, Rolan, and Taylor; thanks for all the good times. To Peter, Beth, and Lisa; my good-natured office mates. To Harvard Memorial Church; my source of illumination. To Annie, Alex, Matt, and Adds; for their advice and friendship during the summer. Finally, to Mom, Dad, Brian, and Caitlin; my love for you transcends all things.

Editor
Arthur Koski-Karell
Associate Editors
Frances Tilney & Peter A. Overland
Managing Editor
Kaya Stone

Publishing Director
Benjamin Wilkinson
Editor-in-Chief
Bentsion Harder
Production Manager
Christian Lorentzen
Cartography Manager
Daniel J. Luskin
Design Managers
Matthew Daniels, Melissa Rudolph
Editorial Managers
Brendan Gibbon, Benjamin Paloff,
Kaya Stone, Taya Weiss
Financial Manager
Kathy Lu
Personnel Manager
Adam Stein
Publicity & Marketing Managers
Sonesh Chainani,
Alexandra Leichtman
New Media Manager
Maryanthe Malliaris
Map Editors
Kurt Mueller, Jon Stein
Production Associates
Steven Aponte, John Fiore
Office Coordinators
Elena Schneider, Vanessa Bertozzi,
Monica Henderson

Director of Advertising Sales
Marta Szabo
Associate Sales Executives
Tamas Eisenberger, Li Ran

President
Noble M. Hansen III
General Managers
Blair Brown, Robert B. Rombauer
Assistant General Manager
Anne E. Chisholm

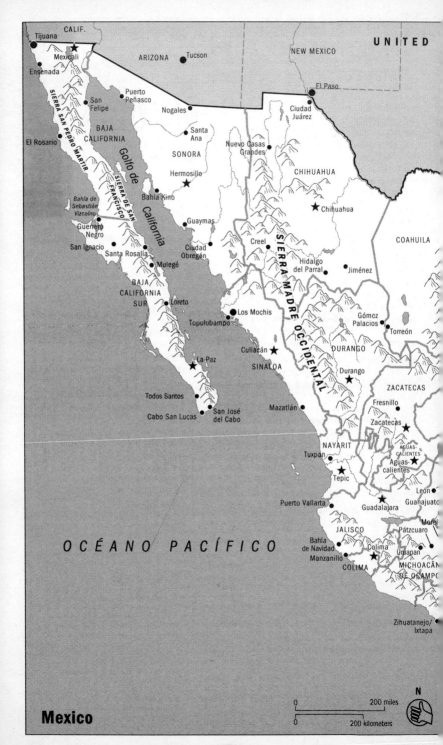

Mexico

XIV

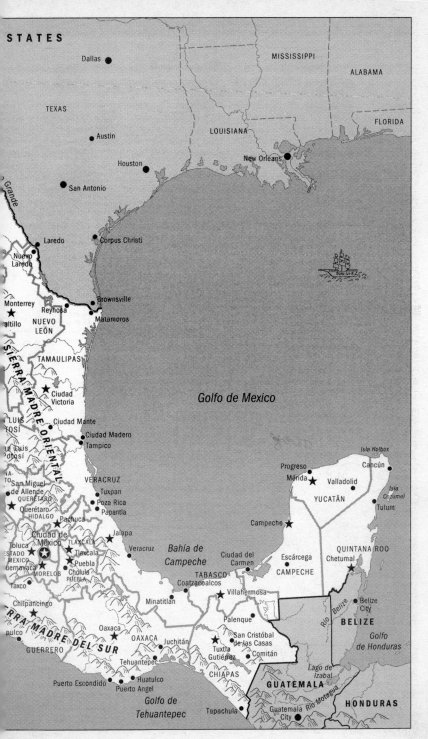

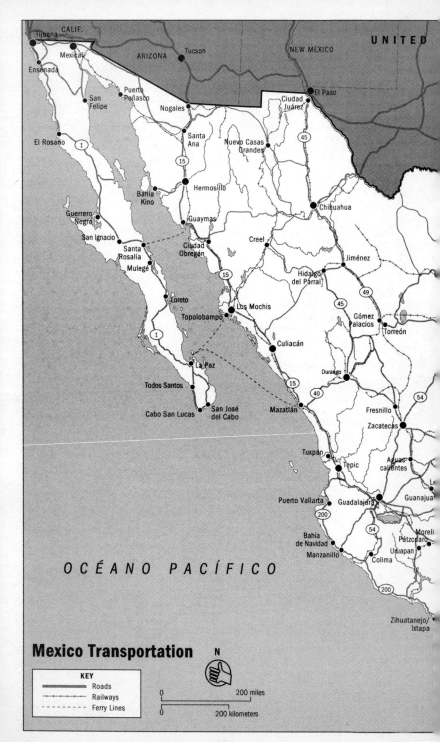

Mexico Transportation

KEY
- Roads
- Railways
- Ferry Lines

0 ——— 200 miles

0 ——— 200 kilometers

N

OCÉANO PACÍFICO

UNITED

CALIF.
ARIZONA
NEW MEXICO

Tijuana
Mexicali
Ensenada
San Felipe
El Rosario
Tucson
Puerto Peñasco
Nogales
Santa Ana
Nuevo Casas Grandes
Ciudad Juárez
El Paso
Bahía Kino
Hermosillo
Chihuahua
Guaymas
Creel
Guerrero Negro
San Ignacio
Santa Rosalía
Ciudad Obregón
Jiménez
Mulegé
Hidalgo del Parral
Loreto
Topolobampo
Los Mochis
Gómez Palacios
Torreón
Culiacán
La Paz
Durango
Todos Santos
Fresnillo
Cabo San Lucas
San José del Cabo
Mazatlán
Zacatecas
Tuxpan
Tepic
Aguas calientes
Puerto Vallarta
Guadalajara
Guanajua
Bahía de Navidad
Manzanillo
Colima
Moreli
Pátzcuaro
Uruapan
Zihuatanejo/ Ixtapa

45
15
49
45
40
54
200
54
200
1

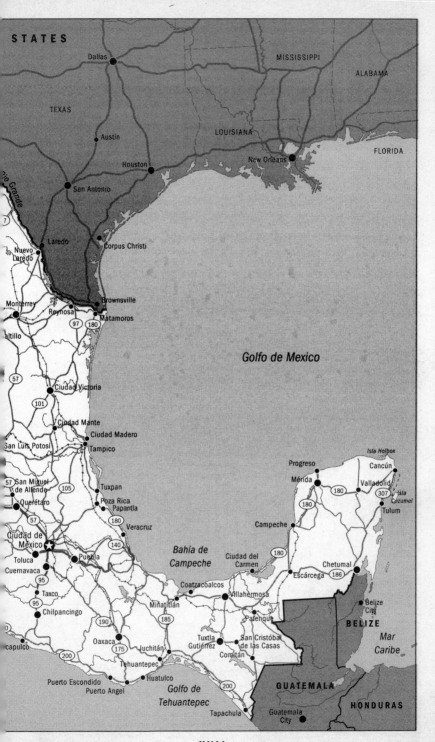

DISCOVER
MEXICO

"Then we'll ride these bikes to Mexico—and freedom, Willie, freedom!"
—Principal Skinner, *Los Simpsons*

While it doesn't take a genius to figure out that Mexico is the best country in the world, it sometimes seems that would-be travelers need reminding. Why else would it be referred to as the ultimate escape—the final destination by so many in song, stage, and screen? Who can forget such illustrious figures as The Grateful Dead, The Beatles, Sean Connery, and Bill Weld longing for the days when they too could roam glinting Pacific beaches, climb cobblestone streets in highland towns, and explore twisting desert canyons. Where, other than Mexico, could they ever hope to find unfrequented amber-based societies, ride rented horses through peyote bush, chauffeur inebriated forest-dwellers over narrow gorges, and befriend enigmatic mechanic Vikings? The sights are often sought after; the experiences are more often accidental. In the end, the freedom granted by a place where the sun will soothe, the food will fill, and the *salsa* will sway, is what satisfies those drawn by countless other reasons to discover Mexico.

FACTS AND FIGURES

- **Capital:** Mexico City
- **Population:** 98,552,776
- **Pop. Growth Rate:** 1.77% per year
- **Religion:** Roman Catholic (89%)
- **Leading Industry:** Food and Beverage
- **GDP per capita:** US$7,700
- **Major Exports:** Oil, Coffee, Silver
- **Independence Day:** Sept. 16, 1810
- **Ethnic Groups:** Mestizo 60%, American Indian 30%, Caucasian 6%

THINGS TO DO

Mexico has no end of attractions. From climbing age-old Maya temples or haggling for silver trinkets in colonial open-air markets, to diving through coral reefs or grooving to *merengue* with margarita in hand, each region has its own cultural allure and culinary appeal. A brief list of popular activities and places follows below. At the beginning of each chapter, there is also a specific **Highlights of the Region** section to help choose the best possible routes and destinations.

SAND AND SURF

Whether you want crashing rollers or lapping waves; miles of soft, empty sand or hordes of beach towels; fiery sunrises or glowing sunsets; Mexico offers every desired beach experience. Many head to the crowded beaches of **Cancún** (p. 621) to soon discover that the less-traveled areas of **Isla Holbox** (p. 627) and **Isla Mujeres** (p. 629) fulfill all sun-cravings without fast-food scenery. **Cabo San Lucas** (p. 184) will sustain the lust for hedonism on its monied coast, but the best surfing in the world can also be found off nearby, deserted shores. For the intrepid adventurers, snorkeling, fishing, diving, and kayaking are readily available along **Baja**, the **southern Pacific coast, Veracruz**, and the eastern **Yucatán**. Those searching for solitude and beauty often migrate to beaches such as **Zihuatanejo** (p. 448) and **Todos Santos** (p. 180); but, if a trip to Mexico is just an excuse to party, stick to the areas where prices are expressed in dollars and all beachside discos are packed by scantily-clad foreigners roused by 2-for-1 Coronas.

MESOAMERICAN METROPOLISES

In unsubtle Conquest symbolism, the Spanish built many Mexican cities on top of Mesoamerican ceremonial centers. Today, it is impossible to miss the Aztec, Maya, Toltec, Olmec, Zapotec, and Mixtec ruins that are scattered throughout the cities and the countryside. Right outside of Mexico City, the holy pyramids of **Teotihuacán** (p. 131) are an awe-inspiring example of the power of pre-Conquest indigenous civilization. In the same central valley of Mexico stands fortified **Tula** (p. 327) while to the south sits multi-layered **Monte Albán** (p. 472). Over the eastern mountains lie some of the most ancient of all Mesoamerican cities, those of the Olmec. Across the Gulf in the Yucatán, **La Ruta Puuc** (p. 587) meanders over kilometer after kilometer of palaces and temples and ballcourts of the Maya—their giant, stone constructions still maintain the carvings and inscriptions of past millennia. If brave enough to fight through the gangs of marauding tourists, soaring **Uxmal** (p. 592) and overwhelming **Chichén Itzá** (p. 608) demonstrate the deep astral knowledge of the Maya along with a wide variety of sculpture and architectural styles. **Tulum** (p. 640), one of the most beautiful sites in all of Mexico, includes a vista of glowing waves and pristine beaches at the foot of a once-grand port called the "City of the Dawn"—just check out the cover of this book.

THE URBAN PULSE

Perhaps the most noticeable of Mexico's attractions is its throbbing city life. Streetside cafes abound in **Oaxaca** (p. 461) and **Cuernavaca** (p. 337) saturating the city with conversation, debate, and the scent of freshly roasting beans. Meanwhile, the sprawling, thriving metropolis of **Mexico City** (p. 78) harbors the most invigorating, iconoclastic nightlife around. Entertainment varies from concerts and *mariachi* performances in the parks, to pulsating bass, flowing tequila, and flashing lights of the world's most renowned *discotecas*. In the beachside cities of **Acapulco** (p. 454), **Cancún,** and **Cabo San Lucas,** the discos stay packed with sunbathers searching to dull the pain of their sunburn with Bacchan revelry. Almost all of the cities in Mexico have myriad museums spilling over with intriguing artifacts, modern art and indigenous representations. **Guanajuato** (p. 302) displays the country's spookiest museum replete with mummified animals, children, and various other characters enshrouded in preserved garments. **Guadalajara** (p. 374), the figurative capital of colonial Mexico, still upholds its legacy through dance and architecture. Urban life in Mexico is not simply contemporary living; it is the manifestation of pre-Hispanic tradition blending with imposed Spanish colonial heritage. The results are as varied as the hedonism of *discotecas* and the intricacy of *ballet folklórico*.

COCA-COLONIZATION...

Unfortunately, U.S. commercialization has sunk its claws into certain areas of Mexico, transforming them into capitals of consumer culture. Some engineered cities-cum-resorts are now defined by golden arches and enclosed by pleasure domes, catering to the rich in utmost style. Luckily, Nike and Coca-Cola have not influenced all of Mexico and most places still retain home-grown cultural ideals. If uninterested in how money can be spent to construct towering hotels along once-pristine shores, steer clear of tourist traps teeming with shopkeepers and taxi-drivers waiting to gouge a profit. The neon necklaces adorning the beaches of **Acapulco,** the avenues of bars in **Tijuana** (p. 140), and the exorbitant prices in **Ixtapa** (p. 448), are to be avoided if you don't want to buy your *enchilada* in dollars rather than pesos. However, many of these venues of over-consumption were chosen by venture capitalists for apt reasons: natural beauty needs no gilded lens. If you can manage to avoid the drunken American teens complaining about a lack of Bud Light, some of these locations should be visited before they are invaded by yet another multinational corporation.

...AND HOW TO AVOID IT

Escaping the excessive displays of wealth is easy. Regardless of the exchange rate, Mexico is rich in natural beauty and constant celebration of culture. The **Copper Canyons** (p. 232) of north-central Mexico is an obvious example of unofficiated, verdant wilderness. The soaring cliffs, narrow trails, and green mountains of this area are saturated by quiet towns, winding rivers, and cascading waterfalls. Granted, this is a choice destination of many foreign backpackers, but the thrill of the canyons is quite a private affair. Elsewhere in the Republic, nature abounds right beyond the towering hotels and neon lights of the cities. In **Baja** and the **Yucatán,** many of the most aesthetically pleasing spots are just down the beach or up the road from the touristy towns and raging clubs—the extra effort is well worth it.

ARTESANÍA

Artistry is one of the most striking legacies and tangible forces in Mexican culture. *Indígena* crafts and textiles, the silver and amber trades of various *pueblos*, and the murals and paintings of politically oriented artists, are all visual representations of life in Mexico. Museums in **Mexico City, Guadalajara,** and **Guanajuato,** display the stunning work of muralists and artists such as **Diego Rivera, Frida Kahlo,** and **José Clemente Orozco.** Kahlo, in her emotionally charged paintings, perhaps best expresses some of the contradictions of Mexican life. Much of her art displays the pull between incoming foreign influence and her *mestizo* heritage. Political thought and artistic expression are combined in most of the mural work found throughout Mexico; these immense works of art show the struggle for independence and the glory of the revolution. *Indígena* artistry is still a strong force in Mexico, where, in many towns, clothing and jewelry reflect ancient design and tradition. In **Semojovel** (p. 540), people toting baskets of amber swaddled in toilet paper, will carefully display shiny bits of the primeval sap carved into beautiful ovals or spheres. **Zacatecas** (p. 273), home of the largest silver mine in Mexico, creates superb jewelry reflecting centuries of craft and design. Even in Baja, the town of **Todos Santos** is home to a colony of artists hoping to recreate the surrounding sea and sunsets.

SUGGESTED ITINERARIES

NORTHWEST MEXICO (2 WEEKS) To begin with cheap, sprawling, unapologetic debauchery, head to **Tijuana.** Recover on the isolated beaches of **Ensenada,** the perfect preparation for the starscapes of hospitable **San Ignacio.** Back on the coast, starfish await under the crystal waters of **Bahía de la Concepción.** The pace of life picks up again in the **Los Cabos** region; whether it's surfing with the beach campers of **Todos Santos,** partying in the laser-lit pleasure palaces of the prodigal **Cabo San Lucas,** or snorkeling off **Cabo San José's** stretches of sand. **La Paz** has perhaps the best of both worlds. Peaceful palms are not swayed by raucous parties in this shimmering oasis of a port. Across the Sea of Cortés, the plunging cliffs and cactus-studded trails of the **Copper Canyons** beckon those in search of more adventure. Heading north, if you manage to leave the mango-scented valleys behind, **Nuevo Casas Grandes** harbors the Mixtec ruins of Paquimé near its lush parks and open markets.

CENTRAL MEXICO (2 WEEKS) The biggest city in the world is home to much more than just smog; glamorous discos, magnificent museums, and historic parks

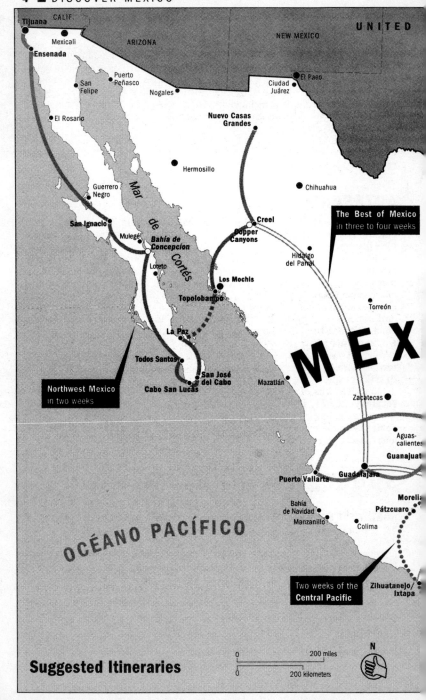

Suggested Itineraries

STATES

MISSISSIPPI

ALABAMA

TEXAS

LOUISIANA

FLORIDA

Houston

New Orleans

San Antonio

Grande

Laredo

Nuevo
Laredo

Brownsville

Monterrey

Matamoros

GOLFO DE MÉXICO

CO

Ciudad Victoria

Central Mexico
in two weeks

Isla
Mujeres

n Luis Potosí

Tampico

Mérida

Cancún

Playa del
Carmen

Tuxpan

Chichén
Itzá

Valladolid

Isla
Cozumel

Papantla

Tulum

Teotihuacan

Veracruz

Campeche

Ciudad de
México

Bahía de
Campeche

Puebla

Chetumal

uernavaca

Cholula

Escárcega

Coatzacoalcos

Taxco

Belize
City

Chiapa de
Corzo

Palenque

BELIZE

pulco

Oaxaca

Juchitán

Tuxtla
Gutiérrez

San Cristóbal
de las Casas

Mar
Caribe

Puerto Escondido

Huatulco

Puerto Ángel

GUATEMALA

HONDURAS

**Three weeks in the
Yucatan and Chiapas**

Tapachula

Guatemala
City

abound in **Mexico City.** The gigantic Temples of the Sun and Moon tower over the nearby Mesoamerican megalopolis of **Teotihuacán,** while to the east, colonial ramparts guard the steamy port of **Veracruz.** Sounds of *marimba* mingle with the scent of grilled snapper and waft up the foothills of the Sierra Madre Oriental to the steep streets of **Paplanta.** The ruins of El Tajín lie a short ride away, while the city itself is home to acrobatic *voladores.* A longer ride takes travelers to silver splendor **San Luís Potosí,** where young and old frolic by lantern-lit cathedrals. Farther west spreads the Pacific and the panoramic beaches of **Puerto Vallarta,** an aphrodesiac for many a torrid love affair. Back inland rises **Guadalajara,** a bastion of folk culture as well as Mexico's second largest city. Next-door is **Tequila,** housing the distilleries of everyone's favorite shot. Down the road is **Guanajuato,** the cradle of the Revolution, now rocking with coffeehouse counterculture and cobbled alleys meant for constant kissing.

CENTRAL PACIFIC (2 WEEKS) Cosmopolitan **Cuernavaca** jumps with hip, artistic culture, while farther south, traditional cafes compete for streetside space with indigenous textiles in **Oaxaca.** Continuing south to the lush coast is a necklace of sapphire beaches including **Huataluco,** bohemian **Puerto Angel,** and *sans*-clothing **Zipolite.** Backpackers congregate under **Puerto Escondido's** *palapas,* while up the beach-studded coast rests **Zihuatanejo,** where the *tranquilo* atmosphere and unspoiled sands are accented by its sophisticated twin, **Ixtapa.** Heading north into the mountains are waves of a different kind, lapping along the misty, lakeside streets of **Pátzcuaro.** Finally, the colonial treasures of highland Michoacán are capped by the rose-colored arcades and cathedrals of **Moreliá.**

YUCATÁN AND CHIAPAS (2-3 WEEKS) The novelty of alcohol-drenched nightlife and crowded sands in **Cancún** dwindles as fast as your pesos; fortunately, the entrancing beaches and pastel clapboards of **Isla Mujeres** are a short ferry ride away. Back on the peninsula, don't skip the colonial spires and cavernous *cenotes* of **Valladolid** on your way to the monumental ruins of Postclassic **Chichén Itzá.** Classy hammocks and *guayaberas* are hawked in the loud markets of French-influenced **Mérida,** while the quieter streets of colonial **Campeche** criss-cross plazas behind pirate-hardened fortress walls. Setting off south into the Chiapan jungle, travelers come upon the soaring temples of **Palenque.** Up in the mountains lies the colonial city of **San Cristóbal de las Casas,** a favorite destination of backpackers for its physical, tile-roofed beauty and indigenous, syncretic culture. To the west sprawls **Tuxtla Gutierréz,** home to the best zoo in Latin America, and near the green walls of the Sumidero Canyon. Back through the Yucatán, **Chetumal** is worth a visit for its world-class Maya museum, while the stark beauty of **Tulum's** temples towering over the Caribbean can be enjoyed from the sea itself. Toast the trip fittingly with a beer on lively **Playa del Carmen.**

THE BEST OF MEXICO (3-4 WEEKS) Landing in Cancún, get your groove on in some of the world's wildest **discos** before heading to **tranquil** Isla Mujeres and simple, beach-loving life. Stop by Chichén Itzá and its **astronomically precise** pyramids and sacrificial *cenote* on the way into otherworldly Chiapas and its cultural capital, San Cristóbal de las Casas. Any stay in the city's **Na Bolom** would be too short, but the aromas of Oaxaca's **cafes** and sights of indigenous **crafts** beckon as well. On the Pacific, Zihuatanejo has one of Mexico's **finest beaches** while neighbor Ixtapa hosts some of its craziest parties. Student-laden Cuernavaca fills with scholarly discussion in its outdoor restaurants by day and energetic **club-hopping** by night. Adjectives fail Mexico City's size as well as the **near-infinite** list of things to see and do. Gaudalajara runs a distant second in those respects, but the home of *mariachis* and **tequila** is still an essential stop for Mexican culture. With all these sights and more to contemplate, it may be a good idea to lose yourself in the **time-worn cliffs** of the expansive Copper Canyons before heading home.

MEXICO

A BRIEF HISTORY

PRE-HISPANIC SOCIETIES

THE BEGINNING. The Olmecs of the Gulf Coast Lowlands are known to be the first large-scale society that developed in Mesoamerica. Although they are no longer thought of as the "mother culture" of the region, they exerted an influence on the culture of later civilizations. The Olmecs inhabited the cities now known as La Venta (see p. 531), San Lorenzo, and Tres Zapotes (see p. 524), spanning the period from 2200 BC to AD 400. However, their existence was not recognized as a distinct civilization until the early 1940s, when an archaeologist stumbled upon an immense basalt head standing several meters tall in the jungles of southern Mexico. In the following years, several more colossal heads were found, all with thick eyelids, big lips, broad noses, and helmet-like head covers. Each depicted a unique individual, and were, in fact, portraits of royal figures; these monumental carvings are indicative of socially stratified communities as well as a highly developed artistic culture.

A symbol of great importance in Olmec cosmology was the **were-jaguar**. These sculpted figures combining the human and jaguar forms reflect the Olmec belief that their lineage originated by the mating between animal and man. Among the most notable Olmec developments was a system of glyphic writing and the invention of the Mesoamerican dating system known as the **Long Count.** The Olmec civilization lasted for over a millennium and eventually came to an end as the result of either internal revolt or invasion from outside. Although the Olmecs perished, many of their cultural achievements were passed on to other Mesoamerican peoples such as the Maya.

THE MAYA DOMINION. The genius of the **Maya** can be seen in the remains of their ancient cities—most notably **Palenque** (see p. 559), **Chichén Itzá** (see p. 608), **Uxmal** (see p. 592), and **Tulum** (see p. 640)—scattered throughout the Yucatán Peninsula and modern-day Chiapas. These cities and smaller sites reflect the high level of cultural and political achievement of the Maya while demonstrating the lack of centralized power. Although no empire ever succeeded in controlling entire Maya settlements, larger sites were connected by upraised roads known as *sacbeob* as well as by trade networks that resulted in continuous contact between polities.

Maya habitation in Mexico and Central America began during the period known as the **Preclassic** (2000 BC to AD 250). By the time of the **Classic Period** (300-900) in Mexico, the Maya had become proficient in engineering, mathematics, art, architecture, calendrical calculations, and astronomy. They also devised a method to predict the movement of celestial bodies with total precision. One of the hallmarks of the Classic Period was the inscription of dates on numerous stone surfaces in one of the two Maya calendars.

Around 900, changes began to take place in the Maya area which led to a transition into what is now called the **Postclassic** (900-1500). This period saw the end of inscribed dates and writing, and it witnessed the dissolution of a substantial number of Maya polities. While this change was referred to as the "Maya Collapse," it is now thought of as the end of a certain type of Maya culture rather than the end of Maya civilization. As 9th century Maya settlements dispersed into modern-day Chiapas, Guatemala, Belize and Honduras, a new style of architectural design, known as the **Puuc** style, emerged at sites such as **Uxmal** in Northern Yucatán and lasted until around 1000. Here, **Chichén Itzá** was the reigning state until falling in 1221. Chichén was followed by the historical site of **Mayapan**, which was abandoned just half a century before the Spanish arrived.

MEXICO

THE DEVELOPMENT OF CENTRAL MEXICO. While Southern Mexico and the Yucatán were dominated by Maya culture, **Central Mexico** harbored other developing societies. One of the grandest examples of civilization in this region is the ruined city of **Teotihuacán** (see p. 131). Built atop a cave, a sacred spot in Mesoamerican cosmology, this pyramid's location was believed by the later Aztec to be the site where the gods met to create the fifth sun. They believed that each cyclical era was recreated with the rebirth of the sun.

The city was abandoned in the 8th century and evidence of fire in the site's core raises the question of whether it was burned by outside conquerors or by restless inhabitants hoping to overthrow the power structure. Images of deities such as **Tlaloc,** the god of rain and lightning, and the feathered serpent are ubiquitous and they appear repeatedly at sites constructed by later peoples. Additionally, the site itself was reused later by the **Toltecs,** who conducted ceremonies in its sacred ruins and buried their leaders in the surroundings.

The Toltecs had established their presence in central Mexico by about 800. They settled cities such as **Xochicalco, Cholula,** and **Tula** during the Postclassic Period. The names of leaders and deities are known both archaeologically and historically, (in the form of legends) and are often confused, since leaders commonly took on the names of deities. The most famous of the Toltec leaders is **Ce Acatl Topiltzin** (renamed **Topiltzin Quetzalcóatl**) who regained the seat of authority in Tula after much infighting. Finding himself immediately confronted by opposition forces led by **Huemac** (renamed **Tezcatlipoca**), he left Tula with a promise to return one day. The legend lived on into the time of the Aztecs, whose emperor at the time of Spanish invasion is said to have believed that Cortés was the returning Quetzalcóatl. Toltec influence can be seen at sites in Yucatán state, most notably **Chichén Itzá,** where Puuc architecture is mixed with a distinctly Toltec style.

By the mid 12th century, Toltec civilization faded from prominence, and the **Aztecs** became the dominant peoples in Central Mexico. Legend has it that the Aztecs, including the Mexica (later called "Mexicans"), arrived at **Lake Texcoco,** an unappealing swamp that remained unclaimed by other groups. They were forewarned by their patron deity, **Huitzilopochtli,** that they would see an eagle perched upon a cactus with a serpent in its talons; when they did, they were to settle in that very spot. Having seen this vision by the side of Lake Texcoco, they succeeded in building a city there called **Tenochtitlán** —a city so prominent that modern-day Mexico City was built atop itsruins. The legend was also so enduring that the eagle and serpent now appear as a symbol of the nation of Mexico, placed centrally on its flag.

The Aztecs practiced a religion derived from their Toltec predecessors; they worshipped a supreme being, the aggregate force of numerous deities. **Quetzalcóatl,** the feathered serpent and god of wisdom, remained a crucial element of religious iconography. The Aztec religion also included a legend of the sun-related warrior-deity **Huitzilopochtli.** His mother, **Coatlicue,** was said to have been a chaste woman; one day, however, she found a ball of feathers which she placed in her pocket which proceeded to impregnate her. Coatlicue already had some 400 sons and a daughter, all of whom were enraged at their mother's pregnancy. They began plotting to kill her to prevent her from giving birth, but while they planned this, Huitzilopochtli spoke to his mother from the womb and promised to protect her once he was born. Soon she gave birth to him, fully armed. Immediately after birth, he saved his mother from the jealous half-siblings by cutting them all into small pieces. Aztec imperialism and violent ascendancy over all other Mesoamerican tribes was justified by the story of Huitzilopochtli, who is memorialized at the principal Aztec temple, **Templo Mayor. Coyolxauhqui,** a half-sister, is depicted with dismembered body parts at the base of the temple.

The Aztec civilization was bloody and hierarchical. Aztec priests practiced human sacrifice on a large scale and rival warriors were regularly dismembered and thrown down the Templo Mayor stairs to honor Huitzilopochtli. Also, in the Aztec view of creation, the fifth sun historical cycle in which they lived was begun by an act of large-scale sacrifice; the gods **Tecuciztecotl** and **Nanahuitzin** sacrificed themselves to become the moon and sun, and the other gods were sacrificed by

Quetzalcóatl in order to set the sun moving through the sky. The Aztec believed they had to replicate the behavior of their creators, and thus they supplied human hearts and blood to the gods in symbolic efforts to keep the sun in its path.

The Aztecs built Mexico's largest pre-Hispanic empire of about five million people. Aztec hegemony consisted of indirect rule over towns that were required to recognize Aztec sovereignty and contribute goods, land, and sacrificial victims to the Aztec rulership. Within the capital city, the Aztecs exerted dominance over their natural environment. *Chinampas* (floating gardens) enabled the Aztecs to cultivate the swamp efficiently, extracting seven rounds of crops per year from each garden. Additionally, the beauty and architectural sophistication of the island city Tenochtitlán, connected to the mainland by a network of canals and causeways, led Western historians to dub it the Venice of the New World. By the 16th century, the city and the empore were thriving and the Aztecs were at the peak of the hierarchy of power in Central Mexico.

CONQUEST AND COLONIZATION

THE ARRIVAL OF CORTÉS. With the arrival of the Europeans in the 16th century, the growth of the Aztec empire came to an abrupt end. After Christopher Columbus inadvertently discovered the islands of the Caribbean in 1492, a wave of explorers flocked to Mesoamerica and began to explore and exploit the new territories. In the early decades of the 1500s, the governor of Cuba, **Diego Velázquez,** launched numerous expeditions to the so-called New World to search for slaves and gold. The natives responded to these new explorers with confusion, awe, and fear. **Hernán Cortés,** who was commissioned by Velázquez to lead an expedition to Cozumel in 1519, bewildered the natives with his large ships and shiny armor. The Spaniards carried "fire-breathing" guns, sat atop armored horses, which the *indigenas* believed to be immortal, and spoke an unknown language. Some communities capitulated instantly and their *caciques* (leaders) showered the Spaniards with fruit, flowers, gold, and women; other towns fought tooth and nail to resist the impending conquest. Cortés sabotaged his own ships to prevent his men from turning back, cut off the feet of those who attempted mutiny, and marched on toward the great Aztec capital of Tenochtitlán with the assistance of **Jerónimo de Aguilar**, a Spaniard who had been held captive by the Maya for eight years and spoke their native language. As the Europeans moved westward they acquired a second interpreter, **La Malinche**—an Aztec princess who became Cortés' mistress and adviser. She is generally considered to be a traitor who sold out the thousands of people who died at Cortés' hand. He recruited 6000 warriors from the Totonacs and Tlaxcalans—enemies of the Aztecs—and massacred 6000 of the Aztecs' allies in a deadly assault; this bloody slaughter was named the **Cholula Massacre.**

Despite the bloodshed Cortés left in his wake, the *indigenas* were not willing to bow to his demands. When the Aztec emperor **Moctezuma II** (1502-1520) received word of Cortés' approach to Tenochtitlán, he had negotiators work with Cortés to discourage his conquest of the capital. Moctezuma also supposedly grappled with rumors that Cortés was the light-skinned, bearded ruler **Quetzalcóatl.** According to the legend, after being banished, Quetzalcóatl declared that he would return in the Maya year "1 Reed." Year-names recured every 52 years in the Maya calendar; the year in which Cortés happened to arrive was also "1 Reed". In the end, Moctezuma decided to welcome the Spaniards into the city. The initial period of peaceful, though tense, relations quickly soured when Moctezuma was kidnapped by the Spanish, and Cortés was driven from the city. Nevertheless, Cortés quickly regrouped and and the Aztecs—who were weakened by plagues and famine and overwhelmed by the Spaniards' military technology—were unable to continue fending off the Spaniards. Finally, on August 13, 1521, the Aztecs, led by their new emperor **Cuauhtémoc**, were soundly defeated at **Tlatelolco.** The empire had fallen.

THE PLAGUES OF MESOAMERICA. As the Spaniards pushed their way through the New World, they left in their wake horrific plagues that killed millions of *indigenas*. The *indigenas* were not naturally resistant to the European diseases such as smallpox, typhoid, and dysentery. The mild childhood diseases of Europe— measles, mumps, and influenza—proved fatal to Mesoamerican peoples. Within 100 years of Cortés' landing, these European diseases had wiped out as much as 96% of the indigenous population—about 24 million people. Smallpox, which caused an eruption of sores on its victims, high fevers and rashes, was by far the biggest killer. Those who lived were sometimes left blind or hideously scarred. Entire villages disappeared from the map and Spaniards simply moved onto the empty lands, called *tierras baldás*, or bought deserted acreage at bargain prices. Settlers grabbed huge estates; by 1618, one family had acquired over 11 million acres on the northern frontier.

LAND AND POWER. The epidemics meant that more land was available for the Spaniards, but it also meant that there were drastic labor shortages. For a time, *conquistadores* enslaved prisoners of war, but due to rampant disease and mal-treatment, *indigena* slavery was abolished in 1542. Instead, royal officials gave Spanish settlers *encomiendas* (labor grants). *Indigena* villages had to send a quota of laborers to work on the Spaniards' farms, and in return, the *encomen-dero* was supposed to Christianize and educate them. The practice of *encomien-das* was first employed in the Caribbean, and it ended in disaster for the *indigenas* who were overworked, abused, cheated, and separated from their fam-ilies. In Mesoamerica, *encomiendas* were replaced by the *repartimiento* system, which required each village to provide a weekly supply of labor to work on projects that included construction and food production. This system led to wide-spread abuses and lasted for most of the colonial era.

Abuses were the most extreme where wealth was greatest—in the mines. Rich veins of silver were discovered in central Mexico in the 1540s and mining camps proliferated rapidly, fueling the growth of colonial boom towns. Miners climbed out of the shafts on ladders made of notched logs, and at night they slept on the same pieces of cloth they used to haul their loads of ore. *Indige-nas* forced to work in the mines died by the thousands, killed by floods, explo-sions, and noxious gases.

THE CHURCH. Christianization was essential to the conquest of Mesoamerica. When the Spaniards took Tenochtitlán, they razed the Aztecs' central temple and built a cathedral atop the rubble. Some communities tried to defend their native religion, but later missionaries were even more successful in their tactics of con-version. *Indigenas* were particularly impressed by the arrival of the first 12 Fran-ciscan friars, who walked barefoot all the way from Veracruz to the capital. Upon their arrival, Cortés bent down at their feet and kissed their robes, making a fan-tastic impression on the awestruck *indigenas* who witnessed the exchange. While the Franciscans concentrated their efforts in the center of the country, the Jesuits pushed north, and the Dominicans moved into the southern regions. Reli-gious services and holidays were the only sanctioned days of rest for many villag-ers, and by the mid-1500s, missionaries had found millions of converts. However, Roman Catholic belief was mixed with traditional practices, creating the religious syncretism that persists today in many rural areas.

Many clergymen tried to protect *indigenas* against exploitation, often locking horns with local *encomenderos* and crown officials. The Dominican friar **Barto-lomé de Las Casas,** a vocal critic of the *encomienda* system, was largely responsi-ble for early laws protecting *indigenas*. The Franciscan, **Juan de Zumárraga,** Mexico's first bishop, personified the best and worst of colonial Catholicism. Zumárraga condemned corrupt judges and lobbied for *indigena* rights—yet he also burned natives at the stake on charges of heresy and regularly boasted that he had razed 500 temples and crushed 20,000 idols.

RACE AND CLASS. When the Spanish built a new city on the ruins of Tenochtitlán, they tried to establish clear racial boundaries. Only whites could live in the city's core; **peninsulares,** whites born in Spain, were at the top of the social hierarchy. **Criollos** (creoles), Spaniards born in Mexico, were considered "second-class" citizens and were overlooked for high positions in the Church and government. **Indígenas** were confined to the fringes and had to commute into the city each day, rowing through narrow canals in dugout canoes. But complete segregation was impossible, and, within a few generations, a huge new racial group had emerged—**mestizos**—children of mixed Spanish and *indigena* parentage. This group would eventually form the entire racial fabric of Mexican civilization. Today, an overwhelming majority of Mexicans are products of this *mestizo* heritage.

INDEPENDENCE AND REFORM

THE FIRST CALLS FOR FREEDOM. The rumblings of rebellion began with **Miguel Hidalgo y Costilla,** an iconoclastic priest in the small parish of Dolores. Always contumacious, Hidalgo was tried by the Inquisition on charges of gambling, dancing, reading forbidden books, fornicating, questioning the immaculate conception, and denouncing the king of Spain but he was acquitted because of insufficient evidence. Hidalgo spent little time proselytizing; instead, he tried to improve his parishioners' economic lot by introducing new trades and crafts to the village of Dolores. He also stockpiled guns. When Spanish officials discovered his hidden reserve, Hidalgo ran to Dolores' church and rang the bells to summon the parishioners. On September 16, 1810, Hidalgo delivered a ringing call to arms—**El Grito de Dolores (The Cry of Dolores)**—to end the rule by Spanish *peninsulares*, to promote the equality of races, and to demand a redistribution of the land. **Mexican Independence Day** commemorates this initial rebellion. Crop shortages, economic disparity and *indigena* resentment against the Spanish fueled the rebellion and Hidalgo's army quickly swelled, capturing several major cities before he was killed in an ambush by Spanish troops in March 1811.

After Hidalgo's death, another parish priest, **José María Morelos y Pavón**—a former student of Hidalgo's—rose to lead the Independence movement. Morelos was unable to rally the support of the *criollos* because they were opposed to the radicalization of the revolution. Morelos thus turned to *mestizos* and *indigenas* to rally against the Spanish and train them in guerrilla warfare tactics. Under his command, the rebels captured Oaxaca, Orizaba, and Acapulco in attempts to cut off the capital from both coasts. Once he isolated the capital, Morelos centered his focus on political reform and convened a meeting of an Athenae Congress to serve as the revolutionary movement's government. On November 6, 1813, the Congress issued Mexico's first formal **Declaration of Independence** declaring Mexico a republic, abolishing slavery, and eliminating all class distinctions. Although the constitution was never put into effect, is served as a model for later reformers.

Meanwhile, Spain was undergoing a profound political change. **King Ferdinand III** reinstated a constitutional monarchy, sovereignty of the people, and freedom of the press. Mexican conservatives and clerical leaders, alarmed by radicalism in Spain, saw that one way to preserve their ideals was to establish an independent Mexico. The movement was spearheaded by **Agustín de Iturbide,** a *criollo* loyalist who had led Spanish troops in battle against Hidalgo. In 1820, he joined forces with rebel leader **Vicente Guerrero.** Reassuringly conservative, Iturbide and Guerrero drafted the **Plan de Iguala,** which is most remembered for its "three guarantees"—independence, religion, and equality. Under the plan, Mexico was to be declared an independent constitutional monarchy and Roman Catholicism was to be the only tolerated state religion. Also, there was to be racial equality for all inhabitants of New Spain, thus making Europeans, Africans, and *indigenas* equal in the eyes of the law. The compromise received widespread support, and, on August 24, 1821, the **Treaty of Córdoba** formalized Mexico's independence forever.

THE FIRST EMPIRE. "He is prompt, bold, and decisive, and not scrupulous about the means he employs to obtain his ends," wrote a U.S. visitor about Iturbide. Iturbide controlled the first Mexican Empire, which only lasted two years during the short transitional period from colony to republic. During this period, Mexico was ruled by a provisional governing *junta* (council) that was presided over by Iturbide. The *junta* arranged for the election of an official Congress made up of conservatives, professionals, elites, and members of the aristocracy; no seats were available to the lower class. Iturbide began vying for control of the throne and congress was reluctant to grant him such power. However, on May 18, 1822, a coup was launched in support of Iturbide's bid for emperor of Mexico; Congress then voted to name him the constitutional emperor.

The first Mexican Empire collapsed within 10 months. After the turbulent previous decade of war, the economy was in shambles, the mining industry was in disarray, and commerce was at a standstill. Iturbide was faced with numerous economic barriers and a discontented nation. The conflicts became more prevalent during his short rule as antagonism arose between him and Congress. On October 31, 1822, Iturbide dismissed Congress and ruled through an appointed 45-man *junta*. This act provided the discontented military men with a pretext to revolt. Anticlericalists, *indigenas*, and *criollos* of modest means rebelled against Iturbide, led by the *criollo* military commander **Antonio López de Santa Anna.** On March 19, 1823, Iturbide finally resigned and left Mexico for Europe. However, when he returned in 1824, claiming to have come back to defend his country against a supposed Spanish plot to reconquer Mexico, he was shot by a firing squad.

In the fighting between 1810 and 1823, half a million people—one in 12 Mexicans—had died, and the fledgling government was flat broke. The political instability that ensued made borrowing abroad an expensive endeavor. But as the national debt increased, so did the nation's problems. Whenever public funds were insufficient to pay the army, its officers revolted, captured the government, and negotiated international loans. In 1824, a new constitution decreed Mexico a federal republic consisting of 19 states, four territories, and a federal district.

THE ERA OF SANTA ANNA. Although the presidency of Mexico officially changed hands 36 times between May 1833 and August 1855, Santa Anna dominated the political scene. Initially elected on a liberal, mildly anticlerical platform, he became a conservative supporter of the Church. Throughout his lifetime, Santa Anna occupied the presidency no fewer than 11 times.

As his cronies grew rich on graft and bribery, Santa Anna drained the state treasuries, desperately levying taxes on everything and everyone to build a huge standing army. Sure enough, Mexico was soon at war again. In 1838, France attacked Veracruz, demanding reparations for property damaged during the war a decade earlier. The conflict was dubbed **"The Pastry War"** in honor of a French pastry cook whose wares had been gobbled by marauding Mexican troops. The attacking French ships were driven back to sea, but Santa Anna lost part of his left leg in the bombardment. Four years later, Santa Anna had his severed leg removed from its grave, carried to the capital in a huge procession, and entombed in an urn atop a towering pillar as the Congress, cabinet, diplomatic corps, and army serenaded the decayed limb.

GRINGO INVASION. Meanwhile, the Mexican army was fighting a losing battle on its northern frontier. Conflict between Texas and Mexico was perpetuated by Anglo settlers in Texas who were resistant to adapting Mexican culture and laws. Angered by Mexico's abolition of slavery in 1829 and under-represented in the legislature, Texan settlers demanded independence. In an effort to quell the rebellion, Santa Anna gathered an army of 6000 men and marched north. In February of 1836, his troops overwhelmed Texan rebels holed up in an old Franciscan monastery called the Alamo. Santa Anna and his troops triumphed, killing all 150 defenders of the fortress. The bloody battle only made the Texans rally together harder;

"Remember the Alamo!" became a universal battle cry. The Texans made a notable comeback and defeated and captured Santa Anna in April 1836. Santa Anna was freed shortly after his capture, but Mexico made no further attempt to reconquer Texas, though it refused to recognize Texas's newly won independence.

Mexico's territorial problems however, were far from over, and when the U.S. annexed Texas in 1845 as part of its doctrine of **Manifest Destiny,** Mexico became entrenched in a drawn-out battle over land. U.S. and Mexican troops clashed over disputed territory and in April 1846, the U.S. formally declared war. U.S. troops captured present-day New Mexico and California and decided that the only way to defeat Mexico was to capture Mexico City. U.S. forces closed in on the capital from the north and east. Young cadets, known as the **Niños Héroes** (Boy Heroes), valiantly fought off U.S. troops from their military school in Chapultepec Castle and then, according to legend, wrapped themselves in the Mexican flag and leapt off the tower when all hope was lost. Things only got worse for the Mexicans when, on April 18, 1847, Santa Anna was defeated in a critical battle at **Cerro Gordo;** Mexico City was captured on September 14th of the same year. Santa Anna went into voluntary exile while the new government negotiated a peace agreement. Under the terms of the **Treaty of Guadalupe Hidalgo,** on February 2, 1848, Mexico sold Texas, New Mexico, and California to the U.S. for a paltry sum. Five years later, Santa Anna returned to Mexico and became dictator. To raise funds for an extended army, he sold off what today is Arizona and southern New Mexico in the **Gadsden Purchase.** Two thousand Mexicans had died in the battle for Mexico City—only to lose half the nation's territory.

While the international turmoil had settled with the Gadsden Purchase, the social and economic conditions for most Mexicans did not. Most Mexicans lived as they had for centuries—poor and isolated. Over one-third of the population lived in remote *indigena* villages. Although *pueblos* were largely self-governed, most villagers lived in extreme poverty. Education was a luxury enjoyed only by the *criollo* elite; only 1% of the total population was enrolled in school.

JUÁREZ AND REFORM. Eventually Santa Anna's regime cracked under enormous opposition. The emerging leader of the reform movement was **Benito Juárez,** who rose from humble roots in a tiny Zapotec *pueblo* in Oaxaca to become one of the more revered presidents in Mexican history. He was exiled to New Orleans by Santa Anna because of his radically egalitarian policies as governor of Oaxaca, but he joined other liberal politicians and journalists in stirring up opposition to Santa Anna abroad while dissidents in Mexico raised rebel armies. In 1855, Santa Anna was forced to resign.

The Juárez administration's policies reflected the ideology of 19th-century liberalism. As the Minister of Justice, Juárez passed the **Ley Juárez,** which abolished the old regulations protecting the military and Church from prosecution under civil laws. He passed a property law intended to weaken the Church, which owned vast rural and urban properties; however, the new law ended up stripping *indigenas* of their lands and livelihoods, since *ejidos* (indigenous communal lands) had to be auctioned off as well.

In 1857, a new constitution was drafted that decreed Mexico to be a representative, democratic, and republican nation with increased rights and liberty. This constitution, which remained in force until it was modified in 1917 after the Revolution, increased the power of the central executive and became the longest-lasting constitution in the Mexican republic's history.

Conservatives, especially high-ranking army officers, were ardently opposed to the new constitution. They supported a revolt in 1858 that became known as the **War of the Reform,** Mexico's bloodiest civil war to date. Conservatives, including the church and military, marched to the capital, dissolved Congress and arrested Juárez. Juárez escaped to Guanajuato, aided by *mestizo* reformers and many *indigena* liberals, .where he assumed the presidency and declared that the constitutional government was reestablished. Both sides committed atrocities; conservatives shot doctors who treated liberal casualties, while liberals defaced churches and executed priests who refused to give the sacrament to their troops. Juárez eventually won the presidential elections in 1861 and the fighting ended, but the country was far from unified. The liberal triumph in the civil war provided only temporary peace, as an international crisis soon erupted.

FRENCH INTERVENTION. After the liberals finally regained the upper hand in 1861, Juárez faced a massive federal budget deficit. He declared a moratorium on the payment of Mexico's foreign debts, prompting Spain, Britain, and France to attack Veracruz once again. Spain and Britain soon pulled out, but Napoleon III sent his troops inland. On May 5, 1862, outnumbered Mexican troops success-fully repelled **French soldiers** from the city of Puebla. **Cinco de Mayo** is now a national holiday that commemorates this triumph over odds; however, the invaders captured the capital a year later.

When Napoleon selected Austrian archduke **Ferdinand Maximilian of Hapsburg** as emperor of Mexico, he made a poor choice. Maximilian was extremely naive; he insisted that the Mexican people approve his ascension. Weirdly idealistic, he did not realize that he was the puppet of European imperialism. The new emperor was moderately liberal and anti-Catholic; instead of rescinding Juárez's anticlerical laws, Maximilian imposed forced loans on the Church to shore up the collapsing treasury. In 1864, he decreed that republicans were to be considered bandits and brigands, subject to extreme penalties. Mexican conservatives were predictably infuriated, and Maximilian's modest popularity evaporated. Meanwhile, liberals stockpiled weapons and hired thousands of U.S. Civil War veterans to fight against the French. Napoleon belatedly withdrew his troops in 1867, and Maximilian sur-rendered himself to Juárez and was promptly shot. The human toll of the war was far higher on the Mexican side—50,000 had died fighting the French.

STRUGGLING TO REBUILD. Juárez returned to the capital to face a dire situa-tion. Unemployment was rampant and to assert the executive's control over the military, Juárez had slashed the size of the Mexican army by two-thirds leaving thousands of decommissioned soldiers wandering through the countryside, raid-ing haciendas and rural villages for food. *Léperos* (beggars) roamed the streets of Mexico City. There were only enough schools for 10% of Mexican children to attend classes; of these students, just 22% were female. In his remaining years, Juárez helped Mexico modernize its economy and some of its social institutions by expanding the rail, road, and telegraph systems, and developing secular education. But despite these innovations, the nation was left in critical condition. When Juárez died in office in July of 1872, Mexico enjoyed peace but not prosperity.

THE PORFIRIATO. The regime of José de la Cruz **Porfirio Díaz,** which lasted from 1876 to 1911, was one of the more colorful and brutal chapters in Mexican history. In the 55 years since Independence, the Mexican presidency had changed hands 75 times; now stability was vital. Díaz's official motto was "Liberty, Order, and Progress"—but for the dictator, the price of order and progress was liberty itself. Elections were rigged, dissident journalists were jailed, and Díaz's strident critics were assassinated in his *pan o palo* (bread or stick) policy. The provinces were controlled by *jefes politicos* (political bosses). When uprisings occurred, they were swiftly smothered by bands of *rurales* (rural police).

Díaz's wealthy, European-trained, *criollo* advisors believed that the nation's problems could be solved with scientific techniques. Under Díaz, Mexico was mechanized, paved, and electrified. Ironically, the regime that brought prosperity to Mexico harbored deeply anti-Mexican prejudices. The Positivist *cientificos*— as Díaz's advisors were called—believed that *indigenas* were weak, immoral, and ineducable. Few of the new schools built during the Porfiriato were located in indigenous *pueblos*. Among the *criollo* elite, French—not Mexican—furniture, food, dance, opera, and fashion were popular .

During Díaz's regime, the Church enjoyed a comeback. The national popula-tion increased by 62% while the growth of the Church and land holdings grew by a much larger percentage. The priesthood more than doubled, and the number of Catholic schools increased sixfold. Additionally, the Porfiriato focused on making drastic improvements in the economy. Under Díaz, the value of exports and imports increased dramatically and the government paid off its past foreign debts, simplified its system of taxation, and increased foreign investment in Mexico. Foreign investors took over the railroad and petroleum industries, creating future problems for Mexico.

As industry prospered and land values skyrocketed, few poor Mexicans profited from the economic boom. Under a new law, *indigenas* could be forced to sell their public lands if they couldn't show a legal title to the plots they farmed. By the turn of the century, most villages saw their *ejidos* taken by wealthy individuals and private companies. In one case, a town was so entirely stripped of its communal lands that it no longer had space to bury its dead. Meanwhile, *científicos* made millions speculating in the volatile land market, manipulating railroad contracts to their own advantage.

Vast haciendas sprung up in the north, some as large as seven million acres, fed by cheap land prices. Half of Mexico's rural population worked as *peones*, legally bound to the *hacienda* owners. But as criticism of the regime increased, so did repression. By 1895, Díaz's popularity began to decline. The hostilities of the people toward the Porfiriato culminated in revolution.

REVOLUTION

CHALLENGES FROM ALL SIDES. Unlike the war for independence, which was ignited by *criollo* discontent, the Revolution began smoldering in the lower levels of Mexican society. In 1906, copper miners in Sonora went on strike, protesting low wages and the discriminatory policies of the mine's U.S. owners. The strike was quashed when Díaz permitted U.S. mercenaries to cross the border and kill strikers in order to protect the interests of U.S. investors. However, similar strikes elsewhere fueled a growing sense of instability and discontent.

In the 1910 presidential election, Díaz faced a vocal opponent. **Francisco I. Madero,** a wealthy *hacienda* owner from Coahuila, was no social revolutionary, but his calls for liberty and democracy were enough cause for Díaz to throw him into jail. Escaping to the U.S., Madero orchestrated a series of grass roots rebellions in northern states from his base in San Antonio. Meanwhile, **Emiliano Zapata** led the revolt against Díaz in the southern state of Morelos. Unlike Madero, Zapata believed that the rebels' first priority was to restore communal lands to the indigenous *pueblos*. Traveling to remote *pueblos* and addressing villagers in their native language, Zapata quickly raised an army of angry *indigenas*. After Madero's troops captured Ciudad Juárez, the 81-year-old Díaz fled to Paris. But once in power, the cautious Madero hesitated to restore any land to the Zapatistas, and he ordered the rebels in the south to disband. Zapata resisted the order, and the Zapatistas tangled with General **Victoriano Huerta's** troops.

THE COALITION COLLAPSES. After fending off rebellions from radical factions, Madero's government finally fell to a conservative uprising. **Venustiano Carranza,** the governor of Coahuila, urged state governors to revolt against the federal government. Guerrilla armies sprung up in the north, led by **Pancho Villa** in Chihuahua and **Alvaro Obregón** in Sonora. Villa worked with **Pascual Orozco** in leading guerrilla forces; by the end of 1910, the two had used the bands to attack federal forces, cut railroad connections, and capture towns and territory in Chihuahua.

In 1911, the Zapata-led and Villa-led revolts flourished. The group of armed peasants that Zapata led took over ancestral lands, destroyed sugar haciendas, and seized several towns. On May 21, 1911, Madero and Díaz signed the **Treaty of Ciudad Juárez,** which provided for the removal of the president and vice president and called for new elections. It left the federal army intact but demanded the disbanding of rebel forces. Zapata followed the new leaders in the beginning but he grew increasingly frustrated with the Madero government. Finally, on November 25, 1911, Zapata proclaimed his own agrarian program, the **Plan of Ayala,** which disavowed Madero as president. Zapata and his revolutionaries rallied together again to fight for *"Tierra y Libertad!"* (Land and Liberty). Provisional governments proliferated; by late 1913, there were more than 25 different types of paper money in circulation. After U.S. troops bombed Veracruz in 1914, Huerta resigned.

Next, Obregón seized the capital; Carranza controlled Veracruz; Villa ruled the north; Zapata held the south. When Villa's troops attacked Obregón's forces at the bloody **Battle of Celaya,** 4000 Villistas were shredded on barbedwire entrenchments, and 5000 more were wounded. As Villistas wreaked havoc on Texas border towns, Carranza's own government found itself hopelessly divided between old-style liberals and radical land reformers. The fighting in the south was the most vicious: thousands of civilians were executed as alleged Zapatista sympathizers; Zapata retaliated by blowing up a train and killing about 400 innocent passengers. In 1919, Carranza's men assassinated Zapata in an ambush, and Carranza assumed the presidency, inaugurating a period of relative calm. One in eight Mexicans had died in the wars of 1910-1920. Since all of the rebel governments had printed their own money, the economy was in ruin. Inflation slashed the real wages of urban laborers; flooding and sabotage put miners out of work, and many Mexicans were on the brink of starvation.

INSTITUTIONALIZED REVOLUTION. In 1917, Carranza gathered delegates to draft a new constitution; the document they produced still governs the Republic today. Zapatistas, Villistas, and Huertistas were barred from the convention, yet delegates outlined a thoroughly radical agenda for the nation. Present was the familiar liberal anticlericalism of the 19th century; more startling were the socialistic articles of the new constitution. Private ownership of land was declared to be a privilege, not a right, and the state was supposed to redistribute lands seized from *pueblos* during the Porfiriato. Workers were guaranteed better conditions and the right to strike. But the moderate Carranza failed to implement most of the radical document, and the Revolution drifted to the right as successive presidents reversed the modest gains.

The **Constitution of 1917** codified the Revolution; the government of the 1920s institutionalized it. **Plutarco Elías Calles,** elected president in 1924, ruled the country for a decade through a series of puppet presidents. Calles, known as the "Jefe Máximo," consolidated the government's support in the new **Partido Nacional Revolucionario (PNR),** which in other forms has run Mexico virtually unopposed since its creation in 1929. In 1934 **Lázaro Cárdenas** took the office and became the first President since the revolution to enforce the Constitution of 1917. His rule marked the beginning of a new era in Mexico.

MODERN MEXICO

CARRYING OUT THE REVOLUTION. The Great Depression hit Mexico in the gut. The value of the peso plummeted, wages dropped, and many Mexicans began to question the direction of the Revolution. Reacting to the mood of the times, Mexico's new president Lázaro Cárdenas seized the reins from his PNR handlers and steered the Revolution sharply to the left. Cárdenas redistributed 44 million acres—twice as many as all of his predecessors combined—to thousands of indigenous *ejidos,* systems in which lands were owned communally. Economically, most *ejidos* were a failure, and agricultural productivity dropped drastically. But the *ejido* program achieved an enormous symbolic goal: worried peasants were given reassurance that the new government intended to meet the goals of the Mexican Revolution.

NEW DIRECTIONS. In addition to drastically increasing the rate of land redistribution, Cárdenas also altered the nature of the government party. Incorporating the peasant, labor, popular, and military sectors into the party, he succeeded in establishing a means by which these groups could be organized under the control of the government. By so doing, Cárdenas immeasurably strengthened the ruling party, which he renamed the **Partido de la Revolución Mexicana (PRM).** To top off Cárdenas's radicalization of Mexico, he took hold of the oil industry in an effort to boost Mexican nationalism. The companies had previously been supported financially by foreign investors, but Cárdenas expropriated them, turning the industry to the hands of Mexican investors. Additionally, he established **Petróleos Mexicanos (PEMEX)** as a means of regulating the oil industry. Unfortunately, due to developing economic woes, PEMEX failed to have the strong impact he had hoped for.

In 1940 **Avila Camacho** was elected president of Mexico. His rule, combined with the onset of World War II, altered any new order Cárdenas had set in motion in Mexico. Camacho's main goal was to modernize the country through industrialization; the war sped up the pace of Mexican development, accelerating the shift from socialism to industrial capitalism. However, the working class didn't share in the new prosperity. Mexican industrialists were urged to keep costs down and, by implication, to keep wages low. Inevitably, oil workers responded to the shift in economic distribution by going on strike in the early 1950s; the army was called in and dozens of union leaders were fired.

THE LEGACY OF THE OFFICIAL GOVERNMENT PARTY. At the end of WWII, the official political party in Mexico, the **Partido Revolucionario Institucional (PRI),** was derived from its PRM predecessor. Under the direction of President **Miguel Alemán,** the PRI integrated the labor, peasant, and popular sectors—a structure it has maintained to this day. Lured by the promise of cushy government jobs, union officials and peasant leaders joined the PRI's swelling political machine. Enjoying wide institutional support, the PRI has not yet lost a presidential election since its inception in 1929.

However, the stability of single-party rule (which is fading in the late 1990s) has come at the price of liberty. Even under president **Adolfo López Mateos**—who between 1958 and 1964 expanded social security coverage and redoubled efforts at land reform—Mexicans were not free to speak their minds. López Mateos removed the Communist leadership of the teachers' and railroad unions and sent in the army to break a railroad-workers' strike in 1959. When the head of the PRI tried to reform the party's nomination process, he was fired by the president under pressure from state political bosses. Student unrest and worker dissatisfaction culminated in 1968 at Mexico City's **Tlatelolco Plaza,** where police killed an estimated 400 peaceful demonstrators and jailed another 2000 protesters just 10 days before the Olympics were to open. Recently, the preferential treatment practiced by the PRI has been scrutinized as the result of the Acteal massacre in Chiapas in the last days of 1997.

SALINAS: TOWARD DEMOCRACY. "The era of one-party rule in Mexico is over," declared PRI presidential candidate **Carlos Salinas de Gortari** during the tense week following the 1988 elections. Salinas officially (and conveniently) received 50.4% of the vote when the final contested results were announced, but many interpreted his remarks and the election itself as a fresh start for Mexican politics.

Mexico's ruling party did not lose a single presidential, senatorial, or gubernatorial race from 1929 to 1988; in the few local elections that it did lose, the PRI often installed its own candidates anyway. Through a combination of patronage, fraud, and ineffectual opposition, the party stayed in power and ran Mexico uncontested. But in the 1982 election, the murmurs of dissent were heard, and the right-of-center **Partido de Acción Nacional (PAN)** won 14% of the vote, most of it in the northern states. In 1983, when the PRI experimented with fraud-free elections, the PAN picked up three mayorships in the state of Chihuahua alone.

When the Harvard-educated Salinas began his six-year term as president on December 1, 1988, the country was faced with numerous problems including high unemployment, a US$105 billion foreign debt, a drug crisis, and a skeptical nation. Salinas instituted wage and price controls to keep inflation down. He then proceeded to boost his popularity with the arrests of a union boss, a fraudulent businessman, and a drug trafficker.

On February 4, 1990, representatives of the Mexican government and its 450 foreign commercial creditors signed a debt reduction agreement designed to ease the U.S. banking crisis and to deflect outlandishly high interest payments. This reprieve, along with Salinas's austerity program, led to growing foreign investment and steady growth (3% per year) in Mexico's gross domestic product. Unemployment, however, remains near 20%. Reduced or not, foreign debt has continued to suck capital out of the country, and a blossoming trade deficit is squeezing out small and medium businesses as foreign franchises muscle their way in.

The fate of these smaller businesses was at the center of the controversial **North American Free Trade Agreement (NAFTA).** The treaty eliminated the tariffs, quotas, and subsidies that had protected Mexican industry and agriculture since the 1940s, by driving up the prices of foreign goods, thus allowing national and local companies to corner certain markets. The implementation of NAFTA meant that smaller Mexican-owned businesses were often driven out of business by *maquiladores*, U.S.-owned assembly and automotive factories. On the other hand, freer trade means cheaper consumer goods for financially strapped Mexicans—a blessing in a nation plagued by constant inflation. Increased competition may eventually reap profits for the Mexican economy, but development is now exacting high human and environmental costs.

In 1992, PRI technocrats dismantled the *ejido* system, which had ostensibly guaranteed communal land rights for rural *campesinos*. Salinas asserted that while redistributing land had served to implement justice in the decades following the Revolution, that program had become unproductive and even detrimental to economic growth by the 1990s. With this constitutional reform and other changes, including rapid privatization, an agrarian culture thousands of years old is being phased out to pave the way for industrialization. Traditional support systems are often lost in urbanization while government safety nets are eliminated; this is all part of an economic streamlining backed by the U.S. and international lenders. The costs of this structural adjustment program (centered around NAFTA) have yet to be determined, but in the meantime they fall on the shoulders of the lower classes.

THE EJÉRCITO ZAPATISTA DE LIBERACIÓN NACIONAL (EZLN). On January 1, 1994, Mexico's government officials were celebrating the implementation of NAFTA, which went into effect that day. In the southern state of Chiapas, however, Mexicans were rallying for a different kind of progress. In the day's early hours, a force of rebels captured the capital city of **San Cristóbal de las Casas** and other strategically chosen cities in the region. Named the **Ejército Zapatista de Liberación Nacional (EZLN),** or **Zapatista National Liberation Army,** this army of over 9000 peasants (mainly Mayas) stepped forward to demand a voice in Mexican politics. Twelve days of fighting ensued, leaving about 150 dead. Months of negotiations followed, and mediator and **Bishop of San Cristóbal Samuel Ruiz** eventually forged a delicate relationship between the government and the rebels. The rebels rejected the government's peace plan and threatened to shatter the fragile cease-fire unless upcoming presidential elections were free and fair.

In an election year that was supposed to express Mexico's material progress and fledgling democracy, the rebels from Chiapas drew attention to the vast inequities that still existed within the Republic. From the first day that the EZLN arrived on the international stage, their spokesman **Subcomandante Marcos** has aired demands for a change in the definition of the Mexican nation. Although many observers have taken the rebellion to be an assertion of indigenous rights, numerous other issues have been brought to the table by the **Zapatista** rebels.

Chiapas is Mexico's poorest state, and President Salinas had poured more "anti-poverty" money into the state than any other—but to little avail. Furthermore, *indigena* rebels clearly harbored deep resentments that no amount of PRI money could assuage. The EZLN not only brought social change to the table—it also demanded political restructuring of the national system. The Zapatista directorate, the **Clandestine Committee,** designed a system in which Mexico would be divided into autonomous regions defined by existing political alliances. Self-determination and autonomy, some of the main demands of the Zapatistas, emphasize their concern with achieving a political structure in which people are guaranteed representation nationally as well as local, individual decision-making.

While the EZLN's goal has been to establish a new structure for the Mexican nation, much of the commentary on the group has focused on the witty, poetic Marcos. Green-eyed and white-skinned, the ski-mask he wears serves only symbolically to hide his identity. Indeed, he has said himself that the mask acts not to protect him but to transform him—to erase the man behind the mask (revealed by President Zedillo on Feb. 9, 1995, to be **Rafael Sebastián Guillén Vicente,** a university-educated Marxist) and to establish, instead, the Marcos who has come to be the voice of the movement. He calls himself a poet; he writes—in addition to lengthy letters to Zedillo, the Mexican nation, and foreign observers—fiction and short stories. In his soft voice, he intertwines Maya oral styles with cunning analyses of his nation. It is no wonder, given his charm and astute speech, that observers are drawn in by him; however, the extent to which discussion of the Zapatistas has focused on Marcos has created a superhero-like aura around him which some observers think diverts important attention from the movement itself.

DEATH AND TRANSFIGURATION. The Zapatista uprising foreshadowed the turmoil to come. On March 23, 1994, the likeable and reform-minded PRI presidential candidate **Luis Donaldo Colosio** of Mexicali was assassinated as he left a rally in Tijuana. Many believe that the leaders of hard-line faction of the PRI killed their own candidate when they found him too radical and conciliatory for their taste; the rumors were fueled by the subsequent murders of the chief investigator of Colosio's assassination and several other officials connected with the investigation. After three years of conflicting investigations by five different prosecutors, Colosio's case remains unsolved.

Meanwhile, the PRI picked Budget and Planning Minister **Ernesto Zedillo** to replace the slain candidate and to rebuild the campaign from scratch. The party relied on more than 800,000 grass roots organizers to comb the country door-to-door, building on an old network of patronage and old-school politics. Sure enough, the PRI won hands-down in a relatively fair election, receiving remarkable support from Mexico's poorer voters.

Just months into his presidency, on December 20, 1994, Zedillo was faced with a precipitous drop in the value of the peso. Spooked by the assassination of Colosio and the unsettling events in Chiapas, foreign investors dumped US$25 billion of Mexican government peso bonds, heralding the imminent monetary devaluation. Aided by the International Monetary Fund (IMF) and the U.S. government, Mexico was salvaged from the depths of economic crisis. Still, severe financial difficulties persisted: in March 1995, interest rates skyrocketed to more than 90%, bringing the banking system to a near collapse. The growing legions of middle-class professionals and entrepreneurs that relied on foreign dollars were left frustrated and frightened. Mexicans have laid the blame on Zedillo, citing his delay in appointing key cabinet posts and in instituting promised economic reforms.

Although the prospect of successfully taming the economy seems distant, Zedillo has sought to pacify the anxious masses with further political reforms. The president has committed himself to decentralizing power and exposing corruption in an attempt to restore the nation's faith in the government. He formally ended the PRI In time for the party primaries for the 2000 presidential elections, he formally ended the PRI tradition of the "degazo," the practice of the incumbent president "pointing out" a handpicked presidential candidate. Elections have slowly become defrauded, and Zedillo has arrested several high-level officials on charges of conspiracy and murder, earning respect and U.S. endorsement as a "partner in the war on drugs."

However, no end to the war is in sight: narcotics and their devastating effects have eaten away at Mexico in recent years. Most disheartening has been the large overlap, only beginning to be exposed, between high-level anti-drug enforcement officials, politicians, and drug lords. In May of 1998, an American undercover operation resulted in the indictment of 26 Mexican bankers who were charged with laundering more than US$110 million in drug profits. Zedillo decried the investigation as a violation of Mexican law. U.S. President Bill Clinton and Zedillo met to try to find a solution to the increasingly problematic relationship between the U.S. and Mexico. Whatever happens, there is no easy solution: more than half of the cocaine smuggled to the United States still travels through Mexico.

MEXICO AT A CROSSROADS. Fortunately, the consolidation of large drug cartels has not been the only Mexican news item fit to print in recent years. Equally newsworthy has been the country's dramatic shift away from one-party rule toward democracy. Under Zedillo's leadership, Mexico has moved toward fair elections that have actually begun to undermine his own party's domination. The PRI once controlled all state governorships; now, several state governors belong to an opposition party, the right-leaning PAN. Furthermore, the liberal Partido de la Revolución Democrática (PRD) party poses a threat from the other side.

In July 1997, Mexico's elections took an unprecedented turn. The PRI, increasingly linked with instability rather than stability, lost its majority in the lower house of Congress for the first time since it took control of the house 68 years ago. PAN and the PRD each took nearly 30% of the Congressional vote, leaving only 41% for the PRI—far from one-party rule. Without a PRI majority supporting Zedillo in Congress, much of the president's power has now passed to that body. But Congress was not the only institution shaken up by the turn of events in the summer of 1997: in the first direct Mexico City mayoral vote since 1928, leftist Cuauhtémoc Cárdenas of the PRD won a landslide victory. Cárdenas is an outspoken opponent of Zedillo's free-market policies. Perhaps following in his father's footsteps, the famous 1930s leader (see p. 16), Cárdenas is said to have his eye on the presidency. For the first time, the prospect of a non-PRI president is a possibility.

But while a victory may have been achieved for liberal democracy, the situation in the southern part of the country is deteriorating rapidly. The long-awaited peace talks between the Zapatista rebels and the government have been stalled since late 1996, while thousands of federal troops are posted throughout the state of Chiapas. The precarious peace has given way to more bloodshed and tragedy. On December 22, 1997, 45 people, including women and children, most of them Zapatista rebel sympathizers, were massacred in the small village of Acteal in Chiapas. Although the government has blamed the massacre on a family feud, there is evidence that state officials had advance knowledge of the **Acteal Massacre** and did nothing to prevent it. In the aftermath of the massacre, the governor of Chiapas, **Julio César Ruiz Ferro,** a member of the PRI, resigned under pressure from the president, the church and opposition leaders. Although federal prosecutors arrested state officials, Zapatista rebels accuse the government of agreeing to peace, while secretly arming paramilitary units.

In the meantime, however, peace is still far from becoming a reality. Less than a month after the Acteal massacre, a police force in Chiapas fired on a crowd of Indians protesting the massacre, killing a defenseless woman and wounding others. In June of 1998, Bishop Samuel Ruiz, a public critic of the government, resigned from his position as the mediator of peace talks between the federal government and the Zapatista rebels. Accused of siding with the Zapatistas and of condoning violence, Ruiz has been the main negotiator between the opposing factions since the initial uprising of January 1994.

MEXICO

June of 1998 also saw seven people dead in a bloody clash in Chiapas, in which the Mexican Army tried to retake control of **El Bosque,** a small town near San Cristóbal that was sympathetic to the Zapatista rebels. The relationship between the government and the rebels is continually tense and exemplifies the problems and paradoxes of current Mexico. Carlos Fuentes, one of Mexico's premier writers and intellectuals, expresses eloquently that "it is impossible for the drama of Chiapas and its democratic solution not to affect the drama of Mexico and the entire's country's democratic solution...if the problems of democracy are not resolved in Chiapas, they will not be resolved in Mexico; if they are not resolved in Mexico, there will be one, two, three Chiapas in Hidalgo, Oaxaca, Michoacán, Guerrero."

CULTURE AND CHARACTER

ART AND ARCHITECTURE

Mexican art is generally classified into three periods: the **Indigenous** (6000 BC-AD 1525), the **Colonial** (1525-1810), and the **Modern** (1810-present). Art createdbefore the Spanish invasion is studied by archaeologists; for the most part, no written commentary on artistic expression exists from the time before the Conquest. With the arrival of the Spanish, Mexican art changed dramatically and was heavily influenced by new styles and interpretations, a trend that has endured through the Modern period.

THE PRE-HISPANIC ERA. Much of the art and architecture from this period has provided the basis for understanding early Mexican history (see **Pre-Hispanic Societies,** p. 7). Some aspects of pre-Hispanic styles were prevalent across Mexico. The use of **stone** is perhaps one of the most noticeable. The Olmecs shaped basalt into the colossal heads for which they are famous. The Maya used limestone and sandstone all over their cities, as building blocks for palaces and temples, stelae (upright stone monuments often inscribed with glyphs and reliefs), and altars. Cities such as Teotihuacán, Tula, and Tenochtitlán show the continued use of monumental stone architecture in their buildings, carved reliefs, and statuary.

On a smaller scale, some of the most impressive pieces of pre-Hispanic art would fit in your hand. **Carved jade** and **ceramic figurines** are plentiful from the very beginnings of Mexican culture through the Colonial period. Maya gods and nobility are often depicted adorned with massive headdresses replete with lengthy feathers, necklaces with beads the size of eggs, and gold and copper bracelets to match the enormous bangles hanging from their earlobes. Much of the information gained from art such as stone monuments or small carved objects pertains only to the elite members of those societies; much less material has been recovered from the non-elite segments of these cultures.

Besides buildings and monuments, a final form of creative expression used by pre-Hispanic peoples is **narrative depiction. Murals** such as those covering the walls at the Maya site of Bonampak reveal scenes of warfare, sacrifice, and celebration. **Frescoes** on interior walls of buildings at Teotihuacán depict, among other subjects, paradise scenes, floral arrangements, religious rituals, and athletic events. Scenes painted onto the **pottery** of all of these cultures depict mythological stories. Other reliefs and objects reveal calendrical events and dates—the famous **Aztec Stone of the Sun** is a prime example. This prophetic calender measures nearly four meters in diameter. Within its concentric rings are contained the four symbols of previous suns—rain, jaguars, wind, and fire, the plagues responsible for the destruction of earlier populations. The Aztecs believed that they were living in the period of the fifth sun, and they expected to be obliterated by an earthquake—the symbol for which also ominously appears on the stone.

THE ARCHITECTURE OF NEW SPAIN. Not surprisingly, the first examples of **colonial art** were created specifically to facilitate religious indoctrination of the *indígenas* as quickly as possible. Churches were often constructed on top of pre-existing temples and pyramids. Volcanic stone, plentiful in most areas, was the main building material. Colonial architecture, recalling **Romanesque** and **Gothic** stylistic elements, is characterized by the use of huge buttresses, arches, and crenulations (indented or embattled moldings). An early architectural development was the open chapel *(capilla abierta)*, a group of arches enclosing an atrium.

Monasteries and churches under the direction of **Franciscan, Dominican,** and **Augustinian** missionaries were built according to climatic and geographic limitations. The Franciscan style tended to be functional and economic, while the Dominican style was more ascetic and harsh, due to earthquake danger and warm weather. Augustinian style was the most free-spirited and grandiose, and architects indulged in gratuitous and excessive decoration whenever possible. Remarkable Augustinian buildings include the **Monastery of St. Augustín of Acolman** near Mexico City and the **Monastery of Actopán** in Hidalgo.

A BLOSSOMING OF THE BAROQUE. The steady growth and spread of the Catholic Church throughout the 17th and 18th centuries necessitated the construction of cathedrals, parochial chapels, and convents. Moreover, this period brought the Baroque style to New Spain. Luxurious **Baroque** facades, teeming with dynamic images of angels and saints, aimed to produce a feeling of awe and respect in the hearts of the recently converted *indígenas*. The narratives set in stone could be understood even by *los analfabetos* (the illiterate people) and easily committed to memory. A look at the cathedrals of Zacatecas and Chihuahua reveals the degree of artistry Baroque ideals encouraged. Baroque painting found its quintessential expression in the works of **Alonso López de Herrera** and **Baltazar de Echave Orio** (the elder).

Sumptuousness, frivolity, and ornamentation became more prevalent in the works of the late 18th-century artists and builders who couldn't get too much of a good thing. During this time, the **Churrigueresque** style was born and **Mexican High Baroque** was carried to the extreme. A hallmark of this style is the intricately decorated *estípites* (pilasters), often installed merely for looks, not support.

20TH CENTURY MURALS AND BEYOND: THE POLITICAL AESTHETIC. As the Revolution reduced their land to shambles, Mexican painters developed an unapologetic national style. This success was made possible by **José Vasconcelos's** Ministry of Education program, which commissioned *muralistas* to create their art on the walls of hospitals, colleges, schools, and ministries. Vasconcelos also sent the artists into the countryside to teach and participate in rural life.

The Mexican **mural,** still unequivocally nationalistic in its current form, dates back to the early days of the Conquest when Catholic evangelists, who could not communicate with the *indígenas*, used allegorical murals to teach them the rudiments of Christian iconography. **Diego Rivera,** the most renowned of the *muralistas*, based his artwork on political themes—land reform, Marxism, and the marginalization of *indígena* life. Rivera used stylized realism to portray the dress, action, and expression of the Mexican people, and natural realism (complete with ugly faces, knotted brows, and angry stances) to represent Spaniards and other oppressors of the *indígenas*. His innovative blend of Mexican history and culture reached a wide audience and embroiled him in international controversy.

Though Rivera is credited as the first to forge the path for *muralistas*, many other artists have contributed to the definition of the art form and have thus achieved national recognition. Some of the best-known *muralistas* include: **David Álfaro Siqueiros,** who brought new materials and dramatic revolutionary themes to his murals; the Cubism-influenced **Rufino Tamayo,** arguably the most abstract of the *muralistas*; and **José Clemente Orozco,** whose murals in Mexico City and lifelike plaster-of-paris skeleton characters have won him a great deal of fame.

Not all 20th-century Mexican artists have exchanged the traditional canvas for walls. **Juan Soriano,** by combining vanguard and traditional Mexican art, forged a name for himself as a painter and sculptor. Due in part to her incredible talent and **Hayden Herrera's** landmark biography, **Frida Kahlo** (1907-54) surpasses many Mexican artists in current worldwide recognition. Kahlo's paintings and self-portraits are icons of pain: the viewer is forced to confront the artist's self-obsession in its most violent and extreme manifestations.

LITERATURE

PRE-HISPANIC WRITING: A MULTI-MEDIA AFFAIR. As far as linguists and archaeologists have been able to tell, three languages were dominant in Mexico before the arrival of the Spanish: **Náhuatl, Mayan,** and **Cakchiquel.** The earliest examples of writing are thought to be the glyphs inscribed at **San José Mogote** and **Monte Albán,** Oaxaca—two sites containing reliefs perhaps dating back to 600 BC. The destructiveness of the Conquest, particulary in its initial years, and the imposition of the Spanish language resulted in the loss of valuable information relating to *indígena* language. Considered a dangerous affront to Christian teachings, Maya and Aztec **codices** (unbound "books" or manuscripts) were fed to the flames. But due to the foresight of some indigenous leaders as well as a handful of missonaries, a number of Maya and Aztec codices did survive. Other historical works such as the **Books of Chilam Balam** (Books of the Jaguar Priest) and the **Annals of the Cakchiquel** cover a range of topics. They are not exclusively historical works, but are instead narrative and poetic, laden with symbolism and lofty metaphor. The **Rabinal Achi** (Knight of Achi), the story of a sacrificed warrior, is considered to be the only surviving example of pre-Hispanic drama.

COLONIAL LITERATURE. Surrounded by a New World, the Spanish were eager to send news home about the land they had conquered and the way of life of Mexico's *indígenas*. These letters home, among them Cortés' **Cartas de Relación** (Letters of Relation), were mainly Crown- and Church-flattering documents detailing the exhaustive ongoing efforts being undertaken to educate and Christianize *indígenas*. Other chronicles, such as the *Nuevo Mundo y Conquista* (New World and Conquest), by **Francisco de Terrazas,** and *Grandeza Mexicana* (Mexican Grandeur), by **Bernardo de Balbuena,** were written in rhyme in order to take the edge off the monotonous melange of factoid stew.

In the caste society of New Spain, only religious orders enjoyed the luxury of genuine intellectual freedom. Many members of the clergy worked to preserve the languages and texts of the *indígenas*, and a handful of universities sprung up. The **Jesuits'** 23 colleges were the best in the colony—until the Crown expelled the Jesuits from the Americas in 1767 because of their growing influence.

Although historical texts dominated Mexico's literary output throughout much of the 16th and 17th centuries, poets made substantial achievements. **Sor Juana Inés de la Cruz** (1648-1695) became a master lyricist known for her razor-sharp wit. A *criolla* of illegitimate birth, Sor Juana turned to the cloistered life and married God, instead of the numerous suitors she undoubtedly had—her beauty was legendary. In the Church she found a moral and physical haven where she produced her most famous works, *Respuesta a Sor Filotea* (Response to Sor Filotea) and *Hombres Necios* (Injudicious Men). Her love poems display a passionate outlook, and many verses display a feminist sensibility ahead of their time.

STRUGGLING FOR A LITERARY IDENTITY. The literary impetus of French Enlightenment philosophical movements eventually gave way to political ones. By the end of the 18th century, the struggle for independence became the singular social fact from which many Mexican texts grew. In 1816, **José Fernández de Lizardi,** a prominent Mexican journalist, wrote the first Latin American novel: **El Periquillo Sarniento** (The Itching Parrot), a tale that revealed Mexican society's displeasure with the status quo.

His ideological, moralizing fiction was very influential. With the Spanish-American modernists of the 19th century, poetry reached a level it had not achieved since Sor Juana. At the same time, **Manuel Gutierrez Nájera** composed the poem *De Blanco* (On Whiteness), a linguistic representation at its most distilled and self-contained.

Many romantic novels of the period used historical themes to introduce sweeping indictments of the military and clergy. Novelists sought to define Mexico's national identity, glorifying strength, secularism, progress, and education. Artists were didactic, producing works with such inspirational titles as *Triumph and Study Over Ignorance*. Whereas European Romanticism was an aesthetic challenge to Neoclassicism, Mexican Romanticism was an artistic response to the country's political and social realities. Shortly after the heyday of the Romantic novel came the popular novel of manners, most notably *El Fistol del Diablo* by **Manuel Payno,** and *Juanita Sousa* and *Antón Pérez* by **Manuel Sánchez Mármol.**

Literature during the **Porfiriato** (1876-1911) abandoned Romanticism for realism, and most writers expressed little sympathy for the poor. Others adopted a Modernist style, emphasizing language and imagery, and replacing didactic social themes with psychological topics. Visual artists, by contrast, began to reject the creed of the *científicos*. Many favored experimental techniques and chose to depict **slums, brothels,** and **scenes from indigenous life.** Their iconoclasm foreshadowed a growing dissatisfaction with the Díaz regime.

20TH-CENTURY GLOBAL PERSPECTIVES. Mexican literature in the post-Revolutionary era is marked by a frustrated desire to forge a national tradition from the vestiges of pre-colonial culture. Nobel prize winner **Octavio Paz,** in such works as *El Laberinto de la Soledad* (The Labyrinth of Solitude), draws on Marxism, Romanticism, and post-Modernism to explore the making and unmaking of a national archetype. Paz, like his equally famous successor **Carlos Fuentes,** concerns himself with myths and legends in an effort to come to terms with Spanish cultural dominance. Fuentes published his first novel, *La region más transparente*, in 1958. Of late, the work of female writers, such as Hollywood darling **Laura Esquivel** *(Like Water for Chocolate*, see p. 26), has been well received both nationally and internationally. Elena Poniatowska, the author of *Tinisma*—a novel about the life of Tina Modotti who was a secret agent for the Soviet Union during the Spanish Civil War—is making a name for herself in the world of Latin American writers. In the past two decades, a new literary movement has emerged from Mexico—the Chicano movement. Chicano literature describes the experiences of Latinos who come to the United States and must overcome numerous barriers to adapt to the new culture. Many Chicano authors are rapidly gaining respect in the international community. **Sandra Cisneros's** *House on Mango Street*—a novel narrated by an eleven-year-old girl who talks about her life on both sides of the Mexican border—has made Cisneros one of the most recognized Chicana authors today. Other Chicano writers such as **Américo Paredes** have used their status as Chicano authors to put traditional Mexican folklore into written form. In *With His Pistol in His Hands*, Paredes put into written form the story of **Gregorio Cortez,** a Mexican who was persecuted by the U.S. judicial system for shooting a sheriff in self-defense. The ballad of Gregorio Cortez has since become an inspirational story to Mexicans.

POPULAR CULTURE

MUSIC. Mexico City has become one of the major recording centers for the Americas. Like most other components of its culture, Mexican music is an eclectic stew of styles and flavors borrowed from across the continent and overseas. Mexico's traditional music is mostly regional, making for a rich and varied collage of styles and artists. Up north, one will hear groups such as **Los Tigres del Norte** sing in the style aptly labeled *norteño*, a border blend of country music. One of the most popular and well-

known styles of traditional Mexican music is **mariachi**, found throughout the country but orginating from west-central states like Jalisco and Michoacan. *Mariachi* songs, commonly called *rancheras*, are usually played live by a sombreroed, gregarious brass-and-string band. The world-famous tradition of women being serenaded by a group of *mariachis* in traditional Mexican garb is seen as an almost obligatory supplement to a romantic evening—foreplay, if you will. Traditional *rancheras* tend to deal with one or several of the following topics: being very drunk, being abandoned by a woman, being cheated on by a woman, getting drunk, leaving a woman, pondering the fidelity of one's horse, loving one's gun, and wanting to get drunk.

Traditional music along the east-central coast continuing into the Yucatán carries a strong dose of Afro-Carribean **rhumba**. In states like Veracruz and Quintana Roo, drum-laden bands often strike up irresistable beats in the sea breeze and evening twilight of central plazas. One of the instruments of this style has inspired countless **marimba** bands, whose popularized music can be found blasting in markets throughout the Republic. Imported from Columbia, **cumbia** has joined **salsa** as the traditional dance music of choice across the central and southern regions of Mexico, which are often jived to with the **merengue** dance step.

Mexico also knows how to rock. The latest alternative groups like **El Nudo** and **Caifanes** provide stiff competition to Spanish and American bands on the radio and on music video channels. Travelers from up north will feel at home, though, as American pop and hip-hop is ubiquitous in bars and *discotecas.* Striving to Mexicanize imports in some way, Mexican artists will often take an American piece and make it their "own" with altered lyrics or a slightly more Latin beat. Domestic cotton-candy pop is sung by such artists as **Luis Miguel, Alejandra Guzmán** (dubbed the *Reina del Rock* (Queen of Rock, in the early 90s) and **Christian Castro. Selena,** the "Latin Madonna" and most beloved of Tejano singers, was born American, but in typical Tejano style, she fused polka, country, Mexican, and R&B. Her bouncy Spanish album *Amor Prohibido* was wildly popular in both Mexico and the U.S., but it didn't hit #1 on the Billboard charts until Selena was murdered—shot in the back by the president of her fan club. After her death, she became even more of an icon for Mexican youth.

TELEVISION. Mexican television can, for the most part, be broken down into four categories: *telenovelas* (soap operas), weekly dramas, sitcoms, and imported American shows. Telenovelas are by far the most popular and widely aired of the bunch. Occupying a huge block of midday air time, these addictive hour-long examples of dramaturgy tend to run for two to four months before being ousted for a fresh group of characters and conflicts. *Catalina y Sebastian* and *Romántica Obsesión* are two of the current favorite *telenovelas* in Mexico. The half-hour sitcoms that are central to American TV are not as popular in Mexico, though there are a few. Popular shows include *Sabado Gigante, Papá Soltero, Chespirito,* and just about anything on the Canal de las Estrellas (Channel of the Stars). When the World Cup is raging, the *fútbol* (soccer) talk shows such as *Los Protagonistas* dominate the airwaves. American shows are often dubbed; as in the U.S., shows such as *Melrose Place* and *Baywatch* are very popular. Cartoons are imported from both the U.S. and Japan. One cannot claim to have *lived* without having watched at least one episode of Los Simpson.

There are about a dozen major national and regional networks that are the most likely to appear on television sets throughout Mexico. The national networks include: XEW 2, which broadcasts its own *telenovelas* and old Mexican movies; XHGC 5, *Televisa,* which airs children's programming, late-night movies, and police, suspense, and horror shows; Canal 7, which broadcasts children's American shows dubbed into Spanish and some movies; Canal 9, which broadcasts mainly syndicated shows including old Mexican comedy shows, old *telenovelas,* and Mexican movies; Canal 11, *Instituto Politécnico Nacional,* which airs mainly culturally oriented shows and movies; and Canal 13, *Television Azteca,* which airs mainly *telenovelas,* particularly from Brazil, Colombia, Venezuela, and Argentina. In many regions, Canal 22, a cultural channel that airs movies and interviews with artists; and Canal 40, which airs news and music shows, have gained immense popularity.

FILM. "Popular cinema is still alive and well in Mexico," wrote one disgruntled director, "mainly as sex comedies and cop dramas." The recent recession has led to an influx of subtitled Hollywood imports and a paucity of quality films. Mexico's golden age of cinema *(cine de oro)* was kicked off in the 1940s and 50s with Emilio "El Indio" Fernández's *Maria Candelaría* (1943), an honoree at the first Cannes Film Festival in 1946, and Luis Buñuel's *Los Olvidados* (1950), a grisly portrait of *barrio* life in Mexico City. During the 1950s, Buñuel went through what were later referred to as his "Mexican years." During this decade, he produced a series of satirical Latin American films, many of which were filmed in Mexico. The films took off with *The Great Madcap* in 1949. In 1952, he directed *Una Mujer Sin Amor*, a film about a married woman who has a passionate affair that later comes back to haunt her. In 1956, Buñuel collaborated on a French and Mexican co-production and filmed *La Muerte de este Jardín* and in 1959, he filmed a political film about fascism in a mythical South American country called *Fever Mounts in El Pao*. In 1960, Mexican cinema reached a new plateau when Roberto Gavalin's *Macario*—a film about a starving woodcutter who cuts a deal with Death and gets the gift of healing—was the first Mexican film to receive an Oscar nomination.

Throughout the 1990s, many Mexican films have achieved international fame and recognition. One of the more famous films from the 90s was **Maria Novaro's** *Danzón*—a critically acclaimed film in 1991 about a Mexican City telephone operator who journeys to Veracruz to find her ballroom dance partner and love. Other Mexican films such as **Robert Rodriguez's** *El Mariachi* have been readily accepted by the international film community, though more for their bloody appeal than for their cultural significance. But the one Mexican film that has enjoyed perhaps the most cross-over success is the delicious romance *Como Agua para Chocolate (Like Water for Chocolate)*, based on the best-selling **Laura Esquivel** novel and directed by **Alfonso Arau,** now Esquivel's ex-husband. The film has the distinction of being the highest-grossing foreign film in U.S. history.

FOOD AND DRINK

Leave your preconceived notions of what constitutes "real Mexican food" behind and prepare your tastebuds for a culinary treat. Regional favorites rarely found outside of Mexico complement the better-known national dishes. With some dedication (and at times, a little courage) the pleasures of Mexican cuisine can be yours.

Mexicans usually have their big meal of the day—*la comida*—between 2 and 4pm. Restaurants often offer *comida corrida* (sometimes called *la comida* or *el menú*), which is a fixed price meal including soup, salad, tea or *agua fresca*, a *plato fuerte* (main dish), and sometimes a dessert. **Guisado,** a soup or stew with meat, is often the main dish, as is **caldo,** a broth-like soup, or a regular meat dish. *Arroz* (rice, sometimes *con huevos*, with chopped eggs), *frijoles* (beans), and tortillas are always included. *Desayuno* (breakfast) can range from a simple continental-style snack to a grandiose meal that rivals *la comida*. Dinner (*cena*) is usually a light meal or snack served around 8pm.

THE STAPLES

Although there is a wide variety of regional cuisine and local favorites, tortillas are the unifying factor. This millenia-old staple is a flat, round, thin pancake made from either *harina* (wheat flour) or *maiz* (corn flour). Fortunately, restaurants almost always give you a choice. *Arroz* and *frijoles* round out the triumvurate of Mexican staples. This tasty, nutritous, and cheap trio is always served together. Rice is usually yellow Spanish or white Mexican rice and prepared with oil, tomato sauce, onions, and garlic. Beans can range from a thick paste to soupy "baked" beans. Expect to see these staples accompany almost every meal—breakfast, lunch or dinner.

ESTOS HUEVOS

Eggs are prepared in any and all conceivable combinations, and are often the first thing to greet travelers in the morning. In addition to breakfast mainstays like *café con leche* and *pan dulce* (sweetened bread), *huevos al gusto* (eggs any style) are usually served *revueltos* (scrambled) with many different kinds of meat or vegetables. *Jamon* (ham), *tocino* (bacon), and *machaca* (dried, shredded beef) are favorite additions. *Huevos rancheros* (fried eggs served on corn tortillas and covered with a spicy red *salsa*), *huevos albañil* (scrambled eggs cooked in a spicy sauce), *huevos motuleños* (eggs served on a fried corn tortilla, topped with green sauce and sour cream), *huevos ahogados* (eggs cooked in simmering red sauce), and *huevos borrachos* (fried eggs cooked in beer and served with beans) are other common ways in which eggs are prepared. In more expensive restaurants omelettes are offered with any of the common meats plus *camarones* (shrimp) or *langosta* (lobster). To round out your *desayuno*, leave room for the plentiful tortillas, *frijoles*, and *arroz*.

ANTOJITOS

Found on almost any Mexican menu, *antojitos* (little cravings) are equivalent to a large snack or small meal. Technically, an *antojito* can be anything but they largely fall into nine categories. Tacos are small, grilled pieces of meat placed on an open, warm tortilla topped with a row of condiments that usually include lettuce, tomato, guacamole, or hot sauce. Burritos, popular in northern Mexico, are thin, rolled tortillas filled with meat, beans, and cooked vegetables. *Enchiladas* are rolled corn tortillas filled with meat or chicken and baked with sauce and cheese. *Quesadillas* are flat tortillas with cheese melted between them; *quesadillas sincronizadas* (sometimes called gringas) are filled with ham or gyro-style pork. *Tostadas* resemble flat, open tacos, topped with raw vegetables, while *chile rellenos* are a large green chile pepper filled with cheese (and occasionally meat), battered, fried, and served with *salsa*. The *chile relleno* is usually mildly spicy and very delicious. *Tamales* are like dumplings, corn husks filled with ground-corn dough, and chicken or beef. *Chimichangas* are similar to burritos but are deep-fried, producing a rich crunchy shell. *Flautas* are similar to *chimichangas* but are rolled very thinly (like a cigar) before being deep-fried.

MAIN COURSE MEATS, POULTRY, SEAFOOD, AND SOUP

Meat platters usually feature beef. **Bistek** is the standard, fried thin cut of beef. *Carne asada* are thin slices of beef that are fried until crispy. Pricier cuts of steak such as T-bone, filet mignon, or New York steak are sometimes available (the English names are frequently used). Meat can be prepared normally (usually well-done), *empanizada* or *milanesa* (breaded and fried), or *a la mexicana* (charred and topped with Mexican red *salsa*). *Encebollado* describes a serving with grilled onions. Meat dishes are usually served with *arroz*, *frijoles*, tortillas, or *papas fritas*. *Pollo* (chicken) is equally common and often served *rostizado* (spit-roasted over an open fire, "rotisserie"-style) or *asado* (grilled).

Mole, which is arguably Mexico's national dish, is a delectable sauce composed of chiles, chocolate, and spices. *Mole* is usually served over chicken. *Mole poblano* is named after its home, the city of Puebla. A typical recipe for *mole poblano* includes turkey, dried chiles, nuts, seeds, vegetables, spices, and melted chocolate (Ibarra Mexican chocolate is almost always used).

Seafood dishes include *pescado* (generic fish fillet, usually a local catch), *camarones* (shrimp), *langosta* (lobster), *calamar* (fillet of squid), scrumptious *jaiba* (crab), and *huachinango* (we-chee-NAAN-go; red snapper). Seafood is usually served either *empanizado* or in garlic (like the delicious *al mojo de ajo*). Many regions have special ways of preparing seafood: one of the most famous is *a la veracruzana*, a method originating in Veracruz to smother the fish in olives, capers, and olive oil. Soups in Mexico are delicious; among others, *sopa de tortilla* made with bits of softened tortilla, and *sopa de lima* flavored with lime.

LIBATIONS

Cerveza (beer) with tortillas and beans on the list of Mexican standbys. It is impossible to drive through any Mexican town without coming across a double-digit number of Tecate and Corona billboards, painted buildings, and cheap beer stores proudly selling their products. **Tecate** is Mexico's version of Budweiser—cheap and widespread. Popular beers in Mexico (listed roughly in order of quality) are **Bohemia** (a world-class lager), **Negra Modelo** (a fine dark beer), **Dos Equis** (a light, smooth lager), **Pacífico, Modelo, Carta Blanca, Superior, Corona Extra,** and **Sol** (watery and light). Mexicans share their love for bargain beer with the world, as demonstrated by the fact that the Mexican-made Corona Extra is a leading export and tops many international charts—including Canada, Australia, New Zealand, France, Italy, Spain, and most European markets—as one of the most popular beers.

Tequila is king when it comes to Mexican liquor, a more refined version of *mezcal* (distilled from the *maguey* cactus). **Herradura, Tres Generaciones, Hornitos** and **Cuervo 1800** are among the more famous, more expensive, and altogether better brands of tequila. Cheap tequila can be bought for prices you wouldn't believe: one Hermosillo supermarket frequently advertises a liter for under US\$1. While many hard-core tequila-lovers will drink the liquor straight, others may prefer a **margarita** (tequila, triple sec, lime juice, and ice) or **tequila sunrise** (tequila, orange juice, and blackberry brandy) to shots. **Mezcal,** coarser than tequila, is sometimes served with the worm native to the plant—upon downing the shot, you are expected to ingest the worm. Some say it induces hallucination; however evidence is to the contrary. If you get a chance to sample **pulque,** the fermented juice of the *maguey*, don't hesitate—it was the sacred drink of the Aztec nobility—for a reason.

Mexican mixed drinks enjoy at least as much recognition worldwide as its beers. Coffee-flavored **Kahlúa,** Mexico's most exported liqueur, deserves its lofty reputation. Enjoy it with cream, with milk, or as part of a **white Russian** or **black Russian.** Bottles are ridiculously cheap below the border. Frozen drinks aren't too shabby, either; well-made **piña coladas** (pineapple juice, cream of coconut, and light rum), or **coco locos** (coconut milk and tequila served in a hollowed-out coconut) are much harder to find outside Mexico.

There are also plenty of popular beverage options that don't include alcohol. Unique Mexican **refrescos** (sodas) often put their Coke and Pepsi counterparts to shame. *Soda de fresa (*strawberry soda) is memorable; also try *soda de piña* (pineapple soda), *toronja* (grapefruit soda—try Kas brand), *manzanita* (apple soda—try Sidral), and Boing! (mango soda). Soda rarely costs more than 8 pesos, even at fancy restaurants, and usually costs 4 pesos for a bottle or can. As for the noncarbonated, **aguas frescas** come in almost any imaginable fruit or vegetable flavor, including *agua de jaimaca* (jamaca) and *agua de horchata* (rice).

RECOMMENDED READING

One of the best ways to learn about a place is to delve head first into its culture. Mexico has a history rich in self-representation: from the ancient texts of the **Books of Chilam Balam** to the poetry of Octavio Paz. Outsiders, as well as the people of Mexico, have continually explored, envisioned, and re-envisioned Mexico: although it is a wasteland at times, and a wonderland at others, it is always a land fertile with possibility. The complexities and excitement of Mexican history have tempted innumerable scholars; there is no dearth of sources on Mexico. Here are some reading suggestions before you venture out on your own and explore.

MEXICAN LITERATURE IN TRANSLATION

Where the Air is Clear, by Carlos Fuentes, trans. Peden (1976). A monumental book that attempts to capture the vast, constantly changing panorama of Mexico City. Fuentes is Mexico's most eminent novelist and one of the world's most celebrated writers. Also be sure to check out **The Death of Artemio Cruz** (1964) and **Terra Nostra** (1976).

THE PARTY LINE "Waiter," you say, "I ordered a bloody Mary, not a Shirley Temple." He smirks and points to the pink fizzy drink in front of you. *"Ley seca,"* he says. "Makealikeawhat?" you ask. But before you get too confused (and annoyed), realize this is a recent tradition. On the day before elections, the national government applies the *ley seca* (dry law). No alcohol may be bought, sold, or consumed the Saturday before elections or election day itself. Need a smoke? Fat chance. Cigarettes are not sold, and shops close early. No movies are shown on public TV. The reason? Explanations vary. One explanation is that the government wants people sober, alert, and completely sane when they vote, hence the prohibitions on "distractions." Another common explanation is that the government is trying to reduce corrupt party practices. In the past, it was not uncommon for party leaders to set up free liquor stands outside election booths and do some "campaigning." Whatever the reason, Mexicans take this law (and their politics) very seriously. So in this election year, if it's Saturday night and you want to rock 'n' roll, remember two words: *ley seca.* Hit the bottled water and save the beer for early Monday morning.

Pedro Páramo, by Juan Rulfo, trans. Peden (1994). The new translation of this 1955 classic is faithful to the stark, concise language of the original. This oft-studied paragon of Mexican novels deals with a young man's search for his roots in the barren town of Comala in the wake of the Revolution.

Selected Poems of Octavio Paz, trans. Aroul (1984). Paz's grandiose poetry is the stuff of which myths are made. His poetry, replete with phalluses and earth-mothers, is about nothing less than...the cosmic soul of Mexico. The Nobel Prize didn't hurt either.

The Underdogs, by Mariano Azuela, trans. Fornoff (1992). One of the earliest novels (1938) and definitely one of the best about the Revolution. Azuela's experiments with form and style (and his clean, unsentimental prose) initiated a mini-revolution within Latin American literature.

Meditation on the Threshold: a Bilingual Anthology of Poetry, by Rosario Castellanos, trans. Palley (1988). Until her death in 1974, Castellanos was one of Mexico's leading feminist voices. Her poetry combines lyricism and acerbic social commentary on what it means to be a woman in Mexico.

LITERATURE ABOUT MEXICO

Under the Volcano, by Malcolm Lowry (1947). Set in Cuernavaca on the Day of the Dead, Lowry's meditative, moody novel about an alcoholic consulate has been compared to Joyce's *Ulysses.*

Stones for Ibarra, by Harriet Doerr (1984). A tender, atmospheric novel about a couple who move from their home in San Francisco to a deserted mining town in Mexico only to confront tragedy. Winner of the United States National Book Award.

Aztec, by Gary Jennings (1980). What *Shogun* did for ancient Japan, this almost-1000-page mass-market paperback does for ancient Mexico. Tons of violence, sex, and sensationalism. And, of course, there's human sacrifice.

The Power and the Glory, by Graham Greene (1940). Greene's famous novel about the fate of a martyred whiskey priest in Mexico. His book explores the fate of a weak-willed but well-intentioned clergyman struggling with God—a tale charged with meaning for modern Mexico.

HISTORY

Mexico: A History, by Robert Miller (1985). One of the best general histories available, this comprehensive and engaging account of Mexican history starts with the ancient Indian civilizations and passes through the centuries to modern day.

Mexico: From the Olmecs to the Aztecs, by Michael Coe (1994). A first-rate account of the habitation of Mexico from the first hunter-gatherers up through the Spanish Conquest. Beautiful photographs of sites and artifacts help guide the reader through the thousands of years covered.

The Ancient Maya, by Robert Sharer (1994). With over 800 pages dedicated to every site in the Maya region from the early Preclassic to the Postclassic periods, you can't find a more comprehensive or precise account of the Maya past.

The Aztecs, by Richard Townsend (1992). A well-researched, well-organized account of Aztec life that is fun to read, containing information not just on history and art but also about daily life and culture.

Zapata and the Mexican Revolution, by John Womack Jr. (1970). This book goes where few historians have gone before; it beautifully recounts the events and people behind the Mexican Revolution. Although it is loaded with precise history, it reads like a novel. You'll cry when Zapata dies.

Mexico Since Independence, by Leslie Bethell (1991). A historical work detailing major events in Mexican history from 1821 to the present day, written by different scholars.

Mexico: A Biography of Power, by Enrique Krauze (1998). A thorough and entertaining account of Mexican history from 1810 to 1996. This indispensable book takes a "great man" approach—it looks at the pattern of Mexican history by focusing on its leaders.

CURRENT EVENTS AND CONTEMPORARY HISTORY

A New Time for Mexico, by Carlos Fuentes, trans. Castañeda and author (1996). Although the book touches on history from pre-Hispanic times to the 1994 peso crisis, Fuentes here concerns himself primarily with Mexico's future. Political commentary, history, poetry and prose, economic prescriptions—a great introduction to modern Mexico.

EZLN web page: www.ezln.org. An absolute must for anyone remotely interested in the Zapatistas, links, articles, essays, quotes from Subcomandante Marcos, and even bilingual translations of EZLN communiques.

First World, Ha Ha Ha! The Zapatista Challenge, by Elaine Katzenberger (1995). This compilation of journals, poems, articles, and essays by Mexican and U.S. writers is a sensitive introduction to the plight of the residents of Chiapas.

CULTURE AND SOCIETY

The Labyrinth of Solitude, by Octavio Paz, trans. Kemp, Milos, and Belash (1990). Although Paz's alpha-male, instant myth-making can grate, he was Mexico's artistic emissary to the world until his death in 1998. Insanely famous, this book of philosophical reflections on Mexican society and character is a literary landmark.

Across the Wire: Life and Hard Times on the Mexican Border, by Luis A. Urrea (1993). A harrowing, true account of life south of the border. His chronicle of poverty and tragedy in modern-day Tijuana is a result of first-hand experience.

Massacre in Mexico, by Elena Poniatowska, trans. Lane (1975). Perhaps the best chronicle of the 1968 Tlatleloco massacre. One of Mexico's greatest writers uses eyewitness accounts and different voices to recreate this important historical event.

ESSENTIALS

FACTS FOR THE TRAVELER

WHEN TO GO

The Tropic of Cancer bisects Mexico into a temperate north and tropical south, but the climate varies considerably even within these belts. **Northwest Mexico** is the driest area of the country but still offers a unique array of desert flora and fauna, as does arid **Baja California,** which separates the cold, rough Pacific from the tranquil and tepid Sea of Cortés. The **Northeast** is a bit more temperate than the Northwest. The **Pacific Coast,** home to Mexico's famed resorts, boasts warm, tropical weather. Pleasant beaches are also scattered throughout the humid, tranquil **Gulf Coast.** The central region north of Mexico City, known as **El Bajío,** and **South Central Mexico** both experience spring-like weather year-round; the cooler climates of the highlands are tempered by coastal warmth, and natural beauty ranges from world-famous beaches to inland forests. Lush, green jungles obscure the ruins of the ancient civilizations of the Yucatán; interior jungles are hot and humid, while trade winds keep the beaches along the Gulf and Caribbean coasts cool and pleasant.

There are two seasons in Mexico: rainy and dry. The rainy season lasts from May until November (with a hurricane season in the south Aug.-Oct.), and rainfall can be as high as 15cm per month. The southern half of the country averages over 250cm of rainfall per year (75% of that during the rainy season), so a summer vacation is likely to be on the damp side. Expect an average of two to three hours of rain every afternoon. The best time to hit the beaches is during the dry season (Nov.-May), when afternoons are sunny, evenings balmy, and nights relatively mosquito-free.

The tourist season consists of December, the entire summer, *Semana Santa* (Holy Week, the week before Easter), and Easter. If you travel to Mexico during this time, you can expect to pay slightly higher prices at hotels and restaurants, The busy seasons vary regionally; in beach towns and resorts on either coast or Baja, the winter season and U.S. spring break (late Mar.-Apr.) are busy times and the summer is less crowded, while the summer is generally heavily touristed in colonial Mexico.

Average Temp. Low-High	January		May		July		November	
	°C	°F	°C	°F	°C	°F	°C	°F
Acapulco	22-31	72-88	25-32	77-90	25-33	77-91	24-32	75-90
Guadalajara	7-23	45-73	14-31	57-88	15-26	59-79	10-25	50-77
La Paz	13-23	55-73	17-33	63-91	23-36	73-97	17-29	63-84
Mérida	18-28	64-82	21-34	70-93	23-33	73-91	19-29	66-84
Mexico City	6-22	43-72	13-27	55-81	13-24	55-75	9-23	48-73
Monterrey	9-20	48-68	20-31	68-88	22-34	72-93	12-23	54-73
Oaxaca	8-28	46-82	15-32	59-90	15-28	59-82	10-28	50-82
San Cristóbal	5-20	41-68	9-22	48-72	10-22	50-72	7-20	45-68
Tijuana	6-20	43-68	12-23	54-73	16-27	61-81	10-23	50-73
Veracruz	18-25	65-77	25-30	77-86	22-31	75-88	21-28	70-82

DOCUMENTS AND FORMALITIES

MEXICO'S EMBASSIES AND CONSULATES

Embassies: Australia, 14 Perth Ave. Yarralumla, Canberra 2600 ACT (tel. (06) 273 3905; fax 273 1190); **Canada,** 45 O'Connor St. #1500, KIP 1A4 Ottawa, ON. (tel. (613) 233-8988 or 235-9123); **U.K.,** 42 Hertford St., Mayfair, W1Y 7TS, London (tel. (0171) 499 8586; fax 495 4035); **U.S.,** 1911 Pennsylvania Ave. NW, Washington, D.C. 20006 (tel. (202) 728-1600; fax 728-1718).

Consulates: Australia, Level 1, 135-153 New South Head Rd., Edgecliff, Sydney 2027 NSW (tel. (02) 326 1311 or 326 1292; fax 327 1110); **Canada,** 199 Bay St., #4440, Commerce Court West, M5L 1E9 Toronto, ON (tel. (416) 368-2875; fax 368-8342; www.canada.org.mex); **U.K.,** 8 Harlkin St., London SW1 X7DW (tel. (0171) 235 6393; fax 235 5480); **U.S.,** 2827 16th St. NW, Washington, D.C. 20036 (tel. (202) 736-1000; fax 797-8458).

Mexican Government Tourism Office (Secretaría de Turismo or **SECTUR**): tel. 800 4463 9426. **Chicago,** 300 N. Michigan Ave. 4th fl., Chicago, IL 60601 (tel. (312) 606-9015 or 606-9252; fax 606-9012); **Houston,** 10103 Fondret Ave. #450, Houston, TX 77069 (tel. (713) 772-2581); **London,** 60/61 Trafalgar Sq., 3rd fl., London WC2N 5DS (tel. (0171) 930 3222; fax 930 9202); **Los Angeles,** 2401 W. 6th St. 5th fl., Los Angeles, CA 90057 (tel. (213) 351-2069); **Miami,** 400 NW 78th Ave. #203, Miami, FL 33126 (tel. (305) 718-4091; fax 718-4098); **Montreal,** 1 Place Ville Marie #1931, Montreal, Québec H3B 2C3 (tel. (514) 871-1053; fax 871-3825); **New York City,** 21 E. 63rd St., 3rd fl., New York, NY 10021 (tel. (212) 821-0304 or 821-8314; fax 821-0367); **Toronto,** 2 Bloor St. W #1502, Toronto, ON M4W 3E2 (tel. (416) 925-0704 or 925-1876; fax 925-2753); **Vancouver,** (also for the Northwest U.S.), 1610-999 W. Hastings #1610, Vancouver, BC V6C 2W2 (tel. (604) 669-2845; fax 669-3498). All have English and Spanish-speaking representatives and provide maps, information and tourist cards.

EMBASSIES AND CONSULATES IN MEXICO

Canada: Colonia Balanco 529, Mexico D.F. 11560 (tel. (5) 724 79 00).

U.K.: Rio Lerma 71, Mexico D.F. 06500 (tel. (5) 207 24 49).

U.S.: Paseo de la Reforma 305, Colonia Cuauhtémoc, Mexico D.F. (tel. (5) 209 91 00 or (5) 207 20 89 or (5) 207 25 69; for visas: (5) 208 80 27).

U.S. CONSULATES

Ciudad Juárez: Av. López Mateos 924N (tel. (16) 11 3000).

Guadalajara: Progreso 175 (tel. (38) 25 2998).

Hermosillo: Av. Monterrey 141 (tel. (62) 17 2375).

Matamoros: Av. Primera 2002 (tel. (88) 12 4402).

Mérida: Paseo Montejo 453 (tel. (99) 25 5011).

Monterrey: Av. Constitución 411, Poniente 64000 (tel. (83) 45 2120).

Nuevo Laredo: Calle Allende 3330, Col. Jardín (tel. (87) 14 0512).

Tijuana: Tapachula 96 (tel. (66) 81 7400).

PASSPORTS

REQUIREMENTS. Citizens of Australia, Canada, Ireland, New Zealand, South Africa, and the U.K., need valid passports to enter Mexico and to re-enter their own country. Mexico does not allow entrance if the holder's passport expires in under six months; returning home with an expired passport is illegal, and may result in a fine. Citizens of the U.S. are recommended to carry a valid passport, but

ENTRANCE REQUIREMENTS.

Passports: Required for citizens of Australia, Canada, Ireland, New Zealand, South Africa, and the U.K. and recommended for citizens of the U.S. (p. 3).

Visas: Businesspeople, missionaries, and students must obtain visas as well as tourists planning to stay over 180 days (p. 35).

Inoculations: None required; many suggested (p. 17).

Work Permit: Required of all foreigners planning to work or live in Mexico (p. 35).

Driving Permit: All foreign licenses are accepted; insurance is recommended (p. 7).

ESSENTIALS

proof of citizenship (such as a U.S. birth certificate, naturalization certificate, consular report of birth abroad, or a certificate of citizenship) and a photo ID will also be accepted by Mexican authorities.

PHOTOCOPIES. It is a good idea to photocopy the page of your passport that contains your photograph, passport number, and other identifying information, along with other important documents such as visas, travel insurance policies, airplane tickets, and traveler's check serial numbers, in case you lose anything. Carry one set of copies in a safe place apart from the originals and leave another set at home. Consulates also recommend that you carry an expired passport or an official copy of your birth certificate in a part of your baggage separate from other documents.

LOST PASSPORTS. If you lose your passport, immediately notify the local police and the nearest embassy or consulate of your home government. To expedite its replacement, you will need to know all information previously recorded and show identification and proof of citizenship. In some cases, a replacement may take weeks to process, and it may be valid only for a limited time. Any visas stamped in your old passport will be irretrievably lost. In an emergency, ask for immediate temporary traveling papers that will permit you to re-enter your home country. Your passport is a public document belonging to your nation's government. You may have to surrender it to a foreign government official, but if you don't get it back in a reasonable amount of time, inform the nearest mission of your home country.

NEW PASSPORTS. All applications for new passports or renewals should be filed several weeks or months in advance of your planned departure date—remember that you are relying on government agencies to complete these transactions. Most passport offices do offer emergency passport services for an extra charge. Citizens residing abroad who need a passport or renewal should contact their nearest embassy or consulate.

Australia Citizens must apply for a passport in person at a post office, a passport office, or an Australian diplomatic mission overseas. Passport offices are located in Adelaide, Brisbane, Canberra, Darwin, Hobart, Melbourne, Newcastle, Perth, and Sydney. New adult passports cost AUS$126 (for a 32-page passport) or AUS$188 (64-page), and a child's is AUS$63 (32-page) or AUS$94 (64-page). Adult passports are valid for 10 years and child passports for 5 years. For more info, call toll-free (in Australia) 13 12 32, or visit www.dfat.gov.au/passports.

Canada Application forms are available at all passport offices, Canadian missions, many travel agencies, and Northern Stores in northern communities. Passports cost CDN$60, plus a CDN$25 consular fee, are valid for 5 years, and are not renewable. For additional info, contact the Canadian Passport Office, Department of Foreign Affairs and International Trade, Ottawa, ON, K1A 0G3 (tel. (613) 994-3500; www.dfait-maeci.gc.ca/passport). Travelers may also call 800-567-6868 (24hr.); in Toronto, (416) 973-3251; in Vancouver, (604) 586-2500; in Montreal, (514) 283-2152.

ESSENTIALS

Ireland Citizens can apply for a passport by mail to either the Department of Foreign Affairs, Passport Office, Setanta Centre, Molesworth St., Dublin 2 (tel. (01) 671 1633; fax 671 1092; www.irlgov.ie/iveagh), or the Passport Office, Irish Life Building, 1A South Mall, Cork (tel. (021) 27 25 25). Obtain an application at a local Garda station or post office, or request one from a passport office. Passports cost IR£45 and are valid for 10 years. Citizens under 18 or over 65 can request a 3-year passport that costs IR£10.

New Zealand Application forms for passports are available in New Zealand from most travel agents. Applications may be forwarded to the Passport Office, P.O. Box 10526, Wellington, New Zealand (tel. 0800 22 50 50; www.govt.nz/agency_info/forms.shtml). Standard processing time in New Zealand is 10 working days for correct applications. The fees are adult NZ$80, and child NZ$40. Children's names can no longer be endorsed on a parent's passport—they must apply for their own, which are valid for up to 5 years. An adult's passport is valid for up to 10 years.

South Africa South African passports are issued only in Pretoria. However, all applications must still be submitted or forwarded to the applicable office of a South African consulate. Tourist passports, valid for 10 years, cost around SAR80. Children under 16 must be issued their own passports, valid for 5 years, which cost around SAR60. Time for the completion of an application is normally 3 months or more from the time of submission. For further information, contact the nearest Department of Home Affairs Office (www.southafrica-newyork.net/passport.htm).

United Kingdom Full passports are valid for 10 years (5 years if under 16). Application forms are available at passport offices, main post offices, and many travel agents. Apply by mail or in person to one of the passport offices, located in London, Liverpool, Newport, Peterborough, Glasgow, or Belfast. The fee is UK£31, UK£11 for children under 16. The process takes about four weeks, but the London office offers a five-day, walk-in rush service; arrive early. The U.K. Passport Agency can be reached by phone at (0870) 521 04 10, and more information is available at www.open.gov.uk/ukpass/ukpass.htm.

United States Citizens may apply for a passport at any federal or state courthouse or post office authorized to accept passport applications, or at a U.S. Passport Agency, located in most major cities. Refer to the "U.S. Government, State Department" section of the telephone directory or the local post office for addresses. Passports are valid for 10 years (5 years if under 18) and cost US$60 (under 18 US$40). Passports may be renewed by mail or in person for US$40. Processing takes 3-4 weeks. For more info, contact the U.S. Passport Information's 24-hour recorded message (tel. (202) 647-0518) or look on the web at http://travel.state.gov/passport_services.html.

VISAS AND WORK PERMITS

VISAS. For stays in Mexico up to 180 days, visas are not necessary for citizens of Australia, Canada, New Zealand, the U.K., the U.S., and most EU countries. Businesspeople, missionaries, and students must obtain appropriate visas. For more information, send for *Foreign Entry Requirements* (US$0.50) from the **Consumer Information Center,** Department 363D, Pueblo, CO 81009 (tel. (719) 948-3334; www.pueblo.gsa.gov), or contact the **Center for International Business and Travel (CIBT),** 25 W. 43rd St. #1420, New York, NY 10036 (tel. 800-925-2428 or (212) 575-2811 from NY), which secures visas for travel to and from all countries for a variable service charge (US$145 for a 1-year multiple entry visa for businesspeople).

WORK PERMITS. Admission as a visitor does not include the right to work, which is authorized only by a work permit, and entering Mexico to study requires a special visa. U.S. citizens planning to work or live in Mexico should apply for the appropriate Mexican visa (FM-2 or 3). U.S. citizens planning to participate in humanitarian aid missions, human rights advocacy groups or international observer delegations should contact a Mexican embassy or consulate to obtain the

ESSENTIALS

necessary visa. This is especially important in light of recent tensions in the state of Chiapas. U.S. citizens have been detained, expelled or deported for violating their tourist visa status or allegedly interfering in Mexican internal politics.

IDENTIFICATION

When you travel, always carry two or more forms of identification on your person, including at least one photo ID. A passport combined with a driver's license or birth certificate usually serves as adequate proof of your identity and citizenship. Many establishments, especially banks, require several IDs before cashing traveler's checks. Never carry all your forms of ID together, however; you risk being left entirely without ID or funds in case of theft or loss. It is useful to carry extra passport-size photos to affix to the various IDs or railpasses you may acquire.

STUDENT IDENTIFICATION. Although the **International Student Identity Card (ISIC)** (www.isic.org) is the most widely accepted form of student identification internationally, it is not particularly useful in Mexico. A regular **university ID card** usually entitles students to whatever discounts are offered to foreign students; it's definitely worth carrying. Many student discounts in Mexico, however, are only offered to students at Mexican universities.

TEACHER IDENTIFICATION. International Teacher Identity Card (ITIC) offers the same insurance coverage as an ISIC card but limited discounts. For more information on these cards, contact the **International Student Travel Confederation (ISTC),** Herengracht 479, 1017 BS Amsterdam, Netherlands (from abroad call 31 20 421 28 00; fax 421 28 10; email istcinfo@istc.org; www.istc.org).

YOUTH IDENTIFICATION. The International Student Travel Confederation also issues a discount card to travelers who are 25 years old or younger but not students. Known as the International Youth Travel Card (IYTC) (formerly the GO25 Card), this one-year card offers many of the same benefits as the ISIC, and most organizations that sell the ISIC also sell the IYTC. To apply, you will need either a passport, valid driver's license, or copy of a birth certificate, and a passport-sized photo with your name printed on the back. The fee is US$20.

TOURIST CARDS

All persons visiting Mexico for tourism or study for up to 180 days must carry a **Tourist Card (FMT,** for *Folleto de Migración Turistica*) in addition to proof of citizenship. U.S. and Canadian citizens don't need the FMT if they are not staying in the country for more than 72 hours. U.S. and Canadian citizens traveling to Baja California will need a card only if they plan to venture beyond Maneadero on the Pacific Coast, south of Mexicali on Rte. 5.

Tourist cards, like all entry documents, are free of charge. Many people get their cards when they cross the border or when they check in at the airline ticket counter for their flight into Mexico; however, you can avoid delays by obtaining one from a Mexican consulate or tourist office before you leave (see **Embassies and Consulates,** p. 32). You will have to present proof of citizenship, and if your financial condition looks suspect, officials will ask you to flash your return ticket. Travelers from outside North America must present a passport. U.S. and Canadian citizens can obtain a tourist card with an original birth certificate, notarized affidavit of citizenship, or naturalization papers, plus some type of photo ID (with the exception of naturalized Canadians, who must carry a passport). But be forewarned: traveling in Mexico without a passport is asking for trouble. A passport carries much more authority with local officials than does a birth certificate, makes returning home by air a lot easier, and is mandatory for anyone going on to Central America.

ESSENTIALS

On the FMT, you must indicate your intended destination and expected length of stay. Tourist cards are usually valid for 90 days and must be returned to border officials upon leaving the country. However, some border crossings and airport officials have been known to provide 30-day visas by default, and stamp 90-day visas only on request; make sure you get a 90-day stamp if you're staying longer than a month. If you stay in Mexico past your 90-day limit, you will be slapped with a fine. Request a special, 180-day **multiple-entry permit** at your point of entry if you plan to leave and re-enter the country several times within a short time period. Otherwise, you must get a new FMT every time you re-enter the country, even if your old one has not expired. Without the multiple-entry permit, **you cannot reenter Mexico** for 3 days after leaving.

Try to get a card that will be valid longer than your projected stay, since obtaining an extension on a 90-day FMT is a huge hassle: you'll need a physician's authorization stating that you are too ill to travel. If you do need an extension, visit a local office of the **Delegación de Servicios Migratorios** several weeks before your card expires. They also take care of lost cards. While in Mexico, you are required by law to carry your tourist card at all times. Make a photocopy and keep it in a separate place. Although it won't replace a lost or stolen tourist card, a copy should facilitate replacement. If you do lose your card, expect hours of delay and bureaucratic inconvenience while immigration verifies your record of entrance.

Special regulations apply if you are entering Mexico on a business trip, or if you expect to study in the country for more than six months (see **Visas,** p. 35). If you're breezing through Mexico *en route* to Guatemala or Belize, ask for a **Transmigrant Form,** which will allow you to remain in Mexico for up to 30 days. You'll need a passport or current photo ID, a Guatemalan or Belizean visa, and proof of sufficient funds. The transmigrant form is not required for U.S. or Canadian citizens.

CUSTOMS: ENTERING MEXICO

Crossing into Mexico by land can be as uneventful or as complicated as the border guards want it to be. You might be waved into the country or directed to the immigration office to procure a tourist card (FMT) if you don't have one already. You also need a car permit if you're driving. Customs officials will then inspect luggage and stamp papers. If there is anything amiss when you reach the immigration checkpoint 22km into the interior, you'll have to turn back.

A clean, neat appearance will help upon your arrival. Don't pass out *mordidas* (bribes; literally "bites"). They may do more harm than good. Border officials may still request a tip, but they're not supposed to. Above all, do not attempt to carry drugs across the border (see **Drugs and Alcohol,** p. 50).

Entering Mexico by air is easier. Agents process forms and examine luggage, using the press-your-luck traffic light system, right in the airport. Electronics, such as personal computers, might make customs officers uneasy; it is a good idea to write a letter explaining that you need to take your precious laptop into the country for personal use and that it will go back home with you and have the document certified by a Mexican consulate.

Mexican regulations limit the value of goods brought into Mexico by U.S. citizens arriving by air or sea to US$300 per person and by land to US$50 per person. Amounts exceeding the duty-free limit are subject to a 32.8% tax. Also, as of July 1st, 1999, the Mexican government charges tourists traveling to Mexico's interior an **entry fee** of $15 dollars per person.

CUSTOMS: LEAVING MEXICO

Getting out of Mexico, especially at the U.S. border, can take five minutes or five hours—the better your paperwork, the shorter your ordeal. Upon returning home, you must declare all articles you acquired abroad and pay a **duty** on the value of those articles that exceed the allowance established by your country's customs

service. Goods and gifts purchased at **duty-free** shops abroad are not exempt from duty or sales tax at your point of return; you must declare these items as well.

"Duty-free" merely means that you do not have to pay a tax in the country of purchase. To establish value when you return home, keep receipts for items purchased abroad. Since you pay no duty on goods brought from home, record the serial numbers of any expensive items (cameras, computers, radios, etc.) you are taking with you before you begin your travels, and check with your country's customs office to see if it has a special form for registering them.

Most countries object to the importation of firearms, explosives, ammunition, obscene literature and films, fireworks, and lottery tickets. Do not try to take illegal drugs out of Mexico. Label prescription drugs clearly and have the prescription or a doctor's certificate ready to show the customs officer. If you have questions, call the **Mexican Customs Office** in the U.S. (tel. (202) 728-1669) or contact your specific embassy or consulate for more information (see **Embassies and Consulates,** p. 32).

If you are a resident alien of the United States or simply have a Latino surname you may receive a lot of hassling from immigration upon your return. You must make up your own mind as to how to react to this unnecessary harassment. Pragmatists answer as straightforwardly as possible any questions the border patrol might ask (they have been known to ask "who won the Civil War?" and other "prove-it" puzzles).

For more specific information on customs requirements, contact the following information centers:

Australia Australian Customs National Information Line 1 300 363; www.customs.gov.au.

Canada Canadian Customs, 2265 St. Laurent Blvd., Ottawa, ON K1G 4K3 (tel. (613) 993-0534 or 24hr. automated service 800-461-9999; www.revcan.ca).

Ireland The Collector of Customs and Excise, The Custom House, Dublin 1 (tel. (01) 679 27 77; fax 671 20 21; email taxes@revenue.iol.ie; www.revenue.ie/customs.htm).

New Zealand New Zealand Customhouse, 17-21 Whitmore St., Box 2218, Wellington (tel. (04) 473 6099; fax 473 7370; www.customs.govt.nz).

South Africa Commissioner for Customs and Excise, Private Bag X47, Pretoria 0001 (tel. 012 314 99 11; fax 328 64 78).

United Kingdom Her Majesty's Customs and Excise, Custom House, Nettleton Rd., Heathrow Airport, Hounslow, Middlesex TW6 2LA (tel. (0181) 910 36 02/35 66; fax 910 37 65; www.hmce.gov.uk).

United States U.S. Customs Service, Box 7407, Washington D.C. 20044 (tel. (202) 927-6724; www.customs.ustreas.gov).

MONEY

If you stay in hostels and prepare your own food, expect to spend anywhere from US$6-10 per person per day. **Hotel accommodations** start at about US$6 per night for a single and can increase in price dramatically. A basic sit-down meal costs US$3. Carrying cash with you, even in a money belt, is risky but necessary; personal checks from home are usually not accepted and even traveler's checks may not be accepted in some locations.

MONEY CAN'T BUY YOU LOVE The Mexican peso isn't always the friendliest of currencies. Coins in 1, 2, 5, and 10 peso denominations quickly become a nuisance as they weigh down your pocket or split your wallet. Don't be tempted to just leave all of your coins in a large mason jar somewhere: they're absolutely necessary. It depends where you are in Mexico, but a general rule is the smaller the denomination, the better. Amazingly, many of the littler establishments will be unable to make change for a 100 or even 50 peso note. Having more of those pesky coins will save headaches in the long run.

Money From Home In Minutes.

If you're stuck for cash on your travels, don't panic. Millions of people trust Western Union to transfer money in minutes to 165 countries and over 50,000 locations worldwide. Our record of safety and reliability is second to none. For more information, call Western Union: USA 1-800-325-6000, Canada 1-800-235-0000. Wherever you are, you're never far from home.

www.westernunion.com

WESTERN UNION | MONEY TRANSFER

The fastest way to send money worldwide:

CURRENCY AND EXCHANGE

The currency chart below is based on published exchange rates from August 1999.

THE PESO

US$1 = 9.32 PESOS	1 PESO = US$0.11
CDN$1 = 6.22 PESOS	1 PESO = CDN$0.16
UK£1 = 14.92 PESOS	1 PESO = UK£0.07
IR£1 = 12.35 PESOS	1 PESO = IR£0.08
AUS$1 = 5.93 PESOS	1 PESO = AUS$0.17
NZ$1 = 4.90 PESOS	1 PESO = NZ$0.20
SAR1= 1.53 PESOS	1 PESO = SAR0.65

ESSENTIALS

It is cheaper to buy pesos than to buy foreign, so as a rule you should convert money after you arrive in Mexico. However, converting some money before you go lets you zip through the airport while others wait in exchange lines. You should buy at least US$75 worth of pesos, including the equivalent of US$1 in change, before leaving home, especially if you will arrive in the afternoon or on a weekend. This will save time and help you avoid the predicament of having no cash after banking hours. It's sometimes very difficult to get change for large Mexican bills in rural areas. Therefore, it's wise to obtain (and hoard) change when you're in a big city. The symbol for pesos is the same as for U.S. dollars (although a "$" with two bars is always a dollar-sign); frequently **"N"** or **"N$"** also stand for the peso.

Changing money in Mexico can be inconvenient. Some banks won't exchange until noon, when the daily peso quotes come out, and then stay open only until 1:30pm and extract a flat commission. You can switch U.S. dollars for pesos anywhere, but some banks refuse to deal with other foreign currencies; non-U.S. travelers would be wise to keep some U.S. dollars on hand. The more money you change at one time, the less you will lose in the transaction (but don't exchange more than you need or you'll be stuck with *muchos* pesos when you return home). The lineup of national banks in Mexico includes **Banamex, Bancomer,** and **Serfín.**

Casas de Cambio (currency exchange booths) may offer better exchange rates than banks and are usually open as long as the stores near which they do business. In most towns, the exchange rates at hotels, restaurants, and airports are extremely unfavorable; avoid them unless it's an emergency. Withdrawing money directly from an **ATM** is perhaps the best exchange rate you'll find; but remember that most ATM cards charge a fee for international withdrawals (US$1-6), so take out a large enough sum of money to make the fee worthwhile (see **Cash Cards,** p. 45).

If you use traveler's checks or bills, carry some in small denominations (US$50 or less), especially for times when you are forced to exchange money at disadvantageous rates. However, it is good to carry a range of denominations since, depending on location, charges may be levied per check cashed.

TRAVELER'S CHECKS

Traveler's checks are one of the safest and least troublesome means of carrying funds, since they can be refunded if stolen. Several agencies and banks sell them, usually for face value plus a small percentage commission. **American Express** and **Visa** are the most widely recognized. If you're ordering checks, do so well in advance, especially if you are requesting large sums.

However, remember that some places (especially in northern Mexico) are accustomed to American dollars and will accept no substitute. Carry traveler's checks in busy towns and cities, but stick to cash, risky though it may be, when traveling through the less touristed spots, particularly small Mexican towns. It's best to buy most of your checks in small denominations (US$20) to minimize your losses at times when you can't avoid a bad exchange rate. Purchase checks in U.S. dollars, since many *casas de cambio* refuse to change other currencies.

Each agency provides refunds if your checks are lost or stolen, and many provide additional services, such as toll-free refund hotlines in the countries you're visiting, emergency message services, and stolen credit card assistance.

In order to collect a **refund for lost or stolen checks,** keep your check receipts separate from your checks and store them in a safe place or with a traveling companion. Record check numbers when you cash them, leave a list of check numbers with someone at home, and ask for a list of refund centers when you buy your checks. Never countersign your checks until you are ready to cash them, and always bring your passport with you when you plan to use the checks.

American Express: Call 800 251 902 in Australia; in New Zealand 0800 441 068; in the U.K. (0800) 52 13 13; in the U.S. and Canada 800-221-7282. Elsewhere, call U.S. collect 1-801-964-6665; www.aexp.com. American Express Traveler's Checks are the most widely recognized in Mexico.

Citicorp: Call 800-645-6556 in the U.S. and Canada; in Europe, the Middle East, or Africa, call the London office at (171) 508 7007; from elsewhere, call U.S. collect 1-813-623-1709. Commission 1-2%. Guaranteed hand-delivery of traveler's checks when a refund location is not convenient. Call 24hr.

Visa: Call 800-227-6811 in the U.S.; in the U.K. (0800) 895 078; from elsewhere, call 44 1733 318 949 and reverse the charges. Any of the above numbers can tell you the location of their nearest office.

CREDIT CARDS

Credit cards are generally accepted in all but the smallest businesses in Mexico. Major credit cards—**MasterCard** and **Visa** are welcomed most often—can be used to extract cash advances in pesos from associated banks and teller machines throughout Mexico. Credit card companies get the wholesale exchange rate, which is generally 5% better than the retail rate used by banks and other currency exchange establishments. **American Express** cards also work in some ATMs, as well as at AmEx offices and major airports.

All such machines require a **Personal Identification Number (PIN).** You must ask your credit card company for a PIN before you leave; without it, you will be unable to withdraw cash with your credit card outside your home country. If you already have a PIN, check with the company to make sure it will work in Mexico. Memorize your **PIN** code in numeral form since machines in Mexico often don't have letters on their keys. Also, if your PIN is longer than four digits, ask your bank whether the first four digits will work, or whether you need a new number. Many ATMs are outdoors; be cautious and aware of your surroundings when making a withdrawal.

CREDIT CARD COMPANIES. Visa (U.S. tel. 800-336-8472) and **MasterCard** (tel. 800-307-7309) are issued in cooperation with individual banks and some other organizations. **American Express** (U.S. tel. 800-843-2273) has an annual fee of up to US$55, depending on the card. Cardholder services include the option of cashing personal checks at AmEx offices, a 24-hour hotline with medical and legal assistance in emergencies (tel. 800-554-2639 in U.S. and Canada; from abroad call collect 1-202-554-2639), and the American Express Travel Service. Benefits include assistance in changing airline, hotel, and car rental reservations, baggage loss and flight insurance, sending mailgrams and international cables, and holding your mail at one of the more than 1700 AmEx offices around the world.

CASH CARDS

Cash cards—popularly called ATM (Automated Teller Machine) cards—are widespread in Mexico. Depending on the system that your home bank uses, you can probably access your own personal bank account whenever you need money.

ATMs get the same wholesale exchange rate as credit cards. Despite these perks, do some research before relying too heavily on automation. There is often a limit on the amount of money you can withdraw per day (usually about US$500, depending on the type of card and account), and computer networks sometimes fail. The two major international money networks are **Cirrus** (tel. 800-4-CIRRUS/424-7787) and **PLUS** (tel. 800-843-7587). To locate ATMs throughout Mexico, use www.visa.com/pd/atm or www.mastercard.com/atm.

GETTING MONEY FROM HOME

If you need to receive emergency money in Mexico, the cheapest thing to do is to have it sent through a large commercial bank that has associated banks within Mexico. The sender must either have an account with the bank or bring in cash or a money order, and some banks cable money only for a fee. Cabled money should arrive in one to three days if the sender can furnish exact information (i.e. recipient's passport number and the Mexican bank's name and address); otherwise, there will be significant delays. To pick up money, you must show some form of positive identification, such as a passport.

AMERICAN EXPRESS. Cardholders can withdraw cash from their checking accounts at any of AmEx's major offices and many of its representatives' offices, up to US$1000 every 21 days (no service charge, no interest). AmEx (www.americanexpress.com) also offers Express Cash at any of their ATMs in Mexico. Express Cash withdrawals are automatically debited from the Cardmember's checking account or line of credit. Green card holders may withdraw up to US$1000 in a seven day period. There is a 2% transaction fee for each cash withdrawal, with a US$2.50 minimum/$20 maximum. To enroll in Express Cash, Cardmembers may call 800-CASH NOW (227-4669) in the U.S.; outside the U.S. call collect 1-336-668-5041. The AmEx national number in Mexico is (5) 326 26 26.

WESTERN UNION. Travelers from the U.S., Canada, and the U.K. can wire money abroad through Western Union's international money transfer services. In the U.S. and Mexico, call 800-325-6000; in the U.K., call (0800) 833 833; in Canada, call 800-235-0000.

U.S. STATE DEPARTMENT (U.S. CITIZENS ONLY). In emergencies, U.S. citizens can have money sent via the State Department. For US$15, they will forward money within hours to the nearest consular office, which will disburse it according to instructions. The office serves only Americans in the direst of straits abroad; non-American travelers should contact their embassies for information on wiring cash. Check with the State Department or the nearest U.S. embassy or consulate for the quickest way to have the money sent. Contact the Overseas Citizens Service, American Citizens Services, Consular Affairs, #4811, U.S. Department of State, Washington, D.C. 20520 (tel. (202) 647-5225; nights, Sundays, and holidays 647-4000; fax (on demand only) 647-3000; http://travel.state.gov).

TIPPING AND BARGAINING

In Mexico, it can often be hard to know when to leave a tip and when to just walk away. Play it safe by handing a couple pesos to anyone who provides you with some sort of service: this includes the bagboy at the supermarket, the shoeshiner, the old man who offers to carry your luggage half a block to your hotel, the young boys who wash your windshield at the carwash, the eager porters who greet you at the bus station, and the street savvy local who shows you the way to the tourist office. Oddly enough, cab drivers (except in Mexico City) aren't tipped since they don't run on meters. In a restaurant, *camareros* are tipped based on the quality of service; good service deserves at least 15%, especially since devaluation makes meals so cheap to begin with. And never, ever leave without saying *gracias*.

In Mexico, skillful bargaining separates the experienced budget traveler from the more timid tourist. While you can't bargain everywhere, it is expected in many places, especially outdoor *mercados* (markets). You will also have ample opportunities to refine your bargaining skills in Mexico City and Mérida. If you're unsure whether bargaining is appropriate, observe the locals and follow their lead. A working knowledge of Spanish will help convince the seller that you are a serious bargainer, thus awarding you with a better deal. Perhaps the most useful skill is a willingness to walk away from the item you were hoping to purchase if the negotiation isn't going anywhere.

SAFETY AND SECURITY

Mexico is relatively safe, although large cities (especially Mexico City) demand extra caution. After dark, keep away from bus and train stations, subways, and public parks. Shun empty train compartments; many travelers avoid the theft-ridden Mexican train system altogether. When on foot, stay out of trouble by sticking to busy, well-lit streets. Many isolated parks and beaches attract unsavory types as soon as night falls.

 NOT THE REAL THING. Warnings are out throughout Mexico City about well-dressed, foreign-looking and foreign-sounding Mexicans who approach tourists saying they work for *Let's Go* or *Lonely Planet* travel guides; they ask for your address and phone number so they can contact you at the end of your trip for comments. (Neither guide actually does this.) If they get this info out of you, they will proceed to contact your address and tell your loved ones they have kidnapped you, in the process extorting high ransoms. Their scheme has worked on numerous travelers, whose terrified parents have indeed paid the faux-ransom. Call home regularly and don't give out your vital stats, especially to people who pretend they're from *Let's Go*. They're NOT the real thing.

The American Embassy strongly recommends that U.S. citizens traveling to the state of **Chiapas** exercise caution. The Mexican military has reestablished authority in rural towns and villages, however, armed rebels still hold some areas of the state. Tension and violence ebb and flow, especially in areas traditionally affected by political conflict. Those areas include the mountain highlands north of **San Cristóbal de las Casas,** the municipality of **Ocosingo,** and the entire southeastern jungle portion of the state cast of **Comitán.** Some segments of the local population resent the presence of foreigners and express their hostility openly. Check the U.S. State Department's Report on Human Rights Practices at www.state.gov.

Kidnapping, including the kidnapping of non-Mexicans is increasing. "Express" kidnappings have reportedly taken place on well-traveled routes such as the **Toluca Route** leading out of Mexico City. These kidnappings are an attempt to get quick cash in exchange for the release of any individual and do not appear to target the wealthy. Tourists and residents should **avoid driving alone** at night anywhere in Mexico City. In a new tactic, thieves stop lone drivers at night, force them to ingest large quantities of alcohol and rob them of their ATM and credit cards.

In Mexico City, as well as most of the larger metropolitan areas, tourists should practice extreme caution in bars and nightclubs where some establishments may **drug the drinks** to gain control of the patron. The most common crimes in the cities are taxi robberies, armed robbery, pickpocketing and purse snatching. In Mexico City, the areas behind the **U.S. Embassy** and around the **Zona Rosa** are frequent sites of street crime against foreigners.

U.S. citizens can refer to the Department of State's pamphlet *A Safe Trip Abroad* or *Tips for Travelers to Mexico*, which are available by mail from the Superintendent of Documents. U.S. Government Printing Office, Washington, D.C. 20402 or at http://www.access.gpo.gov/su_docs, or via the Bureau of Consular Affairs home page at http://travel.state.gov.

BLENDING IN

Tourists are particularly vulnerable to crime because they often carry large amounts of cash and are not as street savvy as locals. To avoid unwanted attention, try to blend in as much as possible. Respecting local customs (in many cases, dressing more conservatively) may placate would-be hecklers. The gawking camera-toter is a more obvious target than the low-profile traveler. Familiarize yourself with your surroundings before setting out; if you must check a map on the street, duck into a cafe or shop. Also, carry yourself with confidence, as an obviously bewildered bodybuilder is more likely to be harassed than a stern and confident 98-pound weakling. If you are traveling alone, be sure that someone at home knows your itinerary and **never admit that you're traveling alone.**

EXPLORING

Extra vigilance is always wise, but there is no need for panic when exploring a new city or region. Find out about unsafe areas from tourist offices, from the manager of your hotel or hostel, or from a local whom you trust. You may want to carry a **whistle** to scare off attackers or attract attention; memorize the emergency number of the city or area. Whenever possible, *Let's Go* warns of unsafe neighborhoods and areas, but there are some good general tips to follow. When walking at night, stick to busy, well-lit streets and avoid dark alleyways. Do not attempt to cross through parks, parking lots or other large, deserted areas. Buildings in disrepair, vacant lots, and unpopulated areas are all bad signs. The distribution of people can reveal a great deal about the relative safety of the area; look for children playing, women walking in the open, and other signs of an active community. Keep in mind that a district can change character drastically between blocks. If you feel uncomfortable, leave as quickly and directly as you can, but don't allow fear of the unknown to turn you into a hermit. Careful, persistent exploration will build confidence and make your stay in an area that much more rewarding.

GETTING AROUND

If you are using a **car,** learn local driving signals and wear a seatbelt. Children under 40 lbs. should ride only in a specially-designed carseat, available for a small fee from most car rental agencies. Study route maps before you hit the road; some roads have poor (or nonexistent) shoulders, few gas stations, and roaming animals. Watch out for open manholes and irregular pavement which are prevalent on Mexican roads. If you plan on spending a lot of time on the road, you may want to bring spare parts. Be sure to park your vehicle in a garage or well-traveled area. Certain roads should be avoided altogether (see **By Car,** p. 68).

Sleeping in your car is one of the most dangerous (and often illegal) ways to get your rest. If your car breaks down, wait for the police to assist you. If you must sleep in your car, do so as close to a police station or a 24hr. service station as possible. Sleeping out in the open can be even more dangerous—camping is recommended only in official, supervised campsites or in wilderness backcountry.

In Mexico City, exercise caution when flagging down **taxis.** Although many travelers still use the ubiquitous lime-green taxis as a form of cheap transportation, the U.S. State Department issued a warning against hailing cabs in 1998. The State Department recommends that tourists get cabs from hotel taxi stands or that they use *sitios* (radio taxis) or airport taxis. *Sitios* tend to cost about twice as much as the lime-green taxis, but travelers should weigh the relative risk against the cost.

Let's Go does not recommend **hitchhiking** under any circumstances, particularly for women—see **Getting Around,** p. 67 for more information.

SELF-DEFENSE

There is no sure-fire set of precautions that will protect you from all of the situations you might encounter when you travel. A good self-defense course will give you more concrete ways to react to different types of aggression. **Impact, Prepare, and Model Mugging** can refer you to local self-defense courses in the U.S. (tel. 800-345-5425) and Vancouver, Canada (tel. (604) 878-3838). Workshops (2-3hr.) start at US$50 and full courses run US$350-500. Both women and men are welcome.

 FURTHER INFORMATION. The following government offices provide travel information and advisories by telephone or on their web sites:

Australian Department of Foreign Affairs and Trade. Tel. (02) 6261 1111. www.dfat.gov.au.

Canadian Department of Foreign Affairs and International Trade (DFAIT). Tel. 800-267-8376 or (613) 944-4000 from Ottawa. www.dfait-maeci.gc.ca. Call for their free booklet, *Bon Voyage...But.*

United Kingdom Foreign and Commonwealth Office. Tel. (0171) 238 4503. www.fco.gov.uk.

United States Department of State. Tel. (202) 647-5225. travel.state.gov. For their publication *A Safe Trip Abroad,* call (202) 512-1800.

FINANCIAL SECURITY

Mexico is a safe country if travelers take precautions and use common sense. The most dangerous locations are usually in the urban centers. To stay safe, simply be aware of your surroundings and protect yourself and your belongings. Try not to travel at night or alone in dangerous locations.

PROTECTING YOUR VALUABLES

To prevent easy theft, don't keep all your valuables (money, important documents) in one place. Photocopies of important documents allow you to recover them in case they are lost or filched. Carry one copy separate from the documents and leave another copy at home. Label every piece of luggage both inside and out. Don't put a wallet with money in your back pocket. Never count your money in public and carry as little as possible. If you carry a purse, buy a sturdy one with a secure clasp, and carry it crosswise on the side, away from the street with the clasp against you. Secure packs with small combination padlocks which slip through the two zippers.

A **money belt** is the best way to carry cash; you can buy one at most camping supply stores. A nylon, zippered pouch with a belt that sits inside the waist of your pants or skirt combines convenience and security. A **neck pouch** is equally safe, although far less accessible. Refrain from pulling out your neck pouch in public; if you must, be very discreet. Avoid keeping anything precious in a fanny-pack (even if it's worn on your stomach): your valuables will be highly visible and easy to steal. Keep some money separate from the rest to use in an emergency or in case of theft.

CON ARTISTS AND PICKPOCKETS

Among the more colorful aspects of large cities in Mexico are **con artists.** Con artists and hustlers often work in groups, and children are among the most effective. They possess an innumerable range of ruses. Be aware of certain classics: sob stories that require money, rolls of bills "found" on the street, mustard spilled (or saliva spit) onto your shoulder distracting you for enough time to snatch your bag. Be especially suspicious in unexpected situations. Do not respond or make eye contact, walk away quickly, and keep a solid grip on your belongings. Contact the police if a hustler is particularly insistent or aggressive.

In city crowds and especially on public transportation, **pickpockets** are amazingly deft at their craft. Rush hour is no excuse for strangers to press up against you on the metro. If someone stands uncomfortably close, move to another car and hold your bags tightly. Also, be alert in public telephone booths. If you must say your calling card number, do so very quietly; if you punch it in, make sure no one can look over your shoulder. Use caution with your credit cards and make sure to keep the account numbers private. Increasingly, thieves will simply steal the credit card number rather than bother with the entire wallet.

ACCOMMODATIONS AND TRANSPORTATION

Never leave your belongings unattended; crime occurs in even the most demure-looking hostel or hotel. If you feel unsafe, look for places with either a curfew or a night attendant. *Let's Go* lists locker availability in hostels and train stations, but you'll need your own **padlock.** Lockers are useful if you plan on sleeping outdoors or don't want to lug everything with you, but don't store valuables in them. Most hotels also provide lock boxes free or for a minimal fee.

Be particularly careful on **buses;** carry your backpack in front of you where you can see it, don't check baggage on trains, and don't trust anyone to "watch your bag for a second." Thieves thrive on **trains;** professionals wait for tourists to fall asleep and then carry off everything they can. When traveling in pairs, sleep in alternating shifts; when alone, use good judgement in selecting a train compartment: never stay in an empty one, and use a lock to secure your pack to the luggage rack. Keep important documents and other valuables on your person and try to sleep on top bunks with your luggage stored above you (if not in bed with you).

If you travel by **car,** try not to leave valuable possessions—such as radios or luggage—in it while you are away. If your tape deck or radio is removable, hide it in the trunk or take it with you. If it isn't, at least conceal it under something else. Similarly, hide baggage in the trunk—although savvy thieves can tell if a car is heavily loaded by the way it sits on its tires.

DRUGS AND ALCOHOL

Drinking in Mexico is not for amateurs; bars and *cantinas* are strongholds of Mexican *machismo*. When someone calls you *amigo* and orders you a beer, bow out quickly unless you want to match him glass for glass in a challenge that could last several days. Avoid public drunkenness—it is against the law. Locals are fed up with teenage (and older) *gringos* who cross the border for nights of debauchery.

Mexico rigorously prosecutes drug cases. Note that a minimum jail sentence awaits anyone found guilty of possessing any drug, and that Mexican law does not distinguish between marijuana and other narcotics. Even if you aren't convicted, arrest and trial will be long, dangerous, and unpleasant. Derived from Roman and Napoleonic law, the Mexican judicial process does not assume that you are innocent until proven guilty but vice versa, and it is not uncommon to be detained for a year before a verdict is reached. Foreigners and suspected drug traffickers are not released on bail. Ignorance of Mexican law is no excuse—"I didn't know it was illegal" won't get you out of jail. Furthermore, there is little your embassy can do other than inform your relatives and bring care packages to you in jail.

Finally, don't even think about bringing drugs back into the U.S.; Customs agents and their perceptive K-9s won't be amused. On the northern routes, especially along the Pacific coast, expect to be stopped repeatedly by burly, humorless troopers looking for contraband. That innocent-looking hitchhiker you were kind enough to pick up may be a drug peddler with a stash of illegal substances. If the police catch it in your car, the drug possession charges will extend to you, and your car may be confiscated. Under no circumstances should you carry **illegal drugs** in any way, shape, or form. If you carry **prescription drugs** while you travel, it is vital to have a copy of the prescriptions themselves readily accessible at country borders.

HEALTH

Before you can say "pass the *jalapeños*," a long-anticipated vacation can turn into an unpleasant study of the wonders of the Mexican health care system. The main plague of many visitors to Mexico results from their drinking anything made with unpurified water. If it's not purified, don't drink it. While illness can typically be fended off with preventive measures (see **Before You Go,** below), local pharmacists can give shots and dispense other remedies should mild illness prove inescapable. Wherever possible, *Let's Go* lists a pharmacy open for extended hours. If none are listed, ask a policeman or cab driver. If you have an emergency and the door is locked, knock loudly; someone is probably sleeping inside.

BEFORE YOU GO

For minor health problems, bring a compact **first-aid kit,** including bandages, aspirin or other pain killer, antibiotic cream, a thermometer, a Swiss army knife with tweezers, moleskin, decongestant for colds, motion sickness remedy, medicine for diarrhea or stomach problems (Pepto Bismol tablets or liquid and Immodium), sunscreen, insect repellent, burn ointment, and a syringe for emergency medical purposes (get a letter of explanation from your doctor). Those using glasses or contact lens should bring adequate supplies and an extra prescription. Mexican equivalents can be hard to find and could irritate your eyes, although almost all pharmacies will carry saline solution. Also, carry an extra prescription and pair of glasses or arrange to have your doctor or a family member send a replacement pair in an emergency.

In your **passport,** write the names of any people you wish to be contacted in case of a medical emergency, and also list any **allergies** or medical conditions you would want doctors to be aware of. Allergy sufferers might want to obtain a full supply of any necessary medication before the trip. Matching a prescription to a Mexican equivalent is not always easy, safe, or possible. Carry up-to-date, legible prescriptions or a statement from your doctor stating the medication's trade name, manufacturer, chemical name, and dosage. While traveling, be sure to keep all medication with you in your carry-on luggage.

IMMUNIZATIONS

Visitors to Mexico do not need to carry vaccination certificates (though anyone entering Mexico from South America or Africa may be asked to show proof of vaccination for yellow fever). No vaccinations are required for U.S.

citizens entering Mexico; however, a few medical precautions can make your trip a safer one. Take a look at your immunization records before you go. Travelers over two years old should be sure that the following vaccines are up to date: MMR (for measles, mumps, and rubella); DTaP or Td (for diptheria, tetanus, and pertussis); OPV (for polio); HbCV (for haemophilus influenza B); and HBV (for hepatitus B). Hepatitis A vaccine and/or immune globulin (IG), as well as rabies vaccine is recommended for travelers to all areas of Mexico. Those traveling in rural areas should also seek typhiod and cholera immunizations Check with a doctor for guidance through this maze of injections.

 INOCULATION REQUIREMENTS. Mexico does not require visitors to carry vaccination certificates. It is advisable, however, for travelers to receive vaccinations for Hepatitis B, rabies, and typhoid fever and malaria tablets.

USEFUL ORGANIZATIONS

The U.S. **Centers for Disease Control and Prevention (CDC)** (888-232-3299; www.cdc.gov) is an excellent source of information for travelers around the world and maintains an international fax information service for travelers. The CDC also publishes the booklet *"Health Information for International Travelers"* (US$20), an annual global rundown of disease, immunization, and general health advice. This book may be purchased by sending a check or money order to the Superintendent of Documents, U.S. Government Printing Office, P.O. Box 371954, Pittsburgh, PA, 15250-7954. Orders can be made by phone (tel. (202) 512-1800) with a major credit card (Visa, MasterCard, or Discover).

The **United States State Department** (http://travel.state.gov) compiles Consular Information Sheets on health, entry requirements, and other issues for all countries of the world. For quick information on travel warnings, call the **Overseas Citizens' Services** (tel. (202) 647-5225; after hrs. 647-4000). To receive the same Consular Information Sheets by fax, dial (202) 647-3000 directly from a fax machine and follow the recorded instructions. The State Department's regional passport agencies in the U.S., field offices of the U.S. Chamber of Commerce, and U.S. embassies and consulates abroad provide the same data, or send a self-addressed, stamped envelope to the Overseas Citizens' Services, Bureau of Consular Affairs, Room 4811, U.S. Department of State, Washington, D.C. 20520.

For **more information**, consult the *International Travel Health Guide*, by Stuart Rose, MD (Travel Medicine; US$20); Travel Medicine at www.travmed.com; or the *First-Aid and Safety Handbook* (Red Cross, 285 Columbus Ave., Boston, MA 02116-5114; tel. 800-564-1234; US$5).

MEDICAL ASSISTANCE ON THE ROAD

The quality of medical care in Mexico often varies directly with the size of the city or town you are visiting. This also goes for the availability of English-speaking medical practitioners. Medical care in Mexico City is first-class, while care in most major cities is quite adequate. Medical care in more rural areas, though, can be spotty and limited. Along with the town clinic (IMSS), local pharmacists can give shots and dispense other remedies should mild illness prove inescapable. Wherever possible, *Let's Go* lists a pharmacy open for extended hours. If one is not listed, ask a policeman or cab driver. If you have an emergency and the door is locked, knock loudly; someone is probably sleeping inside.

If you are concerned about being able to access medical support while traveling, contact one of these two services: **Global Emergency Medical Services (GEMS)** has products called *MedPass* that provide 24-hour international medical assistance and support coordinated through registered nurses who have online access to your medical information, your primary physician, and a worldwide network of screened, credentialed English-speaking doctors and hospitals. Subscribers also receive a personal medical record that contains vital information in case of emergencies, and GEMS will pay for medical evacuation if necessary. Prices start at about US$35 for a 30-day trip and run up to about US$100 for annual services. For more information contact them at 2001 Westside Dr. #120, Alpharetta, GA 30004 (800-860-1111; fax (770) 475-0058; www.globalems.com). The **International Association for Medical Assistance to Travelers (IAMAT)** has free membership and offers a directory of English-speaking doctors around the world who treat members for a set fee schedule, and detailed charts on immunization requirements, various tropical diseases, climate, and sanitation. Chapters include: **U.S.**, 417 Center St., Lewiston, NY 14092 (tel. (716) 754-4883, 8am-4pm; fax (519) 836-3412; email iamat@sentex.net; www.sentex.net/~iamat); **Canada,** 40 Regal Rd., Guelph, ON, N1K 1B5 (tel. (519) 836-0102) or 1287 St. Clair Ave. W., Toronto, ON M6E 1B8 (tel. (416) 652-0137; fax (519) 836-3412); **New Zealand,** P.O. Box 5049, Christchurch 5 (fax (03) 352 4630; email iamat@chch.planet.org.nz).

If your regular **insurance** policy does not cover travel abroad, you may wish to purchase additional coverage, particularly for traveling in Mexico. With the exception of Medicare, most health insurance plans cover members' medical emergencies during trips abroad; check with your insurance carrier to be sure. For more information on, see **Insurance,** p. 56.

MEDICAL CONDITIONS

Those with medical conditions (e.g., diabetes, allergies to antibiotics, epilepsy, heart conditions) may want to obtain a stainless steel **Medic Alert** identification tag (US$35 the first year, and $15 annually thereafter), which identifies the condition and gives a 24-hour collect-call information number. Contact the Medic Alert Foundation, 2323 Colorado Ave., Turlock, CA 95382 (800-825-3785; www.medicalert.org). Diabetics can contact the **American Diabetes Association,** 1660 Duke St., Alexandria, VA 22314 (800-232-3472), to receive copies of the article "Travel and Diabetes" and a diabetic ID card, which carries messages in 18 languages explaining the carrier's diabetic status.

ENVIRONMENTAL HAZARDS

Heat exhaustion and dehydration: Heat exhaustion, characterized by dehydration and salt deficiency, can lead to fatigue, headaches, and wooziness. Avoid heat exhaustion by drinking plenty of clear fluids and eating salty foods, like crackers. Always drink enough liquids to keep your urine clear. Alcoholic beverages are dehydrating, as are coffee, strong tea, and caffeinated sodas. Wear a hat, sunglasses, and a lightweight longsleeve shirt in hot sun, and take time to acclimate to a hot destination before seriously exerting yourself. Continuous heat stress can eventually lead to **heatstroke,** characterized by rising body temperature, severe headache, and cessation of sweating. Heatstroke is rare but serious, and victims must be cooled off with wet towels and taken to a doctor as soon as possible.

Sunburn: If you're prone to sunburn, bring sunscreen with you (don't worry; beach resorts do have an ample supply) and apply it liberally and often to avoid burns and risk of skin cancer. If you are planning on spending time near water, in the desert, or in the mountains, you are at risk of getting burned, even through clouds. Protect your eyes with good sunglasses, since ultraviolet rays can damage the retina of the eye after too much exposure. If you get sunburned, drink more fluids than usual and apply Calamine or an aloe-based lotion.

Hypothermia: While hypothermia may be the last thing on your mind on a sizzling Mexican beach, remember that hypothermia can occur anytime outside air temperature is lower than your internal temperature. Wet conditions greatly exacerbate the risk. A rapid drop in body temperature is the clearest warning sign of overexposure to cold. Victims may also shiver, feel exhausted, have poor coordination or slurred speech, hallucinate, or suffer amnesia. Seek medical help, and *do not let hypothermia victims fall asleep—*their body temperature will continue to drop and they may die. To avoid hypothermia, keep dry, wear layers, and stay out of the wind. In wet weather, wool and synthetics such as pile retain heat. Most other fabric, especially cotton, will make you colder.

PREVENTING DISEASE

INSECT-BORNE DISEASES

Many diseases are transmitted by insects—mainly mosquitoes, fleas, ticks, and lice. Be aware of insects in wet or forested areas, while hiking, and especially while camping. **Mosquitoes** are most active from dusk to dawn. Use insect repellents which have a 30%-35% concentration of DEET (5%-10% is recommended for children). Wear long pants and long sleeves (fabric need not be thick or warm; tropic-weight cottons can keep you comfortable in the heat) and **buy a mosquito net** for travel in rural (especially coastal and jungle) regions. Wear shoes and socks, and tuck long pants into socks. Soak or spray your gear with permethrin, which is licensed in the U.S. for use on clothing. Natural repellents can be useful supplements: taking vitamin B-12 pills regularly can eventually make you smelly to insects, as can garlic pills. Calamine lotion or topical cortisones (like Cortaid) may stop insect bites from itching, as can a bath with a half-cup of baking soda or oatmeal. **Ticks**—responsible for Lyme and other diseases—can be particularly dangerous in rural and forested regions of Mexico. Pause periodically while walking to brush off ticks using a fine-toothed comb on your neck and scalp. Do not try to remove ticks by burning them or coating them with nail polish remover or petroleum jelly.

Malaria is transmitted by *Anopheles* mosquitoes that bite at night, and is a risk in many rural regions of Mexico, particularly along the west and southeastern coasts (Campeche, Chiapas, Colima, Guerrero, Sinaloa, Michoacan, Nayarit, Oaxaca, Tabasco, and Quintana Roo). Incubation period varies; it could take months for an infected person to show symptoms. Early symptoms include fever, chills, aches, and fatigue, followed by high fever and sweating, sometimes with vomiting and diarrhea. See a doctor for any flu-like sickness that occurs after travel in a risk area, and get tested immediately. Left untreated, malaria can cause anemia, kidney failure, coma, and death, and is an especially serious threat to pregnant women. The least danger exists in more urbanized areas. It is advisable to use mosquito repellent in the evenings and when visiting coastal and jungle regions. There are a number of oral prophylactics to protect against the disease. Western Doctors typically prescribe **mefloquine** (sold under the name Lariam) or **doxycycline.** Both these drugs and other malaria treatments can have very serious side effects, including slowed heart rate and nightmares, which your physician can explain.

Dengue fever is an "urban viral infection" transmitted by *Aedes* mosquitoes, which bite during the day rather than at night. Dengue has flu-like symptoms and is often indicated by a rash 3-4 days after the onset of fever. Symptoms for the first 2-4 days include chills, high fever, headaches, swollen lymph nodes, muscle aches, and in some instances, a pink rash on the face. Then the fever quickly disappears, and profuse sweating follows. For 24 hours there is no fever, but a rash appears all over the body. If you think you have contracted dengue fever, see a doctor, drink plenty of liquids, and take fever-reducing medication such as acetaminophen (Tylenol). *Never take aspirin to treat dengue fever.*

FOOD- AND WATER-BORNE DISEASES

One of the biggest health threats in Mexico is the water. Traveler's diarrhea, known in Mexico as *turista*, often lasts two or three days (symptoms include cramps, nausea, vomiting, chills, and a fever as high as 103°F (39°C)) and is the dastardly consequence of ignoring the following advice: never drink unbottled water; ask for *agua purificada* in restaurants and hotels. If you must purify your own water, bring it to a rolling boil (simmering isn't enough) and let it boil for about 30 minutes, or treat it with iodine drops or tablets. Don't brush your teeth with tap water, and don't even rinse your toothbrush under the faucet. Keep your mouth closed in the shower. Many a sorry traveler has been fooled by the clever disguise of impure water—the treacherous ice cube. Stay away from those tasty-looking salads: uncooked vegetables (including lettuce and coleslaw) are a great way to get *turista*. Other culprits are raw shellfish, unpasteurized milk, and sauces containing raw eggs. Peel fruits and vegetables before eating them. Beware of food from markets or street vendors that may have been "washed" in dirty water or fried in rancid oil. Juices, peeled fruits, and exposed coconut slices are all risky. Also beware of frozen treats that may have been made with bad water. A golden rule in Mexico: boil it, peel it, cook it—or forget it. Otherwise, your stomach will not forgive you.

Virtually everyone gets *turista* on their first trip to Mexico; many get it every time they visit, regardless of how careful they are with food; don't fret. A common symptomatic diarrhea-only treatment is **Immodium** (the liquid works faster), but to combat all-out *turista*, forget standard remedies like Pepto-Bismol and take **Lomotil**, a miracle drug sold over the counter in Mexican pharmacies. Avoid anti-diarrheals if you suspect you have been exposed to contaminated food or water, which puts you at risk for other diseases. The most dangerous side effect of diarrhea is dehydration; the simplest and most effective anti-dehydration formula is 8 oz. of (clean) water with a ½ tsp. of sugar or honey and a pinch of salt. Also good are soft drinks without caffeine, and salted crackers. Down several of these remedies a day, rest, and wait for the disease to run its course. If you develop a fever or your symptoms don't go away after four or five days, consult a doctor. Also consult a doctor if children develop traveler's diarrhea, since treatment is different.

Hepatitis A (distinct from B and C, see below) is a high risk in Mexico. The disease is a viral infection of the liver acquired primarily through contaminated water, ice, shellfish, or unpeeled fruits, and vegetables, but also from sexual contact. Symptoms include fatigue, fever, loss of appetite, nausea, dark urine, jaundice, vomiting, aches and pains, and light stools. Ask your doctor about the vaccine called Havrix, or ask to get an injection of immune globulin (IG; formerly called gamma globulin). Risk is highest in rural areas and the countryside, but is also present in urban areas.

Typhoid fever is common in Mexico, especially in rural areas. Transmitted through contaminated food and water and by direct contact, typhoid produces fever, headaches, fatigue, and constipation in its victims. In recent years, **cholera,** caused by bacteria in contaminated food, reached epidemic stages in parts of Mexico. Cholera's symptoms are diarrhea, dehydration, vomiting, and cramps; it can be fatal if untreated. Vaccines are recommended for those planning to travel to rural areas and persons with stomach problems.

OTHER INFECTIOUS DISEASES

Rabies is transmitted through the saliva of infected animals. It is fatal if untreated. Avoid contact with animals, especially strays. If you are bitten, wash the wound thoroughly and seek immediate medical care. Once you begin to show symptoms (thirst and muscle spasms), the disease is in its terminal stage. If possible, try to locate the animal that bit you to determine whether it does indeed have rabies. A rabies vaccine is available but is only semi-effective. Three shots must be administered over one year.

Hepatitis B is a viral infection of the liver transmitted through the transfer of bodily fluids, by sharing needles, or by having unprotected sex. Its incubation period varies and can be much longer than the 30-day incubation period of Hepatitis A. A person may not begin to show symptoms until many years after infection. The CDC recommends the Hepatitis B vaccination for health-care workers, sexually active travelers, and anyone planning to seek medical treatment abroad. Vaccination consists of a 3-shot series given over a period of time, and should begin 6 months before traveling.

Hepatitis C is like Hepatitis B, but the modes of transmission are different. Intravenous drug users, those with occupational exposure to blood, hemodialysis patients, or recipients of blood transfusions are at the highest risk, but the disease can also be spread through sexual contact and sharing of items like razors and toothbrushes, which may have traces of blood on them.

AIDS, HIV, STDS

Acquired Immune Deficiency Syndrome (AIDS) is a growing problem around the world. The World Health Organization estimates that there are around 30 million people infected with the HIV virus, and women now represent 40% of all new HIV infections. Mexico does not require HIV testing for travelers entering the country.

The easiest mode of HIV transmission is through direct blood-to-blood contact with an HIV-positive person; *never* share intravenous drug, tattooing, or other needles. The most common mode of transmission is sexual intercourse. Health professionals recommend the use of latex condoms. Since it isn't always easy to buy condoms when traveling, take a supply with you before you depart for your trip.

For more information on AIDS, call the **U.S. Centers for Disease Control's** 24-hour hotline at 800-342-2437. In Europe, contact the **World Health Organization,** Attn: Global Program on AIDS, Av. Appia 20, 1211 Geneva 27, Switzerland (tel. 44 22 791 21 11, fax 791 31 11), for statistical material on AIDS internationally. Council's brochure, *Travel Safe: AIDS and International Travel,* is available at all Council Travel offices and at their web site (www.ciee.org/study/safety/travelsafe.htm).

Sexually transmitted diseases (STDs) such as gonorrhea, chlamydia, genital warts, syphilis, and herpes are easier to catch than HIV, and some can be just as deadly. Warning signs for STDs include: swelling, sores, bumps, or blisters on sex organs, rectum, or mouth; burning and pain during urination and bowel movements; itching around sex organs; swelling or redness in the throat, flu-like symptoms with fever, chills, and aches. If these symptoms develop, see a doctor immediately. When having sex, condoms may protect you from certain STDs, but oral or even tactile contact can lead to transmission.

WOMEN'S HEALTH

Women traveling in unsanitary conditions are vulnerable to **urinary tract** and **bladder infections,** common and severely uncomfortable bacterial diseases that cause a burning sensation and painful urination. To avoid these infections, drink plenty of vitamin-C-rich juice and plenty of clean water, and urinate frequently, especially right after intercourse. Untreated, these infections can lead to kidney infections, sterility, and even death. If symptoms persist, see a doctor.

Tampons and **pads** that are on sale are unlikely to be your preferred brands, so it may be advisable to take supplies along. **Reliable contraceptive devices** may also be difficult to find. Women on the pill should bring enough to allow for possible loss or extended stays. Bring a prescription, since forms of the pill vary a good deal. Women who use a diaphragm should bring enough contraceptive jelly. Though condoms are increasingly available, you might want to bring your favorite brand before you go, as availability and quality vary.

Abortion is illegal in Mexico; you'll have to cross the border to have one performed legally and safely. In the U.S., the National Abortion Federation Hotline, 1755 Massachusetts Ave. NW, Washington, D.C. 20036 (tel. 800-772-9100; open M-F 9am-7pm) provides referrals. For **more information,** consult the *Handbook for Women Travellers,* by Maggie and Gemma Moss (Piatkus Books; US$15).

INSURANCE

Travel insurance generally covers four basic areas: medical coverage, property loss, trip cancellation/interruption, and emergency evacuation. Although regular policies may extend to travel-related accidents, consider travel insurance if the cost of potential trip cancellation/interruption is greater than you can absorb.

Medical insurance (especially university policies) often covers costs incurred abroad; check with your provider. Canadians are partially protected by their home province's health insurance during travel; check with the provincial Ministry of Health or Health Plan Headquarters for details. **Homeowners' insurance** often covers theft during travel and loss of travel documents up to $500. **ISIC** and **ITIC** provide

ESSENTIALS

basic insurance benefits, including $100 per day of in-hospital sickness for a maximum of 60 days, $3000 of accident-related medical reimbursement, and $25,000 for emergency medical transport (see **Student and Teacher Identification,** p. 37). **American Express** (800-528-4800) grants most cardholders automatic car rental insurance (collision/theft, but not liability) and ground travel accident coverage of $100,000 on flight purchases made with the card. Prices for separately purchased full coverage travel insurance generally runs about $50 per week, while trip cancellation/interruption may be purchased separately for about $5.50 per $100 of coverage.

INSURANCE PROVIDERS. Council and **STA** (see p. 65 for complete listings) offer a range of plans that can supplement your basic insurance coverage. Other private insurance providers in the **U.S.** include: **Access America** (800-284-8300); **Berkely Group/Carefree Travel Insurance** (800-323-3149 or (516) 294-0220; info@berkely.com; www.berkely.com); **Globalcare Travel Insurance** (800-821-2488; www.globalcare-cocco.com); and **Travel Assistance International** (800-821-2828 or (202) 828-5894; email wassist@aol.com; www.worldwide-assistance.com). **U.K.** providers include **Campus Travel** (tel. (01865) 258 000) and **Columbus Travel Insurance** (tel. (0171) 375 0011). In **Australia** try **CIC Insurance** (tel. (02) 9202 8000).

PACKING

Pack according to the extremes of climate you may experience and the type of travel you'll be doing. **Pack light:** a good rule is to lay out only what you absolutely need, then take half the clothes and twice the money. No matter when you're traveling; it's always a good idea to bring a rain jacket (Gore-Tex is a miracle fabric that's both waterproof and breathable), a warm jacket or wool sweater, and sturdy shoes and thick socks. Remember that wool will keep you warm even when soaked through, whereas wet cotton is colder than wearing nothing at all. If you plan to be doing a lot of hiking, see **Camping and the Outdoors,** p. 59.

LUGGAGE. Toting a **suitcase** or **trunk** is fine if you will stay in one or two cities, or if you will be driving a car most of the time, but is less convenient if you will travel frequently on public transportation. If you plan to cover most of your itinerary by foot, a sturdy **frame backpack** is unbeatable (see **Backpacks,** p. 59). In addition to your main bag, a small backpack, rucksack, or courier bag may be useful as a **daypack** for sightseeing trips and can double as an airplane **carry-on.** An empty, lightweight **duffel bag** packed inside your luggage may also be useful so that you can fill your luggage with purchases and keep dirty clothes in the duffel.

SLEEPSACKS. Some youth hostels require that guests bring their own sleepsacks or rent one at the hostel. If you plan to stay in hostels you can avoid linen charges by making the requisite sleepsack yourself: fold a full size sheet in half the long way, and sew it closed along the open long side and one of the short sides. Sleepsacks can also be bought at any Hostelling International outlet store.

ELECTRIC CURRENT. Appliances in Mexico run off the same voltage and plugs as the rest of North America: 110V, parallel plugs. European electrical appliances (220V) don't like 110V current, though. Visit a hardware store for an adapter (which changes the shape of the plug) and a converter (which changes the voltage). Don't make the mistake of using only an adapter (unless appliance instructions explicitly state otherwise).

FILM. Film in Mexico generally costs about 40 pesos for a roll of 24 color exposures. If you're not a serious photographer, you might want to consider bringing a **disposable camera** or two rather than an expensive permanent one. Either way, definitely bring a camera to remember Mexico's natural splendor. Despite disclaimers, airport security X-rays *can* fog film, so either buy a lead-lined pouch, sold at camera stores, or ask the security to hand inspect it. Always pack it in your carry-on luggage, since higher-intensity X-rays are used on checked luggage.

OTHER USEFUL ITEMS. Carry a **first-aid kit** (see p. 51). Other useful items include: vitamins; umbrella; sealable plastic bags (for damp clothes, soap, and spillables); alarm clock; sun hat; sunglasses; needle and thread; safety pins; rubber bands; water bottle; towel; compass; padlock; whistle; flashlight; cold-water soap; earplugs; electrical tape to patch tears; garbage bags; calculator for currency conversion; flip-flops for the shower; money-belt; razors; tampons; and condoms.

ACCOMMODATIONS

HOTELS

Bargain-seekers will not be disappointed with Mexico's selection of hotels. Although some (particularly in resort towns) are among the world's most overpriced, the majority of Mexican accommodations are shockingly affordable. Usually located within a block or two of the *zócalo*, the cheapest hotels rarely provide private bathrooms or air conditioning, though they do often have hot water and/or fans. Slightly higher-priced hotels usually reside in the same district but are much better equipped, including rooms with private bathrooms (often some with and some without). Before accepting any room, ask to see it, and always find out before paying whether the price includes any meals and if there are any extra taxes or surcharges.

All hotels, ranging from luxury resorts in Cancún to dumps in Monterrey, are controlled by the government's **Secretaría de Turismo (SECTUR).** This ensures that hotels of similar quality charge similar prices; you should always ask to see an up-to-date **official tariff sheet** if you doubt the quoted price. Although hotel prices are regulated, proprietors are not prohibited from charging *less* than the official rate. If the hotel looks like it hasn't seen a customer in several weeks, a little bargaining may work wonders, especially if you offer to stay a number of days. For a room with one bed, request *una habitación (un cuarto) con una cama.* If bedding down with a fellow wayfarer, ask for one *con dos camas* (with two beds).

For the bare-bones budget traveler, the hammock is the way to go, particularly on the coast: if you plan to travel on a shoestring, buy one. Most beach towns in Mexico are dotted with *palapas* (palm-tree huts). For a small fee, open-air restaurants double as places to hang your hat and hammock when the sun sets. In small *yucateco* towns, locals often let travelers use hammock hooks for a pittance.

Hotels in Mexico often lock their doors at night, and small-town establishments may do so surprisingly early. A locked door doesn't necessarily mean "closed for the night," as someone is usually on duty. By arriving early in small towns or calling ahead if you can't avoid arriving late, and by checking with the hotel desk before going out for a late night on the town, you'll be able to stay out as late as you want to, and help dispel the Mexican myth of the obnoxious foreigner.

Reservations are absolutely necessary during Christmas, Semana Santa (the week before Easter), and local festivals. However, at most other times, even during the summer season, you need not worry much about reserving budget hotels ahead.

HOSTEL

Hostels in Mexico are generally youth-oriented, dorm-style accommodations, often in large single-sex rooms with bunk beds. With a few exceptions, Mexican hostels tend to be run-down and far from town. Their ban on alcohol, smoking restrictions, and limited hours also deter many budget travelers. Although a bit cheaper than hotels, the couple of dollars you save don't usually make up for the inconvenience. A bed in a hostel will average around 40 pesos. Many are associated with Causa Joven, a government-supported organization which offers discounts (usually 10%-15%) for Hostelling International (HI) members. Email them at biecjuv@causajoven.gob.mx for more information. Another comprehensive web site which includes information on Mexican hostels is www.hostels.com.

CAMPING AND THE OUTDOORS

Camping in Mexico can be relaxing or harrowing, memorable or nondescript (but always cheap). Many people who are accustomed to clean and well-maintained campgrounds may be in for a few surprises. By in large, Mexican national parks exist only in theory. The "protected lands" are often indistinguishable from the surrounding countryside or city. Trails, campgrounds, and park rangers are strictly *gringo* concepts. It is wise to purchase camping equipment before you leave. Any savings you might be expecting in Mexico can be quickly negated by low quality or poor selection.

Camping is always an option, as lax permit laws and public beaches (every meter of beach in Mexico is public property) give campers a wide selection of where to bed down for the night. There has been a sharp rise in robberies and assaults on campers in recent years, though, so safer options short of staying in a hostel or hotel are *cabanas* and trailer parks.

Privately owned **trailer parks** are relatively common on major routes—look for signs with a picture of a trailer, or the words *parque de trailer, campamento,* or *remolques*. These places often allow campers to pitch tents or sling up a hammock. At beaches and some inland towns frequented by backpackers, **cabanas** (cabins, usually simple thatch-roof huts) are common. Many of the restaurants listed throughout the guide will often have space available to put up a hammock, even if there are no *cabanas* in town.

For **more information** consult *Backpacking Mexico*, by Tim Burford (Bradt Publishing; US$17) or *Traveler's Guide to Mexican Camping*, by Mike Church (Rolling Home Press; US$20). Book publishers **Sierra Club Books,** 85 2nd St., 2nd fl., San Francisco, CA 94105-3441 (tel. 800-935-1056 or (415) 977-5500; www.sierraclub.org/books), and **The Mountaineers Books,** 1001 SW Klickitat Way #201, Seattle, WA 98134 (tel. 800-553-4453 or (206) 223-6303; www.mountaineers.org), are great resources for thousands of books on hiking, biking, mountaineering, natural history, and conservation.

CAMPING AND HIKING EQUIPMENT

Good camping equipment is both sturdy and light. Camping equipment is generally more expensive in Australia, New Zealand, and the U.K. than in North America.

Sleeping Bags: Good sleeping bags are rated by the lowest temperature at which they keep you warm ("summer" means 30-40°F at night and "4-season" or "winter" often means below 0°F). Sleeping bags are made either of down (warmer, lighter, and more expensive; miserable when wet) or synthetic material (heavier, more durable, cheaper, and warmer when wet). Prices range from $80-210 for a summer synthetic to $250-500 for a good down winter bag. **Sleeping pads,** including foam pads ($10-20) and air mattresses ($15-50) cushion back and neck and provide insulation from the ground. Bring a **"stuff sack"** lined with a plastic bag to store your sleeping bag and keep it dry.

Tents: The best tents are free-standing, with their own frames and suspension systems; they set up quickly and only require staking in high winds. Low-profile dome tents are the best all-around. When pitched their internal space is almost entirely usable. Tent sizes are misleading: 2 people *can* fit in a 2-person tent, but will find life more pleasant in a 4-person. If traveling by car, buy a bigger tent, but if hiking, get a smaller tent that weighs no more than 5-6 lbs. (2-3kg). Good 2-person tents start at $120, 4-person tents at $300. Waterproof your tent's seams and make sure it has a rain fly. Tent accessories include a **battery-operated lantern,** a **plastic groundcloth,** and a **nylon tarp.**

Backpacks: If you intend to do a lot of hiking, you should have a frame backpack. **Internal-frame packs** mold better to your back, keep a lower center of gravity, and can flex adequately to allow you to hike difficult trails that require a lot of bending and maneuvering. Internal packs are also easier to carry on planes, trains, and buses if your travelling life includes various modes of transport. **External-frame packs** are more comfortable for long hikes over even terrain since they keep the weight higher and distribute it more evenly. Whichever you choose, make sure your pack has a strong, padded hip belt, which transfers the weight from the back to the legs. Serious backpacking requires a pack of at least 4000 cubic in. (16,000cc). Allow an additional 500 cubic in. for your sleeping bag in internal-frame packs. Sturdy backpacks cost $125-420. It doesn't pay to economize—cheaper packs can be less comfortable, and straps are more likely to fray or rip. Before buying a pack, insist on filling it with something heavy and walking around the store to get a sense of how it distributes weight. A **waterproof backpack cover** or plastic garbage bag will prove invaluable. For better protection, store all of your belongings in plastic bags inside your backpack.

Boots: Be sure to wear hiking boots with good **ankle support** appropriate to the terrain you plan to hike. **Gore-Tex** fabric or **part-leather** boots are appropriate for day hikes or 2-3 day overnights over moderate terrain, but for longer trips or trips in mountainous terrain, stiff **leather** boots are highly preferable. Boots should fit snugly and comfortably over one or two wool socks and a thin liner sock. Breaking in boots properly before setting out requires wearing them for several weeks; doing so will spare you from blisters. Treat boots with waterproofing treatment before wearing them.

Other Necessities: Raingear in two pieces, a top and pants, is far superior to a poncho. **Gore-Tex** is the best material for aerobic activity; **rubber** raingear will keep you completely dry but will get clammy if you sweat. Wear warm layers: **synthetics,** like polypropylene tops, socks, and long underwear, along with a pile jacket, are preferable to cotton or because they dry quickly and keep you warm even when wet. **Wool** stays warm when wet, but is much heavier than synthetics. When camping in autumn, winter, or spring, bring along a **"space blanket,"** which retains your body heat and doubles as a groundcloth ($5-15). Plastic **canteens** and water bottles keep water cooler than metal ones, and are virtually shatter- and leak-proof. Large, collapsible **water sacks** significantly improve your situation in primitive campgrounds and weigh practically nothing when empty. Bring **water-purification tablets** for when you can't boil water. Although most campgrounds provide campfire sites, you may want to bring a small **metal grate** or **grill** of your own. In places that forbid fires or the gathering of firewood, use a **camp stove,** such as the propane-powered Coleman stove (from $40) or a **Whisperlite** stove ($60-100), which runs on cleaner-burning white gas; to operate stoves bring waterproof matches or a lighter, and purchase and fill a **fuel bottle.** A **first-aid kit** (see p. 51), **insect repellent,** and **calamine lotion** are other essential camping items.

Mail-order/online companies may have lower prices than retail stores, but going to a camping store helps by giving you a good sense of items' look and weight.

Campmor, Box 700, Upper Saddle River, NJ 07458-0700 (in U.S. 888-226-7667, elsewhere 201-825-8300; email customer-service@campmor.com; www.campmor.com).

Discount Camping, 880 Main North Rd., Pooraka, South Australia 5095, Australia (tel. (08) 8262 3399; www.discountcamping.com.au).

Eastern Mountain Sports (EMS), 327 Jaffrey Rd., Peterborough, NH 03458 (888-463-6367 or (603) 924-7231; email emsmail@emsonline.com; www.emsonline.com). Call to find the branch nearest you.

L.L. Bean, Freeport, ME 04033-0001 (U.S./Canada 800-441-5713; U.K. tel. (0800) 962 954; elsewhere 207-552-6878; www.llbean.com). If your purchase doesn't meet your expectations, they'll replace or refund it. Open 24hr., 365 days a year.

Mountain Designs, P.O. Box 1472, Fortitude Valley, Queensland 4006, Australia (tel. (07) 3252 8894; www.mountaindesign.com.au).

Recreational Equipment, Inc. (REI), Sumner, WA 98352 (800-426-4840 or (253) 891-2500; www.rei.com).

YHA Adventure Shop, 14 Southampton St., London, WC2E 7HA, U.K. (tel. (01718) 36 85 41). The main branch of one of Britain's largest outdoor equipment suppliers.

WILDERNESS SAFETY

If you're planning to get out into the great outdoors it's wise to keep the following tips in mind. Granted, Mexico is a very warm country, but at elevation and in extreme circumstances it is advisable to be well prepared. **Stay warm, stay dry, and stay hydrated.** The vast majority of life-threatening wilderness situations result from a breach of this simple dictum. On any hike, however brief, you should pack enough equipment to keep you alive should disaster befall. This includes raingear, hat and mittens, a first-aid kit, a reflector, a whistle, high energy food, and extra water. Dress in warm layers of synthetic materials designed for the outdoors, or wool. Pile fleece jackets and Gore-Tex raingear are excellent choices. *Never rely on cotton for warmth-* it will be absolutely useless if it gets wet. Make sure to check all equipment for any defects before setting out, and see **Camping and Hiking Equipment,** above, for more information. See **Health,** p. 51 for information about outdoor ailments such as heatstroke, hypothermia, giardia, rabies, and insects, as well as basic medical concerns and first-aid. For **more information,** pick up a copy of *How to Stay Alive in the Woods*, by Bradford Angier (Macmillan; US$8).

KEEPING IN TOUCH

MAIL

SENDING MAIL TO AND RECEIVING MAIL IN MEXICO

Airmail letters under 1 oz. between the U.S. and Canada and Mexico take 8 to 12 days and cost approximately US$0.60 or CDN$1.10. Envelopes should be marked "air mail" or "par avion" to avoid having letters sent by sea. There are several ways to arrange pick-up of letters sent to you by friends and relatives in Mexico.

General Delivery: Mail can be sent to Mexico through **Poste Restante** (the international phrase for General Delivery; **Lista de Correos** in Spanish) to almost any city or town with a post office. Address *Poste Restante* letters to: Jane DOE, Lista de Correos, Calle 65 (street address for post office, or leave it blank), Mérida (city), Yucatán (state), 79000 (postal code), MEXICO. The mail will go to a special desk in the central post office, unless you specify a post office by street address or postal code. As a rule, it is best to use the largest post office in the area, and mail may be sent there regardless of what is written on the envelope. When possible, it is usually safer and quicker to send mail express or registered. When picking up your mail, bring a form of photo ID, preferably a passport. There is generally no surcharge; if there is a charge, it generally does not exceed the cost of domestic postage. If the clerks insist that there is nothing for you, have them check under your first name as well. Letters should be marked *Favor deretener hasta la llegada* (Please hold until arrival); they will be held up to 15 days. If you know people in Mexico, using their addresses may be better. *Let's Go* lists post offices in the **Practical Information** section for each city and most towns.

American Express: AmEx's travel offices throughout the world will act as a mail service for cardholders if you contact them in advance. Under this free **Client Letter Service,** they will hold mail for up to 30 days and forward upon request. Address the letter in the same way shown above. Some offices will offer these services to non-cardholders (especially those who have purchased AmEx Travelers Cheques), but you must call ahead to make sure. Check the **Practical Information** section of the countries you plan to visit; *Let's Go* lists pertinent information for American Express offices in Mexico. A complete list is available free from AmEx (tel. 800-528-4800).

Packages sent via Express Mail International, FedEx, UPS, or other express services might be retained at a different office (often the MexPost office, see below). Be sure to make it clear to officials exactly what type of package you're expecting. It also might be useful to have the express package's tracking number. Also, Express Mail International has lately encountered problems with bandits near Mexico City; some packages are robbed and never arrive. It would be foolish to send anything particularly valuable via any sort of mail to Mexico.

SENDING MAIL HOME FROM MEXICO

Mexican mail service is slow. Although mail usually arrives, it can take anywhere from one to three weeks for *correo aereo* (airmail) to reach the U.S., and at the very least two weeks to reach Europe and other destinations. Official estimates average 40 days by boat, but in reality sea-mail will take months. In Mexico, never deposit anything important in the black hole called mailboxes; take it straight to the **oficina de correos** (post office). There you can buy all the *estampillas* or *timbres* (stamps) that your *carta* (letter) needs. Anything important should be sent *registrado* (registered mail) or in duplicate. For the speediest service possible, **MexPost** works in collaboration with Express Mail International in the U.S. and similar express mail services in other countries to deliver mail quickly and reliably. Three days is the official MexPost delivery time to the U.S., but allow up to a week. In any case, it's much faster than regular or registered mail (but also more expensive). MexPost offices are usually found next to regular post offices, but occasionally they can be located kilometers away. The post office staff can usually give you directions to the nearest MexPost office.

It's wise to use the Spanish abbreviations or names for countries (EE.UU. or EUA for the U.S.). Write *Por Avión* on all postcards and letter not otherwise marked. There is no size limitation for packages, but parcels cannot weigh more than 25kg. Regulations for mailing parcels may vary from state to state. While it is often possible to send packages from smaller towns, post offices in larger cities provide more reliable service. All packages are reopened and inspected by customs at the border, so closing the box with string, not tape, is recommended. In general, in order to send packages you must provide the following: tourist card data (number, duration of validity, date of issue, place of issue), list of contents including estimated value and nature of the package ("Gift" works best), address and return address. It is customary for those mailing parcels to use their home address, or at least some address in the same country as the parcel's destination, as a return address to ensure eventual delivery. In a trade office, you may need to show receipts for each item purchased in Mexico. Postal officials usually record the information from the customs form on the front of the package as well.

Aerogrammes, printed sheets that fold into envelopes and travel via airmail, are available at post offices. It helps to mark *Por Avión* if possible, though "par avion" is universally understood. Most post offices will charge exorbitant fees or simply refuse to send aerogrammes with enclosures. Airmail from Mexico averages 7 to 14 days, although times are more unpredictable from smaller towns.

TELEPHONES

CALLING MEXICO FROM HOME

To call Mexico direct from home, dial:

1. The international access code of your home country. **International access codes** include: Australia 0011; Ireland 00; New Zealand 00; South Africa 09; U.K. 00; U.S. 011. Country codes and city codes are sometimes listed with a zero in front (e.g., 033), but after dialing the international access code, drop successive zeros (with an access code of 011, e.g., 011 33).

2. 052 (Mexico's country code).

3. The city code (see the city's **Practical Information** section) and local number.

CALLING HOME FROM MEXICO

A **calling card** is probably your best and cheapest bet. Calls are billed either collect or to your account. **MCI WorldPhone** also provides access to MCI's Traveler's Assist, which gives legal and medical advice, exchange rate information, and translation services. Other phone companies provide similar services to travelers. **To obtain a calling card** from your national telecommunications service before you leave home, contact the appropriate company below.

USA: AT&T (tel. 888-288-4685); **Sprint** (tel. 800-877-4646); or **MCI** (tel. 800-444-4141; from abroad dial the country's MCI access number).

Canada: Bell Canada **Canada Direct** (tel. 800-565-4708).

U.K.: British Telecom **BT Direct** (tel. (0800) 34 51 44).

Ireland: Telecom Éireann **Ireland Direct** (tel. 800 250 250).

Australia: Telstra **Australia Direct** (tel. 13 22 00).

New Zealand: Telecom New Zealand (tel. (0800) 000 000).

South Africa: Telkom South Africa (tel. 09 03).

To call home with a calling card, contact the Mexico operator for your service provider by dialing:

AT&T: tel. 01 800 288 2872 (using LADATEL phones) or 001 800 462 4240.

Sprint: tel. 001 800 877 8000.

MCI WorldPhone Direct: tel. 01 800 021 8000 (using Avantel phones) or 001 800 674 7000 (using Telmex phones).

That being said, using Mexican telephones is usually a small adventure. Once you are in Mexico, getting lines to foreign countries can be very difficult. Many public phones don't access international lines. Dial 09 for an English-speaking international long-distance operator. If you speak Spanish fluently and can't reach the international operator, dial 07 for the national operator, who will connect you (sometimes even a local operator can help). The term for a collect call is a *llamada por cobrar* or *llamada con cobro revertido*. Calling from hotels is usually faster but beware of exorbitant surcharges.

Taxes and surcharges make it extremely expensive to call abroad from Mexico. Call with a card or collect if you can; not only is it cheaper (about half the price of direct), but you will also avoid enormous surcharges. Remember, however, that there can be a fee of 1-5 pesos for collect calls that are not accepted.

If you do dial direct, you must first insert the appropriate amount of money or a prepaid card, then dial 95 (the international access code for Mexico), and then dial the country code and number of your home. **Country codes** include: Australia 61; Ireland 353; New Zealand 64; South Africa 27; U.K. 44; U.S. and Canada 1.

CALLING WITHIN MEXICO

The simplest way to call within Mexico is to use a coin-operated phone. You can also buy **prepaid phone cards**, which carry a certain amount of phone time depending on the card's denomination. The time is measured in minutes or talk units (e.g. one unit/one minute), and the card usually has a toll-free access telephone number and a personal identification number (PIN). To make a phone call, you dial the access number, enter your PIN, and at the voice prompt, enter the phone number of the party you're trying to reach. A computer tells you how much time or how many units you have left on your card. Be very careful as to the type of card you buy: some operate with a PIN number you must know beforehand, while others contain the pin on the card itself. Phone rates tend to be highest in the morning, lower in the evening, and lowest on Sunday and late at night.

Calls (international and local) using **LADATEL** touch-tone pay phones are cheaper and involve less waiting than any of the alternatives. You can buy LADATEL phone cards at most *papelerias* (stationers) or *abarrotes* (grocers). Without the cards, the challenge is finding enough coins of large denominations: these phones take not more than 10 coins at a time, and some calls require an initial deposit. When dialing, use the station-to-station prefixes. The blue push-button phones do direct dial; the orange old-fashioned ones do not. To reach the English-speaking international operator on a plain old phone, dial 09 and wait until the operator answers (be prepared to wait 30min. or more.) For direct calls, dial 01; for a national operator 02; directory assistance 04; for bilingual emergency operators 06. To make long-distance phone calls within Mexico, dial 91 plus the telephone code and number (station to station), or 92 plus the telephone code and number (person to person). The prefix for calling the U.S. or Canada is 95 for station-to-station; for all other counties the prefix is 98.

If, for example, you want to place a long distance call within Mexico to Frances and Art's Yummy Burrito Emporium in Chihuahua, you would dial the long distance code (92), the telephone code for Chihuahua (14), then the number: (tel. 92 14 65 29 00). If, however, you want to call the Burrito Emporium from another country before you leave, you must dial the long-distance code (011 from the U.S.), the Mexican country code (52), the telephone code for the city (14) and the number (65 29 00). Therefore, the number you would have to dial to call the Burrito Emporium from the U.S. is (tel. 011 52 14 65 29 00). Good luck, be brave.

EMAIL AND INTERNET

With many Mexican businesses, language schools, and individuals now online, the Internet and its email offers a cheap and accessible alternative to pricey phone calls and the less-than-reliable Mexican mail system. There are a number of ways to access the Internet in Mexico. Many employers and schools offer gateways to the Internet, often at no cost. Cybercafes, included in most town listings, are perhaps the most prominent form of Internet access in Mexico. These cafes can be found in even some of the smaller Mexican towns, and they offer access to the Web and the Internet for a nominal fee.

GETTING THERE

BY PLANE

When it comes to airfare, a little effort can save you a bundle. If your plans are flexible enough to deal with the restrictions, courier fares are the cheapest. Tickets bought from consolidators and standby seating are also good deals, but last-minute specials, airfare wars, and charter flights often beat these fares. The key is to hunt around, to be flexible, and to persistently ask about discounts. Students, seniors, and those under 26 should never pay full price for a ticket.

DETAILS AND TIPS

Timing: Airfares to Mexico peak Dec.-May; holidays are also expensive periods in which to travel. Midweek (M-Th morning) round-trip flights run US$40-50 cheaper than weekend flights, but the latter are generally less crowded and more likely to permit frequent-flier upgrades. Return-date flexibility is usually not an option for the budget traveler; traveling with an "open return" ticket can be pricier than fixing a return date when buying the ticket and paying later to change it.

Route: Round-trip flights are by far the cheapest; "open-jaw" (arriving in and departing from different cities) and round-the-world, or RTW, flights are pricier but reasonable alternatives. Patching one-way flights together is the least economical way to travel. Flights between capital cities or regional hubs will offer the most competitive fares.

Boarding: Whenever flying internationally, pick up tickets for international flights well in advance of the departure date, and confirm by phone within 72 hours of departure. Most airlines require that passengers arrive at the airport at least two hours before departure. One carry-on item and two pieces of checked baggage is the norm for non-courier flights. Consult the airline for weight allowances.

Fares: Round-trip fares to Mexico City from New York range from US$300-400; from London, US$1350-1550; from Los Angeles, US$350-450; from Sydney US$2200-2400; from Cancún, US$250-300; from Monterrey, US$150-200.

BUDGET AND STUDENT TRAVEL AGENCIES

A knowledgeable agent specializing in flights to Mexico can make your life easy and help you save, too, but agents may not spend the time to find you the lowest possible fare — they get paid on commission. Students and under-26ers holding **ISIC and IYTC cards** (see **Identification,** p. 37), respectively, qualify for big discounts from student travel agencies. Most flights from budget agencies are on major airlines, but in peak season some may sell seats on less reliable chartered aircraft.

Campus/Usit Youth and Student Travel (www.usitcampus.co.uk). In Europe call (0171) 730 34 02; in North America call (0870) 240 10 10; worldwide call (0171) 730 81 11. Offices include: 19-21 Aston Quay, O'Connell Bridge, **Dublin** 2 (tel. (01) 677 8117; fax 679 8833); 52 Grosvenor Gardens, **London** SW1W 0AG; New York Student Center, 895 Amsterdam Ave., **New York,** NY, 10025 (tel. (212) 663-5435; email usitny@aol.com). Additional offices in Cork, Galway, Limerick, Waterford, Coleraine, Derry, Belfast, and Greece.

Council Travel (www.counciltravel.com). U.S. offices include: Emory Village, 1561 N. Decatur Rd., **Atlanta,** GA 30307 (tel. (404) 377-9997); 273 Newbury St., **Boston,** MA 02116 (tel. (617) 266-1926); 1160 N. State St., **Chicago,** IL 60610 (tel. (312) 951-0585); 10904 Lindbrook Dr., **Los Angeles,** CA 90024 (tel. (310) 208-3551); 205 E. 42nd St., **New York,** NY 10017 (tel. (212) 822-2700); 530 Bush St., **San Francisco,** CA 94108 (tel. (415) 421-3473); 1314 NE 43rd St., #210, **Seattle,** WA 98105 (tel. (206) 632-2448); 3300 M St. NW, **Washington, D.C.** 20007 (tel. (202) 337-6464). **For U.S. cities not listed,** call 800-2-COUNCIL (226-8624). Also 28A Poland St. (Oxford Circus), **London,** W1V 3DB (tel. (0171) 287 3337), **Paris** (tel. 01 44 41 89 89), and **Munich** (tel. (089) 39 50 22).

CTS Travel, 44 Goodge St., W1 (tel. (0171) 636 00 31; fax 637 53 28; email ctsinfo@ctstravel.com.uk).

STA Travel, 6560 Scottsdale Rd. #F100, Scottsdale, AZ 85253 (tel. 800-777-0112 fax 602-922-0793; www.sta-travel.com). A student and youth travel organization with over 150 offices worldwide. Ticket booking, travel insurance, railpasses, and more. U.S. offices include: 297 Newbury Street, **Boston,** MA 02115 (tel. (617) 266-6014); 429 S. Dearborn St., **Chicago,** IL 60605 (tel. (312) 786-9050); 7202 Melrose Ave., **Los Angeles,** CA 90046 (tel. (323) 934-8722); 10 Downing St., **New York,** NY 10014 (tel. 212-627-3111); 4341 University Way NE, **Seattle,** WA 98105 (tel. (206) 633-5000); 2401 Pennsylvania Ave., Ste. G, **Washington, D.C.** 20037 (tel. (202) 887-0912); 51 Grant Ave., **San Francisco,** CA 94108 (tel. (415) 391-8407). In the U.K., 6 Wrights Ln., **London** W8 6TA (tel. (0171) 938 47 11 for North American travel). In New Zealand, 10 High St., **Auckland** (tel. (09) 309 04 58). In Australia, 222 Faraday St., **Melbourne** VIC 3053 (tel. (03) 9349 2411).

Travel CUTS (Canadian Universities Travel Services Limited), 187 College St., Toronto, ON. M5T 1P7 (tel. (416) 979-2406; fax 979-8167; www.travelcuts.com). 40 offices in Canada. Also in the U.K., 295A Regent St., **London** W1R 7YA (tel. (0171) 255 19 44).

Other organizations that specialize in finding cheap fares include:

Cheap Tickets (tel. 800-377-1000) flies worldwide to and from the U.S.

Travel Avenue (tel. 800-333-3335) rebates commercial fares to or from the U.S. and offers low fares for flights anywhere in the world. They also offer package deals, which include car rental and hotel reservations, to many destinations.

COMMERCIAL AIRLINES

The commercial airlines' lowest regular offer is the **APEX** (Advance Purchase Excursion) fare, which provides confirmed reservations and allows "open-jaw" tickets. Generally, reservations must be made 7 to 21 days in advance, with 7- to 14-day minimum and up to 90-day maximum-stay limits, and hefty cancellation and change penalties (fees rise in summer). Book peak-season APEX fares early, since by May you will have a hard time getting the departure date you want.

Although APEX fares are probably not the cheapest possible fares, they will give you a sense of the average commercial price, from which to measure other bargains. Specials advertised in newspapers may be cheaper but have more restrictions and fewer available seats. Popular carriers to Mexico include:

American Airlines (tel. 800-882-8880; www.aa.com) has round-trip offers from the U.S. to many Mexican cities.

Aeroméxico (tel. 800-237-6639; www.aeromexico.com) flies to practically every Mexican city with an airport.

Continental (tel. 800-525-0280; www.continental.com) offers discounts on round-trip flights to Mexico City.

Mexicana (tel. 800-348-6937; www.mexicana.com) is North America's oldest airline, and flies to most major US and European cities.

OTHER CHEAP ALTERNATIVES

AIR COURIER FLIGHTS. Couriers help transport cargo on international flights by guaranteeing delivery of the baggage claim slips from the company to a representative overseas. Generally, couriers must travel light (carry-ons only) and deal with complex restrictions on their flight. Most flights are round-trip only with short fixed-length stays (usually one week) and a limit of a single ticket per issue. Most of these flights also operate only out of the biggest cities, like New York. Generally, you must be over 21 (in some cases 18), have a valid passport, and procure your own visa, if necessary. Groups such as the **Air Courier Association** (tel. 800-282-1202; www.aircourier.org) and the **International Association of Air Travel Couriers,** 220 South Dixie Hwy., P.O. Box 1349, Lake Worth, FL 33460 (tel. (561) 582-8320; email iaatc@courier.org; www.courier.org) provide their members with lists of opportunities and courier brokers worldwide for an annual fee. For **more information,** consult *Air Courier Bargains*, by Kelly Monaghan (The Intrepid Traveler; US$15) or the *Courier Air Travel Handbook*, by Mark Field (Perpetual Press; US$10).

CHARTER FLIGHTS. Charters are flights a tour operator contracts with an airline to fly extra loads of passengers during peak season. Charters can sometimes be cheaper than flights on scheduled airlines, some operate nonstop, and restrictions on minimum advance-purchase and minimum stay are more lenient. However, charter flights fly less frequently than major airlines, make refunds particularly difficult, and are almost always fully booked. Schedules and itineraries may also change or be cancelled at the last moment (as late as 48 hours before the trip, and without a full refund), and check-in, boarding, and baggage claim are often much slower. As always, pay with a credit card if you can, and consider traveler's insurance against trip interruption. **Discount clubs** and **fare brokers** offer members savings on last-minute charter and tour deals. Study their contracts closely; you don't want to end up with an unwanted overnight layover.

TICKET CONSOLIDATORS. Ticket consolidators, or **"bucket shops,"** buy unsold tickets in bulk from commercial airlines and sell them at discounted rates. The best place to look is in the Sunday travel section of any major newspaper, where many bucket shops place tiny ads. Call quickly, as availability is typically extremely limited. Not all bucket shops are reliable establishments, so insist on a receipt that gives full details of restrictions, refunds, and tickets, and pay by credit card. For more information, check the web site **Consolidators FAQ** (www.travel-library.com/air-travel/consolidators.html) or the book *Consolidators: Air Travel's Bargain Basement*, by Kelly Monaghan (Intrepid Traveler; US$8).

BY BUS OR TRAIN

Greyhound (800-231-2222; www.greyhound.com) serves many border towns, including El Paso and Brownsville, Texas. Schedule information is available at any Greyhound terminal, on the web page, or by calling the 800 number. Smaller lines serve other destinations. Buses tend not to cross the border, but at each of these stops you can pick up Mexican bus lines (among them **Tres Estrellas de Oro, Estrella Blanca, ADO,** and **Transportes Del Norte**) on the other side.

By train, you can take **Amtrak** (tel. 800-872-8725) to El Paso, walk across the border to Ciudad Juárez and use other forms of transportation to travel within Mexico. Amtrak also serves San Diego and San Antonio, where you can catch a bus to the border towns (US$285-433 one-way from New York to El Paso, San Diego, or San Antonio). For more information, contact **Amtrak Vacations,** 2211 Butterfield Rd. Downers Grove, IL 60515 (tel. 800-321-8684).

GETTING AROUND

BY BUS

Mexico's extensive, astoundingly cheap bus service never ceases to amaze. Travel luxury class, often called **servicio ejecutivo** (executive service), and you'll get the royal treatment: reclining seats, sandwiches and soda, air-conditioning, and movies galore. Only slightly less fancy is **primera clase** (first-class). Buses are relatively comfortable and efficient; they occasionally even have videos, bathrooms, and functioning air-conditioners (ask at the ticket window). **Segunda clase** (second-class) buses, which are only slightly cheaper than *primera clase*, are sometimes overcrowded, hot, and uncomfortable. To maximize your comfort at night, choose a seat on the right side of the bus (to avoid the constant glare of oncoming headlights); during the day try to get the shady side of the bus. Even on non-air-conditioned buses, drivers or passengers often refuse to drive with the windows open. Don't make a scene. Air-conditioning can be refreshing...until the icicles start forming; bring a sweater or prepare to sniffle.

Buses are either *local* or *de paso* (passing by; you can't buy advance tickets). *Locales* originate at the station from which you leave. If few *locales* leave each day, try to buy your ticket in advance. Once you get on the bus, keep your ticket stub in case you're asked to show it later. *De paso* buses originate elsewhere and pass through your station. First-class *de pasos* sell only as many tickets as there are available seats—when the bus arrives, the driver disembarks to give this information to the ticket seller. When these tickets go on sale, forget civility, chivalry, and anything which might possibly stand between you and a ticket, or plan to spend the greater portion of your vacation in bus stations. You may end up sitting on the floor of a second-class *de paso* bus; ticket sales are based on the number of people with assigned seats who have gotten off the bus. This system does not, unfortunately, take into account the people and packages jammed into the aisle. In any case, if you know when boarding the bus that no seats are available, it's best to wait and board last. That way, while all other passengers without seats have to stand in the aisle, you are able to sit semi-comfortably on the step between the driver's compartment and the aisle.

BY TAXI

Taxis in Mexico are ubiquitous in big cities. Prices are reasonable (by U.S. standards), but since public buses are so frequent and cover so much ground, you shouldn't have to resort to a cab unless it's late at night or you're in a remote part of town. Be careful to avoid getting overcharged by always negotiating a price beforehand (bargaining is the norm) and not agreeing to go by *taxímetro* (metered fare)—it's often more expensive even if legit, but, most importantly, taxi drivers often tamper with the machine to make it charge exorbitant amounts to unsuspecting tourists. Also, the U.S. Department of State (http://www.state.gov) has warned of a rash of reported taxi robberies at gunpoint, particularly in the lime green cabs in Mexico City, but also elsewhere; the best way to avoid this is to only get *sitio* cabs at authorized stands or at hotels instead of flagging them down along the street.

BY CAR

Driving in Mexico is as exciting as swimming in shark-infested waters, and it's much more dangerous. The maximum speed on Mexican routes is 100km per hour (62mph) unless otherwise posted, but it is often ignored. Be especially careful driving during the rainy season (May-Oct.), when roads are often in poor condition, potholes become craters, and landslides are common. When driving on roads near the capital, watch out for fog. A sign warning *Maneje despacio* (drive slowly) should be taken seriously. Dirt roads can mean serious damage for your car if you don't have four-wheel drive. Watch for rocks and gravel and always have a spare tire available.

At night, pedestrians and livestock pop up on the roadway at the most unlikely times. If you can help it, don't drive at night. If you must, beware of oncoming cars without headlights. Whatever you do, never spend the night on the side of the road. When approaching a one-lane bridge, labeled *puente angosto* or *solo carril*, the first driver to flash headlights has the right of way. Lanes are narrow, so if a truck tries to pass your car on a two-lane road, you might need to pull off onto the gravel or graded dirt in order to give the vehicle enough room. (But be careful: the shoulder is often nonexistent or covered with vegetation.)

Check with local authorities or the nearest U.S. consulate for updates on bandit activity and areas of potential danger. Exercise particular caution when driving along Rte. 15 in the state of Sinaloa; Rte. 2 in the vicinity of Carborca, Sonora; Rte. 57 between Matehuala and San Luis Potosí; the route between Palomares and Tuxtepec, Oaxaca; Rte. 3 in Baja (full of potholes); and Rte. 40 between the city of Durango and the Pacific Coast. If possible, avoid Rte. 1 in Sinaloa.

In Baja, if you want to leave your car and go somewhere by public transportation for a few days, you must pay to park in an authorized lot; otherwise, the car will be towed or confiscated. The Motor Vehicle Office will tell you where to leave your car legally. To help reduce the heinous pollution in Mexico City, traffic in the metropolitan area is restricted (see p. 91).

PEMEX (Petroleos Mexicanos) sells two types of gas: Magna (regular) and Premium (unleaded). Unleaded gas is now almost universally available in Mexico; you will find it throughout Baja as well as in Guadalajara, Monterrey, Mexico City, most border towns, and all major metropolitan areas. Both Magna and Premium are extremely cheap by all but Saudi Arabian standards. Don't get overcharged: know how much gas you'll need before you pull in and make sure the register is rung back to zero before pumping begins. PEMEX accepts cash and checks only. When checking the tires, remember that pumps in Mexico are calibrated in kilograms.

The heat, bumpy roads, and fair-to-middling gas may well take a toll on your car. No matter what kind of car you sport, bring spare oil, spark plugs, fan belts and air, a spare tire, and fuel filters—these should take care of all but the biggest problems. If you break down on one of the major toll routes between 8am and

8pm, pull completely off the road, raise the hood, stay with your car, and wait for the **Angeles Verdes** (Green Angels) to come to the rescue. Green Angels are green-and-white emergency trucks dispatched by radio, staffed by almost a thousand mechanics, and equipped for performing common repair jobs, towing, changing tires, and addressing minor medical problems. Your green saviors may take a while to show up, but the service (except for parts, gas, and oil) is free. Tipping is optional but polite. These guardian angels will assist you anywhere but in Mexico City, where you can contact the **Asociación Nacional Automovilística (ANA)** (tel. (5) 597 42 83).

While on the road in Mexico, you'll probably be stopped more than once by agents of the Federal Public Ministry and the Federal Judicial Police for a search of your car and its contents. To avoid being detained or arrested, be as cooperative as possible; they will usually just open your trunk and look around your car and it's fairly painless if you give them no reason to make it painful. Do not carry drugs, firearms, or army surplus in your car.

DRIVER'S LICENSES AND VEHICLE PERMITS

An international driver's license is not necessary for driving in Mexico; any valid driver's license is acceptable. To drive a foreign car into Mexico and beyond the Border Zone or Free Trade Zone (Baja California peninsula and Sonora), you need to obtain a **Vehicle Permit** when you cross the border. The original and a photocopy of the following documents are needed to obtain a vehicle permit: a state vehicle registration certificate and vehicle title, a valid driver's license accompanied by either a passport or a birth certificate, and a Mexican insurance policy, which can be purchased at the border.

If leasing a vehicle, you must provide the contract in your name (also in duplicate). A credit card issued outside Mexico will make your life much easier—simply charge the US$11 fee. Without plastic, you will need to make a cash deposit calculated according to the value of your vehicle. In exchange for all these photocopies, you'll receive two punched stickers bearing the expiration date of your permit. To extend a vehicle permit beyond its original expiration date and to avoid confiscation, contact the temporary importation department of Mexican customs. The maximum permit granted to tourists is six months. Regulations change frequently; for updated information contact a consulate. A vehicle permit is valid only for the person to whom it was issued unless another driver is approved by the federal registry. Violation of this law can result in confiscation of the vehicle or heavy fines. Furthermore, only legitimate drivers may purchase car-ferry tickets.

Resist the temptation to abandon, sell, or give away your car in Mexico. Once you enter the country with a car, your tourist card will be marked such that you will not be allowed to collect the bond or to leave without the vehicle. Even if your car disappears somewhere in Mexico, you must get permission to leave without it; approval can be obtained (for a fee) at either the federal registry of automobiles in Mexico City or a local office of the treasury department.

CAR INSURANCE. Most credit cards cover standard insurance. If you rent, lease, or borrow a car, you will need a **green card,** or **International Insurance Certificate,** to prove that you have liability insurance. Obtain it through the car rental agency; most include coverage in their prices. If you lease a car, you can obtain a green card from the dealer. Some travel agents offer the card; it may also be available at border crossings. Verify whether your auto insurance applies abroad; even if it does, you will still need a green card to certify this to foreign officials. If you have a collision abroad, the accident will show up on your domestic records if you report it to your insurance company. Rental agencies may require you to purchase theft insurance in countries that they consider to have a high risk of auto theft. Ask your rental agency about Mexico.

ESSENTIALS

ESSENTIALS

BY PLANE

Flying within Mexico is more expensive than taking a bus or train, but it is considerably cheaper than comparable flights between U.S. cities. It can be an excellent way of avoiding a 40-hour (or longer) bus ride; many budget travelers rule out the possibility, only to learn later that it would have been much cheaper than they had thought. Check with Mexican airlines for special rates.

BY TRAIN

The Mexican railroads are all government-owned, with most lines operating under the name of **Ferrocarriles Nacionales de Mexico** (National Railways of Mexico, FFNN). The train system is not as extensive, punctual, cheap, comfortable, or efficient as the bus system. Even when they are on time, trains (yes, even the "fast" ones) can take twice as long as buses to reach their destination. Other than the spectacular ride through the **Copper Canyon** (**Los Mochis-Creel;** see p. 232) you probably won't want to rely on trains unless you're nearly broke or crave a leisurely crawl through the country. Don't be surprised if the rail system is privatized and the majority of it axed completely in the next few years—it is already disappearing in most regions.

BY THUMB

 HITCHING CAN BE HAZARDOUS TO YOUR HEALTH. Let's Go urges you to use common sense if you decide to hitch, and to seriously consider all possible risks before you make that decision. The information listed below and throughout the book is not intended to recommend hitchhiking.

The Mexicans who pick up tourists are often friendly, offering meals, tours, or other extras. More often than not, they are generous and well-meaning; in fact, people who *don't* pick you up will often give you an apologetic look or a gesture of explanation. However, always be careful. Women should never hitchhike alone. Hitchhikers should size up the driver and find out where the car is going before getting in. Think twice if a driver opens the door quickly and offers to drive anywhere. Some bandit-ridden routes are particularly dangerous for hitchhikers (see **By Car,** p. 68).

Before getting in, make sure the passenger window or door opens from inside. If there are several people in the car, do not sit in the middle. Assume a quick-exit position, which rules out the back seat of a two-door car. Keep backpacks and other baggage where they are easily accessible—don't let the driver store them in the trunk. If you have trouble getting out for any reason, affecting the pose of someone about to vomit works wonders.

SPECIFIC CONCERNS

WOMEN TRAVELERS

Women who travel through Mexico are often surprised by the unsolicited attention they receive. If you have two X chromosomes, and especially if you look like an *extranjera* (foreigner), you may find it difficult to shake off unwanted companions. Persistent men will insist on joining you; walking down the street, you will hear whistles and propositions. If you're fair-skinned, *"güera, güera"* will follow you everywhere. Offer no response or eye contact. Attention is usually more annoying than dangerous, but in real emergencies scream for help. Don't consider yourself safe just because people in uniform are around.

Awareness of Mexican social standards can prevent unpleasant and dangerous confrontations. Wearing short shorts or halter tops (or not wearing bras) will result in extra harassment; it's best to wear knee-length shorts. Bring a lightweight long skirt to wear in churches or in conservative regions like Chiapas. Almost without exception, *cantinas* are all-male institutions; the only women who ever enter are working, either as servers or as prostitutes.

If you are traveling with a male friend, it may help to pose as a couple: it will make it easier to share rooms and will also chill the blood of horny Romeos. Wearing a **"wedding ring"** on the left hand might also discourage unwanted attention. Northern Mexico, especially the border towns, is less congenial to women travelers. Oaxaca, Chiapas, and the Yucatán are friendlier, safer places. The following resources may prove useful in finding out more information for women travelers.

Don't hesitate to seek out a police officer or a passerby if you are being harassed. *Let's Go* lists emergency numbers in the **Practical Information** listings of most cities. Memorize the emergency numbers in all of the states you are planning to visit in Mexico. Carry a **whistle** or an **airhorn** on your keychain, and don't hesitate to use it in an emergency. A **Model Mugging** course will not only prepare you for a potential mugging, but it will also raise your level of awareness of your surroundings as well as your confidence (see **Safety and Security,** p. 47). Women also face additional health concerns when traveling (see **Health,** p. 51).

When traveling, always carry extra money for a phone call, bus, or taxi. **Hitching** is never safe for lone women, or even for two women traveling together. Look as if you know where you're going (even when you don't) and consider approaching older women or couples for directions if you're lost or feel uncomfortable.

For **more information** consult, *A Journey of One's Own: Uncommon Advice for the Independent Woman Traveler,* by Thalia Zepatos (Eighth Mountain Press; US$17); *Adventures in Good Company: The Complete Guide to Women's Tours and Outdoor Trips,* by Thalia Zepatos (Eighth Mountain Press; US$7); *Active Women Vacation Guide,* by Evelyn Kaye (Blue Panda Publications; US$18); *Travelers' Tales: Gutsy Women, Travel Tips and Wisdom for the Road,* by Marybeth Bond (Traveler's Tales; US$8); *A Foxy Old Woman's Guide to Traveling Alone,* by Jay Ben-Lesser (Crossing Press; US$11).

TRAVELING ALONE

There are many benefits to traveling alone, among them greater independence and challenge. As a lone traveler, you have greater opportunity to interact with the residents of the region you're visiting. Locals are often impressed that you are facing the perils of Mexican travel on your own.

On the other hand, any solo traveler is a more vulnerable target of harassment and street theft. Lone travelers need to be well-organized and look confident at all times. Try not to stand out as a tourist, and be especially careful in deserted or very crowded areas. If questioned, never admit that you are traveling alone. Maintain regular contact with someone at home who knows your itinerary.

A number of organizations supply information for solo travelers, and others find travel companions for those who don't want to go alone. A few are listed here.

American International Homestays, P.O. Box 1754, Nederland, CO 80466 (tel. (303) 642-3088 or 800-876-2048; email ash@igc.apc.org; www.commerce.com/homestays). Lodgings with English-speaking host families around the world.

Connecting: Solo Traveler Network, P.O. Box 29088, 1996 W. Broadway, Vancouver, BC V6J 5C2, Canada (tel. (604) 737-7791; email info@cstn.org; www.cstn.org). Bi-monthly newsletter features going solo tips, single-friendly tips and travel companion ads. Annual directory lists holiday suppliers that avoid single supplement charges. Advice and lodging exchanges facilitated between members. Membership US$25-35.

Travel Companion Exchange, P.O. Box 833, Amityville, NY 11701 (tel. (516) 454-0880 or 800-392-1256; www.travelalone.com). Publishes the pamphlet *Foiling Pickpockets & Bag Snatchers* (US$4) and *Travel Companions,* a bi-monthly newsletter for single travelers seeking a travel partner (subscription US$48).

ESSENTIALS

OLDER TRAVELERS

Senior citizens are eligible for a wide range of discounts on transportation, museums, movies, theaters, concerts, restaurants, and accommodations. If you don't see a senior citizen price listed, ask, and you may be delightfully surprised.

For **more information** consult: *No Problem! Worldwise Tips for Mature Adventurers*, by Janice Kenyon (Orca Books; US$16); or *Unbelievably Good Deals and Great Adventures That You Absolutely Can't Get Unless You're Over 50*, by Joan Rattner Heilman (Contemporary Books; US$13). The following organizations arrange tours or trips for older travelers:

ElderTreks (597 Markham St., Toronto, ON M6G 2L7, tel. 800-741-7956 or (416) 588-5000, fax 588-9839, email passages@inforamp.net; www.eldertreks.com) or **Walking the World** (P.O. Box 1186, Fort Collins, CO 80522, tel. (970) 498-0500; fax 498-9100; email walktworld@aol.com), which sends trips to Mexico and Central America.

Elderhostel, 75 Federal St., 3rd fl., Boston, MA 02110-1941 (tel. (617) 426-7788; email Cadyg@elderhostel.org; http://www.elderhostel.org). For those 55 or over (spouse of any age). Programs at colleges, universities, and other learning centers in Mexico on varied subjects lasting 1-4 weeks.

BISEXUAL, GAY, AND LESBIAN TRAVELERS

Mexican law does not mention homosexuality, and attitudes vary from state to state. While some regions have ongoing campaigns against this "social threat," there is a gay-rights movement in Mexico City and a more rapidly growing movement in Monterrey. Although discreet homosexuality is tolerated in most areas, public displays of gay affection are usually not and might be the quickest way of getting beaten up, especially in smaller Mexican towns. To find cities with **gay and lesbian nightlife** in Mexico, see that index entry.

For **more information** consult: *Gay Mexico* (Ferrari; $18); *Spartacus International Gay Guide*, by Bruno Gmunder Verlag (US$33); *Damron Men's Guide, Damron Road Atlas, Damron's Accommodations,* and *The Women's Traveller* (Damron Travel Guides; 415-255-0404 or 800-462-6654; www.damron.com; US$14-19); *Ferrari Guides' Gay Travel A to Z, Ferrari Guides' Men's Travel in Your Pocket, Ferrari Guides' Women's Travel in Your Pocket,* and *Ferrari Guides' Inn Places* (Ferrari Guides 602-863-2408 or 800-962-2912; www.q-net.com; US$14-16); or *The Gay Vacation Guide: The Best Trips and How to Plan Them,* by Mark Chesnut (Citadel Press; US$15). Listed below are contact organizations, mail-order bookstores and publishers which offer materials addressing some specific concerns.

Giovanni's Room, 345 S. 12th St., Philadelphia, PA 19107 (tel. 215-923-2960; fax 923-0813; email giophilp@netaxs.com). An international feminist, lesbian, and gay bookstore with mail-order service which carries the publications listed below.

International Gay and Lesbian Travel Association, 4331 N. Federal Hwy. #304, Fort Lauderdale, FL 33308 (tel. 954-776-2626 or 800-448-8550; email IGLTA@aol.com; www.iglta.com). An organization of over 1350 companies serving gay and lesbian travelers worldwide. Call for lists of travel agents, accommodations, and events.

International Lesbian and Gay Association (ILGA), 81 rue Marché-au-Charbon, B-1000 Brussels, Belgium (tel./fax 32 2 502 24 71; email ilga@ilga.org; www.ilga.org). Provides political information, such as homosexuality laws of individual countries.

TRAVELERS WITH DISABILITIES

Mexico is becoming increasingly accessible to travelers with disabilities, especially in popular resorts such as Acapulco and Cancún. Northern cities closer to the U.S. also tend to be more accessible; Monterrey and Saltillo might be the most wheelchair-friendly cities in the entire country. Money talks—the more you are willing to spend, the less difficult it is to find accessible facilities. Most public and long-distance modes of transportation and most of the non-luxury hotels don't accommodate wheelchairs. Public bathrooms are almost all inaccessible, as are many ruins, parks, historic buildings, and museums. Still, with some advance planning, an affordable Mexican vacation is not impossible. Those with disabilities should inform airlines and hotels of their disabilities when making arrangements for travel; some time may be needed to prepare special accommodations. For **more information** consult: *Resource Directory for the Disabled*, by Richard Neil Shrout (Facts on File; US$45); *Global Access* (www.geocities.com/Paris/1502/disabilitylinks.html) has links for disabled travelers in Mexico. The following organizations provide useful information:

Mobility International USA (MIUSA), P.O. Box 10767, Eugene, OR 97440 (tel. 541-343-1284 voice and TDD; fax 343-6812; email info@miusa.org; www.miusa.org). Sells *A World of Options: A Guide to International Educational Exchange, Community Service, and Travel for Persons with Disabilities* (US$35).

Moss Rehab Hospital Travel Information Service (tel. 215-456-9600; www.mossresourcenet.org). A telephone and internet information resource center on international travel accessibility and other travel-related concerns for those with disabilities.

Society for the Advancement of Travel for the Handicapped (SATH), 347 Fifth Ave., #610, New York, NY 10016 (tel. 212-447-1928; fax 725-8253; email sathtravel@aol.com; www.sath.org). Advocacy group publishing a quarterly color travel magazine *OPEN WORLD* (free for members or US$13 for nonmembers). Also publishes a wide range of information sheets on disability travel facilitation and accessible destinations. Annual membership US$45, students and seniors US$30.

The Guided Tour Inc., 7900 Old York Rd., #114B, Elkins Park, PA 19027-2339 (tel. 800-783-5841 or 215-782-1370; email gtour400@aol.com; www.guidedtour.com). Travel programs for persons with developmental and physical challenges in Cancún.

MINORITY TRAVELERS

Although culturally diverse, Mexico is largely racially homogeneous. Mexicans are indigenous (called *indígenas*), white, or some mixture of the two (called *mestizo*). The whiter your skin, the better treatment you'll get in larger cities, and the more you'll stand out in rural areas. Speaking English in larger cities may entitle you to royal treatment, whereas in medium to small cities, non-Spanish speakers are immediately viewed as threats. Practically any other ethnicity will mark you as a foreigner in Mexico, and as a result you might receive attention from curious locals, particularly in smaller communities. On most occasions this attention (stares, giggling, questions) is not meant to be hostile; it arises from curiosity rather than racism. Try to be understanding of the excitement produced by difference. In most cases, Mexicans react more strongly to foreignness, particularly Anglophone, than to ethnicity.

TRAVELERS WITH CHILDREN

Children should not be deprived of the wonders of a Mexican vacation; simply slow your pace and plan ahead to accommodate smaller companions. If you plan on going on walking trips, consider bringing along a papoose for carrying your baby. If you rent a car, make sure the company provides a seat for younger children. When deciding where to stay, find child-friendly accommodations. Restaurants often have children's menus and discounts. Virtually all museums and tourist attractions also have a children's rate. Children under two generally fly for 10% of the adult airfare on international flights (this does not necessarily include a seat). International fares are usually discounted 25% for children age two to 11.

For **more information,** consult: *Backpacking with Babies and Small Children*, by Goldie Silverman (Wilderness Press; US$10). *How to take Great Trips with Your Kids*, by Sanford and Jane Portnoy (Harvard Common Press; US $10); *Have Kid, Will Travel: 101 Survival Strategies for Vacationing With Babies and Young Children*, by Claire and Lucille Tristram (Andrews and McMeel; US$9); *Adventuring with Children: An Inspirational Guide to World Travel and the Outdoors*, by Nan Jeffrey (Avalon House Publishing; $15); or *Trouble Free Travel with Children*, by Vicki Lansky (Book Peddlers; US$9).

DIETARY CONCERNS

It's not easy for **vegetarians** in Mexico: most meals include meat or are prepared with animal fat. Always find out if your *frijoles* were prepared using *manteca* (lard). Wherever possible, *Let's Go* includes vegetarian dining options, but if you have any doubts, check with your *mesero* to make sure that your food is completely meat-free. For **more information** contact the **North American Vegetarian Society,** P.O. Box 72, Dolgeville, NY 13329 (tel. (518) 568-7970; email navs@telenet.com; www.cyberveg.org/navs/), which publishes *Transformative Adventures*, a guide to vacations and retreats (US$15).

Travelers who keep **kosher** should contact synagogues in larger cities for information on kosher restaurants; your own synagogue or Hillel should have access to lists of Jewish institutions across the nation. If you are strict in your observance, consider preparing your own food on the road. The **Jewish Travel Guide** lists synagogues, kosher restaurants, and Jewish institutions in over 80 countries. The book is available from Vallentine Mitchell Publishers, Newbury House 890-900, Eastern Ave., Newbury Park, Ilford, Essex, U.K. IG2 7HH (tel. 0181 599 88 66; fax 599 0984).

ALTERNATIVES TO TOURISM

STUDY

Popular in Mexico, foreign study programs vary tremendously in expense, academic quality, living conditions, degree of contact with local students, and exposure to local culture and languages. There is a plethora of exchange programs for high school students. Cuernavaca, San Miguel de Allende, Oaxaca, Guanajuato, and Mexico City are all well known for language programs. Smaller local schools are generally cheaper, but international organizations may be better able to arrange academic credit at your home institution. If your Spanish is already good local universities can be much cheaper than an American university program, though it can be hard to receive academic credit. Applications to Mexican state universities are due in early spring.

UNIVERSITIES

Universidad Nacional Autonoma de Mexico (UNAM) UNAM, Apdo. 70-391, Av. Universidad, Delegacion Coyoacan, Mexico, D.F. 04510 (tel. 5 622 2470; fax 616 2672; www.unam.mx) is the large national university of Mexico (over 100,000 students). It operates the **Centro de Ensenanza para Extranjeros (CEPE)** which provides semester, intensive, and summer programs in Spanish, art, history, literature, and Chicano studies. This program is open only to undergraduate and graduate foreign students. The school also operates a satellite campus in Taxco.

Universidad de las Americas, Ex-Hacienda Santa Catarina Martir, Apartado Postal 100, Cholula, Puebla 72820 (tel. 22 29 20 00) is the only Mexican university that is accredited in the U.S.

American Institute for Foreign Study, College Division, 102 Greenwich Ave., Greenwich, CT 06830 (tel. 800-727-2437, ext. 6084; www.aifs.com). Organizes programs for high school and college study in Mexican universities. Summer, fall, spring, year-long programs, and scholarships available. Contact Dana Maggio at dmaggio@aifs.com.

Council on International Educational Exchange (CIEE), 205 E. 42nd St., New York, NY 10017 (tel. 888-COUNCIL (268-6245); fax (212) 822-2699; www.ciee.org) sponsors work, volunteer, academic, and internship study abroad programs in Mexico.

Language Link Incorporated, P.O. Box 3006, Peoria, IL 61612 (tel. 800-552-2051). Runs the Spanish Language Institute-Center for Latin American Studies in Cuernavaca (US$255 per week) and Mazatlán (US$290 per week). Program offers beginning, intermediate, and advanced level language courses for people of all ages. Students live with Mexican families.

WORK

ESSENTIALS

The Mexican government is wary of giving up precious jobs to foreigners when many of its own people are unemployed. It used to be that only 10% of the employees of foreign firms located in Mexico could have non-Mexican citizenship; now the limit depends on the sector. If you manage to secure a position with a Mexican business, your employer must get you a work permit. It is possible, but illegal, to work without a permit and you risk deportation if caught. Below are some suggestions for further reading about working in Mexico.

For **more information,** consult: *International Jobs: Where they Are, How to Get Them,* by Eric Koocher (Perseus Books; US$16); *Work Abroad,* by Clayton Hubbs (Transitions Abroad; US$16); *International Directory of Voluntary Work,* by Victoria Pybus (Vacation Work Publications; US$16); *Teaching English Abroad,* by Susan Griffin (Vacation Work; US$17); or *Overseas Summer Jobs 1999, Work Your Way Around the World,* and *Directory of Jobs and Careers Abroad* (Peterson's; US$17-18 each).

TEACHING ENGLISH

International Schools Services, Educational Staffing Program, P.O. Box 5910, Princeton, NJ 08543 (tel. (609) 452-0990; email edustaffing@iss.edu; www.iss.edu). Recruits teachers and administrators for American and English schools in Mexico. All instruction in English. Applicants must have a bachelor's degree and 2 years of relevant experience. US$100 application fee. Publishes *The ISS Directory of Overseas Schools* (US$35).

World Teach, Harvard Institute for International Development, 14 Story St., Cambridge, MA 02138 (tel. (617) 495-5527; fax 495-1599; email info@worldteach.org; http://worldteach.org). Volunteers teach English, math, science, and environmental education to students of all ages in Mexico. Bachelor's degree required for 6-month and year-long programs. Room and board are provided during the period of service, but volunteers must pay a fee covering health insurance and training.

ARCHAEOLOGICAL DIGS

Archaeological Institute of America, 656 Beacon St., Boston, MA 02215-2010 (tel. (617) 353-9361; fax 353-6550; email aia@bu.edu; www.archaeological.org), puts out the *Archaeological Fieldwork Opportunities Bulletin* (US$16 for non-members), which lists field sites in Mexico. This can be purchased from Kendall/Hunt Publishing, 4050 Westmark Dr., Dubuque, Iowa 52002 (tel. 800-228-0810).

VOLUNTEER

Volunteer jobs are readily available almost everywhere. You may receive room and board in exchange for your labor. You can sometimes avoid the high application fees charged by the organizations that arrange placement by contacting the individual workcamps directly; check with the organizations.

Volunteers for Peace, 1034 Tiffany Rd., Belmont, VT 05730 (tel. (802) 259-2759; fax 259-2922; email vfp@vfp.org; www.vfp.org). A nonprofit organization that arranges speedy placement in 2-3 week workcamps in Mexico comprising 10-15 people. Most complete and up-to-date listings provided in the annual *International Workcamp Directory* (US$15). Registration fee US$195. Free newsletter.

Global Volunteers, 375 E. Little Canada Rd., St. Paul, MN 55117 (tel. 800-487-1074; fax (612) 482-0915; email email@globalvolunteers.org; www.globalvolunteers.org). Volunteers of all ages spend two weeks in Queretaro, Guanajuato, or Dolores Hidalgo teaching English to students in Guanajuato. Participation fee is $995; includes all expenses except transportation to Mexico.

Los Ninos, 287 G Street, Chula Vista, CA 91910 (tel. 619-426-9110; fax 426-6664).Offers groups of 15-22 opportunities to participate in community projects and education programs near the U.S.-Mexico-border. Participation fees vary.

Transitions Abroad Publishing, Inc., 18 Hulst Rd., P.O. Box 1300, Amherst, MA 01004-1300 (tel. 800-283-0373; fax 413-256-0373; email trabroad@aol.com; www.transa-broad.com). Publishes a bi-monthly magazine listing of opportunities and printed resources for those seeking to study, work, or travel abroad. They also publish *The Alternative Travel Directory*, a comprehensive guide to finding and preparing for a job overseas. For subscriptions (U.S. US$20 for 6 issues), contact them at Transitions Abroad, P.O. Box 1300, Amherst, MA 01003-1400.

OTHER USEFUL RESOURCES

MEXICAN PUBLICATIONS AND ATLASES

Guía Oficial de Hospedaje de Mexico: published for the Secretaría de Turismo by Editorial Limusa, Grupo Noriega Editores, Balderas 95, Mexico, D.F. 06040 Mexico (tel. 5 512 21 05; fax 5 512 29 03). A comprehensive listing of all government registered hotels, in all price ranges. An invaluable resource for travelers heading to small towns not covered by *Let's Go: Mexico 2000*. Available for free from some tourist offices.

Mexico Desconocido: Monte Pelvoux 110-104, Lomas de Chapultepec, Mexico D.F. 11000 (tel. 5 202 65 85; fax 540 17 71). Monthly travel magazines in Spanish and English describe little-known areas and customs of Mexico. Subscriptions to the U.S. cost $50 (call to place an order); subscriptions in Mexico cost 240 pesos.

Rand McNally: 150 S. Wacker Dr., Chicago, IL 60606 (tel. 800-333-0136; www.randmcnally.com), publishes the most comprehensive road atlas of Mexico. Available in most bookstores throughout the U.S. for $10. Phone orders are also available.

INTERNET RESOURCES

The following list of useful Mexico resources on the Web are in English unless otherwise noted. *Let's Go* also lists relevant web sites throughout different sections of the **Essentials** chapter. Keep in mind that web sites come and go very rapidly; a good web site one week might disappear the next. This list is a good departure point for personal cyber-space adventures. Also, *Net Travel: How Travelers Use the Internet* by Michael Shapiro (O'Reilly & Assoc.; US$25) is a very thorough and informative guide to all aspects of travel planning through the Internet.

Consulate General of Mexico: (www.quicklink.com/mexico). Basic information about the Mexican government branches, economic indicators, and links to other Mexico-related sites. In Spanish or English.

El Mundo Maya (www.wotw.com/mundomaya/). Comprehensive coverage of the Maya region of Mexico, including city and regional descriptions, photos, maps, and restaurant and hotel information.

Foreign Language for Travelers: (www.travlang.com) can help you brush up on your Spanish.

Let's Go: (www.letsgo.com) accesses our travel newsletter, updated travel information and links to Mexico.

Mexico City Subway System (http://metro.jussieu.fr:10001/bin/select/english/mexico/mexico). An automated route-finder and map of the Mexico City Metro.

Mexico Reference Desk: (www.lanic.utexas.edu/la/Mexico/). A plethora of hyper-links to sites related to Mexico.

MexWeb (http://mexweb.mty.itesm.mx/) Lots of Mexico-related links by subject. In Spanish.

Microsoft Expedia (http://expedia.msn.com). This mega-site has everything you'd ever need to make travel plans on the web—compare flight fares, look at maps, and book reservations.

The CIA World Factbook (www.odci.gov/cia/publications/factbook/index.html) has tons of vital statistics on Mexico. Check it out for an overview of Mexico economy, and an explanation of its system of government.

Travelocity (www.travelocity.com). Operates a comprehensive network of travel services.

U.S. State Department Travel Advisory for Mexico: (travel.state.gov/mexico.html). The word from above on travel safety and recommended precautions.

Yahoo! Mexico Links (www.yahoo.com/regional/countries/mexico). Well-indexed and searchable database of over 2000 links related to Mexico.

Zapatista Web Page (http://ezln.org). Provides up-to-the-minute information in English and Spanish about Mexico's most prominent rebel group.

ESSENTIALS

MEXICO CITY

The Azeca were the first to settle this troubled and magical valley. These nomadic mercenaries traveled through modern-day northern Mexico worshipping classical Mesoamerican deities including **Quetzalcoatl** (the feathered serpent) and **Tlaloc** (the rain god). There was, however, one god unique to the Aztec—**Huitzilopochitli,** the god of war and day. During their nomadic beginnings, Huitzilopochitli was no more important than the other deities, but he would ultimately play a key role in the future of Aztec society. Huitzilopochitli's priests prophesized that the Aztec's wandering should stop if they were ever to encounter an eagle devouring a snake atop a *nopal* cactus. The eagle was a symbol for the sun and thus represented Huitzilopochitli, while the fruit of the *nopal* (prickly pear) cactus represented the human heart which fed the god of war. The wandering Aztec tribe is said to have encountered the vision of the eagle and the *nopal* on an island in a murky lake nestled in the highland Valley of Mexico, and at this site they dutifully founded the island city of Tenochtitlán, which became the nucleus of the most systematic and dominating empire on the continent. Almost seven centuries and 25 million inhabitants later, the Valley of Mexico now cradles the largest city in the world.

To fathom the size of the city, it helps to see the heart of Mexico from the air. As soon as your jet descends beneath the clouds, urban settlement overflows every angle of the window view. It will soon become clear that the word "city" hardly does justice to the 1480 square kilometers of sprawling humanity enshrouded in a stagnant yellow haze. There appears to be no boundaries, no suburbs, no beginning, no end; buildings tall and short are imbedded into the cupped, drained, saline lake-bed as far as the eye can see.

Mexicans call this cosmopolitan conglomeration **el D.F.** (deh-EFF-ay), short for **Distrito Federal** (Federal District), or simply **México.** The *defectuoso* (defective), as local *chilangos* (Mexico City inhabitants) teasingly call their city, is a breeding ground for staggering statistics. Depending on the statistical interpretation, it is home to between 17 and 30 million people and has over 220 *colonias* (neighborhoods). Virtually the entire federal bureaucracy inhabits the D.F., including the Ministry of the Navy—2240m above sea level. One-quarter of Mexico's entire population lives in the D.F. From the enormous central square to a sprawling governmental palace to 40-story skyscrapers to Parque Chapultepec, the biggest city park in the Americas, everything here is larger than life. First-time visitors stop dead in their tracks when they realize the imposing three-story art-nouveau edifice across from El Palacio de Bellas Artes is simply the post office. No one here buries the ruins of the past nor apologizes for the excesses of the present.

If given a chance, México City will ensure sublime moments amid the overwhelming bustle. While gliding down the floating gardens of Xochimilco, the scent of orchids wafts through the air; meanwhile, the image of young, Mexican patriots wrapped in their country's flag while plummeting from the summit of *el castillo* in Parque Chapultepec as a last stand against the American invasion, prevails. The throngs of devout *chilangos* at the Basílica de Guadalupe surround inconspicuous meandering while the sleepy lie in the shade of the Alameda listening to water rush through the stone fountains. If some of the most exclusive discos in the world won't open their doors to let you catch a glimpse of nocturnal pleasures, be otherwise dazzled by the grandeur of the ancient Templo Mayor, center of the Aztec religious, political, and cultural world. Everywhere you look in the city today, from subway stations to the *zócalo*, such ruins peek out through the centuries of growth and development to catch a breath of fresh smog. Indeed, nowhere else in the world does a country's tumultuous history breathe so heavily down the back of day-to-day life.

After an epic siege and the ultimate defeat of Aztec Emperor Moctezuma II (see p. 9), Cortés and his men purposefully founded the crux of their colonial endeavors directly atop the pantheistic stone monuments in the floating city of Tenochtitlán to symbolize the defeat of Aztec religion. Moctezuma's hubris returned to haunt the colonists when, having destroyed the hydraulic infrastructure, they discovered that their newly won valley, slouching in a huge highland puddle of standing water blocked by mountains, presented a logistical nightmare. After colonization, floods tore through the city again and again, and buildings began to sink into the mud. The *Desagüe General*, a project to drain all of the stagnant water out of the valley, began in 1629 but was not completed until the draining of Lake Texcoco in 1900. When all the water was finally gone, Mexico City—10.33m lower than it was at the time of Conquest and no longer an island—found itself surrounded by infertile salt flats which, as the 20th century progressed, were filled in by miles of straggling shantytowns settled by newcomers from surrounding central Mexico. Landlocked and ringed by mountains, the city lets neither water in nor sewage out.

To make things worse, Aztec legend predicted that the modern world would be destroyed by earthquakes and this almost came true in 1985, when Mexico City was shattered by a massive quake measuring 8.1 on the Richter scale. Tens of thousands of people died and entire neighborhoods were reduced to rubble. In 1997, Armageddon stepped closer when the majestic, snow-capped volcano Popocatépetl awakened to spew ash over the city in late June. Mexico City has also been subjected to its own version of the plagues; among them are huge-scale water shortage (a problem that will soon blossom to epic proportions), volcanic eruptions, massive earthquakes, poverty, the proliferation of petty crime, and the worst air-pollution problem anywhere on earth. The pollution reached new heights of wheezing horror in the summer of 1998; smoke from fires in Chiapas billowed in, and late rains refused to offer any respite. The eye-reddening air is kept in place by the bowl formed by surrounding mountains—some say that just breathing for a day in Mexico City is equivalent to smoking 20 cigarettes. As people from around the country continue to arrive in hopes of finding scarce jobs, Mexico City's infamous demographic crisis becomes more difficult to ignore, and the prospect of feeding everyone becomes increasingly unrealistic.

In the summer of 1998, just one year after the mayoral victory of the PRD (Partido Revolucionario Democrático) ended years of one-party rule, frustration at the lack of any rapid remedy to the city's illnesses is mixed with continued hope, and many still lament that little has changed despite the new leadership. What will this resplendent, rubbish-ridden city accomplish now? Millions each day strut down Paseo de la Reforma, contemplating their sinking city's future under the watchful eye of *El Angel*. Most see the city not as an enemy but as a prodigal son. The *chilangos'* laments are grounded in unconditional love for this apocalyptic metropolis. They are proud of its past, preoccupied with its present, and hopeful about leading their capital to a new and glorious future.

HIGHLIGHTS OF MEXICO CITY

■ Don't miss Mexico City's **zócalo** (p. 105), the center of the country's capital, home to ruins, cathedrals, and government buildings lovingly covered with murals by Rivera, Siquieros, and Orozco—all right next to each other.

■ The **Bosque de Chapultepec** (p. 112) is the biggest urban park in the Americas—it's got everything from panda bears to free concerts to the **Museo Nacional de Antropología** (p. 113), Mexico's biggest and best museum.

■ Wear your fanciest duds to party in the perennially packed bars and discos of the glamorous **Zona Rosa** (p. 125).

■ Flock with the devout to the **Basílica de Guadalupe** (p. 116).

■ Take a nap on the park benches of the gloriously green **Alameda** (p. 107) across from the beautiful, French-inspired **Palacio de Bellas Artes** (p. 108).

■ Some of Mexico City's most fabulous attractions aren't actually in the city—check out our suggestions for **daytrips** (p. 134), especially the nearby pyramids of **Teotihuacán** (p. 131), the most visited ruins in all of Mexico.

⌐ GETTING THERE AND AWAY

All roads lead to Mexico City. Buses, trains, and planes haul passengers from every town in the Republic into the smoggy hyperactivity of the city's many temples of transport—the expanding Benito Juárez International Airport, four crowded bus stations, a desolate train station, and a network of freeways. Fortuitously, airports and stations in Mexico City usually have information booths for frazzled tourists equipped with quasi-English-speaking personnel, free (or cheap) maps, official zone-rated taxi service, and a connected or very nearby Metro station. Except for the typically terrible train service, getting around can even be fun. *Buena suerte* (good luck).

BY AIR

Flying into Mexico City from abroad entails the usual customs and immigration procedures. **Tourist cards (FMTs)** are distributed on the plane and stamped at the airport. Although many border officials are lax about enforcement, the "stoplight" customs system at the airport ensures that a certain percentage of random passengers is inspected—those unlucky enough to get a red light. Be prepared to allow an agent to sift through your silky intimates.

The **Benito Juárez International Airport** (tel. 571 32 95) lies 6.5km east of the *zócalo*, the formal center of the city. Blvd. Capitán Juan Sarabio heads northeast to the airport from Blvd. Puerto Aéreo, one of the major roads circling the city. The surprisingly small airport is expanding at an exponential rate and is jam-packed with facilities, including **24-hour restaurants, cafeterias,** and **ATMs.**

GETTING TO AND FROM THE AIRPORT

Transportation into the city is uncomplicated. Buy a *transporte terrestre* ticket from the *venta de boletos* desk in the airport in *Sala A* and *Sala E,* and present it to any of the white and yellow authorized taxis waiting outside. The price is set by the zone of the city to which you're traveling (63 pesos to the *centro,* 83 pesos to El Monumento de la Revolución; 20% more after hours). Check the map—just because it's an official-looking booth does not mean you won't be overcharged. Avoid people wearing uniforms trying to direct you to a taxi booth or to the taxi stand because they will try to charge large tips for small services. Avoid unauthorized taxis, especially those with bags over the meters. **Taxis** (tel. 784 48 11 or 571 36 00) will also take you to the airport from the city. For more taxi etiquette and warnings, see p. 90.

The Metro is by far the cheapest route to the city (1.50 pesos). The airport subway station, **Terminal Aérea** (Line 5), located at the junction of Capitán Juan Sarabio and Blvd. Puerto Aéreo, is only a 10-minute walk from *Sala E.* Signs will point you in the right direction (for more Metro info, see p. 88). Large bags are officially prohibited, but provided you avoid rush hours and can maneuver through the turnstile, a typical pack should not pose much of a problem. For the comfort of others, and mainly for your own safety, remove the pack from your back when you're on the subway. Also, try to ride in the less crowded cars at the end. If a train appears frighteningly jam-packed, simply let it pass; another will arrive within minutes, and you'll be at the front of the pack. **If you return to the airport by Metro, do not get off at the Aeropuerto stop on line 1. The correct stop Is Terminal Aérea on line 5.**

FLIGHT INFORMATION

Flight Info Hotline: (tel. 5571 36 00). Specify domestic or international flights.

Carriers: Sala A: All **Aeroméxico,** baby. The most complete air transportation throughout the Republic. **Sala B: Mexicana** plays a strong second fiddle, also giving a tiny bit of space to **Aeromar** and **Aerocalifornia,** which really does go to California (Los Angeles) via a variety of Mexican cities (including Tijuana). One of the few airlines with significantly lower prices. **Sala C:** Really tiny, with only Aerolineas Internacionales (don't be

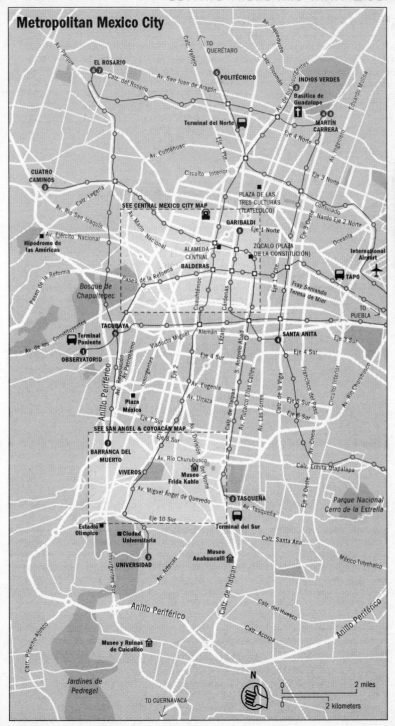

Metropolitan Mexico City

TO QUERÉTARO

Av. Parque

EL ROSARIO
⑥⑦

Calz. del Rosario

Av. San Juan de Aragón

POLITÉCNICO ⑤

Calz. Vallejo

Av. Aducducto

Calz. Ticomán

Av. de los Insurgentes

INDIOS VERDES

Basílica de
Guadalupe

MARTÍN ④⑥
CARRERA

Eduardo Molina

Terminal del Norte

Eje 4 Norte

Av. Cuitláhuac

Av. Ingeniero

Circuito Interior

Eje 3 Norte

Eje 1 Pte.

CUATRO
CAMINOS ②

Calz. Legaria

Av. Río San Joaquín

Av. Martín Nacional

SEE CENTRAL MEXICO CITY MAP

PLAZA DE LAS
TRES CULTURAS
(TLATELOLCO)

Consulado

Nardo Eje 2 Norte

Eje 2 Oeste

Oceanía

Av. Ejército Nacional

GARIBALDI ⑧

Eje 1 Norte

Hipódromo de
las Américas

Paseo de la Reforma

ALAMEDA
CENTRAL

ZÓCALO (PLAZA
DE LA CONSTITUCIÓN)

International
Airport

Bosque de
Chapultepec

Paseo de la Reforma

BALDERAS

Cuauhtémoc

Cárdenas

Eje 1 Oeste

Fray Servando
Teresa de Mier

TAPO ✈

Av. de los Constituyentes

TACUBAYA

Alemán

Lázaro

SANTA ANITA ④

TO
PUEBLA

Terminal
Poniente

Av. Revolución

Viaducto Miguel

Av. Patriotismo

Eje 3 Sur

OBSERVATORIO ①

Insurgentes

Eje 2

Eje 4 Sur

S. Antonio Abad

Eje 4 Sur

Av. Río Churubusco

Anillo Periférico

Av. Eugenia

Calz. de Tlalpan

Av. Plutarco Elías Calles

Calz. de la Viga

Francisco del Paso

Circuito Interior

Plaza
México

Av. Urraza

Av. Las Torres

Eje 5 Sur

Eje 6 Sur

Av. Cinco

Eje 7 Sur

SEE SAN ANGEL & COYOACÁN MAP

Eje 8 Sur

Av. División del Norte

BARRANCA DEL ⑦
MUERTO

VIVEROS

Av. Río Churubusco

Calz. Ermita Iztapalapa

Museo
Frida Kahlo

Eje 3 Oeste

Parque Nacional
Cerro de la Estrella

Av. Miguel Ángel de Quevedo

TASQUEÑA ②

Av. Tasqueña

Eje 10 Sur

Terminal del Sur

Estadio
Olímpico

Calz. Santa Ana

Ciudad
Universitaria

México-Tulyehualco

UNIVERSIDAD ③

Av. Aztecas

Museo
Anahuacalli

Insurgentes Sur

Anillo Periférico

Calz. de Tlalpan

Calz. del Huesco

Calz. Acoxpa

Anillo Periférico

Museo y Ruinas
de Cuicuilco

Calz. Picacho Ajusco

Jardines de
Pedregal

TO CUERNAVACA

N

0   2 miles

0   2 kilometers

fooled by the name—they only offer domestic service) and **AVIACSA. Sala D:** ALLEGRO, TAESA, and charter flights. **Sala E:** International arrivals. **Sala F1:** Aeroméxico (international flights), America West, Avianca, Continental, Delta, Lan Chile, and LAB. **Sala F2:** The big one! Air France, Aviateca, British Airways, Canadian, Copa, Cubana, ETA, JAL, KLM, Lufthansa, Malaysia, Miami Air, Northwest, and Taca. **Sala F3:** American Airlines, Argentinian Airlines, Iberia, and United Airlines.

Domestic Flights: Flight schedules and prices change frequently. Prices are roughly the same from airline to airline. **Aerocalifornia** (tel. 207 13 92), at *Sala B*, tends to be the most competitive. Open daily 7am-7pm. Usually no student discounts, but always ask about *tarifas promocionales*, which can save you up to 50%. Aeroméxico and Mexicana airlines can take you anywhere in the country, provided there's an airport. **Aeroméxico,** (tel. 5726 02 34) Paseo de la Reforma 445 at Mississippi, and Reforma 80 (tel. 566 10 78). Both locations open M-Sa 9am-6:15pm. At the airport, *Sala A* (tel. 13 34 00). Open daily 4:30am-2am. **Mexicana,** Reforma 312 (tel. 5726 02 34), at Amberes in the *Zona Rosa*, and Reforma 107 in the Hotel Sevilla Palace. Both open M-F 9am-6pm. At the airport, *Sala B* (tel. 448 09 04). Open 24hr.

International Flights: Aeroméxico and **Mexicana** fly to Central America and the U.S. **Air France,** Edgar Allen Poe 90 (tel. 627 60 00 or 627 60 60), in Col. Polanco. Open M-F 9am-2pm, 3-6pm. At the airport (tel. 627 60 60) on the 3rd fl. above *Sala F.* Open M 10am-2pm, Tu-Sa 10am-10pm, Su 1:30-10pm. **American,** Reforma 314, first fl. (tel. 5209 14 00). Also at the airport in *Sala F.* Open M-F 9am-6pm, Sa 9am-8:30pm. **British Airways,** Balmes 8, Mez. office #6 (tel. 5785 87 14), in Col. Polanco. **Canadian Airlines,** Reforma 390 (tel. 5208 18 83). **Continental,** (tel. 5283 55 00) at the airport between *Salas D* and *E.* Open M-F 9am-6pm, Sa 10am-2pm. **Delta,** Reforma 381 (tel. 5202 16 08 or 5207 34 11). At the airport (tel. 5279 09 09) in *Sala F.* Open daily 6am-6pm. **Northwest/KLM,** Paseo de las Palmas 735, 7th fl. (tel. 202 44 44 or toll-free 01 800 90 00 800). At the airport (tel. 57 85 16 93) in *Sala F.* Open daily 9am-4pm. **Lufthansa,** Las Palmas 239 (tel. 5230 00 00), at Col. Lomas de Chapultepec. Open M-F 9am-6pm. At airport (tel. 5571 27 02). Open daily 2:30-9:30pm. **Swissair,** Hamburgo 66, 3rd fl. (tel. 5207 24 55), between Niza and Havre in the *Zona Rosa.* Open M-F 9am-6pm. **United,** Hamburgo 213, ground fl. (tel. 5627 02 22 or toll-free 01 800 00 30777). At the airport (tel. 627 02 22 for flight information) in *Sala F.* Open daily 9am-noon, 3-5pm.

AIRPORT SERVICES

Tourist Office: INFOTUR, *Sala A* (tel. 76 27 73). The wonderful staff in this small office has maps and guides of the city, can give you basic info, and can direct you to other resources. There's also a small touch-screen computer replete with info and help with hotel reservations. Open M-F 9am-8pm, Sa-Su 9am-9pm. Other "information" kiosks in *Salas A* and *F* have flight info.

Currency Exchange: Banks exchange currency and traveler's checks in almost all of the *salas.* **ATMs,** accepting a number of cards, are availble in *Sala A,* directly under *Sala B,* and throughout *Salas E* and *F.* **Casas de cambio,** every foot or so, are open 6am-8pm, sometimes later but don't give the best rates in the city.

Car Rental: In *Sala E* (see p. 91), open until about 10:30pm.

Storage Lockers: Next to the snack bar, to the left of the arrival gate in *Sala A* and in *Sala E.* Storage 30 pesos 24hr., 33-60 pesos for larger bags.

Lost and Found: Bags overflow in a small room next to Aeropost in *Sala D.* International carriers have lost luggage offices on the third floor, above *Sala F.*

Bookstore: In *Sala C.* Novels, art, and history books in Spanish and English. Maps available. Open M-Sa 7am-9pm, Su 8am-8pm.

Cultural Information: Instituto Nacional de Antropología e Historia, *Sala A* (tel. 571 02 67). Essentially a bookstore but with free information about archaeological sites and museums throughout the country—currently under construction. Open daily 9am-9pm.

AIRPORT EMERGENCY AND COMMUNICATIONS

Telephones: LADATELs around the airport accept phone cards sold at nearby magazine stands. Some phones take international credit cards. Phone center with **fax** as well as local and international calls between *Salas* D and E. Open 24hr.

Police: (tel. 625 70 07), outside the airport in front of *Sala C.* Open 24hr.

Pharmacy: In *Sala C,* open daily 6am-midnight; in *Sala F,* open daily 6am-11pm.

Post Office: In *Sala A.* Open M-F 8am-7pm, Sa 9am-5pm.

BY TRAIN

Mexican trains tend to be **excruciatingly slow** (for more on that, p. 70). The fastest route—to Veracruz (11hr., 8:45am and 8:15pm daily, 65 pesos)—is barely bearable. Buy tickets for morning trains when the ticket booth (tel. 5547 10 84 or 5547 10 97) opens at 7am. Buy tickets for evening trains by 9am. No advance ticket sales or phone purchases. (Booths open daily 7am-last train.)

   Estación Buenavista of the **Ferrocarriles Nacionales de México** (tel. 547 10 97) is located north of the **Monumento de la Revolución** at the corner of Insurgentes and Mosqueta (Eje 1 Alzate), five long blocks from the nearest Metro station, Revolución (Line 2; open M-F 6am-12:30am, Sa 6am-1:30am). **Taxis** leave from Mosqueta, but be warned these may or may not be *sitio* cabs. Make sure to check for *credenciales* before getting into any taxi.

BY BUS

Mexico City's four main bus stations correspond to the cardinal directions. **Central de Autobuses del Norte** (North Station) serves the Bajío, northern Veracruz, Jalisco, and of northern Mexico; **Terminal Central de Autobuses del Sur** (South Station) launches buses to Guerrero, Morelos, and Oaxaca; **Terminal de Autobuses de Pasajeros de Oriente** (**TAPO;** East Station) sends buses to Puebla, southern Veracruz, Oaxaca, Chiapas, and the Yucatán Peninsula; and the **Terminal de Autobuses del Poniente** (West Station) serves Mexico state and Michoacán. First-class, plus (between first- and second-class), and second-class service are available.

   All stations are served by the Metro and offer an official 24-hour taxi service that charges fixed rates (set by zones) for a ride to any point in the city or adjacent parts of Mexico state. Buy your ticket inside to avoid being ripped off, but be wary of being charged for an extra zone—if you can find it, consult the zone map. *Peseros* (a.k.a. *colectivos*) also serve the four stations. Quality budget hotels near the bus stations are virtually nil (see p. 98) and it's a much safer bet to head toward the city center. **The following bus prices change almost weekly,** and listings are by no means comprehensive. Given the extensive network, it is possible to go almost anywhere at any time.

CENTRAL DE AUTOBUSES DEL NORTE

The Central de Autobuses del Norte (tel. 5587 15 52) is on Cien Metros. Metro: Autobuses del Norte (Line 5). **Banamex ATM, restaurant,** a **luggage storage** (10-20 pesos per 24hr.), **phone** and **fax** offices, and a **pharmacy** are all open around the clock. A **casa de cambio** near the main entrance offers poor rates (open daily 11am-6pm daily). There's also a **post office** (open M-F 8am-7:30pm and Sa 9am-1pm) and a **telegram office** (open M-F 9am-7:30pm, Sa 9am-4:30pm). A hotel **reservations** service booth is occasionally open near the main entrance (supposedly open 8am-9pm). From the **taxi stand,** rides to the *zócalo* or Revolución should be 35 pesos. A plethora of bus companies populate the *Central;* prices are often suspiciously similar, and it's not uncommon for "competing" bus companies to share phone numbers. You've got an infinite but unvaried selection in this terminal/zoo. A few of the perennial faves:

Autobuses de Oriente (ADO; tel. 5133 24 24) serves: **Oaxaca** (6hr., 7 per day 7am-12pm, 211 pesos); **Papantla** (5hr., 6 per day 10:30-12:30am, 110 pesos); **Puebla** (2hr., every 20min. 4am-10pm, 65 pesos); **Tuxpan** (6hr., 12 per day 6am-midnight, 132 pesos); **Veracruz** (7hr., 6 per day 8am-12:15am, 181 pesos); and **Xalapa** (5hr., 2, 3pm and 12:15am, 181 pesos). ADO GL, run by the same company, offers *ejecutivo* service to: **Oaxaca** (6hr., midnight, 247 pesos); **Tampico** (9hr., 10 and 11pm, 261 pesos); **Veracruz** (6hr., 11:30pm, 215 pesos); and **Villahermosa** (10hr., 10pm, 421 pesos). UNO, also run by ADO, goes super-deluxe to **Tampico** (9hr.; 9, 9:45 and 10:15pm; 369 pesos).

Elite (tel. 7529 07 07). The name says it all; posh service to: **Hermosillo** (30hr., every hr. 5:30am-1:15pm, 1530 pesos); **Puerto Vallarta** (14hr., 4 per day 5-11:45pm, 579 pesos); and **Tijuana** (42hr., every hr. 7:15am-10:30pm, 1237 pesos).

Estrella Blanca (tel. 5729 07 07). To: **Chihuahua** (20hr., every hr. 6am-11:30pm, 727 pesos); **Durango** (12hr., 3 per day 7am-11:45pm, 450 pesos); **Torreón** (13hr., every hr., 505 pesos); and **Zacatecas** (7hr., every hr., 316 pesos).

Flecha Amarilla (tel. 5587 52 22). First-class service to: **Guadalajara** (9hr., every hr. 7:30-midnight, 195 pesos); **Guanajuato** (6½hr., 9 per day 1am-6:45pm, 233 pesos); **León** (6½hr., every 30min. 6am-midnight, 214 pesos); **Manzanillo** (16hr.; 9, 10:40, and 11:45pm; 443 pesos); **Morelia** (5hr., every hr., 154 pesos); **Querétaro** (3½hr., every 30min. 5:30am-11:40pm, 120 pesos); **San Luis Potosí** (7hr., 6 per day, 120 pesos); and **San Miguel de Allende** (4½hr.; 7:10, 11:15am and 5:40pm; 140 pesos).

Futura (tel. 729 07 07). To: **Acapulco** (5hr., every 1½hr. 6am-11:30pm, 215 pesos); **Aguascalientes** (6hr., every hr. 7:30am-12:30am, 268 pesos); **Chihuahua** (18hr., every hr. 8:50am-11:30pm, 727 pesos); **Ciudad Valles** (9½hr., 9pm, 246 pesos); **Matamoros** (14hr., 5 per day 2:15-10:30pm, 482 pesos); **Monterrey** (12hr., every hr. 7am-11:55pm, 463 pesos); and **Tampico** (9½hr., every 2hr., 266 pesos).

TERMINAL DE AUTOBUSES DE PASAJEROS DE ORIENTE (TAPO)

The TAPO, General Ignacio Zaragoza 200 (tel. 762 59 77), is behind Metro station San Lázaro (Line 1). To get to the bus station from the Metro, follow the red railings through the store-lined passageway. Helpful **police** booths are scattered throughout the station. Taxi ticket booths are near the entrance to the Metro. Don't try following the signs to the tourist information booth; it no longer exists. The station also contains a 24hr. **ATM, currency exchange** services (open daily 7am-11pm), a **travel agency** (tel. 542 90 92; open M-F 9:30am-2pm and 3-7pm, Sa 10am-1pm.), **food stands**, and a **pharmacy. Luggage storage** is available (tel. 542 23 23; 30 pesos per 24hr., larger pieces 33-60 pesos; open daily 24hr.).

ADO (tel. 542 71 92). First-class to: **Campeche** (18hr., 12:30-11:30pm, 519 pesos); **Cancún** (24hr., 5 per day 8:30am-6:45pm, 690 pesos); **Córdoba** (4½hr., 34 per day, 138 pesos); **Mérida** (20hr., 5 per day 12:30-9:30pm, 586 pesos); **Oaxaca** (6hr., 24 per day, 211 pesos); **Palenque** (12hr., 4 and 6:10pm, 412 pesos); **Veracruz** (5hr., 23 per day, 181 pesos); **Villahermosa** (10½hr., 18 per day, 359 pesos); and **Xalapa** (4½hr., 24 per day, 126 pesos). ADO GL offers *ejecutivo* service to all of the above locations, less frequently and at slightly higher prices.

Autobuses Cristóbal Colón (tel. 133 24 33). First-class to: **Oaxaca** (6hr., 5 per day, 247 pesos); **San Cristóbal de las Casas** (18hr.; 3:30, 5:30, and 7:30pm; 442 pesos); **Tonalá** (13hr.; 5, 7:45, and 10pm; 385 pesos); and **Tuxtla Gutiérrez** (15hr., 5 per day 2:30-9:30pm, 420 pesos).

Autobuses Unidos (AU; tel. 133 24 44). To: **Córdoba** (5hr., 31 per day, 124 pesos); **Oaxaca** (6-9hr., 9 per day, 190 pesos); **San Andrés Tuxtla** (8hr., noon and 9pm, 212 pesos); and **Xalapa** (5hr., 21 per day, 113 pesos).

Estrella Roja (tel. 542 92 00). To **Puebla** (2hr., every 10min. 6am-8pm, 50 pesos).

UNO (tel. 522 11 11). To: **Oaxaca, Tampico, Veracruz, Villahermosa, Xalapa,** and other cities. Only if you must travel in the lap of luxury.

TERMINAL DE AUTOBUSES DEL PONIENTE

The Terminal de Autobuses del Poniente is on Av. Sur 122 (tel. 535 24 52). Metro: Observatorio (Line 1). Follow signs to **Buses Forraneos** and then to **Central Camionero Poniente** as you exit the Metro—a vendor-lined bridge leads to the terminal. From the terminal to the Metro, walk up the large staircase and make a left. Many of these are second-class routes; brace yourself for slow, indirect service. The station is built in the shape of a "V" with the most important services clustered at the vertex. Round-the-clock services include a **restaurant,** long-distance *caseta,* and **luggage storage** (small bags 2.50 pesos for up to 4hr., 5 pesos for 4-8hr., and 7.50 pesos for 8-24hr.; 10 pesos for subjectively determined "larger" bags). There is also a **pharmacy** (open daily 7am-10pm), a **post office** (open M-F 8am-7pm, Sa 9am-1pm), a **phone** and **fax** office (office open daily 6am-10pm), **food stands, shops, newspaper stands,** and a **Western Union.**

Autobuses del Occidente (tel. 271 00 49) sends second-class to: **Guadalajara** (12hr., 4 per day 5:30am-10:20pm, 246 pesos); **Manzanillo** (16hr., 5 per day 1:10am-4:20pm, 383 pesos); **Morelia** (6hr., every 30min., 135 pesos); and **Tuxpan** (4hr., 5 per day 6:15am-11:50pm, 65 pesos).

Caminante has first-class to **Toluca** (1hr., every 5min. 5:30am-10:30pm, 26 pesos).

Elite (tel. 729 07 07 or 729 07 93) travels in style to **Chihuahua** (20hr., 3:30pm, 727 pesos) and **Morelia** (4hr., 4 per day 10:30am-10:30pm, 132 pesos).

ETN (tel. 5567 31 02) has plush luxury service to: **Guadalajara** (7hr., 7 per day, 415 pesos); **Morelia** (4hr., 35 per day, 155 pesos); **Toluca** (1hr., every 30min., 30 pesos); **Uruapan** (5½hr., 6 per day, 265 pesos); and many other cities.

Pegasso Plus (tel. 277 77 61) has first-class trips to **Morelia** (4hr., 15 per day 6am-1am, 160 pesos) and **Pátzcuaro** (5hr., 10 per day 6:30am-midnight, 175 pesos).

Servicios Coordinados has first- and second-class service to: **León** (8hr., 7 and 10:45pm, 177 pesos); **Morelia** (5½hr., every hr. 8am-11:15pm, 135 pesos); and **Querétaro** (6hr., 4 per day 7-10:45pm, 100 pesos), among other destinations.

TERMINAL DE AUTOBUSES DEL SUR (TASQUEÑA)

The Tasqueña terminal, Tasqueña 1320 (tel. 689 97 45), is served by Metro: Tasqueña (Line 2)—exit to the right, through the market. The station has a **post office** (open M-F 8am-7pm, Sa 9am-1pm), long-distance *caseta* with **fax** service (open 24hr.), and **LADATELs** scattered about. There is also a mini-travel agency for **hotel reservations** in select cities (open Su-F 9am-9pm, Sa 9am-3pm), a 24-hour **pharmacy** (tel. 689 08 83) and a round-the-clock **cafeteria. Luggage lockers** (small 10 pesos, large 20 pesos per 24hr.) are near Exit 3. From the **taxi stand,** a trip to the *zócalo* should be 45 pesos and one to the area near Revolución 51 pesos.

ADO, Cristóbal Colón, and **Estrella Roja** sends buses to: **Cuautla** (1½hr., every 15min. 6:10am-10:20pm., 45 pesos); **Oaxaca** (6hr., 7:30am, 4pm, and midnight, 211 pesos); **Oaxtepec** (1½hr., every 15min. 6:10am-10pm, 42 pesos); **Yacutepec** (1½hr., every hr. 6:10am-10:20pm, 42 pesos); and some places in the **Gulf Coast** and **Yucatán.**

Estrella de Oro (tel. 549 85 20). has plus-class to: **Acapulco** (5hr., every hr. 6am-10pm, 205 pesos); and first-class to **Chilpancingo** (3hr., 14 per day, 130 pesos); **Cuernavaca** (1½hr., 3 per day, 35 pesos); **Iguala** (3hr., 10 per day, 72 pesos); **Ixtapa/Zihuatanejo** (9hr.; 8:40, 9:30, and 10pm; 315 pesos); and **Taxco** (2hr., 6 per day 7:40am-8:10pm, 72 pesos).

Futura and **Turistar** (tel. 628 57 71). First-class and *ejecutivo* to **Acapulco** (5hr., 29 per day, 215 pesos) and **Ixtapa/Zihuatanejo** (9hr., every 30min., 332 pesos).

Pullman de Morelos (tel. 549 35 05) sends first-class to: **Cuautla** (1½hr., every 15min. 5am-11pm, 45 pesos); **Cuernavaca** (1¼hr., every 15min. 5:30am-midnight, 40 pesos); **Oaxtepec** (1½hr., every 15min. 5am-11pm, 42 pesos); and **Tepotzlán** (1¼hr., every 15min. 6:30am-8:30pm, 50 pesos).

BY CAR

No other vehicular endeavor matches the experience of driving into Mexico City. Serene mountain roads slowly metamorphose into blaring, bumper-to-bumper, multi-lane routes. Traffic keeps the city crawling from 9 to 11am and 3 to 7pm. Don't expect anyone to drive defensively—welcome to a city where stoplights are occasionally considered optional (see **Getting Around,** p. 88). Remember that because of a desperate attempt to control congestion and contamination, one day of each week your car is not allowed to be driven in the city during the day. This is determined by the last number on your license plate; no one is exempt (see p. 91). Several major routes lead into the city and intersect with the **Circuito Interior,** the route that rings the city, at which point they change names. **Route 57,** from Querétaro and Tepotzlán, becomes **Manuel Avila Camacho** just outside the Circuito. **Route 15,** from Toluca, turns into **Av. Reforma** as it enters the city. **Route 95,** from Cuernavaca and Acapulco, becomes **Av. Insurgentes,** which plugs into the Circuito on the south side. **Route 150,** from Puebla and Texcoco, becomes **Ignacio Zaragoza,** which connects to the Circuito on the east side. **Route 85,** from Pachuca, Teotihuacán, and Texcoco, also becomes **Av. Insurgentes** in the city.

✦ ORIENTATION

The city is difficult to know well; even most *chilangos* don't have it all down pat. It's not uncommon for *taxistas* to ask passengers how to get to their destinations. What's more, many different neighborhoods use the same street name; the 300 Benito Juárez streets in the city attest to this redundant and repetitive tradition. Still, it is only a matter of cardinal directions and good ol' trial and error before you've mastered this megalopolis. The most important thing is to know the name of the **colonia** (neighborhood) to which you're going (common examples are the *centro,* Col. Polanco, *Zona Rosa,* Col. Roma, Col. Juárez). Since street numbers are often useless, cross streets and landmarks are *muy importantes.* Try to locate nearby monuments, museums, *glorietas* (traffic circles), cathedrals, and skyscrapers. It shouldn't be hard—there are loads of them.

More good news: street names tend to be clustered systematically. Streets in the *Zona Rosa* are named after European cities, those directly across Reforma are named after large rivers of the world, and the ones in Polanco are named after famous philosophers. The **Guía Roji Ciudad de México** (80 pesos), a comprehensive street atlas, is a valuable aid for anyone planning to stay in the city for some time. It's available at the airport, most large and English-language bookstores, Sanborn's, museum shops, and at many newspaper stands. Or try the abridged **mini-Guía Roji** (30 pesos).

Mexico City extends outward from the *centro* roughly 20km to the south, 10km to the north, 10km to the west, and 8km to the east. Year after year, the city's boundaries extend hungrily into neighboring communities. There is much debate about where the city actually begins and where it ends. Because of the central location of most sights, few travelers venture past the Bosque de Chapultepec to the west, La Basílica de Guadalupe to the north, the airport to the east, or San Angel and the UNAM to the south. While the best way to navigate the city is by foot, its vast size does not always make it amenable to strolling. A rectangular series of routes **(Circuito Interior)** and a thorough thoroughfare system **(Ejes Viales)** help to make inter-neighborhood travel manageable.

CIRCUITO INTERIOR AND EJES VIALES

The **Circuito Interior** is a roughly rectangular artery made up of several smaller, connected routes. **Blvd. Puerto Aéreo** forms the upper east side of the box, running north from the airport. As it bends left at the northeast corner of the box and heads west, it becomes **Av. Río Consulado.** Río Consulado turns south and becomes **Calzada Melchor Ocampo.** Ocampo heads south until it intersects **Paseo de la Reforma** at Bosque de Chapultepec, after which it continues as **Av. Vasconcelos.**

From Vasconcelos, two roads run to the southwest corner of the Circuito, **Av. Patriotismo** and **Av. Revolución**, either of which could be considered the Circuito at this point. They turn into **Av. Río Mixcoac**, which becomes **Av. Río Churubusco**, running east-west. Río Churubusco is the longest and sneakiest of the routes that constitute the Circuito. It continues east, turns north for a while, heads east again, then turns north once more to connect with Blvd. Puerto Aéreo south of the airport to complete the Circuito.

Aside from the large thoroughfares—Insurgentes, Reforma, Chapultepec, and Miguel Alemán—a system of **Ejes Viales** (axis roads) conducts the majority of traffic within the Circuito. *Ejes* run one way. Running east-west, Eje 1 Nte. and Eje 2 Nte. are north of the *zócalo*, while Ejes 2 through 8 Sur run south of it. The numbers increase heading away from the *zócalo*. **Eje Central Lázaro Cárdenas** runs north-south and bisects the box formed by the Circuito. East of it and parallel lie Ejes 1 through 3 Ote., which veer off to the northwest; west of it are Ejes 1 through 3 Pte. Theoretically, using the Ejes together with the Circuito, any general area of the city can be reached without much delay. Unfortunately, because of heavy traffic and frequent processions, zipping around gleefully is not the norm. The upside is that most travelers' needs are located within the **city center.**

CITY CENTER

As huge as Mexico City is, almost everything of interest to visitors lies within the northern half of the area circumscribed by the Circuito Interior. Moreover, many attractions are within easy reach of **Paseo de la Reforma,** the broad thoroughfare that runs southwest-northeast, or **Av. Insurgentes,** the boulevard running north-south through the city. These two main arteries intersect at the **Glorieta Cuauhtémoc.** The **Bosque de Chapultepec,** home to the principal museums of the city, is served by Metro stops Chapultepec (Line 1) and Auditorio (Line 7). From Chapultepec, Reforma proceeds northeast, punctuated by **glorietas** (traffic circles), each with a monument in the center. Some of the more famous ones, in southwest-to-northeast order, include: **Glorieta Angel de la Independencia, Glorieta Cuauhtémoc,** and the **Glorieta Cristóbal Colón.** Slightly north of the city center lie the **Plaza de Tres Culturas (Tlatelolco)** and the **Basílica de Guadalupe.**

The accommodations and food listings for Mexico City are divided according to the four areas of most interest to tourists. In terms of *barrios,* moving up Reforma from Chapultepec, the **Zona Rosa** is followed by **Buenavista** (near the Monumento a la Revolucíon), **the Alameda,** and, to the east of the Alameda, the *centro*.

CENTRO HISTÓRICO

The *centro* contains most of the historic sights and museums, extensive budget accommodations, and lively inexpensive restaurants. Metro stops Allende (closer to the accommodations and Alameda) and Zócalo (literally the center of México) serve the *centro* (Line 2). This area is bounded by Cárdenas to the west, El Salvador to the south, Pino Suárez to the east, and Rep. de Perú to the north.

ALAMEDA

The Alameda, the central city park, contains budget accommodations and many restaurants. It is accessible by Metro at Hidalgo (Lines 2 and 3), Bellas Artes (Lines 2 and 8; closer to the park, the Palacio de Bellas Artes, and the post office), and San Juan de Letran (Line 8; closer to most food and accommodations listings). The area is bounded by Eje 1 Pte. (known as Rosales, Guerrero, and Bucareli) to the west, Arcos de Belén to the south, Cárdenas to the east, and Pensador Mexicano to the north.

NEAR THE MONUMENTO A LA REVOLUCIÓN/BUENAVISTA

The Monumento a la Revolución/Buenavista area contains perhaps the most copious and inexpensive hotels and eateries. It is bounded by Insurgentes Nte. to the west, Reforma to the south and east, and Mosqueta to the north.

ZONA ROSA

The *Zona Rosa* (Pink Zone) is the capital's most touristy, commercial district, home to some of the country's most exciting nightlife. This neighborhood is accessible by Metro stops Insurgentes (primary location) and Sevilla (both on Line 1). The *Zona Rosa* is bounded by Reforma to the north and west, Av. Chapultepec to the south, and Insurgentes to the east. A few of the area's listings lie just east of Insurgentes, and a string of bars and clubs spill south past Chapultepec along Insurgentes Sur.

SOUTHERN DISTRICTS

The major southern thoroughfare is **Insurgentes Sur.** Most sights to the south, including the suburbs of **San Angel** and **Coyoacán,** as well as **Ciudad Universitaria** and the **Pyramid of Cuicuilco,** lie near or along Insurgentes. Metro Line 3 parallels Insurgentes on Cuauhtémoc and then Universidad, ending at Ciudad Universitaria (Metro: Universidad, Line 3). Two other important avenues are **Av. Revolución,** which runs parallel to Insurgentes, and **Av. Miguel Angel de Quevedo,** which runs parallel to **Francisco Sosa** in Coyoacán. Metro Line 2 runs east of Line 3 and is closer to **Xochimilco,** one of the few southern sights not along Insurgentes.

▐ GETTING AROUND

While most neighborhoods are easily traversed by foot, public transportation is necessary to travel between different areas. The Metro is the fastest, cleanest, and quickest mode of transportation. Unfortunately it becomes inhumanly crowded during rush hour (daily 7:30-9:30am and 6-9pm) and doesn't reach all parts of the city. More extensive are the thousands of white and green mini-buses known as *peseros, micros,* or *colectivos* (1-3 pesos depending on the distance), with stickers marking the route on front. Within the heart of the city, *peseros* are particularly fast and easy to catch along Insurgentes. Taxis, while more expensive, are especially handy for traversing the city late at night and for women traveling alone. However, if you love life, do not ever hail cabs on the street. **Sitio cabs** can be found at official stands or reached by phone. **Use them and them only.** The ancient *tren ligero* (trolley) still travels some routes, mainly at the city's edge and in some suburbs.

BY METRO

The Metro never ceases to amaze visitors—trains come quickly and regularly, the fare is insanely cheap, the crowds are enormous and bizarre, the ride is smooth, the service is extensive, and the stations are immaculate and monumental. Built in the late 1960s, the Metro transports five million people and makes the equivalent of two and a half trips around the earth every day. On top of this, new tracks are laid daily. Mexico's Metro system knows no bounds.

Metro tickets are sold in *taquillas* (booths) at every station. Lines can stretch for huge distances, so buy in bulk. Come prepared with exact change, since the *taquillas* are often short of small denominations. **The 1.50 peso fare includes transfers.** It's simple—you insert a coded ticket and pass through turnstiles. Transfer gates are marked **correspondencia** and exits are marked **salida.** Most transfer stations have information booths to help clueless travelers. If they are not staffed, you can ask the guards standing by the turnstiles to help orient you. A vital resource for all travelers is a color-coded subway guide, available at the tourist office or at Metro Information booths. If you are lost, wander off to a corner and discreetly check your guide. Directions are stated in terms of the station at either end of a given line. Each of the two *andenes* (platforms) has signs indicating the terminus toward which trains are heading. For example, if you are on Line 3 between Indios Verdes and Universidad, you can go either "Dirección Indios Verdes" or "Dirección Universidad." If you realize you are headed in the wrong direction, simply get off and walk under (or sometimes over) to the other side.

EL METROPOLITAN Some Metro stops are sights in their own right. Pino Suárez (Lines 1 and 2) houses a small Aztec building located at mid-transfer. The **Tunel de la Ciencia** (science tunnel) in the marathon transfer at **La Raza** (Lines 3 and 5) is an educational experience: marvel at the nifty fractals, or wear your whites and glow in the dark under a map of the constellations. The stop even has a small **science museum** (open M-Sa10am-6pm). The **Zócalo** stop (Line 2) has scale models of the plaza as it has appeared throughout its history, the *andenes* at **Copilco** (Line 3) are lined with **murals,** and the **Bellas Artes** stop (Lines 2 and 8) houses **Aztec statuettes.** In fact, nearly every Metro transfer stop has some kind of exhibit, from elementary school drawings of the subway system to a re-creation of a London theater.

The first train on all lines runs Monday through Friday at 5am, Saturday at 6am, and Sunday at 7am. The last train runs at midnight from Sunday through Friday, and on Saturday as late as 1am. Try to avoid the Metro from 7:30 to 9:30am and 6 to 9pm on weekdays. Lunch break (2-4pm) during weekdays is also crowded. During these times, huge crowds attract pickpockets. Cars at either end of the train tend to be slightly less crowded and safer.

Safety is a big concern in the Metro. As in many parts of Mexico, being single and having two X chromosomes just isn't a convenient combination. Lewd remarks and stares are a given, and the horrible experience of being groped is a very distinct possibility when the train is crowded or if it stops mid-tunnel between stations. Do not be afraid to call attention to the offender. A loud "*¿No tiene vergüenza?*" (Don't you have any shame?) or, "*¡Déjame!*" (Leave me alone!) tends to be effective. During rush hours, many lines have cars reserved for women and children. They are usually located at the front of the train and designated by a partition labeled *Mujeres y Niños*. Often you will see women and children gathering on a separate part of the platform for the reserved car.

Theft is a chronic problem on the Metro. Carry bags in front of you or on your lap; simply closing the bag does little good because thieves use razors to slit the bag open from the bottom. Subway thieves often work in pairs—one will distract you while the other pulls your wallet. Rear pockets are easy to pick, front pockets are safer; empty pockets are best. If you ride with a backpack on your back, the small pocket is likely to be violated. The safest place in a crowded car is with your back against the wall and your backpack (if you have one) in front of you. Because of overcrowding, large bags or suitcases are not allowed on the Metro. Some travelers have slipped bags past the gate, but on a crowded train, luggage will make fellow passengers uncomfortable and attract thieves. If you are intent on making it on the Metro with that overstuffed pack, come very early or after 10:30pm, when the Metro is fairly empty and guards are more likely to look the other way.

For Metro and bus information, ask at any information booth or contact **COVITUR (Comisión de Vialidad y Transporte Urbano del D.F.;** Public Relations), Felicia 67 (tel. 709 80 36 or 709 11 33), outside the Salto de Agua Metro station (Lines 1 and 8). Nearly all stations have guards and security offices, and all are required to have a *jefe de la estación* (chief of station) in a marked office. These people are valuable resources, ready to deal with questions, complaints, panic attacks, and just about anything else. Further, each train has a red emergency handle, to be pulled in the event of severe harassment or any emergency. Lost belongings can be reported to the **Oficina de Objetos Extraviados** (tel. 542 53 97 or 627 46 43), located in the Candelaria station (Lines 1 and 4), but don't hold your breath (open M-F 9am-8pm).

BY PESERO

Peseros, a.k.a. **colectivos, combis,** or **micros,** are white and green minibuses. The name *pesero* comes from the time when they used to cost one old peso, equivalent to US$0.01 today. Although not quite the steal they used to be, these easily affordable but crowded *peseros* cruise the streets on set routes. No printed information is available, though destinations are either painted or posted on the front window.

In 1997, a great effort was made to establish set *pesero* stops. Look for the traditional bus stand or a little blue sign with a picture of the front of a *pesero*. Most *peseros* now only let you on and off at these stops, but some will still slow down at any corner, and any red light is an excuse for a "stop." Passing *peseros* still need to be hailed even from designated stops. To get off, ring the bell (if there is one) or simply shout loudly *¡Bajan!* (coming down). To prevent a missed stop, pay when you get on and tell the driver your destination. Drivers will honk horns (often rigged to play such perennial faves as "It's a Small World" and the love theme from *The Godfather*) to signal availability during rush hour.

Expect to fork over 1.50-2.50 pesos for cross-city rides and 5 pesos for long-distance trips over 17km (10% more 10pm-6am). Tell the driver your destination as you get on, and he'll tell you the price. Some *peseros* only run until midnight, but the major routes—on Reforma, between Chapultepec and San Angel, and along Insurgentes—run 24 hours. Other well-traveled *pesero* routes travel from Metro: Hidalgo (Lines 2 and 3) to Ciudad Universitaria (via Reforma, Bucareli, and Av. Cuauhtémoc); La Villa to Chapultepec (via Reforma); Reforma to Auditorio (via Reforma and Juárez); the *zócalo* to Chapultepec (via 5 de Mayo and Reforma); San Angel to Izazaga (via 5 de Mayo and Reforma); Bolívar to Ciudad Universitaria/Coyoacán (via Bolívar in the *centro*); and San Angel to Metro: Insurgentes (Line 1; via Av. de la Paz and Insurgentes Sur). Many depart from the Chapultepec Metro station (Line 1) to San Angel, La Merced, and the airport. In heavy rush-hour traffic (7-10am and 6-9pm), even a circuitous Metro ride will often be faster than a *pesero*, but for short, direct trips *peseros* are useful. Check the routes posted on the windshield, but don't be shy about asking the driver personally: "*¿Se va a (La Merced)?*".

BY TAXI

TAXI DRIVER. The U.S. State Department issued a warning about taxis in May 1998 (see p. 68). Heed it. Robberies and rapes in street-hailed taxis are on a rapid rise.

Cabs constantly cruise the major avenues. If you want to be safe, don't hail them, especially not at night. If you have absolutely no other option, make sure that the meter is working and immediately threaten a driver with non-payment if the meter jumps and prices skyrocket. Some taxis have meters that display reference numbers for the driver's price conversion table instead of direct prices. Ask to see the chart before you pay to ensure that the price you're given matches the meter number. Also ask first to see *credenciales* before getting in—all legitimate cab drivers should have large ID badges. Carry small denominations, as drivers will often cite a lack of change as a reason to pocket some extra pesos. Base fares typically begin at 5 pesos, and at night, drivers will add 20% to the meter rate. If a meter is out of order, insist on setting the price before the driver goes anywhere.

The best taxi options, by far, are the official **sitio cabs.** There are several *sitios* (taxi bases) in every neighborhood. *Sitios* will respond to your phone call by sending a car to pick you up. If you're near the *sitio*, walk up to the first cab in line. All restaurants and hotels, as well as most locals, will know the number. Since *sitio* taxis don't use meters, ask the operator what the trip will cost. Prices are set by the zone. Operators will always give you the right price, and drivers very rarely overcharge. Official *sitio* cabs do cost up to twice as much, but it's well worth it. The great advantage of *sitio* taxis, in addition to home pick-up, is that they are much safer than anonymous cabs. Hotel cabs and *turismo* taxis are equally safe but charge more than the *sitio* taxis.

Try to consult a zone map before buying your tickets, and always count your change. If you can't locate a *sitio* number or a hotel cab, try **Servi-taxi** (tel. 271 25 60) or **Taxi Radio Mexicana** (tel. 519 76 90). They offer safe service at *sitio* prices. To get to the airport in a pinch, try calling **Transportación Terrestre al Aeropuerto** (tel. 571 41 93). It is appropriate to tip in either type of taxi especially to cabbies.

BY CAR

You must like pain and be insane. Driving is the most complicated and least economical way to get around the city, not to mention the easiest way to get lost. Mexico City's drivers are notoriously reckless; they became that way in large measure because route engineers did not think about them at all when designing city roads. Route dividers are often absent, and stop signs are planted midstream. Is it any wonder that red lights are routinely defied? Even the fast and free *Angeles Verdes* (see p. 68) do not serve the D.F. If your car should break down within city boundaries, call the **Asociación Nacional Automovilística (ANA;** tel. 5292 19 70 through 77) and request assistance. Wait for them beside your car, with the hood raised. If you leave your car alone, give it a goodbye kiss before you go.

Parking within the city is seldom a problem; parking lots are everywhere (4-8 pesos per hr., depending on the location and condition of the lot). Street parking is difficult to find, and vandalism is extremely common. Never leave anything valuable inside your car. Police will put an *inmobilizador* on your wheels if you park illegally; they will often tow your car. If you return to an empty space, try to locate the nearest police depot (not station) to figure out if your auto has been towed—if it's not there, it was stolen. If anything is missing from your car and you suspect that the police tampered with it, call the English-speaking **LOCATEL** (tel. 658 11 11).

All vehicles, even those of non-Mexican registration, must follow Mexico City's anti-smog regulations. Depending on the last digit of the license plate, cars may not be driven one day per week, according to this schedule: Monday final digits: 5 or 6; Tuesday: 7 or 8; Wednesday: 3 or 4; Thursday: 1 or 2; Friday: 9 or 0. Restrictions apply from 5am to 10pm, and penalties for violations are stiff. There are no limitations on weekdays between 10pm and 5am or on weekends.

Car rental rates are exorbitant, driving is a hassle, and the entire process is draining. Still interested? Then you must have a valid driver's license (from any country), a passport or tourist card, and be at least 25 years old. Prices for rentals at different agencies tend to be similar: a small VW or Nissan with unlimited kilometers, insurance, and tax (which is known as IVA) costs about 330-430 pesos per day or 3000-3300 pesos per week. Most agencies have offices at the airport and in the *Zona Rosa*. **At the airport: Avis,** (tel. 588 88 88 or 786 94 52; open daily 7am-11pm) and at Reforma 308 (tel. 533 13 36; open M-F 7am-10:30pm); **Budget,** (tel. 784 30 11; open daily 24hr.) and at Hamburgo 68 (tel. 533 04 50); **Dollar,** (tel. 207 38 38) and at Av. Chapultépec 322 (open daily 7am-8pm); **Economovil,** (tel. 726 05 90) and at Universidad 749 (tel. 604 59 60), in Colonia de Valle (open daily 7am-11pm); **Hertz,** (tel. 762 83 72; open 7am-10:30pm).

■ SAFETY

Like all large cities, Mexico City presents safety problems to the traveler. Misery-induced crime, corruption, and a lax justice system don't help a bit. In general, the downtown area, where most sights and accommodations are located, tends to be safer, although the back streets near Buenavista and the Alameda are significantly less so. Try to avoid carrying large amounts of cash, and use a money belt or a similar security device that carries valuables inside your clothing, next to your body. Never use a fanny pack. Ignore strangers who seem even slightly suspicious, no matter how friendly their chatter or smiles may seem.

Speaking in Spanish makes would-be attackers far less likely to bother you. Never follow a vendor or shoeshiner out of public view. Don't wear cameras, expensive watches, flashy jewelry, or shorts if you want to be left alone. Sunglasses for men convey don't-mess-with-me *machismo;* for women, they may be less advisable.

Women are, unfortunately, at higher risk of attack. Women in Mexico receive attention that they may not be used to; insistent stares, provocative smiles, whistling, cat-calling, and even extremely vulgar propositions are all part of everyday life. Light hair and skin, revealing or tight clothing, or any sign of foreignness will result in even more attention. Although horribly annoying, most such displays are harmless, provided you take good care of yourself. Stick with other people, especially at night or in isolated areas. A loud, clear *¡Déjame!* (DEH-ha-meh; leave me alone) will make your intentions clear. If in trouble, don't be shy about screaming *¡Ayúdame!* (ah-YOO-dah-may; help me).

The city that used to be known as *la región más transparente del aire* (the most transparent region of air) is now the most polluted in the world. The city's smoggy air may cause problems for contact-lens wearers and people with allergies. Pollution is particularly bad during the winter, due to thermal inversion; the summer rainy season does wonders for air cleanliness. For more information on health, see p. 51.

◪ PRACTICAL INFORMATION

If you come during the summer, keep a light rain poncho or umbrella handy. The rainy season (May-Oct.) features daily one- or two-hour-long rain storms anywhere from 4-6pm. Otherwise, sunny and moderate weather prevails year-round.

PUBLICATIONS

Mexico City Daily Bulletin, includes news, information on tourist sights, and a helpful map of Mexico City. Available free at the City Tourism Office and all over the *Zona Rosa*.

Tiempo Libre (Free Time), is the best resource for truly getting down and dirty in this city. The phenomenal weekly paper is on sale at most corner newsstands and covers movies, galleries, restaurants, dances, museums, and most cultural events (every Th, 7 pesos).

The Mexico City News (an English-language daily; 5 pesos) and **La Jornada** (a top national newspaper; 5 pesos) have film and theater listings as well as extensive international news, in case you miss gossip from the homefront.

Ser Gay, available at newsstands and many gay bars, is less widely distributed but has a complete listing of gay and lesbian nightlife options (for more information, see **Gay and Lesbian Entertainment,** p. 128). Of course, the best way to discover new and exciting bars, restaurants, theaters, and museums is to get out and talk to people.

TOURIST AND FINANCIAL SERVICES

City Tourist Office: Infotur, Amberes 54 (tel. 525 93 80), at Londres in the *Zona Rosa*. Metro: Insurgentes (Line 1). Helpful and friendly. Some officials speak English. The best free maps of the city and Metro upon request. Lists hotels, grouped by region and price range. Open daily 9am-9pm. The office operates information booths at the airport and Terminal Central del Norte bus stations.

Ministry of Tourism: Presidente Masaryk 172 (tel. 250 85 55, ext. 111), at Hegel in Col. Polanco. From Metro: Polanco (Line 7), walk 1 block down Arquímedes, take a left on Masaryk, and walk 3½ blocks—the building is to your right and easy to miss. The tourist information desk gives out copies of *El Mirón,* a free but awful weekly guide with a few poor maps of the downtown area and the Metro. Strangely enough, the staff knows much more about sites outside of Mexico City. At the **reservations desk** (tel. 25 51 06 or 255 31 12), friendly staff makes hotel reservations and offers copious brochures, information, and advice. Office open M-F 8am-9pm, Sa 10am-1pm; 24hr. phone lines.

Tourist Card (FMT) Info: Secretaría de Gobernación, Dirección General de Servicios Migratorios, Homero 1832 (tel. 626 72 00 or 206 05 06), in Col. Palanco. Take the Metro to Polanco, then catch a "Migración" *pesero*. The last stop is at the office. Come here to extend the date on your FMT or to clear up any immigration problems. Arrive early to avoid the long lines and to prepare yourself for Mexican bureaucracy. Open M-F 8am-2pm.

Embassies: Will replace lost passports, issue visas, and provide legal assistance. Visa processing can take up to 24hr.; bring plenty of forms of ID. If you find yourself in an emergency after hours, try contacting the embassy anyway—you could be in luck. **Australia,** 9255 Rubén Darío 55 (tel. 531 52 25; emergency after-hours tel. 905 407 16

98), at Campos Eliseos in Col. Polanco. Open M-Th 8:30am-2pm and 3-5:15pm, F 8:30am-2:15pm. **Belize,** Bernardo de Galvez 215 (tel. 520 12 74), in Col. Lomas de Chapultepec. Metro: Observatorio (Line 1). Open M-F 9am-1:30pm. **Canada,** Schiller 529 (tel. 724 79 00), in Col. Polanco. Metro: Polanco or Auditorio (Line 7). Open M-F 9am-1pm and 2-5pm. **Costa Rica,** Río Po 113 (tel. 525 77 64, 65, or 66), between Río Lerma and Río Panuco, behind the U.S. Embassy. Open M-F 9am-5pm. **Guatemala,** 1025 Av. Explanada (tel. 540 75 20). Metro: Auditorio (Line 7). Open M-F 9am-1:30pm. **Honduras,** Alfonso Reyes 220 (tel. 211 57 47), between Saltillo and Ometusco in Col. Condesa. Open M-F 10am-2pm. **New Zealand,** José Luis Lagrange 103, 10th fl. (tel. 281 54 86). Metro: Polanco (Line 7). Open M-Th 9am-5pm, and F 9am-1:30pm. **Nicaragua,** Payo de Rivera 120 (tel. 540 56 1), between Virreyes and Monte Atos. Open M-F 9:30am-3pm. **U.K.** (tel. 207 21 49, emergency tel. 207 20 89), at Río Lerma Riosena. Open M-F 8:30am-3:30pm. **U.S.,** Reforma 305 (tel. 533 56 93; after-hours tel. 211 00 42), at Glorieta Angel de la Independencia. Open M-F 9am-5pm.

Currency Exchange: *Casas de cambio* keep longer hours than banks, give better exchange rates, and sometimes stay open on Sundays. There are many in the *centro,* along Reforma, and in the *Zona Rosa.* Most can change other currencies in addition to U.S. dollars. Call the **Asociación Mexicana de Casas de Cambio** (tel. 264 08 84 or 264 08 41) to locate the exchange bureau nearest you. **Casa de Cambio Tíber** (tel. 722 08 02 or 722 08 00), is on Río Tíber at Papaloapan, one block from the Angel. Open M-F 8:30am-5pm, Sa 8:30am-2pm. On the south side of the Alameda: **Casa de Cambio Plus,** Juárez 38 (tel. 510 89 53). Open M-F 9am-4pm, Sa 10am-2pm. Near the Monumento a la Revolución/Buenavista: **Casa de Cambio Catorce,** Reforma 51, 4th fl. (tel. 705 24 60), near the Glorieta de Colón. Open M-F 9am-4pm. All banks offer one exchange rate and usually charge commissions.

ATM: The nationwide ATM network, **Red Cajeros Compartidos,** takes Visa for cash advances, and all ATMs work with U.S. system cards. Scores of ATMs are located throughout all major districts. Lost or stolen cards can be reported 24hr. to 227 27 77. **Citibank,** Reforma 390 (tel. 258 32 00 or 227 27 27; open 24hr.), and **Bank of America,** Reforma 265, 22nd fl. (tel. 230 64 00; open M-F 8:30am-5:30pm), can also help in an emergency.

American Express: Reforma 234 (tel. 207 72 82 or 208 60 04), at Havre in the *Zona Rosa.* Cashes personal and traveler's checks and accepts customers' mail and money wires. Report lost credit cards to the main office at Patriotismo 635 (tel. 326 26 66) and lost traveler's checks to either office. Open M-F 9am-6pm, Sa 9am-1pm.

LOCAL SERVICES

English Bookstores: American Bookstore, Madero 25 (tel. 512 03 06), in the *centro,* has an extensive selection of fiction, guidebooks, and a great Latin American history and politics section. Also a branch at Insurgentes Sur 1188 (tel. 575 23 72), in San Angel. Both branches open M-Sa 9:30am-8pm; *centro* store also open Su 10am-3pm. **Pórtico de la Ciudad de México,** Central 124 (tel. 510 96 83), at Carranza. English and Spanish books on Mexican history and guides to archaeological sites. Check out the frescoes while you browse. Open M-F 10am-7pm, Sa 10am-5pm. Also popular is the **Librería Gandhi** (tel. 510 42 31), on Juárez along the Alameda. Open M-Sa 10am-8:45pm, Su 11am-8pm. Another location at M.A. de Quevedo 128 in San Angel.

English Library: Biblioteca Benjamin Franklin, Londres 16 (tel. 209 91 00), at Berlín, 2 blocks southeast of the Cuauhtémoc monument. Books, newspapers, and periodicals. Open M and F 3-7:30pm, Tu-Th 10am-3pm.

Cultural and Arts Info: Palacio Nacional de Bellas Artes (tel. 521 92 51, ext. 132 and 217), Juárez and Eje Central for Bellas Artes info and reservations. Open M-Sa 11am-7pm, Su 9am-7pm. Check *Tiempo Libre* for city-wide listings.

Gay, Lesbian, and Bisexual Information: Colectivo Sol, write to Apdo. 13-320 Av. México 13, D.F. 03500. Has info on upcoming political and social events. Gay bars and clubs publicize events in *Tiempo Libre* and *Ser Gay.* Lesbians and bisexual women can contact **LesVoz** (tel. 399 60 19; email lesvoz@laneta.apc.org), the lesbian journal at Apartado Postal 33-091 Mexico, D.F. 15900. Open M-Th 9am-1pm. Another resource is **El Closet de Sor Juana,** Xola 181, second fl. (tel. 590 24 46), in Col. Alamos, a lesbian and bisexual group that organizes daily activities.

LOCATEL: (tel. 658 11 11). Officially the city's lost-and-found hotline. Call if your car (or friend) is missing. Limited English spoken.

Legal Advice: Organización Nacional Pro-Derechos Humanos de las Mujeres y las Lesbianos (tel. 399 60 19; email proml@laneta.apc.org), gives free legal advice and support to women in cases of sexual discrimination or harassment. Open M-Th 8am-1pm.

Supermarket: Most supermarkets are far from the *centro*, at residential Metro stops. Supermarket prices are higher than *mercados* but lower than corner stores and have it all-in-one. **Mega,** on the way to Tlatelolco from Metro: Tlatelolco (Line 3). Take the González *salida*, turn right on González and walk 3 blocks; it's at the intersection with Cárdenas. Open daily 8am-10pm. **Aurrerá,** 5 blocks north of Puente de Alvarado, on Insurgentes. Metro: M.A. Quevedo. Open daily 7:30am-11pm. **Superama,** Río Sena and Balsas, in the *Zona Rosa*, directly outside the Polanco Metro station (Line 7). Open daily 8am-9pm.

Laundry: Near the Monumento a la Revolución: **Lavandería Automática Edison,** Edison 91. Wash or dry 13 pesos per 3kg. Full-service 42 pesos. Soap 3 pesos. Open M-Sa 10am-7pm, Su 10am-6pm. In the *Zona Rosa*, most hotels have laundry service. Near Metro: Chilpancingo is **Lavandería Automática,** José Martí 224C (tel. 515 07 44). 33 pesos per load full-service or 10 pesos per load self-service. Open M-F 8am-6pm, Sa 8am-4pm. Check with your hotel for the most convenient location.

EMERGENCY AND COMMUNICATIONS

Police: Secretaría General de Protección y Vialidad (tel. 588 51 00). Open 24hr. In case of an **emergency,** dial 08 for the Policía Judicial. Call to report assaults, robberies, crashes, or abandoned vehicles. No English spoken.

Police Aid for Tourists: Patrullas de Auxilio Turístico (tel. 250 82 21), in marked vans in the *Zona Rosa* near el Angel and in the *zócalo*. The police in the vans speak English and are available for any and all help 9am-9pm. Those who answer the phone speak little English and deal primarily with automobile issues (accidents, break-downs, thefts). Phone staffed 24hr. **Procuraduria General de Justicia,** Florencia 20 (tel. 625 76 92 or 625 76 96), in the *Zona Rosa*. A department of justice catering especially to tourists. Go here to file police reports on anything—a minor robbery, a major abuse of power, or a lost or stolen tourist card. Some English spoken. Staffed 24hr.

Emergency Shelter: Casa de Asistencia Social (tel. 744 81 28 for women, 530 47 62 for men), on Calle Santanita in Col. Viaducto Pietá, near the treasury building.

Rape Crisis: Hospital de Traumatología de Balbuena, Cecilio Robelo 103 (tel. 552 16 02 or 764 03 39). Metro: Moctezuma (Line 1). Also call 06 or LOCATEL.

Legal Advice Hotline: Supervisión General de Servicios a la Comunidad, Fray Servando 32 (tel. 625 72 08 or 625 71 84), south of the *centro*. Metro: Isabel la Catolica (Line 1). On José Maria Izagaza, 2 blocks south of the Metro stop. Call the hotline if you are the victim of a robbery or accident and need legal advice. Little to no English spoken. Open daily 9am-9pm.

Sexually Transmitted Disease Info and Innoculation Info: Secretaría de Salud, Benjamin Gil 14 (tel. 277 63 11), in Col. Condensa. Metro: Juanacatlán (Line 1). Open M-F 8am-7pm, Sa 9am-2pm.

AIDS Hotline: TELSIDA/CONASIDA, Florencia 8 Calzada de Tlalpan, 2nd fl. (tel. 207 41 43 or 207 40 77), at Col. Torielo Guerra. From Metro: General Anaya (Line 2), take a *micro* headed for *Zona de Hospitales*. Runs AIDS tests, provides prevention information, and serves as a general help center. Open M-F 9am-9:30pm.

Red Cross: Ejército Nacional 1032 (tel. 395 11 11), at Polanco. Open 24hr.

Pharmacies: Small *farmacias* abound on almost every street corner and are great for most purchases; many drugs requiring prescriptions in the U.S. can be bought over the counter. Rarer drugs and specialized medications should be bought at large, international-looking (and more expensive) pharmacies such as: **Farmacia El Fénix,** Isabel La Católica 15 (tel. 585 04 55), at 5 de Mayo (open M-Sa 9am-10pm); or **VYR,** San Jerónimo 630 (tel. 595 59 83 or 595 59 98), near Perisur shopping center and at other locations (open 24hr.). All **Sanborns** and supermarkets have well-stocked pharmacies.

Medical Care: The **U.S. Embassy** (see p. 92) has a list of doctors with their specialties, addresses, telephone numbers, and languages spoken. **Dirección General de Servicios Médicos** (tel. 518 51 00) has information on all city hospitals. Open M-F 9am-5pm. **American British Cowdray (ABC) Hospital,** Calle Sur 136 (tel. 227 50 00), at Observatorio Col. Las Américas is expensive but generally trustworthy and excellent. No foreign health plans valid, but major credit cards accepted. Open 24hr. **Torre Médica,** José Maria Iglesias 21 (tel. 705 25 77 or 705 18 20), at Revolución Metro station (Line 2), has a few doctors who speak English.

Central Post Office: (tel. 521 73 94). On Lázaro Cárdenas at Tacuba, across from the Palacio de Bellas Artes. Open for stamps and *Lista de Correos* (window 3) M-F 8am-8pm, Sa 9am-5pm, Su 9am-1pm; for registered mail M-F 8am-6pm. Postal museum upstairs with turn-of-the-century mailboxes and other old-school gear. Museum open M-F 8am-10pm, Sa 8am-8pm, Su 8am-4pm. **Postal Code:** 06002.

Courier Services: UPS, Reforma 404 (tel. 228 79 00), and various smaller offices, provides international shipping services and express mail. Open M-F 8am-8pm. **Federal Express,** Reforma 308 (tel. 51 09 96), in Colonia Juárez near the Glorieta Angel de Independencia. Send before 4:30pm M-F, 1:30pm Sa, for overnight service. Open M-F 8am-7pm, Sa 9am-1:30pm.

Fax, Telegrams, and Western Union: Tacuba 8 (tel. 21 20 49; fax 512 18 94), at the Museo Nacional de Arte in the right wing of the building, behind the central post office. Open M-F 9am-11:30pm, Sa 9am-10:30pm, Su 9am-4:30pm. Domestic and international service. Many *papelerías* also offer fax services.

Internet Access: El Universal-Internet Sala, Bucareli 12, across the street from the giant yellow horse sculpture in an unmarked entrance, right next to the main entrance of *El Universal* newspaper office. This service provides absolutely free Internet usage. All you have to do is sign in and leave ID, and then enjoy up to 2hr. of computer escapades. Open M-F 10am-7pm. **Java Chat,** Genova 44K (tel. 514 68 56 or 525 68 53), in the *Zona Rosa.* Enjoy free coffee and soda as you type. 30 pesos per hr. Open M-F 9am-9pm, Sa-Su 10am-9pm. **Cyberspace Cafe,** Mazatlán 148 (tel. 211 68 77), in Col. Condesa. From Metro station: Patriotismo (Line 9), walk down 4 blocks in the direction of traffic, then turn right on Mazatlán—it's 2 blocks down. 30 pesos per hr., 20 pesos per 30min.

Telephones: LADATELs and **Telmexes** are everywhere and can be used for international collect and credit card calls, as well as with a LADATEL card. You need to insert a LADATEL card into the phone in order to make collect and credit card calls, but no money will be deducted from the phone card. For those who miss the golden days of the Mexican phone system, long-distance **casetas** are at the airport between *Salas D* and *E* (open 24hr.) and at Central Camionera del Norte (open daily 8am-9pm).

▛ ACCOMMODATIONS

To give you an idea of the size of this city, there are more than 1000 hotels within its expanse. Rooms abound in the *centro* (between Alameda and the *zócalo*) and near the Alameda Central. Perhaps the best budget bargains are found near El Monumento a la Revolución on the Plaza de la República, which also tends to be the best place to meet wacky locals and tourists alike. Rooms priced at 80 to 100 pesos for one bed and 100 to 130 pesos for two beds should be clean and have carpeting, a TV, and a telephone with free local calls. Some budget hotels charge according to the number of beds needed and not per person; beds tend to be large enough for two. If you don't mind, snuggling is a source of substantial savings.

Avoid the filthier sections of the Alameda and any area that makes you feel uncomfortable—there are plenty more from which to choose. In an attempt to cut down on problems with prostitution, many budget establishments have adopted "No Guests Allowed" policies. Beware of any place where the hotel itself (and not the parking lot) is marked "Hotel Garage." These rooms are frequented by businessfolk "working late at the office" and are designed to allow entry directly from the garage to the room. Figure it out. Always ask to look at a room before you accept it; this is easier to do after check-out time (between noon and 3pm).

CENTRO HISTÓRICO

Situated between the *zócalo* and Alameda Central, this neighborhood is the historic colonial heart of Mexico City. Its hotels are reasonably priced and feel fairly safe, although the streets become empty once locals head home for the night. Still, the *centro* remains an exciting and convenient place to stay. With action inevitably comes noise and congestion. If you crave quieter surroundings, consider moving west to the Alameda or Revolución areas. Many of the hotels listed below are north of Madero and 5 de Mayo, the parallel east-west streets that connect the Alameda with the *zócalo;* and east of Lázaro Cárdenas, the north-south Eje Central that runs one block east of Alameda. Metro stations Bellas Artes (Lines 2 and 8) and Allende (Line 2) are nearby. Hotels on 5 de Mayo, Isabel la Católica, and Uruguay are better served by Metro stations Zócalo (Line 2) and Isabel la Católica (Line 1). Street names change north of Tacuba: Isabel la Católica becomes República de Chile, and Bolívar turns into Allende. Even in the *centro*, most budget hotels **do not accept** credit cards.

■ **Hotel Catedral,** Donceles 95 (tel. 55 18 52 32), is half a block north of the Catedral Metropolitana and offers quiet, comfortable rooms wih TV and phone. The travel agent stationed in the lobby can make arrangements for local sight-seeing trips, and the restaurant offers *comida corrida* for just under 50 pesos. The high prices pay for the 2 huge balconies on the 7th floor, one of which has an unbeatable view of the domes on the cathedral. Singles 245-300 pesos; doubles 350 pesos; each additional person 55 pesos.

■ **Hotel Isabel** (tel. 55 18 12 13), on the corner of El Salvador and Isabel la Catolica, has rooms off an inner and outer courtyard. Each room comes with TV and phone, but what makes this hotel so special is the sheer palacial size of the rooms. 1 person 85 pesos, with bath 140 pesos; 2 people 100 pesos, with bath 170; 3 people with bath 210 pesos.

■ **Hotel Antillas,** Domínguez 34 (tel. 55 26 56 74), between Allende and República de Chile. The colonial exterior promises history-drenched grandeur and the interior does not disappoint. A winding marble staircase leads up to newly renovated (read: extra-clean) modern rooms. Full amenities (TVs, bottled water, and phones) and an eager staff assure a relaxing stay. Ask for a room with a balcony to get the full treatment. 1 person 170 pesos; 2 people 190-200 pesos; 3 people 220 pesos.

Hotel Principal, Bolívar 29 (tel. 55 21 13 33), by the Parilla Leonesa restaurant, which offers room service. Helpful staff bustles down the pale yellow, plant-filled hallways under the enormous skylight. Only the 12 rooms at the front of the hotel have windows, but these rooms have gorgeous high ceilings and little balconies that make the simple rooms feel like grand suites. TV, telephone, bottled water, and a safe are also provided in your room. Rooms without windows are smaller and much darker. Singles 130-150 pesos; doubles 175-210 pesos; triples 210-265 pesos; suites 275-300 pesos.

Hotel San Antonio, on the alleyway off 5 de Mayo called 2 Callejon de 5 de Mayo which leads to Las Palmas. The hotel is #29; knock on the door under the U.S. and Mexican flags to be buzzed in. This hotel has small but extremely clean rooms with TV and phone; make sure to get a room with a window to get the added light. Singles 100 pesos; doubles and triples 130 pesos.

Hotel Monte Carlo, Uruguay 69 (tel. 55 21 25 59). Lots of large, lovingly mismatched rooms have balconies, red carpets, yellow satin furniture and clean tiled bathrooms. There is also a relaxing lounge and top floor skylight. Singles 120-130 pesos; doubles 120-200; suite 130-320. Sharing a bath will save 20-60 pesos.

Hotel Juárez, 1A Callejon de 5 de Mayo 17 (tel. 55 12 69 29 or 55 18 47 18), between Isabel La Católica and Palma. Offers cheap rooms and a great location. Rooms come with TV, radio, and phone, but only half of the 30 small but comfortable rooms have windows; ask for one. Because it is on a side alley, noise shouldn't be a problem. Singles 90-95; doubles 100-120; prices depend on the number of people.

Hotel Buenos Aires, Motolina 21 (tel. 55 18 21 04 or 55 18 21 37). A little fountain in the courtyard adds character to this simple, clean hotel. Each room comes complete with a TV and drinking water. Ask for a window because most rooms don't have them. Singles 80-90 pesos; doubles 100-130 pesos; prices depend on the number of people.

Hotel Atlanta, Domínguez #31 (tel. 55 18 12 00). Offers bright rooms with small, spic'n'span bathrooms, TVs, and phones. Singles 100-110 pesos; doubles 150-200 pesos; triples 200-220; prices depend on the number of people.

ALAMEDA CENTRAL

The expansive Alameda is always throbbing with activity. But the little greenery fades over the course of a few blocks, making way for dirt and danger in some of the surrounding streets. Use caution and use a *sitio* cab. Try to avoid staying in this area—there are nicer parts of the city in which to set up camp.

▨ **Hotel Manolo Primero,** Moya 111 (tel. 521 37 39 or 521 31 49), near Arcos de Belén, halfway between Metros Balderas and Salto del Agua (Lines 1 and 8). Spacious blue hallways and a cavernous lobby lead to spanking new rooms with king-sized beds, TVs, and lounge chairs and clean, large bathrooms with gigantic mirrors. Singles and doubles 120 pesos.

Hotel San Diego, Moya 98 (tel. 55 12 26 53), between Pugibet and Delicias, 6 blocks south of the Alameda. This is a safe second choice if Manolo Primero is full. Mid-size rooms include color TV but no shower curtain. Singles 110 pesos; doubles 160 pesos.

NEAR THE MONUMENTO A LA REVOLUCIÓN/BUENAVISTA

Hotels near the Monumento a la Revolución are cheaper and quieter than their counterparts in the *centro* or the Alameda. Backpackers and bargain-scouting travelers tend to congregate here, particularly in the hotels on Mariscal and Edison. Metro: Revolución (Line 2) serves hotels south of Puente de Alvarado/Hidalgo, while Metro: Guerrero (Line 3) serves those to the north, near the train station.

▨ **Casa de Los Amigos,** Mariscal 132 (tel. 705 05 21 or 705 06 46). Metro: Revolución (Line 2). Originally the home and studio of painter José Clemente Orozco, Los Amigos is now a Quaker-run guest house for tourists and social activists. The 4-day minimum stay is designed to promote understanding and sensitivity among different people in a peaceful environment. Backpackers, grad students, eco-warriors—people from all over the world congregate here. Weekly cultural exchanges, dance lessons, ample library offerings with binders full of volunteer opportunities throughout Latin America (available to non-guests as well), a lively lounge, and kitchen and laundry facilities are all available in this cooperative atmosphere. Dorm rooms 50 pesos; private rooms 65-70 pesos; doubles 110-150 pesos. Breakfast 15 pesos. Key deposit 20 pesos.

Hotel Oxford, Mariscal 67 (tel. 566 05 00), at Alcázar, next to the small park. Metro: Revolución. Large, colorful rooms, many with TV, telephone, great views of the park and inviting bathrooms with huge sinks ideal for laundry. There is also an adjoining bar. Singles 75-85 pesos; doubles 110 pesos; triples 150 pesos; quads 195 pesos.

Hotel Yale, Mosqueta 200 (tel. 591 15 45), between Zaragoza and Guerrero, to the left as you exit the train station. Metro: Guerrero. Recently remodeled rooms and bathrooms, full-length mirrors, TVs, phones, and colorful unmatching furniture all make for an endearing hotel for those who can't get into a better place. 1-2 people 90 pesos; 3-4 people 160 pesos.

Hotel Edison, Edison 106 (tel. 566 09 33), at Iglesias. Luxury at prices that are comparatively high for the area but worth the splurge. Enormous rooms with full amenities surround a beautiful, flower-filled courtyard. Singles 150-170 pesos; doubles 190 pesos.

Hotel Ibiza, Arriaga 22 (tel. 55 66 81 55), between Edison and Mariscal offers small but very clean rooms on a quiet street. All rooms have 1 nice bed. 1 person 90 pesos; 2 people 100 pesos.

NEAR THE BUS STATIONS

There are few good budget accommodations in the vicinity of any of the four bus stations. The areas around these stations generally offer expensive rooms in shabby *barrios*. Even if you arrive late at night, it is not safe to walk a few blocks—you'd do best to catch a cab (and once in a cab, why not head to the center of town?). For travelers just passing through and arrive at the **Central de Autobuses del Norte,** the pricey but comfy **Hotel Brasilia,** Av. de los 100 Mts. 4823 (tel. 587 85 77), is three blocks to the left along the main thoroughfare as you exit the bus station. Rooms are carpeted and clean, with TV, phone, and private safe. (Singles 160 pesos; doubles 220 pesos.) Both the TAPO and Poniente station are in unsafe neighborhoods. If you arrive at the **TAPO,** take the Metro to the *centro*, and if you are at the **Terminal de Autobuses del Poniente,** swing over to the Tacubaya Metro stop (Lines 1, 7, and 9) for the nearest hotels.

◖ FOOD

Options for meals fall into six basic categories: the very cheap (and sometimes risky) vendor stalls scattered about the streets; fast, inexpensive, and generally safe *taquerías;* slightly more formal *cafeterías;* more pricey and decorous Mexican restaurants; locally popular North-Americanized eateries; and expensive international fare. In addition, U.S. fast-food chains mass-produce predictable fare for the timid palate. **VIPS** runs 60 commercialized, Denny's-like eateries throughout the D.F. that are very popular with rich Mexicans (and correspondingly priced); some are open 24 hours. If you're preparing your own food, local neighborhood markets and supermarkets stock almost anything you could need. For a good time, try **La Merced** market (see p. 129), the mother of them all. As always, avoid unpurified water, including ice, uncooked or unpeeled vegetables, and meat that is not fully cooked (see p. 54).

Soda is sold at every corner. *Agua mineral* means mineral water, *sidral* is a great carbonated apple drink, and *refrescos* are your standard soda. Perhaps the best way to combat thirst is through the delicious *aguas* sold everywhere, made with fresh fruit and sugar—just make sure the ice is purified. Bottles are recycled, and patrons pay extra for the privilege of keeping them. If you want your soda to go, try getting it *en una bolsa* (in a plastic bag with a straw).

CENTRO

The historic downtown area of Mexico City offers a wide selection of food at super-low prices. Slick U.S. fast-food establishments, enormous *cafeterías*, and countless small eateries serve inexpensive *comida corrida*, tacos, *tortas*, and other staples. Motolina and Gante host a high concentration of little eateries and there's plenty of good fare for vegetarians.

▧ **Café Tacuba,** Tacuba 28 (tel. 512 84 82). Metro: Allende (Line 2). Tacuba is a bastion of excellent food and engaging conversation in the heart of downtown since 1912. Everyone who's anyone has been here; this place is perennially "in." An amazing combo of camp and class—pure artisanship, brass pitchers, murals, and, if you're lucky, men outside in colonial garb eager to greet you. *Antojitos* 15-42 pesos; entrees 80 pesos; full bar. Be patient—all dishes are made from scratch, and they're well worth the wait. Open daily 8am-11:30pm.

Restaurantes Vegetarianos del Centro, Mata 13 (tel. 510 01 13), between 5 de Mayo and Madero. Shiny, happy, healthy, sunshine-yellow eatery filled with an eclectic group of veggie lovers. *Comida corrida* for 35 pesos. Open daily 8am-8pm.

X-Can-Kin, Motolina 15C (tel. 512 40 68) is a lovely Yucatec eatery with *antojitos* (all 6 pesos each) that will leave you groveling for more. Tasty *comida corrida* 30 pesos. Open M-Sa 9am-9pm.

Restaurant Rincón Mexicano, Uruguay 27 (tel. 512 03 60). From the street you can see only the tiled stove heating fresh tortillas, but the hand-carved wooden chairs and blue tablecloths extend back. Serving only 1 meal, this place produces a scrumptiously home-cooked, 20-peso *comida corrida*. Open M-Sa 1-6pm.

Café Dayi, Isabela la Católica 9-11 (tel. 521 62 03), near Tacuba. Watermelon-ish, kitschy cafeteria decor, but the food—both Chinese and Mexican—is excellent. Chicken and duck dishes 35 pesos; *comida corrida china y mexicana* 40 pesos. Don't be afraid to crane your neck to check out *fútbol* on TV as aproned waitresses refill your *agua de sandía* (watermelon juice). Open daily 8am-11pm.

Restaurant Danubio, Uruguay 3 (tel. 512 09 12), just east of Lázaro Cárdenas. This stately seafood joint boasts its own coat-of-arms and hefty price tags and is always packed, but the good food and drink ain't no laughing matter. Famous artsy types have left their scribblings framed on the walls. Entrees (around 70 pesos) and specials (100 pesos) are big enough for 2. Open daily 1-10pm.

Súper Soya, Tacuba 40 (tel. 510 29 80), and several locations throughout the *centro*. A wildly colorful grocery store/cafe/diner/yogurt stand sells salads (10-23 pesos), vegetarian pizzas (10 pesos), *tacos de guisado* (5 pesos), and an incredible variety of *licuados* for 10 pesos each. Open daily 9am-9pm.

ALAMEDA CENTRAL

The convivial atmosphere that permeates the Alameda carries over to the various restaurants that pepper the area. Gone is the stuffy elitism of the *Zona Rosa* and the frenetic pace of the *centro*. Instead, you'll find good, back-to-basics food. Prices are on the high side, but portions are large. For something a bit different, try one of the Chinese restaurants on Dolores, two blocks west of Cárdenas and one block south of the Alameda. Cheap, small eateries line Independencia, one block south of the Alameda.

■ **Fonda Santa Anita,** Humboldt 48 (tel. 518 46 09). Metro: Juárez (Line 3). Go a block west on Artículo 120, turn right on Humboldt, and continue half a block more. A classic restaurant that has represented Mexico in 5 World's Fairs, this friendly eatery feels no need to dispel stereotypes—the tablecloths are bright pink, and colorful depictions of bullfights and busty women cover the walls. More importantly, it serves incredible versions of old standards and regional specialties from all over the country. *Comida corrida* 38 pesos. Open M-F 1-10pm, Sa-Su 1-8pm.

Oriental (tel. 521 30 99), on a pedestrian walkway at the corner of Dolores and Independencia, on a block of Chinese restaurants. The prices here are slightly lower (45-peso *comida corrida*, and there's an enormous bronze Buddha at the entrance whose belly is sure to bring you good luck. Open daily 10am-11pm.

Energía Natural (tel. 521 20 15), at the corner of 16 de Septiembre and Dolores. The brightest and most beautiful of the bunch, with no walls and healthy touches such as whole wheat bread. Sandwiches and burgers 9-20 pesos. Open daily 8am-7pm.

NEAR THE MONUMENTO A LA REVOLUCIÓN

Without many affluent residents or big tourist draws, this area lacks the snazzy international cuisine of other areas. Instead, homey cafes, *torterías*, and *taquerías* dominate the scene. For hearty portions and low prices, this is the spot.

■ **La Especial de París,** Insurgentes Centro 117 (tel. 703 23 16). This *nevería* has been scooping up ecstasy since 1921. Lots of 100%-natural treats, ranging from *malteadas* (milkshakes; 19 pesos) to *frutas glacé* (fruit ices). Double scoop 15 pesos, triple scoop 18 pesos, 4 scoops 22 pesos. Open daily noon-9pm.

La Taberna (tel. 591 11 00), Arriaga at Ignacio Mariscal, below street level and next to Hotel Pennsylvania. The service is fast and the *ambiente* awesome. The 4-course Italian *comida corrida* (28 pesos) is sure to please. Open M-Sa 8am-6pm.

Super Cocina Los Arcos, Ignacio Mariscal at Iglesias has a homey, cozy atmosphere amid bright orange furnishings. Service is a little slow, but it's worth it—their chicken soups (12-14 pesos) and *alambres con queso* (17 pesos) are the best around. *Comida corrida* 20 pesos. Many dishes are 9-19 pesos. Open M-Sa 8am-11pm.

Restaurant El Paraíso, Orozco y Berra at Gonzales Martinez, across the street from Museo del Chopo. Offers a vegetarian *comida corrida* (18 pesos) in a friendly family atmosphere. Open daily 8am-2am.

ZONA ROSA

The myth: only loaded tourists eat in the *Zona Rosa*. The reality: although the area has some of the city's more expensive restaurants, serving everything from international cuisine to traditional Mexican cooking, many eateries cater chiefly to clerks from the scores of surrounding office buildings. But don't think you won't see more tourists here than anywhere. The *Zona Rosa* also has more fast-food joints than any other area of the city. If you're more interested in the *Zona Rosa*'s slick party atmosphere than in filling your stomach, skip dinner and settle for a drawn-out evening appetizer.

Ricocina, Londres 168 (tel. 514 06 48), east of Florencia. Once the *Zona Rosa*'s best-kept secret, this wonderful family-owned restaurant is quickly becoming the joint *du jour*. Still, the food is the best around. Soft peach surroundings help you enjoy a delicious *menú del día* (30 pesos). Open daily 9am-6pm.

Saint Moritz, Genova 44, next to Java Chat. This tiny, lively restaurant offers the *Zona Rosa*'s best prices for great eats. *Menú del día* 16 pesos. Open daily 1-6pm.

La Luna, Oslo 11, on the narrow walkway between Niza and Copenhagen. Beautiful sketches of *indígenas* grace the walls of this cozy, popular restaurant. The *comida corrida* (24 pesos) includes soup, a small and large entree, and a beverage—a great budget value. Avoid the 2-3pm lunch rush. Open M-Sa 7am-9pm.

Vegetariano Yug, Varsovia 3 (tel. 526 53 30), near Reforma. Dig the classy Indian furnishings, plants, and erotic Hindu sculpture, then sample the *carnitas vegetarianas* (vegetarian pork bits; 32 pesos). The fab buffet starting at 1pm features Indian, French, and other cuisines (46 pesos). Open M-F 7am-10pm, Sa 8:30am-8pm, Su 1-8pm.

Coffee House, Londres 102 (tel. 525 40 34), is a great place to sip a cappuccino (11 pesos), munch on a salad, sandwich, or crepe (18 pesos), and gawk at/fantasize about Mexico's most fashionable couples strolling the street. Open daily 8am-9pm.

Kai Lam, Londres 114 (tel. 514 58 37). This homey restaurant serves both *comida mexicana* (*menú del día* 36 pesos) and *comida china* (24-38 pesos). Open doors and location make it a good place to chill. Open daily 8am-10:30pm.

Teriyaki San, Niza 22 (tel. 207 24 07), makes trendy but affordable Japanese food, now the rage in Mexico City (dishes 18-38 pesos). This low-key establishment serves your meal fast-food style. While the eco-minded may flinch at the styrofoam containers, most savor their sushi while watching Mexican TV. Open daily 11am-8pm.

NEAR CHAPULTEPEC

Inside the Bosque de Chapultepec, sidewalk stands offer an enormous variety of snacks. Should you want a sit-down eatery, the immediate vicinity of the Chapultepec Metro station, just outside the park, is cluttered with vendors and small restaurants offering popular and mundane *tortas* and *super-tortas* (not for the weak of stomach). A bit farther east, however, lie a few more adventurous options easily accessible from Metro: Sevilla (Line 1). A ritzier alternative might be *antojitos* in beautiful Colonia Polanco, north of the Anthropology Museum, which is also accessible by Metro: Polanco (Line 7).

Los Sauces, Av. Chapultepec 530 (tel. 28 67 05), at Acapulco Roma, 1½ blocks east of Metro: Chapultepec (Line 1). The uniquely tiled bar and grill is cluttered with pictures of Mexican politicians and stars. There are lots of choices regarding entertainment: zone out to *telenovelas* on TV, listen to the blaring radio, or watch chefs chopping onions and peppers for your 18-25-peso meal. Open daily 9am-9pm.

El Kioskito (tel. 553 30 55), on Chapultepec, at the corner with Sonora, serves succulent specimens (*antojitos* 12-20 pesos, specialties 32-40 pesos) in a classy, but relaxed atmosphere with a tiled fountain and old photos of the city. The guacamole (9 pesos) has pizazz. Open daily 8am-9pm.

COYOACÁN

The southern suburb of Coyoacán attracts students, young couples, and literati to its restaurants. If you crave brie, cheesecake, or pesto, spend an afternoon here. Outdoor cafes and ice cream shops fill the colonial buildings that line the cobbled streets. For some sweet scoops, try **Santa Clara,** at Allende and Cuauhtémoc (12 pesos per scoop), and **La Siberia,** on the northeast corner of Jardín Centenario (13 pesos per scoop, floats 15 pesos). For a cheap, excellent meal, try the **food court** on Hijuera, just south of Plaza Hidalgo. Populated almost exclusively by locals, these tiny restaurants offer home-cooked food at un-Coyoacán-like prices. (Open M-Sa 9am-9pm.)

Café El Parnaso, Carrillo Puerto 2 (tel. 554 22 25 or 658 3195), on Jardín Centenario, across from the cathedral. A celebrated book and record store with an outdoor cafe in a prime locale on the plaza's edge. Although the food is a bit pricey, the people-watching and eavesdropping here are unbeatable. Coffee and cheesecake with strawberries (20-30 pesos). Open daily 8:30am-10:30pm.

El Guarache (tel. 554 45 06), on the south side of Jardín Centenario, offers *jardín*-sitting and Mexican tasties at wonderfully reasonable prices (*antojitos* 13-25 pesos, meals 29-40 pesos). Open daily 10am-10pm.

Café Kowloon (tel. 554 78 90 or 554 62 65), on the southeast side of Jardín Centenario. A Chinese joint with pastel decor, bubbling fish tanks, and startlingly good *menús del día* (30-45 pesos). Open Su-Th 7:30am-11pm, F-Sa 7:30am-1am.

El Jarocho (tel. 568 50 29), on Allende, 1 block north of Pl. Hidalgo. The aroma of freshly ground coffee and the long line will lead you to this legendary corner stand. The Jarocho has been serving some of the best java in the city since 1953. Cappuccino, mocha, and hot chocolate for under 7 pesos each. Open daily 7am-midnight.

SAN ANGEL

The chic restaurants and *típico* taco stands of San Angel pack 'em in, especially on Saturdays, when crowds of well-to-do tourists and Mexicans are drawn to the booths of overpriced art in the Bazaar Sábado. If you want to dine in style, Plaza San Jacinto is the place to be. Many places will empty out your wallet in five seconds flat, but a few budget gems can be easily discovered.

La Mora, Madro 2 (tel. 616 20 80), offers a great view of the plaza from its spiffy upstairs patio. The brick walls are hung with flowering gardenias and cacti for atmosphere, and the food is finger-lickin' good. *Comida corrida* during the week is only 22 pesos and includes a jar of *agua purificada* and dessert. Prices rise on the weekends to 30 pesos. Open daily 10am-8pm.

Chucho el Roto, Madero 8 (tel. 616 20 41). A simple, deliciously inexpensive spot situated just steps from the action. This daytime diner serves up *menú del día* of soup, rice, an entree, and dessert for 22 pesos. Breakfast specials 20 pesos. Open daily 9am-5:30pm.

Restaurante Hasti Bhawan: La Casona del Elefante, Pl. San Jacinto 9 (tel. 616 16 01). This unbelievable restaurant has Indian ambience and scrumptious fare. Indo-Thai chicken 45 pesos; vegetarian platter 35 pesos; *pakoras* or *samosas* 12 pesos. Treat yourself to a *lassi*, a thick yogurt drink (10 pesos). F-Sa live jazz. Open Tu-Th 2-11pm, F-Sa 2pm-midnight, Su 1-6:30pm.

El Rincón de La Lechuza, Miguel Angel de Quevedo 34 (tel. 661 00 50), straight down from Metro: M. A. Quevedo (Line 3), just past La Paz remains joyfully crowded and decorated in yellow and white with wood tables. Tasty tacos 18-25 pesos; specials 29-45 pesos. Open daily 10am-1am.

La Finca Café de Dios (tel. 550 94 82), on Madero right off the Pl. de San Jacinto. This hole-in-the-wall coffee stand only serves coffee that is 100% Mexican grown...and it kicks Colombia's butt. All mocha, espresso, and other pipin' hot treats under 5 pesos. If you're truly hard-core, check out the kilos of coffee beans (50-82 pesos) grown in Chiapas. Open daily 8am-8pm.

MEXICO CITY

Central Mexico City

SIGHTS

Casa de los Azulejos, **35**
Catedral Metropolitana, **44**
Centro Cultural José Martí, **23**
Fonart, **26**
Glorieta Ángel de la Independencia, **8**
Glorieta Cristóbal Colón, **16**
Glorieta Cuauhtémoc, **14**
Iglesia de San Francisco, **37**
La Lagunilla, **46**

Mercado de Artesanías de la Ciudadela, **27**
Mercado San Juan Artesanías, **28**
Monumento a la Revolución, **17**
Monumento de los Niños Héroes, **7**
Museo de Arte Moderno, **6**
Museo del Chopo, **18**
Museo del Claustro de Sor Juana, **40**
Museo Diego Rivera, **24**
Museo de la Ciudad de México, **41**
Museo de la Charreria, **39**
Museo del Ejército, **33**

Museo Franz Mayer, **29**
Museo Nacional de Antropología, **3**
Museo Nacional de Arte, **34**
Museo Nacional de Historia, **5**
Museo Nacional de la Estampa, **30**
Museo San Carlos, **20**
Museo Siqueiros, **2**
Museo Tamayo, **4**
Palacio de Bellas Artes, **31**
Palacio Iturbide, **38**
Palacio Nacional, **43**

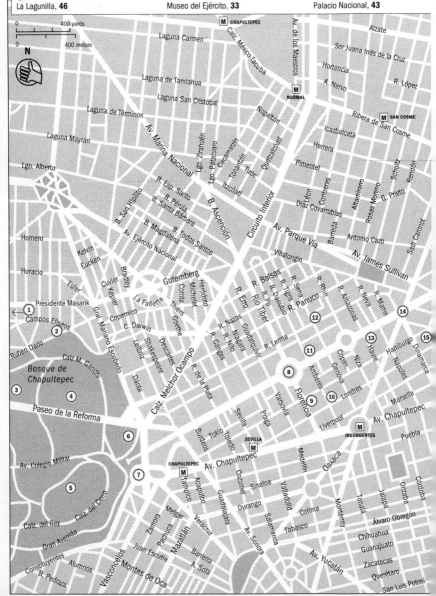

Pinacoteca Virreinal de San Diego, **25**
Suprema Corte de Justicia, **42**
Templo Mayor, **45**
Tianguis del Chopo, **22**
Torre Latinoamericana, **36**

SERVICES
American Express, **13**
Biblioteca Ben Franklin, **15**
Central Post Office, **32**
Federal Tourist Office, **10**

Ministry of Tourism, **1**
Procedura General de Justicia, **9**
Torre Medica, **19**
Train Station, **21**
U.S. Embassy, **11**
U.K. Embassy, **12**

HOTELS
Hotel Edison, **A**
Casa de los Amigos, **B**
Hotel Oxford, **C**

Hotel Buena Vista, **D**
Hotel Yale, **E**
Hotel Hidalgo, **F**
Hotel la Marina, **G**
Hotel Atlanta, **H**
Hotel Antillas, **I**
Hotel Monte Carlo, **J**
Hotel Buenos Aires, **K**
Hotel Principal, **L**
Hotel Sevillano, **M**
Hotel Manolo Primero, **N**

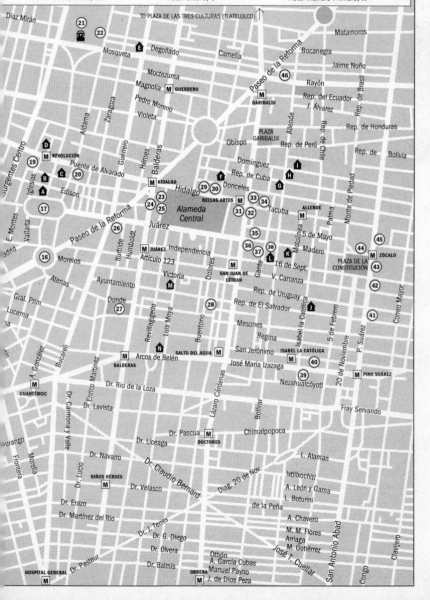

👁 SIGHTS

It would be impossible to find an appetite that couldn't be satiated by Mexico City's incredibly diverse range of sights and attractions. Getting a well-rounded picture of Mexico City will require a week at the very least, but it would take a lifetime to truly learn this metropolis's ins and outs.

If you're in town for more than a day or two, you'll want to check out the incredible ruins at **Teotihuacán,** also known as **Las Pirámides** (see p. 134), the most visited archaeological site in the country, only a short bus ride away. Mexico City's location also makes it an ideal base for exploring much of central Mexico. See the suggestions for **daytrips** (see p. 134), at the end of this chapter.

Still, the typical visitor won't want to leave the city right away. Here's a quick, handy list of some of the metropolis's major sights:

CENTRO

Mexico City spans hundreds of kilometers and thousands of years, but it is all drawn together in the *centro*. On the city's main plaza, known as the **zócalo,** the Aztec **Templo Mayor,** the gargantuan **Catedral Metropolitana,** and the **Palacio Nacional,** decorated with the work of Mexico's great leftist muralists, sit serenely side by side. It's not just the architecture that's eclectic; the space is shared by street vendors hawking everything from handwoven bags to used-looking razors, AK-47-sporting soldiers reading adult comic books, permanent political protestors, and endless lines of unemployed men advertising their skills on cardboard scraps. The crowds of tourists who come here daily don't even begin to compare to the number of Mexicans who pass through or work in this center of the center. If you have time for only one area in Mexico City, make it here. To reach the *zócalo* by Metro, take Line 2 to Metro: Zócalo. The station's entrance sits on the east side of the square, in front of the Palacio Nacional. The Catedral Metropolitana lies to the north, the Federal District offices to the south, and the Suprema Corte de Justicia (Supreme Court) to the southeast.

THE ZÓCALO

Officially known as the **Plaza de la Constitución,** the *zócalo* is the principal square of Mexico City. Now surrounded by imposing colonial monuments, the plaza was once the nucleus of **Tenochtitlán,** the Aztec island-capital and later the center of the entire Aztec empire. Cortés's men razed the city and, atop the ruins, built the power center from which they would rule New Spain (see p. 9 and p. 78). To the southwest of the **Templo Mayor—**the Aztecs' principal place of worship, which they called Teocalli—was the Aztec marketplace and major square. The space was rebuilt and renamed several times, becoming the Plaza de la Constitución in 1812. In 1843, the dictator Santa Anna ordered that a monument to independence be constructed in the center of the square. Only the monument's *zócalo* (pedestal) was in place when the project was abandoned. The citizens of Mexico City began to refer to the square as the *zócalo,* which has become the generic name for the central plazas that mark most of the cities and towns in Mexico. Modern-day urban life has emerged out of this past. Now, indigenous drummers vie with *chicle* (gum) sellers to be heard. The *zócalo* gets hectic and confusing during the day; it becomes deserted and dreamlike at night.

PALACIO NACIONAL

Location: *on the east side of the zócalo.* **Open:** *daily 9am-5pm.* **Free,** *but you must trade a piece of ID for a big red "turista" badge at the entrance.* **Tours:** *ask local officials and tour guides about prices; you should be able to get a guided tour (M-F 10am-4pm) for 60-70 pesos. Then again, joining a tour that has already begun is free.* **Museum:** *open M-F 9am-5pm. Free.*

Stretching the entire length of the enormous *zócalo,* the **Palacio Nacional** is a sight to behold. Over 200m long, this regal mammoth of a government palace is as over-the-top as Mexico City itself. It's hard to believe the *palacio* could have ever been anything else. Its history, however, is more fantastic and fairy tale-ish than the armed guards standing outside would make you think. Completely demolished during the riots of 1692, the *palacio* had been the site of an Aztec ruler's (Moctezuma II) palace, Hernán Cortés's house, and the palace of the king of Spain's viceroys. Now the chief executive center of the Republic, the *palacio* houses monumental murals and a museum honoring Benito Juárez.

It took Diego Rivera from 1929 to 1951 to sketch and paint the **frescoes** on the *palacio*'s western and northern walls. **Mexico Through the Centuries,** one of his most famous works, is on the west wall of the *palacio,* at the top of the grand staircase. The mural is divided into eight smaller scenes, each of which depicts an event in the social history of Mexico. Each of the five arches at the top of the mural deals with the Mexican nation—from the beginning of the fight for independence in 1810 to the start of the Mexican Revolution in 1910. These colorful, larger-than-life murals tackle such varied themes as the horror of the slave trade, the early-20th-century class struggle, and the legendary Aztec priest-king Quetzalcóatl. At times, his murals look like an illustrated *Who's Who?* of famous people. Look for his famous wife, Frida Kahlo, hidden in the frescoes. Guides to the murals wait at the central staircase trying to charge exorbitant fees.

The *palacio* also contains the **Bell of Dolores,** which was brought to the capital in 1896 from Dolores Hidalgo (see p. 317). It can be seen from outside, at the top of the *palacio's* Baroque facade. Miguel Hidalgo rang this bell on September 16, 1810, summoning Mexicans to fight for their independence. Every year on that date it rings in memory of the occasion, and the Mexican president repeats the words once shouted by the father of independence. On the east side of the *palacio's* second floor is the **Museo del Recinto del Parliamento,** dedicated to the one and only Benito Juárez.

CATEDRAL METROPOLITANA

Tel.: 521 76 37. *Location:* on the north side of the zócalo. *Hours:* open daily 10am-6pm. Exact schedules posted on the westernmost door.

In the wake of Cortés' military triumphs, a land devoted to Quetzalcóatl, Tlaloc, and Huitzilopochtli became a stronghold of Christianity. The third cathedral built in New Spain was the **Catedral Metropolitana**, a mish-mash of architectural styles from three different centuries that somehow turned out beautifully. Construction started in 1562 but wasn't completed until 1813. Modeled after the cathedral in Sevilla, Spain, its scalloped walls and high arches give it a Moorish feel. Overwhelmingly gold altars maintain the Baroque influence. Unfortunately, the splendor of the cathedral is occluded by the green support structures placed to combat the ongoing floor damage—the temple, along with the rest of the city, is sinking into the murky ground. Ongoing renovations mean scaffolding and partitions occasionally obscure parts of both the exterior and the interior. If you use your imagination and block out the ugly green and yellow supports, the cathedral still glows. Attached to it are several annexes. The main one, with its door to the left of the cathedral, holds the **Altar de Perdón** (Forgiveness), a replica of an altarpiece built by Jerónimo de Balbás between 1731 and 1736, and destroyed by fire in 1967. The cedar interior of the choir gallery, constructed in 1695 by Juan de Rojas, boasts an elegant grille of gold, silver, and bronze, and Juan Correa's murals of dragon-slaying and prophet-hailing cover the sacristy walls. Perhaps the most magnificent part of the cathedral is the **Altar de los Reyes,** dedicated to those kings who were also saints—not a common occurrence. Two chapels near the entrance honor Mexico's patron, the Virgin of Guadalupe (also honored in the **Basílica de Guadalupe,** see p. 116). Mass takes place almost hourly on weekends; visitors should take extra care to show respect and be silent during these times.

TEMPLO MAYOR (TEOCALLI)

Tel.: 542 47 84 or 542 06 06. *Location:* on the corner of Seminario and República de Guatemala. Just east of the cathedral and north of the Palacio Nacional. *Hours:* museum and ruins open Tu-Su 9am-5pm. Guided tours in Spanish free, in English 10 pesos per person. *Admission:* 16 pesos, free for under 13 and all on Su. 10 pesos for camera permit.

According to legend, Tenochtitlán was the first place that the Aztecs, having wandered for hundreds of years, could call home. When they arrived on this spot, they saw, as the war god Huitzilopochtli had predicted, an eagle perched on a cactus eating a snake (see the Mexican flag and p. 8). **Teocalli** is now an astonishingly huge excavated archaeological site in the middle of the world's largest city. Although work was initiated at the beginning of this century, the excavation was completed only in 1982. At first, the site appears to be little more than the foundation of a demolished modern complex. Before making any judgments, however, have a look inside. The excavated ruins reveal five layers of pyramids, each one built on top of the others as the Aztec empire grew, topped off by structures added by the conquistadors to mark their domination. Over 7000 artifacts, including sculpture, jewelry, and pottery, have been found in the ruins. Highlights include the enormous flat, round sculpture of **Coyolxauhqui,** the moon goddess.

The extraordinary **Museo del Templo Mayor,** now part of the archaeological complex, houses this unique collection. A must-see stop even for visitors on a whirlwind tour of Mexico City, the museum is divided into eight *salas* that are meant to imitate the layout of the original temple, and the artifacts found in the excavation are accompanied not only by dry museum inscriptions (in Spanish) but also by excerpts from the ancient Aztec texts which describe them (also in Spanish).

SOUTH OF THE ZÓCALO

SUPREMA CORTE DE JUSTICIA. Aside from the spectacle of manacled foreigners pleading that they don't know who planted cannabis in their socks, the Supreme Court draws tourists because of its murals. Four frightening murals by José Clemente Orozco cover the second-floor walls of the present-day Supreme Court, built in 1929 on the spot where the southern half of Moctezuma's royal palace once stood. Filled with roaring tigers, masked evildoers, bolts of hellish flame, and a thuggish Mr. Justice himself wielding a huge axe, the murals are not to be missed. If nothing else, they'll make you think twice about breaking the law. *(Tel. 522 15 00. On the corner of Pino Suárez and Corregidora. Officially, murals can be viewed only 9am-noon or by appointment; call M-F 10am-2pm to schedule a free visit; however, lucky visitors should be able to wheel and deal their way in any time of the day, provided a really big case is not being tried. Bring an ID to leave at the entrance.)*

MUSEO DE LA CIUDAD DE MÉXICO. The museum features a random assortment of modern Mexican art and temporary exhibits focusing on the city's colonial history. The spacious courtyard is a good place to rest, and the store has excellent information not only on the city, but on all of Mexico. *(Pino Suárez 30, at República del Salvador, 3 blocks south of the zócalo's southeast corner. Tel. 542 00 83. Museum and store open Tu-Su 10am-6pm. Admission 5 pesos. Free guided tours available by appointment.)*

MUSEO DEL CLAUSTRO DE SOR JUANA. Located at the very spot where, as a plaque states, this "most illustrious poetess, literate, and philosopher of Hispano-American thought" actually lived and worked, the buildings are used today primarily as a private university. However, the small chapel holding Sor Juana's remains can be visited, as can several rooms inside the Gran Claustro. No plaques in the museum tell the story of this outstanding 17th-century woman who dressed as a man for several years in order to attend university classes. Sor Juana entered the convent in order to escape marriage. There, she produced some of Latin America's most famous and most beautiful literature. *(Tel. 709 59 89. On José Maria Izagaza, between Isabel la Católica and 5 de Febrero. Open Tu-Su 10am-5pm. Free.)*

MUSEO DE LA CHARRERIA. The wild collection of saddles, spurs, and ropes, proudly explains in Spanish, English, and French, the development of *charreria* (being-a-cowboy; rodeoing) and its ultimate incarnation as Mexico's national sport. Learn how quintessentially Mexican the cowboy, his clothes, and his sport are as you marvel at tons of artifacts. *(Across the street from the Claustro, at the corner of Izagaza and Isabel la Católica. Open M-F 10am-7pm. Free.)*

ALAMEDA

The area around the Alameda Central is doubly blessed, filled with must-see sights and easily accessible by public transportation. It's within walking distance of the *centro* and the Monumento a la Revolución, and it has the best crafts market in the city, **La Ciudadela** (see p. 129). Near the park are three Metro stations: Hidalgo (Lines 2 and 3), at the intersection of Hidalgo and Paseo de la Reforma, one block west from the park; Bellas Artes (Lines 2 and 8), one block east of the park's northeast corner, between the park and Bellas Artes itself; and San Juan de Letrán (Line 8), one block south of the **Torre Latinoamericana.**

ALAMEDA CENTRAL

Amid the howling sprawl that is downtown Mexico City, the Alameda is an oasis of sanity and photosynthesis. But while the Alameda can feel like an island, it is not impervious to the urban life that bustles around it—three major thoroughfares (Avenidas Hidalgo, Juárez, and Lázaro Cárdenas) flank the Alameda, and the park is packed with mimes, young lovers, protesters, *comerciantes* selling their trinkets, and pick-pockets. The Alameda was originally an Aztec marketplace and then the site at which heretics were burnt at the stake under the Inquisition; it was finally turned into a park in 1592 by Don Luis de Velasco II, who intended it to be a place where the city's elite could meander peacefully. Enlarged in 1769 to its actual size, the park was repaired after the 1985 earthquake, and in 1997 the sidewalks were restored by the city government. The park takes its name from the rows of shady *alamos* (poplars) that flood it. Since it was opened to the public in this century, Mexico City has fallen in love with the park; Mexicans of all sorts enjoy the Alameda, and even in a city with soaring real estate prices and overcrowding, no one ever considers paving over the park.

At the center of the Alameda's southern side is the **Monumento a Juárez,** a semicircular marble monument constructed in 1910 to honor the revered former president on the 100th anniversary of Mexican Independence. A somber-faced Benito Juárez sits on a central pedestal among 12 doric columns. On July 19 of each year, a civic ceremony commemorates the anniversary of Juárez's death.

PALACIO DE BELLAS ARTES

Location: *Juárez and Eje Central, at the northeast corner of Alameda Central complex. It's hard to miss.* **Hours:** *Open Tu-Su 10am-6pm.* **Admission:** *15 pesos to see the murals and art exhibits on the upper floors, free for students and teachers with ID. Temporary exhibits on the first floor are generally free for all.*

This impressive Art Nouveau palace is perhaps one of the most obvious (and one of the only) beautiful things to come out of Porfirio Díaz's dictatorship (1876-1911; see **The Porfiriato,** p. 14). Soon after construction began in 1900, the theater started to sink into the city's soft ground—it now sits many meters lower than when it was built. Most tourists, however, come to the palace to see the second and third floors, where the walls have been painted by the most celebrated Mexican muralists of the 20th century. If you have time for only one mural, see Diego Rivera's, on the west wall of the third floor. John D. Rockefeller commissioned Rivera to paint a mural depicting the topic "Man at Crossroads Looking with Hope and High Vision to the Choosing of a New and Better Future" in New York City's Rockefeller Center. Rivera, however, was dismissed from the project when Rockefeller discovered Lenin's portrait in the foreground. The Mexican government allowed Rivera to duplicate the work in the *palacio*. The result, **El Hombre, Controlador del Universo, 1934,** includes an unflattering portrayal of John D. Rockefeller looking like a mad scientist, his hands on various technological instruments designed to rule the world. The second floor also has a permanent collection of less-well-known pieces by Rivera, Kahlo, Tamayo, and others, as well as space for temporary exhibits by well-known artists.

On the east wall of the third floor, murals by the leftist José Clemente Orozco depict the supposed tension between natural human characteristics and industrialization. In addition to Orozco's work, the *palacio* displays the frescoes of David Alfaro Siqueiros, the 20th-century Mexican muralist, Stalinist, nationalist, and would-be assassin of Leon Trotsky. Look for his work on the third floor. Like his contemporary Diego Rivera, Siqueiros favored overt themes of class struggle and social injustice; he flaunted a cavalier disregard for topical subtlety. His *Tormento de Cuauhtémoc* describes Cortés's attack on the last vestiges of the Aztec nation.

On the fourth floor of the palace is the **Museo Nacional de Arquitectura** (tel. 709 31 11). It exhibits early sketches and blueprints for the most architecturally distinctive buildings in the city, including the Teatro Nacional, and the *palacio* itself.

The **Ballet Folklórico de México** performs regional dances in the Palacio de Bellas Artes and in the **Teatro Ferrocarrilero** (tel. 529 17 01), near the Revolución Metro station. Two companies, one resident and one traveling, are world-renowned for their choreographic and theatrical skill. Their program combines folk and *indígena* dancing with the formal aspects of traditional ballet. Bellas Artes performances are the only way to see the crystal curtain designed by Gerardo Murelli, made up of almost one million pieces of multicolored crystal which, when illuminated from behind, represent the Valley of Mexico at twilight. *(Dance performances W 8:30pm, Su 9:30am and 8:30pm. Tickets 140-250 pesos. Sold 3 or 4 days in advance at Bellas Artes.)* The Bellas Artes **ticket office** sells tickets for these and other artistic performances throughout the city. *(Ticket booth open M-Sa 11am-7pm, Su 9am-7pm.)* An **information booth** (tel. 521 92 51 ext. 132 and 217), up the first set of stairs next to the ticket booth, has information on all performances in Mexico City, and the staff speaks some English (open daily 11am-7pm). Travel agencies snatch up a lot of tickets during Christmas, *Semana Santa,* and summer; check first at Bellas Artes, then try along Reforma or in the *Zona Rosa.*

MUSEO NACIONAL DE ARTE

Tel.: 512 32 24. *Location:* Tacuba 8, Half a block east of the palacio's north side. *Hours:* Open Tu-Su 10am-5:30pm. *Admission:* 20 pesos, free for students and teachers with ID, adults over 60, children under 13, and for all on Sundays. Camera permits 5 pesos, video 30 pesos.

The **Museo Nacional de Arte,** half a block east of the *palacio*'s north side, was built during the Porfiriato to house the Secretary of Communications. In 1982, it was inaugurated as a museum. The building's architect, Silvio Conti, paid particular attention to the central staircase—its sculpted Baroque handrails were crafted by artists in Florence. The museum is not as frequented as the *palacio* or other nearby *museos,* despite its enormity. Because of this and its spacious design, the museum has an empty feel; footsteps echo through the galleries. The museum contains works from the stylistic and ideological schools of every era in Mexican history. Look for Guerra's *Monumento a José Martí,* a celebration not only of the young revolutionary's life, but also of color and space. The museum displays everything from *arte deco* (art deco) to *retrato popular del siglo XIX* (popular portraits of the 19th century); current exhibits are listed in the *sala* downstairs.

NEAR ALAMEDA CENTRAL

MUSEO MURAL DIEGO RIVERA

Tel.: 510 23 29. *Location:* Calzada Colón and Balderas, facing the small park at the west end of the Alameda. *Hours:* Tu-Su 10am-6pm. *Admission:* 10 pesos; free on Sundays and for Mexican national students and teachers with ID.

Also known as **Museo de la Alameda,** this fascinating building holds Diego Rivera's masterpiece, **Sueño de un Tarde Dominical en la Alameda Central** (Sunday Afternoon Dream at the Alameda Central). The work was originally commissioned by the Hotel del Prado in 1946, but when the hotel proudly hung the just-finished work in 1948, a national controversy ensued over the figure of Ignacio Ramírez, who is shown holding up a pad of paper that reads "God does not exist," an excerpt from a speech he gave in 1836. The archbishop of Mexico refused to bless the hotel, and on June 4th at dawn, more than 100 angry students broke into the hotel, erased the "does not exist" fragment from the original phrase, and damaged the face of the young Diego Rivera in the center of the mural. After the 1985 quake, the mural was moved to the museum, which was constructed solely to showcase this piece. The key in front of the mural points out the portrayal of historical figures woven into the crowd: Frida Kahlo, José Martí, and a chubby young Rivera, among others. José Guadalupe Posada's *La Calavera Catrina,* the central figure in the mural (the smiling skeleton wearing the boa), mocks the aristocratic pretentions under the Díaz presidency. Along with the mural, the museum displays original clippings of 1948 describing the

MURALISTS In the period between the First and Second World War and continuing into the 1960's, an artistic movement in Mexico flourished and eventually impacted the world. The movement was dominated by three men: **Diego Rivera, José Clemente Orozco,** and **David Alfaro Siqueiros.** Each one had a distinct technique and personality, but they all shared common aspirations. The three muralists worked during the time of liberation after the suffocating regime of Porfirio Díaz in 1911 and towards a new spirit of nationalism encouraged by the 1917 constitution. The three artists received government commissions to decorate public buildings with themes that glorified the revolution and pre-colonial history of Mexico. The principal artistic and political message of the murals was expected to be easily understood by any Mexican citizen. Rivero, Orozco, and Siqueiros believed that Europeans had strangled the art of Mexico and they vowed to return to *indígena* themes. Tending to focus their work on the "common man," they shunned the elaborate decorations of colonial Mexico and especially exaultations of the church. With their grand scope and political expression, murals became the silent voice of the populace throughout all of Mexico.

vandalism. It also has Rivera's original notes regarding plans for the reconstruction, as well as extensive information (in Spanish) on Rivera's life and the cultural scene of the time. Changing exhibits upstairs also relate to Rivera's life and work.

WEST OF THE ALAMEDA

CENTRO CULTURAL JOSÉ MARTÍ. The poet José Martí was a leader of the Cuban independence movement in the late 19th century. He dreamed of a united and free Latin America, led by Mexico, and he repeatedly warned of the dangers of North American imperialism. This center features a rainbow-colored mural depicting Martí's poetry as well as Martí himself and the people of Latin America. A tally sheet in the corner of the mural records Spanish, British, French, and U.S. interventions in Latin America from 1800 to 1969; the grand total is a staggering 784. Temporary exhibits on Cuba share the space. Movies and other cultural events take place in the adjoining theater. Stop by or call the Centro Cultural to see what's on the program. *(Dr. Mora 2 at Hidalgo, on the Alameda's west end. Tel. 518 14 96. Open M-F 9am-9pm, Sa 9am-3pm. Free.)*

PINACOTECA VIRREINAL DE SAN DIEGO. Constructed between 1591 and 1621. as a churcht, the huge rooms with high, decorated ceilings and wooden floors now contain an extensive collection of Baroque and Mannerist paintings that are almost exclusively religious. Don't miss the almost endless spiral staircase leading up to a second floor balcony to the left of the entrance. *(Dr. Mora 7, next door to Centro Cultural José Martí. Tel. 510 27 93. Open Tu-Su 9am-5pm. Admission 10 pesos, students with ID 5 pesos. Free for all on Su.)*

EAST OF THE ALAMEDA

TORRE LATINOAMERICANA. As the second-tallest building in the city at 181m and 44 stories high, the tower's 44th-floor observatory, 2422m above sea level, commands a startling view of the sprawling city on a clear day: all you can see in any direction is city, city, and more city. At night, the *torre* is positively sexy, with city lights sparkling for miles in every direction. *(Lázaro Cárdenas and Madero (the continuation of Juárez), 1 block east of Alameda Central's southeast corner. Top -floor observatory open daily 9:30am-11pm. Admission 32 pesos, children under 12 26 pesos. Telescope fee 5 pesos.)* The 38th floor holds the gimmicky and depressing **"highest aquarium in the world."** *(Open daily 9:30am-10pm: Admission 21 pesos, children 18 pesos.)*

LA IGLESIA DE SAN FRANCISCO. The first and largest Franciscan convent in Mexico City was once a vast Franciscan complex that included several churches, a school, and a hospital built in the early 1500s and visited by Hernán Cortés. Two fragments of the original cloisters can be seen at Gante 5, on the east side of the church, and at Lázaro Cárdenas 8, behind a vacant lot. Holy water runs freely from a tap inside and is quickly put into bottles by locals. *(Just east of the Torre LatinoAmericana on Madero. Open M-F 9am-1pm and 5-7pm, Sa 9am-1pm.)*

CASA DE LOS AZULEJOS. The *casa* is an early 17th-century building covered with *azulejos* (blue and white tiles) from Puebla. To be able to afford even a token few of these tiles was a mark of considerable status. This mansion was festooned by an insulted son who set out to prove his worth to his father. An Orozco mural is on the staircase wall; check out the great view of the building from the second-floor balcony. Go through **Sanborn's** (tel. 512 13 31) to view them. *(Across the street from San Francisco. Both the Casa and Sanborn's open daily 7:30am-10pm.)*

PALACIO ITURBIDE. A great place to chill, the grand 18th-century *palacio*, in recent years, has been taken over by Banamex (Banco de México); before that it was the residence of Mexico's old Emperor, the despotic Agustín Iturbide. There is a gallery on the ground floor with exhibitions that change every three months. *(Madero 17, between Bolívar and Gante, 1½ blocks east of Lázaro Cárdenas, near the Iglesia de San Francisco. Tel. 225 24 71. Open daily 10am-7pm.)*

NORTH OF THE ALAMEDA

MUSEO FRANZ MAYER. In the small, sunken Plaza de Santa Veracruz, flanked by the beautifully aging facades of the churches of San Juan de Dios and Santa Veracruz, lies one of the loveliest sights in this area. The museum was formerly the Hospital de San Juan de Dios, but the building has been expertly restored and now houses an extensive collection of ceramics, colonial furniture, and religious paintings. Plush red velvet, gleaming display cases, and an ultra-professional staff make wandering through the lavish display cases a joy. The old cloister of San Juan de Dios lies inside the first entrance to the left; its courtyard holds benches, trees, and a fountain, and its upper level holds more exhibits. *(Hidalgo 45. Tel. 518 22 65. Open Tu-Su 10am-5pm. Admission 15 pesos to the museum, 10 pesos to the cloister, 10 and 5 pesos for students with ID, free for all on Tu. Guided tours Tu-F 10am-2pm, 10 pesos.)*

MUSEO NACIONAL DE LA ESTAMPA. Here lies the National Institute of Fine Arts's graphic arts and engraving collection, tracing the art of printmaking from pre-Hispanic seals to contemporary engravings. The highlight of the museum is the work of the acclaimed José Guadalupe Posada, Mexico's foremost engraver and print-maker. His woodcuts depict skeletons dancing, singing, and cavorting in ridiculous costumes—a truly graphic indictment of the Porfiriato's excesses. Catch an excellent view of the Alameda from the second floor. *(Hidalgo 39, next door to the Franz Mayer museum in the pretty pink building. Tel. 521 22 44 or 510 49 05. Open Tu-Su 10am-6pm. Admission 10 pesos, free on Su and for students with ID.)*

NEAR THE MONUMENTO A LA REVOLUCIÓN

MONUMENTO A LA REVOLUCIÓN AND MUSEO NACIONAL DE LA REVOLUCIÓN

Tel.: 546 21 15. *Location:* At the Plaza de la República. The museum is just northeast of the monument, in a blackstone park. *Hours:* Museum open Tu-Sa 9am-5pm, Su 9am-3pm. *Admission:* 5 pesos, for students and teachers with ID 2.50 pesos. Call to arrange a tour.

Díaz originally planned the site as the seat of Congress, but progress halted as revolutionary fighting entered the city streets, and the dome was left only half-completed. It wasn't until the 1930s that the monument and the space below were finally dedicated to the memory of the Revolution. Today, 32 flag poles representing the Mexican states line the pathway to this marmoreal dome. The entrance to the subterranean exhibition is just northeast of the monument. Inside the doors, a thorough chronology of the Revolution unfolds. Although everything is in Spanish, great collections of Revolutionary artifacts (cars, clothing, guns) will interest all. Temporary exhibits reach beyond the Revolution; they comment on and connect contemporary artistic expression and politics.

OTHER MUSEUMS

MUSEO DEL CHOPO. The modern, relatively tourist-free Chopo (as it's commonly called) displays the works of up-and-coming modern Mexican artists in every medium. Every mid-June to mid-July, for 12 years running, they have proudly hosted a show of uncensored gay and lesbian photography, sculpture, and painting—passionate pictures of pain and love. *(Dr. Enrique Gonzalez Martinez 10. Just after Puente de Alvarado turns into San Cosme, turn right on Dr. Enrique Gonzalez Martinez—it's 1 block up on the left. Open Tu-Su 10am-2pm and 3-7pm. Admission 6 pesos, 3 pesos for students with ID, free on Tuesdays. Free guided visits Tu-F 10:30am, noon, 4:30, and 6pm.)*

MUSEO SAN CARLOS. The museum lets you feel as though you've gone to Spain instead of Mexico. Housing an old art school and an impressive collection of European paintings spanning the 16th to 19th centuries, the eclectic museum features excellent work by minor artists, as well as standards by artists like Rubens and Goya. Temporary exhibits often highlight certain themes in post-Renaissance European art. *(At the corner of Puente de Alvarado and Ramos Arizpe, 3 blocks north of the Monumento a la Revolución. Tel. 566 85 22. Open M and W-Su 10am-6pm. Admission 20 pesos, students and teachers 10 pesos, Su free.)*

BOSQUE DE CHAPULTEPEC

Mexico City has to do everything a little bigger and better than everywhere else, and this, the D.F.'s major park and recreational area, is no exception. Literally "Forest of Grasshoppers," this 1000-acre green expanse on the western side of the *centro* is the biggest urban-situated park in all the Americas and one of the older natural parks in the New World. With its manifold museums, hiking paths, zoos, bikes, amusement parks, castles, balloon vendors, and modern sports facilities, one could easily spend several days in the Bosque. Mexico's most famous museum, the **Museo Nacional de Antropología,** sits among the hills of the park.

The area that is officially the Bosque is open only 5am to 5pm daily. During this time, it is fairly safe (as safe as anywhere in the city). Hordes of cleanup crews emerge at 5pm to ensure the Bosque will be bright and beautiful each morning. The areas north of Reforma near the Museo Nacional de Antropología are open 24 hours. They tend to be a little dirtier and, while full of happy families during the day, should be avoided after nightfall, especially by women. Helpful signs point you toward major sites, but the Bosque's myriad paths wind and curve without warning; keep a close watch on your bearings. Try to visit on Sunday, when families flock here for the cheap entertainment. Musical spectacles and open-air concerts enliven the park. Best of all, the zoo and all of the museums in the area are **free on Sundays.**

All the museums and sights listed are in Old Chapultepec, the eastern half of the park, which fans out to the west of the *Zona Rosa.* To reach the park, take the Metro to Auditorio (Line 7, closer to the **zoo**), to the more convenient Chapultepec (Line 1, closer to the **Niños Héroes** monument and the museums), or take any *pesero* going down Reforma to Auditorio or Chapultepec.

ANGELS AND INSECTS One kilometer east of Chapultepec Park is the **Angel de la Independencia.** Situated at the fourth traffic circle on the Paseo de la Reforma, the Angel soars 50m above passing cars. Designed by Antonio Rivas Mercado, the monument is a stone column capped by a golden angel; its round-terraced base holds the remains of Hidalgo, Allende, and other national heroes. The original angel fell during an earthquake in 1957, and the head was so mangled that a new one had to be cast. Solid ever since, the Angel stands erect as a symbol of Mexican victory, and crowds often converge here after major *fútbol* triumphs. The view at night, when the angel is embraced by the surrounding lights and skyline of the city, is magnificent. There are also a lot of Volkswagen **bugs** driving around.

MUSEO NACIONAL DE ANTROPOLOGÍA

Tel.: 553 62 66. *Location:* Paseo de la Reforma and Gandhi—you can't miss it. Take an audi-torio pesero (2 pesos) southwest on Reforma and signal the driver to let you off at the second stop after entering the park. By Metro, take Line 7 to the Auditorio station; the museum is just east down Reforma. *Hours:* Tu-Su 9am-7pm. *Admission:* 25 pesos, free for national students and teachers (try your luck with international student or teacher's card; they sometimes work), free for all on Sundays. Audio guides in Spanish 30 pesos, in English 36 pesos. Cam-era permits 10 pesos.

Some journey to Mexico just to consult this magnificent and massive mega-museum, considered by many to be the best of its kind in the world. This mini-universe houses 4km of Mexico's most exquisite archaeological and ethno-graphic treasures; it's the yardstick by which all other Mexican museums are mea-sured. Constructed of volcanic rock, wood, and marble, the museum opened in 1964. A huge stone image of the goggle-eyed rain god Tlaloc hails you outside, and 23 exhibition halls await within. Poems from ancient texts and epics grace the entrances from the main courtyard. In the center of the courtyard, a stout column covered with symbolic carvings supports a vast, water-spouting aluminum pavil-ion. Although guards may give you menacing looks, it is quite all right to run through this refreshing liquid cylinder—as long as you don't look like you're going to stay and bathe.

It would take about three days to pay proper homage to the entire museum, though some visitors are afflicted with pottery overload after a few hours. As you enter on the right side of the ground floor, a general introduction to anthropology precedes a series of chronologically arranged galleries moving from the right to the left wings of the building. These trace the histories of many central Mexican groups, from the first migrations to the Americas up to the Spanish Conquest. Among the highlights not to be missed: the **Sala Teotihuacana,** with detailed models of the amazing city of Teotihuacán; the **Sala Toltec,** with huge statues of Quetzal-cóatl; the museum's crown jewel, the **Sala Mexica,** with the world-famous **Aztec Cal-endar Stone (Sun Stone),** featuring Tonatiuh, the Aztec god of the sun, tongue stuck out, and an enormous statue of Coatlicue ("the one with the skirt of snakes"), god-dess of life and death; the **Sala Golfo de Mexico,** with colossal stone Olmec heads; and the **Sala Maya,** where you can descend into a model of the tomb of King Pacal. The museum also contains a **restaurant** (open Tu-Su 9am-6pm) and a large **book-shop** that sells English guides to archaeological sites around the country, as well as histories and ethnographies of Mexico's indigenous populations. Some of these guides are not available at the sites themselves, so plan ahead.

MUSEO RUFINO TAMAYO (MUSEO ARTE CONTEMPORÁNEO)

Tel.: 286 65 19. *Location:* Just to the east of the Museo Nacional de Antropología, on the corner of Reforma and Gandhi. Take the first right on Gandhi from the Chapultepec Metro stop (Line 1). After a five-minute walk on Gandhi, the museum lies to the left down a small, semi-hidden path through the trees. Alternatively, walk due east (straight ahead as you exit) from the entrance of the anthropology museum into the woods; Tamayo is 100m straight ahead. *Hours:* Tu-Su 10am-5:45pm. *Admission:* 20 pesos, free on Sundays and for students and teachers with ID.

The Mexican government created the nine halls of the museum after Rufino and Olga Tamayo donated their international collection to the Mexican people. The murals of Rufino Tamayo were much criticized in the wake of the Revolution of 1910 for not being sufficiently nationalistic. Since the museum's opening in 1981, however, his reputation has been rehabilitated, and he has taken his place with Rivera, Siqueiros, and Orozco as one of the omnipresent bad boys of modern Mex-ican art. The museum, opened in 1981, houses a large permanent collection of Tamayo's work, as well as important works by Willem de Kooning and surrealists Joan Miró and Max Ernst. Although some of the *salas* are currently closed for ren-ovation, the museum is still a worthwhile visit, featuring exhibits by top interna-tional artists and filmmakers.

MUSEO DE ARTE MODERNO

*Tel.: 553 62 33. **Location:** On Reforma and Gandhi, north of the Monumento a los Niños Héroes and on the opposite side of Reforma from the anthropology museum. **Open:** Tu-Su 10am-6pm. **Admission:** 20 pesos, free on Sundays and for students and teachers with ID.*

This wonderful museum houses a fine collection of contemporary paintings by Kahlo, including perhaps her most famous work: the exquisite **Las Dos Fridas.** Works by Siqueiros, José Luis Cuevas, Rivera, Orozco, Velasco, Angelina Beloff (supposedly a lover of Rivera's), and Remedios Varo (the only well-known female Spanish surrealist painter) are also on display. Temporary exhibits feature other up-and-coming, extremely talented Mexican artists, and the biggest in traveling exhibits. The museum is linked to **Galería Fernando Camboa,** a remarkable outdoor sculpture garden with pieces by Moore, Giacometti, and others.

MUSEO NACIONAL DE HISTORIA

*Tel: 286 99 20. **Location:** Inside the Castillo de Chapultepec, on top of the hill behind the Monumento a los Niños Héroes. To get to the top, walk up (way up) the road directly behind the Niños Héroes monument and be prepared to open your bag for the guard. **Hours:** Tu-Su 9am-5pm; tickets sold until 4pm. **Admission:** 20 pesos, free on Sundays, but all second-floor salas are closed Sundays. Camera permit 10 pesos.*

This fascinating museum lives up to its name; it exhaustively narrates the history of Mexico from before the time of the Conquest. An immense portrait of King Ferdinand and Queen Isabella of Spain greets visitors in the first *sala* before they meander through the excellent exhibits on the not-so-distant past. Galleries contain displays on Mexican economic and social structure during the War for Independence, the Porfiriato, and the Revolution. The particularly interesting upper level exhibits Mexican art and dress from the viceroyalty through the 20th century. The walls of *Sala 13* are completely covered by Siqueiros's *Del Porfirismo a la Revolución*, a pictoral cheat-sheet to modern Mexican history. Admission to the museum also allows you a peek at some of the castle's interior.

MUSEO DEL CARACOL (GALERIA DE HISTORIA)

*Tel.: 553 62 85. **Location:** On the southern side of Chapultepec hill. On the road up to the castle, turn right just before the castle itself, at the sign. **Hours:** daily 9am-5:30pm. **Admission:** 16 pesos, free on Sundays and for students and teachers with ID.*

The official name for this museum is **Museo Galería de la Lucha del Pueblo Mexicano por su Libertad** (Museum of the Struggle of the Mexican People for Liberty), but it's more commonly known as **Museo del Caracol (Snail Museum)** because of its spiral design. The gallery consists of 12 halls dedicated to the greatest hits of Mexican history from the early 19th to the early 20th century. A quotation at the entrance urges visiting Mexicans to live up to the legacy embodied in the museum. From the start of your downward spiral, the gist of the museum's message is clear: foreign intervention has made Mexico's fight for liberty an uphill battle. There are especially interesting exhibitions on the executions of Hidalgo and Morelos, the execution of Maximilian, and the battles of Villa, Zapata, and Obregón. A whole room is dedicated to "remembering the Alamo." The museum's exhibitions consist of amazingly life-like mini-dioramas, documentary videos, paintings, and various other historical artifacts. The staircase leads to a beautiful, round, skylit hall that holds a copy of the Constitution of 1917 handwritten by Venustiano Carranza himself. Visitors less familiar with the contours of Mexican history, however, will be bewildered by the Spanish-only explanations written next to each piece. Spanish also blares from speakers in each room; visitors are treated to an annoying audio tour complete with mini-dramatizations.

ELSEWHERE IN CHAPULTEPEC

MONUMENTO A LOS NIÑOS HÉROES. At the end of the long walkway just inside the park on the east side stands six white pillars capped with monoliths and teased by small fountains. The monument is dedicated to the young cadets of the 19th-century military academy, now known as the **Castillo de Chapultepec.** In 1847, during the last major battle of the war with the U.S., the Niños Héroes fought the advancing army of General Winfield Scott. As the invaders closed to within a matter of yards, the last five boys and their lieutenant wrapped themselves in Mexican flag before throwing themselves from the castle wall, refusing to surrender.

TREE OF MOCTEZUMA. The tree boasts a circumference of 13m and is reputed to have been around since the time of the Aztecs. Behind the monument, Av. Gran cuts through the park. Walk west on this street and take the second right on Gandhi. A five-minute stroll north takes you to Reforma and the Museo Nacional de Antropología. On weekends, indigenous groups perform traditional dances in front of the museum and welcome donations.

MUSEO SALA DE ARTE PÚBLICO DAVID ALFARO SIQUIEROS. Twenty-five days before his death in January 1974, famed fanatic, muralist, and would-be Trotsky assassin David Álfaro Siqueiros donated his house and studio to the people of Mexico. In compliance with his will, the government created this museum. Siqueiros was not only an artist, but also a revolutionary soldier, propagandist, communist, republican, Stalinist, and anti-fascist. Fifteen thousand murals, lithographs, photographs, drawings, and documents recount his fascinating life. *(Tres Picos 29 at Hegel, just outside the park. Walk north from the Museo Nacional de Antropología to Rubén Darío. Tres Picos forks off to the northwest on the left; follow it for 1 block. The quirky little museum is on the right. Tel. 531 33 94. Open Tu-Su 10am-3pm. Admission 10 pesos, free for students with ID and free on Su. Call to arrange a guided tour.)*

PARQUE ZOOLÓGICO DE CHAPULTEPEC. Although animal lovers might shed a tear or two over some of the humbler habitats, the zoo is surprisingly excellent, mostly shunning the small-cage approach for larger, more amenable tracts of land. Everyone's favorites—those huggable pandas—have survived quite well here. *(Accessible from the entrance on Reforma, east of Calzado Chivatitio. From the Auditorio Metro Station exit, it is in the opposite direction from the National Auditorium. Tel. 553 62 63. Open Tu-Su 9am-4:30pm. Free.)*

OTHER SIGHTS. West of the Siqueiros museum, up Reforma past the Auditorio Metro station, is the **Jardín de la Tercera Edad,** reserved for visitors over age 50. It contains the **Jardín Escultórico,** a sculpture park full of realist and symbolist statues, as well as the **Jardín Botánico,** a botanical garden with a little lake (botanical garden open daily 9am-5pm; free). The big lake is the **Lago de Chapultepec,** situated at the heart of the park; it has rowboats for rent that fit up to five people (rowboat rentals open daily 7:30am-4:30pm; 6 pesos per hr.).

TLATELOLCO

Tlatelolco lies north of the *centro.* To get to Tlatelolco, take the Metro to the Tlatelolco stop (Line 3) and exit through the Gonzalez *salida.* From the exit, turn right on Gonzalez, walk three blocks east until you reach Cárdenas (Eje 2 Norte), cross the street here and then turn right to follow it one long block up. The plaza will be on your left. Archaeological work has shown that the city of Tlatelolco ("Mound of Sand" in Náhuatl) existed long before the great Aztec capital of Tenochtitlán. By 1463, the Tlatelolco king, Moquíhuix, had built his city into a busy trading center coveted by the Aztec ruler, Axayácatl. Tension mounted over territorial and fishing boundaries, and soon Moquíhuix learned that the Aztecs were preparing to attack his city. Even forewarned, Moquíhuix couldn't handle the Aztec war machine, and Tlatelolco was absorbed into the huge empire.

Today, a monstrous state low-income housing project looms over the 17th-century church that stands on the grounds of Tlatelolco's ancient temple. Three cultures—ancient Aztec, colonial Spanish, and modern Mexican—have left their mark on this square, giving rise to the name **Plaza de las Tres Culturas,** at the corner of Lázaro Cárdenas and Ricardo Flores Magón, 13 blocks north of the Palacio de Bellas Artes. Today the three "cultures" are represented by ancient ruins, a mammoth church, and the nearby ultra-modern Ministry of Foreign Affairs, also known as the **Relaciones Exteriores** building. With stoic optimism, a plaque in the southwest corner of the plaza asserts: "On August 13, 1521, heroically defended by Cuauhtémoc, Tlatelolco fell to Hernán Cortés. It was neither a triumph nor a defeat, but the birth of the *mestizo* city that is the México of today." That battle marked the last serious armed resistance to the *conquista*.

More than 400 years later, the plaza witnessed another gruesome and bloody event, for which it is, sadly enough, most famous: the **Tlatelolco Massacre** of October 2, 1968. An adolescent rivalry between two secondary schools led to fighting in the streets; with the Mexico City Olympic games just a few months away, the government thought it necessary to quell all disturbances forcefully. Fueled by anger at the government's violence and at President Díaz Ordaz's militant anti-protest laws (as well as the city's debt incursion for the upcoming Summer Olympics), the street fighting gave way to protests, which were answered with even more violence—in September the national university was occupied by soldiers. On October 2, a silent pro-peace sit-in was held at the Plaza de Las Tres Culturas. Toward the end of the day, government troops descended on the plaza, shooting and killing hundreds of protesters; prisoners were taken and tortured to death. In memory of the victims of the massacre, a **simple sandstone monument** was erected in the plaza and dedicated in 1993, on the 25th anniversary of the incident—before then, the government had repressed any mention of the event, going so far as to remove related newspaper articles from all national archives. The humble monument lists the names of the dead, and a small plaque on the back of the monolith explains that the present monument, already dirtied and defaced, is just temporary construction—a more fitting memorial will be built when more funds are collected. In the summer of 1998, PRD members of Congress proposed a reopening of the investigation of the army's actions on that fateful day.

In the plaza, parts of the **Pyramid of Tlatelolco** (also known as the **Templo Mayor**) and its ceremonial square remain dutifully well kept. Enter from the southwest corner, in front of the Iglesia de Santiago, and walk alongside the ruins, down a steel and concrete path that overlooks the eight building stages of the main pyramid. At the time of the Conquest, the base of the pyramid extended from Insurgentes to the Iglesia de Santiago. The pyramid was second in importance to the great Teocalli of the Aztec capital, and its summit reached nearly as high as the skyscraper just to the south (the Relaciones Exteriores building). During the Spanish blockade of Tenochtitlán, the Aztecs heaved the freshly sacrificed bodies of Cortés's forces down the temple steps, within sight of the *conquistadores* camped to the west at Tacuba. Aztec priests collected the leftover body parts at the foot of the steps; food was scarce during the siege and all meat was valuable. Another notable structure is the **Templo Calendárico "M,"** an M-shaped building used by the Aztecs to keep time. Scores of skeletons were discovered near its base. A male and female pair that were found facing each other upon excavation have been dubbed "The Lovers of Tlatelolco."

On the east side of the plaza is the simple **Iglesia de Santiago,** an enormous, fortress-like church erected in 1609 to replace a structure built in 1543. This church was designed to fit in with the surrounding ruins, and with its stonework and solid, plain masonry, it does. *(Open daily 8am-1pm and 4-7pm.)*

LA BASÍLICA DE GUADALUPE

To get to the Villa de Guadalupe, take the Metro to La Villa Basílica (Line 6), go past the vendor stands, and take a right on Calzada de Guadalupe. A small raised walkway between the two lanes of traffic leads directly to the Basílica.

Ever since the legend of Juan Diego and his mantle, Our Lady of Guadalupe has since been the patron of Mexico, an icon of the nation's religious culture.

Diego's mantle can be seen in **La Basílica de Guadalupe,** north of the city center. Designed by the venerated Pedro Ramírez Vásquez in the 1970s, the new basilica is an immense, aggressively modern structure. Although the flags from different cultures inside of the basilica make it feel more like the United Nations than a church, crowds of thousands flock daily to the Virgin's miraculous likeness. *(Open daily 5am-9pm.)*

The devout and the curious alike throng around the central altar and impressive organ to step onto the **basilica's moving sidewalk**—it allows for easier (and faster) viewing of Diego's holy cloak. On December 12th, the Virgin's name day, pilgrims from throughout the country march on their knees up to the altar. Perhaps the most striking feature of the basilica is the set of huge, haunting words written in gold Byzantine script across the top of the edifice: "*¿Aqui no estoy yo que soy tu madre?*" ("Am I not here, I who am your mother?").

Next to the new basilica is the **old basilica,** built at the end of the 17th century. These days, the old basilica houses the **Museo de la Basílica de Guadalupe.** This gorgeous, lavish museum makes you wonder why they built the new, ungainly basilica. The colonial paintings dedicated to the Virgin pale beside the intensely emotional collection of *ex votos* (small paintings made by the devout to express their thanks to the Virgin of Guadalupe for coming to their assistance) in the entryway. A room at the base of the staircase contains a pair of golden *fútbol* shoes offered to the Virgin before the 1994 World Cup by the Mexican star Hugo Sánchez. *(Plaza Hidalgo 1, in the Villa de Guadalupe. Tel. 781 68 10. Open Tu-Su 10am-6pm. Admission 3 pesos.)*

Behind the basilica, winding steps lead up the side of a small hill, past lush gardens, crowds of the faithful, and cascading waterfalls. A small chapel dedicated to the Virgin of Guadalupe, the **Panteón del Tepeyac,** sits on top of the hill. The bronze and polished wood interior of the chapel depicts the apparitions witnessed by Juan Diego. Upon entering, one can stop in front of a priest to be blessed with holy water. From the steps beside the church, one can absorb a breathtaking panoramic view of the city framed by the hillsides and distant mountains. Descending the other side of the hill, past the spouting gargoyles, statues of Juan Diego and a group of *indígenas* kneel before a gleaming Virgin doused with the spray from a rushing waterfall. Vendors, both in and around the basilica's grounds, hawk religious paraphernalia: holy water, holy shoes, holy T-shirts, holy jeans, and more.

MEXICO CITY

THE DARK VIRGIN Probably the most important figure in Mexican Catholicism is the **Virgen de Guadalupe.** She first appeared as a vision on a hill to the *indígena* peasant Juan Diego in December 1531. When Juan Diego informed the bishop of his vision, the clergyman was dubious. Juan Diego returned to the hill and had another vision of the Virgin; she told him that on the hill he would find a great variety of roses (in December!) that he should gather and bring to the bishop as proof. The Virgin also instructed Juan Diego to build her a shrine at that very spot. Juan Diego gathered the roses in his cloak, and when he let them fall at the feet of the bishop, an **image of the Virgin** remained emblazoned on the cloak. The bishop was convinced, and the shrine was built.

The image was of a woman with brown skin, an *indígena.* She quickly became a symbol of religious fusion between the *indígenas* and Christians for the people of Mexico. Depictions of La Virgen of Guadalupe have maintained her dark skin and indigenous features, and she is often referred to proudly as the **Dark Virgin.** A plaque on the Old Basílica of Guadalupe in Mexico City commemorating her words to Juan Diego sums up her enormous importance. It reads: "I am the eternal Virgin Mary, mother of the true God, author of life, creator of all...I ardently desire that here a temple to me be raised...I will show you my clemency and the compassion I have for all natural things and for those who love and seek me."

COYOACÁN

To reach Coyoacán from downtown, take the Metro directly to the Coyoacán station (Line 3). Taxis cost about 10 pesos. It's also a pleasant walk.

The Toltecs founded **Coyoacán** (Place of the Skinny Coyotes, in Náhuatl) between the 10th and 12th centuries. Cortés later established the seat of the colonial government here, and, after the fall of Tlatelolco, had Cuauhtémoc tortured; he hoped the Aztec leader would reveal the hiding place of the legendary Aztec treasure. Although no longer a refuge for the aforementioned "skinny coyotes," it is a haven for "English-speaking tourists." South of the center, wealthy Coyoacán today is the city's most attractive suburb. Well-maintained and peaceful, it is worth visiting for its museums or simply for a stroll in beautiful **Plaza Hidalgo**, neighboring **Jardín Centenario**, or nearby **Placita de la Conchita.** Come to Coyoacán for a respite from the hurried *centro;* the pace is slower and life a little easier here. Coyoacán is centered around the Plaza Hidalgo, which is bounded by the cathedral and the Casa de Cortés. The two parks are split by Calle Carrillo Puerto, which runs north-south just west of the church.

Coyoacán's center of **tourist info** (tel. 659 22 56 ext. 181) is found in the **Casa de Cortés,** the big red building on the north side of Plaza Hidalgo. From here, **free guided tours of Coyoacán** leave whenever a few people gather. On Saturday mornings from 8am to noon, **free tours** of various other areas also leave from here. Originally Cortés's administrative building, the *casa* now houses the municipal government. Inside are murals by local artist Diego Rosales, a student of Diego Rivera's, showing scenes from the Conquest. *(Open daily 8am-8pm.)*

MUSEO FRIDA KAHLO

Tel: 554 59 99. *Location:* Londres 247. On Allende, five blocks north of Plaza Hidalgo's northeast corner, in the colorful indigo and red building at the northeast corner of the intersection. *Hours:* Open Tu-Su 10am-6pm. *Admission:* 20 pesos.

Perhaps Coyoacán's most wonderful and moving sight is the **Museo Frida Kahlo.** Works by Rivera, Orozco, Duchamp, and Klee hang in this restored colonial house, the birthplace and home of Frida Kahlo (1907-1954). Kahlo's disturbingly exquisite work and traumatic life story have been growing in international renown since Andre Breton proclaimed her a surrealist during one of his visits to Mexico. She was impaled by a post during a trolley accident when she was a teenager, suffered innumerable complications, and was confined to a wheelchair and bed for most of her life. She married Diego Rivera twice, and became a celebrated artist in her own right. Kahlo was notorious for her numerous affairs, most famously with Leon Trotsky. Those looking for loads of her work will be disappointed (only a few paintings and early sketches are around), but the museum still has much to offer. Wandering through the house is an emotionally wrenching experience: witness the bed on which Frida suffered, the words "Diego" and "Frida" lovingly scrawled on the kitchen wall, and Diego's painting of his "little girl" Frida hanging next to sultry portraits of various women (many of whom were his lovers). Those looking for insight into Kahlo's morbid work will find it in this house, full of reminders about her chronic health problems and her obsession with adultery. Read (or have someone translate) the excerpts of her diary and her letters hanging on the walls. They eloquently and intimately explain her childhood dreams and the inspiration for some of her work. The house also hides a gorgeous garden full of flowering lilies and hidden pre-Hispanic artifacts.

MUSEO Y CASA DE LEON TROTSKY

Tel: 658 87 32. *Locations:* Río Churubusco 410. Continue north on Allende toward the route and make a right on Viena. The entrance is around back. *Hours:* Tu-Su 10am-5pm. *Admission:* 10 pesos, students with ID 5 pesos.

After Leon Trotsky was expelled from the USSR by Stalin in 1927, he wandered in exile until Mexico's president Lázaro Cárdenas granted him political asylum at the suggestion of Trotsky's friends, muralist Diego Rivera and his wife Frida Kahlo. Trotsky arrived in 1937 with his wife and first lived in the "Casa Hazel," now the

San Angel & Coyoacán

MEXICO CITY

Museo Frida Kahlo (see above). A falling out with Rivera in 1939 led the Trotskys to relocate to the house on Curubusco. Bunny rabbits nibble peacefully in the gardens while bullet holes riddle the interior walls—relics of an attack on Trotsky's life led by the Stalinist muralist David Alfaro Siqueiros on May 24, 1940. Perhaps because this self-proclaimed "man of the people" living in a posh house in a posh suburb feared Stalinist wrath, Trotsky had **bullet-proof bathroom doors** created. Apparently, this paranoia wasn't enough; Trotsky was eventually assassinated by a Spanish Communist posing as a Belgian journalist-in-search-of-a-mentor who buried an axe in his skull. For more cool details of Trotsky's life and work, Jesús the English-speaking goth tour guide and the kitty he saved from the street will be happy to accommodate you.

OTHER SIGHTS

PARROQUIA DE SAN JUAN BAUTISTA. South of the plaza is the 16th-century park bordered by Plaza Hidalgo on the north and Jardín Centenario on the west. The church interior is elaborately decorated with gold and bronze. Enter south of the church's main door. *(Open Tu-Sa 5:30am-8:30pm, M 5:30am-7:30pm.)*

CASA COLORADA. Cortés built the house for La Malinche, his Aztec lover. When Cortés's wife arrived from Spain, she stayed here briefly with her husband, but soon disappeared without a trace. It is believed that Cortés murdered his spouse because of his passion for La Malinche (see p. 8), although he later gave her away as loot to another *conquistador*. The *casa* is now a private residence and cannot be visited. *(Higuera 57, a few blocks southeast of Plaza Hidalgo, facing the Placita de la Conchita and marked by the gardened plaza at the end of Higuera.)*

MUSEO NACIONAL DE LAS CULTURAS POPULARES. Listen to hundreds of tunes, watch videos of dances, and, if you read Spanish, learn an overwhelming amount about instruments and rhythms from all over the country; the permanent exhibit deals with indigenous music. Temporary exhibits usually feature specific regions of the country or specific mediums of artistic expression. *(Tel. 554 86 10. On Hidalgo between Allende and Abasolo, 2 blocks east of Plaza Hidalgo. Open Tu-Th 10am-6pm, F-Su 10am-8pm. Free.)*

CONVENTO DE NUESTRA SEÑORA DE LOS ANGELES DE CHURUBUSCO. Built in 1524 over the ruins of a pyramid dedicated to the Aztec war god Huitzilopochtli, the present structure was not built until 1668. The walls near the main gate are riddled with bullet holes from the U.S. invasion of Mexico in 1917. Commemorating Mexico's valiant defense and the many before is the **Museo Nacional de las Intervenciones** inside the ex-convent. This tremendous nationalistic homage to the Mexican military is set in one of the most serene and peaceful buildings in the D.F. The museum's halls cover four eras, from the late 18th century to 1917. A few rooms are also dedicated to exhibitions on North American expansionism and cruelty to *indígenas*, U.S. slavery and its significance for Mexico, and European imperialism. This excellent museum really makes its point: international "interference" (whether in peace or war) has done Mexico more harm than help. *(Tel. 604 06 99. 20 de Agosto and General Anaya. To get to the convent from Coyoacán, walk 4 blocks down Hidalgo and then follow Anaya as it branches left; it's 4 blocks farther to the convent grounds. The General Anaya Metro stop (Line 2) is only 2 blocks east of the convent along 20 de Agosto. The Gen. Anaya pesero goes from Plaza Hidalgo to the museum (2 pesos); the Sto. Domingo goes back. Museum open Tu-Su 9am-6pm. Admission 20 pesos, free on Su and for students with ID.)*

MUSEO ANAHUACALLI. Designed by Diego Rivera with Aztec and Maya architectural motifs, the building is an exhibit in and of itself. To reach the museum from Plaza Hidalgo or Churubusco, take a "Huipulco" or "Huayamilpa" *pesero* going south on Av. División del Nte. and get off at Calle Museo. You might want to ask the driver to point out the stop; it is not visible immediately. Turn right onto Museo, and soon you'll reach the place. It houses Rivera's huge collection of pre-Hispanic art. Built atop a hill, Anahuacalli commands one of the best views in Mexico, comparable to those of the Torre LatinoAmericana and Castillo de Chapultepec. *(Tel. 617 43 10. On Calle Museo. Open Tu-Su 10am-2pm and 3-6pm. Free.)*

SAN ANGEL

South of Mexico City near Coyoacán is the wealthy community of San Angel. Neither as artsy or bohemian as Coyoacán, San Angel's main appeal is that, quite simply, it's beautiful. Dotted with churches and exquisite colonial homes, this mecca of Mexican suburbia is a great place for a stroll. To reach the area, 10km south of the *centro* along Insurgentes, take the Metro to the M.A. Quevedo station (Line 3). Head west on Quevedo (away from the big Santo Domingo bakery) for three blocks; when it forks, take a left onto Av. La Paz, and continue along the very green (but sometimes trash-laden) Parque de la Bombilla.

PARQUE DE LA BOMBILLA. The centerpiece of this park is the **Monumento al General Álvaro Obregón.** Obregón was one of the Revolution leaders who united against Huerta, the usurper who executed President Madero and seized power in 1913. During the Revolution, Obregón lost an arm. The statue in the monument shows him thus, while a separate statue of the severed limb can be viewed on the lower level of the monument. In 1920, Obregón became the first president of the post-revolutionary era. The inscription in the sunken lower level reads, "I die blessing the Revolution." *(Open daily 7am-4:30pm. Free.)*

IGLESIA DEL CARMEN. Designed and built between 1615 and 1626 by Fray Andrés de San Miguel of the Carmelite order, the church and adjacent ex-convent are decorated with tiles and paintings. An outstanding statue of Christ the Nazarene is located in the Capilla del Señor Contreras. *(Open daily 7am-1pm and 5-9pm.)* The **Museo del Carmen** (tel. 550 48 96) is located in the converted ex-convent next to the church. The museum tells the history of the barefoot Carmelites in the New World—they were the first order to renounce missionary work—and displays colonial art, crucifixes galore, and portraits of various holy figures. Also exhibited are typical convent rooms—look out for the flat wooden bed and oh-so-comfy log pillow. Most tourists come to see the **mummies,** located in an underground crypt; the grotesque cadavers were originally found in 1916 when the Zapatistas arrived in search of treasure. *(At Revolución and Monasterio. Open Tu-Su 10am-5pm. Admission 14 pesos, free for all Su.)*

CASA DE RISCO. The well-preserved 17th-century house holds an important collection of 14th- through 18th-century European art. The whitewashed inner courtyard contains an exquisitely tiled fountain made of pieces of bowls and plates (called *riscos*) that were collected from around the world. Also look out for *Crisol de las Razas,* a painted colonial chart that lists racial combinations with names like *lobo* (wolf) and *salto atrás* (a step backwards). *(Plaza San Jacinto 15, on the north side of the zócalo. Tel. 550 92 86. Open Tu-Su 10am-5pm. Free.)*

MUSEO CARRILLO GIL. The small, modern building houses the contemporary art collection of the late Carillo Gil, including works by Siqueiros, Orozco, and the young Rivera. Siqueiros's famous *Caín en los Estados Unidos* (Cain in the United States) is on the third floor, revealing the potential whereabouts of this biblical bad boy. The top two floors house temporary exhibits. *(Revolución 1608, 3 blocks north on Revolución from the intersection with La Paz, to the right if coming from the Parque de la Bombilla. Tel. 550 39 83. Open Tu-Su 10am-6pm. Admission 10 pesos, students with ID 6 pesos; free for all on Su.)*

MUSEO ESTUDIO DIEGO RIVERA. This wild and windy studio-turned-museum houses a tiny but phenomenal collection of Rivera's *Niños Indígenas* with a commentary by Rigoberta Menchú. On the top floors, you can see where this great artist worked and comment on his taste in furniture. Even his left-over paints are lying around untouched. *(Tel. 550 15 18. Follow the signs 5 blocks up Altavista, which crosses Revolución. Open Tu-Su 10am-6pm. Admission 10 pesos; students and Su free.)*

OTHER SIGHTS. Across the street from the Iglesia del Carmen is the **Centro Cultural** (tel. 616 12 54 or 616 20 97), which borders the lovely **Plaza del Carmen.** Besides hosting changing art exhibits and plays, this building displays billboards that explain what's hip and hot in the Mexican art world. *(Open Tu-Sa 10am-8pm, Su 10am-7pm.)* One block up Madero, which runs along the left side of the Casa de Cultura (as you face the Casa), is the **Plaza de San Jacinto,** at San Francisco and Juárez. Every Saturday, the plaza fills up with ritzy shoppers scoping out pricey arts and crafts at the **Bazaar Sábado** (see p. 130). A gazebo in the center frequently hosts orchestras and big bands, and plastic chairs and peanut vendors span the plaza. One block past the Casa de Risco on Juárez lies the beautiful **Iglesia de San Jacinto,** a 16th-century church with an ancient orange facade, beautifully carved wooden doors, and a peaceful courtyard (open daily 8am-8pm). This neighborhood, the oldest in San Angel, contains some obscenely swank and impressive modern mansions. Come see how the *ricos* (rich) live, Mexican style.

CIUDAD UNIVERSITARIA

Metro: Universidad (Line 3) lets you off (via *Salidas D* and *E*) in front of the free shuttle service. The shuttles are limited and irregular when classes are not in session (Jul. 5-Aug. 15), but still available to all campus areas.

UNIVERSIDAD NACIONAL AUTÓNOMA DE MEXICO (UNAM)

The **Universidad Nacional Autónoma de México** (National Autonomous University of Mexico), or **UNAM,** is the largest university in Latin America, boasting a staggering enrollment of over 100,000. Immediately after the new colonial regime was established, the religious orders that arrived in Mexico built elementary and secondary schools to indoctrinate new converts and to educate young men who had come over from Spain. After petitioning the king of Spain, the first university was established in 1553 in the building at the corner of Moneda and Seminario, just off the *zócalo.* As the university grew, classes were moved to the building that now houses the Monte de Piedad, on the west side of the *zócalo,* and then to a building at the east end of the Plaza del Volador, where the Supreme Court now stands. In 1954, the **Ciudad Universitaria (C.U.)** reached its present size of **7.3 million square meters.** This veritable "city" boasts 26km of paved roads, 430,000 square meters of greenery, and four million planted trees—and it's not even residential. With all of the modern architecture around, it's easy to forget that UNAM is one of the three oldest universities in the Americas.

Its size makes UNAM a little difficult to navigate on foot unless you have plenty of time to wander. Luckily, a continuous flow of free buses circulate throughout the C.U.'s many streets from the Universidad Metro stop. Routes do not always overlap—your best bet to get from one campus location to the next is usually to ride back to the Metro station and catch a new bus from there. Pick up a map of the C.U. (20 pesos) at the photocopy store across the greenery from the library (store open M-F 8am-7pm). Should you have any serious problems, call **university security** (tel. 55 from a university phone, tel. 616 09 14 from an outside phone).

Despite the rock-bottom tuition (something like US$5 per semester), the university is still able to support an amazingly varied collection of student groups, activities, and social and cultural events. Films, shows, and club meetings abound. You name it, it's here—from a Tae Kwon Do club to a film about young gay Mexicans to local bands playing Mexican alternative rock to tribal dances that explore the country's indigenous heritage. **Tiempo Libre** magazine and the leaflets **Cartelera** and **Los Universitarios** provide comprehensive schedules; hundreds of other events are posted on kiosks around campus. The most notable bulletin board is in the **Centro Cultural Universitario (CCU).** This large, modern complex houses the **Teatro Juan Ruíz de Alarcón,** the **Foro Sor Juana Inés de la Cruz** (tel. 665 65 83; ticket booth open Tu and F 10am-2pm and 5-9pm; tickets 50 pesos, students 25 pesos), the **Sala Netzahualcóyotl** (tel. 622 71 11; shows Saturdays 8pm and Sundays noon; tickets 50-100 pesos, students 50% off), several other concert halls, and two movie theaters, **Salas José Revueltas** and **Julio Bracho** (tel. 665 28 50; tickets 20 pesos, students 10 pesos). The CCU is accessible by Line 3 of the UNAM shuttle which leaves from the Universidad Metro station.

Just outside the CCU is the impressive **Espacio Escultórico.** Out of a huge lava bed and surrounding cave formations rises a pan-chromatic collection of metal, cement, and wood sculptures constructed in the early 1980s. The artists strove to revive the architectural traditions of pre-Hispanic ceremonial centers through modern techniques. The Espacio Escultórico should only be visited during the day; its secluded location makes it dangerous after nightfall.

Hop on another yellow and blue UNAM shuttle to get to the heart of the campus. The **Estadio Olímpico 1968** is located on the opposite side of Insurgentes Sur from the Jardín Central; cross via the pedestrian underpass. The stadium, built in the 1950s, was appropriately designed to resemble a volcano with a huge crater—lava coats the ground on which it is built. The impressive mosaic that covers the stadium was made by the unstoppable Rivera using large colored rocks; it depicts a man and a woman holding two torches, a symbol of the 1968 Olympics, which were held in the stadium.

Although the university's architecture is impressive, most visitors come to see the mosaic murals that cover its larger buildings. From the stadium, cross Insurgentes (use the pedestrian tunnel), and continue east (straight ahead) to the Jardín Central. West of the Jardín Central's southern half, the university's administrative building is distinguished by a 3-D Siqueiros mosaic on the south wall, which shows students studying at desks supported by society. One of the world's larger mosaics, the work of Juan O'Gorman, wraps around the university **library** (tel. 622 16 13), a breathtaking, nearly windowless box next to the rectory tower ahead and to your left as you come out from under Insurgentes. A pre-Hispanic eagle and Aztec warriors peer out from the side facing the philosophy department. The side facing the esplanade shows the Spaniards' first encounter with the natives; the opposite side depicts a huge atom and its whirling components. *(Library open daily 8:30am-7pm.)* Across the *jardín* from the library, the **Museo Universitario de Arte Contemporáneo** has single-artist exhibits that change every three months. Guided tours by art students are available in the mornings for only 5 pesos; most speak English. *(Open Tu-F 10am-noon for guided visits and noon-2pm for regular visits, Sa-Su 10am-6pm. Admission 6 pesos, students 3 pesos. Museum closes during school break, July 5-Aug.15.)*

A beautiful and pleasantly secluded attraction is the **Jardín Botánico,** a stop on the free UNAM shuttle leaving from the Metro station. From the endless species of cactus to the shady arboretum to the tropical plants pavilion, the *jardín* is a welcome change from the city's urban sprawl; it offers a peek into the Valley of Mexico as it was hundreds of years ago. The trails of red volcanic sediment that wander past lagoons and glens and a helpful map at the entrance provide guidance. You must leave your bags with the guard at the entrance. *(Open M-F 9am-4:30pm. Free.)*

CUICUILCO ARCHAEOLOGICAL ZONE

Tel.: 553 22 63. *Location:* On the southeast corner at the intersection of Insurgentes Sur and Anillo Periférico. Take the "Huipulco" pesero (1 peso) from Metro: Universidad to the entrance on the west side of Insurgentes Sur, south of the Periférico. Most peseros will let you off on the other side of Insurgentes. Cross over on one of the yellow pedestrian bridges and head right (away from the Escuela Nacional de Arqueología) to the entrance. *Hours:* daily 9am-4pm. *Admission:* free.

Near the end of the pre-Classic Period, the tiny volcano **Xitle** erupted, leaving eight square kilometers covered with several meters of hardened lava. The lava flow preserved one of the first pyramids constructed in the Valley of Mexico and formed what is now the archaeological zone. The **Pyramid of Cuicuilco,** which means "Place of the Many-Colored Jasper," was built between 600 and 200 BC by the early inhabitants of the Valley of Mexico, when ceremonial centers first began to spring up in Mesoamerica, and their priests gained extraordinary powers. Measuring 125m across at its base and 20m in height, Cuicuilco consists of five layers, with an altar to the god of fire at its summit. The lava rock around the base has been removed, allowing visitors to walk along it up to the altar. However, very little other restoration has taken place. On a clear day, you can faintly see Xitle to the south and Popoc-atépetl to the east from the pyramid. These volcanoes are far from "dead." One night in 1997, Popocatépetl threw a temper tantrum that sent ash and debris over 100km. *Chilangos* were distressed to find their roofs covered in silt of a natural origin.

XOCHIMILCO

To get to Xochimilco, take the Metro to Tasqueña (Line 2) and then ride the *tren ligero* (trolley, 3 pesos; follow the *correspondencia* signs) in the *Embarcadero* direction and get off at that stop. Numerous signs labeled "Embarcadero" and white-shirted boat owners will direct you to the boats. *Peseros* below the station will also take you there; ask to be let off at *las canoas* (the canoes).

The **floating gardens** were not designed by nautical engineers—they are remnants of the Aztec agricultural system. In fact, this tourist trap was once an important center of Aztec life. In the Aztec's brilliantly conceived system, *chinampas* (artificial islands) were made by piling soil and mud onto floating rafts. These rafts were held firm by wooden stakes until the crops planted on top eventually sprouted roots, reaching through the base of the canals. They became fertile breeding grounds, supporting several crops a year. Although polluted today, the canals still bear the waterborne commerce they did centuries ago.

Multicolored *chalupa* boats crowd the maze of fairly filthy canals, ferrying passengers past a **floating market** offering food, flowers, and music. The market is especially popular on Sundays, when hordes of city dwellers and tourists pack the hand-poled *chalupas*. Visitors lounge and listen to the waterborne *mariachis* and *marimba* players, and celebrate Mexico City's aquatic past as they munch goodies from the floating taco bars that tie up pirate-style to the passenger boats. Although nothing of great quality or value is sold (no crafts, *artesanías*, cultural relics, or clothes), you can buy delicate orchids and bubbly beer, and the festive mood is more than enough to make Xochimilco a popular Sunday afternoon spot.

The key word for almost anything you do in Xochimilco is **bargaining.** From markets to boats, this is the only way to get around in this overly popular tourist spot. Be aware that if you come earlier, you'll find a much emptier Xochimilco, with far fewer boats and much higher prices. For a private boat for two people, expect to pay about 70 pesos per hour with bargaining; consult the official diagram for prices, as boat owners will try to charge eight or 10 times as much. On weekend afternoons, *colectivo* boats are cheaper (8 pesos) and more fun than the private boats. The standard price for *mariachis* is 35 pesos per song.

Xochimilco also offers two enormous land-bound markets, one with the usual food and household items, the other lusciously filled with live plants and animals. To reach the marketplace from the *tren ligero*, turn left on any street within three blocks of the station as you walk away from it, and then walk until you hit the market just beyond the **Iglesia de San Bernandino de Cera.**

◨ NIGHTLIFE

As the sun sets, storefronts pull their shutters closed and a new street scene begins to emerge. The city doesn't stop hopping until 6 or 7am on weekends, when the last pooped partiers stumble out of tired taxis. Be it the Ballet Folklórico at Bellas Artes, an old film at an art cinema, a bullfight, someone playing the blues in a smoke-filled bar, or some down-and-dirty techno in a three-story warehouse, Mexico City has something for everyone; this crazy chameleon of a city shows it true colors in the entertainment department.

Different areas of the city boast different entertainment specialties. As a general rule, the best *discotecas* are found along Insurgentes Sur and in the *Zona Rosa*. Rock clubs with young, hip crowds abound in the *Zona Rosa*, and a few exist around the Alameda. More posh bars and discos in the *centro* cater to an older, business-oriented crowd. *Mariachi* bands teem in Garibaldi Plaza, while merengue and *salsa* clubs cluster near the *zócalo* and in San Angel and Coyoacán. Jazz bands, *salsa*, and traditional Mexican music can also be found in the city's southern suburbs. Topless bars disguised as traditional bars abound in the *Zona Rosa*—double-check at the door if you don't see enough women entering.

Tourists and Mexicans alike flood the streets in the evenings, dressed to kill, and determined to have a good time. Bars and discos clog the streets, each attempting to outdo the others in flashiness and decibel output. Although the Alameda and other areas also have some places to dance, discos in more run-down parts of town can get seedy. Women venturing out alone should be aware that they will most likely be approached by men offering drinks, dances, and much, much more.

At many large nightclubs, in the *centro* and *Zona Rosa*, men are unofficially required to have a female date for admission. If you're pushy enough, foreign, and appropriately attired, this unwritten rule shouldn't apply to you. Cover charges range anywhere from 10 to 150 pesos, but women are often admitted free or at reduced prices. A very steep cover charge may signify an open bar; be sure to ask. Places with no cover often have minimum consumption requirements and high drink prices. Covers magically drop during the week when business is scarce, especially for *norteamericanos*, reputed to have hearty appetites and deep pockets. If prices are not listed, be sure to ask before ordering, lest you be charged exorbitant gringo prices. Be aware that *bebidas nacionales* (Mexican-made drinks, from Kahlúa to *sangría*) are considerably cheaper than imported ones. In fact, *barra libre* (open bar) often means *barra libre nacional* (open bar including only nationally made drinks). No biggie, though. Settling for Mexican beer or tequila is hardly settling for second-best. **Cantinas,** bars with dimly lit interiors, no windows, or swinging doors reminiscent of Wild West saloons are often not safe for unaccompanied women. For safety, the *Zona Rosa* offers the best lighting and least lonely streets, which are problems in other areas. Taxis run all night and are the safest way of getting from bar to disco to breakfast to hotel, but—especially after dark—do not flag a cab on the street. Ask any bartender, bouncer, or waiter to call or give you the number for a local *sitio* taxi company.

Mexico City also has more clubs, bars, and discos that cater to gay and lesbian travelers than anywhere else in the country (see **Gay and Lesbian Entertainment,** p. 128).

ZONA ROSA

BARS

While cover charges get steeper and steeper (and drinks weaker and weaker) as the 90s progress, the *Zona Rosa* is still a bar-hopper's dream come true. The high price tags often mean live performers and tasty *botanas* (appetizers). *Zona Rosa* bars cater to all ages and tastes, from teenybopper *fresas* to elderly intellectual. Many feature live music or, at the very least, beamed-in video entertainment. Women will probably feel safer in this area than elsewhere in the city, but men still aggressively try to pick up any female who comes along. Catch a ride home in a *pesero* running all night along Reforma or Insurgentes Sur (3 pesos). Or better yet, call a *sitio* cab.

🦋 **Luna Bar,** Insurgentes Sur 123 (tel. 208 87 21), at the corner of Liverpool, has two floors of intimate tables lit with glowing black light. The blaring music may not facilitate deep conversation, but it creates a great atmosphere for relaxing, drinking, and people-watching—this place draws a snazzy crowd of all ages. Beers are a hefty 35 pesos, but no cover. Open daily 5pm-4am.

🦋 **Bar Osiris,** Niza 22 (tel. 525 66 84). Suffers from mid-week attendance problems, but on weekends, this small, dark second-floor bar turns into a throbbing dance pit. Live rock bands perform after 8pm. 1 beer 20 pesos, a pitcher 90 pesos. Cover F-Sa 25 pesos. Open W-Su 7pm-4am.

El Chato, Londres 117 (tel. 511 17 58), with a stained-glass doorway. This splendid faux old-Euro bar has a dark smokey rear piano bar with fittingly beat tunes. No glitz, no booming beat, but the somewhat older crowd likes it that way. Beer 20 pesos, tequila 25 pesos. Occasionally visited by musicians from the Yucatán, when a 30-peso cover charge takes effect. Open M-Sa 6pm-2am.

El Tlacoache, Londres 142 (tel. 514 31 68), at Ambres. Step upstairs into this brand-new, cool, classy restaurant/bar where chairs are pushed aside to make room for dancing as the night progresses. All ages and all types of music. Starts to fill up by 8pm and closes only after you leave—don't rush.

Melodika, Florencia 52 (tel. 208 01 98). This 3-part bar is host to everything from rave music to karaoke. Make lots of young local friends as you all huddle together and croon everybody's favorite ballads. Karaoke every night to your favorite Mexican, American, or even French hits. Cover 25 pesos. Open Th-Sa 7pm-2am.

DISCOS

The *Zona Rosa* has some of the Republic's flashiest discos and highest cover charges—on weekend nights, the *Zona* can seem like the center of the entire universe. Club-hopping, however, is becoming more difficult, as many discos are moving over to the high cover charge and open bar system. Long lines around the block mean a club is *de moda* (in); expect tons of trendy teens and Armani-clad young couples eager to pay *muchos pesos* in order to get down. If being seen in the hippest nighttime hangouts isn't terribly important to you, try hitting a less populated, slightly *de paso* (out) club and hold out for a deal. Even in the *Zona Rosa*, some clubs offer entrance and open bar for under 40 pesos. Sidewalk recruiters will likely try to lure in groups, especially those with high female-to-male ratios; hold out and you just might be offered a deal. Dress codes of sorts apply: if you look particularly foreign, it is unlikely that you'll be turned away by the fashion police, but it still does happen. If you can't find something to your liking here, keep on truckin' south on Insurgentes Sur and then along the thoroughfare—you'll run across the whole gamut of clubs.

🖎 **Rock Stock Bar & Disco,** Reforma 260 (tel. 533 09 07), at Niza. Clubs come and go, but *el estok* remains packed and fun year after year. Follow the street signs through the rotating darkroom-style doors upstairs into a huge open-attic room in which railings, scaffolding, and metal cages are doused in fluorescent paint. Lively action, with everything from rave to underground rhythms. Two shifts of music and shows. 3-9pm is cheaper and less crowded (40-60 pesos; women free 3-4pm). Come early if you want to be part of the 10pm-to-late crowd—later, swarms of people wait outside, hoping to be let in. Being foreign and/or being a young female (especially in tight clothes) helps. Cover with open bar 150 pesos men, women free. Open M-Sa 3pm-late.

🖎 **Mecano** (tel. 208 96 11), on Genova, near the corner with Hamburg, up the spiral staircase. Blasting dance music reverberates off the metal floor and walls of this enormous industrial-themed disco. Crowds fill up two floors worth of dance space while they shake and shimmy. Cover (including *barra libre*) for men 170 pesos; women free until 11pm, after 11pm 70 pesos. Open Th-Sa 9pm-3am.

🖎 **Urano,** Hamburgo 115 (tel. 514 74 18). At the end of a long metal hallway, a deep high-ceilinged dance floor features caged dancers (ahem...they are clothed) at one end and on the upper balcony. Get into their groove and let the music move you and hundreds of beautiful, hip young Mexicans to the bar. *Barra libre* comes with the 20 pesos cover for men, 15 pesos cover for women. Open Th-Su 9pm-2am.

Celebration, Florencia 56 (tel. 541 64 15). Rigged with speakers heard 'round the world. A combination of disco, techno, *salsa*, merengue, and house accompanies a stylish set and varied theme nights. Scattered tables provide an oasis from the active dance action. A slightly older, more dressy crowd celebrates here. Cover (including *barra libre*) 150 pesos. Women often get in for free, and covers drop during the less crowded weeknights. Don't be afraid to bargain (this is Mexico—you even haggle for nightlife) with the men outside. Open daily 7pm-3am.

Yarda's, Niza 42, is a restaurant/bar during the day and a booming disco after 8pm. With an enormous dance floor and disco, house, and techno music, everyone from young adults to 40-somethings keep this place packed with dancers. Cover 50 pesos.

CENTRO

A hop, skip, and a jump away from the *zócalo*, a testament to the proud and complex history of the Mexican people, lies a slew of nightclubs, testaments to something even grander: people here sure know how to party. The clubs in the *centro* are elegant and upscale (most have valet parking), but this doesn't stop 1600 corporate executives from cramming into a three-story disco and "workin' it." Most of the clubs have terraces with fully stocked bars and smashing skyline views.

■ **Opulencia,** Católica 26 (tel. 512 04 17), on the corner of Madero. What's in a name? A heck of a lot, in this case. Spic-and-span elevator and velvet curtains are just the beginning. The enormous dance floor features big bouncers, black lights, video screens, headsets, and the best of 1980s dance music. Check out the zany living room on the 3rd floor with plush couches and silly furnishings a la Lewis Carroll. Totally decadent. Totally cool. Cover (including open bar) for men 130 pesos Th, 170 pesos F-Sa. No cover for women. Open Th-Sa 10pm-4:30am.

■ **La Ópera,** 5 de Mayo 10 (tel. 355 34 36), just west of Filomeno Mata. A restaurant and bar since 1807 with Baroque ceilings, mirrored walls, a grandfather clock, and dark wooden booths. While it's relatively low-key today, government alliances were made and betrayed within these walls. A great place to grab a whiskey and soda and talk politics. Drinks 20-32 pesos. Open M-Sa 1pm-midnight, Su 1-6pm.

El Bar Mata (tel. 518 02 37), Filomeno Mata at 5 de Mayo. For the *centro,* it packs in a youthful crowd ready to party. Take the elevator or walk up 5 flights to check out the sophisticated design with mood lighting and hip architecture. Equals nearly everything the *Zona Rosa* has to offer mid-week, although on non-band nights (no cover) the clientele noticeably thins out. Live bands Wednesdays and Saturdays. Mixed drinks 20-25 pesos. Cover 50 pesos on Wednesday. Open Tu-Sa 8pm-3am.

ALAMEDA CENTRAL

While bars and discos near the Alameda can't compare in luster to those in the *Zona Rosa*, prices are refreshingly low. Unfortunately, surrounding neighborhoods may be dangerous, especially late at night. Although Metro stops are abundant, taxis are somewhat less so, so you'll want to ask for the phone number of a nearby *sitio* (it's safer, anyway).

Especially noteworthy is the **Hostería del Bohemio,** Hidalgo 107 (tel. 512 83 28), just west of Reforma. Leave the Hidalgo Metro stop (Lines 2 and 3) from the Av. Hidalgo/Calle de Héroes exit and turn left. Situated in the cloister of the ex-convent of San Hipólito, this romantic cafe is saturated with music, singing, and poetry in the evenings. Seating is on the outdoor terraces of both levels and on all four sides of a lush, two-tiered courtyard with a gurgling central fountain. At night, thousands of Christmas lights only add to the already unparalleled ambience. The slice-of-a-tree tables and chairs are lit by old-fashioned lanterns, making it the perfect spot for intimate conversations. Guitars strum in the background. You're guaranteed to fall in love here, if not with the attractive, googly-eyed *joven* sitting next to you, then with the amazing assortment of coffee, cake, and ice cream. (Every single gosh-darn thing on the menu is exactly 16 pesos, except for cigarettes at a whopping 12 pesos. No cover. Open daily 5-11pm.)

GARIBALDI PLAZA

Garibaldi Plaza hosts some of Mexico City's gaudiest, seediest, and funniest nightlife. The plaza is at the intersection of Lázaro Cárdenas and República de Honduras, north of Reforma. Take the Metro to the Bellas Artes stop (Lines 2 and 8), and walk three blocks north along Cárdenas; Garibaldi is the plaza on your right. Metro: Garibaldi (Line 8) takes you three blocks north of the plaza. Exit to your left from the stop and walk south. By 5pm, wandering *mariachis* fill the plaza, striking up as it gets dark to compete with each other while roving *ranchero* groups play your favorite tune for 30-40 pesos (foreigners often get the privilege of paying more). Tourists, locals, prostitutes, musicians, vendors, transvestites, young kids—just about anybody and everybody mingles here, many reeling, dancing, and screaming in the street because of the copious amounts of liquor they've just downed. Big nightclubs surrounding the plaza, each with its own *mariachi*, do their best to lure the crowds. Although they advertise no cover, per-drink prices are staggeringly high. Don't wander too far away from the plaza looking for cheaper options; you'll find only strip joints and dangerous *cantinas*. Beware of pickpockets, purse-snatchers, and prostitutes (or some combination of the three); it's best to leave your credit card, wallet, and purse at home. The best time to visit Garibaldi is from 8pm to 2am on weekends, but it's also the least safe then. Prostitutes turn tricks here, and the neighboring streets, strip joints, and *cantinas* can be dangerous. Women should be particularly cautious.

COYOACÁN AND SAN ANGEL

While generally very safe sections of town, these two southern suburbs fall just outside many of Mexico City's public transportation axes. The Metro serves both until midnight, after which a taxi is the best option. Most moderately- to high-priced restaurants have live jazz at night. Coyoacán and San Angel are infamous for their slews of moody gringos getting drunk and wistful to blues and rock. For a good time, hang out in Coyoacán's main plaza and soak up all the noise from comedians and musicians as you think deep thoughts. An option is **El Hijo del Cuervo** (tel. 658 78 24), on the north side of the Jardín Centenario, in Coyoacán. A motley international crue of people-watching, liquor-downing folks crowd here weekend nights for live rock and Latin music. (Open daily 1pm-2am.)

GAY AND LESBIAN ENTERTAINMENT

Mexico City offers the full range of social and cultural activities for gays and lesbians. There is an active gay rights movement in Mexico City, even though the general tolerance of public homosexual activity is still very low. Although not illegal, public displays of affection by gay and lesbian couples on the Metro and in other public places often results in harrassment, especially by the police. Gay men will have a much easier time finding bars and discos, although more and more venues integrate lesbians. For exclusively lesbian activities, contact the lesbian groups (see p. 93). The free pamphlet *Ser Gay* is an information-laden resource: it details gay entertainment and art events in the city and provides a complete listing of all the gay bars in town and many throughout the country. Copies are available at all the clubs listed below. Often, clubs will waive cover provided you show a copy of *Ser Gay*. In June, Mexico's gay pride month, an inordinate number of parties, rallies, art exhibits, marches, and fun *fiesta*-type events occur throughout the city.

■ **El Antro,** Londres 77 (tel. 511 16 13), near the intersection with Insurgentes. This enormous, tasteful new club occupies a prime spot in the *Zona Rosa*. Only men are allowed to enjoy the multiple bars, pianos, dance floors, private rooms, video screens, and just about anything (and everything) else. Men of all ages come here to check out the acclaimed stripper shows or get down to hard-core disco. Check *Ser Gay* for schedules that include play-money casino night, social/cocktail night, and "all fun" night (Saturdays). Cover W 20 pesos, Th-Sa 40 pesos with 1 drink, Sunday 20 pesos. Open Tu-Sa 7pm-late, Su 6pm-2am.

■ **Anyway, Exacto, and the Doors,** Monterrey 47 (tel. 533 16 19), half a block from Durango in Col. Roma, just south of the *Zona Rosa*. A 3-part party. Food and drink are offered at The Doors, while dancing, more drinks, and dancing are offered at the other two. On Thursdays, Exacto offers the only all-women's disco in the city, and on other days, it caters to a high concentration of lesbians. Cover W-Th 20 pesos includes 1 drink, F-Sa 55 pesos includes 2 drinks. Open daily 8pm-late

■ **El Celo,** Londres 104 (tel. 514 43 09), in the *Zona Rosa*. A gay-friendly restaurant during the day, this candle-lit restaurant/bar is filled by an exclusively gay and lesbian clientele after 7pm. The 20-peso beers are 2-for-1 from 9-11pm, and there's no cover. Later in the evening, tables are pushed aside and the bouncing begins.

Butterfly, Izazaga 9 (tel. 761 18 61), near Metro Salto del Agua (Lines 1 and 8), half a block east of Lázaro Cárdenas, just south of the cathedral. Although no signs point out this club, don't be afraid to ask. This big, brash gay nightspot is worth the searching. Lesbians are also beginning to come out. Video screens and a superb lighting system. Male revue late on weekend nights. Cover Tu-Th Free, F-Sa 65 pesos with 2 drinks. Gay events throughout the city are advertised from here. Open Tu-Su 9pm-3:30am.

El Almacen, Florencia 37 (tel. 207 69 56). A bar that serves Mediterranean food and plays 1980s pop. A growing number of lesbians are joining the men kicking back beers on their way to the high-octane gay male dance club in the basement, **El Taller.** Open daily noon-late.

El Taller, Florencia 37A (tel. 533 49 84), in the *Zona Rosa.* Underground; watch carefully or you'll miss the entrance. Well-known hangout for blue-collar gay men. Wednesdays and Sundays attract a twentyish crowd; private barroom attracts an older crowd. Throbbing dance music, faux construction-site decorations and dark, private alcoves make for an intense men-only pickup scene. Check *Ser Gay* for schedules; Saturday is usually theme night. Cover Th-Su 40 pesos includes 1 drink. Open Tu-Su 8pm-5am.

La Estación, Hamburgo 234 (tel. 514 47 07), in the *Zona Rosa.* A brand new all-men leather bar—wear your leather or latex to get into this enormous 2-floor bar. Open daily 4pm-2am.

La Cantina de Vaquero, Algeciras 26, Col. Insurgentes, near el Parque Hundido, between Metro: Mixcoáo and Metro: Zapata. This was the first openly gay *cantina* in Mexico—it just celebrated its 24th anniversary. Working-class gay men still flock to "El Vaquero," a low-profile bar in a commercial center, to watch XXX videos, sample the "darkroom," or, simply grab a beer and *parlar* (chat). Videos screened daily 5-11pm. 2 beers included with the 35-peso cover. Open daily 5pm-late.

■ SHOPPING

While most Mexican cities have a single central market, Mexico City has one specializing in every retail good. These markets are relatively cheap. Each *colonia* has its own market, but the major marketplaces are all in the center of town. Shopping throughout the *centro* and the Alameda proceeds thematically: there is a wedding dress street, a lighting fixtures street, a lingerie street, a windowpanes street, a power tools street, a military paraphernalia street, and so on.

Mercado de La Ciudadela, 2 blocks north of Metro: Balderas (Lines 1 and 3) off Av. Balderas. An incredible array of *artesanías,* crafts, and traditional clothing at low prices. Its reputation as the biggest and best *artesanía* market in the city makes tourist traffic rampant. Open daily 8am-7pm.

San Juan Artesanías, Plaza El Buen Tono, 4 blocks south of Alameda Central, 2 blocks west of Lázaro Cárdenas. Bounded by Ayuntamiento, Aranda, Pugibet, and Dolores. From Metro: Salto de Agua, walk up López 4 blocks and make a left on Ayuntamiento; 3 floors of artisanry from all over Mexico will greet you. The typical mix of mold-made cheesy tourist items and handmade treasures. Prices are similar to La Ciudadela (see above), but comparison shopping always helps. Fewer tourists wander around here. Open M-Sa 9am-7pm, Su 9am-4pm.

La Merced, Circunvalación at Anaya, east of the *zócalo.* Metro: Merced (Line 1). Not just a market but a way of life. The **largest market in the Americas,** it has a ridiculously wide selection of fresh produce from all over the country at rock-bottom prices. You'll find every kind of fruit imaginable, and crayfish abound. The **Mercado de Dulces** (candy market) can't help but cause candy-lovers' sweet teeth quiver in ecstasy. Between the two lies the **Mercado de Flores** (flower market). All three markets open daily 8am-7pm.

FONART, Patriotismo 691 (tel. 563 40 60), Juárez 89 (tel. 521 01 71), and Carranza 115 (tel. 554 62 70) in Coyoacán. A national project to protect and market traditional crafts. *Artesanías* from all over the country: giant tapestries, Oaxacan rugs, silver jewelry, pottery, and colorful embroidery. Regulated prices are not quite as low as the markets, but if you're not in the mood for crowds and haggling, come here and pay only a little more. Open M-Sa 10am-7pm.

Sonora, Teresa de Mier and Cabaña, 2 blocks south of La Merced. Specializes in witch-craft, medicinal teas and spices, figurines, and ceremonial images. Search no further for lucky cows' feet, shrunken heads, eagle claws, black salt (for nosy neighbors), powdered skull (for the domination of one's enemies), and dead butterflies, among other useful things. Cures are prescribed for almost any illness—bee venom cream supposedly works wonders on arthritis. Open daily 8am-7pm.

La Lagunilla, Comonfort at Rayón, east of the intersection of Lázaro Cárdenas and Reforma. Two large yellow buildings on either side of the street with stands spilling out-side. Although now a daily vending site, this market really gets going on Sundays when it turns into a gargantuan flea market, most notable for its antique books. Feel completely authentic as you browse and get battered by the throngs of wise locals looking for the real deal. The rest of the week, their specialty is communion and party dresses. Taffeta, anyone? Open daily 8am-7pm.

Bazaar del Sabado, Plaza San Jacinto, in the center of San Angel. Saturdays only, this market opens up and spills onto the plaza with arts and crafts. It tends to be pricey and touristy, but it's one of the few markets to which contemporary artists bring their work. This posh market is the equivalent of a nightclub to which "everyone who's anyone" goes. Open Saturday 9am-6pm.

Jamaica, Congreso and Morelos (Eje 3 Sur). Metro: Jamaica (Lines 4 and 9). Immediately as you exit the subway station, there is a clump of vendor stalls selling cheap eats and some of the juiciest mangos and *piñas* in town. The real pride and joy of the market is the assortment of fragrant and brightly colored flowers, including, of course, the deep-red Jamaica flower, source of the lip-smacking *agua de Jamaica* sold at many stands. Also be sure to check out live animals and exotic birds (all for sale) squawking and screaming in their confining cages. Open M-Sa 8am-6pm.

SPORTS

Whether consumed by their passion for bullfighting, soccer *(fútbol)*, jai alai, or horse racing, Mexican fans share an almost religious devotion to *deportes*. If sweaty discos and cavernous museums have you craving a change of pace, follow the crowds to an athletic event and prepare yourself for a rip-roarin' rowdy good time. *Andale!*

The famous **Frontón Mexico,** facing the north side of the Revolution monument, as well as the **Hipódromo de las Américas,** beyond the Tacuba Metro station, are usually the sites of the popular **jai alai** matches, while the Hipódromo houses a **racetrack.** Check local newspapers for game times and venues.

Aztec Stadium, Calz. de Tlalpan 3465 (tel. 617 80 80 or 617 20 88). Take a *pesero* or *tren ligero* (trolley) directly from the Metro: Tasqueña station (Line 2). The Azteca is the greatest of many Mexican stadiums where professional *fútbol* is played and one of the largest in the world (capacity nearly 100,000). Read the sports pages of any newspa-

GOOOL-LASSO! Although *charretería* (horsemanship, rodeo, and bull-fighting) may be the official national sport of Mexico, *fútbol* (soccer) is by far the most popular. If you want to check out the *fútbol* phenomenon, you're in luck—*fútbol* matches take place year-round. Mexico has two professional soccer leagues: the Winter League (season runs July-Dec.) and the Summer League (season runs Jan.-May). In addition, there are countless minor and amateur *fútbol* leagues throughout the nation. Each of the professional leagues has 17 regular games in its season, excluding the playoffs, semifinals, and finals. Every fourth June, the World Cup takes Mexico by storm—even gas and water delivery stops as soccer fans throughout the country pack bars and restaurants to watch the games. Whenever Mexico scores a goal, the entire country shakes from the shout of the word "GOAL!" that rings out from every bar, business, and bus.

per for information on games, and keep your eye out for any **Mexico-Brazil** matches. These teams are fierce rivals and any match at the Azteca promises to be frighteningly exciting and overpopulated; good luck trying to get tickets. Many bars, though, have 2-for-1 *fútbol* specials with the game on TV. The only better thing than *fútbol* is *fútbol* with beer. Season runs Oct.-July. Tickets run from 50-1200 pesos.

◪ **Plaza México** (tel. 563 39 59), on Insurgentes Sur. Accessible by Metro: San Antonio station (Line 7). Mexico's principal bullring, seating 40,000 fans. Bullfights on Sundays. Professionals fight only late July-Nov.; *novilladas* (young *toreros* and bulls) Nov.-Feb. Tickets run 25-150 pesos. Prices depend on the seats' proximity to the ring and whether they fall on the *sombra* (shady) or *sol* (sunny) side. If you're going cheap, bring sunglasses, a hat, and a pair of binoculars.

NEAR MEXICO CITY

TEOTIHUACÁN

For about 1000 years, a consummately organized, theocratic society thrived in the Valley of Mexico, then disappeared as mysteriously as it had arisen. The cultural and commercial center of this society was Teotihuacán (teh-oh-tee-wah-KAN), founded in 200 BC. An important holy city, Teotihuacán drew hundreds of pilgrims and became something of a market town in order to accommodate their needs. Its influence on architecture and art was so great that many of the styles developed here can be found in Maya civilizations' ruins as far south as Guatemala.

Much about Teotihuacán is a mystery. Probably built by the Olmeca-Xicalanca, a Mixtec-speaking group, the city eventually became an international cosmopolitan center, inhabited by a diversity of geographical and linguistic groups. Little can be said for certain, however, about the inhabitants of Teotihuacán or its rise to prosperity and sudden decline. Some scholars speculate that the city eventually collapsed under its own weight, having grown so unwieldy that it could no longer produce enough food to keep its inhabitants properly fed. Evidence of a tremendous fire around 800 can be found in layers of blackened stone, but the city had experienced significant decline before that time. At its heyday between 150 and 250, Teotihuacán covered nearly 22.5 sq. km and accommodated a population of nearly 200,000. Overcrowding resulted in construction on older buildings during the twilight of the city.

By 850, only a trickle of people was left in the enormous urban complex. When the Aztecs founded Tenochtitlán in 1325, Teotihuacán, 50km northeast of their capital, lay in ruins. The Aztecs adopted the area as ceremonial grounds and believed its huge structures had been built by gods who sacrificed themselves here so that the sun would shine on the Aztec world. Believing that those buried in this hallowed place were of some superhuman order, the Aztecs called the area Teotihuacán, meaning "Place Where Men Become Gods."

THE ARCHAEOLOGICAL SITE OF TEOTIHUACÁN

Teotihuacán (tel. 6 01 88 or 6 00 52; from Mexico City add the prefix 91 595) has some of the most enormous ruins in the country. (*Site open daily 7am-6pm. Admission 20 pesos, free on Sundays for national students and children under 13. Free parking.*) There are five entrances to the site. Buses drop visitors off by *Puerta 1*, the main entrance, surrounded by souvenir stalls. *Puerta 5*, the easternmost entrance, is by the Pirámide del Sol. Free guided tours for groups of five or more can be arranged at the administration building by *Puerta 1* (southwest corner). The museum and souvenir stalls sell guidebooks for about 40 pesos. Expect to spend about 30 minutes at the museum and another three to four hours exploring the ruins. Be sure to bring plenty of water, a hat, and sunglasses. Rapacious vendors descend upon the slew of international tourists offering water, as well as hats, silver, and *"piezas* *originales"* (original pieces). A firm *"¡No, gracias!"* will sometimes help keep vendors away; if it doesn't suffice, try to avoid eye contact. If you want to eat more than peanuts, splurge on a rare fancy meal just outside *Puerta 5*—**La Gruta** (tel. 9 15 95) is located inside a real natural cave, with tables lining the sides and floor. *(Open daily 10am-10pm.)* La Gruta offers tourists traditional dance shows and truly delicious gourmet Mexican dishes. It does, however, come with a price tag. Meals run 54-70 pesos.

The ceremonial center, a 13 sq. km expanse, was built along a 2km stretch now called **Calle de los Muertos** (Avenue of the Dead) for the countless human skeletons that were discovered alongside it. Since the Teotihuacanos planned their community around the four cardinal points, this main road runs in what is almost a perfectly straight north-south line from the **Pirámide de la Luna** (Pyramid of the Moon) to the **Templo de Quetzalcóatl**. The main structure, the **Pirámide del Sol** (Pyramid of the Sun), is on the east side and is squared with the point on the horizon where the sun sets at the summer solstice.

Las Pirámides, as the place is commonly called, is the **most visited archaeological site** in the Republic for a reason. The pyramids themselves loom over a vast expanse of traipsing tourists (both Mexican and international) and vying vendors; off in the distance, wildflowers and rolling hills metamorphose into majestic mountains. Don't turn the scaling of the pyramids into a chore or a race. Take some time, savor the view, and hang out.

GUIDE TO THE RUINS

The best way to explore the ruins is from south to north, starting your visit at the expansive **Ciudadela,** where priests and government officials once lived. At the center of the Ciudadela is the **Templo de Quetzalcóatl,** once a giant walled-in stadium sheltering a group of ancient temples. Beside the temple's stairway wind enormous stone carvings of the serpent whose great toothed head emerges from flowers at regular intervals. The red paint that originally decorated these sculptures (look for the remaining traces) was made by cutting off nopal leaves into which tiny bugs had burrowed, carving out the colorful critters, and smashing them. Just southeast of the Pirámide del Sol is the **Museo de Sitio.** This beautifully designed museum's marble tiling and design imitate the forms and colors used by the site's ancient inhabitants. Displays compare the size of the ancient city to various present-day cities, illustrate the architecture and technology of the pyramids, describe the social, religious, and economic organization of the society, and exhibit *indígena* art. The museum's high point is an enormous floor model of Teotihuacán at the height of its glory. All of the pieces in the museum are replicas. The originals are at the Museo Nacional de Antropología in Mexico City (see p. 113).

Continuing north along the Calle de los Muertos, you will cross what was once the San Juan river. On the west side of the street are the remains of two temples, known as the **Edificios Superpuestos,** that were built in two phases, 200 to 400 and 400 to 750, atop older, partially demolished temples.

Farther to the north and east is the **Pirámide del Sol,** the most massive single structure in the ceremonial area. Second in size only to the pyramid at Cholula, its base measures 222m by 225m—dimensions comparable to those of Cheops in Egypt. The pyramid rises 63m, but the grand temple that once crowned its summit is missing. Smokers and slowpokes: don't quit. Although the climb to the top may leave you out of breath, a rope rail runs the length of the pyramid, and the platforms of the multitiered pyramid make convenient rest stops. Unfortunately, the ubiquitous vendors are everywhere, even on the peak of this mammoth pyramid. As soon as you reach the top, weary and awe-struck, be prepared to say, "No, I don't need any more obsidian turtles, thank you." (In Spanish: *"No me faltan tortugas de obsidiana, gracias."*) For quieter contemplation, walk around a terrace to the back side.

Between the Pyramid of the Sun and the Pyramid of the Moon on the west side of the street is the **Palacio de Quetzalpapalotl** (Palace of the Quetzal Butterfly). This

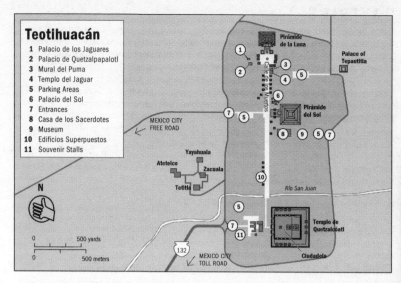

Teotihuacán

1 Palacio de los Jaguares
2 Palacio de Quetzalpapalotl
3 Mural del Puma
4 Templo del Jaguar
5 Parking Areas
6 Palacio del Sol
7 Entrances
8 Casa de los Sacerdotes
9 Museum
10 Edificios Superpuestos
11 Souvenir Stalls

MEXICO CITY

columned structure was the residence of nobles who staked out an area next to the ceremonial space, far from the residential complexes of the common folk. The inner patio is one of the most beautiful sights of the ancient city; the colored frescoes and bird glyphs have survived years of decay and retain much of their intricate detail.

Behind the first palace is the **Palacio de los Jaguares** (Palace of the Jaguars) and the now-subterranean **Palacio de las Conchas Emplumadas** (Palace of the Feathered Seashells). This palace dedicated to jaguars is entirely restored, complete with fluorescent lights and plastic handrails, and some of the original frescoes remain, adorned with red, green, yellow, and white symbols representing birds, corn, and water. This palace is a prime example of multi-level construction; it was built over another temple in which patterns of plumed seashells adorn the walls.

At the northern end of the Calle de los Muertos is the stunning **Pirámide de la Luna.** A sculpture of **Chalchiutlicue,** a water goddess and important Aztec deity, was found here during excavations. Although the climb is not as steep as the one up the Pyramid of the Sun, there are fewer vendors here to greet you and the view is even more magnificent. You will have a stunning view of the Calle de los Muertos and Teotihuacán in all its glory.

If you still have the energy, on the northeast side of the Pyramid of the Sun near *Puerta 4* is the **Palacio de Tepantitla,** which has some of the best-preserved frescoes on the site complete with a full range of colors. You can still see priests with elaborate headdresses and representations of Tlaloc. His goggle-eyes and snaky hair identify him as the god of water, important stuff. The lower part of the mural displays the Teotihuacano ideal of paradise where butterflies abound.

Getting There: Direct bus service from Mexico City to the pyramids is available from **Autobuses Teotihuacán** (1hr., every 30min. 5am-6pm, 13 pesos), located in the Terminal de Autobuses del Norte (tel. 781 18 12 or 587 05 01) at *Sala* 8. Alternatively, buses marked "Teotihuacán" (13 pesos) leave from outside the Indios Verdes Metro station (Line 3) every 20 minutes or so from opening until closing. The last bus back from the pyramids to Mexico City leaves the main entrance at 6pm. A few kilometers before reaching Teotihuacán, the bus passes just to the right of the town of **Acolmán,** founded shortly after the Conquest by Franciscans. The majestic lines of the ex-monastery of Acolmán rise skyward, breaking the monotony of the corn fields. To stop at the ex-monastery on your way back to Mexico City, take the "Indios Verdes" bus from the main entrance and get off at Acolmán.

DAYTRIPS

Even those who've fallen in love with Mexico City need some time away. Fortunately, its great location makes it easy to escape (but who can escape it for long?). From small towns to not-so-small towns and from posh getaways to volcanoes, all of these places make cool and convenient daytrips.

YET MORE FUN

CUERNAVACA, MORELOS

This lovely-colonial-town-turned-chic-upperclass-getaway still hits the mark every time. The large number of expats and language school students testify to the fact that people can't stay away. Despite its gaggle of gringos and high prices, it's worth saving up for this one. Come check out lush greenery, luxurious living, and trendy nightlife *a la mexicana* (distance: 85km; see p. 337).

DESIERTO DE LOS LEONES, ESTADO DE MEXICO

Don't worry—this isn't a desert. It's a pine forest (go figure). Just outside of Mexico City, this "desierto" offers gorgeous hiking and fresh, pine-scented air; it's the perfect antidote to the smog and congestion of the city. The 2000-hectare park is also host to a Carmelite convent with lovely gardens. Free music and theater events take place on Sundays, when the park is filled with picnickers (distance: 25km; see p. 334).

GRUTAS DE CACAHUAMILPA, GUERRERO

Have you ever wanted to see rock formations shaped like people making out? Well, these enormous, impressive caverns provide the opportunity for much merriment. Let your imagination run wild here through stalagmites, stalactites, and caves, some over 85m high. Raucous tour guides lead you through the underground wonderland (distance: 130km; see p. 447).

IXTAPAN DE LA SAL, ESTADO DE MEXICO

Despite the presence of nearby Disneyland-ish waterparks and resorts, Ixtapan couldn't be lovelier or more good-natured if it tried. The Mediterranean-style plaza and church are one of a kind. This is a good place to check out rustic life and take long mid-afternoon siestas (distance: 117km; p. 330)

PACHUCA, ESTADO DE MÉXICO

An important center for silver mining and processing since the 16th century, Pachuca offers several lovely plazas, a few worthwhile museums, extremely friendly inhabitants, and invigoratingly crisp mountain air. The city exudes a sense of prosperity and contentment that is infectious, and the delightful streets are mostly free of tourists, making Pachuca a refreshing daytrip from the D.F. (distance: 90km; p. 325).

POPOCATÉPETL AND IXTACCÍHUATL, ESTADO DE MEXICO

Veiled in Aztec mythology, the snow-capped Popocatépetl (Smoking Mountain) and Ixtaccíhuatl (Sleeping Woman) volcanoes overlook the state of Morelos and nearby Puebla. The volcanoes look like calmly majestic mountains when you see them from Mexico City (on a clear day), but they are really just slumbering beasts. In June 1997, Popocatépetl "smoked" more than it had in decades, dumping tons of ash and debris on nearby areas, including Mexico City. Although Popo is closed to hikers, some of Ixta can be climbed on well-marked tourist trails, or higher up in organized tour groups (distance: 60km; see p. 336).

TAXCO, GUERRERO

You've heard about the silver. Have you heard about the cable cars, stunning vistas, and fab church? Taxco boasts more than tourist treasures—it is a picturesque

Near Mexico City N

20 miles

20 kilometers

TO ATLACOMULCO
AND QUERÉTARO

TO ZITÁCUARO

TO PACHUCA

TO TULA AND
QUERÉTARO

TO CUAUTLA

TO XOCHICALCO

TO VALLE
DE BRAVO

TO IXTAPAN
DE LA SAL

TO VERACRUZ

HIDALGO

MEXICO

PUEBLA

FEDERAL
DISTRICT

MORELOS

MEXICO

Santa Rosa

Apan

Calpulalpan

Santiago
Cuautla

San Martín
de las Pirámides

Teotihuacán

Acolman

Tepexpan

Nanacamilpa

Hueyotipan

Tlaxcala

Cacaxtla

Tenancingo

Puebla

Cholula

Texmelucan

Huejotzingo

San N. de
los Ranchos

Parque
Nacional
Zoquiapan

Parque
Nacional
Ixta Popo

Tlamacas

Tlalmanalco

Amecameca

Ozumba

Chalco

CD.
NEZAHUALCÓYOTL

TLALNEPANTLA

Mexico
City

NAUCALPAN

Tepotzotlán

Parque
Nacional
Desierto de
los Leones

Parque
Nacional
Lagunas de
Zempoalá

Parque
Nacional El
Tepozteco

Tepoztlán

Cuernavaca

Xonacatlán

Metepec

Mexicaltzingo

Joquicingo

Malinalco

Toluca

San Diego

Tenancingo

Parque Nacional
Nevado de Toluca

white pearl of a town way up in the hills. Its pink stone Catedral de Santa Prisca ranks among the loveliest in Mexico (distance: 180km; see p. 442).

TEPOTZOTLÁN, ESTADO DE MÉXICO

On the route from Mexico City to Tula and Querétaro, Tepotzotlán offers a glimpse of small-town life, and its church and monastery house some of the country's most exquisite religious art. The beautiful *zócalo* and religious museum can be comfortably enjoyed in a couple of hours, and the comparatively smog-free air might make you crave even more of this town (distance: 36km, see p. 335).

TEPOZTLÁN, MORELOS

Surrounded by towering cliffs, this quiet *pueblo* occupies one of Morelos' more scenic sites. The cobbled *indígena* village preserves a colonial feel amid growing modernization, and many indigenous people still speak Náhuatl. Bring plenty of spirit (and bottled water and sunscreen) if you plan to scale Tepoztlán's "mother" hill. On Sundays, the *zócalo* comes alive with vibrant market activity. Quetzal-cóatl, however, who was supposedly born in this sacred place, would be disturbed by the tons of *turistas* and gradual gringo-ization (distance: 70km; see p. 345).

TULA, HIDALGO

Tula itself offers not much more than a cute plaza, a good meal, and a bed, which may be why the fascinating ruins a 10-peso taxi ride away are relatively tourist free. The archaeological site at Tula houses the ruins of what was the capital city of the Toltec civilization. A great combination of desert-like and hilly terrain makes for picturesque ruins. Particularly interesting are the famous **Atlantes,** 10-meter tall massive stone statues of warriors with bad attitudes (distance: 65km; see p. 327).

VALLE DE BRAVO, ESTADO DE MEXICO

Wealthy Mexico City residents go to play in the beautiful town of Valle de Bravo and the surrounding area are where. The lake may be man-made, but the beautiful red-roofed white stucco houses, cobblestone streets, and blossoming bougainvillea are irresistible. You don't have to jet-ski or golf to enjoy Valle; grab a picnic basket and loll around on the grassy hills (distance: 140km; see p. 329).

XOCHICALCO, MORELOS

Ceremonial center, fortress, and trading post rolled into one, Xochicalco (Náhuatl for Place of the Flowers) is the most impressive archaeological site in the state. Because it has not gotten as much hype as other places, Xochicalco's beauty lies quiet and deserted in the rolling green hills. Aside from the occasional busload of screaming children, only swarms of dragonflies can be heard for miles. Photographers will writhe in ecstasy here, as will museum-lovers—the site's museum is truly phenomenal (distance: 120km; see p. 344).

BAJA CALIFORNIA

The peninsula of Baja California is cradled by the warm, tranquil Sea of Cortés on the east and the cold, raging Pacific Ocean on the west. Baja claims one of the most spectacular and diverse landscapes in the world—sparse expanses of sandy deserts give way to barren mountains jutting into Baja's traditionally azure, cloudless sky at incredible angles. The high-altitude national parks of northern Baja are home to seemingly out-of-place evergreens and snow during the winter months. And then, of course, there's the bizarrely blue-green water slapping at Baja's miles of uninhabited shore. This Crayola-aqua liquid flows past coral reefs, bats around in rocky storybook coves, and laps at the white sandy shores of thousands of miles of paradisiacal beaches lining both coasts. Meanwhile, the sands and outcrops of areas such as the bucolic Bahía de Concepción are watched over from above by many thousands of species of cacti that thrive on Baja's otherwise barren hillsides.

Called "el otro Mexico" (the other Mexico), Baja is neither here nor there, not at all California, yet nothing like mainland Mexico. Even its history is different—it was permanently settled by the Franciscans and Jesuits in the 1600s. Mainland Mexico has massive Aztec and Maya temples; Baja has serene little Jesuit missions. The peninsula's tradition of carefully blending wildness and tranquility, domesticity and simplicity, are emblematized by the Jesuit legacy in sleepy towns like San Ignacio.

Until relatively recently, Baja was an unknown frontier of sorts; the only way to reach its rugged desert terrain was by plane or boat. With the completion of the Transpeninsular Highway (Rte. 1) in 1973, and the addition of better toll roads and ferry service, Baja has become a popular vacation spot among Californians, Arizonans, Mexicans, and others. Vacationers range in type from hardy campers setting out to tame the savage deserts of central Baja to families living in one of Baja's many RV parks to the ubiquitous U.S. tourists who prefer a day on the beach, an evening when they can drown their inhibitions in many a *cerveza* and *margarita*, and a night of posh resort life, all without the inconvenience of changing currency.

Large resort hotels and condominium complexes are sprouting like grass to house these human torrents in the south. The heavily Americanized Los Cabos on the southern tip now have almost as little integrity and authenticity as Tijuana, the bawdy border wasteland of the **Baja California** state, wedged in the hilly crevices of the peninsula's northern extreme. The honest Mexican city of La Paz, the capital of **Baja California Sur,** is a southern beacon of beauty for resort-weary port-seekers. But it is Baja's southern midsection—from the tranquility of Mulegé to the palm-laden oasis town of San Ignacio to the thousands of undisturbed beaches beneath sheer cliffs—that is most pristine and mysterious. Most of Baja is still somewhat of an undiscovered country, prime for the hearty budget traveler to explore.

HIGHLIGHTS OF BAJA CALIFORNIA

■ Explore the secluded and beautiful beaches of **Bahía de La Concepción** (p. 170), 48km of turquoise water, coves, powdery sand, bubbly springs, and abundant marine life.

■ Sleep under a million stars in **San Ignacio** (p. 164), a tiny leafy Northern Baja town/oasis with a remarkable **mission** (see p. 166).

■ Hike through the amazing **Parque Sierra Nacional San Pedro Mártir** (p. 159), home to mountains, valleys, waterfalls, and Mexico's **National Observatory** (p. 159).

■ Despite over-development, **Los Cabos** (p. 183) still draws curious U.S. travelers: lie on the peaceful beaches of **San José del Cabo** (p. 189) by day, party with reckless abandon in **Cabo San Lucas** (p. 184) by night.

■ Stroll down the gulf side boardwalk of breezy, beautiful **La Paz** (p. 175), the good-natured capital of Baja Sur, and a favorite Mexican vacation destination.

GETTING AROUND

BY LAND

Driving through Baja is far from easy. The road was not designed for high-speed driving; often you'll be safely cruising along at 60mph and suddenly careen into a hidden, poorly banked, rutted curve that can only be taken at 30mph. Beware of potholes—some of the biggest and baddest in Mexico lurk on the roads leading off the Transpeninsular Highway. They will rock your world and eat your tires for breakfast; always be sure to have a good spare tire.

Still, a car (especially if it's four-wheel drive) is the only way to get close to the more beautiful and secluded areas of Baja, opening up an entire world of hiking and camping opportunities. The ride through Baja is probably one of the more beautiful in Mexico. During the journey, you will see vast deserts filled with cacti, gigantic mountains with ominous peaks, and stupendous cliffs that will make you hold on to your seat. If you need roadside assistance, the *Angeles Verdes* (Green Angels) pass along Rte. 1 twice per day. Unleaded gas may be in short supply along this highway, so don't pass a PEMEX station without filling your tank. All of Baja is in the *Zona Libre* (Free Zone), so strict vehicle permits are not required. If you will be driving in Baja for more than 72 hours, you only need to get a free permit at the border; to do this, show the vehicle's title and proof of registration. For more information on driving in Mexico, see p. 68.

If you plan to navigate the peninsula by bus, be forewarned that almost all *camiones* between Ensenada and La Paz are *de paso*. This means you have to leave at inconvenient times, fight to procure a ticket, and then probably stand the whole way. A much better idea is to buy a reserved seat in Tijuana, Ensenada, La Paz, or Los Cabos, and traverse the peninsula in one shot while seated. Unfortunately, you'll miss the fantastic Mulegé-Loreto beaches (for more info on buses, see p. 67).

Anyway you cut it, Baja's beaches and other points of interest off the main highway are often inaccessible via public transportation. Some swear by hitching— PEMEX stations are thick with rides (for more info on hitchhiking, see p. 70). *Let's Go* does not recommend hitchhiking; it's unpredictable and potentially hazardous.

BY SEA

Ferry service was instituted in the mid-1960s as a means of supplying Baja with food and supplies, not as a way for tourists to get from here to there—passenger vehicles may take up only the ferry space left over by the top-priority commercial vehicles. There are three different ferry routes: Santa Rosalía to Guaymas (8hr.), La Paz to Topolobampo/Los Mochis (9hr.), and La Paz to Mazatlán (17hr.). The La Paz to Topolobampo/Los Mochis route provides direct access to the train from Los Mochis through the Barrancas del Cobre (Copper Canyon).

Ferry tickets are generally expensive, even for *turista*-class berths, which cram two travelers into a cabin outfitted with a sink; bathrooms and showers are down the hall. It's extremely difficult to find tickets for *turista* and *cabina* class, and snagging an *especial* berth (a real hotel room) is as likely as stumbling upon a snowball in the central Baja desert—there are only two such suites on each ferry. This leaves the bottom-of-the-line *salón* ticket, which entitles you to a bus-style seat in a large room with few communal baths. If, as is likely, you find yourself traveling *salón*-class at night, ditch your seat early on and stake out a spot on the floor, or outside on the deck—simply spread out your sleeping bag and snooze. A small room is available to store your belongings, but once they're secured there is no way of retrieving any items, so make sure you take what you'll need during the trip. A doctor or nurse is always on board in the (rare) event that someone gets seasick. For those who plan to take their car aboard a ferry, it's a good idea to make reservations a month in advance; consult a travel agent or contact the ferry office directly. For further ferry information, contact a **Sematur** office, listed in the **Practical Information** sections of the cities from which the ferry departs.

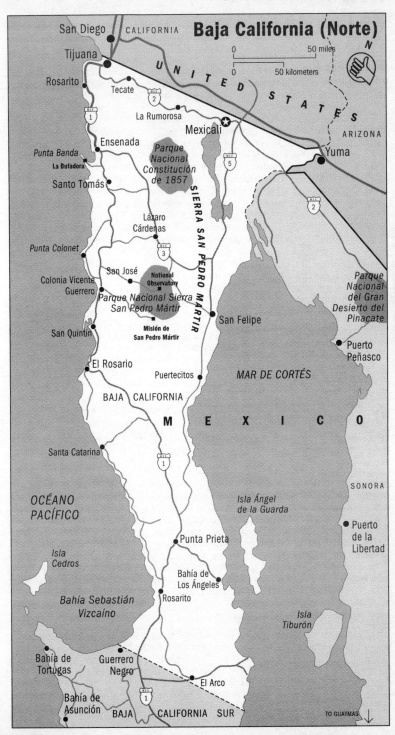

Baja California (Norte)

BAJA CALIFORNIA NORTE

TIJUANA

In the shadow of swollen, sulphur-spewing factories smeared across a topographical nightmare of gorges and promontories lies the most notorious specimen of the peculiar border subculture: Tijuana (pop. 2.5 million)—the most visited border town in the world. By day, swarms of tourists cross the border to explore the curio-filled alleys, haggle with street vendors, gulp cheap margaritas, and get their picture taken with donkeys painted as zebras. By night, Av. Revolución, the city's wide main drag, becomes a big, bad party. *Mariachi* bands triumph over the thumping dance beats blaring from the city's many clubs as bottle rockets explode in the near distance. This three-ringed, duty-free extravaganza comes complete with English-speaking, patronizing club promoters and every decadent way of blowing money, from *jai-alai* to dark, dingy strip joints, from mega-curio shops to Las Vegas-style hotels. And this is exactly how most of its 30 million yearly tourists would have it. A short distance from where U.S. dollars are exchanged for shots of tequila poured down tourists' throats, thousands of undocumented emigrants leave their tin shacks and make a midnight run for the U.S. in a perpetual and deadly game of tag. But with the fastest growth rate (13.6%) of all the world's major cities, Mexico's fourth-largest metropolis (founded in 1829 when Don Santiago Argüello received the title to Tía Juana—Aunt Jane's—ranch) continues to proliferate at an alarming rate. Beyond the gaudy neon lights and curio shops of Av. Revolución, Tijuana does offer some more refined attractions such as cultural museums, palm-shaded *parques*, and a winery. However, it's hard to say whether it's the city's strange charm, its cheap booze, or its sprawling, unapologetic hedonism that attracts tourists to Tijuana like flies.

▟ ORIENTATION

From San Diego to Tijuana, take the red **Mexicoach** bus (tel. 85 14 70 or 619-428-9517 in the U.S.) from its terminal at the border (every 30min., 9am-9pm; US$1). It passes **Plaza Pueblo Amigo** on the Mexican side and leaves you on Revolución between Calles 6 and 7 in the heart of the *centro*. Alternatively, grab a **trolley** to San Ysidro, at Kettner and Broadway in downtown San Diego (US$2), and walk across the border. Transfers from airport buses are also available.

If you arrive at the central bus station, avoid the cab drivers' high rates (up to 80 pesos to downtown) and head for the **public bus** (30min., every 5min. 5am-10pm; 4 pesos). When you exit the terminal, turn left, walk to the end of the building, and hop on a bus marked "Centro Línea." It will let you off on **Calle 3** and **Constitución,** one block from **Revolución.** In Tijuana, *calles* run east-west; *avenidas* run north-south. The avenidas in the *centro* area are (from east to west) **Mutualismo, Martínez, Niños Héroes, Constitución, Revolución** (the main tourist drag), **Madero, Negrete,** and **Ocampo.** *Calles* in the *centro* area are both named and numbered. Beginning at the north, they are **Artículo 123** (Calle 1), **Benito Juárez** (Calle 2), **Carrillo Puerto** (Calle 3), **Díaz Mirón** (Calle 4), **Zapata** (Calle 5), **Magón** (Calle 6), **Galeana** (Calle 7), **Hidalgo** (Calle 8), and **Zaragoza** (Calle 9).

▚ CROSSING THE BORDER

Driving across the border is fairly hassle-free, though traffic can be heavy at times, especially on weekends. A quick wave of the hand will usually notify you that you are no longer in the United States. However, driving in Tijuana can be harrowing: many traffic lights function merely as stop signs, four-way stop signs act as traffic lights, and the crowded streets can leave you ready to turn around (for more info on driving into Mexico). If you're only in Tijuana for a day, it's a better idea to leave your car in a lot on the U.S. side and join the throngs of people walking

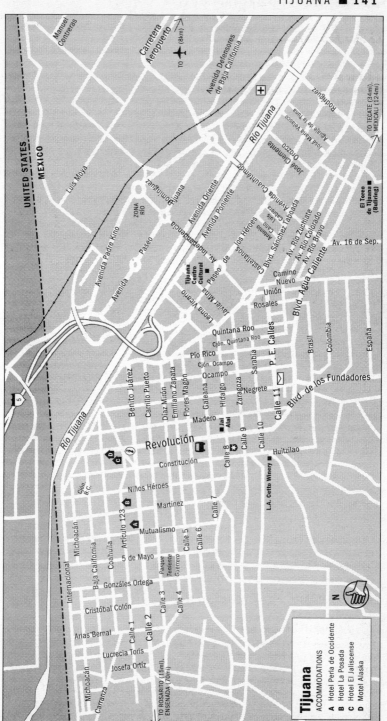

Tijuana

ACCOMMODATIONS

A Hotel Perla de Occidente
B Hotel La Posada
C Hotel El Jaliscense
D Motel Alaska

across the border. Parking rates start at US$3 per day and increase as you move closer to Mexico. Bring proper ID to re-enter the U.S. While a driver's license or other photo ID is acceptable, a passport ensures the speediest passage. Leave fruits, veggies, and weapons behind.

⑦ PRACTICAL INFORMATION

TRANSPORTATION

Buses: To reach the bus station (tel. 21 29 83 or 21 29 84) from downtown, board the blue-and-white buses marked "Buena Vista" or "Camionera" on Niños Héroes between Calles 3 and 4 (5 pesos), or jump in a brown-and-white communal cab on Madero between Calles 2 and 3 (5 pesos). Autotransportes de Baja California (tel. 21 29 82 through 87) runs to: **Ensenada** (1½hr.; every hr. 5-9am, every 30min. 9am-9pm; 73 pesos); **La Paz** (24hr., 4 per day 8am-9pm; 649 pesos); **Loreto** (18hr., 4 per day 8am-9pm; 494 pesos); **Mexicali** (3hr., every 30min.; 84 pesos); **San Felipe** (5hr., 4 per day 5am-4pm; 192 pesos); and **Santa Rosalía** (15hr., 4 and 6:30pm; 390 pesos). Elite (tel. 21 29 48) serves: **Guadalajara** (36hr., every 30min.; 1096 pesos); and **Hermosillo** (12hr., every 30min.; 470 pesos). Greyhound (tel. 21 29 82) runs to **Los Angeles** (3hr., every hr. 5am-11:05pm; US$18), and connects to other locations in the U.S. **Communal cabs** are all over town; some go to **Rosarito** (30min.)

Car Rental: Central Rent de Mexicali (tel. 84 28 52), Héroes 104, Zona del Río, open daily 9am-3pm. **Bargain Auto Rentals,** 3860 Rosecrans St. (tel. 619- 299-0009); in San Diego, is fairly priced, and you only have to be 18 to rent. Credit card required. Open daily 8am-6pm. If you'll be driving in Mexico, spend US$5 per day in San Ysidro to get **car insurance.** There are several drive-through insurance vendors just before the border at Sycamore and Primero, who distribute free booklets with maps and travel tips.

TOURIST, FINANCIAL, AND LOCAL SERVICES

Tourist Office: Revolución 711 (tel. 88 05 55), at Calle 1. Friendly English-speaking staff doles out maps and advice. Open M-Sa 8am-5pm, Su 10am-5pm.

Customs Office: (tel. 83 13 90) at the border on the Mexican side, after crossing the San Ysidro bridge. Open M-F 8am-3pm.

Consulates: Canada, German Gedovius 5-202 (tel. 84 04 61), in the Zona del Río. Open M-F 9am-1pm. **U.K.,** Blvd. Salinas 1500 (tel. 81 73 23), in Fracc. Aviacón, La Mesa. Open M-F 8am-3pm. **U.S.,** Tapachula Sur 96 (tel. 81 74 00), in Col. Hipódromo, adjacent to the Agua Caliente racetrack southeast of town. In an emergency, call the U.S. Duty Officer (tel. 28 17 62). After hours, leave a message and they'll respond shortly. Open M-F 8am-4:30pm.

Currency Exchange: Banks along Constitución exchange currency at the same rate. **Banamex** (tel. 88 00 21 or 88 00 22), Constitución at Calle 4. Open for exchange M-F 9am-5pm with a 24hr. **ATM. Bital,** Revolución at Calle 2 also has a 24hr. **ATM.** *Casas de cambio* all over town offer better rates but generally do not exchange traveler's checks. Ask if there is commission and stay away from the lower-numbered streets (such as Calle 1 and 2) because the exchange rates are atrocious.

Supermarket: Calimax (tel. 88 08 94), Calle 2 at Constitución. Open 24hr.

EMERGENCY AND COMMUNICATIONS

Emergency: dial 060.

Police: (tel. 38 51 68), Constitución at Calle 8.

Red Cross: (tel. 21 77 87, emergency 066) Calle Alfonso Gamboa at E. Silvestre, across from the Price Club.

Pharmacy: Farmacia Vida (tel. 85 14 61), Calle 3 at Revolución. Some English spoken. Open 24hr. **Discount Pharmacy,** Revolución 615 (tel. 88 31 31), between Calle 2 and Calle 3. Open Su-F 8am-8pm and Sa 8am-9pm.

Hospital: Centenario 10851 (tel. 84 02 37 or 84 00 78), in the Zona del Río.

Post Office: (tel. 84 79 50) on Negrete at Calle 11. Open M-F 8am-7pm, Sa-Su 9am-1pm. **Postal Code:** 22001.

Fax: Telecomm (tel. 84 79 02; fax 84 77 50), to the right of the post office, in the same building. Open M-F 7am-7:30pm, Sa-Su 8am-1pm.

Telephones: Tijuana's streets are paved with **LADATELS.** There is a reasonably priced **caseta** at Motel Díaz, Av. Revolución 650 at Calle 1 (open daily 24hr.), and at Hotel San Jorge, Calle 1 at Constitución. Calls within Mexico 4 pesos per min., to the U.S. 10 pesos per min. Open daily 8am-9pm.

Phone Code: 66.

ACCOMMODATIONS

There's no shortage of budget hotels in Tijuana. You'll find plenty on Calle 1 between Revolución and Mutualismo, and they tend to be towards the roachy side. Ask to see rooms before paying. The area teems with people during the day and is relatively safe; however, come nightfall, it becomes something of a red-light district, especially on Calle 1 between Revolución and Constitución. Everyone should be extremely cautious when walking in this area at night; to return to your hotel, head down Calles 2 or 3, or take a taxi (US$2) from anywhere on Revolución.

Hotel Perla de Occidente, Mutualismo 758 (tel. 85 13 58), between Calles 1 and 2, 4 blocks from the bedlam of Revolución. Multicolored translucent roofing over the central hallway casts beautiful rays of light along the tiled floor. An odd picture of a chimp smoking a joint hangs two doors down from a mosaic of Jesus. Large, soft beds, roomy bathrooms, and fans on request. Singles 120 pesos; doubles 140 pesos.

Hotel El Jaliscense, Calle 1 #7925 (tel. 85 34 91), between Niños Héroes and Martínez. A great deal with clean, small rooms with high, resilient beds, private baths, fans, and phones. Ask for a room that doesn't face Calle 1, that is, unless you don't like to sleep soundly. Singles 120 pesos; doubles 140 pesos.

Hotel La Posada, Calle 1 #8190 (tel. 85 41 54 or 85 83 91), at Revolución, just seconds away from all the drunken, debaucherous action. Select your room carefully—the good ones have fans, comfy beds, and bathrooms even your mother would approve of. Singles 60 pesos, with bath 105 pesos; doubles 170 pesos.

Motel Alaska, Revolución 1950 (tel. 85 36 81), at Calle 1, smack in the middle of smack central. Simple clean rooms with comfy beds and small showers. Parking lot. Singles 170 pesos; doubles 220 pesos.

FOOD

Tijuana's touristy eats are essentially Tex-Mex, but some cheap *típico* restaurants line Constitución and the streets leading from **Revolución** to **Constitución.** Even cheaper are the mom-and-pop mini-restaurants all over town. If you choose the myriad taco stands, select carefully. Slightly more expensive tourist restaurants and U.S. fast-food chains crowd Revolución. To save money, pay in pesos, even if the menu quotes prices in dollars.

El Pipirín Antojitos, Constitución 878 (tel. 88 16 02), between Calles 2 and 3. Sit at orange tables under orange brick arches and enjoy great food with friendly service. *Burritos de pollo con arroz y frijoles* (chicken burritos with rice and beans) all for 25 pesos. Open daily 8:30am-9pm.

Los Panchos Taco Shop (tel. 85 72 77), Revolución at Calle 3. Orange plastic booths are packed with hungry locals munching on ultra-fresh tortillas. Since it's open late during the summer months, this is a good place to satisfy those nighttime munchies. Steak taco US$1, bean burritos US$2. Open Su-Th 8am-4pm, F-Sa 8am-2am (8am-4am in summer).

Hotel Nelson Restaurant (tel. 85 77 50), Revolución at Calle 1, under the hotel. Good, cheap food in a clean, fan-cooled, coffee-shop atmosphere. Jukebox blares Mexican oldies. Gringo breakfast (eggs, hotcakes, ham) 26 pesos; 3 enchiladas 18 pesos. Open daily 7am-11pm.

Lonchería Tico-Tico, Madero 688 (tel. 85 06 16), on the corner of Calle 1. Provides homey service—both the cooks and the clients enjoy themselves. *Batido de platano* (banana milkshake) 15 pesos; 4 *tacos dorados* 23 pesos; liver and onions (yum!) 20 pesos. Open daily 6am-5pm.

◼ SIGHTS

In the 1920s, when prohibition laws were enacted in the U.S., many of its citizens crossed the border to revel in the forbidden nectars of cacti (tequila), grapes (wine), and hops (beer). Ever since, Tijuana has had a reputation for being the venue for nights of debauchery. Although Tijuana still has the ability to satiate the wildest of party animals, it has a great deal to offer the sober tourist as well. Try **people-watching** while strolling down **Revolución;** you'll see plenty of surprising sights, including tourists having their pictures taken while wearing oversized sombreros. *Mariachis* serenade as they explore the **artisan's market** on Calle 1. The beautiful and shady **Parque Teniente Guerrero,** Calle 3 and 5 de Mayo, is a nice place to relax and it's in one of the safer, more pleasant parts of town. The **cathedral,** with its massive chandelier, is nearby at Niños Héroes and Calle 2. **Morelos State Park,** Blvd. de los Insurgentes 26000, features an exotic bird exhibition and picnic area. To get to the park, board the green-and-white bus on Calle 5 and Constitución. (Tel. 25 24 70. Open Tu-Su 9am-5pm. Admission 5 pesos, children 2 pesos.)

Since 1926, the Cetto family has been churning out wine made from grapes grown in the Valle de Guadalupe, northeast of Ensenada. The family-owned **L.A. Cetto Winery,** Cañón Johnson 2108 at Calle 10, is just off Constitución. Tours are available; just don't try to remove a bottle from the storeroom—one American woman tried it and caused a wine avalanche that destroyed 30 cases of bottles. A **harvest festival** is held in the Cetto vineyards every August. Make reservations from January to June. (Tel. 85 30 31. Tours M-Sa every 30min. 10am-5pm. US$1, with wine-tasting US$2, with wine-tasting and souvenir goblet US$3.)

Walk off your wine buzz with a visit to one of Tijuana's museums. The **Museo de Cera,** on Calle 1 between Revolución and Madero, is home to a motley crew of wax figures, including such strange bedfellows as Tía Juana, Gandhi, Michael Jackson, and Marilyn Monroe (Tel. 88 24 78. Open daily 10am-7pm. Admission US$1.10, under 6 free.) Nearby, **Mexitlán,** Benito Juárez 8901, at Calle 2 and Ocampo, is home to over 200 miniatures depicting famous Mexican historical, religious, and cultural monuments. Absorb Maya architecture, Mexico City's Paseo de la Reforma, and Teotihuacán without having to consult a single bus schedule. Mexican folk art is also sold. (Tel. 38 41 01. Open W-Su 9am-7pm. Admission US$1.50.)

SPORTS

Jai alai is played in the majestic **Frontón Palacio,** Revolución at Calle 7. Two to four players take to the three-sided court at once, using arm-baskets to catch and throw a Brazilian ball of rubber and yarn encased in goatskin. The ball travels at speeds reaching 180mph; jai alai is reputedly the world's fastest game. After each point, the winning one- or two-player team stays on the court, while the losing team rotates out in king-of-the-hill style. The first team to score seven points wins; after the first rotation through the entire eight team lineup, rallies are worth two points, not one. If you can, try to catch a doubles match—the points are longer and require more finesse. Players are treated like horses, with betting and odds. All employees are bilingual, and the gambling is carried out in greenbacks. (Tel. 85 78 33. Open F-Sa at 7pm for viewing of practice matches. Free.)

If you're in town on the right Sunday, you can watch the graceful and savage dance of a bullfight in one of Tijuana's two bullrings. **El Toreo de Tijuana** (tel. 80 18 08), downtown to the east of Agua Caliente and Cuauhtémoc, hosts *corridas* (bullfights) on chosen Sundays at 4:30pm from early May to July. The more modern **Plaza Monumental,** northwest of the city near *Las Playas de Tijuana* (follow Calle 2 west), employs famous *matadores* and hosts fights from August to mid-September. Tickets to both rings are sold at the gate and at the ticket window at Mexicoac, on Revolución between Calles 6 and 7. To get to the Plaza Monumental, catch a blue-and-white bus on Calle 3 between Constitución and Niños Héroes.

🎵 ENTERTAINMENT

If bullfighting turns your stomach, stroll over to the **Tijuana Centro Cultural** (tel. 84 11 11), on Paseo de los Héroes at Mina (open daily 10am-9pm). The monumental sphere in the plaza houses the **Space Theater,** an auditorium with a giant 180° screen that shows American OmniMax movies dubbed in Spanish (shows Tu-F every hr. 3-9pm; Sa-Su every 2hr. 11am-9pm; admission 38 pesos, children 16 pesos). A *Sala de Espectáculos* (performance center) and *Caracol al Aire Libre* (open-air theater) host visiting cultural attractions, including the **Ballet Folklórico.** The **Sala de Video** screens free documentaries, and the **Ciclo de Cine Extranjero** shows foreign films (W-F 6 and 8pm, Sa-Su 4, 6, and 8pm; 25 pesos). Children's films are shown on weekends (Sa-Su 10am, noon, and 2pm; free). The *Centro Cultural* also serves as a gallery for local and visiting art exhibits. Pick up a monthly calendar at the information booth in the *Centro's* art gallery.

While all of this is just swell, if you've come to party, brace yourself for a raucous good time. Strolling down Revolución after dusk, you'll be bombarded by thumping music, neon lights, and abrasive club promoters hawking "two-for-one" margaritas (most places listed below charge US$4 for 2 of the fine concoctions). All clubs check ID (18+), with varying criteria of what's acceptable; many frisk for firearms. If you'd like to check out a more local scene, peek into the small clubs on Calle 6 off Revolución.

■ **Iguanas-Ranas** (tel. 85 14 22), Revolución at Calle 3. Drink your beers (US$2.25) in the school bus or raise hell on the all-encompassing dance floor. Lively on weeknights; packed on weekends. Constellations of margarita-drinking iguanas and *ranas* (frogs) adorn the walls. A twentyish crowd of both *norteños* and *norteamericanos* breaks it down. Open M-Th 10-2am, F-Su 10-5am.

Tilly's 5th Avenue (tel. 85 90 15), at Revolución and Calle 5. The tiny wooden dance floor in the center of this upscale, balloon-filled restaurant/bar resembles a boxing ring, but rest assured—there's only room for dancing. The reflections from the disco ball are enhanced by the mirrored walls and the dance-happy staff. Tilly's is packed on weekends. Beer US$2, but fear not; Wednesday is US$1-beer night. Open M-Th 10:30am-2am, F-Sa 10:30am-5am.

Caves (tel. 88 06 09), Revolución and Calle 5. Dinosaurs and prehistoric beasts perched on a rock facade lead to a dark but airy bar and disco with orange decor, stalactites, and blacklights. Drink 2 beers for US$3.50 with the blond/e clientele. No cover. Open daily 11am-2am.

The Vibe, Revolución by Calle 6. Prepare yourself for this 3-tiered party palace. Miami-esque neon decor and pool tables bring in the masses. Toss back those US$2 margaritas. Cover F-Sa.

El Ranchero Bar (tel. 85 28 00), in front of the fountain in Plaza Santa Cecilia on Calle 1 and Revolución. Red, white, and green paper hangs from the ceiling of this dimly lit gay bar. Beer 10 pesos. Open M-W 10am-2am, Th-Su 10am-3am.

ROSARITO

Once a little-known playground for the rich and famous, the beach haven of Rosarito (pop. 120,000) has expanded at breakneck speed to accommodate the throngs of northern sun-seekers who have discovered its hotels, restaurants, shops, and beaches. Hollywood has also discovered Rosarito. The largest grossing movie of all time, *Titanic*, was filmed here. Giant 10-story hotels and posh resorts cater to the tastes of American tourists. Most of the visitors are from the north or are semi-permanent U.S. expats. English is everywhere and prices are quoted in dollars. On weekends, the sands and surf overflow with people, volleyball games, and horses; finding a place for your towel may be a struggle.

⊠ ORIENTATION AND PRACTICAL INFORMATION. Rosarito lies about 27km south of Tijuana and stretches along the shore. Virtually everything in town is on the main street, **Blvd. Juárez,** upon which street numbers are non-sequential. Most of the action can be found on the southern half of Juárez and you can pick up a map at the tourist office. Most of what is listed below is near the purple Ortega's Restaurant at the Oceana Plaza. To get to Rosarito from **Tijuana,** grab a yellow and white *taxi de ruta* (30min., 9 pesos) that leaves from Madero, between Calles 5 and 6. To return to Tijuana, flag down a *taxi de ruta* along Juárez or at its starting point in front of the Rosarito Beach Hotel. To go to **Ensenada,** take a blue-and-white striped cab marked "Primo Tapia" from Festival Plaza, north of the Rosarito Beach Hotel, to the toll booth *(caseta de cobro)* on Rte. 1 (4 pesos). From there, buses leave for Ensenada (every 30min. until about 9pm, 25 pesos).

The **tourist office** (tel. 2 02 00), on Juárez at Centro Comercio Villa Floreta at the beginning of Juárez, has tons of brochures and a friendly, helpful staff. Some English is spoken. (Open M-F 8am-5pm, Sa-Su 10am-3pm.) **Banamex:** (tel. 2 15 56) on Juárez at Ortiz (open for exchange M-F 8:30am-4:30pm). On weekends, you'll have to go to one of the *casa de cambios* scattered along Juárez, which charge commission. **Calimax** (tel. 2 15 69), at Lázaro Cárdenas and Juárez, just before Quinta del Mar heading south on Juárez, has plenty of foodstuffs (open 24hr.). **Lavamática Moderna** is on Juárez at Acacias (wash and dry 10 pesos; open M-Sa 8am-8pm, Su 8am-6pm). **Emergency:** dial 006. **Police:** (tel. 2 11 10) at Juárez and Acacias. **Red Cross:** (tel. 132) on Juárez at Ortiz, just around the corner from the police. **Farmacia Roma** (tel. 2 35 00; open daily 24hr.), **IMSS Hospital** (tel. 2 10 21; open 24hr.), and the **post office** (tel. 2 13 55; open M-F 8am-3pm) are on Juárez, near its intersection with Acacias. **Postal code:** 22710. **Phone code:** 61.

⌐⌐ ACCOMMODATIONS AND FOOD. Budget hotels in Rosarito are either inconvenient or cramped, with the exception of the outstanding **Hotel Palmas Quintero** (tel. 2 13 59), on Lázaro Cárdenas near the Hotel Quinta del Mar, three blocks inland from north Juárez. A helpful staff and a dog welcome tourists to giant rooms with double beds and clean, private baths. Cool down in the patio under the palm trees. (Singles US$20; doubles US$40.) **Rosarito Beach Rental Cabins** (tel. 2 09 68), on Lázaro Cárdenas two blocks toward the water, are the cheapest housing in Rosarito. You get what you pay for—each small cabin contains bunk beds, a toilet, and a sink. Disney-castle spires make the cabins hard to miss. (Key deposit US$5. Erratic reception 8am-2pm and 4-7pm. Singles US$5, with shower US$10; doubles US$10, with shower US$15.)

Fresh produce and seafood abound in the restaurants that line Juárez. For an economic seafood dinner, head to **Vince's Restaurant** (tel. 2 12 53), on Juárez between Acacias and Robie, across from the police station. Enjoy a feast of soup, salad, rice, potatoes, tortillas, and an entree—*filete especial* (50 pesos), shrimp burrito (40 pesos) or octopus-any-style (50 pesos; open daily 8am-10pm). **La Flor de Michoacán,** Juárez 306 (tel. 3 02 78), serves up fresh tacos filled with the meat of your choice (5.50 pesos, with beans 10 pesos; open daily 10am-8pm). Filling morning grub can be had at **Ortega's Restaurant at the Oceana Plaza,** Juárez 200 (tel. 2 27 91), in a gaudy pink building, where appetites are often pricked by a cactus omelette (US$2; open Su-Th 8am-10pm, F-Sa 8am-11pm).

SEEKING PETITE, DANGEROUS SCORPIO

"Scorpions? But this isn't the jungle," you gasp, "this is Baja." Tough break. These nasty little pests (known in Spanish as *alacranes*) frequent Baja, especially around Mulegé and the mid-peninsula. Unless you are allergic to them, don't worry about a slow, painful death—these aren't the fatal black scorpions that are found in Asia and Africa. These are beige, desert-and-beach-camouflaged scorpions. The smaller (and lighter-colored) the scorpion, the bigger the bite. Most scorpion-bite victims experience intense pain for a day or two. These critters like dark, warm, damp places, so be sure to shake your shoes and clothing before you put 'em on. Ice packs help to alleviate the pain, although locals swear that garlic is the best relief. If you wake up in the middle of the night and a scorpion is crawling up your chest, don't try to flatten or squash it; it will just get angry and sting your hand. Because of their hard protective armor, scorpions are hard to crush. The best thing to do is to give it a hard flick from the side and watch it fly far, far away.

🔲 🔲 **SIGHTS AND ENTERTAINMENT.** Rosarito attracts tourists with its fancy resorts, beautiful shores, and rollicking nightlife. **Rosarito Beach** boasts soft sand and gently rolling surf. The **Museo de Historia Wa Kutay,** on Juárez just south of the Rosarito Beach Hotel, showcases folk art and history of the area. **Fox Studios Baja** (tel. 4 01 10), 2km south of Rosarito on the Tijuana-Ensenada road, offers a short film and tour (US$5) of some of the set and props used in the movie *Titanic* (open Sa-Su 10am-6pm). Once the sun goes down, travelers live the dream at **Papas and Beer,** Calle de Coronales 400 (tel. 2 04 44), one block north of the Rosarito Beach Hotel and two blocks toward the sea. Reminiscent of a giant wooden jungle gym, the open-air dance floor, bar, and sandy volleyball courts are packed with revelers on the weekends. Beer is 15 pesos, and mixed drinks run 18-27 pesos. Don't forget the ID; they take carding very seriously. (Cover US$15-20 on Sa and holidays. Open daily 11am-3am.) Or follow the striped sidewalk outside **Festival Plaza,** on South Juárez at Nogal, to **ChaChaCha's,** where you can dance the night away (beers 18 pesos, mixed drinks 24 pesos; open daily 6pm-3am).

MEXICALI

The highly industrialized capital of Baja California, Mexicali (pop. 1.2 million) straddles both the U.S. and the Mexican mainland. From the cheap, duty-free stands on the border to the 11 industrial plants that ring the city, Mexicali is large, loud, and rapidly growing. As a result, the city is heavily polluted and there's not much tourism here. Some portions of Mexicali, including the mall and surrounding plaza, wear the U.S. facade so well that if not for the language, they could be across the border. Still, Mexicali is a good place to stock up on supplies, check out the local Chinese cuisine or catch a case of the Mexicali Blues. Because of turn-of-the-century immigration, thousands of Chinese live in Mexicali; Chinese food is more popular than Mexican food, and a Chinese-influenced dialect has emerged in the city center.

⚡ ORIENTATION

Although far from the beaten path between the U.S. and Mexico, Mexicali can still serve as a starting point for travelers heading south. The city lies on the California border 189km inland from Tijuana, with Calexico and the Imperial Valley immediately to the north. Its valley location subjects Mexicali to chilly winters and hot summers. Mexicali is one of the more difficult cities in Mexico to navigate. Run directly to the **tourist office** and pick up a deluxe **map.** Mexicali is plagued with haphazardly numbered, zig-zagging streets. The main boulevard leading away from the border is **López Mateos,** which heads southeast, cutting through the downtown area. North-south *calles* and east-west *avenidas* both intersect Mateos, causing even more confusion. **Cristóbal Colón** (also known as Blvd. Internacional), **Madero, Reforma, Obregón, Lerdo,** and **Zaragoza** (in that order from the border) run east-west. **Azueta, Altamirano, Morelos, México, Bravo, Del Comercio,** and streets **A-L** (in that order from west to east) run north-south, starting from where Mateos meets the border (a gigantic green canopy marks the spot). Although the border area can be confusing, a few well-directed questions will set you on the right path. To reach the border from the bus station, take the local bus marked "Centro" (every 10min. 5am-11pm, 4 pesos) from outside the bus terminal, just across the footbridge. Ride past the Vicente Guerrero monument and the enormous new mall, get off at López Mateos, and walk until the border crossing.

◪ PRACTICAL INFORMATION

Buses: The station (tel. 57 24 10 or 57 24 15) is near the intersection of Mateos and Independencia, about 4km south of the border. A blue-and-white bus will take you to the station from the border (4 pesos). Autotransportes de Baja California (tel. 57 24 51) sends buses to: **Ensenada** (14hr., 4 per day; 162 pesos); **Puerto Peñasco** (5hr.; 9am, 2, and 8pm; 149 pesos); **San Felipe** (2hr., 5 per day 8am-8pm; 93 pesos); and **Tijuana** (3hr., every hr.; 110 pesos). Elite (tel. 56 01 10) sends buses to most of the above locations at higher prices, plus: **Chihuahua** (17hr., 11am and 2:20pm; 623 pesos); **Juárez** (14-16hr.; 3:20, 4, and 8:15pm; 550 pesos); and **Nogales** (9hr., 11:15pm; 297 pesos). Golden State (tel. 53 61 69) sends buses to Californian cities, including: **Los Angeles, CA** (4½hr., 8am, 2:30, and 10pm; US$28); and **Ontario, CA** (8am, 2:30, 10:30pm; US$30). Transportes del Pacífico (tel. 57 24 61) offers *de paso* service to most of the above locations for slightly higher fares than Norte de Sonora, as well as second-class buses for around 15% less that take 2-6hr. longer. Service to: **Guaymas** (305 pesos); and **Tijuana** (*primera clase* 100 pesos). Transportes Norte de Sonora (tel. 57 24 10) sends buses to: **Guaymas** (11hr., every hr.; 330 pesos); **Hermosillo** (9hr., every hr.; 262 pesos), and **Los Mochis** (17hr., every hr.; 372 pesos).

Tourist Office: Comité de Turismo y Convenciones (tel. 57 23 76; fax 52 58 77), a white building at Mateos and Camelias facing the Vicente Guerrero monument and park, 3km from the border. Lots of brochures, huge maps, and a friendly English-speaking staff. Open daily Aug. 8am-5pm; Sept.-July M-F 8am-6pm. **Tourist cards** are available at the Federal Immigration office at the border.

Currency Exchange: Exchange currency at any *casa de cambio* along Madero, or try **Banamex** (tel. 54 28 00), at Altamirano and Lerdo, with a 24hr. **ATM** (open M-F 9am-5pm). The **Bital** across the street from the post office also has a 24hr. **ATM** and exchanges traveler's checks. Open M-F 8am-7pm, Sa 8am-5:30pm.

Emergency: dial 060.

Police: (tel. 58 17 00) at Calle Sur and Mateos. English spoken.

Pharmacy: Farmacia Genéricos (tel. 52 29 88) at López Mateos and Morelos. Open daily 8am-10pm.

Hospital: IMSS Centro de Salud (tel. 51 51 50), Lerdo at Calle F, has an English-speaking staff. Otherwise, try the **Hospital Civil** (tel. 53 11 23).

Post Office: Madero 491 (tel. 52 25 08), at Morelos. Open M-F 8am-6:30pm, Sa 9am-1pm. **Postal Code:** 21000.

Fax: Telecomm (tel. 52 20 02) is in the same building as the post office. Service to the U.S. (13 pesos per page) and within Mexico (10 pesos per page). Open M-F 8am-6:30pm, Sa 8am-3pm.

Telephones: LADATELS can be found all over the city as well as *casetas*. Local calls 1 peso; long-distance within Mexico 3 pesos per min.; calls to U.S. 7-11 pesos per min.

Phone Code: 65.

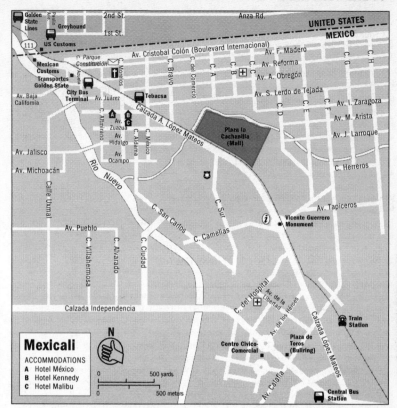

Mexicali

ACCOMMODATIONS
A Hotel México
B Hotel Kennedy
C Hotel Malibu

BAJA CALIFORNIA

ACCOMMODATIONS

Budget hotels crowd the noisy bar strip on Altamirano between Reforma and Lerdo and line Morelos south of Mateos. Hotels on Madero close to Mateos will dig deeper into your wallet but tend to be cleaner.

Hotel Málibu, (tel. 52 80 88), on Morelos near Lerdo. Look out for the big sign. Although the hotel doesn't quite live up to its name, the worn rooms are clean and come with the basics. Windows and light-colored rooms help a bit. One of the cheapest joints in town, it's ideal for the hard-core budget traveler. Singles with bath 100 pesos; doubles with bath 140 pesos; each additional person 50 pesos.

Hotel Kennedy, Morelos 415 (tel. 54 90 62), between Lerdo and Zoazua. Color TV, A/C, and a phone grace the sparkling rooms of this hotel. Singles (1-2 people) 190 pesos, with carpet 210 pesos.

Hotel México, Lerdo 476 (tel. 54 06 69), at Morelos. This hotel offers clean, pink rooms that not only have color TV and super-cold A/C but also overlook a central patio. Bathrooms are small but clean. The office doubles as a grocery store, and the staff is *muy simpático.* Singles 230 pesos; doubles 250 pesos.

FOOD

Some of the best and cheapest food in town is at the food court in Mexicali's huge mall on López Mateos. Here, cheap Chinese cuisine is bountiful, but the constant crowds make it a challenge to find a seat. Most places have combination plates that offer three entrees for 15 pesos or four entrees for 25 pesos.

Restaurant Hollis (tel. 52 66 96), Morelos and Mateos opposite Farma Genéricos. Select your meal from the choices of Chinese, Mexican, or American cuisine. Lots of locals converse casually as they enjoy home-cooked meals. Chinese combo plates 35 pesos. Filling steak sandwiches 20 pesos. Open daily 9am-10pm.

Restaurant Buendía, Altamirano 263 (tel. 52 69 25). Despite sharing a name with the illustrious family of Gabriel García Márquez's epic, Buendía specializes in Chinese cuisine—but chefs are always happy to whip up some *antojitos*. Try a heaping plate of beef with broccoli, fried rice, egg roll, and fried chicken (29 pesos). Three burritos 38 pesos. Vegetarians can delight in a veggie combo for only 32 pesos. Open daily 7am-9pm.

Tortas El Chavo, Reforma 414 at Altamirano, off Mateos, 3 blocks from the border. A fast food joint with mirrored walls that reflect its bright green and yellow booths. *Tortas* are 18-20 pesos; *tacos de machaca* (tacos filled with strips of beef) go for a mere 4.5 pesos. Open daily 8:30am-8pm *(más o menos)*.

■ ♫ SIGHTS AND ENTERTAINMENT

Mexicali's **park, forest, lake,** and **zoo** are located on Alvarado between San Marcos and Lázaro Cárdenas in the southwestern part of town. Children and adults alike wink at the birds in the aviary, pedal paddleboats on the lake, or admire lions and tigers from the train that circles the park and nature reserve. The grounds contain carousels, bumper cars, a pool, and a **science museum.** To reach the park area, board a black-and-white *colectivo* marked "Calle 3" downtown. (Tel. 55 28 33. Zoo open Tu-Su 9am-5pm. Admission 4 pesos, children 3 pesos.) If you've got wheels, drive south on Azueta over the Río Nuevo. The road becomes Uxmal south of the river; turn left on Independencia, then right on Victoria. The city's **Parque Vicente Guerrero**, off Calle López Mateos and next door to the mall, has jungle gyms as well as picnic spots and party space rentals (Tel. 54 55 63. Open daily 8am-9pm).

Plaza de Toros Calafia (tel. 54 43 73), on Calafia at Independencia in the *centro* is host to regularly scheduled bullfights in the fall. Take a 10-min. ride on the blue-and-white bus (4 pesos) from the *centro* to the plaza, which holds up to 11,500 people (11,499 if the bull's having a good day). Wild and crazy rodeos rampage in the winter and spring at **Lienzo Charro del Cetys,** at Cetys and Ordente. Check with the tourist office for schedules. Good, clean fun awaits at **Mundo Divertido,** an amusement park at Mateos 850 (tel. 52 56 75), across from the mall. To get to the park, board a blue-and-white bus marked "Centro Cívico" departing from Madero and Altamirano (every 10min. 5am-11pm; 4 pesos; park open M-F noon-9pm, Sa-Su 10am-10pm). For a film, check out **Cinema Gemelos** in the mall (25 pesos).

TECATE

Any one who has spent any time in Mexico will recognize the name of this small border town. Indeed, the ubiquitous brand of Mexican beer is named after this town and is brewed here at Cervecería Cuauhtémoc Moctezuma. However, Tecate's alcoholic creations are not its only claim to fame—it also serves as one of the quickest border crossings in Baja California, especially for those headed to Ensenada. Unlike its industrialized neighbors, Tijuana and Mexicali, Tecate's air is refreshingly clean (albeit it smells like beer in some parts) and the town's central park is among the more pleasant in Baja California. Street vendors and curio shops are absent here, making it the ideal destination for a daytrip from the frenzied streets of Tijuana.

■ ORIENTATION AND PRACTICAL INFORMATION. Tecate lies 49km east of Tijuana on **Rte. 2.** If you drive in from Tijuana, you'll be on **Av. Benito Juárez** (the main street); from the U.S. you'll drive in on the palm-tree lined **Calle Lázaro Cárdenas.** These two streets intersect at the northwest corner of **Parque Hidalgo,** the hub of activity. The entire town slants north (uphill is north; downhill is south). *Aveni-*

das and *callejones* run east-to-west parallel to the border and *calles* run north to south. Starting from the north, the streets are **Callejón Madero, Av. Revolución, Callejón Reforma, Av. Benito Juárez, Callejón Libertad,** and **Av. Hidalgo.** Starting from the east, the *calles* are **Portes Gil, Rodriguez, Ortiz Rubio, Lázaro Cárdenas, Elias Calles, Obregón, De la Huerta, Carranza,** and **Aldrete.** Simple maps of the town are available at the **tourist office,** Libertad Alley 1305 (tel. 4 10 95), located on the south side of Parque Hidalgo (open daily 8am-7pm).

The **bus station** is two blocks east of the park on Av. Juárez. Autotransportes de Baja California (tel. 4 12 21) sends buses to: **Ensenada** (5 per day 8am-7pm, 35 pesos); **Mexicali** (every hr. 6:30am-10pm; 76 pesos); and **Tijuana** (every 20min. 5am-9pm; 22 pesos). Elite and Transportes Norte De Sonora (tel. 4 23 43) share a ticket window and jointly send buses to: **Guaymas** (13hr., 300 pesos); **Hermosillo** (12hr., 259 pesos); **Mazatlán** (24hr., 539 pesos); **Mexicali** (2hr., 50 pesos); and **Sonoita** (6hr., 132 pesos). All buses are *de paso* and leave every hour beginning at 7am. **Bancomer** (tel. 4 14 50 or 4 13 49), on the corner of Cárdenas and Av. Juárez, exchanges traveler's checks and has a 24hr. **ATM** (open M-F 8:30am-4pm, Sa 10am-2pm). A **Banamex** (tel. 4 11 88) at Av. Juárez and Obregón, across from the PEMEX station, with 24hr. **ATM** also exchanges traveler's checks (open M-F 9am-4pm, Sa 9am-2pm). **Calimax** (tel. 4 00 39), on Av. Juárez between Carranza and Aldrete, sells groceries and more (open daily 6am-11pm). **Emergency and Police:** dial 060. **Red Cross** can be reached in an emergency by dialing 066. **Farmacia Santa Lucia,** Av. Juárez 45 (tel. 4 32 00), next to the Calimax, (open M-Sa 9am-9pm, Su 9am-7pm). **Post office:** Ortiz Rubio 147 (tel. 4 12 45), two blocks north off Av. Juárez (open M-F 8am-3pm). **Postal code:** 21400. **Faxes** can be sent from **Telecomm** (tel. 4 13 75), next door to the post office (open M-F 8am-6pm, Sa 8am-11am). There is a long distance **caseta** in the bus station and **LADATEL** line Av. Juárez. **Phone code:** 665.

▐▛▟ ACCOMMODATIONS AND FOOD. Although most visitors to Tecate do not spend the night, there are a few places for budget travelers to rest. **Hotel Tecate** (tel. 4 11 16), on Libertad at Cárdenas around the corner from the tourist office, is centrally located and offers simple, clean rooms with bathrooms and fans (singles and doubles 160 pesos, with TV 200 pesos). Farther from the center of activity is **Motel Paraíso,** Aldrete 83 (tel. 4 17 16), one block north of Av. Juárez, with clean, but worn, rooms. (1-2 people 145 pesos; 2-3 people 190 pesos; each additional person 55 pesos). **Hotel Juárez,** Juárez 230 (tel. 4 16 17), about two blocks east of the park, offers small, clean rooms with tile floors. An open air hallway lets in cool breezes and glittering sunlight. (Singles 110 pesos; doubles 140 pesos; towel deposit 10 pesos.)

As usual, the cheapest eats in town are in *taquerías,* which line Av. Juárez between the park and the bus station. **Cafe de Pollo,** Juárez 170 (tel. 4 07 46), one block west of the park, serves *tortas* of many varieties (16-24 pesos) in a turquoise environment. At the **Restaurant Jardín Tecate** (tel. 4 34 53), on the south side of the park next to the tourist office, you can enjoy your meal under the shade of park trees as you watch the world go by (*quesadillas* 25 pesos, Mexican combo 40 pesos; open daily 7am-10pm).

◙ SIGHTS. Undoubtedly, the **Tecate Brewery** is the biggest attraction in town, on Av. Hidalgo two blocks west of Cárdenas. The brewery was started in 1944 and was the first *maquiladora* in Baja California. Today it pumps out 20 million liters of amber-colored beer per month. The **Jardín Cerveza Tecate** (tel. 4 20 11), in front of the brewery, offers a free beer to anyone who wants one (ages 18 and older, of course). The garden was opened in 1994 to commemorate the company's 50th anniversary. Besides Tecate, the company also produces Bohemia, Carta Blanca, Superior, Sol, Dos Equis Amber and Dos Equis Lager. After your beer, check out the art galleries that line the south side of the park, or just sidle up to a bench and relax under the palm trees. (Open M-F 10am-5:30pm, Sa-Su 10am-4pm. Free tours are offered for groups of 5 or more M-F 11am and 3pm, Sa 11am.)

BAJA CALIFORNIA

ENSENADA

The secret is out—beachless Ensenada (pop. 72,000) is fast becoming a weekend hot spot. The masses of Californians that arrive every Friday evening have gringo-ized the town to an incredible degree; everyone speaks some English and store clerks turn to their calculators if you try to buy something with pesos. Street vendors wander up and down the main drag, Av. López Mateos, dressed in bright colors and quoting prices. Stores in all sizes and shapes populate the streets. Fear not, Ensenada is nothing like its brash and raucous cousin to the north, the infamous Tijuana. Ensenada's cool sea breezes, warm hospitality, and vast assortment of activities all contribute to its allure. However, the city is more pleasant during the week when fewer tourist-consumers populate the city.

The 90-minute ride from Tijuana to Ensenada offers continuous views of the Pacific, and the last 20 minutes are breathtaking on the Ensenada *cuota* (toll road), the road buses take. Three toll gates along the way each charge 16 pesos. Don't begrudge the money, though; you'll enjoy a phenomenal view of the ocean, large sand dunes, stark cliffs, and broad mesas—if busing it, try to grab a seat on the right-hand side. The *cuota* is also the safer of the two roads, with a breakdown lane and emergency phones about every 10 miles. The less scenic *libre* (free road) is a poorly maintained two-lane highway that parallels the toll road to La Misión, then cuts inland for the remaining 40km to Ensenada. If you're coming by car, drive during the day—there are no streetlights and many tight curves. Most driving is done in the right lane; the left is for passing only. Keep an eye out for rest spots along the road; they provide the perfect chance to enjoy a fantastic view or take a short hike along the lonely cliffs.

◈ ORIENTATION

Ensenada is 108km south of Tijuana on **Rte. 1.** If you're driving, follow signs on Rte. 1 to the *centro.* You'll come into town on **Azueta,** which later becomes **Gastelum.** Buses from Tijuana arrive at the main terminal, at Calle 11 and Riveroll. Turn right as you come out of the station, walk 10 blocks, and you'll be at **López Mateos** (also called **Primera**), the main tourist drag. **Juárez (Calle 5)** runs parallel to Mateos, while from north to south, **Av. Ryerson, Moctezuma, Obregón, Ruíz, Gastelum, Miramar, Riveroll, Alvarado, Blancarte,** and **Castillo** are perpendicular to it north of the *arroyo,* a grassy trench crossed by small bridges; below the *arroyo,* **Av. Espinoza, Floresta, Guadalupe, Hidalgo, Iturbide,** and (later) **Balboa** also run perpendicular to Mateos. **Blvd. Costero** traces the shoreline, parallel to (and west of) Mateos. *Calles* are numbered, *avenidas* are named; together they form a grid. *Calles* run northwest-southeast, while most *avenidas* run northeast-southwest (Juárez and Mateos are exceptions). After sundown, avoid the area near the shoreline, and use caution while navigating the regions bounded by Av. Miramar and Macheros, and Mateos and Cuarta. While orienting yourself, keep in mind that the large residential Chapultepec Hills lie to the north and the water to the west.

◨ PRACTICAL INFORMATION

Buses: Transportes Norte de Sonora (tel. 78 67 70) sends buses to: **Guaymas** (16hr., 437 pesos) and **Los Mochis** (20hr., 6 per day 7am-9:30pm, 525 pesos). Autotransportes de Baja California (tel. 78 66 80) runs to several destinations: **Guerrero Negro** (10hr., 6 per day 10am-11pm, 90 pesos); La Paz (22hr., 4 per day 10am-11pm, 438 pesos); **Loreto** (16hr., 6 per day 10am-11pm, 322 pesos); **Mexicali** (4hr., 4 per day 5:30am-8pm, 107 pesos); **San Felipe** (3hr., 8am and 6pm, 103 pesos); **Santa Rosalía** (13hr., 7 and 9:30pm, 251 pesos); and **Tijuana** (1½hr., every 30min., 55 pesos). Transportes Aragón (tel. 74 07 17), on Riveroll between Calles 8 and 9, rolls to: **Tijuana** (every hr. 5am-9pm, 48 pesos). Local *urbano* buses (tel. 78 25 94) leave from Juárez at Calle 6, and from Calle 2 at Macheros (every 8-15min., 3 pesos). **Luggage storage** is 7 pesos for the first 5hr., 0.50 pesos each additional hr.

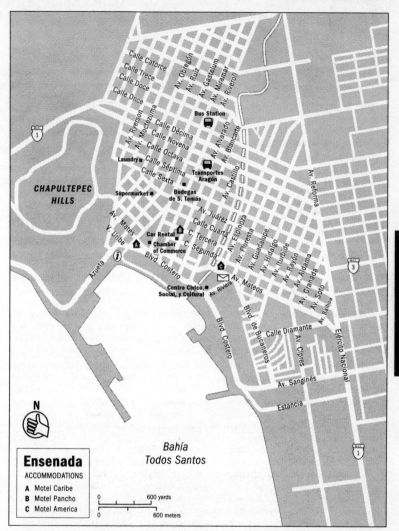

Ensenada

ACCOMMODATIONS

A Motel Caribe
B Motel Pancho
C Motel America

Bahía Todos Santos

Car Rental: Hertz (tel. 78 29 82), Calle 2 at Riveroll, rents cars, but they aren't cheap US$51 per day with unlimited km. Open M-F 9am-6pm, Sa 9am-1pm.

Tourist Office, Blvd. Costero 540 (tel. 78 24 11; fax 78 36 75), at Azueta, has friendly, English-speaking staff members who dole out plenty of helpful information about Ensenada and the surrounding area as well as maps and pamphlets in English. Open M-F 9am-7pm, Sa-Su 11am-3pm. The **Chamber of Commerce,** Mateos 693, 2nd floor (tel. 78 37 70, or 74 09 96), at Macheros, is closer to the center of town and provides brochures and city maps. Open M-F 8:30am-2pm and 4-6:30pm.

Currency Exchange: Banks cluster along Juárez at Av. Ruíz. **Bancomer** (tel. 78 18 01), on Juárez at Av. Ruíz, exchanges dollars and traveler's checks. Open M-F 8:30am-4pm, Sa 10am-2pm. **ATMs** are along Juárez in the bank district, including one at **Serfín,** on Juárez at Gastelum.

Supermarket: Supermarket Calimax (tel. 78 33 97), Gastelum at Calle 4. Open daily 6am-midnight.

Laundry: Lavandería Lavadero (tel. 78 27 37), on Obregón between Calles 6 and 7, across from Parque Revolución. Open M-Sa 8am-7pm, Su 8am-4pm.

Emergency: dial 060.

Police: (tel. 76 24 21) at Calle 9 at Espinoza.

Red Cross: (tel. 74 45 85, emergency 066) on Blvd. de Jesús Clark at Flores.

Farmacia San Martín: (tel. 78 35 30), at Av. Ruíz and Calle 8. Open 24hr.

Hospital General: (tel. 76 78 00 or 76 77 00), on the Transpeninsular Highway at km 111. Open 24hr.

Post office: (tel. 76 10 88), on Mateos and Espinoza. Open M-F 8am-7pm, Sa 8am-noon. **Postal code:** 22800.

Telephones: Faxes can be sent from **Telecomm** (tel. 77 05 45), Av. Floresta at Calle 3. Open M-F 8am-6pm, Sa 8am-11am. **Cafe Internet** (tel. 76 13 31), at Juárez and Floresta. 30 pesos per hr. Open M-F 9am-6:30pm, Sa 9:30am-2pm. **Phone code:** 61.

ACCOMMODATIONS

Budget hotels line Mateos between Espinoza and Riveroll and at Miramar. Most rooms are a 15-minute stroll from the beachfront "boardwalk" and the popular clubs. Although many owners quote prices in greenbacks, paying in pesos means saving cash. The beach between Tijuana and Ensenada is lined with RV parks; one near Ensenada is **Ramona RV Park** (tel. 74 60 45), on km 104 of the Transpeninsular Highway. (US$10 for full hookup).

Motel Caribe, Av. López Mateos 627 (tel. 78 34 81). Great rooms and a superb location: it's right on the main drag and one block from some of Ensenada's popular dance clubs and bars. Singles 220 pesos; doubles 320 pesos; key deposit 50 pesos; rates go up on weekends. Cheaper, more modest rooms are available across the street if you request.

Motel America (tel. 76 13 33), on López Mateos at Espinoza, is a little farther from the action, but its rooms have kitchens, fans, and TVs. Singles for 1-2 people 220 pesos; doubles 340 pesos.

Motel Pancho (tel. 78 23 44), on Alvarado at Calle 2, one block off López Mateos (in line with the giant flagpole) has large rooms and clean baths with tiny showers. The hospitable staff will direct you to neighborhood bars. Singles 120 pesos; doubles 200 pesos.

FOOD

The cheaper restaurants in town line Juárez and Espinoza; those on Mateos jack up their prices. The eateries along the waterfront near the fish market compete fiercely for their customers and offer good, cheap, fresh seafood. Fruit, seafood, and taco stands abound, but be wary of how the food is handled. If you have a kitchen, the best bargains are at the **supermarkets** on Gastelum.

Mary's Restaurant, Av. Miramar 609 between Costero and López Mateos. Serves scrumptious seaside fare, with good old down-home hospitality. Fish filets start at 30 pesos, and a whopping portion of *huevos rancheros* with an ice-cold Coke goes for just 20 pesos. Snack on homemade tortilla chips and peruse the wall of foreign money or the various knick-knacks caught in the fish nets on the walls.

Cafetería Monique Colonial (tel. 76 40 41), Calle 9 at Espinoza. Friendly atmosphere makes it a local favorite. Diners sit in anxious anticipation of their breaded steak with salad and fries (42 pesos). The *Galeria Infantil* over the kitchen displays the masterful artwork of local school children. Open M-Sa 6am-10pm, Su 6am-5pm.

Las Parrillas (tel. 76 17 28), Espinoza at Calle 6. Chefs grill up fresh meat cutlets on the flaming pit as customers drool like Pavlov's dogs. Squeeze onto a counter stool and scarf down burritos (28 pesos) and *súper hamburgesas* with veggies, avocado, and chile (28.50 pesos). Open daily 7am-10pm.

SIGHTS

Seeing Ensenada requires more than a quick cruise down López Mateos. For a spectacular view of the entire city, climb the **Chapultepec Hills.** The steep road to the top begins at the foot of Calle 2; expect a 10- to 15-min. hike. Or take a stroll down **Av. López Mateos,** where herds of curio shops allow for endless shopping. Many of the outdoor cafes are perfect for people-watching.

The mild, dry climate of northern Baja's Pacific coast has made it Mexico's prime grape-growing area. **Bodegas de Santo Tomás,** Miramar 666 (tel. 78 33 33), at Calle 7, located in a less-visited part of town, has produced wine since 1888. Today, the *bodegas* distill over 500,000 cases of wine and champagne per year. Tours include free wine tasting and an assortment of breads and cheeses. (Tours daily 11am, 1, and 3pm. Admission US$3.)

The larger-than-life golden busts of Venustiano Carranza, Miguel Hidalgo, and Benito Juárez stare seriously onto **Plaza Cívica.** Grab an ice cream cone, strut over to the *Ventana al Mar* (window to the sea) next to the Plaza Civica, and marvel at the **largest flag** in Mexico. The nearby gardens of the **Centro Cívico, Social, y Cultural de Ensenada** (tel. 76 43 10 or 76 42 33) are one block from Costero (US$1 entrance fee). Once a world-famous casino built in 1930, the *centro* is now a shrine to Ensenada's archaeological and social history. The architecture and gardens alone make a visit worthwhile. The **Instituto Nacional de Antropología e Historia,** Ryerson 99 (tel. 78 25 31), at Virgilio Uribe, is the oldest building in town. There are numerous artifacts and images of the earliest missionary settlements in Baja including several mission church bells. (Open M-F 9am-4pm. Free.) Nearby, the **Museo Histórico Regional** (tel. 78 25 31), on Gastelum between Virgillo Uribe and López Mateos, houses artifacts from all over Baja, including a charming photograph of two elderly *Cucapa* men standing next to their shared young wife, whom they acquired during a robbery in a nearby town. Originally built in 1886 as barracks, it is the **oldest public building** in the state. The building was converted to a jail in 1914 and served as such until 1986. (Open Tu-Su 10am-5pm. Admission US$1.) A 15-min. walk from Mateos is the **Museo de Ciencias,** Obregón 1463 (tel. 78 71 92), at Catorce. Housed in an old wooden boat, the museum displays photographs of and information about the endangered species of Baja. (Open Tu-F 9am-5pm, Sa noon-5pm. Admission 12 pesos, children 10 pesos.)

 ENTERTAINMENT

Most of the popular hangouts along López Mateos are members of the hybrid species known as the restaurant/bar/disco. Food and drinks are served only until 8pm or so, when the eateries metamorphose into full-fledged dance club monsters. On weekends, almost every place is packed with festive tourists. Better known than Ensenada itself is **Hussong's Cantina** (tel. 78 32 10), on Ruíz between Mateos and Calle 2. Now 106 years old, Hussong's is the prototypical Mexican watering hole: dark, wood-paneled walls adorned with deer heads and sawdust on the floor, deliver the true *cantina* flavor with your Tecate. Gulp down beer (12 pesos) or a margarita (16 pesos) at the long, shiny bar. (Open daily 10am-2am.) When you tire of the continuous stream of *mariachis*, cross the street to **Papas and Beer** (tel. 74 01 45), a frenetic high-tech music emporium popular with a young crowd that swigs large margaritas (21 pesos) and spends horse-choking wads of cash. Escape the congestion and whistle-blowing staff by stepping onto the terrace, where hockey-rink-like plexiglass boards prevent carousers from cross-checking each other off the balcony to the street below. Thursday night is theme night (birthday, pajamas, whatever) and Friday is ladies' night, when men aren't let in until 10pm (cover US$3-5; open Su-Th noon-3am, F-Sa 10am-2am).

If you're looking for a less alcohol-centered evening, join the gyrating mass of teens whirling to late-80s pop hits at **Roller Ensenada** (tel. 76 11 59), a roller rink on Mateos at Hidalgo (open Tu-Th 2-10pm, F-Su noon-10pm; admission 13 pesos with or without skates). If you just want to zone out in front of a big screen, **Cinema**

Gemelos (tel. 76 36 16 or 76 36 13), on Balboa and Mateos, at the southern end of town, screens subtitled U.S. features (shows daily 4-10pm; admission 20 pesos).

NEAR ENSENADA

Ensenada is an excellent base from which to explore Baja's natural wonders. Unfortunately, to reach most of them, you'll need some wheels, particularly a four-wheel-drive or all-terrain vehicle. Try Hertz in Ensenada, or, better yet (if you're driving down from Cali), Bargain Auto Rentals in San Diego (see **Tijuana: Car Rental,** p. 142).

BEACHES

Good sand to accompany your swim in the bucolic Bahía de Todos Santos can only be found outside of the city. To the north, **Playa San Miguel,** with its rocky coastlines and large waves, is great for surfers but might not be ideal for others. To get there, drive north up Calle 10 to the toll gate; turn left at the sign marked "Playa San Miguel." Buses also run to this beach—catch a bus marked "San Miguel" departing from Gastelum at Costero (3 pesos). Buses back must be flagged down.

Somewhat more frequented beaches lie 8km south of Ensenada off the Transpeninsular Highway. Probably the nicest beach around is **Playa Estero,** dominated by the Estero Beach Resort. Volleyball courts fill the beach's clean but hard and unforgiving sand. You can rent water skis, banana boats, or bicycles (US$5 per hr.) and sea lions can be spotted off the coast during low tide. The **Estero Beach Museum** (tel. 6 62 35), located in the Estero Beach Resort, has an impressive display of Mexican folk art (open daily W-M 9am-6pm; free). To get there, take a right at the "Estero Beach" sign on Rte. 1 heading south. Free parking is available in the first lot of the hotel. Alternatively, catch a bus marked "Aeropuerto," "Zorrillo," "Maneadero," or "Chapultepec" from Pl. Cívica. **Playa El Faro** (tel. 77 46 30), 10km south of town, is similarly rife with volleyball courts and Americans but has slightly better sand and offers camping on the beach (camp space, parking, and bathroom privileges US$7 for 4 people; full RV hookup US$10; rooms with bath US$30 for 2 people). Another nearby beach is **Playa Santa María,** where you can rent a horse (US$9 per hr.) and ride around the bay.

Heading onto the Punta Banda peninsula (continuing south from Ensenada, take the paved road BCN 23, which splits west off Rte. 1 north of Maneadero), you'll find lonelier beaches along the stretch known as **Baja Beach.** Horses are available for rent, and you can swim anywhere along the clean, soft, white sand in front of a quiet scattering of Americans in semi-permanent RV parks. The rolling hills and marshes provide a pleasant backdrop. The Baja Beach Resort also runs a pool of hot springs, located on Rte. 1 on the left, 2km before turning off onto the Punta Banda peninsula. To get to Baja Beach, walk down a dirt road after the sign, on the right-hand side. By car, bear right at the first fork in the road after turning onto the peninsula and proceed with caution; this road is very poorly maintained. Look for "Horses for Rent" and "Aguacaliente" signs. Beautiful hiking spots are nearby. You can also take a bus to La Bufadora and ask the driver to let you off, but don't count on a ride back.

⚠ HIKING

The area's most beautiful spots remain essentially undiscovered by most tourists. Breathtaking hikes on well-kept trails can be completed around the mountains of the **Punta Banda** peninsula near La Bufadora. Bring a snack, as there are some good spots with spectacular view of cliffs and never-ending blue sea to stop and picnic. Bathing suits are key—when you reach the bottom, you can relieve your sweaty body with a dip amid the rocks in the chilly Pacific. Most of the trails consist of unmarked footpaths and dirt roads. Be sure to stay on a path once you've chosen it; trail blazing will damage the surrounding flora.

The best spot to enter the trails is **Cerro de la Punta,** on the road to La Bufadora near the end of the Punta Banda peninsula. Turn right up a long driveway at the "Cerro de la Punta" sign (parking 10 pesos). You'll see a small clearing and a large house on the cliffs; here, you can hike up among the cacti to the top of the mountains for views of the surrounding area or down beautiful trails on the oceanside.

Other stops earlier along the road to La Bufadora are equally scenic. The bus to La Bufadora (see below) will drop you off anywhere along this road, including Cerro de la Punta, but you may wait quite a while for the bus back. **Punta Banda** itself has a roadside **grocery market** and **post office** (open M-F 8am-3pm; but, honestly, go to Ensenada) on the main road after the turn-off for Baja Beach. You can camp or park an RV in Punta Banda at **Villarino** (tel. 54 20 45; fax 54 20 44), adjacent to the plaza, which has modern shower and bathroom facilities and full hookups (1-2 people US$10; $5 every extra person per night; call for reservations).

Hiking farther inland offers completely different terrain, ranging from deep lagoons and cactus forests to ponderosa pine. The rugged mountain range east of Ensenada is the solitary **Sierra de Juárez,** where **Parque Nacional Constitución de 1857** is located. Be forewarned that you'll need an all-terrain vehicle or pickup truck to make the trek. If you can afford it, find a guide who can show you the correct paths to take once off the main roads. Dirt roads and brush make these paths difficult to navigate. To get there, follow **Highway 3** east from Av. Juárez in Ensenada all the way past **Ojos Negros.** At about km 58, turn left onto the dirt road leading into the park. Follow signs (or, better, ask a guide for help); after about one hour and 20 minutes, you will find yourself at **Laguna Hanson,** a little lake surrounded by basic camping spots. **Ecotur** Espinoza 1251 (tel. 76 44 15; fax 74 67 78), at Calle 9, offers excursions to those without wheels. The owner, Francisco Detrell, also leads tours in Ensenada and parts of Baja. Call or fax at least three days in advance to book a tour.

LA BUFADORA

La Bufadora, the largest geyser on the Pacific coast, is 30km south of Ensenada. On a good day, the "Blowhole" shoots water 40m into the air out of a water-carved cave. On a bad day, visitors will have to be satisfied with the beautiful view from the Bufadora peak. The area is crowded with droves of visitors, cheesy curio shops, and food vendors. Be sure to try the *churros.* In spite of the bustling buzz of the area, the geyser makes the trip worthwhile. To get there, drive south on the Transpeninsular Highway. (take a right onto the highway off López Mateos at the southern end of town), head straight past exits for the airport, military base, and Playa Estero, and take a right after about 20 minutes at the sign marked "La Bufadora." Continue on that road until its end. You'll know you're there when you've finished a brain-numbing series of road loops and you find yourself on a small street with multi-colored vending stalls (parking US$1 or 8 pesos). Alternatively, you can take a yellow *microbús* from Ensenada to **Maneadero** (3 pesos) and a connecting bus to La Bufadora (2 pesos).

VALLE DE SAN QUINTÍN

Occupying the lonely mid-Pacific coast of northern Baja, San Quintín Valley (pop. 30,000) is the lifeblood of the peninsula's agricultural production. Driving south from Ensenada on Rte. 1 (the Transpeninsular Highway) for 180km, you'll encounter a series of small, bland towns bordered by the ocean on the west and the mountains on the east—farmland lies everywhere in between. The valley's settlement is made up of numerous ranches belonging to gallant *vaqueros* (cowboys) and three tiny towns (listed north to south): **San Quintín, Lázaro Cárdenas** (not to be confused with its same-named neighbor only about 100km to the northeast), and **El Eje del Papaloto.** What brings most people here, however, is the superb fishing off the small *bahía.* Americans and other foreigners are hard to find in the area's main strip (as is virtually everything). The summer morning fogs and the cool bay breezes of the old port area give way to hot afternoon sun and vistas of desert and cacti. Above all, the town makes a good rest stop on the way to points farther south, or a convenient place to stock up on supplies for a camping excursion to the nearby **Parque Nacional Sierra San Pedro Mártir** (see p. 159).

◪ ORIENTATION AND PRACTICAL INFORMATION. All three towns border **Rte. 1,** Mexico's **Transpeninsular Highway.** Small streets off the highway have neither street signs nor common-use names. Addresses are designated by highway location. The beaches are all west of the highway, off small dirt and sand roads. Coming from the north, San Quintín is the first town, Cárdenas (as it is known in the region) is second, and little Eje comes last. The Valle de San Quintín **tourist office** (tel. 6 27 28) actually comes before the towns themselves at km 178 in Col. Vicente Guerrero—look for signs. The friendly staff will provide plenty of info about the valley and the surrounding area. (Open M-F 8am-5pm, Sa-Su 10am-3pm.) To **exchange currency** and traveler's checks, head to **BITAL,** the Valle's bank, located in Lázaro Cárdenas behind the PEMEX station (open M-F 8am-7pm, Sa 9am-2:30pm). **Emergency:** dial 134. **Police:** in Cárdenas, east of the highway. **Farmacia Baja California:** (tel. 5 24 38) in Cárdenas, Rte.1 at km 195 (open daily 8am-10pm). **Clínica Santa María:** (tel. 75 22 63 or 75 22 12) in San Quintín, on a dirt road off Rte. 1 at km 190. **Post office:** a gray building next to the Farmacia Baja California in Cárdenas (open M-F 8am-3pm). **Postal code:** 22930. **LADATELS** are in all three towns and a **caseta** is in Cárdenas. **Phone code:** 616.

▐ ◪ ACCOMMODATIONS AND FOOD. Sleeping arrangements in the Valle are minimal but, for the most part, comfortable. In San Quintín, **Hotel Chavez** (tel. 5 20 05), on Rte. 1 at km 194 just before the bridge, offers large, airy rooms, soft beds, and cable TV in the main lobby (singles 180 pesos; doubles 240 pesos; call ahead for reservations). In Lázaro Cárdenas, **Motel Romo** (tel. 5 23 96), at km 196 on the west side of Rte. 1, has almost-new carpeted rooms. Clean bathrooms border on Art Deco and large windows let in the sunlight. (Singles 110 pesos; doubles 130 pesos.) About 3km down a dirt road just south of Lázaro Cárdenas lies **Motel San Carlos** (follow signs for the Old Mill). Situated near the old pier on San Quintín Bay, its carpeted rooms with baths offer guests a nightly serenade of wind and waves lapping at the shore. (Singles US$20; doubles US$25.) Cheap eats aren't tough to find in San Quintín. Small *loncherías* along both sides of Rte. 1 serve tacos for 9 pesos. Enjoy a *bistec milanesa* (49 pesos) among framed portraits of John Wayne, Clint Eastwood, and other *vaqueros* in the air-conditioned **Asadero El Alazán** in San Quintín, at km 190 on Rte. 1.

◙ ◪ SIGHTS AND ENTERTAINMENT. San Quintín is best known for the fishing off the San Quintín bay. You can drive out to the **Molino Viejo** (Old Pier) and to the **Old Mill Hotel** (U.S. tel. 619-428-2779 or 800-479-7962), where you can get a fishing permit, hire a boat for the day, and catch a glimpse of some original mill machinery of the failed 19th-century English colony. The surrounding mountains and peaceful bay waters will soothe the worn traveler. The Old Mill itself is a semi-permanent American expat community. To get there, turn west on a sand and dirt road on km 198 and head down about 4km (signs will point you in the right direction). Or, if you'd like something a little different, check out the salt lakes formed on the edge of the sea, west of Cárdenas. To get there, turn left at the corner of the military base. Head down a dirt and sand road for approximately 8.2km. You don't need an ATV, but follow the sand paths very carefully. Although San Quintín's nightlife is hardly hoppin', those in search of spirits can wet their whistle at **Bar Romo** (tel. 5 23 96), on Rte. 1 in Cárdenas, where *mariachis* and local singers are cheered on by catcalls until the late hours. In San Quintín, grab a chilly *cerveza* (about 12 pesos) or margarita (20 pesos) at the friendly tourist-oriented **Restaurant Bar San Quintín** (tel. 5 23 76) on Rte. 1 next to Hotel Chavez. The well-stocked bar and weekend *mariachis* will help you strum a buzz in no time. (Open daily 7:30am-1am.)

PARQUE NACIONAL SIERRA SAN PEDRO MÁRTIR

Although the trippy towns of the Valle de San Quintín appeal mostly to anglers, the nearby **Parque Nacional Sierra San Pedro Mártir** has enough canyons, peaks, and waterfalls to satisfy the urges of the most zealous land lover. Founded in 1947, the park occupies the highest zone on the peninsula and is home to **Picacio del Diablo** (also known as **Cerro de la Encantada** or **La Providencia**), the highest peak in Baja at 3086m above sea level. From its peak on a clear day, you can admire the aquamarine waters of the Sea of Cortés, turn around, and check out the vast Pacific Ocean. The climb to the peak is rated three to five and is said to be one of the most challenging climbs in Mexico. For those uninterested in scaling mountains, the park has three canyons to explore as well as the San Pedro Mártir Falls, an 800m fall accessible only with an authorized guide. Check out the tourist office in San Quintín or contact **Ecotur** (see **Hiking** in Ensenada, p. 157). The park is situated on a plateau, and because of its elevation, it has considerably more rainfall than its lowland desert surroundings—it even snows in the winter here. As a result, the park is beautifully shaded by evergreens (pines and junipers abound) and is host to a vast array of wildlife including deer, puma, eagles, not-so-wild cows, and the Nelson rainbow trout (a species endemic to the region). The park's isolated location makes it one of the least-visited parks in Mexico and a prime destination for backpackers and hikers who wish to be alone to commune with nature. There are several tent site locations, but none for trailer or car camping. A few trails leading to viewpoints and wilderness campsites are nominally maintained and can be accessed off the park's only road. See a ranger at the entrance to the park for information and help with orientation.

The park is also home to Mexico's **National Observatory.** Founded in 1967, the observatory is one of the most important in all of Latin America; it houses both reflecting telescopes and a new state-of-the-art telescope that utilizes infrared technology. The observatory lies at the end of the road leading into the park and tours are given on Saturdays from 11am to 1pm (by appointment).

Getting There: The road leading to the park and observatory lies approximately 51km north of San Quintín and runs east of the highway for 100km. Be forewarned—this road is not for the faint of heart. The ride to the park is approximately 2½ hours on a poorly maintained dirt road (due to heavy rainfall, the road may be temporarily closed). You can make the trek in a passenger vehicle, but it is highly recommended to go with four-wheel-drive. Be careful of oncoming traffic as the road is narrow and the cliffs steep. Also watch out for cattle; local *vaqueros* use the road to herd their cows to greener pastures. In spite of the dangerous curves, the views from the road are unparalleled—breathtaking vistas of canyons and hills tinted yellow and red by wildflowers are some of the best in all of Baja. The trails in the park are not well marked, and it is advisable to bring a compass and, for some trails, mandatory to bring along an authorized guide. If you plan on backpacking or spending the night in the park, bring plenty of safe drinking water.

BAHÍA DE LOS ANGELES

The village of Bahía de los Angeles is quiet, peaceful, and the perfect place to sip a margarita while watching the sunset. Wedged between steep rocky hills to the west and the Sea of Cortés to the east, the Bahía is home to a rich variety of marine life. Hunchback and finback whales can be spotted during the summer, while whale sharks cruise the bays around October. Dolphins, both common and bottlenose, as well as sea lions, are present all year. Several small rock islands guard the entrance to the bay and provide beautiful scenery. You won't find any dance clubs or *mariachis* in this little Baja town; most visitors come to fish or just relax—modern amenities are not yet universal here.

Bahía de los Angeles is very small and easily navigable by foot. The road that leads from the Transpeninsular Highway to the bay becomes the town's main road. None of the streets are named, but everything is right off the main strip. The owner of **Guill-**

ermo's, a *mercado*/restaurant/RV park/motel, serves as the official **tourist** liaison. There are no banks; exchange your traveler's checks before you drive into town (you will be driving—there is no bus service). A **public phone** can be found in the office of Hotel Costa Azul on the main road (12 pesos per min.). The **police** are behind the park across from Guillermo's. The cheapest way to stay in the Bahía is to camp, and the best place to do that is at **Daggett's Campground.** Follow the signs from the main road just before entering town. Situated right on the beach, each space comes with a small *palapa* and barbecue pit. The campground has bathrooms, hot showers, and a great view. (US$6 per couple; US$2 each additional person.) The owner, **Ruben,** is a great source of information and he also leads fishing and diving tours (half-day US$85). **Hotel las Hamacas** in town off the main road has very clean rooms with concrete floors, A/C, and fans (singles 150 pesos; doubles 200 pesos). Park your RV at **Guillermos,** off the main road (an unbeatable US$3 per person per night for a full hookup). Because of its isolated location, food in town is not so cheap. Your best bet is to grill up your catch of the day. If the fish just aren't biting, head to the **Restaurante las Hamacas,** in front of the hotel. The simple, trophy-adorned dining room is cooled by fans and ice-cold *cerveza.* Try the Mexican combo for 30 pesos. (Open 8am-8pm.) **Restaurante Isla** has a great view of the bay from its second floor *palapa*-roofed patio. Silk flowers peeking out of tinfoiled beer bottles grace the tables along with delicious *tacos de pescado* (35 pesos; open 7am-9pm).

Although Bahía de los Angeles is small and relatively undeveloped, it has a rich history. The area was originally inhabited by the **Cochimi,** a group of Native Americans that were prevalent in this area of Baja. A Jesuit mission built in 1697 introduced ranching to the area. More information about the town, its history, and its natural surroundings can be found at the small but exquisite **Museo de Historia y Cultura,** located directly behind the police office; look for the large white skeleton in front. The well-maintained wooden museum holds detailed exhibits on the Cochimi and local wildlife, fossils, stuffed animal specimens, and a collection of old photographs of the town in its previous incarnations as mining town and fishery. It's well worth the visit. (Open in summer daily 9am-noon and 3-5pm; in winter daily 9am-noon and 2-4pm. Free, but donations accepted.)

Most visitors to Bahía de los Angeles come to catch fish and many come with their own boats. If you plan to fish, be sure to bring (or borrow) your own supplies—there is no place to pick up fishing supplies in town. Ruben Daggett of Daggett's Campground will take you fishing on his diving boat (half-day US$85). Fill your dive tank or rent your dive gear at the only dive shop in town, **Larry and Raquel's,** next to Daggett's Campground. They also rent kayaks for the day (US$15). The best beaches lie north of town along Ensenada la Gringa. Permanent RVs park along the coast, but you can access the beach via dirt paths off the unpaved road leading to **Punta la Gringa,** the northern lip of the Bahía. The road to la Gringa can be accessed by following signs to Daggett's Campground. Once on the dirt road outlined by white stones, follow it north for about 4km until it ends.

SAN FELIPE

San Felipe may put on Mexican airs, but it's a tourist-oriented beach town at heart, complete with high prices, sandy volleyball courts, and vendors selling shell sculptures. From October to April, San Felipe's 200 RV parks are packed with northerners. Northerners claimed the area as a regular hangout in the 50s, bringing with them handfuls of greenbacks and a new industry—tourism. Cashiers look positively perplexed if you try to pay in pesos. However, San Felipe offers a stellar selection of seafood and a beautiful stretch of beach teased by the warm, shallow waters of the Gulf. The town is laid-back and scenic, and provides the perfect place to relax for a day or 10, and grab a drink or 20. As one local bar has written on the wall, "No worries—be happy."

■ **ORIENTATION.** San Felipe is 198km south of Mexicali at the end of sizzling-hot Rte. 5. The town is also accessible via Rte. 3 from Ensenada, a poorly maintained jacuzzi-sized pothole-infested paved road. If coming from Tijuana, the latter makes for a more pleasant ride despite the treacherous potholes. A dirt and gravel road connects San Felipe to points farther south (attempt with four-wheel drive only). **Los Arcos** (a tall arched structure) is immediately recognizable when entering the village; **Chetumal** is the street continuing straight from the arch toward the sea. Hotels and restaurants cluster on **Mar de Cortés,** one block from the beach. The **Malecón,** lined with seafood stands, is right on the beach. Almost all of the "action" (restaurants, hotels, services) is on these two streets. All cross-streets named "Mar" run parallel to the beach; from west to east they are **Malecón, Mar de Cortés, Mar Baltico, Mar Tasmania, Man Cantabrico, Mar Negro,** and **Mar Blanco.** From south to north, **Manzanillo, Topolobampo, Ensenada, Chetumal,** and **Acapulco** run perpendicular to the beach. To get downtown from the **bus station,** walk north on Mar Caribe to Manzanillo and turn right toward the water. Hike until you see the Hotel Costa Azul, and you're on Mar del Caribe, one block from the beach.

🛈 **PRACTICAL INFORMATION.** Catch **buses** at the terminal on Mar del Caribe (tel. 7 15 16), a 15-min. walk from the center of action. Autotransportes de Baja California runs buses to: **Ensenada** (3½hr., 8am and 6pm, 135 pesos); **Mexicali** (2½hr., 5 per day 6am-8pm, 96 pesos); and **Tijuana** (5 per day 6am-4pm, 207 pesos). Tickets are on sale daily from 5:30am to 10:30pm. The air-conditioned **tourist office,** Mar de Cortés 300 (tel. 7 18 65) at Manzanillo, has English-speaking staffers and handy maps and brochures (open M-F 8am-7pm, Sa 9am-3pm, Su 10am-1pm). The only bank in town, **Bancomer** (tel./fax 7 10 90), Mar de Cortés Nte. at Acapulco, near Rockodile Bar and has a 24-hour **ATM** (open M-F 8:30am-4pm, Sa 10am-2pm).

In an **emergency,** dial 134. **Police:** (tel. 7 13 50 or 7 11 34), Mar Negro Sur, just south of Chetumal. **Red Cross:** (tel. 7 15 44) at Mar Bermejo and Peñasco, has English-speaking staff (open 24hr.). **Farmacia San José,** Pto. Mazatlán 523 (tel. 7 13 87; open 24 hours). The **Centro de Salud** (tel. 7 15 21) is on Chetumal, near the fire and police station (English spoken; open 24hr.). **Post office:** (tel. 7 13 30) Mar Blanco across from city hall, five blocks inland from Cortés (open M-F 8am-3pm, Sa 9am-noon). **Postal code:** 21850. **Faxes** can be sent from **Copicentro** (tel. 7 14 02) on Chetumal across from Mercado Palillo (open daily 8am-9pm; 20 pesos for 1st min., 15 pesos for each additional min.). Some **LADATELS** line Mar del Caribe. **Phone code** is 657.

🛏 **ACCOMMODATIONS.** There are two kinds of accommodations in San Felipe: those with air-conditioning and those without. Travelers who prefer the former will end up paying *mucho dinero* for mediocre rooms (although during summer it might be worth it). Sadly enough, San Felipe is one of the most expensive cities in one of the most expensive parts of the country; serious penny-pinchers will not find any cheap lodging. Those who plan on staying in this expensive little town should consider camping. A cheaper option is to rent a room in a private residence; check with the tourist office for a list. **Carmelita** (tel. 7 18 31), across from the Chapala Motel, is one of the private residences renting out rooms with air-conditioning and private bath and a whole bunch of birds. Four rooms are available, housing single people or married couples only (US$25 per room). Free wake-up calls. Crammed between curio shops and administered from the liquor store next door, **Motel El Pescador** (tel. 7 26 48), on Mar de Cortés at Chetumal, offers spacious and nicely furnished rooms overlooking the beach with air-conditioning, color TV, and private baths. It's a real bargain, at least by San Felipe standards. (Singles 250 pesos; doubles 350 pesos.) RV parks abound in San Felipe and are the most economical way (besides camping) to spend the night. The best known is **Ruben's** (tel. 7 20 21), toward the end of Av. Golfo de California in Playa Norte. To reach Ruben's, turn left from Chetumal onto Mar de Cortés, and follow the signs on the short drive up. Individual beachfront parking spaces are topped with two-story, open-air bungalows that look like *palapa* tree-forts. Each spot easily accommodates carloads of folks with sleeping bags. RVs can hook up to electricity, hot water, and sewer connections. (2 people in summer US$15, in winter US$12; US$2 per extra person; office open daily 7am-7pm.) **Campo San Felipe** (tel. 7 10 12), on Mar de Cortés just south of Chetumal, lures campers with a fabulous beachfront location. A thatched roof shelters each fully loaded trailer spot. (Most spots US$15-20, a few US$10, depending on location and proximity to the beach; US$2 per extra person, children under 6 free; tent space US$10.)

⏶ FOOD. Mar de Cortés is crammed with restaurants advertising air-conditioned relief. The beach, Malecón, is lined with fish taquerías serving up inexpensive fresh seafood under shady thatched roofs. Shrimp tacos are US$1, while full shrimp dinners run US$5-6. **Los Gemelos** (tel. 7 10 63), on Mar de Cortés between Acapulco and Chetumal, near Bancomer, serves tasty huevos rancheros for US$2.50 (open daily 6am-10am). Enjoy beef, chicken, or shrimp enchiladas (23 pesos) and a calming view of the sea at **Restaurant El Club** (tel. 7 11 75) on the Malecón at Acapulco. Shark fins and plastic turtles hang over bright multicolored table cloths. The camarones al mojo de ajo (garlic shrimp; 75 pesos) is one of the world's most perfect meals. Ice-cold agua purificada available free. (Open daily 7am-11pm.)

⏴ SIGHTS AND SAND. People come to San Felipe to swim in the warm, tranquil, and invitingly blue Gulf waters. The beach in town follows along the Malecón and gets crowded on weekends. Try the beaches farther south for scuba and snorkeling—the water's clearer. A booth that rents **ATV's** is located right next to Motel El Pescador (US$20 per hr., open 8am-6pm). **Banana boats** wait along the beach in front of Bar Miramar, ready to take you for a 20-min. spin (boats run 9am-6pm, 30 pesos per person, min. 5 people).

The whole Bahía is generally clean, safe, and appealing; beaches outside of town are more isolated, but might require a long walk or a drive. Every beach is accompanied by a commercialized RV trailer park, but, as always, beaches are free—you only need to pay if you're parking.

Take time to visit the **Altar de la Virgen de Guadalupe,** a shrine to the virgin at the top of the hill near the lighthouse. After a short hike, you'll be rewarded with a spectacular view of San Felipe and the blue bay. Sixty-four kilometers south of San Felipe is the **Valle de los Gigantes National Park.** With cacti up to 15m tall, the park was the original home of the giant cactus that represented Mexico at the 1992 World's Fair in Seville, Spain. Fossil hunters will be elated to find a vast array of petrified sea life. Ask at the tourist office about guided dune buggy tours of the park.

⏵ ENTERTAINMENT. San Felipe merrily courts throngs of migrant snowbirds and tourists with its picturesque beaches and a variety of venues to get tipsy or blasted. The high-priced, high-profile bar **Rockodile** (tel. 7 12 19), on Malecón at Acapulco, caters to a younger crowd and has a full line of Rockodile beachwear at its souvenir store on Mar de Cortés. Drunk customers write their names with magic marker on dollar bills and paste them up. Check out the volleyball court, pool table, and outdoor terrace. It's mellow during the day, but on weekend nights, it's a sweaty dance party. To begin inducing amnesia, try the electric-blue king-sized beverage, the "Adios motherfucker" (US$4). (F-Sa cover $3-4. Half-price Happy Hour Su-F 11am-7pm; open daily 11am-3am.) Seasoned veterans nurse drinks at **Bar Miramar,** Mar de Cortés 486 (tel. 7 11 92). The oldest bar in San Felipe may look like a *cantina* from the 60s, but the patrons come for company, not glitz. Push a few cues over green felt on the pool tables out front (beer US$1.50, margaritas US$2.50; open daily 10am-2am). **Beachcomber** (tel. 7 21 22), on Malecón and Chetumal, always has sports on TV and tourists tranquilly nursing a buzz. A well-stocked bar, long wooden counter, and jukebox makes this a quiet, understated place to get trashed—and one of the cheapest (beer US$1.50 pesos, margaritas 20 pesos, flavored drinks 30 pesos; Su karaoke at 8pm; open daily 10am-2am).

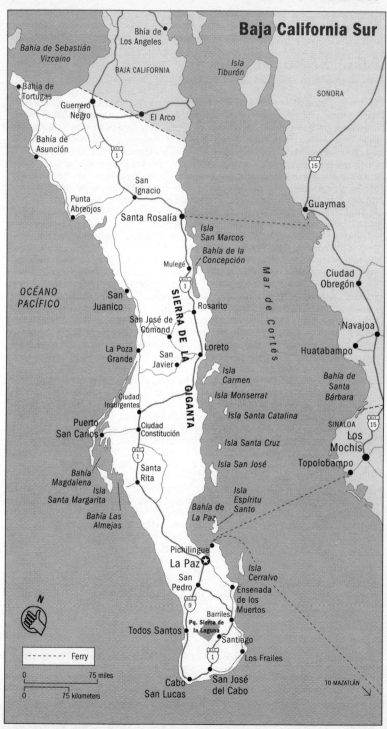

Baja California Sur

Bhía de
Los Angeles

Bahía de Sebastián
Vizcaíno

BAJA CALIFORNIA

Isla
Tiburón

SONORA

Bahía de
Tortugas

Guerrero
Negro

El Arco

Bahía de
Asunción

1

San
Ignacio

Santa Rosalía

Punta
Abreojos

Isla
San Marcos

Bahía de la
Concepción

Mulegé

15

Guaymas

OCÉANO
PACÍFICO

San
Juanico

SIERRA DE LA GIGANTA

1

Rosarito

Ciudad
Obregón

San José de
Comond

Navajoa

La Poza
Grande

San
Javier

Loreto

Huatabampo

Mar de Cortés

Isla
Carmen

Bahía de
Santa
Bárbara

Ciudad
Insurgentes

Isla Monserrat

Puerto
San Carlos

Ciudad
Constitución

Isla Santa Catalina

SINALOA

15

1

Isla Santa Cruz

Los
Mochis

Bahía
Magdalena

Santa
Rita

Isla San José

Topolobampo

Isla
Santa Margarita

Bahía Las
Almejas

Isla
Espíritu
Santo

Bahía
de La Paz

Pichilingue

La Paz

Isla
Cerralvo

San
Pedro

Ensenada
de los
Muertos

9

Barriles

Pq. Sierra de
la Laguna

Todos Santos

Santiago

1

Los Frailes

Cabo
San Lucas

San José
del Cabo

TO MAZATLÁN

N

- - - - Ferry

0   75 miles

0   75 kilometers

BAJA CALIFORNIA

BAJA CALIFORNIA SUR

GUERRERO NEGRO

Twenty degrees cooler than the bleak Desierto de Vizcaíno to the southeast, Guerrero Negro (pop. 10,000), though dusty and painfully industrial, might earn a soft spot in the hearts of heat-weary northbound travelers. There's always a cool breeze here, and even late summer nights can be positively chilly. The town is named for a whaling boat, "Black Warrior," that wrecked in the town's lagoon in 1858. In Guerrero Negro, salt is God, king, and country. So saline-ridden is Guerrero Negro that even a deep breath of the town's air can send the hypochondriac's blood pressure soaring. The salt plant is now the **world's largest,** dominating the town's economy and attracting job-seekers from throughout the region. Although the locals are friendly and the cool breezes cathartic, Guerrero Negro's most attractive feature is its **gas station,** a beautiful **PEMEX** wonder. Be prepared for lots of wind and gray—Guerrero Negro resembles a beach town without the beach. Fill up that tank, and burn, baby, burn.

Guerrero Negro sprawls along a 3km strip west of the Transpeninsular highway. Its two main roads, **Blvd. Zapata** and **Av. Baja California,** are home to basically all of the town's industrial and commercial centers. The **ABC Autotransportes de Baja California** terminal (tel. 7 06 11) is one of the first buildings from the highway on Blvd. Zapata as you come from the highway. ABC sends **buses** north (6 per day 7:30pm-8:30am) to El Rosario (6hr., 122 pesos), Ensenada (10hr., 218 pesos), Lázaro Cárdenas (7hr., 142 pesos), Punta Prieta (4hr., 55 pesos), Rosarito (2hr., 37 pesos), San Quintín (8hr., 149 pesos), and Tijuana (11hr., 264 pesos); and south to La Paz (11hr., 5 per day 4:30pm-8:30am, 288 pesos), Mulegé (4hr., 5 per day, 115 pesos), Santa Rosalía (3hr., 7 per day, 86 pesos), and points in between. Yellow **minivans** run up and down the Transpeninsular highway (every 15min. 7am-10pm, 6 pesos). Change money at **Banamex** (tel. 7 05 55), on Av. Baja California in front of the plant (bank open M-F 9:30am-3pm). Travelers heading south should change currency here, as 24-hour **ATMs** and bank services become sparse. The **police** (tel. 7 00 22) are in the Delegación Municipal, a few hundred meters before the salt plant, on the left. The **post office** (tel. 7 03 44) is off Av. Baja California. Go two blocks past the church, and turn left onto a dirt road just before the basketball courts (open M-F 8am-3pm). The **Postal code:** 23940. The **Phone code:** 115.

The best bargain in town is the **Motel Las Dunas** (tel. 7 00 55) on Zapata, below the water tank and a short walk north from the bus station. Immaculate rooms with large showers are as worthy as those at more expensive spots, and the extremely courteous staff helps in every way possible. (Singles 66 pesos; doubles 77 pesos; triples 81 pesos; key deposit 10 pesos.) Many aspects of Guerrero Negro are a little hard to swallow, and the city's food is no exception. If you like entertainment while you eat, try **Cocina Económica Letty,** on the south side of Zapata before the water tower. Diners feast on the scrumptious *bistec milanesa* (35 pesos) as they gaze at the mounted TV. (Open M-Sa 8am-8pm.)

SAN IGNACIO

More than any other stop on the arid Baja Peninsula, San Ignacio (pop. 2000) seems like a tropical oasis. From a distance, the town appears to be a cruel illusion, a mirage of the mind—leafy date palms, flowering bushes, and broad swaths of green appear magically in the middle of the blistering desert. Pinch yourself—you're not dreaming. The area around San Ignacio is blessed with the most plentiful underground freshwater supply in all of Baja California Sur; of late, it's been dammed up to form a murky lake used for swimming and irrigating local orchards.

Although it's hot during summer days, San Ignacio earns points for just about everything else. Locals are extremely amiable, and the whole town is one big, happy, close-knit family that is hospitable to the few gringos who disrupt the solitude. San Ignacio's intimate atmosphere, nighttime starscapes, and historic mission overlooking the *zócalo* are just a few of the reasons why so many of the pleasure-seekers who set eyes on the town end up settling down here. San Ignacio is also a prime point of departure for cave painting and whale-watching tours.

⁊ ORIENTATION AND PRACTICAL INFORMATION. A winding road canopied by swaying date palms leads south from the Transpeninsular Highway. and becomes **Juan Bautista Luyando** at the *zócalo*. Within minutes of pulling in, you'll know tiny San Ignacio better than your hometown. Life revolves around the wonderfully tranquil *zócalo*, which is delineated by Juan Bautista Luyando and the mission to the north, **Morelos** to the south, **Juárez** to the east, and **Hidalgo** to the west. Locals are more than happy to give directions.

Buses pick up passengers at the sheltered bench across from the PEMEX, 2km from San Ignacio on the Transpeninsular Highway. *De paso* buses head north at 7pm to: **Guerrero Negro** (3hr., 78 pesos); **Ensenada** (13hr., 312 pesos); and **Tijuana** (14hr., 372 pesos); buses also head south at 10am and 6pm for: **La Paz** (8hr., 278 pesos); **Mulegé** and **Rosarita** (1hr., 43 pesos); and **Loreto** (1hr., 124 pesos) all via **Santa Rosalía.** There's no official **tourist office** in town, but to hear informative chatter about San Ignacio, visit **Jorge Antonio Fischer** (tel. 4 01 50 or 4 01 90), the owner of the mini-mart next to Restaurant Chalita on Hidalgo (open M-Sa 7am-6pm, Su 7am-1pm). He also leads whale expeditions and tours to the cave paintings. Nuevos Almacenes Meza S.A., a good-sized **grocery store** (tel. 4 01 22), is on the corner of Juárez and Luyando, facing the *zócalo* (open M-Sa 8am-noon and 2-7pm, Su 8am-noon). The **police** are in the Delegación Municipal on Ocampo and Zaragoza (open daily 8am-3pm). The **Boticas Ceseña pharmacy,** Madero 24A (tel. 4 00 76, after hours 4 00 75), parallel to and east of Juárez and Hidalgo, is unmarked (open daily 8:30am-1pm and 2-9pm; available 24hr. in case of emergency). To reach the **Centro de Salud,** walk away from the mission down Hidalgo and turn right on Cipris, a tiny dirt road; when you reach the auto parts shop, turn right and take a quick left just after the tin-roofed warehouse. Continue straight for two blocks; it's the white building with the white flag on the right-hand side. (Open M-Sa 8am-4pm.) If you have a **medical emergency** after hours, call **Lourdes Rouzaud** (tel. 4 00 81) the local nurse. **Post office:** in the gray stone building on Juárez next to the *zócalo* (open M-F 8am-3pm). **Postal code:** 23930. **LADATEL:** at all four corners of the *zócalo* and in front of Restaurant-Bar Rene's. You can place calls and send **faxes** at a pricier **caseta,** Hidalgo 24 (tel. 4 02 50; open M-Sa 8am-1pm and 3-6pm). **Phone code:** 115.

⌘ ACCOMMODATIONS. San Ignacio has few hotels, and they don't come cheap. Make reservations or call early if you're going to be in town during *Semana Santa* or the week-long celebration of El Día de San Ignacio (July 30). The town is converted into a giant *fiesta* complete with horse races, dances, fireworks, and lots of fun. The family living in **Restaurant Chalita,** Hidalgo 9 (tel. 4 00 82), rents bedrooms that ooze with local culture and have fans and black and white TVs (singles 130 pesos). **Hotel Posada** (tel. 4 03 13), on Ocampo and Independencia, a 3-min. walk down Ciprés from Hidalgo, has remarkably clean rooms with standing fans, private baths, and a family-type atmosphere (singles and doubles US$20). **El Padrino RV Park** (tel. 4 00 89) is 500m from the *zócalo* on the road connecting San Ignacio to the highway. A full trailer hookup costs US$10; a hookup without electricity runs US$7. Motorcycles cost US$3 to park. El Padrino also offers four new rooms with private baths and A/C. (Singles US$10; doubles US$20.)

◖ FOOD. There are few places to dine in San Ignacio, but not to worry. All of the restaurants are within a stone's throw of the *zócalo* and serve delectable and affordable cuisine. Seafood dishes receive top billing on restaurant menus. Eat outdoors under the starry sky at **Restaurant-Bar Rene's** (tel. 4 02 56), just outside the *zócalo*, off Hidalgo. If you'd rather eat under a roof, head into their round stone-floored thatched hut. Inside you can enjoy your meal under the cooling breeze of a ceiling fan and listen to the soothing sounds of the 80s while staring out at the small adjoining pond. Wash down the house special, the *calamar empanizado* (breaded squid, 50 pesos) with a beer (10 pesos), or try the delicious *filete pescado* for 50 pesos. (Open daily 7am-10pm.) **Restaurant Chalita,** Hidalgo 9 (tel. 4 00 82), is housed in an old-fashioned Mexican kitchen. Listen to the caged birds sing, and find salvation in a warm plate of *pescado al mojo de ajo* (40 pesos), enchiladas (30 pesos), or *chiles rellenos* (35 pesos; open daily 7:30am-10pm). **Flojo's Restaurant/Bar** (tel. 4 00 89) is part of El Padrino RV Park (see above) and a 5-min. walk from town. You'll be full for days when you overstuff yourself with three chicken burritos with rice and beans (30 pesos) or breaded Italian meat (45 pesos). Open daily 7am-10:30pm.

■ **SIGHTS.** A colonial colossus towering over wild, leafy vegetation, the **Mission of San Ignacio,** on the northern side of the *zócalo*, was founded in 1728 by Jesuit missionary Juan Bautista Luyando. The construction of the mission proved a logistical nightmare: wood had to be hauled in from the Guadalupe mission in the Sierras, furniture was brought from Mulegé after a scorching four-day mule ride through the unpaved desert, and the paintings were carried by boat from the mainland. Its walls, over 1m thick, are made from blocks of volcanic rock. Despite the problems its construction imposed, the mission is a beautiful achievement—magnificent on the outside, cool on the inside, and heavenly at night when illuminated by outdoor spotlights. The majestic stone exterior has aged well; it is one of the most fantastic of the Baja missions. When you are inside, look up to see a flying gold angel suspended in the dome. From halfway between the *zócalo* and Hotel Posada, on Cipris, the evening view of the mission poking above palms and huts is particularly striking. The newly opened **Mission Museum** (tel. 4 02 22), on Luyando, 30m west of the mission, tells the story of the nearby cave paintings and even has its own huge faux cave painting (open Tu-Sa 8am-3pm; free).

The main tourist draw near San Ignacio is the **painted caves,** 75km away in the **Sierra de San Francisco.** Five hundred paintings, probably more than 10,000 years old, reside within a 12 sq. km area. **Oscar Fischer** of Hotel Posada and his son Dagoberto (tel. 4 03 13 or 4 01 00) offer various tours to the caves. During the tourist season, US$25 gets you a nine-hour trip to one cave and two petroglyphic zones. The tour leaves at around 8am and makes as many stops as requested. A two-day tour will take you to the impressive **La Pintada** and the minor **El Ratón** caves. For US$15 per person per day you'll get transportation, a guide, and a mule. Some adventurous travelers make the trip between caves on foot (about 8km each way), saving all mule costs but leaving their bodies worn. US$80 plus the cost of a tent and a mule gets you the grandest tour of all: a three-day, eight-cave extravaganza that will show you more indigenous paintings than you probably ever wanted to see—all but the most resilient travelers will feel battle-worn. All trips must be cleared with the Mexican government, so call well in advance. The managers also run trips to the Laguna San Ignacio to spy on **gray whales.** The trips leave before 7am and cost US$55 per person. Note that prices for all tours (caves and whales) assume groups of six or more; smaller parties can expect to pay more. Tours of the painted caves and whale watching expeditions are also led by the owner of **Flojos Restaurant/Bar** and **El Padrino RV Park** (tel. 4 00 89).

SANTA ROSALÍA

Santa Rosalía is not only a convenient transportation hub for buses and ferries but also the heir to a rich and colorful history. After enormously rich copper ore was discovered here in 1868, a French-owned mining company settled Santa Rosalía. The French built the town on the sides of the mountain in an orderly fashion according to rank; the wealthier, higher-ranking officials lived at the top of the mountain, overlooking the "lower" classes below. Santa Rosalía is not nearly as picturesque as its history might suggest—today, mountains of abandoned machinery and railroad cars bristle with rust, returning their metals to the ground. Even the public beaches are somewhat dirty and deserted. If you're planning to visit, keep in mind that the town is unbearably hot and humid in the summer and that the entire town shuts down by 9pm. Still, Santa Rosalía isn't a bad stopover—you'll get a chance to see jarring European architecture in the middle of Baja; the town's cast-iron church, Iglesia Santa Bárbara, was designed by Gustave Eiffel (of Tower fame). The town is often used as a departure or arrival point for the cross-Gulf ferry to and from Guaymas, Sonora.

⚡ ORIENTATION AND PRACTICAL INFORMATION. To get from the **ferry** to **Obregón,** Santa Rosalía's main strip, turn right as you leave the ferry compound (from the bus station, take a left); walk along the water toward town until you come to the old train engine in front of the town's two main streets—the one on the left is Constitución, and the one on the right is Obregón.

Most **buses** depart from the ABC station (tel. 2 01 50), across the street from the ferry office. Buses travel north (7 per day, 3pm-5am) to: **San Ignacio** (1hr., 43 pesos); **Guerrero Negro** (3½hr., 102 pesos); **Punta Prieta** (7hr., 145 pesos); **El Rosario** (9hr., 230 pesos); **San Quintín** (9½hr., 249 pesos); **Ensenada** (13½hr., 340 pesos); **Tijuana** (15hr., 390 pesos); and **Mexicali** (18½hr., 510 pesos). Heading south (7 per day 9:30am-3am), all buses go to: **Mulegé** (1hr., 35 pesos); **Loreto** (3hr., 91 pesos); **El Insurgentes** (4hr., 137 pesos), **Ciudad Constitución** (4½hr., 151 pesos); and **La Paz** (7hr., 213 pesos). From Santa Rosalía, you can catch the **ferry** connecting Baja to Guaymas on the mainland (8hr.; Tu and F 11pm; *salón* 140 pesos, *turista* 278 pesos, *cabina* 415 pesos, *especial* 552 pesos). The boat leaves from the modern, blue and green **Sematur** office (tel. 2 00 13) on Rte. 1 (the Transpeninsular Highway.), just south of town. To reach the docks, catch a bus from the **ABC Autotransportes** station, about 200m south of the ferry. Those with **cars** must purchase tickets in advance and show a tourist card, registration, and proof of their Mexican insurance (cars 1578 pesos, motorcycles 398 pesos; office open M, W-Th, and Sa 8am-3pm, Tu and F 8am-1pm and 3-6pm). Departure days and times, prices, and office hours are constantly in flux, so be sure to call the office or talk to a travel agent to confirm the schedule.

Banamex (tel. 2 01 60), on Obregón and Calle 5, changes traveler's checks, has a 24-hour **ATM** (open M-F 9am-3pm). **Farmacia Central** (tel. 2 20 70), on Obregón at Plaza, is owned by the English-speaking Dr. Chang Tam (open M-Sa 9am-10pm, Su 9am-1pm). **Centro de Salud Hospital:** (tel. 2 21 80) at Juan Michel Costeau. **Red Cross:** (tel. 2 06 40) on Calle 2 and Carranza, right off of Constitución (Nelson Romero speaks English; open 24hr). **Post office:** (tel. 2 03 45) on Constitución, between Calle 2 and Altamirano (open M-F 8am-3pm). **Postal code:** 23920. **Phone code:** 115.

⚑⚑ ACCOMMODATIONS AND FOOD. If you're going to stay in sweltering Santa Rosalía, consider popping the few extra pesos for A/C. Constitución is lined with cheap and good *taquerías* and several *comida corrida* joints. The budget standout is **Hotel Olvera,** Calle Plaza 14 (tel. 2 00 57 or 2 02 67), about three blocks from the shore on Constitución, just right of the foot bridge. Enjoy spacious bathrooms, large double beds, and free lukewarm *agua purificada.* (Singles 100 pesos, with A/C 130 pesos; doubles 130 pesos, with A/C 150 pesos.) Perhaps the cheapest room in town can be found at the **Hotel Playa,** on Calle 1 off Constitución behind the Hotel Olvera. There are only 12 rooms, and though they're rundown, the mattresses are soft. (Singles 50 pesos; doubles 80 pesos; triples 110 pesos.) **RV Park Las Palmas,** 3.5km south of town, has 32 spots with full hookups, a laundromat, and a restaurant (2 people US$10, additional person US$2). Santa Rosalía's best-known establishment, **El Boleo Bakery** (tel. 2 03 10), on Obregón at Calle 4, renowned for its French architecture, deserves a visit for its excellent baked goods as well. Fabulous French bread (1.60 pesos), *pan dulce* (1.80 pesos), and turnovers (2.60 pesos) thrill customers. (Open M-Sa 8am-9pm.)

🔆 **SIGHTS.** Travelers looking for fun in the sun and abundant water sports would do better to make tracks south for the heavenly beaches in Bahía de la Concepción. The wooden houses, general stores, and saloons along Santa Rosalía's streets recall the town's mining-boom days. Startling specimens of 19th-century French architecture include the long and many-windowed **Palacio Municipal,** the **Hotel Francés,** and **El Boleo Bakery** with their pure colors, simplicity of form, and modern use of glass and steel. The most serendipitous of artifacts is the pre-fabricated, white, cast-iron **Iglesia Santa Bárbara,** at Obregón and Calle 1. Designed by Gustave Eiffel for a mission in Africa, the church was never picked up by the company that had commissioned it. French mining *concessionaires* spotted the church at the 1889 Exhibition Universale de Paris and decided Santa Rosalía couldn't do without it. Observers either love it or hate it; the outside panels look like they fell off an industrial washing machine. The purple stained-glass windows are "interesting." For a great view of the church and all of Santa Rosalía, climb the decrepit stone steps just off the beginning of Obregón. The steps lead to the new **Museo Histórico Minero de Santa Rosalía.** The museum, housed in the old office building of the Compagnie du Boleo, exhibits journals, photographs, and mining equipment. (Open M-F 9am-3pm; 10 pesos.)

MULEGÉ

Although many are inclined to keep driving when they reach Mulegé, a small town dominated by desert, palm trees, and a winding river, it actually has much more to offer visitors than may meet the eye. Mulegé is one of Baja's best-kept secrets, bursting with good food and warmhearted people. Best of all, Mulegé, located 136km north of Loreto and 300km south of Guerrero Negro, is the ideal place from which to explore the glistening beaches and storybook-blue sea of **Bahía de la Concepción** to the south (see p. 170). By day, most of the town's visitors—and many of its expats—abandon the little parcel of preciousness that is Mulegé proper and head for the heavenly sands of the Bahía.

🚩 **ORIENTATION AND PRACTICAL INFORMATION.** Soon after bearing left off the Transpeninsular Highway. the road into Mulegé forks. To the left is **Moctezuma;** to the right is **Martínez.** Both are soon crossed by **Zaragoza;** take a right onto Zaragoza to get to the *zócalo,* which is one block away. **Madero** heads east from the *zócalo* (away from the highway) and, after following the Mulegé River for about 3km, hits the water at the town beach, **Playa de Mulegé.** You can pick up a sketch map of the town from Cortez Explorers on Moctezuma (see p. 170).

    El Candil restaurant serves as the unofficial **tourist office.** English-speaking **Kerry "El Vikingo" Otterstrom** has written and published a 160-page book on Mulegé (50 pesos). Look for him at El Candil after 2:30pm. The **Hotel Las Casitas,** Madero 50 (tel. 3 00 19), also has tourist info. Ask for Javier—besides leading tours, he also has info on beaches, camping, and fishing. The **"Igriega" bus station** is simply a sheltered blue bench at the turn-off to Mulegé from Rte. 1. All buses are *de paso,* a phrase that might roughly be translated as "inevitably arrives late and full." Northbound buses stop by daily at 4:30, 10:30am, 4, 7, and 10:30pm and head to: **Mexicali** (19½hr., 529 pesos) via **Santa Rosalía** (1hr., 40 pesos); **San Ignacio** (2hr., 61 pesos); **Rosarito** (6hr., 157 pesos); **Punta Prieta** (8hr., 294 pesos); **El Rosario** (10hr., 258 pesos); **San Quintín** (10½hr., 290 pesos); **Lázaro Cárdenas** (11hr., 283 pesos); **Ensenada** (14½hr., 375 pesos); **Tijuana** (16hr., 432 pesos); and **Tecate** (17hr., 457 pesos). Southbound buses stop by daily at 10 and 11:30am and go to: **La Paz** (6hr., 198 pesos) via **Loreto** (2hr., 60 pesos); **Insurgentes** (3hr., 66 pesos); and **Ciudad Constitución** (3½hr., 85 pesos). **Police:** (tel. 3 00 49) in the old Pinatel de Educacion building on Martínez, across from the PEMEX station. **Red Cross:** (tel. 3 01 10) on Madero, on the Transpeninsular Highway. 20m past the turn-off into town. **Farmacia Moderna:** (tel. 3 00 42) at Madero on the plaza (open daily 8am-1pm and 4-10pm). **Centro de Salud B (ISSTE),** Madero 28 (tel. 3 02 98), treats **medical emergen-**

cies (open 8am-2:30pm). **Post office:** (tel. 3 02 05) in the same building with the police (see above; open M-F 8am-3pm). **Postal code:** 23900. **Minisúper Padilla** (tel./ fax 3 01 90), on Zaragoza at Martínez, one block north of plaza, has many **phones** for international calls and now offers fax service. **Phone code:** 115.

⌐ ACCOMMODATIONS. Although Mulegé has plenty of cheap rooms, those with sleeping bags can find the best deals on the shore. Unfortunately, all accommodations in town are far from the beaches. The most economical hotels crowd the center of town. **Casa de Huéspedes Manuelita** (tel. 3 01 75), on Moctezuma, next to Los Equipales, around the corner from Zaragoza, has clean rooms with soft beds, table fans, and private showers. Campers who simply need to use the bathroom and shower pay 15 pesos. (Singles 80 pesos; doubles 120 pesos; all prices negotiable.) The brand new **Hotel Mulegé** (tel. 3 00 90) is right near the bus station, on your left as you head into town. Live in luxury—all of the big, white-tiled rooms with spotless bathrooms come with TVs and remote controls. (Singles 205 pesos; doubles 255 pesos.) **Orchard RV Park** and **María Isabel RV Park,** both just south of town and accessible from the Transpeninsular Highway., are on the Mulegé River (US$16 per night; tents US$4; each additional person US$1.50).

◖ FOOD. For something informal and delicious, try **Taquería Doney,** known more commonly as **Doney's,** near the bus station, across the street from Hotel Mulegé. Locals cram both the indoor tables and outdoor stools, wolfing down delicious tacos (8 pesos) or huge steak *tortas* (17 pesos; open daily 8am-10pm). **Restaurant La Almeja,** at the end of Madero near the lighthouse, about 3km from the center of town, is right on the beach. It offers a great view and outstanding seafood, including the tasty and filling *sopa de siete mares* ("soup of the 7 seas", which includes just about every creature that ever swam in the sea; 60 pesos; open daily 8am-11pm). The newly renovated **El Candil Restaurant,** on Zaragoza near Martínez north of the plaza, serves an enormous Mexican combination platter with rice, beans, *chiles rellenos*, and tacos (50 pesos) and an excellent fish fillet (35 pesos). (Open daily 7am-10pm.)

◢ SIGHTS AND SAND. Mulegé's lovely **Misión Santa Rosalía de Mulegé** sits on a hill to the west. To get there, walk down Zaragoza away from the *zócalo*, go under the bridge, and turn right on the shaded lane with all the palms. Although not quite as impressive as the Mission of San Ignacio, the church's massive stone facade is imposing and its interior is beautiful and quiet. The small hill behind the missionary affords a great view of the whole town, river, and palms. Despite the fact that the paths are not lit at night, the mission is a perfect place for a meditative stroll; walk where you will be immediately visible to cars. Mass is still held every Sunday at the mission.

Over 700 14,000-year-old pre-Hispanic cave paintings are located at **La Trinidad** and the **Cuevas de San Borjita.** Salvador Castro of **Castro Tours** at Hotel Las Casitas (tel. 3 02 32) leads hiking tours to La Trinidad that include a 200m swim in a narrow canyon to San Borjita (US$55 per person). During the high season, Salvador recommends making tour reservations a week in advance but you can probably drop into a group on short notice. If you plan to bring a camera you must have a permit issued at the INAH office; Salvador will direct you.

Although they are conveniently located—3km from the center of town— Mulegé's two beaches can't hold a candle to those 18km south in Bahía de la Concepción (see p. 170). **El Faro** is at the end of Madero, which becomes a dirt road long before you reach the beach. Alternatively, reach the **public beach** by following the Mulegé River to the Sea of Cortés, where it drains. For a more isolated beach, walk to the PEMEX station about 4km south on the highway, continue about 20m south, and take the dirt road leading to the left until you reach a lonely beach with sand dunes and desert hills overlooking somewhat rocky sand. Locals say this area is quite safe, but watch out for **jellyfish,** especially in June and July. **Scorpions** sometimes stalk unsuspecting tourists in Mulegé; they like warm, moist places (like shoes), so look before you slip your feet in. Scorpions will attack even if unprovoked; if you cross paths with one, give it plenty of room.

Mulegé's abundance of sea life makes for great **sport-fishing** and **clamming**. Alejandro Bukobek leads tours to do both and can usually be found at the **Hotel Serenidad** (tel. 3 03 11 or 3 01 11) on the Mulegé River. Fishing usually runs US$100 for three to four people. He also offers kayak trips which include lunch for US$40 per person. If you just want to look at all the marine life, head over to **Cortez Explorers**, Moctezuma 75A (tel. 3 05 00), just past the entrance to town. This newly opened dive shop is the only one in Mulegé. They **rent snorkel and scuba equipment**, lead boat excursions into Bahía de la Concepción, and rent mountain bikes (US$15 per day, US$10 per day for 4 days). If you already know how to scuba dive and brought your own equipment, try the five-hour trip (US$40, 2 person min.); otherwise, an instruction course helps you get your feet wet (US$70). They also organize five-hour **snorkeling** excursions (US$25 including equipment, 2 person min.). All excursions leave at 8am. Make reservations at least one day in advance. (Open M-Sa 10am-1pm and 4-7pm.) The best snorkeling is at nearby **Islas Pitahaya, San Ramón, Liebre, Blanca, Coyote,** and **Guapa.** Ask at the tourist office or the dive shop for maps.

The **Museo Comunitario Mulegé** just opened and is really worth a visit. To get to the museum, walk down Moctezuma away from the highway until you reach a steep set of stairs on your left. The museum is housed in the town's old prison, once known as the "prison without doors." Each day, the inmates were allowed to leave their cells to work in town on the condition that they would return at the end of the work day. The exhibit includes artifacts of the Cohimi and displays of local marine life. (Open M-Sa 9am-1pm; 10 pesos.)

BAHÍA DE LA CONCEPCIÓN

Heaven on earth may just be the 48km arc of rocky outcrops, shimmering beaches, and bright-blue sea known as the Bahía de la Concepción. Cactus-studded hills and stark cliffs drop straight down to white sand, translucent waters, and coves, creating the most breathtaking beaches in Baja. Grown sport-fishers and shell collectors weep for joy at the variety and sheer size of the specimens caught here, and divers fall under the spell of underwater sights. As if this isn't enough, the Bahía remains relatively quiet and virginal, still untouched by running water and permanent electricity. While the Bahía is generally blissfully noiseless, Christmas holidays and *Semana Santa* bring strewn beer cans and noisy rows of RVs stretching from the highway to the beach. Although the beer cans and bottles have accumulated into unsightly meter-high mounds of refuse along the access roads to some of the beaches, the *playas* are still some of the most beautiful in all Baja. During the high season, come early to find some peace and a place to put your towel. At other times, Bahía de la Concepción might just be Mexico's most secret treasure.

To get there from Mulegé (or from anywhere north of Mulegé), check at the bus station for the next *de paso* bus south (10:30, 11am and noon). Wait to pay the fare until the bus arrives; check with the bus driver to ensure that he will stop at one of the beaches. But don't count on a bus to take you back; service to the beaches is infrequent, and bus drivers may not stop along the busy highway. Beach-hoppers might consider renting a car for the day, as access to and from the beaches farther south is limited. Many nomadic travelers hitch (known in Americanized Spanish as "*pedir* ride") from Mulegé to the beaches, catching one of the RVs or produce trucks barreling down the Transpeninsular Highway toward the bay. While *Let's Go* does not recommend hitching, those who hitch are most successful getting rides right across the island from the bus stop, and telling the driver exactly where they are heading. Hitching back to Mulegé is reputedly even easier, since many people go in that direction.

◙ THE BEACHES

Illuminated by millions of stars, the beaches of Bahía are otherworldly after dark. Only come at night if you plan to camp out or if you're equipped with wheels; it's impossible to hitch back, no buses run, and oncoming cars spell disaster for would-be pedestrians.

PLAYA PUNTA ARENA. Sixteen kilometers south of Mulegé, Punta Arena is far enough from the road that the roar of the waves drowns out the noise from muffler-less trucks. From the highway, travel 2km down a rocky dirt road. Bear right at all forks in the road. A dozen palm-frond *palapas* line the beach with sand-flush toilets in back (cabanas US$6; parking US$4). The waters near the shore are great for **clam fishing,** but beware of the manta rays that lurk under the water's surface. If you walk down the dirt road to Playa Punta Arena, take a left instead of a right at the 2nd fork, and you'll end up at **Playa San Pedro** and **Los Naranjos RV Park,** where payments for your space may be made with freshly caught fish.

PLAYA SANTISPAC. The most popular beach on the Bahía, Santispac is connected to Playa Punta Arena by a dirt path that winds through mountains for a grueling 1km. The beach is most easily accessible by the highway (about 20km south of Mulegé), where it is visible and clearly marked. During the winter, Santispac is the liveliest beach on the bay. In the summer, however, the sands are sparsely populated by laid-back sunbathers. If you drive in a vehicle, it will cost you 60 pesos to park it on the beach for the day. On Playa Santispac, **Las Palapas Trailer Park** rents *palapas* and tent space (both US$6 per night; use of bathrooms and showers US$1). **Ray's Place,** a *palapa*-roofed place for eats with a TV-equiped bar, draws a distinctly American crowd for good reason. Try their "three fish tacos and a beer" for 50 pesos and hang with Cuban-born Ray himself and the local ratpack of ex-pats who frequently drop by. (Open daily 2-10pm; closed Su in summer, M in winter.) At **Ana's Restaurant,** guests enjoy fried fish (30 pesos) and shrimp omelettes (32 pesos) while marveling at the exotic shells on sale to the right of the counter (2 for US$1). The restaurant doubles as a bakery and sells cakes, huge loaves of bread (13 pesos), and *pan dulce* (15 pesos; open daily in summer 7am-7pm, high season 7am-10pm). Watch out in the water—there are mating sting rays in the spring and manta rays in the summer. In case of a sting, some locals recommend treating the affected area with hot, salty water. Such a treatment can be found in the warm, bubbly (though somewhat dirty) **hot springs** on the south end of Playa Santispac.

PLAYA LA POSADA. La Posada is the next accessible beach south of Santispac which looks essentially like a minuscule RV village complete with its own tennis court. **Eco-Mundo** (tel. 3 04 09) on the south side of the beach, can be reached from the highway a few hundred meters beyond the entrance for La Posada and rents *palapas* for US$12 per night that come with two hammocks and solar powered fans. This eco-friendly center also rents kayaks (US$25) and mask-snorkel-fin sets (US$5). Eco-Mundo has a *palapa*-style restaurant right on the beach that serves up smoothies (20 pesos) or veggie omelettes (28 pesos) with most of the veggies grown on the premise.

PLAYA ESCONDIDA. "Hidden Beach" is at the end of a 500m dirt path winding through the valley between two hills; look for a white sign with black letters at the southern end of Playa Concepción. True to its name, the short, facility-less Escondida is refreshingly secluded from civilization affording great views and stunning shoreline reef snorkeling. There is a good snorkeling island about a 30-min. swim away. **Playa Los Cocos** is identified by its white garbage cans adorned with palm trees. Access to the beaches is free, but use of the facilities is not. The cabanas that line the shallow beach can be rented for approx. US$4. A grove of trees and shrubs separates the strip from the highway. At **Playa El Burro,** you can rent a *palapa* next to hordes of RVs for US$5 per day.

PLAYA EL COYOTE. Coyote is perhaps the most populated beach after Santispac. Shelter and camping space can be rented for reasonable, completely negotiable prices; the better sands and *palapas* are down on the southern end. Down the road 15km is the exquisite (and even less populated) **Playa Resquesón** and its neighbor to the south, **La Perlita,** which also has a few *palapas* (US$4 per night). Park your car and rent a *palapa* for the day for US$4, or just park and enjoy the beach for US$3. While there, visitors can check out the natural rock formations on the mountain to the southwest that were outlined in cal (the material chalk is made from) by students from the University of Tijuana. Even farther south, two more spots—**La Ramada** and **Santa Bárbara**—are currently undergoing development and are closed to the public, though *palapas* have been built. Another nearly deserted stretch of sand separating Mulegé from Loreto is the last before Rte. 1 climbs into the mountains. All of these beaches are marked from the highway.

LORETO

Founded by Jesuit missionaries in 1697, Loreto (pop. 12,000) was the first capital of the Californias, and its mission was the first in a chain of Jesuit missions along the west coast of Baja. Although the town was wiped out by a freakish combination of hurricanes and earthquakes in the late 19th century, Loreto's loveliness didn't languor for long. The Jesuits were no aesthetic dummies—300 years after settlement, the town is quiet, restful, and a great place to adore nature. Sandwiched between the calm blue waters of the Sea of Cortés and golden mountains, Loreto remains an unassuming, simple town with a long, tranquil *malecón* (pier, beachside road) shaded by rows of palm trees and sprinkled with stone benches overlooking the rocky shore. You won't find any raucous dance clubs here; the few visitors are mostly laid-back *norteamericanos* who come to fish and enjoy Happy Hour at small local bars.

◪ ORIENTATION AND PRACTICAL INFORMATION. The town is easy to navigate; almost everything of interest is on the main road. The principal street in Loreto is **Salvatierra,** which connects the Carretera Transpeninsular to the Gulf. When Salvatierra becomes a pedestrian walkway, **Hidalgo** roughly becomes its continuation. **Allende, León,** and **Ayuntamiento** run north-south (roughly) and intersect Salvatierra. **Independencia** intersects Salvatierra just as it turns into Hidalgo, and **Madero** intersects Hidalgo closer to the water. **Malecón,** which leads north to the beach and outlines the entire width of the city at the coast, runs perpendicular to Hidalgo where Hidalgo ends. **Juárez** runs parallel to, and north of, Salvatierra and Hidalgo. The **zócalo** is at Hidalgo and Madero. To get to the *centro* from the **bus station,** walk down Salvatierra toward the distant cathedral (10min.) or indulge in a taxi (18 pesos).

Aguila **buses** stop by Terminal E (tel. 5 07 67), on Salvatierra two blocks west of Allende near the highway, about 2km from Madero (ticket office open daily 7-10:30am, noon-5pm, and 6:30pm-1am). Northbound buses leave at 2:30am, 3, 9, and 11pm, heading to **San Ignacio** (5hr., 143 pesos) and **Guerrero Negro** (7½hr., 200 pesos); **Mulegé** (2½hr., 2 and 5pm, 60 pesos) and **Santa Rosalía** (4hr., 2 and 5pm, 77 pesos). Southbound buses go to: **La Paz** (5hr.; 2, 8am, 1, 2:30, and 11pm; 137 pesos). **Budget** (tel. 5 10 90) rents cars for US$55 per day including insurance, tax, and unlimited mileage (open M-Sa 8am-1pm and 3-6pm, Su 8am-1pm). The Palacio Municipal, on Madero, between Salvatierra and Comercio, facing the *zócalo*, houses the air-conditioned **tourist info center** (tel. 5 04 11); English is spoken (open M-F 8am-3pm). The only bank in town, **Bancomer** (tel. 5 00 14 or 5 09 10), on Madero across from the *zócalo*, exchanges dollars (open M-F 8:30am-2:30pm). **Supermarket El Pescador:** (tel. 5 00 60) on Salvatierra and Independencia (open daily 7:30am-10:30pm). **Red Cross:** (tel. 5 11 11) on Salvatierra at Deportiva (open daily 9am-1pm and 3-8pm). **Farmacia Flores** (tel. 5 03 21), on Salvatierra, between Ayuntamiento and Independencia (open daily 8am-10pm). **Hospital: Centro de Salud** (tel. 5 00 39) is on Salvatierra, one block from the bus terminal (open 24hr.). **Medical emergencies:** dial 5 03 97 or 5 09 06 (to reach Red Cross volunteers). **Post office:** (tel. 5 06 47) on Salvatierra and Deportiva, near the bus station, behind the Red Cross (open M-F 8am-3pm). **Postal code:** 23880. **Fax:** Telecom (tel. 5 03 87), next to the post office (open M-F 8am-2pm, Sa 8-11am). **Internet access: The Internet Café** (tel. 5 12 39) on Salvatierra near Ayuntamiento has two computers available for 30 pesos per half hour. (Open M-F 9am-5pm, Sa 10am-2pm). **LADATEL:** along Salvatierra. **Phone code:** 113.

▛▟ ACCOMMODATIONS AND FOOD. Motel Salvatierra (tel. 5 00 21), on Salvatierra, across from the PEMEX and close to the bus station, has clean rooms with A/C that are a bit small but mercifully cold (singles 170 pesos; doubles 190 pesos). The most economical hotel in town is the **Motel Davis** on Calle Davis, about four blocks north of the *zócalo*. Both the unmarked motel and street are difficult to find, so don't be afraid to ask. If you can put up with the muddy courtyard and slightly worn-down rooms, it's a real deal. Rooms are small and clean, with beds, baths, and not much else. (All rooms 100 pesos.) **El Moro RV Park,** Robles 8 (tel. 5 05 42), though not on the water, allows you to hook up a trailer (US$10) or just camp out (US$4). If no one is there, you can park on the honor system and leave your payment under the door. (Showers are US$2. Office open daily 7am-midnight.)

Decent, cheap meals are served in establishments up and down Salvatierra, and a number of restaurants cluster conveniently near the bus terminal, offering roast chicken and the like for good prices. *Palapa*-roofed **Café Olé**, Madero 14 (tel. 5 04 96), south of the *zócalo* and across from Bancomer, offers huge portions, great food, excellent prices, and amazing gossip. Both tourists and locals chatter salaciously over their jumbo burritos (28 pesos) or fresh fish fillet with fries and *frijoles* (40 pesos). Huge omelettes with sides of beans and fries (22-29 pesos) will make breakfast buffs roar like the morning tigers they are. (Open M-Sa 7am-10pm, Su 7am-2pm.) The popular **Restaurant-Bar La Palapa** (tel. 5 11 01), on Hidalgo between Madero and López Mateos, fills the bellies of hungry diners with beef or fish tacos for 42 pesos (open M-Sa 1-10pm).

◙ SIGHTS. With shaded benches along the water and the sidewalk, the **Malecón** is a popular place for an evening stroll. Loreto's **public beach,** a few blocks north of Hidalgo, is nice enough. Although the beach is often crowded, the gray sand and the yellow and black fish that practically swim to shore can amuse you for hours as you soak up the sun. Equally enjoyable is the **Museo de las Misiones** next to the reconstructed mission, one block west of the plaza. The museum recounts the complete history of the European conquest of Baja California. Here you can also receive information on Loreto's mission, built in 1697, and on other missions scattered throughout the peninsula. (Tel. 5 04 41. Open Tu-Su 9am-1pm and 1:45-6pm. Admission 17 pesos.) The **Misión de Nuestra Señora de Loreto** is home to eerie, yet beautiful, life-sized statues of Jesus, Mary, and other saints.

If you're angling for a fresh seafood meal, rent a fishing boat and a guide (7hr., US$125 for up to 3 people), or go at it alone with some fishing equipment (US$5 per day) from **Alfredo's** (tel. 5 01 32) on the Malecon at Agua Dulce near the pier. **Arturo's Sports Fishing Fleet** (tel. 5 07 66), on Hidalgo, half a block from the beach, offers five-hour snorkeling trips (2 people US$80, each additional person US$15). Any of the above options may take you on a trip to **Isla Coronado,** where wide, sandy beaches and herds of sea lions await. **Isla Carmen,** another popular destination, contains an eerie ghost town and abandoned salt mines. North of Loreto the road passes the beautiful **Bahía de la Concepción** (see p. 170), with its incredible expanse of coves, blue-green water, and barren, cacti-dotted mountains. South of Loreto, the road winds away from the coast into rugged mountains and the **Planicie Magdalena,** an irrigated and cultivated plain. The striking white stripes on the first hillside beyond town are formed by millions of clams, conch, oyster, and scallop shells—refuse left by the region's Paleolithic inhabitants. Some caves on the hillside, inhabited as recently as 300 years ago, contain shells and polished stone.

BAJA CALIFORNIA

PUERTO SAN CARLOS

Puerto San Carlos (pop. 4500) is a strange little town. Completely seasonal, it hosts pods of tourists from around the world during whale watching season and then settles down for an insanely quiet summer featuring boarded-up restaurants, vacant dirt roads, and the town's two policemen playing dominoes in the heat. There is little of anything to do here during the summer months. Visit Puerto San Carlos from November to March, when an estimated 18,000 gray whales migrate yearly from the Bering Sea southward through the Pacific to **Bahías Magdalena and Almejas,** just south of town and easily accessible by boat. During mating season (mid-January to mid-March), the lovestruck creatures wow crowds with aquatic acrobatics. Few travelers have discovered Puerto San Carlos, and locals observe *extranjeros* with the same bemused fascination with which tourists view whales.

⛴ ORIENTATION AND PRACTICAL INFORMATION. To get to San Carlos, take a transfer bus from **Ciudad Constitución** (1hr., 22 pesos), a nondescript tumbleweed town that has connections on **Autotransportes Águila** south to La Paz (3hr., every hr. 5am-11pm) and points in between, and north to Tijuana (19hr., every hr. 5am-11pm) and points in between. In Ciudad Constitución, basic hotels and restaurants abound; try the **Hotel Conchita** and the 24-hour **Ricos Tacos,** both on Olachea at Hidalgo, if you're stuck in town.

In Puerto San Carlos, most services are on the two main streets, **La Paz** and **Morelos,** which are perpendicular to each other. Both of these major roads are made of sand and marked by illegible street signs. Don't fret if the bus drops you off in what seems like the middle of nowhere—you're actually smack in the middle of town. If you have a car, drive carefully, as it is easy to become stuck in the sand roads. **Autotransportes Aguila buses** leave from the small white terminal on La Paz and Morelos. Buses are few and far between, heading to: **Constitución** (45min., 7:30am and 1:45pm, 22 pesos); **La Paz** (3½hr., 7:30am and 1:45pm, 96 pesos); and **Cabo San Lucas** (7hr., 1:45pm, 192 pesos). The **tourist office** is on La Paz (tel. 6 02 53), in a house next to the **IMSS Hospital,** marked by a cardboard sign. The extremely helpful English-speaking staff also leads **whale-watching tours** (open 24hr.; just don't ring late at night and wake them). The pink **information booth** at the edge of town near the PEMEX station provides maps of the bay and islands (closed in summer).

⬛⬛ ACCOMODATIONS AND FOOD. Finding budget rooms in San Carlos isn't easy. This town has few hotels, and they're pricey; come whale-watching season, the town becomes a tourist trap. Possibly the best deal in town is the **Motel Las Brisas** (tel. (113) 6 01 52 or (113) 6 01 59). To get there from the bus station, turn right on La Paz, then left on Madero; the hotel will be on your left. Clean, yellow rooms with large fans surround a somewhat stark courtyard. If, for some strange reason, you're here when the whales aren't, console yourself by studying the fading courtyard mural dedicated to these gentle giants. (Singles 100 pesos; doubles 120 pesos.) A **trailer park** at Playa la Curva outside of town offers full hookups for US$10. Dining in San Carlos is homey—literally. A string of combination restaurant-living rooms along La Paz and Morelos allows you to meet locals, their kids, and their pets while you enjoy remarkably fresh delicacies from the sea. **El Patio Restaurant-Bar** (tel. 113 6 00 17), in front of Hotel Alcatraz on La Paz, welcomes you into white plastic Corona chairs under open skies. They also offer tourist info. Enjoy a roasted chicken (70 pesos) or a *bistec ranchero* (50 pesos). (Open daily 7am-10pm.)

⬛ SIGHTS. The islands and bays surrounding Puerto San Carlos teem with life. The cheapest way to explore the islands is to make an ad-hoc deal with one of the fishermen departing from Playa la Curva in front of the PEMEX station. Unless you plan to camp out on the islands, make definite pick-up plans before you disembark. Both **Bahía Magdalena** and **Bahía Almeja** lie just south of Puerto San Carlos

It's a **big world.**

And **we've got the network** to cover it.

Use **AT&T Direct**® Service
when you're out exploring the world.

 **AT&T**

and are home to some of the best **whale watching** in the world. The tourist office offers whale watching trips for US$45 per hour for a boat fitting up to six people. From January to March, enormous numbers of whales have sex with each other. In a peculiar maneuver called "spy hopping," a huge hormonal whale pops its head out of the water, fixes an enormous eye on whatever strikes its fancy, and remains transfixed for minutes on end, staring hypnotically like a submarine periscope.

Feisty Pacific waves at **Cabo San Lázaro** and **Point Hughes,** both on the western tip of **Isla Magdalena,** will keep even veteran surfers on their toes. Reed huts scattered along the beach offer protection from the oppressive midday sun. Fifteen species of clams and starfish inhabit the waters of these immaculate beaches. Farther south, the island narrows to less than 50m in width, tapering off into perfectly white sand tufted with occasional bits of foliage, unusual flowers, and cacti. An enormous colony of *lobos marinos* (sea lions) lives near the island's southern tip.

LA PAZ

The eclectic capital of Baja California Sur, La Paz (pop. 170,000) is part port, party town, and peaceful paradise. Home to 10 tranquil beaches along the Sea of Cortés, this is where true Mexicans vacation, leaving the honky-tonk Cabos to U.S. tourists. In a past life, La Paz was a quiet fishing village, frequently harassed by pirates for the iridescent white spheres concealed in the oysters off its coast; John Steinbeck's *The Pearl* depicted the town as a tiny, unworldly treasure chest. La Paz's hour of reckoning came in the 1940s, when the oysters got sick and died, wiping out the town's pearl industry. Within two decades after the completion of the Transpeninsular Highway in the late 1960s and the institution of Baja ferries, La Paz was reborn. Now, the row of nightclubs along the beach may make La Paz (The Peace) feel sheepish about its name. No worries, though: the days are still hot and nonchalant and the fishermen are still friendly. At night, despite the bass beats issuing from semi-gringoized dance clubs, pelicans still skip along the lamp-lit water, and a merciful breeze ruffles the hair of couples strolling along the rocky beach and the serene boardwalk at sunset.

ORIENTATION

La Paz lies 222km north of Cabo San Lucas and 1496km southeast of Tijuana on the Transpeninsular Highway. (Rte. 1), and overlooks the **Bahía de la Paz** on Baja's east coast. The city's main street and loveliest lane for a stroll is **Av. Obregón,** more commonly known as the **Malecón,** which runs along alternately sandy and rocky shore. Activity centers around the area delineated by **Constitución, Ocampo, Serdán,** and the shore. The **municipal bus system** in La Paz serves the city sporadically (approximately every 30min. 6am-10pm, 4-5 pesos). Flag buses down anywhere, or wait by the stop on Revolución and Degollado, next to the market. From the station, try to convince your driver to drop you off in the *centro.* If you're in the center of activity, you need not worry about the buses; it's all easily navigable on foot.

CROSSING THE GULF

Ferries leave from the suburb of **Pichilingue;** they're the best way to get from La Paz to the mainland. Buy tickets at the **Sematur Company office** (tel. 5 46 66), on 5 de Mayo at Prieto (open M-F 8am-6pm, Sa-Su 8am-4pm). Ferries go to **Mazatlán** (15hr.; daily 3pm; 209-831 pesos, cars 2243 pesos, motorcycles 396 pesos) and **Topolobampo,** a suburb of Los Mochis (9hr.; daily 10pm except for "cargo only" days; *salón* (third-class) 140 pesos; cars 1089 pesos, motorcycles 305 pesos). The dock office is open daily from 8am to 10pm.

In order to secure a ticket, be sure to get to the Sematur main office early, ideally right after it opens. Acquiring a *salón* ticket should be no problem on the day of departure, but for other classes, call and make reservations one day ahead. During holidays, competition for ferry tickets is fierce, and Sematur doesn't give a damn whether you have been naughty or nice.

In order to get a vehicle on the ferry, you will need (at the very least) proof of Mexican insurance (or a major credit card with the car owner's name on it), car registration, permission for the importation of a car into Mexico, and a tourist card. Oh, and **three photocopies** of each. You can get a permit at **Banjército** (tel. 2 11 16), at the ferry stop in Pichilingue for US$11, or through **AAA** in the U.S. (for more info on bringing your car into Mexico, see p. 69). Regardless of whether you have a car or not, you will need to obtain a **tourist card (FMT)** if you entered Mexico via Baja and are mainland-bound; get one from **Servicios Migratorios** (see p. 176). Clear all of the paperwork before purchasing the ticket; otherwise, Sematur will deny you a spot whether or not you hold reservations. For more information on ferries, see p. 138.

You need not hike 17km to the ferry dock in Pichilingue—**Autotransportes Aguila** buses run between the dock and the downtown terminal on Obregón, between Independencia and 5 de Mayo (M-F 9:30am and every hr. 11:30am-5:30pm, 15 pesos). When you get off the ferry, hurry to catch the 9:30am bus to the *centro;* otherwise you'll have to wait for two hours. A taxi from the dock to downtown, or vice versa, will set you back a good 100 pesos.

🔢 PRACTICAL INFORMATION

TRANSPORTATION

Airport: West of La Paz, accessible only by taxi (80 pesos). If heading from the airport to the *centro,* buy taxi tickets inside to avoid being swindled. Served by **Aeroméxico** (tel. 4 62 88), at Obregón, between Hidalgo and Morelos (open M-F 8:45am-7pm, Sa 9am-2pm) and **Aerocalifornia** (tel. 4 62 88), between Ocampo and Bravo.

Buses: There are 3 stations. The **main station** is on Jalisco and Independencia, about 25 blocks southeast of downtown. Two municipal buses, "Central Camionera" and "Urbano," head to the terminal; catch them near the public market at Degollado and Revolución. **Taxis** cost 30 pesos. Aguila and ABC (tel. 2 42 70) provide service to points north, including: **Loreto** (5hr., 8 per day 9am-10pm, 137 pesos); **Mulegé** (7hr., 8 per day 9am-10pm, 197 pesos); **Santa Rosalía** (8hr., 8 per day 9am-10pm, 213 pesos); **San Ignacio** (9hr., 5 per day 10am-10pm, 278 pesos); **Ensenada** (19½hr., 4 per day 10am-10pm, 592 pesos); **Tijuana** (21hr., 4 per day 10am-10pm, 649 pesos); and **Mexicali** (24½hr., 4pm, 746 pesos). A bus from the **Aguila Malecón station** (tel. 2 78 98), on Independencia at Obregón, is the best way to get to nearby beaches. Buses run to: **El Carmancito, El Coramuel, Playas Palmira, Tesoro,** and **Pichilingue** (up to 30min., 11 per day 7am-7:30pm, 6-11 pesos), and to **Playas Balandras** and **Tecolote** (45min., Sa-Su only, every hr. 8am-6pm, 15 pesos). The last bus back to La Paz leaves Tecolote M-F 7pm only and Pichilingue M-F 6pm, Sa-Su 7pm; but, be sure to ask the driver before you get off the bus. The new **Enlaces Terrestres station** (tel. 3 31 80), on Degollado at Serdán, is convenient for heading south. Buses run to: **Todos Santos** (2hr., 9 per day 7am-8pm, 35 pesos); **Cabo San Lucas** (3hr., 7 per day 6:30am-7pm, 72 pesos); and **San José del Cabo** (3½hr., 7 per day 6:30am-7pm, 82 pesos).

TOURIST AND FINANCIAL SERVICES

Tourist Office: (tel. 2 59 39), Obregón at 16 de Septiembre, in a pavilion on the water. Excellent city maps and information about Baja Sur, especially Los Cabos. English-speaking staff. Open M-F 8am-8pm.

Tourist Police: Fabulous folks recognizable by their starched white uniforms and big grins. Their job is "protection and orientation," but they will also give recommendations for hiking, beaches, hotels, restaurants, and barbers.

Immigration Office: Servicios Migratorios, Obregón 2140 (tel. 5 34 93; fax 2 04 29), between Juárez and Allende. You must stop here to obtain a tourist card if you entered Mexico via Baja and are mainland-bound. Open M-F 9am-6pm. After hours, head to the airport outpost outside of town (tel. 4 63 49). Open daily 7am-11pm.

La Paz

ACCOMMODATIONS

A Hotel Posada San Miguel
B Hotel Yeneka
C Hotel San Carlos
D Hostería del Convento
E Pensión California

Bahía
de La Paz

LOCAL SERVICES

Currency Exchange: Bancomer (tel. 5 42 48), on 16 de Septiembre, half a block from the waterfront has a 24hr. **ATM.** Open for exchange M-F 8:30am-2:30pm, Sa 9am-2:30pm. **BITAL,** (tel. 2 22 89) 5 de Mayo, at Madero, has a 24hr. **ATM** and talking doors. Open for exchange M-Sa 8am-7pm.

American Express: (tel. 2 86 66) 5 de Mayo at Domínguez. Open daily 8am-8pm.

Laundry: Lavandería Yoli (tel. 2 10 01), 5 de Mayo at Rubio, across the street from the stadium. Wash and dry a big load 18 pesos. Open M-Sa 7am-9pm, Su 8am-3pm.

EMERGENCY AND COMMUNICATIONS

Emergency: dial 060 or 080.

Police: (tel. 2 07 81) on Colima at México. Open 24hr.

Red Cross: Reforma 1091 (tel. 2 12 22), between Isabel la Católica and Ortega. Open 24hr.

Pharmacy: Farmacia Bravo (tel. 2 69 33), next to the hospital. Open 24hr.

Hospital: Salvatierra (tel. 2 14 96 or 2 14 97), on Bravo at Verdad, between Domínguez and the Oncological Institute.

Post Office: (tel. 2 03 88 or 5 23 58) on Revolución at Constitución. Open M-F 8am-3pm, Sa 9am-1pm. **Postal Code:** 23000.

Fax: TELECOM (tel. 2 67 07; fax 5 08 09), upstairs from the post office. Open M-Sa 8am-7pm, Su 8:30am-11:30pm.

Internet: Baja Net Cafe Internet, Madero 430 (tel. 5 93 80), between Hidalgo and Constitución. Enjoy free coffee and A/C. 20-30 pesos per 30min. Open M-Sa 8am-8pm.

Telephones: Sexy young **LADATELS,** as well as older, more mature pay phones, pepper the downtown area and *zócalo.*

Phone Code: 112

ACCOMMODATIONS

The city is full of inexpensive establishments bound to satisfy even the most finicky of travelers. The cluttered artistic look, however, seems to be making a resurgence in the budget hotels of La Paz. A student of Mexican folk art could skip the Museo Antropológico and tour the lobbies of these hotels instead. Many economical lodgings cluster in the downtown area.

Hotel Yeneka, Madero 1520 (tel. 5 46 88), between 16 de Septiembre and Independencia. Quite possibly the most unique hotel in all of Baja. Doubles as a museum of eccentric items, including a 1916 Model-T Ford, a pet hawk, and a stuffed monkey. Each Tarzan-hut room has been remodeled in matching twig furniture and painted with rainbow colors. You can see the painted handprints of the owner's little son on the walls and the green hallways are a labor of love. All rooms come with fans and foam mattresses laid on concrete frames. Laundry, fax, bike rentals, and a restaurant are but a few of the services this budget bunkhouse offers. Singles 160 pesos; doubles 230 pesos; triples 300 pesos.

Pensión California Casa de Huéspedes (tel. 2 28 96), on Degollado at Madero. Bungalow rooms have concrete floors and concrete-slab beds. You can't help but admire the plastic turtle sculpture, seashells, washing machine, picture mural of past guests, and unique shower-toilet-sink combo. Prices include use of the communal kitchen and TV. Bring your own blanket and towel. Padlocks on the doors provide security. Singles 100 pesos; doubles 130 pesos; triples 160 pesos. **Hostería del Convento** (tel. 2 35 08), across the street, which is under the same ownership, has an almost identical, but cheaper set-up. Singles 85 pesos.

Hotel Posada San Miguel, Domínguez 1510 (tel. 5 88 88), just off 16 de Septiembre. Step back in time as you enter the beautiful fountained courtyard. Oversized framed black-and-white photographs of La Paz in its early days, tiled arches, and wrought-iron scrollwork on windows and railings help to create a feeling of an earlier, simpler time. Cubical rooms with sinks and large, comfortable beds. Singles 100 pesos; doubles 120 pesos; triples 140 pesos.

Hotel San Carlos (tel. 2 04 44), on 16 de Septiembre between Revolución and Serdán, is worn with pink, peach, and oh-so-clean rooms. The staff is prompt and helpful. Singles and doubles 100 pesos, with a view 130 pesos.

FOOD

On the waterfront you'll find decor, menus, and prices geared toward peso-spewing tourists. Move inland a few blocks and watch the prices plunge. Seafood meals are generally fresh. The **public market,** at Degollado and Revolución, offers a cheap selection of fruits, veggies, and fresh fish.

Restaurante El Quinto Sol (tel. 2 16 92), on Domínguez at Independencia. One of the few vegetarian joints in Baja has a menu including sausage à la soybean and an assortment of juices. Luscious yogurt smoothie with fruit 15 pesos; vegetarian steak 45 pesos; tasty pastries 12 pesos. Open M-Sa 7am-10pm.

Restaurant Palapa Adriana (tel. 2 83 29), on the beach off Obregón at Constitución. Not just on the water, but practically in the water. *Huachinango* (red snapper) 50 pesos; *pollo con mole* 35 pesos; *pulpo al ajo* 60 pesos. Great view and sea breeze *gratis.* Open daily 10am-10pm.

La Luna Bruja, on Playa Pichilingue, the second *cabaña* on shore, farthest from the ferry dock. Defying the stereotype of the overpriced beachfront *palapa,* this quiet restaurant offers amazing seafood at good prices. *Tostados de ceviche* 30 pesos; fish about 50 pesos. Ice-cold beer 15 pesos or a 40 oz. for 25 pesos—a real deal when it's hand-delivered to you on the beach. Open daily 12-10pm.

La Fuente, on Obregón at Bañuelos, across from the big arch. What better way to battle the heat than with a few scoops of ice cream? This local *nevería* is always buzzing—during the day with little kids, at night with eager clubgoers. Open daily 8am-midnight.

◢ SAND AND SIGHTS

Instead of curving around long expanses of wave-washed sand, the beaches of La Paz snuggle into small coves sandwiched between cactus-studded hills and calm, transparent water. This is prime windsurfing territory. But be careful—La Paz lifeguards make appearances only on weekends and at popular beaches.

The best beach near La Paz is **Playa Tecolote** (Owl Beach), 25km northeast of town. A quiet extension of the Sea of Cortés laps against this gorgeous stretch of gleaming white sand near tall, craggy mountains. Even though there are no bathrooms, Tecolote is terrific for **camping.** Several spots on the eastern side of the beach along the road to the more secluded **Playa El Coyote** come equipped with a stone barbecue pit. **Actividades Aquatica,** on Tecolote, rents **snorkeling** gear (50 pesos per day), **kayaks,** and **paddle boats** and organizes trips to **Isla Espiritu Santo** (300 pesos per person, min. 4 people). The snorkeling off **Playa Balandra,** just south of Tecolote, is excellent. Balandra is actually a cove with almost no view of the sea; it resembles a big blue swimming pool with rocky hills instead of cement walls. Because facilities are sparse and sporadically open, it is best to rent equipment either in the city or at nearby Pichilingue or Tecolote. You may not be able to reach Tecolote or Balandra during the week without a car; **Autotransportes Aguila** buses get you there from the mini-station on Obregón and Independencia (spring break and July-Aug. daily, in the low season Sa-Su only; 12 pesos).

Plenty of other beaches are easily accessible by taking the "Pichilingue" bus up the coast (10 pesos). Be forewarned that neither of these buses run back to La Paz after 6:30 or 7pm. The "Pichilingue" bus goes as far as the ferry dock, at which point you need to walk 1km farther on the paved road to **Playa de Pichilingue.** This beach is the most crowded and a favorite among the teen set, who splash in the shallow waters and ride **paddleboats** in the winter (30 pesos per hr.). Unfortunately, the view from Pichilingue is corrupted by the ferry docks and the nearby power plant. Along the same bus route lies **Playa El Coromuel,** near La Concha Hotel, where visitors and locals congregate on weekends. All of the above beaches are out of walking distance from the city center, though a short ride away. The farther you venture from La Paz, the prettier and more secluded the beaches get.

The aquatic fun in this city doesn't stop at the shoreline; many popular dive spots are located around La Paz. North of La Paz is **Salvatierra Wreck,** a dive spot where a 100m boat sank in 1976. Also popular is the huge **Cerraluo Island,** east of La Paz. This popular destination promises reefs, huge fish, and untouched wilderness. Both of these destinations (and many others) require guides because of strong currents, fluctuating weather conditions, and inaccessibility.

Baja Diving and Service, Obregón 1665 (tel. 2 18 26; fax 2 86 44), between 16 de Septiembre and Callejón La Paz, organizes daily scuba and snorkeling trips to nearby reefs, wrecks, and islands, where you can mingle with hammerheads, manta rays, giant turtles, and other exotica (scuba trips US$77 per day without equipment, US$15 extra for equipment, snorkeling US$40 per day). Trips leave at 7am and return before 5pm. Nearby, **Sea & Scuba** (tel. 3 52 33), at the corner of Obregón and Ocampo, offers similar activities and rates. Forty-five kilometers south of La Paz along the Transpeninsular Highway is **El Triunfo,** an abandoned mining town. Marked by a huge tower/chimney, this lonely desert town offers lovely views, solitude, and a chance to see local artwork done in shell or stone.

NIGHTLIFE

Structure (tel. 2 45 44), Obregón and Ocampo, 3 blocks east of the center, is a new, hoppin' disco with a dim interior and loud, terrific techno. The dance floor looks like a boxing ring. Some Thursdays feature live karate and sporting events while young couples drink beer (15 pesos) and watch Mexico's version of MTV on scattered screens. Cover F men 70 pesos, women 30 pesos, includes open bar; Sa 2-for-1 specials. Open Th-Su 10pm-late.

La Cabaña, Obregón 1570, on the 2nd fl. of Hotel Perla, offers something a bit more mature. Every night, live music and bands crooning favorite Mexican ballads entertain a dressy, scotch-sipping, over-35 crowd. This joint is bizarre, kitschy, and rockin'. Wednesday nights you can catch a boxing match, and on Sunday nights you can two-step to good ol' country tunes. Grab a tall, cool *cerveza* from the long dark bar and knock yourself out. Cover F-Sa 30 pesos. Open W-Su 9pm-3am.

Carlos 'n' Charlie's/La Paz-Lapa, Obregón and 16 de Septiembre, is the most central and noticeable structure in town. You can savor a staple of gringo nightlife in the form of huge margaritas (32 pesos), or go buck-wild at the La Paz-Lapa, an outdoor booze and rockfest. U.S. and Mexican teens get down and sing along to Aerosmith amid giant palm trees and an imposing bar. Tongue-in-cheek signs like "Do not dive from balcony" turn into real warnings after 3am. Cover and drink prices vary. Women usually pay much less; sometimes before 10pm they can enter and drink free. Cover Th men 40 pesos, includes open bar. Open daily 10:30pm-late.

TODOS SANTOS

Dick and Jane have moved to Todos Santos. She runs an outdoor fish market and has started surfing—at age 47. He got his ear pierced (three times), and now makes sculptures out of chrome and cactus flowers. And yes, of course, they've never been happier. Todos Santos (pop. 3700) is paradise for the frugal surfer/ painter/zoned-out, vacationer/nature-lover, Deadhead/elderly, mellow/expat set. Halfway between La Paz and Cabo San Lucas, Todos Santos is one of the few serene and sophisticated towns on the southern Baja coast and is accessible by bus, offers budget accommodations, and is unmutilated by resort development.

John Steinbeck used to hang his hat here; a number of lesser-known (but more ecologically concerned) U.S. expats have recently fallen in love with Todos Santos' rolling cactus hills, killer surf, dusty roads, and laid-back demeanor. Their presence is revealed by the myriad gourmet shops, classy restaurants, and art galleries that now inhabit the buildings whose large brick chimneys are all that remain of the town's sugarcane-producing past. Still, expats and locals seem to coexist in harmony; the result is a hospitable and lively environment. It's OK to ogle art, but don't think too hard; follow Dick and Jane's example and rediscover yourself—slowly.

■ **ORIENTATION AND PRACTICAL INFORMATION.** Todos Santos's two main streets, running parallel and north-south, are **Colegio Militar** and **Benito Juárez.** Juárez is just west of Militar; west of and parallel to Juárez run **Centenario** and **Legaspi.** East of Militar and parallel, runs **Rangel** and **Cuauhtérloc.** From north to south, **Ocampo, Obregón, Topete, Hidalgo, Márquez de León, Morelos, Zaragoza,** and **Degollado** run east-west. Activity centers around the area between **Legaspi, Militar, Zaragoza, and Topete;** León crosses Legaspi and Centenario at the church and main plaza. You may be dropped off near Degollado and Militar, as this is where the **Transpeninsular Highway.** (from La Paz) turns to head toward Los Cabos.

The **bus** stop (tel. 5 01 70) is at Pilar's taco stand, on the corner of Zaragoza and Colegio Militar. If you have any questions about bus times or anything else, Pilar is an excellent person to talk to. *De paso* **buses** run north to **La Paz** (1hr., 8 per day 7am-8pm, 55 pesos) and south to **Cabo San Lucas** (1½hr., 8 per day 8am-10pm, 60 pesos) and **San José del Cabo** (2hr., 8 per day 8am-10pm, 60 pesos). Todos Santos has no tourist office, but the American-owned **El Tecolote Libros**, on Juárez and Hidalgo, sells English-language magazines, maps, and a comprehensive book on the town (100 pesos; open July-Oct. M-F 10am-5pm, Nov.-June M-Sa 9am-5pm, Su 10am-3pm). To exchange currency or use the 24hr. **ATM**, try the **Bancrecer**, the only bank in town, on the corner of Obregón and Juárez (open M-F 9am-2pm). **Faxes** can be sent and received at **The Message Center** (tel. 5 00 03; fax 5 02 88) at Juárez and Hidalgo right next to El Tecolote Libros (open M-F 8am-6pm, Sa 8am-2pm). Meet your recommended daily nutritional allowances at **Mercado Guluarte** (tel. 5 00 06), on Morelos between Colegio Militar and Juárez (open M-Sa 7:30am-9pm, Su 7:30am-2pm). Other markets are on Degollado and Juárez. **Police:** in the Delegación Municipal complex on Legaspi between León and Hidalgo. **Farmacia de Guadalupe:** (tel. 5 00 06) on Juárez at Zaragoza (open Su-Th 8am-11pm, F-Sa 8am-2am). **Emergencies:** call the **hospital** (tel. 5 00 95) on Juárez at Degollado (open 24hr.). **Post office:** (tel. 5 03 30) on Colegio Militar at León (open M-F 8am-3pm). **Postal code:** 23300. **Phone code:** 114.

⌐ ACCOMMODATIONS AND CAMPING. The town has four main hotels; two are in the center of town, and the other two are a 15-min. jaunt away. Beware: red ants are everywhere. The best deal in town is the centrally located **Motel Guluarte** (tel. 5 00 06), on Juárez at Morelos. This tiny motel is run out of a grocery store in the Mercado Guluarte (see above). The pool is well-suited to those who enjoy bathing in full view of the street. Clean, cozy rooms have TVs, fans, and refrigerators. (Singles 150 pesos; doubles 230 pesos.) The **Way of Nature Bed and Breakfast,** half a mile down a dirt road directly next to Farmacia de Guadalupe, is a cool, breezy, and secluded hotel/campsite run by the Perkins family. Wake up to breakfast, yoga, or tai chi lessons, then head to the beach for body-boarding, surfing, or a sail to La Paz in the owner's SunFish and end your day with a dip in the small pool. Every evening, guests bang away in drum circles—a great place to meet people if you are traveling alone. No one is pressured to participate in any of the activities offered by this unique, mellow and centrally located hotel with four superclean rooms and shared bathrooms. (Camping in provided tents 80 pesos; singles 250 pesos, doubles 350 pesos.)

The best deals in town are the campgrounds and if you have the equipment, Todos Santos is a great place to camp, with plenty of gorgeous beaches, scenic views of rolling hills, and pot-smoking, Kerouac-reading, surfing-hard bodies. **San Pedrito Trailer Park** (tel. 7 92 09), the closest beachfront RV park to town, offers great facilities and has a prime location. Turn right off the Transpeninsular Highway., 6km south of town—you can't miss the giant welcome sign and arch. Pass under the arch, drive 3km, bear left at the fork, and you're there. The beach here is beautiful and has prime surfing waves. (RV hookups US$15; simple, semi-sheltered *cabañas* where you can pitch your tent US$3.50; full-size, indoor cabanas with amenities US$45; open 7am-9pm.)

⌐ FOOD. Good budget eats aren't hard to find in Todos Santos. Several **loncherías** line Colegio Militar near the bus station, offering triple tacos for 10-12 pesos. **Pilar's Taco Stand** (tel. 5 03 52), on the corner of Zaragoza and Colegio Militar, is not only the town's de facto bus station but also an excellent place to indulge in glorious fish tacos (14 pesos) or fries (8 pesos; open daily 7am-9pm). **Restaurant Santa Monica** (tel. 5 02 04), on Degollado and Colegio Militar, has been open for 26 years—try their *pescado a la veracruzana* (50 pesos) and you'll know why. Simple yet elegant decorations, giant potted cacti, and tiny birds playing in the next room create a pleasurable eatery. (Open daily 7am-10pm.) Locals love **Carnitas Barajas,** an outdoor stand on Degollado and Chauetemoc past the PEMEX, with excellent meat tacos (7 pesos).

⌐ ART GALLERIES. Modern art lovers are sure to be wowed by the surfeit and high quality of galleries. Todos Santos's new pride and joy (among art fans, at

STEALING HOME If you're feeling energetic at night, you might want to take in a **baseball game** at the local stadium, off Degollado to the south. Follow the light towers—any local will show you the way. Admission is only 10 pesos, though a cold Tecate is another 10 pesos. Root, root, root for the home team—**Los Tiburones** (the Sharks); while analyzing the odder aspects of Mexican League professional baseball: you'll see an all-sand playing field, umpires in bright blue pants, baserunners without batting helmets, players trading gloves between batters, lots of submarine-ball pitchers, players on the same team in different uniforms, and huge crowds dancing between innings to popular dance music. Oh, and if, by chance, you catch a ball, don't even think about keeping it as a souvenir—you will first be swarmed by young children paid by commission for every ball (and crushed beer can) they recover, and eventually you'll even be bothered by the police. Games are at 7pm some weeknights and 1 or 2pm on weekends.

least) is the **Todos Santos Gallery** (tel. 5 05 00), on Legaspi and Topete, opened in 1995 by artist Michael Cope. (Open M and W-Sa 10am-5pm.) The gallery is devoted to the work of artists who reside in Mexico—approximately half of them Mexican and the other half from the U.S. and other countries. Futuristic bronze and clay sculptures, off-the-wall wall clocks, and ornate mirrors are on parade at the **Santa Fe Art Gallery,** Centario 4, between Hidalgo and Márquez de León (open W-M 10am-5pm). **Casa Franco Gallery** (tel./fax 5 03 56), on Juárez at Morelos, has furniture and bowls from Todos Santos, Guadalajara, and all over Mexico; the staff will be happy to tell you more (open M-Sa 9am-5pm). It's worth peeking into the **Charles Stewart Gallery and Studio** (tel. 5 02 65), on Obregón at Centenario, which is both Mr. Stewart's home and his studio (open 10am-4pm).

⬢ **BEACHES.** If you overdose on art, don't forget that Todos Santos is surrounded by some of the region's most unspoiled (and unexplored) beaches. **La Posa,** only 2km from town, is perfect for that romantic stroll or uplifting solitary walk. To get there, go up Juárez and turn left on Topete. Follow the road as it winds across the valley and past a white building, and....*voilà!* Unfortunately, vicious undercurrents and powerful waves make this beach unequivocally unsuitable for swimming. To reach **Punta Lobos,** the stomping ground of the local sea lion population and a beach popular with locals, turn left onto Degollado as you walk away from the town center. Roughly six blocks later, the city limits end. Around km 54, turn right and follow the terrible washboard road until you come to the beach. To catch a spectacular arial view, turn right 1.5km south on the highway at the first possible fork in the road. Follow the main dirt path east for 2.5km; the path will bear left past an old fish plant and continue up a hill, with steep drop-offs to the seashore. Most other beaches are accessible via the Transpeninsular Highway. south of town. These sights are isolated, and therefore both attractive and hazardous. Bring a friend, and plan to return before nightfall.

The only beaches considered suitable for swimming are **Playa de las Palmas** and **Playa los Cerritos,** although beware of the mating shoreline sting-rays in June. Los Cerritos, a popular picnic spot and family beach, lies approximately 14km south of Todos Santos. Look for a turn-off on the right side of the Transpeninsular Highway. Head south about 3km past the signs for Gypsy's Bed and Breakfast. The current is tamer here than elsewhere, but the waves are just as big, and there's always some sort of party going on. The Todos Santos Surf Shop on the right side of the beach can give the day's conditions and rent surfboards (100 pesos per day) or a Boogie board (50 pesos per day). To reach the appropriately named **Playa de las Palmas** (Beach of the Palm Trees), travel 5km south from town on the highway, and turn right when you see the white Campo Experimental buildings on the left. Travel another 2.6km and you'll be bowled over by palm trees; just past these is the beach. The serene and deserted shore here is excellent for swimming and the hollow waves are perfect for body surfing.

A quiet and lovely beach by the highway is **San Pedrito,** 8.2km south of town. Lots of surfing and hangin' loose goes on here. It's easy to find a sunbathing spot, and on these bohemian beaches, nobody cares if you bare all. However, San Pedrito is really unsuitable for swimming; the rocky bottom, big waves, swift currents and steep beach slope are the classic conditions to get yourself killed if you don't know what you are doing. To get there, just turn off at the sign for San Pedrito RV Park.

Sierra de la Laguna, a beautiful lake atop a mountain, is accessible only by car (it's a 1½hr. drive). One kilometer south down the highway, past the Punta Lobos turn-off, turn left at the fenced-off cattle ranch. A 45-min. drive brings you to **Rancho La Burera,** which serves as the trailhead for the *laguna.* Be social and make friends in town; they'll be happy to show you the way.

NEAR TODOS SANTOS: SIERRA DE LA LAGUNA

Sierra de la Laguna, the mountain range that fills the foot of Baja, is visible from virtually all beaches around Los Cabos and Todos Santos. Dark rain clouds hovering above the Sierra rarely make their way to the beaches but induce the growth of some of the most exotic and varied flora and fauna in Baja. The climate of the mountains is completely different than the surrounding coastal areas and can, in the winter, drop below freezing.

La Laguna, the Sierra's most popular hiking destination is a meadow of about one square mile perched at an altitude of 5,600 ft. amid the jagged peaks of **Picacho la Laguna** and **Cerro las Casitas.** Once a lake, erosion destroyed its edges in the late 19th century, transforming La Laguna into a grassy meadow. The climb up to the meadow is a grueling eight hours with steep inclines towards the end of the hike. However, the climb is rewarding as the mountain range is unspoiled and there are many beautiful vistas and rest-stops along the way—one is about three hours into the hike from where it is possible to view the entire width of the penninsula. The trail is well-marked and there are several rustic campsites along the way.

For more information about Sierra de la Laguna, visit **Johnny** at the **Todos Santos Hostel,** two blocks up from the PEMEX on Degollado on the left. He organizes multiple day trips to La Laguna and is a great source of local lore. Sierra de la Laguna is worth checking out if just for the stunning view at the trailhead. It's also a nice change from the touristy areas of Todos Santos and Los Cabos.

Getting There: To get to the trailhead, drive south out of Todos Santos. After passing the marker for km 53 and climbing a small hill you will see the turn-off on the left at the top of the hill. Drive down this dirt road through a fenced off cattle ranch bearing right at the first unmarked major fork in the road and follow signs for about 40 minutes until you reach a locked gate and suprisingly, the end of the road. There is a small dirt lot to park your car. Beware of the numerous flies which will no doubt bother you during the first hour or so of the hike (that is unless you unleash a battalion of bullfrogs to trailblaze in front of you).

LOS CABOS

The towns of **Cabo San Lucas** and **San José del Cabo** comprise the southwestern part of the Los Cabos district (pop. 80,000), which includes most of the coastline of Baja California's southern end. Los Cabos (the capes) is the most tourist-oriented area in all of Baja outside of Tijuana. Million-dollar resorts and golf courses infest the otherwise heavenly natural elements of the tip of Baja—spectacular rock formations, surf that is said to occasionally compare with the waves in Hawaii, and vast expanses of fine white-sand beaches. Visitors are drawn here by the stretch of beach leading from San José del Cabo to Cabo San Lucas, where luxury hotels form a glittering strip between the desert and the ocean. Don't expect wilderness or hidden pirate plunder: Bud-guzzling, sunbathing, sightseeing, gift-buying, jet-skiing *norteamericanos* congregate by the thousands. The *vía corta* bus from La Paz first heads to Cabo San Lucas, then to San José del Cabo, then back to La Paz.

CABO SAN LUCAS

Perched on the southern tip of Baja, Cabo San Lucas (a.k.a. Land's End or, in Latin, the Time-share capital of the world) is a reflection of the heavy U.S. influence on the resort industry of Mexico. Although small (pop. 10,000), the town has surpassed such classic resorts as Acapulco in popularity among honeymooners and U.S. college spring-breakers due to its peaceful waters and ultra-modern pleasure domes. A favorite vacation spot among families looking for an easy, pampered escape from stress, Cabo is best suited to those who desire neither a peek into Mexican culture nor the "inconvenience" of changing their dollars into pesos—or even of learning what a peso is. Cabo San Lucas now has one of the country's highest costs of living, and it is quickly turning into a city dominated by endless neon-lit, fog-machined discotheques, cigar shops, and U.S. fast-food joints.

If all this sounds like it's not for you, then Cabo can be depressing. Tensions between maltreated Mexicans, elderly resident U.S. expats, and carefree tourists run high. Local fishermen are finding it increasingly hard to survive, and the dolphins and whales that once flourished near the coast have all but disappeared. Recent legislation to reduce pollution may be just a little too late. Outside of the natural beauty that surrounds Cabo San Lucas, the town itself is nothing to write home about. The many resort hotels try hard to distinguish themselves from one another. The result: bizarrely shaped buildings and a gimmicky faux lighthouse that gives the town the feel of a giant mini-golf course.

Despite its influx of dollar-rich, culture-poor tourists, Cabo San Lucas holds some appeal for the budget traveler, mostly due to its superb beaches and picturesque rock formations: El Arco is the famous arch rock that marks the very tip of the Californias. Cabo San Lucas has yet to develop extensive facilities for budget travelers and if you don't plan to spend a lot of money, stay in town only for the day and camp on the beach, or simply treat the town as a big supermarket—buy your sunscreen and make tracks for cheaper San José del Cabo. If you've come to party, you're knocking on the right door. Break out your wallet and brace yourself for a rollicking good time.

■ ORIENTATION

Lázaro Cárdenas is the main street in Cabo San Lucas. It runs roughly southwest-northeast, diagonally through the town's grid of streets. **Paseo de la Marina** forks off Cárdenas where the resort zone begins, continues south, and winds around the marina. From west to east, north-south streets (all branching off Cárdenas) include **Ocampo, Zaragoza, Morelos, Vicario,** and **Mendoza.** Farther west, **Cabo San Lucas, Hidalgo, Matamoros,** and **Abasolo** cross Cárdenas and continue south into the resort zone, eventually meeting Marina. From north to south, the following east-west streets are perpendicular to those above: **Obregón, Carranza, Revolución, 20 de Noviembre, Libertad, 16 de Septiembre, Niños Héroes, Constitución,** and **5 de Mayo.** South of Cárdenas, **Madero, Zapata,** and **Domínguez** run east-west in the resort area. Continuing south on Marina, you'll pass the posh resorts, and eventually arrive at **Playa de Médano.** Restaurants and bars are concentrated on Cárdenas between Morelos and the mountains on the western edge of town. To get to the center of the town from the bus station, follow Zaragoza for two blocks toward the water to Cárdenas.

■ PRACTICAL INFORMATION

ABC Autotransportes and Aguila **buses** (tel. 3 04 00) are located at Zaragoza and 16 de Septiembre. They head to: **San José del Cabo** (30min., every hr. 7am-10pm, 15 pesos); and **La Paz** (3hr., 11 per day 6am-7pm, 70 pesos) via **Todos Santos** (1½hr., 45 pesos). One *de paso* bus per day leaves at 4:30pm and heads north, stopping at: **La Paz** (3hr., 70 pesos); **Cd. Constitución** (6hr., 170 pesos); **Loreto** (8½hr., 219 pesos); **Mulegé** (10½hr., 250 pesos); **Santa Rosalía** (11½hr., 315 pesos); **San Ignacio** (12½hr.,

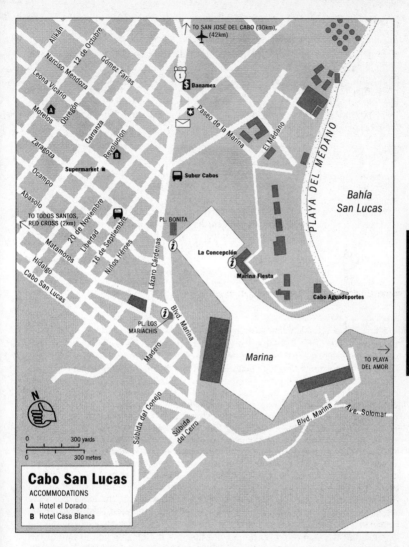

340 pesos); **Guerrero Negro** (14½hr., 400 pesos); **San Quintín** (19hr., 554 pesos); **Ensenada** (23hr., 680 pesos); and **Tijuana** (26½hr., 732 pesos). **Avis Rent-a-Car** (tel. 3 46 07) at Plaza Los Mariachis, across from Pizza Hut, on Paseo de la Marina rents tiny Chevys, including insurance and unlimited kilometers, for US$46 per day (open daily 9am-5pm).

Tourist information and **maps** are dispensed by time-share hawkers all over the center of town. The "Marina Fiesta" and "Plaza Los Mariachis" salespeople have the best of the lot. To exchange money, try **Banamex** (tel. 3 36 68 or 3 36 69) on Cardenas between Farias and 16 de Septiembre (open M-F 8:30am-4:30pm, Sa 9am-2pm.) It also has a friendly **ATM** that's fluent in English. Most hotels and restaurants will exchange dollars at lower rates. **American Express** (tel. 3 57 88) services can be found at the Plaza Bonita at Cardenas and Morelos (open M-F 9am-6pm, Sa 9am-1pm). Get your groceries at **Almacenes Grupo Castro,** on Morelos and

Revolución 1910 (open 7am-11pm). **Police:** (tel. 3 39 77) on Cárdenas, two blocks
north of Morelos. **Farmacia Aramburo:** (tel. 3 14 89) on Zaragoza and Cárdenas, at
Plaza Aramburo (open 8am-11pm). **Red Cross:** (tel. 3 33 02) in front of the Delegación Municipal on the outskirts of town toward Todos Santos, 200m from the gas
station. **Post office:** (tel. 3 00 48) next to the police station (open M-F 9am-5pm, Sa
9am-noon). **Postal code:** 23410. **Faxes: Telecomm** (tel. 3 19 68; fax 3 02 31) next to the
post office (open M-F 8am-7:30pm, Sa 8-11am, Su 8am-3pm). **Internet access: Cabo-
net** (tel. 3 01 20), on Blvd. Lázaro Cárdenas at Paseo de la Marina, across from the
PEMEX station (40 pesos per hr.; open M-F 9am-2pm and 4-7pm, Sa 9am-2pm).
Phone code: 114.

ACCOMMODATIONS

Multi-million-dollar resorts with every service imaginable dominate San Lucas's
coast; as a result, simple, cheap beds are seriously lacking. During the winter high
season, make reservations early and be prepared to shell out more *pesos* than you
would during the slower summer months. The only legitimate budget accommodation remaining may be the **Hotel Casa Blanca** (tel. 3 53 60), on Revolución at Morelos. Slightly less luxurious than its name implies, the hotel provides clean and
simple rooms with fans and functional private bathrooms (singles 160 pesos; doubles 180 pesos; 50 peso towel deposit). The next best deal in town is **Hotel El Dorado**
(tel. 3 28 10), on Morelos about two blocks north of Casa Blanca. The spotless
gigantic tiled rooms are almost as luxurious. (Singles or doubles with TV and fan
200 pesos, with TV and A/C 300 pesos.)

FOOD

Restaurant-bars along the water gang up on tourists; the cheap spots line Morelos,
a safe distance from the million-dollar yachts. Growling stomachs gravitate
toward the enormous rotating chickens at **El Pollo de Oro** (tel. 3 03 10), Cárdenas at
Morelos. Enjoy a half-chicken for 35 pesos or a quarter bird for 22 pesos. (Open
daily 6am-11pm.) King of *taquerías*, **Asadero 3 Hermanos,** Morelos at 20 de Noviembre, serves up scrumptious, cheap, and safe tacos and quesadillas (9-10 pesos;
open 24hr.). Although it's not a bargain eatery (85-110 pesos per entree), you will
not find better seafood in all of San Lucas than at **Mariscos Mocambo** (tel. 3 60 70),
on Vicario at 20 de Noviembre. The atmosphere and decor are simple, and ceiling
fans cool the hungry masses who crowd the wooden tables every night. If you plan
to eat with a big group, it would be wise to call ahead. (Open daily 11am-11pm.)

SIGHTS AND SAND

All major activity in Cabo San Lucas revolves around the pristine waters off the
coast. **Playa del Médano,** one of the area's better beaches, stretches east along the
bay around the corner from the marina. Escape the blazing sun in one of the
beach's many restaurants or *palapas*. The waters of the Playa de Médano are alive
with parasailers and motorboats full of lobster-red, beer-guzzling vacationers.
Cabo Acuadeportes (tel. 3 01 17), in front of the Hotel Hacienda, rents **water equipment** (open 9am-5pm), as does **JT Watersports** (tel. 7 55 43), adjacent to Hotel Plaza
Las Glorias Beach Club (snorkeling gear US$10 per day, wave runners US$40 per
30min., SunFish US$20 per hr.; open 9am-6pm).

   The famous **Arch Rock** (El Arco) of Cabo San Lucas is only a short boat ride from
the marina. The rocks around the arch are home to about 40 sea lions who can
usually be seen hanging out, sunning themselves, or swimming alongside the taxis
checking out the funny-looking passengers. To get there, walk through the Plaza
Las Glorias hotel or the big Mexican crafts market farther down Paseo Marina to
the docks. Eager, English-speaking boat captains will be happy to take you on a
45-min. glass-bottom **boat ride** to El Arco and back (US$7). In addition to the pic-
turesque Arch and the creatures that visit it, you may catch a glimpse of the sum-

THE PLAYER Time-share vendors disguised as "tourist officials" roam the streets of Cabo San Lucas. If you want to take advantage of what they have to offer for free, you must be at least 28-30 years old and possess a major credit card. If you qualify and have a free afternoon, it's quite possible to go on the Arco boat ride for free and order anything you want at an expensive restaurant in exchange for an hour and a half of "listening," ears closed but eyes open, mouth pleasantly grinning, and head nodding to the English-speaking con man's pitch. He will try to convince you to dump US$15,000 into his hands in exchange for yearly time at an exclusive, American-oriented resort in Cabo. Don't admit until after dinner that you're not prepared to spend $15,000 (unless you want a struggle). Other lures include a free car rental and a free day at a resort.

mer dwellings of Sly Stallone, Michael Jackson, Madonna, Eddie Van Halen, and others (or so they'll tell you). The boat also stops at **La Playa del Amor** (yes, that's the Beach of Loooove) right near El Arco and allows you to get out and head back later on a different boat for no additional charge. At high tide, the light, tranquil Sea of Cortés meets the rough, deep blue Pacific, and the two bodies of water kiss. Swimming is good on the gulf side, but beware of the Pacific's currents; two unlucky swimmers died after being dragged out to sea on this side. To get to the water taxis (US$7) which will take you there, walk along the east side of the marina until you come to the beach by JT Watersports. A beautiful and more secluded Pacific beach where you shouldn't swim is **Playa del Divorcio** (Beach of Divorce). To get there, hop on a yellow bus (3 pesos) or walk out on Marina and turn right across from the Mexican crafts market. Slip out to the beach between massive condo complexes right after you pass the Terra Sol Hotel.

Snorkeling is popular on La Playa del Amor and around the rocks between the marina and the beach, where tropical fish abound. Bring your own gear or pay the pesos for rented equipment from one of the vendors in the marina area (see above). Although pricey, the snorkeling here is some of the best you'll find in Mexico; once you've seen the incredible array of angelfish, rays, and octopus, you'll be glad you did it. The best snorkeling beach is said to be **Playa Santa María,** 13km from Cabo San Lucas, on the highway between San Lucas and San José del Cabo (see p. 188).

🎵 NIGHTLIFE

If you want to go buck-wild, you couldn't pick a better place. At night, the couple of streets near the sea turn into a huge laser-lit party ground, and everyone stumbles down the street smoking Cuban cigars and shrieking. You too can join rich Americans and hip Mexican teens in the nightly ritual of alcohol-induced gastro intestinal reversal. Typical Cabo San Lucas bar decor is in the same booze-can-punish vein—signs like "Sorry, We're Open" and "Wrong Way—Do Not Exit" vie for space with assorted driver's licenses. Cabo is a great place to cut loose; just don't expect cheap booze—this ain't Tijuana. Here, those who play hard pay hard.

La Concepción (tel. 3 49 63), north of the Marina, next to Hotel Marina Fiesta is probably Los Cabos's best-kept secret. The ambience is amazing—sit outside in old hanging boats, listen to the latest in Mexican reggae, or sample one of 105 different tequilas. They'll give you a oral history of the drink and explain tequila from A (agave) to W (worm). Check out the ceiling, which is a rendition of an old pirate's map, while you nibble on delicious *botanas* or down tequila shots (28-500 pesos). The house drink, *La Concepción,* contains cranberry and pineapple juice, tequila, and *creme de cacao* (45 pesos). Open daily 5pm-2am.

Squid Roe (tel. 3 06 55), Cárdenas at Zaragoza, is the undisputed heavyweight champion of the loud, beer-guzzling, dance clubs in Los Cabos—the most popular spot in town, especially around 1am, when tourists from other clubs flock here to end their night (hopefully not alone). The pick-up scene is frantic. Conga lines, tequila everywhere, and short-skirted, jello-shot-peddling salesgirls dancing on any and all surfaces. When things get too hot, the MC sprays the crowd with ice-cold water. Tons of hookers, pimps, and *tamale* stands await outside if you come up empty handed. Beer 30 pesos; mixed drinks 28 pesos. Open daily noon-3am.

Kokomo's (tel. 3 52 52), on Blvd. Marina, across the street from Squid Roe. Although tamer than its rowdier neighbor, things get pumping at 10:30pm, when this new club starts spouting fog from all corners, and the lights really start acting up. The music is "contemporary"—late 80s Top-40 abounds, and there's plenty of room to dance on the mosaic tile dance floor. Beer 26 pesos, margaritas 26 pesos. Open daily 11am-3am.

Carlos 'n' Charlie's, Blvd. Marina 20 (tel. 3 12 80 or 3 21 80), near Zaragoza. This club (owned by the Squid Roe franchise) is hip, loud, and happening. A young crowd drinks and dances to U.S. pop tunes from the 80s and 90s. Choreographed "waiter show" at 9 and 11pm. Beer 30 pesos; huge margaritas 60 pesos. Open daily 10am-1am.

Cool Hippo's, on Blvd. Marina, in the Plaza de los Mariachis has both an outdoor and indoor bar and dining area. Casual and fun: impromptu dancing occurs whenever the urge (or the beer rush) hits you. Not as taxing as some of the other nightspots. Specials include 4 tacos and a beer for US$6. Comparatively inexpensive drinks (beer 10 pesos, margaritas 15-20 pesos) and 80s background music attract a young, mellow crowd and make this a great place to chill. Open daily 8am-3am; kitchen closes at 1am.

CABO SAN LUCAS TO SAN JOSÉ DEL CABO

The 30km stretch of coast between Cabo San Lucas and San José del Cabo is dotted with many beautiful beaches. Unfortunately, development is creeping over the small strip of land from both sides. The only pristine beaches are those that lie in the middle; you have to maneuver around condos and resorts to access the beaches closer to the two towns. Despite the expansion of touristy resorts, the beaches in between San José and San Lucas are far less crowded than those in Cabo San Lucas.

All of the following beaches are accessible from the Transpeninsular Highway. Many lie at the end of winding, sandy access bars, and all are easily maneuverable in passenger vehicles. Access roads to some beaches are identified by blue and white palm tree signs—the Los Cabos symbol for *playa*. Others are marked by an entrance to a dirt road and little else. Although the easiest way to get to the private little oasis is to drive there, the "Subur Cabos" buses that run between San José and Cabo San Lucas will leave you at any of the listed beaches (8-15 pesos). Getting a bus ride back into town is slightly more difficult as it has to be flagged down.

Starting from San José del Cabo, the first beach of note is **Playa Barco Varada** (Shipwreck Beach) at km 9. Ideal for scuba diving, this beach is home to a sunken tuna boat that lies just 27m below the water's surface. There's no beach sign; look for the access road around the 9km marker. The access road to **Playa Twin Dolphin** lies just south of the entrance to the eponymous resort. The rough sandy road leads to a small, secluded, rocky beach. Unfortunately, the rough break and rocky shore make it unsuitable for swimming.

Playa Santa María is just past the Twin Dolphin Resort at km 12. This small clear water beach is protected from harsh waves by a slight cove; and is the perfect place to spend the day in solitude swimming and **snorkeling** which is said to be the best in Los Cabos. You can rent gear for US$10 or bring your own. Next is **Chileno Bay,** at the 14km marker, a popular swimming spot. Chileno comes complete with public baths and showers, as well as a small dock. **Kayaks** (US$10-15 per hr.) and **snorkel** gear (US$10 per day) are available for rent from **Cabo Acuadeportes** (open daily 9am-5pm). The snorkeling here is adventurous because the rocks and reefs are more varied; however, Santa Maria has overall better visibility and more fish.

Although there are no signs pointing the way to **Playa del Tule**, it's easy enough to find. Just past the entrance to Hotel Cabo San Lucas (around km 15), there are signs for Punta del Tule and when the road drops level with the sand and there's a bridge on your left, pull off to the right—you're there. The shore is rocky and not suitable for swimming. Surfers, however, abound. From km 16 to km 20 are *playas* **Canta Mar, Costa Brava, El Zalate, San Carlos,** and **El Mirador.** Unfortunately, these areas are under heavy construction, and access is obscured by bulldozers and concrete walls. **Playa Buenos Aires** comes next, at km 22. It too is under development but is accessible by a crude sand and dirt road. The waves are rough but the beach is long and desolate.

Under the shadow of Hotel Palmilia, the first resort hotel in Los Cabos, **Playa Punta Palmilia** offers smooth, gentle waves and great swimming. There are plenty of fishing *pangas* for hire, and if you get thirsty, you can pop into Restaurant/Bar Pepes. **Playa Acapulquito,** at km 27, is easy to miss. Look for cars parked on the side of the highway just before the Acapulquito Scenic Overlook. Walk down the steep dirt path and slip through the condos; great waves make this a popular surfers' beach. The last beach before San José del Cabo is **Costa Azul,** the best **surfing beach** in all of Los Cabos. Swim if you dare; this beach belongs to surfers. You can rent a board for the day (US$15), or, for virgin surfers, get a lesson for US$25 from **Playa Costa Azul Rentals** (tel. 7 00 71) on the beach, located around km 28 in the Playa Costa Azul, right across the highway from Zippers, a beachside restaurant (open daily 8:30am-6:30pm).

SAN JOSÉ DEL CABO

If Los Cabos were two brothers, then José would be the more sedate of the two: unlike his ill-fated, party-animal, bad-boy younger brother Lucas, José would be better-looking, charming, sincere, and polite, yet still lots of fun. Although, due to a genetic defect, José would be more humid than his brother and consequently hotter. It's sad but true. José suffers from a rare congenital disease known as "Closer-to-the-Sea-of-Cortés-and-thus-more-humid-and-less-pleasant."

San José del Cabo remains relatively untouristed and peacefully Mexican, a haven from the Resortville that dominates the rest of the cape. While the town may be larger than Lucas, San José is strikingly tranquil and collected. Elegant colonial architecture adds to the simple charm of this town. Religious services with hymns are held in the plaza every Wednesday, and snorkel shops snuggle peacefully with the *loncherías* next door.

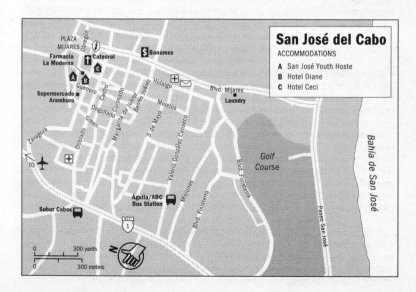

San José del Cabo

ACCOMMODATIONS

A San José Youth Hoste
B Hotel Diane
C Hotel Ceci

■ **ORIENTATION.** The **Transpeninsular Highway** on the west and **Blvd. Mijares** on the east, both running north-south, connect the town with San José's broad sweep of beautiful beach 2km away. From north to south, cross-streets, running east-west between the above two include **Obregón, Zaragoza, Doblado, Castro, Coronado, González,** and, much farther south along the resort-laden beach, **Paseo San José.** Between the two main north-south streets, **Green, Degollado, Guerrero, Morelos,** and **Hidalgo** run parallel from west to east. The conspicuous cathedral and *zócalo* are on Zaragoza near Hidalgo. To get to town from the **Aguila/ABC bus station,** turn left out of the station, and walk eight to 10 minutes down González until it hits Mijares (shaded by palm trees). Turn left on Mijares, walk three blocks and make another left on Zaragoza, to the *zócalo.*

■ **PRACTICAL INFORMATION.** Although another is under construction, San José de Cabo currently has only one **bus station** (tel. 2 11 00)—on González, two blocks from the highway. Aguila and ABC Autotransportes launch **buses** to: **Cabo San Lucas** (30min., every 1½hr., 16 pesos); **La Paz** (3hr., every hr. 6am-7pm, 95 pesos); and **Todos Santos** (1½hr., 8 per day, 60 pesos). **Thrifty Rent-A-Car** (tel. 2 41 51) on Mirajes at Doblado will rent VW Jalopy's with insurance and unlimited kilometers for US$50 per day. If you didn't have at least 25 candles on your last birthday cake, you will be charged a bit more (open daily 8am-10pm). The **tourist center** (tel. 2 29 60 ext. 150), on Zaragoza and Mijares, in the beige building next to the *zócalo,* offers a valuable map as well as plenty of brochures and info (open M-F 8am-3pm). Change money or use the **ATM** at **Banamex** (tel. 2 31 84) on Mijares, two blocks south of the *zócalo* (open M-F 8:30am-4:30pm, Sa 9am-2pm); traveler's checks can be cashed at most of the **casas de cambio** that line Mijares. **Laundry: Cabomatic** (tel. 2 29 33), five blocks south of the *zócalo* on Mijares in the same complex as the Bital Bank; (wash 10 pesos, dry 10 pesos; open M-Sa 7:30am-8pm, Su 9am-5pm.) **Emergency:** dial 060. **Police:** (tel. 2 03 61) in the City Hall at Zaragoza and Mijares. **Red Cross:** (tel. 2 03 16) on Mijares in the same complex as the post office (24hr. ambulance service). **Hospital:** (tel. 2 37 13 or 2 38 13) on Retorno Atunero, in Col. Clamizal. **Centro de Salud:** at Manuel Doblado 39 (tel. 2 02 41). **Farmacia La Moderna:** (tel. 2 00 50) on Zaragoza between Degollado and Guerrero (open daily 8am-9pm). **Post office:** (tel. 2 09 11) on Mijares and González, several blocks toward the beach on the right-hand side (open M-F 9am-4pm, Sa 9am-1pm). **Postal code:** 23400. **Internet access: CafeNet** (www.cafe.net.mx), follow Zaragoza north out of town past the PEMEX station. Approaching the Transpeninsular Highway., you'll see a sign for a big pharmacy on the left; CafeNet is in that complex. **Phone code:** 114.

■ **ACCOMMODATIONS.** With the approach of the mega-resorts, room prices in the center of town have been slowly increasing. However, compared to Cabo San Lucas, San José is a virtual heaven for the seeker of budget accommodations. Several economical hotels can be found along Zaragoza. You can enjoy multi-colored bedspreads and ancient paint jobs at **Hotel Ceci,** Zaragoza 22, 1½ blocks up from Mijares. Clean, cold rooms put guests in a positive mood and the bathrooms have colored glass windows—take a shower while admiring the cathedral. (Singles 100 pesos, with A/C 130 pesos; triples with A/C 150 pesos.) **The Hotel Diana** (tel. 2 04 90), on Zaragoza near the *centro,* has big, clean rooms with TVs and A/C. All rooms have one king-sized bed and one single bed. (All rooms 200 pesos.) **San José Youth Hostel** (tel. 2 24 64), on Obregón and Guerrero, has relatively clean and spacious pink rooms with fans, thick mattresses, and warm water. Although the hotel offers mail service, bike rentals, and long-distance phone calls, it can be a little desolate at times. (Singles and doubles 100 pesos, with color TV 180 pesos.) **Trailer Park Brisa del Mar** (tel. 2 39 99), just off the highway to San Lucas when it reaches the coast, provides beach campers, communal bathrooms, and a bar with TV (winter prices: beachfront hookup US$30 per day, back row spots US$18.50; summer prices: beachfront US$25 per day, back row US$18.50; tents US$10).

⌐⌐ **FOOD.** Budget restaurants in San José del Cabo are being pushed out by real estate offices and fancy tourist eateries, leaving few options between taco stands and *filet mignon*. A healthy suspicion of anglophone restaurants will save you money: if the menus are printed in flawless English, the food is probably more expensive than it ought to be. Good, moderately priced meals hide on Doblado and along Zaragoza, between the cathedral and the banks. The food at **Cafetería Rosy,** on Zaragoza and Green, is riveting. Seafood dishes such as *sopa de camarones* (shrimp soup; 35 pesos), *pescado en mantequilla* and *al mojo de ajo* (fish in butter or garlic sauce; 50 pesos), or *pollo a la naranja* (chicken in orange sauce; 45 pesos) will knock your socks off. (Open M-Sa 8am-5pm.) Follow locals to **El Nuevo Imperial,** Zaragoza and Green, a Chinese restaurant with great food and low prices. Entrees are usually below 30 pesos, and even the frighteningly named *paquete turístico* (tourist package) offers egg rolls, fried rice, and an entree for 35 pesos. People-watch on the outdoor patio, but if you must catch some sun, take your meal to go. (Open daily 8am-9:30pm.) For a cheap, delicious lunch, head to **Super Tortas** (tel. 2 31 05) on Doblado between Morelos and Hidalgo. This small restaurant serves a variety of tasty *tortas* (surprise!) starting at 28 pesos and *sabrosa* smoothies for 28 pesos—some people drive all the way from San Lucas simply to savor the smoothness. (Open M-Sa 7am-8pm.)

▣ **SIGHTS.** The most popular beach in town (for surfing, if not swimming) is **Costa Azul,** on Palmilla Pt., 1km south of the Brisa del Mar trailer park. To get there, take a bus headed for San Lucas (every 15min.) from Doblado and Highway. 1 and ask the driver to drop you off at Costa Azul. A 15-min. walk down Mijares leads to good beaches much closer to town. The newer luxury hotels mar the sand in spots, but there's plenty of natural, clean coastline in the stretches between the artificial structures. If you've got time between trips to the beach, stop by the **Huichol Gallery** (tel. 2 37 99), on Zaragoza and Mijares. It features beautiful handicrafts by local Huichols, who have lived centuries without much outside influence. (Open daily 8am-10pm.)

▣ **ENTERTAINMENT.** San José del Cabo can't compete with its noisy neighbor, but it's still possible to have a good time here—just kick back, relax, and don't expect conga lines and table dancing. **Piso #2,** Zaragoza 71, two blocks from the church, is even mellower. Red chairs, palm trees, and neon lights help you digest your Dos Equis (20 pesos). Huge mixed drinks are 20 pesos but don't try hitting the bar's pool tables after you've had one (W open bar). Downstairs, **Piso #1** offers the same prices and a similar atmosphere. (F 9-11pm free, open bar for women; W 9pm-2am men pay 120 pesos, women drink for free; open in summer daily 6pm-3am; in winter noon-3am.)

NEAR SAN JOSÉ DEL CABO: SANTIAGO

Although Santiago (57km from San José, pop. 4,500) may appear ordinary and uneventful upon entering, it is home to the only Siberian Tiger and Bald Eagle south of Mexicali. Believe it or not, this small town has the only **zoo** in Baja. The zoo is small, but it still houses interesting animals and a collection of labeled cacti. (Open daily 6am-6pm. Free, but donations are gladly accepted.) To get there, follow the main road in from the route and make a left at the far side of the *zócalo*. Follow this road towards Palomar's restaurant until it ends, then turn right and continue down until the Parque Zoológico appears on the right.

The real reason, however, to come to Santiageo is for the nearby **hotsprings** in the town of **Chorro.** Some rustic pools await the wearied traveler, and in the high season, the springs are diverted into more luxurious artificial tubs. To get to the pools, follow the directions to the zoo and continue on the road past the zoo for 7km until you arrive in the town of **Agua Caliente.** Bear right when you encounter the Casa de Salud and follow this road for 5km until it ends at a dam. Get out of the car and sniff the sulfur—you're there. Depending on the level of recent rainfall, you may have to hike up the stream for about 40 minutes to find larger pools; the tranquility and beauty is well worth the effort.

NORTHWEST MEXICO

Northwest Mexico is home to raucous border towns, calm fishing villages, vast expanses of desert, and warm water beaches along the alluring Sea of Cortés. For many, the first taste of life south of the border consists of nights of debauchery, rounds of tequila shots, oversized straw sombreros, and blistering heat. But in the midst of all this madness, many tourists overlook the rows of shantytowns, border-patrol battles, and miles of industrial wasteland that consume a large part of the cities. Things calm down considerably as you venture farther south. The grime and frenetic madness of Ciudad Juárez and Nogales, Mexico's brawny border towns, give way to bustling markets, colonial mansions, iconoclastic museums, and a surreal cactus-studded landscape. In some towns, things slow to a virtual standstill—you can hear the flies buzz and the wind whistle through the desert. The condominiums, time-shares, and resort hotels that cast their shadows over the *palapas* gracing the light-colored sands mark the presence of the U.S. citizens and Canadians who have discovered the elegant beaches of Sonora. Despite the gentrification of some of its beach towns, swaggering *vaqueros* clad in tight jeans can still be spotted in Sonora's smaller towns (like Kino Viejo). You may want to bring along a pair of cowboy boots and a wide-brimmed sombrero of your own—the rugged terrain requires a lot of stamina, and the *noroeste* sun is merciless.

The Sierra Madre Occidental rips through the heart of Northwest Mexico. To the east of the mountains, the parched desert gives even the larger cities in Chihuahua the feel of dusty frontier; frequent sandstorms enhance the mood. Along the coast, in the states of **Sonora** and **Sinaloa,** a melange of commercial ports, quiet fishing villages, and sprawling beaches overlook the warm waters of the Sea of Cortés. Landlocked **Durango,** traversed by the Sierra Madres, thrives on mining and is known for its Old-West ruggedness. But the most stunning sight in the *noroeste* are the **Barrancas del Cobre (Copper Canyons),** a spectacular series of deep gorges and unusual rock formations in **Chihuahua** brimming with tropical vegetation, all cut through by the Río Urique far below. The caves in the area are home to the reclusive Tarahumara Indians. The Northwest's diverse landscape and natural wonders are overlooked by most tourists, but those who look past the border towns and into the region's heartland and coast will reap the rewards.

HIGHLIGHTS OF NORTHWEST MEXICO

■ Mexico's best-kept secret are the **Barrancas del Cobre** (**Copper Canyons;** p. 232), which provide some of the most awe-inspiring vistas in the world—these canyons are four times the size of Arizona's Grand Canyon. Most travelers use the gorgeous town of **Creel** (p. 228) as a base from which to explore.

■ Take long, placid naps on the beaches of **Bahía Kino** (p. 204), a pair of tiny laid-back fishing towns.

■ **El Pinocate** (p. 197) is a four million-acre volcanic preserve and one of the most spectacular biospheres in the world. NASA trained astronauts for the Apollo moon mission here because the terrain is so similar.

SONORA

NOGALES

Pushed up against the border and straddled by steep hills covered with tin houses and block-long Corona signs, Nogales (pop. 300,000) is an archetypal border town

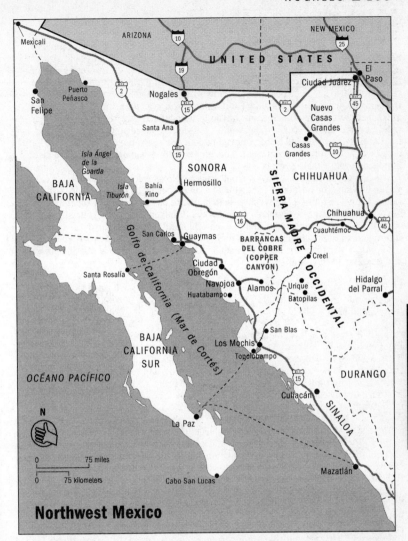

Northwest Mexico

with cheap curio shops and cheesy bars. The streets are crowded with street vendors actively promoting their merchandise to everyone and their mother. On shack-lined, candle-lit dirt roads far above the border bustle, entire blocks of families watch TV and cook together each evening. Born out of the 1848 Mexican-American War as something of an unarmed fortress, Nogales is rapidly growing as a result of the influx of U.S.-owned *maquiladoras* (factories). More than 100 U.S. companies have established production centers in the hills outside the downtown area, attracting Mexicans from across the Republic. However, in spite of its swelling population, Nogales remains a friendly place to get a good meal and enjoy the thrill of old-fashioned bargaining.

■ **ORIENTATION.** If you plan to venture beyond Nogales, obtain a **FMT/tourist card** (see **Tourist Cards,** p. 37) at the border and have your passport on hand. It's much simpler to get the card here than farther south. When you cross the border through the arched crossing complex, turn right into the **tourist office,** the first building on the right and to the left of the immigration center.

The **bus terminal** and **train station** are directly across from each other on **Carretera Internacional,** 4.5km from town. A taxi from the bus station to the center of twn will cost an exorbitant 50 pesos; instead cross the street and walk north to the end of the block, where you can catch one of the local white buses (3 pesos) marked "Parque Industrial" or "Villa Sonora." Downtown Nogales is the last stop. To get from downtown to the bus terminal and train station, wait at the bus stop on **Juárez** and **López Mateos,** one block south of the tourist office. Take the "Parque Industrial" bus and ask the driver to let you off before the bus terminal. A large supermarket called *Ley* should be to your right when you reach the correct stop on the corner of Carretera International. There is a second, smaller bus station two blocks before the main station.

The downtown area is relatively small, making Nogales fairly easy to navigate. If you're crossing the border by foot, you'll be on **Pesqueira;** by car, you'll drive in on López Mateos. From east to west, **Pesqueira, Juárez** (which becomes **López Mateos** several blocks south), **Morelos** (a walkway), **Obregón** (the main tourist drag), **Hidalgo,** and **Ingenieros** run parallel to each other and perpendicular to the border. Internacional runs parallel to the tall picket fence that marks the border. Proceeding south, away from the border, **Campillo, Ochoa, Pierson, Aguirre, Vázquez, Díaz,** and **González** all run parallel.

⚡ PRACTICAL INFORMATION. Elite (tel. 3 16 03) sends posh **buses** to: **Guadalajara** (666 pesos), **Hermosillo** (106 pesos), **Los Mochis** (292 pesos), **Mazatlán** (610 pesos), and **Mexico City** (1133 pesos). Call for schedules. Greyhound buses (tel. in Tucson, USA ((520) 287-5628) leave for **Tucson** (every hr.; 7am-7pm and 9pm; US$7) from their station half a block from the U.S. side of the border. Transportes del Pacífico (tel. 3 16 06) has buses *de paso* that leave every two hours from 8am to 8:30pm and go to: **Guaymas** (5hr.; 157 pesos); **Hermosillo** (3hr.; 106 pesos); **Puerto Vallarta** (26hr.; 570 pesos); **Querétaro** (33hr.; 1069 pesos); and **Tepic** (22hr.; 500 pesos). Prices listed are for first class fares. Transportes Norte de Sonora (tel. 3 16 03) runs buses to: **Guadalajara** (26hr.; 762 pesos); **Hermosillo** (3hr.; every hr. 8:30am-6:30pm; 96 pesos); **Los Mochis** (11hr.; 7:30am-11:30pm; 257 pesos); **Mazatlán** (16hr.; 531 pesos); and **Mexico City** (32hr.; 3 per day; 739 pesos). Check schedules for changes.

The **tourist office** (tel. 2 06 66) is to the left of the border from the Mexican side, in the Edificio Puerta de México #1. The friendly, English-speaking staff can provide maps of the downtown area. (Open daily 8:30am-7 or 8pm.) **Banks** line Obregón near the border. **Banamex** has two locations: one at Obregón and Ochoa (tel. 2 07 80 or 2 55 05; open M-Th 8:30am-4:30pm, F 8:30am-5:30pm); the other a 10-minute walk farther south on Obregón (tel. 2 12 51 or 2 10 65; open M-F 8:30am-4:30pm, Sa 9am-3:30pm). Both exchange dollars and traveler's checks and have 24-hour **ATMs. Luggage storage** is available from 6am to 10pm at the bus terminal (1 peso per hr.). Buy munchies at **VH Supermarket,** Obregón 475 (tel. 2 48 00), between Ramos and Rodríguez, and 10 minutes from Av. Juárez (open daily 8am-10pm).

Emergency: dial 060. **Police:** (tel. 2 01 29 or 2 01 14) at González and Leal with English speakers on hand in the afternoon (open 24hr.). **Highway Patrol:** dial (tel. 4 18 30 or 4 18 33). **Red Cross:** (tel. 3 58 00 or 3 58 01) on Elías Calles and Providencia (open 24hr). **Medical assistance: Seguro Social,** Escobedo 756 (tel. 3 59 85), at Obregón (take the "Parque Industrial" bus). English is spoken (open 24hr). Some English is spoken at the **Hospital Básico,** Dr. Francisco Arriola 1277 (tel. 3 06 71 or 3 34 65 or 3 34 60; open 24hr). There are many pharmacies, but for late night needs try, **Farmacia San Xavier,** Campillo 73 (tel. 2 55 03), between Juárez and Morelos (open 24hr). The bus terminal **caseta** (see below) has fax machines. Downtown Nogales has a high concentration of **LADATELs.** Look for them at Obregón and Campillo, Obregón and Flores Guerra, and at the border in front of the tourist office. The **caseta** in the bus terminal (tel. 3 50 81; fax 3 50 82) offers overpriced international calls, but collect calls are free from the marked phone next to the *caseta* (open 24hr). **Post office:** on Juárez 52 (tel. 2 12 47), at Campillo. **Postal code:** 84000. **Phone code:** 631.

█▐ ACCOMMODATIONS AND FOOD. Relative to towns farther south in Mexico, rates in Nogales are steep. The most economical budget hotels can be found on the block behind the tourist office on Av. Juárez. The **Hotel San Carlos,** Juárez 22 (tel. 2 13 46 or 2 14 09; fax 2 15 57), between Internacional and Campillo, features a lobby with an ice-cold purified water dispenser and a mural of San Carlos. Large, clean rooms have A/C, color TVs with U.S. cable, massage-showers, and phones. (Singles 190 pesos; doubles 290 pesos.) Right next door is the **Hotel Regis** (tel. 2 51 81 or 2 55 35). Clean, peach-colored rooms have A/C, phones, and TV. If you're afraid you'll oversleep, don't worry—*norteño* tunes are piped in through the speakers in each room's ceiling. (Singles 235 pesos; doubles 250 pesos.)

There are oodles of overpriced restaurants that cater to daytrippers from the U.S. Ditch the tourist traps and head straight for **La Posada Restaurant,** Pierson 116 (tel. 2 04 39), off Obregón, where you can mingle with the town's *petit-bourgeois.* Tiny birds chirp quietly in the cool breeze provided by the ceiling fans. Painted tiles and miniature clay pots adorn the walls, while *burritos de machaca* (dried beef, 19 pesos) and *chimichangas* (15 pesos) grace the tables. (Open daily 7:30am-10pm.) **Café Ajijic,** Obregón 182 (tel. 2 50 74), features a picturesque fountain in the middle of its red-tiled patio and is a perfect place to relax under the shade of a table umbrella with an espresso or cappuccino (both US$1.50; open 9am-midnight).

▣▐ SIGHTS AND ENTERTAINMENT. Most of the curio and craft shops line Obregón. You may get good deals if you bargain and know something about quality. In fact, vendors expect shoppers to ask for a lower price, but obnoxious haggling is frowned upon. Before buying, ask turquoise vendors to put the rocks to "the lighter test." Plastic or synthetic material will quickly melt under a flame. Likewise, when buying silver, look for a ".925" stamp on the piece; if it's not there, the goods are bad.

At night, the bars on Obregón are filled with a mix of locals and tourists. **Bora Bora,** Obregón 38, between Campillo and Internacional, offers live music at night and drinks from 10 to 30 pesos (open W-Su noon-3am). Across the street, giant metal palm trees greet you at the entrance to **Kookaracha's,** Obregón 1 (tel. 2 47 73), where you can dance the night away and down US$1 tequila shots or chill with a *cerveza* by the fountain in the "roach's" techno-colored courtyard (open W, F, Sa 10pm-3am). There is a US$5 minimum on Saturdays at **Catoche Cafe Bar** (tel. 2 31 10), on López Mateos but with it comes three beers and...karaoke! (happy hour M-F 6-8pm; open M-Sa 1pm-2:30am).

Not in the mood to get intoxicated? **Cinemas Gemelos,** Obregón 368 (tel. 2 50 02) between González and Torres, shows first- and second-run American films (open M-F 3:30pm-midnight, Sa-Su 1:30pm-midnight; tickets 30 pesos. Either dubbed or subtitled in Spanish). For those looking for more culture, the new **Teatro Auditorio de Nogales,** on Obregón between Vásquez and González brings live performances from Mexico City. The box office has showtimes and prices. Feeling lucky? **Casino de Nogales,** on Campillo between López Mateos and Elias Calles may be the place for you.

PUERTO PEÑASCO

Once a launching pad for shrimp boats, Puerto Peñasco dried up when overfishing decimated the shrimp population in the Sea of Cortés. Economically widowed, the town now courts investors with a dowry of tax breaks and other incentives. Just 105km from the border, the town with the English nickname "Rocky Point" attracts a fair share of weekenders, much like neighboring northern Baja. Despite the throngs of gringos, somewhat tranquil beaches and clean streets make this dusty port worth a trip. Budget travelers, however, should beware of the special "tourist pricing." For the better bargain, always ask for prices in pesos instead of in dollars, even if the seller is reluctant. Fifty kilometers north on the road to Sonoita lies the fascinating **El Pinacate** volcanic area.

⚐ ORIENTATION AND PRACTICAL INFORMATION. To reach the *centro* from the bus station, take a left past PEMEX and walk nine blocks down Puerto Peñasco's main road, **Blvd. Juárez;** continue south on Juárez past the **Dársena**—the port area—and eventually to **Malecón** (or Old Port), Peñasco's old section, on the western edge of town. **Playa Hermosa** (Beautiful Beach) lies to the northwest, and **Playa Miramar** lies to the south. Town activity centers around two intersections: **Fremont** and **Juárez** and **Constitución** and **Juárez.** Numbered *calles* run east-west and start with 1 at **Playa Miramar** (southernmost); boulevards run north-south.

Buses depart from Juárez and Calle 24. Autotransportes de Baja California (tel. 3 20 19) sends buses to: **Ensenada** (10hr., 260 pesos); **Mexicali** (5hr., 150 pesos); **San Luis** (3hr., 100 pesos); **Sonoita** (1hr., 40 pesos); **Tecate** (6hr., 212 pesos); and **Tijuana** (8hr., 232 pesos). All buses are *de paso;* buses leave for **Mexicali** at 8:30am and 5pm while those headed for **Tijuana** and farther leave at 8:30am and 1am. Transportes Norte de Sonora (tel. 3 36 40) sends buses to **Guaymas** (9hr., 4 per day, 249 pesos) and **Hermosillo** (7hr., 5 per day, 214 pesos).

Puerto Peñasco's **tourist office** (tel. 3 35 55), Blvd. Benito Juárez on the northern outskirts of town is a tiny green shack where little English is spoken (open daily 9am to mid-afternoon). **Bancomer** (tel. 3 24 30), just past Jim Bur Plaza heading south on Juárez exchanges currency and traveler's checks (open M-F 8:30am-4pm, Sa 10am-2pm). **Banamex,** on Juárez at Freemont, provides the same services (open M-F 8:30am-4:30pm). Both have 24 hour **ATMs.**

Stock up at **Supermarket Jim Bur** (tel. 3 25 61), on Juárez in the Jim Bur Plaza (open M-Sa 8am-9pm, Su 8am-4pm). At **Lavamática Peñasco** on Constitución at Morúa across from Hotel Paraíso del Desierto, a wash costs 8 pesos; a dry costs 7 pesos (open M-Sa 8am-7pm). **Police** (tel. 3 26 26) wait at Fremont and Juárez but speak little English (open 24hr.). The **Red Cross** (tel. 3 22 66), on Fremont at Chiapas, is open 24 hours. Little English is spoken. **Farmacia Botica Lux:** Ocampo 146 (tel. 3 28 81), two blocks east of Blvd. Juárez (open daily 7:30am-midnight). **Farmacia 24 Horas:** (tel. 3 54 45), don't be fooled by the name, it's only open 7am-11pm, on Calle 13 between Francisco Villa and Pino Suarez. **Hospital Municipal:** (tel. 3 21 10) Morúa and Juárez; little English is spoken (open 24hr.). **Post office,** (tel. 3 27 82) Chiapas, two blocks east of Juárez on Fremont (open M-F 8am-3pm). **Postal code:** 83550. The **fax** and **telegram office** (tel. 3 27 82) is in the same building (open M-F 8am-6pm, Sa 9am-noon). **Internet access** can be found at **Infotec** (tel. 3 64 60), at Juárez and Ocampo, for US$3 per hour (open M-F 9am-9pm). **Phone code:** 638.

⚐⌂ ACCOMMODATIONS AND FOOD. Budget rooms in Puerto Peñasco are a rare commodity, since cheap accommodations are being torn down left and right to clear space for expensive resorts, condos, and time-shares. The most economical way to spend the night is to camp in your tent or RV. Trailer parks abound in the south around Playa Miramar. **Playa Miramar RV Park** (tel. 3 25 87), on Playa Miramar (go figure), rents scenic spots year-round with cable TV, and full hookup. Washers, dryers, and showers are also available. (Check-out noon. 1-2 people US$13; each additional person US$2; weekly US$80 with beachfront spaces slightly higher.) Otherwise, one of the last remaining quasi-budget hotels is the **Motel Playa Azul** (tel. 3 62 96), Calle 13 and Pino Suárez, about two blocks from Playa Hermosa. It offers nicely furnished rooms with ancient TVs that receive a single channel, generous A/C, and yes, private bathrooms with hot water. Bargain with the manager. (Singles 250 pesos; doubles 350 pesos.)

As always, *taquerías* are the spot for budget grub; find some at Juárez between Constitución and Calle 24, near the bus station and the Old Port area. Most beachside restaurants cater to gringos, with their (high) prices quoted in U.S. dollars; insist on paying in good ol' *moneda nacional.* For traditional Mexican cuisine, head east on Calle 13 and turn left onto Blvd. Kino to **La Curva** (tel. 3 34 70). This family owned restaurant will treat you right and satiate your appetite. The *combinación grande* includes chips-'n-*salsa,* rice, beans, and your choice of entree for 45 pesos. (Open M-Th 8am-10:30pm, F-Su 8am-11pm.) **Gamma's** (tel. 3 56 80), on

Calle 13, in front of Plaza Las Glorias Hotel, specializes in fried fish. Dine at picnic tables under an open air *palapa* and gaze at the sunbathers on Playa Hermosa. A plate of fried shrimp goes for US$3 and a grilled steak for US$3.50. (Open daily 8am-11pm.)

🔲🔳 **SIGHTS AND ENTERTAINMENT.** Puerto Peñasco's clean and rarely crowded beaches are blessed with clear, warm waters. Shallow tide pools cradle clams, small fish, and colorful shells. **Sandy Beach** and **Playa Hermosa** are the best choices for swimming; both have curio shops, restaurants, and hotels galore. The beaches around **Rocky Point** and **Playa Miramar**, at the southern end of town, are less crowded but also rockier and rougher. Playa Miramar also brims with RV parks and condominiums. For those interested in sand-and-sea research and conservation, the **Intercultural Center for the Study of Deserts and Oceans** (**CEDO;** tel. 2 01 13), at Playa Las Concaas, 9km from town (taxi 40 pesos), gives free tours of its wet lab and museum Tuesdays at 2pm and Saturdays at 4pm (open M-Sa 9am-5pm, Su 10am-2pm). **Excursions Paraiso,** Victor Estrella 14 (tel. 3 62 09), across from Thrifty Ice Cream in the Old Port, rents sea kayaks (single kayaks US$35; double kayaks US$40; weekend rates US$5 more; boogie boards US$10 per day). The friendly folks at **Sun 'n' Fun** (tel. 3 54 50), on Juárez at the entrance to the Old Port, will teach you how to go clamming and give you tips on how to prepare your catch, all for US$10 (open M-Th 7am-6pm, F-Sa 7am-7pm, Su 7am-5pm).

To get to Playa Hermosa, turn right on Calle 13 when heading south on Juárez; the beach is straight ahead five or six blocks down. To reach Playa Miramar, head south on Juárez, and turn left onto Campeche near the Benito Juárez monument. Continue uphill for three blocks; Playa Miramar will be on your left. To reach Playa Las Conchas, head south on Juárez, turn left on Fremont near the Plaza del Camaronero, take a right onto Camino a las Conchas, and follow the rock-slab road for 3 or 4km. To reach Sandy Beach, head north on Encinas or Juárez until the intersection with Camino a Bahía Choya. Take a left and follow the road; turn left on the road labeled "To Sandy Beach."

NEAR PUERTO PEÑASCO: EL PINACATE

Forty-eight kilometers north of Puerto Peñasco on Rte. 8 to Sonora is the **El Pinacate** volcanic preserve, one of the largest and most spectacular biospheres in the world. Encompassing more than four million acres, and extending to the upper reaches of the Sea of Cortés, the biosphere was created in June 1992 to limit volcanic rock excavation and protect endangered species. Pockmarked by over 600 craters and 400 cinder cones, the Pinacate lava fields form 30,000-year-old islands in a vast sea of sand. From inside the park, the only thing visible for kilometers around are fields of igneous rock and monochromatic moonscape (NASA trained astronauts here for the Apollo moon mission because the terrain is so similar). The people of the Tohono O'odham nation have lived in this region for tens of thousands of years, crossing the desert on foot from Arizona to bathe in the waters they consider to be sacred and healing. They also extract fresh water from *saguaro* cacti.

Ecoturismo Peñasco (tel./fax 3 32 09) leads tours into the area; ask at the tourist office for details or talk to Peggy at **CEDO** (see above; 1-2 people US$50 per person, 3-4 people US$40 per person, 5 or more people US$35 per person). The vast, isolated, climatically harsh region makes a guide necessary. If you do decide to tough it out alone, four-wheel-drive, high-clearance vehicles with partially deflated tires are a must. Bring tons of water, a shovel, a spare tire, and firewood. Camping is permitted, but don't leave anything behind and don't remove any souvenirs. The ideal time to visit is from November to March, when temperatures range from approximately 15 to 32°C, as opposed to summer months, when temperatures can exceed 47°C.

CABORCA

About halfway between Hemosillo and Puerto Peñasco rises the agricultural metropolis of Caborca (pop. 200,000). Surrounded by desert and pastures of cattle,

Caborca is virtually void of tourists year-round. While Caborca is no Cancún, it does offer simple pleasures for the itinerant traveler and merits a stop if not only for a meal at the city's top *asadero*. If you're on your way to the beaches or coming back and need a rest stop, fear not, as Caborca has all your needs covered—especially if you've experienced a gringo overload or your carnivorous tastebuds beckon.

◪ **ORIENTATION AND PRACTICAL INFORMATION.** Caborca lies 269km northwest of Hermosillo on **Rte. 2.** Its main street, **Obregón** or **Calle 5,** runs east-west and is lined with shops and *asderos*. Running parallel to Obregón are **Calle 1, Calle 2,** etc. Perpendicular to *los calles* run *avenidas* which are lettered A-Z. The center of the city is around **Obregón** and **Quiroz y Mora,** or **Calle E.** Although the *calles* and *avenidas* intersect nicely at right angles, they can be extremely confusing and some of the letter and numbers have been replaced by extended street names. For instance, Av. B is also **Av. Padre Gónzalez,** and Calle 8 is **Blvd. Benito Juárez.** So be sure to know the alphabet backwards and forwards if you plan to navigate the streets.

To get to Obregón from the **Transportes Norte de Sonora** bus station, turn right as you exit the station and make your first right onto Calle 8. Walk about three blocks to Av. Padre Gonzalez, turn left and walk three more blocks and you'll be at Obregón. From the **Transportes del Pacifico** station, walk left as you exit the station one block and turn left at Av. Padre Gonzalez. In three blocks you'll be at Obregón.

Transportes de Pacifico (tel. 2 35 59), on Calle 8 and Av. A, sends **buses** to: **Tijuana** (9hr., 284 pesos); **Hermosillo** (3hr., 118 pesos); **Guadalajara** (24hr., 774 pesos); **Guaymas** (6hr., 167 pesos); **Mexico City** (32hr., 1030 pesos); **Mexicali** (7½hr., 180 pesos). All buses are *de paso* and leave every hour. Transportes Norte de Sonora (tel. 2 12 32) on La Carretera and Calle 8 next to Motel Los Arcos sends buses to: **Tijuana** (9hr., 304 pesos); **Hermosillo** (3hr., 126 pesos); **Mexicali** (7½hr., 193 pesos); **Guadalajara** (24hr., 828 pesos); **Puerto Peñasco** (2½hr.; 2, 6:30, and 9pm; 100 pesos); and **Mexico City** (32hr., 1102 pesos). Again, all buses are *de paso* and leave every hour.

Bancomer (tel. 2 06 16 or 2 06 17), at Obregón and Sotelo, exchanges only American Express traveler's checks (open M-F 8:30am-3pm; with 24hr. **ATM**). Stock up on foodstuffs at **PH Supermarket** (tel. 2 06 00), at 6 de Abril between Calle 8 and 7 (open daily 7am-10pm). **Lavamatica,** Quiroz y Mora #52 between Calle 7 and 8, offers self or full-service laundry (open M-Sa 9am-9pm, Su 9am-3pm). **Emergencies: 08. Police:** 2 08 69. **Red Cross:** 2 11 77. **Hospital:** (tel. 2 08 98) Calle 1 and Av. K. **Farmacia Principal** (tel. 2 25 79) at Calle Obregón and Av. M, has the best hours of the town's drug stores (open daily 8am-midnight). **Post Office:** (tel. 2 01 16) Av. Pereida and Av. Guillermo (open M-F 8am-3pm). **Postal Code:** 83600. The **Telecomm** (tel. 2 03 55), at Quiroz y Mora, one block north of Obregón, sends and receives faxes (open M-F 8am-6pm, Sa-Su 9am-noon). To check email or surf *el red* visit **Sistemas Modernos de Caborca** (tel. 2 34 34) Blvd. Juárez #225 between Av. P and Q, charges 25 pesos per hour or 20 pesos for 30 minutes. (open M-F 9am-1pm and 3-7pm). **Phone code:** 637.

▐▐ **ACCOMMODATIONS AND FOOD.** If you decide to spend the night in Caborca, you will be in good hands, as there are several solid, centrally located hotels. **Motel Jesusita** (tel. 2 17 51), Av. B at Calle 4, offers clean rooms with A/C, cable TV, and super high pressure showers (singles 160 pesos; doubles 180 pesos; triples 211; key deposit 50 pesos). **Hotel La Rivera** (tel. 2 13 90), on Av. H between Calle 6 and Calle 5, has A/C, private baths, and TVs that receive four channels (singles 140 pesos; doubles 170 pesos). Caborca also serves as the mecca for carnivorous tourists. **Asadero Bífalo** (tel. 2 27 35), Obregón and Av. K, is the town's best budget eatery, serving tasty fresh tacos (8 pesos each). If you're in the mood to splurge, treat yourself to an *order de carne* complete with broiled meat, ribs, veggies, quesadillas, beans, tortilla chips, and fresh guacamole plus *salsa* for 67

COCO LOCO About twelve miles off Route 1 on the way to San Luis Gonzaga, lives a one-legged man named Coco. Besides being the proprietor of a bar/hotel/restaurant appropriately named "Coco's," he gets his kicks from hauling pathetic gringos and their vehicles from the muck of Baja's infamous roads. Constantly the subject of the English Baja newsletter, Coco rescues the inane from the dirt-death-trap running south from Puertocitos to Rte. 1. Besides being a wizard mechanic, Coco is seemingly an aspiring short-story writer. If stymied by multiple flat tires, Coco may come to your rescue but retain the story of your vehicular debacle in a 2-inch-thick tome of roadside rescues. Who knows? You too may be imortalized in the book-of-big-mistakes if you rest too much faith in the power of your S.U.V.

pesos. (Open daily 10am-midnight.) **Pepe's Burger 3** (tel. 2 63 27), Obregón at Calle H, is an all-you-can-eat buffet for 35 pesos (open M-Sa 10am-5pm).

🔲🔲 **SIGHTS AND ENTERTAINMENT.** Besides Asadero Bífalo, Caborca's main attraction is **La Concepción de Nuestra Señora de Caborca.** This church, which was constructed in 1809, served as a defense outpost against invading American filibusters in 1857. Every year on April 6, the locals commemorate their victory with a fiesta. La Concepción lies on 6 de Abril, about 1mi. south from Obregón.

While the locals claim there is little to do in Caborca at night except sleep, and weekend entertainment consists of heading to Puerto Peñasco, Caborca manages to hold its own thanks to **Dunas Discoteca Bar** (tel. 2 70 00 ext. 173), the town's main nighttime hot spot. Located on Quiroz y Mora at the corner of Calle 10, Dunas has 15 peso beers and live music (F-Sa 11pm-2am). On Thursday traditional *folklorico* music hits the stand. (Open Th-Su 9pm-2am. Cover F-Sa 40 pesos.)

HERMOSILLO

The capital city of Sonora, named after the famous Mexican general, is an expansive metropolis and a center for commerce and education. With glorious cathedrals, majestic government palaces, stylish open-air malls, an endearing *zócalo*, and an incredible ecological research center and zoo, areas of Hermosillo (pop. 700,000) are certainly worth exploring. Daytrippers to the beaches of Kino will find hopping university-spurred nightlife in Hermosillo. However, not all of this huge city boasts such allure. The crowded, dusty thoroughfares of the *centro* scream during the day with the frenzied activity of urban life and are left by sundown without much more than garbage on the streets. The low-slung architecture of the *centro* affords a clear view of the *Cerro de la Campana* (a tall mountain cluttered with radio towers and satellite dishes) from practically every street corner. If you get an early start and the buses run on time, you can breeze from Tucson to the beaches of Guaymas or Mazatlán in a single day (or vice versa), and skip the lonelier parts of Sonora entirely. Although much of Hermosillo is unsavory and unsafe at night, a layover in this lively city can add a pleasant surprise to your trip.

ORIENTATION

Hermosillo lies 271km south of the border on **Rte. 15,** the main route connecting the western U.S. and central Mexico. **Buses** depart from the main terminal on **Blvd. Encinas,** 2km east of the city center. To get from the bus station to the center of town, catch a bus marked "Circuito Norte-Mendoza" or "Centro" (every 10min. 5am-10:30pm, 3 pesos). Taxis will ask 45 pesos for a trip to the *centro* but may go lower; don't get in until settling a price. To get to the bus station from town, wait for a bus at Elías Calles and Matamoros, across from Óptica Morfín.

At the junction of **Blvd. Luis Encinas** and **Rosales,** the **Hermosillo Flash** (an electronic bulletin board displaying daily news) helps the mapless orient themselves. Most of the activity lies inside the square area (the *centro*) bordered by **Rosales** on the west, **Juárez** on the east, **Serdán** on the south, and **Encinas** on the north. Jardín Juárez is bounded by **Colosio, Sonora, Matamoros,** and **Juárez.** The area surrounding Sonora west of the park should be avoided by lone travelers, especially women, at night. Listed from west to east, the principal north-south streets are **Rosales, Pino Suárez, Yañez, García Morales, Garmendia, Guerrero, Matamoros, Juárez,** and **González.** Listed from north to south, the east-west streets are **Encinas, Niños Héroes, Oaxaca, Sonora, Colosio, Dr. Noriega, Morelia, Monterrey, Plutarco Elías Calles,** and **Serdán.** If you get lost, remember that the antenna-capped mountain is always to the south if you're in the *centro*.

▌ PRACTICAL INFORMATION

TRANSPORTATION

Airport: (tel. 61 00 08) 10km west of town on Transversal toward Bahía Kino. Get there with the help of a small red bus called a *taxi colectivo;* it departs from the bus or train station (3 pesos). Aeroméxico (tel. 16 82 59) goes to: **Guadalajara** (2hr.; 8:15am and 3:25pm; 1514 pesos); **Mexico City** (2½hr.; 8:15, 11:10am, 3:25, and 7:20pm; 1837 pesos); **Tijuana** (1hr.; 10:50am; 750 pesos), and other destinations. Mexicana (tel. 61 01 12) will carry you to: **Mexico City** (2hr.; 3:15 and 7:20pm; 1306 pesos) and more. Times and flights vary.

Buses: All service out of Hermosillo is *de paso;* during holidays and weekends you'll need to lace up your boxing gloves in order to win a seat. Buses to **Tijuana** and **Mexico City** fill up early, so buy tickets at least a day ahead. The cheapest carrier is Transportes del Pacífico (tel. 12 50 91), including buses to: **Guadalajara** (22hr.; every hr.; 747 pesos); **Guaymas** (1½hr.; every hr.; 52 pesos); **Los Mochis** (7hr.; every hr.; 180 pesos); **Mazatlán** (13hr.; every hr.; 482 pesos; or 14hr.; 280 pesos); **Mexicali** (9hr.; every hr.; 316 pesos); **Mexico City** (30hr.; every hr.; 1077 pesos; or 32hr.; 710 pesos); **Nogales** (4hr.; 3 per day; 106 pesos; or 4hr.; 70 pesos); and **Tijuana** (12hr.; every hr.; 427 pesos; or 12hr.; 280 pesos). Transportes Norte de Sonora (tel. 13 40 50) goes to most of the above, plus **Acapulco.**

Car Rental: Budget, Garmendia 46 and Tamaulipas (tel. 14 30 33 or 14 38 05). Open M-F 8am-6pm, Sa-Su 8am-3pm. **Hertz,** Blvd. Rodríguez and Guerrero (tel. 14 85 00 or 14 85 03). Open M-F 8am-6pm, Sa, Su 8am-3pm.

TOURIST AND FINANCIAL SERVICES

Tourist Office: (tel. 17 29 64; fax 17 00 60), on the 3rd fl. of the **Centro de Gobierno de Sonora** at Cultura and Rosales. Walk south on Rosales over the canal, turn right, then walk 1 block west. Look for the buildings crowned with indigenous drawings. If you need help, ask one of the officers wearing gray-and-brown camouflage. Open M-F 8am-5pm.

Currency Exchange: Banks line Encinas and Serdán. **Bancomer** (tel. 59 33 43), on Serdán at Yañez, cashes traveler's checks. Open M-F 8am-4pm. The **casa de cambio** is open Sa 10am-2:30pm. **Banamex** (tel. 14 76 15), on Serdán at Matamoros, is closer to the center. Open M-F 8:30am-4:30pm, Sa 9am-3:30pm. There are 24hr. **ATMs** at both. There's also **Bital** on the 1st fl. of the Centro de Gobierno (see above), open M-F 8:30am-5pm.

American Express: Hermex Travel (tel. 17 17 18), on Rosales at Monterrey. Open M-F 8:30am-1pm and 3-6:30pm, Sa 9am-1pm.

LOCAL SERVICES

Supermarket: Ley Centro (tel. 17 32 94), on Juárez at Morelia. Absolutely huge. Public toilets. Takes U.S. dollars at a good exchange rate. Open daily 6:30am-10pm.

Laundry: La Burbuja, on Guerrero and Niños Heroes. Open daily 8am-1pm and 3-7pm.

EMERGENCY AND COMMUNICATIONS

Emergency: dial 08.

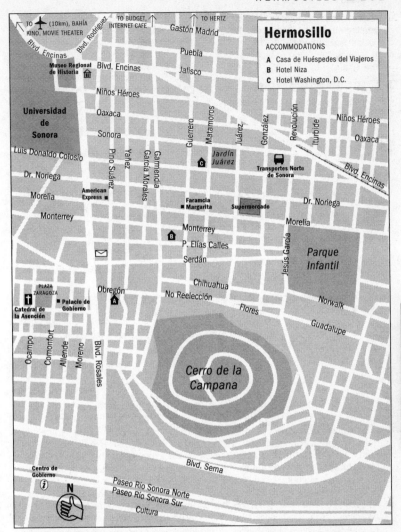

Ambulance: dial 10 04 00 or 17 11 26.

Police: (tel. 18 55 64), at Periférico Nte. and Solidaridad. Some English spoken. Open 24hr.

Transit Police: (tel. 16 08 77).

Red Cross: (tel. 14 07 69), on Encina at 14 de Abril. Open 24hr. Barely English-speaking staff on hand daily 9am-5pm.

Pharmacy: Farmacia Margarita, Morelia 93 (tel. 13 15 90), at Guerrero. Open 24hr.

Hospital: (tel. 13 25 56), on Transversal at Reyes. Open 24hr. English spoken.

Post Office: (tel. 12 00 11), on Elías Calles at Rosales. Open M-F 8am-7pm, Sa-Su 8am-noon. **Postal Code:** 83000.

Fax: Telecomm (tel. 17 21 50 or 12 03 56), in the same building as the post office on Blvd. Rosales side. Also **telegram** service. Open M-F 8am-7pm, Sa 8:30am-4pm, Su 9am-12:30pm.

Internet Access: Arroba Café, Blvd. Rodríguez 96, (tel. 14 50 70) on the corner of Garmendia. Open M-F 9am-11pm, Su 2-11pm. 30 pesos per hr. Minimum 30 minutes. Credit cards accepted.

Phone Code: 62.

ACCOMMODATIONS

Hermosillo has its fair share of budget hotels, allowing those who must watch every peso they spend to sleep comfortably and safely. Air conditioning is costly but sometimes indispensable, especially in the blistering summer heat.

◼ **Hotel Washington, D.C.,** Dr. Noriega 68 Pte. (tel. 13 11 83) between Matamoros and Guerrero. This place has nothing to do with the capital of the U.S. It does have helpful management, good-sized rooms with A/C, clean bathrooms and no red tape. The gated entrance provides solid security, and the open air hallways and red clay tiles are reminiscent of a Spanish villa. The only drawback is that the "D.C." can get a little loud sometimes. Singles 115 pesos; each additional person 25 pesos.

Hotel Niza, Elías Calles 66 (tel. 17 20 28 or 17 20 35) between Guerrero and Garmendia. A grandiose Art Deco hotel, with a pink atrium graced with murals and a colossal stained glass globe. Rooms branching off this centerpiece have A/C, color TV, and comfy beds. Singles 170 pesos; doubles 200 pesos. There is a convenient restaurant in the lobby with *comida corrida* for 21 pesos.

Casa de Huéspedes del Viajero, Sufragio Efectivo 90, between Pino Suárez and Yañez. Walk south on Suárez; as you pass Extasis Nite Club, turn left onto S. Efectivo. Unbelievably large rooms in an 84-year-old building. Adobe construction and fans keep the rooms cool. Aging outdoor bathroom. Lock your bags, since there's only someone at the entrance 7am-7pm. Singles 60 pesos.

FOOD

For cheap refueling, head for the *taco* and *torta* places around **Serdán** and **Guerrero**, where *taquitos* and quesadillas cost 7 or 8 pesos and *comida corrida* goes for around 15-20 pesos. Alternatively, try the counters lining the inside of the *mercado* at **Matamoros, Guerrero,** and **Elías Calles.** Although busy and smelly, some are sufficiently sanitary and above all, it's cool inside. Choose wisely: look out for flies and dirty pans and tabletops. Most offer tacos for a paltry sum, but both *Let's Go* and your mother do not recommend eating foods containing uncooked vegetables in these establishments.

◼ **Mi Cocina,** Obregón 84 (tel. 17 55 38), between Pino Suárez and Yañez. Omar opens his *cocina* (kitchen) to budget travelers, serving up a mean 2-course home-cooked meal for only 25 pesos and making great conversation all the while. Open M-F 7:30am-6pm.

Restaurant "My Friend" (tel. 13 10 44), Elías Calles at Yañez. This restaurant is definitely trying to make some American *amigos*. A framed photo of a cheeseburger (20 pesos), fries, and a soft drink beckons to starved and homesick gringos. Otherwise, enjoy delicious *huevos al gusto* (eggs how ya like 'em) for 15 pesos or a platter of 3 *tacos de cabeza y barbacoa* (BBQ pig snouts) for 15 pesos. Open M-Sa 7am-6pm.

Restaurant Jung, Niños Héroes 75 (tel. 13 28 81), at Encinas. A new-age vegetarian restaurant a mere 6 blocks from the center of town? Yes indeed. Relax to soothing music and the faint smell of incense as you savor the rejuvenating *comida corrida*, which comes with wheat rolls, soup, fruit juice, an entree, *frijoles*, whole-grain rice, and dessert (whew!...55 pesos). Jung also offers an assortment of cereals with fruit (16-25 pesos) or Belgian waffles with pure maple syrup (25 pesos) for breakfast. The adjoining herbal medicine, Eastern philosophy, and pseudo-psychology store has a wide assortment of natural products from ginseng to sesame candy (plus *agua purificada*). Happy Hour M-Sa 5-7pm. Open M-Sa 7:30am-8pm, Su 9am-5pm.

Fonda Chapala (tel. 12 39 92), on Guerrero between Sonora and Oaxaca. Mexican golden oldies blare from the jukebox while throngs of middle-aged men drown their sorrows in 40s of Tecate. Chicken, fish, or meat dishes come fried to crispy perfection and served with french fries, *frijoles*, tortillas, side salad, and a drink (35-38 pesos). The tipsy men aside, you might as well be in your Mexican aunt's house—if you're Mexican and if you have an aunt, that is. Open daily 7am-10pm.

SIGHTS AND ENTERTAINMENT

Look for the cross-capped spires of the architecturally eclectic and beautifully adorned **Catedral de la Asunción** (tel. 12 05 01), as you walk south on Rosales past the post office on Hidalgo and Ocampo (office and gift shop open M-F 8am-7pm, Sa 8am-4pm). Fugitives from the blistering sun can find refuge in the bee-yoo-tiful and refreshingly shady **Plaza Zaragoza,** where looming trees surround an open-air bandstand. Other shady parks line the streets near the plaza, making this one of the more peaceful areas of Hermosillo and a welcome change from the dusty, filth-ridden streets of the *centro*. This area is well lit at night, making it safer than the lonely *centro*. For the kids, a **playground,** complete with basketball courts, dwells on the corner of Pino Suárez and Elías Calles, adjacent to the post office.

The **Museo Regional de Historia,** on Rosales at Encinas by the University of Sonora, which contains exhibits on pre-Hispanic and colonial history (open M-F 9am-1pm, 4-6pm, Sa 9am-1pm; free). **Cuartel Catorce** (tel. 17 12 41) is a rough structure with walls of brown brick on Guerrero and Colosio. The colonnaded inner courtyard is an oasis; the room in the back of the courtyard was once home to the army's cavalry (for Sec. de Intercambios try ext. 122. Open M-F 8am-3pm).

Across the street from the Plaza Zaragoza and facing the cathedral is the majestic, gray-and-white **Palacio de Gobierno.** The *palacio*, from which the state of Sonora is governed, should not be confused with the pink brick **Palacio Municipal** nearby, where city government functions are carried out. Both are worth investigating for their architecture. The Palacio de Gobierno contains four fascinating and detailed murals surrounding its beautiful, tree-laden inner courtyard, where statues immortalize Sonoran patriots and senators.

Those in need of a bit more levity can head to **Multicinemas,** Blvd. Encinas 227 (tel. 14 09 70), to absorb U.S. movies with Spanish subtitles. The theater is located on Transversal at Reforma, a 5min. bus ride from the center of town. (Open daily 3-9pm. 26 pesos.) There is not a great deal of nightlife in Hermosillo. However, if you're in the mood for a drink or two, a couple of watering holes can be found on Rosales south of Colosio. Go with caution, though; many of the bars are situated in less than desirable areas.

Bars include **La Fogata** at Dr. Noriega, **La Bella Epoca** at Morelia, and **Fook Lam Moon** (tel. 12 77 17), a Chinese restaurant and bar also at Morelia (open daily noon-11:30pm). For a tougher bar-going experience, try **La Verbena** or **El Grito del Callejón** (literally, "the Cry of the Alley"), both at Obregón and Pino Suárez—La Verbena to the south and El Grito to the north. Adjacent to La Verbena is **Extasis Night Club,** located in what would be a beautiful colonial building if it weren't for the neon green glow.

NEAR HERMOSILLO

CENTRO ECOLÓGICO DE SONORA. Lions and tigers and bears and emus...oh my! This is more than just your token neighborhood **zoo**: it is host to an impressive array of animal life, a mini-aquarium (complete with outdoor sea lions), and hundreds of plant species from Sonora and elsewhere. Founded in 1985, the *Centro* is also home to groundbreaking biological research. A clean and clearly marked walkway guides visitors through the exhibits and aviaries and often affords a spectacular view of Hermosillo and its surrounding mountains.

Among the animal exhibits, the sea lions, desert owls, and noisy wild boars stand out; there is also a *basura* (garbage) exhibit with some crazy *cucarachas* (cockroaches). The most spectacular feature of the Centro Ecológico, however, is its incredible collection of cacti—over 340 species are labeled and displayed throughout the animal exhibits or just outside the main pavilion. Keep your eyes peeled for the rare and beautiful *cina* and *biznaga*, from which fruit and candy are made, and the *maguey bacanora*, the fanned-out, spiked cactus that is the source of all those tequilas you've been downing.

The *Centro* is an excellent place for children; they delight in the clowns and Disney or Disney-esque flicks shown every Saturday and Sunday in the air-conditioned movie theater (noon-6pm; free). The enthusiastic and knowledgeable staff is happy to answer any questions about the *Centro* and its flora and fauna. Cafeterias and *agua purificada* can be found throughout the park, and there is a LADA-TEL at the entrance.

To get to the *Centro*, grab the orange-and-green bus marked "Luis Orci" from the corner of Guerrero and Dr. Noriega at the "Ruta 20" stop (20min., 3 pesos). Ask the driver to let you off at the Centro Ecológico since there is no sign—it actually lies about a ¼ mi. from the bus stop. If the driver ignores you, walk south along the dirt path. (Tel. 50 12 25. Open in summer W-Su 8am-7pm; in winter W-Su 8am-5pm. Admission 10 pesos, students 5 pesos, children 7 pesos.)

BAHÍA KINO

Bahía Kino, a 20km stretch of glistening sand, blue water, and radiant sun, is comprised of a pair of beach towns on the beautiful Sea of Cortés (or Golfo de California). **Kino Viejo,** a dusty, quiet fishing village, lies down the road from **Kino Nuevo,** a 4km-long strip of posh, secluded homes and condos where the satellite dishes are as abundant as the pelicans overhead. As the residents of Hermosillo who flock there on weekends will tell you, Kino (as the two towns are collectively known) is an ideal destination for a daytrip escape from the urban desert to the beach. Soothing breezes, warm waters, and vast expanses of sand make the rickety ride from the city worthwhile.

🛈 ORIENTATION AND PRACTICAL INFORMATION. Bahía Kino is located 107km west of Hermosillo. **Buses** in Hermosillo leave from the old blue-and-red-striped **Transportes Norte de Sonora** station on Sonora between Jesús García and González, near the Jardín Juárez (2hr., 10 per day 5:40am-5:30pm, 38 pesos one way). The bus stops in **Kino Viejo** before going on to **Kino Nuevo.** Look for water on your left and get off wherever you'd like. Early birds catch the daytrip-to-Kino worms—get an early bus from Hermosillo and sleep (if you can) during the ride. Missing the 5:30pm bus back to Hermosillo means spending the night in Kino.

To get from one Kino to the other or back to Hermosillo, flag down the bus (every hr., 4 pesos between Kinos) on Nuevo's main (and only) road, **Av. Mar de Cortés,** or on **Blvd. Kino** in Kino Viejo. If you choose to walk the 6km, be sure to keep plenty of water or other hydrants on hand as well as adequate sun protection. Some travelers have been able to hitch rides between the two towns.

Public bathrooms are on the beach in Kino Nuevo, at the end closer to Kino Viejo. In Kino Viejo itself, some downright pleasant potties are available at the **Centro de Salud** at Tampico and Kino. Bring your own toilet paper. In any type of **emergency,** your best bet might be to look for the American-run **Club Deportivo** on the right side of Monaco off of Mar De Cortéz and knock on the door; the friendly expatriate community takes good care of foreign visitors. Another option is to dial the **emergency phone number,** 08. The **police** (tel. 2 00 67) are available at Santa Catalina and Av. Mar de Cortés in Kino Viejo or at Kino and Cruz (tel. 2 00 32) in Kino Nuevo. Near the post office and the police in Kino Viejo is the **Red Cross,** at Kino and Manzanillo, which has no phone but can be contacted via the Hermosillo emergency number. For medical services, call **Dr. José Luís** (tel. 2 03 95), who speaks English. Next to the police in Nuevo is the **post office** (open M-F 8am-3pm). Small markets dot the road through Kino Nuevo under inviting "Tecate" signs. **Long-distance**

phones are available at the clothing shop at Kino and Tampico in Kino Viejo. **LADA-TEL's** dot Mar de Cortés in Kino Nuevo. **Phone code:** 624.

█ ACCOMMODATIONS AND FOOD. If you plan to spend the night in Kino, bring your tent or RV; most of the hotel prices are geared toward wealthy northerners. Nearby Hermosillo provides more choices for the budget traveler. If you miss the bus, **Islanda Marina** (tel. 2 00 81), on Guaymas at Puerto Peñasco just off Blvd. Kino. It is run by two Arizona women who own a purified water plant—you'll never be short on that precious commodity. You can also rent cabins there (150 pesos for 4 people; 30 pesos for each additional person). In Kino Nuevo, **Hotel Posada del Mar** (tel. 2 01 55), Mar de Cortés at the beginning of Kino Nuevo, is the cheapest you'll find (singles 300 pesos with A/C, private bath, TV, and use of the pool; doubles 350 pesos); call ahead to reserve a room. **Caverna del Seri,** at the end of Mar de Cortés, offers full RV hookups for US$14 a day and rents tent space for US$8 a day. The more adventurous traveler can camp for free under one of the many *palapas* (thatched umbrella structures) on the Kino Nuevo beach.

For a meal that's as economical as you want it to be, do as the *hermosillanos* do and pack a lunch to enjoy under a beach *palapa*. Otherwise, a decent budget meal can be found in Kino Viejo. Try the nice 'n' spicy **Dorita,** Av. Eusebio Kino and Sabina Cruz (tel. 2 03 49), decorated with "Spice Girls" paraphernalia and paintings of Jésus; they have relatively inexpensive breakfasts (27-30 pesos) and delicious *carne asada* (30 pesos). Fill up on free purified water. There is a huge variance in price between the *mariscos* (shellfish), *pescado* (fish), and lobster (ranging 10-140 pesos). (Open daily 7am-8pm.) In Kino Nuevo, **Restaurante la Palapa** serves up decent *hamburguesas* (25 pesos) and *mariscos* starting at 55 pesos.

◪ SAND AND SIGHTS. The **beaches** of Kino are peacefully deserted early in the week, but as the weekend approaches, so does the maddening crowd. Fortunately, the masses of Kino are nothing compared to the masses at many other beach towns. Gringos with homes in Kino tend to populate the beaches during the winter, making for some long, lonely stretches of sand during the summer months. In general, the beaches are better in Kino Nuevo.

For water fun in Kino Nuevo, ask at **Hotel La Posada** on Av. Mar de Cortés toward Kino Viejo, just before Kino Nuevo's main strip begins, for the names of people renting out scuba/snorkeling gear. For non-beach entertainment, the **Museo de los Seris,** on **Mar de Cortés** at Progreso near the end of Kino Nuevo, offers air-conditioned refuge from shade-free Kino and teaches you more than you ever thought you'd learn about the Seris, a once-nomadic indigenous tribe whose specialty was fishing (open W-Su 9am-4pm; admission 3 pesos, children 2 pesos).

In Kino Nuevo about 300 yards past the Museo de los Seris, you'll see a giant image of *La Virgén Maria* painted on the face of a hill. The short pilgrimage up to her perch is worth the hike—it affords a breathtaking view of Bahía Kino.

GUAYMAS

Nestled by steep, rocky hills to the north and the Sea of Cortés to the east, Guaymas (pop. 150,000) is the principal port in Sonora and the proud home of an active shrimping fleet and busy seafood-processing plants. Nearby, beachy **San Carlos** wins the prize as destination-of-choice for many *norteamericano* tourists while the other neighboring beach town of **Miramar** draws a distinctly Mexican crowd. However, Guaymas itself is no schmaltzy resort venue. The port area does offer a pleasant view of some of Mexico's most scintillating sunsets (over docked shrimping boats, the sea, and nearby mountains nonethelss), while its charming cathedral and companion park all serve as havens for weary travelers. The town suffers from an acute lack of convenient beaches but is still a nice place to rest on the trip south to the more alluring resorts at **Mazatlán, San Blas,** and **Puerto Vallarta;** its civility and cool ocean breezes give it a decided advantage over Hermosillo.

 ORIENTATION

Guaymas is 407km south of Nogales on Rte. 15. Municipal buses (2.5 pesos) cruise its main strip, **Av. Serdán.** Running perpendicular to Av. Serdán are **Calle 1, Calle 2, Calle 3**...well, you get the idea. If you're walking along Av. Serdán and the numbers of the intersecting streets are increasing, you know you're headed east toward the waterfront. The center of the city lies around the crossings of Calles in the low 20s and Serdán, and buses arrive right in the thick of things at Calle 14, right off (surprise) Serdán. To get to Serdán from the bus station, turn left if you're coming out of the **Transportes del Norte** station and turn right if you're coming out of the **Transportes del Pacífico** or the **Transportes Baldomero Corral** stations. Women should not walk alone more than two blocks south of Serdán after dark. The waterfront begins around Calle 23 and Serdán; coming up to the water, the many public plazas and the cool ocean breeze will immediately provide relief from the heat.

Northbound vehicles, including buses, are often stopped by narcotics police. Have your identification ready and let them search whatever they want; it's better not to assert the right to privacy when dealing with humorless armed *federales*. Along Serdán, you can also catch buses marked "Miramar" (4 pesos) and "San Carlos" (7 pesos) to reach the beaches north of the city; both buses run frequently between 6am and 8pm.

🔃 PRACTICAL INFORMATION

TRANSPORTATION

Airport: To reach the airport, catch a bus marked "San José" along Serdán (3 pesos). Aeroméxico (tel. 2 01 23), Serdán at Calle 16, has daily flights to: **La Paz** (1hr., 3:30pm, 932 pesos); **Mexico City** (2½hr., 3pm, 1698 pesos); and **Phoenix, Arizona** (2hr., 11:50 am, 1644 pesos). Open daily 6am-6pm.

Buses: The town's 3 bus terminals are on opposite sides of the street at Calle 14 and Rodríguez. Transportes Norte de Sonora (tel. 2 12 71) goes to: **Ciudad Juárez** (13hr., 2:30pm, 380 pesos); **Culiacán** (9hr., every hr., 190 pesos); **Guadalajara** (23hr., every hr., 600 pesos); **Hermosillo** (1¾hr., every hr., 45 pesos); **Los Mochis** (6hr., every hr., 120 pesos); **Mazatlán** (12hr., every hr., 350 pesos); **Mexicali** (12hr., every hr., 330 pesos); **Mexico City** (31hr., every 2hr., 890 pesos); **Nogales** (10hr., every hr., 136 pesos); **Obregón** (1¾hr., every hr., 45 pesos); **Puerto Peñasco** (9hr., 11am, 209 pesos); **San Luis** (6hr., every hr., 290 pesos); **Tepic** (18hr., every hr., 470 pesos); and **Tijuana** (15hr., every hr., 400 pesos). Transportes del Pacífico (tel. 4 05 76), offers fares to most of the above destinations for about 10% more than Transportes Norte del Sonora, while its 2nd-class service runs 3-5% less. Transportes Baldomero Corral, across the street, offers service to **Nogales** (5hr., every 2hr., 147 pesos) and **Navojoa** (4hr., every hr. 8:45am-midnight, 48 pesos).

Ferries: Terminal (tel. 2 23 24) on Serdán, about 1km past Electricidad. The boat steams to **Santa Rosalía** Tu and F at 9am (arriving at 4pm). Tickets may be bought on the day of departure from 6-8am or on M, W, or Th 8am-2pm. (*Salón* 140 pesos, *turista* 268 pesos.) To get to the terminal, hop on a bus heading away from the Carretera Internacional and get off at the "Transbordador" sign, on your right

TOURIST AND FINANCIAL SERVICES

Currency Exchange: Banks are located along Serdán. **Banamex** (tel. 4 01 23), Serdán at Calle 20, exchanges traveler's checks and greenbacks, and has 2 24hr. **ATMs**. Open M-F 8:30am-4:30pm.

Luggage Storage: Lockers are available at the **Transportes Norte de Sonora** bus terminal. 12 pesos for 1st 8hr., 5 pesos each additional hr. Open 24hr.

LOCAL SERVICES

Market: VH Supermarket (tel. 4 19 49), on Serdán between Calles 19 and 20. You can't miss it. Open M-Sa 7am-11:30pm, Su 7am-8:30pm.

EMERGENCY AND COMMUNICATIONS

Police: (tel. 4 01 04 or 4 01 05), on Calle 11 at Av. 9, near the Villa School. Some English spoken. Open 24hr.

Pharmacy: Farmacia Sonora (tel. 2 11 00), Serdán at Calle 15. Open 24hr.

Hospital: Hospital Municipal (tel. 4 21 38), on Calle 12 between Av. 6 and 7. Some English spoken. Open 24hr.

Post Office: (tel. 2 07 57), Av. 10 between Calle 19 and 20, next to the pink Luis G. Davila School. Open M-F 8am-7pm, Sa 8am-noon. **Postal Code:** 85400.

Fax: Telecomm (tel. 2 02 92), next to post office. Open M-F 8am-7:30pm, Sa-Su 9am-noon.

Phone Code: 622.

ACCOMMODATIONS

Accommodations in Guaymas cluster around **Av. Serdán,** where tourists will find a handful of relatively inexpensive hotels and motels. A few *casas de huéspedes* can be found on streets off Serdán.

Casa de Huéspedes Lupita, Calle 15 #125 (tel. 2 84 09), 2 blocks south of Serdán and across from the castle-like *cárcel* (jail). The 30 rooms and 12 communal baths all open onto the tree-shaded courtyard. Birds in the trees will serenade you until the sun goes down. Fans in every room provide relief from the relentless heat outside; an ice-cold *agua purificada* dispenser awaits downstairs at the office. Singles 50 pesos, with bath 60 pesos, with A/C 100 pesos; doubles with bath 140 pesos, with A/C 180 pesos.

Motel del Puerto, Yañez 92 (tel. 4 34 08 or 2 24 91), 5 blocks south of Serdan on Calle 17. Reminiscent of a beachfront motel (without the beach), it offers super- clean rooms with satellite TV and A/C at an affordable rate. Singles 150 pesos; doubles 170 pesos; triples 200 pesos.

Hotel Impala, Calle 21 #40 (tel. 4 09 22), 1 block south of Serdán. The hotel revels in its antiquity through the photos of Guaymas's past gracing the walls. Rooms, however, have been modernized with polyester bedspreads and curtains, A/C, and TV. Singles 140 pesos; doubles 180 pesos; triples 220 pesos.

FOOD

Seafood is the Guaymas specialty. Local favorites include *ancas de rana* (frog's legs), *cahuna* (turtle steaks), and *ostiones* (oysters) in a garlic and chile sauce. Unfortunately, if you want to sample these local delicacies, you're going to have to pay a fair sum for them. Otherwise, the **Mercado Municipal,** on Calle 20, one block from Serdán, sells fresh produce; and there are an abundance of *comida corrida* joints on Serdán.

Restaurant Todos Comen (tel. 2 11 00), Serdán between Calles 15 and 16. Dark draperies extend outward from a central ceiling fan, creating a cool and cozy atmosphere. Try the *pescado al plancha* (40 pesos) or the *Camarones Boston* (55 pesos). Open daily 7am-midnight.

Los Barcos (tel. 2 76 50), Malecón at Calle 22. Gaze at the sea and nearby mountain peaks from inside the restaurant or enjoy the sea breeze of its open-air annex as you savor a seafood meal that won't bust your budget. Ubiquitous platters of *chimichangas de camarón* (shrimp), *pescado* (fish), *pulpo* (octopus), *jaiba* (crab; 50 pesos), or the *machaca* (shredded beef; 51-55 pesos). Open daily 10am-10:30pm.

Las 1000 Tortas, Serdán 188, between Calles 17 and 18. The *torta* rules at this family-run joint (12 pesos each). Three types of delicious *comida corrida* (27 pesos) are prepared daily and served from noon-4pm. Energetic customers sit upright in orthopedic wooden chairs while tired neighbors slouch in brown vinyl booths, but everyone munches on enchiladas and *gorditas* (20 pesos). Tasty *burritos de machaca con frijoles* just 20 pesos. Open daily 8am-11pm.

S. E. Pizza Buffet (tel. 2 24 46), Serdán at Calle 20. Disney images and framed posters of American cars and athletes decorate the walls. Satisfy your appetite with the all-you-can-eat buffet of pizza, spaghetti, and salad (20 pesos). Open daily 11am-11pm.

👁 🎵 SIGHTS AND ENTERTAINMENT

Guaymas's **beaches,** popular with tourists and locals alike, are located to the north in **San Carlos** (see p. 208) and **Miramar;** both are accessible by a 15 minute bus ride. The nicer (but smaller) beaches in Miramar are back along the bus route in front of the fancy villas. The beaches are safe, although camping in this area is not advisable; if you absolutely must, opt for San Carlos over Miramar.

Most of the scenic places in Guaymas lie on the east side of town near the waterfront. For the best view in town—of Guaymas, the mountains, the port, and the bay—seek out the shady benches of the **Plaza del Pescador,** just off Serdán toward the water, between Calles 24 and 25. While you're in the area, take a stroll in the **Plaza de los Tres Presidentes,** on Calle 23 at Serdán, in front of the **Palacio Municipal,** a classic Colonial-style structure built in 1899. The blue bay waters, the towering green-and-white **Catedral de San Fernando,** and three bronze statues of (rather obscure) Mexican presidents complete the scene. The small park directly in front of the cathedral has benches and many leafy trees which provide cool shade. **Cine Guaymas Plus** (tel. 2 14 00), Av. 11 (the Malecón) at Calle 20, two blocks off Serdán, shows U.S. films with Spanish subtitles daily between 3:30 and 11pm (admission 25 pesos, double features on Wednesday).

Travesty shows—transvestite acts imitating popular Mexican singers—are big in Guaymas. You can find them at **Charles Baby Disco Video,** a club near the waterfront on Serdán, between Calle 16 and 17, and at **Cyrus**—the club with the wolf facade also near the waterfront. Cover varies according to the popularity of the acts, but it's usually about 20 pesos for men and free for women. If you're just looking for a drink without the frills, head to **Sahuaro Piano Bar** or **Zodiakos,** next to Charles Baby Disco Video, where beers run about 10 pesos.

SAN CARLOS

San Carlos is quickly becoming a major destination for Americans and Canadians. Condominiums, hotels, and malls are sprouting like wildflowers to accommodate the increasing influx of tourists. Just 12 mi. outside Guaymas, San Carlos boasts a country club with an 18-hole golf course, the only five-star hotel in Sonora, and the largest, shallowest, albeit artificial, shipwreck in the world. The unmistakable Tetakawi (*Las Tetas de Cabra,* literally "Teats of the Goat") overlook majestic cliffside homes and the Sea of Cortés. Although accommodations for the budget traveler are limited, and the best beaches are accessible only by car, a stop in San Carlos is worth it, if only for the views and a bath in the warm waters.

🚩 ORIENTATION AND PRACTICAL INFORMATION. The main (and basically only) road in San Carlos, **Blvd. Manlio F. Beltrones** runs east-west. Most of the shops, restaurants, and accommodations lie on Blvd. Beltrones between Hacienda Tetakawi Hotel and Trailer Park to the east and the San Carlos Country Club to the west. Green-and-white **buses** from Guaymas run the boulevard about every 10 minutes (6am-11pm) to the Marinas and Plaza Las Glorias but don't go to the **Playa Algodones** (7 pesos to Guaymas, 3 within San Carlos).

The **tourist office** can be found in **Hacienda Tours** (tel. 6 02 02), at Luna and Beltrones (open M-F 9am-5pm, Sa-Su 9am-2pm). **Banamex** (tel. 6 12 40), on Beltrones next to the PEMEX station, exchanges **traveler's checks** and has a convenient 24-hour **ATM** (open M-F 8:30am-4:30pm). Buy your groceries at **San Carlos Super Mercado** (tel. 6 00 43) in front of the Catholic Church at Plaza Comercial 2 (open 7am-

9pm). **Lavandería San Carlos** (tel. 6 00 13), across the street from the post office and Ana Maria's Beauty Shop, offers full or self-service (open M-Sa 9am-5pm). For **emergencies,** call **Rescate** (tel. 6 01 01 or 6 01 58). **Police:** (tel. 6 14 00) across the street from Plaza Las Glorias Hotel and Condos on Plaza Comercial. **Farmacia Bahia San Carlos** (tel. 6 00 97 or 6 02 42), across the street from Motel Creston, can satisfy your pharmaceutical needs (open M-Sa 8am-7pm). **Post office:** (tel. 6 05 06) next to Ana Maria's Beauty Shop. **Copicentro** (tel. 6 11 80), next to Rosa's Cantina, sends and receives **faxes** (open M-F 9am-6pm, Sa 9am-1pm). **Cafe de Internet** (tel. 6 13 63), across the street from the San Carlos Bowling Lanes on Beltrones, offers internet access (open daily 8am-11pm, 15 pesos for 15min.). **Phone code:** 622.

▐▐ ACCOMMODATIONS AND FOOD. The best way to stay in San Carlos cheaply is to bring a tent or RV. **Hacienda Tetakawi** (tel. 6 02 20), on Beltrones, km 8.5, at the beginning of the main strip, offers full RV hookups (US$20 per day, US$126 per week) and rents tent spaces (US$10 for 1-2 people, US$3 each additional person). **Motel Creston** (tel. 6 00 20), across the street from Jax Snax, is the cheapest you'll find at 350 pesos for a room with two beds, A/C, bath, and a shower made for people 4ft. (1.3m) tall.

Many of the restaurants cater to tourists; it's evident from their prices. However, there are still a few places that appeal to the budget traveler. An eclectic collection of unframed paintings by local artists adorn the walls of **Banana's Restaurant,** just past El Mar Diving Center, which offers US$1 breakfasts (1 egg, toast, and hash browns) and Happy Hours from 10-11am and 4-5pm. Decorated with *atarrayas* (fishing nets), **La Tarray Restaurant,** just past the police station on the opposite side of Plaza Comercial, serves up big portions of *tacos de carne asada* (10 pesos) and daily lunch specialties; beer and wine is available. (Open daily 8am-9pm.)

◪ SIGHTS AND SAND. Dining and sport fishing are the main attractions in San Carlos. The Sea of Cortés is home to a vast array of underwater wildlife. Nearby is **San Pedro Nolasco Island,** a popular dive site where sea lions and hundreds of marine birds coexist in harmony. The state of Sonora recently spent a large sum of money to sink a 120ft. tuna boat and 300ft. passenger liner, creating artificial reefs for scuba divers to explore. Dive shops along Beltrones rent scuba gear and sea kayaks and lead guided dives for a pretty penny. **El Mar Diving Center** (tel. 6 04 04), also rents bikes (US$10 for 8hr. on a cruiser; US$25 for 8hr. on a mountain bike; open daily in summer 7am-6:30pm; in winter 7:30am-5:30pm).

If fishing is your thing, pick up a license (58 pesos per day) at the **Secretaria de Pesca** on Beltrones just before the turn-off to Plaza Las Glorias; it's illegal to fish without one (open 9am-3pm). In San Carlos, the beach gets better past the end of the bus route near Club Med and Howard Johnson's. There are two main beaches in this town: San Fransisco and Playa Los Algodones. **San Francisco,** beginning at Condominios Pilar and extending to about Hotel Fiesta, tends to be pretty rocky. The most beautiful beach, **Playa Los Algodones** (Cotton Beach), once used as a set for the American movie *Catch 22*, is the most difficult to get to without a car; it lies west of Tetakawi. The beachs are about 8km from the end of the bus route.

ALAMOS

The sleepy little town of Alamos (pop. 8000), in the scenic foothills of the Sierra Madre Occidental at the edge of the Sonoran desert, is a rambling collection of handsome colonial *haciendas*. Founded by Coronado in 1531, Alamos produced more silver than any area in the world during its mining peak in the 1790s. But when the silver veins ran dry at the turn of the century, Alamos shrank to ghost-town proportions. In the last 50 years, Alamos has returned to its architectural glory days with the arrival of wealthy gringos in search of winter homes. The refurbished *haciendas* and cobblestone streets organized around the massive cathedral give Alamos a bygone feel unlike any in northwest Mexico.

⚠ ORIENTATION AND PRACTICAL INFORMATION. Alamos is a comfortable size—you can explore the small and compact town on foot. As you come into town on **Calle Madero,** you'll reach a fork in the road at the bronzed statue of Benito Juárez and the PEMEX station; the left branch leads to **Plaza Alameda,** the commercial center (where the bus stops), and the right branch leads to **Plaza de Armas** in the historic district. A small alley known as the **Callejón del Beso** connects the Plaza de Armas with the market behind the Plaza Alameda. The **cathedral** south of Plaza de Armas marks the northern edge of the **Barrio La Colorada,** where most of the *norteamericanos* have concentrated their *hacienda*-restoring efforts.

All **bus service** to Alamos passes through **Navojoa,** 53km southwest of Alamos. From the Transportes Norte de Sonora and Elite bus stations in Navojoa, stand at the corner of Allende and Ferrocarril, looking down Ferrocarril as you face the bus stations. Then, walk one block to the Transportes del Pacífico station, and turn left (toward the center of town) onto Guerrero. Six blocks along Guerrero (passing the Transportes de Baja California bus station after 3 blocks) is the Los Mayitos bus station at Rincón, where you can catch a bus to **Alamos** (1hr., every hr. 6am-6:30pm, 18 pesos). The return trip from Alamos starts from the bus station at Plaza Alameda (same times and price).

The **tourist office,** Calle Juárez 6 (tel. 8 04 50), is under the Hotel Los Portales on the west side of the Plaza de Armas (open M-F 9am-2pm and 4-7pm, Sa 9am-2pm), although it's anyone's guess when the eccentric tour guide will be around. He may be sitting on a bench in the plaza across from the office. Currency can be exchanged at **Bancrecer** (tel. 8 03 57), on Madero before the fork in the road (open M-F 8:30am-3pm, Sa 10am-2pm). A 24hr. **ATM** is right next door. Pick up some prescription drugs, a side of bacon, and a bottle of tequila at **SuperTito's** (tel. 8 05 12), at the fork in Calle Maderos, which operates as a pharmacy, grocery store, and a liquor store (open daily 7:30am-10:30pm). Farther out of the center of town on Madero is the **Hospital Básico** (tel. 8 00 25 or 8 00 26). The **Post office** (tel. 8 00 09) is also on Madero, between the Bancrecer and the hospital (open M-F 8am-3pm). The **Postal code:** 85763. The **Phone code:** 642.

⌂ ACCOMMODATIONS. Unless you rediscover silver on your way into town, you'll probably have to turn away from the lush garden courtyards of the *hacienda*-hotels and head toward the outskirts for hotels whose courtyards look more like parking lots. For a hair-raising experience, head to the **Hotel Enrique** (tel. 8 03 10), next to the Hotel Los Portales on Juárez, on the west side of the Plaza de Armas. Don't be alarmed by the tame wolf that lives on the grounds; the owners say it just wandered down from the hills. Fans will help keep your cool and the communal bathroom is irreproachable. (Singles 90 pesos; doubles 150 pesos). **Motel Somar,** Madero 110 (tel. 8 01 95), near the Plaza Alameda, offers clean rooms with showers and a chance to sit and chat with locals in the lobby. All rooms have fans and a few come with TV and A/C. (Singles 130 pesos; doubles 150 pesos.)

⌂ FOOD. True peso-pinchers patronize the taco stands, such as **Taquería Blanquita,** in the Mercado Municipal by Plaza Alameda (open daily 7am-10:30pm). In

---

LIKE WATER FOR CHICHARRONES In Mexico,

there's no escaping the *chicharrones* (pork rinds), and in some towns the popular snack has become...an ice cream flavor! On sweltering hot days, vendors push long carts loaded with rows of metal casks and scoop out ice cold salvation in a crazy variety of flavors—*elote* (cornmeal), *cerveza* (beer), *aguacate* (avocado), and tequila. Hand a vendor 5 pesos and he'll cram a mammoth portion into a cone or plastic cup. Mexican ice cream is known to harbor more than a few nasty amoebas, so verify the product's hygienic integrity by looking at the cleanliness of the stand before placing that spoon in your mouth. Once you're assured of your food's safety, tuck a napkin into your shirt front, close your eyes, and lick away.

the market, you can choose from various delectable fruits and vegetables sold within walking distance of where they were grown. **Polo's Restaurant** (tel. 8 00 03) is a short distance away from las Palmeras at Zaragoza 4, right off the Plaza de Armas. Friendly service, paintings of local sights, and good food at hefty prices (entrees start at 38 pesos). Open daily 7am-9:30pm. For a good view of the Plaza de Armas, the distant foothills, and an *hacienda* or two, eat outside under the arches at **Restaurant Las Palmeras,** Cárdenas 9 (tel. 8 00 65), northeast of the Plaza de Armas. Here, you're likely to run into some U.S. expats and any number of local officials. (Breakfasts 20-30 pesos, antojitos 20-35; open daily 7am-10pm.)

SIGHTS. The main reason to visit Alamos is to get a glimpse of the glory days of the *hacienda* in Mexico. Learn about the history of the town by strolling along narrow streets and by peeking into as many buildings as possible. Don't be hesitant to ask shop owners if you can look around their buildings and courtyards. If you're lucky, you'll run across a *hacienda* being renovated and be able to see the inner workings of the fabulous architecture. One of the grandest homes in town was constructed in 1720 and refinished in the 19th century, when it became the home of Don José María, owner of one of the world's richest silver mines. The **Hotel Las Portales** now occupies most of the building, including Don Alameda's foyer and overgrown courtyard. Several other impressive restored homes, many of which are now hotels, can be found around the cathedral, including the **Casa de los Tesoros** (a former convent), the **Hotel La Mansión,** and the **Casa Encantada.**

Today, the town **jail** and the **mirador** offer excellent views from the site Coronado chose for a fort in 1531. To get to the jail, walk along Madero west of the center of town and follow the signs. The current **cathedral** dates from 1805. In the mid-19th century, many Asians arrived in Alamos to work in the mines and to foster the growing silk industry. The only remainders from this period are a few mulberry trees and the **old silk factory** currently being restored as a private residence. To learn more about the history of Alamos, visit the **Museo Costanmbrista,** the yellow and white building across from Las Palmeras in the Plaza de Armas. *(Tel. 8 00 53; open 9am-6pm, W-Su. Admission 15 pesos.)*

CHIHUAHUA

EL PASO, TEXAS

The largest of the U.S. border towns, El Paso (pop. 700,000) boomed in the 17th century as a passageway on an important east-west wagon route that followed the Río Grande through "the pass" (*el paso*) between the Rockies and the Sierra Madres. Today, modern El Paso sits in the midst of rocks and sagebrush, and it serves as a stop-over between the U.S. and Mexico. Influenced by Mexican culture as much as that of the U.S., this border town gives those crossing over into Mexico a first glimpse of what awaits them. After dark, central El Paso becomes a ghost town: most activity leaves the center and heads to the University of Texas at El Paso (UTEP) or south of the border to El Paso's raucous sister city, Ciudad Juárez. It's difficult to find a party without a car, as many clubs and casinos are located a fair distance from downtown.

ORIENTATION

Before leaving the airport, be sure to pick up maps and information from the **visitor's center** located at the bottom of the right-hand side of the escalators descending from the arrival gates. To get to the city from the airport, take **Sun Metro bus** #33. The stop is located on a traffic island outside the air terminal building (50min. to downtown; every hr. M-F 5:54am-8:59pm, Sa 7:24am-8:59pm, Su 8:12am-7:12pm. US$1, students and ages 6-13 US¢50, seniors US¢30, transfer tickets US¢10; exact change only). Get off when the bus arrives at San Jacinto Plaza and you'll be right in the thick of things, near most of the hotels and restaurants.

When the bus stops running late at night, the only way to get to the city is to take a taxi (approximately US$20-25). Alternative approaches include **I-10** (running east-west) and **U.S. 54** (north-south). El Paso is divided into east and west by **Santa Fe Ave.** and into north and south by **San Antonio Ave.** Tourists should be wary of the streets between San Antonio and the border late at night.

☒ CROSSING THE BORDER

The best way to cross the border, unless you are traveling by car, is to walk. To reach the border from El Paso, take the north-south #8 green trolley operated by Sun Metro to the **Santa Fe Bridge,** its last stop before turning around (every 15min. M-F 6:15am-8:15pm, Sa 7:45am-8:15pm, Su 8:45am-7:15pm, US¢25). For information about **FMT/tourist cards,** see **Documents and Formalities,** p. 7.

Do not confuse the inexpensive #8 trolley with the more costly trolley. Two pedestrian and motor roads cross the Río Grande: **El Paso Ave.,** a crowded one-way street, and **Stanton Ave.,** a parallel road lined with Western-wear stores, clothing shops, and decent restaurants. Entering Mexico costs US¢25; the return trip costs US$0.45.

If entering Mexico by foot, walk to the right side of the Stanton Bridge and pay the quarter to cross. Daytrippers, including foreign travelers with multi-entry visas, should be prepared to flash their documents of citizenship in order to pass in and out of Mexico. You might get your bag searched by a guard, but usually you won't even have to show ID. If you need a tourist card, stop in at the Mexican immigration office, directly to your right as you enter into Juárez. Continue walking two blocks west to the corner of Juárez and Azucenas, where you'll find the air-conditioned Juárez **tourist office,** and where friendly, English-speaking employees await with maps and info.

To enter the United States, cross over the Santa Fe Bridge near the large *"Feliz Viaje"* sign. Be ready to deal with U.S. border guards and to show a valid visa or proof of citizenship. You may be searched or asked to answer a few questions to prove your identity. Once in El Paso, wait at the bus stop on the right-hand sidewalk just across from the bridge. The north-south bus runs until 8:15pm to San Jacinto Plaza.

🛈 PRACTICAL INFORMATION

TRANSPORTATION

Airport: Northeast of the city center; to reach it, take bus #33 from San Jacinto Square or any other central location.

Buses: Greyhound, 200 W. San Antonio (tel. 532-2365 or 800-231-2222), across from the Civic Center between Santa Fe and Chihuahua. Daily service to and from: **Dallas** (10hr.; 7 per day; US$76), **Los Angeles** (16hr.; 6 per day; US$39), **New York** (48hr.; 7 per day; US$99), **Phoenix,** and other U.S. cities. **Storage lockers** US$2 per hr. Open 24hr.

Public Transportation: Sun Metro (tel. 533-3333), departing from San Jacinto Plaza, at the corner of Main and Oregon. US$1, students and children US$0.50, seniors US$0.30, transfer US$0.10.

Car Rental: Avis (tel. 753-6050), **Budget** (tel. 778-5287), **Dollar** (tel. 881-1500), **Hertz** (tel. 772-4255), **National** (tel. 778-9417), **Thrifty** (tel. 779-7171), and more, all at the airport.

TOURIST AND FINANCIAL SERVICES

Tourist Office: 1 Civic Center Plaza (tel. 544-0062; www.VisitElPaso.com), a small round building next to the Chamber of Commerce at the intersection of Santa Fe and San Francisco. Maps and brochures available. Also sells **El Paso-Juárez Trolley Co.** tickets

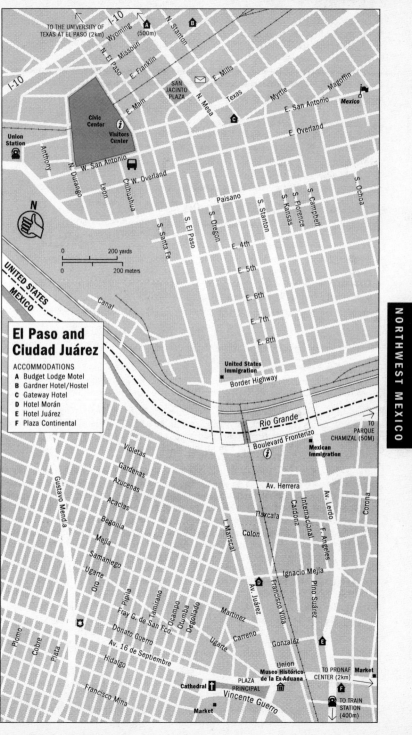

TO THE UNIVERSITY OF TEXAS AT EL PASO (2km)

I-10
I-10

Wyoming
Missouri
E. Franklin
E. Main
E. Mills
E. Texas

N. Stanton
N. El Paso
N. Mesa
N. Durango
Anthony
Leon
Chihuahua

A (500m)
B

SAN JACINTO PLAZA

Myrtle
E. San Antonio
Magoffin

Mexico

Civic Center

Visitors Center

Union Station

W. San Antonio
W. Overland

E. Overland

G

Paisano
S. Santa Fe
S. El Paso
S. Oregon
S. Stanton
S. Kansas
S. Florence
S. Campbell
S. Ochoa

E. 4th
E. 5th
E. 6th
E. 7th
E. 8th

N

0   200 yards
0   200 meters

Canal

UNITED STATES
MEXICO

El Paso and Ciudad Juárez

ACCOMMODATIONS
A Budget Lodge Motel
B Gardner Hotel/Hostel
C Gateway Hotel
D Hotel Morán
E Hotel Juárez
F Plaza Continental

United States Immigration

Border Highway

Rio Grande

Boulevard Fronterizo

Mexican Immigration

TO PARQUE CHAMIZAL (50M)

Violetas
Gardenas
Azucenas
Acacias
Begonia
Mejia
Samaniego
Ugarte
Oro

Gustavo Menda

Av. Herrera

Tlaxcala
Colon

Internacional
Cardone
Av. Lerdo
F. Angeles
Corona

I. Mariscal

Ignacio Mejia

Pino Suárez

D

Av. Juárez
Francisco Villa

Martinez
Carreno
González

E

Plomo
Cobre
Plata
Pipila
Tamirano
Ocampo
Orumba
Degollado
Fray G. de San Fco.
Donato Guerro
Av. 16 de Septiembre
Hidalgo
Francisco Mina

Ugarte

Union
Museo Histórico de la Ex-Aduana
PLAZA PRINCIPAL

Cathedral

Vincente Guerro

Market

TO PRONAF CENTER (2km)
Market

F

TO TRAIN STATION (400m)

for day-long tours across the border leaving on the hour from the Convention Center. Tickets US$11, ages 4-12 US$8.50, under 4 free. Trolleys run daily Apr.-Oct 10am-5pm and Nov.-Mar 10am-4pm. Call for reservations at 544-0062, which are recommended, or 544-0061 for recorded info.

Mexican Consulate: 910 E. San Antonio (tel. 533-3644), on the corner of Virginia. Dispenses **FMT/tourist cards** (see p. 37). Open M-F 9am-4:30pm.

Currency Exchange: Valuta, 307 E. Paisano (tel. 544-1152), at Mesa St. Conveniently near the border and open 24hr. **Melek,** 306 E. Paisano Dr. (tel. 532-4283), next to Valuta. Rates are worse than those at the banks. Most banks change cash and traveler's checks, but for the best rates try **Bank of the West,** 500 N. Mesa St. (tel. 532-1000), on the corner of Missouri. Open M-Th 9am-4pm, F 9am-5pm.

ATM: All of the banks in the downtown area around San Jacinto Plaza have them. Plan ahead because the banks close by 5pm and other ATMs are scarce.

American Express Office: 3100 N. Mesa (tel. 532-8900). Open M-F 8am-5pm.

EMERGENCY AND COMMUNICATIONS

Hospital: Providence Memorial Hospital, 2001 N. Oregon (tel. 577-6011), at Hague near UTEP. Open 24hr. Immunizations recommended but not required to enter Mexico. Call the immunization department (tel. 591-2050) of the **El Paso City County Health District,** 222 S. Campbell (tel. 543-3560), at First St. When approaching the Mexican border, turn left on Paisano St. and walk 3 blocks.

Post Office: 219 E. Mills (tel. 532-2652), between Mesa and Stanton. Open M-F 9am-5pm, Sa 8am-noon. **Postal code:** 79901.

Internet Access: Cybersmith Internet Cafe (tel. 845-1440), located at Sunland Park Mall, offers connections to the Internet at a rate of US¢20 per minute, US$5 per 30min., and US$9 per hr. Take Sun Metro Bus #12, 14, or 16, from San Jacinto Plaza to the Sunland Park Mall stop (approximately 20min.).

Phone Code: 915.

█ ACCOMMODATIONS

El Paso offers safer, more appealing places to stay than Juárez. Apart from the usual hotel chains (La Quinta, Days Inn, etc.) lining **I-10** and some more upper-end establishments near the airport, several great budget hotels cluster around the center of town near **Main St.** and **San Jacinto Square.**

Gardner Hotel/Hostel, 311 E. Franklin (tel. 532-3661; fax 532-3661; email epihostl@whc.net), between Stanton and Kansas. From the airport, take bus #33 to San Jacinto Park, walk 2 blocks north to Franklin, turn right, and head east 1½ blocks. With a helpful staff, an authentically decorated lobby, and cozy rooms, the Gardner is an oasis in the gritty, desert environment of downtown El Paso. **Hotel:** All rooms have color TV with cable and a phone. Check-out 1pm. Singles US$20, US$30 with bath; doubles and triples US$32.50, with bath US$45. **Hostel:** Small, 4-person dorm rooms and shared bathrooms. Locker rental US¢75, US¢50 for four or more days. Linen US$2. Laundry US$1.50 per load. Reception 24hr. Check-out 10am for hostel, 1pm for hotel. US$15 with AYH membership, valid US college ID, ISIC, CIEE, or ISTC, US$17.50 w/o membership.

Budget Lodge Motel, 1301 N. Mesa (tel. 533-6821; fax 534-9130), at California across from Cathedral H.S., a 10min. walk from San Jacinto Square up Mesa St. Even though it is more removed from downtown, it is only 6 blocks from UTEP. Rooms have A/C and cable TV. Small cafe, conveniently located on the 1st fl., serves breakfast and lunch at good rates. Outdoor swimming pool open May-Sept. Singles US$25 plus US$4 for each additional person.

Gateway Hotel, 104 S. Stanton (tel. 532-2611; fax 533-8100), at San Antonio Ave. A stone's throw from San Jacinto Square and a favorite stop for middle-class Mexicans. Spacious rooms, large beds and closets, and bathrooms, some with bathtubs. A/C upstairs; diner and small pharmacy downstairs; continental breakfast included. Parking US$1.50 for 24hr. Nice late checkout at 4pm. Singles US$23, with TV US$30; doubles US$35, with TV US$37.

◌ FOOD

El Paso has many small mom-and-pop diners that prepare a wide variety of tasty, homemade Mexican and American dishes. Burritos are the undisputed local specialty, and the array of places that serve 'em up hot is almost dizzying. Unfortunately, many places close early, so your options may be more limited after 6pm on weekdays.

La Malinche, (tel. 544-8785) N. Stanton St., at the corner of Texas near San Jacinto Square. Authentic Mexican fare in a brightly colored, cool environment. Burritos of all types US$1.75; breakfast and lunch menu US$3.50-6. Open M-Sa 7:30am-4pm.

Manolo's Café, 122 S. Mesa (tel. 532-7661), between Overland and San Antonio. Try the *menudo* (US$2), burritos (US$1), or the generous *comida corrida* (US$3.75) while checking out the bullfighter posters on the walls. Friendly service, free refills, and large portions make Manolo's a popular local hangout. Open M-Sa 7am-5pm, Su 8am-3pm.

Back Door Grill and Bar, 916 N. Mesa St. (tel. 546-9190; fax 532-3859). This local hangout is famous for its Philly cheese steak sandwich, but its best feature is a free draft beer if you mention that you're staying at the Gardner Hotel.

The Tap, 408 E. San Antonio (tel. 532-1848), at Stanton. You can't miss the big lightbulb sign. This bar/restaurant serves up authentic Tex-Mex to a local clientele and has a major advantage: it's open late. Breakfast US$3, lunch specials US$4, and dinner plates US$4-7. US$1 tequila or beer. Th 12-6pm, Sa 10:30-11:30pm. Open M-Sa 9am-2am, Su noon-2am.

◉ ♪ SIGHTS AND ENTERTAINMENT

The majority of visitors to El Paso are either stopping off on the long drive through the desert or heading south to Ciudad Juárez and beyond. For a whirlwind tour of the city and its southern neighbor, hop aboard the **Border Jumper Trolleys** that depart every hour from El Paso (see **Tourist Office,** p. 212).

Historic **San Jacinto Plaza** is the heart of El Paso and swarms with daily activity. The plaza is the main bus stop for all San Metro buses, and there you can take advantage of the shade of some of El Paso's only trees. South of the square on **El Paso St.** you can find countless small shops and open air stands, mostly along Stanton, San Antonio, and El Paso streets. Expect the normal goods such as clothing, food, and souvenirs. A savvy negotiator can find tons of bargains along the bustling thoroughfare. To take in a complete picture of the Río Grande Valley, head northeast of downtown along Stanton and take a right on Rim Rd. (which becomes Scenic Dr.); **Murchinson Park,** at the base of the ridge, offers a commanding vista of El Paso, Juárez, and the Sierra Madres. Take Sun Metro bus #63 from San Jacinto Plaza to catch a movie at **Cinema 6.** For museum enthusiasts, the area around the Civic Center on Santa Fe Ave. contains a renowned **Americana Museum,** as well as the **El Paso Museum of Art** (tel. 541-4040), located next to the tourist office.

For nightlife, try **The Palace,** 209 S. El Paso St. (tel. 532-6000), which pumps dance music to a packed house in a trendy, neon setting. (2nd fl. jazz lounge. 18+ admitted. US$5 cover. Open F and Sa until 2am.) **Club 101,** 500 San Francisco (tel. 544-2101), is El Paso's oldest club and boasts two dance floors (21+). An emerging gay scene is headed by **OP,** 301 S. Ochoa (tel. 533-6055), located 1 block north of Paisano. (Open Th and Su 9pm-2am, F-Sa 9pm-4am.) If you've had enough of the less-than-stellar evening pursuits in El Paso, head to Juárez for more rowdiness, a minimum drinking age of 18 and ubiquitous nightlife. Remember: both cities can be dangerous at night.

From April to September, the **El Paso Diablos** (tel. 755-2000) will make your trip to the stadium as much fun as one to the major league, but for minor league prices. To reach the home of the Diablos, **Cohen Stadium,** 9700 Gateway, take Sun Metro bus #42 from San Jacinto Plaza as far north as it goes and walk the rest of the way. Ask the driver for directions. (General admission US$3, box seats US$4.75.)

If munching on crackerjacks under the kleig lights of the stadium isn't your idea of outdoor activity, there's plenty of hiking opportunities outside of town like the **Mission Trail.** The tourist office will be happy to provide trail info. If you are driving and are feeling lucky, check out **Speaking Rock Casino** (tel. 860-7777).

CIUDAD JUÁREZ

Although Ciudad Juárez (pop. 1 million) is separated from El Paso only by the narrow Río Grande, the two cities are worlds apart. Visitors to Juárez are immediately bombarded with commotion on all sides and beset by a collage of bright paint and neon. Enterprising locals are eager to hawk their wares to anyone with a pulse. Near the border, the city is hectic, loud, dirty, and cheap. Many locals seem eager to help confused tourists, but they often expect a tip for leading you to your destination. Don't be surprised by the cab drivers who constantly ask you if you need a ride. The incredibly high concentration of junkyards on the southern fringes of the city and the nearby dilapidated ghettos provide a sharp contrast to the calm, ritzy, and pricey ProNaf area. Fleeing in the face of the American advance, Mexican culture can be found in the city's cathedral square and Parque Chamizal, pleasant respites from the sprawling industrial production centers and poor residential shantytowns that dot most of the cityscape.

✦ ORIENTATION

Most of Old Juárez (the area immediately adjoining the Santa Fe and Stanton Bridges) can be covered on foot. Street numbers start in the 600s near the two border bridges and descend to zero at **16 de Septiembre,** where **Av. Juárez** (the main street) ends. Both **Lerdo** and **Francisco Villa** run north/south, parallel to Juárez. To reach the **ProNaf Center,** take public bus "Ruta 8A" (2.80 pesos), which leaves from the intersection of Presidencia and Juárez near the border. Most city buses leave from the intersection of **V. Guererro** and Francisco Villa or thereabouts; ask the driver whether your bus will take you to your destination. It's a good idea to grab a map from the **tourist office** (see below) because outside of Old Juárez the streets get convoluted and you don't want to be in the wrong part of town. **Taxis** are always downtown, but fees are steep; negotiate before getting in. To get from the bus station to downtown, walk out the left-most door (if you're facing the main station entrance) and up to the street. Don't be satisfied with just any bus that will take you to the *centro;* get on an old converted school bus labeled "Ruta 1A" or "Ruta 6," both of which go to Av. Juárez, or you'll be left a few blocks outside the real center.

During the day, Juárez is relatively safe for the alert traveler. As darkness increases, however, so does the ratio of drunk to sober people wandering the streets. Be wary of people loitering about late at night, which large numbers of men have a tendency to do. Juárez is not the safest of places, especially after dark, so be careful and avoid places that look at all suspicious. Additionally, be wary of suspicious cab drivers. Don't go out unaccompanied. For information on entering and leaving Mexico, see **El Paso: Crossing the Border** (see p. 212) and **Entering and Leaving Mexico** (see p. 39). Women should not walk alone or in dark places; everyone should avoid the area more than 2 blocks west of Av. Juárez. The **police station** is on the corner of 16 de Septiembre and Juárez, and there is usually an abundance of police officers patrolling the downtown steets during the day.

🔃 PRACTICAL INFORMATION

TRANSPORTATION

Airport: (tel. 33 09 34), about 17km out on Rte. 45 *(Carretera Panorámica)*. Catch the crowded "Ruta 4" bus and get off at the San Lorenzo Church; then board the "Ruta Aeropuerto" (1.80 pesos). **Aeroméxico** (tel. 13 80 89 or 13 87 19) flies to Chihuahua, Mexico City, Monterrey, and a few close U.S. locations.

Buses: Central Camionera, Blvd. Oscar Flores 4010, (tel. 13 20 83), north of the ProNaf Center and next to the Río Grande Mall. To get there, take the Chihuahuenses bus from the El Paso terminal to Juárez (US$7), or cram into the "Ruta 1A" (red and white) or Permisionairos Unidos (blue) near F. Villa and V. Guererro (2.80 pesos). Be sure to ask the bus driver whether it is going to the bus station, since not all do. Chihuahuenses (tel. 29 22 29), Estrella Blanca (tel. 13 83 02), Ominbus de México (tel. 10 74 04 or 10 72 97), and others offer service to: **Chihuahua** (7hr.; every 30min.; 168 pesos); **Guadalajara** (24hr.; 10am, 1 and 10pm; 723 pesos); **Hermosillo** (10hr.; 290 pesos); **Mazatlán** (24hr.; 440 pesos); **Mexico City** (26hr.; 6 per day; 851 pesos); **Nogales** (8hr.; 6pm; 250 pesos); and more. Greyhound serves the U.S., including: **Dallas** (US$75); **El Paso** (50min.; every hr.; US$7); **Los Angeles** (US$45); **San Antonio** (US$79).

TOURIST AND FINANCIAL SERVICES

Tourist Office: The most conveniently located branch, the **Caseta de Información Turística** (tel. 14 92 56; main office, tel. 29 33 40, ext. 5160 or 5649; fax ext. 5648), can be found on Av. Juárez Azucenas, 2 blocks from the border. Few helpful brochures, but an amiable English-speaking staff. Open M-F 8:30am-2pm and 4-6pm.

U.S. Consulate: López Mateos Nte. 924 (tel. 13 40 48 or 13 40 50), at Hermanos Escobar. From Av. Juárez, turn left on 16 de Septiembre, right on López Mateos, and then walk for 15-20min. Closed Sa-Su. In an emergency, call the El Paso tourist office in the U.S. (tel. (915) 544-0062).

Currency Exchange: Banks congregate near the bus station, on Juárez and on 16 de Septiembre. Most are open M-F 9am-3pm. Traveler's checks can be cashed by **Comisiones San Luis** (tel. 14 20 33), on the corner of 16 de Septiembre and Juárez. Open M-Th 9am-7pm, F-Sa 9am-8pm, Su 9am-6:15pm. Also try **Chequerama** (tel. 12 35 99), at Unión and Juárez. Open M-Sa 10am-6pm. There are also numerous currency exchange booths with varying hours, rates, and services available on many major streets.

LOCAL SERVICES

Supermarket: Smart, López Mateos and Carretera Casas Grandes, a 15min. ride from Av. Juárez. The **Río Grande Mall,** at Guerrero and López Mateos, sells groceries, clothes, furniture, and much, much more.

Laundry: Lavasolas (tel. 12 54 61), Tlaxcala and 5 de Mayo. 12 other locations in town. Large washers 9 pesos, small 8 pesos; dryers 9 pesos. Open M-Sa 9am-9pm, Su 8am-5pm.

EMERGENCY AND COMMUNICATIONS

Emergency: dial 060.

Police: (tel. 15 15 51), Oro and 16 de Septiembre, near Juárez. English spoken.

Transit Police: (tel. 12 31 97 or 41 10 28), English spoken.

Red Cross: (tel. 16 58 06), in the ProNaf Center next to the OK Corral. English spoken. Open 24hr.

Pharmacy: El Félix Super Farmacia (tel. 14 43 31), 16 de Septiembre and Noche Triste, across from the cathedral. Turn right from Juárez. Open daily 8am-9pm.

Hospital: Hospital Latinoamericano, 250 N. López Mateos (tel. 16 14 67 or 16 14 15; fax 16 13 75), in the ProNaf area. English spoken. Open 24hr. Take "Ruta 8A."

Post Office: Lerdo at Ignacio Peña. Open M-F 8am-5pm, Sa-Su 9am-1pm.

Postal Code: 32000.

Fax: Secrefax (tel. 15 15 10 or 15 20 49; fax 15 16 11), on Av. Juárez near the Santa Fe Bridge, partially obscured under a white awning. Open 24hr.

Phone Code: 16.

ACCOMMODATIONS

In Juárez, a typical cheap hotel meets only minimal standards and charges some of the highest "budget" rates in Mexico. Even a moderate increase in quality means a huge jump in prices. Relatively inexpensive lodging can be found along the main strip, **Av. Juárez**; pricier places are located in ProNaf, around **López Mateos** and **Av. de las Américas.**

Hotel Juárez, Lerdo 143 Nte. (tel. 15 02 98 or 15 03 58), at 16 de Septiembre. Simple, small rooms in an old, yellow building, but one of the best deals you'll find in downtown Juárez–if you can deal without A/C. Its popularity means that Hotel Juárez is often full, even by early afternoons or on weekends. You can call ahead on the same day to reserve a room. Rates vary by season. Singles 112 pesos; doubles 116 pesos; triples 131 pesos; quads 145 pesos.

Hotel Morán, Av. Juárez 264 (tel. 15 08 02; fax 14 12 42), near Mr. Fog Bar. Located in the heart of Juárez, patrons of this hotel don't have to venture far for excitement. Reasonable rooms with A/C, color TV, and private baths provide all of the necessities. Singles 200 pesos; doubles 250 pesos.

Hotel San Carlos, Av. Juárez 131 Nte. (tel. 15 04 19 or 15 04 79). One of the cheaper hotels in downtown Juárez, its has all the basic amenities: TV, bathroom, phone, A/C. Hotel San Carlos slaps a higher price on married couples. Singles 135 pesos; married 185 pesos; doubles 205 pesos; married 220 pesos.

FOOD

Eateries vary from clean, air-conditioned tourist restaurants to roadside shacks with picnic tables and open pit grills on street corners. Travelers should avoid shacks, and in general should stick to restaurants on **Av. Juárez** and **Lerdo** or to the ProNaf Center. In general, *mariscos* (shellfish) are overpriced and less than fresh. As always, be cautious of foods that might have been washed in unclean water.

Cafetería El Coyote Inválido, Av. Juárez 615 (tel. 14 27 27), at Colón. Its name means "the crippled coyote," but this place is anything but weak when it comes to food and decor. A bustling, clean, American-style diner with heavenly A/C. Hamburgers (16 pesos), burritos (16 pesos), and an array of Mexican plates (16-32 pesos). Open Su-Th 8am-11pm, F-Sa 24hr.

Restaurant Guadalajara, Av. Juárez 222 Nte. (tel. 15 20 02), between Gonzáles and Carreño–the place with the open-air facade. The special Juárez tacos are excellent, and come with soup and baked potatoes all for 30 pesos. The service, though, is so slow you should make sure to savor every bite. Open daily 9am-9pm.

Hotel Santa Fé Restaurante, Lerdo 675 Nte. (tel. 15 15 22), at Tlaxcala, in the Hotel Santa Fe. Roll from here to there on the wheeled chairs. Sample chicken enchiladas or club sandwiches (25 pesos) and wash 'em down with a beer (12 pesos). Open daily 7am-11pm.

SIGHTS

The **Aduana Fronteriza** (tel. 12 47 07) stands in the *centro*, where Juárez and 16 de Septiembre cross (open Tu-Su 10am-6pm; free.) Built in 1889 as a trading outpost and later used for customs, it now houses the **Museo Histórico de Ciudad Juárez,** which chronicles the region's history from the begining of indigenous civilization up to the 20th century. The **Museo de Arte e Historia** (tel. 16 74 14), at the ProNaf

Center, exhibits Mexican art of the past and present (open Tu-Su 11am-5pm; admission 8 pesos, students free). Also at the ProNaf Center, the **Centro Artesanal** sells handmade goods at sky-high prices; you'd be crazy not to haggle here. The "Ruta 8" bus will take you from the *centro* to ProNaf for 2.80 pesos; a taxi charges much more.

The deforested **Parque Chamizal,** near the Córdova Bridge, down Av. Presidencia east of the Stanton Bridge, is a chance to escape from the clamor and commotion of downtown Juárez also see the newly inaugurated Mexican flag is said to be as large as an American football field. The **Museo Arqueológico** (tel. 11 10 48 or 13 69 83), Av. Pellicer in Parque Chamizal, houses plastic facsimiles of pre-Hispanic sculptures as well as trilobite fossils, rocks, and bones (open Tu-F 11am-8pm, Sa-Su 10am-8pm). The **Misión de Nuestra Señora de Guadalupe** (tel. 15 55 02), on 16 de Septiembre and Mariscal, is the oldest building on either side of the border for kilometers around features antique paintings and altars.

🎵 ENTERTAINMENT

Downtown Juárez was built for partying. It seems that every establishment along Av. Juárez that isn't selling booze or pulling teeth is a club or a bar; counting them could make you dizzy before you start drinking. Many establishments are unsavory, however, and even some of the better ones can become dangerous. Moderately safer and higher scale clubs such as **Chihua Charlie's, Amaryonos,** and **Ayinas** can be found in the ProNaf area. On weekends, gringos swarm to Juárez in a 48-hour quest for fun, fights, and fiestas. At **Mr. Fog Bar,** Av. Juárez Nte. 140 (tel. 14 29 48), at González, you can enjoy the atomosphere of a "ladies piano bar," meaning female bartenders and live music (beer and liquor 12 pesos). The dance floor is in the back. (Open daily 11am-midnight).

Juárez offers visitors more than just bars and clubs. If you enjoy bullfights or have never seen one, you can find them at the **Plaza Monumental de Toros** (tel. 13 16 56), Paseo Triunfo de la República at López Mateos. They usually occur at 5:30pm on Sundays from April to September. Prices go from 70 pesos in the sun to 95 pesos for nice seats in the shade. The **Lienzo Charro** (tel. 27 05 55), on Av. Charro off República, also hosts bullfights and a *charreada* (rodeo) on Sunday afternoons during the summer. At the western edge of town, **Galgódromo** (also known as the **Juárez Racetrack** (tel. 25 53 94) rises from Vicente Guerrero. Dogs run Wednesday through Sunday at 7:30pm and a Sunday matinees at 2:30pm. Also during the summer, there is a traveling carnival which periodically sets up on the soccer fields next to Parque Chamizal.

NUEVO CASAS GRANDES AND PAQUIMÉ

Nuevo Casas Grandes belongs to a time when cowboys ruled the land. A quiet town (pop. 80,000) in the expansive Chihuahuan desert, this community arose at the beginning of this century after a group of pioneering families from (Viejo) Casas Grandes decided to move to the newly constructed railroad station. Nuevo Casas Grandes is still an agricultural center and a great place to pick up a *vaquero* hat and boots. The town has clean streets, shaded parks, and friendly citizens—a welcome departure from the craziness of Juárez. Casas Grandes and the ruins of **Paquimé**(pah-kee-MEH)—one of the most important cities in pre-Hispanic northern Mexico—lie 8km to the southwest.

📍 ORIENTATION AND PRACTICAL INFORMATION. From the **Estrella Blanca** and **Omnibus Mexico** bus station on Obregón and 16 de Septiembre, walk one block down 16 de Septiembre to reach **Constitución,** which runs along the railroad tracks. One block further is **Juárez.** Two main streets in town; **5 de Mayo** and **16 de Septiembre** each run perpendicular to Juárez and Constitución and are the heart of the city. The main park in town, **Plaza Juárez,** is at the intersection of Juárez and 5 de

Mayo. **Taxis** loiter on 16 de Septiembre at Constitución and on Minerva at Obregón. Everything listed below lies within the nine-block downtown area.

Buses: Estrella Blanca and Caballero Azteca (tel. 4 07 80) running to: **Chihuahua** (4hr.; 6 per day 2am-midnight; 132 pesos); **Ciudad Juárez** (3½hr.; 12 per day 5am-9pm; 80 pesos); and **Cuauhtémoc** (6½hr.; 3 per day; 95 pesos). Chihuahuenses (tel. 4 14 75) runs buses all the way to: **Hermosillo** (8hr.; 6:30pm and midnight; 181 pesos); **Monterrey** (16 hr.; 3 per day; 390 pesos); and **Tijuana** (16hr.; 3 per day; 375 pesos).

The **tourist office** (tel./fax 4 64 73), on the corner of Juárez and Domínguez, is on the second floor of the Cámara de Comercios office, across from La Mansión (open M-F 9am-4pm). Change money at **Casa de Cambio California**, Constitución 207 (tel. 4 32 32 or 4 45 45), at 5 de Mayo (open M-F 9am-2pm and 3:30-7pm, Sa 9am-2pm and 3:30-6pm). **Bancomer** (tel. 4 61 18), 16 de Septiembre at Constitución, has a 24-hour **ATM** (bank open M-F 9am-3pm, Sa 10am-2pm). Stock up on groceries at **Hiperama** (tel. 9 21 04), Juárez at Minerva (open daily 9am-9pm). **Police:** (tel. 4 09 75) on Blanco and Obregón. **Red Cross:** (tel. 4 20 20) Carranza, at Constitución (open 24hr.). **Farmacia Benavides:** (tel. 4 55 55) Obregón, at 5 de Mayo (open daily 8am-10pm). **Post office:** (tel. 4 20 16) 16 de Septiembre and Madero (open M-F 8am-6pm, Sa 8am-1pm). **Postal code:** 31700. **LADATELs** cluster around the central square. **Phone code:** 169.

⊓⊡ ACCOMMODATIONS AND FOOD. Despite its small size, Nuevo Casas Grandes has plenty of great hotel and restaurant options. Accommodations with modern conveniences cluster on Constitución and on Juárez between 5 de Mayo and Jesús Urueta. The **Hotel Juárez,** Obregón 110 (tel. 4 02 33), is just a block from the bus station. Owner Mario is super-friendly and speaks flawless English. Small rooms with a fan are available upon request. Questionable plumbing and an odd bathroom set-up doesn't take away from the fact that it's one of the best deals in town. (Singles 60 pesos; doubles 70 pesos; triples 80 pesos.) At the **Hotel Paquimé,** Juárez 401 (tel. 4 13 20; fax 4 47 20; email npinon@paquinet.com.mx), a block from the plaza, rooms with extra large beds, cable TV, A/C, and carpeting make for a comfortable, though slightly pricey, option. (Singles 179 pesos; doubles 213 pesos.) They won't keep you, but if you can afford it, you may never want to leave the **Hotel California,** Constitución 209 (tel. 4 22 14), next to 5 de Mayo. A first-class joint with spacious, clean, air-conditioned rooms and tiled bathrooms. (Singles 210 pesos; doubles 250 pesos; triples 275 pesos; quads 300 pesos.)

The low tourist count means that the food is cheap and the nightlife soporific. **Restaurante Constantino** (tel. 4 10 05), at the corner of Juárez and Minerva, has great complete meals for under 30 pesos. Family owned for over 45 years, the service is as good as the food. (Open daily 7:30am-midnight.) **Dinno's Pizza** (tel. 4 02 40), Minerva and Constitución, has jalapeño, cherry, pineapple, and coconut pizzas (small 35 pesos, medium 40 pesos, large 50 pesos; open daily 8am-11:30pm).

⊡ SIGHTS. Surrounding Nuevo Casas Grandes are many archeological points of interest, including the **Cueva de Olla** (75km southwest), the **Arroyo de los Monos** (35km southeast), and **Mata Ortiz** (40km south). About 254km southeast of Nuevo Casas Grandes is **Madera,** from which the **Cuarenta Casas** archaeological site can be reached (54km north). Ask at the tourist office for more info. The most accessible and significant site, however, is the pre-Conquest city of **Paquimé.**

Paquimé (Casas Grandes) (tel. 2 41 46) is 8km southwest of Nuevo Casas Grandes and its architecture suggests that it grew out of two different cultures: its many-storied *pueblos* resemble those in the southwestern U.S., but other structures show the influence of central and southern Mexico. From 1000-1200, Paquimé was the most important agricultural and trading center in northern Mexico. The inhabitants kept snakes, macaws, and parrots, the latter two of which they used for decapitation rituals. They earned their livelihoods by farming and trading sea shells brought from the Pacific coast. The decline of Paquimé began about 1400 AD, and the settlement was completely destroyed by a fire caused by enemy attack. Be sure to visit the museum which displays artifacts found on the site and explains history and layout of the labyrinth of ruins.

On summer afternoons, the dry and shadeless ruins can become a blazing inferno, as temperatures approach or exceed 100°F (38°C). Be sure to bring sun protection, a broad-brimmed hat (cheap *sombreros* are available in town), and, most importantly, plenty of water. It might be a good idea to visit during the early morning or late afternoon when the temperatures aren't intolerable. From Nuevo Casas Grandes, take the beige and blue **municipal bus** at the corner of Constitución and 16 de Septiembre across from the furniture store (10min., 1 per hr., 3.80 pesos). Get off at the main plaza of Casas Grandes and walk back in the direction the bus just came from on Constitución. This road quickly turns into a dirt road which rounds a bend and goes straight to Paquimé (a 10min. walk). Almost any **taxi** driver will take you to the site from Nuevo Casas Grandes and walk around with you for about 70 pesos per hour. (Ruins open Tu-Su approximately 9am-5pm. Free. Museum open Tu- Su 10am-5pm. Admission 25 pesos; free Su.)

CHIHUAHUA

The capital of the Republic's largest state, Chihuahua (pop. 800,000) is a culturally vibrant and historically rich outpost secluded in the vast northern desert. The seclusion of Chihuahua convinced Pancho Villa to establish the headquarters of his revolutionary *División del Norte* here. His rebel troops staged attacks against the Porfiriato, using Chihuahua as their base. Dilapidated shacks with crumbling adobe walls stretch as far as the eye can see, but then give way to a modern, bustling downtown and beautiful villas on the southern side of the city. As the cultural center of northern Mexico, Chihuahua attracts a wide array of people, from Mennonites to the *indígena* Tarahumara people living isolated in the nearby Sierra Madres, who venture into the city only on market day to sell handmade crafts. The plentiful plazas, *parques*, and vendors liven up the streets of downtown Chihuahua.

◤ ORIENTATION

¡Ay! Chihuahua sprawls in every direction. Sliced in half by **Rte. 45** (the Pan-American Highway), the city serves as an important transportation hub for northern Mexico. Trains arrive at the **Estación Central de los FFNN,** just north of downtown. Trains headed for Los Mochis and Creel via the Barrancas del Cobre leave from the **Chihuahua al Pacífico** station, south of the city center off Ocampo and two blocks from **20 de Noviembre.** To shorten the 20-minute walk to the *centro*, hop on one of the **public buses** (2.80 pesos) that run up and down Ocampo to Libertad, but be prepared for a ride—the old school buses can be an adventure. Alternatively, snag a **cab** at the *centro* or the airport (about 25 pesos), but set the price before you step in. From the bus station, a municipal bus (2.80 pesos) will take you to the cathedral. Ask for information regarding municipal bus routes and cab prices at the information booth in the bus station.

Libertad is a pedestrian-only shopping arcade between **Independencia** and **Guerrero.** The two other main streets, **Victoria** and **Juárez,** run parallel to Libertad. **Av. Ocampo** crosses Juárez one block southwest of the cathedral. Starting with Av. Independencia, parallel streets *(calles)* have ascending even numbers to the south and ascending odd numbers to the north. *Avenidas* such as Victoria and Juárez that run north-south are named. Don't let Chihuahua's sheer size intimidate you; while the city is large, most sights are within walking distance of the **cathedral.** Budget hotels and restaurants cluster on the streets behind the cathedral. With the exception of Av. Victoria—the hub of Chihuahua's nightlife—the streets in Chihuahua are poorly lit. Women should avoid walking alone after dark.

⁊ PRACTICAL INFORMATION

TRANSPORTATION

Airport: (tel. 20 06 16 or 20 09 18), 14km from town. **Aerolitoral,** Victoria 106 (tel. 20 06 16). **Aeroméxico,** Victoria 106 (tel. 15 63 03). **Aerovías de México,** Bolívar 405 (tel. 16 35 47). **Transportes Aéreos Ejecutivos,** Jiménez 1204 (tel. 16 02 37). All are open M-F 9am-6:30pm. "Aeropuerto" buses get you there from Ocampo. Buses heading downtown wait outside of the baggage area at the airport.

Buses: To get to the main station (tel. 20 22 86), catch the "Aeropuerto" bus near Niños Heroes and Independencia. Ómnibus de México (tel. 20 15 80) sends its luxurious fleet to: **Aguascalientes** (every 2hr.; 444 pesos); **Casas Grandes** (6 per day; 132 pesos); **Durango** (7 per day; 272 pesos); **Guadalajara** (2:40am, 3, and 7:05pm; 553 pesos); **Matamoros** (2 per day; 495 pesos); **Mexico City** (7 per day; 678 pesos); **Monterrey** (4 per day; 370 pesos); **Querétaro** (1 per day; 574 pesos); and **Saltillo** (4 per day; 304 pesos). Transportes Caballero Azteca (tel. 29 02 42) sends buses to: **Hermosillo** (14hr.; 2, 7:30, and 10pm; 468 pesos); **Tijuana** (22hr.; 6:30 and 10pm; 735 pesos); and **Zacatecas** (12hr.; 14 per day 6am-11pm; 385 pesos). Transportes Chihuahuenses (tel. 29 02 42) sends buses daily to **Cd. Juárez** (5hr.; every hr. until 9pm; 168 pesos); **Mazatlán** (18hr.; 10:15am and 5:30pm; 413 pesos). Turismos Rápidos Cuauhtémoc-Anáhuac (tel. 10 44 33) has service to: **Cuauhtémoc** (1½hr.; every 30min. 5am-midnight; 45 pesos). Estrella Blanca has a slightly older fleet of buses that chugs to nearly all of the above cities for lower prices but requires more travel time and has a limited departure schedule.

Car Rental: Hertz, Av. Revolución 514 (tel. 16 64 73; fax 15 78 18), at José Nari Santos. VW Beetle with insurance and 300km per day costs 351 pesos per day.

TOURIST AND FINANCIAL SERVICES

Tourist Office: (tel. 10 10 77; fax 16 00 32), on Aldama between Carranza and Guerrero, in the Palacio del Gobierno across from the Plaza Hidalgo. Helpful, English-speaking staff dispenses maps and brochures. Open daily 9am-7pm.

Currency Exchange: BanPaís, Victoria 104 (tel. 16 16 59 or 10 15 93), 1 block from the cathedral past Independencia. No exchange fee for traveler's checks. Open M-F 9am-2:30pm. **Hotel San Francisco** (tel. 16 75 50), across the street, has 24hr. exchange. **ATMs** near the lobbies of all the tall banks downtown near the *zócalo.*

American Express: Vicente Guerrero 1207 (tel. 15 58 58; fax 16 77 70), past Allendex where Guerrero curves to become Bolívar. Open M-F 9am-6pm, Sa 9am-noon.

EMERGENCY AND COMMUNICATIONS

Emergency: dial 060.

Police: Av. Homero 540 (tel. 81 28 88 or 21 35 75), across from the Ford plant, at the exit to Juárez.

Red Cross: (tel. 11 22 11 or 11 14 84), Calle 24 and Revolución. Open 24hr.

Pharmacy: Farmacia Mendoza, Calle Aldama 1901 (tel. 16 69 32 or 16 66 38), at Calle 19, away from the cathedral past Plaza de Hidalgo. Open 24hr. **Farmacia Hidalgo** (tel. 10 65 08), at Guerrero and Aldama.

Hospital: Hospital General (tel. 16 00 22 or 15 60 84), Revolución and Colón, in Colonia Centro. **Clínica del Centro,** Ojinaga 816 (tel. 16 00 22).

Post Office: (tel. 37 12 00), on Libertad between Guerrero and Carranza, in the Palacio Federal. Open M-F 8am-7pm, Sa 9am-1pm. **Postal Code:** 31000.

Telephones: Silver **LADATELs** gleam in the sun all over the *zócalo.* Long distance service available in expensive hotels and at the plaza, in front of the cathedral.

Phone Code: 14.

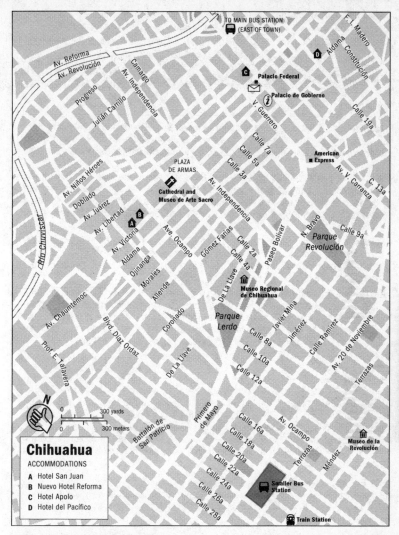

Chihuahua

ACCOMMODATIONS

A Hotel San Juan
B Nuevo Hotel Reforma
C Hotel Apolo
D Hotel del Pacífico

■ ACCOMMODATIONS

Hotels in Chihuahua are like the city itself—charm smiling through the grit. Economical hotels lie in the area behind (southwest of) the cathedral between **Victoria** and **Juárez.** More luxurious accommodations are available, but for much more than the comfortable economical hotels.

Nuevo Hotel Reforma, Victoria 823 (tel. 10 00 48; fax 16 08 35). Unique and delightful architecture. The old courtyard is covered by a warehouse-like roof and is connected to the 2nd fl. by an X-shaped staircase. The bug-free rooms have fans, soft beds, clean tile bathrooms, and incredibly tall ceilings. Singles 100 pesos; doubles 130 pesos.

Hotel Apolo, (tel. 16 11 00 or 16 11 01; fax 16 11 02; email hapolo@chihu.telmex.net.mx), Juárez at Carranza, in the *centro*. Travel back in time to the splendor of ancient Greece at the Hotel Apolo. Dark but majestic lobby with sculptures, chandeliers, and paintings. All clean, bright rooms have TV, A/C and nice, tiled bathrooms. Cafeteria, bar, and parking. Singles 250 pesos; doubles 280 pesos, triples 300 pesos. Discounts for large groups.

Hotel del Pacífico, Aldama 1911 (tel. 10 59 13), at Calle 21, a few blocks from the Palacio de Gobierno. Although the lobby is dark and musty, the clean rooms have A/C, large bathrooms, and decent foam mattresses with cement bases. Gregarious management. Singles 120 pesos; doubles 150 pesos; triples 180 pesos. Checkout 2pm.

◖ FOOD

Most eateries in Chihuahua are not geared toward tourists. Some of the best meals can be found in small *cantinas*, where bands serenade drunken (and often rowdy) men. However, women should be careful in the *cantinas* alone.

Mi Café, Victoria 1000 (tel. 10 12 38), at Calle 10, across from Hotel San Juan. If you like big portions and the color orange, then *Mi Café es su café.* The ceiling, chairs, even sugar container tops are *naranjado* (orange). A 40 peso order of *milanesa* (thinly sliced steak) comes with soup, beans, salad, and dessert. Breakfast platter 30 pesos. Open daily 9am-11pm.

Rosticería Los Pollos, Aldama 702 (tel. 10 59 77), between Calle 7 and Guerrero. Cafeteria-style dining at its best. Plastic booths, mirrored walls, and A/C spice up your excellent *pollo en mole* with rice and tortillas (only 20 pesos). For dessert, try some sweet *arroz con leche* (5 pesos). Open 9:30am-5:15pm.

Restaurant-Bar Degá, Victoria 409 (tel. 16 77 70), at Hotel San Francisco near the *zócalo.* Oozing with class, this joint offers a rare (if pricey) chance at a vegetarian meal. The *plato vegetariano* (45 pesos) includes vegetarian soup, a soy steak, avocado, and white rice; the *ceviche vegetariano* (30 pesos) has mushrooms and olive oil. Fresh carrot, papaya, or grapefruit juice costs 15 pesos. Open daily 7am-10:30pm.

◖ SIGHTS

PALACIO DE GOBIERNO. The stately and regal 19th-century palace stands in the center of Chihuahua on Aldama and Victoria. Inside, Aarón Piña Mora's beautiful murals tell the story of Chihuahua and Mexico. Look for a nude Emiliano Zapata, whose modesty is maintained by another soldier's conveniently placed rifle. The **Palacio Federal,** behind the Palacio de Gobierno was the jail of Miguel Hidalgo, where he was detained before being shot by a firing squad. Now, it houses the post office.

CATHEDRAL. A few blocks from the Palacio de Gobiero, on Victoria and Calle 2, is the giant cathedral. While construction began in 1725, the church was actually finished more than a century later in 1826. The unique stone facade is from the Baroque period.

MUSEO DE LA REVOLUCIÓN. Also known as Pancho Villa's House, visitors can relive the turbulence of the revolution by looking through an extensive collection of documents and photographs, paintings of Señor Villa, the bullet-ridden Dodge in which he was assassinated, his household furnishings, and his vast collection of weapons. Soldiers outside stand at attention. *(Tel. 16 29 58. To reach the museum at Quinta Luz, hike 1.5km south on Ocampo, turn left on 20 de Noviembre, and go two blocks to Calle 10 and Méndez. Turn right, and Villa's house is two blocks down. Open daily 9am-1pm and 3-7pm. Admission 10 pesos.)*

QUINTA GAMEROS CENTRO CULTURAL UNIVERSITARIO. Also called the Museo Regional de Chihuahua, this amazing architectural feat is one of the more stunning mansions in Mexico. Mining engineer Don Manuel Gameros, the aristocrat who had it built, never lived in it—the Revolution drove him to El Paso, Texas. The house was seized by revolutionaries and at one point served as Pancho Villa's barracks. Some astounding art-nouveau furniture and rooms now wow observers;

look for the 3m-high toilet and the Little Red Riding Hood building. Upstairs is an impressive collection of modern Mexican art, while the downstairs houses a Japanese doll collection. *(Tel. 16 66 84. On the corner of Calle 4 and Paseo Bolívar, about a 10min walk from the cathedral. Open Tu-Su 11am-2pm and 4-7pm. Admission 20 pesos, students, teachers, senior cititzens, and children,10 pesos. Half-price Wednesdays.)*

MUSEO DE ARTE SACRO. The museum houses pastoral religious paintings from the 18th century mingling with photos and portraits from the Pope's most recent visit to Chihuahua. *(Located in the SE corner of the cathedral, Libertad and Calle 2. Open M-F 10am-2pm and 4-6pm. Admission 9 pesos, students 6 pesos, children 4 pesos.)*

MUSEO DE ARTE CONTEMPORÁNEO. Sebastián's geometrical sculptures and Diego Rivera's sketch of a two-headed man/beast are among the highlights of this formidable collection of modern art. *(Tel. 29 33 00, ext. 3700. At Carranza and Aldama, kitty-corner to the Palacio del Gobierno. Open Tu-Su 10am-8pm. Admission 5 pesos, students and teachers 3 pesos. Free Wednesdays.)*

🎦 ENTERTAINMENT

At night, catch a flick at **Cinépolis** (tel. 17 52 22), Vallarta at Zaragoza *(Shows 3-9:30pm; 20 pesos, first show 15 pesos, Wednesdays 12 pesos).* To get there, hop on a "Cerro de la Cruz" bus in front of the Héroes de la Revolución building, in the *centro* (15min., every 8min. until 9:30pm, 2.80 pesos). If the buses have stopped running, you'll have to take a 20-peso cab back. **Café Calicanto,** Aldama 411 (tel. 10 44 52), serves local specialties and a wide selection of coffees and beers. Live Latin American music on the weekends on a beautiful outdoor stage surrounded by citrus trees. (Open Su-Th 4pm-2am, F-Sa 5pm-3am.) **La Casa de Los Milagros,** (tel. 37 06 93) on Victoria across from the Hotel Reforma, serves up an array of drinks in a classy courtyard setting (live Cuban music M and F-Sa; open Su-W 3pm-midnight; F-Sa 3pm-2am.) Nightclubs tend to be far from the center, but taxis will get you there. **Quinto Sofía,** in front of Lerdo Park, brings out a twenty-something crowd to listen to live Spanish rock (beers 12 pesos; cover 15 pesos after 10:30pm). A somewhat older crowd flocks to **Old Town,** Juárez 3331 (tel. 10 32 71), between Colón and Calle 39 (cover F-Sa 30 pesos; open Th 9pm-1am, F-Sa 9pm-2:30am).

HIDALGO DE PARRAL

Forget New York, London, or Paris, the capital of the world is Hidalgo de Parral. Dubbed "The Silver Capital of the World" by King Phillip IV of Spain in 1640, the name has stuck. The La Negrita silver mine was founded in 1631. The mine, now known as La Prieta, has been closed more than 10 years but still sits on the hills above town, keeping watch over the city to which it gave birth. With very little tourist activity, Parral (as it is affectionately known) is not only one of the cleanest cities in northwest Mexico, but also one of the most relaxed. The Río Parral, which hasn't seen water for five years, winds through downtown and "laps" up against the backsides of shops and hotels.

🚩 ORIENTATION AND PRACTICAL INFORMATION. From the bus station, exit the main doors and go left on Pedro de Sille, which runs into **Av. Independencia.** Turn left and you are on the main strip headed toward downtown. The routes which intersect in Parral also empty onto Av. Independencia; from the junction, turn right to get to downtown. Parral's city center is compact and made for walking. There are municipal buses which stop at the corner of **Mercedes** and **Pedro Gomez** downtown, or you can always hail a cab from downtown or along Independencia. The river runs through the center of downtown, and while streets zig-zag haphazardly, you're never far from the center if you stay near the river. Just after Av. Independencia crosses the river, it runs beside the **cathedral plaza,** where it intersects **Calle Benitez** and **Calle Hernandez,** the two other largest streets in town.

There is no tourist office, but you can call 2 02 21 for info, and residents are happy to point you in the right direction. Buses leave from the Parral bus terminal off Av. Independencia near the Motel El Camino Real. Ómnibus de México and Estrella Blanca run buses to: **Chihuahua** (4hr.; 5 per day; 96 pesos); **Juárez** (7hr.; 2 per day; 270 pesos); and **Mexico City** (20hr.; 2 per day; 670 pesos). To **exchange currency,** the easiest place to go is **Banco Serfín** near the cathedral plaza. The largest **grocery store** in town is **El Camino,** on Av. Independencia just outside of downtown, next to Hotel Margarita's. **Post office:** on the corner of Rago and Libertad, a few blocks from the cathedral plaza (open M-F 8am-3pm). **Postal code:** 33800. **Phone code:** 152.

■✆ **ACCOMMODATIONS AND FOOD.** Parral has some very stately old hotels left over from its mining boomtown days. The **Hotel Turista,** Independencia 12 (tel. 3 40 70 or 3 40 24), is well worth the 15-minute walk from the bus station; turn left on Independencia and follow it until you run into the hotel. Large, spotless rooms with a view come with A/C, TV, phone and tiled bathrooms. Incredible rooms for the price. (Singles 133 pesos, doubles 163 pesos, triples 193 pesos.) For a true dining experience, head to **Restaurante el Aseradero,** where you can watch your food being cooked over a wood fire. Heading towards the *centro,* the restaurant is on the left side of Independencia after Calle Primavera. Great chicken, beef, and *cabrito* (young goat) for 25-35 pesos (open daily 10am-10pm). Fantastic *comida corrida* (25 pesos) in cool, clean surroundings, can be found at the **Restaurant Turista,** right next to the hotel of the same name (open daily 7:30am-10:30pm). The true hidden culinary treasures, however, are the many family-run **taquerías** that dot the downtown area. While sitting at the tables along the sidewalk you can watch all of Parral stroll by and chow down on an order of tacos (10 pesos) or a burrito (6 pesos). The different homemade *salsas* at each stand will light up your life—and set your mouth on fire (most stands open about 10am-10pm.)

■♫ **SIGHTS AND ENTERTAINMENT.** Home to Pancho Villa during the last years of his life, Parral has many museums and sights dedicated to this hero of the Revolution. Chief among them is the **Museo de General Francisco Villa,** upstairs in the town library (open M-F 9am-8pm, Sa 9am-1pm; free). It's somewhat difficult to find, but if you turn right on Calle Hernandez, heading away from the Cathedral, you should be there in about 10 minutes. A bronze plaque marks the spot where Villa was assassinated when his car came to rest after being riddled by over 150 bullets. Although Villa's body rests in the **Cementerio Municipal,** on the outskirts of town, many of Parral's residents believe that, through a government conspiracy, his body has been robbed from the grave and moved to Mexico City. Other noteworthy sites in Parral include some of the magnificent buildings built with mining money. The interior of the **Catedral de San José,** dazzling in its immensity, is decorated with ore from local mines and contains the remains of the founder of the mines. The **Templo de la Virgen de Fátima,** on a hill by the mine overlooking the city, even has pews made from local ore. The **Palacio Alvarado,** constructed by one of the mine owners, is an mansion that rises up from among the ordinary houses on the city's northern side. If you stop to gawk, don't go in—part of the family still lives there. Nearby are the mining towns of Santa Barbara and San Francis de Oro; the bus station is happy to give information on trips to the nearby areas.

Besides the usual cinder block *cantinas,* nightlife can be found at **J. Quísseme,** a lounge/dance club on Av. Independencia near the bus station that starts hoppin' after 10pm (beer 10 pesos; cover 10 pesos; open Th-Sa 8pm-3am). The **Lone Star** club by the stadium is also a local favorite (open W-Sa 9pm-3am). If you are lucky enough to be in town at the right time, there are **bullfights** two weekends each summer (usually in mid-July and late-August), complete with carnivals and day-long parties. To get there, follow the noise to the stadium, a few blocks left of Independencia. Turn left near Pedro de Lille as you are heading out of town.

CUAUHTÉMOC MENNONITE COLONIES

As you explore downtown Cuauhtémoc, don't look twice if you pass a blond-haired, blue-eyed Caucasian in overalls or a long dress—hardly a typical sight in northwest Mexico. It's not surprising in Cuauhtémoc, the town and surrounding communities are home to about 40,000 Mennonites. The Mennonites are a pacifist religious group founded in the 16th century in Germany. After being expelled from virtually every country in Europe due to their refusal to serve in the military and their steadfast determination to educate their children privately, a large number of Mennonites settled in the agricultural fields just outside Cuauhtémoc. The hard-working, almost compulsively clean group of Mennonites that now inhabits the area is renowned for the cheese that they produce. Most Cuauhtémoc Mennonites have abandoned most of the traditional tenants of their religion, such as the prohibition of the use of electricity or mechanization, but traditional dress is still standard: hats, hair plastered to their heads, and long dresses for the women; overalls or jeans and work-shirts for the men.

🖈 **ORIENTATION AND PRACTICAL INFORMATION.** Cuauhtémoc lies midway between Creel and Chihuahua and is a two and a half-hour bus ride from each. The route into Cuauhtémoc from Chihuahua continues past the city and into the **Mennonite area,** organized in small communities called **campos.** Each *campo* has a number and is laid out in an orderly manner, with a main street, several farms, a creamery, a church, and a school. *Campos* are organized by number: on the left of the route, numbers start at one and go up, on the right they start in the mid-20s and count down, and after a certain point, the field numbers switch to the 100s. The center of Cuauhtémoc is at the *zócalo.* The cross-streets running east-west, Allende and Morelos, are the main streets in town.

You can ask for tourist info at the travel agency/**Mennonite tour headquarters,** Calle 3A 466, (tel. 2 30 64; fax 2 40 60) between Guerrero and Rayón. (Open M-F 9am-7pm, Sa 9am-1pm. Mennonite tours are approximately 150 pesos and departure times are flexible.) The Estrella Blanca **bus station** (tel. 2 10 18), Allende at Calle 9, runs buses to: **Basaseachi** (5hr., 8am, 12:30, and 4:30pm, 70 pesos); **Casas Grandes** (5hr., 4 per day, 90 pesos); **Chihuahua** (1½hr., every 30min. 8:30am-9:40pm, 35 pesos); **Cd. Juárez** (9hr., 2 per day, 155 pesos); and **Creel** (3½hr., every 2hr. 7:30am-7:30pm, 64 pesos). **Public buses** run all over the city and stop at blue bus stop signs—the main stop is on Calle 3 between Allende and Guerrero (2 pesos). **Banco Serfín** Melgar (Calle 1) at Allende, (tel. 2 63 33), has a 24-hour **ATM** and **changes money** at very good rates (open M-F 9am-5pm). The **Super Bonanza** (tel. 2 18 60), on Morelos between Calle 5 and 7, is a gigantic **supermarket** (open M-Sa 8am-9pm, Su 8am-2pm). The **police** (tel. 1 26 50), and the **Red Cross** (tel. 2 06 87) can be reached round the clock. **Farmacia Cuauhtémoc:** Morelos 321 (tel. 1 48 77) between Calle 3 and 5 (open M-Sa 8am-midnight, Su 10am-6pm). **Emergency:** dial 060. **Post office:** (tel. 2 03 14), Calle 4 at Guerrero, 1 block south of Allende (open M-F 8am-3pm). **Postal code:** 31500. **Phone code:** 158.

🖪🖹 **ACCOMMODATIONS AND FOOD.** Most hotels line Allende and cluster near the *zócalo.* **Hotel Princessa,** Allende 204 (tel. 2 07 83), one block west of the *zócalo,* has clean rooms with carpeted floors, beautiful furniture, A/C, TVs, and phones (singles 107 pesos; doubles 120 pesos; triples 134 pesos). **Nuevo Hotel Gran Visión,** (tel. 1 20 75), on Allende between Calles 7 and 9, across from the bus station, offers small tidy rooms with A/C, TVs, and phones (singles 130 pesos; doubles 140 pesos; triples 160 pesos). Those looking for nothing but the bare essentials should head to **Hotel Romo,** (tel. 2 11 31) at Calle 4a and Allende. Clean rooms come with solid beds and good plumbing. (Singles 55 pesos; doubles 110 pesos.) To sample Mennonite cuisine, try the **Travelers Restaurant** (tel. 2 64 70), between *Campo* 3B and *Campo* 19 near the Motel Gasthaus. Traditional Mennonite foods are quite rich, such as the *empanadas de requesón* (dough filled with cottage cheese and covered with cream sauce; 21 pesos) and *fideos con crema* (noodles with ham or sausage, also drowned in cream sauce; 30 pesos). Eat here more than twice, however, and your cholesterol count may hit quadruple digits. (Open daily 8am-9pm.) The **Restaurant Mennonita** (tel. 9 25 46), just up the road towards Cuauhetémoc from the Traveler's Restaurant, offers full buffet meals. A hefty price (45 pesos) buys all you can eat of a delicious combination of Mexican and Mennonite foods. (Open M-Sa 8am-8pm, but don't expect a full buffet until lunchtime.) **El Chalet,** Allende 544 (tel. 2 44 4 3), serves Mexican cuisine in a Spanish mission setting (open M-Sa 8am-8pm).

⬛ THE COLONIES. Exploring the Mennonite communities of Cuauhtémoc is very difficult unless you have a car. The Estrella Blanca bus heads to Casas Grandes from the bus station (11 pesos): it stops at Campo 6.5. The Motel Gasthaus and Restaurant are earlier in the route so be sure to tell the bus driver if you want to get off there. Taxis will also take you there for a high price. Hitchhikers report success on and off the main route, but drivers are scarce on the desolate dirt roads between colonies removed from the route. If you want to stay in the colonies, the **Motel Gasthaus,** (tel. 1 43 33) also called Motel 12, has big, bright, squeaky-clean rooms and tiled bathrooms (checkout 10am; singles 150 pesos; doubles 200 pesos). They'll also provide you with a tour of the colonies for about 180 pesos. Tours typically include a look inside an authentic Mennonite home, a tour of a cheese factory and a machinery plant, and a meal (at your expense) at a Mennonite restaurant. To check out the Mennonite colony on your own, you'll need a car to get from place to place. To see a Mennonite cheese factory in action, take a left at the 2-B/22 sign and follow the road heading down into the village. After passing a school and church (Su only) on your left, take a right into the **Quesería América,** one of the 20 to 25 cheese factories in the 80 or so Mennonite villages in the area. Try visiting in the morning, when the cheese is actually made.

CREEL

High amid the stunning peaks and gorges of the Sierra Madres lies the small village of Creel (pop. 5000, elevation 2340m) which welcomes travelers with natural beauty and refreshing mountain air. Cabins dot the hillsides, the train rumbles through town two or three times a day, animals freely roam the streets, and the town's residents are friendly and rugged. Creel is most popular as a base from which to explore the stunning **Copper Canyon** (see p. 232). Although tourism to Creel has increased lately, it hasn't damaged the unique ambience of the town nor has it substantially altered the lives of the 50,000 Tarahumara Indians living in the mountains surrounding Creel. Like many of Mexico's *indígena* groups, the Tarahumara have warded off modern Mexican culture. They are famous for their non-stop long-distance sacred foot races, which last up to 72 hours. The countryside around Creel is also home to a number of other *indígena* groups, including the Pima to the northwest, the Northern Tepehuan to the south, and the Guarojio to the west.

⬛ ORIENTATION

The railroad tracks function as a rough compass: toward Chihuahua is north and toward Los Mochis is south. The *zócalo* is the center of town and the best place from which to get your bearings. With your back to the **bus station** and facing the **train station,** the *zócalo* is down a small hill in front of you and a bit to the right. The main street, **Mateos,** runs parallel to the trains on the opposite side of the *zócalo* and is the only street around the *zócalo* that extends any distance in one direction. Everything you need can be found on or near Mateos. **East Batista Caro,** farther south, runs parallel to Mateos and up to the tracks. **Avenida Ferrocarril** and **Avenida Francisco Villa** run parallel to the train tracks on the opposite side of Mateos. Be sure to check out the map next to Banca Serfín.

✷ PRACTICAL INFORMATION

TRANSPORTATION

Trains: Av. Tarahumara 57 (tel. 6 00 15), right in town on the tracks across from the Estrella Blanca bus station. Trains leave daily for **Chihuahua** (first-class 6hr., 3pm, 188 pesos; second-class 7hr., 4pm, 55 pesos), and **Los Mochis** (first-class 9hr., 11:30am, 225 pesos; second-class 10hr., M, W, F at 1pm, 67 pesos). You can get off anywhere along the way and avoid paying full price. Tickets aren't sold in advance, so scramble on quickly when your train pulls up and elbow for a seat, then pay the conductor as he comes around. See **The Train Through the Canyons,** p. 232.

Buses: Estrella Blanca (tel. 6 00 73), in a small white-and-green building across the tracks from the *zócalo,* sends buses to: **Chihuahua** (5hr., 7 per day, 122 pesos); **Cuauhtémoc** (3hr., 5 per day, 80 pesos); and **Parral** (71 pesos). From the **Hotel Piños** office at Mateos 39, **Canyon buses** (tel. 6 02 79 or 6 02 30) leave for **Batopilas** (6hr.; Tu, Th, and Sa 7:15am; 120 pesos; return trip leaves Batopilas M, W, and F 5am). From the ticket office (tel. 6 01 77), on Francisco Villa behind the Hotel Posada, buses run from Creel to **San Rafael** departing at 4pm daily (40 pesos).

Bike Rental: Expediciones Umarie, south along the tracks next to the 2-story cabin. Rents bikes (65-80 pesos per day, 40-50 pesos per half-day, 12 pesos per hr.) as well as helmet and gloves (15 pesos); they also offer a half-day introductory **rock climbing** course (150 pesos per person, min. 2 people). Bikes can also be rented from **Complejo Turístico Arareco,** Mateos 33 (tel. 6 01 26), south of the *zócalo* for 20 pesos an hr. They also have horses available for hire (60 pesos per hr.).

TOURIST AND FINANCIAL SERVICES

Tourist Information: Artesanías Misión (tel. 6 00 97), on the north side of the *zócalo.* Not an official tourist office, but the best source of information on Creel and the surrounding area. Sells maps along with Tarahumaran books and crafts. Proceeds donated to the Tarahumaran Children's hospital fund. English spoken. Open M-Sa 9:30am-1pm and 3-6pm, Su 9:30am-1pm.

Currency Exchange: Banco Serfín, Plaza 201 (tel. 6 02 50 or 6 00 60), next door to the Misión. Dollars exchanged M-F 9am- 1:30pm. Open M-F 9am-3pm. 24hr. **ATM.**

LOCAL SERVICES

Market: Abarrotes Pérez, on Mateos next to Cabañas Bertis. Fruit, vegetables, and purified water. (Open daily 9am-9pm.)

Laundry: Lavandería Veno, Francisco Villa 112 (tel. 6 01 39). Around the back of the 2-story blue house, behind the Casa de los Artesanios del Estado. 30 pesos per load for wash and dry. Same-day service ends at 6pm. Open daily 9am-8pm.

EMERGENCY AND COMMUNICATIONS

Police: (tel. 6 04 50), in the Presidencia Seccional, on the south side of the *zócalo.*

Pharmacy: Farmacia Rodríguez, Mateos 43 (tel. 6 00 52). Open M-Sa 9am-2pm and 3:30-9pm, Su 10am-1pm.

Medical Services: Clínica Santa Teresita, (tel. 6 01 05), on Calle Parroquia at the end of the street, 2 blocks from Mateos. Little English spoken. Open M-F 10am-1pm and 3-5pm, Sa 10am-1pm). Open for emergencies 24hr.

Post Office: (tel. 6 02 58), in the Presidencia Seccional, on the south side of the *zócalo.* Open M-F 9am-3pm. **Postal Code:** 33200.

Fax: In Papeleria de Todo, Mateos 30. Open daily 9am-8pm.

Telephones: LADATELs are located around the *zócalo* and on Mateos and Francisco Villa.

Phone Code: 145.

ACCOMMODATIONS AND CAMPING

Due to Creel's flourishing popularity, there are a large number of hotels competing for tourists' pesos. Prices may be negotiable during low season, and budget rooms are plentiful. Most budget rooms are a block or two from the *zócalo*.

Margarita's Casa de Huéspedes, Mateos 11 (tel. 6 00 45), kitty corner from the zócalo. An international backpacker's mecca. You'll have no trouble finding it—a young emissary meets almost every train and bus to lead you to the house, where you mingle with Margarita's family, friends, and guests, who come from every corner of the globe. Most conversations gravitate towards English and the staff speaks it fluently. Make it clear that you want to go to the *casa,* not the hotel. Clean, fresh rooms. Tours offered. Dorms 50 pesos; singles 150 pesos, doubles 200 pesos with a private bathroom. Best of all, prices include breakfast and dinner.

Cabañas Bertis, Mateos 31 (tel. 6 00 86). Rooms are much nicer than one would expect from the exterior. Several even come with a fireplace and TV. A/C and heater. Tours offered. Singles 120 pesos; doubles 180 pesos; triples 240 pesos. For reservations, call 18 49 60.

Hotel Korachi, Francisco Villa (tel. 6 02 07), across the tracks from the train station. A wanna-be hunting lodge. Clean bedrooms with dark, wood-paneled walls and comfy beds, and wood or gas heaters in the bathroom. Singles 120 pesos; doubles 160 pesos; triples 200 pesos; quads 220 pesos. *Cabañas* with animal skins on the walls include private bath and wood supply. Singles are not available; doubles 250 pesos; triples 300 pesos; quads 350 pesos.

For the adventurous type, the campground and lodges around **Lago Arareco** are the way to go. A scenic **campground** can be found on the northwestern shore, on a hill overlooking the lake. The site sports 31 barbecue and fire pits, 12 latrines, hot showers, and picnic areas. You'll need a car to get there. Drive down Av. Mateos until you hit the route and turn left towards Cusárare. The campground is 8km down on the left. (10 pesos per person.) The **Batosárachi Lodge** (tel. 6 01 26), on the southeast corner of this vast body of water, houses up to 50 in the three Tarahumara-style cabins (each has bunk beds, a common room, heaters, and hot water). At both places, guests can cook their own meals or let themselves be served. Both are located next to the campground. A **KOA Campground,** (tel. 14 21 70 88) is just a few blocks south on Mateos from Cusárare (camp sites 50 pesos per person; RVs 180 pesos and up; hotel rooms for 4 590 pesos; tours offered).

FOOD

There are several inexpensive restaurants along **Mateos** with friendly atmospheres and home-cooked fare. Almost everything is cheap, but quality varies. Picnicking spots lie on the quiet hillsides and are reachable by car or hiking.

Cafeteria Gaby, Mateos 48, across from the grocery store, serves up various home-cooked meals. Sit in Gaby's kitchen and enjoy out-of-this-world food. Breakfast 15-20 pesos; lunch 25 pesos; dinner 30 pesos. If you're confused by the door, just pull the string. Open daily 7am-10pm.

Restaurante Todo Rico, Mateos 37 (tel. 6 02 05), at E. B. Caro. Good food served up in a friendly atmosphere. *Comida corrida* 25 pesos; 2 hamburgers and fries are only 23 pesos. Open daily 7:30am-11pm.

Restaurante Veronica, Mateos 34. This simple joint is a local favorite. Enjoy an order of eggs any style (19 pesos) or the *comida corrida* (28 pesos). Open daily 7am-10:30pm.

SIGHTS AND ENTERTAINMENT

Creel's real draw is the canyon and surrounding countryside. To explore the beautiful and wild surroundings, you'll need a car, a tour guide, or a brave heart and a strong pair of legs to get there (see **Near Creel** and **Barrancas del Cobre,** p. 232).

The **Casa de las Artesanías del Estado de Chihuahua** (tel. 6 00 80) is on Av. Ferro-carril 178, in the old railroad station across from the *zócalo*, displays local and Tarahumara arts, crafts, and a random assortment of historical relics. What really steals the show is the mummy in the back room, which may be an ancestor of the Tarahumara. (Open Tu-Sa 9am-5pm, Su 9am-1pm. Admission 5 pesos.)

Most of Creel's sights lie just outside of the city. **Lago Arareco** is 8km down the route toward Cusárare and has a variety of trails— perfect for a day hike. Day tours leaving from the *zócalo* (hours are flexible and prices vary) venture into the nearby Barrancas del Cobre. Exploring the countryside with a **bike** is also a good option (see **Practical Information,** p. 229).

At night, **Laylo's Lounge and Bar,** López Mateos 25 (tel. 6 01 36), inside **El Caballo Bayo** restaurant and hotel, is a local *cantina* with a touch of class. Its male-dominated crowd is classic *cantina*, but the comfy lounge chairs and nice decor outdo most watering holes. (Open daily 3pm-1am.) **Tio Molcas,** Mateos 35, at Batiste Caro, also breaks *cantina* stereotypes and has a laid-back lounge atmosphere. Satisfy a late night craving here—the place doubles as a restaurant during the day. (Open daily 11am-1am.) One of the most happening places in town is the bar at **Margarita's Plaza Hotel.** turn left on E. B. Caro heading away from the *zócalo*, and then right into the hotel courtyard. Happy Hour lasts from 7 to 10pm and includes a **free tequila shot** with every beer. While most establishments in Creel close before 9pm, a few are open late, and the town usually has a few tourists roaming the streets or people strumming guitars until midnight. On Saturday nights, the **Casino de Creel,** in front of the plaza, offers outdoor and indoor dances, to which both locals and tourists are welcome (men 15 pesos, women 10 pesos; festivities 8pm-1am).

TOURS

Tours of the surrounding sights make Creel tick, so you'll never have trouble finding one. One of the best ways to see the surrounding canyons necessitates forking out a little cash—but it's worth it. The more expensive hotels also offers tours as do some local residents.

Casa Margaritas: 5 tours. Reasonable prices with lunch included.

Cabanas Bertis: 10 tours. Various combinations of sights.

KOA Campground: 7 tours. Higher prices but modern transportation.

Compleja Turistico Arenero: Tours of sights near the *Laguna Arareco*.

Tarahumara Tours: Located at a booth in the center of the *zócalo*. Competitive prices.

NEAR CREEL

For great excursions in the surrounding Sierra Tarahumara/Copper Canyon region, see **The Canyons: North of Creel to Basaseachi Falls** (p. 234), **The Canyons: South of Creel to Urique** (p. 235), **The Canyons: The Road to South to Batopilas** (p. 235), **Batopilas and Satevó** (p. 236).

SAN IGNACIO MISSION. Much of the immediate area around Creel is also very beautiful and worth exploring. To reach the San Ignacio Mission, walk south on Mateos until the road forks and stay to the left. The road forks again shortly; again, take the left path. To enter the area of the Mission and lake, you'll need to pay 15 pesos. From this check point, the Mission is about 1km straight ahead and there are signs directing you to the other sights. The mission was constructed in 1744 and is still in use today—services are conducted Sundays at 12pm in Rarámuri, the native language of the Tarahumara. Nearby is the **Valle de los Hongos** (Valley of the Mushrooms) and the **Valle de las Ramas** (Frogs) and the **Valle de las Chichis** (Breasts) along with the cave of Sebastion. Don't ask about that last valley.

LAGUNA ARARECO. Travelers can also hike to the man-made lake 3km long and eight acres in area. Just bear right when the road forks past Mateos and follow the path 7km southeast. To reach the lake from the Mission, follow the path up the mountain, jump the fence and veer to the right through two large fields. The water here is cold and contains dangerous weeds below the surface. From the small station next to the lake you can rent paddle boats for 60 pesos. Nearby is Recohuata Hot Springs, where you can take a break from a long day of hiking in the soothing, warm waters (admission 10 pesos). If you take a tour, it's a 40-minute ride from Creel and a 600m hike down into the canyon (around 60 pesos). The **Valle de las Monjas** (Valley of the Nuns), 9km away, makes a great daytrip on horseback.

BARRANCAS DEL COBRE

Covering an area four times the size of Arizona's Grand Canyon, the **Copper Canyon region,** hidden deep within the Sierra Madres, is one of the most spectacular sights in all of Mexico. The Barrancas, comprised of five interlocking canyons in an area more generally known as the **Sierra Tarahumara,** hibernate under drifts of snow during the winter months and explode with color during the rainy season (July-Sept.) when the canyon's plants are in full bloom. The Copper Canyons, so-named for the minerals in the rock that give the canyon walls a copper color, is transversed on the western side by the tracks of the **Chihuahua-Pacífico Railroad;** trains career along canyon walls at death-defying angles, plunge into tunnels (there are 96 of them), and briefly skim the rim of the *barrancas*. The railroad stretches from Chihuahua to Los Mochis, crossing the Continental Divide three times and soaring to a height of 2240m. Passengers peering from train windows can see a breathtaking series of landscapes—cactus-covered plateaus, mountains covered with pine, unusual rock formations, endless blue skies, and canyon floors teeming with tropical vegetation.

Perhaps the most amazing feature of the expansive and magnificent Barrancas is what a well-kept secret they are. Few foreigners, even those familiar with Mexico, have ever heard of the Copper Canyons, and still fewer could place it. The immense area and singularity of the canyons means there is a wealth of breathtaking vistas, but with little infrastructure around the canyons, they are hard to explore, especially without a car. Dirt roads wind through remote corners of the canyons, but travelers without cars must rely on kind-hearted locals to give them a lift, or else they must really enjoy walking many miles. It almost doesn't matter where one goes—in this beautiful country, adventure awaits everywhere.

THE TRAIN THROUGH THE CANYONS

Two types of trains make the daily journey between Los Mochis and Chihuahua. The **first-class train** is for tourists; equipped with bathrooms and A/C, and blessed with large, comfortable, tilt-o-matic seats. The **second-class train** screeches along the same tracks carrying both passengers and livestock; it's a much slower, sweatier ride. Trains go from Los Mochis to Chihuahua (first-class 13hr., 6am, 415 pesos; second-class 16hr., 7am, 85 pesos) and vice-versa (first-class 7am; second-class 8am). Creel is the most noteworthy stop along the way, and makes the best base from which to explore the canyon (first-class Chihuahua to Creel 6hr., 188 pesos; Los Mochis to Creel 10hr., 225 pesos; second-class 13hr., 50 pesos). The serious mountain scenery lies between Creel and El Fuerte, so if you take the second-class Los Mochis-bound train, you'll zoom by some great views in the dark. For more expansive natural spectacles, grab a seat on the **left side** of the train heading toward Los Mochis, and the **right side** if you're on the way to Chihuahua. For more information, see Creel (p. 228). Since the train only comes through any town twice a day if you get off you'll be there at least 12 hours—it's important to get off at the right place.

DIVISADERO STATION

At the **Divisadero Station,** the jagged mountain edges overlap to create a maze of gorges at the rim of the Barrancas del Cobre. Eight hours out of Los Mochis and two hours out of Creel, the first-class train stops here for 15 minutes of sightseeing. As you get off, you'll be bombarded by people selling local Tarahumara crafts

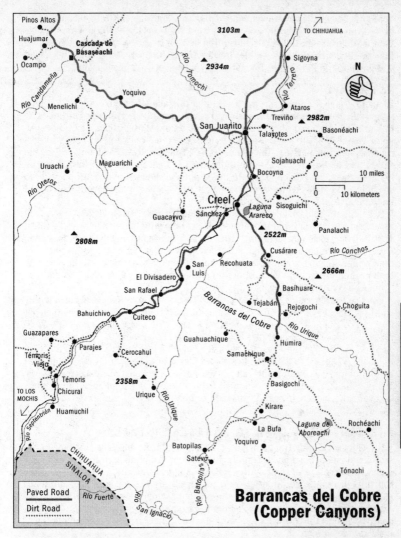

Barrancas del Cobre (Copper Canyons)

Paved Road
Dirt Road

as well as *gorditas* and *burritos* (about 8 pesos). If you've got a few pesos to burn, Divisadero is well worth spending a day around. There are three resort-type hotels near the train station, which offer tours (about 300 pesos per person) and horseback riding. Several trails of varying difficulty also begin at El Divisadero. The best bet for maps or information is to ask at one of the local hotels. For a day hike, trek down to **Las Cuevas** (the caves) and back (about 8hr.). Guides are recommended for the other overnight trail trips. Plenty of people roaming around the train stop will be willing to help you out. Don't worry, they'll find you. **Margarita's** (see p. 230) charges 120 pesos per person for an excursion. Aside from claiming an amazing vista of the canyon (perhaps the fullest view of the Barrancas anywhere), Divisadero is also home to **La Piedra Volada,** a large, precariously balanced stone. It is technically possible (though quite difficult) to attempt a full-day hike between Cusárare and Divisadero, but an experienced guide is a must. A far more manageable and popular hike from Divisadero (which might force you to stay at a pricey hotel, as camping is not recommended) is down into the canyon—you can go as far as you want. A six-hour, 4km round trip hike leads to the Tarahumara village **Bacajipare,** while the 27km descent to the bottom of the canyon from Divisadero takes eight hours each way. Guides for hire hang around the hotel, and they'll take you down to the Río Urique, Bacajipare, or wherever your heart desires.

SAN RAFAEL

Eleven kilometers down the tracks from **El Divisadero** lies the dusty and nondescript village of **San Rafael.** The town sprung up on the hillsides around the saw mill outside town and offers a rare peek into an older way of life. San Rafael has just a handful of phones and all cooking is still done on wood-burning stoves—running water is a luxury few people have. From San Rafael, continue down the tracks and marvel at the 300-year-old church at **Cuiteco,** but do it from the train because there is no place to stay in Cuiteco. **Bahuichivo** is the take-off point to go south into the canyons toward Urique (see p. 235), and it has several hotels and restaurants to offer the budget traveler.

San Rafael's two main streets are **Av. Centro** and **Av. Linda Vista.** As you face Mochis at the railroad station, the best hikes are to your left up and over the ridge. Just follow Av. Linda Vista until it ends and then start heading up the ridge. Because San Rafael is situated in the crook of two intersecting ridges, the views of the Copper Canyons are not that spectacular from the town itself; the surrounding high ground around the town offers much better vistas. There is no set path, so bringing a compass is advisable.

Hotel de Los Magnolias, Av. Linda Vista 18, just down from the plaza, has not only spotless rooms, real beds, and a patio and deck that look out over the canyons, but flushing toilets and—be still, my beating heart—hot water showers (singles 200 pesos; doubles 220 pesos; triples 300 pesos). Two hotels next to each other on Av. Centro have beds in the 40 to 50 peso price range but are not as luxurious the Magnolia. A good place to eat is the **Restaurant Cierra,** at the edge of town on the road to Bahiochino. At **Restaurant Nalby,** Av. Centro, across from Restaurant Doris, Nalby cooks up a huge Mexican meal for her family and some local single men, and you are welcome to eat all you want for just 12 pesos (meals served daily 8am, 1 and 7pm).

THE CANYONS: NORTH TO BASASEACHI FALLS

With water cascading from a height of 246m, the **Basaseachi Falls** are some of the world's most spectacular waterfalls. Basaseachi (Tarahumaran for "place of the cascade" or "place of the coyotes") is the highest waterfall in Mexico and the fourth highest in North America. Few waterfalls are blessed with such gorgeous surroundings. Tucked away back in the corner of Canyon Candameña, the falls are undisturbed and don't get many visitors because of their remoteness, but any person who makes the trip will be rewarded with scenery from a postcard photographer's wildest dream.

Getting to Basaseachi can be a little tricky unless you have a car. With a car, just pick up a map in Creel and enjoy the drive on the newly paved road. Without one, there are a few options. **Margarita's, Cabañas Bertis,** and **Tarahumara Tours** (see p. 230), in Creel, run tours to Basaseachi. Another cheaper and just as easy option (since trails are well marked and a guide isn't necessary) is to take an **Estrella Blanca** bus to Basaseachi from either Cuauhtémoc (2 per day, 80 pesos) or Creel (5hr., 3 per day, 91 pesos). The bus from Creel stops at a pair of tiny crossroads called San Pedro where you'll have to change buses to get to Basaseachi.

Along the way to Basaseachi, you'll pass through some of the most sparsely populated areas of the Sierra Tarahumara area. **San Juanito** is the only town along the road with gasoline, reliable telephones, and decent restaurants and hotels (most of them near the bus station). If you are forced to stay, **Hotel San Juanito** is a mere two blocks from the bus station; it has humble but clean rooms (singles 70 pesos; doubles 90 pesos; triples 110 pesos).

Once in Basaseachi, walk 3km down the paved road that runs through town to the trailhead to see the falls. The path is clearly marked and leads to the top of the falls after about a 30-minute walk. You won't have much of a view from the top of the falls, so hike down the steep path to the natural *ventana* (window), which gives a breathtaking view of the falls and surrounding canyon. The hike takes about 45 minutes each way. Adventurous spirits can trek to the bottom of the falls by following the path. The hike is difficult and takes about another hour from the "window," but you'll be alone at the bottom in a sub-tropical paradise.

Back in Basaseachi, there is only one indoor accommodation—**Hotel Nena**, on the corner of the route and the road to the falls. The rooms have private baths and comfy beds. (Singles 50 pesos; doubles 70 pesos; triples 100 pesos.) A **long distance telephone** can be found across the street at **Restaurant Betty**, which serves up quick and cheap burritos (7 pesos) and *chile rellenos* (8 pesos; open daily 7am-9pm). Restaurant Betty is also the place to buy **bus tickets** and wait for the bus.

THE CANYONS: SOUTH TO URIQUE

It's a 154km jaunt from Creel to Urique. **Bahuichivo,** in a clearing in the forest, is 97km south of Creel. There's not much to see there, but it's often used as a departure point for spots deeper in the canyon or for Cerocahui and Urique, farther south. The mountain village of **Cerocahui** (pop. 600, elevation 1525m) is 17km southeast of Bahuichivo. The main attraction in Cerocahui is the **Jesuit Mission**, founded in 1681 by the priest Juan María de Salvatierra. **Sangre de Cristo** (gold and silver mines), the **Gallego Mountain** (38km away), the **Misión Churo,** and the **Yeparavo Waterfall** (4km south) are among the possible excursions from Cerocahui. The **grocery store** at the fork in the road has all the information about excursions from Cerocahui. Several locals offer tours for steep prices, and unless you know the way yourself, they are your best bet.

The village of **Urique** sits at bottom of the **Barranca de Urique,** the deepest of the canyons. Both the drives into Urique and Batopilas are very difficult and almost impossible without 4WD drive. The hairpin turns and unstable bumpy road means that you're better off going with a tour if you're not familiar with the road. The three-hour, 54km, edge-of-your-seat dirt road ride from Bahuichivo to Urique takes you from a cool, frontier-like town in the forest to a warm, tropical village where the mango trees share the same humid air as the cacti beside them. About halfway down to Urique, the canyon opens up to reveal magnificent cliffs. You can see the village of Urique far below on the canyon floor. The lookout point rivals Divisadero as the best place to take in the Copper Canyons. There's always a posse of vehicles waiting at the train station in Bahuichivo going to Urique for about 50 to 60 pesos. If a man with a brown van offers to take you to Urique for 20 pesos, don't get in. You'll never get where you want to go. **Alfredo,** however, who drives a brown and tan StatusUtilityVehicle, is a reliable ride on the way back.

Calle Principal is the main street in Urique and runs parallel to the river; you'll drive into it at a "T" intersection and the hotel is on the left. The limited services available in Urique are all along Calle Principal, including the **police** (at the pink building) and **caseta** (in the green-and-white municipal building; open M-Sa 8am-1pm and 2-7pm, Su 8am-noon). Accommodations in Urique are fairly cheap; options include the **campgrounds** on Calle Principal, on the edge of town (15 pesos per person), and the only hotel in town, the **Hotel Cañon Urique** (tel. 6 03 08). The rooms have bare bones necessities and leaky, crumbly bathrooms and come cheaply (singles 50 pesos; doubles 100 pesos). If you're hungry, the **Restaurant Plaza,** on Calle Principal, has a mango-tree-shaded patio where you can indulge. There is no menu; simply tell the cook what you want (meals 15-25 pesos). Don't expect any raging nightlife in Urique because electricity is never a certainty.

THE CANYONS: SOUTH TO BATOPILAS

Heading south from Creel, a road winds through the more scenic parts of the Copper Canyons. Buses rumble around nail-biting hairpin turns along the edges of steep cliffs that will make your heart pound both from excitement (at the view) and nervousness (your life is in the hands of a stranger). The road has been called North America's most spectacular by many, but, unpaved most of the way, it is also one of the continent's most treacherous. The first 75km section of the road just south of Creel is happily two-laned and paved.

Margarita's, in Creel (see p. 230), offers trips that cover **Cusárare** (mission and falls), Lake Arareco (see p. 231), a Tarahumara cave, and the **Elephant Rock.** It's a four-hour trip and costs around 90 pesos per person for at least five people. **Cabanas Berti's** send trips to Lake Arareco and the Valley of the Nuns for 60 pesos and Cusárare for 80 pesos. Tours that go as far as La Bufa run 220 pesos per person from Margarita's and 150 pesos from Cabañas Bertis (minimum 6 people; 10hr. round trip). On any trip, remember to bring plenty of water and food, adequate footwear, and protection from the sun. If you're averse to walking, you can arrange to navigate on bikes, horses, or even donkeys. **Hotel Nuevo,** and **Motel Parador,** Mateos 44 (tel. 6 00 75; fax 6 00 85), offer somewhat more expensive tours, and locals hanging around the kiosk in the Creel *zócalo* will make cheaper offers than anyone. You can also catch the local bus from Creel to Batopilas (a red-and-white striped converted schoolbus), which leaves once a day sometime before 9am from in front of the train station (30 pesos); ask someone in the train station what time it leaves. Be warned that once in Cusárare, getting around is difficult—not having a car limits your options and your speed of travel.

On the right side heading south, still-inhabited **Tarahumara caves** are within view of the road if you search very hard. On tours, it's possible to go in and visit the homes for a small donation. Beds and other furniture, woodstoves with chimneys, and kerosene lamps adorn the insides of many of the dim caves.

Twenty-two kilometers from Creel down the road to Batopilas is the town of **Cusárare,** which features its very own 18th-century Jesuit mission. Check out the mission's Tarahumara interior, with its wood floors and indigenous designs. There are no pews—people sit on the floor when it's used on Sundays. A boardinghouse for children and a small Tarahumara craft museum are nearby, but the most popular attraction in the town's vicinity is the **Cusárare Falls,** a 3km hike uphill through a pine forest.

Another 20 kilometers beyond Cusárare on the road to Batopilas is **Basíhuare,** an old overnight stop once frequented by silver carriers en route to Batopilas. Further on, the road weaves around the narrowing canyon, offering spectacular vistas as it crawls by the **Cerro de Siete Pisos** (Seven-Floor Hill), so named for the seven distinct layers of earth that lead up along the rocky inner walls of the canyon on the most frightening stretch of this incredible one-lane path. The seven steps can best be seen from **La Bufa,** 60km from Basíhuare, a scenic lookout that has the most magnificent view of all. You can make out the Río Urique far, far below and the yellow wooden bridge that runs across it. If you go left at the fork in the road before La Bufa, you'll come to **Norogachi,** a Tarahumara mission center at the river with beautiful (but touristy) *Semana Santa* services, and **Guachochi,** a rocky, frontier-like village with both colonial and Tarahumara influences.

The right fork will take you to the more impressive town of **Batopilas** (see below). On the way you'll pass over the bridge that spans the Urique; you can get out and walk down into the bushes for a smashing view of the waterfall down below. Keep your eyes peeled for **Tescalama trees,** which have yellow flowers and grow right out of sheer rock. The last quarter of the ride to Batopilas has plenty of **piedra cobriza** (copper rock), which gives the canyon its colorful tint.

THE CANYONS: BATOPILAS AND SATEVÓ

Batopilas (pop. 1200), a tiny village nestled in the depths of the canyons, is a mile below the rest of civilization. The village lies along the river, a rough 35km from La Bufa and a thrilling but scary 140km (6hr. by van, 8hr. by bus) from Creel. Batopilas was a silver-mining boom town founded in 1708. Its rich silver supply lasted until the late 1800s, which is why such a secluded place was the second city in all of Mexico (after Mexico City) to receive electricity. Ironically, the availability of electricity in the town today is anything but a sure thing.

Take the local bus from Creel to Batopilas (see p. 229). The bus makes a couple of stops during the six-hour trip, allowing you to grab a bite to eat or simply to gape at spectacular scenery (the La Bufa stop is mind-blowing). **Casa Margarita's** and **Cabanas Berti's** (see p. 34) send tours to Batopilas. Both are two days in length, and while Margarita's seems pricey at 320 pesos, Berti will set you back a cool 2,300 pesos. It's possible, but difficult, to get from Batopilas to Urique and vice versa on a treacherous road that takes about an hour to traverse.

Everything in Batopilas centers around the **old stone plaza,** referred to as the **parque.** Streets do have names, but locals don't use them. The main street (which connects Batopilas to Creel and the rest of the world) splits off into two streets, one of which encounters a dead end while the other becomes Juárez. As you drive into town, take a left both times the road forks to get to the main plaza. Here, Juárez splits off into two more streets. At the end of the northernmost of these (farther from the river) is a second, **smaller plaza** dedicated to Don Manuel Gómez Marín, founder of the PAN political party. For medical attention, try the **Red Cross** on the main street. The lonely **caseta** (tel. 6 06 32 or 6 06 33) is on the east side of the main plaza kitty corner from the police station. Calls cost 3 pesos per minute (open M-Sa 9am-1pm and 3-7pm, Su 9am-1pm, 7-8pm). **Police:** across from the north side of the plaza in the Presidencia Municipal. **Post office:** close to where the main street first forks (open M-F 9am-4pm). **Postal code:** 33400. **Phone code:** 145.

A good choice for lodging in town is the **Hotel Mary,** Juárez 15, next to the church near the plaza. Large, rustic adobe rooms come with refreshing ceiling fans (singles 70 pesos; doubles 120 pesos). During low season, restaurants' opening and closing times are left to the whims of visitors. For a home cooked meal, head to **Señora Che's** house located in the smaller plaza. Bring your appetite as it's the same price regardless of how many helpings you have. A more conventional eatery in town that is usually open is the Hotel Mary's **Quinto Patio.** Enchiladas with fresh cheese (22 pesos), an order of tacos (20 pesos), and *bistek* (27 pesos) are on the menu, but you're limited to whatever happens to be in the refrigerator at the time. Check out the old lightbulbs converted into flowerpots. (Open daily 7am-10pm.)

The magnificent **haciendas** lying in ruins along the river recall of the excesses of the owners in the silver-mining days in Batopilas. The brown, castle-like **Hacienda Shepard** belonged to an American, and its ruins now stand in contrast to the green of the surrounding trees and canyon. Look for the *tescalama* trees with their mass of yellow roots growing directly out of the *hacienda* walls. Hikes from Batopilas leave daily for the **Porfirio Díaz mine** in town and for the more interesting **Peñasquito,** both an hour hike up a steep hill; for **Cerro Colorado,** a section of the old Camino Real during the mining boom, a 12-hour hike; and for the lost mission of **Satevó** (see below). The best source of information about departing tours is the **Riverside Lodge,** in town diagonally across from the plaza on the bench side (not the basketball-court side). A restored *hacienda,* the lodge is now an incredibly posh package-tour inn—stop by and visit the luxuriant piano room and the view from the rooftop. The historical photos on the walls may be the most interesting exhibits. Don't miss an 1899 shot of Pancho Villa at age 22, a photo of gold bars stacked to the ceiling, and another of the day the river ran as high as the hotel wall. **Artesanías Monse,** on the south side of the plaza next to the Hotel Juanita, offers the opportunity to view and purchase handicrafts from Tarahumara gentiles—supposedly the least Christianized of the Tarahumara. You might get a chance to meet the artists who often hang out in the garden in the back.

The most fascinating excursion from Batopilas is to **Satevó,** a minuscule town with a spooky and beautiful mission. It's a 40-minute drive (you'll need 4WD or, better yet, pixie dust) or a two-hour walk. In the middle of a fertile valley straddled by the towering canyon rises a lonesome, round mission shrouded in mystery. Why was it built here, of all places? When was it built? (The 15th or 16th century are the best guesses, but no one knows.) And finally, how did the Tarahumara, barely able to find shelter for themselves, gather up the energy and desire to build such a thing? In any case, it's a sight to behold, especially at sunset, when the rays play off the red bricks of the roundhouse-like construction, combining with the clouds and valley to create a supernatural scene. In order to take a peek inside the mission, you'll have to tip the **family living next door;** they have the key. The inside of the mission is even eerier, with ancient tombs below and darkness above.

SINALOA

LOS MOCHIS

Just 15 minutes from the ocean and linked to the Baja Peninsula (by a ferry departing from Topolobampo to La Paz) and the major cities of Mexico by rail and route, Los Mochis (pop. 300,000) has sprung up as a bustling center of trade and commerce. The strategic location also make Los Mochis (or just "Mochis" to locals) an important stop-over for travelers. The open-air markets and tree-lined boulevards make Mochis a pleasant place to wander and shop for a day. While not the bastion of Mexican culture or the showcase of cutting-edge entertainment, relatively new Los Mochis, founded in 1903, is a good departure point to more exciting destinations, such as the **Las Barrancas del Cobre** (see p. 232).

TRANSPORTATION. Transportes Norte de Sonora (tel. 12 17 57) and Elite (tel. 18 49 67) **buses** operate out of the modern terminal at the corner of Juárez and Degollado. Transportes Norte de Sonora, usually the cheapest carrier, runs buses to: **Guaymas** (5hr., every hr., 120 pesos); **Mazatlán** (5½hr., every hr. 5am-5pm, 178 pesos); **Mexicali** (18hr., 7 and 8:15am, 490 pesos); **Mexico City** (24hr., 6pm, 730 pesos) via **Culiacán** (3hr., 70 pesos); and **Tijuana** (22hr., 4, 7, and 8:15pm, 585 pesos) via **Hermosillo** (7hr., 166 pesos) and **Navajoa** (2hr., every 2hr., 60 pesos). Transportes del Pacífico, on Morelos between Leyva and Zaragoza (tel. 12 03 47 and 12 03 41), sends *de paso* buses south to **Mazatlán** and north through **Guaymas, Hermosillo,** and **Mexicali** to **Tijuana.** These buses are relatively cheap, but often packed by the time they reach Los Mochis. Seats are easier to obtain on the slower local buses to **Guadalajara, Mazatlán,** and **Tijuana** (approximately 3 per day). Buses to **El Fuerte** and other nearby destinations leave from Zaragoza, between Ordoñez and Cuauhtémoc. Norte de Sinaloa (tel. 18 03 57) sends a large fleet of rickety green buses every 15 minutes to **Culiacán** (3½hr., 45 pesos), **Guamuchil** (2hr., 25 pesos), and **Guasave** (1hr., 20 pesos).

The **ferry** to **La Paz** leaves from Topolobampo daily at 10pm and arrives at 8am the next day (*salón*-class tickets 140 pesos per person, 1500 pesos per car). Buy tickets at the **Sematur** office, Rendón 519 (tel. 686 2 01 41; fax 686 2 00 35). (Open M-F 8am-1pm and 3-7pm, Su 9am-1pm; hrs. erratic.) Tickets go on sale at 6pm every evening or can be purchased on the ferry at Topolobampo. To get to the office, walk nine blocks from Juárez on Flores, then turn left on Rendón. **Bus service** to Topolobampo begins every morning at 6am (every 20min., 10 pesos). The bus leaves from a stop on Cuauhtémoc between Prieta and Zaragoza, one block north of Obregón. Buses to other parts of Los Mochis run throughout the city and cost 2.60 pesos. The main stop is on Zaragoza at Obregón. Ask the driver if he goes where you need to go. For **taxis,** call 12 02 83.

The **Chihuahua al Pacífico train** (tel. 12 08 47) runs back and forth from Los Mochis to Chihuahua, passing through the **Copper Canyon.** At the Divisadero stop, just south of Creel, tourists are allowed to get off the train and gape for 15 minutes. Unfortunately, the train can be unreliable due to frequent problems on the one set of tracks that carries trains in two directions simultaneously—if one train is late, they all are. The first-class train passes through daily at 6am (225 pesos to Creel; 414 pesos to Chihuahua). **Tickets** are sold on the train or from a travel agency in advance. The train arrives in Creel around 4pm. A second-class train is supposed to leave daily at 7am and arrive in Creel around 8pm. After dark, or early in the morning, those who rely on the train become the captives of cagey taxi drivers (40 pesos to downtown). **Group rates** can be much cheaper, so find a buddy and save some pesos. A free bus carries guests to and from the Hotel Santa Anita. No official documentation of guest status is generally required to get on board. To catch a public bus from the station back to town during the daylight hours (every 15min., 3 pesos), just walk away from the station down the road about 100m. If you miss the train and must get to Chihuahua or Creel, the best alternative is to get a bus to Hermosillo (8hr., 100 pesos) and then catch the overnight Hermosillo-Chihuahua bus (14hr., 8pm, 217 pesos). From Chihuahua, buses run regularly to Creel (5hr., 80 pesos).

🚩 ORIENTATION AND PRACTICAL INFORMATION. The city is laid out in a simple grid. Downtown, principal avenues parallel to one another are (from south to north) **Blvd. Degollado, Av. Zaragoza, Av. Leyva, Av. Guerrero, and Blvd. Rosales.** Perpendicular to these (from east to west) are **Blvd. Juan de Batiz, Av. Cardenas, Av. Morelos, Av. Independencia, Blvd. Castro,** and **Av. Ordoñez.** The boulevards frame the rectangle of the downtown district.

Set office hours are the butt of town jokes. The **tourist office,** on Obregón and Allende (tel. 15 10 90), is near the **Palacio Gobierno** in the Unidad Administrativa. Somewhat difficult to find; go in the side entrance off of Ordonez (open M-F 9am-3pm). Stop by and pick up a free map and billions of brochures. To purchase bus, plane, or train tickets in advance, try **Viajes Conelva,** Leyva 525 (tel. 15 60 90 or 15 80 90) at Valdez, inside Hotel El Dorado (open M-Sa 8am-7pm, Su 9am-2pm). Given the number of travel agencies in town, the residents of Los Mochis seem to be aware that their role in tourism is to help visitors get somewhere else. For your banking needs, try the **Bancomer** (tel. 12 23 23) on Leyva and Juárez (open M-F 8:30am-4pm and 3:30-7pm, Sa 9am-1:30pm). Four 24-hour **ATMs** are at your disposal.

For fresh fish, fruit, and vegetables, check out the **market** in the area around Zaragoza, between Castro and Ordoñez; on weekends it bustles with activity (most stores close around 7pm). Los Mochis's hippest threads get washed and dried at **Lavamatic,** Allende 228, just before Juárez (wash 9 pesos, dry 13 pesos; open M-Sa 7am-7pm, Su 7am-1pm). The **Red Cross** (tel. 15 08 08 or 12 02 92), Tenochtitlán and Prieto, one block off Castro, has 24-hour ambulance service. **Tourist Security:** 91 800 90 392. **Emergency:** dial 060. **Police:** (tel. 12 00 33), Degollado at Cuauhtémoc in the Presidencia Municipal. No English is spoken. **Super Farmacia San Jorge:** (tel. 18 18 19), at Juárez and Degollado, is open 24 hours. **Hospital Fátima:** Blvd. Jiquilpán Pte. 639 (tel. 12 33 12). No English is spoken. **Centro de Salud:** (tel. 12 07 74). **Post office:** Ordoñez 226 (tel. 12 08 23), two blocks off Castro, between Prieta and Zaragoza (open M-F 8am-7pm). **Postal code** is 81200. **LADATELs** are scattered throughout downtown. When making local calls within the city, add "1" before any number with only five digits. **Phone code:** 68.

🏠 ACCOMMODATIONS. Budget hotels of variable quality are sprinkled throughout the downtown area demarcated by Castro, Juárez, Leyva, and Constitución. **Hotel Montecarlo,** Flores 322 Sur (tel. 12 18 18), a gracefully aging blue building at the corner of Independencia, comes with large rooms surrounding a quiet, palatial indoor courtyard. Air-conditioning, fans, and cable TV make life much easier. It still helps to take a cooler room downstairs. (Singles 165 pesos, 2-person singles 175 pesos; doubles 200 pesos; triples 220 pesos.) The **Hotel Lorena** Obregón 186 (tel. 12 02 39 or 12 09 58), across from the market, offers rooms furnished with everything but a butler. Huge windows give a great view of the city, air-conditioning keeps you from melting, and cable TV and phones keep you entertained. (Singles 165 pesos; doubles 200 pesos; triples 230 pesos.) At **Hotel Hidalgo,** Hidalgo 260 Pte. (tel. 18 34 53), between Prieta and Zaragoza, ceiling fans and chilly colors (deep blue furniture and baby-blue walls) cool the small rooms. If there's a soccer game on the tube, the lobby becomes a local hang-out. (Singles 110 pesos, with A/C 130 pesos; doubles 150 pesos; triples 170 pesos.)

⚑ FOOD. The crowning virtue of this farming region is the daily **public market** along Zaragoza, between Castro and Ordoñez, where prices are low and quality is high. Stores start to close around 7pm. The *taquerías* and *loncherías* in the market dish out cheap, home-brewed enigmas, many of which pack quite a wallop. Except for the *cantinas* (which women should avoid) and the corner *taquerías*, just about everything in town shuts down at 9pm. Good, cheap *tortas* can be found on Independencia and Hidalgo. Try **Tortas Moka,** Independencia 216 (tel. 12 39 41), at Prieto, where you can enjoy a *torta* (8 pesos) while you people-watch. At **El Taquito,** on Leyva between Hidalgo and Independencia (tel. 2 81 19), pink window shades provide shade from the offending sun, and air-conditioning dries your sweaty skin and prevents the vinyl booths from sticking to your thighs. A bit pricey, but that's what you get for waiters in red jackets serving up *enchiladas suizas* (27 pesos), hamburgers and fries (20 pesos), and cheese-filled shrimp wrapped in bacon (42 pesos). Open 24hr.

◉ ♫ SIGHTS AND ENTERTAINMENT. Los Mochis boasts a few modest amusements, but if you can, head to **Topolobampo.** Catch the bus at Prieto and Cuauhtémoc (every 20min., 10 pesos). Those that stick around can visit the extraordinary collection of trees and plants assembled in **Sinaloa Park,** on Rosales and Castro. Walk to the end of the Castro and turn left, the entrance is about half a block down on Rosales. Hundreds of species of flora inhabit this outdoor forest museum. Check out the stump at the entrance to the park; a harem of wild animals and the insignia of the state of Sinaloa have been gouged into its roughened surface. The **Museo Regional del Valle del Fuerte,** near the end of Obregón towards the park and Rosales, was the home of an early settler whose guns and personal diary are now housed there. Photographs documenting the growth and development of Northern Mexico are also on display. (Tel. 2 46 92. Open Tu-Sa 10am-1pm and 4-7pm, Su 10am-1pm. Admission 5 pesos, free on Su and holidays.)

For a schedule of upcoming festivals and musical events at the **Pl. Solidaridad** and the nearby **Plazuela 27 de Septiembre,** consult the **Secretaria de Cultura y Acción Social** (tel. 5 04 05, ext. 38 or 39). Adjoining the Plaza Solidaridad is the **Santuario del Sagrado Corazón de Jesús,** Los Mochis's oldest church, which was built after Johnston's wife donated the land to the people. Many locals find it ironic that she was not even Catholic. The **Cinema 70** is on Blvd. de la Plaza. If you spend the night in Mochis, head to the **Rodeo Bar,** on Obregón and Constitución, where you can down a few beers and take the mechanical horse for a ride. The whole town comes out for live music on the weekends, when cover is 60 pesos. (Open 9pm-3am).

EL FUERTE

Founded in 1564 by conquistador Don Francisco de Ibarra, this city of 30,000 people overlooks the Rio Fuerte. In 1824, it became the capital of an area including present-day Sinaloa, Sonora, and part of Arizona. It's now one of the first stops in Sinaloa on the train to Los Mochis, and a good place to prepare for a journey into or out of the canyons.

▤ ORIENTATION AND PRACTICAL INFORMATION. From the train station, you'll have a hard time getting to El Fuerte without taking a cab; the city is about 7km from the station. **Calle Júarez** is the main street in town. Walk west and turn left onto **5 de Mayo** and continue walking about a block south to reach the walkway along the river.

Trains leave daily for **Los Mochis** (first class 1½ hr., 7:30 pm; second class 2 hr., 8:30pm), and **Chiuhuahua** (first class 6am, second class 7am). **Taxis** gather on Júarez to take you to the train station. **Buses** depart to: **Los Mochis** (every ½ hr., every 30 min., 30 pesos) and leave from the corner of Júarez and 16 de Septiembre. There is no official **Tourist Office,** but you can inquire at the **Hotel Posada,** 5 de Mayo and Hidalgo for information. **Pharmacies** and **markets** can be found up and down Júarez. **Currency exchange: Bancamex,** at Júarez and 16 de Septiembre (open M-F 8:30am-2:30pm). There is also a 24hr. **ATM. Post Office:** in the Palacio Gobierno in the Playuela. Open M-F with varying hrs). **Postal code:** 81820. **Telephones: LADATEL's** along Júarez and in the Playuela. **Caseta:** at Mariela, Júarez and 16 de Septiembre (open M-Sa 8am-1pm, 4-6pm, Su 8am-1pm). **Phone code:** 689.

■ ◨ **ACCOMODATIONS AND FOOD.** El Fuerte has few budget accomodations, but **Hotel San José,** Júarez 108 (tel. 3 08 45) has some of the lowest rates around. Enormous rooms with cement floors and high ceilings, but don't look up if you have arachnophobia. If you're willing to sleep on a cot without a bathroom, you can stay for as cheaply as 20 pesos. (Single beds with bathroom 50 pesos; doubles 80 pesos.) **Restaurant Yerbia,** located on Júarez right next to the Hotel San José, offers complete meals for 15-16 pesos. (open daily 7am-7pm). Also try the good food of **Restaurant Economica,** on Júarez past 16 de Septiembre.

◧ ◪ **SIGHTS AND ENTERTAINMENT.** No one will mistake El Fuerte for the tourist capital of the world, but it does have some worthwhile attractions. The **Hotel Posada** always has information about local sights. Stroll along the **Río Fuerte** and keep your eyes peeled for native birds such as the **Crested Caracara,** the **Mexican Blue-Rumped Parrotelet,** and the **Plain-Capped Starthroat.** Also keep your eyes on the path ahead of you: it's a frequently used cow path. A beautiful view of the river and city can be found at the hilltop Hotel Rio Vista; follow 5 de Mayo to the river and walk up the hill. *Combis* from town can take you to the nearby Tehuero Mayo Indian Mission, the ancient Mayo Indian village of Capomos, or the 1500-year-old Nahuatl Petroglyphs. Information can be had at the Hotel Posada.

MAZATLÁN

Mazatlán (pop. 315,000) means "place of the deer" in Náhuatl. A less appropriate name can hardly be imagined, since there is nothing even remotely pastoral about this city. The only wildlife present roams the beaches and nightclubs in large herds.

Mazatlán is truly a city divided. The **old city** is traditionally Mexican, with a shady *zócalo,* busy streets, and bustling markets that lend it a genuine charm. Nearby on the shore is the **Olas Altas** (Tall waves) neighborhood, with a peaceful, nearly empty beach, pleasant streets, and faded resorts of yesteryear that evoke Mazatlán's glory days. The breezy Malecón connects the old city with the more expensive and touristy northern part of town, and is a favorite destination of Mexicans and the few foreign tourists out for strolls along the beach. The city welcomes visitors with a huge sign that reads: "One destination, a thousand vacations," an estimate that understates the importance tourism has taken on for Mazatlán.

Eight kilometers or so up the Avenida del Mar lies another city entirely—the **Zona Dorada** (Golden Zone), home to high-rise hotels, Disney-castle clubs and pleasure palaces, dollar-dishing Americans, time-share condos, trinket shops, and patronizingly friendly tourism agents. Budget travelers can save money by heading south and avoiding the swarms of tourists and fast-food franchises concentrated in this part of town.

Mazatlán offers little of historical or cultural interest to the traveler. The city's greatest assets are gifts of nature—glorious sunsets, a glittering ocean, and wide beaches. The *Zona Dorada* is the most popular, but not necessarily the best, way to appreciate those assets. **Old Mazatlán,** with its nearly abandoned shore and its fading, grand old hotels, is what stirs the *mariachis* to sing the classic bittersweet song of lost youth in Sinaloa.

⚡ ORIENTATION

Built on a rocky spur jutting southwest into the Pacific, Old Mazatlán's downtown area lies north of the *zócalo*. The main street running east-west is **Angel Flores,** the southern boundary of the *zócalo*. Farther south, the **Malecón** follows the shore line. It starts as **Olas Altas** on the south end near **Old Mazatlán,** then runs to the **Zona Dorada** 8km north, serving as the *Zona Dorada's* one main street; there it is called **Avenida del Mar.** In between the two areas, to the south of the fisherman's statue and north of Olas Altas, it is called **Paseo Claussen;** and to the far north, past Valentino's in the *Zona Dorada*, it's known as **Camaron Sábalo.** Since Mazatlán is very spread out, the easiest way to navigate the city is by bus.

Mazatlán's **bus station** is three blocks behind the Sands Hotel, and about 2km north of Old Mazatlán, in Olas Altas. To head downtown from the bus station, catch any of the red buses with "centro" or "mercado" written on their windshields. Avoid the "sabado-coco" bus, as it goes downtown eventually, but not before making an enormous loop around the city. The place to catch the bus is one block west of the bus station and about a block down to your right along **Av. Benemerito de las Américas.** Buses cost 2.60 pesos and 3 pesos after 9pm; they stop running at 10pm. A cab will make the trip for 25 pesos or more. The area around the bus station, with several reasonably priced hotels and restaurants, along with a good beach and the vital "Sábalo" bus line nearby, makes a convenient home base. From the **train station,** on the far eastern edge of Mazatlán, the "Insurgentes" or the "Cerritos-Juárez" buses will take you downtown. From the **airport,** 18km south of the city, the "Central Camionera" bus makes the trip; the only way to get back to the airport from downtown is a 70-peso cab ride. It's a grueling 20-minute walk from the *centro* to the **ferry** docks; the blue "Playa Sur" school bus (2.60 pesos) makes the trip, and, for 15 pesos, so will a taxi.

Mazatlán's efficient **bus system** makes getting around the city a breeze. At some point, all municipal buses pass the public market on Juárez, 3 blocks north of the *zócalo* at Ocampo. The most useful bus line is the **"Sábalo-Centro,"** which runs from the downtown market with stops a few blocks from the Malecón in **Olas Altas** and at Playa Sábalo in the *Zona Dorada*. The **"Cerritos-Juárez"** bus continues up to Playa Bruja at Puerta Cerritos. The **"Insurgentes"** route services the bus and train stations, and **"Playa Sur"** goes to the ferry dock and lighthouse (every 15min. 5am-10pm, 2.60 pesos).

For late-night disco hopping, you'll have to take a cab or a *pulmonía* (pneumonia), which you might actually have a chance of catching if the temperature ever dipped below 70°F, an open vehicle that resembles a golf cart or a sawed-off Volkswagon and putters along blasting raucous music. Always set the price before you commit yourself to a ride; standard fare between Old Mazatlán and the *Zona Dorada* is 20-24 pesos, depending on the time of night (later gets more expensive). Don't be afraid to haggle with the *pulmonía* drivers—there are usually plenty of them to choose from. If you want to save the fare, it'll take you over an hour to walk the long path between the two sections. Olas Altas and the *centro* both make convenient home bases. Olas Altas is a 10-minute walk to the *centro* (take a right on Angel Flores from the Malecón), and is also well connected by bus.

⚡ PRACTICAL INFORMATION

TRANSPORTATION

Airport: Rafael Buelna International Airport (tel. 82 23 99), 18km south of the city. Served by **AeroCalifornia** (tel. 13 20 42), El Cid Resort; **Aeroméxico,** Sábalo 310A (tel. 14 11 11 or 91 800 36 202); **Alaska Airlines** (tel. 95 800 426 0333; fax 85 27 30); **Mexicana,** B. Domínguez and Av. del Mar (tel./fax 82 77 22).

Buses: The Mazatlán bus station looks like a primitive space station and is about as simple to navigate as the solar system. Norte del Sonora sends buses north to: **Monterrey**

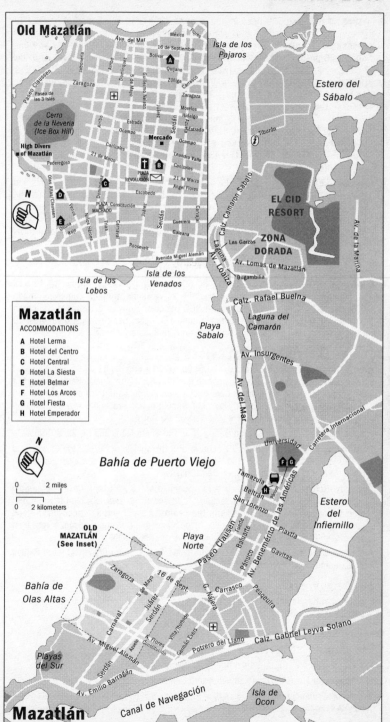

Old Mazatlán

Isla de los Pájaros

Estero del Sábalo

Paseo Claussen
Paseo de las 3 Islas

Cerro de la Nevería (Ice Box Hill)

High Divers of Mazatlán

Pederegoso

Ave. del Mar
México
Flores
16 de Septiembre
Bolívar
Quijano
Zúñiga
Carrasco
Zaragoza
Morelos
Hidalgo
Estrada
Ocampo

Estrada
Ocampo
Canizales
Leandro Valle
Canizales
21 de Marzo
Ángel Flores
Escobedo

Zaragoza

Mercado

PLAZA REVOLUCIÓN

PLAZA Constitución MACHADO

Guerrero
Galeana

Roosevelt

Avenida Miguel Alemán

EL CID RESORT

ZONA DORADA

Las Garzas

Av. Lomas de Mazatlán

Bugambilia

Calz. Rafael Buelna

Laguna del Camarón

Av. de la Marina

Tiburón

Calz. Camarón Sábalo

Laguna del Infiernillo

Av. Loaiza

Isla de los Lobos

Isla de los Venados

Mazatlán

ACCOMMODATIONS

A Hotel Lerma
B Hotel del Centro
C Hotel Central
D Hotel La Siesta
E Hotel Belmar
F Hotel Los Arcos
G Hotel Fiesta
H Hotel Emperador

N

0   2 miles
0   2 kilometers

Bahía de Puerto Viejo

Playa Sabalo

Av. Insurgentes

Av. del Mar

Universidad

Carretera Internacional

Tamazula
Beltrán
San Lorenzo

Av. Benemérito de las Américas

Estero del Infiernillo

Pánuco
Fuerte
Balluarte
Plaxtla
Gavitas

OLD MAZATLÁN (See Inset)

Playa Norte

Paseo Claussen

Zaragoza
5 de Mayo
Juárez
Serdán
16 de Sept.

G. Nájera
Carrasco
Pesquería

Bahía de Olas Altas

Carnaval

Av. Miguel Alemán

Serdán

Villa Iturbide
Germán Evers
Constitución
A. Flores

Potrero del Llano

Calz. Gabriel Leyva Solano

Playas del Sur

Av. Emilio Barragán

Canal de Navegación

Isla de Ocon

Mazatlán

(17hr., 7 per day, 629 pesos); and **Tijuana** (26hr., 11am, 2, and 6:30pm, 847 pesos). Transpacífico (tel. 81 38 01) serves: **Culiacán** (2½hr., 5, 6, and 8:30pm, 60 pesos); **Durango** (7hr., 5 per day, 152 pesos); **Los Mochis** (6½hr., every hr. 6am-4pm, 186 pesos); and **Puerto Vallarta** (7hr., 7:30am, 241 pesos). Transportes del Pacífico (tel. 81 51 56) has service to: **Guadalajara** (7hr., almost every hr., 271 pesos); and **Tepic** (5hr., every hr., 141 pesos). Elite (81 38 11) has service to: **Aguascalientes** (14hr., 4 per day, 379 pesos), **Hermosillo** (4½hr., every hr., 471 pesos). Transportes Chihuahuauses (tel. 81 53 81) runs to: **Ciudad Juárez** (24hr., 2pm and midnight, 577 pesos). Transportes del Norte (tel. 81 23 35) has 1st-class service to: **Saltillo** (16hr., noon, 5, 7, and 10pm, 426 pesos). The Tropicales line in the other terminal will take you to nearby locations such as **El Quelite.** The **Transporte Rapido de Sud terminal** is a block away from the station on Av. Benemerito de las Américas.

Ferry: Sematur (tel. 81 70 20 or 21), at the end of Carnaval, south of Angel Flores and the *centro*. Tickets are sold only on the day of departure. Arrive at the office at least 2hr. early to procure a spot, as capacity is very limited. You can buy tickets on the ferry, but you aren't guaranteed a spot, since they let ticketed passengers board first. Ticket office open daily Su-F 8am-3pm, Sa 9am-1pm. Purchase tickets in advance at a local travel agency. During the high season (Dec. and July-Aug.), make reservations at least 2 weeks ahead. Travels every day to La Paz, arriving around 8am (*salón* 17hr., 3pm, 163 pesos; *turista* 400 pesos; children 2-11 half-price).

Car Rental: Hertz, Sábalo 314 (tel. 13 60 60, airport office 85 05 48; fax 13 49 55). Starting around 300 pesos per day. Must be 21 years old. **Budget,** Camarón Sábado 402 (tel. 13 20 00), starting around 200 pesos per day and **National,** Camarón Sábado 7000 (tel. 13 60 00), starting around 150 pesos per day. Must be at least 25 years old and have a valid driver's license and credit card for both.

TOURIST AND FINANCIAL SERVICES

Tourist Office: (tel. 16 51 60 or 16 51 65; fax 16 51 66 or 16 51 67) on Av. Camarón Sábalo at Tiburón, in the *Zona Dorada,* on the 4th floor of the pinkish Banrural building past El Cid resort on the "Sábalo Centro" bus line. Helpful staff doles out much-needed Mazatlán maps. English spoken. Open M-F 9am-5pm and reachable only by phone on Sa 9am-1pm. **Tourist Assistance:** (tel. 91 800 90 392).

Tourist Police: (tel. 14 84 44), on Gabriel Ruíz and Santa Mónica in the Zona Dorada.

Consulates: Canada (tel. 13 73 20), Loaiza at Bugambiliain in Hotel Playa Mazatlán in the *Zona Dorada*. Open daily 9am-1pm. **U.S.** (tel. 16 58 89), Loaiza at Bugambilia in front of Hotel Playa Mazatlán. Open daily 9am-1pm.

Currency Exchange: Most banks open for exchange M-F 8:30-11am. *Casas de cambio* are open all day in the northern section of the downtown area, but tend to sport less than thrilling rates. Stick to banks in the *centro* to avoid getting ripped off. A good option is **Banca Serfin** (tel. 82 66 66), 21 de Marzo and Gillerman Nelson, across from the *zócalo*. Open M-F 8:30am-5pm, Sa 10am-2pm. 24hr. **ATM.**

American Express: (tel. 13 06 00; fax 16 59 08), in the Centro Comercial Plaza Balboa on Camarón Sábalo. Open daily 9am-5pm.

LOCAL SERVICES

Laundry: Lavamatic del Centro, Serdán 2914 (tel. 81 35 56), on the Malecón. Will wash and dry 3kg in a few hr. for 24 pesos. Open M-Sa 8am-7:30pm.

EMERGENCY AND COMMUNICATIONS

Emergency: (tel. 81 36 90), open 24hr. Or just dial 060.

Police: (tel. 83 45 10), on Rafael Buelna in Colonia Juárez.

Red Cross: (tel. 85 14 51), on Zaragoza and Corona.

Pharmacy: Farmacia Ibael (tel. 822 62 49), on Angel Flores and Campana. English spoken. Open daily 8:30am-10:30pm.

Hospital: Sharp Hospital (tel. 86 56 76), on Dr. Jesús Kumate and Rafael Buelna, near Zaragoza park. English spoken.

Post Office: (tel. 81 21 21), on 21 de Marzo and Juárez, across from the *zócalo*. Open M-F 8am-6pm. **Postal Code:** 82000.

Fax: (tel. 81 22 20), in the same building as the post office. Open M-F 8am-7pm, Sa-Su 8-11am. Also at the *caseta* below.

Internet Access: The *caseta* at Serdán 1510 and 21 de Marzo has Internet access for 20 pesos for 30min. Open M-Sa 8am-8:30pm, Su 9am-2pm. You can surf the web at **Mail Boxes Etc.** (tel. 16 40 10), on Av. Camarón Sabado in the *Zona Dorada*. 30 pesos per 30min. Open M-Sa 9am-5pm. **Cyber Café Mazatlan** (tel. 14 00 08), is across the street. 25 pesos per 30min., 40 pesos per hr. Open daily 11am-9pm.

Phone Code: 69.

ACCOMMODATIONS AND CAMPING

High-quality cheap rooms do exist; simply avoid the *Zona Dorada*, where rates are exorbitant even at the shabbier joints. Budget hotels cluster in three areas: in Old Mazatlán along the two avenues east of the main square (Juárez and Serdán), in the noisy area around the bus station, and on the pleasant waterfront along Olas Altas, southwest of the center of Old Mazatlán. The cheapest rooms are by the bus station, the most affordable nice rooms are in the *centro* and Olas Altas, and the posh resorts are in the *Zona Dorada*. The busiest seasons in Mazatlán are Christmas and the month following *Semana Santa*—check in early. There's a trailer park, **La Posta** (tel. 83 53 10), on Av. Rafael Buelna (full hook-up 85 pesos).

OLAS ALTAS. Back in the 1950s, long before wily developers began constructing multi-million-dollar pleasure pits along the north shore, the focal point of Mazatlán's fledgling resort scene was Olas Altas. The area has something of a deserted feel, although several restoration projects are currently underway. Although the majority of tourists now opt to stay in the flashy hotels to the north, Olas Altas is a place to avoid the steep prices and clamor of the *Zona Dorada*. It's only a 10 min. walk from the *centro* and connected to the rest of Mazatlán by several buses.

Hotel Belmar, Olas Altas 166 (tel. 85 11 12), at Osuna. A resort of yesteryear, the Belmar glows with hazy marble floors, luxuriant dark wood paneling, and arches lined with colorful tiles. Let the elevator take you up to your spacious room and large bathroom. Match other guests ping for pong at the table downstairs, take a dip in the pool, or crawl into an antique rocker with an English book in hand (they have a small library—mostly romances and thrillers, but a few good reads). Singles with A/C and TV 130 pesos, with an ocean view (no A/C) 130 pesos; doubles with A/C and TV 160 pesos, with ocean view (no A/C) 160 pesos.

Hotel La Siesta, Olas Altas Sur 11 (tel. 81 26 40 or 81 23 34, toll-free 01 800 71 229), at Escobedo. Next door to the Belmar, the Siesta is a newer, more modern clone. The beautiful courtyard and state-of-the-art amenities will cost you. Ocean view singles 235 pesos, doubles 281 pesos; interior room singles 170 pesos, doubles 200 pesos.

OLD MAZATLÁN. Downtown is a bit noisier during the day, and the hotels here are farther from the beach so rooms are usually cheaper. While everyone vanishes after dark and most streets are poorly lit, the area is generally considered safe.

Hotel Lerma, Simón Bolívar 622 (tel. 81 24 36), at Serdán. Riotously bright colors, centrally located, and clean. Ceiling fans make the heat bearable. Popular among those who know a good deal when they see one. Singles 60 pesos; doubles 80 pesos; triples 100 pesos.

Hotel del Centro, Canizales 705 (tel. 81 26 73), between Serdán and Juárez smack dab in the middle of things. A/C or ceiling fans, some rooms with balconies with a lovely street view, and TV. Singles 122 pesos, doubles 142 pesos, triples 163 pesos, quads 183 pesos.

Hotel Central, Domínguez 2 Sur (tel. 82 18 88), at Escobedo. Spotless rooms decorated with funky wood carvings. Phone, TV, A/C, and sparkling bathrooms make this hotel a smart choice for larger groups. Singles 170 pesos, doubles 200 pesos, and triples 233 pesos.

NEAR THE BUS STATION. Hotels in this area are closer to the ritzy *Zona Dorada* in proximity, but not in quality. The places are a little more run-down and a little older. Convenient location, but bear in mind that buses never sleep, so you might not either. Competitive hotels located a block away along Av. Benemérito de las Américas.

Hotel Los Arcos, Río Panoco 1006 (tel. 81 06 75), just around the block to your left from the the main exit of the bus station. Very basic rooms, with ceiling fans and a private bath. Singles 80 pesos, doubles 100 pesos; add 30 pesos for A/C.

Hotel Fiesta, (tel. 81 78 88) Ferrosquila 306, in front of the bus station. Clean rooms have bathrooms, firm mattresses, and purified water. Aquamarine halls with fluorescent lights make you feel like you're in a fishbowl. Singles 110 pesos, doubles 140 pesos; 10 pesos extra for A/C or TV.

Hotel Emperador, Río Panoco 1000 (tel. 82 67 24), next to Hotel Los Arcos. The high-rise style hotel has a top-notch cleaning crew, tile floors, and fans. Singles 110 pesos; doubles 130 pesos; 10 pesos extra A/C or TV.

◖ FOOD

Mazatlán's restaurants serve up everything from *comida corrida* to charbroiled T-bone steak to *mariscos* (seafood). Prices escalate as you get sucked toward the *Zona Dorada* with its fast food restaurants and tourist geared establishments. Mazatlán's *centro* is the place to be for quality budget meals. The busy **public market,** between Juárez and Serdán, three blocks north of the *zócalo,* serves the cheapest food in the area. If you need a **headless pig,** look no further. Jumbo shrimp, *antojito* platters, and steak are available for staggeringly low prices. Snacking opportunities exist outside in the **loncherías** and **taco stands.** For a more formal meal, try one of the *centro's* many inexpensive restaurants or, for the view, a joint along the Malecón in Olas Altas. Enjoy your meal with **Pacífico** beer, the pride of Mazatlán.

Restaurante Karica Vegetariano Angel Flores 601 (tel. 81 79 52), at Frías. A great place even for the non-vegetarian—phenomenal cuisine at unbeatable prices. Enjoy the enormous *comida corrida,* which includes salad, soup, a hearty main course, fresh wheat bread, a pitcherful of juice, and dessert, all for only 30 pesos. A family joint. Open daily 8am-4:30pm.

Restaurant la Cocina de Esther, Serdán 1605 at Canizales. Tucked back in from the street, Esther serves up a large selection of entrees and a *comida corrida* for 26 pesos. Try the *licuado de platano* for a sweet, palate pleasing beverage (8 pesos). Open daily 7am-10pm.

Cafe Machado, Constitución 515 (tel. 81 73 31), on the Plaza Machado. Shady outdoor seating to enjoy 2 for 1 beers until 7pm (18 pesos) If you've never had marlin, sample the *Marlin in estotado* (marlin stew) for 35 pesos—it's a very tasty fish. Open daily 12pm-2am.

Cafe Pacífico, Constitución 501 (tel. 81 39 72), across from the Plazuela Machado. This famous pub is a relic, with an odd assortment of animal skins, rifles, beautiful stained glass windows, big screen TV's and U.S. country western music. You can get away from the above by eating at the outdoor tables and enjoying the tuna salad (25 pesos), marlin burritos (50 pesos), or cheese plate (50 pesos). Open daily 9am-2am.

Cafeteria, at the corner of Juárez and Bolivar, just downt he street form the Hotel Lerma. Gawk at the beautiful poster of Marilyn Monroe as you enjoy some of the cheapest eats around. Full breakfast with coffee (10 pesos), *comida corrida* (12 pesos). Not impeccably clean, but very serviceable. Open M-Sa 8am-5pm, Su 8am-3pm.

◢ SAND AND SIGHTS

Mazatlán's greatest asset is its 16km of beach stretching from just north of Olas Altas to well north of the *Zona Dorada*. Just north of Old Mazatlán and along Av. del Mar is **Playa Norte,** a decent stretch of sand, if you don't mind small waves and the stares of local *machos* who play soccer here. Solo women should consider doing their swimming farther north. As you hone in on the *Zona Dorada*, the beach gets cleaner, the waves larger, and Playa Norte eases into **Playa Las Gaviotas.** Just past Punta Sábalo, in the lee of the islands, is **Playa Sábalo,** whose great waves and golden sand are enjoyed to the point of abuse by crowds of *norteamericanos*. Most area beaches are patrolled by lifeguards, who use color-coded flags to inform bathers of conditions: green, yellow, and red flags respectively indicate the level of undertow (green being little undertow, red meaning strong undertow); white flags mean *quemadores* (jellyfish) are around. "Sábalo-Centro" buses pass by all of these beaches. To spice up your time at the beach, boogie boards and sailboats are available for 300 pesos per hour.

As Playa Sábalo recedes to the north, crowds thin rapidly and you can frolic on the glorious beaches all by yourself. Take the "Cerritos-Juárez" bus to the last stop and walk left (if you walk straight ahead you'll end up at a rocky outcropping with a few restaurants but little sand); you'll soon reach nearly deserted **Playa Bruja** (Witch Beach), with tons of beautiful sand and 1 to 2m waves. Camping is permitted, but be cautious after dark, and camp in groups whenever possible. Solo women should be especially cautious. For a 360° view of Mazatlán, the sea, and the surrounding hills, climb to the top of **El Faro, the second-tallest lighthouse in the world.** It's located near the ferry to Isla de las Piedras at the end of the "Playa Sur" bus route. The hike (about 30min.) is almost unbearable in the summer; avoid the heat by ascending in the early morning or late evening.

The **Acuario Mazatlán,** Av. de los Deportes 111 (tel. 81 78 15 or 81 78 16), off Av. del Mar, keeps piranhas and other feisty fish (up to 250 breeds in all) in a slew of cloudy tanks. The aquarium, supposedly the largest in Latin America, also hosts performing sea lions and birds. In the aviary, check out the hooded orioles, barvented wren, and social flycatchers in the trees. The Acuario is one block back from the beach and north of the Sands Hotel; the turn-off is marked by a shimmering blue sign. *(Open daily 9:30am-6:30pm. Admission 40 pesos, children 5-10 20 pesos.)*

Mazatlán's **tower divers** may not have their heads screwed on straight, but their acrobatic and dangerous plunges into the rocky surf from an 18m high ledge are nevertheless very entertaining. Performances take place during the day, but be forewarned that the divers will not perform unless they can pull in a sufficient amount of money beforehand. They usually won't dive for less than 70 pesos total. If you come at this time and hang around for awhile, you may get to see a dive for free, funded by other tourists. The best time to watch the divers is 10-11am and 4:30-6:30pm, when guided tour buses arrive and tourists fork over their pesos. The best viewing spots are located just south of the towers. On days when the water is too rough for diving, climb the tower to watch the waves break below. The diving platform is on Paseo Claussen, just south of Zaragoza and north of La Siesta Hotel.

William Blake saw the universe in a grain of sand and eternity in an hour. You too may get bored at the beach. When the throngs of tourists and street vendors hawking plastic sunglasses get on your nerves, hop on one of the boats to **Isla de la Piedra** (see p. 249), where locals go to escape the crowds. Boats leave from the wharf on Av. del Puerto at Gutiérrez Najera. Buses to the wharf depart from near the public market (2.50 pesos) on Serdan. To walk there, take 21 de Marzo from the cathedral past Serdán to the water, and then turn left on Emilio Barragan (7 pesos round-trip; last boat back leaves at 5pm). **Islas Venados** (Deer Island) is a relatively deserted scrap of land with fine diving; catamaran boats leave for the island from the Agua Sports Center in the **El Cid Resort** in the *Zona Dorada (Tel. 13 33 33, ext. 341. Open daily 10am, noon, 2, and 4pm, 35 pesos).* Waterpark mania has hit Mazatlán with the new **Mazagua** located north of the *Zona Dorada* near Puerta Cerritos. To get there, take a "Cerritos Juárez" bus (2.20 pesos). Go bonkers in the wave pool or shoot down slippery slides. *(Tel. 88 00 41. Open Mar.-Oct. daily 10am-6pm. Admission 35 pesos, children under 4 free).*

The newly restored and luxurious **Teatro Angela Peralta,** at Carnaval and Libertad near the Plaza Machado, hosts an impressive variety of cultural programs and has a fascinating history to boot.

♫ ENTERTAINMENT AND NIGHTLIFE

Hordes of *norteamericano* high schoolers ditch the prom and hit Mazatlán yearly to twist, shout, and drink. Supply rises to meet demand, and more than a dozen discos and bars clamor for gringo dollars. Inside, only the occasional Mexican rock tune reminds you that you're in a foreign country. Most of the hot clubs are in the area known as **Fiesta Land,** in the *Zona Dorada,* a block from Paseo del Mar. If you address bartenders or bouncers in Spanish, they'll smile, pat you on the head, and answer in near-perfect English, never forgetting to address you as *amigo.* Prices can vary wildly (especially during high season and holidays such as *Semana Santa* and Christmas) and a few hours of open bar can cost as much as 120 pesos. However, many clubs cut their high prices in half at midnight, so come late and save a few pesos.

El Caracol (tel. 13 32 38), located in the El Cid Hotel on Camarón Sábado. One of Mazatlán's premier dance clubs with four levels and crazy lights that rise out of the floor. Beer runs at 19 pesos and mixed drinks are 30 pesos. Cover 50 pesos F-Su, 35 pesos M-Th. Open 9pm-4am daily.

Joe's Oyster Bar, Louiza 100 (tel. 83 53 53), next to the Los Sabados Hotel. A good place to put away a few beers before hitting the club scene (2 beers for 20 pesos from 5-7pm and 10pm-2am). The Oysters usually turn into a dance floor after a while. No cover. Open 11am-2am daily.

Señor Frog's (tel. 85 11 10), on Paseo del Mar, several blocks south of Bora-Bora. A chain establishment, but nonetheless a place to shake that booty. American pop and dance music blast from a wall of speakers as youngsters wriggle in a wall of flesh. Cover F-Su 45 pesos. Open daily 9pm-4am.

Bora-Bora (tel. 86 49 49), on Paseo del Mar at the southern end of the *Zona Dorada,* next to the beach. Always jam-packed with touring (and local) teenagers clad in neon (or nothing at all). Those so inclined may dance in cages. Clubbers in search of more wholesome activities can head for the volleyball court and swimming pool. Order your beer (22 pesos) or mixed drink (30-35 pesos) at the bar, then jump up on top of it (the bar) to bust some serious moves. Cover F-Su 20-40 pesos, including beer. Open daily 9pm-4am.

Valentino's (tel. 86 49 49), in the same complex as Bora-Bora. Valentino's attracts a more sophisticated, late-20s crowd, which would rather lounge on leather couches and bob their heads to the music than get naked and procreate to it. Cover F-Su 40 pesos, beer 12 pesos, mixed drinks 20 pesos. Open daily 9pm-4am.

Chaos and **Club Venus,** both on Camarón Sábado. Chaos gets chaotic with a wet T-shirt contest and Venus boasts the largest music collection of any club in Mexico, with over 11,000 CDs. Before moving south of the border, its owners were working in the Seattle club that broke bands like *Soundgarden* and *Alice in Chains*.

NEAR MAZATLÁN: ISLA DE LA PIEDRA

Just a five-minute boat ride from the mainland, Isla de la Piedra consists of 10km of glistening sand, crashing waves, and rustling palm trees. Imagine drinking out of a coconut while lying in a hammock and feeling like you're in a postcard—that's Isla de la Piedra. Less crowded and less shamelessly developed than mainland beaches, the island is an unspoiled haven of sunshine and ocean popular among Mexican families. Isla de Piedra's beaches don't have the intimidating undertow of the mainland, either.

The main attractions are, of course, the beautiful **beaches.** Wriggle your toes in the cool sand, duck the waves, or bask in the radiant sun. You won't have any trouble finding a place to spread your towel. Bring a frisbee or a kite or a surf board—you'd have to try to not have a good time at this beach. If you're into water sports, try a trip on a banana boat (40 pesos), rent snorkeling equipment (90 pesos per hr.), or borrow a boogie board (10 pesos per hr.). The restaurants will point you in the right direction. Aging horses may also be hired (60 pesos per hr.) farther up the beach.Obtain **tourist information** at any of the restaurants near the beaches; most owners have been on the island for ages and are more than willing to help. The island's one **telephone** (tel. 85 44 50) is located across from the dock

The island is perfect for a daytrip or for camping. **Carmelita's,** a few meters from the shore, offers space for tents, sturdy trees for hammock slinging, and use of the bathroom and grill free of charge. If you can't camp out, Carmelita also offers clean rooms with the basics: electricity and private bathrooms with running water (80 pesos for 1-3 people). **Lety's,** adjacent to Carmelita's, offers similar free lodging. It also has spacious rooms with modern bathrooms, desks, lighting, two beds, and a sofa-bed (85 pesos for 1-3 people). There's nothing nicer than camping out on a secluded beach and gazing at the stars, but be careful and don't stray too far from the center. Seafood rules on the island. **Carmelita's** serves shrimp platters and fish fillets, both with *frijoles,* tortillas, salad, and rice (25 pesos; open 9am-6pm). If you're tired of seafood, head to **Lety's** for a quarter-chicken (25 pesos) or quesadillas (20 pesos; open 9am-7pm). Listen to the cool tunes and watch folks play volleyball by the shore at **Restaurant Estebin,** a two-minute walk from Carmelita's. You'll find the same ol' grub: fish fillets (25 pesos) and chicken (22 pesos; open daily 9am-7pm).

Getting There: To get to the island, take a green "Independencia" **bus** (2.60 pesos) from the *mercado* at Serdan to the **Embarcadero de la Isla de la Piedra.** From there, take a **boat** (5min., every 10min., 8 pesos round-trip) to the island. Remember that the last boat back to the mainland leaves at 5pm; **trucks** (2 pesos) and **taxis** (6 pesos) will be waiting to take passengers to the *playa* from the ferry landing. Alternatively, walk straight away from the boat landing and follow the concrete path across the island for about 15 minutes. All the restaurants and stores (all three of them) are in a cluster on the beach.

DURANGO

DURANGO

State capital and commercial center, Durango (pop. 490,000) is a busy city caught up in the heavy traffic of Mexico's push toward industrialization. However, it's still surrounded by the pristine countryside that caused Hollywood producers to flock there during the mid-20th century. The city's collection of colonial architecture and its worthwhile museums offer more than enough to hold your interest for a day or so, although it certainly isn't a thriving tourist mecca. You'll definitely appreciate the cooler climate if you're coming from the muggy coastal area, and a light jacket or pullover may come in handy at night.

⚐ ORIENTATION AND PRACTICAL INFORMATION. Durango's **bus station** is located on the eastern outskirts of town. To reach the *centro*, catch one of the red buses in front of the station (2.60 pesos); **taxis** are also available, thankfully with meters to avoid the usual tourist rip-off (fare about 12 pesos). After dark, a taxi is the only way to travel. The suburbs and outskirts of Durango are full of tractor-trailers and warehouses; to find fun, culture, and amenities, you'll have to head downtown. Most sites of interest lie within a few blocks of the cathedral and its **Plaza de Armas. 20 de Noviembre** is a major east-west thoroughfare passing in front of the cathedral; **Juárez** runs north-south. Navigating downtown is fairly simple; the streets are in a grid and rarely change names.

Estrella Blanca and Rojo de los Altos (tel. 18 30 61) send buses to: **Aguascalientes** (6hr., 6 per day 5:30am-7pm, 185 pesos); **Guadalajara** (9½hr., 5 per day 7:15am-7pm, 264 pesos); and **Mazatlán** (7hr., 5 per day 10am-10pm, 150 pesos). Transportes Chihuahuenses rolls to: **Mexico City** (11hr., 4 per day 4-10pm, 420 pesos); **Monterrey** (8½hr., 9 per day, 284 pesos); **Torreón** (3hr., 18 per day, 118 pesos); and **Zacatecas** (4½hr., 6 per day 8am-11:15pm, 130 pesos). Omnibus (tel. 18 33 61) speeds to: **Ciudad Juárez** (8hr., 3 per day 6-10pm, 447 pesos; nondirect 12hr., 5 per day 8am-11:05pm, 250 pesos); **Matamoros** (13hr., 7:35 and 9:15pm, 310 pesos); **San Luis Potosí** (6hr., 7 per day 7:30am-11pm, 154 pesos); and **Zacatecas** (6hr., on the ½hr. 7:30am-9:30pm, 130 pesos). Turistar Ejecutivo and Futura (tel. 18 37 84) serve **Nuevo Laredo** (12hr., 8 and 9:30pm, 300 pesos). Transportes del Valle Poanas and Transportes de Durango send buses throughout the state of Durango, including: **Agua Vieja** (2½hr., every hr. 7am-8pm, 28 pesos); **Los Angeles** (1¼hr., about every hr. 7am-8pm, 19 pesos); and **Villa Unión** (2hr., every 30min 7am-8pm, 25 pesos).

Tourist information can be found at the **Dirección de Turismo y Cinematografía,** Florida 100, at the intersection of 20 de Noviembre and Independencia. Tourist info is located through a door around the side of the building, and up the stairs. Helpful staff provides maps and brochures. **Banco Serfín** (tel. 12 80 33), on the plaza, has great **exchange** rates, as well as a 24-hour **ATM** (open M-F 9am-5pm, exchange 9am-3pm). **Emergency:** dial 060. **Police:** (tel. 17 54 06 or 17 55 50) at Felipe Pescador and Independencia. **Hospital General:** (tel. 11 91 15) on 5 de Febrero and Norman Fuentes (open 24 hr.). **Post office:** (tel. 11 41 05) at 20 de Noviembre and Roncal, 12 long blocks from the Plaza de Armas (open M-F 8am-7pm, Sa 9am-1pm). **Postal code:** 34000. **Fax: Telecomm,** at Felipe Pescada and Zaragoya, about eight blocks from the plaza (open M-F 8am-8pm, Sa 9am-4pm). **Caseta:** at 5 de Febrero 106 Pte. (open daily 8am-10pm). **Internet access: Cybercom** (tel. 11 37 01), 5 de Febrero 1302 (15 pesos per hr.). **Phone code:** 118.

⌐ ACCOMMODATIONS. Inexpensive accommodations can be found near the market, along 5 de Febrero a few blocks west of the Plaza de Armas. The **Hotelito La Casa de Huéspedes,** Progresso 102 Sur (tel. 12 31 81), near the market, has clean, basic rooms with TVs and bathrooms. The *casa* is simple and gives you exactly what you pay for. The elderly *dueña* also rents large furnished apartments with kitchens. (Singles 60 pesos; 1-person apartments 100 pesos; doubles 80 pesos; 2-person apartments 120 pesos.) For a step up in comfort (and also in price), the **Hotel Plaza Catedral,** Constitución 216 Sur (tel. 13 26 60), right off 20 de Noviembre and next door to the cathedral, will fix you right up. The old convent has a dark, mysterious charm. Rooms are carpeted and have phones and cable TVs. (Singles 150 pesos; doubles 180 pesos; triples 200 pesos; 2 room suites with refrigerator 200 pesos.) Clean rooms come dirt cheap **Hotel Gallo,** 5 de Febrero 117 (tel. 11 52 90), near the market. Catch a *telenovela* on the lobby TV or admire the many colorful pet birds. (Singles 45 pesos; doubles 60 pesos, with TV 70 pesos.)

◨ **FOOD.** Inexpensive meals aren't hard to rustle up in Durango. The few blocks of 5 de Febrero before Juárez contain a wide variety of restaurants with everything from cheap fast food to more expensive, family-style dining, to soda fountains. Somehow the cafe **Al Grano,** at Negrete and Zaragoza, a few blocks west of the cathedral, manages to cram giant feline masks, a blow-up of a tarot magician, a ceramic clown, a wooden Don Quixote, and countless plants into its small space. Specialties include breakfast plates with fresh squeezed orange juice (20 pesos) along with vegetarian fare. (Open M-Sa 8am-8pm.) The family-run **Cafe de la Mancha,** 20 de Noviembre 807 Pte., at Zaragoza, prepares your meal in front of your eyes. Laid-back atmosphere; family members are sometimes among the clientele and the occasional pigeon strolls through the dining room. (*Comida corrida* 22 pesos; *gorditas* 4 pesos. Open daily 9am-8pm.) What do you get when you combine red-and-white streamers, a glass design with a rooster in the middle left over from the 1970s and garish neon lighting? Why, the perfect place to listen to *mariachi* music of course. **La Terraza,** 5 de Febrero 603 (tel. 11 60 50), across from the Plaza de Armas has a full menu of Mexican and American dishes (entrees around 32 pesos; beer 16 pesos; mixed drinks 22 pesos). Nightly *mariachi* madness around 11pm. (Open daily 8am-1am.)

▣ **SIGHTS.** The most imposing building in town is the enormous **cathedral** overlooking the Plaza de Armas. The carved Baroque facade is marred by an ugly modern clock, and the facade rests under two enormous bell towers including figures of angels, an eagle, and a heavy iron cross. The dim interior is filled with marble pillars, carved wood, and wrought iron. Just west of the cathedral on 20 de Noviembre stands the white brick **Teatro Ricardo Castro.** Construction of the building began in 1900; on its centennial it houses temporary exhibitions, and hosts theatrical productions and film screenings. Its hours are irregular, so don't be too disappointed if it's closed. The huge **Palacio de Gobierno,** on 5 de Febrero between Martinez and Zaragoza, was built by a Spanish mining tycoon and expropriated by the government after Mexico gained independence. Inside, a bronze likeness of Benito Juárez glares amid colorful murals depicting the city's history.

Durango has several worthwhile museums including the **Museo de las Culturas Populares,** Juárez 302 at Barreda, which displays ceramics, and textiles. The *museo* also hosts talks, dances, and other events. (Open Tu-F 9am-6pm, Sa 10am-6pm, Su noon-7pm. Admission 3 pesos.) The **Museo Regional de Durango,** at Serdán and Victoria, known as **El Aguacate** (the Avocado) for its unique shape and texture, at Serdán and Victoria, houses some paintings by Miguel Cabrera, as well as exhibits on the state's history, indigenous groups, paleontology, and natural resources (open Tu-Su 9am-4pm; admission 1 peso; Su free). The **Museo de Arte Contemporanea,** 301 Negrete at Pasteur, hosts well put together, temporary exhibits of local and national artists (open Tu-Su 10am-6pm; free).

◧ **ENTERTAINMENT.** Come sundown, throw your hands in the air at La Covacha, Pino Suárez 500 Pte. (tel. 12 39 69), at Madero, where locals dance to international and Latin hits (cover 25 pesos; open Th-Su 9pm-4am). Excalibur, at Mascareñas and Cárdenas, is a mellower hangout, with pool tables and live *mariachi* music on weekends (open daily 4pm-late). **Cinetecha Municipal,** Juárez 217 at Coronado, screens artsy flicks. Several showings daily of classic, foreign, and art films (tickets 10 pesos).

On Sundays, head to **Parque Guadiana** to celebrate *Domingo Familiar,* where vendors hawk kid-pleasing treats and street performers play to the crowds. For 10 days at the beginning of July, Durango commemorates the city's founding with the **Feria Nacional.** Parades and fireworks liven things up and reservations become a must. Fans of Westerns may be keen to note that over 200 films, including several John Wayne classics, have been shot in the desert around Durango. Some of the **movie sets** have been left standing and are now tourist attractions. The tourist office organizes trips to visit the sets. You can try a do-it-yourself version by taking a Chihuahuenses bus to **Chupaderos** (30min., every 25min., 7 pesos). Ask the driver to let you off on the route near the sets.

NORTHEAST MEXICO

Dust-swept border towns, former colonial settlements, old mining hotspots, and congested urban centers dot the expansive deserts and occasional rich forests of Northeast Mexico. The incredible lack of tourists—one of the most constant features across the disparate towns and cities of the Northeast—creates a paradisiacal sense of calm among the proud, parched-white missions and wide streets. Eager for the industry and not (yet) inundated with tourists, Northeast-

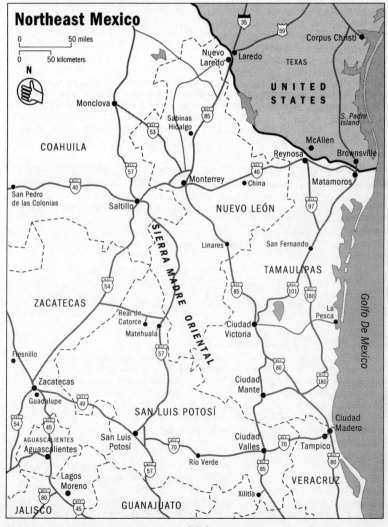

Northeast Mexico

0   50 miles

0   50 kilometers

N

ern Mexicans welcome the few travelers who do trickle through with boundless hospitality, always open to share the culture of which they are so proud.

This description, though, does not apply to the border towns of **Tamaulipas** and **Nuevo León.** Not for the faint of heart, these towns are replete with money-dropping, booze-guzzling day-trippers, lost souls, industrious young men and women from all over Mexico and Central America eager for access to the American Dream (or just a full day's work), and U.S. border police determined to keep them out.

Farther south, however, the gringo influence and grubbiness fade. In Monterrey, a metropolis of millions, lovely cathedrals and gorgeous parks peek out of a sea of gray skyscrapers; Monterrey has become a chic city without catering to tacky tourists and is one of the most gay-friendly cities outside the D.F. If it's beach you crave, the *noreste* offers little more than a taste. Fresh, salty Tampico has never been able to draw flocks of tourists: you can swim, tan on the sand, and munch on fresh seafood, but it's far from picturesque.

Perhaps the most wonderful part of the Northeast lies within the state of **San Luis Potosí.** Even the town of Real de Catorce, ridden with peyote-hungry back-packers, is largely untouched by modernity, with one phone, hundreds of bur-ros, and mountain views. Xilitla offers the eco-warrior caves, waterfalls, rivers, wild parrots, semi-tropical rainforests, and ruins an hour or two from congested city centers. The city of San Luis Potosí is a quiet jewel—the capital of the state, it is a playground of regional culture, awesome architecture, and colonial appeal. The **Zacatecas** state was blessed with a location smack in the middle of Mexico's legendary silver store; as a result, its capital, now a university town, is far more classically colonial, commercial, and cosmopolitan than is customary for the Northeast. While the *noreste* might not feature prominently in the plans of most tourists, the quiet appeal and dry charm of its towns and cities might surprise you.

HIGHLIGHTS OF NORTHEAST MEXICO

■ Despite incongruous architecture, the eclectic, fast-paced city of **Monterrey** (see p. 266) is still beautiful. Rage with the best of them in the one-of-a-kind **Barrio Antiguo** (see p. 271). Monterrey also has a **thriving gay scene** (see p. 271).

■ The tiny, lush town of **Xilitla** (see p. 296) might very well be Eden. Be sure to check out **Las Pozas** (see p. 297), a gorgeous expanse of jungle "ruins" built early this century by a crazy Englishman.

■ Dubbed "City of Plazas," **San Luis Potosí** (see p. 285) is one of the most beautiful and tourist-free cities in Mexico.

■ **Real de Catorce** (see p. 293) is a tiny ex-mining town high in the Sierra Madres that now specializes in gorgeous mountain views and peyote.

BROWNSVILLE, TEXAS

The license plates might read "Texas" and the street signs might be in English but Brownsville (pop. 135,000) may as well be a city in Mexico. Here, lanky men sporting cowboy hats and driving late-model American cars are as likely to speak to you in Spanish as in English. A nearly 90% Hispanic population and wholesale markets blaring Mexican top-40 hits will serve as a gentle bilingual introduction to life in Mexico. Few tourists come to Brownsville, and for good reason: despite its incredibly friendly and helpful residents, this border town offers little to interest tourists.

■ **ORIENTATION.** Most points of interest lie northwest of **International Blvd.,** which traverses the city before turning into the **Gateway Bridge** that leads to the city of Matamoros, Mexico. Numbered streets run parallel to International Blvd., beginning at **First St.** on either side of **Palm Blvd.** both eastward and westward. Running perpendicular to the numbered streets, **Elizabeth St.** is the city's main commercial thoroughfare and precedes the streets named after American Presidents in order, with **Washington** and **Adams** encompassing the greatest tourist interest. Street numbers correspond to location—770 Elizabeth is between 7th and 8th. The few tourists who do visit Brownsville are often drawn to the old city near the border and the swanky suburban hotel strip in the southeastern part of town. At night, the area around the border is desolate; women and solo travelers should avoid it. The cautious traveler should also think twice before entering **Southmost Rd.**, perpendicular to and east of International Blvd., late at night. Brownsville is not a city to explore by night. Downtown empties out by 9pm during the week and by 10:30pm on Friday and Saturday. After that, traveling in groups or in cabs is advisable. **Local buses,** which travel long routes throughout Brownsville, run from 6am to 7pm and cost US75¢ (seniors US15¢); all buses leave on the hour or the half-hour from **City Hall** on E. Washington St. between E. 11th and E. 12th. Bus maps and schedules are available for free at the station at City Hall. If you're planning to stay more than a day or two, it is worthwhile to invest in a 20-ride pass for US$12.

⁷ PRACTICAL INFORMATION. Brownsville and South Padre International Airport, 700 S. Minnesota (tel. 542-4373), is served by Continental (tel. 541-2200 or (800) 231-0856), which offers eight flights per day to and from **Houston** (8:25am-7:30pm; US$97 one way with early reservation). The Greyhound station, 1134 E. Charles St. (tel. 546-7171), two blocks from the International Bridge runs **buses** to: **Dallas** (13hr., 11 per day 7am-10:15pm, US$43); **Houston** (8hr., 14 per day 7am-9:45pm, US$20); **Laredo** (5hr., 8:15am and 11:30pm, US$24); and **San Antonio** (7hr., 11 per day 5am-10:15pm, US$31). Trailways (tel. 504-2351), at the corner of E. Adams and International, offers even faster, cheaper service to: **Houston** (6½hr., 4 per day 8am-10pm, US$20), as well as comparable service to other points north and south. **Taxis** to downtown run US$9-11. **Bus #7** passes by the airport every hour and 10 minutes starting at 6:23am, with the last bus at 7:13pm. It takes about 40 minutes to go downtown. **Car rentals** are also available at the airport. **Dollar** (tel. 982-2006) is US$45 per day plus an extra US$15 if you're under 25 (but over 21).

The **Chamber of Commerce,** 1600 E. Elizabeth (tel. 542-4341), has maps (US$1) and city guides, complete with every business in Brownsville. These guides also cover Matamoros, Brownsville's southern neighbor (open M-F 8am-5pm). The **tourist office** (tel. 800-626-2639 or 546-3721), across the street from Sunrise Mall, on bus routes #2 and #4, offers little more info than the Chamber of Commerce, but call if you're in a pinch for a hotel (open daily 8:30am-5pm.) You can also check out the **Brownsville City Web Page** (www.brownsville.org) before you go. **Casas de cambio** line International Blvd.; rates are approximately the same in banks, if not better, but if you want to exchange **traveler's checks** you'll have to use a bank—look for them on Elizabeth St. and in the lower numbers on the East Side. The best rates for exchanging dollars into pesos, though, are found across the border. **Police:** 600 E. Jackson (tel. 548-7000). **Emergency: Brownsville Medical Center,** 1040 W. Jefferson (tel. 544-1400), at Central. **Post office:** Elizabeth and E. 10th, is in the beautiful brick masonry courthouse building (counter open M-F 9am-5pm). **ZIP Code:** 78520. **Area code:** 956.

⌐ ACCOMMODATIONS. Lodging in Brownsville—besides the pricey national chains—gently prepares the southbound traveler for the hotel life that is to come. Brownsville prices, however, certainly are American. Although more expensive, the downtown area is more convenient than the distant area along **Central Blvd.** If you don't mind the trek, cheaper motels line Central Blvd. on the Los Ebanos and Jefferson and Central bus lines. But remember, you get what you pay for—rooms start at about US$29. For a comfortable and reasonable place to stay downtown, the **Cameron Motor Hotel,** 912 E. Washington (tel. 542-3551), has rooms with bath, cable TV, A/C, and telephones. Hotel Cameron is often full so it's a good idea to call ahead. (Singles US$36; doubles US$41 plus tax.) The **Hotel Colonial,** 1147 Levee St. (tel. 541-9176), the street next to Elizabeth, offers refuge from the interminable heat in a cool lobby. Bright rooms come with full amenities and a friendly staff awaits you in the quiet, cool lounge. (Singles US$36; doubles US$41.)

█ FOOD. Catering primarily to local residents, Brownsville restaurants serve a combination of simple Mexican dishes and hamburgers. Downtown, cafes open and close early—most shut down by 5:30pm—all offer similar menus of burgers and burritos. For a late snack, **Lucio's Cafe,** 1041 E. Washington, is a comfortable place to hang out with meals running about US$5 (open Su-Th until 10pm, F-Sa 24 hr). Diners should also seek out the friendly, red dining room of **Restaurant Nuevo Leon,** 1203 E. Adams St. (tel. 541-9522; open daily until 6:30pm). For the *salsa*-weary, **Artichoke Deli,** 108 E. Elizabeth (tel. 544-7636), is a 10-minute walk from downtown and on the #1 bus line. Perhaps the closest thing in Brownsville to a vegetarian-friendly eatery, the deli features salads and sandwiches for about US$5, and the largest selection of beer south of San Antonio. On the weekends, it turns into one of the most happening places in town when local classic rock bands draw in fun-loving crowds. (Open M-Th 11am-4pm, F 11am-midnight and Sa 11am-1am.)

◙ █ SIGHTS AND ENTERTAINMENT. Brownsville may look like a non-descript border town, but it boasts one of the top zoos in the nation for rare and endangered species, as well as several museums honoring the city's role in American history. The **Gladys Porter Zoo,** 500 Ringgold St. (tel. 546-7187), off E. 6th on the #2 ("Los Ebanos") bus line, offers a 31-acre tropical sanctuary where most animals live in open quarters surrounded only by waterways. The collection includes lowland gorillas, infant Sumatran orangutans, and white rhinos. (Open daily 9am-7:30pm. Tickets sold until 5pm; extended to 6pm during summer weekends. Admission US$6, children US$3.)

If a long, hot day of wholesale shopping and exchanging money leaves you longing for a yuppified evening, kick back at the **Artemis Sports Bar and Grille,** 1200 Central Blvd. (tel. 542-2361), a five-minute walk from the medical center. The Artemis is hip, clean, and relatively safe—even at night. TVs blare football games, and on Fridays and Saturdays, live bands play everything from alterna-rock to Spanish pop. (Happy Hour 11am-7pm. Open M-F 11am-2am, Sa-Su noon-2am; kitchen closes at midnight.)

TAMAULIPAS

MATAMOROS

While border-patrol jeeps line the Brownsville side of the Río Grande, cows quietly stare across the river from Matamoros. Calmer than its sister city to the north, Matamoros offers numerous tree-and-bench-lined squares for the weary traveler and store-lined walking streets for the exuberant shopper. But lest this sound too peaceful, don't worry: the town has enough booze and border brawls (especially at night) that you won't need to dream up your own reasons to stay out after dark.

▄ ORIENTATION. To reach Matamoros from Brownsville, walk or drive (bring along all documentation and check your insurance policy's validity in Mexico—see p. 69) across the **International Bridge.** Pedestrians pay a budget-busting US$0.35 or 2 pesos to leave either country. Autos pay US$1.25. From the border crossing, the city extends out in a V-shape following the bend in the **Río Bravo;** the left (eastern) arm of the V is defined by **Calle 1,** which runs parallel to the river and leads directly to the **Central de Autobuses,** 2km down in the southeast corner of the city. As the city opens up to the right (west) toward **Calle Hidalgo,** the street numbers increase. Heading south of the border, the main area of activity and importance is the *centro,* focused in the area between Calles 5 and Calles 11, and between **Bravo** and **Abasolo.**

⑦ PRACTICAL INFORMATION. To reach the center of town from the border area, take one of the yellow minibuses labeled "Centro" on the hood (US45¢ or 3 pesos). "Central" minibuses go to the **bus station,** the Central de Autobuses. Returning to the border, catch a minibus marked "Puente." Minibuses really do make *paradas continuas;* just wave your index finger at them and they'll stop almost anywhere (local transport info tel. 17 88 80). **Bus** traffic flows through the Central de Autobuses, on **Canales** at **Aguilar,** off Calle 1 (station closed Su). ADO (tel. 12 01 81) goes to: **Tampico** (7hr., 7 per day 3:10-11:30pm, 202 pesos); **Tuxpan** (11hr., 3 per day 3:10-10pm, 298 pesos); and **Veracruz** (16 hrs., 4 per day 4-10pm, 355 pesos) with numerous stops in between. Noreste (tel. 13 27 68) services: **Monterrey** (6hr., 11 per day 1-7:40pm, 161 pesos); and **Reynosa** (2hr., every 2hr., 31 pesos). Transportes del Norte (tel. 16 66 15 or 16 65 80) runs to: **Mexico City** (14hr., 1 *ejecutivo* per day 6:40pm, 517 pesos; 4 1st-class buses per day, 383 pesos); **Saltillo** (7hr., 6 per day, 184 pesos); and **San Luis Potosí** (10hr., 11 per day, 305 pesos). Omnibus de México (tel. 13 76 93), sends buses to **Reynosa** (44 pesos), **Saltillo** (182 pesos), **Monterrey** (161 pesos), and **Río Bravo** (31 pesos) every hour on the hour or on the half-hour between 7am and midnight. **Check your baggage** at the bus station for as long as you want (1st hr. 2 pesos, each additional hr. 1 peso).

On the right, just past the turnstile marking entry into Mexico, lies the **tourist office** (tel. 12 36 30), which offers a few general pamphlets about Mexico, and lots of friendly advice. Matamoros maps are available from the Brownsville **Chamber of Commerce. Casas de cambio** dot the *centro,* particularly along Calles 5 and 6, but the best exchange rates await in the bus station or from **ATMs** like the one at **Bancomer** (tel. 16 30 67) at Matamoros and Calle 6. Bancomer, also exchanges **traveler's checks** (open M-F 9am-6pm, Sa 9am-5pm). **Emergency:** dial 060. **Police:** (tel. 16 20 21, 17 22 05, or 17 22 05) always stationed around International Bridge and the border 24hr. **Post office:** in the bus station (open M-Sa 9am-3:30pm). **Postal code:** 87370. **Phone code:** 891.

🍴 ACCOMMODATIONS AND FOOD. Although prices in Matamoros are reasonable, expect little more than the basics. The market area, where most of the budget accommodations are located, quickly loses its bustling crowds after nightfall—be very careful. **Hotel Majestic** (tel. 13 36 80), on the pedestrian mall on Abasalo between Calles 8 and 9, offers simple, clean, bright rooms with private bath (singles 80 pesos; doubles 125 pesos; each additional person 20 pesos). **Hotel Sexta Avenida** (tel. 16 66 66 or 16 66 96), on Calle 6 between Zaragoza and Terán, is a bit more expensive and farther from the *centro,* but worth it for the rare quiet and comfort (one person 300 pesos; each additional person 50 pesos).

The food in Matamoros is typically overpriced and border-town bland. If you choose to follow the crowds heading to delectable **outdoor stands,** try to avoid the generic nachos and look instead for **brisket.** Also be sure to check for proper cleanliness and hygiene. There are some great small **cafes** on the streets surrounding the pedestrian mall. **Café y Restaurant Frontera** (tel. 546 71 87), on Calle 6 between N. Bravo and Matamoros with a heart-shaped sign, is filled with locals soaking in the air-conditioning and enjoying the optical-illusion floor while digging into Mexican specialties for 25-29 pesos (open daily 7am-10pm). Slip into an upstairs booth at **Cafeteria Deli,** 1307 Calle 7 (tel. 13 93 87), between Abasolo and Matamoros, to escape the bright sun and to enjoy a range of *antojitos* (15-25 pesos; open daily 6am-9pm).

PUMP UP THE VOLUME On the bus rides, in local bars, and on the street, you will hear three major types of Mexican music. **Corridas** are laments of love gone wrong, sung to a plaintive slow tune. Vincente Fernandez's "Volver, volver, volver a tus brazos otra vez" (roughly trans: "to return, to return, to return to your arms again) is one of the most famous *corridas*. Sung by *gauchos*, the original cowboys, **rancheros,** always accompanied by accordion, celebrate the fruits of the earth or pray for God to bless or save crops and livestock. Young and old Mexicans alike belt out or quietly whistle *corridas* and *rancheros* on a regular basis. The black-and-red-clad men with bells and capes, the same ones that appear on tequila ads outside of Mexico, are **mariachis**. The most traditional Mexican music, *mariachi* is lively and light-hearted. Wandering *mariachis* will strike up in front of restaurants and always play at traditional *fiestas*. When you feel moved by the spirit (or the tequila), feel free to stand with your legs shoulder-width apart, throw your head back, and cry "ay, ay ay ay..." along with any music.

📷 🎵 SIGHTS AND ENTERTAINMENT. Matamoros and **Abasolo,** pedestrian streets between **Calles 6** and **11,** are lined with shops and vendors; closer to Calle 6 is modern clothing, while crafts abound around Calle 9. Brash vendors pounce upon any sign of interest, so be wary and look weary. For even more condensed browsing, the old market, **Pasaje Juárez,** has entrances on both Matamoros and Bravo between Calles 8 and 9. Bright piñatas and rows of glittering jewelry illuminate the dim interior of **Mercado Juárez,** the new market on Abasolo between Calles 9 and 10. Markets farther south offer higher quality and lower prices. For a cultured evening, stop by the **Teatro de la Reforma** (tel. 12 51 21), on Calle 6 between González and Abasolo. Renovated in 1992, this beautiful colonial brick building is home to everything from classical drama to contemporary Mexican theater. (Adults 120 pesos.) If you're in the mood to bar-hop, boogie, and booze, think twice. Most reasonably priced **bars** and **discos** near the border are very unsafe at night. More upscale drinking occurs in bars attached to fancy hotels.

REYNOSA

Horse-drawn carts share the streets with 16-wheelers in Reynosa (pop. 600,000) as pushcarts sell fruit cups outside American 7-11 mini-marts. Reynosa, just across the border from McAllen, Texas, still exudes the atmosphere of a small border town, despite its growing population. There isn't a lot to see or do in Reynosa, but with a walkable, well-planned center, wide clean streets, a shady plaza, and plenty of shopping, Reynosa is a tiny gem by border town standards.

🛬 ORIENTATION. Reynosa is 150km from Monterrey and 645km from Mexico City; it can be reached from McAllen by taking **23rd St.** 12km south into **Hidalgo** and then over the **International Bridge. Rtes. 2** and **40** from Matamoros and Monterrey respectively, both lead straight into town. The city forms a square with the **International Bridge** border crossing at the northeast corner. The city rises to the **central plaza,** one square block bounded by **Zaragoza** on the north, **Hidalgo** on the west, **Morelos** on the south, and **Juárez** on the east. The main city is a very walkable 10 blocks by 12 blocks, but if you get tired, *peseros* run in nearly all directions for about 1 peso; **taxis** will try to overcharge, so try and bargain before getting in.

🛈 PRACTICAL INFORMATION. The **bus station** is on Colón in the southwest corner of town. To reach the center, turn left as you exit the station and walk until you hit Colón. Then take any city bus labeled "Centro" or turn left on Colón, walk five blocks to Juárez, and go right on Juárez; the plaza is six blocks down. Among the many companies servicing the Reynosa station, ADO (tel. 22 87 13) offers primarily evening service with routes to: **Tampico** (7hr., 5 per day 4:30pm-11pm, 205 pesos); **Veracruz** (16hr., 2 per day 8:30pm and 11pm, 358 pesos); and **Villahermosa** (24hr., 11pm, 534 pesos). Futurama (tel. 22 14 52) offers *ejecutivo* service to: **Monterrey** (3hr., 1-11pm, 113 pesos); **Mexico City** (15hr., 2:30-10pm, 480 pesos); and **Guadalajara** (15hr., 6:15-9pm, 450 pesos). Omnibus de México (tel. 22 33 07) runs to: **Monterrey** (3hr., every hour, 113 pesos); **Saltillo** (5hr., 8 per day 3:30am-4:30pm, 108 pesos); and **Chihuahua** (15hr., 9am and 10:30pm, 438 pesos). Noreste (tel. 22 02 06) offers the most extensive service including: **San Luis Potosí** (11½hr., 9 per day 4:20am-10:30pm, 210 pesos); **Matamoros** (2hr., every 45min. 5:22am-10:05pm, 47 pesos); **Monterrey** (3hr., every hour 6am-8:45pm, 113 pesos); and **Nuevo Laredo** (4hr., 9 per day, 117 pesos).

The **Cámara de Comercio,** on Chapa at Allende, one block north of Zaragoza and one block east of Juárez, has free pamphlets with maps and brochures (open M-F 9am-5pm). **Casas de cambio** are scattered all along Hidalgo and the plaza area, but none accept traveler's checks. **Banorte,** on Morelos at Hidalgo (open M-F 9am-2:30pm) and **Bancomer** (tel. 22 81 01), opposite Banorte on Zaragoza, have competitive rates, accept traveler's checks, and also offer 24hr (bank open M-F 9am-5:30pm, Sa 10am-2pm). **ATMs. Exchange office** in the bank (open M-F 9am-6pm, Sa 9am-5pm). **Police:** (tel. 22 00 88 or 22 07 90) southwest across Canal Anzaldvas. **Post office:** (tel. 22 01 10) on the corner of Díaz and Colón (open M-F 8am-4pm, Sa 9am-1pm). **Postal code:** 88500. **Phone code:** 89.

▐. ACCOMMODATIONS. The many hotels around the plaza are pricey. The cheapest are around south **Díaz** and **Hidalgo St.** Although boisterous and congested during the day, this area becomes desolate and even a little scary at night. *Cuídate.* **Hotel Avenida,** Zaragoza 885 Ote. (tel. 22 05 92), sets its sparkling clean, carpeted rooms around a beautiful leafy patio complete with chirping birds. With its proximity to the main plaza, A/C-TV combo, and the occasional antique piece of furniture, you can't lose. (1 person 190 pesos; 2 people 230 pesos; 3 people 300 pesos; 4 people 350 pesos.) For about the same prices, **Hotel Rey** (tel. 22 26 32), on Díaz between Mendez and Madero, has TV and A/C fit for a budget king. (1 person 190 pesos; 2 people 230 pesos; 3 people 260 pesos; 4 people 270 pesos.)

▐ FOOD. Locals at the outdoor stands or at open-air family-run cafeterias know exactly where to enjoy delicious, super-cheap fare. There are many stands near the bus station and the plaza. To sit down and escape the heat, you don't need to go far either. Despite the classy paintings by Frida Kahlo and Diego Rivera in the immaculate and cool **Café Sánchez** (tel. 22 16 65), on Morelos off Hidalgo at the southwest corner of the plaza, it's really the food that lures in the diverse crowd of businessmen, bus drivers, and families of 10. Entrees (26-60 pesos) are *riquisimos.* (Open daily 7am-8pm.) **Café Paris,** Hidalgo 815 (tel. 22 55 35), just past Morelos, is as gorgeous inside as it is out and offers super-reasonable fixed-price meals (breakfast 16.50 pesos, entrees 14-38 pesos; open daily 7am-10pm).

▣▐ SIGHTS AND ENTERTAINMENT. At nightfall, the main plaza hosts congregating couples, young and old. The **Hidalgo Marketplace** may not offer any substantial deals, but it is a great spot for people-watching. For an abridged history lesson, check out the beautiful storefront mural on the corner of Zaragoza one block east of Canales, just a few blocks south of the border crossing. It was funded by Bacardi (their billboard forms the last scene of the mural). Yet all is not civic altruism; enough rum 'n' cokes and *Cuba libres* more than cover the cost for the landmark. Drinking in Reynosa is serious stuff. Most bars tend to be near the border. Most brawls and brain damage occur near the border. Coincidence? You decide. Clustered along Ocampo near the border, most nightspots have on- and off-seasons. For a month during U.S. spring breaks (Feb.-Mar.), Reynosa turns into a miniature Cancún. The off-season, on the other hand, is a mellow time. Young people head year-round to the **Alaska Grill,** on Ocampo between Allende and Zaragosa, a dark, cold discotheque with two levels, an enormous dance floor, and a fully-stocked bar. In summer, Happy "Hour" (1pm-1am) means no cover with all beers US$1, and all shots and mixed drinks US$1.50.

Check out Reynosa's community theater at one of **La Casa de la Cultura's** free productions (tel. 22 99 89), next door to the tourist bureau, or just drop in to find out about cultural events (open M-F 9am-2pm, 3-7pm).

LAREDO, TEXAS

Having served under seven flags during its history, Laredo is growing at a mad pace. The strip malls and interminable suburban sprawl of Laredo are offset somewhat by its beautiful central square and the surrounding historic districts. The recent growth of this once-small town is exemplified by a modern bus station and the invasion of fast food chains.

■ ORIENTATION. Laredo's downtown centers around **International Bridge #1,** which becomes **Convent St.** on the U.S. side and runs north. Seven blocks north of the border and one block west of Convent is **Jarvis Plaza,** surrounded by all the main government buildings and delimited by **Matamoros, Farragut, Salinas,** and **Juárez.** The other main thoroughfare is **San Bernardo,** which originates near the border three blocks east of Convent and stretches north past the **Laredo Civic Center** and **Chamber of Commerce,** as well as most of the motels and restaurants. One block east lies **I-35,** which used to be the eastern border of town for most travelers. Many newer hotels and nightspots, however, now lie miles north and east of Jarvis Plaza and the border, most are accessible only by car and taxi. East-west streets are named after American and Mexican military and political figures.

⌗ PRACTICAL INFORMATION. The airport (tel. 795-2000) is on Maher, northeast of town. American Eagle (tel. 800-433-7300) serves **Dallas** (2hr., 6 per day); Continental Express (tel. 800-523-3273 and 723-3402) covers **Houston** (1½hr., 10 per day); and Taesa (tel. 800-328-2372 and 956-725-1022) goes to **Mexico City** (2hr., M-Tu, and Th-F). The **bus station** (tel. 723-4325) on San Bernardo and Matamoros runs Greyhound-affiliated buses to cities throughout the U.S., and sends daily buses to: **Aguascalientes** and **León** (14hr., 5pm, US$55-61); **Monterrey** (3hr., 5 per day, US$23); **San Luis Potosí** (11hr., 2 per day 7am-8pm, US$52); and **Querétaro** (13hr., 3 per day 3:30-8pm, US$72). However, traveling south from Nuevo Laredo is much cheaper than leaving from Laredo and provides more destinations and departures as well as **luggage lockers.** Scoot around town on **El Metro city buses** (tel. 795-2280), which run from Matamoros and Farragut streets on Jarvis Plaza (every 30min. daily 6am-9pm, US75¢, children US25¢, seniors US10¢). Schedules are avaliable from their office in the **Laredo Intermodal Transit Center** on the south side of the plaza.

The **tourist office,** 501 San Agustin (tel. 800-361-3360 or 795-2200), offers colorful, informative, and easy-to-read maps and brochures directing you to a plethora of sights and eateries in the downtown area (open M-Sa 8:30am-5pm). Currency can be exchanged at **casas de cambio** all along Convent and the few that are sprinkled throughout downtown. **Laredo National Bank,** 700 San Bernardo (tel. 723-1151), at the corner of Farragut, has both a bubbling fountain and a 24hr. **ATM** (bank open M-F 9am-4pm, Sa 9am-3pm). A good **supermarket** is **HEB,** 1002 Farragut (tel. 791-3571), two blocks south of the courthouse downtown (open daily 7am-10pm). **Sunshine Laundromat,** 2900 San Bernardo (tel. 722-8403), north of the Chamber of Commerce, has do-it-yourself (US$1 per wash, US25¢ per 10min. of drying, detergent available) or same-day full service (small load US$5, large load US$7; open daily 8am-10pm). The main **police** department (tel. 795-2800), near the airport and the foot/bike station (tel. 795-2650), is on Farragut next to HEB market (open daily 10am-5pm). **J&A Pharmacy,** 201 West Del Mar Blvd. (tel. 717-3839), lies to the far northeast of town (open M-F 9am-8pm, Sa 9am-4pm). Medical emergencies can be treated at **Mercy Regional Medical Center,** 1515 Logan Ave. (tel. 718-6222). **Post office:** 1300 Matamoros (tel. 723-3643), on Jarvis Plaza, (open M-F 8:30am-5pm, Sa 9am-noon). **Postal code:** 78040. You can **fax** at the **Western Union,** 711 Salinas (tel./fax 722-08-50), by Jarvis Plaza. UPS and pool cues are also available. Look for more Western Unions in the bus station and in every HEB supermarket. **Internet access: Laredo Times,** 111 Esperanza Dr. (tel. 729-2500 or 728-2504), off San Dario, accessible by the San Bernardo bus, 3 mi. north of downtown. **Phone code:** 956.

ACCOMMODATIONS. Nice hotels in Nuevo Laredo are cheaper than the most inexpensive Laredo lodgings. Nevertheless, those who value American motel amenities (drinkable tap water, carpets, newer furniture) will find an ample selection along San Bernardo north of the Chamber of Commerce, where budget hotels (U.S. style) are a dime-a-dozen. Expect good deals and nice, standard rooms from such big names as **Days Inn,** 4820 San Bernardo (tel. 722-6321); **Best Western Fiesta Inn,** 5240 San Bernardo (tel. 723-3603); or **Motel 6,** 5310 San Bernardo (tel. 725-8187). Most lodgings are accessible by the #2 El Metro city bus. For relatively closer access to the center, try the **Cortez Hotel,** 3113 San Bernardo (tel. 727-1001), but the entrance is a block over on Santa Ursula. With jungle-print bedsheets, dark wood paneling, hanging Tiffany-style lamps, and wrought-iron decorated mini-patios, these are perhaps the kitschiest rooms around. (Singles US$34; doubles US$39.) Another great bargain is **EconoLodge,** 2620

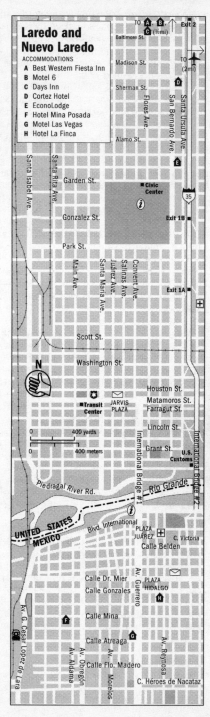

Laredo and Nuevo Laredo

ACCOMMODATIONS
A Best Western Fiesta Inn
B Motel 6
C Days Inn
D Cortez Hotel
E EconoLodge
F Hotel Mina Posada
G Motel Las Vegas
H Hotel La Finca

NORTHEAST MEXICO

Santa Ursula (tel. 722-6321) at the corner of San Bernardo, one block past the Chamber of Commerce. The friendly staff transforms it from a chain to a local joint. (Ultra-clean singles US$40; doubles US$50.)

◩ **FOOD.** Head downtown for a copious culinary selection with a strong emphasis on Tex-Mex cuisine (who knew?). *Salsa*-phobes can always order good burgers or find salvation in seafood restaurants and Chinese buffets. Fast-food joints and tasty *taquerías* line **San Bernardo**. Great food awaits you at **Tacolare**, 1206 San Bernardo (tel. 727-5115), just north of the railroad tracks. The small storefront disguises a large and inviting restaurant, a favorite among locals. (Great selection under US$5; open M-Sa 11am-10pm.) **Danny's Restaurant**, 802 Juárez (tel. 724-3185), on Jarvis Plaza near the courthouse building, has modern southwest art that adds color to Danny's decor. The food unquestionably sets it apart from the fast-food chains in that it's good! Lunch specials include Mexican brisket and mushroom burgers (US$4-6). Danny encourages you to eat three balanced meals a day—heaping breakfast specials served from 6-11am (US$3.50; open daily 6am-11pm).

▨◪ **SIGHTS AND ENTERTAINMENT.** The **Civic Center**, on **San Bernardo** next to the Chamber of Commerce, is the place to catch traveling performances or the **Laredo Philarmonic Orchestra** (tel. 727-8886; concerts some nights Oct.-May at 8pm). Every February, Laredo turns into one big **Washington's Birthday Celebration**, which includes a parade, led by the town princess dressed as Pocahontas, and the **Martha Washington Ball**. For a dose of the occult, get a consultation, a palm-reading, or a cure at **Yerbería de San Judas**, 711 Salinas (tel. 725-8336), a witchcraft store selling herbs and religious charms.

"Entertainment" in Laredo (e.g. drinking yourself into a stupor and losing $150 to a pool shark) is complicated by the large distances between establishments and the relative scarcity of taxis—most people drive into Laredo from the route. On top of this, police are cautious and alert, especially at night, frequently arresting people for public drunkenness and drunk driving.

NUEVO LAREDO

Nuevo Laredo pulses with commerce, from small souvenir shops to enormous trailers passing through with NAFTA-spurred trade. Today, pesos and dollars pour through Nuevo Laredo (pop. 420,000) at a dizzying pace, leaving many of its residents to snatch the crumbs that fall through the cracks. Nuevo Laredo's cheap liquor, abundant artisans, and easily accessible city center attract over-the-border-for-an-afternoon tourists, but the city's many plazas and friendly inhabitants make it more desirable than most Mexican border towns.

◪ **ORIENTATION. International Bridge #1** is the main way for pedestrians to go into Mexico; simply plunk down the US35¢ (for information on crossing the border, see p. 39). Travelers stick to the *centro*. **Av. Guerrero** emerges from International Bridge #1 as the main thoroughfare running south from the border. Three plazas along Guerrero define the downtown. Small, inviting **Plaza Juárez** lies just two blocks from the border, large, central **Plaza Hidalgo** adjoins the **Palacio Federal** in the heart of the city. **Plaza Mexico**, farthest south, is bordered on the southern end by Gonzales. The bus station lies to the far south of town. Areas of interest extend approximately seven blocks east and west of Guerrero.

◪ **PRACTICAL INFORMATION.** The **airport** (tel. 14 07 05), is in the extreme southwest of the city, off Rte. 2. Purchase **Mexicana** tickets at **Viajes Furesa**, Guerrero 830 (tel. 12 96 68), for the flight to **Mexico City** (11am and 5pm M-Sa). Also purchase tickets here for U.S. destinations leaving from the Laredo airport. (Office open M-F 9am-7pm.) **Buses:** Station is at Refugio Romo 3800, southwest of the city and quite a trek from the *centro*. To get to the border, take any blue-and-white or green-and-white bus marked *"Puente."* Hop off when you cross Gonzáles if you're going to the *centro*. To get to the station from the border, take the bus marked "Central." Around the clock **luggage storage** is also available (2 pesos per hr., or storage lockers for 22 pesos, but you have to drop off your bags before you exit the station; head toward the waiting room as if you were going to catch another bus rather than out the *salida)*. Omnibus de México (tel. 14 06 17) goes afternoons and evenings to: **Aguascalientes** (8hr., 3 per day, 295 pesos); **Leon** (12hr., 3 per day, 390 pesos); **Saltillo** (3½hr., 150 pesos); and **Zacatecas** (8hr., 2 per day, 280 pesos). Noreste (tel. 14 21 00) travels to: **Matamoros** (6hr., 8 per day 7am-midnight, 120 pesos) and **Reynosa** (4hr., 10 per day, 90pesos). Turistar, Futura, and Transportes del Norte share an information line (tel. 14 06 70) and a counter, but they maintain separate routes and services. Transportes del Norte boasts a bus to: **Monterrey** (3hr., every 30min., 120 pesos).

The **tourist office, Delegación Turismo** (tel. 12 01 04), at the Nuevo Laredo tip of the bridge before Mexican customs, provides an extensive supply of brochures in both Spanish and English (open M-Sa 8am-8pm). If you miss the *delegación*, call the Consultario de Turismo (tel. 12 73 97; open M-F 8am-8pm, Sa 9am-3pm). As usual, **casas de cambio** (especially the one at the border) offer the best exchange rates. Major banks line Guerrero near Plaza Hidalgo. **Banamex and Serfin** (tel. 12 15 02), on Canales and Guerrero, each have a 24hr. **ATM** (open M-F 9am-5pm). Supermarket **Gigante,** Reforma 4243, is located on the southern extension of Guerrero; take a bus toward the *centro* and get off when you see the enormous pink complex. For an **emergency:** dial 06. **Emergency:** dial 060. **Police:** tel. 12 21 46. **Farmacia Calderón:** (tel.12 55 63), on Guerrero west of Plaza Hidalgo. Open 24hr. **Medical Services,** at **ISSTE** (tel. 12 34 91), on Victoria and Reynosa to the east of Plaza Juárez has limited English-speaking staff. **Post office:** (tel. 12 21 00), in the back of the Palacio Federal, on the northeast corner of Dr. Mier and Camargo with **fax** and **telegram** service (open M-F 8am-6pm, Sa 9am-noon). **Mexpost** (tel. 13 47 17) is located on the opposite side of the *palacio*. Open M-F 9am-6pm, Sa 9am-1pm. **Telephones: LADATELs** and **Telmexs** are throughout the downtown border area, particularly near Plaza Hidalgo and Plaza Juárez. **Phone code:** 87.

▐ ACCOMMODATIONS. Most hotels of all prices are found within a few blocks of the city's main plazas. There are some great bargains if you're willing to look around. With just six rooms, **Hotel Posada Mina,** Mina 3521 (tel. 13 14 73), six blocks west of Guerrero has charming and quiet better-than-U.S. lodgings at slightly less-than-U.S. prices. The individually decorated rooms have carpet, TV, A/C, telephones, and lush flora. The two-person staff offers great service and conversation. (Singles 330 pesos; doubles 380 pesos.) **Hotel La Finca,** Reynosa 811 (tel. 12 88 83), just off Gonzalez by the southeast corner of Plaza Hidalgo is on a quiet street smack in the *centro*. Spacious, clean rooms rise above a cool, red-tile patio and offer a great value complete with A/C, TV, and phone. (Singles 180 pesos; doubles 230 pesos; 20 pesos each additional person.) **Motel Las Vegas,** Arteaga 3017 (tel. 12 20 30), 1½ blocks west of Guerrero and four blocks south of Plaza Hidalgo has cellar-like rooms featuring A/C, TV, and clean bathrooms. The smell of the extra cash in your pocket may mask the slightly dank odor of some of the rooms. (Singles 60 pesos; doubles 75 pesos.)

▝▏ FOOD. Home to the oft-imitated, never duplicated fajita, Nuevo Laredo's culinary fortes are meat and seafood. **Cabrito,** the roasted goat kid found throughout the northeast, and fajitas, often sold by the kilo, are well worth the extra money. Eating establishments are often similar in quality, price, and plenitude. Most of the good stuff is south of Herrera, around Guerrero 1700. **Playa Azul** (tel. 14 55 35, ext. 735), around Guerrero 2001 is a great place to kick back and relax as you enjoy *ceviche* (marinated fish cocktail with lime juice) and *telenovelas* (soap operas). Inviting dining room decorated with tasteful *campesino* furniture and a selection of seafood specialties (25-45 pesos) will blow your mind. There's also a full traditional Mexican menu with entrees going for 60-85 pesos (open daily 8am-11pm). **Cafeteria los Pinos,** on the east side of Plaza Juárez, is a hidden gem for travelers who find themselves getting hungry a little later than the rest. The slow fan may leave you hotter than the delicious *salsa verde* at noon, but after many places close up after dusk, it should be no problem (open 9am-11pm).

SIGHTS AND ENTERTAINMENT. The largest (and most expensive) *mercados* are concentrated around **Guerrero** near the border. With an ample selection of sturdy wooden furniture, pottery, and practical goods, this may be just the place to load up on souvenirs. Although better prices and higher-quality goods can be found further south, Nuevo Laredo has a tantalizing and terrific supply of liquor stores. Along Guerrero, for blocks south of the border, stores carrying lavish varieties of liquor all advertise the lowest prices in town. Pick up 750mL of Kahlua for US$7 or a liter of Cuervo Gold for US$4.50.

Those in search of cultural titillation can head to the **Teatro de la Ciudad** on Guatemala near Aguirre in the southeast corner of town, accessible via the "Viveros" buses. Strolling up and down Guerrero can be relaxing in the evenings when the three plazas fill with people gaily chatting and pleasantly passing time; the fountain on Nacatez and Guerrero is a favorite resting spot. If all this ambling about is not your style, then head to **Señor Frog's** (tel. 13 30 11), the self-proclaimed "Home of the Mother Margarita," just blocks south of the border on Belden at the corner of Ocampo. Although beers and tequila shooters are steeply priced (US$2 or 20 pesos), the lack of cover charge, the expert bartending, and the wonderfully campy cartoons and comics that adorn every inch of the restaurant/bar never cease to amaze.

TAMPICO

If you've seen Humphrey Bogart in *The Treasure of the Sierra Madre*, you might think of contemporary Tampico (pop. 434,000) as the hot, dirty, unfriendly oil town that every gringo is itching to skip. Although it is somewhat dirty and crowded and incredibly hot, Tampico is anything but unfriendly. The pleasant nearby beach is often uncrowded on weekdays, and Tampico's two main plazas are full of intriguing architecture and much-needed greenery. Founded in the 16th century on the ruins of an Aztec village, Tampico was destroyed by crazy pirates in 1623. Two hundred years later, Santa Anna ordered the city re-settled, and it soon grew into one of the most important oil ports in the world. Despite the ominous oil tankers and loads of litter, Tampico is trying to carve out a new identity: *tampiqueños* built the first beach resort in all of Tamaulipas, and their seafood is ridiculously fresh. Tampico may not be terrific yet, but at least it's trying to be.

■ **ORIENTATION.** The town centers around the **Plaza de Armas,** south of which is the **Plaza de la Libertad.** To the north of the Plaza de Armas is **Calle Carranza,** to the east is **Olmos,** and to the south is **Díaz Mirón.** Juárez runs parallel to Olmos one block east and along the western side of Plaza de la Libertad. One block south of Diaz Mirón, **Madero** is the northern border of Plaza de la Libertad. Continuing east and parallel to Olmos, you'll find **Aduana** and **López de Lara;** to the west, and running parallel to Olmos, you'll find **Colón, 20 de Noviembre,** and **Sor Juana Ines de la Cruz.** To get to the city center from the bus stop, take a yellow taxi (35 pesos), minibus (3.50 pesos), or *colectivo* (3.50 pesos, with luggage 5 pesos).

⊠ PRACTICAL INFORMATION. The **bus station,** on Zapotal north of the city, has just completed renovations. Omnibus de México (tel. 13 43 49) serves: **Ciudad Valles** (2½hr., 4 per day, 73 pesos); **Monterrey** (7hr.,11:30pm, 240 pesos); **Saltillo** (8½hr., 11:30pm, 257 pesos); and **Tuxpan** (3½hr., 4 per day, 95 pesos). ADO (tel. 13 55 12) rolls to: **Matamoros** (7hr., 7 per day, 202 pesos); **Puebla** (10hr., 4 per day, 220 pesos); and **Xalapa** (9hr., 2 per day, 216 pesos). Futura and Frontera (tel. 13 42 55) keeps truckin' to: **Monterrey** (7½hr., 12 per day, 240 pesos); **Ciudad Mante** (2½hr., 5 per day, 63 pesos); **Guadalajara** (12hr., 4 per day, 383 pesos); and **Reynosa** (7½hr., 8 per day, 150 pesos). Estrella Blanca, Del Norte, Oriente, and Turistar (tel. 13 46 55) unite to travel to **Mexico City** (9 or 12hr., 8 per day, 226 pesos).

The **tourist office,** 20 de Noviembre 218 Nte. (tel. 12 26 68 or 12 00 07), one block west and two blocks north of Plaza de Armas, is very easy to miss but has the goods—maps 'n' guides to the city (open M-F 8am-7pm, Sa 9am-2pm). **Exchange currency** or traveler's checks at **Central de Divisa,** Juárez 215 Sur (tel. 12 90 00; open M-F 9am-6pm, Sa 9am-1:30pm). **Bancrecer** (tel. 12 20 32 or 14 26 21), on Díaz Mirón next door to Sixpack, also exchanges traveler's checks (open M-F 9am-5pm, Sa 10am-2pm) and has a 24hr. **ATM.** The **Sixpack,** Díaz Mirón 405 Ote. (tel. 12 24 15), three blocks east of the southeast corner of the Plaza de Armas, is a **supermarket** that sells more than just beer (open daily 8am-10pm).

English-speaking doctors can be found at the **Hospital General de Tampico,** Ejército Nacional 1403 (tel. 15 22 20 or 13 20 35), near the bus station. Medical and legal aid for tourists is available toll-free (tel. 91 or 01 800 90 392). **Emergency:** 060. **Police:** (tel. 12 10 32 or 12 11 57) on Tamaulipas at Sor Juana de la Cruz. **Red Cross:** (tel. 12 13 33 or 12 19 46), 24hr. ambulance service. **Farmacia el Fenix:** (tel. 12 43 51), at the corner of Díaz Mirón and Olmos (open daily 8am-11pm). **Post office:** Madero 309 Ote. (tel. 12 19 27), in the yellow building on Plaza de la Libertad (open M-F 8am-7pm, Sa 9am-1pm) also has a **Mexpost** office (tel. 12 34 81) inside. **Postal code:** 89000. **Internet access:** at the **video arcade** at Juárez 102 Nte. (tel. 12 44 43) for 20 pesos per hour (open M-Sa 9:30am-8:30pm, Su 10:30am-8pm). **LADATELs** that work well are clustered around the corners of the Plaza de Armas. **Phone code:** 12.

⌐⌐ ACCOMMODATIONS AND FOOD. Quality budget hotels are rare in Tampico, but for those willing to pay 100-300 pesos, many of the larger hotels on Madero and Díaz Mirón near the plazas provide excellent rooms. **Hotel Capri,** Juárez 202 Nte. (tel. 12 26 80), sits between Calles Altamira and Obregón. Clean, no-frills rooms with fans and some with TVs are pleasant, except for the noise from the street below. (Singles 100 pesos; doubles 120 pesos; each additional person 10 pesos.) For those willing to spend a bit more, the **Hotel Posada del Rey,** Madero 218 (tel. 14 10 24), two doors east of Hotel Plaza, offers a few more amenities. Rooms with a view on the Plaza de la Libertad have balconies for late night lounging. (Singles 260 pesos; doubles 280 pesos; each additonal person 20 pesos.)

Seafood is the standard fare in Tampico, with such specialties as *jaiba* (blue crab). If you're feeling adventurous, try eating at a seaside stand or at the covered food court near the river (a few blocks from Plaza de la Libertad). As you walk upstairs, you will be accosted by small "restaurant" (read: moving countertop) owners pushing their fresh food and fab prices. Have fun—but investigate the kitchen before chowing down. **Naturaleza,** Aduana 107 Nte. (tel. 12 85 56), one of Tampico's vegetarian restaurants, offers excellent options and wonderful conversation with the owner, Catalina Durán Raigoza, in Spanish, English, or French (open M-Sa noon-8:30pm). Locals don't mind the wait at **Restaurant Lucy** to savor traditional dishes. This tiny place, on Altamira a half block past López de Lara, is always packed for a reason. *Comida corrida* costs 12-15 pesos, and *antojitos* run 7-14 pesos. (Open daily 12:30-4pm and 6-11pm.) The local contingent of Tampico's up-and-coming yuppie community hang out at **VIP's** on Hidalgo at the northeast corner of the Plaza de la Libertad. The international fare ranges from 20 to 30 pesos, but it's the people-watching that makes this a very important "place" to be near the action of the *centro*.

■ ▣ **SIGHTS AND ENTERTAINMENT.** For a seaside getaway, **Playa Miramar** is accessible by either the "Playa" or "Escollera" bus (3.50 pesos from López de Lara and Madero). By bus, the beach is about 30 minutes away. You can also hop into any taxi that is beeping and shouting "playa" to share the shortened ride for 15 pesos. You can lie out on the sand or rent a palm-frond umbrella, chairs, and a table (30 pesos per day).

In the *centro*, join romantically minded young couples at **Boys and Girls,** 316 Olmos, as they make out and get their groove on. Be there Saturday at midnight for a moment of lively *norteño*. (Cover 20 pesos. Open W-Su 8pm-late.) If you really want to rock out, catch a taxi to **Byblos** (cover 30 pesos; open F-Su). A gay-friendly vibe welcomes you at **Obsession** and **Fiesta;** ask any taxi driver to take you there. Cab drivers also know the current "it" clubs—don't be timid about asking.

NUEVO LEÓN

MONTERREY

The words fast, frenetic, and fried (baking at an average summer temperature of 34°C) sum up this city of three million people and growing. Mexico's third-largest city and industrial leader has expanded aggressively at the foot of **Cerro de la Silla** (Saddle Mountain). Although Monterrey is decked out with the unfortunate raiment of "progress" (traffic, pollution, and a sobering belt of factories and dingy, impoverished huts), the *centro* is a pleasantly cosmopolitan surprise. Gorgeous parks, chic, smoke-filled cafes, sun-drenched plazas, and modern art are all here—and all right next door to each other. Backed by some of the country's wealthiest corporations and families, modern development has given Monterrey a look that is at times incongruous: across the street from the old yellow cathedral, a 30-story red monolith pays tribute to Monterrey's budding business sense as it shoots fluorescent blue laser beams into the semi-peaceful night. The city is an eclectic mix of European cobblestone streets, American capitalism, and Mexican spirit.

◾ ORIENTATION

As the largest city in northern Mexico, Monterrey serves as an important transportation hub. The bus and train stations are in the northern part of town, 3km north of the *centro*. All buses in and out of the city pass through Monterrey's huge **Central de Autobuses** at Colón and Villagrán. To reach the city center from the **bus station,** take any bus going south on Pino Suárez, the thoroughfare to the left as you exit the station (#18 lets you off at the central Gran Plaza), or walk two blocks east to the gray subway station at Cuauhtémoc and Colón, and take the **metro** (Line 2; 3 pesos) to Padre Mier or Zaragoza.

Downtown, **Av. Constitución** runs east-west along the Río Catarina, a 10km long dry river bed that has been converted into a series of athletic fields. From west to east, the most important streets running north-south across **Constitución** are **Gonzalitos, Pino Suárez, Cuauhtémoc, Av. Benito Juárez, Zaragoza, Zuazúa,** and **Dr. Coss.** From north to south, running east-west and parallel to Constitución are **Colón, Madero,** and farther south, **Washington, 5 de Mayo, 15 de Mayo, Matamoros, Padre Mier, Hidalgo,** and **Ocampo.** The upscale **Zona Rosa** is bounded by Padre Mier to the north, Zaragoza to the east, Ocampo to the south, and Juárez to the west, with Morelos at its center, open only to foot traffic. The historic **Barrio Antiguo** is centered between Zaragoza and Constitución, east of Dr. Coss.

⚡ PRACTICAL INFORMATION

TRANSPORTATION

Airport: Taxis charge 80-130 pesos for the 4km trip (20-30min.) to the center. **Tourism Universo,** 844 Matamoros (tel. 344 93 74), can help with reservations (open M-F 9:30am-7pm, Sa 9:30am-1pm). Some English spoken. **Aerómexico** (tel. 343 55 60) or **Mexicana** (tel. 340 55 11) require 2-3 day advance reservations, more for weekends.

Buses: Station at Colón and Villagrán. Ómnibus de México (tel. 374 07 16) departs for: **Aguascalientes** (8hr., 3 per day, 275 pesos); **Chihuahua** (12hr., 4 per day, 370 pesos); **Guadalajara** (12hr., 4 per day, 365 pesos); **Mexico City** (12hr., 3 per day, 370 pesos); **Querétaro** (8hr., 10:30pm, 326 pesos); **Zacatecas** (6hr., 3 per day, 198 pesos); and more. Sendor, Tamaulipas, and Noreste share offices (tel. 375 00 14). Noreste heads to **Nuevo Laredo** (3hr., 12 per day, 121 pesos) and **Matehuala** (4hr., every hr., 144 pesos). Frontera (tel. 375 09 87) rolls to **Saltillo** (1½hr., every hr., 40 pesos) and **León** (10 hr., 5 per day, 321 pesos). Similar service provided by Estrella Blanca (tel. 318 37 37), Líneas Americanas, and luxurious Futura and Turistar. **Luggage storage:** 2 pesos per hr. for up to 30 days; 24hr. lockers 22 pesos.

Local Transportation: Monterrey's amazing **subway** system has all but replaced the large and confusing bus system. Although buses are useful in providing transportation to points far from the *centro* and near the city's periphery, the subway system is new, clean, and efficient—only 7min. from the bus station to the Gran Plaza. Signs are clear and everywhere (subway runs daily 6:30am-midnight, 3 pesos). **Local buses** usually head in only one direction on any given street except for Constitución and Juárez (6am-midnight, 3 pesos). Popular routes include stops at the Gran Plaza (#18 or 42), points along Padre Mier and Hidalgo (#15), and along the perimeter of the downtown area (#69). To get from the budget hotel area to the city center, take the #1 Central or #17 Pío X bus, both of which run the lengths of Pino Suárez and Cuauhtémoc. For more detailed route information, ask locals or the English-speaking staff at the tourist office.

TOURIST AND FINANCIAL SERVICES

Tourist Office: Oficina de Turismo, Hidalgo 477 (tel. 345 08 70 or 345 09 02), just before Escobedo in the *Zona Rosa,* 1 block down from Morelos. Helpful staff, with abundant maps and bilingual brochures. Open Tu-Su 10am-5pm. There also are enlarged maps and miniature information booths at various points along Morelos.

Consulates: Canada, 1300 Zaragosa (tel. 344 32 00). Open M-F 9am-5:30pm. **U.K.,** Priv. Tamazunchale 104 (tel. 333 75 98). Open M-F 8am-5pm. **U.S.,** Constitución Pte. 411 (tel. 345 21 20), downtown. Open M-F 8am-1pm for passports and citizen's concerns, 9am-5pm for telephone information; 24hr. guard and emergency service.

Currency Exchange: Banks dot Madero near the budget hotels and flood the *Zona Rosa,* lining Padre Mier in particular, but many refuse to cash traveler's checks and most of those who do charge high service fees (10%). All have 24hr. **ATMs.** Most open M-F 9am-1:30pm. **Mexdollar Internacional,** 1136 Av. Pino Suárez (tel. 374 43 11), right by the bus station and Cuauhtémoc subway stop, offers 24hr. currency and traveler's check exchange at a great rate without service charges. They also exchange traveler's checks at a lower rate. **Eurodivisas** (tel. 340 16 83) in Plaza Mexico on Morelos and Padre Mier near Galeana exchanges traveler's checks at low rates but charges no commission. Open M-F 10:30am-8:30pm, Sa 10am-9pm, Su 11am-8pm.

American Express: San Pedro 215 Nte. (tel. 318 33 04). Catch bus #214 headed for "San Pedro" on Av. Pino Suárez at the stop just past Ocampo with benches and an awning. Get off at the stop before Calzada de Valle and cross the street. Open M-F 9am-6pm, Sa 9am-1pm.

LOCAL SERVICES

Supermarket: Gigante, on Colón across from the bus station, offers clothes, food items, *panadería,* and an adjoining **pharmacy.** Open daily 8am-10pm. **Mercado del Norte,** also known as La Pulga, is an endless maze of vendor stalls covering Reforma, the street just south of Colón; enter on Colón, 2 blocks east of the bus station. Open from morning to dusk.

Laundry: Laundry services available at most hotels for about 40 pesos per load.

EMERGENCY AND COMMUNICATIONS

Emergency: dial 060.

Police: (tel. 345 54 19), on the corner of Carranza and Espinosa or at the 24hr. stand on Morelos at Paraz in the *Zona Rosa*. For missing persons call **Locatel** (340 77 77). Little English spoken.

Medical Assistance: Red Cross, Alfonso Reyes 2503 Nte. (tel. 375 11 77 or 375 12 12), at Henry. Open 24hr. **Cruz Verde** (tel. 371 50 50 or 371 52 06), at Ciudad Madero and Ciudad Victoria. Open 24hr. English spoken.

Pharmacy: In the bus station or **Benavides,** Pino Suárez at 15 de Mayo or on Morelos past Zaragoza. Open 24hr.

Post Office: (tel. 342 40 03) on Zaragoza at Washington, inside the Palacio Federal. Open M-F 8am-7pm, Sa 9am-1pm. Another option is the 2nd fl. of the bus station near Sala 3. Open M-F 9am-4pm, Sa 9am-1pm. **Postal Code:** 64000.

Fax: In the bus station next to the post office. Open M-F 7am-11pm, Sa-Su 9am-4pm.

Internet Access: Cybercafé El Alebrije, Padre Mier 827 (tel. 333 88 43), inside La Tumba Cafe/Bar in the *Barrio Antiguo* (25 pesos per hr.). Open M-Sa noon-9pm.

Telephones: LADATELs in the *Zona Rosa* and in every metro stop.

Phone Code: 8.

▛ ACCOMMODATIONS

Hotels conveniently located near the *Zona Rosa* tend to be four-star or five-star hotels, and even the three-star ones inflate their rates to exploit tourists. Budget accommodations are sprinkled throughout the underdeveloped area near the bus stations. Many rooms are full by early afternoon. If you feel like splurging 400 to 500 pesos, a hotel downtown will give you what you pay for. Take precautions when walking in this area at night.

Hotel Mundo, Reforma 736 (tel. 374 68 50), just off Amado Nervo. Slightly more luxurious than other hotels near the bus station: the A/C works well, the TVs are newer, the floors shine a bit more brightly. 1-2 people 170 pesos, with A/C 200 pesos; 3-4 people 225 pesos, with A/C 250 pesos.

Hotel Posada, Amado Nervo 1138 (tel. 372 39 08), across from the bus station. Cross the overhead walkway on Colón and expect wonderfully quiet rooms and a staff willing to do its best to combat the endless stream of bugs. 1-2 people 145 pesos, with A/C 170 pesos; 3-4 people 170 pesos, with A/C 200 pesos.

▛ FOOD

Barbecued meats, especially *cabrito* (goat kid), are a specialty of northern Mexico; other popular dishes include *agujas* (collar bone), *frijoles a la charra* (beans cooked with pork skin, coriander, tomato, peppers, and onions), *machacado con huevos* (scrambled eggs mixed with dried, shredded beef), hot *tamales,* and for dessert, *piloncillo con nuez* (hardened brown sugar candy with pecans) or heavenly *glorias* (candy balls of goat's milk and nuts). Although the *Zona Rosa* is home to some of Monterrey's most expensive shopping (and some of northern Mexico's most expensive hotels), for food, it can't be beat. Catering mainly to businesspeople on their lunch breaks or avid shoppers, the service is good, the food *sabroso,* and the prices more than reasonable. *Buen Provecho.*

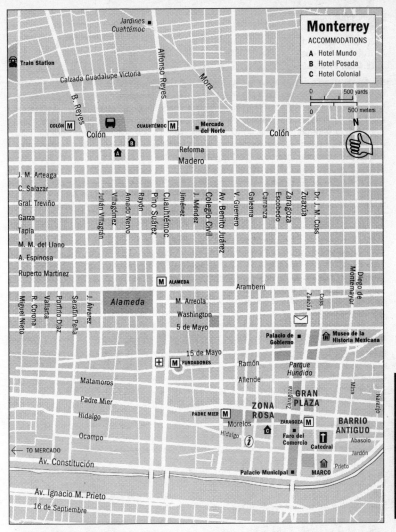

Restaurante El Cabrito, Padre Mier 276 Pte. (tel. 345 12 28), offers an elegant, delicious meal right in the heart of the *Zona Rosa*. Although you'll pay a bit more (entrees 70-90 pesos), it's well worth the expense. Try the *cabrito;* it's the house specialty.

Casa de Maíz, Abasolo 870B (tel. 40 43 32), in the *Barrio Antiguo*. Each table is a masterpiece painted by local artists; their work also covers the walls at this health food restaurant. Savor traditional Mexican dishes made with whole wheat flour, or try vegetarian versions such as tofu in red sauce (22 pesos). Open Tu-Th 1-10:30pm, F 1-11:30pm, Sa 2-11:30pm, Su 1-7:30pm.

Cafe Paraíso, on Morelos and Mina. A great place to take a break from sightseeing and relax in the heart of the *Barrio Antiguo*. Its huge 15-peso frappuccinos will reaffirm your caffeine addiction. This hip little spot also serves tasty French cuisine for 20-35 pesos. Open daily 9am-midnight.

👁 SIGHTS

Monterrey's architects were kind to tourists. They jam-packed virtually all of Monterrey's sights, art, and historical relics (both new and old) into the 40-acre **Gran Plaza** and in the *Barrio Antiguo* across the street.

EL GRAN PLAZA. Bounded by Washington on the north, Constitución on the south, Zaragoza on the west, and Dr. Coss on the east, the Grand Plaza is host to a slew of government buildings. Also known as the Macroplaza, it includes the **Palacio Federal,** the **Palacio del Gobierno** at the north end of the plaza, and the **Palacio Municipal** at the southern end. Just east of the Palacio Federal lies the **Plaza 400 Años** with a man-made river on the lower level with paddle boats for rent. If the sun is too much for you, try dozing in the cool garden paradise of the **Parque Hundido** (Sunken Park), just south of the Palacio del Gobierno. One of Mexico's most notorious centers of public affection, the *parque* looks like Noah's Ark, with groups of two napping, nuzzling, and often just plain necking all over the place. Farther along the Gran Plaza lies the **Fuente de La Vida** (Fountain of Life) which douses an immense statue of Neptune surrounded by cavorting nymphs and naiads. The most striking construction, however, is the bright orange **Faro del Comercio** (Commerce Lighthouse) topped with a laser beacon that circles the skies at night. The lighthouse serves a purely symbolic purpose; it is a testament to the economic ambitions of Monterrey's leaders. The laser doesn't begin to pulse until after 10pm, when hundreds pack the adjoining *Barrio Antiguo* in search of some late-night fun. Just across Zuazúa from the Faro de Comercio is the resplendent, pale yellow **Catedral de Monterrey.** If you tire of planting yourself in front of *palacios* or watching couples go at it in the parks, though, a shot of culture in one of its museums is never far away.

MUSEO DE HISTORIA MEXICANA. The *museo* offers a permanent collection that has something for everyone, including state-of-the-art audio/visual resources, intriguing artifacts, and informative exhibitions, as well as evening movies and many daytime shows. *(Dr. Coss 445 Sur at the far end of the Plaza 400 Años. Tel. 345 98 98. Open Tu-Th 11am-7pm, F-Su 11am-8pm. Admission 20 pesos, students with ID 10 pesos. Tu free, Sa 5 pesos, Su 1 peso. Shows often free.)*

MUSEO DE ARTE CONTEMPORÁNEO (MARCO). To cool off and relax while you view, slip into the MARCO. Avoid the pedantic placards in the museum and focus on some of the best exhibits of Mexico's truly great and innovative modern artists, or just recline by the enormous decorative pool in the center of the museum and watch for the periodic water shows. *(Tel. 342 48 20. At the southern end of Dr. Coss across from the Palacio Municipal. Open Tu and Th-Sa 11am-7pm, W and Su 11am-9pm. Admission 20 pesos, students with ID 10 pesos, W free.)*

STRANGE BREW What do Mexican *beisból*, gardens, Monterrey's leading producer of beer, and modern art have to do with each other? If you said "nothing," you are 100% incorrect, as proven by **El Cuauhtémoc,** 1½ blocks south of the General Anaya subway stop on Line 2. Featuring gardens, a **Hall of Fame** (tel. 528 57 96) that commemorates Mexican baseball legends, and the **Museo Deportivo,** (a shrine to rodeos, boxing, and soccer), the complex also houses a beer museum foaming over with beer-related artifacts (don't miss the mugs). Perhaps the most interesting part is the **Museo de Monterrey** (tel. 328 60 60), covered wall to wall with the best in modern Mexican art. The museum cafe serves (what else?) Carta Blanca beer along with many others. This is your chance to sample 30 different kinds of beer and then proceed to observe and analyze modern art. (Open Tu-Su 11am-8pm.) Every spring, Banamex, a large national bank, funds a competition including painting and sculpture. Each year thousands of top-notch artists compete for the honor of having their work judged by a bank and displayed in an old beer factory. Go figure.

OBISPADO. The former palace of the bishop of Monterrey is now a state museum displaying artifacts from the colonial era. The museum itself may not be worth the half-hour bus ride from the *centro*, but the view and cool breeze are nice. Bring a picnic and enjoy a break from the city on the wandering terraces. *(Tel. 346 04 04. Take bus #1 from Dr. Coss along the Macroplaza, ask the driver to point out the stop, and hike up to the very top of the hill. Open Tu-Sa 10am-6pm, Su 10am-5pm. Admission 10 pesos.)*

GRUTAS DE GARCÍA. Also worth a visit are the Caves of García, 45km northwest of the city and accessible by car or bus. The *grutas* are a network of natural chambers; the dozens of sedimentary layers in their walls reveal that 50 or 60 million years ago, the caves lay on the ocean floor. The easiest way to get to the *grutas* is on a three-hour **Grayline** tour (tel. 345 49 56 for reservations; 120 pesos, children 100 pesos) leaving from the Hotel Monterrey at 3pm on Thursdays, Saturdays, and Sundays. A cheaper alternative is to take an **Estrella Blanca** bus from the central bus station (every 20min., 16 pesos). Once there, take the cable car railway to avoid the steep 700m uphill climb. *(Open daily 9am-5pm. Admission, including cable car, 30 pesos, children 18 pesos.)*

🎵 ENTERTAINMENT

The **Barrio Antiguo** is a beautiful and quiet place to wander away from the mobs in the **Zona Rosa** during the day, but if you want to party, head there at night for a totally different scene. After sundown, police cordon off the area to cars, and although the action doesn't get started until 10:30pm or so (9:30pm on weekends), many places have no cover if you come early enough. For a calmer night out, try calling the **Teatro Municipal** (tel. 43 89 74), or stop by the immense theater on the **Gran Plaza** to see what is playing. Show types, times, and prices vary greatly, but there is always an early afternoon kids' show on Sundays.

El Infinito, Raymundo Jardón 904 Ote. (tel. 340 36 34). For something a bit mellow and beat, try this cafe-cum-used-bookstore-cum-art-house movie theater promising radical politics and challenging conversation. Although no alcohol is served, if you donate a book, you get a free cup of coffee. Th and Sa, art-house international films are shown. Open daily 5pm-midnight.

Real de Catorce, Padre Mier 1062, is a club featuring live music—everything from hard rock to sweet ballads. Things get a little louder in this small, neat, and classy space with 7-8 peso drinks. Cover 20-25 pesos after 10pm. Open daily 9:30pm-3am.

Hemispherio, on Padre Mier, cranks it a couple decibels higher, as it thumps with live rock, pop, and *manacos*. Beer 15 pesos. Cover 30 pesos. Open Th-Sa 9pm-3am.

El Reloj, also on Padre Mier, will get your engines a-pumpin' and hearts a-thumpin'. With a young (read: teen to 30-year-old) contingent, Reloj always has long lines and loud U.S. and Spanish rock reverberating. People-watching outside may be even better than groovin' inside—your call. Cover 30 pesos. Open daily 9pm-late.

🏳️ GAY AND LESBIAN NIGHTLIFE

After its first-ever Pride March in the summer of 1997, Monterrey is quickly becoming one of the most gay- and lesbian-friendly cities in Mexico. Young same-sex couples walk the streets of the *Zona Rosa* and the *Barrio Antiguo* day and night, and gay clubs are sprouting up and overflowing daily. Although most nightspots cater primarily to men, women are more than welcome.

Club Vongole, Blvd. Pedreras 300, east of *Barrio Antiguo*, is the most hip-hop, be-bop, and happening gay and lesbian night spot in town, with over 1000 people W, F, and Sa.

Charao's, at the corner of Garza and Zaragoza, closer to the *centro*. Open every night to an exciting, young crowd. Cover 35 pesos. Ask for a copy of the free gay and lesbian monthly magazine *New Concept Gay* at any of these bars for more listings.

COAHUILA

SALTILLO

Only 1½ hours from Monterrey, Saltillo is a treat for the tired traveler. Once past the enormous dusty expansion that houses most of the 850,000 inhabitants as well as the industrial, mostly foreign car companies, the *centro* is surprisingly clean, relaxed, and easily walkable. Early to bed and early to rise, *saltillenses* are proud of their dry climate and pretty spot in the Sierra Madres. Although the limited sights and nightlife do not draw many tourists, excellent budget lodgings, good food, and cool afternoon breezes await those who do come. Saltillo was once known throughout Mexico for its wool *sarapes*, so much so that their *sarape* style was known as a "saltillo." These intricate *sarapes* are worth the 300 to 1500 pesos spent (the wool ones are of much higher quality).

■ **ORIENTATION.** Saltillo, located in a valley between the jagged Sierra Madre mountains, lies 87km southwest of Monterrey, along desolate **Rte. 40.** The **bus station** is about 3km southwest of the city center on **Blvd. Echeverría Sur.** To get to the *centro*, exit the terminal, cross the pedestrian overpass, and catch minibus #10 from the small street perpendicular to Echeverría, across the street from the Restaurant Jaslo. All local buses cost 3 pesos and run daily 6:30am to 11pm. Catch a return bus (#9) at the corner of **Aldama** and **Hidalgo**, a block down the street from the cathedral, in front of the entrance to the furniture store. The *centro's* streets form a slightly distorted grid not quite aligned with the four cardinal directions. The quiet **Plaza de Armas** is home to the cathedral and is bordered by **Juárez** to the south (or right, facing the cathedral) and **Hidalgo** to the east (between the plaza and cathedral). Walk one block to the west, past the **Palacio de Gobierno**, and one block north (or left, facing the cathedral) to arrive at **Plaza Acuña**, bordered on its west (far side) by the narrow **Padre Flores**, on the east by **Allende**, on the south by **Victoria**, and on the north by **Aldama.**

■ **PRACTICAL INFORMATION.** The **Central de Autobuses**, at Echeverría Sur and Garza, is accessible by minibus #9. Frontera runs buses to: **Matamoros** (5hr., 10am, 185 pesos) and **Monterrey** (every 30min., 40 pesos). Òmnibus de México (tel. 17 03 15) serves **Aguascalientes** (7hr., 7 per day, 219 pesos) and **Reynosa** (5hr., every hr. noon-9pm, 140 pesos). Transportes del Norte (tel. 17 09 02) runs to: **Guadalajara** (10hr., 5 per day, 325 pesos); **Mexico City** (10hr., 5 per day 6am-9pm, 391 pesos); **San Luis Potosí** (5hr., 7 per day 6am-11pm, 180 pesos); and **Zacatecas** (5hr., 6 per day, 164 pesos).

Wonderful maps of the city stand outside the bus station and dot the *centro*. They should be enough to orient you, but if you want your own map, go to the **tourist office** (tel. 12 51 22), at the corner of Acuña and Coss. Little English is spoken. (Open M-F 9am-5pm). **Banamex**, at Allende and Ocampo, behind the Palacio de Gobierno, has a 24hr. **ATM. Police:** (tel. 14 45 50) at Treviño and Echeverría Ote. **Post office:** at Victoria 453 after Urdiñola (tel. 14 90 97; open M-F 9am-4pm, Sa 9am-1pm). **MexPost:** (tel. 14 18 90) in one corner (open M-F 9am-4pm, Sa 9am-2pm). **Postal code:** 25000. **Phone code:** 84.

■ **ACCOMMODATIONS.** Blvd. Luis Echeverría, which runs along the bus station, teems with cheap places to rest your head, and the *centro* is full of lower-to-medium range, clean, comfortable spots. There are also a few higher-end hotels with accompanying quality. ■ **Hotel Urdiñola**, Victoria 207 (tel. 14 09 40), behind the Palacio del Gobierno, is very swank, with an exquisite marble staircase, beautiful stained-glass windows, and a charming courtyard. This elegant retreat is also equipped with *agua purificada*, cable TVs, and phones; unfortunately, such grandeur is reflected in the prices. (Singles 236 pesos; doubles 260 pesos.) At the modern **Hotel Saade,** Aldama Pte. 397 (tel. 12 91 20 or 12 91 21), a block west of Plaza Acuña, earth tones dominate the clean, well-furnished, and quiet rooms in the heart of it all. The rooftop restaurant offers a stunning panorama of the city and the Sierra, and a semi-useful tourist office awaits you in the lobby. Rooms come in three styles, from *económico* with bed and bath, to *ejecutivo* with bed, bath, TV, and phone. (Reception M-F 9:30am-1:30pm and 3:30-7pm. Single *económico* 190 pesos, standard 220 pesos, *ejecutivo* 240 pesos.)

◘ **FOOD.** Be sure to sample delicious *pan de pulque* (bread made with tequila-like fermented cactus juice), a Saltillo specialty. For more upscale dining and more adventuresome dishes, head to the cheerful ▩ **Restaurant Principal,** Allende Nte. 702 (tel. 14 33 84), seven blocks north of the Palacio de Gobierno. Their *cabecito* (28 pesos) will leave you with that invigorating after-the-hunt feel, as will a splurge on grilled ram (69 pesos). (Open daily 8am-midnight.) Restaurants on Allende and Carranza cater more to tourists, while the cafes on smaller streets remain local picks. **Café and Restaurant Arcasa,** Victoria 263 (tel. 12 64 24), is a family-run cafe that draws locals in with delicious food and fast breakfasts (19-29 pesos), and 3-course *menú del días* (30 pesos). (Open daily 7:30am-midnight.)

▣▩ **SIGHTS AND FESTIVALS.** Weary travelers rest assured: Saltillo does not lend itself to much sightseeing. Saltillo's streets burst with artistry and cultural pride (the town even host a series of rodeos and bullfights) during **Feria de Saltillo** from late July to early August. Otherwise, the most alluring site in town is probably the **Museo de las Aves** (tel. 14 01 68), on Hidalgo three blocks south (up) from the cathedral and one block past Escobedo. The *museo* is home to a multitude of bird species. If you're determined to find more, call **Salvador Medina** (tel. 17 42 55), who, for US$10 per hour, will take you around, tell you in English or Spanish the history of Saltillo, and if you're lucky, let you up into the cathedral's bell tower.

    Plaza Acuña, two blocks northwest of the Plaza de Armas, is a good place to people-watch. Vendors spill out of the **Mercado Juárez** in the northwest corner of the plaza, the place to look for reasonably priced *serapes*, or drop in to the **Serape Factory** on Hidalgo just before the Museo de las Aves. Perched on a hill overlooking the city, **Plaza México** (or **El Mirador**) offers a smashing view of the whole area and the unconquerable mountains beyond. Follow Miguel Hidalgo uphill, take your first left after the Museo de las Aves, and continue for another four blocks, turning onto the winding Gustavo Espinoza and heading up to the small plaza with benches and old street lamps.

ZACATECAS

ZACATECAS

At approximately 2400m above sea level, Zacatecas (pop. 118,000) is the second-highest city in Mexico after Toluca. The lifeblood of Zacatecas once flowed through rich veins of silver, and shopowners still cater to that legacy. A silver trinket, given to early Spanish colonists by an indigenous Cascane in the mid-1500s, triggered the mining frenzy that eventually stripped the surrounding hills of 6000 tons of silver. As far as mining towns go, Zacatecas was unusually fortunate: the arts flourished under the patronage of affluent silver barons, and the rows of grand colonial mansions downtown testify to an era of lavish consumption. As a result of silver money, Zacatecas is home to beautiful parks, elaborate cathedrals, cobblestone streets, and some of the most nationally renowned museums in all of Mexico. When the mines ran dry, Zacatecas distinguished itself as a busy university town and a center of commerce and tourism. The town's colonial beauty continues to attract a large number of tourists. They also enjoy plenty of Corona beer, home brewed in the state of Zacatecas.

☀ ORIENTATION

Zacatecas is 347km north of Guadalajara, 135km south of Aguascalientes, and 832km south of Chihuahua. All buses arrive and depart from the **central bus terminal** on the outskirts of town. City buses (2 pesos; Ruta 8 to the *centro*) and taxis (20 pesos to the *centro*) wait outside. After dark, a taxi is the only option.

Zacatecas has no identifiable city center. Activity revolves around two streets, **Juárez** and **Hidalgo** (called **González Ortega** southwest of Juárez). Use the Juárez-Hidalgo intersection, which falls one block northwest of **Jardín Independencia,** as your point of orientation. Shops, restaurants, and clubs also cluster on Hidalgo, as well as many of the city's colonial monuments. The temperature in Zacatecas dips during the evening (even in summer), so consider packing a sweater.

⊞ PRACTICAL INFORMATION

TRANSPORTATION

Airport: (tel. 498 03 38), accessible by *combis* (tel. 2 59 46) departing from the Mexicana office (20min., leave 1¼hr. before flight, 30 pesos). **Mexicana,** Hidalgo 406 (tel. 2 32 48). Open M-F 9am-7pm. **Taesa,** Hidalgo 306 (tel. 2 00 50 or 2 02 12). Open M-F 9am-7pm, Sa 10am-6pm.

Buses: Central de Autobuses (tel. 2 11 12), Lomas de la Isabélica, at Tránsito Pesado. From the *centro*, take the Ruta 7 or 8 bus on González Ortega (1 block from Juárez). Rojos de los Altos (tel. 2 06 84) travels to **Aguascalientes** (3hr., every 30min. 6am-8:30pm, 48 pesos). Estrella Blanca (tel. 2 06 84) buses to **Mexico City** (8hr., 4 per day 3:20am-10:05pm, 295 pesos) and **Torreon** (6hr., about every hr. 6am-8:30pm, 154 pesos). Ómnibus de México (tel. 2 54 95) drives to: **San Juan** (4hr., 1:50am and noon, 89 pesos); **Reynosa** (9hr., 8:15 and 10:30pm, 332 pesos); **León** (4hr., 10:30am, 107 pesos); **Durango** (6hr., 11 per day, 127 pesos); **Guadalajara** (5hr., 16 per day, 167 pesos); **Matamoros** (11hr., 6 per day 4:30am-1am, 339 pesos); and **Mexico City** (8hr., 11 per day 1am-10:50pm, 295 pesos). Transportes Chihuahuenses (tel. 2 00 42) calls on: **Chihuahua** (12hr., about every 45min., 383 pesos); **Irapuato** (4hr., 5 per day 1:15pm-12:30am, 143 pesos); and **Puerto Vallarta** (12hr., 1am, and 5pm, 342 pesos). Futura (Fresnillo 22N) sends buses to **Fresnillo** (45min., 10 per day, 22 pesos). Transportes del Norte (tel. 2 00 42) sends buses to: **Monterrey** (6hr., 5 per day 11:30am-5pm, 198 pesos); **Nuevo Laredo** (11hr., 7:30, 9:30, and 10pm, 341 pesos); and **Piedras Negras** (11hr.; 4:30am, 7:45, and 9:15pm; 331 pesos).

Car Rental: Budget, Mateos 104 (tel. 2 94 58). 410 pesos per day including insurance, taxes, and 200km daily. Must be age 25 with valid credit card and driver's license. Open M-F 9am-2pm and 4-8pm, Sa 9am-2pm.

TOURIST AND FINANCIAL SERVICES

Tourist Office: Hidalgo 403, on the 2nd fl. Helpful staff distributes useful maps and brochures. Little English spoken. Open daily 8am-8pm. *TIPS,* a Spanish-language weekly, listing cultural events and tourist services, is available during high season at hotels and newsstands.

Guided Tours: Servicios Turisticos El Vergel, Julian Adame 305 (tel. 4 18 07; email elvergel@logicnet.com.mx), offers tours of local attractions.

Currency Exchange: Banca Promex, González Ortega 122 (tel. 2 22 40), has good rates and a 24hr. **ATM.** Open M-F 8:30am-5:30pm, Sa 10am-2pm. The first blocks of González Ortega and Hidalgo away from Juárez are inundated with banking options.

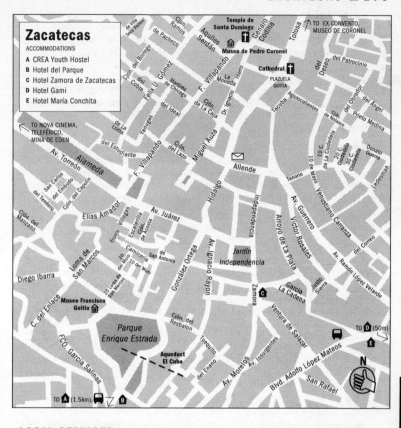

Zacatecas

ACCOMMODATIONS

A CREA Youth Hostel
B Hotel del Parque
C Hotel Zamora de Zacatecas
D Hotel Gami
E Hotel María Conchita

LOCAL SERVICES

Luggage Storage: Located at the bus station. 1.50 pesos per hr. Open 24hr.

Laundry: Lavandería del Indio Triste, Juan de Tolosa 826, an extension of Hidalgo, about 3 blocks past the cathedral. 8 pesos per kg. Same-day service if dropped off before 5pm. Open M-Sa 9am-9pm.

EMERGENCY AND COMMUNICATIONS

Emergency: dial 060.

Police: Héroes de Chapultepec 1000 (tel. 2 05 07 or 2 43 79). No English spoken.

Red Cross: Calzada de la Cruz Roja 100 (tel. 2 30 05 or 2 33 23), off Héroes de Chapultepec, near the exit to Fresnillo. English spoken. Open 24hr.

Pharmacy: Farmacia La Perla de Zacatecas, Hidalgo 131. Open daily 9am-11pm. **Farmacia Isstezac,** Callejón de las Campañas 103 (tel. 4 37 25, ext. 19), on the right side of the cathedral. Open 24hr.

Hospital: Hospital General, García Salinas 707 (tel. 3 30 04, 3 30 05, or 3 30 06). Open 24hr. **Dr. José Cruz de la Torre González** (tel. 4 07 03) speaks English.

Post Office: Allende 111 (tel. 2 01 96), off Hidalgo. Open M-F 8am-7pm, Sa 9am-1pm. **Postal Code:** 98000.

Fax: Telecomm (tel. 2 00 60; fax 2 17 96), on Hidalgo at Juárez sends telegrams too. Open M-F 8am-7:30pm, Sa-Su 9am-noon.

Internet Access: Public library, at the end of Av. Juárez across from Jardín Independencia, provides free service (30min. limit if someone's waiting). Open daily 9am-9pm.

Phone Code: 492.

ACCOMMODATIONS

Budget hotels aren't in abundance in downtown Zacatecas, but they can be found. One price you pay for the convenient downtown location is frequent traffic noise.

Hotel Zamora de Zacatecas, Plazuela de Zamora 303 (tel. 2 12 00), near the Jardín Independencia opposite Juárez. Zamora boasts a central location and unbeatable prices for the area. Clean rooms painted in unbelievably bright colors. Singles 50 pesos; doubles 60 pesos.

Hotel María Conchita, Av. López Mateos 401 (tel. 2 14 94 or 2 14 96), 3 blocks south of the Jardín Independencia. Distinctive architecture with private bathrooms. Rooms have tiny TVs and phones. Singles 80 pesos; doubles 95 pesos; triples 120 pesos; quads 140 pesos. New 4th and 5th fl. rooms for an additional 60 pesos.

Hotel del Parque, González Ortega 302 (tel. 2 04 79), near the aqueduct. Appropriately named, as the Parque Enrique Estrada is practically the hotel's backyard. The clean rooms are sort of dark, although the TVs brighten things up. Singles 85 pesos; doubles 95 pesos; triples 125 pesos; quads 145 pesos.

CREA Hostel (tel. 2 02 23, ext. 7), in the Parque La Encantada, southwest of the city. Take the Ruta 8 bus on González Ortega (2 pesos) from Jardín Independencia or the bus station, and get off after about 10min. at the sign for La Encantada. Walk down Calle 5 Señores for about 15min., turn left on Calle Ancha, and walk up the hill until you see the grounds of the youth camp. Veer right around the red building; the white hostel is behind the pool to the left. Well removed from the center of city life, although relatively near the bus station, it's not the best option unless you absolutely must have the cheapest room in town. Small, sterile quads and single-sex floors with clean communal bathrooms. Breakfast or dinner 18 pesos; lunch 28 pesos. 35 pesos per person.

FOOD

Zacatecas has some good eats that won't break the bank. Fantastic restaurants are tucked in between shops along **Hidalgo** near the cathedral. Get that sugar rush with a chunk of *dulce con leche*, *camote* (a fruit), *coco* (coconut), or *batata* (sweet potato) peddled by vendors throughout the *centro* (2 pesos).

El Pueblito, Av. Hidalgo 403 (tel. 4 38 18), near Gorditas Doña Julia. Specializing in Zacatecan food in an old renovated *hacienda,* Try the *Reliquia Zacatecana* (39 pesos). A classy place, but a bit pricey. Open daily 1-11pm.

Restaurant Parrilla La Villa Real, C. Tacuba 6 (tel. 2 14 37), under La Terraza. All of your grill favorites; steaks starting at 40 pesos. Live Latin American music Th-Sa begins at 10pm. Open daily noon-3am.

Gorditas Doña Julia, Av. Hidalgo 409 (tel. 3 79 55), 1 block from the cathedral. Locals devour delicious *gorditas* (4.50 pesos) of all kinds. If you can't find a table at the restaurant, ask for your *gorditas para llevar* (to go). Open daily 8am-9pm.

Mesón La Mina, Av. Juárez 15 (tel. 2 27 73), just off the Jardín Independencia. This spacious local favorite serves up solid Mexican fare. *Enchiladas verdes* 30 pesos; *comida corrida* 35 pesos. Full breakfast menu. Open daily 8am-11pm.

La Terraza (tel. 2 32 70), in the shopping mall next to the cathedral. A lovely outdoor cafe where you can order traditional fare such as coffee, ice cream, and fountain drinks, or grab a beer (10 pesos) and a burger (12 pesos). Watch the shadows get long and creep up the walls of the cathedral. Open daily 11am-9:30pm.

👁 SIGHTS

There are enough churches, museums, and lookout points in Zacatecas to make travelers want to keep busy despite any sore feet. Fortunately they are found in a couple of clusters, cutting back on the otherwise ample walking time.

CATHEDRAL. The 18th-century cathedral, four blocks northeast of Juárez, on Hidalgo, has an intricately sculpted facade representing the Eucharist. Zacatecans proudly claim it as the most beautiful cathedral in all of the Americas. Apostles, doctors, and angels jostle for space above the cathedral's main entrance. The northern facade bears a representation of Christ on the cross, and the European Baroque southern facade pays homage to Nuestra Señora de las Zacatecas. The interior of the cathedral, in contrast to its lavish exterior, is surprisingly plain. *(Open daily 7am-1pm and 3-9pm.)* Next to the cathedral, the **Palacio de Gobierno** distinguishes itself with the mural that surrounds its interior stairwell. Painted in 1970 by Antonio Pintor Rodríguez, the work traces the history of Zacatecas from the pre-Hispanic era until the present. *(Open M-F 9am-8pm.)*

MUSEO DE PEDRO CORONEL. Next door to the cathedral is a building whose past incarnations include a monastery and a jail. Housing the tomb, sculptures, and paintings of the Zacatecan artist Pedro Coronel, the museum has one of the best modern art collections in Latin America, and is the pride of Zacatecas. The museum includes works by such varied artists as Picasso, Braque, Chagall, Miró, Goya, and William Hogarth; as well as African and Far East pieces. *(Tel. 2 80 21. Open F-W 9:30am-5pm. Admission 15 pesos, students and seniors 5 pesos, under 10 free.)*

TEMPLO DE SANTO DOMINGO. Built by the Jesuits in 1746. The Temple contains nine impressive Baroque gilded wood altars and a rare 18th-century German pipe organ. *(Across Hidalgo and up the steep Callejón de Veyna. Open daily 7am-1pm and 5-8pm.)*

MUSEO RAFAEL CORONEL. Housed in the dramatic **Ex-Convento de San Francisco,** an attraction in itself, the museum showcases an impressive collection of masks, figurines, pottery, and puppets. *(To reach the museum from the cathedral, follow Hidalgo, bearing left at the first fork, at the fountain, and right at the second. Museum and ex-convent open Tu-Th 10am-5pm. Admission 15 pesos; students and seniors 7.50 pesos, under 10 free).*

MINA DE EDÉN. One of the region's most productive silver mines until about 30 years ago, the mine closed when continual flooding made mineral extraction futile. Today, tour groups cross rope bridges and learn about the haunting myths of the mine. The mine can be entered from either the top or the side and the top entrance is 100m to the right as you leave the *teleférico.* From there, walk into the mountain, take the elevator down, and begin the tour. Otherwise, follow Juárez northwest along the Alameda, a tree-and-fountain-filled park lined by some of Zacatecas's grandest colonial mansions. Continue along Torreón until it ends, and then turn right and walk one block, veering to the left. From there, a mini-locomotive whisks tourists into the mountain to start a one-hour guided tour (in Spanish) of the cool subterranean tunnels. *(Tel. 2 30 02. Open daily 10:30am-6:30pm. Admission 15 pesos.)*

ON CERRO DE LA BUFA. Named for its resemblance to a Spanish wineskin, the *cerro* peers down on Zacatecas from the city's highest crag. La Bufa is lit by floodlights at night and is a favorite lookout point for the spectacular view it offers of Zacatecas and the surrounding area. The **Museo de la Toma de Zacatecas** is adjacent to the Cerro. Erected to commemorate Pancho Villa's decisive victory over federal troops in the summer of 1914, the museum displays an array of revolutionary memorabilia, including photographs, displays, cannon, and small arms. *(Tel. 2 80 66. Open Tu-Su 10am-4:30pm. Admission 10 pesos; students and seniors 5 pesos; under 12 free.)* On one side of the museum lies the 18th-century **Capilla del Patrocinio,** whose graceful facade and cloistered courtyards are carved from deep-red stone. Nearby shops sell arts, crafts, and loads of geodes. A short, but steep walk up the hill leads to the Moorish **Mausoleo de los Hombres Ilustres de Zacatecas** (Tomb of the Famous Men of Zacatecas), worth the hike if only for the view of the city. There's an even better vista from the **Meteorological Observatory** behind the museum.

Getting There: Public buses run to La Bufa (daily 8am-7pm) only on Sundays and holidays (take Ruta 9 from the Plaza de Armas). The most appealing way to make the trip if you aren't claustrophobic or afraid of heights is by *teleférico* (suspended cable car), which runs between the peak of El Grillo and La Bufa every 10 minutes. (tel. 2 01 70; runs daily 10am-6pm; 10 pesos each way). Follow García Rojas northwest up a steep incline to its end to reach the cable car stop, or take the lengthy and convoluted Ruta 7 bus from González Ortega. The **Teleférico** doesn't run in rain or high winds.

OTHER SIGHTS. Southeast of the downtown area, 39 pink stone arches mark the end of Zacatecas's famous colonial aqueduct, **El Cubo.** Beside the aqueduct, the verdant **Parque Enrique Estrada** has a little bit of everything, with beautiful flowers and green grass alongside barbed wire, numerous dead tree trunks, and a dry cement stream bed. The park borders the former governor's mansion, now the **Museo de Francisco Goitia,** Enrique Estrada 101. The museum displays regional historical artifacts and gives a good account of the history of Mexico. *(Tel. 2 02 11. Open Tu-Su 9:30am-3pm. Admission 10 pesos, seniors and under 13 free.)*

🎵 ENTERTAINMENT

Zacatecas has two completely cool nightlife hot-spots. The first is **El Malacate** (tel. 2 30 02), located 600m in from the side entrance of the Mina de Edén (see above for directions). You've never really experienced a bass beat until you hear it reverberating off the solid stone walls of this former mine shaft. Buy your tickets at the entrance to the mine shaft, take the train the dance floor, and sit back and enjoy the mellow, slow music (not the club in which to practice your head-banging or moshing) and drinks served by waiters in hard hats. (Cover 50 pesos. Beer 20 pesos; mixed drinks 30 pesos. Open Th-Su 9pm-3am.)

The newest and most popular club in town is **Casa de Sueños** Av. Hidalgo 716, a block past the cathedral on the right—keep your eyes out for people socializing on the street because there's no sign. Everyone who's anyone in Zacatecas can be found dancing to the latest Mexican and American dance beats in the two-story converted mansion. (Cover 20 pesos, 80 pesos when open bar. Open Th-Sa 9pm-3am.) Escape the pressure to dance at **Cactus,** Hidalgo 111 (tel. 2 05 09), at the Juárez intersection. The well-decorated interior is suitable for lounging with a beer (12 pesos), dancing on the faux-cathedral dance floor, or going upstairs to shoot some pool. Happy Hour, with 2-for-1 drinks, lasts from 8 to 10pm. (Cover F-Sa 30 pesos. Open M-Sa 9pm-3am.) As always, be cautious walking alone at night; streets are fairly well lit, but practically deserted.

If you're feeling a bit more mellow, the **Nova Cinema,** Constituyentes 300 (tel. 2 54 04), reels through the latest in Mexican and American films. On Thursdays at 6pm and Saturdays at 7pm, take advantage of the free performance by the **Banda del Estado** in the Plazuela Goitia, next to the cathedral.

The yearly cultural highlight is **Zacatecas en la Cultura,** a festival during **Semana Santa** in which concerts and artistic activities are held in the elegant **Teatro Calderón,** on Hidalgo near the cathedral, and throughout the city. From September 8-22, the city celebrates the **Feria Nacional de Zacatecas** with musical and theatrical events, bullfights, agricultural and crafts shows, and sporting events.

NEAR ZACATECAS

GUADALUPE

The village of Guadalupe is home to the famous **Virgin of Guadalupe,** located above the altar in the town **cathedral.** The Virgin may be admired at Mass (M-Sa 7, 8am, noon, 6:30, and 7:30pm) or Sunday Mass (9 throughout the day). Right next to the cathedral is the **Museo de Guadalupe.** This museum contains paintings depicting scenes from the life of St. Francis, as well as nearly every known incident in the life of Christ. Especially impressive are the huge and daunting paintings on the first stairwell—you can walk away with your very own souvenir poster of *La Virgen del Apocalisis* (Virgin of the Apocalypse) for 60 pesos. Those yearning for some medieval misadventure can walk into the museum courtyard, around to the other side of the stone block, and down the steps into the dank, dark cistern. (Open daily 10am-4:30pm. Admission 20 pesos; students, under 13, students, and teachers 10 pesos.)

Getting There: From Zacatecas, you can catch a **Transportes Guadalupe bus** from the bus station or the smaller bus station behind the Howard Johnson hotel on López Mateos (30 min., 2 pesos). It's difficult to discern when Zacatecas ends and Guadalupe begins, so be sure to tell the bus driver you want to get off in the *centro* in Guadalupe. From the bus station in Guadalupe, walk a short distance to you left along Mateos and turn right on Constitución at the monument in the center of the street. The cathedral is a couple blocks in front of you. Catch a return bus to Zacatecas from the same bus station.

JEREZ AND LA QUEMADA

About an hour's bus ride from Zacatecas lies the rapidly expanding colonial town of **Jerez** (pop. 12,500). From the bus station in Jerez, turn right on the street directly ahead and you'll eventually get to the *centro.* It's a good 20- to 30-minute walk, so consider taking a cab or a bus (if you can find one). From closest to furthest from the bus station, the sights in Jerez are: **Casa-Museo Ramon López Velarde, Santuario de Soledad, Edificio de la Torre,** built by architect Dámaso Muñetón in 1896, the **Iglesia Parroquia,** and the **Teatro Hinojosa,** built in 1878 as a replica of New York City's Lincoln Center. All of the sights are clustered together to the left of the main plaza as you come from the bus station. You can find **tourist info** at the Edificio de la Torre across from the Iglesia Parroquia. Jerez is large enough to offer several decent hotel and restaurant options if you wish to stay overnight.

Nearby lie the ruins of **La Quemada.** The origins and inhabitants of this northernmost Mesoamerican city remain shrouded in mystery. Some postulate that it was the site of the legendary Aztec city *Chicomóstoc.* Said to have been occupied from about 500 to 900 A.D., La Quemada has been well preserved and offers a beautiful view of the surrounding area. There's a museum at the beginning of the site which gives visitors the low-down on its history. The site, with its unique rotund ruins, can be thoroughly viewed in about an hour. Some of the trails are very steep and are not recommended for very young children, the elderly, or the mobility impaired. If you're brave enough, venture off the trail a bit—it's the only way to reach the part of the ruins on the second hill, which has no official trail. (Site open daily 10am-4:30pm. Admission 20 pesos. Museum open daily 10am-4pm. Admission 7 pesos. Site and museum free on Su.)

Getting There: It's possible, but a little tricky, to see both Jerez and La Quemada in one day. First, take a Camiones de los Altos bus from the main bus station in Zacatecas (you can also reach Jerez and La Quemada from a smaller bus station located on López Mateos near the Howard Johnson motel) to La Quemada (40min., every 30min. half-hour 6am-10pm, 17 pesos). Be sure to specify that you want to get off at the ruins, not the city itself. The road to the ruins is on the left of the main route, right after the white, yellow, and blue **Res-**

taurant de 7 Cuevas with the Corona sign. Walk about 3km along this road to reach the entrance of the ruins. To head to Jerez, walk back to the main route and hop on a bus heading back to Zacatecas. You'll have to get off in **Malpaso** and change buses to get to Jerez. Ask the bus driver where to get off to wait for the Jerez bus. If you just want to get to Jerez from Zacatecas, catch a Camiones de los Altos bus (1hr., every 30min. 5:15am-10pm, 20 pesos).

AGUASCALIENTES

AGUASCALIENTES

The city of Aguascalientes (pop. 520,000) has a marvelous Plaza de la Patria, numerous churches and palaces, and a wealth of cultural sites. The pride and joy of the city is the eagerly anticipated *Feria de San Marcos*, a three-week long party during the last two weeks of April and the first week of May. Residents claim it as the biggest, best, and wildest festival in all of Mexico—come see for yourself. Aside from its yearly extravaganza, Aguascalientes offers a range of attractions, including the impressive colonial architecture of its *centro histórico* and several worthwhile museums. Just wandering the tree-lined street is a pleasant way to spend a day. Aguascalientes is a thoroughly modern city with the laid-back attitude one would expect of a smaller Mexican town.

✈ ORIENTATION

Aguascalientes is 168km west of San Luis Potosí, 128km south of Zacatecas, and 252km northeast of Guadalajara. **Av. Circunvalación** encircles the city, while **Av. López Mateos** cuts through town east to west. The **bus station** is on **Av. Convención,** a few blocks west from **Av. José María Chávez.** Most city buses are green and white, and most buses with numbers in the 20s or 30s (2.20 pesos) run from outside the bus station to the Mercado Morelos, two blocks north of the **Plaza de la Patria,** the center of town. "Central Camionera" buses traverse the length of **Madero,** the main road downtown that runs along the north side of the *centro* and changes names to **Carranza** west of the plaza. These buses also will return you to the bus station. Enjoy passing through the turnstiles on the city buses—one way to make sure that everybody gets off through the back door. Due to a city ordinance, some taxi drivers here actually wear their seat belts. The strapped-in *taxistas* charge about 20 pesos from the bus terminal to the center of town. From the Plaza de la Patria, most sights are within walking distance either on **Montoro** (the street that runs east from the southeast corner of the plaza) or on Carranza, which begins to the west of the plaza, behind the *basílica*. When planning your days in Aguas, keep in mind that the city takes its siestas quite seriously; many sights and businesses close from 2 to 4pm. ·

🛈 PRACTICAL INFORMATION

TRANSPORTATION

Buses: The bus station is on Av. Circunvalación south of town near Blvd. Chávez. Take the "Central Camionera" or a 20-peso cab to get there. Estrella Blanca and its subsidiaries Rojo de los Altos, Transportes Chihuahuenses, and Transportes de Norte (tel. 78 27 58) team up to serve: **Chihuahua** (10hr., 4 per day, 443 pesos); **Ciudad Juárez** (16hr., 2 per day, 614 pesos); **Fresnillo** (2½hr., 8 per day, 81 pesos); **Matamoros** (9hr., 2 per day, 402 pesos); **Monterrey** (8hr., 12 per day 9am-midnight, 255 pesos); **Saltillo** (6hr., 11 per day 9am-midnight, 219 pesos); **Durango** (first-class 7hr., 4 per day 3:30pm-midnight, 160 pesos; second-class 8hr., 4 per day 9am-5:20pm, 134 pesos);

NORTHEAST MEXICO

Aguascalientes

ACCOMMODATIONS

A Hotel Rosales
B Hotel Señorial
C Hotel San José
D Posada San Rafael

Zaragoza

Museo de Aguascalientes
Templo de San Antonio

Prmo Verdad

Saracho

Madero

Parga

Hidalgo

16 de Septiembre

Montoro

Wasco

TO PLAZA KRISTAL (300m)

5 de Febrero

Mina

TO MUSEO DE GUADALUPE POSADA (50m)

Velarde

Hospitalidad

Díaz de León

Morelos

Colón

Palmira

Mercado Morelos

Juárez

Obregón

Riviero Y Gutiérrez

5 de Mayo

Basílica de la Asunción

PLAZA DE LA PATRIA

Colón

Homedo

José María Chávez

Héroes de Chapultepec

Unión

Victoria

Galeana N.

Galeana Sur

Casa de la Cultura

Altende

Insurgentes

López Mateos

Gorostiza

Guerrero Norte

Guerrero Sur

Alarcon

Matamoros Norte

Matamoros Sur

Libertad

Nieto

Pocitos

Rayón

Macias

Carranza

Elizondo Norte

Las Américas

Correa

TO

Zapata

Jardín de San Marcos

Bernal

Pani

Azteca

Contreras

Templo de San Marcos

Ponce

Expo Plaza

Plaza de Toros

250 yards

250 meters

N

Mexico City (6hr. direct, every hr. 7am-4pm and 10pm-12:30am, 151 pesos); **San Luis Potosí** (3hr., 8 per day, 66 pesos); **Torreon** (6hr., 4 per day, 172 pesos); **Zacatecas** (2½hr., every 30min. 6am-8:30pm, 42 pesos); and nearby villages including **San Juan** and **Xalapa** (1hr., every hr., 24 pesos). Flecha Amarilla (tel. 78 26 61) rolls second-class service to: **Guanajuato** (3½hr., 7:10, 9:10am, 7:30, and 8:30pm; 73 pesos); **Irapuato** (3½hr., 12 per day, 80 pesos); **Mexico City** (8hr., 5 per day 6am-11:25pm, 214 pesos); and **Uruapan** (8½hr., 11:30am and 3:30pm, 182 pesos). Futura sends first-class buses to: **Mexico City** (6hr., every 2hr., 250 pesos); and **San Luis Potosí** (3hr., 12 per day 6am-11pm, 92 pesos). Omnibus de México (tel. 78 27 70) provides first-class service to: **Acapulco** (11hr., 11:30pm, 485 pesos); **Ciudad Juárez** (15hr., 7 per day, 614 pesos); **Leon** (2hr., 7 per day, 65 pesos); **Cuernavaca** (6½hr., 5 per day, 305 pesos); **Durango** (6hr., 7 per day, 186 pesos); **Guadalajara** (3hr., 14 per day, 118 pesos); **Mexico City** (6hr., every hr., 250 pesos); **Monterrey** (8hr., 4 per day, 254 pesos); and **Zacatecas** (2hr., 5 per day 6am-6pm, 58 pesos).

TOURIST AND FINANCIAL SERVICES

Tourist Office: (tel. 15 11 55 or 16 03 47), off the Plaza de la Patria, on the 1st fl. of the Palacio de Gobierno, the first door to the right of the main entrance. Grab a decent map and as many brochures (some in English) as you want Open M-F 8am-7:30pm, Sa-Su 9am-6pm.

Currency Exchange: Moneytron, Montoro 120 (tel. 15 79 79), 1 block from the *zócalo,* has excellent rates and charges no commission. In addition to changing currency, you can also pawn your precious metals. Open M-F 9am-5pm. **Bancomer,** 5 de Mayo 112 (tel. 15 51 15), one block from the plaza, also offers good rates. Open M-F 8:30am-5:30pm, Sa 10am-2pm.

EMERGENCY AND COMMUNICATIONS

Emergency: dial 060.

Police: (tel. 14 20 50 or 14 30 43) at the corner of Libertad and Gómez Orozco.

Pharmacy: Farmacia Sánchez, Madero 213 (tel. 15 35 50), 1 block from the plaza. Open 24hr.

Hospital: Hospital Hidalgo, Galeana 465 (tel. 17 19 30 or 17 29 83). Open 24hr.

Post Office: at Hospitalidad 108 (tel. 15 21 18). Open M-F 8am-3pm, Sa 9am-1pm. **Postal Code:** 20000.

Telephones, Fax, and Internet Access: Telecomm (tel. 16 14 27), Galeana at Nieto, provides telegram, fax, and money wiring service as well as **Internet access** for 25 pesos per hr. Open M-F 8am-7pm, Sa 9am-1pm, Su 9am-noon. **LADATELS** may be found along the plaza and throughout town; there is a **caseta** (along with a good cigar selection) at the Tabaquería Plaza, Colón 102, on the corner of the plaza. Open daily 9am-9pm.

Phone Code: 49.

◤ ACCOMMODATIONS

Budget accommodations in Aguascalientes will satisfy the most finicky of travelers, but you have to know where to look. Everything is tucked away on side streets around the plaza. As a general rule, stay in the *centro* rather than near the bus station; it's a much nicer part of town. The hotels are better, the prices are about the same, and it's not far away. During the Feria de San Marcos (mid-Apr. to early May), reservations are a must.

Hotel Señorial, Colón 104 (tel. 15 16 30) at the corner of Montoro, is located on the Plaza de la Patria. There couldn't be a better location. Nice rooms with cable TV, telephones, and a supply of purified water. Singles 115 pesos; doubles 145 pesos; triples 185 pesos.

Posada San Rafael, Hidalgo 205 (tel. 15 77 61), at Madero, 3 blocks from the plaza. Ceiling fans, cable TV, free parking, and complimentary coffee or tea in the morning. Singles 100 pesos; doubles 110 pesos; triples 130 pesos; quads 150 pesos.

Hotel San José, Hidalgo 207 (tel. 15 51 30 or 15 14 31), next to Posada San Rafael, has somewhat institutional rooms with TV, telephones, and ceiling fan along with aqua blue-tiled bathrooms. Singles 105 pesos; doubles 125 pesos; triples 145 pesos.

Hotel Rosales, Victoria 104 (tel. 15 21 65), off Madero, right across from the *basílica* and Plaza Patria. Simple, clean rooms. Run by a nice old couple and a courtyard with like phones and TV. Singles 70 pesos; doubles 100 pesos; triples 120 pesos.

◐ FOOD

Cheap eats are spread out in San Marcos Plaza in the shopping area north of the Plaza Patria across Madero, and on Madero itself.

Restaurant Vegetariano, Madero 409 (tel. 15 79 89), 4 blocks from the *zócalo*. A different entree daily for 23 pesos. Besides veggie fare, it also offers yoga classes and a nutritional supplement store. Restaurant open daily 1:30-8pm.

El Zodiaco, Galeana Sur 113 (tel. 15 31 81). Combines an open kitchen, bright orange chairs, formica tables, live canaries, and a painted shrine to the Virgin. Popular local place with a large menu—get yourself a sandwich (7 pesos), or a hamburger (8 pesos). Open daily 8:30am-11pm.

Gorditas Victoria, Victoria 108 (tel. 18 17 92), next door to Hotel Rosales. This ever-popular restaurant serves up every kind of *gordita* (7.50 pesos) imaginable. Grab your grub *para llevar* (to go) and eat in the plaza. Open daily 9am-9pm.

Sanfer Restaurant, Victoria 204 (tel. 15 45 88). A cozy little place with prices that are hard to beat. Breakfasts (10-20 pesos), chicken tacos (20 pesos), and *milanesa* (30 pesos) are all on the menu. Open daily 9am-10pm.

La Fogata, Moctezuma 111, across the street from the cathedral in the Plaza Patria. Those looking to satisfy a late-night craving for red meat should make tracks to La Fogata. Savor the mammoth homemade tortillas—you'll need them to tackle your steak (22 pesos) as there is no silverware in the house. Eclectic decor to say the least, with a copy of Da Vinci's *Last Supper* hanging next to a shot of a '69 Corvette. You wouldn't want to eat off the floor here, so just keep your eyes fixed on the beautiful food. Open daily 5:30pm-2am.

◉ SIGHTS

Visitors fortunate enough to have the time should explore the outskirts of the city, where an increasing number of attractions can be found—from theme parks to outdoor activities. Those with less time should not worry. Aguascalientes is host to a plethora of important historical and cultural landmarks within easy reach of the central district.

MUSEO DE GUADALUPE POSADA. The *museo* displays morbidly witty turn-of-the-century political cartoons, replete with skulls and skeletons. Inside are 220 original works by Mexico's most famous printmaker, including many figures caricaturing dictator Porfirio Díaz. The most familiar image is that of La Catrina, a society lady-calavera (skull) wearing an outlandish hat. Diego Rivera used her figure in *Sueño de Una Tarde Dominical en la Alameda*, now on display in Mexico City (see p. 109). The museum also shows 100 works by Posada's mentor, Manuel Manilla, and has rotating exhibits of contemporary art. On León, next to the Templo del Encino, and four blocks south of López Mateos. *(Tel. 15 45 56. Open Tu-Su 10am-6pm. Admission 5 pesos, students 2.50 pesos, children free; Su free.)*

BASÍLICA DE LA ASUNCIÓN DE LAS AGUASCALIENTES. The soft grays and rose-colored Solomonic Baroque facade of the *basílica* make it the most remarkable structure in the city. Located in the center of the Plaza de la Patria, the *basílica* is the most recognizable landmark in town and is the center of daily activity. Look for the sculptures of church patrons San Gregorio, San Jerónimo, and San Agustín. The cathedral's interior is graced with high ceilings, gold trimmings, and ornate icons, as well as paintings by José de Alcíbar, Andrés López, and Miguel Cabrera. *(Open daily approximately 7am-2pm and 4-9pm.)*

TEMPLO DE SAN ANTONIO. Every inch of the interior is painstakingly decorated with a collage of soft blues, pinks, and gold leaf. The mix of patterns on the murals, frescoes, oil paintings, and delicate stained-glass windows matches the eclectic exterior. The church was built by a local self-taught architect. *(On Pedro Parga and Zaragoza; from the plaza walk 3 blocks down Madero, then 3 blocks left on Zaragoza. Open daily approximately 7am-1pm and 5-9pm.)*

INSTITUTO CULTURAL DE AGUASCALIENTES. Popularly known as the Casa de la Cultura, the institute hosts temporary sculpture, painting, and photography exhibits in another old *hacienda* that boggles the mind with its complexity and beauty. Kiosks in the courtyard drip with listings of cultural events; you can also check the Casa's monthly bulletin or call 16 62 70. *(Carranza 101 at Galeana. Tel. 15 34 43. Open M-F 10am-2pm and 5-9pm, Sa-Su 10am-2pm and 5pm-8pm. Free.)*

CENTRO CULTURAL LOS ARQUITOS. Serving as a public bathroom from 1821 until 1973, the building became a beautiful cultural center in 1994 after a magnificent restoration process. Houses a bookshop, a video room that shows children's movies (F 5pm), and a small museum, on the Alameda at Héroes de Nacozari. *(Tel. 17 00 23. Open M-F 9am-1pm and 3-8pm, Sa 9am-1pm and 3-6pm, Su 9am-2pm.)*

MUSEO DE AGUASCALIENTES. A showcase of local and national art (along with a strange collection of classical busts tucked away in a corner) in a stunning building. *(On Parga and Zaragoza across from Templo de San Antonio. Open Tu-Su 11am-6pm. Admission 5 pesos, students and seniors 2.50 pesos; Su free.)*

JARDÍN DE SAN MARCOS. The area around the *jardín* was originally an Indian pueblo, but around the year 1600, *indígenas* erected the Templo Evangelista San Marcos at the site. The small church still has services today and is the center of a crowded pedestrian thoroughfare popular with Mexican families in the evenings. *(The jardín is a 5- to 10-minute walk on Carranza from the Plaza de la Patria. Church open daily 7am-2pm and 4-9pm).*

OTHER SIGHTS. Clustering around the *centro* are some other museums worth a look They include the Museo de Arte Contemporaneo at the corner of Morelos and P. Verdad *(open Tu-Su 10am-6pm);* and the Museo Regional de Historia, Carranza 118 *(open daily 10am-2pm and 5-10:30pm).*

🎵 ENTERTAINMENT

Aguascalientes is not a beacon of wild nightlife, but the intrepid partier can still find a good time. By city ordinance, *discotecas* in Aguascalientes aren't allowed in the *centro histórico* around the Plaza Patria and can only open their doors Thursday to Saturday; bars are open every night of the week. Cabs are your best bet to and from the relatively distant clubs; buses stop running around 10pm.

> **Disco El Cabús** (tel. 73 04 32), Blvd. Zacatecas at Colosia in the Hotel Las Trojes. A good place to shake your caboose amid the usual flashing lights and bass-heavy dance beats. Don't wear shorts, or the fashion police may apprehend you. Cover Th-F 30 pesos, Sa 40 pesos. Open Th-Sa 9pm-3am.

IOS, Av. Miguel de la Madrid 1821 (tel. 12 65 76). The young crowd dances the night away. On Thursdays and Fridays ladies get in for free, but the cover is 30 pesos for *cabelleros* (men) and on Saturdays no one gets through the door without forking over *el dinero*. Open Sa-Th 9pm-3am.

Jubilee, Calle Laureles 602-101 (tel. 17 05 07 or 18 04 94). Where to go if you value drinking over dancing. All drinks cost about half as much as those at other *discotecas*, and the lounging areas are more happening than the dance floor, which features live music and dancing Th-Sa until 3am. No cover.

To show off that golden voice you always knew you had, head to **El Sotano,** Madero 341, for a little karaoke action (open daily 5pm-midnight). Be part of Mexican League *beisbol* with the hometown Rieleros (www.rieleros.com.mx). To get to the stadium, catch a #12, 24, or 25 bus heading east on López Mateos. Snag a bleacher seat in the sun for just 7 pesos and compete with local kids in chasing down home run balls. (Games Apr.-Sept.) **Bol Kristal,** inside the Centro Comercial Plaza Kristal, offers billiards, bowling, and dominos without the usual *cantina* atmosphere. To reach it on foot, walk east on López Mateos until you reach the Don Quixote fountain; it's about a 30-minute walk from the *centro*. Grab a bowling ball and lace up those slick shoes for 22 pesos per game. There is also a seven-screen movie theater next door in the Plaza Kristal. (Open daily 10am-1am.)

■ **SEASONAL EVENTS.** During the **Feria de San Marcos** (mid-Apr. to early May), everything from cockfights to milking contests takes place in the Jardín de San Marcos. Walk two blocks to the left down the pedestrian route as you face the *templo* to reach the Expo Plaza, filled with shops and restaurants. The expansive plaza has everything from a 10-screen movie theater to upscale dining and accommodations, to great shopping, to cheap eats, to a rose garden. If you can't stomach a real bullfight in the adjacent **Plaza de Toros** (most Sundays in Sept. and Dec.), just watch the little gold matador and shiny black bull exit the clock of Fiesta America (just behind the statue of the horseman and running bulls)—they do their passes daily at noon, 3, 5, 7, and 9pm. The festival of the patron saint of Aguascalientes, **La Romería de la Asunción,** takes place August 1-15, with dances, processions, and fireworks. The **Festival de las Calaveras,** the last week of October and the first week of November, is another occasion for the city to cut loose and celebrate.

SAN LUIS POTOSÍ

SAN LUIS POTOSÍ

In San Luis Potosí (pop. 820,000), everyone smiles a lot. And there's a lot to smile about; *potosinos* are truly, madly, deeply in love with their city. With plazas galore, plenty of pedestrian walkways, and innumerable cathedrals naturally dotting the landscape as easily as overgrown trees, San Luis is a crash course in urban planning. Founded in 1592 after Franciscan missionaries began to convert local Guachichil and Tlaxcaltec tribes, and then discovered silver and gold, San Luis Potosí has twice served as the capital of Mexico. Also serving as the site for many pivotal events of the Independence and Revolutionary wars, Emperor Maximilian's death sentence and the 1910 "Plan of San Luis" were both signed in the city. The "downtown," with bright, squat buildings and wide median strips harboring pineapple palms, is downright inviting, and the residents of San Luis set the city apart by their eager and friendly embrace of the surprisingly few tourists who arrive. As lanterns dot the cathedrals and fountains, bands, magicians, and soap-bubble blowers gather in the town plazas at dusk to entertain assembled crowds of young and old. On a warm evening, it's hard not to feel that San Luis Potosí is the quiet capital of some magical world.

◢ ORIENTATION

San Luis Potosí is at the center of a triangle formed by Mexico's three largest cities—Monterrey, Guadalajara, and Mexico City. Five main routes **(Rte. 57, 85, 70, 49, and 80)** snake their way into the city. To get downtown from the **bus station,** catch an "Alameda" or "Centro" bus (5:30am-10:30pm, 1.90 pesos) and hop off at **Parque Alameda,** the first big stretch of green. Continue walking in the direction the bus was going, as straight as you can, past the **Plaza del Carmen** on your left, and you'll end up in the **Plaza de Armas.** A **taxi** costs 20 pesos.

San Luis's main street, **Av. Carranza,** runs east-west and passes the north side of the city's historic center, the Plaza de Armas (along which it is also known as **Jardín Hidalgo**). East of the plaza, Carranza is called **Los Bravos. Madero** runs parallel to Carranza one block south, touching the Plaza de Armas's south side. East of the plaza, Madero goes by **Othón.** Running parallel to Carranza one block north is **Av. Obregón. Zaragoza** forms the east side of Plaza de Armas; north of the plaza, the name changes to **Hidalgo.** Parallel and one block east of Hidalgo is Morelos, which further north turns into **Moctezuma**—this is where most of the shopping in the *centro* is done. On the west side of the plaza is **5 de Mayo,** known as **Allende** farther north. **Aldama** is one block west of 5 de Mayo. The Plaza del Carmen is two blocks east of the plaza on Madero. A block farther east lies the Alameda, where the bus from the station drops off visitors. The **train station** is on Othón opposite the Alameda. Most city buses exiting the *centro* can be caught on **Ponciano Arriaga,** which runs north-south along the Alameda (back to the Central de Transportes Terrestres) or else on Othón in front of the train station.

🛈 PRACTICAL INFORMATION

TRANSPORTATION

Airport: (tel. 22 00 95) 25min. north of the city. Tickets can be purchased at **2001 Viajes,** Obregón 604 (tel. 12 29 53). Open M-F 9am-2pm and 4-8pm, Sa 9:30am-2pm. Flights to **Mexico City** begin at 480 pesos with Aerocalifornia (tel. 18 80 50), and flights to **Monterrey** start at 1450 pesos with AeroLiteral (tel. 13 33 99). Mexicana (tel. 17 89 20) also flies to various destinations.

Trains: The station (tel. 12 36 41) is on Othón near the north side of the Alameda. To **Mexico City** (6hr., W, F, and Su 10:30am; 80 pesos) and **Monterrey** (8hr.; M, W, and F 5:30pm; 80 pesos). The ticket booth opens just before trains leave.

Buses: Central de Transportes Terrestres is 2 blocks south of the chaotic convergence of routes that wrap around the Glorieta Benito Juárez, 4km east of the city center along Av. Universidad. Not to be confused with the old *central* which is now shut down. When going to the *central* from the *centro*, be sure to take only the *peseros* labeled "Central TT" or to ask the driver for the *central nuevo*. The *pesero* will let you off at the back side of the station. **24hr. luggage storage** in Sala 1 (3 pesos per hr. or 30 pesos per day). Del Norte (tel. 16 55 43) goes to: **Acapulco** (12hr., 3 per day, 320 pesos); **Querétaro** (2½hr., every hr., 100 pesos); and **Uruapán** (7hr., 2 per day, 210 pesos). Estrella Blanca (tel. 16 54 77) goes to: **Aguascalientes** (3hr., 7 per day, 90 pesos); **Chihuahua** (14hr., 10 per day, 372 pesos); **Cuernavaca** (6hr., 3 per day in the evenings, 198 pesos); **Monterrey** (7hr., every hr., 142 pesos); **Querétaro** (2½hr., every hr., 105 pesos); and **Zacatecas** (3hr., every hr., 62 pesos). Omnibus de México (tel. 16 81 61), sends buses to: **Reynosa** (9hr.,

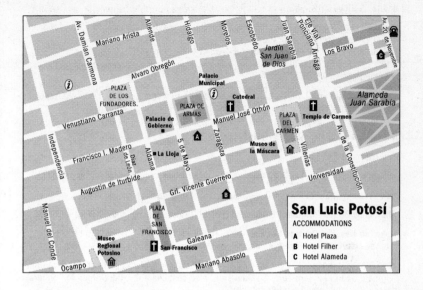

San Luis Potosí
ACCOMMODATIONS
A Hotel Plaza
B Hotel Filher
C Hotel Alameda

8pm, 245 pesos); **Saltillo** (5hr., 2 per day, 141 pesos); and **Tampico** (7hr., 3 per day in the evenings, 147 pesos). Oriente serves **Río Verde** (2-3hr., every hr., 51 pesos) and **Tampico** (7hr., 7 per day, 149 pesos). Transportes Tamaulipas and Noreste (tel. 16 69 64) jointly trek to: **Matehuala** (2hr., 14 per day, 75 pesos); **Monterrey** (6hr., 12 per day, 188 pesos); and **Reynosa** via **Linares** or **Monterrey** (9hr., 6 per day, 210 pesos).

Car Rental: Hertz, Obregón 670 (tel. 12 95 00). Cars cost 280 pesos per day plus insurance and mileage. Must be 25. Open M-F 9am-2pm and 4-8pm, Sa 9am-2pm.

TOURIST AND FINANCIAL SERVICES

Tourist Office: A city **turismo municipal** (tel. 12 27 70), on the 1st fl. of the Palacio Municipal, at the northeast corner of Plaza de Armas. Excellent city maps and guides (20 pesos) are provided as well as a friendly staff eager to help; English and some French spoken. Open M-F 8am-3pm. The **state tourist office,** Obregón 520 (tel. 12 99 06 or 12 23 57), 1 block west of the Pl. de los Fundadores, also has city maps with suggested walking tours and explanations in English, in addition to information about the rest of the state. Open M-Sa 8am-8pm.

Consulate: U.S., Mariel 103 (tel. 12 15 28); take the "Morales" bus. Open M-F 8:30am-1:30pm, but sometimes available in the afternoons. The police and the tourist office have consulate employees' home numbers in case of emergency.

Currency Exchange: Casas de Cambio can be found all along Morelos a few blocks north of Plaza de Armas. **San Luis Divisas** (tel. 12 66 06), at the corner of Morelos and Bocanegra, usually accepts traveler's checks. Open M-Sa 9am-8pm. Several other banks are around Plaza de Armas and are open M-F 9am-1:30pm. **Banamex,** at Allende and Obregón, 1 block east of Pl. de Armas, has a 24hr. **ATM** and exchanges traveler's checks with no commission. Get there early; by noon the lines are endless.

American Express: Grandes Viajes, Carranza 1077 (tel. 11 11 27), will help you out with lost or stolen checks or cards and will sell checks; they do not cash American Express traveler's checks. Open M-F 9am-2pm and 4-6pm.

NORTHEAST MEXICO

LOCAL SERVICES

Supermarket: Gigante is enormous. Cross the treacherous route from the bus station, turn left, and follow the curve until you see the sign. Open M-F 9am-10pm, Sa-Su 9am-8pm. In the *centro*, the **Mercado Hidalgo,** on Morelos and Mier 3 blocks north of the Plaza de Armas, sells fruit, bread, and candy as well as an extensive selection of crafts. Open daily 8am-8pm.

Laundry: Lavandería La Gotita, on 5 de Mayo and Hernandez. Full service only. Takes approximately 8hr. 16 pesos for a medium load. Open M-Sa 10am-8pm.

EMERGENCY AND COMMUNICATIONS

Emergency: dial 060.

Police: (tel. 12 54 76 or 12 25 82) can always be found in the Palacio Municipal.

Red Cross: (tel. 15 36 35 or 20 39 02), on Juárez at Díaz Gutiérrez.

Pharmacy: Botica Mexicana, Othón 180 (tel. 12 38 80), near the cathedral. Open 24hr.

Hospital: Hospital Central, Carranza 2395 (tel. 13 03 43 or 17 01 64), 20 blocks west of the *centro*. Some English spoken. Open 24hr.

Post Office: Morelos 235 (tel. 2 27 40), 1 block east and 3 blocks north of the Plaza de Armas. Open M-F 8am-7pm, Sa 9am-1pm. Also contains a **MexPost.** Open M-F 9am-6pm, Sa 9am-1pm. **Postal Code:** 78000.

Internet Access: Escobedo 335 on Plaza del Carmen. To enter, walk past the green gates into what looks like a garage. Go up the marble stairs at the back. Computers with Internet 12 pesos per hr. Open M-Sa 10am-10pm.

Telephones: LADATELs are scattered throughout the plazas, particularly on Av. Obregón and Carranza near the Plaza de las Armas and the Plaza de los Fundadores. **Computel,** Carranza 360 (tel.12 01 89 or 12 01 13), opposite the Hotel Panorama, allows international collect calls and has a **fax** (fax 12 01 86). Open M-Sa 7:30am-9pm.

Phone Code: 48.

ACCOMMODATIONS

Some good, cheap accommodations can be found near the bus station, but they fill up very quickly. Past-their-prime hotels close to the *centro* still boast somewhat commodious rooms, plaza views, and low prices. Alternatively, spring for a more expensive room in the *centro* and get a real treat.

Hotel Plaza, Jardín Hidalgo 22 (tel. 12 46 31), on the south side of the Plaza de Armas. This hotel, the first in San Luis Potosí, has seen better days, but the clean rooms maintain a funny sort of charm. Ask for a room facing the plaza or with a balcony. One person 130 pesos; 2 people 140 pesos; each additional person 10 pesos.

Hotel Filher, Universidad 335 (tel. 12 15 62 or 12 15 63), at the corner of Zaragoza 3 blocks south of the Plaza de Armas. Boasts bright, clean rooms with beautiful wooden furniture, TVs, phones, fans, and big bathrooms inside a renovated colonial building. One person 217 pesos; 2 people 281 pesos; 3 people 322 pesos.

Hotel Alameda, Callejón La Perla 3 (tel. 18 06 06), next to the Pemex gas station on the northwest corner of the Alameda, is the cheapest option in San Luis Potosí. Rooms are small, dark and in minor disrepair, but the plumbing is new, the water is hot, the manager is accommodating. One person 65 pesos, 2 people 75 pesos.

◖ FOOD

Although they are plentiful, restaurants in the *centro* often offer mediocre or bland dishes and poor service. The further you stray, the better your chances of bumping into a gem. Both *tacos potosinos* and *enchiladas potosinas* are stuffed with cheese and vegetables, then fried. *Nopalitos* are tender and absolutely delicious pieces of cactus (spines removed) cooked in a salty green sauce of garlic, onion, and tomato. *Chongos coronados* (curdled milk in sweet maple water) is a popular dessert.

La Güera, Tata Nacho 800 (tel. 11 87 28), on the left as you approach the Parque Tangamanga, in the block before the entrance. This traditionally decorated treasure offers some of the best meals in all of Northeast Mexico. Serving only breakfast specials (18-21 pesos, 8am-1:30pm) and *comida corrida* (28 pesos, 1:30-6pm), La Güera assures groans of delight at every bite. From the pickled *nopalito* garnish served with chips to the homemade *mole* (only one main entree option among many), everything here is scrumptious. Open Tu-Su 8am-6pm.

Restaurant Cafeteria (tel. 12 29 57), with the bright orange doors on Madero just west of the Plaza de Armas. Delicious odors waft from this bright hole in the wall. At 1 of just 3 tiny tables, you will be served breakfast, lunch, or dinner (*tortas* 9-20 pesos, meals 15-55 pesos), as well as rare and scrumptious desserts (5-10 pesos) and espresso. Open daily 8am-10:30pm.

Tokio, Zaragosa 305 (tel. 14 61 89). Only the jade-colored decor reflects the quasi-Japanese name. Tokio serves tasty Mexican dishes in a cool, modern atmosphere. *Comida corrida* (23 pesos) starts at 1:30pm. Open daily 7:30am-1am.

Yu Ne Nisa, Arista 360 (tel. 14 36 31). This Yucatec celebration of vegetarianism has a bright eating area decorated with plants and matching green chairs. Veggie burgers are 20 pesos, and the *quesadillas* are a rock-bottom 12 pesos. Luscious *licuados* are freshly squeezed behind the counter. Adjoins an herbal/homeopathic/vegetarian store. Large variety of fruit juices, yogurt concoctions, and whole wheat breads. *Comida corrida* (30 pesos) starts at 1:30pm. Open M-Sa 9am-8pm.

◖ SIGHTS

San Luis Potosí has so many beautiful buildings and fascinating sights that it's almost intimidating; the great majority have historical markers in both English and Spanish.

PLAZA DE ARMAS. Dubbed the "City of Plazas," San Luis Potosí has three main town squares. The most central of these is the Plaza de Armas, replete with trees and *potosinos*. At the beginning of the 17th century, residents watched bullfights from the balconies of the surrounding buildings. Since 1848, a red sandstone gazebo bearing the names of famous Mexican musicians has graced the plaza; on Thursday and Sunday evenings, it hosts local bands attracting large crowds.

PALACIO DEL GOBIERNO. The west side of the Plaza de Armas is marked by the Neoclassical facade of the Palacio del Gobierno. Constructed in 1798 and briefly serving as the capital of the country and the seat of the presidency in 1863, the structure was renovated in 1950 and continues to serve as San Luis Potosí's administrative seat. The building has interesting *salas* (living rooms) on the second floor filled with murals, statues, plaques, and legends. Ask the guard to unlock the *salas* if the rooms are closed. *(Open M-F 9am-2:30pm. Free.)*

CATHEDRAL. Opposite the Palacio de Gobierno stands the cathedral, with two bell towers that toll a different melody every 15 minutes. Both magnificent and ominous, the cathedral was completed in 1710, but in 1855, when San Luis became a diocese, the building was "upgraded." Miners are said to have donated gold and silver to glorify the interior, and marble statues of the apostles (small copies of those at the Basilica of San Juan de Letrán in Rome) were placed in the niches between the Solomonic columns of the Baroque facade. *(Open daily 8am-7pm. Avoid visiting on Sunday or during Mass.)*

JARDÍN DE SAN FRANCISCO. The *jardín* is distinguished by its bronze fountain, quaint cobblestone streets, and red sandstone buildings. Elderly *potosinos* often congregate on the shady benches carrying grandkids and tossing crumbs to the pigeons. Book stalls line the east side of the plaza while artisan sellers extend down Universidad, off the west side.

IGLESIA DE SAN FRANCISCO. Soon after the city's founding, construction began on the Iglesia de San Francisco, on the plaza's west side. Less ornate than its nearby counterparts, the orange stucco facade still displays a highly Baroque interior beautifully accentuated by the flickering votives at each altar. *(Open daily 6:30am-1:30pm and 4:30-9pm.)*

MUSEO DE LAS CULTURAS POPULARES. Parque Tangamanga also houses this *museo*. It houses a great exhibit of indigenous handcrafts as well as rare photo exhibitions of indigenous communities and ceremonies. *(Tel. 12 29 76. Open Tu-Su 10am-5pm; Admission 1 peso.)*

MUSEO NACIONAL DE LA MÁSCARA. The pink sandstone *museo* displays hundreds of ancient and modern masks from every Mexican region, from *diablos* (devils) to dancing cows. This is a fascinating place; be sure to check out all of the oversized *mojigangas* in the hall—these enormous, eccentric representations are taken out of the museum and paraded around the streets during seasonal festivals. *(Located at Villerías 2, in the Palacio Federal, half a block south of Pl. del Carmen along Villerías. Tel. 12 30 25. Open Tu-F 10am-2pm and 4-6pm, Sa-Su 10am-2pm. Admission 2 pesos.)*

MUSEO REGIONAL POTOSINO. On Independencia near the corner of Galeana, the *museo* occupies the grounds of the former Franciscan convent. The government seized the land in 1950 and converted part of it into a museum. The first floor contains artifacts from all of Mexico, including a collection of artifacts of the Huasteca, natives of the region and contemporaries of the Maya. On the museum's second floor is the marvelous **Baroque Capilla a la Virgen de Aranzazu.** A shepherd found the altar's image of the Virgin in a prickly thicket, hence the name—*aranzazu* means "from within the thorns". *(Tel. 12 51 85. Open Tu-Su 10am-7pms. Admission 10 pesos, free on Su.)*

OTHER SIGHTS. The bright, lively **Plaza de Carmen** with its Sunday festivals is host to the serene **Templo de Carmen** on its northeast corner, two blocks east of the Plaza de Armas. Many *potosinos* claim that the church is the most beautiful religious building in the city; it features hanging chandeliers, golden altars, and a huge mural of the crucifixion. During the day, the light filters in and the place glows. *(Open daily 7am-1:30pm and 4-9pm. Avoid visiting during mass.)* Three blocks east along Manuel Othón from the Plaza de Armas is the expansive **Alameda Juan Sarabia** with artisans and trinket-vendors as well as game operators along the western side. Avoid the Alameda at night when drunks and pickpockets roam. **Parque Tangamanga,** with lakes for paddle-boating and fishing, a baseball field, electric cars, and bike paths is a great place to bring a blanket and a picnic and spend the day lounging, or rent a bike (400m into the park on the main drag; 17 pesos per hour) and explore it all. *(To get to the park, catch a "Perimetral" bus (1.90 pesos) on Constitución across from the Alameda. Get off at the Monumento a la Revolución which is in the middle of a large rotary and looks like Mexican soldiers firing rifles from a bunker. Walk south from the monument for three blocks. Open Tu-Su 9am-6pm.)*

♫ ENTERTAINMENT AND SEASONAL EVENTS

Taxis are nearly impossible to catch on Saturday nights and few discos are in the *centro*, so if you plan on hitting the clubs, leave early. Both **Dulcinea** (tel. 18 13 12), Carretera Mexico km 5, inside the five-star Holiday Inn del Quixote, and **Oasis** (tel. 22 18 82), Carretera Mexico km 1, in the Hotel Maria Dolores, attract a young, stylish crowd (cover 40 pesos; both open Th-Sa 10pm-late). A little closer to the *centro* is **Staff**, Carranza 423 (tel. 14 30 74), where a young, gay-friendly crowd grooves to Latin and dance music (cover 25 pesos; open F-Su).

For those itching for a bit of visual arts, **El Teatro de La Paz** (tel. 12 26 98), behind the Templo de Carmen, is one of the four most famous and fabulously constructed theaters in Mexico—many performers don't even need microphones. The salon holds a collection of modern art, the foyer has lovely sculptures and murals, and the theater plays everything from traditional Mexican fare to *101 Dalmatians*. The best news? Prices tend to be below 30 pesos. Pick up a *guía* at the city tourist office to see what's playing, or look at the posters outside the *teatro*.

Sip an espresso with theater-going types for only eight pesos at the **Café del Teatro** in the same building as the *teatro* (open Tu-Su 10am-10pm). If you'd rather spend money shopping and be completely hip, the area along Carranza west of the *centro* teems with trendy restaurants and clubs. Here, the swank **Jardín de Tequis** is a great place to relax and listen to the trickle of four beautiful fountains. This area is accessible via the "Morales" bus.

Finally, the last two weeks of August mark the **Fiesta Nacional Potosina.** Concerts, bullfights, fireworks, and a parade guarantee that great times are had by all.

MATEHUALA

Although Matehuala derives its name from a Huachichil phrase meaning "don't come," the town is anything but unfriendly. The few tourists who do trickle in are often hallucinogen-hungry backpackers en route to Real de Catorce. They may be surprised to find that this town of 100,000, once a base for Spanish silver and gold mining, is relaxing, open, and beautiful—well worth a stay.

⊞ ORIENTATION. Matehuala is 261km from Saltillo and 191km from San Luis Potosí. The **Central de Autobuses** is located on Calle 5 de Mayo, just south of the city and near the large, red Arco de Bienvenida. **Calle 5 de Mayo** runs north-south through the center of town. Across the street from the station, a *pesera* labeled "Centro" will take you to the downtown area for two pesos—ask the driver to let you off near the cathedral, or easier still, get off at Hidalgo, next to the Chalita market. **Taxis** charge 20 pesos for the trip.

Constantly forking or changing names, the streets of Matehuala are confusing, but they are so short and close together that you'll never be lost for long. Maps can be obtained at the **tourist office** on Rte. 57 or at the blue **Papeleteria Corias** on Morelos, next door to #510 (8 pesos; open M-F 8am-9pm), but if you speak any Spanish, asking directions is easier than reading the maps. **Miguel Hidalgo** runs north-south through most of the city; **Benito Juárez** runs parallel to it, one block west; and **Morelos** runs one block east. **Betancourt** forks off Morelos one block past Hotel del Valle. At the end of its 400 block, Morelos ends up perpendicular to Madero. **Constitución** runs up one side of the *templo*, and **Reyes** runs perpendicular to Hidalgo starting directly in front of the *templo*. Most points of interest lie somewhere on or between these streets.

◪ PRACTICAL INFORMATION. Central de Autobuses (tel. 2 26 50), on 5 de Mayo south of the downtown area, provides a consolidated service of Transportes del Norte, Frontera, Estrella Blanca and El Aguila to: **Mexico City** (7hr.; 11 per day; first class 281 pesos, second class 241 pesos); **Monterrey** (4hr., every hr.,

144 pesos); **Nuevo Laredo** (7hr., 11 per day, 265 pesos); **Querétaro** (6hr., 3 per day, 173 pesos); **Saltillo** (3hr., every hr., 115 pesos); and **San Luis Potosí** (2hr., every hr., 81 pesos). Noreste (tel. 2 09 97) serves **Monterrey** (4hr., every hr., 144 pesos) and **Reynosa** (7hr., 8 per day, 222 pesos). Tamaulipas (tel. 2 27 77) heads to **Real de Catorce** (5 per day, 28 pesos); and **San Luis Potosí** (2 hr., 18 per day, 81 pesos).

For **tourist information,** head over to the **Cámara de Comercio,** Morelos 427 (tel. 2 01 10), one block east of Hidalgo. Low on maps, but high on knowledge, they also offer Internet connection for 1.70 pesos per minute. (Open M-F 9am-1:30pm and 4-7pm.) **Maps** are for sale (8 pesos) at the blue **Papelería Corias** on Morelos next door to #510. There is a small-scale **tourist office** (tel. 2 12 81) next to the Padregal Motel on Rte. 57, north of the city and accessible only by car or taxi (open M-F 10am-4pm). **Casas de cambio** dot the *centro,* all offering good rates. **Biotal,** 111 Reyes (tel. 2 48 18), exchanges cash and traveler's checks and has a 24hr. **ATM** (bank open M-Sa 8am-9pm). The **indoor market** next to the Templo de la Imaculada Concepción sells crafts and produce (open daily 9am-6pm). The **Lavandería Acuario** (tel. 2 70 88), Betancourt and Madero, offers self-service wash and dry of 5kg for 30 pesos (open daily 8:30am-2pm and 4-8pm).

Emergency: dial 06. **Police station:** (tel. 2 06 47), next to the bus station. **Red Cross:** (tel. 2 07 26), at Ignacio y Ramírez and Betancourt about eight blocks east of Betancourt's original fork from Morelos. **Farmacia del Centro:** Morelos 623 (tel. 2 05 92); open daily 9am to midnight; English spoken). **Hospital General:** (tel. 2 04 45), on Hidalgo a few blocks north of *el centro* (open 24hr.; little to no English spoken). **Post office:** (tel. 2 00 71), at Leandro Valle and Negrete. Walk up Constitución, turn right on Independencia one block before the Iglesia Santo Niño, turn right again on Negrete, and it's on your left at the corner. (Open M-F 8am-3pm, Sa 9am-1pm.) **Postal code:** 78700. **Fax:** can be sent from most *papelerías* or from **Telecomm,** 5 de Febrero at Juárez (tel. 2 00 08), a few blocks east of the *centro.* Also houses a **Western Union** office. (Open M-F 9am-7pm.) **LADATELs** are not as common in Matehuala as in other cities but can still be found throughout the *centro.* **Phone code:** 488.

⌐ **ACCOMMODATIONS.** Budget accommodations dot the *centro.* The *casas de huéspedes* on Calle Bocanegra are the cheapest options (singles 30 pesos; doubles 40 pesos with shared bathrooms), but by spending more you'll get some pretty luxurious rooms in a central location.

▧ **Hotel y Casino Del Valle** (tel. 2 37 70), on Morelos right off the Plaza de Armas, provides its customers comfortable and fun doubles for reasonable prices. The lobby greets you with a counter of opaque glass and sandstone, black velour loveseats, and pink walls. Hyperactive ceiling fans, TVs in the rooms, and an attached dance hall make this hotel as swank as a Vegas casino. (All rooms are doubles; max 4 to a room. 1 person 160 pesos; each additional person 20 pesos.) **Hotel del Parque** (tel. 2 55 10), on the corner of Rayon and Bocanegra, offers some luxury digs close to the *centro* and right next to the Parque Vicente Guerrero. For 250 pesos for one person, you definitely get what you pay for with spacious rooms that boast TV and A/C. For much less money, **Hotel Matehuala,** Bustamante 134 (tel. 2 06 80), just north of the Plaza de Armas, features a huge and empty tiled courtyard, decidedly monastic in the best way. Though the rooms are dark as confessional booths, the 6m ceilings with wooden rafters, white walls, and rust color bureaus are strangely appealing. Ask for a room with windows to the outside and a balcony. (Singles 100 pesos; doubles 120 pesos.) **Hotel Blanca Estela,** Morelos 406 (tel. 2 23 00), next to the video store, has smaller rooms for a bit less. Fans cool small, super-clean, colorful rooms with TVs and beautiful wooden furnishings lend a classy feel to the rooms in this narrow, small hotel. Check in early; this may well be the most crowded place in town. (Singles 90 pesos; doubles 110 pesos.)

FOOD. The few restaurants in Matehuala are family-owned, family-prone cafeteria types with good food and low prices. Get ready to practice your hardcore menu-ordering Spanish. **Restaurant Fontella,** Morelos 618 (tel. 2 02 93) cooks up some of the best food in town. The murals of the city evoke a sense of yesteryear, while the food is the best of today. Charcoal-roasted specialties are 27 to 34 pesos and *comida corrida* offers copious servings of fresh vegetable soup, rice, chicken or steak, and dessert for 23 pesos. (Open daily 7:30am-4am.) **Restaurant Video Bar House Rock** (tel. 2 20 08), on Hidalgo directly across from the *templo*, offers exquisite simple fare in a cool, family-style restaurant upstairs with *comida corrida* for only 22 pesos, while the hippest 20-30 year-olds hang out in the video bar downstairs where antique decorations mix with modern music (beer 10 pesos; restaurant open daily 9am-11pm; bar open W-Sa 7pm-1am). **La Cava,** Callejón del Arte 1 (tel. 2 28 88), between Hidalgo and Morelos just east of Hotel Matehuala is a pleasant escape from the merciless sun in an elegant dining room. A mix of Mexican, French, American, and Russian cuisine goes for 33 to 50 pesos. The cocktails here are especially smooth. (Open daily 1:30-10:30pm.)

SIGHTS. While there are not a lot of big-name sights in Matehuala, every wide street and little park seems ripe for reclining. Standing solemnly at the center of Matehuala between Calles Juárez and Hidalgo is the almost completed **Templo de la Inmaculada Concepción,** a copy of Saint Joseph's cathedral in Lyon, France. Construction began in 1905, and although poor funding has slowed progress on the project, more than 90 years of Matehualans are proud of their all-but-finished cathedral. The large clock and seemingly impenetrable gray exterior of this Gothic-style edifice belie a beautiful interior flooded with light. Just in front of the main cathedral is the **Plaza Juárez,** now permanently occupied by vendor stalls and small, makeshift cafes. Sprawling out onto adjoining streets, the bazaar is collectively known as **Mercado Arista,** selling leather and ceramic goods as well as the usual slew of cheap plastic toys and trinkets. The **Alameda,** a few blocks south of the main plaza, offers lots of shade and jungle-like lushness.

Two other large parks stand at the northeast and southeast corners of the downtown area. Approximately three blocks east of Hidalgo, between Bocanegra and Altamirano, is the soothing **Parque Vicente Guerrero** (also called the **Parque del Pueblo**). Vicente Guerrero's counterpart is the more lively **Parque Álvaro Obregón,** just south of Insurgentes. With basketball courts and benches aplenty, Álvaro Obregón draws entire families in the early evening hours.

REAL DE CATORCE

Once a thriving mining town with 30,000 inhabitants, Real de Catorce now looms mysteriously on the side of a mountain, a veritable ghost town with a population of barely 1500 people. Still, backpackers come from all over to see this town's *burro*-trodden paths and brick ruins rising up from the Sierra Madre like desert flowers. The cobblestone streets and carts full of holy candles may not seem like much, but Real de Catorce is a Mexican miracle—the little town was left behind by time. Tourists from all over Mexico travel to Real de Catorce to investigate this dusty anachronism of a town, to explore hallucinogens, and to pray to Saint Francis. Its history and natural beauty may soon be threatened by the increasing investment in Real de Catorce by wealthy Mexicans bent on creating another resort town. The silent magic in the air in Real is not to be missed before it's lost.

ORIENTATION AND PRACTICAL INFORMATION. The town's main thoroughfare (path) is **Calle Lanzagorta,** which runs from the **bus stop** past the famed **cathedral** and a few hotels and restaurants to a little town square with a gazebo.

Calle Constitución runs parallel to Lanzagorta up the hill, through the **Plaza Princi-pal.** For transportation, Autobuses Tamaulipas (tel. 2 08 40) runs **buses** from **Matehuala** to **Real de Catorce** (1¼hr., during peak season every 2hr. 6am-6pm, round-trip 56 pesos; fewer buses during the rest of the year). Passengers should always check with the bus driver about the schedules and arrive 15-30 minutes early. Also be sure to check which bus your return ticket is for. Although you'll always be let on a bus out of Real de Catorce, it may be standing-room only. Buses from Matehuala leave from a **station** at **Guerrero** and **Méndez** near the *centro* and always stop at the smaller station on **Parque Vicente Guerrero.** From the cathedral, walk down Reyes, turn left on Rayón, and follow it to the park. The station will be on your right. Tickets are sold here, or catch a shuttle bus from the **Central de Autobuses,** the central bus station on **5 de Mayo,** for free. The ride to "Real de 14" is guaranteed to whiten the knuckles of the timid traveler: the bus rambles along a cobblestone road and a winding path chiseled into the mountainside, and riders change to a lower bus for the seven-minute tunnel at the end of the ride. Self-appointed guides, offering **tourist information,** can be found as you get off the bus or in the back streets of the city. Most services (i.e. the civil registry, **police** station, and municipal government) are run out of the **Presidencia Municipal,** just by the Plaza Principal. **Post office:** on Calle Consti-tución to the right of the Presidencia as you are facing it, on the right side of the street (open M-F 9am-1pm and 3-6pm). The town's single **telephone** (tel. 2 37 33), is on a side street running perpendicular to Calle Constitucion next to the Presidencia Municipal.

▐▐ ACCOMMODATIONS AND FOOD. Real de Catorce has a number of good budget accommodations; look for the *casas de huéspedes* on the side streets runing off of Lanzagorta. Singles with bathrooms usually are no more than 80 pesos. Most of the hotels are beautiful and, if not equipped with the latest electronics, richly decorated. For considerably less than other accommodations and at no cost to quality is the ▧ **Hotel San Francisco,** on Teran right off Constitución. The family-run gem only has a few rooms but it is clean and very comfortable (50 pesos, with bath 70 pesos). Another option is **El Mesón de la Abundancia,** Langazorta #11. The oldest edifice in town (it used to be the town treasury in the 1880s), this hotel is also an exercise in historical recreation. Most furniture is handmade and the blankets are made of superior wool, and some rooms have private terraces and sitting rooms. (1 person 250 pesos, each additional person 50 pesos.) At the adjoining restaurant/bar a full meal runs 28 pesos and the menu includes vegetarian options. **Hotel Providencia,** Lanzagorta 29, offers a few bare-boned cheaper rooms (singles 60 pesos; doubles 130 pesos) and a few expensive ultra-modern rooms whose biggest draws are bathtubs and telephones (doubles 250 pesos, but prices may be negotiable). They also serve *comidas corridas* with delicious homemade tortillas in the restaurant downstairs for 25 pesos. Many restaurants are open only during tourist season, which is late June through August. Real has some great Italian food because of a number of Italians who have settled here. Prices everywhere go down off-season.

▧ SIGHTS. Calle Lanzagorta runs past most major sights. The **Templo de la Purísima Concepción** is down the road on the right; ascend the white walkway to reach the entrance. Inside, the floor seems to be composed of rectangular blocks of wood which are actually doors to subterranean **tombs.** The cathedral resembles a brightly colored Fabergé egg, with pastel decor and plastic figu-rines. It houses a lifelike image of St. Francis, whose miracles have created a devoted following. On October 4, the saint's feast day, the town attracts a flock of pious visitors hoping to pray at the cathedral. The most amazing part of the cathedral is a side room filled with **letters** of thanks and devotion to St. Francis for everything from visa waivers to cures from fatal diseases. Often hand-painted, stenciled, or filled with photographs, these thousands of letters spanning decades are full of hope and meticulously crafted. Uphill, on the right after the cathedral (a steep climb), is the **Plaza Principal,** where today only a crumbling fountain remains. Next to the plaza is the **Casa de Moneda,** formerly a mint, whose third floor houses a photography exhibit of Real de Catorce. The museum entrance is by the plaza. (Open daily noon-2pm. Free.) You can also check out artifacts from Real de Catorce's past at the **Museo Parroquial** on Lanzagorta across from the cathedral. If you read Spanish, you can buy a series of written guides on the area for 8-40 pesos. (Open F-Su 9:30am-4:30pm. Admission 2 pesos, children 1 peso.)

Turning right immediately after the *jardín,* continue two blocks uphill, then head one painfully uphill block to the left. There, the terraced steps of the **Palenque de Gallos** (cock-fight ring) replicate the layout of a classical Athenian theater (ask someone in the Casa de Moneda to unlock it for you). At the high end of Constitución lies **El Mirador,** a little area of ruins offering a view of the city. The surrounding cliff known as **El Voladero** offers breathtaking views of the nearby mountains and valleys. To reach it, walk downhill on Calle Constitución and you'll be rewarded with visions of 300m drops, dry riverbeds crackling with heat, and herds of cows on distant hilltops. At the top of Calle Zaragoza stands the stark white **Capilla de Guadalupe** (also called the *Panteón*), which overlooks a cemetery tightly paved with the graves of local saints. For a **horseback tour** of the region, walk from the bus stop down Lanzagorta until you reach the Plaza Hidalgo. To the left across Lanzagorta is a stable that will rent horses for 30 pesos per hour to any number of destinations. If you're feeling more adventurous, try a two-day trip to a nearby *rancho,* down into the desert valley, or up toward the **Ciudad de las Fantasmas,** straight up off the end of Lanzagorta nearest the bus station. The guides expect a tip of 50 to 70 pesos. Try to arrange a fixed price before the trip to avoid a hassle. The trip into the desert is breathtaking and well worth the six-hour horse ride.

CIUDAD VALLES

Ciudad Valles (pop. 350,000) is a major crossroads between the *noreste* and central Mexico. Commonly known as Valles, the hot (the average summer temperature is 110°F/43°C) and dirty city, is the second largest in the state after the capital; however, it lacks the charm, culture, and beauty of San Luis Potosí. Unfortunately it doesn't hint at the rich Huastecan culture surrounding the area—Valles feels more like Industrytown, Anywhere.

🖪 ORIENTATION AND PRACTICAL INFORMATION. Ciudad Valles's main thoroughfare is **Calle Hidalgo. Carranza** runs perpendicular to Hidalgo and connects it to the city bus station, four blocks down Carranza from Hidalgo. **Juárez** runs parallel to Hidalgo one block south. Hidalgo and Juárez end at **Jardín Hidalgo,** Valle's only plaza, bordered on the west by the **Parque Colosio** and **Río Valles.** Most accommodations and points of interest lie along Hidalgo and Juárez.

The **Central de Autobuses,** on the outskirts of town, is accessible by bus from Calle Hidalgo (2 pesos) or taxi (20 pesos). Oriente (tel. 2 39 02) serves: **Guadalajara** (10hr., 8 per day, 253 pesos); **Matamoros** (8hr., 7 per day, 228 pesos); **Querétaro** (8hr., 10:30pm, 193 pesos); **San Luis Potosí** (5hr., 11 per day, 141 pesos); **Tampico** (2½hr., every hr. 73 pesos); and **Xilitla** (1½hr., 3 per day, 25 pesos). Transpaís (tel. 2 38 59) runs buses to: **Monterrey** (7½hr., 10 per day, 231 pesos); **Reynosa** (7½hr., 5 per day, 231 pesos); and **Ciudad Victoria** (4hr., 5pm, 97 pesos).

Terrific maps of the town can be purchased for 8 pesos at the **Cámara de Comercio,** Carranza Sur 53 (tel. 2 45 11), half a block north of Hidalgo (open M-F 9am-1pm and 4:30-8:30pm), and at the Hotel Piña. The Cámara de Comercio is also happy to provide info on local and regional sights. **Banamex** (tel. 2 02 12), on Hidalgo at Madero, exchanges traveler's checks and has a 24-hour **ATM** (open M-F 9am-3pm). **Red Cross:** (tel. 2 00 56) **Police:** (tel. 2 53 53). **Post office:** Juárez 520 (tel. 2 01 04), with a **Mexpost** office inside (open M-F 8am-7pm, Sa 9am-1pm). **Postal code:** 79000. **Phone code:** 138.

▮▮ ACCOMMODATIONS AND FOOD. Several hotels dot the *centro.* **Hotel Piña,** Juárez 210 (tel. 2 01 83), offers clean rooms with private baths and enormous empty closets with no apparent purpose. Piña offers three different ranges of rooms—some have TVs or the much-needed A/C (singles 110-171 pesos; doubles 137-212 pesos). **La Troje** (tel. 2 48 80), adjoining Hotel Piña, offers *comida corrida* for only 20 pesos as well as a tasty variety of *antojitos* (10-50 pesos) in brightly decorated and marvelously air-conditioned comfort.

XILITLA

A serpentine road winds through the rocky *huasteca* highlands to the tiny, lush hamlet of Xilitla, 1½ hours from and 1000m above Ciudad Valles. The town itself (pop. 10,000) consists of dozens of sidewalk stores and a tiny market offering staples to locals and crafts to tourists. Xilitla's main attraction, however, is its incredible beauty; the town rises to a picturesque central plaza with phenomenal views. The area has over 150 caves, including El Sótano de las Golondrinas, a spelunker's dream, over 450m deep with a cave floor covering approximately six acres. Xilitla's most fabulous and notable attraction is the beautiful and bizarre "ruins" built by Edward James early this century, known locally as Las Pozas. The natural splendor of dozens of waterfalls, rivers ripe for rafting, horseback trails, unofficial sanctuaries of wild orchids, and rare animals are accessible from Xilitla.

▐ ORIENTATION AND PRACTICAL INFORMATION. The bus station sits just below town. It is served by Vencedor, with buses rolling to: **Ciudad Valles** (1½hr., every hr. 5:30am-7pm, 30 pesos); **Jalpan** (45min., every hr., 32 pesos); **San Luis Potosí** (6½hr.; 5am, 12:30 and 1:30pm; 143 pesos); and **Tampico** (4½hr., 6 per day, 93 pesos). Flecha Amarilla (tel. 5 02 33) goes to: **Jalpan** (2hr., 4 per day, 28 pesos); **Mexico City** (8hr., 3 per day, 116 pesos); and **Querétaro** (6½hr., 8 per day, 92 pesos). To get to the **Plaza Central,** officially named **Jardín Hidalgo,** go up the stairs to the right of the bus station and turn right on Zaragosa. Exchange currency or traveler's checks at the **Centro de Cambio** (tel. 5 02 81), on the right-hand side of Zaragosa as you go toward the plaza (open daily 8am-8pm). **Banorte** (tel. 5 00 29), on the Zaragosa side of the plaza, also exchanges currency and checks and has a 24 hour **ATM** (open M-F 9am-2:30pm). **Police:** on the plaza, in the Palacio Municipal. **Red Cross:** (tel. 5 01 25) on the road descending from Xilitla. **Farmacia San Augustín:** (tel. 5 00 11) on Hidalgo, at the northwest corner of the Plaza Principal (open daily 8:30am-9pm). **Post office:** behind the Palacio on Calle Zaragoza (south side of the plaza), on the 2nd floor (open M-F 9am-3pm). **Postal code:** 79902. **Long-distance public phone:** Hotel Ziyaquetzas on the Zaragosa side of the plaza. **Phone code:** 136.

▮▮ ACCOMMODATIONS AND FOOD. In mid-summer, Xilitla's few and wonderful hotels fill up fast and require reservations. Along Jardín Hidalgo, **Hotel Ziyaquetzas** (tel. 5 00 81 or 5 02 45) offers ultra-clean rooms with fans and astounding views (singles 100 pesos; doubles 120 pesos). Nature-lovers will be happy to spend the extra pesos to **sleep in the forest** in **Las Pozas** (tel. 5 02 03). Rooms are as wild and varied as you can imagine. They range in price from 180 pesos for a room that holds two people to 400 pesos for a room that holds four. Las Pozas also has a little **restaurant** where you can eat to the sound of the waterfalls for 15-50 pesos (open daily 9am-5pm). In town, tiny restaurants line Escobedo just past the plaza, all offering delicious meals at rock-bottom prices (10-16 pesos; open from about 7am until no one is left on the streets).

⚙ SIGHTS. Xilitla's main attraction is **Las Pozas** (the pools), formally called the **Enchanted Garden of Edward James.** To get there, walk down Ocampo, at the northwest corner of the plaza. Continue as it veers right and turns into a path. This path lets you out onto the main road at a white bridge. Cross the bridge and take your first left, following the upward dirt path until you get to a gravel road; make a left and walk on for about 2km. The breathtaking (seriously, it will physically take your breath away) walk is about 45 minutes long. Las Pozas will be on your right. Those with sore feet can take a *combi* (5 pesos) from the top of the stairs near the bus station to the white bridge, or find a taxi to take you right to the gates (45 pesos).

The son of a wealthy nobleman, James was a good old-fashioned English eccentric, obsessed with cleanliness and tissue paper and sometimes requiring his secretaries to work in the buff. After early experiments with poetry and art, James created a universe of concrete, steel, and stone in wild colors and even wilder shapes throughout the jungle. James' melange of bridges, arches, and artistic relics recalls *Alice in Wonderland*, with winding staircases that lead to nowhere, a library without books, and other touches of madness. Wander for hours through the forest to run into wild blue and pink flowers as well as crazily shaped houses now inhabited by older men who used to work for Señor Edward. James channeled the waterfall running through Las Pozas's 36 structures into the nine pools themselves. They're safe for swimming—bring your bathing suit.(Open daily 9am-8pm. Admission 10 pesos.)

For more information about what else to do in the area, contact Avery and Lenore Danziger, owners of El Castillo, a resort down the hill from Xilitla's main plaza. This infinitely wise and fabulously friendly couple (tel. 5 00 38) is best contacted through email: junglegossip@compuserve.com, where they can direct you to their soon-to-be-finalized web site. Besides running a lovely resort, these folks can provide information about nearby sites, Huastecan culture, hiking, rafting, and other outdoor opportunities. If they're not in, ask whoever answers the door for their pamphlets, which offer some guidance.

In town, Xilitla's historical claim to fame is the quietly graying **Ex-Convento Agostino,** on the western side of the plaza. Built between 1550 and 1557, the ex-convent is the oldest colonial building in the state. Although the exterior could use a good white-washing, the interior is beautifully preserved. A large, quiet courtyard is surrounded by little altars, childrens' creations, and, to one side, a never-empty church.

For the commercially inclined, shops and stands selling fruit, shoes, crafts, and trinkets line either side of the plaza on Zaragoza and Escobedo. Enter the shop on the southwest corner of the plaza to find beautiful *artesenia* from all over Mexico at astoundingly low prices or just chow on some *comida corrida* for 25 pesos.

CIUDAD VICTORIA

Ciudad Victoria (pop. 245,000) may be the sleepiest state capital in Mexico. On the edge of the Sierra Gorda, Ciudad Victoria makes an ideal stopping point when traveling to and from the border. The city also serves as a good starting point for those intent on diving into nature. Among the natural sights a short ride away from the city, are the Cañón del Novillo—a glorious spot for hiking and camping, and the Boca de San Juan Capitán—a stream of unmatched beauty. Ardent hikers or those simply looking to escape may want to visit the Reserva de la Biosfera El Cielo, 50 km from the city. Although Ciudad Victoria is relatively nondescript, it offers a mild climate and a relaxed, welcoming environment for the weary traveller. The Ciudad Victoria Expo takes place during the second week of October. It features live music, dancing, and artisanry from the surrounding areas.

NORTHEAST MEXICO

⁊ ORIENTATION AND PRACTICAL INFORMATION

Ciudad Victoria's main attractions can be found centered around the **Plaza Hidalgo** (all north of the **Río San Marcos**) which is bordered by **Morelos** to the north and **Hidalgo** to the south. The streets running north to south are numbered. **Calle 8,** otherwise known as **Tijerina,** is on the east side of the plaza and **Calle 9,** otherwise known as **Colón,** is on the west side. The **Catedral del Refugio** is facing the east side of the plaza with the **Museo de Antropología e Historía** facing the north side.

The **Central de Autobuses,** northeast of the *centro*, off Calle Torres, is accesible from the plaza for three pesos in a *combi*, or 30 pesos in a taxi. Sendor Tamaulipas (tel. 6 72 42) serves **Monterrey** (4hr., every hr., 129 pesos) and **Nuevo Laredo** (7hr., every 4 hrs., 250 pesos). Transpaiz (tel. 6 77 99) runs to: **Matamoros** (4hr., every hr., 131 pesos); **Reynosa** (4hr., every hr., 134 pesos); **Ciudad Valles** (4hr., every hr., 97 pesos); and **Tampico** (3½hr. every hr, 100 pesos). Transporte del Norte (tel. 6 01 38) has a line to **San Luis Potosí** (10hr., every hr., 166 pesos). There is a **luggage storage** in the bus station (open daily 7am-10:30pm; 3.50 pesos per hr.).

The **tourist office,** 272 Calle Rosales (tel. 2 50 84 or 2 50 17), near the Paseo Pedro J. Mendez and just west off of Blvd. Balboa (which runs adjacent to Río San Marcos), provides everything you need to know about the city and the marvelous state of Tamaulipas (open M-F 8am-8pm). **Exchange currency** or traveler's checks at **BanCrecer** (tel. 2 75 88) on the corner of Hidalgo and Nafarrette with a 24 hour **ATM.** Or try the handful of banks along Hidalgo.

Emergency: 060. **Police:** (tel. 3 50 47) or, if you need to locate a missing person, call **Locatel** (tel. 2 20 20). **Red Cross:** (tel. 6 20 77). **Hospital General Libramiento Fidel:** at 1845 Velázquez Ote. (tel. 6 21 97 or 6 22 57) **Post office:** (tel. 2 12 85) on Tijenna between Morelos and Matamoros. (Open M-F 8am-7pm and Sa 8am-12pm.) **Phone code:** 131.

⌂ ACCOMMODATIONS

There are a number of expensive luxury hotels in Ciudad Victoria while the cheaper lodgings vary in quality. **Hotel Fiesta Plaza,** Juárez 401 (tel. 2 78 77), just off Calle 14 (Nafarrelle), offers bright, spacious rooms. The friendly staff makes the stay worth the extra pesos as does the cable TV and A/C. (Singles 250 pesos; doubles 280 pesos; triples 340 pesos.) For a bit more you can bask in luxury at the **Hotel Sierra Gorda** (tel. 2 20 10), right on the south side of Plaza Hidalgo. The hotel has a barber, a restaurant (*Las Candiles* open daily 7am-1:30pm), and a game room under construction. All rooms come with A/C and cable TV and some have a VCR for which you can rent videos in the lobby. (Splurge on a single 355 pesos; doubles 398 pesos; triples 428 pesos.)

◖ FOOD

If an urge hits you to rip off the Tevas and don your wingtips, try some of the fancy restaurants in the even fancier hotels around the *centro*. But for a filling *comida corrida* (28 pesos), **Café Canton,** Colón 114 (tel. 2 21 77) just south of the plaza, soothes the palate while helping you beat the empty-wallet blues. (Entrees 15-28 pesos.) To enjoy some unbelievable *gorditas*, the local favorite, **Doña Tota's,** Juárez 205, will serve up 4 to 5 *gorditas* that will leave you panting with an uncontrollable need for more. This glorified taco stand offers all the taste of a street-side vendor but cleaner; for just a bit more money— your satisfied stomach will thank you. (Open daily 9am-11pm.)

👁️ 🎵 SIGHTS AND ENTERTAINMENT

As the state capital, Ciudad Victoria's **Palacio de Gobierno,** on the corner of Hidalgo and Calle 17 (Madero), is fittingly grandiose and harbors large, impressive murals. The **mercado** north of Hidalgo between Calle 5 and 6, offers everything from artistry to goat liver. For those perpetually craving knowledge, the **Museo de Antropología e Historía,** on the north side of Plaza Hidalgo is allegedly open Monday through Friday 9am to 7pm but seems to close unexpectedly and sporadically. The collection boasts *indígena* art and artifacts, historical photographs, and a small fossil collection. For those bound to the biological reserve of **El Cielo,** red-tape must first be slashed and burned. To receive the necessary permission from *el gobierno*, **Sra. Ivonne Lana** (tel. 2 97 77), on the 9th floor of the Torre Gobierno on Blvd. Balboa, needs to give the big OK. If possible, call early because the bureaucracy takes more than a week. This office will also be happy to help with lodgings within the park.

CENTRAL MEXICO

The states of **Guanajuato** and **Querétaro** form a vast, bowl-shaped plateau of fertile soil, rolling farms, and verdant hillsides, all home to some of Mexico's most exquisite colonial *pueblos* and cities. Since the 16th century, its silver-rich underground has brought the region prosperity and shaped its history. In the 18th century, the city of Guanajuato supplied most of Mexico's minting silver, and the area became one of the wealthier and more influential in the country. Guanajuato later became the commercial and banking center of this thriving region. Today, the region is home to a growing expatriot population in and around San Miguel de Allende, one of the most lively and culturally charged cities in Mexico. Nearby **Hidalgo,** one of the most mountainous states in Mexico and home to the pine-laden edge of the Sierra Madre Oriental, also lived on silver for much of its colonial history. Although best known for its archaeological sites, like Tula, Hidalgo is home to slow-paced colonial towns including the pleasant Pachuca.

Although Veracruz was the first part of Mexico to bear the colonial mark of Hernán Cortés, the Conquest did not really pick up steam until his group ventured inland to **Puebla** and **Tlaxcala,** where many local tribes joined the entourage. A glimpse into one of the region's 16th-century temples, where images from *indígena* mythology mingle with Catholic icons, indicates the pervasiveness of elements from indigenous cultures, despite missionaries and 'conquistadors' attempts at complete subjugation.

Contrary to popular belief, the **Estado de México** has more to offer than easy access to insanely populated Mexico City. In the area outside Mexico City's smog cloud, green plains creep up snowy volcanoes and swollen towns continue to grow, pushing against their natural barriers. The state is speckled with stellar archaeological sites, solemn convents, and vestiges of the colonial era. Forests seem to stretch forever, and small towns and villages within appear untouched by modernity.

After Emperor Maximilian built his summer home in Cuernavaca, thousands of Mexicans followed him and **Morelos** became a prime vacation spot. Once again, the state enjoyed the same interest that had first brought the Olmecs from the Gulf Coast nearly 3000 years earlier. These days, Mexicans and foreigners alike march to Morelos to take advantage of Cuernavaca's "eternal spring," Xochicalco's beautifully desolate ruins, and Tepoztlán's striking landscape. Unlike the overpopulated Federal District, parts of Morelos remain undeveloped, with plentiful tree-covered vistas and unspoiled streams. Morelos is just a short jaunt from the D.F.; you can easily spend a day in Cuernavaca or Tepoztlán and return to the capital in the evening.

HIGHLIGHTS OF CENTRAL MEXICO

■ **Guanajuato** (see p. 302) and **San Miguel de Allende** (see p. 309) are two of Mexico's most perfect and picturesque colonial towns. They've got everything from cobblestone streets to mountain views to huge international student populations. Guanajuato is especially notable during its yearly festival in October, **El Cervantino** (see p. 309). You'll come for a day and stay for a month.

■ The **great pyramid of Cholula** (see p. 365) is one of the largest in the world, rivaling those at Giza, Egypt.

■ Learn to *salsa* with thousands of language-school students in **Cuernavaca** (see p. 337), a lively, posh city with an impressive array of **nightclubs** (see p. 343).

■ Check out the **massive statues of warriors** (the Atlantes; see p. 329) at the archaeological site of **Tula** (see p. 328), once the capital of the Toltec Empire.

■ Stuff your face with delicious **mole dishes** and **sweets** in the modern metropolis of **Puebla** (see p. 354).

Central Mexico

N

75 miles
0
75 kilometers
0

Golfo De Mexico

SIERRA MADRE ORIENTAL

SAN LUIS POTOSÍ

QUERÉTARO

HIDALGO

GUANAJUATO

JALISCO

COLIMA

MICHOACÁN

MEXICO

TLAXCALA

PUEBLA

VERACRUZ

OAXACA

MORELOS

GUERRERO

OCÉANO PACÍFICO

Tuxpan

Papantla
El Tajín

Xalapa

Veracruz
150

Córdoba
150

Tehuacán
125

Huajuapan
de León

San Andrés
Tuxtla
Catemaco
145

Santiago
Tuxtla

Huautla

Tuxtepec

Pachuca
105

Tula

Tequisquiapan

Querétaro

57

Mexico City
Netzahualcóyotl
15
Toluca

Popocatépetl

Cholula
Puebla
190

Cuautla
Cuernavaca
Cacahuamilpa
Taxco
Iguala
95

Tlaxcala

Zitácuaro

Dolores
Hidalgo
Guanajuato
San Miguel
de Allende
Salamanca
45

Morelia

Pátzcuaro

Uruapan

Zamora
15

La Piedad

León
57

Lagos de
Moreno

Aguascalientes
45

AGUASCALIENTES
Aguascalientes

80

Lázaro
Cárdenas

GUANAJUATO

GUANAJUATO

Guanajuato (gwa-nah-WAH-toh) was the former capital of the Republic under the presidency of Benito Juárez. Now, it is not only a bastion of cultural, historical, and natural wealth but also a captivating colonial town. The road into the city winds through sloping mountains dotted with rows of *nopales* (prickly-pear cacti) contrasting with the bright, red soil. The hills gradually give way to the city where the legacy of colonial days can still be observed in the rich culture and architecture. Serpentine slate streets overflow with monuments to the silver barons who made Guanajuato one of the richest mining towns in North America, while *callejones* (stone alleyways) sneak through Spanish archways and court-yards and lead to the city's myriad of museums, theaters, and cathedrals. Though the mining boom days are over, Guanajuato is now livelier than ever. University students and musicians promote an animated and light-hearted lifestyle, and the city continues to enjoy its status as a favorite destination among Mexican and foreign tourists.

■ ORIENTATION

Guanajuato lies 380km northwest of Mexico City. Navigating the city's tangled maze of streets and *callejones* can lead people in circles even with the best of maps. The **Plaza de la Paz,** the **Basílica,** and the **Jardín Unión** mark the center of town. **Av. Juárez** climbs eastward past the *mercado* and Plaza de la Paz. Just past the *basílica,* the street becomes **Luis Obregón;** past Teatro Juárez, it turns into **Av. Sopeña.** The **Subterránea,** which roughly follows the path of Juárez/Sopeña, is an underground avenue built beneath the former riverbed. When you become lost (and you will), remember that the tunnel is always downhill from you.

Guanajuato's **bus station** is 3km west of town; from there, the "El Centro" bus takes you to the heart of the city, while the "Mercado" bus takes you to the market. Buses cross the city running westward above ground and eastward underground (every 5 min., daily 6am-10:30pm, 1 peso). A **taxi** from the bus station to the *centro* costs 15 pesos. Taxis within the city cost about 10 pesos. The bus system is easy to follow, but make sure to request a stop from the driver because they shout out locations rapidly and incoherently.

■ PRACTICAL INFORMATION

TRANSPORTATION

Buses: Central de Autobuses, west of the *centro.* Take the "Central de Autobuses" bus from Plaza de la Paz to the station (1.50 pesos). Flecha Amarilla (tel. 3 13 33), sends buses to: **Aguascalientes** (3hr.; 8:30am, 4:40, and 5:50pm; 55 pesos); **Celaya** (2hr; every 40 min. 6am-8:40 pm; 33 pesos); **León** (1hr.; every 10 min. 5:40am-10:30pm; 15 pesos); **San Luis Potosí** (4hr.; 7:20am, 1pm; 75 pesos); and **San Miguel de Allende** (1hr.; 8 per day 7am-6pm; 29 pesos). Futura (tel 3 13 44) sends 1st-class buses to: **Mexico City** (5hr.; 4 per day 10:20am-midnight; 135 pesos); and **Monterrey** (11hr.; 6:30pm; 269 pesos). ETN (tel. 3 02 89) sends luxury buses to: **Guadalajara** (3¾hr.; 8am, 12:30, and 5:30pm; 160 pesos); **Irapuato** (45min.; 5:30, 8:30am, and 6:30pm; 22 pesos); and other destinations. Servicios Coordinados (3 13 33) and Omnibus Mexico (3 13 56) both sell tickets in **Guanajuato** and offer 1st-class bus service out of nearby **León.**

Guanajuato

ACCOMMODATIONS

A Posada Hidalgo
B Hotel Posada San Francisco
C Hotel La Condesa
D Casa Kloster

TO CASA DE LEYENDAS

Carretera Panorámica

Temezcuitate

Sangre de Cristo

Cjón. Espinazo

Túnel del Barretero

Miguel Hidalgo

Manuel Matavacas

Campanero

Tecolote

Doblado

Perros Muertos

Tambores

Cantaramas

Sopeña

Potrero

Museo Iconográfico del Quijote

Antiguo Camino a Guanajuato

Cjón. Buenavista

Cjón. Domínico

Glor. de la Alameda

Cjón. Cascarones

Cjón. Papudo

Mextamora

Teatro Juárez

Pochote

Cancela

Túnel La Galereña

Maria

Jardín Unión

Obregón

Constancia

San Miguel

Carretera panorámica

Cámbio Navarro

Ayuntamiento

Truco

San Diego

Basílica de Nuestra Señora de Guanajuato

Alonso

Guadalupe

Templo de la Compañia

Reforma

Ponciano

Aguilar

De Sopeña

Alonso

Santo del Monte

Zapote

Peñascos

Universidad de Guanajuato

Museo del Pueblo de Guanajuato

PLAZA DE LA PAZ

Túnel Miguel Hidalgo

Quebradita

Mulas

Pocitos

Cerro del Cuarto

Juan Valle

Cjón. Calixto

Zavala

León de Bronce

Túnel Los Ángeles

Cjón. Moyas

Museo y Casa de Diego Rivera

Juárez

Callejón del Beso

Subida Cerro del Cuarto

Túnel Santa Fe

Pocitos

Galarza

San Miguel

Jardín de la Reforma

Av. Juárez

Rosarito

Cjón. Guadalupe

C. Pozuelos

Cjón. Graiero

Mendizabal

Mercado Hidalgo

Gavira

Peñas

Cuatro Vientos

Cjón. Chilito

Terremoto

28 de Septiembre

Museo de la Alhóndiga de Granaditas

5 de Mayo

Hidalgo

Juárez

Cienfuegos

Cantador

De La Alhóndiga

C. Apartado

Llantos de Salgado

Insurgencia

Túnel Tamazuca

Insurgencia

Hidalgo

Tepetapa

Cjón. Griteria

TOURIST AND FINANCIAL SERVICES

Tourist Office: Coordinación de Turismo, Plaza de la Paz 14 (tel. 2 15 74 or 2 19 82; fax 2 42 51; email turismo@quijote.ugto.mx.), on your right as you head up Juárez from the market to the *Basílica*. English-speaking staff distributes *folletos* (brochures) and mediocre maps. Open M-W 9am-7pm, Th-F 9am-8pm, Sa 10am-4pm, Su 10am-2pm.

Currency Exchange: Banks line Juárez and Plaza de la Paz. **BITAL,** Plaza de la Paz 59 (tel. 2 00 18; fax 2 25 07), is open for exchange M-Sa 8am-7pm. **Banco Bilbao Vizcaya,** Plaza de la Paz 69 (tel. 2 94 78 or 2 94 79), is open for exchange M-F 9am-5pm. **ATM** inside same building as **Fax** (below).

Laundry: Lavandería Automática, Manuel Doblado 28 (tel. 2 67 18). Self- and full-service. Open M-Sa 9am-2pm and 4-8pm.

EMERGENCY AND COMMUNICATIONS

Emergency: dial 060.

Police: Alhóndiga 8 (tel. 2 02 66 or 2 27 17), close to Calle Juárez. Open 24hr.

Red Cross: (tel. 2 04 87), on Juárez, 2 blocks beyond the *mercado*. Open for emergencies 24hr. Some English spoken.

Pharmacy: San Francisco de Asis, Ponciano Aguilar 15 (tel. 2 89 16), just off the Plaza de la Paz. Open daily 7am-10:30pm.

Hospital: Clinica Hospital de Especialidades (tel. 2 23 05 or 2 13 38), Plaza de la Paz. English spoken by Dr. Sanchez Leyva and Dr. López Márquez. Open 24hr.

Post Office: Ayuntamiento 25 (tel. 2 03 85), across from the Templo de la Compañía. Follow Truco, the street running behind the *Basílica*, for 1 block and turn left. Open M-F 8am-7pm, Sa 9am-1pm. **Postal Code:** 36000.

Fax: Sopeña 1 (tel. 2 69 91), to your left facing Teatro Juárez. Open M-F 8am-7pm, Sa-Su 9am-noon. Also in **Computel** (see below).

Internet Access: Redes Internet Guanajuato, Alonso 70 (tel. 2 06 11; email root@redes.int.com.mx). Email 20 pesos per 30min., 30 pesos per hr. MC, Visa, AmEx. Open M-F 9am-8pm and Sa 9am-2pm. More access can be found at **Cantananas 5** near the Teatro Principal. Email 20 pesos per hour.

Telephones: LADATELs are around Plaza de la Paz and throughout the city. **Lonchería y Caseta de Larga Distancia Pípila,** Constancia 9 (tel. 2 00 75), behind the Templo de San Diego. Open M-Sa 10am-9pm, Su 11am-3pm.

Phone Code: 473.

ACCOMMODATIONS

The neighborhood around the *basílica* is home to some inexpensive hotels, often occupied by young people from every corner of the globe. More economic lodgings cluster near the *mercado* and the **Alhóndiga.** Those visiting Guanajuato on weekends, during the *Festival Cervantino* in October, or during *Semana Santa* in April, should make hotel reservations far in advance and expect prices to rise dramatically. The tourist office keeps a list of families who rent out rooms during the festival. Most hotels do not take credit cards.

 Casa Kloster, Alonso 32 (tel. 2 00 88). As you leave the *Basílica* and pass the Plaza de la Paz, turn left on Callejón de las Estrellas and follow it to Alonso. Clean, airy rooms overlook an open courtyard filled with flowers and chirping birds. Sparkling communal bathrooms. Friendly guests include mostly traveling international students and the management is extremely helpful. 70 pesos per person. Reservations recommended.

Posada Hidalgo, Juárez 220 (tel. 2 31 45), 1 block past the *mercado*. The simple rooms have faux wood paneling and very small bathrooms. The restaurant inside serves breakfast and lunch specials: all-you-can-eat for 30 pesos. Singles are 80 pesos.

Hotel La Condesa, Plaza de la Paz 60 (tel. 2 14 62), nestled in the corner of the plaza, is a great base for exploring the attractions of Guanajuato. Neon signs and suits of armor brighten up the spooky but fun lobby. Each room's door is emblazoned with grim black-and-white scenes from around Guanajuato. Never fear, rooms are old but clean and have bathrooms; all have bottled water. Expect noise from the *discoteca* downstairs. Singles 80 pesos; doubles 110 pesos; 2 beds 120 pesos.

Hotel Posada San Francisco, Juárez 178 (tel. 2 24 67 or 2 20 84), at Plaza Gavira, the big green hotel next to the market. Clean, brightly colored bedrooms with shiny, white bathrooms and an antechamber for entertaining guests. All rooms come with TV, but if you feel lonely (which is hard to feel right on the noisy *calle*) you can watch in the 2nd fl. lounge, with a suit of armor to keep you company. All rooms contain bottled water. Singles 125 pesos; doubles 150 pesos throughout the year.

◖ FOOD

Inexpensive restaurants cluster around Guanajuato's plazas and near the *Basílica*. Prices rise near the **Jardín Unión**, as does the gringos-per-square-inch ratio. There are affordable fruit and taco stands all over the city as well as many small snack shops selling *dulces* (candy) and *refrescos* (beverages).

Truco No. 7, Truco 7 (tel. 2 83 74), the 1st left beyond the *basílica* heading towards the jardín. Artsy, funky, dark, and immensely popular with both local and foreign students and families. International pop music fills the air of this dimly lit, soothing environment. Breakfast 11 pesos. *Antojitos* and *comida corrida* 13-40 pesos. Open daily 8:30am-11:30pm.

Panadería Purisima, Juárez 138 on the right side of the street heading to Plaza de la Paz, 1 block past the Mercado. This *panaderia* (bakery) lacks a sign but travelers will have no trouble finding it: just follow the wafting scents of fresh baked rolls, *galletas* (cookies) and pastries (.5-1 pesos each) and the steady crowd of patrons flowing in and out of its doors. A cheap and delicious way to fulfill morning and afternoon cravings.

El Retiro, Sopeña 12 (tel. 2 06 22), across from the Teatro Juárez. Escape from the crowded *jardín* to join families and young couples feasting on breakfast (17-22 pesos), Mexican specialties (15-30 pesos), or the *menú del día* (26 pesos). Top off your meal with a cold beer (14-18 pesos) or a drink (14-28 pesos) from the fully stocked bar. Vegetarian selections are available. Open daily 8am-11pm.

La Loca Rana, Pozitos 32 (tel. 2 13 25), across the street from Diego Rivera's house. After you have worked up an appetite leering at the relics of Rivera's youth, catch a *fútbol* game on the tube with local students filling up on the tasty 3 course *menú del día* (15 pesos), *chilaquiles* (14 pesos), or *flautas* (5 pesos). Breakfast 12-15 pesos. Open M-F 8am-midnight, Sa 8am-5pm.

◉ SIGHTS

JARDÍN UNIÓN. In the heart of the city and one block east of the *Basílica*, the Jardín is the town's social center. This triangular plaza boasts enough shops, cafes, and guitar-strumming locals to satisfy any tourist. During the afternoons and evenings, crowds gather to relax on the benches under the shade of the surrounding trees or listen to the state band perform every Thursday and Sunday.

TEATRO JUÁREZ. Built in 1903 for dictator Porfirio Díaz, the theater has an unabashedly ornate facade—columns, lampposts, statues, bronze lions and eight staring muses. The auditorium betrays its Moorish design: half-circles, arabesques, and endlessly weaving frescoed flowers in green, red, yellow, and brown make the interior seem overwhelmingly colorful. In addition to housing government offices, the Teatro Juárez still hosts plays, operas, ballets, classical music concerts, and the main events of the Festival Cervantino. *(Tel. 2 01 83. Faces*

1 corner of Jardín Unión. Open Tu-Su 9am-1:45pm and 5-7:45pm, except on days of perfor-mances. Admission 5 pesos. Cameras 2 pesos. Video cameras 5 pesos. Performance tickets 30-50 pesos.)

BASÍLICA DE NUESTRA SEÑORA DE GUANAJUATO. This elegant Baroque structure was started in 1671 and took 25 years to construct. Dozens of candela-bra illuminate the Doric interior, including fine ornamental frescoes and paintings of the Madonna by Miguel Cabrera. The wooden image of the city's protectress, Nuestra Señora de Guanajuato, rests on a pure silver base and is believed to be the **oldest piece of Christian art in Mexico.** The *Basílica* rises above Guanajuato's central plaza, the Plaza de la Paz. The large square, lovely outdoor cafes and itinerant vendors make this a popular gathering place. *(Basílica open daily 8am-9pm.)*

TEMPLO DE LA COMPAÑÍA. Completed in 1765, the Jesuit temple was shut down just two years later when the Jesuits were expelled from Spanish America. The ornate stone exterior is one of the most striking in the region, and it still has four of the original five Churrigueresque facades. Life-size and life-like statues of the *Virgén* and the apostles as well as gruesome representations of Christ surround the interior. There is an art exhibit containing an original collection, including a 17th-century painting of San Ignacio de Loyola and an 18th-century representation of San Francisco de Asis. At the end of the exhibit is a spooky *relicario*, a wooden shelf enveloped in gold leaf, holding a collection of human bones. *(Tel. 2 18 27. Next to the university and one block north of the Basílica. Open daily 7am-9pm. 5 peso donation requested to support the restoration process.)*

MUSEO ICONOGRÁFICO DEL QUIJOTE. One of the best museums in Guanajuato is housed in a gorgeous colonial mansion reminiscent of 18th-century Spanish architecture. Ten large galleries contain over 600 works of art inspired by Cer-vantes's anti-hero Don Quijote, including paintings, sculptures, stained-glass win-dows, clocks, and even chess pieces. Artists such as Dalí, Picasso, Daumier, Ocampo, and Coronel have all interpreted Quijote. *(Manuel Doblado 1. East of the Jardín Unión following Calle Sopeña. Tel. 2 33 76 or 2 67 21; fax 2 61 17; www.guana-juato.gob.mx/mquijote. Open Tu-Sa 10am-6:30pm, Su 10am-2:30pm. Free.)*

MUSEO DE LA ALHÓNDIGA DE GRANADITAS. Constructed as a granary between 1797 and 1809, this building witnessed some of the more crucial and bloody battles of the fight for Mexican independence. Today, the Alhóndiga is an ethnographic, archaeological, and historical museum. A chamber on the first floor charts the course of Mexican nationhood. Other exhibits display the work of *indígena* artisans of the Bajío region: masks, firecrackers, engraved machetes, tapestries, and candy horse skeletons designed for consumption on *El Día de los Muertos* (The Day of the Dead). Another gallery shows Romualdo García's photographs of Mexicans on the eve of the 1910 Revolution. While the hall, containing sculpted faces of the heroes of 1910, is nothing short of stunning, the museum's finest exhibition traces the social history of Guanajuato from the Conquest through the Revolution. Captivating murals overwhelm the ceiling and sides of the stairwells and are often mistaken for those of José Clemente Orozco or Diego Rivera; the true painter, José Chávez Morado, was a contemporary of both artists. *Abolición de Esclavitud* (1955), the earliest of these murals, follows Mexico's history from the Conquest and Indian encomienda slavery, on to the Revolution, by which time native groups had regained some measure of power. *(Tel. 2 11 12. At the west end of Pozitos on the corner of Calle Mendizabal. Open Tu-Sa 10am-1:30pm and 4-5:30pm, Su 10am-2:30pm. Admission 14 pesos, free for students, seniors, under 13, and on Su. Cameras 1 peso. Video camera 30 pesos.)*

MUSEO Y CASA DE DIEGO RIVERA. The museum chronicles the life of Guana-juato's most famous native son; he was born in 1886 in this house, which was converted to a museum after his death. Works reveal the influence of Picasso, from landscapes to Cubist sketches and elongated nudes, as well as Rivera's later fascination with Maya art. Visitors can admire furniture from his childhood home and then move upstairs to study works arranged chronologically and representatively of his different artistic periods. Don't miss the outstanding watercolor illustrations for the *Popol Vuh* (the sacred book of the Maya), which imitate Maya iconography, as well as Rivera's sketch for a section of the mural commissioned in 1933 by New York's Rockefeller Center—the mural was destroyed after a portrait of Lenin was discovered in it. This sketch, which portrays a woman enslaved by a machine with the head of Adolf Hitler, was not incorporated into the final composition. The museum also holds several photos of Rivera and his wife of 22 years, fellow artist Frida Kahlo. *(Pocitos 47. Tel. 2 11 97. Open Tu-Sa 10am-6:30pm, Su 10am-2:30pm. Admission 8 pesos, students and teachers 5 pesos, seniors and children free.)*

MUSEO DEL PUEBLO DE GUANAJUATO. The museum houses a permanent collection of 18th- and 19th- century works by Mexican artists and rotating exhibits of work by contemporary Mexican artists. *(Pocitos 7, next to the university. Tel. 2 29 90. Open Tu-Su 10am-6:30pm. Admission 8 pesos, students and teachers with ID 5 pesos, seniors and children free.)*

MONUMENTO AL PÍPILA. Museums and churches are not the only sites of interest in Guanajuato. Looking down on the *jardín* from the nearby hill is the Monumento al Pípila which commemorates the miner who torched the Alhóndiga's front door. This lookout site is not to be missed. For a panoramic view of the city while descending the hill, follow the even steeper path down the west side which ends near the *Tunel de los Angeles*. If you're planning to walk up at night, take a friend. The titanic Pípila looks most impressive at night, when he is illuminated by spotlights. While the view of Pípila from below is striking, the monument itself affords a magnificent panoramic vista of the city and the surrounding mountains. To ascend even higher, pay one peso to climb the narrow staircase inside the monument to a small platform behind the back of the infamous miner. *(Open daily 8am-8pm. To reach the statue, follow Sopeña to the east and take the steep but manageable Callejón del Calvario to your right (a 5min. climb), or hop a bus marked "Pípila" from Plaza de la Paz (every 20min., 6am-10pm, 1.5 pesos.)*

CALLEJÓN DEL BESO. The most famous alley in the city, "Kiss Alley," is off Juárez, about two blocks down from the *Basílica* off the Plaza de Los Angeles, just as Juárez curves right towards the market. Local lore has it that a Spanish aristocrat living on one side of the Callejón surprised his daughter one night while she was kissing her lover, a poor miner. Enraged by the lover's low breeding and occupation, the father cursed his daughter and forbade her to see her lover ever again. Ignoring her father, the young woman returned to her lover. When he discovered her insubordination, the Spaniard flew into a rage and stabbed his daughter to death. The alley is so narrow that people can literally lean out their windows and kiss each other.

MERCADO HIDALGO. Constructed in 1910 in honor of the 100th anniversary of the struggle for national independence, the *mercado's* entrance is a monumental Neoclassical arch another block farther down Juárez from the Callejón del Beso. The stands sell everything from *carne* (meat) to small, hand-crafted woolen dolls; most of the fun is haggling over *los precios. (Most stalls open daily 11am-9pm.)*

CASA DE LEYENDAS. Guanajuato has many attractions that are just a short bus ride from the center of town (2 pesos). This museum aims to convey and preserve Guanajuatense legend. Dioramas complete with moving figures and special effects recreate Guanajuato's many legends. Cringe as you watch the father of the famous lover from *Callejón del Beso* violently stab his daughter, then enter an elevator and "descend" into a mine filled with snakes, skeletons, and miners' unrealized

MUMMY DEAREST Museums in Guanajuato explore the historical, the artistic, the monumental, and the macabre. A museum of the latter variety is the **Museo de las Momias.** The mix of minerals in Guanajuato's soil naturally mummified the 122 corpses now on display in the museum. Cautiously tread through the catacombs, such as the *Salon de Culto a la Muerte,* and view morbid holograms, a mummified fetus, and torture weapons of the colonial era complete with the skulls of victims. Gag at the purplish, inflated body of a drowning victim; a woman buried alive, frozen in her attempt to scratch her way out of the coffin; two fashionable Frenchmen; a man who died by hanging; and another who was stabbed. The museum's oldest mummy has been around for 132 years, while its youngest has been on display for 12. The mummies are the most popular sight in Guanajuato, drawing a larger crowd than the less gory museums downtown. At the exit, vendors hawk 5 peso candy figurines of the more memorable mummies, some wearing little sombreros. *(Tel. 2 06 39. Next to the city cemetery west of town. To get to the museum, catch a "Las Momias" bus (1.50 pesos) in front of the Basílica or the market. To catch the bus back, go up the hill to your right as you exit the museum and follow it as it goes downhill. At the bottom of the hill, take a left and walk to the end of the street. Museum open daily 9am-6pm. 20 pesos. 14 pesos for students and seniors. Salon de Culto open daily 9am-6pm. 20 pesos.)*

dreams. Displays and guides in Spanish. *(Tel. 1 01 92. To get there, catch a "La Presa" bus for 1.50 pesos in the Subterránea or across from the Basílica and ask the driver to let you off at the Escuela Normal. From the Escuela, walk up the unmarked street to your left for two blocks, veering left at the fork. The museum will be directly in front of you at Súbida del Molino and Panorámica. Open Th-Tu 10am-2pm and 4-7pm. Admission 25 pesos.)*

EX-HACIENDA DE SAN GABRIEL DE BARRERA. Seventeen glorious gardens, each laid out in a different style, cover about three acres and are perhaps the most beautiful of Guanajuato's many natural attractions. Cobbled paths, well-groomed flora, and whistling birds are perfect impeti for a dreamy stroll. The ex-hacienda itself, a 16th-century structure, borders the gardens; its rooms contain furniture, silverware, and paintings from the era in which it was built. *(To get there, hop on a bus marked "Noria Alta/Marfil" across from the mercado (every 15min. 7am-9pm, 2 pesos), and tell the driver you're headed to San Gabriel de la Barrera. Tel. 2 06 19. Open daily Jan. 2-Dec.24 9am-6pm. Admission 10 pesos, students and seniors 5 pesos.)*

MONUMENTO A CRISTO REY. The monument stands atop a mountain 2850m above sea level about 20km from Guanajuato. The mountain, called the **Cerro del Cubilete,** is considered the geographical center of Mexico. The dark bronze statue of Jesus that lords over it is 16m tall and weighs more than 80 tons. Although the statue is striking, you may spend more time observing the surrounding landscape; long stretches of blue hills are visible from the summit. *(Take the "Cristo Rey" bus from the bus station (1hr., 7 per day 6am-4pm, 7 pesos). Arrive 15 min early to be safe.)*

 ENTERTAINMENT

The core of Guanajuato's nightlife rests in the bar/cafe scene. The venues in the vicinity of the **Jardín Unión** are friendly and relaxed, even for single women.

Damas de las Camelias es Él, Sopeña 32. A sophisticated crowd of local professionals groove to late-night Latin rhythms, while downing *cerveza* (15 pesos) and mixed drinks (25 pesos). Decorated by Juan Ibañez, a student of the Spanish director Luis Buñuel (see p. 26), the bar's tall yellow walls are covered with impressive cave-style paintings awkwardly juxtaposed with large portraits. A wide selection of flamenco, jazz, *salsa,* Cuban, Peruvian, and Portuguese music. Open daily 8pm-4am.

Chez Santos, Juan Valle 19. Located off Juárez just before turning up into Plaza de la Paz, the bar is set in a former horse stable—its dark red carpet and stone walls make it feel like a strange, romantic dungeon. The dark, moody, and mellow atmosphere calls for candlelight. Strangely enough, there is none, so it's a bit hard to see, which explains its reputation as a romantic rendezvous. The bar features a bargain 2 beers for 15 pesos and mixed drinks running from 12-18 pesos.

Café Dada, Baratillo 16. Follow Truco until it meets Calle Nuevo, then head down Nuevo until Baratillo, a small avenue that extends upward to your left. A much more casual hangout to play chess or chat with a whole range of clientele over an espresso for 5 pesos or cappuccino for 6 pesos while enjoying the work of local artists. Open daily 8:30am-11pm.

Guanajuato Grill, Alonso 20 (tel. 2 02 87), one block behind the Jardín Union. Neon palm trees mix with scantily clad men and women who surround the center bar before hitting one of the many dance floors. Thirsty students and eager dancers flock around the entrance and have the Grill bursting at the seams while the booming bass shakes the block. Beer costs 10 pesos. Open bar Tu and Th 9-10pm. No cover. Open Tu and Th-Sa 9pm-2am, but people still pack it in until 4am.

El Capitolio, (tel. 2 08 10) Plaza de la Paz, next door to Hotel La Condesa. Similar clientele and music to the Grill (techno, dance, etc.) but in a larger and darker room. Don't show up in sneakers and cut-offs or the bouncer will turn nasty. Beer 10 pesos, drinks 18-22 pesos. Open bar Sa 9pm-12:30am. Occasional cover. Open Tu-Sa 9pm-3am.

❋ FESTIVALS AND SEASONAL EVENTS

Guanajuato explodes during the **Festival Internacional Cervantino** for two weeks in October. The city invites repertory groups from all over the world to make merry with the *estudiantinas* (strolling student minstrels). The festivities take place mostly at local theaters, but many museums and churches are also transformed into stages for the events. Dramatic productions are always sold out. Tickets are sold by TicketMaster a month in advance and sell rapidly. The **Office of the Festival Internacional Cervantino** (tel. 2 11 69; fax 2 67 75) provides more information.

On June 24 of each year, Guanajuato celebrates the **Feria de San Juan,** at the Presa de la Olla, with dancing, cultural events, fireworks, and sports. Shorter celebrations occur on **Día de la Cueva** (July 31), when residents walk to a cave's entrance to honor San Ignacio de Loyola, first patron saint of Guanajuato and founder of the *Compañía de Jesús.* After the worshippers hold mass, they party. December religious celebrations include the famous *posadas,* which re-create Mary and Joseph's search for budget accommodations in Bethlehem. Other smaller festivals include **Viernes de Dolores,** which occurs a week before Good Friday, **Apertura de la Presa** on the first Monday of July, and **Las Iluminaciones** in November.

For the rest of the year, theater, dance, and music performances abound; check the tourist office for information or consult posters around town. On Thursday and Sunday nights in the Jardín Unión, the state band performs at about 7pm. *Callejonadas* (sing-alongs with the minstrels down Guanajuato's winding alleys) are organized on Friday and Saturday nights at 8:30pm and depart from the Teatro Juárez. Student groups present films almost every day of the week. Call the **Teatro Principal,** Hidalgo 18 (tel. 2 15 26; admission 16 pesos, students and seniors 8 pesos) or the **Teatro Cervantes,** on Plaza Cervantes (tel. 2 11 69; admission 14 pesos, students and seniors 12 pesos).

SAN MIGUEL DE ALLENDE

The plethora of expatriates and long-term tourists who have settled in San Miguel de Allende (pop. 80,000) have made their presence evident. Shopkeepers are happy to humor customers itching to practice their Spanish, yuppies bring their children in for a painless injection of Spanish skills and cultural consciousness, and travelers come to relax among the mostly welcoming locals in the city's shady plazas, colonial churches, and quiet green gardens. Throughout the year, tourists

CENTRAL MEXICO

and inhabitants alike can enjoy outdoor concerts and other performances along the city's cobblestone streets.

San Miguel boasts impressive colonial architecture and a number of exquisite churches. The town was founded by the Franciscan friar Juan de San Miguel in 1542 and soon became an important stop on the route that connected the Zacatecas silver mines with Mexico City. San Miguel's character is shaped as much by its reign as a bustling commercial center in the 18th century as by its pivotal role in the struggle for Mexican independence in the following century. On September 16, 1810, when Hidalgo, the priest of nearby Dolores, led his rebel army into the city, the town rallied in opposition to Spanish rule under the leadership of the patriot Ignacio Allende. In 1826, the infant republic recognized Allende's role in the drive for independence by adding his name to San Miguel's.

Rather than its rebellious history, San Miguel has now gained a reputation for artistry and academics. Beware the doldrums of June and July, when cold afternoon drizzle or day-long downpours from the rolling highlands can turn the cobblestone streets into gushing streams. The temperate climate, the impressive colonial architecture embodied in stunning churches, and renowned foreign language institutes account for San Miguel's large expatriate resident population and booming tourist industry.

☀ ORIENTATION

San Miguel is 94km southeast of Guanajuato and 428km northwest of Mexico City. To get from the **bus station** to the center (known as the **Jardín Allende** or **Plaza de Allende),** take a "Centro" bus to the corner of **Colegio** and **Mesones,** near the statue of Allende on horseback (every 15min. 7am-10pm, 1.80 pesos, exact change required). Walk two blocks down Mesones, then left one block on **Reloj** to the Plaza Allende. Alternatively, take a taxi (20 pesos). The **train station** lies 1km west of the bus station on the same road as the bus route.

Most attractions are within walking distance of the *jardín*, and the streets form a near-grid. **San Francisco, Reloj, Correo,** and **Hidalgo** border the *jardín*. West of the *jardín*, San Francisco becomes **Canal** and Correo becomes **Umarán.** East-west streets that run south of the *jardín* change their names every few blocks. The streets are relatively easy to follow if you keep an eye on the changing names on the corners of buildings. The always-visible, towering *Basílica* in the Jardín Allende can orient even the most frustrated of travelers.

☷ PRACTICAL INFORMATION

TRANSPORTATION

Buses: On Calzada de la Estación, 1km west of the *centro.* Catch a "Central Estación" bus on Colegio at Mesones near the Plaza Cívica or on Insurgentes near the public library (1.80 pesos). Ómnibus (tel. 2 32 18) sends buses to: **Guanajuato** (1¼hr.; 11:15am; 35 pesos). Primera Plus (tel. 2 73 23) runs to: **Guadalajara** (7:30, 9:30am, and 5:30pm; 218 pesos), **Guanajuato** (1¼hr.; 7:30am and noon; 50 pesos), **León** (2¼hr.; 7:30am, 9:30am, and 5:30pm; 80 pesos), and **Mexico City** (3¼hr.; 9:40am and 4pm; 130 pesos). Herradura de Plata (tel. 2 07 25) runs to: **Dolores Hidalgo** (1hr.; every 40min. 6am-10:55pm; 13 pesos), **México City** (4hr.; every 40min. 5am-7:40pm; 86 pesos), and **Querétaro** (1¼hr.; every 40min. 5am-7:40pm; 20 pesos). Also has 1st-class service to: **Mexico City** (3½hr.; 6am, 1pm; 105 pesos). Transportes del Norte (tel. 2 22 37) serves: **Monterrey** (10hr.; 10:30am, 1:30 and 7pm; 253 pesos), and **Nuevo Laredo** (12hr.; 7pm; 290 pesos), and also sells tickets to various destinations in **Texas** (call for more information). Flecha Amarilla (tel. 2 73 23) has service to: **Aguascalientes** (3¼hr.; 12:35 and 2:35pm; 80 pesos), **Dolores Hidalgo** (every 15 mins 5:15am to 10:05; 16 pesos), **Guanajuato** (10 departures per day, 6:45am to 5:00pm; 36 pesos), **Mexico City** (5:20am; 107 pesos), **Queretaro** (every 40min.; 26 pesos), and **San Luís Potosí** (4 hr.; 7:40, 8:55, 11:15am, 12:25, 3:20 and 5:50pm, 78 pesos).

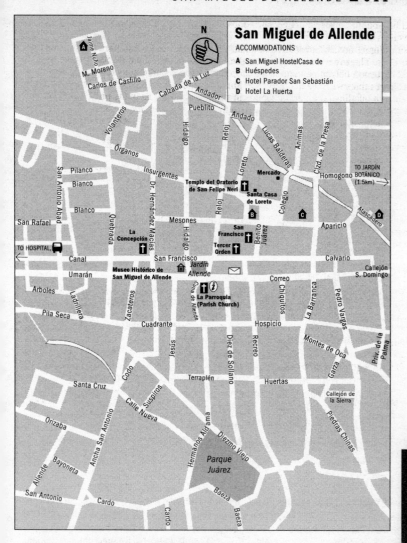

San Miguel de Allende

ACCOMMODATIONS

A San Miguel HostelCasa de
B Huéspedes
C Hotel Parador San Sebastián
D Hotel La Huerta

TOURIST AND FINANCIAL SERVICES

Tourist Office: Delegación Regional de Turismo (tel./fax 2 65 65), on Pl. de Allende, to your left as you face the Parroquia. Knowledgeable and helpful staff speaks English and distributes maps. Also sells posters and the guidebook *The Insider's Guide to San Miguel de Allende* (150 pesos) useful for an extended stay. Open M-F 10am-7pm, Sa 10am-3pm, Su 10am-2pm.

Tours: During high season, groups gather in front of the church in the jardín for 1½ hr. tours of the city (20 pesos per person). Tours are erratic; call the tourist office for more information. The public library gives 2 hr. guided **home and garden bus tours** of the city in English (Su noon; arrive 30min. early; US$15). San Miguel boasts some beautiful orchid-filled courtyards, but some say the tours are something of a real estate pitch.

Consulates: U.S., Macías 72 (tel. 2 23 57, after hours emergencies only: 2 00 68 or 2 06 53; fax 2 15 88), across the street from Bellas Artes. Open M and W 9am-1pm and

4-7pm, Tu and Th 4-7pm, or by appointment. For other countries, or to extend visas or visitors' permits, contact the **Delegación Regional de Servicios Migratorios,** Pl. Real del Conde Shopping Center, 2nd fl. (tel. 2 25 42 or 2 28 35). Catch the "Gigante" bus from the corner of Colegio and Mesons or from Juárez. Documents may be dropped off 9am-12:30pm and picked up 1:30-3pm. Processing takes at least 1 day. Open M-F 9am-3pm.

Currency Exchange: Exchange spots abound. **Deal** (tel. 2 29 32, 2 17 06, or 2 34 22) at Correo 15, San Francisco 4, and Juárez 27, has great rates. All open M-F 9am-6pm, Sa 9am-2pm. **Helados Holanda** Juárez 1 (tel. 2 05 67), at San Francisco, not only serves tasty ice cream but also doubles as a *casa de cambio* with excellent rates. (Open M-F 10:30am-3:30pm, Sa-Su 11am-2pm.) **Banamex,** on the west side of the *jardín*, has 24hr. **ATMs,** as does **Bancomer,** at Juárez 11.

American Express: Hidalgo 1 (tel. 2 18 56 or 2 16 95; fax 2 04 99). Full financial and travel services. Open M-F 9am-2pm and 4-6:30pm, Sa 10am-2pm.

LOCAL SERVICES

English Bookstore: El Colibrí, Sollano 30 (tel. 2 07 51), near Cuadrante. Paperback fiction and art supplies, some in French and German. Open M-Sa 10am-2pm and 4-7pm. **Lagundi,** Umarán 17 (tel. 2 08 30), at Macíashas a large selection of English magazines and some in other languages, as well as books and art supplies. Open M-Sa 10am-2pm and 4-8pm, Su 11am-3pm.

Public Library: Insurgentes 25 (tel. 2 02 93), between Reloj and Hidalgo. Art-filled courtyard serves as a gathering place for expatriates and students. Wide selection in both English and Spanish. Sells old paperbacks (4-5 pesos), postcards, and posters. Open M-F 10am-2pm and 4-7pm, Sa 10am-2pm. The building is also home to **Café Santa Ana,** which serves breakfast and lunch (19-25 pesos). Open M-F 9am-6pm, Sa 9am-2pm.

Market: Bonanza, Mesones 43A (tel. 2 12 60), has a good selection of Mexican and American groceries. Open M-Sa 8am-3pm and 4-9pm, Su 8am-5pm.

Laundry: Lavandería El Reloj, Reloj 34 (tel. 2 38 43), in between Mesones and Insurgentes. Wash and dry 4kg for 25 pesos. Open M-F 8am-8pm, Sa 8am-5pm.

Public Toilets: Cuna de Allende, 2 pesos.

EMERGENCY AND COMMUNICATIONS

Emergency: (tel. 2 09 11). Direct contact with Red Cross, fire department, police. A few dispatchers speak English.

Red Cross: (tel. 2 16 16) 1km on the Carretera Celaya. 24hr. emergency service.

Pharmacy: Botica Agundis, Canal 26 (tel. 2 11 98), at Macías. Knowledgeable and helpful staff. Open daily 9am-11pm. Call police to find out which pharmacy is on call 24hr.

Hospital: Hospital de la Fe San Miguel (tel. 2 22 33 or 2 23 20; 24hr. emergency line 2 25 45; fax 2 29 00), Libramiento Rte. 43 to Dolores Hidalgo, near the bus station. English spoken.

Post Office: Correo 16 (tel. 2 00 89), 1 block east of the *jardín*. Open M-F 8am-7pm, Sa 9am-1pm. **Postal Code:** 37700.

Fax: Telecomm, Correo 16-B (tel. 2 32 15; fax 2 00 81), adjacent to the post office. Open M-F 9am-5pm, Sa-Su 9am-noon. Also telegrams and money wiring.

Internet Access: Estación Internet, Recreo 11 2nd fl. (tel. 2 73 12), between Correo and Hospicio right above Mailboxes Etc. 1 peso per min. for email and Internet use; minimum charge of 10 pesos; 5hr. 250 pesos. Open M-F 9am-2pm and 4-8pm, Sa 9am-2pm. **Unísono Net,** Macías 72 2nd fl. (tel. 2 63 31; fax 2 49 58; email info@unisono.ciateq.mx; http://unisono.net.mx), across the street from Bellas Artes. 5 pesos per 10min. of email use, 30 pesos to surf the net for 30min. Open M-F 9am-2pm and 4-6pm. Unísono also runs a **San Miguel de Allende web page:** unisono.net.mx/sanmignew.html.

Telephones: LADATELs are scattered throughout town. **La Esquinita,** Correo at Recreo (tel. 2 36 21 or 2 39 39), charges 5 pesos for international collect calls. Open M-Sa 10am-2:30pm and 5-9pm, Su 10am-2:30pm. **El Toro Caseta,** Macías 58A (tel. 2 11 00), charges 4 pesos. Open M-Sa 8am-8:30pm, Su 8am-2pm.

Phone Code: 415.

 ACCOMMODATIONS

As with many hot spots on the gringo trail, budget accommodations can be hard to find in San Miguel, particularly during the winter, *Semana Santa*, and the month of September, when San Miguel throws a huge fiesta in honor of Independence Day (Sept. 15-16) and the city's founding. Reservations (if possible) are strongly recommended during these times.

The San Miguel International Hostel, Jaime Nuno 28. From the corner of Quebrada and Organos take Volanteros until it reaches Calzada de Luz. Turn left, walk one block and turn right onto Jaime Nuno and the red hostel is 3½ blocks on the left. Students and young travelers from all over the world engage in afternoon discussions around the shady courtyard. Free kitchen use, large and clean communal bathrooms, and washing machines (20 pesos per load including soap). Reservations are not accepted; key deposit 20 pesos. Open daily from 7am-11pm. Quick morning chores required. 60 pesos per person, 50 pesos with an ISIC card, including breakfast.

Hotel Parador San Sebastián, Mesones 7 (tel. 2 70 84), about 6 blocks from the *jardín;* take Reloj away from the *jardín,* turn right onto Mesones and the hotel is on the left. Vibrant bougainvillea spill over arched stone walls enclosing the sunny courtyard of this friendly, family-owned and operated establishment. Pleasant rooms with tiled bathrooms. Common sitting room off the courtyard is filled with books and has a TV. Spacious singles 117 pesos; doubles 140 pesos.

Casa de Huéspedes, Mesones 27 (tel. 2 13 78) across from Juárez. More than just your generic "guest house." Serene, flower-filled patio and rooftop complete with ivy-covered arches, lounge chairs, and back issues of *National Geographic.* Wonderfully friendly staff. Rooms offer private bath with 24hr. hot water. Some rooms have kitchens. Singles 120 pesos; doubles 160 pesos. Monthly 1950 pesos, with kitchen 2200 pesos.

Hotel La Huerta, Callejon de Atascarero 9 (tel. 4 44 65). Walk up Mesones, 3 blocks past Colegio; when you see a stream to your left, turn right onto Atascadero. Follow the stone path about 1 block uphill—the hotel is the large, blue building on your left. Just outside the main avenues of the town, this tranquil and colorful hotel rests in a lovely Rooms have great views of the town, *agua purificada,* and a large bathroom. Reservations accepted. Singles 120 pesos; doubles 150 pesos.

 FOOD

The sweet aroma of international cuisine wafts through the cobbled streets of San Miguel, and restaurants and cafes grace almost every corner. Unfortunately, their prices can be as *norteamericano* as their clientele. However, restaurants around the *jardín* offer sunny, flower-filled courtyards that make the occasional splurge well worth it. For cheap eats, try **Calle Insurgentes** and the streets around the *mercado* on **Colegio.**

La Villa de Pancho, Quebrada 12 (tel. 2 12 47). From the corner of Hidalgo and Insurgentes, follow Insurgentes 3 blocks down to the west until it meets Quebrada. Continue to follow Quebrada for a half block to your left. Welcome to the kitchen of Cristina, the bubbly owner enormously popular among backpackers. *Comida corrida* 25-40 pesos, breakfast 18 pesos, and *cerveza* 10 pesos. Open daily 9am-9pm. Cristina can also show you the 3 spacious rooms connected by a communal bathroom on the 2nd floor. An extremely welcoming, friendly atmosphere for any lonely traveler. 60 pesos per person.

La Piñata, (tel. 2 20 60), on the corner of Jesús and Umarán, 1 block from the *jardín*. A favorite among locals and travelers alike, this vegetarian-friendly restaurant serves devourable food at prices that won't devour your wallet. Escape from the crowded *jardín* and join a mellow mix of artists, students, backpackers, and Mexican families feasting upon *tostadas* (4 pesos), *tacos de guisado* (3 pesos), and sandwiches (10-15 pesos). Open daily W-M 9am-8pm.

Casa María, Hidalgo 15. Hungry from a morning of exploring? This conveniently located restaurant offers large *carne* (meat) dishes for 30 pesos as well as filling burritos for 10 pesos. Their specialties, *pollo en mojo* and tasty *puerco* (pork) *cubano* both for 35 pesos.

Los Burritos, Mesones 69 (tel. 2 32 22), between Hidalgo and Reloj. Watch while cooks prepare tasty and economical *comida rápida* that would make "los burritos" (whoever they are) proud. *Burritacos* or *burriquesos* (less than 10 pesos) and for the gigantic and ravenous traveler, the *burrito gigante* (15 pesos) will really make a meal. Open M-Sa 10:30am-6pm.

El Tomato, Mesones 62B (tel. 2 03 25). This all-natural, all-organic restaurant allows crunchy customers to sip luscious fruit juices for 10 pesos or eat a scrumptious salad for 30 pesos in a very clean and modern atmosphere. The *especial del día* offers a 3 course meal for 45 pesos and is a break from typical taco fare. Open M-Sa noon-9pm.

🕶 SIGHTS

The cheapest and most effective way to experience San Miguel is on your own two feet. Nearly all sites of interest (and there are many) lie within walking distance of the *jardín*, and San Miguel's cobbled streets are easy to navigate.

LA PARROQUIA. The neo-Gothic facade and tower were designed in 1890 by *indígena* mason Zeferino Gutiérrez, who is said to have learned the style from postcards of French cathedrals. La Parroquia, located next to the *jardín*, is one of the most distinctive churches in central México. The pointed arches and flute-like towers attract eyes upward and inside the ceilings are graced by glittering chandeliers and gold trim catching the sunlight from the tower windows. At the front is a tremendous four piece, gold-leaf altar. Former President Bustamante is buried in the basement. *(Tel. 2 41 97 or 2 05 44. Open daily 5:30am-9:30pm. Mass M-F 6-8am, noon-1pm, and 7-9pm; Sa 6-8am and 11am-1:30pm; all day Su.)*

MUSEO HISTÓRICO DE SAN MIGUEL DE ALLENDE. Although some exhibits have not been completed, the museum has a respectable collection of ancient ceramics, pre-classical artifacts, exhibits on the history of the region, and, of course, a tribute to the man known about town. *(Cuna de Allende 1 at Umarán, is just across the street from La Parroquia and is built on Allende's birthplace. Tel. 2 24 99. Open Tu-Su 10am-4pm. Free.)*

TEMPLO DEL ORATORIO DE SAN FELIPE NERI. Founded in 1712 and rebuilt many times, the church is an amalgamation of styles; its interior is mainly Neoclassical but its engraved Baroque facade shows syncretic *indígena* influences. The interior is incredibly ornate with pale pink walls, gold inlay, sparkling chandeliers, and a beautiful pink-and-mauve-toned dome. The altar holds a figure of Christ in red robes standing upon red carpets, surrounded by gold-leaf and marble pillars; it looks like a giant wedding cake. On the west side of the church, the towers and the dome belong to the *Santa Casa de Loreto*, a reproduction of the building of the same name in Italy; enter on the right side of the altar in San Felipe Neri. The floors and the lower wall are covered with glazed tiles from China, Spain, and faraway Puebla. *(Tel. 2 05 21. At the corner of Insurgentes and Loreto, 2 blocks east of the library. Open daily 6:30am-1pm and 6:30-8:30pm. Santa Casa open daily M-Su 8am-2pm.)*

IGLESIA DE LA CONCEPCIÓN. The enormous church with its crumbling brick exterior towers in decaying grandeur. Graced by the representation of the Immaculate Conception crowning its two-story dome, the church was finished in 1891.

The breathtaking interior boasts an ornate gold altar with a likeness of the *Virgén* in blue metallic robes. *(At the corner of Canal and Macías, one block west of the jardín. Tel. 2 01 48. Open daily 7:30am-7pm. Mass M-F 7:30am and 7pm, Su 9:30, 11:30am, and 7pm.)*

BELLAS ARTES. Housed in an 18th-century former convent, this cultural center and art school all rolled into one has galleries with rotating exhibits and a concert hall. The stunning murals echo the impressive talent of the students and enliven the walls surrounding the peaceful, perfectly manicured courtyard—look for *campesina* L. R. Santos lassoing a dreaded purple *chupacabras* (a monster that sucks the blood of goats). The school offers classes in ceramics, dance, art, guitar, and more, with a few in English. European and American films are occasionally screened. *(Macías 75, next door to the Iglesia de la Concepción. Tel. 2 49 46. Open M-Sa 9am-8pm, Su 10am-2pm.)*

OTHER SITES NEAR THE CENTRO. The **Instituto de Allende** also houses several galleries with exhibits by local artists and offers art, Spanish, and social studies classes. *(Ancha de San Antonio 20 about a 15 min. walk up Zacateros from Iglesia de la Concepción. Tel. 2 01 90. Open M-F 8am-6pm, Sa 9am-1pm.)* Every Tuesday, vendors from all around San Miguel converge upon the **Tianguis del Martes** (Tuesday market) near the municipal stadium to hawk their wares. Clothing, groceries, old doorknobs, and assorted odds and ends await the adventurous shopper. To get there, take a bus marked "Gigante" from Calle Juárez (1.80 pesos) or take a taxi (10 pesos). Most vendors set up around 7am and leave around 4pm. Reverberating with the calls of tropical birds, **Parque Juárez** is a large, lush garden just south of the *centro*. From the jardín, head down Luna de Allende until it meets Cuadrante. Follow Cuadrante for one short block to your left, and take your first right on Hermanos Aldama.

OTHER SITES AWAY FROM THE CENTRO. Not to be missed is **Jardín Botánico Cante,** San Miguel's spectacular home to a dazzling array of cacti and succulents. About 1,300 species grow along the *jardín's* 8km of walking paths. Walk past the Mercado Ignacio Ramirez, then turn right at Homobono, and continue on a steep uphill incline that flattens after about 10 minutes. Then walk straight for 20 minutes, following the signs; the jardín will be to the left. Or take a taxi from Jardín Allende for 12 pesos. *(Mesones 71. Tel. 2 29 90; fax 2 40 15. Open daily sunrise-sunset. Admission 7 pesos, children 4 pesos. Proceeds benefit Cantes, a nonprofit conservation group.)*

There is a breathtaking view of San Miguel and the surrounding mountains by visiting the **mirador** above the city. To get there from the *jardín*, walk two blocks up Correo to Recreo. Take a right and walk about 10 minutes. One block past the Plaza de Toros, take a left and walk uphill three blocks until the street ends at the main road, called Salida a Querétaro. The *mirador* is a few minutes to your right. Or take the bus labeled "Gigante" from Colegio and Mesones or Juárez and ask to be let off at the *mirador* (1 peso there; 1.80 pesos back).

Hot springs fans will find their paradise at **La Gruta,** a 10-minute bus ride from San Miguel (6 pesos). Catch the Dolores Hidalgo bus and let the driver know that you want to go to La Gruta, but look out for the stop yourself. Ask to be let off at a hotel near a billboard that says "La Gruta". Walk in the direction of the billboard and take a left on the dirt road directly ahead. To reach the springs, veer to your left. When returning to San Miguel, wait on the side of the router-oute for one of the numerous buses to stop. *(Open daily 8am-5pm. Admission 40 pesos.)* **Centro de Crecimiento,** organizes trips to San Miguel's surroundings and the profits benefit children in need of health care. *(Zamora Ríos 6. Tel. 2 03 18. Sa 10:30am. 100 pesos.)*

🎵 ENTERTAINMENT AND NIGHTLIFE

Did you think all these students came here just to learn? There are as many clubs as churches in San Miguel, and the music pumps through the city's veins daily. The magazine *Atención*, available every Monday in the tourist office and in local newsstands, is the best source of information on upcoming concerts, theatrical productions, and lectures by both locals and *extranjeros* (5 pesos). **Bellas Artes** and the **Instituto Allende** also have bulletin boards crammed with posters advertising art exhibits, openings, and other events.

Tourists permeate the nightlife scene, which centers around drinking and dancing. A warning—San Miguel is not cheap: don't expect bars to serve beer for under 15 pesos. Expect cover charges at clubs to skyrocket during fiesta times, especially *Semana Santa*. The listings below are for clubs, but if you're not up for such a boisterous evening, there are *cantinas* all around town—though women may feel more comfortable elsewhere *(cerveza* about 7-8 pesos).

Mama Mía, Umarán 8 (tel. 2 20 63), just off the *jardín,* is a favorite destination of foreigners and friendly (especially *gringita*-friendly) locals. Restaurant, bar, and *discoteca* in one, this enormous building is divided into several smaller establishments. **Mama Mía Bar,** to your right as you enter, attracts a twenty-something crowd and features jazz, soul, and rock music M-W, *salsa* Th-Su. Open M-Th 9pm-2am, F-Sa 9pm-3am. **Leonardo's,** across the entryway, scores points for its heavy bar stools and big-screen TV. Techno music blares as college-age customers crowd the bar. Open M-W 7pm-2am, Th-Sa 7pm-3am. Directly in front of the entrance is a rather pricey restaurant appealing mainly to tourists and hosting nightly *música folklorica* (traditional music performances). Open M-W 8am-midnight, Th-F 8am-1am. The **terrace** upstairs often pulses to the beat of live and loud rock performances F-Sa. When there is no live music, a young crowd enjoys the view of the city and makes conversation over a couple of beers (15 pesos). Open F-Sa 9pm-2am.

Pancho and Lefty's, Mesones 99 (tel. 2 19 58), provides hours of entertainment for students craving a pounding beat and a big drink from the well-stocked bar. Loud rock and cover bands or DJs spinning techno, disco, and Mexican pop songs thrill the young and tightly packed crowd every night. Sa cover 20 pesos. 2-for-1 beers Wednesday. Open W, F-Sa 8pm-3am.

La Coronela, San Francisco 2 (tel. 2 27 46), on the corner of the *jardín,* has decor that is as eclectic as its fabulous jukebox. A large-screen television, shotguns, and numerous posters of Mexican movie stars grace the walls while U.S. musicians such as Michael Jackson and George Michael play on the jukebox mixed with classic Mexican hits. The 16 peso beers are compensated for by the ultra-friendly staff. M-Tu 2-for-1 Coronas. Open M-Tu 2-9pm, W-Sa noon-1am. This place really picks up by midnight, so go and get your groove on.

El Ring, Hidalgo 25 (tel. 2 19 98 or 2 67 89), features standard *discoteca* fare and a late, lively, and very young Mexican crowd. Latin and U.S. dance hits will keep even the weariest club-hopper bouncing until the wee hours. Drinks are 20-50 pesos. Cover F 30 pesos, Sa 50 pesos, free on W-Th. Open W 8pm-3am, Th-Sa 10pm-4:30am, Su 5:30-10:30pm; July open nightly.

100 Angeles, Mesones 97 (tel. 2 59 37), next door to Ponchos, is a private club that caters to a strictly gay and lesbian clientele. Disco balls illuminate the otherwise dark dance floor as the all-ages crowd gets down to tunes from the 70s and 90s. Cover 35 pesos on Sa with one drink, F free. Open F-Sa 10pm-4am.

Char Rock, Correo 7, 2nd fl. (tel. 2 73 73), right off the *jardín.* The best part about this relaxed and casual bar is not the cheap drinks from the well-stocked bar, but the fabulous view from the top floor terrace. Live music every night as well as a happy hour. No cover. Open daily 6:30pm-2am.

▧ FESTIVALS AND SEASONAL EVENTS

San Miguel is reputed to have more *fiestas* than any other town in Mexico. A celebration of some sort takes place nearly every weekend. In addition to national and religious holidays, San Miguel celebrates the birthday of **Ignacio Allende** on January 21 with parades and fireworks. The **Fiesta de la Candelaria,** which marks the start of spring, takes place each February 2. Nearly all of September is a party as San Miguel celebrates its independence and founding. On the third Saturday in September, the city emulates Spanish tradition and hosts **San Miguelada,** a running of the bulls in the *jardín.* The impressive **International Chamber Music Festival** is held in August at Bellas Artes, Macías 75 (tel./fax 2 02 89). Ticket packages start at 900 pesos and go on sale at the end of February. Other festivals include the **Jazz Festival** in November and **El Día de San Antonio** and **El Festival de Locos** on June 13. Hotels tend to fill up during festivals, so tourists should plan accordingly.

NEAR SAN MIGUEL: DOLORES HIDALGO

"Mexicanos, viva México!"
—Miguel Hidalgo, "Grito de Dolores"

Nearly 200 years later, Hidalgo's rousing words still echo through Mexico's dusty "Cradle of Independence." Best seen as a daytrip from San Miguel, the small town of Dolores Hidalgo (pop. 40,000) has little more to offer than hot, dirty streets, a thriving ceramics industry, and an amazing story. On Sunday, September 16, 1810, Don Miguel Hidalgo y Costilla, the town's priest, learned that the pro-independence conspiracy in which he had taken part had been discovered by the government. He decided to take decisive action and at 5am woke the entire town by tolling the parish church bell. The town's residents tumbled out of bed and gathered at the church; Hidalgo delivered a ringing speech proclaiming Mexico's independence from Spain—the *Grito de Dolores.* Then, calling his flock to arms, Hidalgo rallied an army to march on to Mexico City. Thus, the priest signed his own death warrant and paved the way for an independent Mexico years later. Today, Hidalgo is one of Mexico's most admired heroes, second only to Benito Juárez in the number of statues, streets, and plazas commemorating his heroism.

⚑ ORIENTATION AND PRACTICAL INFORMATION. Dolores Hidalgo sits 50km northeast of Guanajuato and 40km north of San Miguel de Allende. To get downtown from the **Flecha Amarilla** bus station, walk straight out the door and take a left on **Hidalgo.** Three blocks down the street are the **Jardín,** the tourist office, **Plaza Principal,** and the **Parroquia.** To get to the Plaza Principal from the **Herradura de Plata** bus station, go out the door on your left as you face **Yucatán.** Go down Chiapas, which turns into Tabasco, take a left on Hidalgo and follow it into the plaza. Streets have different names on opposite sides of the plaza. The town's points of interest all lie within a few blocks of the center.

Flecha Amarilla (tel. 2 06 39), sends **buses** from the station on Hidalgo at Chiapas to: **Guanajuato** (1½hr.; every 20min. 5:20am-9pm; 29 pesos) and **San Miguel de Allende** (40min.; every 20min. 5am-8:45pm; 13 pesos). Herradura de Plata (tel. 2 29 37) has buses at the corner of Yucatán and Chiapas that go to: **Mexico City** (5hr.; every 40min. 5:20am-6:40pm; 96 pesos) and **San Miguel de Allende.**

The **tourist office** (tel./fax 2 11 64), in the Presidencia Municipal, is the large yellow building on the left side of the Plaza Principal as you face the Parroquia (open M-F 10am-3pm and 5-7pm, Sa-Su 10am-6pm). The **Casa de Cambio,** Plaza Principal 22 (tel. 4 15 86), has good exchange rates (open M-Sa 9am-6pm) and the **Bancomer** on Dolores Hidalgo has **ATM** access (M-F 8:30am-5:30pm). **Post office:** (tel. 2 08 07) Puebla 22 at Jalisco, one block from the Plaza Principal (open M-F 9am-4pm, Sa 9am-1pm). **Postal code:** 37800. **Phone code:** 418.

⚑⚑ ACCOMMODATIONS AND FOOD. Quality budget rooms are rather scarce in Dolores Hidalgo. Expect prices to rise dramatically and rooms to fill up during the *Semana Santa* in March and April between September 8 and 17 when Dolores is overrun by Independence Day celebrants. Dolores is also crowded from December 15 to 31; reservations are advised. **Hotel Posada Cocomacán,** Plaza Principal 4 (tel. 2 00 18), on the *jardín*, has rooms with wooden floors, red brick walls, and tiled bathrooms. You might just stay in the room Benito Juárez used, but regardless, every room is fit for a *Presidente*. The sunny courtyard is a perfect place to put your feet up, and the rooms on the west side have balconies overlooking the Plaza Principal. Every room has a nice bathroom. Reservations strongly recommended. Singles are a pricey 135 pesos, doubles are 160 pesos, and quads escalate to 250 pesos.

Around the *jardín*, most restaurants are reasonably priced, and those that aren't betray themselves by their touristy clienteles. **Torticlán,** Plaza Principal 28 (tel. 2 26 76), on the west end of the plaza, serves inexpensive and tasty food in a cafeteria-style setting. Join families and fellow tourists as you munch on *tortas* (7 pesos) with juice (3 pesos) or a beer (5-8 pesos). Vegetarians can get soyburgers for 10 pesos. (Open daily 7:30am-7pm.)

🔘 **SIGHTS.** Most of Dolores's sights lie within four blocks of the bus station, and they revolve around the *Grito de Dolores*. The beautiful **Parroquia de Nuestra Señora de los Dolores,** where the *Grito* was sounded, still stands in the Plaza Principal, although the original bell now graces Mexico City's Palacio de Gobierno. Constructed between 1712 and 1778, the church, with an intricate facade and towers of rose stone, is the by far the most striking building in town. The lavish interior features a main altar surrounded by columns beautifully ornamented with gold leaf, and two side altars—one Churrigueresque and the other ultrabaroque. Dress appropriately—no shorts or tight dresses are allowed. (Open daily 9am-2pm and 4-8pm.)

On the west side of the plaza is the **Casa de Visitas,** built in 1786 and now host to each president of the Republic for a visit during his last year in office, when he reissues the *Grito*. In the center of the plaza is a huge bronze statue of Hidalgo, the man who made Dolores Hidalgo *la cuna de la independencia nacional* (the cradle of national independence).

Museo de la Independencia, Zacatecas 6, lies less than one block northwest of the Parroquia. Gory technicolor paintings detailing the material and spiritual conquest that characterized life under Spanish rule and the fight for independence add a twist to Mexico's already tumultuous history. Relive Hidalgo's *Grito* in an eerie life-sized diorama with wooden statues of an inspired Hidalgo and anxious *mexicanos*. The museum also includes Mexican *artesanía* and a shrine to Dolores Hidalgo's favorite musical son, mariachi legend José Alfredo Jiménez. (Open daily F-W 9am-5pm. Admission 5 pesos, students free, teachers with ID, seniors, and children under 13; free Su.)

Hidalgo's home from 1804 until 1810, the **Museo Casa Hidalgo** (tel. 2 01 71), at Morelos and Hidalgo one block from the Plaza Principal, is less than thrilling. The collection housed in it is comprised of contemporary religious paraphernalia, documents, and artwork relating to the independence movement. (Open Tu-Sa 10am-6pm, Su and holidays 10am-5pm. Admission 14 pesos, free Sunday and holidays, free for teachers and students with ID, children under 13, and seniors.)

QUERÉTARO

Situated between Mexico City and Guadalajara on the busiest stretch of route in the Republic, Querétaro (pop. 870,000) lies at the crossroads of Mexico's geography and history. As the prosperous agricultural and industrial center of the Bajío, the outskirts of Querétaro assault the senses with whining grain elevators, monstrous warehouses, and truckloads of squealing pigs. Inside the commercial ring, however, the city center is a colonial wonder, with lantern-lit squares and an 18th-century aqueduct formed by 74 graceful arches. In Querétaro's heart, university students and entrepreneurs bustle past one another on centuries-old brick streets and *andares* (pedestrian walkways).

Querétaro's central role in modern Mexican history began with the death of Emperor Maximilian. Abandoned by Louis Napoleon and captured by Juárez's

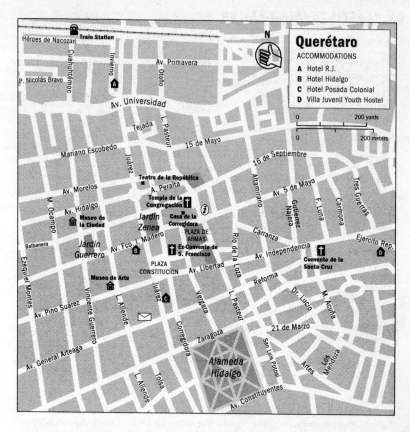

Querétaro

ACCOMMODATIONS

A Hotel R.J.
B Hotel Hidalgo
C Hotel Posada Colonial
D Villa Juvenil Youth Hostel

troops, it was here that he ascended the *Cerro de las Campañas* (Hill of the Bells) and uttered his famous last words: "Mexicans, I am going to die for a just cause: the liberty and independence of Mexico." In the subsequent 50 years, Mexico was plagued by violence until the victorious Carranza drafted the new constitution in Querétaro. While Mexico relinquished a great deal of its power and land in this city (the Treaty of Guadalupe Hidalgo, which compelled the Republic to cede its northern territories to the U.S., was signed in Querétaro) the many museums and monuments nevertheless indicate the city's pride in its history. Querétaro's historical and cultural offerings are frequently overlooked by foreign travelers, although it is a popular destination among Mexican tourists.

⬥ ORIENTATION

Querétaro's streets form a grid, and nearly all important sights are within walking distance of the **Jardín Zenea**. The *jardín* is bounded by **16 de Septiembre** (north), **Madero** (south), **Corregidora** (east), and **Juárez** (west). The modern **bus station** is on the south side of town. To catch a bus to the *centro*, follow the signs marked "Transporte Urbano" to *Salida A*, on the left-hand side of building "C" (mercado) as you face it. A taxi will whisk you to your destination for 18 pesos— tickets can be bought inside the station and handed to the driver. The many parks provide ample places to rest, but the city blocks are long.

⁊ PRACTICAL INFORMATION

TRANSPORTATION

Buses: Station accessible via the "Ruta 25" bus on Allende and Zaragoza; "Ruta 8" on Ocampo and Constituyentes; "Ruta 19" at the corner of Madero and Guerrero; and "Ruta 72" on Universidad—all are labeled "Central" (every 5-10min. 5:30am-11pm, 2.50 pesos). **First-class service** in *Acesos* 1 and 2. ETN (tel. 29 00 17) sends plush buses to: **San Luis Potosí** (2½hr., 1 and 1:30pm, 110 pesos); and **San Miguel de Allende** (1hr., 5 per day 10:30am-8:15pm, 49 pesos). Primera Plus (tel. 11 40 01) serves: **León** (2hr., 16 per day, 90 pesos); **Mexico City** (30min., every 20min. 6am-midnight, 113pesos); **Irapuato** (2½hr., 7 per day 1am-10:30pm, 50 pesos); and **Guadalajara** (4½hr., 5 per day noon-10:10pm, 180 pesos). Ómnibus (tel. 29 00 29) serves **Aguascalientes** (5hr., 1:15pm and 2:15am, 141 pesos). Servicios Coordinados (tel. 11 40 01) runs to: **Guanajuato** (3hr., 7 per day 8am-5:30pm, 68 pesos); and **Toluca** (3½hr., 4 per day 11am-9:50pm, 80 pesos). **Second-class service** in Acesos 3 and 4. Estrella Blanca (tel. 29 00 22) has service to: **Ixmiquilpan** (3hr., every hr. 6:15am-6:15pm, 54 pesos); **Pachuca** (5hr., every hr. 6:15am-6:15pm, 78 pesos); and **Poza Rica** (6hr., 9:15pm, 125 pesos). Oriente (tel. 29 02 02) runs to: **Matamoros** (12hr. 6 per day 5-10:30pm, 340 pesos); and **Salamanca** (1½hr., every 20min. 5am-8:30pm, 31 pesos). Flecha Amarilla (tel. 11 40 01) whisks passengers to: **Manzanillo** (12hr.; 1:45am, 7:45am, and 7:40pm; 223 pesos); and **San Luis Potosí** (3hr., 6 per day 2:15am-9:15pm, 79 pesos). Flecha Roja (tel. 29 00 01) sends buses to **San Mateo** (4hr., every 20min. 2:30am-2:30pm, 72 pesos). Flecha Verde (tel. 29 00 02) serves **Misión de Palmas** (4hr.; 8, 10am, and 4pm; 28 pesos). Herradura de Plata (tel. 29 02 45) runs to: **San Miguel de Allende** (1¼hr., every 40min. 6am-10:10pm, 26 pesos); and **Toluca** (3½hr., 6 per day, 71 pesos). Transportes Amealcences (tel. 29 00 15) runs to: **Amealco** (every hr. 6:30am-8:30pm, 21 pesos); and **San Juan del Río** (1hr., every 15min. 6am-10:30pm, 19 pesos). Finally, Flecha Azul (tel. 29 03 22) serves: **Higuerillas** (3hr., 12:30 and 3:30pm, 39 pesos); **San Joaquín** (3hr., 6 per day 6:20am-4:20pm, 41 pesos); and **Tequisquiapan** (1hr., every 30min. 6:30am-8:15pm, 22 pesos).

TOURIST AND FINANCIAL SERVICES

Tourist Office: State Tourist Office, Pasteur Nte. 4 (tel. 12 14 12 or 12 09 07; email turismo@ciateq.mx). From the *jardín,* take 5 de Mayo; the office is to the left at the end of the Plaza de Armas. Maps and lists of local cultural events are available. City tours in English or Spanish depart at 9, 10, 11am, 4, 5, and 6pm (15 pesos). Open daily 8am-8pm.

Currency Exchange: Casa de cambio, Corregidora 108 (tel. 12 80 86), 2 long blocks south of the Jardín Zenea. Open M-Sa 9am-5pm. **ATM** next to the tourist office door on Pasteur Nte.; others by the *jardín.*

Laundry: Lavandería Veronica, Av. Hidalgo 153 (tel. 2 16 61 68), at Ignacio Pérez. From Teatro de la República, turn left onto Hidalgo and walk for 20min.

EMERGENCY AND COMMUNICATIONS

Emergency: dial 080. **LOCATEL** finds lost people (tel. 214 33 11).

Police: Pie de la Cuesta 107 (tel. 20 83 83 or 20 83 03), in Colonia Desarrollo San Pablo. **Angeles Verdes** (tel. 13 84 24) rescues stranded motorists.

Red Cross: (tel. 29 06 65 or 29 07 29), at Balaustradas and Circuito Estadio, near the Estadio Corregidora.

Pharmacy: Súper Farmacia Querétaro, Av. Constituyentes Pte. 17 (tel. 12 44 23), 5 blocks south of the *jardín.* Open 24hr.

Hospitals: Sanatorio San José, Ezequiel Montes Sur 34 (tel. 12 61 36 or 12 30 13); English spoken by **Dr. Encorrada** of **Grupo Médico Zaragoza,** Zaragoza Pte. 39B (tel. 16 76 38 or 16 57 86), between N. Campa and E. Montes.

Post Office: Arteaga Pte. 5 (tel. 12 01 12), between Juárez and Allende, 2 blocks south of the *jardín*. Open M-F 8am-7pm, Sa 9am-1pm. **Postal Code:** 76000.

Fax: Telecomm, Allende Nte. 4 (tel. 12 01 63; fax 14 39 48), 1 block west of the *jardín*. **Telegrams** and **Western Union,** too. Open M-F 8am-6pm, Sa-Su 9am-4pm.

Telephones: LADATELs abound. Also make long-distance calls from the "Larga Distancia" *caseta*, 5 de Mayo 33 (tel. 12 11 67), half a block from the *jardín*. Open M-Sa 9am-7pm. Collect calls 10 pesos.

Phone Code: 42.

ACCOMMODATIONS

Despite the small-scale tourist industry, there are a handful of colorful places to lay your head near Querétaro's *jardín*. The cheapest accommodations, though, are a walk from the center of action.

Hotel Hidalgo, Madero Pte. 11 (tel. 12 00 81 or 12 81 02), half a block from the *jardín*. Comfortable rooms with small bathrooms and cable TV. The attached restaurant serves inexpensive and tasty food (*menú del día* 25 pesos; open M-Sa 8am-10pm, Su 8am-8pm). Singles 105 pesos; doubles with 1 bed 120 pesos, 2 beds 105 pesos.

Hotel del Márquez, Juárez Nte. 104 (tel. 12 04 14 or 12 05 54), 4 long blocks north of the *jardín*. An enormous stained-glass depiction of Querétaro's aqueduct welcomes guests to this hotel. *Agua purificada* in the lobby and from dispensers on each floor. Carpeted rooms have cable TV, telephones, and sparkling clean tiled bathrooms. Check-out 1pm. 1 person 100 pesos; 2 people 125 pesos; 3 people 145 pesos.

Villa Juvenil Youth Hostel (tel. 23 31 42), Av. Ejército Republicano. From the *jardín*, walk 1 block south on Corregidora, then walk left on Independencia for 8 blocks. Veer right onto Ejército Republicano, just past the Convento de Santa Cruz. Follow the stone wall on the right side of the street until you reach the entrance to the sports and recreation complex. The hostel is inside next to the swimming pool. While a bit remote, it's a bargain—large groups of athletes fill the rooms quickly so call ahead. No drinking or smoking. Single-sex dorms with 8 bunks per room. 20 pesos per person. 15 pesos with HI card. Linen deposit 20-peso. Reception 7am-10:30pm; call if arriving later.

Hotel R.J., Invierno 21 (tel. 12 04 88). Walk 5 long blocks north of the garden up Juárez to Universidad, cross the bridge onto Invierno and continue for half a block and the hotel is on the left. While you certainly will not be living in the lap of luxury, this fairly clean hotel will go easy on your wallet. 60 pesos for 1 or 2 people; 3 people 85 pesos.

Posada Colonial, Juárez 9 (tel. 12 02 39). This conveniently located hotel is just two blocks south of the *jardín* on the left side of Juárez. 10 rooms, 5 with shared bathroom. Reception 24hr. The prices vary depending on whether you choose a room with a *baño* or TV but the prices are more or less 50-70 pesos for 1 to 2 people.

FOOD

Inexpensive restaurants face the Jardín Zenea; pricier *loncherías* and outdoor cafes rim the nearby Plaza Corregidora; and taco, *torta*, and other fast-food stands line **5 de Mayo** and **Calle Juárez** north of the *teatro*. Many restaurants stop serving their *menú del día* at 5 or 6pm.

La Mariposa, Angela Peralta 7 (tel. 12 11 66), at Juárez. This cafeteria and *pastelería* has been a local favorite for 57 years and counting. Enjoy *enchiladas verdes* (with green *salsa*; 21 pesos), fresh fruit juice (7 pesos), or a banana split (14 pesos). Get a quick bite to go or take time to eat in the spacious dining area. Open daily 8am-9:30pm.

Restaurante de la Rosa, Juárez Nte. 24 (tel. 12 87 84), at Peralta, across from the Teatro Republicano. Tasty Mexican cuisine seasoned to perfection. Red wooden chairs, plaid tablecloths, and brick floors are nice, but it's the food that gets rave reviews from locals and tourists. *Enchiladas queretanas* 15 pesos; 4-course *menú del día* 18-20 pesos. Open M-Sa 9am-9pm, Su 9am-1pm (breakfast only on Su).

Café del Fondo, Av. Pino Suárez 9 (tel. 12 09 05), between Juárez and Allende 1 block south of the *jardín*. Good food and great prices make this local hangout an enticing stop for the budget traveler craving quesadillas (7.50 pesos) or sandwiches (6 pesos). The cafe also boasts one of the largest coffee grinders you'll find anywhere, which is the key behind the strong, fresh exotic coffee drinks (around 15 pesos). Try the *Queretano*—coffee, brandy, vodka, chantilly cream, and cinnamon. Hearty breakfast specials 11-15 pesos. Open daily 7:30am-10pm.

Ibis Natura Vegetariana, Juárez Nte. 47 (tel. 14 22 12), half a block north of the *jardín*. Despite what you've heard, Mexican veggies can be delicious and nutritious. Try a lip-smacking veggie cheeseburger (8 pesos), or the hearty *menú del día* (22 pesos) with an energizing glass of freshly made fruit and vegetable juice (7 pesos). The social staff also sells numerous vitamins and supplements in case your diet has consisted too long of meat and *frijoles*. Open daily 8am-9:30pm.

▓ SIGHTS

Querétaro has more to see and to do than most colonial towns. For those tired of historical museums and Churrigueresque churches, Querétaro offers plazas and walkways perfect for a post-meal, pre-siesta stroll.

CONVENTO DE LA SANTA CRUZ. The most intriguing sight in Querétaro is the *convento*. Built on the site where Spaniards defeated Chichimeca Indians, this convent was an integral part of the evangelistic movement throughout Mexico and lower California. Nearly everything inside Santa Cruz (founded in 1683) is original—the clay pipes and water-catching system date from the city's aqueduct days. On the second floor of the convent is the cell in where Maximilian spent his last minutes; it has been left exactly as it was on the day of his execution. In one courtyard, trees grow thorns in the form of crucifixes. According to legend, the thorns began growing into crosses after a friar stuck his cane into the ground near the trees. The tree is a mimosa and is known simply as the **Arbol de la Cruz** (Tree of the Cross), and it is said that these are the only trees of their kind in the world; attempts to plant seedlings elsewhere have supposedly failed. *(Tel. 12 02 35. South of Jardín Zenea. Follow Corregidora to Independencia and turn left. After walking about five blocks, you'll reach the convent, which occupies a plaza dedicated to the founders of the city. Open Tu-F 9am-2pm, Sa-Su, and holidays 9am-4:30pm. Free, but a small donation is requested for the convent. 20min. guided tours in Spanish, English, French, or Italian.)*

CERRO DE LAS CAMPAÑAS (HILL OF THE BELLS). Named for the peculiar sound its rocks make when they collide, this hill is where Emperor Maximilian first established his military headquarters and later surrendered his sword to General Escobedo in 1867. To the left of the *Cerro de las Campañas* and up a low hill, Maximilian's family built a small **chapel** over the ground where the emperor and two of his generals were shot. If the rich historical atmosphere isn't enough to tempt a sojourn to this place then the peaceful, well-kept garden that surrounds the hill is well worth it. Flowering trees and quiet paths lead the way to an impressive panoramic view of Querétaro. Up the stairs to the left of the chapel stands a large stone sculpture of Benito Juárez, the man responsible for Maximilian's execution. *(To reach the monument, walk a few blocks north of the Jardín Zenea on Corregidora and turn left onto General Escobedo. Proceed until the Escobedo ends at Tecnológico, then take a right and you will come to the monument on the left side of the street after about 30min. Otherwise, catch the "Ruta 45" bus headed west on Zaragoza. Open Tu-Su 7am-6pm. Admission 1 peso.)*

TEATRO DE LA REPÚBLICA. Newly remodeled, the *teatro* has borne witness to many historic events: in 1867, the final decision on Emperor Maximilian's fate; in 1917, the drafting of the constitution in the **Sala de Constituyentes** upstairs; and in

1929, the founding of the Partido Nacional de la Revolución (PNR), the precursor of today's Partido Revolucionario Institucional (PRI). The *sala* is closed to the public, so the theatre is best viewed in passing. But there are numerous performances that let visitors enjoy the rich velvet seats. Look for a copy of *Tesoro Turístico* in the lobby to learn about upcoming events. *(Tel. 24 00 40. At Angela Peralta and Juárez, just one block up from the jardín. Open Tu-Su 10am-3pm and 5-8pm. Free.)*

MUSEO DE ARTE DE QUERÉTARO. The original edifice, an 18th-century Augustinian monastery, was rebuilt in 1889 and the beautiful courtyard makes this building truly worthy of the impressive pieces it holds. An exhibition on local architecture supplements the bounty of Baroque paintings. European canvasses, 19th- and 20th-century Mexican art, and Cristóbal de Villa Pando's 19th-century depictions of the 12 apostles round out the formidable collection. *(Allende 14, between Madero and Pino Suárez. Two blocks south of the jardín, turn right on Independencia and the museum is 1 block on the right. Tel. 12 35 23. Open Tu-Su 11am-7pm. Admission 10 pesos; students with ID, seniors, and children under 12 free; free all on Tu.)*

MUSEO REGIONAL. Housed in the **Ex-Convento de San Francisco,** this impressively modern museum brings visitors through the highlights of Mexican history with numerous pre-Hispanic Indian artifacts as well as colonial period pieces such as the table upon which the 1848 Treaty of Guadalupe Hidalgo was signed with the U.S. The second floor is devoted to colonial-era religious paintings and artifacts relating to Querétaro's military and political history. *(Tel. 12 20 31. At Corregidora and Madero, on the east side of the Jardín Zenea. Open Tu-Su 10am-6pm. Admission 14 pesos; seniors, students with ID, children under 12 free; free for all on Sundays.)*

TEMPLO DE LA CONGREGACIÓN. This church's two white towers and central dome rise above all the other buildings in the area. The stained-glass windows toward the top of the church let in dim light, and delicate chandeliers are suspended against a backdrop of pillars and frescoes. The image of *La Guadalupana* is by Miguel Cabrera. *(Tel. 12 07 32. One block north of the Casa de la Corregidora, at Pasteur and 16 de Septiembre. Open daily 7am-9pm. Mass M-F at 8, 10am, and 8pm, Sa-Su more frequently.)*

OTHER SIGHTS. Querétaro's fascinating **Acueducto** stretches along Calzada de los Arcos west of the *centro*. This distinctive structure, with its 74 arches of pink sandstone, was constructed in 1735 as a gift to a perpetually parched community from the Marqués de Villas del Águila. A *mirador* overlooking all 1280m of the aqueduct is located on Av. Ejército Republicano, about three blocks past the Convento de la Santa Cruz. From the *mirador*, the arched aqueduct blends into the surroundings in contrast to the increasing modernization of the city that lies below. Up 5 de Mayo to the east of the *jardín* is the **Plaza de la Independencia (Plaza de Armas),** a monument to the aforementioned Marqués. Faithful stone dogs surround his statue, drooling respectfully into a fountain. The plaza is bordered by old square-rimmed trees, colorful cafés, shaded benches, and beautiful colonial buildings, including the **Casa de la Corregidora,** home of Doña Josefa Ortíz de Domínguez, heroine of the Independence movement. The *casa* is now the seat of the state government, so only the courtyard may be viewed; it's less than thrilling. *(Open M-F 8am-9pm, Sa 9am-2pm.)* The **Museo de La Ciudad** served as the final prison of Emperor Maximilian and contains a well-organized display of religious art and an ever-changing exhibit of contemporary art. To reach the museum, take a left on Hidalgo as you face the Teatro de la República and walk three blocks; turn left on Guerrero. *(Vicente Guerrero 29, between Hidalgo and 16 de Septiembre. Tel. 24 37 56. Open Tu-Su 11am-5pm. Admission 10 pesos, students and seniors free.)*

For lazing around, nothing beats the shady trees of the **Alameda Hidalgo,** three blocks down Corregidora. The Alameda, which was built in 1790, includes a duck pond, green lawns, tree-lined paths, a skating rink, and a monument honoring

Hidalgo. The **Andador Libertad,** two blocks from the *jardín* and connecting the Plaza de la Independencía and Av. Corregidora, is host to a slew of mellow vendors and *artesanía* shops. *(Open daily from about 10:30am-9:30pm.)* **Andador 5 de Mayo,** off the *jardín,* has several galleries with local artwork for sale.

📻 ENTERTAINMENT AND SEASONAL EVENTS

Local entertainment, like almost everything else in Querétaro, revolves around the *Jardín Zenea,* with spectacular people-watching each evening. Open-air brass-band concerts are given in the gazebo Sunday evenings from 6 to 8pm, and myriad jugglers, *mariachis,* and magicians perform there less regularly. Balloons in bunches big enough to fly you around the world and back are sold around the *jardín,* brightening the already-festive plaza. **Jardín de los Platitos,** where Juárez meets Av. Universidad north of the *zócalo,* dances to mariachi music. Things start to heat up at about 11pm on Fridays and Saturdays. The *Cartelera de Eventos,* published monthly by the tourist office, is an excellent source of information about cultural events, concerts, performances, and festivals. The **Academia de Bellas Artes** (tel. 12 05 70), Juárez Sur at Independencía, has information on what the carousing and performing students of the Universidad Autónoma de Querétaro have in store for the public. If you're lucky, you might catch a ballet recital, piano concert, theatrical event, or even a folk dance presentation. Performances usually begin at 5pm. Ready for the millennium, **Querétaro 2000** (tel. 20 68 10 or 20 68 13), on Blvd. Bernardo Quintana, is a huge stretch of parks and facilities, including a pool, football field, basketball court, amusement park, library, open theater, and camping area (open daily 7am-7:30pm).

Restaurant/bar **El Portal de Querétaro,** Corredor a N. 25 (tel. 24 03 95). This establishment is located on the east side of the Plaza Constitución two blocks south of the *jardín.* A lively hangout for local professionals, it features a simple menu of Mexican favorites (16-25 pesos) as well as a loaded bar. (Beer 15 pesos. Open daily 9am-1am.) A more relaxing atmosphere can be found at **Quadros,** Andador 5 de Mayo 16 (tel. 12 04 45), on the walkway just north of the Ex-Convento de San Francisco. Local artwork decorates the walls of this spacious but intimate cafe-bar, and each night starting at 8pm, musicians play hour-long sets of anything from blues to *trova.* Friday and Saturday nights, twentyish would-be Selenas compete for drinks and prizes. Appetizers and a small menu as well as drinks are served. (Thur. 2-for-1 drinks. Beer 9-17 pesos. Cover 20 pesos F-Sa. Open Tu-Su 6pm-2am.)

PEEL IT, SLICE IT, SUCK IT, DICE IT Mangoes

may be one of Mexico's more delicious offerings, but the fruit's sumptuous flavor is often passed over by foreigners who can't figure out how to eat it. There are many types of mangoes, but the two most popular are the *paraiso,* which is the larger of the two and red and green, and the yellow *manila.* Mexicans often eat mango seasoned with chile powder and fresh lime juice, but for those with less adventurous taste buds, they can also be consumed straight-up. The easiest way to eat a mango is to pluck an end with your fingernail or a fork, peel it like a banana, and suck away. But for hygiene's sake, consider a fancier option; cut along both sides of the seed, leaving yourself with two pieces and a seed with some fruit around the edges. then take your two bowl-shaped pieces and cut down into the fruit, creating a grid in the pulp. Turn the skin inside out and scrape the pieces onto a plate. Diced mango! Alternatively, cut the fruit into strips, shove them into your mouth, and use your teeth to scrape off the pulp. Mangoes are sometimes sold on a stick, and one can eat the fruit like ice cream by turning and sucking—be sure to lean over as you eat or you will soon be wearing your mango. If you want to savor the flavor of a mango without all the hassle of eating the fruit itself, an excellent way is to sip a freshly-made drink. Juice stands are found in almost all *mercados* and will whip you up a banana-mango-orange drink that is delicious, safe and, of course, healthy.

The local twenty-something crowd hits the dance floor hard at **JBJ,** Blvd. Bernardo Quintana 109 (tel. 13 72 13 or 13 43 07). Booming rhythms and a merciless strobe light will keep you movin'. (Open W-Sa 10pm-2am; live music.) Next to the disco is the **JBJ Bar,** which has karaoke and pool tables. Live music is played to an eclectic audience while friendly waiters serve margaritas prepared with purified ice. (Open W-Sa 8pm-2am.) Keep your ear open for the beats eminating from the disco **Van Gogh,** Prolongación Pasteur Sur 285 (tel. 12 65 75; cover 20-25 pesos; open Th-Sa 9pm-2am).

The annual **Feria de Querétaro** usually takes place during the second week of December. The **Feria de Santa Ana,** complete with bulls running through congested streets, takes place every July 26. The whole town dances during the **Celebración de la Santa Cruz de los Milagros** and the *Fiestas Patrias*, which take place during the second or third week of September. Other festivals include the **Feria International del Queso y del Vino** in May or July, the festival commemorating the founding of the city on July 25, and, of course, **Semana Santa** in March and April.

HIDALGO

PACHUCA

Hidalgo's capital city, Pachuca (pop. 220,000) offers fresh mountain air and a crowded city with a few sights that chronicle its importance as a center for silver mining processing since the 16th-century. There are also several daytrips available from Pachuca that let visitors see the breathtaking mountain scenery and vistas that are often blocked by Pachuca's congested downtown. Pachuca itself, only one hour by bus from Mexico City, makes for an easy daytrip.

◪ **ORIENTATION AND PRACTICAL INFORMATION.** Getting oriented is a bit difficult, as many streets curve and change names. The bus station is a fair distance from downtown. Frequent *combis* run from the bus station to the **Plaza de la Constitución** (6am-10pm, 2 pesos). To get from there to the *zócalo,* also known as **Plaza de la Independencia,** make a left on Hidalgo and a right on Ocampo. This will put you at the northeastern corner of the plaza. The street forming the eastern boundary of the square is **Matamoros;** it runs parallel to **Allende** (across the plaza) and **Guerrero** (1 block west of the plaza). Matamoros and Allende converge a few blocks to the south at **Plaza Juárez. Juárez** and **Revolución** both begin at Plaza Juárez and run parallel to the south.

ADO runs first-class **buses** to: **Mexico City's** North Station (1¼hr.; every 15min. M-F 4:45am-10:15pm, Sa-Su 5:45am-10:15pm; 25 pesos); **Poza Rica** (5hr., 4 per day 8:30am-8:45pm, 53 pesos); and **Tuxpan** (7hr., 8:30am and 8:45pm, 69 pesos). Flecha Roja (tel. 3 27 94) has second-class buses to: **Mexico City** (1½hr., every 10min. 4am-10pm, 23 pesos). Estrella Blanca (tel. 3 27 47) provides second-class service to **Querétaro** (4½hr., every hr. 5:15am-6:15pm, 66 pesos) and **San Juan del Río** (3½hr., every hr. 5:15am-6:15pm, 46 pesos). Pachuca's **tourist office** (tel. 5 14 11) lies in the bottom of the huge clock tower, on Plaza de la Independencia (open M-F 9am-3pm, Sa-Su and festivals 10am-6pm). **Bancomer** (tel. 3 06 00 and 3 06 09), on the west side of the plaza on Allende, changes money (open M-F 8:30am-5:30pm). There is a **market** on the north side of Plaza de la Constitución. **Emergency:** 060. **Police:** (tel. 1 18 80) in Plaza Juárez. The **Red Cross** (tel. 4 17 20) provides 24-hour ambulance service (tel. 4 17 20). **Farmacia Rex Reloj,** Plaza de la Independencia 106 (tel. 5 00 52; fax 5 56 82), can help you with your pharmaceutical needs (open M-Sa 8am-10pm, Su 8am-8pm). For medical care, try **Clínica IMSS** (tel. 3 78 33), off Maderos, although it is a bit far from downtown. **Post office:** (tel. 3 25 92), Juárez at Iglesias, two blocks south of Plaza Juárez (open M-F 8am-7pm, Sa 9am-1pm). **Postal code:** 42070. **Phone code:** 771.

ACCOMMODATIONS AND FOOD. There is a dearth of true budget establishments in the immediate area. A couple blocks farther south on Matamoros is **Hotel Hidalgo,** Matamoros 503 (tel. 5 17 35). Rooms feature carpet, cable TV, friendly staff and flowered bedspreads. (Singles 100 pesos; doubles 145 pesos.) One block south of the main square, **Hotel Noriega,** Matamoros 305 (tel. 5 15 55), is a slightly budget hotel offering phones and private bathrooms (singles 100 pesos; doubles 120 pesos; triples 130 pesos).

In the 19th-century there was an influx of Cornish miners to the Pachuca area. Their two lasting legacies are *fútbol* and *pastes*—pastry shells filled with meat, potatoes, and onions, with a dash of chile to keep it all tasting Mexican. The filling snacks are sold all over town for 2-4 pesos. Try the **market** on the north side of Plaza de la Constitución for other inexpensive bites. For a hearty, sit-down meal, make your way over to **Lisú Vegetariano,** Revolución 903 (tel. 4 78 73; owned by a fellow *Let's Go* aficionado), 8 blocks from Plaza Juárez. Feast on disinfected fruits and veggies before you dig into a hefty serving of eggplant lasagna (20 pesos; open M-Sa 8am-7pm). On the east side of the *zócalo* is **Restaurante La Blanca,** Matamoros 201 (tel. 5 18 96). This friendly spot, named in honor of the mine that furnished the stone for the Reloj Monumental, is popular with locals of all ages, and the airy interior is the perfect place to enjoy breakfast (22-34 pesos) or *antojitos* (9-24 pesos). Tasty *pastes* (3 pesos) are available to go. (Open daily 8am-10pm.) A bit of a walk south from downtown is **Girasol Restaurant and Bar,** Revolución 1107 (tel. 8 30 97), about 10 blocks south of Plaza Juárez, across from the Revolución market. The lively ambience attracts a younger crowd, and the jazzy music keeps patrons happy while they munch on their *antojitos* (15-23 pesos; open M-Sa 8:30am-11pm, Su 8:30am-6pm).

SIGHTS. The Plaza de la Independencia is dominated by the impressive **Reloj Monumental,** built in celebration of 100 years of Mexican independence. This huge clock tower is a prime example of the French architecture that was popular during the Porfirio Díaz regime. Female statues represent Independence, Liberation, Constitution, and Reform. The clock and bell were made in England by the manufacturers of Big Ben. Funded by local mining companies, the **Reloj** was fashioned out of white stone brought from nearby Tezoantla de Mineral del Monte. To reach the **Archivo Histórico and Museo de Minería,** Mina 110, walk down Matamoros one block past the Plaza de la Independencía, take your first left onto Mina and follow it up 1½ blocks. The museum, a former mining company office, holds an impressive collection of rocks, minerals, mining tools, and heavy machinery. (Tel. 5 09 72. Open Tu-Su 10am-2pm and 3-6pm. Admission 4 pesos, students and teachers with ID 2 pesos. Video in English and Spanish at 11am, noon, 1, 4, and 5pm.)

The **Centro Cultural Hidalgo** is in the **Ex-Convento de San Francisco.** To get there from the *zócalo*, take Matamoros south of the square for one block then turn left on Mina, take it for two blocks and turn right on Hidalgo (not to be confused with Viaducto Hidalgo) and after three blocks you'll be in front of the *centro.* The cultural center contains the **Museo Nacional de la Fotografía,** an impressive survey of the technological history of photography. The museum boasts a fascinating collection of Mexican photographs, such as the triumph of Pancho Villa and Emiliano Zapata as they marched into Mexico City in 1914. The center also contains the **Museo Regional de Hidalgo,** featuring exhibits on archaeology, history, crafts, and indigenous cultures. (Both museums open Tu-Su 9am-6pm. Free.) Adjoining the cultural center is the **Church of San Francisco.** One block past the Ex-Convento de San Francisco is **Parque Hidalgo,** favorite hang-out spot for local teens.

NEAR PACHUCA

MINERAL DEL CHICO
Forty minutes of breathtaking scenery separate Pachuca from the tiny town of **Mineral del Chico** (pop. 500). Nestled in the **Parque Nacional el Chico,** the town

has only a couple of restaurants, a small church, and a few houses. The striking views of nearby rock formations and numerous hikes make it a great natural escape for those sick of urban congestion and noise. Follow the road that runs uphill to the right from the *combi* stop to reach the spectacular vista point at **Peña del Cuervo** (6km). Walking past the church and heading downhill to the left will take you through some old silver mines. That trail eventually leads up to the craggy rock formation dubbed **Tres Monjas** because of its resemblance to nuns bowed in prayer. Locals are very friendly and will happily suggest other trails to explore.

Getting There: *Combis* run from Pachuca to Mineral el Chico (40min., every 30min. 7am-8:30pm, 10 pesos). They leave from Galeana; to get there, follow Guerrero north of the *zócalo* and make a left on Galeana. Head uphill for about two blocks. If there isn't a *combi* waiting, one will be along shortly.

REAL DEL MONTE

Real del Monte, whose streets used to hum and reverberate with the sounds of nearby mines, is now a colorful idyllic little town located just 9km north of Pachuca. **Mina Acosta,** a 15-minute walk down Guerrero north of the Plaza Principal, stands as a testament to Real's rich mining history. This mine passed through the hands of Spanish, English (who built the edifice, on your right as you enter, in 1874), Mexican, and North American owners before finally coming under government control. The silver from Acosta was taken to Guerrero to be melted and molded. The building on the left housed the mine managers, and the obsidian shards that line the tops of the walls surrounding the mine served to keep silver-hungry intruders out. Real del Monte also offers offers good hiking and climbing opportunities. *Combis* depart from "La Madre" in front of the Deportivo de la Ciudad for **Peñas Cargadas,** a massive rock formation 16km from town (every 30min. 6am-7pm, 5 pesos). Follow the sign for Peñas Cargadas (1km). *La cargada mayor* on your left stands 100m tall. Directly to its right is *cargada menor*, at a mere 80m. Next to the *menor* stands *el pilón*, just 70m tall. And on the far right is *cerrote*, 30m high. Multiple hiking paths surround *las peñas*. Climbers must come prepared with proper equipment (crosses at the bottom of *las peñas* mark the spots where unprepared climbers were also unlucky). Interested climbers should contact Lucio Ramirez, Club Alpino, Lerdo de Tejada #4, Mineral del Monte, Hidalgo 42130; or stop by the Club Alpino headquarters in the Deportivo de la Ciudad (open M-Sa 6am-8pm).

Getting There: To reach Real del Monte from Pachuca, hop in a shared taxi in front of the **Iglesia de la Asunción** on the corner of Carranza and Villigran (near the east side of the Plaza de la Constitución; 3 pesos).

TULA

Tula (pop. 90,000) is not much to look at, but she's got a great personality. Her **excellent ruins** (see **The Archaeological Site of Tula,** below) lure daytrippers from Mexico City (80km) and Pachuca (75km). Unfortunately, she herself is—well, to put it bluntly—unexciting at best.

Downtown Tula consists of a few commercial streets, a semi-central *zócalo* and a centrally located cathedral with an uncanny exterior resemblance to a prison. To reach the *centro* from the **bus station,** turn right down Xicoténcatl and then left at Ocampo. Take a left down Zaragoza, and then a right on Hidalgo. Thoroughly confused? Another option is to head toward the cathedral by whatever route pleases you—it's visible from anywhere and is near to everything. Juárez runs past the side of the cathedral to the *zócalo*. 5 de Mayo runs parallel to Juárez, one block from the *zócalo*. To get to Tula from Mexico City, take an **AVM** bus from the Central de Autobuses del Norte *Sala 8* (second-class 2hr., every 20min. 8am-8pm, 20 pesos; first-class 1½hr., every hr. 8am-8pm, 27 pesos).

Buses run out of the **AVM** terminal (tel. 2 02 25 or 2 02 64), on Xicoténcatl, to Mexico City (second-class 2hr., every 20min. 6am-8pm, 25 pesos; first-class 1½hr.,

CENTRAL MEXICO

every 40min. 6am-8pm, 35 pesos), Pachuca (1½hr., every hr., 305 pesos), and Querétaro (2hr., 9 per day 7am-7pm, 40 pesos). Currency and traveler's checks can be exchanged at **Banamex,** (tel. 2 37 72) Leandro Valle and Juárez, down from the *zócalo* (open M-F 9am-5pm, Sa 10am-2pm). It also has a 24-hour **ATM.** The **police** (tel. 2 01 85) are at 5 de Mayo 408. Lovely **LADATELs** are found near the bus station and on Zaragoza and Hidalgo near the *centro.* **Phone code:** 773.

Because Tula is a small town and the few travelers that show up only come to see the ruins, budget rooms don't come easy. The best deal in town is the **Auto Hotel Cuéllar,** 5 de Mayo 23 (tel. 2 04 42). Here, your car will have a place to sleep, too. Cute rooms with phone and TV and slightly worn bathrooms surround a quiet courtyard full of flowering plants and singing birds. (Singles 100 pesos; doubles 130 pesos.) **Restaurante Casa Blanca,** Hidalgo 114 (tel. 2 22 74), serves up a cheap five-course *comida corrida* (35 pesos) in a bright, traditional atmosphere (open daily 8am-9pm). Some of the best and cheapest food in town is cooked at the **Restaurante El Ranchito,** on Zaragoza, half a block before Hidalgo, a family-owned, family-style restaurant. *Comida corrida* goes for 15 pesos. (Open daily 7am-2am.)

THE ARCHAEOLOGICAL SITE OF TULA

Tula is one of the most-studied sites in the Republic; archaeologists from all over the world have visited it. *(Site open daily 9am-5pm. Admission 20 pesos, free for children under 13, students and teachers with ID, seniors, and for all on Sundays and holidays. Museum free).* During the week, few people come, and it is possible to scale hills without seeing anyone. Taxis (tel. 2 05 65) will take you from the *sitio* stand on Zaragoza at Hidalgo in Tula (16 pesos). Taxis aren't available at the site for the return, but *peseros* stopping near the *central camionera* (bus station) and then the *centro* (3 pesos) pass frequently on the route.

HISTORY

The first large settlement in northern Mesoamerican and once the Toltecs' greatest city, Tula was reputedly founded during the 9th century by the legendary **Ce Acatl Topiltzin** (a.k.a. **Quetzalcóatl**). Ce Acatl Topiltzin is the most venerated king in *indígena* history and mythology. Under his rule, Tula grew to hold thousands of inhabitants and developed an architecture that would serve as the prototype for Aztec cities. After many years at Tula, the story goes, strife arose with neighbors who took issue with his peaceful ways, and he abandoned the city in 884 and led many of his followers to the Gulf coast, supposedly heading out to sea off the coast of Veracruz and vowing to return in the year "1 Reed." In the following years, several kings expanded Tula into the center of the mighty Toltec empire. Hundreds of years later, Cortés arrived in Veracruz on the year "1 Reed." Legend had it that because of his skin color and this strange coincidence, the Aztecs believed the conquistador was the same light-skinned Quetzalcóatl who had fled to the east so many years before, causing Aztec Emperor Moctezuma to welcome Cortés with open arms.

The Toltecs (see p. 8), whose name means "builders" in Náhuatl, relied on irrigation for their agricultural success and modeled their architecture after the style of Teotihuacán. During the 200-year-long Toltec heyday, the kingdom abandoned its once-peaceful stance for violence and viciousness. When crop failures and droughts weakened the Toltec capital in 1165, the Chichimecs lashed out and destroyed Tula. The ruins of the city (approx. 17 sq. km have been excavated) are eroded due to the poor quality of the materials (rock) found in this area, as well as to poor maintenance and the Toltecs' sporadic internal instability—at one point Quetzalcóatl urged the Toltecs to evacuate the city, prompting some residents to bury their belongings and move to the region called Tlapallan. Tula was eventually absorbed by the Aztec empire, and Aztec ceramics and pottery can be found scattered among the ruins.

GUIDE TO THE RUINS

From the entrance area, a 600m dirt path zigzags past super-prickly cacti through two sets of vendor stalls before arriving at the main plaza. Amid much junk, they sell some delicate and "authentic" reproductions at super-low (they get even lower if you bargain) prices. Illegal vendors inside the site will try to sell you the same pieces at much higher prices, claiming they are real Toltec pieces found in the fields—a highly unlikely story if they offer you anything other than tiny fragments or obsidian shards. The first structure you see to your right (north) as you reach the main plaza is **Ballcourt #1,** just north of the large **Edificio de los Atlantes.** This court, nearly 70m long, once held a depiction of a ball player in ritual dress, which is now located in the archaeological sponge that is the Museo Nacional de Antropología in Mexico City (see p. 113). To the left (south) is the monumental **Edificio de los Atlantes (Pyramid B).** Standing starkly against the horizon high above the rest of the site, **the Atlantes** emblemize Tula on covers of *National Geographic* and on posters hanging in tourist offices throughout the country. Close inspection of these statues (each a whopping 9.6m tall) reveals traces of red pigment, the only remnant of the many colors the statues once wore. Representing warriors, and originally standing inside a temple that had formerly held religious figures, the Atlantes are evidence of the change from theocratic to militaristic rule in Tula during the Postclassic period. Along the pyramid's northern side and currently covered by a tin roof is **El Coatepantli** (The Wall of Snakes). This wall, which depicts jaguars and serpents in procession, so impressed the Aztecs that they built copies of it around the plazas of their cities. Reliefs of serpents feasting on humans adorn the adjacent wall.

Immediately west of the Edifico de los Atlantes is the **Palacio Quemado** (Burnt Palace). It is thought to have been an administrative center in ancient Tula. A **chacmool** (messenger to the gods) was originally found in the central patio; now the black figure with a gaping mouth reclines near the steps to the Edifico de los Atlantes, under the awning. Like many other indigenous cultures, the Toltecs built their largest buildings on the eastern boundary of the plaza as witnesses to the sunrise. In this manner, Toltec leaders attempted to maintain sociopolitical control by inspiring awe and linking natural phenomena to the government. Tula's **Templo Principal** once towered over the others. The object of deliberate destruction by the Chicimecs and others following Tula's abandonment at the end of the 12th century, it now pales in comparison to the Edificio de los Atlantes. Not fully excavated and still overgrown with weeds, the Templo Principal can't be climbed from the front, but you can scramble up a steep rocky path in its southeast corner. It was most likely once adorned with a massive sculptural slab found nearby, covered with images of Quetzalcóatl in his manifestation as Tlahuizcaltec Uhtli, "the morning star." Adjoining the ballcourt on the interior of the plaza is **El Tzompantli,** a small platform built by the Aztecs. Tzompantli means "place of skulls" and was used to display the victims of sacrifice.

ESTADO DE MÉXICO

VALLE DE BRAVO

Everything about this 16th-century town is perfect and picturesque, from the mountain views at the end of every cobblestone street to the luscious fruit sold at the market by traditionally clad *indígenas*. Wealthy Chilangos keep resplendent vacation homes on the edges of Valle, and although enough business is brought in to make this town feel newly wealthy, it still has a cozy, tiny, traditional feel. This is probably due in part to Valle de Bravo's having been declared a "typical town" in 1972; among other things, construction on new buildings is heavily restricted. Even the stray dogs look healthy and well-fed. You don't come to Valle to "do" anything but rather to wander and marvel at the beauty of it all. Relax in the leafy par-

CENTRAL MEXICO

adise of the plaza while you sip an *agua de fruta* or lick a *paleta* (frozen fruit bar). In the afternoons and on weekends, craftspeople from all over the country set up booths around the plaza. Quality and prices are both surprisingly good.

From the **Central de Autobuses Poniente** in Mexico City, Autobuses Mexico-Toluca-Zinacantepey sends buses to Valle de Bravo (3hr., every 20min., 46 pesos). They're almost all second-class, but mercifully they're rarely full. To return to the D.F., buses leave from the Central in Valle de Bravo twice every hour: on the hour and at 40 minutes past the hour.

To get to the *centro* from the bus station, turn right as you exit the station, walk downhill one block, and make a right on Zaragoza. Follow it two blocks until you see the Centro Comercial Isseymym, and turn left. You'll see the church at the end of the street. One block before the church, on the right, stretches the market. Just to the right of the cathedral as you face it, the **Plaza Independencia** overflows with well-trimmed greenery and the songs of tropical birds. Still facing the cathedral, the road running along the far side of the plaza is **Bocanegra**. On the far right corner, you will find **Joaquín A. Pagaza. Biotal,** Bocanegra 205 (tel. 2 44 04), has a 24hr. **ATM** and exchanges currency and traveler's checks during business hours (open M-Sa 8am-7pm). The **Farmacia Paty is o**n the right-hand side of the plaza, facing the church (open daily 9am-3pm and 4-9pm). The **post office** is on Joaquín A. Pagaza 200 (tel. 2 03 73; open M-F 9am-4pm, Sa 9am-1pm). **Telmex** phones are easy to find around the plaza.**Phone code:** 726.

A few expensive luxury hotels can be found on Bocanegra. **Hotel Mary,** Plaza Independencia 1 (tel. 2 29 67), however, offers a prime location and totally affordable prices. Clean and comfortable rooms are very simple with a random smattering of mismatched decorations. Try to get one of the two with a view of the plaza. (Singles 170 pesos; doubles 235 pesos, triples 250 pesos.) When you get hungry for something small, cheap, and quick, try any of the hole-in-the-walls between the bus station and the *centro*. Big, beautiful, expensive restaurants can be found on and around the *zócalo*. For something in between, duck into **La Parilla,** Bocanegra 104. This tiny, bright restaurant serves mouth-watering food in a sweet, homey atmosphere. *Comida corrida* is 35 pesos. (Open Tu, Th-Su 9am-9pm.) If you want to throw back a beer (or five) with the locals, check out **Restaurant Bar Los Torres,** across the street from the Centro Vocacional Isseymym, on the route from the bus station to the *centro*. *Comida corrida* costs only 25 pesos. See if you run into anyone who's brought a guitar along and after a few more beers, join in the singing. (Open daily 8am-11pm.)

IXTAPAN DE LA SAL

Most people go to Ixtapan de la Sal for three reasons: the $200-per-day resorts, the upscale spas, and the water park. There is one reason why you should go: *everything else*. Ixtapan de la Sal (pop. 40,000) welcomes its visitors with clean, quiet streets, rustic life, and smells of home-cooked meals and fresh fruit wafting from doorways and markets. The gorgeous and refreshingly simple rust and white-washed cathedral and *zócalo* are beautiful to behold. Only a quarter of a mile of road links Ixtapan's *centro* to the ritzy slew of resorts and natural spas that have made this sleepy little town famous, but in Ixtapan proper, horses and *burros* still amble down the streets while people arrange flower offerings for the Virgin Mary. Come quickly, before resorts swallow the town itself, but once you're here, rest easy—life is slow, and good.

🔁 ORIENTATION AND PRACTICAL INFORMATION. The bus station is actually in Tonatico, a small town just to the south of Ixtapan. Leave the front of the bus station and take a *combi* (2 pesos) with Ixtapan written on the windshield. The main street in Ixtapan is Juárez, the same street that almost 500m ahead, ends in the huge *balneario* (spa and waterpark) and chain of resorts. Running parallel to Juárez is **Allende.** Some of the main streets that run perpendicular to Juárez (listed in order, from the south end of town the resorts): **20 de Noviembre, Independencia,**

16 de Septiembre, Ignacio Aldama, Constitución. There is no tourist office, but an excellent **information booth** can be found at the end of Juárez, on the north side of the market in front of the water park. The **bus station** (tel. 3 05 12) sends first-class buses to: **Mexico City** (2hr., every hr. M-Sa 6am-6pm; Su 6am-4pm, 40 pesos). It also runs second-class service to: **Acapulco** (6hr., 10:50am, 1:20, and 5:20pm, 128 pesos); **Cuernavaca** (3hr., 8 per day, 5am-6pm, 27 pesos); **Toluca** (1:30pm, 3:30pm, 28 pesos); **Taxco** (10:50am, 1:20, and 5:20pm, 27 pesos); and **Mexico City** (3hr., M-Sa every 15min. 3am-7:30pm; Su every 30min. 6am-7:30pm, 35 pesos). The **police** (tel. 3 02 44) can be reached 24 hours. The **Red Cross** (tel. 3 19 39), on the route before the sports complex, has 24-hour emergency service (complex open from 9am-9pm). Buy shampoo at **Farmacia El Fénix,** Plaza de Mártires 1, on the *zócalo* (open M-F 8am-10pm, Sa-Su 9am-3pm and 5-9pm). **Post office:** located on 16 de Septiembre, two blocks from the cathedral (open M-F 9am-4pm). **Postal code:** 51900. **Phone code:** 713.

▚▞ ACCOMMODATIONS AND FOOD. If you stay away from the obscenely high-priced resorts and spas, some real deals await you in Ixtapan. **Casa de Huéspedes Sofia,** 20 de Noviembre 4 (tel. 3 18 51), is a short walk from the bus station. Go up Juárez three-quarters of a block, make your first right, and continue two blocks. Pink walls, fluffy floral bedspreads, and large bathrooms with purple fixtures make this place a winner (50 pesos per person). The pleasant **Casa de Huéspedes Francis,** Obregón 6 (tel. 3 04 03), near the cathedral, has a large, fern-filled lobby and a friendly dog. Rooms provide the basics, including 24-hour hot water. (60 pesos per person.) The **Hotel Casa Sarita,** Obregón 1512 (tel. 3 01 72), is refreshingly posh. This 11-room hotel features soft beds and rocking chairs! Prices include three phenomenal home-cooked meals and excellent service (230 pesos per person, 115 without meals).

For one of the best meals in town, eat at **Restaurante Yolis,** Juárez 33. The menu is posted every day. The huge *comida corrida* costs 30 pesos—breakfast *cual quiere* (as you like it), and *cena* (dinner) each go for 25 pesos (open daily 8am-7pm). **Fonda Jardín,** Plaza 7 (tel. 3 02 74), offers both central location off the lovely plaza and cheap and yummy eats. The 15-peso enchiladas and ice-cold 5-peso beers (believe it) will make you want to wander around drunk and full for the rest of your days in Ixtapan. For the do-it-yourself traveler, **Panificadora Ixtapan,** Obregón 101 near Allende, offers freshly baked bread at 0.70 pesos per loaf. Or spring for the most expensive thing in the bakery—a 2.50 peso cream-filled *barkillo* (pastry; open daily 5am-9:30pm).

⬛ SIGHTS. Most people come to Ixtapan to enjoy the massive water park/spa/thermal springs complex appropriately named **Ixtapan** (tel. 3 22 00), located at the end of Juárez (open daily 7am-7pm; admission 70 pesos, children 3-10 yrs. 35 pesos). For a less expensive tryst in soothing thermal springs, check out the **balneario** back in town at the corner of Allende and 20 de Noviembre. (Tel. 3 02 97. Open daily 7am-6pm. Admission 10 pesos, children 2-10 7 pesos.) Splurge on a massage (35 pesos, 25min.) or apply mud masks, courtesy of the management, as you soak. To get to the **Plaza de los Mártires,** make a right from Juárez (facing the water park) onto Independencia and continue straight for three or four blocks. This center of town life is surprisingly modern and clean, with plenty of recycling bins and a new obelisk-like monument dedicated to all the martyrs of the revolution. Adjoining the plaza is the **Santuario de la Asunción de Maria,** an astonishing white church with burgundy and rust trim. This cathedral with its little plaza-like "yard" is a veritable feast for the eyes. Inlaid mosaic benches surround the garden, while gold ornamentation, stained glass windows, and intricate murals adorn the inside of the church. Completely open and airy, the church has a bulletin board filled with news of local weddings and a garden that sounds of buzzing bees and songbirds. Adjoining this Mediterranean-like cathedral is the **Capilla del Santísima y del Perdón,** in which a glass case holds a silver Christ. (Open daily 7am-8pm.)

MALINALCO

Malinalco's Aztec ruins contain **one of four monolithic pyramids in the world**—the other three are in India, Jordan, and Egypt. Malinalco is easily accessible. Buses from Cuernavaca head to **Chalma** at 7:15 and 9:15am (Flecha Roja, 25 pesos), so the best way to get there is to take a bus to **Santa Marta** (1hr., Flecha Roja, every 30 min., 5am-7:30pm, 15 pesos) and then wait there for a bus to Chalma (every 30 min., 10 pesos). To get there, take a bus to Chalma. Once you've arrived at Chalma, and no doubt marveled at the rocky mountain scenery, there, hail a taxi to Malinalco (20min., 30-35 pesos for *taxi especial*, 5 pesos if shared). To get to the ruins from the *zócalo*, follow the blue pyramid signs along Guerrero and go straight. Take a left on Milgar, a right at the next blue arrow, and another right at the blue sign that appears to lead visitors into someone's driveway. (Open Tu-Su 9am-6pm. Admission 16 pesos, free on Sundays.) Malinalco's helpful **tourist office** is a red building located on one corner or the *zócalo*. (Open M-F, 9am-3pm, Sa 9am-1pm).

Malinalco was the sacred ground for the rituals that officially transformed an Aztec youth into a *guerrero tigre* or *guerrero águila* (tiger or eagle warrior). Because of the importance of these rituals and the ground they were performed on, the area was terraced and completely fortified from the outside. On the open circular stone platform—the first structure on the right as you enter—prisoners were bound to a pole with only their arms left free and made to wrestle the recently initiated warriors. If the prisoner won consecutive bouts with two *águila* and two *tigre* warriors, he was matched against a left-hander. If the prisoner defeated the lefty, he was granted freedom. Defeat, on the other hand, had more unpleasant consequences; the small rectangular basin in front of the entryway to the pyramid was used to hold the prisoner's blood after his ritual sacrifice. Behind the pyramid, the bodies of the sacrificed were burned to ashes on the oval bed of rock. The **Templo de la Iniciación** (Temple of the Initiation) for eagle and tiger warriors is a massive monolithic structure. All of its statues, rooms, and facades were carved from one giant slab of stone, and it was originally painted a brilliant crimson. To the right of the Templo de la Iniciación stand the remains of a **temascal,** the ancient predecessor to the sauna.

TOLUCA

Capital of the Estado de México since 1846, Toluca (pop. 500,000) embodies many of the qualities that define the country as a whole. Industry is rapidly expanding on the outskirts of town, traffic congestion and pollution is becoming a serious problem, and the not-so-invisible hand of American economic hegemony has replaced simple colonial beauty with a host of billboards, supermarkets and vendors pushing *helado* carts. But while these signs of the changing times may not always please tourists, they are indicators of a city eagerly moving forward. Toluca's downtown area remains truly striking for its beautifully preserved colonial architecture, as elegant cathedrals strongly assert their timeless grandeur. Toluca is also rich with museums that present historical, cultural and intellectual triumphs. Its beautiful botanical garden enclosed in an enormous stained-glass mural along with the surrounding mountains that scrape the clouds make Toluca a fitting escape from the sprawl of Mexico City, only an hour away.

■ **ORIENTATION.** Toluca is connected to Mexico City by the routeroute **Paseo Tollocan**. The *zócalo*, cathedral, and Portales shopping market constitute the *centro* and are bounded by **Av. Hidalgo** on the south, **Lerdo de Tejada** on the north, **Juárez** on the east, and **Bravo** on the west. **Independencia** runs parallel to Hidalgo one block to the north and forms the south side of the *zócalo*, a large, paved area with fountains in its stretched corners. The **Alameda** lies three blocks west of the *centro* on Av. Hidalgo. The amazing, stained-glass **Cosmovitral** is one block east of the *centro* on Lerdo de Tejada. **Taxis** (20-30 pesos) and **buses** (3 pesos) link the bus station to the *centro*.

◪ PRACTICAL INFORMATION. The **bus terminal** in Toluca is tucked between Paseo Tollocan and Felipe Berriozabal, southeast of the *centro*. Tons of buses run to the *centro* from the terminal, and return trips can be caught on Juárez north of Independencía on any bus marked "Terminal" (3 pesos). Flecha Roja serves: **La Marquesa** (30min., every 10min. 6am-10:30pm, 10 pesos); **Mexico City** (1hr., every 5min. 5am-8pm, 20 pesos); and **Querétaro** (3hr., every 1½hr. 4:40am-7:20pm, 56 pesos). Naucalpan goes straight to **Mexico City's Metro** stop "Torero: Linea 2" (1½hr., every 5min. 5am-8:30pm, 20 pesos). Herradura de Plata (tel. 17 00 24) heads for **Jilotepec** (2½hr., every hr. 7am-5pm, 26 pesos) and **Morelia** (4hr., every hr. 6:15am-5:15pm and 6:30pm, 75 pesos).

The **State Tourist Office**, Urawa 100, #110, (tel. 12 60 48, or toll free 01 800 8 49 13 33 00), at Paseo Tollocan, about six blocks toward town from the bus station, in the large yellow municipal government building behind the Clínica IMSS and Wal-Mart (yes, unfortunately), accesible by taking any bus marked "Wal-Mart" (open M-F 9am-3pm and 5-8pm) Change money at **Bancomer** (tel. 14 37 00), on the corner of Juárez and Hidalgo, which also has a 24-hour **ATM** (open M-F 8:30am-5:30pm, Sa 10am-2pm). For a **market**, try **Mercado 16 de Septiembre** (tel. 14 52 47), Manuel Gómez Pedraza between Ignacio Rayón and Sor Juana Inés de la Cruz, two blocks north of the Cosmovitral (open M-Sa 8am-7:30pm, Su 8am-6:30pm). *Artesanías* also set up their handicrafts in the square directly west of the Cosmovitral (usually 9am-7pm). **Emergency:** 060 or call **LOCATEL** (tel. 13 31 83). **Police:** Morelos 1300 (tel. 14 93 51). **Red Cross:** (tel. 17 25 40) Jesús Carranza, one block south of Paseo Tollocan and one block west of Paseo Colón, southwest of the *centro* (open 24 hr.). **Pharmacy:** (tel. 17 94 44) the corner of Hidalgo and 5 de Febrero (open daily 7am-11pm). For 24-hour **medical care**, go to **Clínica IMSS**, Paseo Tollocan 620 (tel. 17 07 33), about five blocks from the bus station. Some English is spoken. **Post office:** Av. Hidalgo 300 (tel. 14 90 68), just east of Sor Juana Inés de la Cruz, two blocks east of Juárez (open M-F 8am-7pm, Sa 9am-1pm). A small branch in the bus station (tel. 17 08 85) has the same hours. **Postal code:** 50141. **Telecomm** (tel. 17 07 74), in the bus station, offers **fax, telegram,** and money wiring services (open M-F 9am-3pm, Sa-Su 9am-1pm). **Phone code:** 72.

▚◌ ACCOMMODATIONS AND FOOD. Mid-range accommodations surround the *centro*, which are a far cry from the noise and filth of rooms near the bus station. The centrally located **Hotel Maya,** Hidalgo 413 (tel. 14 48 00), a few blocks west of the *centro*, is small and homey. Quirky homespun quilts, clean communal bathrooms, and a flower-laden courtyard are welcome touches. (Singles 35 pesos; doubles 35 pesos, with 2 beds 70 pesos.)

Restaurants and cheap stalls clutter the storefronts of the *portales*. *Chorizo* (sausage), the local specialty, makes an appearance in everything from *queso fundido* (melted cheese) to *tortas*. Also popular are traditional candies including *palanquetas* (peanut brittle), candied fruits, and *dulces de leche* (burnt milk candy). **Restaurant Ambia** (tel. 15 33 93), right across Hidalgo from the *Portales*, serves simple but cheap cuisine, consisting of a *menu del día* (20 pesos), within its warm pink walls. Vegetarian options are available. (Open daily 9am-9pm.) **Taquería Las Brisas del Sur,** on Morelos, one block south of Hidalgo, between Juárez and Aldama, is not for vegetarians. This carnivorous paradise specializes in *carnes al carbon* (24-28 pesos). Plastic tables and chairs may not excite you, but the mouth-watering smell wafting onto the sidewalk is a veritable temptation. (Tacos 12-16 pesos, drinks 4-7 pesos. Open daily noon-midnight.)

▣ SIGHTS. The bulk of Toluca's offerings are found in the *centro*. The **Cosmovitral** and **Jardín Botánico** (tel. 14 67 85) are housed one block east of the northeast corner of the *zócalo* in a building dating back to the turn of the century. The Cosmovitral, a stained-glass mural designed by Mexican artist **Leopoldo Flores,** occupies 3000 square meters and is made of half a million pieces of glass. It depicts the timeless struggle between universal binaries; good and evil, light and dark. Its beauty enhances that of the many plants and pools of the *jardín*. A small plaque and friendship lantern commemorate Toluca's sister city, Saitama, in Japan. (Open daily 9am-5pm. Admission 5 pesos, children 2 pesos.)

Toluca is bursting at the seams with museums. Happily, they are universally well maintained and present their contents in easily digestible forms. The museum motherlode lies 8km out of town; the **Centro Cultural Mexiquense** is accessible by buses that say "C. Cultural" and run along Lerdo de Tejada (2.50 pesos). The complex houses three museums. The **Museo de Culturas Populares** is a beautifully restored *hacienda* with a large collection of folk art and colorful, traditional Mexican crafts, including an impressive Metepec Tree of Life, a large tree-like structure composed of clay figures incorporating Christian symbolism, Baroque style, and fantastical elements. The **Museo de Antropología e Historia** offers a large and informative collection of assorted Mexican artifacts and exhibits. Don't miss the hair-raising collection of preserved animals, including cats, dogs, snakes, and **a pig with two snouts** (in a jar). The **Museo de Arte Moderno,** housed in an edifice that's a far cry from colonial architecture, provides a potpourri of modern art. (All museums open Tu-Su 10:15am-5:45pm. Admission 5 pesos each, all 3 for 10 pesos; free W and Su; purchase tickets at the kiosk in the parking lot.)

The **Museo José María Velasco,** Hidalgo 400 (tel. 13 28 14), and the **Museo Felipe S. Gutiérrez,** Bravo 303, are housed in adjoining restored colonial structures off the northwest corner of the *zócalo*. Both artists were important 19th-century Mexican naturalists, and the museums maintain their permanent collections, as well as visiting exhibitions. (Both open Tu-Su 10am-6pm. Free.) The **Museo de la Acuarela,** Pedro Asencio 13 (tel. 14 73 04), two blocks west of the *portales*, is splashed with all watercolors imaginable.

DESIERTO DE LOS LEONES

Just outside of the city, this breathtaking park, **El Desierto de Los Leones (Desert of the Lions),** offers solace and clean air among millions of pines. Hundreds of paths wind through the woods for hiking, walking, or jogging; the longest is 30km. The beauty of the trails here, perched on the mountains above the urban sprawl, will take your breath away, and each inhalation will fill your chest with fresh, clean, pine-smelling air. This gorgeous park is one of Mexico City's main oxygen sources. At the heart of the park sit the pristine remains of the **Convento Santo Desierto,** for which the park is named. There was never a desert here; like all Barefoot Carmelite convents, this one was purposefully placed in a desolate area to facilitate the extreme self-abnegation practiced by its inhabitants. The woods may never have held lions, but they were home to hundreds of pumas. (Park open daily 6am-5pm. Convent open for visits Tu-Su 10am-5pm. Convent admission 5 pesos. Guided tours Sa-Su 11am-3pm, around 15 pesos.)

Desierto de Los Leones makes a wonderful daytrip from Mexico City. From Metro: Observatorio in Mexico City, exit to your right; you will see tons of *autobuses urbanos*. Take any one going to San Angel. Get off in front of the Centro Cultural San Angel, just past the flower market to your left and the PEMEX station to your right. Whenever 10 people for Desierto de Leones gather, a bus (1hr., 10 pesos per person) will head off. The bus dispatcher, checking off sheets of paper and yelling out destinations, will be happy to help. If people are slow to gather, you can pay for the empty seats. The last stop is in front of the convent. To return to the city, *colectivos* to San Angel or Tacubaya Metro stops leave from the entrance approximately every hour. The last bus leaves at 5pm.

The **convent** was originally built between 1606 and 1611. Exactly 100 years later, it was demolished by an earthquake. The re-building was completed in 1723. Between 1780 and 1801, however, the monks moved to another convent in the Nixcongo mountains due to harsh weather conditions. Wander through the immense corridors to catch a glimpse of a bedroom as it was left in 1801. Bring a flashlight or buy a candle (5 pesos) to descend into the basements. Shrouded in complete darkness under the entire structure, the winding basement passages are not for the claustrophobic.

On Saturdays and Sundays from noon until 3 pm, the church hosts free (with the entrance fee) **theater,** ranging from passion plays to the avant garde works of Federico García Lorca (shows change weekly). The **convent cafeteria** serves scrumptious savories. Another food option is at **Los Leones,** restaurant, just outside the convent, which serves delicious *conejo* (rabbit) and *trucha* (trout) specialties (35-55 pesos), homemade *mezcal,* and Mexican traditionals (from 8 pesos).

TEPOTZOTLÁN

On the route from Mexico City to Tula and Querétaro, the terrifically tiny town of Tepotzotlán (pop. 14,000) makes an easy and worthwhile daytrip from Mexico City. For those itching to escape the smog and bustle of the city, Tepotzotlán offers a beautifully masoned central plaza and an extensive church and monastery housing exquisite examples of religious art.

To get to Tepotzotlán from Mexico City, hop onto one of the AVMs' indirect second-class Tula buses (every 20min., 15 pesos) at the Central de Autobuses Norte and ask to be left off at the "*caseta* Tepotzotlán" (1hr.). Alternately, take the Metro to Cuatro Caminos (Line 2), then the yellow or blue bus from *salida H* (buses leave about every 30min. 6am-10pm, 10 pesos). Both will leave you at the *caseta.* The *zócalo* is half a mile up Insurgentes. A 10-peso cab ride will get you there, or follow the signs around the corner and just keep walking or flag any *pesero* (2 pesos). To get back to Mexico City, grab a bus across the street from Hotel Posada San José to "Toreos" which will let you off at the *Cuatro Caminos* metro station (1hr., every 15-20min., 12 pesos). From there you can walk or take a 14-peso cab ride to the *zócalo.*

MUSEO DEL VIRREINATO

Tel.: 876 02 45 ext. 120. On the plaza. *Hours:* Tu-Su 9am-5:45pm. *Admission:* 22 pesos, free for seniors, national students with ID, children, and for all on Sundays.

In the 16th century, Jesuits established a convent in Tepotzotlán where *indígenas* could study language, art, theology, and mathematics. Martín Maldonado, an *indígena* convert, donated the land to the missionaries in 1582. Construction of the buildings continued until the end of the following century, and the huge bell in the tower was added in 1762. After the 1767 expulsion of the Jesuits, the church and buildings became a reform school for priests. Early this century, they were returned to the Jesuits, and the whole complex of buildings became the **Museo del Virreinato.** This church-turned-museum is a masterpiece of the Churrigueresque style; the craftsmanship is among the most well preserved in all of Mexico. Clerical vestments, murals lining the inner courtyard, and faded frescoes further enhance this divine religious collection. Look out for *El Crucifijo,* a 17th-century sculpture of Christ on the cross carved from a single piece of wood.

Exhibitions chronicle pre-Hispanic culture, colonial expansion, and missionary activities in the Republic. Jesuit imagery dominates the monastery's halls—St. Ignatius busts out all over the place, and St. Francis Xavier is only slightly less ubiquitous. Gregorian chants echo faintly throughout the halls, fitting the mood perfectly. Don't miss the concealed entrance to the upper floor near the exit; the hall contains more artifacts, and the balcony provides a great view of the surrounding area. Delight in the monastery's sweet-smelling orchard, criss-crossed by cobblestone paths. The high point of it all is the lavishly ornate Churrigueresque **Iglesia de San Francisco Javier** with the **Capilla de la Virgen de Loreto** as well as the astounding **Camarín de la Virgen** (altar room). Not a single millimeter is left unsculptured or uncolored here. The interplay between sunlight and gold leaf is perhaps the most wonderful relic of Baroque godliness and glitz.

POPOCATÉPETL AND IXTACCÍHUATL

Overlooking Morelos and Puebla are two snow-capped volcanoes veiled in Aztec mythology, **Popocatépetl** (5452m) and **Ixtaccíhuatl** (5282m), the second- and third-largest peaks in the country. These magnificent mountains are shrouded in indigenous mythology. Legend has it that the warrior Popocatépetl ("Smoking Mountain" in Náhuatl) loved Ixtaccíhuatl ("Sleeping Woman"), the emperor's daughter. Once, when Popocatépetl went off to battle, Ixtaccíhuatl came to believe that he had been killed; she subsequently died of grief. When Popo (as he was known to friends) learned of his lover's death, he built the two great mountains. On the northern one he placed her body (which you can see by looking at Ixtaccíhuatl from afar, with a little imagination), and on the southern one he stood vigil with a torch. Locals pay their respects to the supine, death-pale Ixtaccíhuatl on the mountain's snowy summit. The passage between the two is called *Paso de Cortés* because it is the route the Spanish conqueror took to the valley of Tenochtitlán.

From Mexico City's TAPO bus station, several bus lines go to **Amecameca**, the best jumping-off point for Ixta. **Volcanos** has the most frequent service (1½hr., every 30min. 5:30am-10pm, 12 pesos). **Taxis** located in front of Hotel San Carlos on the plaza can take you to the La Joya trailhead, and they'll charge an arm and a leg for it. Expect to pay about 300 pesos for a round-trip fare including waiting time while you hike. A one-way trip runs 130 pesos, but no return taxi is guaranteed, and public transportation is not available. If you decide to visit Ixta via **San Rafael**, catch a *pesero* from **Tlalmanalco** (5am-7pm, 5 pesos) and get off in front of **La Fábrica**, a printing press. From there, another *pesero* (6 pesos) will take you to the San Rafael trailhead. To return to Mexico City, hop onto a **Volcano** bus or any bus labeled **Metro San Lázaro**. They stop along the plaza in Amecameca or on the road labeled "Mexico" in Tlalmanalco (daily every 30min. 6am-8pm).

From Cuernavaca, you'll want to take Estrella Roja to **Cuautla** (every 15 min. from 6am-10pm), then walk to the Cristóbal Colón bus station (go right on Ing. Mongoy as you exit the station, walk one block and turn left on 5 de Mayo; the station is half a block ahead on your left), and catch a Volcanos bus to Amecameca (1hr., every 15min. 5am-7pm, 8 pesos). Buses return to Cuernavaca from Cuautla (1½hr., every 15min. 5am-7pm, 14 pesos).

Due to its increasingly active status, Popocatépetl has been closed to hikers since 1994; in June 1997, it spat out enough volcanic ash to reach Mexico City. Parts of Ixtaccíhuatl can be explored on easy daytrips, but to reach the peak you'll need to be a seriously seasoned backpacker or else travel with a tour group. Signs pointing to *Rutas de Evacuación* (escape routes) in all nearby towns remind of the omnipresent danger.

The Federación Mexicana de Alpinismo, all Mexican officials, and *Let's Go* strongly recommend against making even a daytrip when the **Socorro Alpino** (**Alpine Assistance**; tel. 531 14 01) is not nearby; no season is free from rapid meteorological change. Always bring both warm clothes and raingear. By taking all the right precautions, you can have a superb adventure hiking the volcano. The Socorro Alpino is at the Paraje la Joya trailhead every weekend to provide guidance and ensure safety. Although Ixta is most easily reached from San Rafael via Tlalmanalco, a safe hike is well worth the extra pesos it takes to get to La Joya. Arrangements can be made with Socorro Alpino from Mexico City or they can be met at the trailhead on Saturday or Sunday. If you are planning a longer or non-weekend trip, be certain to register with the Socorro Alpino before you go. Should you have an accident or **medical emergency** in the mountains, do your best to reach Danton Valle Negrete, Socorro Alpino's medical director in Mexico City (tel. 740 67 82; beeper 227 79 79, code 553 17 73).

MORELOS

CUERNAVACA

Whether you're ambling around Jardín Juárez, fruit drink in hand, or moving your hips to a *salsa* beat in one of the hot clubs, Cuernavaca will have you on your feet. This once mellow colonial town is alive with nonstop activity enjoyed by its inhabitents and visitors alike. The capital of Morelos, Cuernavaca (pop. 2 million) has earned the nickname "City of Eternal Spring" for its temperature, which hovers around 20°C year-round. Situated in an enviable place in the hills and strewn with classic colonial architecture and serpentine streets, Cuernavaca has long been a popular destination for American expats. A victim of its own good graces, the city has become more noisy and industrialized in the past 10 years, and chaos, commotion, and construction dominate its ambience. For such a center of movement, however, Cuernavaca still has plenty of shady places to relax, grab a beer, and meditate.

Before there were gringos here, or even Mexicans, there were Aztecs. The valley was first populated by the Tlahuica, an Aztec tribe; the city that grew up in the valley was called Cuauhnahuac (Place on the Outskirts of the Grove). Mexico's *criollo* elite transformed the city into their private summer camp, and the name was corrupted into the Spanish quasi-homonym Cuernavaca. As word spread of the allure of Eternal Spring, Cuernavaca became a magnet for famous visitors like Cortés, García Marquez, Muhammad Ali, and the Shah of Iran; magnificent haciendas with vined fences too high for peeking began to radiate from the *zócalo*. Lately, the city's center of gravity has shifted away from the famous and toward the rich—wealthy Mexicans flock to Cuernavaca, and the city functions as a springtime playground for upper-class Mexico City residents fleeing bigger-city hassles. This surge has been accompanied by equal, if not greater, swarms of foreigners (both tourists and residents), with innumerable foreign-language schools now drawing them in by the bushel.

While penny-pinchers might snarl at Cuernavaca's cost of living, there's a reason people can't stay away—bars and clubs throb with nightly excitement, scores of fine restaurants pepper the streets, and an entire gringo scene has emerged. The city is hip, young, international, and full of art, culture, and Spanish instruction.

✦ ORIENTATION

Route 95 from Mexico City intersects many of Cuernavaca's main avenues. To get to the city center, exit onto **Domingo Díaz** if coming from Mexico City, or **Emiliano Zapata,** which splits into the northbound **José María Morelos** and the southbound **Avenida Obregón.** Morelos is the main street in Cuernavaca and runs straight through the center of town after which it is know as **Morelos Sur. Benito Juárez** runs parallel to Morelos a couple of streets to the east and forms the eastern side of the *zócalo*. On the southern side is **Hidalgo**, which runs from Morelos to Juárez. **Matamoros** forms the western side.

The *zócalo* is comprised of **Plaza de la Constitución** and the smaller **Jardín Juárez** one block north. Cuernavaca is not an easy city to navigate—expect irregularities, random turns, and sudden name changes, especially near the plaza. Even and odd numbers usually stay on different sides of the street but, because of two different numbering systems, buildings opposite each other may have addresses several hundred numbers apart. As if this isn't headache enough, by some strange governmental decree, the official address system was changed. On Morelos and nearby streets, it's not uncommon to see two addresses on each building. "400/antes 17" means that the old address was 17 and the new "official" one is 400.

CENTRAL MEXICO

To reach the *centro* from the **Flecha Roja bus station,** take a right at the exit and head south on Morelos. Turn left onto Rayón, Hidalgo, or any nearby cross-street. If you arrive via **Pullman de Morelos** (make sure it's **terminal #1, Terminal del Centro;** if it's not, ask the bus driver to take you there), head straight uphill on Netzahualcóyotl to Hidalgo; most major sights can be accessed from there. Those arriving via **Estrella de Oro** should cross the street and flag down any northbound minibus on Morelos (2.50 pesos)—they all run past the center of town.

Frequent local buses (2.40-3.50 pesos) called **rutas** run up and down Morelos; the final destination of the bus is painted on the windshield. Taxis will go almost anywhere in the city for 12-20 pesos. After dark, because of Cuernavaca's active and spread-out nightlife, cabs charge 20-25% more. In any case, set prices before hopping in.

🛈 PRACTICAL INFORMATION

TRANSPORTATION
Buses: Flecha Roja, Morelos 503 (tel. 12 81 90), 4 long blocks north of Jardín Borda. First-class service to: **Taxco** (1¾hr., 14 per day 7am-8:35pm, 32 pesos); **Acapulco** (4hr., every 2 hr. noon-midnight, 170 pesos); **Mexico City** (1¼hr., every 30min. 5:30am-4pm, 37 pesos); and **Guadalajara** (8½hr., 4 per day, 313 pesos). Estrella de Oro rolls to: **Iguala** (2hr., 12 per day 6am-10pm, 31 pesos); **Chilpancingo** (2hr., 8 per day 6am-3:30pm, 61 pesos); and **Acapulco** (4½hr., 8 per day 6am-3:30pm, 109 pesos). Plus packs it to: **Querétaro** (6hr., 10pm only, 140 pesos); and **Aguascalientes** (9hr., 10pm only, 305 pesos). Pullmande Morelos trucks to: **Mexico City** (1hr., every 15 min., 5:15am-9:30pm, 37 pesos); **Jojutta** (½hr., every 30min., 6:16am-10:16pm, 13 pesos); and **Ixtapa/Zihuatanejo** (8:20, 10:10pm, 232 pesos). **Estrella Roja** shoots to: **Matamoros** (1½hr., every hr., 5am-7pm, 16 pesos); and **Cuautla** (½hr., every 15min., 6am-10pm, 10 pesos).

TOURIST AND FINANCIAL SERVICES
Tourist Offices: State Office, Morelos Sur 187/antes 802 (tel. 14 38 72), a 15min. walk south from Hidalgo and Morelos. Look for a yellow wall on the right side of the street. A somewhat helpful staff doles out info about language schools and study options. Open M-F 9am-9pm, Sa-Su 10am-6pm. The informal white **info booth** on the north side of the cathedral also has brochures. Open daily 7am-7pm.

Currency Exchange: Try **Banca Serfín** (tel. 14 08 88), on the northwest corner of Jardín Juárez. Currency exchange M-F 9am-5pm; 24hr. **ATM. Gold and Silver,** Morrow 9 (tel./fax 10 00 34), at Comonfort, is one of the many *casas de cambio* that line Morrow and offer good exchange rates. Open daily 9am-7pm.

American Express: Marín Agencia de Viajes (tel. 14 22 66), in Las Plazas shopping mall on the *zócalo.* Holds mail and provides travel services. Open M-F 9am-2pm and 4-6pm, Sa 10am-1pm.

LOCAL SERVICES
Supermarket: Superama (tel. 12 81 20) at Morelos, just behind Helados Holanda, north of the cathedral and south of the Flecha Roja bus station. Huge grocery and **pharmacy.** Open daily 7am-midnight. The **market** on Blvd. Alfonso López Mateos sells excellent produce. Head east on Degollado, up the pedestrian bridge, and past the vendor stands.

Laundry: Lavandería Obregón (tel. 12 94 98), on Obregón and Salinas. Head down Morelos past the *centro* and make a left on Salinas—the laundry is at the bottom of the hill to your left. 6 pesos per kilo. Open M-F 9am-7pm, Sa 9am-2pm.

EMERGENCY AND COMMUNICATIONS
Emergency: dial 08 or 060.

Pericon
Fabregas
Av. José María Morelos
Madero
Chamilpa
Leandro Valle
Balsas
Melchor Ocampo
Guerrero

Train Station

Linares Guemez
G. Farías
Ayuntamiento
Victoria
Ave. López Mateos
Plan de Ayala
Popocatépetl

Flecha Roja
Arista
No. Reelección
Guerrero
Matamoros
Blvd. López Mateos

Degollado
Salinas
B Aragón y León
Morrow
C
Arteaga
Clavijero
F. Zarco
Gutenberg

Tejada
Rayón
Jardín Borda
Jardín Juárez
PLAZA CONSTITUCIÓN
Hidalgo
Ballejón Borda

Cuauhtémoc

T **Catedral de la Asunción**
20 de Nov.
Fray Bartolome de Las Casas
Museo de Cuauhnáhuac/ Palacio de Cortés

Abasolo
Autobuses Pullman de Morelos & Autobuses Zacatepec

Álvaro Obregón
Netzahualcóyotl
Blvd. Juárez
Motolinía
Humbolt Palmira
Atlacomulco

Cuauhtémotzin
Estrella Roja
González Bocanegra
Hidalgo

Amates
Morelos
Galeana
Leyva
Tamayo
Morelos
Giro
16 de Septiembre

Av. Chufavista
Laurel

0 ___ yards ___ 550
0 ___ meters ___ 500

Himno Nacional
Montealban
Plande Ayutla

N

San Juan
Jalisco
Autobuses Estrellas de Oro

Cuernavaca
ACCOMMODATIONS
A Los Canarios
B Hotel America
C Hotel Colonial

Police: Emiliano Zapata 803 (tel. 17 11 15 or 17 10 00). Take Morelos north until it becomes Zapata; it's a bit farther up on the left. For something more heavy-duty, call the **Policía Judicial** (tel. 17 17 19).

Red Cross: (tel. 15 05 51 or 15 35 55), on Ixtaccíhuatl at Río Panuco.

Pharmacy: Farmacia del Ahorro, Hidalgo 7 at Galeana, has English-speaking staff and a large selection. Open daily 7am-10:45pm.

Medical Assistance: Centro Quirúrgico, Juárez 507B (tel. 14 23 38). A pricey doctor for every ailment. No English spoken. Free help at **IMSS** (tel. 15 50 00).

Hospital: Hospital Civil Domingo Diez (tel. 11 22 10), in the Colonia de Empleado. Some English spoken.

Fax: Telecomm, Plaza de la Constitución 3 (tel. 14 31 81; fax 18 00 77), to the right of the post office. **Telegrams** and fax M-F 8am-7pm, Sa 9am-5pm, Su 9am-noon.

Internet Access: Sports and Internet Café, Morelos Sur 178 (tel. 12 16 56). Facing the Jardín Borda, turn right on Morelos and walk a few blocks—the café is on your left, across from a huge supermarket. 20 pesos per 30min.

Post Office: Plaza de la Constitución 3 (tel. 12 43 79), on the southwest corner in the *zócalo.* Open M-F 8am-7pm, Sa 9am-1pm. **Postal Code:** 62001.

Telephones: LADATELs are easy to find around the *zócalo,* along Morelos Sur, and in the bus stations. For a good, old-fashioned **caseta,** there's **Telecomm,** Salazar 8, on the eastern edge of the *zócalo.* Open M-F 8am-8pm, Sa 9am-1pm.

Phone Code: 73.

▌ ACCOMMODATIONS

Although Cuernavaca's status as an upper-class getaway does not necessarily affect one's peaceful meanderings through town, it does reveal itself in the hotel department. Simply put, rooms are chronically overpriced. The cloud has a silver lining, though—even the barest of hotels is often outfitted with a swimming pool or a lush courtyard. There are also some less glamorous but cheap *casa de huespedes* on Aragón y León between Matamoros and Morelos. Luckily there are numerous hotels located within a short walking distance of Cuernavaca's center.

For an extended stay (a couple of weeks or more), it's possible to lodge with a local family through one of the city's Spanish language schools. Students choose from a list of families willing to provide room, board, and language practice. **Cuauhnahuac,** Morelos Sur 123/antes 1414 (tel. 12 36 73), is especially willing to lend their family list to backpacking visitors who wish to spend time with *cuernavaquenses.* Sharing a room with a student costs US$18 per day for room and board; for a private single, you pay US$25 (contact José Camacho at Cuauhnahuac).

▨ **Villa Calmecac,** Zacatecas 114 (tel. 13 21 46; email meliton@mail.giga.com), in Col. Buenavista. From the *centro,* hop on a Ruta 1, 3 or 12 bus (2.40 pesos) and head north up Morelos/Zapata. Get off at the statue of Zapata (known as *Glorieta a Zapata*) and continue on the road that leads past the statue, taking your first right on Zacatecas. Don't worry—it's worth the trip. Billing itself as an "ecotourist hostel," this unbelievable place offers lodging as well as numerous opportunities to bicycle, kayak, and generally participate in the great outdoors. With vegetable gardens, an art gallery, and ultra high-tech recycling and waste-management disposal, it's an earth-lover's dream. Facilities are new and well-maintained. Squeaky-clean communal baths. 10% discount with HI or ISIC. Reception open 8am-8pm; call before arrival. Dorms 100 pesos, 110 pesos with breakfast; private doubles, with breakfast 210 pesos.

Hotel Colonial, Aragón y León 19 (tel. 18 64 14), uphill between Matamoros and Morelos. Despite the presence of nearby sketchy "hotels," this one is a gem. Pretty orange colonial home with a relaxing central courtyard and hospitable staff. Front door closes at 11pm but a bell summons the person at the desk. Singles 120 pesos, with TV 150 pesos; doubles 140 pesos, with TV 160 pesos.

Los Canarios, Morelos 369/antes 713 (tel. 13 00 00), 5 long blocks north of the *centro* (not to be confused with the restaurant "El Canario" a few doors before). Although some *cuernavaquenses* say this motor lodge is *de paso* (past its prime), it still offers colorful rooms with bathrooms, 2 swimming pools, and a restaurant 15% student discount, except during high season and festivals; credit cards and reservations accepted. Singles 85 pesos; doubles 160 pesos.

Mesón Las Hortensias, Hidalgo 13 Col. Centro (tel. 18 52 65), right near the Catedral, across the street from the plaza. The key word is location, which helps explain the price. Step outside and you're in the middle of everything. One can't complain about the clean green rooms and gorgeous outdoor patio (also green). Charge your way into continual cleanliness but hurry—the 23 rooms go fast. Singles 154 pesos; 1-bed doubles 168 pesos; 2-bed doubles 188 pesos.

🍴 FOOD

Overflowing with tourists, Cuernavaca has more than its share of budget eateries. For your main meal, take advantage of one of the excellent restaurants around the plaza. Head up the side streets or larger thoroughfares Galeana and Juárez for lighter, less expensive fare. In the market, a *comida corrida* costs about 13-15 pesos *con refresco*. Along Guerrero, north of the plaza, street vendors sell mangoes, *piñas* (pineapples), and *elotes* (corn on the cob). The health drinks sold at the Eiffel kiosk in the Jardín Juárez include everything from the standard fruit and milk *licuados* to a spinach concoction not even Popeye could love (6-12 pesos).

Trattoria Marco Polo Pizzería, Hidalgo 30 (tel. 12 34 84), on the 2nd floor. The hanging geraniums, dinner by candlelight, and sweet music put Italy in the heart of Mexico. This elegant restaraunt will seat you in a breezy scenic balcony or in the softly-lit interior. The food is delicious; pizzas, simply smothered in thick cheese, come in 4 sizes starting at 25 pesos. Credit cards and reservations accepted. Open M-Th 1:30-10:30pm, F-Sa 1:30-midnight, Su 1:30-10pm.

Restaurante Los Arcos, Jardín de Los Héroes 4 (tel. 12 15 10), on the south side of the *zócalo*. Flanked by lush plants and a bubbling fountain, mosaic-inlaid outdoor tables are ideal for watching the day slip by. Musicians of varying ages and abilities serenade the clientele. *Comida corrida* 35 pesos, breakfast 35-45 pesos, *antojitos* 30-40 pesos. Open daily 7am-midnight.

Gin Gen, Rayón 13 (tel. 18 60 46), 2 blocks west of the Jardín Borda at Morelos. Fans, lanterns, and pictures of Chinese pop stars adorn the walls. From 1-5pm, the super-filling *guisados del día* provide soup, rice, 2 entrees, and dessert for only 35 pesos. Great tofu and vegetarian options too (17-29 pesos). They also boast a small bakery and sell green tea. Open M-Sa 8am-9pm, Su 8am-6pm.

👁 SIGHTS

Cuernavaca's popularity has little to do with scintillating sights, but there is a lot to see in the city of eternal spring besides the city's sunglasses-clad elite sipping iced tea and speaking in newly acquired Spanish or English .

For starters, the city's main square, the **Plaza de la Constitución,** is shaded by trees colored by fiery red *flamboyanes* (royal poinciana) and speckled with cafes and wrought-iron benches. Extending east from the Palacio de Gobierno, the plaza the heart and soul of the city as well. Food vendors, *mariachis* and shoe shiners loudly tempt passersby. A kiosk designed by Gustave Eiffel and commissioned by Cuernavaca's Viennese community stands in the **Jardín Juárez,** at the northwest corner of the Pl. de la Constitución, north of the Palacio de Gobierno. Thursdays and Sundays at 6pm, a mediocre but merry local band commandeers the kiosk and belts out polkas, classical music, and Mexican country music. The kiosk alsohouses a multitude of nutritionally sound fruit drink stands. Those with adventurous tastebuds should try "La Bomba," a concoction of various fruits, grains, chocolate, and eggs (12 pesos).

CENTRAL MEXICO

MUSEO CUAUHNAHUAC (PALACIO DE CORTÉS). The Palacio de Cortés stands as a stately reminder of the city's grim history—Cortés set Cuernavaca on fire in 1521, then built this two-story fortress from the remains of local buildings, situating the fortress atop a sacred pyramid. It was completed in 1524 when Cortés craved another conquest; the building functioned as a prison in the 18th century and as the Palacio de Gobierno during the dictatorship of Porfirio Díaz. A grant from the former British ambassador to Mexico (none other than Charles Lindbergh's father-in-law) transformed the Palacio de Cortés into the Museo Cuauhnahuac. On the first floor of the museum, archaeological and anthropological exhibits explore pre-Hispanic cultures. One of the more interesting displays is the collection of indigenous drawings and depictions of the Spanish arrival, in which valiant eagle and tiger warriors in full regalia battle the invaders. Second-floor exhibits on the Conquest and Mexican history include the first public clock ever to toll in Mesoamerica. The western balcony of the second floor is covered by a mural painted by the ubiquitous and astonishing Diego Rivera. The mural, commissioned by then-U.S. ambassador to Mexico Dwight D. Morrow as a gift to the people of Cuernavaca, depicts Mexico's history from the Conquest until the Revolution of 1910, proceeding chronologically from right to left. *(Southeast corner of the Plaza de la Constitución, east of Juárez. Open Tu-Su 10am-5pm. Admission 20 pesos; free on Sundays and for Mexican students with ID.)*

CATEDRAL DE LA ASUNCIÓN. Black soot has darkened the tall walls and towers of the Catedral de la Asunción, three blocks down Hidalgo from the *zócalo*, at Morelos. Although it's one of the oldest churches in the Americas (construction began in 1525), it was only 20 years ago that the removal of the aisle altars revealed some fabulous Japanese frescoes depicting the persecution and martyrdom of Christian missionaries in Sokori, Japan. Historians speculate that these startling frescoes were painted in the early 17th century by a converted Japanese artist who had settled in Cuernavaca. But ultimately, the simple altar makes this church special (and very unusual in a country of gold and gilded centerpieces). Here, seven plain baskets holding candles hang within a faceless box. *(Open daily 7am-2pm and 4-8pm.)*

JARDÍN BORDA. The Jardín Borda, once the site of glamorous soirees during the French occupation of Mexico, is now a Sunday gathering spot for young couples and families on picnics. The stone entrance is on Morelos, across from the cathedral. In 1783, the priest Manuel de la Borda built a garden of magnificent pools and fountains and, in 1864, Emperor Maximilian and his wife Carlota established a summer residence here. Today, it takes a vivid imagination to recognize the park's faded splendor amid the sometimes non-functional fountains and cracked sidewalks. Unlike the fountains and sidewalks, the flora—mango trees, tropical ferns, ornamental plants, and giant palm trees—have flourished through the years, accounting for the garden's heavy, overripe smell. Its modern amenities—an art collection near the entrance, a small theater, and a museum near the emperor's old summer home significantly add to the gardens attractions. **Rowboats** are also available on the small duck pond. (10 pesos for 15min., 15 pesos for 30min., 20 pesos for 1hr.). *(Tel. 12 92 37. Open Tu-Su 10am-5:30pm. Admission 10 pesos; all students, teachers, and children 5 pesos; free on Sundays.)*

PYRAMID OF TEOPANZOLCO. The Pyramid is on a glistening green lawn at the center of a public park near the southern end of Teopanzolco, southeast of the market on Guerrero. To get to the site from the marketplace or along Morelos, take a taxi (12 pesos) or hop on local bus #10 at the corner of Degollado and No Reelección (3 pesos) and ask the driver to let you off at the *pirámide*. Strangely deserted and unkempt, the pyramid consists of two pyramids, one within the other. The first stairway leads to a ledge, at the bottom of which a second stairway, belonging to the second pyramid, begins. An eerie partial staircase suggests that the new pyramid was unfinished when Cortés arrived. *(Open daily 9am-6pm. Admission 14 pesos, free Su and festivals.)*

THESE AIN'T THE SUNDAY FUNNIES As you are waiting for the bus, you notice that the teenage boys standing next to you are completely absorbed in the small comic books in their hands. Your curiosity wins out and you take a closer look—they're reading pocket-sized comic books with pictures of scantily clad couples doing things you thought couldn't be done by two-dimensional characters. Surprised, but amused, you shrug it off (after all, boys will be boys), and turn away. Suddenly you spot an elderly woman reading the comics. Now you're getting worried. Don't worry, you haven't entered the twilight zone. These little comics (called *revistas*) are all the rage in Mexico. Each book graphically weaves tales of romance, passion, and lust, leaving little to the imagination. You'll find someone selling them and someone reading them on virtually every street corner and at every bus stop in Mexico. Although they may seem a little strange at first glance, the comics are harmless and often even amusing. Check one out—if nothing else, they're bound to teach you some new slang.

🎵 ENTERTAINMENT AND SEASONAL EVENTS

Cuernavaca's popularity as a vacation spot fuels a fairly glitzy nightlife, and the city's *norteamericano* expatriates, now over 20,000 strong, as well as its plethora of studying-to-be bilingual students from the U.S., lend a north-of-the-border feel to many festivities. Bars and clubs go to expensive lengths to attract and please their customers while the clubgoers and bar hoppers, dressed to the hilt, enjoy themselves immensely regardless of high cover charges. If you're up to it, a night on the town here promises a sleek, sophisticated time. Several of the clubs have live nightly entertainment and practically all of them offer a spectacular decor.

Discos are typically open from 9 or 10pm to 5am on Friday and Saturday. To deter the fistfights and *broncas* (brawls) that used to plague Cuernavaca's clubs, some now officially admit only male-female couples and require reservations; most, however, do not enforce these rules. The more popular discos in town are not on the *zócalo* but in different *colonias*. Most lie beyond walking distance (especially at night) and are best reached by *rutas* or a taxi after 9pm. Most *rutas* stop running around 10:30pm, and Cuernavaca is nationally notorious for nightly rains. During the wet season (May-Nov.), it rains at least an-hour-and-a-half during the late afternoon or evening; cabs are your best bet. All the spots listed are familiar to cab drivers. Only Kaova is within walking distance of the *zócalo*.

If you're in the mood for something more artistic, catch a flick for 10-12 pesos. Try **Cinema Las Plazas** (tel. 14 07 93), downtown, across from the Jardín Juárez, screening imports and high-quality Mexican films. On Saturday and Sunday, the **market** in the Jardín Juárez specializes in silver jewelry; don't be afraid to bargain. The **Feria de la Primavera** (Festival of Spring) brings parades and costumes for 10 days a year at the vernal equinox (March 21-22).

🎵 **Zúmbale,** Chapultepec 13A (tel. 22 53 43 or 22 53 44), next to Ta'izz. This 4-story *salsa* club is unbelievable—an indoor waterfall, amazing live music, and some of the best Latin dancing around (*salsa*, rumba, merengue)—watch practiced pelvises grind. Don't worry, though—the friendly atmosphere (and copious bar service) encourages gringos of all ages to give it a go. Great fun. No cover Thursday. Open bar 9-10pm. Cover 80 pesos F-Sa for men, women free. Beer 20 pesos, national drinks 30 pesos and up. Open Th 9pm-4:30am, F-Sa 9pm-5am.

🎵 **La Casa del Dictador,** Jacarandas 4 (tel. 17 31 86), a few blocks south of the Zapata statue, on the corner of Zapata in Col. Buenavista. Raging dance music welcomes a strictly gay clientele. Cover 30 pesos. Beer 15 pesos. Open F-Sa 10pm-4am.

Barbazul, Prado 10 (tel. 13 19 76). This club with long lines out the door would make Bluebeard shake his "booty." Good lighting and continually hip. A staple of Cuernavacan nightlife, popular with the early-20s, hard-hitting techno crowd. Drinks 16 pesos and up. Cover on Saturday 50 pesos for men, women free. Open W and F-Sa 10pm-late.

Kaova, Av. Morelos Sur 241 (tel. 18 43 80), 3 blocks south of the cathedral. Rock-dance hybrid. Starts off mellow and turns into a full-fledged dance party later. Not many tourists here—senior citizens and college kids alike hit the small dance pit as waiters clad in bowties and suspenders clamor about. You, however, can come as bare as you dare. 50 peso cover F and Sa with bar tab up to 50 pesos on Friday only. 2 for 1 beers W 10-11pm. Beer 18 pesos. Domestic drinks 25 pesos. Open W-Sa 9pm-late.

NEAR CUERNAVACA

XOCHICALCO

Placed atop a steep hill with a view to hundreds of surrounding acres, **Xochicalco** (ho-chee-CAL-co) dominates its terrain. Built in 200B.C., this fortress reached its zenith almost 10 centuries later, from 700 to 900B.C. Under the Aztecs, it became a center for trade, religious observation, and an extremely successful weapon of defense for its inhabitants. Xochicalco's ruins and central location explain the similarities in ruins as far apart as Teotihuacán and Tula. Besides being a center of Toltec culture, it is also thought that Xochicalco was a Maya outpost, thus explaining its influence on architecture as far south as Central America. Archaeologists speculate that the site may even be the mythical city of **Tamoanchan,** the place where wise men of different cultures, including Maya and Zapotec sages, came to begin the cult of the new god Quetzalcóatl, as well as to synchronize civil and religious calendars. (*Museum and site open daily 10am-5pm. Admission 25 pesos, free for children, students, and on Sunday.*)

ARCHAEOLOGICAL SITE OF XOCHICALCO

Before entering the ruins, visit the **Museo del Sitio de Xochicalco** that lies to the right of the site entrance. This museum was designed to mimic the ruins, greenery, and lush flora that pervades the area. It succeeds brilliantly; inaugurated in April 1996, the museum's beautiful marble tiling and wall frescoes complement the site, and a gorgeous pyramidal motif is carried throughout the museum's skylights, tiling, and structure. Comprehensive exhibits on the site, invaluable brochures on the ruins (5 pesos), and the tickets allowing admission to the ruins make the museum a necessary stop before climbing on to the site itself.

GUIDE TO THE RUINS

From the museum, a rocky path leads to the ruins. The ruins are best explored in a generally circular manner; start at the elevated plaza up to the left of the first patch of greenery. On the right side of the first plain, the **Pirámide de las Estelas** (Structure A) and the **Gran Pirámide** (Structure E) just south of it nearly dwarf the three smaller structures on the left. Remember, guards (when they're present) are strict about climbing in non-designated areas. Anyway, later on you can scale the back stairs and see the view. The Gran Pirámide forms the northern boundary of the **Plaza Central,** which can be reached by continuing straight (south) and taking the small slope down to the left. This area was most likely a trading center for the local and regional populations—many ancient roads converge here. Twin pyramids on the east and the west sides of the plaza, labeled **Structure C** and **Structure D,** were used in the worship of the sun, with one oriented toward the sunrise, the other toward the sunset. At the center of the plaza is a carved obelisk that bears two hieroglyphs related to the god Quetzalcóatl. Sadly, the coded inscriptions are faded and hard to see. Apparently, priests plotted the sun's trajectory over the pyramids by tracing the obelisk's shadow.

The southwest corner of this plaza offers a great overhead view of the **Juego de Pelota** (ballcourt) below. To reach it, walk down the stone steps between **Structures C and D.** Straight ahead and off to the left lie unexcavated remnants of this sprawling city. Continue down the narrow rocky path directly to the right for the **ballcourt.** Many experts believe that this ballcourt was the earliest one built;

ballcourts as far south as Guatemala show signs of the heavy influence of Xochicalco's. In fact, a statue found here bears a remarkable likeness to another found in Copán, Honduras.

After heading back up the hill to the central plaza, make your way to the base of the **Gran Pirámide (Structure E),** atop which rest the remains of an even more ancient structure. Follow the path down to the left (west) and over to the stairway/portico section. This area was used to limit access to the main part of the city in case of invasion, a design ineffective in preventing Xochicalco from falling prey to a revolution.

Past the portico and up two sets of impressive stairways rebuilt in 1994, find the **Plaza Ceremonial,** which served as the main ceremonial center of the city. As you enter, the top of the Pirámide de las Estelas is accessible, enclosing a huge pit in the center that was the burial site for high priests and a place for ritual offerings. In the center of the plaza is the renowned **Pirámide de la Serpiente Emplumada** (Pyramid of the Plumed Serpent). Haphazardly reconstructed in 1910, it bears carved reliefs of Quetzalcóatl, the great feathered serpent who was a god-hero to a plethora of Indian groups, including the Toltecs and the Aztecs.

On the rear (west) end of the plaza is the tremendous **Montículo 2,** the highest area of the site, and supposedly the spot where the rulers of Xochicalco lived. The eastern side was intended for daily activities, while the west end was exclusively ceremonial. Exit the Plaza Ceremonial on the north side and head west down the slope to the **Hall of the Polichrome Altar,** where a colored altar rests beneath an authentic reconstruction of the roofing used by the Toltecs. Farther down is a cistern used for water storage, a sauna used for pre-game initiation rites, and **Teotlachtli,** the northern ballcourt. Here, two massive rings of rock are attached in the middle, unlike most ballcourts in Mesoamerica, which have only one ring. Teams competed for the privilege of being sacrificed atop the Pyramid of Quetzalcóatl, a true honor and a sign of good sportsmanship. Nearby remain the foundations of the **Calmecac,** the palace in which Toltec and Aztec priests underwent training and initiation.

Continue west along the weed-ridden path, around the back of the base of Montículo 2 until you reach a large stone amalgamation. A small opening in the corner (with steps leading up) allows access to the stuccoed interior of the underground **Observatorio,** where ancient astronomers followed the cosmos. On summer solstices, Aztec sages and stargazers peered through a shaft in the ceiling to trace the path of the sun; by doing so, they hoped to verify and adjust the Aztec calendar. A guide gives periodic presentations in Spanish/English as soon as a group has assembled. The tours start in the museum. *(Observatory open 11am-4pm.)*

Getting There: From Cuernavaca, both **Flecha Roja** and **Autos Pullman** stations run buses that will take you to the *Crucero de Xochicalco.* Either wait at this intersection for a taxi to take you to the site (10 pesos) or start the climb yourself. The road to the site is 4km, uphill, and takes about an hour. Bring a hat, sunblock, and some water. Coming home is easier, as small buses come by the site every hour to take people back to Cuernavaca (7 pesos). Wait by the green refreshment stand and be prepared for buses to run a little late.

TEPOZTLÁN

In northern Morelos, the quiet *pueblo* of Tepoztlán occupies one of the state's more scenic and impenetrable sites—towering cliffs form a natural fortress that allows entrance only from the south. Proceeding along Rte. 95D toward Tepoztlán, keep your eyes peeled for **Popocatépetl**, a presently active volcano peak towers over the surrounding mountains. The *indígena* village with cobbled streets preserves a colonial feel despite the pool maintenance and satellite television stores. Some indigenous people still speak Náhuatl, and many of Tepoztlán's youth are learning to speak it, even in the town's schools. On Sundays, the *zócalo* comes alive with vibrant market activity. During the rest of the week, however, the town is quieter. Perched on a peak 360m above the village are the archaeological sites for which the town is famous. The thin air may leave you breathless and thirsty, so prepare accordingly.

The valley of Tepoztlán is charged with the myth, legend, and magic of ages gone by. It is thought that the god-hero of the Toltecs (and the Aztecs, and almost every other pre-Hispanic *indígena* group), Quetzalcóatl, was born here about 1200 years ago. Celebrations still take place every September 8, when the *pulque* flows and the dance floor fills in honor of Tepozécatl. *Los chinelos*—colorfully attired folk dancers—may invite you to join their traditional dance, *el salto*. Don't be shy; after pounding a couple of *pulques*, you'll be weeping cactus tears and dying to dance.

Tepoztlán's main draw is the **Pirámide del Tepozteco,** perched on the northern ridge of the cliffs that rise above one end of town, about 3km above the valley. Some say the pyramid was a Tlahuica observatory and defense post for the valley, while others swear it served as an Aztec sacrificial temple. The 10m structure has a porch inscribed with barely discernible Tlahuica glyphs. To reach the pyramid, follow Av. 5 de Mayo north out of town (passing the *zócalo* on your right) until you reach its end. The hour-long climb is steep and strenuous, but it's made bearable by the cooling shade of trees. If you intend to climb, equip yourself with appropriate footwear, water, and spirit. If you can't make it all the way up, don't worry - there are numerous views that reward you along the way. Sunday excursions offer a fabulous people-watching experience; whole families, from newborns to great-grandfathers, don their Sunday best and hike up this holy hill. Don't be surprised to see an eight-year-old carrying an ice chest overtake you. (Open daily 9am-5:30pm. Admission 17 pesos, free Su, for children under 13, national students, and teachers with ID. Video cameras 30 pesos.)

The **Museo de Arte Prehispánico** (more commonly known as the **Museo Carlos Pellicer;** tel. 5 10 98), at the rear of Capilla Asunción, holds a collection donated to the city by the nationally renowned poet Carlos Pellicer. The impressive display includes masks, pottery pieces, and clay figures of Olmec, Zapotec, Maya, Totonac, and Aztec origin, as well as many objects from Teotihuacán. *(Open Tu-Su 10am-6pm. Admission 4 pesos.)*

Because of its natural beauty, vernal climate, and proximity to Mexico City, the area around Tepoztlán attracts an ever-growing population of wealthy *norteamericanos*. While the town and surrounding area are still lovely, prices are incredibly steep. Tepoztlán lacks moderately priced anything—forget budget accommodations. Though expensive, your best bet is **Casa Iccemanyan,** Calle de Olvido 26 (tel. 5 08 99 or 5 00 96; fax 5 21 59), on the first cross street after the Pullman de Morelos station, all the way down the hill. This joint offers six bungalows for extended stays and gives travelers studying at neighboring language schools a chance to practice their skills with a welcoming Mexican family. Well-maintained and well-decorated rooms come with clean bathrooms and lots of privacy. Beautiful pool, lawn, and unlimited use of kitchen facilities offer additional perks. Call before you arrive. Tepozteco vistas are a plus. (Singles 180 pesos, with 3 meals 250 pesos; doubles 250 pesos, with 3 meals 350 pesos.) Budget restaurants are likewise a scarcity in popular Tepotzlan. If you are willing to splurge, grab a bite to eat in one of the many vegetarian-friendly international restaurants that line Av. 5 de Mayo. If not, head for the market or for **La Parilla de Tepotzlan,** Av. 5 de Mayo #6A (tel. 5 10 73). Don't be dissuaded by the tacky plastic tablecloths—the *menú del día* (24 pesos) is delicious. (Open daily 9am-8pm.)

Getting There: From Cuernavaca, **Ometochtli** buses leave from the market (40min., every 15min. 5:45am-10pm, 8 pesos). You can also take a *pesero* (5 pesos). If you arrive at the Ometochtli depot, follow the main road; it will curve to become Av. 5 de Mayo.

TLAXCALA

TLAXCALA

There is no better place to sit in all of Mexico than the colonial city of Tlaxcala, whose glittering *Talvera* architecture fills the basin and sides of a small valley just beyond the last saggling remains of Poblano sprawl. The city's quiet, sunny streets are filled with cheap *taquerias* and juice stands that lead towards a meticulously manicured city center. The mango exterior of the **Parroquia San José** glows beside gurgling fountains near the ornate pavillion accentuating the detail and design of the *zócalo* and wrought-iron benches adorn the supremely peaceful, adjoining **Plaza Xicoténcatl**—better seating arrangements are hard to find.

Though Tlaxcala has an intruiging collection of colonial buildings, mingled with a fascinating history and culture, its most precious commodity is the all-pervasive *tranquilidad*, which draws world-weary refugees from Mexico City and Puebla on weekends throughout the year. If anything, the tired urbanites slow down an already moderate pace of life—while their money supports lots of good restaurants and small, fashionable clothing stores.

Tlaxcala may be relaxing but it's hardly a dead end. The best place to begin to explore a state full of now-deserted convents, untouristed *indígena* communities and well-preserved ruins; Tlaxcala's museums, helpful tourist office, art galleries and cultural center make accessible an unpackaged portion of Mexico's heartland.

✴ ORIENTATION

Most services can be found in and around **Plaza de la Constitución** (the *zócalo*), and **Plaza Xicoténcatl,** diagonally adjacent to it. You'll know you're there when you see the blue-and-white tiled dome of the orange **Parroquia de San José.** To get there from the bus station, exit through the glass doors to a swarm of idling *colectivos.* Those facing the right go to the downtown area, the market, and the hotel district on the northern edge of the city (2-3 pesos). To return to the bus station, take a "Central" *colectivo* from the market at **20 de Noviembre** and **Alonso Escalona,** or flag one down behind San José at 20 de Noviembre and **1 de Mayo.**

Facing the back of the church (the yellow side), the street behind you is 20 de Noviembre and the street on the left is **Lardizábal.** Going around the church to the right will bring the entrance to the *zócalo* into view. The **Palacio de Gobierno** takes up the whole north side of the *zócalo* and will be on your left. At the end of the Palacio del Gobierno, **Av. Benito Juárez** begins as the *zócalo's* eastern boundary, and continues north, constituting the city's main commercial strip. After four blocks, Juárez veers right and becomes **Av. Guillermo Valle.** Several cheap hotels are on the northern edge of town, where Guillermo Valle angles to the right and becomes **Blvd. Revolución.** To get there, catch a "Santa Ana" *colectivo* at 20 de Noviembre, three blocks from the *zócalo,* behind San José (2-3 pesos); it's a 40-minute walk from the *zócalo.* Despite the large number of pushy, beeping *colectivos,* Tlaxcala is a very walkable city. Distances are manageable, and it's often more direct and always cheaper to climb the stairs up the hillsides yourself than it is to ride in the VW vans, whose 1600cc engines can't handle the steep grades, forcing drivers to take longer, more roundabout routes.

▐ PRACTICAL INFORMATION

TRANSPORTATION

Buses: From the **Central Camionera,** Autotransportes Tlaxcala (tel. 2 02 17) runs to **Mexico City** (1½hr., every 30min. 6am-8:30pm, 60 pesos) and **Veracruz,** stopping in **Xalapa** (6hr., 10:30am and 3:30pm, 37 and 58 pesos respectively). Autotransportes

México-Texcoco has similar first-class service to **Mexico City.** Flecha Azul buses run to **Puebla** (30min., every 5min. 5:45am-10pm, 7-8 pesos).

TOURIST AND FINANCIAL SERVICES

Tourist Office: Av. Benito Juárez 18 (tel. 2 00 27). From the beautiful turn-of-the-century office at the central intersection of Juárez and Lardizábal, the state tourist office carries out carefully orchestrated plans designed to make the area a visitor's haven. Besides providing many free and helpful maps and pamphlets, the office sponsors cheap tours of **Tlaxala** and the surrounding area every Saturday and **Cacaxtla** and **Xochiténcatl** every Sunday. The comprehensive tours leave at 10:30am from the Hotel Plaza San Francisco on the south side of the *zócalo* with a knowledgeable guide (15 pesos). A gold mine of information from a friendly, English-speaking staff. Open M-F 9am-7pm, Sa-Su 10am-6pm.

Currency Exchange: Banamex, Plaza Xicoténcatl 8 (tel. 2 20 55 or 2 25 36), and **Banca Serfín,** Av. Independencia 4 (tel. 2 62 42), in Plaza Xicoténcatl, have 24hr. **ATMs.** Open M-F 9am-5pm. There are also several banks on Av. Juárez past the tourist office. The **Centro de Cambio Tlaxcala** (tel. 290 85), Av. Independencia, at the corner of Calle Guerrero, buys or sells cash, money orders, and traveler's checks. Open M-F 9am-4pm.

LOCAL SERVICES

Cultural Center: Palacio de la Cultura, Av. Benito Juárez 62 (tel. 2 60 69), 4 blocks from the *zócalo* at the corner of Av. Justo Sierra. Stages concerts, exhibits, and performances all over town. Open daily 10am-6pm.

Markets: The entire street of **Alonso Escalona** teems with *mercado* activity. From San José, cross to Lira y Ortega and walk 3 blocks, keeping the church behind you. Open daily 8am-8pm. On weekends, vendors sell *artesenias* from throughout Mexico in Plaza Xicoténcatl. Practical goods can be found at **Gigante,** the city's behemoth supermarket on Blvd. Guillermo Valle, in the shopping center on the corner of Arévalo Vera. Open daily 8am-8pm.

Laundry: Lavandería de Autoservicio Acuario, Alonso y Escalona 13A (tel. 2 62 92). Walk 4 blocks north from the *zócalo* on Juárez and turn left: it's a half block down on the left side. Full-service 30 pesos per 3kg., self-service 8 pesos per 10min. 1hr. service available. Open M-Sa 8:30am-8pm.

EMERGENCY AND COMMUNICATIONS

Emergency: dial 060.

Police: (tel. 2 07 35 or 2 10 79) on Av. Lardizábal, 1 block past the tourist office, at the corner with Calle Xicoténcatl. Open 24hr. No English spoken.

Red Cross: Allende Nte. 48 (tel. 2 09 20 or 2 47 05). Go 2 blocks behind San José to Av. Ignacio Allende, then turn left and continue 1½ blocks past Muñoz Camargo. 24hr. walk-in emergency service. No English spoken.

Pharmacy: Farmacia Ocotlán, Av. Juárez No. 33 (tel. 2 04 50), on the corner of Guridi y Alcocer. Open daily 9am-7pm.

Hospital: Hospital General, Jardín de la Corregidora 1 (tel. 2 00 30 or 2 35 55), 4½ blocks from the *zócalo* down Av. Muñoz Camargo, past the post office. No English spoken. Open 24hr. **IMSS** (tel. 2 34 00 or 2 34 22), Blvd. Guillermo Valle, across the street from the stadium. Take Av. Juárez from the *zócalo* until it turns into Blvd. G. Valle; the hospital is right after the Nestlé factory. Open 24hr.

Post Office: Plaza de la Constitución 20 (tel. 2 00 04), on the corner with Av. Muñoz Camargo. Open M-F 8am-8pm, Sa 9am-1pm.

Postal Code: 90000.

Fax: Telecomm, Porfirio Díaz 6 (tel. 2 55 87), behind the post office. **Telegraph** service as well. Open M-F 8am-6pm, Sa-Su 9am-noon.

Internet Access: Planet Systems, Juárez 30-B (6 16 75) has a solid connection and 7 servicible computers. 20 pesos per hr. Open M-Sa 9am-8pm. The busier **Internet Café,** Av.

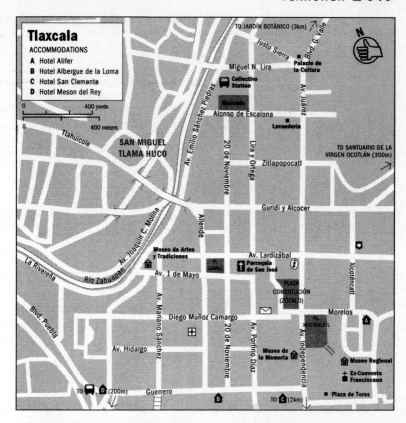

Tlaxcala

ACCOMMODATIONS

A Hotel Alifer
B Hotel Albergue de la Loma
C Hotel San Clemente
D Hotel Meson del Rey

Independencia No. 21 (tel. 2 44 64), east of the Plaza Xicoténcatl, offers a speedier connection for the same price. Open M-Sa 9am-8pm, Su 10am-8pm.

Telephones: LADATELs under the arches along the *zócalo*. **Coin-operated phones** in front of and behind Parroquia de San José, northwest of the *zócalo*.

Phone Code: 246.

ACCOMMODATIONS

Truly cheap accomodations in Tlaxcala are available, but the only sights you'll find near these backstreet bargains are the local *farmacia*, *miscellaneria*, and the *michoacana*. Those willing to fork over 150 pesos for a double and slightly less for a single will be able to stay close to the *zócalo* in very comfortable rooms, often with a view of the city. Be sure to make reservations for the weekend, though, since the lower range hotels at good locations fill up quickly.

Hotel Albergue de la Loma, Calle Guerrero 58 (tel. 2 04 24). From the bus station, walk downhill following the street's curve to the right, and continue along Calle Guerrero until just past Allende. A rustic wood-covered stairway leads up the hill on the right to a white-washed building with wide balconies and picture windows, which, if you plead for them, can be yours. The views of San José, Ocotlán and the surrounding valley make it hard to go to sleep at night, and the vista at daybreak is even more spectacular. Rooms have phones, TVs, and private bathrooms. The downstairs restaurant serves up good, cheap food every day from 8-10pm. Don't miss the *tlacloyos*, covered with delectable, sunset-colored *salsa*. Singles 138 pesos; doubles 167 pesos. Reservations recommended for weekend stays.

Hotel Alifer, Morelos 11 (tel. 2 56 78; email alifer@tlax.net.mx). A pastel-colored hotel conveniently located about a 2min. walk from the *zócalo*. From the *zócalo*, take Av. Morelos past Plaza Xochiténcatl and up the hill until you reach the hotel on the right. The modern rooms are a tad expensive, but they feature wall-to-wall carpeting, cable TV, phone, and a full bath. The only drawback? The bells of the neighboring *Ex-Convento* start ringing at 6am. 1 double bed 150 pesos; 2 beds 260 pesos.

Hotel San Clemente, Av. Independencia 58 (tel. 2 19 89). In the same price range but further afield, San Clemente makes up for the trek with a fountain, an outdoor BBQ area, and tiled quartz bathrooms. To reach the hotel, follow Av. Independencia south past Plaza Xicoténcatl for about 2km. The bright yellow hotel is on the left .8km after Av. Independencia starts to curve. 1 double bed 150 pesos; 2 beds 180 pesos.

Hotel Meson del Rey, Calle 3 #1009 (tel. 2 90 55) is across the intersection to the left when one exits the bus station doors. Clean, upholstered rooms with TV/phone and super-easy public transportation counterbalance the admittedly unglamorous locale. 1 bed 80 pesos; two beds 150 pesos.

⌐◙ FOOD

Regional specialties include *pollo en xoma* (chicken stuffed with fruits and other meats), *barbacoa en mixiote* (meat cooked in *maguey* leaves), and *pulque*, an ancient, unrefined alcoholic drink made from the *maguey* cactus. You can either drink *pulque* straight, eat it with your chicken, or try *pulque verde*, a drink made with honeywater, *yerba buena* (spearmint), and lemon juice. With all these culinary extravaganzas, it's hard to go wrong when picking a place to eat in Tlaxcala. For delicious midday meals, duck into one of the small family-run restaurants on **Juárez** between **Zitlalpopocatl** and **Alonsa de Escalona,** where *comida corrida* is usually 20 pesos or less. Around the *zócalo*, 30-40 pesos translates into a very quality meal, often served by intimidatingly classy waiters.

Los Portales Restaurant-Bar, Plaza Constitución 8 (tel. 2 54 19), on the side of the *zócalo* under the arches. Los Portales can afford to be a little bit pricier than its *zócalo* competition. With the most fashionable clientele on Juárez, paying the extra 5-10 pesos to dine there is to make a social statement. Good, standard *antojitos* start at 25 pesos, with sandwiches and pastas around the same price. Open Su-Th 7am-11pm, F-Sa 24hr.

Restaurant El Tirol, Av. Independencia #7A (tel. 2 37 54), rises above the rest...aurants along Plaza Xicoténcatl. Impeccable service and fancy tale settings belie the completely reasonable prices. Self-conciously Mexican, this colorful restaurant caters to weekday business luncheons and hip evening and weekend clientele. For authentic Tlaxcalan food, try the *sopa Tlaxcalteca*. Also try the *gusanos de maguey,* but only if you're daring. *Comida corrida* from 25 pesos. Open daily 7:30am-midnight.

El Quinto Sol, on Av. Juárez diagonally across from the tourist office. A popular vegetarian joint full of tempting fruits matching the orange walls outside. Sprinkled with grains and smothered with fresh fruit, their yogurt will leave your tastebuds begging for more. Breakfasts include coffee, yogurt, eggs, and juice (18-20 pesos). Cheese or soybean *tortas* 7-9 pesos; specialty cure-all juices 7-10 pesos. Open M-Sa 8am-8pm.

◉ SIGHTS

PLAZA DE LA CONSTITUCIÓN. Filled with ornate stone carvings and orange tile, the *zócalo*, also called the Plaza de la Constitución, is the obvious hotbed of Tlaxcala's historical and cultural sights. While meandering through this pain-stakingly pruned symbol of Renaissance civilization, keep an eye out for the octagonal fountain of Santa Cruz in the center by the bandstand. Built in Europe during the 14th century, it was given to the city by King Phillip IV in 1676—no small token when

STUDENT TRAVEL

Planning Trips for Generations X, Y and Z.

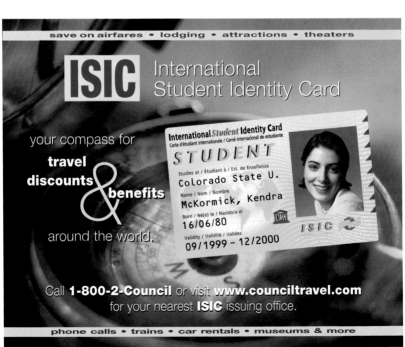

one considers the distance those stones were hauled, and symbollic of the Spanish gratitude towards *El Leal Ciudad* (the loyal city) and their instrumental role in Mexico's colonization.

CAPILLA REAL DE INDIOS. On the plaza's eastern boundary, directly across from the fountain, the octagonal design continues in the bright, orange tiling of the Capilla Real de Indios (today's **Palacio de Justicia**). When Cortéz and Co. arrived in the region in 1519, they found a quasi-Republican alliance of four lordships that had existed since the 13th century, all of which were struggling to stave off an encroaching Aztec tide. Seeing that it would be mutually advantageous, Cortés and the Confederation of Tlaxcala formed an alliance which ultimately helped defeat the the Aztecs, and colonize much of the land to the north. Tlaxcalans participated in a variety of colonizing crusades throughout the 10th and 17th centuries, founding cities and subduing the natives. The Capilla Real was founded by the four chieftans that headed the Tlacxalan *vicerealties* allied with Spain. The side towers were constructed later, but the Capilla remains an interesting symbol of Tlaxcala's important alliance.

PALACIO DE GOBIERNO. Among other things, Tlaxcala's unique history can be followed in the huge, 450m, electric, jam-packed murals by **Desederio Hernández Xochitiotzin** covering the interior walls of the 16th century *palacio* on the plaza's north side. If you had visited the city in the 17th century you would have stayed in the elaborate upper chambers on the left hand side of the building, joining in the long history of red carpet treatment for visitors to the city. Be sure to get someone to explain the murals to you, or read about them yourself using the coded number system called, "The History of Tlaxcala and Its Contribution to What is Mexican"—much is explained in its complex narrative. *(Open daily 10am-6pm; free.)*

PLAZA XICOTÉNCATL. Cutting back through the *zócalo* and past the fountain is Plaza Xicoténcatl. The plaza was dedicated to the young Tlaxcalan warrior **Xicoténcatl Axayacatzin,** who was among the few Tlaxcalans violently opposed to Cortés as the *conquistador* successfully seduced Tlaxcala into joining him against the Aztecs. Today Xicoténcatl is a hero, and his fierce-looking statue commands the center spot in the plaza. Normally a tranquil area, the plaza livens up on weekends as a carousel and small artisan markets occupy Xicoténcatl's grounds.

EX-CONVENTO FRANCISCANO DE NUESTRA SEÑORA DE LA ASUNCIÓN. On the southeast side of Plaza Xicoténcatl, a 400-year-old cobblestone way leads about 200m up to the ex-convento. Built in 1525 and one of the first convents in North America, the ex-convent is one of the most beautiful structures of New Spain. The thick, wooden door of the cathedral opens into a beautifully simple romanesque nave and a ceiling of intricate Islamic influenced *mudéjar* (woodwork) highlighted with gilded stars. The storied main altar contains, among other relics, *la conquistadora*—a canvas of the virgin Cortés is said to have kept between his armor and his breast. The side chapel closest to the altar, **La Capilla de la Teresa Orden,** contains the basin used to baptize the four Tlaxcalteco chieftains at the time of their alliance.

MUSEO REGIONAL DE TLAXCALA. The small museum presents artifacts from nearby archaeological zones, exhibitions of Spanish colonial art, and boasts a library specializing in Tlaxcalan history and anthropology. Take a peek through the fence across from the ex-convent to discover one of Tlaxcala's pride and joys, the **Plaza de Toros.** Named after the famous *torero* Jorge "El Ranchero" Aguilar, the beautiful plaza has been in use since 1788 and comes to life during the last week of October and first week of November when Tlaxcala celebrates its annual fair. *(Tel. 2 02 62. Museum next door to the ex-convento. Open Tu-Su 10am-5pm. Admission 20 pesos.)*

CHURCH OF CHRIST THE GOOD NEIGHBOR. Branching off from the ex-convent is a striking stone staircase. At the top stands the derilict 16th-centrury church of Christ the Good Neighbor, which opens only on July 1st for the *Día de la*

Purisima Sangre de Cristo. The rest of the year, the hill offers one of the most spectacular views of the city of Tlaxcala.

PARROQUIA SAN JOSÉ AND THE SANTUARIO DE LA VIRGÉN DE OCTOLANA. Tlaxcala's skyline is defined by the city's two most glorious churches, the towering Parroquia San José in the city center and the shining white tours of the Santuario de la Virgén de Octolana that rise up from the ridge of the basin. While San José takes on the role of Tlaxcala's main place of worship, Octolana has unmatchable religious, symbolic and historical significance. A Virgén de Guadalupe Tlaxcala-style, Ocotlán appeared in 1541 to an ailing Indian named Juan Diego Bernadino, curing him and ordering him to build a church at the spot (which at the time, held the ruins of an ancient pyramid). The modern day church was finished in 1723 and holds the 16th-century wooden image of the Virgen, which appeard in one of the hills famous pine tress, and which is carried through the city streets on the first Monday of May every year. In the interior, golden conch shells top the pilasters and another giant shell frames the end of the nave. The star of the show, however, is the *camarín*, the small octagonal room off to the side where the Virgin is "dressed" for important festivals. (*To get there, take an "Ocotlán" colectivo (1.50 pesos). It stops right in front of the church, where it waits to go back into town. To hike there, take a right on Av. Benito Juárez, head one block past the tourist office, and hang another right on Guridi y Alcocer. When the road forks, follow it up the hill to the left. The road climbs to a small Capilla del Pocito de Agua Santa, where it becomes a cobblestone street with a staircase alongside; the stairs lead directly to the square of the church.*)

MUSEO DE ARTES Y TRADICIONES POPULARES DE TLAXCALA. The museum is across the street on the left. In nine exhibition halls, artisans demonstrate the technicalities of their crafts in real-life displays. Presentations include a tour of a traditional indigenous kitchen, an explanation of textile production, and perhaps most interestingly, a discourse on how the state's famous *pulque* is made. (*Tel. 2 23 37. Go west on Lardizábal until it ends at Blvd. Mariano Sanchez, about 4 blocks from the tourist office. Open Tu-Su 10am-6pm. Admission 6 pesos, students 4 pesos.*)

JARDÍN BOTÁNICO DE TIZATLÁN. For more indigenous beauty without the tourist packaging, the *jardín* delivers Mexican plants in an otherwordly setting. No bikes, balls, radios, or beer are allowed in this pastoral paradise. The rocky paths meander across a stagnant creek to reveal a tucked-away greenhouse. (*From the hotel district on Blvd. Revolución, turn left at Camino Real before the brick bridge passes over the road.Tel. 2 65 46. Open daily 6am-11pm. Free.*)

THE RUINS OF TIZATLÁN. Located about 4km outside of Tlaxcala, these tiny ruins compose all that is left of one of Tlaxcala's four *señoríos* (warrior city-states). (*Take a colectivo from 20 de Noviembre labeled "Tizatlán." Get off in front of the golden-domed church and walk to the left until you reach the ruins, lying near the back of a beautiful church that is also worth visiting. Site open Tu-Su 10am-5pm. Admission 12 pesos.*)

🎵 ENTERTAINMENT

Tlaxcala has become something of a nightspot, at least on weekends. **Royal Adler's Disco,** Blvd. Revolución 4 (tel. 2 18 42), at the Hotel Jeroc, plays current hits (cover 15 pesos; open F-Sa 10pm-3am). Another local hotspot is **Burladero,** 1 de Mayo 9 (tel. 2 64 57), a disco bar just two blocks west of the *zócalo* (cover 17 pesos; open M-W noon-7pm, Th-Sa 9pm-3am). Many of the restaurants and bars in the arcades feature live music on weekend nights as well. On weekdays, finding entertainment becomes a more difficult task, since much of the city shuts down by 10:30pm. However, **La Revolución Discoteca,** on the 2nd fl. of the East Portal towards Plaza Xicoténcatl, plays loud pop-rock music and serves somewhat expensive drinks (open Tu-Su 5pm-5am). **Cines 1 y 2,** Guillermo Valle 113 and Calle de Bosque 1 (tel. 2 35 44), and **Cinema Tlaxcala** (tel. 2 19 62), on the south side of the *zócalo* across the street from the post office, show first-run American movies (15 pesos).

NEAR TLAXCALA

CACAXTLA

One of the best-preserved and best-presented archaeological sites in the country is the hilltop ruin of Cacaxtla (kah-KASH-tla), 19km southwest of Tlaxcala. The Olmecas-Xicalancas, who once dominated the southwest corner of Tlaxcala State and most of the Puebla Valley, built and expanded the city between 600 and 750. Cacaxtla was abandoned by 1000, and its inhabitants were finally driven from the area by Toltec-Chichimec invaders in 1168. Excavation began at Cacaxtla in 1975, and the area is now reconstructed as the ceremonial center it once was, complete with more modern additions such as a restaurant and gift shop.

Upon entering the site, visit the **museum** on the right. It contains artifacts and bones collected from the site and serves as a good intro to the area. From the small museum, a dirt path leads toward the pyramid by way of the **Gran Basamento,** the thick platform upon which the center was built. The pyramid is covered by the **world's second largest archaeological roof** in order to prevent the erosion of the adobe structures, and it makes for a refreshingly cool viewing experience. Once upstairs, visitors move clockwise around the excavations of ceremonial court-yards, temples, tombs, and what appears to have been a palace.

Two discoveries distinguish this site from others. One is a **latticework window** on the west side, opposite the entrance. The window, a free-standing fence, is the only one of its kind. It was produced by surrounding a latticework of twigs and branches with mud and stucco. Cacaxtla's other chief attraction is a series of murals scattered about the site, considered some of the best-preserved pre-His-panic paintings in Mesoamerica. The largest of them, the **Battle Mural,** depicts a historical-mythological battle in which an army dressed in jaguar skins crushes the skulls of an army dressed as birds. The murals appear in all the glory of their orig-inal mineral-based colors, which are still amazingly bright and gruesome.

From the Battle Mural, the official circuit takes you to an area whose bland name, **Building A,** belies its beauty. Five of the site's murals stand together, united by color and imagery into a symbolic unit. The leftmost mural depicts the god Quetzalcóatl and a human figure in a jaguar skins, while the right-most one shows a bird-man surrounded by symbols of rain god Tlaloc. (Open daily 9am-6pm. Admission 14 pesos; free Sunday. Guides are available for 30 pesos per person, with reduced rates for large groups, but few speak English.)

XOCHITÉNCATL

The civilization at Xochiténcatl (o-chee-TEN-cahtl) predates Cacaxtla by several hundred years, and its ruins are located on a hill just opposite Cacaxtla. Public transportation that runs between Cacaxtla and Xochiténcatl is difficult to find. Follow the signs around the Cacaxtla pyramid to the path that leads up the hill (about a 2km walk). In 300, the inhabitants of Xochiténcatl were conquered by the Olmecas-Xicalancas, who also took up residence at Cacaxtla. The site features four pyramids, the largest of which, **The Pyramid of Flowers,** is actually a pyramid on top of a pyramid. The **spiral pyramid,** the one farthest from the entrance, is also worth a look. Dedicated to the wind god Ehecatl, it is the only such spiral pyramid known to exist. Other interesting finds include a large snake sculpture and several large basalt pilars. These pilars are impressive considering that they were made from a single large piece of stone without any steel tools. The site also offers a spectacular view of the surrounding volcanoes: **Popocatépetel, Ixtaccihuatl,** and **La Malinche.**

Getting There: From Tlaxcala, take one of the *colectivos* labeled "Texoloc-Tlax-cala" or buses marked "Nativitas" that leave from the bus plaza on 20 de Noviem-bre next to the market or along 20 de Noviembre behind San José. Ask whether the bus goes to Cacaxtla. Some go to the town of San Miguel del Milagro (San Miguelito) at the base of the site; others travel past the main entrance (40 min., 5 pesos). If you're dropped off in town, walk up the windy road, following the signs to the entrance. To return to Tlaxcala, walk downhill from the ticket booth and turn right to go down to San Martín. From Tlaxcala, *colectivos* go to Xochiténcatl; across the street, "Tlaxcala" *colectivos* return to the bus plaza next to the market (5 pesos). The tourist office offers guided trips to the two zones every Sunday for 15 pesos. The trips include transportation and usually an English-speaking guide. These tours are an excellent way to visit the sites.

PUEBLA

PUEBLA

Puebla (pop. 2 million) was a great social experiment; Renaissance meets ruffian—the ultimate test of Enlightenment ideals concerning cities and civilization. Conceived by a group of humanist Spaniards, Puebla was to be a city of faith and education, with libraries, schools and administrative buidings contrived to civilize troublesome compatriots. Though it would take several centuries to pacify Mexico's wild west, Puebla, suprisingly enough, was completed as planned, and to this day is a mix of 17th-and-18th centrury European art and ideals with a uniquely passionate and colorful Mexican energy.

Unlike many colonial cities in the New World, Puebla was planned meticuously. Built on dry, solid ground (rather than on a lake or over the ruins of a Mesoamerican city as with many Mexican metropoli), Puebla is said to have been designed by angels who flew down and streaked ribbons across the land, forming the grid that makes the city so simple to navigate.

Angels or not, the cityscape was defined by holy visitors. Franciscans built hospitals, libraries and orphanages for the illegitimate children of ruffians, while nuns from a variety of orders set up cloisters and kitchens, where they invented some of Mexico's most glorious dishes and a genius of sugar-candy sweets which are one of the city's major selling points to this day.

Today, Puebla is one of the most important cities in the country. Despite its size, the city elegantly combines gilded churches and trendy clothing stores, while in the shady *zócalo* both teen hipsters and older locals relax together. And while the Bishop's angels may choke on the exhaust fumes or balk at the upsurge in fast food restaurants, they must still smile down on the amorous couples in the *zócalo*, foreign students exercising their new-found language skills at local discos, and tourists immersing themselves in a little Mexican history.

✸ ORIENTATION

Puebla, capital of Puebla state, is connected through an extensive route network to **Mexico City** (125km northwest along Rte. 150), **Oaxaca** (Rte. 190, 125, or 131), **Tlaxcala** (Rte. 119), **Veracruz** (Rte. 150), and countless other cities. All **bus** companies operate out of the **CAPU (Central de Autobuses Puebla)** on Blvd. Norte and Tlaxcala, in the northwest corner of the city.

The *avenidas* and *calles* of Puebla form a near-perfect grid, with the northwest corner of the *zócalo* in the center. Everything changes names at that point; the main north-south street is called **5 de Mayo** north of the *zócalo* and **16 de Septiembre** south of it; the main east-west drag is **Avenida Reforma** to the west, and **Avenida Máximo Ávila Camacho** to the east. *Avenidas* run east-west and are designated either *Poniente* (*Pte.*, west) or *Oriente* (*Ote.*, east), depending on where they lie with respect to that intersection. Similarly, *calles* run north-south and are labeled *Norte* (*Nte.*) or *Sur* with respect to the critical point. Numerical addresses correspond to the order of the block away from the city center. For example, 4 Ote. 212 is located on the second block of the street, in the section bounded by Calle 2 Nte. and Calle 4 Nte. On the following block away from the center, addresses will be in the 400s.

Puebla

ACCOMMODATIONS
A Hotel Cathedral
B Hotel Teresita
C Hotel Avenida
D Hotel Imperial
E Hotel del Parián

0   300 yards
0   300 meters

Red Cross

Av. 20 Oriente
Av. 18 Oriente
Av. 16 Oriente
Av. 12 Oriente
Av. 8 Oriente
Av. 4 Oriente
Av. 2 Oriente
Av. 5 Oriente
Av. 7 Oriente

Mercado el Alto Garibaldi

Iglesia de San Francisco

Blvd. Héroes del 5 de Mayo

TO CENTRO CIVICO 5 DE MAYO, FORTS (1km)

Calle 6 Norte

Teatro Principal

Av. 6 Oriente
Av. 2 Oriente

Mercado el Parián

North Office

Av. Maximino Ávila Camacho

Universidad Autónoma de Puebla

de la Compañía

Av. 3 Oriente

Calle del Sapo

TO AFRICAN SAFARI (16km)

Calle 4 Norte

Av. 16 Oriente
Av. 14 Oriente
Av. 12 Oriente
Av. 10 Oriente
Av. 8 Oriente
Av. 4 Oriente

Casa de Aquiles Serdán

La Casa de los Muñecos

Calle 2 Sur

Av. 5 Oriente

Museo Amparo

Av. 18 Ote.

Calle 2 Sur

ZÓCALO

Casa de Cultura and Biblioteca Palafoxiana

Av. 9 Oriente

Av. 5 de Mayo
Av. 16 de Septiembre

Exconvento de Santa Mónica

Mercado 5 de Mayo

Exconvento de Santa Rosa

Calle 3 Norte

Catedral Basílica de Puebla

COMERCIAL CENTER

Santo Domingo

Museo UPAEP

Museo Bello

A
B
C

Calle 3 Sur

Av. 10 Poniente
Av. 8 Poniente

Calle 5 Norte

Calle 5 Sur

Calle 7 Norte

Calle 16 Poniente
Calle 14 Poniente
Calle 12 Poniente

Av. 10 Poniente
Av. 8 Poniente
Av. 6 Poniente
Av. 4 Poniente
Av. 2 Poniente
Av. Reforma
Av. 3 Poniente
Av. 5 Poniente
Av. 7 Poniente
Av. 9 Poniente

Calle 9 Norte

TO CAPU BUS STATION (4km)

Calle 11 Norte

Juárez

TO ZONA ESMERELDA (1km), AIRPORT (22km)

PASEO BRAVO

Calle 11 Sur

Calle 13 Sur

N

Official yellow **taxis** labeled *taxis controlados* will take you to the *zócalo* from the bus station for about 20 pesos (24 pesos at night). If traveling with an independent *taxista*, set a price before getting in and don't be shy about haggling. Cabs from the train station to the *zócalo* run about 15 pesos. **Municipal buses** and *micros* (also known as *combis*), white Volkswagen vans that operate like buses, cost 3 pesos. Anything labeled "Centro" should take you close to the *zócalo*. On Calle 9 Nte.-Sur you can catch buses to the bus station (marked "CAPU"), or to the train station (marked *"Estación Nueva Popular"*). CAPU buses also run along Blvd. Héroes de 5 de Mayo.

🔢 PRACTICAL INFORMATION

TRANSPORTATION

Airport: In **Huejotzingo,** 22km away (tel. 32 00 32). Regional airlines fly to Guadalajara, Monterrey, and Tijuana.

Buses: CAPU (Central de Autobuses Puebla; tel. 49 72 11) at Blvd. Norte and Tlaxcala is one of the largest bus stations in the country, with buses regularly traveling to all parts of the Republic. Prices and routes change frequently and vary from carrier to carrier, so the following is just a guideline. ADO (tel. 25 90 01), has many first-class destinations including: **Cancún** (24hr., 11:45am, 636 pesos); **Mérida** (21hr., 7:55pm, 533 pesos); **Mexico City** (2½hr., every 20min., 60 pesos); **Oaxaca** (4½hr., 7 per day, 158 pesos); **Veracruz** (3½hr., 7 per day, 127 pesos); **Xalapa** (3hr., every 2hr. 6:45am-9:15pm, 72 pesos). Cristóbal Colón (tel. 49 75 68), rolls to: **Huatulco** (13hr., 7:30, 8:30 and 9:55 pm, 303 pesos); **Puerto Escondido** (15hr., 7:30 and 8:30pm, 305 pesos); **Tehuantepec** (9hr., 8:15pm, 280 pesos); and other resort cities. Estrella Roja (tel. 40 76 96), sends first-class service to: **Mexico City** (2hr., every 15min. 5am-9pm, 38-60 pesos). Estrella Blanca (tel. 45 74 33), first class to: **Acapulco** (7hr., 5 per day, 250 pesos); **Chilpancingo** (6hr., 5 per day, 124 pesos); and **Taxco** (5hr., 8am, 80 pesos). Flecha Azul (tel. 49 73 55), leaves for **Tlaxcala** (50min., 4:40am-10pm, 10 pesos). Smaller bus lines also serve the CAPU bus station.

TOURIST AND FINANCIAL SERVICES

Tourist Office: State Office, Av. 5 Ote. 3 (tel. 46 12 85 or 46 20 44), facing the cathedral's southern side, 1 block from the *zócalo*. Free maps and a monthly guide to cultural events in Puebla. The staff is highly melodramatic and wears trendy apparel. Open M-Sa 9am-8:30pm, Su 9am-2pm. There is also a **booth** at the bus station.

Currency Exchange: Banks line Av. Reforma and Av. 16 de Septiembre around the *centro;* most have 24hr. **ATMs. Bital,** Reforma 126 (tel. 46 30 50), changes money M-F 8am-7pm and Sa 8am-5pm. **Casas de cambio** offer slightly better rates and cluster in the Zona Esmeralda along Av. Juárez further from the *zócalo*. Try **Casa de Cambio Puebla,** Av. 29 Sur. 316A (tel. 48 01 99) at Juárez. Open M-F 9am-6:30pm.

American Express: Díaz Ordaz 6A Sur 2914, #301 (tel. 24 75 12 or 24 75 13), in the Plaza Dorada. Best bet for cashing and replacing AmEx checks; holds client mail for 10 days. Open M-F 9am-6pm.

LOCAL SERVICES

Markets: Puebla's squawking **Mercado 5 de Mayo,** located on 3 Nte. between 16 and 18 Pte. has stentorian bartering that spills over into the adjoining streets. Frantic commerce extends across the length and breadth of Av. 5 de Mayo (closed to traffic); prices tend to fall as you go north. For jangling trinkets and crafts that span the gamut of quality, **Mercado El Parian** Calle 6 Nte. 200, will fulfill your every desire. If you seek A/C and order, head for **Gigante,** 4 Nte. and Blvd. Héroes del 5 de Mayo, to the north of Templo de San Francisco. Open daily 9am-9pm.

Laundry: Lavandería Roly, Calle 7 Nte. 404 (tel. 32 93 07). 30 pesos for 3kg self-service. Open M-Sa 8am-9pm, Su 8am-3pm.

EMERGENCY AND COMMUNICATIONS

Emergency: dial 060. Also try the **Policía Auxiliar** (tel. 88 18 63), open 24hr. or the **Escuadrón S.O.S.** (tel. 40 67 91).

Police: Dirección de Policía, (tel. 32 22 23 or 32 22 22).

Red Cross: 20 Ote. and 10 Nte. (tel. 35 80 40, 35 86 31, or 34 00 00). 24hr. ambulance service. Some English spoken.

Pharmacies: Farmacias del Ahorro, (tel. 31 33 83) in Plaza San Pedro. Open 24hr. **Sanborn's,** Av. 2 Ote. 6 (tel. 43 43 00). Open daily 7am-1am.

Hospital: Hospital UPAEP, Av. 5 Pte. 715 (tel. 42 02 52 and 32 32 21), at 39 Sur. **Hospital Universitario,** (tel. 46 64 64) Calle 13 Sur at Av. 25 Pte., 10 blocks south and 7 blocks west of the *zócalo*. 24hr. emergency service. Some English spoken.

Post Office: 16 de Septiembre at Av. 5 Ote. (tel. 42 64 48), 1 block south of the cathedral, just around the corner from the state tourist office. Open M-F 8am-8pm, Sa 9am-1pm. **Northern office,** Av. 2 Ote. 411 2nd fl.(tel. 42 11 36). Open M-F 8am-7pm, Sa 9am-noon. The 2 branches have separate *Lista de Correos,* so make sure you know where your mail waits. **Postal Code:** 72000.

Fax: Telecomm, 16 de Septiembre 504 (tel. 32 17 79), just south of the post office. Western Union, telegrams, fax. Open M-F 8am-6pm, Sa-Su 9am-1pm.

Internet Access: Cybercafes line Calle 2 Sur. **Internet Cyber-Byte,** Calle 2 Sur 505B, across from the Lion's Club has lots of computers, fast connection, and cool drinks for 20 pesos per hr. Open M-Sa 10am-9pm. **Cyber-Café** (tel. 42 27 04), 1 block down from 2 Sur at 907C is a café with computer screens imbeded in rustic, wooden tables. Reasonably quick service is 20 pesos per hour and for the craving, *Café Americano* is 8 pesos. Open M-Sa 9am-9pm, Su 11am-4pm.

Telephones: LADATELs are easy to find along 5 de Mayo and around the *zócalo*.

Phone Code: 22.

ACCOMMODATIONS

Puebla is well stocked with budget hotels, and most are within a five- or six-block radius of the *zócalo*. When walking around the *zócalo*, be on the lookout for large signs with a red "H" jutting out of the packed buildings. These signs, friends of the weary traveler, indicate that a hotel—often a cheap one—is near.

Hotel Imperial, Av. 4 Ote. 212 (tel. 42 49 80). On the expensive side, but oh, the amenities! Telephone and TV in all rooms, a mini-golf course, workout area, purified plumbing (you can guzzle the shower water), laundry service, pool table, and a Hershey's kiss on your pillow every night. Breakfast in the downstairs cafe (open 7:30am-9:30pm) is included. Five stars—budget style. A **30% discount** for proud *Let's Go* owners makes the Imperial's luxury more affordable. One double bed 185 pesos; 2 beds 275 pesos.

Hotel Avenida, Av. 5 Pte 336 (tel. 32 21 04), is arguably the cheapest hotel in Puebla. Bedrooms are clean and pleasant, but this hotel will not suffice for people in need of the luxury toilette. Hot water is only turned on from 6am-6:30pm and while the private baths are nice, the shared ones are decidedly icky. Still, friendly staff and a good location, not to mention the incredibly low prices, make Hotel Avenida an unbelievable bargain for the budget traveler. Singles 40 pesos; doubles 60 pesos; prices for the larger rooms depend on the number of guests; private bathrooms cost 20 pesos more.

Hotel Real del Parián, 2 Ote. 601 (tel. 46 19 68), 2 blocks away from the *zócalo*, directly across the street from the *mercado*, and upstairs from some of Puebla's best bargain restaurants. From the clean, colorful rooms with private baths, you can use your bird's-eye view to pick out a cheap *talvera* pattern in the stands below, and head across the street for a filling 10 peso meal at Mercado el Alto. Drinking water, laundry facilities and accomodating staff is icing on the proverbial cake. One double bed 80 pesos; 2 beds 115 pesos; 3 beds 170 pesos.

CENTRAL MEXICO

Hotel Cathedral, Av. 3 Pte. 310 (tel. 32 23 60). If you liked *A Room with a View,* this is your *pensione.* The romance of the early 19th-century home's high ceilings and glowing hardwood floors can warm even the coolest shared showers (bathrooms are communal), and the sun helps as well when it shines on the balconies, planted courtyards and spectacular *techo con vista* (roof with a view) accessible by ancient spiral staircases. Super-clean, friendly and casual—the aesthete's thumbs up. Singles 100 pesos.

☕ FOOD

Culinarily-speaking, Puebla is very much like Wonka-land, only the river that runs through this food factory's arteries is **mole poblano**, not Wonka-chocolate. This rich, dark chocolate sauce can be found slathered on chicken, beef and just about everything else edible in town—especially during the annual *mole* cook-off where antique family recipes compete for the civic glory of *Mole Ambassador.* While it's fun to try a different version of *mole poblano* at every meal, don't miss Puebla's other secret sauces—*mole pipian* containing pumpkin seeds and chiles, and *mole adobo,* a spicier blend of cumin powder. Most restaurants will let you sample the offerings before you decide.

The munchkins behind the menu-madness are several centuries worth of *poblano* nuns, who quietly concocted delicacies in their cloistered and often clandestine kitchens. Their creative genius can best be witnessed in the *dulcerías* along Av. 6 Ote., which are filled with delicate, colorful candies, some of which are still named after the convents of their origin. The nun's penchant for sweetness spilled over into their meal preparation. You should be sure to try the *Chiles en Nogada,* a green pepper stuffed with a complicated beef and fruit filling, and smothered in white walnut sauce, devised by the nuns of Santa Monica as a birthday present for Augustín de Iturbide when he visited the city in 1821. The food is still eaten in August—Iturbide's birth month.

Puebla is also a breeding ground for that wonderful culinary *burro*—the taco stand-restaurant. These cheap, tasty joints have menus based around *tortas,* tacos and the *cemita* (A sandwich made with a special long-lasting bread that colonial Puebla exported to Veracruz, where it was put on ships to Spain as sustenance for the transatlantic deck-set; have no fear: it's much better than hardtack). These places also invariably serve a rendition of *mole poblano*—always the most expensive thing on the menu. To find these filling, 10-peso meals, look to the outlying *colonias,* to **5 de Mayo** at **14 Ote.,** to **Av. 2 Ote.** near **El Parián Mercado** and to **Mercado Alto Caribaldi** on the far side of La Iglesía de San Francisco. Though they usually close by 8 or 9pm, they usually serve fruit breakfast too.

▧ Restaurant Del Parián, 6 Nte. 5 (tel. 46 47 98), near the **Mercado el Parián.** One of the cheaper restaurants offering *comidas regionales.* The open-air, blue-tiled kitchen lets you get a glimpse of the mystic rituals of Mexican cooking while you sample the restaurant's much-touted *mole poblano* (40 pesos for 2 meat chunks, 30 pesos for 1 meat chunk). Seating in the back room was clearly designed for the tourist gaze, but it is charming and quiet nonetheless. Open daily 9am-7pm.

▧ Restaurant El Vegetariano, Av. 3 Pte. 525 (tel. 46 54 62). While the Vege's cafeteria-style 1950s decor may make you worry that you've come to the wrong place, stay cool—the *chorizo* and *jámon* on this menu are made of spiced soy. Amazing fruit drinks (9 pesos) and gigantic salads (20 pesos) bulk up the menu. Their *energetica,* a plateful of tropical fruits topped with yogurt and granola, will make you wish for a franchise in your neighborhood. Open daily 7:30am-9:30pm.

La Fonda Santa Clara, Av. 3 Pte. 307 (tel. 42 26 59). Expensive and touristy, but *the* place to try the regional cuisine. Ask locals where to find good *mole* and they'll often point you in the direction of Santa Clara where *mole poblano* is a pricey 68 pesos. All the nice touches, including *talvera* and waitresses in traditional dress. Serves harder-to-find seasonal dishes like *chiles en nogada* (65 pesos).

Restaurant Santa Lucia, 4 Nte. between 6 and 8 Ote. Serves up some of the best and cheapest *comida corrida* in Puebla for 12 pesos. The mid-afternoon meal fills the tables with locals and businessmen, making dining more of an event than a bland chewing of food. Once you get a grasp on your Spanish, put it to the test by trying to hold your own with some of Santa Lucia's hyper-opinionated clientele. Open daily 7am-11pm.

Tepoznieves, Av. 3 Pte. 150 (tel. 42 64 29). Serves the strangest ice cream and sherbet flavors imaginable. Corn lovers will crave their *nieve de elote* (corn ice cream), and for veggies, they also serve lettuce, beet, and celery ice cream. The more adventurous might want to try the spicy ice creams (such as *mango con chile*) or the alcoholic ice creams (popular flavors include tequila and pineapple rum). Those who don't feel daring enough to try the rice ice cream and other such flavors, have no fear. Tepoznieves also serves old favorites such as chocolate and vanilla. Open daily 10am-9pm.

◉ SIGHTS

From the stern gray of the tremendous cathedral to the brilliant *talvera* tile of the restaurants and copolas, one only need wander to encounter the Oz-like civic majesty at every corner. If you have only a short time in Puebla, the **Museo Amparo, Capilla del Rosario,** and **Casa de Aquiles Serdán** should top your list. There are also a slew of museums in the nearby **Centro Cívico 5 de Mayo.** For those interested in churches, the **cathedral** and **Ex-Convento de Santa Mónica** should not be missed. There are also several important sights lying outside the city, including **Tlachichuca,** 80km away and the town closest to Mexico's highest peak. The **Pico de Orizaba** is a 5747m volcano, the **third-tallest mountain in North America.** To get to Tlachichuca, head to the CAPU.

CATEDRAL BASÍLICA DE PUEBLA. Visible from all angles and directions, the cathedral is the obvious starting point for any tour of the city. Constructed by an entirely *indígena* labor force working under Spanish direction between 1575 and 1649, the building set an architectural precedent whose effect can be seen throughout Puebla's monumental colonial structures—solid Baroque purity enlivened by *talvera* domes. Though the exterior is an impressive testament to how fast the Spanish got moving, the interior is also worth a visit. Be sure not to miss the ornate, inlaid choir stalls behind the freestanding octagonal main altar, the Altar of the Kings which has a number of famous paintings, and a statue of the Virgin known as *la conquistadora* because she arrived with the first Spaniards. *(Guided tours start at 30 pesos. Open daily 10am-12:30pm and 4-6pm.)*

CASA DE LOS MUÑECOS. One of Puebla's most entertaining buildings is this "House of the Dolls" decorated on the outside with *talvera* renditions of the labors of Hercules; the building's highlight is the white ceramic men who have been straining to hold up the eves of the house for the last 200 years. According to some, the men are the architectural rivals of the designer, while others say that they are the city aldermen who were not consulted when the *casa* was built higher than the municipal palace. Today, this refreshing bit of secular architecture hosts the **University Museum** in which random exhibits on regional technological and natural history are redeemed by the collection of luminous martyrs, who stare out from over 200 dusty, unrestored canvasses on the third floor. If you read Spanish, be sure to check out the religious orders in Puebla on the second floor—it helps explain how all the saintly-types got here. *(Tel. 46 28 99. On Calle 2 Nte. at the zócalo's northeast corner. Open Tu-Su 10am-5pm. Admission 10 pesos, with student ID 5 pesos.)*

MUSEO BELLO. In the 1999 earthquake, the stairs and part of the second floor of the Museo Bello caved in; due to damage, it may be closed for the better part of 2000. The art collection of the late textile magnate José Luis Bello is crammed with ivory, iron, porcelain, earthenware, and *talvera* artifacts from different places and periods in world history; highlights include a collection of decorative keys and locks, a musical crystal door, and voluminous books of Gregorian chants from the 16th, 17th, and 18th centuries. A knowledgeable tour guide will spit out information about prominent pieces and answer questions in a strange robot-like voice. Guided tours are offered in Spanish and English, but tours in English can be rather indecipherable. (Tel. 32 94 75. Av. 3 Pte. at Calle 3 Sur 1 block west of the southeast corner of the zócalo. Open Tu-Su 10am-5pm; last entry 4:30pm. Admission 10 pesos, students with ID 5 pesos. Tu free.)

IGLESIA DE SANTO DOMINGO. The extravagant, gilded church is one of the most important examples of not only the Spanish but also the international Baroque; the building was constructed by the Dominican's brood of rural converts between 1571 and 1611. Statues of saints and angels adorn the fantastic altar, but the church's real attraction is the exuberant **Capilla del Rosario,** laden with enough 23½-karat gold to make the King of Spain jealous. Masks depicting an *indígena*, a *conquistador* in armor, and a *mestizo* hang above each of the three doors along each side of the chapel. On the ceiling, three statues represent Faith, Hope, and Charity. The 12 pillars represent the 12 apostles; the six on the upper level are each made from a single onyx stone. Since there was no room for a real choir, designers painted a chorus of angels with guitars and woodwinds on the wall over the door. (Between Av. 4 and 6 Pte. on 16 de Septiembre. Open daily 10am-2pm and 4-8pm.)

MUSEO REGIONAL DE LA REVOLUCIÓN MEXICANA. The **Casa de Aquiles Serdán,** originally the home of the eponymous printer, patriot, and martyr of the 1910 *Revolución*, serves today as the Museo Regional de la Revolución Mexicana. Hundreds of bullet holes, both inside and out, bear witness to Serdán's assassination. The museum includes photos of Serdán, of the bloody battles of the Revolution, of the bedraggled battalions of Reyes and Obregón, and of the dead Zapata and Carranza. One room is dedicated to Carmen Serdán and *las carabineras* (other female revolutionaries). (Av. 6 Ote. 206. Tel 32 10 76. Open Tu-Su 10am-4:30pm. Admission 20 pesos, children 10 pesos.)

CONVENTO DE SANTA MÓNICA. When Benito Juárez's Reform Laws went into effect in 1857, they not only weakened the power of the Church but also forced the nuns at the *convento* into hiding. The convent operated in secrecy for 77 years before it was accidentally discovered. Today's *ex-convento* serves as a museum of curious and sporadically-labeled religious art, much of which was produced by the nuns themselves. One particularly eerie holding is a life-sized re-enactment of the Last Supper, where plaster apostles in real robes sit around a colonial dinner table in one of the side rooms adjoining the convent's edenic courtyard. Even more unnerving is the nun's crypt where those who died during the period of hiding were quietly plastered into the walls. Also open to visitors are the nun's beautiful kitchen (and sometimes a laboratory), where many famous *poblano* dishes got their start. (At 5 de Mayo and 16 Pte. Open Tu-Su 10am-5pm. Admission 7 pesos. Su free.)

TEMPLO DE SAN FRANCISCO. Across 5 de Mayo from El Parián is one of Puebla's oldest neighborhoods, and its oldest church. Built by the fast-moving Franciscans between 1535 and 1585, the building's incredible *talvera* facade radiates against what is probably the world's most ominous bell tower. Expect the apocalypse to begin here. (Av. 14 Ote. and Calle 10 Nte. Open daily 10am-5pm.)

CASA DE LA CULTURA. One block from the *zócalo* behind the cathedral, in the same building as the tourist office, the *casa* is a great place to start when visiting Puebla. Have a very good cup of coffee in the courtyard (10 pesos; open daily 10am-8:30pm) before perusing the traveling art exhibits on the second floor. Folk dances are performed every Saturday and Sunday; movies are shown Thursday through Sunday. Check the board on the right as you walk in from the street for the latest schedules. The same building houses the impressive **Biblioteca Palafoxiana,** a beautiful library holding 43,000 16th-century volumes. Belonging to no specific religious order himself, Don Juan de Palafox was a vocal critic of the Jesuits, condemning their aspirations to power, land, and money. His 6000-book library, which he donated to the city in 1646, includes an illuminated copy of the **Nuremberg Chronicle** from 1493. The library was also severely damaged in the earthquake of 1999 and is expected to be under reconstruction for a year. *(Av. 5 Ote. 5. Casa de la Cultura. Tel. 42 29 11. Biblioteca tel. 46 56 13. Open Tu-Su 10am-5pm. Admission 10 pesos.)*

MUSEO AMPARO. Around the corner from the Casa de la Cultura, and two blocks away from the *zócalo*, is the Museo Amparo. The exhibits begin with a timeline comparing the development of Mesoamerican art with that of Oceania, Asia, Africa, and Europe from 2400 BC to AD 1500. From there, the rooms guide you through the techniques, uses, and trends in the art of dozens of Mesoamerican indigenous groups without losing the global perspective. Objects are presented in the context of their original use, in relation to other cultures, and finally as individual masterpieces. The last rooms of the museum jump to the colonial era, recreating the house as it once looked. Headphones provide visitors with more information on the pieces from the monitors in each room of the museum; explanations come in five languages. *(Calle 2 Sur 708. Tel. 46 46 46. Open W-M 10am-6pm. Admission 16 pesos, students 8 pesos. M free. Guided tour Su at noon. Headphones 8 pesos with 8-peso deposit.)*

MERCADOS. On the way back to the *zócalo*, be sure to check out the **Mercado 5 de Mayo** and the surrounding area, which is usually piled high with spices, fruit and consumers. A more touristy, less utilitarian experience can be had at **Mercado El Parián,** just northeast of the *zócalo*, which sells keychains, *talvera*, and everything in between.

⚑ SIGHTS IN THE OUTSKIRTS OF PUEBLA

CENTRO CÍVICO 5 DE MAYO. A short trip from the *centro*, the Centro Cívico 5 de Mayo commemorates the Mexican army's victory over the French, which took place in these fields in 1862. To reach this historic site, walk to Blvd. Héroes del 5 de Mayo, about three blocks to the east of the *zócalo*, where you can catch a #72 bus or #8 *colectivo* (both 3 pesos). Get off by the large, multi-armed cement monument which sits alone on an empty-looking glorieta. (You know you're there when you look out the window and wonder out loud, "What's that?") Although some think the monument resembles an octopus, it is a dignified remembrance to Ignacio Zaragoza, the Mexican general who led the defeat of the French troops. Facing the monument, cross the street to the left and walk uphill. Past a now defunct information center, a large concrete representation of the Mexican flag marks a fork in the road. To the right is the **Fuerte de Loreto,** which now houses the **Museo de La No Intervención.** The oddly named museum houses artifacts, paintings, and documents dealing with the May 5th battle and, in particular, the actions of the courageous General Zaragoza. The museum also features a panoramic recreation of the battlefield as it might have looked in 1862 and more exhibits dealing with French rule in Mexico downstairs. *(Both open Tu-Su 10am-4pm. Admission 10 pesos. Su and holidays free.)*

MUSEO DE HISTORIA NATURAL. The Museo de Historia Natural is full of fossils, live snakes, and well-behaved school kids. Life-sized—but out of date—dinosaur models command a spot in the foyer while a spectacular butterfly collection lights up the left exhibition wing. The museum also boasts the largest collection of stuffed deer heads you'll ever see under one roof. The **Planetarium,** next to the Museum of Natural History, takes the shape of a giant, glittering, silver pyramid. Inside, it features the usual slew of space exhibits and an **Omnimax Theater.** Across from the Museum of Natural History is the **Recinto Ferial,** an exposition center and fairgrounds. *(Tel. 35 34 19. Natural History Museum open Tu-Su 7am-5pm. Admission 11 pesos, children 8 pesos. Tu free. Planetarium and Omnimax open daily 10am-5pm. Tel. 35 20 99. Admission including Omnimax 20 pesos. Shows vary and play approx. every hr.)*

PARQUE RAFAELA PADILLA DE ZARAGOZA. The *parque* provides a large, nature-filled oasis with rambling trails descending to a theater, a playground, and benches that beckon to picnickers. The administration building near the entrance shows National Geographic-style videos, and the immersion in nature would be complete save for the oversized statues of animals and piped-in radio shows. *(Open daily 9am-10pm. Videos 1 peso.)*

FUERTE DE GUADALUPE. At the tip of the loop, about a 10-minute walk from the rest of the museums, is "Guadalupe's fort," "an altar to the patriotism of the heroes of the Fifth of May." This *fuerte* offers a view of Puebla. Finally, the **Museo Regional de Antropología,** on your right as you leave the fort. The museum features clothing, artifacts, and information about the historic state of Puebla. *(Museum open Tu-Su 10am-5pm. Admission 10 pesos. Su and holidays free.)*

AFRICAN SAFARI. A somewhat longer trip from the *centro* takes you to African Safari, an ecological zoo dedicated to conservation and recreation. Once inside the park, you will be greeted by over 3000 animals representing approximately 250 species. Organized by geographical area, the park encompasses areas such as Asia, America, and Antarctica, as well as specialized African areas such as Uganda, Kenya, Mombasa, and Botswana. But what makes the African Safari unique is that the animals roam freely. Visitors can drive through the park and get off at certain locations to take photos and to mingle with the animals. Located about 16km southeast of Puebla, the easiest way to get to African Safari is by bus. *Estrella Roja* offers packages that include round-trip bus service from the CAPU and park admission at about 82 pesos for adults and 65 pesos for children. Bus service alone is 20 pesos for adults and 16 pesos for children. Buses depart every two hours on weekdays and every 45 minutes on weekends and major holidays starting at 10:45am and continuing until 2:45pm. If driving, head to the south of the city and then go east, following the signs to **Valsequillo.** *(Tel. 35 88 29 or 35 87 18. Open daily 10am-5pm. Admission varies; call for more information.)*

🎵 ENTERTAINMENT

For evening entertainment, take a stroll along the **Zona Esmeralda,** on Av. Juárez, west of Calle 13 Sur. Enjoy the collection of movie theaters, shops, restaurants, and bars. A youngish Mexican crowd boogies to the beat of *salsa* and disco at **Pagaia,** Juárez 1906 (tel. 32 46 85), after Calle 19 (cover 30 pesos; open Su-Th 4pm-2am, F-Sa 4pm-3am). If you're feeling mellower, the **Italian Coffee Company** (tel. 46 28 26) is just across Av. Juárez from Charlie's. A sophisticated set sits on the patio enjoying espresso and pastries. (Open daily 9am-9:30pm.)

For those who prefer to hear both sides of the conversation, bookstore/cafe **Teorema,** Reforma 540 (tel. 42 10 14), at Calle 7, is a hip hangout. Lively banter and nightly live music pervade this literary lair. (Cover F-Sa 20 pesos. Open 9:30am-2:30pm and 4:30pm-2am; bookstore closes and music starts at 9:30pm.)

PUEBLA'S PRIDE AND JOY Where have all the Beetles gone? They're all in Mexico—1.1 million of them. More than every one in eight passenger vehicles in Mexico is a classic style VW Beetle, and Puebla is the last place on Earth to manufacture them. The VW factory on the outskirts of town employs more than 16,000 workers and churns out 1,000 cars each day. Many of these are the chic, US$20,000 New Beetle, but almost all are shipped north. Mexican drivers still overwhelmingly prefer the US$6,700 classic model, affectionately known as "Vochos," and it shows. Souped-up Beetles often sport chrome fenders, oversize tires, and mini steering wheels, while many of Mexico City's 35,000 Beetle taxis are meticulously customized. No need to call shotgun in these cabs; most are missing the front passenger seat to make room for car-less teens, commuters, and tourists.

If you're interested in nightlife, though, nearby **Cholula** has some of the best in the area, especially along **Recta Cholula**, the route that connects Puebla and Cholula. It is best to take a taxi there; ask to be let off by the clubs near UDLA.

CHOLULA

Cholula (pop. 70,000) is the perfect opening shot for a documentary on Mexico—the kind with a warbly 70s soundtrack and a booming announcer who begins: "In 1519, Hernán Cortés arrived..." The camera pans across a flat civic plain, and then a huge mountain looms up in the middle of the city. As the aerial shot closes in, you notice that what you're looking at isn't a mountain at all, but an immense, overgrown stone pyramid. Crowning its top is a delicate little pastry of a church—in its incongruity, perhaps the most succinct statement of Spanish conquest imaginable.

A sacred place of pilgrimage for over 2000 years, every civilization to control the valley added a tier to the **Teneapa Pyramid,** which was ultimately crowned by the small but triumphant shrine of **La Virgén de Remedios,** the petite, foot-high, decked-out icon who is the city's most recent *conquistador*. Her sanctuary, along with the other 365 churches built by devout Christians to counterbalance the girth of Cholula's pagan past have secured the city's continued importance as a place of pilgrimage for both the faithful and the curious.

Though it's an easy daytrip from Puebla, the huge number of sacred idiosyncracies that litter the town, its beautiful weather, and its happening *portal* attract weekend daytrippers from Puebla and restless students from the nearby **Universidad de las Americas (UDLA)** Party along the *Recta Cholula* on Saturday evening, but don't expect to get much sleep—bells from the 365 church towers start ringing early on Sunday morning.

⚡ ORIENTATION

Cholula is on **Rte. 150,** 122km east of Mexico City and 8km west of Puebla. The Estrella Roja **bus station** is located on **Av. 12 Pte.** near the intersection with **Av. 3 Nte.** The bus station is tiny and poorly marked. Go down one block to the intersection of **12 Pte.** and **5 de Mayo.** To get to the *centro*, walk four blocks downhill toward the large yellow church of San Pedro on the right side of the street. *Colectivos* to Puebla can be flagged down at a variety of locations in the city center, including the corner of **Av. 4 Pte.** and **Calle 3 Nte.**, as well as at **Morelos** and **Calle 4 Sur** (30 min. to Puebla's CAPU, 2 pesos). After the *colectivos* stop running at 8pm, you'll have to negotiate a price with a local taxi (30 pesos or more).

The numbered streets in Cholula form a grid with the *zócalo* roughly at the center. But beware: the municipality of Cholula encompasses two towns—**San Pedro Cholula** and **San Andrés Cholula.** The *zócalo*, tourist office, and the majority of the restaurants are located in San Pedro; everything on the other side of the Great Pyramid is in San Andrés. As usual in Mexico, the same street may go by different names along different stretches. Streets change name at **Av. Miguel Alemán** (also **5 de Mayo**) and **Av. Hidalgo** (**Av. Morelos** or **Av. 14 Oriente** in San Andrés).

Though Cholultecos say that the little crime the city does have is more often directed at business establishments than at individuals, travelers should always exercise caution, especially when walking alone at night. The walk from San Andrés to Cholula past the pyramid can be uncomfortably lonely; cabs travel the distance for 20 pesos.

🛈 PRACTICAL INFORMATION

Buses: Estrella Roja, at Av. 12 Pte. between 5 de Mayo and 3 Nte., runs buses to: **Mexico City** via **Puebla** (2hr., every 30min. 5am-8:30pm, 49-57 pesos); **Puebla** (30 min., every 30min. 5am-8:30pm, 3 pesos). Other destinations through Puebla's CAPU.

Tourist Office: Av. 4 Pte. 103 (tel. 47 18 97). From the end of the *portales* at 3 Norte, walk down the street and take the first right. The tourist office is the white building a block down on the right. Books and pamphlets on Cholula and its history are available, as well as a somewhat confusing free map. Open M-F 10am-6:30pm.

Currency Exchange: Casa de Cambio Azteca, 2 Sur 104 (tel. 47 21 90; open M-F 9am-7pm, Sa 9am-2pm). Though they have more limited hours, the banks on Morelos at the *zócalo* offer comparable rates and all have **ATMs**. **Bancomer,** Morelos 10, in the arcade on the side of the *zócalo* near the Church of San Pedro. Open for exchange M-F 8:30am-5:30pm, Sa 10am-2pm.

Market: Cosme del Razo, Av. Hidalgo between Av. 3 and 5 Nte., also in the *zócalo*. Cheap prices for meat, fruit, flowers, and clothing. W and Su are *días de plaza* when the already crowded market swells with even more merchants.

Laundry: Lavandería Burbujas, on Av. 14 Ote. 103 (tel. 47 37 66), 1 block toward the *zócalo* from 5 de Mayo in San Andrés. 1kg for 7 pesos. Open M-Sa 9am-7pm.

Emergency: dial 060.

Police: At the Presidencia Municipal, Portal Guerrero 1 (tel. 47 05 62), in the arcade under the arches on the side of the *zócalo*. The station itself is at the intersection of Av. Hidalgo and Calle 7 Sur.

Red Cross: Calle 7 Sur at Av. 3 Pte. (tel. 47 03 93), a bit of a hike from the *centro*. Walk-in service. Open 24hr. No English spoken.

Pharmacy: Farmacia San Juan Bautista, at Calle 3 Nte. 405 on the corner of Av. 6 Pte. (tel. 47 34 45). Open daily 8am-11pm.

Hospital: Clínica de IMSS (tel. 47 53 14), Calle 4 Nte. and Av. 10 Ote. Open 24hr. **Hospital San Gabriel,** Av. 4 Pte. 503 (tel. 47 00 14), 2 blocks west of the *zócalo*. No English spoken.

Post Office: At the intersection of Av. 7 and Av. 5 Pte. Open M-F 8am-7pm, Saturdays and holidays 8am-noon. **Postal Code:** 72760.

Fax: Telecomm, Av. Portal 9 (tel. 47 01 30). Telegrams, fax, Western Union. Open M-F 8am-7:30pm, Sa-Su 9am-noon. **Centro de Copiado Cholula,** Morelos 8B (tel./fax 47 14 72), on the south side of the *zócalo*. Open daily 8am-9pm.

Telephones: LADATELs line the west side of the *zócalo*, and phone cards are readily available in nearby stores. Or try the phone inside the **Casa de la Cultura,** which takes coins.

Phone Code: 22.

▗ ACCOMMODATIONS

While there are several hotels beyond the bus station, there is a very limited choice of budget hotels near the *zócalo* and the ruins. Visitors have a larger choice 30 minutes away in Puebla.

Hotel Reforma, Calle 4 Sur 101 (tel. 47 01 49), near the corner of Av. Morelos and Calle 4 Sur. From the *zócalo*, walk 2 blocks on Morelos towards the Great Pyramid, then turn right. While the economy of Cholula's other budget options is severly mitigated by the taxi fares you'll pay to get from the nightlife to your bed, Hotel Reform is but a short stumble from the *portales*. Typical low-budget Mexican comfort is supplemented by private bathrooms, colorful bedspreads, and a chipper courtyard cactus garden. Singles 80 pesos; doubles 130 pesos. The front gate is locked after 10:30pm; ring to enter.

Hotel Las Américas, Av. 14 Ote. 6 (tel. 47 09 91). To reach the hotel from the *zócalo*, take Av. Morelos and walk past the pyramid approximately 4 blocks—the hotel is on the right after 5 de Mayo. A machine-for-living in transition, Las Américas' time-capsule 70s architecture is being slowly overgown by the grass that frames the yet-empty courtyard swimming pool. Rooms have lots of dark colored upholstery, TVs and phones, and the curtain-less private bathrooms are one giant shower-fest. Comparatively commodious, it may be worth the treacherous walk past the Temple of Doom. Singles 60 pesos; doubles 80 pesos.

FOOD

Unlike some Mexican *zócalos* whose restaurants tend to price locals out of the market, many of Cholula's cheapest eats can be found at its center on **Hidalgo,** perpendicular to the *portales*. Towards the bus station, family-owned *torta* shops and market stands offer even better prices, but eating in the *zócalo* is a great way to meet laid-back locals, and the *charla* (chat) is worth the few extra pesos.

Güeros, Av. Hidalgo 101 (tel. 47 21 88). Güeros' flourescent lighting, and glowing BBQ shine like beacons across the *zócalo*, promising good grub for *güeros* and non-*güeros* alike. The restaurant serves everything hot, cheap and tasty, and has the best local following in town.

El Pecas Parilla, Av. Miguel Alemán (tel. 47 16 18), at 7 Pte. This restaurant offers all the savory meat, nice services, and colorful ambience of the touristy restaurants at slightly lower prices. Tacos hover around 5 pesos, and for 40 pesos, you can have really tender *Aranchadas* complete with excellent guacamole.

Los Tulipanes, Portal Guerrero 13, on the side of the *zócalo* near the Church of San Pedro. You can watch the traffic of the *zócalo* go by as you munch on breakfast (starting at 16 pesos), *antojitos* (13-23 pesos), *comida corrida* (33 pesos), or meat and fish entrees (18-43 pesos). Open Tu-Su 8:30am-9pm.

 SIGHTS

When visitors arrive in Cholula, their gaze invariably turns to two things: the city's churches and the huge hill near the *zócalo* called the **Great Pyramid.**

GREAT PYRAMID. When Cortés destroyed the Toltec temple atop the misshapen hill that dominates Cholula, he was unaware that the hump of earth was actually the giant pyramid of a culture that had dominated the area more than eight centuries before. This ancient civilization mysteriously collapsed in 700, and since then, the pyramid's outer layers of adobe brick have disintegrated and sprouted trees. When the Toltec-Chichimec groups settled in Cholula in the 12th century, they named the pyramid **Tlachiaualtepetl,** or "man-made hill," and are believed to have practiced human sacrifice atop it. Twentieth-century archaeologists tunneled into the "hill," discovering three other pyramids built one on top of the other, the oldest of which dates from roughly 200. Sophisticated drainage systems preserved the structure, which is volumetrically **the largest pyramid in the world.** Today, the archaeological tunnels and some excavations on the south and west sides of the pyramid are open to visitors. Due to a lack of funding, only 5% of Cholula's ruins have been uncovered. (*In the center of town. Entrance is on Morelos, across from the railroad. Ruins and tunnels open daily 9am-6pm. Admission 20 pesos, Su free.*)

MUSEO AL SITIO. Before entering the Indiana-Jones-style tunnels at the pyramid's base, get a feel for what you're looking at by visiting the museum just across the street from the ticket booth. The museum centers around a surprisingly helpful diorama of the pyramid (guaranteed to convince skeptics that it is not, in fact, a hill), and also features a good collection of artifacts from the area. The highlight is the spooky back chamber, painted with reproductions of the site's famous frescoes. Puzzle over a fluid depiction of drunken revelers and the strange Toltec rendition of *chapulines* (grasshoppers) in this refreshingly cool faux-storeroom. (*Open Tu-Su 10-5pm. Free with tickets to the pyramid.*)

EXCAVATIONS AND TUNNELS. To get to the open-air excavations on the side of the pyramid opposite the entrance, most visitors walk throught the labyrinthine archaeological tunnels that riddle Teneapa's base. Deeper, darker side tunnels can be explored with a guide who will explain the outdoor excavations as well, but a similar effect can be had by walking through yourself. Look for a

CENTRAL MEXICO

particularly stunning section of one of the interior pyramid's main staircase, which has been excavated from bottom to top. The underground adventure ends at the south side of the pyramid in a complex, large, and still mostly unexplored outdoor archaeological site. English language pamphlets explaining the ruins can be purchased at the bookstore near the exit, though the bare essentials can also be gleaned form the explanatory markers in front of each structure. *(Guide 30-35 pesos.)*

SANTUARIO DE NUESTRA SEÑORA DE LOS REMEDIOS. Follow the path as it takes you back to the railroad tracks; make an immediate right outside the fence where it ends, and begin climbing. No ticket is required to reach the Santuario de Nuestra Señora de los Remedios, the church built atop the pyramid in 1594 and the highlight of the archaeological zone. Trekking up the pyramid demands as much effort as a Stairmaster workout, but you will be rewarded with a superb view of Cholula and its many churches. On Sunday, the path fills with visitors and the hill rumbles with crackling pyrotechnic displays and the sound of church bells from neighborhoods below. It may be difficult to locate Remedios in her ornate baroque shrine. Look for the neon purple lettering around the altar area—she's well labeled. The original church was built in 1594 and dedicated to the most important Spanish virgin—La Virgen de los Remedios—as a safeguard against the return of the gods from whose ruined temple the walls of the sanctuary had been constucted. Destroyed by an earthquake in 1864, the structure was re-built using much of the original material. The present day shrine, an elaborate fabrege jewelry box with Remedios as the principal gem, was seriously damaged in the 1999 earthquake and is awaiting reparis and possible reconstruction. The Aztec empire was a hard conquest but nature has proven the more formidable enemy. On a clear day, the snowcapped volcanoes **Popocatépetl** and **Ixtaccíhuatl** are visible in the distance. Although the church is small, it offers a stunning view on the inside as well: ornate gold decorations and fresh flowers for the daily mass.

CHURCHES IN THE ZÓCALO. Three of Cholula's most spectacular churches are also the easiest to find, as they border the immense *zócalo*. On the side opposite the *portales*, the church on the right is the **Convento de San Gabriel,** the home of Cholula's busiest clergy and an impressive symbol of power built on top of the **Templo de Quetzalcóatl.** Constructed in the 16th century under the direction of the Franciscans and with a completely *indígena* labor force, the church was intended as the great factory for the conversion of the Cholutecos. The altar in today's chapel was built in 1897 and has a neoclassical solemnity that emphasizes the mass of the already weightly church. Despite San Gabriel's imposing size, though, the Franciscans found it too small for their epic conversion campaign, and in 1575 they began work on the church next door, today's beautiful **Capilla Real.** Possibly the most striking of the city's churches, the 49 domed structure was finished in the early 1600s, finally becoming the long awaited auditorium where thousands of *indígenas* could hear mass at once. Dedicated to the Virgén, the wall behind the splendid altar is covered with three famous paintings which depict the story of the **Virgén de Guadalupe.** The third painting in the series (on the left) is a particularly vivid portrayal of the flabbergasted Spanish clergy, kneeling at the image of the *indígena* virgin emblazoned on Juan Diego's cloak. The *Capilla Real* lacks the ornate gold filigré of the surrounding churches, and has a startlingly beautiful simplicity defined by the ever-changing panorama of whitewashed arches, soaring domes, and uniquely decorated side-chapels.

SANTA MARÍA TONANTZINLA. Almost as famous as Cholula itself are two churches in the surrounding villages, particularly the church of Santa María Tonantzinla. Built in the 10th century on yet another pre-Hispanic temple, the church's bright saffron facade covers a startling interior where over 450 stucco faces stare out from every spare inch of wall and ceiling. Saints, musicians, and chiefs congregate with animals and flowers in an explosion of iconography; it is the handiwork of the same indigenous artisan who executed the plans of European artists in Puebla's *Capilla del Rosario*. Here, the artisan reinterprets the colonial style with his own fascinating fusion of indigenous and rococo art. Only a 15 minute walk away (or an even shorter 1-peso minibus ride) lies the town, and 15th-century church of **San Francisco Acatapec.**

SAN FRANCISCO ACATAPEC. Built in 1588, the facade of the church is almost as ornate as Tonantintla's walls. Entirely covered in brilliant *Falvera* tile, the concentration of color on the front of the church is perhaps the most exquisite applicatoin the famous tiles have yet found. *(Take a colectivo marked "Chipilo" at Av. 6 Ote. and 5 de Mayo for 1.50 pesos. On the way, you may see on the right the castillo of Cholula's famous fortune teller Diego Gaona, where he lives with his 9 wives.)*

UNIVERSIDAD DE LOS AMÉRICAS. UDLA, (pronounced OOHD-LAH), a short bus ride up Av. 14 Ote., provides a perfect example of the universality of university culture. This elite college campus offers cultivated respite from the city's dusty mayhem. Guards at the clearly marked gate will ask you to leave a form of ID before entering the lush flower laden campus inside the gates. Cheap diversion can be found on weekends when the schools's extensive sports facilites host *fútbol* tournaments and pick-up basketball. The Mexican version of institutionalized cafeteria food is served up at **Cafeteria Santa Catrina** (open daily 7am-9pm) and soveniers are available in the nearby social center kiosk.

🎵 ENTERTAINMENT

Cholula's entertainment comes in both the high impact and low impact varieties. For a madly intense workout, hit the dancefloors along the **Recta Cholula,** just beyond UDLA en route to Puebla. Warehouse sized *discotecas* provide industrial strength evenings, powered by the energy of both cities. Clubgoers should dress well and fill their wallets with cash—this isn't the boonies. Though bars and *discotecas* in this area frequently re-invent themselves in attempt to get an edge on the market, for the most part you'll find the same scene packaged in several different ways. To get there, take a Puebla-bound bus from Av. 14 Ote. past UDLA. The return trip, especially if it's late at night, is best made in a taxi—a pricey finish for a pricey evening.

Cholula proper offers lost of cheaper, more sedentary options. Under the *portales*, **Bar-Restaurant Enamorada** feeds and inebriates a diverse, sociable crowd. Though it closes at midnight, the live music is good, and those who wish to continue their evening past the witching hour will find that it's a good place to pick up companions for the scene along the Recta. Also under the *portales* is the ubiquitous **Italian Coffee Company,** a quieter, conversational place to caffeinate, which has recently become famous for their delicious, cream-covered cappuccino *granitas* (14 pesos for a small splurge). On Av. 14 Ote., between the *zócalo* and the Hotel Las Américas, are a number of other bars offering reasonable prices and more local, slightly older clientele. The exception is **Club Keops,** on the corner of 5 de Mayo, whose young, mostly gay clientele keeps it jamming to a techno beat. Don't miss *Travesty*, the drag show put on at midnight Friday and Saturday. (Open Th-Sa 9pm-2am; cover 30 pesos.)

✳ FESTIVALS

On a normal day, Cholula's religious presence is overwhelming. If your visit coincides with one of the many *Días de Fiesta*, you'll be witness to an even more intense experience. There are two different celebrations which feature the Virgén de Remedios. Every June, since 1640, Cholula has celebrated the **Bajada de la Virgén,** when Remedios comes down from her celestial sanctuary and visits the city and the surrounding towns. These days she travels by motorcycle through the streets every morning at 7am during the week of the festival, heralded by the ringing of church bells and shouts of her devotees. During the evenings the town of San Andres celebrates in her honor under the elaborate gateways of flowers, seeds, and glitter that deck the *Virgén's* route. An even bigger party is held in San Pedro in August for Remedios' *Día Santa*. More universal celebrations for *Carnaval, Semana Santa,* and Christmas are also big events in the city, which fills with visitors from Puebla, Mexico City and the surrounding villages.

CENTRAL PACIFIC COAST

Stretching from the quiet fishing villages near San Blas to the busy port of Manzanillo, the central Pacific coast is lined by kilometer after kilometer of smooth sand massaged by the ebb and flow of the tide. Hot but comfortably dry, the weather is beautiful and the sun rarely fails to illuminate the azure skies. Priding itself on diversity, the central Pacific states range from vibrant Jalisco, the birthplace of *mariachi* and tequila, to the jungles and fertile land of Nayarit, and the quiet beachtowns of Colima.

A state with varied terrain, **Nayarit** is marked by volcanic highlands, tropical jungles, and a network of lakes and rivers. This verdant and fertile region grows the lion's share of the nation's marijuana and is home to the oldest native group in Mexico, the Huichol. It is not uncommon to see Huichols in colorful native dress, even in the state's larger cities. Men typically wear light-colored pants and light, wide shirts belted at the waist, all brilliantly embroidered with religious figures and eye-catching designs. Peyote may be carried in colorfully woven knit or stitched bags worn across the shoulders. Women's traditional clothing consists of a similarly colorful embroidered blouse and long skirt.

South of Nayarit lies **Jalisco,** the most touristed state along the central Pacific coast. Much of the world's Mexican pop culture image could be stamped "Hecho en Jalisco"—the *jarabe tapatío* (hat dance), *mariachis*, *charros*, and tequila all originated in this state. For much of its history, though, this province remained isolated from the rest of the Republic, possessing neither silver nor gold, jewels nor water, fertile land nor agricultural climate. It wasn't until the 1920s, when railroad tracks extended to Guadalajara, that this Sierran town (elevation 1552m) began to grow into a metropolis; today, it is Mexico's second-largest city.

Tiny **Colima** boasts spectacular beaches as well as thoroughly pleasant towns where tourists can escape the resort scene and rest in the cool mountain air. The state is also home to the city of Colima, a sparkling, untouristed gem, and Manzanillo, the workhorse of Mexico's Pacific coast. This port has not paused once in 700 years of commerce with Asia to wipe its sweaty brow, and only recently has it attempted to polish its image for the benefit of visitors.

HIGHLIGHTS OF THE CENTRAL PACIFIC COAST

■ **Guadalajara** (see p. 374), Mexico's second-largest city, is clean and green and comes complete with great **museums** (see p. 381) and exciting **nightlife** (see p. 384).

■ No longer the quiet, secluded paradise of the 1960s, **Puerto Vallarta** (see p. 391) has a thriving tourist industry due to its glitzy nightlife, luxury hotels, and shop-crowded streets. There is also a booming **gay scene** p. 397. The **best beaches,** however, lie south of the city (see p. 397).

■ The **Bahía de Navidad** (see p. 400) isn't hyper developed—yet. Swim, surf, sunbathe on your choice of beautiful beach, quickly, before word gets out. Both Bahía de Navidad and **Melaque** (see p. 400), located on the bay, offer budget accommodations and gorgeous beaches.

■ The small villages **near Guadalajara** (see p. 386) are renowned throughout the country for their individualized artesanía and markets.

■ The city is hot and crowded, but **Manzanillo** (see p. 403) does boast the best beaches in Colima state. However, it's nearby **Cuyutlán** (see p. 407) that dazzles tourists: solitude, black-sand beaches, and a wondrous lagoon.

■ Tired of "authenticity"? Travel to **Tequila** (see p. 388), the touristy and fun home of your favorite liquor.

NAYARIT

SAN BLAS

San Blas (pop. 19,000) is a small, dusty fishing village that feeds off its ecological wealth: huge beaches and over 300 species of birds. Although there is not much to see or do in the town itself, the nearby jungle attracts *norteamericano* expatriates, birdwatchers, and tourists en route to Puerto Vallarta, while the smooth sand beaches and long waves make San Blas a mecca for surfers. Bring plenty of bug repellent; ravenous mosquitoes are everywhere .

⚐ ORIENTATION AND PRACTICAL INFORMATION. San Blas is 69km northeast of Tepic by Rte. 15 and 54. **Calle Juárez**, the town's main drag, runs parallel to the bus station on the south side of the *zócalo*. **Batallón** runs perpendicular to Juárez from the *zócalo*'s center and leads to the closest beach, **Playa Borrego.**

Transportes Norte de Sonora (tel. 5 00 43) has **buses** that run to: **Guadalajara** (6hr., 7am, 118 pesos); **Mazatlán** (5hr., 7:30am and 5pm, 107 pesos); **Puerto Vallarta** (3hr., 7 and 10am, 70 pesos); **Santiago Ixcuintla** (1¾hr., 7:30am and 4pm, 27 pesos); and **Tepic** (1¾hr., every hr. 6am-7pm, 35 pesos). The **tourist office** (tel. 5 03 81) Mercado, one street west of Juárez, provides maps and information about trips to La Tovara (see p. 372) and hikes to some of Nayarit's waterfalls (office open daily 9am-1pm and 6-8pm). Change money or use the 24-hour. **ATM** at **Banamex** (tel. 5 00 30), on Juárez east of the *zócalo* (open M-F 8am-2pm).

Police: (tel. 5 00 28) on Sinaloa opposite the bus station; the last door in the Palacio Municipal as you walk away from the *zócalo* (open 24hr.). **Farmacia Económica:** at Batallón 49 (tel./fax 5 01 11; open daily 8:30am-2pm and 4:30-9:30pm). **Centro de Salud:** (tel. 5 02 32) on Batallón and Campeche, five blocks south of the *zócalo;* (no English spoken; open 24hr.). **Clínica IMSS:** (tel. 5 02 27) at Batallón and Guerrero (open daily 7am-6pm; at other times, enter on Canalizo). **Post office:** (tel. 5 02 95) at Sonora and Echeverría, one block north and one block east of the northeast corner of the *zócalo* (open M-F 8am-2pm, Sa 8am-noon). **Postal code:** 63740. Make long-distance **phone** calls from the *caseta de larga distancia* at Juárez 4. The **caseta** also has **fax** service (open daily 8am-10pm). **Phone code:** 328.

▐▜ ACCOMMODATIONS AND FOOD. Finding a place to sleep in San Blas isn't difficult during the offseason, but autumn storms bring mile-long waves and bed-seeking surfers. During September, October, *Semana Santa*, and Christmas, make reservations and expect higher prices. The blood-sucking mosquitoes near the water make camping difficult; rooms inland are the best choice. **El Bucanero,** Juárez 75 (tel. 5 01 01), is reminiscent of a creaky pirate ship. It offers large, dim rooms with high ceilings, clean bathrooms, a swimming pool, and a huge, fading crocodile in the lobby. Hot water and fans make things comfy, but the adjoining disco is a little noisy on the weekends. (Singles 100 pesos; doubles 150 pesos.) To reach **Bungalows Portolá,** Paredes 118 (tel. 5 03 86), at Yucatán, turn right out of the bus station and then past the *zócalo* turn right again on Paredes. The hotel is about three blocks down on the right side. Clean, floral, furnished bungalows come complete with fans, baths, and kitchens for up to four people. The owner offers laundry services, rents bicycles, and trades English books. (Bungalows 160 pesos; singles 80 pesos, high season 150 pesos.)

La Isla (tel. 5 04 07), on Mercado and Paredes, lives up to its name—every space, crack, and crevice of "the island" is covered with shells and the food will knock you out (fried fish 30-35 pesos; open Tu-Su 2-10pm). **La Familia**, Batallón 18 (tel. 5 02 58), is a family joint, right down to the conversation-starting, wall-mounted shark's teeth, sea bottles, old drums, and provocative cow statue. A full breakfast goes for 15-25 pesos and fresh fish for 37-40 pesos. (Open daily 8am-10pm.)

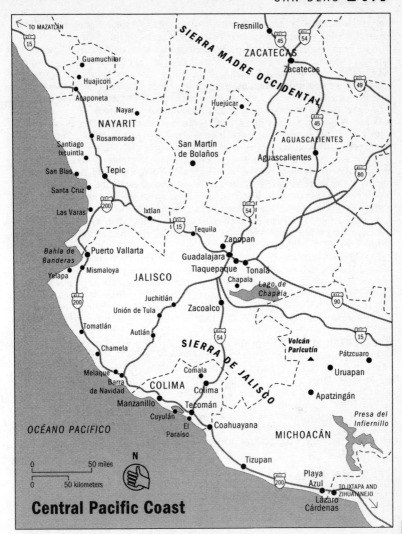

TO MAZATLÁN

15

Guamuchilar

Huajicori

Acaponeta

Nayar

NAYARIT

Rosamorada

Santiago
Ixcuintla

San Blas

Santa Cruz

Las Varas

Tepic

Ixtlan

15

Tequila

Fresnillo

SIERRA MADRE OCCIDENTAL

45   54

ZACATECAS

Zacatecas

49

Huejúcar

45

AGUASCALIENTES

San Martín
de Bolaños

Aguascalientes

80

200

Bahía de
Banderas

Yelapa

Puerto Vallarta

Mismaloya

JALISCO

200

Juchitlán

Unión de Tula

Tomatlán

Autlán

Chamela

Melaque

Barra
de Navidad

Manzanillo

Cuyulán

OCÉANO PACÍFICO

El
Paraíso

Zapopan

Guadalajara

Tlaquepaque   Tonalá

Chapala

Lago de
Chapala

Zacoalco

90

SIERRA DE JALISCO

54

Comala

COLIMA   Colima

Tecomán

Coahuayana

Volcán
Paricutín

Pátzcuaro

Uruapan

Apatzingán

MICHOACÁN

Presa del
Infiernillo

15

Tizupan

0   50 miles

0   50 kilometers

N

Central Pacific Coast

Playa
Azul

Lázaro
Cárdenas

200

TO IXTAPA AND
ZIHUATANEJO

◪ **SAND AND SIGHTS.** San Blas, known for its perfectly symmetric waves and safe, sandy bottom, has churned out many a surfing champ. To rent surfing equipment or take lessons, **La Tumba de Yako,** Batallón 219 (tel. 5 04 62), about six blocks from the *zócalo*, run by Juan García, president of San Blas's surfing club and technical director of Mexico's surf team, has more than enough experience to help.

San Blas's main attractions are the smooth water, packed sand, and long waves of **Playa Las Islitas.** During the stormy months of September and October, surfers flock to San Blas in hopes of catching the famous, yearly mile-long wave that carries them from Las Islitas all the way to Playa Matanchén. To reach Las Islitas, you can take a bus from the station (every hr. 6am-5pm, returning 7:30am-4pm, 5 pesos) or from the corner of Sinaloa and Paredes in front of the green trim building (15min., 4 per day 8:30am-2:30pm, 5 pesos). The latter bus continues to other beaches, passing by Las Islitas on its way back to town about one hour later. A taxi to Las Islitas costs 50 pesos. The first few stretches of sand that greet you are lovely, but seclusion and prettier coves await farther along the shore.

At the southern end of Batallón, **Playa Borrego** is easily accessible from town and offers a relaxing, though somewhat bland, view of the coast. Borrego's sand is gray, and mosquitoes feast on those who dare to venture outside around sunrise or sunset. Quiet and pretty **Playa del Rey,** off the coast of Borrego, has somewhat stronger currents. A *lancha* will take you there from the pier at the west end of Juárez (round-trip about 5 pesos; boats run daily about 7am-4pm).

Locals hype the springs of **La Tovara**—not the beaches—as San Blas's main attraction. While the winding jungle boat ride to La Tovara springs can be expensive, seeing a live crocodile just might make it worthwhile. Guides navigate the shallow, swampy waters, pointing out rare and interesting birds and the stilted huts left over from the set of the film *Cabeza de Vaca.* The path clears to reveal hordes of turtles and huge fish. Trips can be arranged through the tourist office or directly with a boat owner; they're found at the small docking area on Juárez's eastern end. Trips last 1½-2½ hours and can be made any day between 7am and 4pm, but it's best to journey to La Tovara early in the morning, when the water is still calm and the birds undisturbed by the *lanchas*. Depending on the tour, groups of four cost 160 to 240 pesos.

The short hike to the top of **La Contaduría,** the hill near town, affords a beautiful view of the city and coast. The splintering stone fortress that protected the city rests impressively above, while an 18th-century church stands farther downhill. To get there, head east on Juárez as if leaving town. Just before the bridge and the sign that reads "Cape Victoria 7," turn right onto the dirt road behind the houses and restaurants, and veer right off that road onto the stone path that winds uphill.

■ **ENTERTAINMENT.** Except for bands of youths crowded in the *zócalo* on weekends, nights in San Blas are about as *tranquilo* as the days. **Mike's Cant-aBar** (tel. 5 04 32), rarely gets wild or crazy, but it's an interesting place to pass the evening. Mike no longer performs vintage rock, but he sings live *salsa* in what looks like an antique airport lounge. (No cover. Live music Th-Su starting around 10pm. Open daily 6pm-1am.) If you are in the mood for something more upbeat and raucous, join the teen and pre-teen population of San Blas at **Disco Voga,** Juárez 75 (tel. 5 01 01), next to Hotel El Bucanero offers standard *discoteca* fare to get you into the groove (beer 6 pesos; cover 15-20 pesos; open F-Su 9pm-4am).

NEAR SAN BLAS: EL CUSTODIO DE LAS TORTUGAS

El Custodio de las Tortugas (The Guardian of the Turtles; tel. 329 2 29 54; www.methow.com/~custodio) is an eco-resort in the tiny village of **Platanitos,** 1½ hours south of San Blas and two hours north of Puerto Vallarta. The villa, run by owners Min and Mona, is perched on a precipice and overlooks 20km of virgin beach and the longest stretch of turtle camp in Nayarit. Between July and August, the Mexican government and several ecological organizations collect turtle eggs, protecting them from thieves and predators. Two elegant three-bedroom villas and one two-bedroom villa have TVs, A/C, and huge breezy terraces for whale watching and sunset-worshipping. The gorgeous pool perched on the overlook offers a respite from salty water. Don't miss going into town to try the local specialty, *pescado sarandeado* (mesquite grilled fish, 80 pesos per kilo—enough to feed 3-4 people). (Villa rental low season US$650-750 per week, high season US$800-900 per week; US$15 per night to help out and bunk in the turtle camp; some meals and kayak trips to the lagoon included.)

Getting There: Transportes Norte de Sonora (tel. 5 00 43) gets you there from Puerto Vallarta (2hr., noon and 2:30pm, 55 pesos) or San Blas (1½hr., 6 per day 6am-2pm, 18 pesos). Ask the bus driver to let you off at Platanitos, then walk down the road and up the hill on your right.

TEPIC

The steam-belching, tree-guzzling woodchip plant directly across from Tepic's bus station provides an appropriate introduction to this hard working city. Once called *Tepique* (the Place Between the Hills) by its pre-Hispanic inhabitants, Tepic became an important center for trade and commerce under the Spanish in the 16th and 17th centuries. Today, this city of around half a million people retains the duty of housing the Nayarit state government as well as remaining an important crossroads for the entire region. However, there is not yet much of tourist interest here. Some shady parks and a few museums will satisfy those who come through Tepic to connect to another city, a use which brings most tourists here in the first place.

■ **ORIENTATION.** Tepic is in a strategic location 170km north of Puerto Vallarta, 230km northwest of Guadalajara, and 280km south of Mazatlán. The large bus station is east of the *centro* following the **Insurgentes** route. As you leave the station, cross the street and catch one of the yellow buses (6am-10pm, 2 pesos). Hustling *taxistas* charge around 15 pesos for the short trip to the *centro*. **Av. México,** running north-south six blocks west of the bus station, is downtown Tepic's main drag. Addresses on Av. México change from *norte* to *sur* about four blocks north of Insurgentes, which is the largest east-west street. The yellow minivan *combis* (6am-midnight, 1.50-3 pesos) run back and forth daily along Av. México and Insurgentes. At its northern terminus, the many-fountained **Plaza Principal** (officially the **Centro Histórico**) is dominated on one end by the cathedral and on the other by the **Palacio Municipal.** Six blocks to the south, **Plaza Constituyente** appears to be shockingly desolate. Most tourist services lie on or near Av. México.

■ **PRACTICAL INFORMATION. Buses** leave Tepic from the newer long-distance station (the smaller one downtown, 3 blocks north of the plaza on Victoria serves local destinations). To get to the new station, take a "Central" or "Mololoa Llanitos" bus from the corner of México Sur and Hidalgo. Estrella Blanca (tel. 13 13 28) serves: **Aguascalientes** (6hr., 4:30 and 7:45pm, 235 pesos); **Monterrey** (15hr., 4:30, 445 pesos); and **Zacatecas** (10hr., 4:30 and 7:45pm, 260 pesos). Norte de Sonora (tel. 13 23 15) speeds toward: **Culiacán** (6hr., every hr., 220 pesos); **Guadalajara** (3hr., 10 per day 5:30am-5pm, 128 pesos); **Mazatlán** (5hr., 9:30am, 119 pesos); **San Blas** (1½hr., every hr. 5am-7pm, 34 pesos); **Santiago** (1½hr., every 45min. 5:30am-8pm, 34 pesos); and **Tuxpan** (1½hr., every hr. 6:15am-8:15pm, 27 pesos). Transportes del Pacífico (tel. 13 23 20) provides first-class service to: **Mexico City** (10hr., every hr. 3pm-7am, 357 pesos) and **Tijuana** (29hr., every hr., 864 pesos); and second-class service to **Puerto Vallarta** (3½hr., 19 per day 1:30am-10pm, 98 pesos).

Dirección de Turismo Municipal (tel. 16 56 61), Av. Puebla at the corner of Amado Nervo, one block from the cathedral, hands out maps and brochures (open daily 8am-8pm). **Banks** (most open M-F 8am-1:30pm) and **casas de cambio** (commonly open M-Sa 9am-2pm and 4-7pm) clutter Av. México Nte. Both **Banamex** and **Bancomer,** on Av. México Nte., a few blocks south of the plaza, have **ATMs.** For faxes, try **Telecomm,** Av. México Nte. 50 (tel. 12 96 55), about one block from the cathedral (open M-F 8am-7pm, Sa-Su 8am-4pm). The station has **luggage storage** (1.50 pesos per hr.).

Police station: Av. Tecnolópgica 3200 Ote. (tel. 11 58 51); accessible by cab only (8 pesos). **Farmacia CMQ:** Insurgentes at Av. Mexico (open 24hr.). **Hospital General:** (tel. 13 79 37) on Paseo de la Loma next to La Loma Park. From the bus station, take a left as you leave the building and another left on Av. México. After three blocks, take the right-hand fork at the rotary; the hospital is two blocks down on the left. Taxis to the hospital cost 10 pesos from the *centro* (open 24hr.). **Post office:** (tel. 12 01 30) at Durango Nte. 33, between Allende and Morelos (open M-F 8am-7pm, Sa 8am-noon). **Postal code:** 63000. **Phone code:** 321.

█:█ ACCOMMODATIONS AND FOOD. Besides the large four-star behmouths that seem to cover whole city blocks, Tepic has several smaller, affordable hotels that hide in their shadows. Hotels in the *centro* are closer to Tepic's few sights, but those near the bus station are more convenient for those who anticipate a short stay. **Hotel Las Americas,** Puebla 317 (tel. 16 32 85), at Zaragoza, provides clean rooms with TVs, fans, and tiled bathrooms. Wooden furniture and sunny patchwork quilts ensure a comfortable stay in a great location. (Singles 80 pesos; doubles 100 pesos.)

Mangos and *guanábanas* (soursops) make their way to the stalls at the **mercado,** on Mérida and Zaragoza, four blocks south and three blocks east of the Museo Regional (see below). For a more formal meal, head to **Restaurant Vegetariano Quetzalcóatl,** León Nte. 224 (tel. 12 99 66), at Lerdo, four blocks west of Plaza Principal. *Tranquilo* waiters serve good vegetarian food in a leafy courtyard decorated with local indigenous artwork and vibrant tablecloths. Sample the *comida corrida* (28 pesos) or stuff yourself with the Saturday buffet (32 pesos; open M-Sa 8:30am-6:30pm).

█ SIGHTS. In front of the Plaza Principal is the **Catedral de la Purísima Concepción de María,** a church marked by twin 40m-tall towers. The **Museo Regional de Antropología e Historia,** México Nte. 91, south of the Plaza Principal at Zapata houses a small collection of Toltec and Aztec bones, pottery, and artifacts, as well as a stuffed 6m-long crocodile and a collection of religious works from the 16th to 19th centuries (tel. 12 19 00; open M-F 9am-7pm, Sa 9am-3pm; free). The **Museo Casa de los Cuatro Pueblos,** Hidalgo Ote. 60, displays the colorful artwork, embroidery, and beadwork of Nayarit's four indigenous groups: the Coras, Huichols, Náhuatls, and Tepehuanos (tel. 12 17 05; open M-F 9am-2pm and 4-7pm, Sa 9am-2pm; free). Also south of the plaza, at Av. México and Abasolo, is the **state capitol,** a gracefully domed structure dating from the 1870s. At Av. México's southern end, turn west (uphill) on Insurgentes and you'll come to **La Loma,** a huge and enchanting park. If in service, a miniature train will take you through the park's many playgrounds (3 pesos).

JALISCO

GUADALAJARA

Guadalajara (pop. 5 million) is the crossroads of Mexico. The capital of the state of Jalisco and the second-largest city in the Republic, Guadalajara is where north meets south, colonial meets modern, and traditional meets cutting-edge. This crowning achievement of Spanish colonial urbanity has spawned many of Mexico's most marketable icons: bittersweet *mariachi* music, the *jarabe tapatío* (the Mexican hat dance), and tequila. These icons, now important symbols of the entire Republic, grew out of the distinctive culture forged by Spanish colonists who wanted to be far from the capital in a comfortably Spanish environment after pro-Independence convulsions disrupted life in 19th-century Mexico City. Founded by Nuño de Guzmán, the most brutal of the *conquistadores*, the city was created out of a bloodbath; most of the region's *indígenas* were killed and very few pre-Hispanic traditions survived. However, for better or for worse, it is this enduring and alluring *tapatío* legacy that colors even the most idealized images of colonial Mexico, Guadalajara is the image's finest incarnation.

Green, mostly clean, and accessible, Guadalajara is an urban traveler's dream. The city's *centro*, with its wide, tree-lined avenues, parks, and plazas, is wonderful for walking or simply passing time. When your legs get tired, turn to the excellent local bus system and speedy subways that connect the metropolis's sprawling suburbs with its *centro*—most sights in the city can be reached in 20 minutes or less. Kamikaze bus drivers zoom by on streets designed to preserve the splendor of

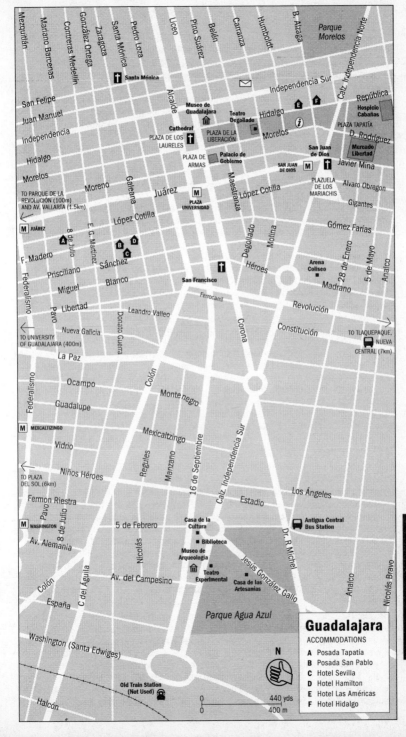

Guadalajara

ACCOMMODATIONS

A Posada Tapatía
B Posada San Pablo
C Hotel Sevilla
D Hotel Hamilton
E Hotel Las Américas
F Hotel Hidalgo

N

0   440 yds
0   400 m

Guadalajara's past; streets have been widened on one side, wisely sparing the buildings that have since become architectural treasures. The historic district, with its rich collection of colonial palaces and cathedrals, is the heart of the city, and industrial giants have been pushed into the suburbs where endless rows of flat, unspectacular, one-story houses reach far into the surrounding countryside.

Guadalajara is a cultural mecca as well—a collage of colonial and modern worlds. Dozens of museums attest to Mexico and Guadalajara's rich history, culture, and glory. Markets in and out of the city provide an abundance of *jalisciense* crafts, and local artists, street performers, thespians, and dancers (including the renowned *ballet folklórico*) continue to celebrate Guadalajara's fine artistic tradition. Meanwhile, the university, the second-oldest in Mexico, keeps Guadalajara young and tints the urban bustle with high-brow intellectual sophistication.

ORIENTATION

Step 1: Take a deep breath and try not to panic. Step 2: Get a detailed map. The tourist office has a good one, stores in the bus station and airport sell them, and you'll need one to navigate Guadalajara's sprawl. The heart of the city is the *centro histórico* around **Plaza Tapatía** and **Plaza de la Liberación.** Many accommodations and restaurants as well as the main shopping district, cathedral, and museums cluster around this area. Guadalajara is divided into quadrants more or less along the major streets **Hidalgo,** known as **República** east of Calzada Independencia, and **Calzada Independencia Norte and Sur.** Streets change names at the borders between these quadrants. A good place to get your bearings is at the intersection of **Juárez** and **Alcalde/16 de Septiembre.** Most bus routes stop there or a block away. The area west of Tapatía and the University of Guadalajara, known as the **Zona Rosa,** is home to many of the most expensive hotels and restaurants, modern buildings, and the U.S. consulate.

The poorer *colonias* (suburbs) can be dangerous at any time of day. Check with the tourist office before blazing new trails. Throughout Guadalajara, it is wise to stick to lit streets after dark and to take taxis after 10pm. Solo women travelers may want to avoid **Calzada Independencia** after this hour as well; the street has a magnetic field that attracts raucous, drunken men and supports a thriving prostitution trade at all hours of the day and night. Moving east from Calzada Independencia, conditions deteriorate—use common sense when deciding where to walk.

PRACTICAL INFORMATION

TRANSPORTATION

Airport: Aeropuerto Internacional Miguel Hidalgo (tel. 688 51 20 or 688 51 27), 17km south of town on the road to Chapala. *Combis* (tel. 688 59 25 or 812 43 08) run 24hr. and will pick you up from your hotel (40min., 60 pesos). A yellow-and-white "Aeropuerto" bus passes through the *centro* on Independencia at Los Angeles (every hr. 5:45am-8:45pm, 8 pesos) and makes the trip back from outside "Sala Nacional." Get off at 16 de Septiembre and Constituyentes. Don't pay more than 85 pesos for a cab—some are metered, some aren't. Served by **AeroCalifornia** (tel. 616 25 25), **Aeroméxico** (tel. 669 02 02), **American** (tel. 616 40 90), **Continental** (tel. 647 42 51), **Delta** (tel. 630 35 30), **Mexicana** (tel. 678 76 76), **Taesa** (tel. 679 09 00), and **United** (tel. 616 94 89).

Buses: The station, **Nueva Central Camionera,** is in nearby Tlaquepaque. Fixed-fare buses and taxis (15-40 pesos) head downtown frequently, as do "Centro" buses (2.50 pesos). From downtown, catch a #275, 275A, or "Nueva Central" bus on Av. Revolución or Av. 16 de Septiembre, across from the cathedral. In a taxi, be sure to specify the *new* bus station. Unless you're partial to a particular bus line, you can pretty much get where you're going from any of the 7 terminals. Only partial listings provided; call for more info. **Terminal 1:** Primera Plus and Flecha Amarilla (tel. 600 02 70) provide first-class service to: **Aguascalientes** (3hr., 4 and 8:15pm, 128 pesos); **Guanajuato** (4hr., 5 per day 11am-8pm, 197 pesos); **Mexico City** (10hr., every hr., 300 pesos); **Morelia** (6hr., 8 per day 4:30am-9:30pm, 140 pesos); **Querétaro** (8hr., every hr., 180 pesos); and **San Miguel de Allende** (5hr., 1 and 3pm, 218 pesos). **Terminal 2:** Autobuses de Occidente (tel. 600 00 55) travel to: **Manzanillo** (4hr., 14 per day 4am-11:45pm, 138 pesos), via **Colima** (3hr., 90 pesos); **Pátzcuaro** (7hr., 6 per day, 110 pesos); **Toluca** (11hr., 8 per day 3:30am-8pm, 183 pesos); and **Uruapan** (5hr., 7 per day 4:45am-5:15pm, 90 pesos). **Terminal 3:** Transportes del Pacífico (tel. 600 08 54) speeds to: **Culiacán** (10hr., 6 per day, 404 pesos); **Mazatlán** (8hr., 6 per day, 271 pesos); **Mexico City** (8hr., 7 per day 5am-1pm, 276 pesos); and **Puerto Vallarta** (6hr., 11 per day 4:30am-midnight, 216 pesos). **Terminal 4:** Transportes de Sonora (tel. 679 04 63) rumbles to: **Hermosillo** (24hr., every hr., 649 pesos), via **Mazatlán** (8hr., every hr., 235 pesos); and points in between. **Terminal 5:** Línea Azul (tel. 679 04 43) makes haste to **San Luis Potosí** (first-class 5hr., 8 per day, 166 pesos; second-class 6hr., every 30min. 7am-11:30pm, 146 pesos). **Terminal 6:** Ómnibus de México (tel. 600 02 91 or 600 04 69) beats tracks to: **Aguascalientes** (3hr., every hr., 118 pesos); **Ciudad Juárez** (24hr., 5 per day 7am-10:30pm, 773 pesos); **Durango** (10hr., 7 per day 7:30am-midnight, 307 pesos); **Mexico City** (8hr., every 30min., 278 pesos); **Querétaro** (8hr., 4 per day, 167 pesos); and **Zacatecas** (5hr., 19 per day 6:30am-midnight, 177 pesos). **Terminal 7:** Estrella Blanca (tel. 679 04 04) is the parent company of numerous smaller lines, including Rojo de los Altos and Transportes del Norte. This is the biggest terminal and it serves almost every major city in the Republic for competitive prices.

Local Buses: Though usually crowded, always noisy, and sometimes uncomfortable, **mini-buses** and **regular buses** (2.50 pesos), and the big blue **TUR** buses (5 pesos) are an excellent way to get just about anywhere in the city. Drivers all seem to dream of being on a racetrack, so trips can be short and exciting. Always be sure to check what letter (A, B, C, or D) the bus is—in general, the C and D buses have very different routes out into the residential neighborhoods. Buses **#60** and **#62** run the length of Calzada Independencia, from the train station past the zoo and Plaza de Toros. The electrically wired **"Par Vial"** bus runs west on Independencia, then Hidalgo, before turning onto Vallarta, just short of López Mateos. Coming back eastward, it cruises Hidalgo, 3 blocks north of Juárez. Bus **#258** from San Felipe, 3 blocks north of Hidalgo, runs from near the Plaza Tapatía down López Mateos to the Plaza del Sol—nightclub central. Bus **#52** is a direct link to downtown along 16 de Septiembre from locations north and south of the city. Bus **#24A** runs the length of López Mateos, from Zapopan to beyond the Plaza del Sol, in both directions. TUR bus **#707A** circles from the *centro* on Juárez west to López Mateos, down to Mariano Otero at the Plaza del Sol, up to Niños Héroes, and north on 16 de Septiembre and Corona to the start of the route. The big red **Cardenal** bus runs west on Madero to Av. Chapultepec along which is the **Zona Rosa**, the upscale shopping district west of the *centro*. The **aqua** TUR bus and Rte. **#45** return east on López Cotilla. Bus Rte. **#51** runs up and down Av. La Paz. Buses run from 6:30am-10pm; TUR buses run slightly later.

Subway: (tel. 853 75 70). Two lines run smoothly (every 5-10min. 6am-10:30pm, 3 pesos) and are a great alternative to the bus system if you're tired of breathing exhaust, however, they are not so helpful if you don't know the stops. The tourist office hands out a good map. **Line 1** runs from the northern boundary of the city, Anillo Periférico Nte., more or less along Federalismo to Anillo Periférico Sur. There is a stop at Federalismo and Juárez. **Line 2** runs from Juárez and Av. Alcalde/16 de Septiembre to Av. Patria in the east. The limited coverage of the 2 lines doesn't make the subway as practical as the bus for most destinations, but if it goes where you want to, it's a good option.

Car Rental: Dollar, Av. Federalismo Sur 540A (tel. 826 79 59, at the airport 688 56 89; fax 826 42 21), at Mexicaltizingo. Renters must be at least 21 years old and have a driver's license and major credit card. Prices start at 325 pesos per day plus 8% tax, including insurance and 300km. Staff delivers cars free of charge. Open daily 7am-9pm. **Hertz** (tel. 688 54 83), at the airport (open 24hr.) and at Av. 16 de Septiembre and Niños Héroes, has similar rates for drivers over 25. Several other options can be found on Niños Héroes at Av. 16 de Septiembre.

TOURIST AND FINANCIAL SERVICES

Tourist Office: State Office, Morelos 102 (tel. 613 03 06, or toll-free within Mexico 91 800 363 22), in Pl. Tapatía. In addition to helpful information and maps, super friendly and helpful staff distributes *Guadalajara Weekly* (free tourist paper), and *Mexico Living and Travel Update* (detailed information for living in Mexico). English spoken; ask about tours. Open M-F 9am-8pm, Sa-Su and holidays 9am-1pm. Another office in the Palacio de Gobierno. Open daily 9:30am-3pm and 4-7:30pm.

Tours: Panoramex, Federalismo 944 (tel. 810 51 09 or 810 50 05), at España runs tours to **Guadalajara** and **Tlaquepaque** (5hr., M-Sa 9:30am, 90 pesos); **Chapala** and **Ajijic** (6hr.; Tu, Th, and Sa-Su 9:30am; 110 pesos); and **Tequila** (6½hr.; M,W,F 9:30am; 120 pesos). Tours with English-speaking guides leave from the Jardín de San Francisco at 9:30am and from the Arcos de Vallarta at 9:45am. Tickets available either at the tourist office or at Panoramex. Office open M-F 9am-2pm and 4-7pm, Sa 9am-2pm.

Consulates: Guadalajara is home to a diplomatic diaspora. **Australia,** López Cotilla 2030 (tel. 615 74 18; fax 818 33 90), between López de Vega and Calserón de la Bara. Open M-F 8am-1:30pm and 3-6pm. **Canada,** Local 30 (tel. 615 62 70 or emergency 01 800 706 29 00; fax 615 86 65), at Hotel Fiesta Americana, on the Minerva traffic circle (catch a "Par Vial" bus). Open M-F 8:30am-5pm. **U.K.,** Eulogio Parra 2339 (tel. 616 06 29; fax 615 01 97). Open M-F 9am-3pm, and 5-8pm. **U.S.,** Progreso 175 (tel. 825 27 00 or 825 29 98; fax 826 65 49). Open M-F 8am-4:30pm. The **Oficina de la Asociación Consular,** at the U.K. consulate, can provide listings for other consulates.

Currency Exchange: The block of López Cotilla between Degollado and Molina is a *mercado* with only one product: money. Rates don't vary much. **Bancapromex** is on Corona at Juárez. Open M-F 8:30am-5:30pm, Sa 10am-2pm.

American Express: Vallarta 2440 (tel. 615 89 10), at Plaza los Arcos. Take the "Par Vial" bus. Open M-F 9am-2:30pm and 4-6pm, Sa 9am-1pm.

LOCAL SERVICES

English Bookstores: Sandi Bookstore, Tepeyac 718 (tel. 121 08 63), near the corner of Av. de las Rosas in Colonia Chapalita. Take bus #50 from Garibaldi or the green "Plus" bus from Juárez. Extensive selection of new books and newspapers. Open M-F 9:30am-2:30pm and 3:30-7pm, Sa 9:30am-2pm. The **Hyatt** at López Mateos and Mexico, carries day-old copies of the *New York Times.* **Sanborn's** department store, at Juárez and Corona, stocks a wide range of English-language magazines.

Cultural Information: Dirección de Educación y Cultura, 5 de Febrero and Analco (tel. 669 13 80 ext. 1487). **Instituto Cultural Cabañas,** Hospico Cabañas 8 (tel. 617 43 22), in Pl. Tapatía. Open M-F 9am-3pm and 6-9pm. Blue and yellow Ayuntamiento stands in the major plazas also field cultural and tourist queries. Open daily 8am-8pm.

Supermarket: Gigante, Juárez 573 (tel. 613 86 38) between E.G. Martinez and 8 de Julio. It has just about everything. Open M-Sa 8am-10pm, Su 8am-9pm.

Laundry: Lavandería Canadá, Patria 1123 (tel. 628 74 34), at Tepeyac. Open M-Sa 8am-8pm.

EMERGENCY AND COMMUNICATIONS

Emergency: dial 080.

Police: Independencia Nte. 840 (tel. 617 60 60 ext. 126 and 143) just before the *fuente olympica.*

Red Cross: (tel. 613 15 50 or 614 27 07), at Juan Manuel and San Felipe, on the 1st fl., behind Parque Morelos. Some English spoken. Open 24hr.

Pharmacy: Farmacia Guadalajara, Javier Mina 221 (tel. 617 85 55), at Cabañas. Minimal English spoken. Open 24hr.

Hospitals: México Americano (tel. 641 31 41 or 641 44 58), Colones and América. English spoken. **Green Cross Hospital** (tel. 614 52 52 or 643 71 90), Barcenas and Veracruz. English spoken.

Fax: Palacio Federal (tel. 614 26 64; fax 613 99 15), Alcalde and Álvarez and at the airport. Open M-F 8am-7pm, Sa 9am-noon.

Internet Access: Café Internet, Madero 413, just a few blocks from the *centro*. You can also grab a bite to eat here. 20 pesos per hr. Open M-Sa 10am-9pm. Another option might be **PC Express,** 2077 López Mateos (tel. 647 69 20); take the #258 bus from the corner of Madero and 16 de Septiembre downtown and get off 3 blocks past Cárdenas. 12 pesos per 30min. Open M-Sa 9am-9pm.

Post Office: (tel. 614 74 25), on Carranza between Juan Manuel and Calle de Independencia (not Independencia Sur). Open M-F 8am-7pm, Sa 9am-1pm.

Postal Code: 44100.

Telephones: LADATELs in the *centro*. **Caseta** in Nueva Central bus station. Open 24hr.

Phone Code: 3.

▊ ACCOMMODATIONS

Guadalajara is full of cheap places to stay. *Posadas* are an intriguing option—they're small, family-run establishments, often in beautiful, remodeled homes, that provide large, well-furnished rooms and good security. Some have curfews and in general are less private than a typical hotel. However, it's wise to call ahead if possible; many places tend to fill up early in the day. Check the tourist office for a list. Guadalajara also has an excellent hostel. For hotels, reservations are only necessary in the festival seasons of February and October.

NEAR THE CENTRO HISTÓRICO

The widest variety of rooms, the best location, and the safest spots are in this area. From *posadas* to standard hotel rooms, budget accommodations won't disappoint, but you do get what you pay for at most of the cheaper options.

Posada San Pablo, Madero 429 (tel. 614 28 11), between Ocampo and Donato Guerra. There is no sign and the door is always closed; ring the bell to enter this budget traveler's dream. Enormous rooms, an attractive courtyard, a small library, kitchen access, a chess set, and a friendly dog are a few of the highlights. Laundry service (40 pesos). Extremely popular with travelers from all over the world; call ahead if possible. Singles 70 pesos, with bath 90 pesos; doubles 120 pesos; triples 150 pesos.

Hotel Las Américas, Hidalgo 76 (tel. 613 96 22), at Humboldt. Comfortably carpeted rooms with TV, phone and fans as well as a great location and reasonable prices. Singles 100 pesos; doubles 110 pesos; triples 150 pesos.

Posada Tapatía, López Cotilla 619 (tel. 614 91 46). A beautiful old mansion with peachy walls and brightly colored trim, fucshia sofas and spreads, and a leafy courtyard has clean rooms with private baths and fans (singles 120 pesos; doubles 150 pesos).

Hotel Sevilla, Sánchez 413 (tel. 614 91 72), between Ocampo and Donato Guerra. Rooms have TVs, phones, and sky-blue bathrooms, and are graced by landscape photos to make up for the lack of a view in this old but clean hotel. Singles 90 pesos; 1-bed doubles 100 pesos, 2-bed doubles 120 pesos.

CODE Youth Hostel, Av. Prolongación Alcalde 1360 (tel. 624 65 15). Take bus #52 or #54 from the Jardín de San Francisco or anywhere on Alcalde. The CODE is just past the traffic circle, across from the Foro de Arte y Cultura in a blue fence encircled sports complex. Clean, single-sex rooms hold 20 metal bunks each. Bedding, pillows, and lockers provided, but bring your own lock. Reception M-F 8am-2pm and 4-9pm, Sa-Su 9am-3pm and 5-9pm. Curfew 11pm. Hostel closed during *Semana Santa* and Christmas. 35 pesos per person. 25% discount with HI membership.

Hotel Hidalgo, Hidalgo 14 (tel. 613 50 67), a block from Hotel Las Americas. Offers basic rooms in a less than appealing building in a good location going for a price hard to find anywhere else in the city. Singles and doubles 65 pesos; triples 70 pesos. If you don't mind them, there are rooms with permanent cockroach residents (40 pesos).

EAST ON JAVIER MINA

Hotels in this area are close to the Mercado Libertad, the Hospico Cabañas, and the Plaza de los Mariachis. Some of the surrounding areas require extra caution at night. If the establishments above don't work out (or if you just want to be closer to Plaza de los Mariachis), these hotels are basic, modern, and clean.

Hotel México 70, Javier Mina 230 (tel. 617 99 78), at Cabañas. White tile floors, red bedspreads, aqua tile bathrooms, and dark hallways make up this mysteriously-named hotel. Singles 90 pesos; doubles 110 pesos, triples 120 pesos. TV 15 pesos extra.

Hotel Imperio, Javier Mina 170 (tel. 617 50 42). Large rooms with dark red and gold overtones lend the place the feel of either a centurion's quarters or a love-naysium, or both. Singles 80 pesos; doubles 90 pesos; triples 100 pesos; TV 10 pesos extra.

Hotel San Jorge, Javier Mina 284 (tel. 617 79 97). Plain but comfortable rooms with tile bathrooms and dark hallways. Singles 80 pesos; doubles 90 pesos. Patrons can pay another 15 pesos to enslave themselves to a TV, the bane of our modern existence.

Hotel Ana Ísabel, Javier Mina 164 (tel. 617 79 20 or 617 48 59), at Cabañas. Clean, small, somewhat dark rooms with ceiling fans and TVs overlook a green courtyard. Singles 115 pesos; doubles 135 pesos.

ZONA ROSA

Hotels in the **Zona Rosa,** the wealthiest area of Guadalajara, are predictably fancy and pricey. One option between the *centro* and the more expensive Av. Chapultepec is **Hotel La Paz,** La Paz 1091 (tel. 613 30 07), between Donato Guerra and 8 de Julio, on bus Rte. #51 or #321. New-looking rooms are decorated in blue and have lovely faux marble countertops and phones. (Singles 100 pesos; doubles 140 pesos; triples 165 pesos.) If you have spare pesos and want a really classy, quiet lodging, the *Zona Rosa* has an abundance and is only a short bus ride from the heart of the action in the *centro*.

◖ FOOD

Guadalajara has tons of budget eateries as well as many expensive, upscale restaurants serving French, Italian, and Japanese cuisine. *Birria* is a hearty local specialty made by stewing meat (typically pork) in tomato broth thickened with cornmeal and spiced with garlic, onions, and chiles. Quench your thirst with Estrella beer, brewed *clara dorada* (golden clear) right here in Guadalajara. The city is also famous for its *taquerías* and the number of ingredients that can be wrapped in tortillas here.

NEAR THE CENTRO HISTORICO

This is a great place to snack or fill up with a huge meal. Ice cream and fast food is everywhere and *panaderías* (bakeries) cluster around the area southwest of the plaza, primarily on the blocks enclosed by Pavo, Sánchez, Galeana, and Juárez.

La Zanahoria, Hidalgo 112, near the Teatro Degollado has no sign, so look for the brown awning. This glorified juice bar with pine tables and traditional blue glasses is fantastically cheap and very popular. Large fruit yogurt with granola (7.50 pesos); or whole wheat quesadillas (3 pesos). Open M-Sa 9am-7pm, Su 7am-5pm.

El Farol, Moreno 466 (613 03 49), at Galeana, 2nd fl. has *comida típica* at rock-bottom prices. The friendly owner makes a mean *chile relleno*. Complementary *buñuelos*, a fried dough dessert dripping with sugary syrup. Entrees 15-20 pesos; tacos 3 pesos; beer 10 pesos. Open daily 10am-8pm.

Restaurant Acuarius, Sánchez 416 (tel. 613 62 77), across from Hotel Sevilla. The age of Restaurant Acuarius dawned in that heavy hip year of 1974 and has been raising the general cosmic consciousness of Guadalajara ever since. *Jugo verde* 9 pesos; and vegetarian *comida corrida* 36 pesos. Open M-Sa 9:30am-6pm.

Café Madrid, Juárez 264 (614 95 04), at Corona. This pricey American 1950s diner flourishing in the *centro* has waiters sporting white jackets and bowties serving breakfast (36 pesos), enchiladas (36 pesos), and divine cappuccino (13 pesos) to patrons seated on stools along the formica counter or at tables beneath an enormous Alfredo Santos mural. Open daily 7:30am-10:30pm.

Restaurant Villa Madrid, López Cotilla 553 (tel. 613 42 50). The large displays of fresh fruit scream vegetarian, but this place combines both veggie and traditional fare without the self-righteous pretense of many vegetarian restaurants. Burritos are 26 pesos and salads are 39 pesos, but the real bargain are the lunches; your choice of sandwich and every vegetable imaginable for just 19 pesos. Open M-F 8am-9pm, Sa noon-8pm.

Taco Cabaña, on the corner of Moreno and Maestranza near the Palacio de Gobierno by the Plaza Tapatía. Cheap beer and tacos amid the *mariachi*-filled jukebox and a panel of TVs tuned to *fútbol*. Two beers 13 pesos; tacos 3 pesos. Open daily 9am-9pm.

Mercado Libertad, Calle Independencia, next to the plaza. The enormous market has an entire wing dedicated to family-run restaurants. Watch food be cooked before your eyes as you sit in the frenetic market atmosphere. You can find anything to eat here from *birria* to fried chicken at prices that'll leave you with plenty of pesos for shopping (huge meals average 25 pesos). Open daily 8am-9pm.

ZONA ROSA

Most of the places listed below are near the intersection of Vallarta and Chapultepec, on the "Par Vial" and bus Rte. #321. It's worth the trip—the extra pesos buy excellent food and even a measure of elegance.

▧ Restaurant Samurai, Vidrio 1929 (tel. 826 35 54), ¼ block north and to the right of the Niños Héroes monument on Chapultepec has authentic Japanese-Mexican cuisine. While waiting for the food to arrive, you can meditate on the goldfish pond, rock garden, and hummingbirds. Japanese *comida corrida* with rice, soup, and main course is 24 pesos. Samurai *especial* includes a huge teriyaki steak, fish, shrimp, and more for 56 pesos. Many vegetarian options. Open M-Sa noon-10pm, Su noon-7pm.

Naló Cafe, Justo Sierra 2046 (tel. 615 27 15), just off Chapultepec Nte. Outside seating under a big umbrella, the better to sample the delicious breakfast and lunch specials (15-25 pesos). Menu changes daily but the friendly servers and relaxing atmosphere don't. Fettucine alfredo 25 pesos; salads 15 pesos; carrot cake 12 pesos. Open daily 8am-9pm.

Café Don Luis, Chapultepec 215 (tel. 625 65 99), at Av. de la Paz, has a large coffee and drink selection with just a few desserts. A great place to revive your sleepy bones after a *siesta; a Beso de Angel* (Angel's Kiss) is more than just a peck on the cheek (made with rum, Kahlúa, and egg nog; 17 pesos). Open daily 8:30am-3pm and 5pm-midnight.

◉ SIGHTS

A great city for walking, Guadalajara fills with families out for a stroll in the cool evening air. But don't limit your exploration to the *centro* alone—efficient bus and subway systems make getting around fairly easy. The sheer number of monuments testifies to the rich history and culture of Guadalajara and statues commemorating everyone from the Niños Héroes to (who else?) Benito Juárez are plentiful. Guadalajara's plazas are clean, crowded, and often visited by party-hardy *mariachis*. The city's museums are a great introduction to Mexican culture and history outside of Mexico City.

DOWNTOWN

PLAZA DE LA LIBERACIÓN. La Liberación is one of downtown Guadalajara's four plazas which punctuate the city's concrete sidewalks with splashes of greenery. Horse-drawn carriages sit near the **Museo Regional** across from the cathedral, waiting to whisk you around the city (45 min. 120 pesos). The spacious plaza, with its large, bubbling fountain and enormous Mexican flag that eclipses the sun, is surrounded by the cathedral, Museo Regional, Palacio de Gobierno, and Teatro Degollado. Daily at 6pm, military personnel ceremonially retire the colors. An enormous sculpture in the plaza depicts Hidalgo breaking the chains of servitude in commemoration of his 1810 decree abolishing the slave trade, which was signed in Guadalajara. Always bustling with activity, the Plaza de la Liberación is the effective center of historic Guadalajara.

PALACIO DE GOBIERNO. On the plaza's south side, the palace was built in 1774, and is graced by a José Clemente Orozco mural punctuated by Miguel Hidalgo's feverish eyes glaring down at the passers-by. A second Orozco mural, covering the ceiling in the echoing **Sala de Congreso,** on the second floor of the palace, depicts enslaved *indígenas* and the heroism of Hidalgo and Juárez. Climb to the roof for a great view. *(Palacio open M-F 9am-8:30pm, Sa-Su 9am-3pm. Guided tours in English available for a few pesos.)*

CATHEDRAL. This imposing structure faces the Teatro Degollado across Plaza de la Liberación. Begun in 1558 and completed 60 years later, the cathedral is a melange of architectural styles. After an 1848 earthquake destroyed its original towers, ambitious architects replaced them with much taller ones. Fernando VII of Spain donated the cathedral's 11 richly ornamented altars in appreciation of Guadalajara's aid during the Napoleonic Wars. One of the remaining original altars is dedicated to Our Lady of the Roses; it is this altar that gave Guadalajara its nickname "City of Roses." Inside the sacristy is the *Assumption of the Virgin*, painted by the 17th-century painter Bartolomé Murillo. The towers, known as the *cornucopías*, can be climbed with the permission of the cathedral's administrators, who hole up in the side of the building facing the Teatro Degollado. Decend into the semi-spooky area underneath the altar (take the steps down on the right-hand side) where the remains of three cardinals and two bishops will keep you company. The 60-meter jaunt to the top of the towers affords the best view in town. On the cathedral's west side is the arboreal Plaza de los Laureles; to the north, the Plaza de los Mártires commemorates *tapatíos* who have died in various wars. *(Open daily 7:30am-7:30pm. Visit after 2pm on Su so as not to intrude on Mass.)*

MUSEO REGIONAL DE GUADALAJARA. This *museo* chronicles the history of western Mexico, beginning with the Big Bang. The most popular museum around, it's always crowded with field-tripping students and tourists. The first floor spans the country's pre-Hispanic history. Collections of colonial art, modern paintings, and an exhibit on the history of the Revolution occupy the second floor. Artsy and educational movie screenings, plays, and lectures take place in the museum's auditorium—inquire within or at the tourist office. *(Calle Liceo 60 at Hidalgo. On the north side of the Plaza de la Liberación. Tel. 614 99 57 or 614 52 64. Calle Liceo 60 at Hidalgo. Open Tu-Sa 9am-5:45pm, Su 9am-3:15pm. Admission 20 pesos; seniors, children under 12, and Tu Su, free.)*

TEATRO DEGOLLADO. Attend the *ballet folklórico* on Sunday mornings at 10am to get a good look at the breathtaking Teatro Degollado, a neoclassical structure on the Plaza de la Liberación's east end. The gold and red balconies, a sculpted allegory of the seven muses, and Gerardo Suárez's depiction of Dante's Paradiso on the ceiling may compete with what's on stage for your attention; the theater plays host to amateur acts of sometimes dubious skill during the week. *(Tel. 614 47 73. Open sporadically for non-ticket holders. Tickets available at the theater box office.)*

PLAZUELA DE LOS MARIACHIS. On the south side of San Juan de Dios, the church with the righteously funky blue neon cross on Independencia at Javier

Mina. Immediately after sitting down in the crowded plaza, roving musicians will pounce. Using every trick in their musical bag, the *mariachis* will try to separate you from your pesos. Prices for songs are completely variable; a good *mariachi* who likes you or a bad one without much choice may perform a song for only 20-25 pesos, post-haggling. The *mariachis* continue playing long into the night, but you probably don't want to be around to hear them—the Plazuela becomes a stage for roving unsavories who may also try to get you to part ways with your pesos. And if they offer music in return, it isn't the kind you listen to.

HOSPICIO CABAÑAS. Also known as the Casa de Cultura Cabañas, at the corner of Hospicio and Cabañas, three blocks east of Independencia. It was here that Hidalgo signed his proclamation against slavery in 1810; the building has since served as an orphanage and as an art school. For its main chapel, Orozco painted a nightmarish and brilliant rendition of the **Four Riders of the Apocalypse;** some regard the contorted, fiery shape as his best work. *Espejos* (mirrors) are available free for those who don't want to strain their necks; alternatively, lie down on one of the many benches set up for reclined viewing. The *hospicio* also hosts photography and sculpture exhibits. *(Open Tu-Sa 10am-6pm, Su 10am-3pm. Admission 8 pesos, with student ID 4 pesos, children under 12, and Su free. 10 pesos for camera rights—no flash.)*

MERCADO LIBERTAD. At Javier Mina and Independencia, the cavernous *mercado* is touted as the largest covered market in the Americas. Although its size may be exaggerated, there are still oodles of sandals, *sarapes*, jewelry, guitars, dried iguanas, and other witchcraft supplies filling tier after tier of booths. Don't be afraid to get good and lost among all the merchandise or to bargain with savvy merchants. You can get a great deal on that purple sombrero you've always wanted if you're willing to get in the trenches and haggle. *(Open daily roughly 9am-8pm, but some merchants don't open on Su.)* The Sunday market **El Baratillo** on Javier Mina, approximately 15 blocks east of Mercado Libertad, offers bargain hunters even more temptations. From Mercado Libertad, walk two blocks north to Hidalgo and catch bus #40 heading east or a "Par Vial" bus on Morelos. El Baratillo lasts all day Sunday and sometimes sprawls out over 30 or 40 blocks. If you thought the Mercado Libertad was huge, wait until you see its daddy. Everything imaginable is peddled here, from hot *tamales* to houses.

SOUTH

PARQUE AGUA AZUL. If you're tired of the hustle and bustle of the city streets, take a stroll in the lavish green park with tropical bird aviaries, an orchid greenhouse, a butterfly house, and a sports complex. *(South of the centro on Calzada Independencia; take bus #60 or #62 heading south along this main street. Open Tu-Su 10am-6pm. Admission 4 pesos, children 2 pesos.)*

CASA DE LAS ARTESANÍAS DE JALISCO. Everything is for sale inside the *Casa*, but prices can be 50% higher here than in the surrounding villages. High quality pottery, jewelry, clocks, hammocks, china, blankets, *equipales*, chessboards, shirts, and purses have been carted over from Tlaquepaque and Tonalá. *(Tel. 619 46 64. On González Gallo, the street bisecting Parque Agua Azul. Open M-F 10am-6pm, Sa 10am-5pm, Su 10am-3pm.)*

ZONA ROSA

Cultural activity in the city's wealthier area focuses on the **Plaza del Arte,** on Chapultepec, one block south from its intersection with Niños Héroes.

GALERÍA DE ARTE MODERNO. National artists bare their souls on a rotating basis in the plaza's *galería*, although the artwork displayed is often of dubious quality. It's worth it to stop in if you're in the area, but definitely don't bother with a special trip out here. *(Tel. 616 32 66. On Mariano Ote. and España. Open Tu-F 10am-7pm, Sa-Su 10am-2pm. Free.)*

TEATRO JAIME TORRES BODET. The theater hosts everything from book expositions and wind concerts to theatrical productions. Stand-up comedy and performance art enliven the premises with laughter and pretension. *(Tel. 615 12 69. In the Plaza del Arte, at Chapultepec and España. Open M-F 9am-9pm.)*

NORTH

For the sights listed below, take Ruta #60 or #62 north on Calzada Independencia.

ZOOLÓGICO GUADALAJARA. To visit furry and feathered friends, head to the Zoológico Guadalajara, featuring an especially impressive collection of tropical birds. At the far end of the zoo is a spectacular view of the Barranca de Huentitán, a deep ravine. *(Tel. 674 44 88 or 674 43 60. Continue north on Calzada Independencia past the Plaza de Toros. It's a good 1½ km. walk to the entrance of the zoo from the bus stop on Independencia. Open W-Su 10am-6pm. Admission 22 pesos, ages 12 and under 12 pesos.)*

CENTRO DE CIENCIA Y TECNOLOGÍA. The center houses a planetarium, exhibits on astronomy, aeronautics, and geological formations, and a sculpted plant garden out back. *(Tel. 674 41 06. A 20min. walk from the zoo. Open Tu-Su 9am-7pm. Museum admission 2 pesos, planetarium 4 pesos.)*

🎵 ENTERTAINMENT

Guadalajara is known for its cultural sophistication and dizzying variety of entertainment options; you'd have to bury your head in the sand to miss them. To keep abreast of Guadalajara's goings-on, from avant-garde film festivals to bullfights, check listings of clubs and cultural events in *The Guadalajara Weekly*, *Vuelo Libre*, (a monthly calendar of events), and the kiosks and bulletin boards of places like Hospicio Cabañas. Be prepared to take a taxi after 10pm (when buses stop running), but provided you use caution, walking about in most places in the *centro historico* at night should not pose a problem.

BARS

Guadalajara has a thriving nightlife; determined partiers can find something going on every night of the week. If you're not big on the club scene, there's a wide array of bars from the traditional cantina to the corporate commercial American imports. Live entertainment in these hotspots ranges from punk to *mariachi*.

La Maestranza, Maestranza 179 (tel. 613 20 85), at López Cortilla, in the *centro*. If you think you've seen bullfighting posters and regalia before, wait until you get a load of this. It's a vertible shrine to the "tragedy" no bullfighting aficionado should miss. The food and the beer are good too. Enchiladas 24 pesos. Beer 8 pesos. Live trio daily 3-5pm. No cover. Open daily 10am-3am.

Copenhagen, upstairs at Marcos Castellanos 120-2 (tel. 825 28 03), between Juárez and López Cortilla. A jazz haven. Come to hear a few good bop rhythms and beats. Live music M-Sa 9pm-12:30am. Open M-Sa 2pm-1am, Su 1-6pm.

Bananas Café, Chapultepec 330 (tel. 615 41 91), at Lerdo dc Tejada. If you've ever wanted to step up to a bar and order a Metallica, Rolling Stones, or Doors, this is your chance to do it. The walls are decked out with U.S. and British pop stars and the DJ will play favorite tunes. Crazy mixed drinks have low, low prices (10-15 pesos), and alcohol contents to match. Beer 10 pesos. Open daily noon-midnight.

La Cripta, Tepeyac 4038 (tel. 647 62 07), at Niño Obrero. Cool locals, mostly university types, down *cerveza* to live alternative tunes. Cover 20-40 pesos. Open daily 8pm-3am.

NIGHTCLUBS

Elegantly dressed partygoers line up to get into the classy joints along **Av. Vallarta** (taxi 35 pesos from the *centro*), while more classic discotheques with sophisticated track lighting and elevated dance floors cluster around **Plaza del Sol** (taxi 50 pesos). On Friday and Saturday nights, when many bars and discos offer drink specials, the crowds come out in droves. In general, Guadalajara discos are fancy; most won't let you in with blue jeans or without leather shoes, so dress to the nines and get ready to shake, shake, shake; shake, shake, shake; shake your booty.

Pixie, Vallarta 2503 (tel 658 10 80), near Los Arcos. The young and happening put on a little pixie dust and float into Never-Neverland (not in the hallucinogenic sense) at this new disco. The DJ throws out a batch of heavy techno and electronica sprinkled with a few pop tunes. Cover 40 pesos. Open W, F-Sa 10pm-3am.

La Marcha, Vallarta 2648 (tel. 615 89 99), at Los Arcos, has fancy artwork, fountains, and pretension, oh my. March on to electronic beats in this converted 19th century mansion. Cover men 100 pesos, women 60 pesos. Open W-Sa 10pm-4am.

Lado B, Vallarta 2451 (tel. 616 20 96), at Queredo at Plaza Los Arcos. This blazing inferno full of creepy murals has images of the sphinx and phoenix hovering over the metal and wire furniture. Cover 120 pesos, women 60 pesos. Open bar nightly. Open W, F-Sa 9pm-4am

Dany Rock, Mariano Otero 1989 (tel. 121 13 63), by the Plaza de Sol. A brand new place appealing to a somewhat older crowd, with plenty of tables to sit and listen to music from the 60s to 90s. Cover 50 pesos, women 40 pesos. Open W-Su 9pm-3am.

GAY AND LESBIAN NIGHTLIFE

There is more gay nightlife here than anywhere in the Republic except Mexico City, mostly along Chapultepec, in the upscale *Zona Rosa*, and at the Plaza de los Mariachis. Many of the drag shows are popular and are attended by people of all sexual orientations.

Sahara, Mariano Otero 3445 (tel. 621 88 40), 2 blocks from Pasaje in the Plaza del Sol. The latest in lights, glitz, and racy drag shows pack a full house. Cover 25 pesos. Shows 10:30pm and 1:30am. Open W-Su 9pm-4am.

S.O.S., La Paz 1413 (tel. 826 41 79), at Camarena. Incredibly vibrant drag shows. Cover 30 pesos. Shows W-Su midnight. Disco open W-Su 10pm-4am.

Caudillós, Sanchez 407 (tel. 613 54 45), near Hotel Cervantes, about 3 blocks from the *centro*. A small bar and disco that draws loyal regulars who enjoy the 2-for-1 brew (14 pesos), free cover, spirited dance floor, and occasional live "sensual performance." Open Th-Su 3pm-3am; music starts at 8:30pm.

Mascara's, Maestranza 238 (tel. 614 81 03), at Madero. A popular gay bar with 2-for-1 beers (16 pesos). Don your favorite mask (optional) and step into the fun. Open daily 9am-midnight.

CULTURAL EVENTS

The **Ballet Folklórico** dazzles the world with precise rhythmic dance, regional garb, and amusing stage antics. There are two troupes in Guadalajara, one affiliated with the University of Guadalajara and the other with the state of Jalisco. The former, reputedly better, performs Sundays at 10am in the **Teatro Degollado** (tel. 614 47 73; box office open daily 10am-1pm and 4-7pm). Tickets (25-120 pesos) can be purchased on the day of the performance or one day in advance, which usually is not necessary. The **Ballet Folklórico de Cabañas,** the state troupe, performs Wednesdays at 8:30pm in the Hospicio Cabañas (tickets 40 pesos). If you arrive before 8pm, you can take a tour of some of the murals of the Hospicio. The Hospicio also shows premieres of Mexican films to much fanfare (shows daily at noon, 3:50, 6:50, and 9pm; tickets 10 pesos). The **Instituto Cultural Cabañas** presents live music on an open-air stage in the Hospicio Cabañas at least once a week; for schedules, drop by the their ticket counter (see p. 383) or look for their flyers with the Cabañas insignia (a building with a dome and pillars) for schedules.

University facilities, scattered throughout the city, have created a market for high culture on a low budget. The **Departamento de Bellas Artes,** García 720, coordinates activities at a large number of stages, auditoriums, and movie screens throughout the city. The best source of information on cultural events is the blackboard in the lobby, which lists each day's attractions.

For both modern and cultural artistic films, head to the **Cinematógrafo,** Vallarta 1102 (tel. 825 05 14), just west of the university. A different film is presented each week (showings at 4, 6, 8, and 10pm; tickets 25 pesos). Guadalajara has dozens of other cinemas with admission around 20 pesos; check the newspapers for listings.

Although they close earlier than bars, many **cafes** are still happening nighttime spots. **Café La Paloma,** López Cotilla 1855 (tel. 630 00 91), at Miguel de Cervantes, is a rendezvous point for the young and hip university crowd. The cool patio filled with wicker chairs is a welcome respite from the hustle of downtown. Local artwork spanks the imagination while the body enjoys dishes and desserts including *cafe de olla* (14 pesos) and chocolate cheesecake (19 pesos). (Open M-Sa 8:30am-11pm, Su 9am-10pm.)

▧ FESTIVALS

Finding a bench in the Plaza de Armas, across from the Palacio de Gobierno, on Tuesday, Thursday and Sunday nights is a tricky task—the **Jalisco State Band** draws crowds of locals for free performances. The music doesn't get going until about 6:30pm, but seat-seekers should arrive before 6pm (see next page). The **Plaza de los Fundadores,** behind the Teatro Degollado, serves as a stage every afternoon and evening for the clown-mimes. Watch and give tips, but unless you like being the butt of jokes, keep out of the mime's eye. On any given day, the entire area around the *centro* is crowded with pedestrians and the artists, clowns, and actors who come to entertain them.

Every October, Guadalajara explodes with the traditional **Fiestas de Octubre,** a surreal, month-long bacchanal of parades, dancing, bullfights, fireworks, food, and fun. Each day of the month is dedicated to a different one of Mexico's 29 states or its two territories. Revelers are treated to regional dance performances, concerts, and cultural celebrations for 31 consecutive days. The small communities around Guadalajara also celebrate huge festivals during different parts of the year. Keep your eyes open for the copious advertisements that coat the city.

SPORTS

Bullfights take place almost every Sunday from October through March in the **Plaza de Toros** (tel. 637 99 82 or 651 85 06), on Nuevo Progreso at the northern end of Independencia (take Ruta #60 or 62 north). Tickets (25-180 pesos) can be purchased at the Plaza de Toros. (Open M-Sa 10am-2pm and 4-6pm.)

Even by Mexican standards, *fútbol* is huge in Guadalajara. The Chivas, the local professional team, are perennial contenders for the national championship; conversations turn nasty, brutish, and short at the mention of the Pumas, the rival team for Mexico City. Matches are held September through May in **Jalisco Stadium** (tel. 637 05 63 or 637 02 99), at Calzada Independencia North in front of the Plaza de Toros (on the #60 or 62 bus Rte.), and in **Estadio 3 de Marzo** (tel. 641 50 51), at the Universidad Autónoma (ticket office is at Colomos Pte. 2339).

NEAR GUADALAJARA

As if Guadalajara weren't overwhelming enough, its surrounding area is home to more exciting tourist options. From evenings spent hiking around Mexico's second-largest lake to mornings spent slugging your favorite liquor out of a bullhorn, adventure outside of the city boundaries is quickly and cheaply accessible by the local bus system.

LAGO DE CHAPALA AND CHAPALA

Forty kilometers from the hustle and bustle of Guadalajara lies **Lago de Chapala,** Mexico's second-largest lake. Although industrial waste has made swimming in the lake a bad idea, a visit to the small villages of **Chapala** and **Ajijic** (see p. 388) is still a good option. Home to a peaceful mix of Mexican tourists, *norteamericano* retirees, local artists, and residents, these villages lie tucked between the lake's serene northern shore and surrounding mist-cloaked mountains. Chapala is a bit less developed than Ajijic, but neither of them can escape the tourist feel. It's still possible to enjoy these towns, you just have to look a little harder and always look at signs in English as a red flag indicating inflated tourist prices.

Chapala is named after the Tecuexe Indian chief Capalac, who founded the village on the banks of the lagoon in 1510. The town's mix of history and geographic beauty has inspired artists for centuries; its charm shines through its growing size and modernity. Reeds thriving in the lake's now-polluted waters have caused the lake to shrink, but the beautiful walkways bordering the old water line are still perfect for a stroll. Otherwise, there really aren't any trails along the lakes. You can walk or take a bus (suggested donation 10 pesos) from the edge of town to the waterfront, but there isn't much to see there. Nobody in Chapala is in a hurry to get anywhere, and cars on the main north-south drag, **Madero,** putter along, making the markets great places to wander.

🚩 ORIENTATION AND PRACTICAL INFORMATION. The **bus station's** main entrance lies on Madero and Martinez. Turn left on Madero as you walk out of the bus station to reach the lake. The lake is Chapala's southern and eastern boundary. **Hidalgo** (known as **Morelos** east of Madero) runs west to Ajijic from two blocks north of the lake. **Banamex** (tel. (376) 5 22 71), on Madero and Hidalgo, exchanges money and has an **ATM** (open M-F 9am-3:30pm). The **mercado de artesanías** is on the waterfront and extends four blocks east of Madero's end, on Ramón Corona. **D.H. Lawrence** lived in Chapala during the 1920s and 1930s, and it was here that he began writing *The Plumed Serpent.* For a spectacular view of Chapala, Ajijic, and the surrounding countryside, walk up the stone stairway that winds up the hills from Madero, about four blocks from the lake.

🛏🍴 ACCOMMODATIONS AND FOOD. If you plan on spending the night in Chapala, the **Hotel Nido,** Madero 202 (tel. (376) 5 21 16), which once played host to dictator Díaz's weekend soirées, offers the most comfortable rooms. The airy hotel has clean, simple rooms with cable TV, a pretty courtyard, and a pool. (Parking available; singles 178 pesos; doubles 218 pesos.) The hotel also has a somewhat pricey restaurant. A much cheaper (and the only other) option is **Hotel Cardilejas,** at López Cotilla 363 (tel. (376) 5 22 79), with a red and white sign one block off Madero near the bus station. Rooms are small but clean and the rooftop patio has a view of the lake. (Singles 100 pesos; doubles 120; triples 200 pesos.) For dining options, follow Madero or walk along the waterfront to **Restaurant Superior,** Madero 415 (tel. (376) 5 21 80) offering a full bar, steaks (26-35 pesos), hamburgers (12 pesos), and breakfasts (12-24 pesos; open W-M 8am-10pm, Tu 8am-5pm). More *típico* food including a 25 peso *pescado* (fish) specialty is served at **Chabela's Fonda,** Encarnación Rosa 62 (tel. (376) 5 43 80), at the far right corner of the plaza (open daily 8am-6pm).

Getting There: From the *antigua* bus station in Guadalajara, take a **Guadalajara-Chapala** bus (tel. (376) 617 56 75, 45min., every 30 min. 6am-9pm, 20 pesos). Buses back to Guadalajara leave from the station on roughly the same schedule. Otherwise, Guadalajara's new bus station has service to Chapala (1¼hr., every hr. 7:45am-5:45pm, 12 pesos). From Ajijic, hop on any bus; all roads lead through Chapala (20min., every 20min., 3 pesos).

CENTRAL PACIFIC COAST

AJIJIC

Hugging the shore of Lake Chapala and commanding a beautiful view of the surrounding mountains, the village of Ajijic is unfortunately a minefield of money-hungry establishments ready to pounce on unsuspecting gringos. Because of this fact (and the fact that the lake is the only attraction) you might want to avoid Ajijic completely or at the very least spend as little time in the actual village as possible.

◪ ORIENTATION AND PRACTICAL INFORMATION. The only paved street in Ajijic is the route Carretera Chapala, which divides the town into north and south. Buses down to Chapala or Guadalajara can be flagged down along it. The town's north-south strip is **Colón. Constitución** changes its name to **Ocampo.** The plaza is several blocks towards the lake from the route on Colón. While Ajijic lacks an official tourist office, longtime resident **Beverly Hunt,** owner of **Laguna Axixic Realty,** Carretera 24 (tel. (376) 6 11 74; fax 6 11 88), gets the job done, providing maps, brochures, English newsletters, and a friendly cup of coffee. **Bancapromex** (tel. (376) 6 05 46), on Hidalgo at Morelos, exchanges money and has a 24hr. **ATM** (open M-F 9am-5pm, Sa 9am-1pm). English is spoken at **Farmacia Jessica,** Parroquia 18 (tel. (376) 6 11 91), on the plaza (open daily 9am-10pm). **Post office:** Colón 23 (tel. (376) 6 18 88), at Constitución (open M-F 8am-3pm, Sa 9am-1pm).

◪◪◪ ACCOMMODATIONS, FOOD, AND ENTERTAINMENT. Prices   for accomodations in Ajijic may be out of reach of the budget-conscious. **Las Casitas,** Carretera Chapala Pte. 20 (tel. (376) 6 11 45), has red tile floors, a little kitchen, and a cozy living room with fold-out couch and chimney (bungalows for 2 people 180 pesos). At the **Posada Las Calandrías,** Carretera Chapala Pte. 8 (tel. (376) 6 10 52), there is a flower-filled garden, barbecue space, and a great view of the *laguna* from the terraces (small bungalow with 2 single beds 300 pesos; large bungalow with 4 single beds are also available). Both establishments have pools. It's difficult to find a good place to eat in Ajijic; tourist traps like **El Serape** on the Carretera Chapala should be avoided because of ridiculously high prices and American-style food. On weekends, live Latin rhythms spice up the old **Posada Ajijic** on the *laguna* at Colón (live music F-Sa 9pm-1:30am; cover 15 pesos).

Getting There: From the *antigua* bus station in Guadalajara, take a **Guadalajara-Chapala** bus (tel. 376 56 75, 45min., every 30min. 6am-9:40pm, 15pesos); ask to be dropped off at Ajijic. Buses back to Chapala or Guadalajara can be caught along the route (45min., every hr. 6am-8:30pm, 15 pesos). From Chapala, take the bus to Ajijic from the bus station on Madero and Martinez (20min., every 15min. 6:15am-8:30pm, 3 pesos). It first weaves through the village of San Antonio, then goes on to Ajijic.

TEQUILA

Surrounded by gentle mountains and prickly, blue-green *agave* plants stretching as far as the eye can see, Tequila is a typical Mexican *pueblo* with a difference: since the 17th century, Tequila has been dedicated solely to the production and sale of its namesake. The town is home to 16 tequila distilleries, and nearly every business in town is linked to the liquor in some way. Tourism sustains a slew of t-shirt and souvenir shops as well as numerous liquor stores in the *centro* and along the route just outside of town. Although touristy (surprise!), the town is lots of fun and makes a great daytrip from Guadalajara.

◪ ORIENTATION AND PRACTICAL INFORMATION. The town is organized around the main plaza; all roads lead to and from it. From the bus station, follow the same road into town, turn right and then take your 1st left at the cathedral to reach the plaza. The distilleries are all within easy walking distance from downtown. The José Cuervo and Sauza plants, the two biggest distilleries, are next door to each other two blocks north of the plaza. Tequila's **tourist office** is located on the

TEQUILA TIME The best tequila, as the tour guides will tell you, bears a label boasting its content: 100% *agave*. Around 1600 varieties of this cactus exist in Mexico but only the blue *agave* is used to make tequila. Plants take eight to 12 years to mature, at which point their huge, dense centers (called *piñas*—pineapples—for their appearance) weigh 35-45kg. Once harvested, each plant provides around 5L of tequila. Not bad for a cactus. From the field, the *piñas* are taken to the factory where they are cooked for 36 hours in enormous traditional ovens, or for 12 hours in the modern and speedy autoclave. You can take a taste of a cooked *piña* on the factory tour—it's similar to a sweet potato. *Piñas* are then chopped and mixed with water and the stringy pulp that's strained off is used for rugs, animal food, and stuffing furniture. The remaining mixture is poured into huge tubs where it ferments, attracting bees, flies, ants, and other bugs that inevitably join this not-so-appetizing concoction. Only 10% of this mixture will actually become tequila. Be thankful for modern yeast fermentation—in the old days the options included naked, sweaty workers sitting in the vats, or throwing in a piece of animal dung wrapped in cloth. The tequila then goes through two distillations to remove the methanol and lower the alcohol content. The tequila is then aged in white oak barrels; the longer, the smoother. In the factory, you can take a sip of tequila after its first distillation, with an alcohol content as high as 80%. The whole process can only happen here: it's against the law to produce tequila anywhere but Jalisco and a few surrounding areas.

town's main plaza across from the Presidencia Municipal (open daily 10am-5pm). The staff will arrange tours of the distilleries and the museum. **Banamex**, at Sixto Gorjón and Juárez, has an **ATM** and exchanges money. The **police** wait on the Plaza Principal at José Cuervo 33, next to the tourist office.

☐ **FOOD.** Rather then spending the night and enjoying a Tequila sunrise, it's wiser to head back to Guadalajara at dusk. There's not a whole lot of choice in the dining department, either. One option is **Restaurant Bar El Sauzal**, Juárez 45, between Gorjón and Cuervo, home to a garish mural and beer-drinking locals (*bistec ranchero* 30 pesos; quesadillas 5 pesos; beer 8 pesos; open daily noon-11pm). True budget hunters will love the *pollo* roaster **Aricola**, Sixto Gorjón 20, where a roasted half-chicken goes for about 25 pesos (open daily 7:30am-4pm). Tortillas are available at the *tortillería* next door.

▣ **SIGHTS.** There's not much to do here other than drink or take a **tequila factory tour.** But hey, why else did you come to a town called Tequila? The tourist office will take you on a tour pretty much whenever you show up (daily 10am-5pm; 20 pesos), while the **Sauza** and **José Cuervo tours** kick off at the respective plants every hour (daily 9am-6pm; 20 pesos). To really see a factory in action, try to get there as early in the morning as possible and also avoid the *siesta* (2-4pm). For the price of a few shots, you'll learn more than you ever wanted to know about *agave* (the plant from which tequila is distilled), the distillation and aging processes, and the history of every *mariachi's* favorite liquor. The tourist office outing includes a stop in a small **tequila museum** and gift shop (open M-F 9am-2pm, Sa 9am-4pm), where you can sample the town's finest. The private tours end in the factories' very own bars, where the **first three shots** of assorted varieties of tequila are free; subsequent lip-puckering doses will run you 6-15 pesos. Those who can spare the pesos will find good deals on hard-to-find varieties and tequila-related knick-knacks for the folks back home.

✹ **FESTIVALS.** For 15 days beginning with a huge parade on the last Saturday of November, Tequila celebrates its **Feria Nacional del Tequila.** Each of the town's factories has its own day on which it holds rodeos, concerts, cockfights, fireworks, and other festivities. And of course, there are always plenty of drinks to go around.

Getting There: Buses to Tequila leave from Guadalajara's Antigua Central (2hr., about every 15min. 5:40am-9:15pm, 22 pesos) and return on the same schedule.

TLAQUEPAQUE

The "village" of Tlaquepaque is little more than the strip along Independencia and Av. Juárez, where upscale shops set in old colonial mansions sell silver, handicrafts, leather, ceramics, and other artistic objects. Although completely geared toward tourists, Tlaquepaque offers the best quality and prices for *artesanías* in the Guadalajara area (other than Tonalá). Just off its main square lies the *mercado*, where you can find cheaper goods of lesser quality.

Tlaquepaque was made for shopping, so bring your credit card and a big bag to carry your loot. The **Museo Regional de las Cerámicas y los Artes Populares de Jalisco,** Independencia 237 (tel. 635 54 04), at Alfareros, sells an interesting collection of antique regional crafts as well as newer pieces (open Tu-Sa 10am-6pm, Su 10am-3pm; free). Another fun, if touristy, spot is **La Rosa de Cristal,** Independencia 232 (tel. 639 71 80), at Alfareros, where artisans blow glass by hand and then sell their work at inflated prices (glass-blowing M-F 10:30am-1:30pm, Sa 10:30am-noon; shop open M-Sa 10am-6pm, Su 10am-2pm). There is a small **tourist information** booth on Independencia at the **Parque Hidalgo** (tel. 635 57 56). Fancy restaurants dot Independencia and offer menus in English, outside seating, and delicious food. More affordable meals can be found near the *mercado*. Forget about accommodations: come to Tlaquepaque during the day; sleep in Guadalajara at night.

Getting There: Take the local #275 or 275A bus or the "Tlaquepaque" TUR bus (30min. from Av. 16 de Septiembre). For the main markets, get off at Independencia, by the Pollo-Chicken joint on the left; if the driver turns left off Niños Héroes, you've gone too far. To get back to downtown Guadalajara, hop back on a #275 or TUR bus at the corner of Niños Héroes and Constitución, two blocks north of Independencia.

ZAPOPAN

Northwest of Guadalajara, the town of Zapopan is famous for the **Basílica de la Virgen de Zapopan,** a giant 16th-century edifice erected to commemorate a peasant's vision of the Virgin. The walls of the church are hung with many decades' worth of *ex votos,* small paintings on sheet metal recognizing the Virgin's aid in curing diseases. The image of the Virgin was made by natives from corn stalks in the 16th century. Pope John Paul II visited the shrine in 1979, and a statue of the pontiff holding hands with a beaming *campesino* boy now stands in the courtyard in front of the church. During the early fall, the figure of Our Lady of Zapopan is frequently exchanged from church to church throughout the state—each move occasions serious partying. On October 12 (*Día de la Raza,* the day Columbus landed in America), the figure makes her way from Guadalajara's cathedral to Zapopan, in the midst of a large procession. The impressive cathedral and spectacular plaza are the only real points of interest. The *mercado* adjacent to the fountain and tree-adorned plaza is the best place to take a break from lounging and grab a cheap taco or roasted chicken. Again, head back to Guadalajara to spend the night. The last bus leaves around 10pm.

Getting There: To reach Zapopan, catch the local #275A bus northbound on Av. 16 de Septiembre (40min., 3 pesos); ask the bus driver when to get off as the village is fairly non-descript.

TONALÁ

A shopper's paradise, **Tonalá** is a less accessible, mercifully less touristed version of Tlaquepaque and is most fun on market days (Th and Su). Activity centers around the **Plaza Principal** and spills out west to Av. Tonaltecas. Merchants, vendors, and restaurant owners sit around with their feet up and invite tourists in to scope their ornate metal or glassware. Women weave multi-colored rugs and sew dolls, while patient ceramics merchants paint personalized messages on their products. Here, the soft sell rules; merchants will take the time to talk with you, and you won't feel obliged to purchase anything. Tonalá specializes in inexpensive, decorated ceramics, high quality, low-priced silver, and glass dishes.

When you get tired of shopping, walk north of the city up the **Cerro de la Reina** for an astonishing view of Guadalajara. The **tourist office,** Zapata 275A (tel. 683 60 47 or 683 17 40; open M-F 9am-3pm), one block off the plaza, will be able to direct you to other worthy sights, such as the **Museo Nacional de la Cerámica,** where you can see how the beautiful pot you bought was made. The only hotel in town is **Hotel Tonalá,** Calle Madero 22 (tel 683 05 95), a block away from the plaza. Clean, airy rooms have fans and TV. Not surprisingly, the lobby is also an art gallery. (Singles 110 pesos; doubles 120 pesos; triples 160 pesos.)

Getting There: Local bus #275 or TUR bus #706, which run along Av. 16 de Septiembre, are the best ways to reach Tonalá (30min., 2 pesos). Get off at the intersection of Av. Tonalá and Tonaltecas. The rows of pottery stores will indicate that you've arrived. Tonaltecas is a main drag; bear right to reach the plaza.

PUERTO VALLARTA

Puerto Vallarta (pop. 150,000) is hard to compare to any other Mexican city because it really is nothing like a Mexican city. Its dependence on tourism has perfected its image into an expensive retreat that gift wraps a cushy and entertaining vacation for its visitors. But its success as a resort town, its upscale clubs and restaurants, and its nice hotels set it apart from the crumbling glamour of resorts like Acapulco. In 1956, tabloid headlines had the world fantasizing about Puerto Vallarta. The torrid affair between Richard Burton and Elizabeth Taylor while Burton was on location shooting John Huston's *Night of the Iguana* helped paint the city as the world headquarters of sensuality. At that time, Vallarta was still a remote and mysterious *pueblo* without phonelines or routes connecting it to the outside world. Forty years later, the city has become a world-class resort rife with showy mansions and groomed beaches—not quite the place to immerse yourself in Mexican culture.

The south end of town has virtually all the cheap hotels, best beaches, budget restaurants, and dance clubs. To the north, the hotels get more extravagant, and boutiques and restaurants cater almost exclusively to the thick-walleted. Farther north, international resorts line the route. On the outskirts, the mansions and property that are the fodder of glossy brochures sparkle in sensual luxuriance.

ORIENTATION

Running roughly east-west, **Río Cuale** bisects Puerto Vallarta before hitting the ocean. The main streets in the southern half of town are **Insurgentes** and **Vallarta,** which run north-south two blocks apart, and **Francisco Madero** and **Lázaro Cárdenas,** which run east-west one block apart. Most buses and *combis* pass along Insurgentes between Madero and Lázaro Cárdenas at some point on their route. Rte. 200 from Manzanillo runs into town south of the river, becoming Insurgentes. Insurgentes and Vallarta run north from Lázaro Cárdenas to the two bridges that link the south and north sections. The main streets in the northern section are **Morelos,** the continuation of Vallarta, and **Juárez,** one block east. Four blocks north of the river is the **Plaza Mayor;** its cathedral is an excellent landmark. The ritzy waterfront between Plaza Mayor and 31 de Octubre, called the **Malecón,** contains overpriced restaurants, clubs, and tacky shirt shops. **Paseo Díaz Ordaz** runs parallel to the Malecón, becoming **Av. México** to the north. North of the Malecón, Morelos becomes **Perú** and before joining the coastal route. North along the route lie the **airport,** the **marina,** and the **bus station.**

Taxis charge about 10 pesos to drive customers within the *centro* and about 32 pesos to go from the *centro* to the Marina Vallarta or to the airport in the north. **Buses** enter the city on Av. México, which becomes Díaz Ordaz. Any municipal bus operating south of the Sheraton or labeled "Centro" and all *cmbis* pass the plaza. Buses and *combis* labeled "Hoteles" pass the hotel strip. For the most part, buses stop only at the clearly marked *parada* signs and at the covered benches (buses and *combis* operate daily 6am-10:30pm; 2.50 pesos). To get downtown from the airport or the bus station, take a "Centro" or "Olas Altas" bus or a taxi. To get to the airport or the bus station from town, catch a "Novia Alta," "Marfil," or "Aeropuerto" bus on Lázaro Cárdenas, Insurgentes, or Juárez.

▚ PRACTICAL INFORMATION

TRANSPORTATION

Airport: 8km north of town via the route. Served by **Alaska** (tel. 1 13 50 or toll-free 95 800 426 0333), **American** (tel. 1 17 99 or toll-free 01 800 904 6000), **Continental** (tel. 1 10 25), **Mexicana** (tel. 4 89 00), and **Taesa** (tel. 1 15 31 or toll-free 01 800 904 6300).

Buses: The modern, mammoth, air-conditioned bus station is located north of the *centro*, just beyond the airport. Autocamiones Cihuatlán (tel. 1 00 21) has service south to: **Manzanillo** (5-6½hr., 12 per day 5am-11:30pm, 140 pesos). Second-class buses pass through: **Barra de Navidad** (5hr., 78 pesos); **Chamela** (3½hr., 52 pesos); **Melaque** (5hr., 77 pesos); and **Perula** (3½hr., 50 pesos). First-class service to: **Manzanillo** also stops in **Barra de Navidad** (3½hr., 92 pesos); and **Melaque** (3½hr., 91 pesos). Elite/Estrella Bianca (tel. 1 08 48 or 1 08 50) provides first-class service to: **Acapulco** (18hr., 1am, 418 pesos); **Aguascalientes** (9hr., 5:30pm, 353 pesos); **Ciudad Juárez** (36hr.) and 21 points in-between (5pm, 995 pesos); **Guadalajara** (5½hr., every hr. 6am-1:30am, 231 pesos); **Mexico City** (13hr., 5 per day 5:15-9pm, 519 pesos); and **San Blas** (3hr., 12:15 and 2:30pm, 89 pesos). ETN (tel. 1 05 50) serves: **Guadalajara** (5hr., 15 per day 12:30-11:15pm, 315 pesos); and **Mexico City** (12hr., 6:30 and 9pm, 710 pesos). Primera Plus (tel. 1 00 95) serves: **Aguascalientes** (9hr.; 2:30, 3:30, and 4:30pm; 380 pesos); **Colima** (7hr., 7:45am and 12:30pm, 165 pesos); **León** (9hr.; 12:45am, 10pm, and midnight; 405 pesos); **Manzanillo** (5-7hr., 6 per day 7am-10pm, 98-118 pesos) via **Melaque** (4hr., 96 pesos) or **Bahía de Navidad** (98 pesos); and **Querétaro** (12hr., 9pm, 340 pesos). Transportes de Pacífico (tel. 1 08 69), sends buses to: **Mexico City** (13hr., 6pm, 526 pesos) and **Tepic** (3½hr., every 30min. 4:15am-8pm and 10:30pm, 78 pesos).

Car Rental: Almost all car rental companies have offices on Calle Francisco Medina Ascencio, the hotel strip. Prices are high. **National,** Medina Ascencio km 1.5 (tel. 2 27 42 or 1 12 26 at the airport), has the lowest rates—a VW with tax, insurance, and 200km goes for US$45. **Thrifty,** Medina Ascencio km 5.5 (tel. 4 07 76 or 4 92 80), rents VWs for US$50 per day, including tax, insurance, and unlimited kilometers.

TOURIST AND FINANCIAL SERVICES

Tourist Office: (tel. 2 02 4), in the Presidencia Municipal, on the north side of the Pl. Mayor (enter on Juárez), and at Av. Medina Ascencio 1712 (tel. 3 07 44 or 3 08 44; tel./fax 2 02 43); the street is also known as Av. Las Palmas. Free maps, brochures, and *Passport,* a publication that lists bars and restaurants (only with American Express card). English spoken. Open M-F 9am-5pm.

Consulates: Canada (tel. 2 53 98; fax 2 35 17; open M-F 9am-5pm) and **U.S.** (tel. 2 00 69; fax 3 00 74; open M-F 10am-2pm) are both at Zaragoza 160 in the Vallarta Plaza, on the Pl. Mayor above "Subway."

Currency Exchange: Banamex (tel. 6 61 10), at Juárez and Zaragoza, in front of the Presidencia Municipal. Open M-F 9am-5pm, Sa 9am-2pm. **Bancrecer,** Olas Altas 246 (tel. 3 04 84), between Carranca and Badillo. Open M-F 9am-5pm, Sa 9am-2pm. Both banks have **ATMs.** *Casas de cambio* are everywhere, especially near the Malecón. Their rates are lower than the banks; better deals are generally found away from the beach. Usually open daily 9am-9pm.

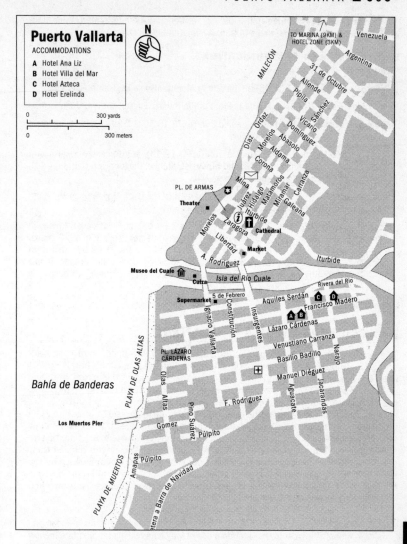

Puerto Vallarta

ACCOMMODATIONS

A Hotel Ana Liz
B Hotel Villa del Mar
C Hotel Azteca
D Hotel Erelinda

American Express: Morelos 660 (tel. 3 29 55; fax 3 29 26), at Abasolo. English spoken. Open M-F 9am-6pm, Sa 9am-1pm.

LOCAL SERVICES

Laundry: Laundry Aguamatic, Constitución 275 (tel. 2 59 78), between Lázaro Cárdenas and Carranza, charges 21 pesos to clean 3kg. Open M-Sa 9am-8pm.

📖 **Bookstore: Señor Book Café,** Olas Altas 490 (tel. 2 03 24), at Rodolfo Gómez. They exchange a used English book of theirs for two of yours or buy books for 10-20 pesos. Also serves coffee and cold drinks (12-16 pesos). Open daily 7am-11:30pm. Or try right up the street at **Una Página en el Sol,** Olas Alta 339 at Diéguez. They sell used English books for 20-30 pesos and serve terrific banana splits (25 pesos) or veggie sandwiches (20 pesos). Open daily 7:30am-midnight.

Supermarket: Gutiérrez Rico (tel. 2 02 22), at Constitución and Serdán. Open daily 6:30am-11pm. **La Ley,** México and Uruguay, is even bigger. Open 24hr.

EMERGENCY AND COMMUNICATIONS

Emergency: dial 060.

Police: (tel. 2 01 23 or 2 01 06) on Iturbide at Morelos. Some English. On-call 24hr.

Red Cross: (tel. 2 15 33) on Río de la Plata at Río Balsas. English spoken. Open 24hr.

Pharmacy: Farmacia CMQ, Basilio Badillo 365 (tel. 2 13 30 or 2 29 41), at Insurgentes, plus 4 other locations. All open 24hr.

Hospital: CMQ Hospital, Basilio Badillo 365 (tel. 3 19 19), at Insurgentes. English spoken. Open 24hr. Up the hill is **Hospital Medasist,** Manuel Diéguez 360 (tel. 3 04 44), at Aguacate. Some English spoken. Open 24hr.

Post Office: Mina 188 (tel. 2 18 88), left off Juárez past the Plaza Mayor. Open M-F 8am-7:30pm, Sa 9am-1pm. **Postal Code:** 48300.

Internet Access: Cafe.com, Olas Altas 250 (tel.fax 2 00 92), at F. Rodríguez. Chic café and small bar, plush sofas and fax and copy service. Internet use 5-30min. 20 pesos; 46-60min. 40 pesos. **The Net House,** Ignacio Vallarts 232 (tel. 2 69 53), at Lázaro Cárdenas. Email 1hr. 45 pesos, students with ID 30 pesos. Open 24hr. **Eclipse,** Juaréz 208 (tel. 4 49 50), by Plaza de Armas. Email use 15 pesos per 15min., 45 pesos per hr. English spoken at all 3 places.

Phone Code: 322.

▐ ACCOMMODATIONS AND CAMPING

The best budget hotels in Puerto Vallarta are south of Río Cuale, on or near Madero, and, although they are relatively cheap for Vallarta, almost all hotels cost at least 100 pesos per night. Make sure the fan in your room works before whipping out your wallet. Prices vary with the season: June is the least expensive month of the year, December the most expensive. Reservations for November through January should be made two months in advance. Even in July, reservations should be made a few days ahead of time. Officially, Vallarta frowns on shiftless beach bums, but most travelers who choose to camp encounter few problems. Some beachfront clubs have night guards who may keep an eye on those who request their permission before bedding down—a tip is appropriate. Many people sleep on the sand behind the Hotel Los Arcos or the Castle Pelícanos, or on the open space between the J. Newcombe tennis courts and the Sheraton. Exercise caution when selecting any camping site.

Hotel Azteca, Madero 473 (tel. 2 27 50), between Jacarandas and Naranjo. Clean and simple rooms at a great price. An abundance of long-term *huéspedes* lend to a friendly atmosphere. The brick and wrought-iron exterior and the giant leafy jungle plants set it apart. Fans and *agua purificada.* Long-distance phone for patrons. Singles 100 pesos; doubles 130 pesos; triples 160 pesos. Small suites with kitchen 200-250 pesos. Towel deposit 30 pesos.

Hotel Villa del Mar, Madero 440 (tel. 2 07 85 or 2 28 85), 2 blocks east of Insurgentes. Brick detailing, wooden doors, and lanterns hanging over brightly colored bedspreads give the well-scrubbed rooms a rustic feel. Spiral staircases wind around Mexican and Cuban flags to a rooftop terrace with a fabulous view of the *centro.* Try for a room with a balcony. Singles 100 pesos; doubles 120 pesos. Towel deposit 15 pesos.

Hotel Ana Liz, Madero 429 (tel. 2 17 57), at Jacarandas, has basic, small, dim rooms with tiny bathrooms. Tasteful landscape photos do their best to brighten up the place. Singles 100 pesos; doubles 130 pesos; triples 150 pesos. Towel deposit 40 pesos.

🌀 FOOD

Puerto Vallarta's Malecón specializes in tourist traps with *norteamericano* cuisine, but some excellent, decently priced restaurants can be found elsewhere on the north side. Near the beach on the south side, many upscale restaurants are built especially for gringos, particularly on the blocks enclosed by Basilio Badillo to the south, Olas Altas (the beachfront) to the east, Lázaro Cárdenas to the west, and Constitución to the south. Cheaper down-home eateries cluster along Madero, in the **market** (open M-Sa 8am-8pm) on the north side, where Insurgentes crosses Río Cuale, and along Calle México to the north. Taco and quesadilla stands thrive south of the river.

🍴 La Casa de los Hot Cakes, Badillo 289 (tel. 2 62 72), at Constitución has a stupendously good breakfast. Indulge in the specialty pancake or waffle platters (22-30 pesos) or delectable cheese blintzes (33 pesos). Also serves lighter fare (scrambled egg whites 20 pesos) and traditional Mexican *desayunos* (*chilaquiles* 23 pesos). Open daily 8am-2pm.

La Fonda China Poblana Restaurante y Bar, Insurgentes 222 (tel. 2 31 70), between Cárdenas and Carranza. An open-air ground floor with wood and wicker tables to prop up the weary in the wee hours gives way to an airy second floor with a balcony. Breakfast 15-20 pesos; *enchiladas suizas* 35 pesos; beer 10 pesos. Open 7am-2am.

Restaurant Buffet Vegetariano, Iturbide 270 (tel. 2 30 73), at Hidalgo, a few blocks inland from Plaza Mayor and up the steep steps of Iturbide. 100% vegetarian cuisine, with a strong Indian influence. Brightly painted yellow walls decorated with designs provide solace for hungry businesspeople and tourists. Buffet includes beans, rice, and soy patties (35 pesos). Open M-Sa noon-7pm.

Café de Olla, Basilio Badillo 168 (tel. 3 16 26), 1 block from the beach. A tourist joint with attentive waiters, reasonable prices (for Vallarta, that is), and exceptional food. *Mariachis* weave between tables to serenade vacationers. Beautiful burgers 35 pesos; *chiles rellenos* 35 pesos. Open daily M and W-Su 10am-11pm.

La Fonda Dianita, Madero 243 and Vallarta. Find a table (if you can) in this teensy local favorite, and enjoy tasty and filling *comida corrida* (25 pesos). Clean and cheap. Open daily 8am-6pm.

🏖 SAND AND SIGHTS

Although the veneer of tourism detracts somewhat from Puerto Vallarta's natural beauty, the panorama of the city's 40km of coastline and surrounding palm-tree covered mountains is still enchanting. Some of the least crowded and most gorgeous beaches stretch along the coast south of town on the road to **Mismaloya** (see p. 398) and north into Nayarit. The most popular beach within the Puerto Vallarta city limits is **Playa de los Muertos** (Beach of the Dead), a strip in front of the south side's costliest hotels. It begins at its southern end with a rocky cliff spotted with small white homes, and north to a small dock that separates it from the **Playa de Olas Altas** (High Waves Beach). To get there, walk all the way west on Lázaro Cárdenas and then south along Playa de Olas Altas which continues to the Río Cuale, then becomes the rocky **Malecón** (boardwalk). Near the southern end of Playa de los Muertos is a small section of the beach known as **Las Sillas Azules** (the blue chairs), one of Mexico's only **gay (male) beaches.**

Water sports are very popular, particularly during the morning hours. This is your chance to go **parasailing** (US$30 a shot, prices negotiable); parachutes are scattered on the Playa de Olas Altas and the beaches along the hotel strip, and owners will descend upon you like vultures if you look even remotely interested. **Wave runners** (doubles 250 pesos for 30min.), **banana boat** rides (50 pesos per person), **kayaks** (80 pesos per hr.), and **waterskiing** (500 pesos per hr.) are also there for the taking. **Bahía Deportes Aquaticos,** Olas Altas 477A (tel./fax 3 24 94), across from Señor Book Café, offers scuba certification classes (1 week, 8hr. per day,

US$350), and introductory scuba diving classes (1½hr., US$15). Ask about renting cheaper scuba equipment, snorkeling equipment, and boats for excursions. (Open daily 7am-7pm.) Equestrian fanatics can boot the shore and take to the hills on **horseback;** rentals are available near Daiquiri Dick's on Olas Altas, at Carranza (horses 70-80 pesos per hr.; open daily around 7am-5:30pm).

   Isla Río Cuale lies between and underneath two bridges spanning the ponderous **Río Cuale.** A cool pathway runs the length of the verdant island among small stores selling postcards, jewelry, and souvenirs. The **Museo del Cuale,** at the seaward end of the island, houses interesting displays on Mesoamerican culture and the region's history (open Tu-Sa 10am-7pm, Su 10am-2pm; free). During the day, the walk along the river is pleasant, but do not try it alone after dark. The river can also be reached from the north via Zaragoza. Stairs, beginning behind the Church of Guadalupe, lead up the mini-mountain amid bougainvillea and hibiscus into the wealthy **Zaragoza** neighborhood, known locally as **Gringo Gulch.** The prominent bridge spanning the apex of the street connects Elizabeth Taylor's humble pad with Richard Burton's.

◪ NIGHTLIFE

After dark, Puerto Vallarta offers something for everyone, whether it's a cocktail in the moonlight or the chance to thrash across a crowded dance floor. The **Malecón** swarms with hundreds of young Mexicans and Americans batting eyelashes and showcasing their newly tanned bods. Most of the action is along **Díaz Ordaz** on the northern waterfront, where clubs and restaurants cater to suntanned professionals quaffing pricey rum drinks and dancing to U.S. Top-40 tunes. Discos are aimed at those who don't mind dropping 50-70 pesos for cover and 15-20 pesos for a drink. For those clubs with covers, save a small fortune by obtaining free passes (which may not be honored during peak tourist season) from the condo-hawkers who lurk around the Malecón. Most discos aren't worth visiting until 11pm or midnight; the time before then is better spent tossing back drinks in cheap bars. Vallarta has sprouted a thriving **gay scene,** and boasts several clubs catering exclusively to gay men and, occasionally, to lesbians.

   Nightlife transportation is greatly aided by the "Marina Vallarta" bus, which goes to the marina, and the "Pitillal" bus, which will take you just past the hotel strip. After 11pm, you're stuck with a cab (about 40 pesos to the *centro*). For some entertaining air-conditioning, take in a movie (20 pesos) at **Cine Bahía,** Insurgentes 189 (tel. 2 17 17), between Madero and Serdán.

BARS AND CLUBS

   Carlos O'Brian's Bar & Grill & Clothesline (tel. 2 14 44), Díaz Ordaz at Pípila. The only things hanging out to dry here are totally trashed high-school students who've forgotten the names of their hotels. Teens bounce between here, **Kahlúa** (tel. 2 24 86), a few blocks south on the waterfront, and the **Zoo,** Díaz Ordaz 638 (tel. 2 49 45), next door (high-season weekend cover 50 pesos). It's the biggest party in town—block-long lines wrap around the building all night. There is even a taxi stand in front to help you avoid a long, stumbling walk home. Open daily 9am-4am.

   Collage (tel. 1 08 61 62), next to Marina Vallarta, is big enough to house all of Vallarta. Bowling, pool tables, video games, a sushi bar (with cholera-free fish shipped from abroad), a sports bar in back, temporary tattoo parlors, an Internet cafe, bars, and a high-tech dance floor. Cover 50 pesos after 9pm. No cover M; no cover W for women; open bar Th. Cover 80 pesos for women, 120 pesos for men. Open daily 11am-6am.

   J & B (tel. 4 46 16), Medina Ascencio km 2.5 toward the hotel zone. An older crowd dances to live *salsa*, merengue, and the occasional Michael Jackson tune. The raised dance floor makes it impossible to be shy, and fun to be bold. Those determined not to dance can play pool instead. Cover 50 pesos. Open daily 10pm-5am.

El Faro (tel. 1 05 41), in the Marina Vallarta. An elegant lighthouse bar 35m above ground provides a fantastic view of Puerto Vallarta, especially at sunset. Live music M-Sa after 10:30pm. 2-drink minimum. Open daily 5pm-2am.

Club Roxy, Ignacio de Vallarta 217, between Madero and Carranza. A clientele of *extranjeros* jams to live reggae, blues, and rock and roll. Santana and Bob Marley covers are skillfully sung to a crowd of beer guzzlers (15 pesos) of all ages. No cover. Open M-Sa 8am-3am.

Cuiza (tel. 2 56 46), on Isla Río Cuale, at the foot of the *puente nuevo.* Doesn't get any mellower than this: find a table on the shady patio, order a margarita, and listen to the jazz. Mexican professionals and lots of new-waveish gringo couples. Live music daily 8pm-closing. Open daily 9am-1am; low season 5pm-midnight.

GAY NIGHTLIFE

A **gay cruise,** departing daily at noon from the Los Muertos pier, takes partners Noah's ark-style to a private gay beach (includes drinks, snorkeling, and table dancing; around US$45). Tickets are available from travel agents or time-share hawkers; for more info, ask at Paco Paco (below), or see www.pacopaco.com.

🖎 **Paco Paco,** Ignacio Vallarta 278 at Lázaro Cárdenas. Vallarta's hottest gay disco, with great music, lots of floor space, mirrors, strobe lights, and aquariums has a rooftop bar for a relaxing view of the sunset before kicking-off the night. The friendly owner is a fount of information on Vallarta's gay scene. It's also home to Paco's Tanch, around the corner on Carranza, a "man's bar" that hosts different theme nights as well as stripper dance shows at midnight. Ladies pay 80 pesos to enter. Cover Th-Su 30 peso for men, 60 pesos for women with 1 drink. Open daily noon-6am.

Porque No, Morelos 101 (tel. 2 63 92), on the Plaza Río next to the Vallarta Bridge. Art Deco coffee and video bar (with pool tables) sits above the vibrations of a rocking basement below. Wall-to-wall dancing—perhaps because there's no room at the bar. Almost exclusively gay men. Happy Hour noon-8pm. Open daily noon-4am.

Los Balcones, Juárez 182 (tel. 2 46 71), at Libertad. International gay crowd practices looking languid on the balconies. Scantily dressed patrons sizzle on the neon-lit dance floor. Starts hopping at 11:30pm. F mixed drinks half-off. M beer 10 pesos. Cover F-Sa 10-15 pesos. Open daily 9pm-4am.

NEAR PUERTO VALLARTA

SOUTHERN COAST

Vallarta's most popular beaches lie a few kilometers south of the city itself. The first few you'll come across are monopolized by resorts and condos, and though they're nicer and quieter than the ones back in town, access to them is usually only through the hotels. Farther down the coast lies **Los Arcos,** a group of pretty rock islands hollowed out in some spots by pounding waves. The coastline here lacks sand, but it still serves as a platform from which to start the 150m swim to the islands. Bring a mask or goggles, or risk missing the tropical fish that flit through the underwater reefscape. Flippers are useful against the heavy currents but mind your step—the coral is sharp enough to draw blood; use caution and swim with a friend. To get to Los Arcos, take the bus to Mismaloya and ask the driver to stop at Hotel de los Arcos. The beautiful crescent beach of **Mismaloya** lies just around the bend to the south. Best known as the setting of *Night of the Iguana* and Arnold Schwarzenegger's *cinéma vérité* classic, *Predator*, Mismaloya has recently been encircled by large hotels and is only slightly less crowded than the beaches in town. **Xanadu** is a gay club near this beach. Farther down, the road veers away from the coast just beyond the **Boca de Tomatlán;** this narrow cove contains only a small beach but offers a breather from the touristy hubbub of the northern coastline. The last place to check out on the southern road is **Chico's Paradise,** 5km inland from the Boca de Tomatlán. Wash down the view of the **Tomatlán Falls** with a drink at Chico's huge, airy *palapas.*

South along the coast lies the beaches of Las Ánimas, Quimixto, and Yelapa, all of which are only accessible from the ocean. That doesn't stop hordes of tourists from visiting the lovely beaches, accessible by cruise boats from Vallarta. **Las Ánimas** and **Quimixto** are twins, both boasting long stretches of unoccupied sand backed by small villages and a few *palapas*. Quimixto also offers a small waterfall as an alternative to the beach-weary. The trip can be made in an hour by foot from the beach or in 30 minutes by rented mule. **Scuba** trips (organized by Outcast) also make their way from downtown Vallarta and Mismaloya to these beaches. **Yelapa,** a destination of the popular boat ride and highly touted by locals, is a bit of a fake. Supposedly a secluded peasant fishing village, its seemingly simple *palapa* huts were designed by a *norteamericano* architect whose definition of "rustic" apparently included interior plumbing and hot water. Many of these *palapas* are occupied for only part of the year, and short- and long-term rentals can be arranged easily for varying and sometimes surprisingly low prices. The beach fills with hawkers and parasailers during the day, but the town, a 15-minute walk from the beach, remains *tranquilo*, with waterfalls and nude bathing upstream and poetry readings downstream. Don't miss the secluded swimming hole at the top of the stream that runs through town; follow the path along the stream uphill; just before the restaurant, duck under the water pipes to the right of the trail and head up the track. About 15m before it rejoins the stream, an inconspicuous trail leads off to the left to a deep pool that overlooks the bay.

Getting There: Buses run to Mismaloya from the corner of Constitución and Badillo in Puerto Vallarta (every 10min. 6:20am-10:30pm, 3 pesos; returning on the same schedule). Taxis to Mismaloya cost 50 pesos. Buses labeled "Tuito" run to Chico's Paradise from the corner of Carranza and Aguacate (every 30min. 5am-9pm, 8 pesos). **Taxis Acuáticos** are the cheapest way to get to the boats-only beaches. They leave from the Muelle de los Muertos and stop at Las Ánimas, Quimixto, and Yelapa (45min.; departs at 11am, returns at 4pm; 60 pesos each way). If you prefer something more organized, **cruises** to points south of Vallarta leave the marina every day starting at 9am and return around 4pm. The cheapest cruises to Yelapa are 180 pesos, including breakfast and music. The more expensive cruises include dinner and an open bar. Information about these ritzy tours can be found in the tourist office, at any large hotel, or at the marina.

NORTHERN COAST

Bahía de Banderas (Bay of Flags), the bay that Puerto Vallarta calls home, owes its name to a blunder: when Nuño Beltrán de Guzmán sailed here in 1532, he mistook the colorful headdresses of the thousands of natives awaiting him for flags. The northern edge of the bay has some of the prettiest and least-exploited beaches on Mexico's central Pacific coast. Nuevo Vallarta, the largest and southernmost of nine small towns on the north bay, is 150km south of Tepic and 20km north of Puerto Vallarta.

Protected by a sandy cove, **Playa Piedra Blanca** has wonderfully calm waters. Farther north along the bay is **Playa las Destiladeras,** named for the freshwater pools formed by water trickling through the rocky cliff. Although the sandy bottom is colored with occasional rocks, the rougher waves make this strip of beach perfect for body-surfers and boogie boarders. **Punta de Mita,** the northernmost point along the bay, is a lagoon sheltered by two rock islets. It is marked by the **Corral de Riscos,** a living reef. Freshwater showers (2 pesos) in Destiladeras make the bus ride home more comfortable. Bring a bag lunch to avoid inflated prices in beachside *palapas*.

Getting There: From Puerto Vallarta, flag down a Camiones del Pacífico "Punta de Mita" second-class bus on Lázaro Cárdenas, Insurgentes, Juárez, or Medino Ascencio (every 20min. 9am-5pm, returning until 5pm; to **Piedra Blanca** 40min., 10 pesos; to **Destiladeras** 1hr., 13 pesos; to **Punta de Mita** 1¼hr. plus a 4km walk, 15 pesos).

BAHÍA DE CHAMELA

The tranquil and secluded Bahía de Chamela, 60km northwest of Melaque, marks the northern point of Jalisco's "Ecological Tourism Corridor." A chain of small rocky islands breaks the horizon, while 11km of golden-brown sand dotted with gnarled driftwood and the occasional *palapa* beckon to the pensive beachcomber. Although Chamela receives its share of tourism, especially in December and April, the Midas touch has yet to spoil the natural beauty and seclusion of the bay. This, however, presents other problems; lone travelers (particularly women) and small groups should use common sense in deciding which beaches to visit, particularly during the low season.

🔃 ORIENTATION AND PRACTICAL INFORMATION. Second-class buses from **Puerto Vallarta** to **Manzanillo** (3½hr., 40 pesos) pass through **Perula,** as do buses going from **Melaque** or **Barra de Navidad** to **Puerto Vallarta** (1½hr., 29 pesos) or **Manzanillo** (3hr., 53 pesos). Always tell the bus driver where you're going in advance so you don't miss the stop. To get to Playa Perula, get off by the big white "Playa Dorada" sign and walk 30 minutes down a winding dirt road—don't be surprised if friendly locals offer you a ride. To get to Playa Chamela, get off farther south at "El Súper," marked by the colorful figure directing passersby to the Villa Polinesia; walk 15 minutes down the country road until you hit the beach. Perula is a 30 minute walk along the shore. Hotels in Perula will also come pick you up or send a taxi. Unfortunately, there's only a **LADATEL** phone outside the Primera Plus Station; your best bet for placing a long-distance call is cajoling one of the hotel or restaurant owners into letting you call collect. To get back, catch a Primera Plus bus from that station. They head to: **Guadalajara** (3hr.; 8, 10:30am, and 4pm; 50 pesos); **Manzanillo** (2½-5hr., every hr. 7:30am-10:30pm, 50-65 pesos) via **Melaque** (1½hr., 27-35 pesos); and **Puerto Vallarta** (every hr., 7:30am-10:30pm, 65 pesos).

🔃 ACCOMMODATIONS AND FOOD. The **Hotel Punta Perula** (tel. 328 5 50 20) the corner of Juárez and Tiburón, two blocks from the beach, features a massive courtyard laden with trees and overhanging hammocks that eclipse the comfortable, floral rooms (low season singles 110 pesos, doubles 170 pesos; high season singles 140 pesos doubles 190 pesos). In Perula, **Tejamar Restaurante y Cuartos** (tel. 328 5 53 61), on the corner of Independencia and the *carretera* (route) on the *jardín*, one block south of Hotel Punta Perula and less than a block from the beach, is a small, family-run taco restaurant and *posada*. Its basic rooms have ceiling fans and open onto a small courtyard. Friendly owners are eager to accommodate guests with bargain meals, trips to the nearby islands, and weekly discounts. (Singles and doubles with communal bath 90 pesos; private bath 110 pesos.) Feast on the catch of the day as you relax under palm frond umbrellas at **Mariscos La Sirena** (tel. 328 5 51 14), one of the several *palapas* along the shore. La Sirena serves shrimp (45 pesos) and fish (40 pesos) and a cold one costs 8 well-spent pesos. (Open daily 7am-8pm, or until the last person leaves.)

🔃 BEACHES. Punta de Perula, the bay's northernmost point, shelters **Playa Perula,** making it perfect for swimming. A 30-minute walk down the coast along completely virgin beach will bring you to the **Villa Polinesia Motel and Campsite,** marking **Playa Chamela.** Here, and farther south, the rougher waves invite bodysurfing and boogie-boarding, but watch out for a frequent and powerful undertow. **Perula** is a tiny fishing *pueblo* that lacks most services beyond a few hotels and seafood *palapas* but still keeps its visitors content with a charming beach. Continuing south will bring you to **Playa Rosada** and even more secluded beaches. The occasional *palapa* refreshes the parched and weary body-surfer, and *lanchas* from Playa Perula transport wannabe Crusoes to the nearby islands (round-trip about 250 pesos).

BAHÍA DE NAVIDAD

Along with Guadalajara and Puerto Vallarta, Bahía de Navidad forms one vertex of Jalisco's "Tourist Triangle." Power is not shared equally within the triumvirate, however. With the exception of December and *Semana Santa*, few tourists are spotted on the placid shores of Bahía de Navidad. The *bahía*, a sheltered cove of talcum sand and shimmering water, is home to the towns of **Melaque** and **Barra de Navidad**. It is a wonder that more vacationers don't come here year-round—the water is gorgeous, the beach long and empty, and the whole bay is enclosed by scenic, rocky cliffs. During high season, however, growing pains are more evident—the beach between the towns is transformed into a river of bronzed bodies, and hotels in both towns overflow with tourists. Change is in the air: restaurants, hotels, and clubs are sprouting with greater frequency; a Xanadu-esque hotel at the end of the bay opened in early 1997, and a 300-boat marina under construction threatens to overwhelm the bay with hordes of yachting foreigners.

Although Barra and Melaque lie only five kilometers from each other, they are worlds apart. Barra offers few places to eat and sleep and a steep beach with powerful undertow (better for surfing or boogie-boarding than swimming), but the town itself is pretty. Melaque treats visitors to gentle, choppy waves and an abundance of budget accommodations. However, it is hot and dusty and tends to be full of shell and bikini shops unlike the artisan stores of nearby Barra.

Melaque and Barra de Navidad are 55km northwest of Manzanillo on Rte. 200 and 240km southwest of Guadalajara on Rte. 54. Melaque is the northernmost of the two. They're well-connected by road: **municipal buses** shuttle between the two towns (20min., every 15min. 6:20am-9:30pm, 1-1.50 pesos). Larger buses head to Manzanillo on the hour and are slightly more expensive (around 5 pesos) but faster and more comfortable. Of course, the 40-minute walk along the beach is the hard-core budget option. Don't walk after sunset; some dangerous encounters have been reported. **Taxis** cost 25 pesos.

BAHÍA DE NAVIDAD: MELAQUE

The placid town of Melaque offers little besides ambling through the *zócalo*, splashing around in the waves, and nibbling on fresh fish as you watch the sunset from a beachside restaurant, but no one seems to complain. There's not much to do in beautiful Melaque, which suits the place just fine.

⊓ ORIENTATION AND PRACTICAL INFORMATION. Melaque's bus station (tel. 5 50 03) is on **Gómez Farías**, the parallel-to-the-beach main drag. From the bus station, turn left on Gómez Farías and walk two blocks to reach **López Mateos**. Another left turn takes you to the plaza, a few blocks inland. López Mateos and **Hidalgo** are the main cross-streets toward the ocean.

Autocamiones Cihuatlán (tel. 5 50 03) sends **buses** to: **Guadalajara** (6½hr., 21 per day 12:15am-10:30pm, 130 pesos); **Manzanillo** (1½hr., every 30min. 5:30am-9:30pm, 22-27 pesos); and **Puerto Vallarta** (5hr., 12 per day 3am-11:30pm, 77-91 pesos) via **Chamela** (1½hr., 22 pesos) and **Perula** (1½hr., 27 pesos). A few doors down, Primera Plus, Gómez Farías 34 (tel. 5 61 10), has service to: **Guadalajara** (5hr., 7 per day 9:15am-1:15am, 130-155 pesos); **Manzanillo** (1½hr., 15 per day 2am-10:30pm, 22-27 pesos); and **Puerto Vallarta** (5½hr., 8 per day 1:45pm-9pm, 91-107 pesos); second-class service passes through **Chamela** (1½hr., 25 pesos) and **Perula** (1½hr., 29 pesos).

Banamex (tel. 5 52 77 or 5 53 52) is on Gómez Farías, across from the bus station and has a 24-hour. **ATM** (open M-F 9am-3pm, Sa 9am-2pm; changes traveler's checks daily 9am-noon). **Police:** Upstairs at López Mateos 52 (tel. 5 50 80), north of the plaza. **Red Cross:** (tel. 5 23 00) 15km away in Cihuatlán, accessible by buses that leave from the plaza (every 15min. 6am-8pm, 4 pesos) or by taxi (50 pesos). **Supermarket: Súper Farmacia Plaza**, López Mateos 48 (tel. 5 51 67), on the south side of the plaza (open M-Sa 8am-3pm and 5-10pm, Su 8am-2:30pm and 6:30-10pm). **Medical Assistance: Clínica de Urgencias**, Carranza 22 (tel. 5 61 44), two blocks from the bus station. **Post office:** Orozco 13 (tel. 5 52 30), two blocks left of the plaza as you face the beach, in the green building on your left (open M-F 8am-3pm, Sa 8am-noon). **Postal code:** 48980. **Internet access:** available inside the *centro commercial*, Gómez Farías 27A (tel. 5 59 19), next to the *casa de cambio* (open M-Sa noon-2:30pm, 4-6pm, and 8:30-10pm). **Casetas:** next to the bus station is **Yimmi's,** Gómez Farías 34 (tel. 5 63 10; fax 5 54 52; open M-Sa 8:30am-9pm, Su 8:30am-3pm; in high season open daily until 10pm). The public telephones by the bus station can be used for **long-distance collect calls. Phone code:** 335.

⌐⌐ ACCOMMODATIONS AND FOOD. Melaque boasts a crop of snazzy hotels, but few of them are legitimate budget accommodations (good bargains occasionally lurk among the beachside bungalows). Expect rates to rise, of course, during high season. If you don't mind a little innocent proselytizing, **Hotel Emanuel,** Bugambilias 89 (tel. 5 61 07), is half a block from the beach and has clean rooms or bungalows. Turn right on Gómez Farías from the bus station and walk about five blocks turning left after the large blue house; look for the "Abarrotes Emanuel" sign. Spacious rooms have floral decor and clean, white-tile bathrooms. (Singles 70 pesos, with kitchen 120 pesos; doubles 90 pesos, with kitchen 160 pesos.) **Casa de Huéspedes San Juan,** Gomez Fariás 24 (tel. 5 52 70), is right out of the bus station and on the first block across from the bank. The rooms are a bit old and worn, but they're the best deal in town. There is a large, sunny courtyard and kitchen units are in some rooms. (Singles 50 pesos; 4-person bedroom with kitchen 250 pesos.)

During the summer, restaurants ship in shrimp from the north, but come high season, local fishing boats catch everything that is served on the waterfront. Cheaper, more authentic Mexican places are near the central plaza. Cheaper still are the sidewalk food stands that materialize after sunset and the unnamed, dirt-floored eateries in the *mercado*. On the *zócalo* sits **Cafeteria Siete,** López Mateos (tel. 5 64 21). It's not much, but this small joint offers terrific food at incredibly low prices. Try a filling *comida corrida* (15 pesos) or hot *tortas* for about 12 pesos. A happening place to grab dinner is **Caxcan Restaurant** on the corner of the *zócalo* above the pharmacy as you enter from López Mateos. While munching on seafood specialties, the bar hands out cheap two-for-one drinks to wash back the fishies. (Open daily 6pm-1am.)

◪ SAND, SURF, AND ENTERTAINMENT. The main attraction in Melaque is, of course, the beach. Waves get smaller and the beach more crowded toward the western end of Melaque's sandy strip. Rent **jet-skis** at the Restaurant Moyo (tel. 7 11 04), on the far west end of the beach (200 pesos for 30min., 2-person maximum; available daily 10am-7pm). Be prepared to get wet if you go for a spin in a **banana boat** (25 pesos). Drivers regularly dump unsuspecting riders into the ocean. Nightlife in Melaque focuses on the beach until 9:30 or 10 in the evening when people still swim and stroll along the sand while enjoying the remnants of the glorious sunset. The after-hours oasis of Melaque's under-30 tourist crowd is **Disco Tanga** (tel. 5 54 72 or 5 54 75), on Gómez Farías,. Multicolored walls and stairs lined by strip lights create a game show effect. (Cover 20-30 pesos. Open daily in high season, F-Sa off-season, 9pm-2am.) For something a bit more mellow and smoky, you can always twirl cues with the middle-aged men at **Billiard San Patricio,** Melaque's pool hall, on Orozco and Juárez, up the street from the post office, three blocks from the *zócalo* (pool and *carambola* 10 pesos per hr., dominoes 3 pesos per hr.; open daily 11am-11pm). This is exactly the place women might want to avoid. Don't get your hopes up during the low season, though; nightlife just about dies for those months of the year.

BAHÍA DE NAVIDAD: BARRA DE NAVIDAD

Of the two cities, Barra is smaller and has less crowded beaches (due to the strong undertow) than its sister Melaque. However, its shaded streets, numerous sidewalk eateries and popular seaside bars give it a vitality that Melaque lacks. The saltwater *lagún* at the end of town also makes a great place to swim, play volleyball, or sunbathe. Barra doesn't offer much, but who could ask for more?

🔢 ORIENTATION AND PRACTICAL INFORMATION. Barra de Navidad is a narrow peninsula flanked on its eastern shore by a salty, sleeping *laguna* while the restless waves tug at its western shore. Virtually everything closes during low season. **Veracruz,** the main street, runs towards the southeast, angling off at its end. There it meets **Legazpi,** another main street, which runs north-south, hugging the beach. Barra de Navidad's bus stop is at Veracruz 226, on the corner of Nayarit. Turn left on Veracruz from the bus station to get to the *centro*. **Buses** depart from Autocamiones Cihuatlán, Veracruz 228 (tel. 5 52 65), at Michoacán, to: **Guadalajara** (6hr., 17 per day 3:15am-10:20, 131 pesos), and **Puerto Vallarta** (5½hr., 10 per day 7am-9:15pm, 78-93 pesos); second-class buses pass through **Chanela** (1½hr., 25 pesos), and **Perula** (1½hr., 27 pesos). Primera Plus/Costa Alegre, Veracruz 269 (tel. 5 61 11), at Filipinas, has service to: **Guadalajara** (6½hr., 9 per day 8:15am-10:15pm, 156 pesos), and **Manzanillo** (1¼-5hr., 6 per day 11:45am-7:30pm, 26-78 pesos). Second-class buses stop at **Chamela** (1½hr., 22 pesos), and **Perula** (1½hr., 27 pesos).

The **tourist office** is at Jalisco 67 (tel. 5 51 00; open M-F 9am-5pm). The friendly Texans at **Crazy Cactus** (tel. 5 60 99), next to the church on Jalisco, between Legazpi and Veracruz, can help with insider's advice. The **travel agency,** Veracruz 204A (tel. 5 56 65, 66; fax 5 56 67), sells tickets for ETN buses departing from Manzanillo (open M-Sa 9am-8pm). Barra has no bank, but a **casa de cambio,** Veracruz 212C (tel. 5 61 77), exchanges money at a less-than-ideal rate (open M-Sa 9am-2pm and 4-7pm, Su 9am-2pm). Barra de Navidad is without a *caseta*, so your best long-distance calling option is to use LADATEL calling cards. **Emergency:** dial 060. **Police:** Veracruz 179 (tel. 5 53 99). **Centro de Salud:** (tel. 5 62 20), on Puerto de la Navidad down Veracruz, just out of town. Make a right just after the signs for El Márquez, just before Veracruz becomes a route; the *Centro* is the second building on the right, with the red-and-white gate. **Postal code:** 48987. **Phone code:** 335.

🛏 ACCOMMODATIONS AND CAMPING. Budget accommodations in Barra are available only to the keen-eyed traveler but reasonable accommodations are sometimes available in private residences—ask around and look for signs in restaurants. All prices are subject to hikes during the high season. It's no longer possible to camp in Barra de Navidad; try Melaque instead. **Hotel Caribe,** Sonora 15 (tel. 5 57 48), has decent pastel rooms with fans and fluorescent-lit desks. The large lobby is enlivened by socializing elderly ladies. (Singles 110 pesos; doubles 150 pesos.) **Bungalows Karelia,** the large aqua-colored building on Legazpi, is a good deal for three or more people. Airy but worn suites house a refrigerator, table, stove, fan, and kitchen utensils. The romantic little loveseats aren't shabby either. (Suites for 2 people 220 pesos, each extra person 20 pesos.)

For delicious, inexpensive Mexican food in a pleasant atmosphere, try **Restaurant Paty,** Jalisco 52 at Veracruz—red tablecloths are even brighter in the outdoor sunshine (grilled *pollo* 23 pesos, enchiladas 12 pesos; open daily 7am-11pm). A good place for some serious eating is **Bananas** (tel. 5 6 16 63), on Legazpi, which serves hearty American-style breakfasts and dinners.

🎿🏄 SIGHTS AND ENTERTAINMENT. Crazy Cactus (tel. 5 60 99), at the corner of Jalisco and Veracruz, is closed during the summer months but rents equipment during the rest of the year. **Snorkeling equipment** and **boogie boards** are 50 pesos for a half-day and 80 pesos for a full day. **Surfboards** are 70 pesos for a half-day and 120 pesos for a full day; **bikes** are 100 pesos for a full day. Serious fishers will want to call **Z Pesca,** Legazpi 213 (tel. 5 64 64 www.zpesca.com), for a day-long **deep-sea fishing** expedition (1200 pesos per day for up to 4 people; 4hr. 900 pesos. Open daily 9am-9pm, low season 9am-7pm).

The short trip across the lagoon to the village of **Colimilla** is pleasant; a *lancha* will deposit up to 10 passengers at the far end of the lagoon or amid Colimilla's palms, pigs, cows, and open-air restaurants (60 pesos). Deserted **Playa de los Cocos,** 1km away, has larger breakers than those in Barra. If you don't want to swim back,

TELENOVELA, ANYONE? Every evening, grown men and women across Mexico will be found glued to their TV sets, clutching boxes of tissues and seeming impervious to the outside world. Why? They are watching *telenovelas*, the strange hybrids between soap operas and mini-series that monopolize Mexico's airwaves from afternoon to late night. Mexico has made a name for itself internationally with these heart-wrenching and addictive shows. Each *telenovela* lasts between six months and one year and contains enough cliched love stories, tragedies, and cliffhangers to put all other series to shame. In fact, characters and story lines are added and removed according to ratings; as a result, each show's plot is, in part, guided by audience response. This explains why the protagonist of a poorly watched show might suddenly get hit by a 4x4 truck and his younger, sexier brother will be called upon to assume the leading role. Having celebrated its 40th birthday in 1998, the *telenovela* looks like it's here to stay.

remember to set a time to be picked up. Up to eight people can tour the lagoon behind Barra for 80 pesos. For 150 pesos per hour, up to four people can take a fully equipped *lancha* for tuna or marlin fishing. Operators formed a cooperative, so prices are fixed. Their office and docks lie at the end of Veracruz (office open daily 7am-7pm). Bibliophiles should not miss **Beer Bob's Book Exchange,** Mazatlán 61, a few blocks to the right as you face the Posada Pacífico. It's purely a book *exchange*—no cash involved. It's quite a collection. In the back room sit Bob and company, watching TV, playing cards, or engaging in "some serious beer-drinking." (Usually open M-F 1-4pm.)

Everyone out past midnight parties at **El Galeón Disco,** Morelos 24 (tel. 5 50 18), in Hotel Sand's. Sit on cushioned horseshoe-shaped benches as you down a beer for 8 pesos or a mixed drink for 16 pesos. (Cover 10-20 pesos; open daily 9pm-3am, F-Sa during low season.) Those who prefer singing to dancing may want to mellow out at the **Terraza Bar Jardín,** Jalisco 70 (tel. 5 61 35), a **karaoke** bar. Somebody will sing "New York, New York" all night if you won't. Beer goes for 8 pesos. (Open daily 6pm-2am.) If you just want to concentrate your efforts on drinking, make your way to **Piper Lovers,** Legazpi 138A (tel. 5 64 34), where drinks are cheap and **pool** and **ping-pong** are free for customers. (Beer 10-12 pesos, mixed drinks start at 10 pesos. Open daily 9pm-2am.) If you tire of Lovers, the many two-for-one Happy Hours along Legazpi make the giddy trip toward inebriation that much cheaper.

COLIMA

MANZANILLO

Manzanillo (pop. 115,000) is home to the state's finest beaches, but the only beaches are located along the resort strip west of the dynamic, sweaty *centro* where barges and cranes are the only things that swim in the water. Reasonably priced hotels lie in the midst of the loud and brazen port action—those seeking only sand and surf would do better to retreat to some secluded village, such as Cuyutlán or Barra de Navidad, where there is no metropolis between the hotels and the Pacific. But for those excited by the prospect of beautiful, immensely popular beaches—and a real city—Manzanillo delivers.

■ ORIENTATION

Manzanillo lies 98km west of Colima and 355km south of Guadalajara. The city is separated into a *centro* at its southern end and a long strip of resort hotels and beaches that run along **Blvd. Costera Miguel de la Madrid** about 5-6km to the north. White and blue "Miramar" and "Centro" buses run back and forth between the areas (about every 15min. 5am-11pm; price varies by destination). In the *centro*, **Jardín Obregó**, the *zócalo*, is the most useful orientation point. It faces north onto the harbor, but boxcars often obstruct the glorious view of oil tankers. **Morelos** runs east-west along the north (waterfront) edge of the plaza; **Dávalos**, which becomes **Juárez**, runs along the south. **Av. México**, Manzanillo's main street, runs south from the plaza; most hotels and services are nearby. The bus terminal is in the *centro* at the east end of **Calle Hidalgo**, three streets south of the *zócalo*. **Taxis** from the terminal to the *centro* cost 8-10 pesos or a "Centro" bus can take you into town for 2.50 pesos.

⁊ PRACTICAL INFORMATION

TRANSPORTATION

Airport: (tel. 3 11 19 or 3 25 25), Playa de Oro, on the route between Barra de Navidad and Manzanillo. Airlines include: **Aerocalifornia** (tel. 4 14 14), **Aeromar** (tel. 3 01 51), and **Mexicana** (tel. 3 23 23). **Viajes Vamos a...**, Carrillo Puerto 259 (tel. 2 17 11), 1 block west of México and 3 blocks south of the *zócalo*, can facilitate ticket purchase. Open M-F 9am-2pm and 4-7pm, Sa 9am-2pm. **Colectivos** (60 pesos) transport passengers to the airport 2hr. before take-off (45min., daily 9am-1:30pm and 5-7pm); call the airport to make arrangements. **Taxis** from the airport to the *zócalo* cost 120 pesos. Taxis back to the airport cost 165 pesos.

Buses: The station lies on Hidalgo, in the outskirts of town between Laguna Cuyutlán and the ocean. Taxis to the *centro* 8-10 pesos. Autobuses de Occidente (tel. 2 01 23) serves: **Mexico City** (16hr., 6 per day 2:45am-7:30pm, 269 pesos). Autobuses de Jalisco (tel. 2 01 23) provides first-class service to: **Colima** (1hr., 8 per day 4:45am-9:30pm, 26 pesos); **Guadalajara** (4hr., 8 per day 1am-11:30pm, 103 pesos); **Morelia** (8hr., 10:45pm, 167 pesos); and **Uruapan** (8hr., 8:30pm, 130 pesos). Autocamiones Cihuatlán (tel. 2 05 15) provides second-class service to: **Guadalajara** (6hr., 6 per day 9am-midnight, 130 pesos); and **Puerto Vallarta** (6½hr., 10 per day 7:30am-10pm, 100-120 pesos) stopping at **Melaque** and **Barra de Navidad** (1½hr., 27 pesos). Autotransportes Sur de Jalisco (tel. 2 10 03) serves: **Colima** (1½hr., 2:45pm, 32 pesos). Primera Plus (tel. 2 02 10) sends buses to **Puerto Vallarta** (5hr., 12:30am, 125 pesos) and **Querétaro** (12hr., 6:15pm, 220 pesos). Transportes Costa Alegre (tel. 2 02 10) runs buses to **Melaque** and **Barra de Navidad** (1½hr., every hr. 4am-12:30am, 26 pesos). Elite (tel. 2 04 32) provides cushy service to: **Acapulco** (12hr., 6am, 275 pesos); **Mexico City** (21hr., 7:30pm, 340 pesos); **Zihuatanejo** (8hr., 6am, 155 pesos); and **Tijuana** (36hr., 4 and 9pm, 910 pesos) via **Hermosillo** (24hr., 711 pesos); **Mazatlán** (12hr., 303 pesos); and **Tepic** (7hr., 195 pesos). There is a 24hr. **luggage storage** booth in the bus station (6 pesos per day).

TOURIST AND FINANCIAL SERVICES

Tourist Office: Blvd. Costera Miguel de la Madrid 1033 (tel. 3 22 64 or 3 22 77; fax 3 14 26; email sectur@bay.net.mx), 2 blocks past Fiesta Mexicana. Catch a "Miramar" bus (2.50 pesos) and tell the driver where you're headed. Open M-F 9am-3pm and 5-7:30pm. Helpful **tourist police** (tel. 2 10 02) reside in the Palacio Municipal on the *zócalo* and distribute maps and brochures about Manzanillo and other locations throughout the state of Colima. **Information booths** are in front of the *palacio*, around town, and along the beaches (Open daily 9am-7pm, M-F in lowseason).

Currency Exchange: Bital, México 99 (tel. 2 21 50 or 2 09 50), at 10 de Mayo, has slightly better rates and longer hours than most banks. Open M-Sa 8am-7pm. **ATM** across the street at **Banamex.**

Laundry: Lavi-Matic, Hidalgo 1 (tel. 2 08 44), down Av. México across the small plaza. Wash and dry 3 kilos for 24 pesos. Open M-Sa 8am-7pm.

EMERGENCY AND COMMUNICATIONS

Emergency: dial 06.

Police: (tel. 2 10 02 or 2 10 04) on Juárez in the Palacio Municipal, facing the *jardín*.

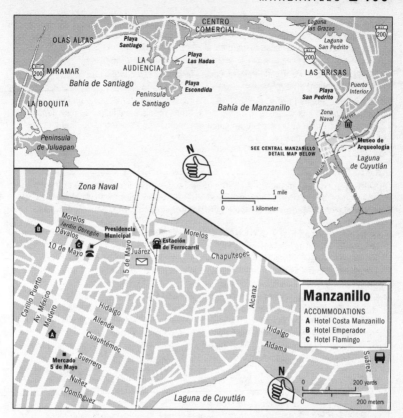

Red Cross: (tel. 6 57 70) on Av. Barotes. Open 24hr.

Pharmacy: Farmacia Manzanillo, Juárez 10 (tel. 2 01 85 or 3 24 11), on the south side of the *zócalo*. English spoken. Open daily 8:30am-midnight.

Hospital: (tel. 2 00 29) in the Colonia San Pedrito, Sector 7. English spoken. Open 24hr.

Post Office: Calle Miguel Galindo 30 (tel. 2 00 22), 3 blocks down México from the *zócalo*. Open M-F 8am-7pm, Sa 9am-1pm. **Postal Code:** 28200.

Fax: Telecomm (tel. 2 30 30), in the Palacio Municipal, to the left of the stairs as you enter. Also sends **telegrams.** Open M-F 8am-6pm and Sa-Su 9am-12:30pm.

Internet Access: Juárez 115, 2nd fl. (tel. 2 26 60), a half block down from the *zócalo*. 13 pesos for 30min. Open M-F 10am-2pm and 5-9pm, Sa 5-9pm.

Telephones: Computel, México 302 (tel. 2 39 26), at Galindo; another on Morelos, a half block east of the *zócalo*, next to Banca Serfín. Both open daily 7am-10pm.

Phone Code: 333.

ACCOMMODATIONS

Manzanillo's budget accommodations tend to be basic and plain, but you'll be on the beach the whole time anyway. Hotels near the *zócalo* are in a safer area than those near the bus station. **Camping** on Playa Miramar is feasible during *Semana Santa* and in December, when bathroom facilities are available and security is heightened.

Hotel Flamingo, Madero 72 (tel. 2 10 37), 1 block south of the *zócalo*. Old Spanish-style rooms with stucco walls and heavy wooden furniture; fans and large windows keep it cool at night. *Agua purificada* available. Singles 70 pesos; doubles 90-100 pesos.

Hotel Emperador, Dávalos 69 (tel. 2 23 74), 1 block west of the plaza. Small rooms enlivened by rustic wooden furniture, ceiling fans, and *agua purificada*. Singles 80-100 pesos; doubles 100-120 pesos.

Casa de Huéspedes Perlita, (tel. 2 01 87), 4 blocks south of the *zócalo* on México, turn left on Allende and the *casa* is on the right. Small rooms are cheap and have fans but seem to be made of plywood. Communal bathrooms don't make this hotel any quieter. Singles 50 pesos; doubles 70 pesos.

ⓕ FOOD

Since tourists mostly stake their claims closer to the beach, food at the market and in downtown restaurants is simple and cheap. A few blocks from the plaza, at Cuauhtémoc and Madero, is a market with family-run and inexpensive *fondas*.

Restaurante Chantilly (tel. 2 01 94), at Juárez and Moreno, on the plaza. Crowds of newspaper-reading professionals, flocks of families, and stragglers off the *zócalo* munch on fantastically good Mexican staples in a diner-like setting. Enchiladas (22-25 pesos) and mango *licuados* (10 pesos) are as good as it gets. Open Su-F 7:30am-10:30pm.

Restaurant Emperador, Dávalos 69 (tel. 2 23 74), below the eponymous hotel. The blank walls, white tablecloths, and fluorescent lights aren't nearly as pleasing to the eye as the food is to the palate. Gargantuan *comida corrida* for a mere 20 pesos. *Chiles rellenos* only 20 pesos; hotcakes 8 pesos. Open daily 8am-10pm.

Restaurant Del Rio, México 330, is a small, cheap place that will fill you up in no time with delicious *comida corrida* (20 pesos) or Mexican specialties for 12-17 pesos. Try a barbecued taco for 3 pesos and wash it down with a chilly beer (8 pesos) or a thick 'n' tasty *licuados* (7 pesos).

ⓑ BEACHES

Manzanillo's beaches stretch from west to east along two bays, **Bahía de Manzanillo** and **Bahía de Santiago,** formed by the Santiago and Juluapan Peninsulas. The Bahía de Manzanillo has more expensive hotels and cleaner golden sand. Unfortunately, its beach slopes steeply, creating a strong and sometimes dangerous undertow. The beaches at Bahía Santiago are better protected by the Juluapan peninsula and are ideal for swimming, water sports, and sun worshipping.

The most accessible beach from the *centro* is **Playa Las Brisas** on Bahía Manzanillo. It has a few secluded spots, but for the most part is crowded with luxurious hotels and bungalows. To get to Las Brisas from downtown Manzanillo, take a taxi (25 pesos) or the "Las Brisas" bus (3 pesos) or, alternatively, catch the "Miramar" bus and ask the driver to let you off at the *crucero* (crossroads), then turn left to populated shores or stake out a private piece of beach right at the junction.

Along the rest of the bay, west of Peninsula Santiago, lies cleaner water and excellent beaches. Beyond **Olas Altas,** a beach popular with experienced (largely American) surfers and infamous for its powerful waves and dangerous undertow, is **Miramar Beach.** Get off where the footbridge crosses the route. This is the most crowded section of the beach, but it boasts top-notch beachfront restaurants from which you can **rent bodyboards** and **surfboards** (15 pesos per hr.). Crowds thin out 20m to the east or west.

The calmer waters of the *palapa*-lined **Playa la Boquita,** the westernmost point on the Juluapan Peninsula, make this a popular spot for children and water sports. **Club Eureka** (tel. 6 57 02) is the last *palapa* on the shore. It offers **banana boat** rides (20 pesos, price negotiable), **water skiing** (US$20 per hr.), **snorkeling gear** (90 pesos for full-day use), **snorkeling excursions** (2hr., 200 pesos), **sky riding** (2 people, US$50), **deep sea fishing excursions** (4hr., US$100), and deep sea fishing, sightseeing, and snorkeling all in one (2hr., 200 pesos; open daily 9am-5pm). If you're not much of a deep-sea enthusiast, try taking a **horse,** available near Club Eureka, for a sandy jaunt (30 pesos per 30min.). To get to Playa La Boquita, take a "Miramar" bus to Club Santiago (4 pesos, 40min.). Walk through the white arches along the cobblestone and palm-lined street, which becomes a dirt road; you'll hit the road after 25 minutes (taxis 13 pesos). Also reveling in its tranquility is **Playa Audiencia,** a small but magnificent cove with calm waters, light brown sand, a few small boats, and a gorgeous, rocky vista. To reach the *playa*, take a "Las Hadas" bus from Niños Héroes or anywhere on Miramar Rte. to the Sierra Radison (4 pesos), then follow the path to the beach. The bus ride back to town offers a spectacular view of the peninsula.

◪ NIGHTLIFE

Manzanillo doesn't sleep when the sun sets. "Miramar" buses run down the hotel strip and taxis back to the *centro* cost 35-40 pesos. After frolicking in the sun and splashing in the sea, those ready to rumble head over to **Tropigala,** Blvd. Miguel de la Madrid km 14.5 (tel. 3 24 74), to get down to live tropical music. The mixed age crowd shows off their groove and works up appetites to gorge on hot dogs, *frijoles*, chicken, and potatoes from the all-you-can eat buffet (included in cover). Ladies who have a special place in their hearts for the big and brawny should watch for the occasional Chippendale's night where oiled-up men strut their stuff. On Wednesdays and Thursdays, women drink for free. (Cover 30 pesos. Open W-Su 9pm-4am.) Next door at the cavernous **Baby Rock** (tel. 3 28 39), a young crowd gets down to popular Mexican and U.S. disco hits. As if dancing weren't enough, a large-screen TV and extensive lights stimulate the senses. (Open bar W and Th. 30 peso cover for men with 2 drinks Tu, F-Sa; 60 peso cover for men, 30 peso for women W-Th; Su 20 peso cover for all; open in high season Tu-Sa; low season Th-Su.) Locals and tourists show off their tans and threads at **Vog,** Av. Miguel de la Madrid km 9.2, on the hotel strip. At 11:30pm, sophisticated track lighting rhythmically sprays beams across prehistoric walls. Men, leave your tank tops, shorts, and sandals at the beach. (Cover 40 pesos. Open W-Sa 10pm-4am, daily during high season.) Next door at the **Bar de Felix** (tel. 3 18 75), funky topiaries welcome an older crowd. Weary revelers recline in plush chairs while the packed dance floor pulsates to a melange of disco and Latin rhythms. (Open Tu-Su 9pm-4am.)

NEAR MANZANILLO

CUYUTLÁN

With its lush vegetation, breathtaking black-sand beach, and mysterious lagoon, quiet **Cuyutlán** (pop. 1650) offers the traveler a few days of solitude. Medium waves roll up on the shore, making for fairly safe and exciting swimming. In the low season, closed buildings and silent streets give the place a ghost-town feel, and the huge golden head of Benito Juárez amid the palm trees of Cuyutlán's green and white *zócalo* is often the only face visible. Summer weekends are slightly busier, but it is only during the high tourist season (December and *Semana Santa*) that Cuyutlán truly comes to life.

◪ ORIENTATION AND PRACTICAL INFORMATION. The road from Armería, 15km from Cuyutlán, runs parallel to the coast and becomes **Yavaros** as it enters town. It intersects **Hidalgo,** which runs along the east side of the town square; a left at this intersection takes you to the beach. **Veracruz,** Cuyutlán's other mighty boulevard, runs parallel to Yavaros, one block off the beach. Most of Cuyutlán's municipal services are within one block of the *zócalo*. The bilingual owners of the **Hotel Fenix** will **change money** if they have the cash. The only long-distance **caseta** is at Hidalgo 47 (tel. 6 40 00), one block inland from the *zócalo* (open M-Sa 9am-1pm and 4-8pm, Su 9am-1pm). **LADATELs** are located around the *zócalo* and the intersection of Hidalgo and Veracruz. **Phone code:** 332.

▮▯ ACCOMMODATIONS AND FOOD. Waves lap at the doorsteps of most nearby budget hotels. Most are well-maintained and affordable. During high season (mainly in December and *Semana Santa*), expect rates to skyrocket to 130-150 pesos per person, with meals included to help justify the price. Make reservations a month in advance during this time. **Hotel Morelos,** Hidalgo 185 (tel. 6 40 13), at Veracruz, offers plush rooms with clean bathrooms and carved wooden furniture. Tiled floors, festive colors, and all the artificial flowers in Cuyutlán give the place pizazz; a small, refreshing pool and a restaurant just add more. (70 pesos per person.) The rooms at **Hotel Fenix,** Hidalgo 201 (tel. 6 40 82), at Veracruz, may be taller than they are wide, but the rooms are cooled by fans and the second-story abodes open to a breezy, beach-view balcony complete with hammocks. The friendly English-speaking owners run a popular bar that serves as the town watering hole. (Rooms 40-60 pesos per person.) Unofficial camping sites lie 200m from Cuyutlán's hotels, in a private patch of black sand. Some travelers string up hammocks in one of the *palapas* near the hotels. For 5 pesos, campers and daytrippers can use the toilets and showers at Hotel Fenix. For 10 pesos, you can use the pool at Hotel Morelos. Almost all of the food in Cuyutlán is served up in the **hotel restaurants,** and seafood is the obvious specialty.

▰ SIGHTS, SURF AND FIESTAS. Aside from its gorgeous beach, Cuyutlán's biggest claim to fame is its **green wave,** a phenomenon that occurs regularly in April or May. Quirky currents and phosphorescent marine life combine to produce 10m swells that glow an unearthly green. The town itself reaches high tide during the **Festival de la Virgen de Guadalupe** (the first 12 days of December), when twice a day—at 6am and 6pm— men, women, and children clad in traditional dress walk 5km to the town's blue church. The celebrations peak on the twelfth day, when *mariachis* accompany the procession, and the marchers sing tributes to the Virgin. Cuyutlán's **Tortugario,** 3.5km east of town along Veracruz, is a combination wildlife preserve and zoo. (Open daily 10am-6pm; admission 5 pesos; taxi to the camp 30 pesos.) The Tortugario is home to hordes of turtles, iguanas, and crocodiles. The camp also has saltwater pools for (human) swimming.

Getting There: The only way to get to Cuyutlán is from Armería. From Manzanillo, take a "Colima" bus (45min., every 15min. 4:20am-10:30pm, 13 pesos) lined up at the entrance of the station and ask to be let off at Armería. To arrive at the Terminal Sub-Urbana, get off at the blue "Paraíso" sign and follow the street to the left. Buses to Cuyutlán leave from here every 30 minutes or so (7am-7:30pm, 5 pesos). Buses return to Armería on the same schedule and pick up people around the *zócalo*. The trip is about 20 minutes.

PARAÍSO

Paraíso may soon be destroyed by the gods for its hubris, but for now it outclasses its unsightly sister city, nearby **Armería.** A well-paved road connects the two towns, cutting through 7km of banana and coconut plantations before it dead-ends at the lava-black sands that surround Paraíso's few hotels and thatched, beachfront restaurants. A shoreline strewn with endless lawn chairs and umbrellas backs the emerald-green surf. Paraíso is popular among Mexicans for daytrips and weekend vacations; during the high season and on Sundays, the beachfront has a true family atmosphere and the town's single dirt road is often crammed with buses and cars blaring music. But on lazy summer weekdays, the beach is almost deserted, and a few lucky swimmers have the warm black sand and green water all to themselves. Long-distance **phone** calls can be made from **Abarrotes Valdovinos** (tel. 2 00 25), next to the bus stop (open daily 7am-10pm).

The main road comes into town from Armería 7km away and ends at the black sand beach. Paraíso's other street is the dirt road **Av. de la Juventud** (also called **Calle Adán y Eva**) which runs along the back of the beachfront restaurants. The first building on the beach to your left is **Hotel Equipales,** where you'll find no-frills rooms with a view of the shore. The cramped and dingy bathrooms leave much to be desired. (Singles and doubles 50 pesos.) Farther to the left lies **Hotel Paraíso** (tel. 7 18 25), a cut above Equipales, but pricier. Spacious beachfront rooms have yellow-tiled floors, ceiling fans, and cold showers. A jungle-theme mural adds a splash of color to the popular pool. (Singles and doubles 195 pesos.) At the opposite end of the strip lies **Posada Valencia,** where the beds are waist-high and the rooms are clean (singles 50 pesos; doubles 100 pesos). Paraíso's extensive **beach** makes a soft pillow for **campers,** and the Hotel Paraíso provides showers (5 pesos) and free access to bathrooms. Hotel Equipales also offers bathroom (1 peso) and shower use (5 pesos). Some *enramada* owners may let you hang your **hammock** under their thatched roofs. During the high season (December and April), rooms may be available in **private houses;** ask in stores or at the town's *caseta*.

Restaurants run the slim gamut from rustic *enramadas* to cement-floored *comedores*. Locally caught seafood dominates menus. **Restaurant Paraíso,** in the Hotel Paraíso, at the east end of Av. de la Juventud, is more popular than the hotel pool. Uniformed waiters provide snazzy service, and string quartets and *mariachis* sometimes appear in the afternoon. Breakfast goes for 20 pesos and tasty shrimp dishes cost 45 pesos. (Open daily 8am-6pm.) The restaurant at Hotel Equipales also offers a pleasant atmosphere and reasonable prices.

Getting There: Follow the same directions to get to Cuyutlán but take a "Paraíso" bus (15min., every 30min. 6:30am-7:30pm, 4 pesos) from Armería's Terminal Sub-Urbano. Buses return to Armería on the same schedule and honk as they slowly leave town.

COLIMA

With 160,000 residents, the capital of the Colima state can hardly be called a *pueblo*, but it does manage to maintain a certain benevolence and informality. The streets and parks are magnificently groomed, the civic-minded inhabitants are remarkably friendly, and on Sundays, slews of stores close shop as families attend Mass, walk in the park or sit and listen to a *mariachi* band in the gazebo of the Plaza Principal. Blessed with cool mountain air, pleasant budget lodgings, a string of museums, theaters, and a university, under-touristed Colima is a beautiful place to spend a couple of days on your way to or from the coast.

◼ ORIENTATION

A string of plazas runs east to west across downtown Colima. The shady **Plaza Principal,** flanked by the cathedral and the Palacio de Gobierno on the east side, is the business center of town. The Plaza Principal is bordered by **Degollado** on the west, **16 de Septiembre** on the south, **Madero** on the north, and **Reforma** on the east. Just past the cathedral and *palacio* is the smaller, quieter **Jardín Quintero,** marked by the large fountain in its center. Three blocks farther east on Madero is the large, lush **Jardín Núñez,** the other significant reference point in town. Madero also forms the northern border of the Jardín Nuñez with Juárez on the west, **Morelos** on the south, and **Revolución** on the east. Many tourist services are on **Hidalgo,** which runs parallel to Madero one block to the south. The main **bus station** is on the northeast side of town about 2km from the center, but minibuses zip by every five minutes (6am-8:30pm, 2 pesos). **Taxis** charge 8.50 pesos to destinations within the *centro*, and 9 pesos to the outskirts.

◼ PRACTICAL INFORMATION

TRANSPORTATION

Buses: The bus station can be reached by "Bital" or "Ruta 5" on Bravo or "Ruta 4" on Zaragoza (2 pesos). Autobuses de Occidente (tel. 4 81 79) has service to: **Lázaro Cárdenas** (6hr., 12:10 and 3:20am, 93-108 pesos) and **Uruapan** (6-8hr., 11am and 10:45pm, 94-100 pesos); and second-class service to **Mexico City** (13hr., 6 per day

5am-10pm, 240 pesos) via **Morelia** (8hr. 116 pesos). Autotransportes Sur de Jalisco (tel. 2 03 16) has second-class service to **Manzanillo** (1hr., 4 per day 6-11:40am, 24 pesos) via **Armería** (45min., 13 pesos). Elite (tel. 2 84 99) sends first-class buses to **Hermosillo** (27hr., 5pm, 698 pesos); **Mazatlán** (12hr., 5pm, 310 pesos); **Mexico City** (10hr., 9:30 and 11pm, 306 pesos); and **Tijuana** (36hr., 5pm, 897 pesos) via **Tepic** (6hr., 213 pesos). ETN (tel. 2 58 99) sends plush buses to the **Guadalajara airport** (3hr., 3 and 9:30am, 132 pesos) and **Morelia** (6hr., 11:45pm, 195 pesos). Flecha Amarilla (tel. 2 11 35) rolls to **Guzman** (2hr., 5 per day 7am-5:30pm, 32 pesos). Omnibus de Mexico (tel. 4 71 90) heads to: **Aguascalientes** (6½hr., 3:20pm, 188 pesos); **Mexico City** (10hr.; 7:45, 8:30, and 10pm; 306 pesos); and **Monterrey** (15hr., 6:50pm, 390 pesos). Primera Plus (tel. 4 80 67) sends first-class buses to **Aguascalientes** (6hr., 12:30pm, 186 pesos); **Guadalajara** (3hr., 11 per day 5am-7:40pm, 87 pesos); **Manzanillo** (1¼hr., 11 per day 1:50am-11:30pm, 30 pesos); and **Mexico City** (10hr., 9 and 11:30pm, 326 pesos); and second-class buses to **Querétaro** (8hr., 3:30 and 8:30pm, 169 pesos).

TOURIST AND FINANCIAL SERVICES

Tourist Office: Hidalgo 96 (tel. 2 43 60; fax 2 83 60; email turiscol@palmera.colima-net.com), on the corner of Hidalgo and Ocampo, halfway between the Plaza Principal and Jardín Nuñez. Helpful staff provide you with pamphlets and maps. Open M-F 8:30am-3pm and 6-8pm, Sa 10am-2pm.

Currency Exchange: Banamex, Hidalgo 90 (tel. 2 01 03), 1 block east of Pl. Principal, has an **ATM.** Open M-F 9am-5pm. **Majapara Casa de Cambio,** Morelos 200 (tel. 4 89 98; fax 4 89 66), on the corner of Juárez at Jardín Núñez, has slightly better rates. Open M-Sa 9am-2pm and 4:30-7pm.

Luggage Storage: At the bus station. 2 pesos per bag for 6hr., 0.50 pesos each additional hr. Open daily 6am-10pm. 24hr. restaurant can assist after hours.

Laundry: Lavandería Automática Amana, Domínguez 147, behind Hospedajes del Rey. 24 pesos to wash and dry 3kg. Open M-Sa 8am-9pm.

EMERGENCY AND COMMUNICATIONS

Emergency: dial 06.

Police: (tel. 2 09 67 or 2 25 66) Juárez at 20 de Noviembre.

Red Cross: (tel. 2 14 51) Aldama at Obregón. Some English spoken. Open 24hr.

Pharmacy: Sangre de Cristo (tel. 4 74 74), Obregón at Madero, 1 block northwest of Jardín Núñez. Some English spoken. Open 24hr.

Hospitals: Hospital Civil (tel. 2 02 27 or 2 09 11), San Fernando at Ignacio Zandoval. **Centro de Salud** (tel. 2 00 64 or 2 32 38), Juárez at 20 de Noviembre. **Dr. Armando López** speaks English. Open M-F 7am-2:30pm, Sa 7am-1:30pm.

Fax: Madero 243 (tel. 2 60 64), next to the post office. **Telegram** service also available. Open M-F 8am-6pm, Sa 9am-noon.

Post Office: Madero 247 (tel. 2 00 33), on the northeast corner of the Jardín Núñez. Open M-F 8am-7pm, Sa 8am-noon. **Postal Code:** 28000.

Telephones: LADATELs abound in the plazas. The **caseta,** Revolución 99 (tel. 3 83 70 fax 2 71 14), on the southeast corner of Jardín Núñez, is open daily 8am-10pm with long distance phone calls 14.50 pesos per minute to the US.

Internet: CiberCafe, Av. F. Sevilla del Rio 80 (tel. 4 23 39), on the second floor of Plaza Country Mall next to the movie theater. Follow Calle Sandoval past Fernando and turn left on Sevilla del Rio. 18 pesos for 30 min. students with I.D. 15 pesos.

Phone Code: 331.

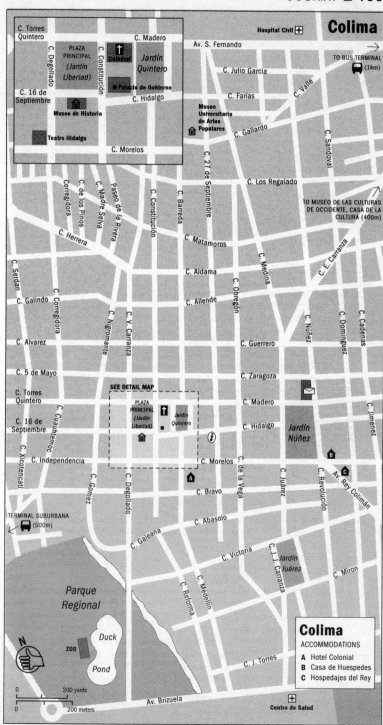

Colima

C. Torres
Quintero

Hospital Civil ⊞

Av. S. Fernando

TO BUS TERMINAL
🚌 (1km)

PLAZA
PRINCIPAL
(Jardín
Libertad)

C. Madero

Jardín
Quintero

C. Julio Garcia

C. Valle

C. Degollado

C. Constitución

† Catedral

C. Farías

C. Sandoval

C. 16 de
Septiembre

■ Palacio de Gobierno

C. Hidalgo

Museo
Universitario
de Artes
Populares

C. Gallardo

🏛 Museo de Historia

C. Los Regalado

TO MUSEO DE LAS CULTURAS
DE OCCIDENTE, CASA DE LA
CULTURA (400m)

■ Teatro Hidalgo

C. Morelos

C. 27 de Septiembre

C. Barreda

C. Matamoros

C. Medina

C. E. Carranza

Corregiadora

C. de los Pinos

C. Madre Selva

paseo de la Rivera

C. Constitución

C. Herrera

C. Aldama

C. Obregón

C. Serdan

C. Galindo

Corregidora

C. Nigromante

C. V. Carranza

C. Allende

C. Guerrero

C. Núñez

C. Dominguez

C. Cadenas

C. Alvarez

C. Zaragoza

C. 5 de Mayo

C. Madero

✉

C. Jimenez

C. Torres
Quintero

SEE DETAIL MAP

PLAZA
PRINCIPAL
(Jardín
Libertad)

†

Jardín
Quintero

C. Hidalgo

Jardín
Núñez

C. 16 de
Septiembre

C. Cuauhtemoc

🏛

ⓘ

B

C. Independencia

C. Morelos

C. de la Vega

C. Juárez

C. Revolución

Av. Rey Colimán

C

C. Xicotencatl

A

C. Bravo

C. Gomez

C. Degollado

TERMINAL SUBURBANA
🚌 (500m)

C. Abasolo

C. Galeana

C. Victoria

Jardín
Juárez

C. J. J. Carranza

C. Miron

Parque
Regional

C. Medellin

C. Reforma

Duck

N

ZOO

Pond

C. J. Torres

Colima

ACCOMMODATIONS

A Hotel Colonial
B Casa de Huespedes
C Hospedajes del Rey

0   200 yards

0   200 meters

Av. Brizuela

⊞
Centro de Salud

ACCOMMODATIONS

Cheap lodging may be found near the Jardín Núñez while higher-priced hotels tend to cluster around the university.

■ **Hospedajes del Rey,** Rey Colimán 125 (tel. 3 36 83), a half block from the southeast corner of the Jardín Núñez. "Fit for a king" couldn't describe it better: enormous, plush rooms have fans, TVs, and wall-to-wall windows; hardwood floors and a beveled-glass dining table and chairs complete the royal ensemble. Bathroom floors are clean enough to eat from. Singles 140 pesos; doubles with 1 bed 140 pesos, with 2 beds 180 pesos.

Hotel Colonial, Medellín 142F (tel. 3 08 77), between Morelos and Nicolás Bravo, 1 block from the Plaza Principal. Rooms have fans, wicker chairs, wrought-iron beds, wide TVs, and spotless, flower-tiled baths. (Singles 80-100 pesos; doubles 110 pesos).

Casa de Huéspedes, Morelos 265 (tel. 2 34 67), off the southeast corner of Jardín Núñez. A friendly family-run *posada* with breezy but decaying rooms and spades of blooming plants. The bathrooms, however, could use a good scrub. Singles 50 pesos, with bath 60 pesos; doubles 60 pesos, with bath 70 pesos.

FOOD

Restaurant fare in Colima reflects the town's dearth of tourism; inexpensive and authentic Mexican meals consist of traditional faves like *pozole blanco* and *sopitos*. A few pricey joints cluster around the Plaza Principal, but a jaunt down the smaller side streets will lead to budget meals aplenty.

■ **Samadhi,** Medina 125 (tel. 3 24 98), 2½ blocks north of Jardín Núñez. Walk down Juárez (the western border of the *jardín*); Samadhi is next to the red and white church. Delicious, vegetarian-friendly cuisine served with new-age music in a leafy courtyard with soothing pastel walls. Breakfast buffet 30 pesos; soy burger with mushrooms and fries 15 pesos. Open F-W 8am-10pm, Th 8am-5pm.

Comedor Familiar El Trébol, 16 de Septiembre 59 (tel. 2 29 00), at Degollado on the Pl. Principal. Colima at its best: popular and cheap. A family spot packed with kids laughing and stuffing their faces amid the festive decor. *Comida corrida* 18 pesos; breakfast 10-18 pesos; beer 9 pesos. Open Su-F 8am-11pm.

Los Naranjos, Barreda 34 (tel. 2 00 29), almost a block north of Madero, northeast of the Plaza Principal. A classy but comfortable restaurant, popular with those in the know. *Periódico*-perusing middle-aged men sip coffee over bright orange tablecloths while glass vases and wicker chairs add charm. Breakfast 10-25 pesos; *pollo a la mexicana* 23 pesos; *antojitos* 7-22 pesos. Open daily 8am-11:30pm.

Cenaduría Selecta de Colima, Morelos 299 (tel. 2 93 32), at Domínguez, 1 block off the southeast corner of Jardín Núñez. Try one of Colima's regional specialties at this cheap joint. *Pozole* (pork stew), is a delicious dish or try *enchiladas dulces* (sweet enchiladas) served with a mountain of diced onion and hot-ass sauce (entrees 10-15 pesos). Cool it off with a beer (7-8 pesos) and top it off with a sweet serving of *flan* (6 pesos). Open Tu-Sa 1:30-11pm.

SIGHTS

PLAZA PRINCIPAL. The gazebo and fountains of the **Jardín Libertad** lure bureaucrats on their lunch breaks to the garden's ornate white wrought-iron benches. The double arcade around the plaza encompasses the **Museo Regional de Historia de Colima.** *(Tel. 2 92 28. In Colima's main plaza. Admission 17 pesos, Free for all students and teachers with I.D., video cameras 35 pesos.)*

SANTA IGLESIA CATHEDRAL. Adjoining Colima's Palacio de Gobierno on the east side of the plaza is the Cathedral; a pawn in the battle between humanity and nature—or, depending on your perspective, between Catholicism and the ghost of indigenous religions. The Spanish first built a church on this spot in 1527, but an earthquake destroyed the original wood-and-palm structure and a fire destroyed its replacement. Undeterred, the Spanish built yet another church. The cathedral's neoclassical interior sparkles with gilt paint, chandeliers, polished marble, and statues. A statue of San Felipe de Jesús, the city's patron saint, resides in the pulpit designed by Othón Bustos. *(Tel. 2 02 00. Open daily 6am-2pm and 4:30-8:30pm.)*

MUSEO DE HISTORIA. This is the city's newest museum, home to a respectable collection of pre-Hispanic ceramics and a creepy replica of a western Mesoamerican burial site, complete with two real skeletons. In the same courtyard is an eclectic gallery of art. *(Tel. 2 92 28. Portal Morelos 1 at 16 de Septiembre and Reforma, on the south side of the Plaza Principal. Open Tu-Sa 9am-6pm, Su 5-8pm. Free.)*

TEATRO HIDALGO. The theater is one block down Degollado, to your left as you face away from the Cathedral. Completed in 1883, yet unmarred by the passage of time, the theater's four tiers of side-seating almost touch the high ceiling, and its swooping red curtains lend the stage a 19th-century ambience. Occasional performances enliven the majestic interior beyond those large wooden doors; inquire at the tourist office.

MUSEO DE LAS CULTURAS DE OCCIDENTE. Calle Calzada Galván at Ejército Nacional, a short ride away from the city center, this museum is devoted to local pre-Hispanic art. Rarely seen outside the state, the Colima ceramic figurines displayed here, with their exaggerated, disproportionate bodies, are among the most playful and captivating artifacts in Mexico. The museum provides an excellent narrative of the artifacts' meaning and of their role in indigenous culture. To get there, take the yellow "Ruta #3 Sur" bus (2 pesos) on Av. Rey Colimán at Jardín Núñez. Taxis from the *centro* cost 5 pesos. *(Tel. 2 31 55. Open Tu-Su 9am-6:30pm. Admission 17 pesos, students with ID 5 pesos.)* The Casa de la Cultura, the university's cultural center, is the best source of information on cultural events in Colima *(same tel.; open daily 8:30am-9pm).*

MUSEO UNIVERSITARIO DE ARTES POPULARES. At Barreda and Gallardo, this museum displays collections of traditional dresses and masks, figurines recovered from nearby tombs, and descriptions of the pre-Aztec western coast. A gift shop sells handmade reproductions of local ceramics. The museum is an easy 15-minute walk north on 27 de Septiembre from the Plaza Principal; alternatively, catch the #7 bus (2.50 pesos) on Gabino Barreda between Zaragoza and Guerrero, and take it to the corner of Barreda and Gallardo. *(Tel. 2 68 69. Museum open Tu-Sa 10am-2pm and 5-8pm, Su 10am-1pm. Free.)*

PARQUE REGIONAL METROPOLITANO. This park offers nature-lovers an afternoon stroll along a manmade duck pond and is home to two absurdly large pelicans who pester young children for fish. A miniature **zoo** houses monkeys, crocodiles, and lions. Children feed ice cream cones to the zoo's deer through the wire fences and frolic in the pool, zooming down the waterslide. On Degollado, 4 blocks south of the Plaza Principal. *(Tel. 4 16 76. Zoo open daily 7am-6:30pm. Admission 1 peso. Pool and waterslide open W-Su 10:30am-4:30pm. Admission 5 pesos, children 3 pesos. Waterslide and boat rides 6 pesos per hr., children 4 pesos.)*

⚓ NIGHTLIFE

Erupting volcanoes aren't the things shaking in Colima. Hot nightclubs offer cheap beer and kicking dance music that brings young locals and students out to party.

Bariloche, Av. Rey de Colimán 440 (tel. 4 55 00), near the Monumento Rey Colimán. May be the hottest spot in town. Big-screen videos, pool tables, and wandering entertainers keep 'em coming. Cover W 100 pesos for men, free for women; F 70 pesos for men, 30 pesos for women; Sa 45 pesos including 2 drinks. Open W-Sa 10pm-3am.

Splash, Av. Benito Juárez 4 (tel. 3 65 07), is a dimly lit, ever-packed gay and lesbian bar where clientele get down on the dance floor in between transvestite lip-synching shows. No cover Th; Friday 25 pesos, free beer 10pm-1am; Saturday 20 peso cover; Sunday 20 pesos with one free beer. Open Th-Su 10pm-3:30am.

Collash, Zaragosa 521 (tel. 4 47 00). Try working your way through the smoke as you gyrate to popular Mexican dance music. If you're not up to dancing, play some pool as you sip a beer (10 pesos) or a mixed drink (18 pesos and up). Cover Saturday 15 pesos, open 11pm-3am; Sunday—under 18 night—cover 10 pesos; open 6-10pm).

Dalí, the Casa de la Cultura's cafe, is a great place to drop by for a slower atmosphere, including melancholy tunes that pierce the air and wrench the heart. Prints from the master of surrealism drip from the walls under dim, smoky lights. The food isn't exactly cheap, but it's worth it just to drink *cervezas* or smoke cigars while, a *mariachi* stands on the cafe's small platform wailing love songs, a guitar cradled in his arms (9-11pm). *Muy romántico.* Beer (9 pesos), *bebidas nacionales* (18 pesos and up). Open M-F 1:15pm-midnight, Sa-Su 5:30pm-midnight.

NEAR COLIMA

This is where the wild things are. If you want to commune with nature, feel the heat of the nearby indignant volcanoes, or relax by serene lakes and quiet towns, Colima serves as an ideal base for daytrips to numerous sites. The soaring peaks of the **volcanoes** 25km away and the large **lakes** overflowing with wildlife send their siren calls to curious visitors and draw them in by the busload. The neighboring town of **Comala** provides another outlet for travelers who want to leave the hordes of humanity in Colima behind, but are unwilling to march through flora to do it.

VOLCANOES

In Náhuatl, Colima means "place where the old god is dominant." The old god is **El Volcán de Fuego** (3960m), 25km from Colima City. Puffs of white smoke continuously billow from the volcano; recorded eruptions date back to the pre-Hispanic era. Lava was visible from the capital once again in 1994, when El Fuego reasserted its status as an active volcano (the tourist office assures visitors that the volcano is not a threat to the city). The nearby and slightly taller **El Nevado de Colima** (4335m) earned its name from the blanket of snow that drapes it in the winter. This dormant volcano also provides an advanced trail to the top. The **Joya Cabin,** near the summit, lacks all amenities except a roof. The park is open sporadically; if you're planning a trip to the top, call the **police** ahead of time (tel. 2 18 01). As always, be cautious. The ascent should not be attempted by solo travelers or by those without sufficent hiking experience.

Getting There: Guadalajara-bound *locales* (from the new bus station) pass through the town of **Atenquique,** 57km away. From here, a 27km dirt road runs to the summit of El Fuego. The trip is only recommended for four-wheel-drive vehicles, although logging trucks based at the factory in Atenquique make trips to spots near the summit. You can get to El Nevado by car or by bus. Flecha Amarilla (tel. 4 80 67) runs buses from Colima to **Guzmán,** 83km away (2hr., 5 per day 7am-5:30pm, 35-40 pesos). Buses from Guzmán limp up to Joya, where you can make your epic assault on the summit.

LAGUNA CARRIZALILLO

The waters and banks of **Laguna Carrizalillo** are teeming with life. Birds keep up a constant jabber in the trees while lizards and frogs jump about underfoot. But even with the hyperactive wilderness, this beautiful spot 27km north of Colima is still a peaceful retreat from the city. Larger, closer to the volcanoes, and more visited is **Laguna La María,** whose calm, green waters surrounded by a dense wall of plant life attract flocks of ornithologists in search of tiny yellow Singing Henkins. The lake also offers equipment to fish, either from the shore or from a rented *lancha* (25-30 pesos per hour).

Getting There: Green buses destined for San Antonio or Zapotitlán leave from the suburban bus station and chug up and down the mountain road to La María (1½hr.; 7:10am, 2:40, and 5pm; 6 pesos; buses return at 7:30am, 3, and 4pm). Survivors of the painfully bumpy ride are rewarded with a magnificent view of the mountains just before the lagoon. To get to the entrance from the bus stop, follow the wooden sign that says "La María" (a 15-min. hike). The bus back leaves from the same crossroads on the opposite side of the street. To reach Terminal Suburbano from the *centro* of Colima, catch a "Ruta 2" bus labeled "Los Rojos" on Morelos (2 pesos).

COMALA

South of the lagoons and just 9km north of Colima is the picturesque *pueblo* of **Comala**. This town is known as "El Pueblo Blanco de America" (The White Town of America) because originally, all the facades in town were white, with red-tiled roofs, huge porches, and windows filled with flowers. Comala's *zócalo* is surrounded by cobblestone streets with white benches, fountains, and orange trees. The south side of the *zócalo* is lined by lively restaurants where *mariachis* perform and waiters supply patrons with a steady stream of free *botanas* (Mexican appetizers) to whet the appetite for *ponche* (warm rum-and-fruit-punch), one of the region's traditional drinks.

Comala's main claim to fame is its colony of *indígena* artisans who craft wooden furniture and bamboo baskets. The **Cooperativa Artesenal Pueblo Blanco** (tel. 5 56 00), a small *tianguis* (market), stands just outside Comala's *centro*, 200m past the restaurants on Progreso; it's a 20-minute walk from the *zócalo* (open M-Sa 8am-4pm).

To the east of the *zócalo* lies the **Iglesia San Miguel del Espíritu Santo,** whose unfinished bare-bricked rear gives it character. The interior of the cathedral is shadowed by a beautiful, sky-blue vaulted ceiling. The nave unfortunately became home to dozens of pigeons that keep the walls echoing and ringing with their deafening cacophony. On the other side of the *zócalo* are the city offices, where a four-wall mural commemorates Comala's 130 years as a city and celebrates the "richness of its soil." Unfortunately, the birds who now control the church have also settled across the way and have graciously added their own artistic expression to the mural. For more information, contact Ignacio Zamora, Director of Education, Culture, and Tourism (tel. 5 55 47), next door in the municipal building (available M-F 8:30am-2:30pm and 5-8pm).

Getting There: Green buses head to Comala from the far right end of Colima's suburban bus station (30min., every 15min. 6am-10pm, 2.50 pesos). Taxis charge about 30 pesos from Colima and, if you ask, the *taxista* may show you Colima's famous *magnético*—a segment of the road where cars can have their engines turned off but still appear to run uphill. Optical illusion or miracle of science, it's loads o' fun.

FROM OVER THE HILLS You have probably marveled at the intricate beadwork designs on carved bowls and masks. Although the artwork is sold in quality shops around the state of Nayarit, the masters behind the beautiful artwork are from the Huichol natives who are considered Mexico's oldest Indian group. More than 15,000 Huichol still live in rural mountain regions, entering towns to sell their work. For centuries, they have created unique crafts depicting mythological scenes. The **Comunidad Cultural Huichol** in San Blas is a non-profit organization that provides a non-exploitative forum for expressions for the Huichol Artists, an attempt to perpetuate a market for their products. The best prices for the beautiful bowls and decorated works are buying them straight from the artist stands themselves, not expensive stores.

ZAMORA

Founded in 1574, Zamora is affectionately known as the *Cuna de Hombres Ilustres* (Cradle of Illustrious Men). The list includes figures such as Manuel Martinez de Navarrete and Nobel Peace Price winner Alfonso García Robles. These illustrious men also apparently aided the valley of Zamora to become the leading producer of potatoes in all of Mexico. Besides potatoes, Zamora yields strawberries and manufactures many famous varieties of *dulces* (candy)—especially *chongos*. While not exactly bursting at the seams with tourist offering, Zamora is a quiet, pleasant place to pass a day and is a convenient stop between Guadalajara (176km) and Morelia (152km).

◪ ORIENTATION AND PRACTICAL INFORMATION

Almost everything needed can be found in or around the *centro* bordered by **Amado Nervo** and **Guerrero** running east-west, and **Morelos** and **Allende** running north-south. The bus station is on Juárez at the edge of town. Take a "Central" bus (2.80 pesos) from Colón and Hidalgo near the *centro*, or splurge on a cab (12 pesos from the *centro*). Autobúses de Occidente and La Linea (tel. 5 11 29) send buses to: **Guadalajara** (13 per day, 60 pesos); **Morelia** (4 per day, 44 pesos); **Toluca** (8hr., 14 per day, 137 pesos); **Mexico City** (9 hr., 13 per day, 180 pesos); **Uruapan** (2hr., 6 per day, 43 pesos); and **Patzcuaro** (2½ hr., 11am, 54 pesos). For an expanded schedule of destinations and departures along with higher prices, try Elite or Flecha Amarilla bus lines. The **Tourist Office**, Morelos Sur 76 (tel. 2 40 15) a few blocks from the *centro* provides a good map and plenty of oral info (open daily 9am-3pm and 5-8pm). **Bancomer**, Morelos 250 in the *centro* has a 24hr **ATM** (open M-F 8:30am-5:30pm, Sa 10am-2pm; currency exchange open M-F 8:30am-3pm). **Emergency:** dial 060. **Police:** dial 2 00 22. **Red Cross:** dial 2 05 35. **Hospital: San José:** Colón Ote. 320, (tel. 2 15 96). **Post Office:** Hidalgo 112 in the Palacio Federal (open M-F 8am-4pm). **Internet access:** At the Biblioteca Publica, Morelos 339 Sur (tel. 2 23 56), one block off the *centro* (15 pesos per hr.; open M-F 9am-8pm, Sa 9am-2pm). **LADATELSs** are thick as molasses in the *centro* along with a few **casetas;** Morelos 375 has phone and **fax** service (open M-Sa 9:30am-2:30pm and 4:30-8pm). **Phone code:** 351

▮ ACCOMMODATIONS

There are no earth shattering places here, but Zamora has plenty of decent hotels at affordable prices. **Hotel Nacional**, Corregidora 106 (tel. 2 42 24), just off the *centro* has cramped but clean rooms with tiny bathrooms. A nice balcony juts off the 4th floor and a TV blares in the lobby. (Singles 90 pesos; doubles 110 pesos; triples 130 pesos; TV extra 20 pesos.) **Hotel 5 de Mayo,** at (surprise!) Av. 5 de Mayo 352, doesn't have the most appealing lobby, but rooms are serviceable and some of the cheapest in town. (Singles 60 pesos; doubles 70 pesos; triples 80 pesos.)

▧ FOOD

Zamora has an even larger than average number of small restaurants and stands with delicious food and prices to match. For cinnamon-roll-minded folks, there's a small bakery on Hidalgo behind the Cathedral. **Centro Comercial (Mercado) Morelos,** just off the *centro* across from the cathedral is the place to go for cheap eats and local sweets as well. Restaurants close around 6 or 7pm; candy shops are open until about 9pm. Don't expect any heavy metal thrash by this *pantera*, **La Pantera Rosa,** Hidalgo 234 Sur (tel. 2 18 66), but do look for the *carnes asados en su jugo* (grilled beef with beans and tortillas; small 23 pesos, medium 25 pesos, large 27 pesos; open daily noon-9pm).

NEAR ZAMORA

LA PIEDAD

An hour bus ride and 45km away from Zamora lies the town of La Piedad. Although fairly large, the town has little to offer tourists except for the archaeological zone **Zaragoza.** The 1st Sunday of October is the **Santo Cristo Rey Festival,** where the streets and everything else are literally covered with statues and designs all made from flower petals.

⚡ ORIENTATION AND PRACTICAL INFORMATION

The La Piedad **bus station** is located on the outskirts of town on **Blvd. Lazaro Cardenas,** the main road running through town. Most of what you need in La Piedad can be found in or around the **Jardín Principal** at the **Parroquia Sr. de La Piedad.** Flecha Amarilla sends buses to: **Irapuato** (2hr., 5 per day, 50 pesos); **Morelia** (3½ hr., 6 per day, 90 pesos); **Uruapan** (3hr., 2 per day, 86 pesos); and **Zamora** (1hr., 7 per day, 21 pesos). **Tourist information** is available on the 2nd floor of the Presidencia Municipal in the Jardín (tel. 2 91 19; open M-F 9am-2pm and 6-8pm). **Bancapromex,** (tel. 2 00 05) at Hidalgo 1 in the corner of the Jardín, exchanges money (open M-F 8:30am-5:30pm, Sa 10am-2pm). **Post office:** in the Sorrento building, #9 in the plaza (open M-F 8am-4pm). **Postal code:** 59300. **Café Internet:** Hidalgo 220, a few blocks from the Jardín (open M-Sa 10am-2pm and 4-7pm). For **police** and **medical emergencies,** dial 2 30 30. **LADATELs** are everywhere in the *centro* and a **caseta** and **fax** can be found at Communitel, Morelos 74, just off the Jardín (open 8:30am-8pm). **Phone code:** 52.

🍴 ACCOMMODATIONS AND FOOD

If heading to La Piedad, your best bet is to make it a day trip. If you must stay overnight, **El Gran Hotel** or **Hotel El Eden,** both located on Blvd. L. Cardenás a few blocks northwest of the Jardín Principal, should do. The choices for eating in La Piedad are considerably better. **Restaurant Del Portal,** Portal Abasolo 19 (tel. 2 10 79), overlooks the *Jardín* and serves a large *comida corrida* (36 pesos) with a full bar in the background (open daily 2-10pm). **Fiesta Restaurant** offers a hamburger with fries (15 pesos), beer (12 pesos), and nice outdoor seating (open daily 24hr.). Across the street, **Restaurante El Patio** is another option offering good breakfast specials (20-28 pesos) and quesadillas (28 pesos; open daily 9am-10:30pm).

ZARAGOZA ARCHAEOLOGICAL ZONE

To explore Zaragoza, it's almost imperative to have a guide of some sort. If nothing else, boys from the nearby village are often eager to accompany tourists for a small fee. Guides will be able to point out many etchings and carvings in boulders made by ancient indigenous peoples, several small coves, and a shrine to the *Virgén de Guadalupe.* There is no trail to speak of and scaling the side of the mountain can be precarious, but the reward is a spectacular vista of the surrounding area. Before departing, try to find **Fernando Tejera** in the **Museo Zaragoza** located next to the Presidencia Municipal in the *Jardín* of La Piedad. He may be willing to show you around the archaeological zone and at the very least, he will point you in the right direction. (Open M-F 10am-5pm; free.)

Getting There: From the bus stop along Blvd. L. Cardenás near the Jardín, catch the Zaragoza bus (30min, every hr., 5 pesos). The bus bounces along over unpaved roads to the village of Zaragoza, where it's a short walk to the start of the archaeological zone.

LAGO CAMECUARO

The peaceful little Lake Camecuaro is just 15 minutes by bus from Zamora. A haven for outdoor recreation, the lake offers rowboats (50 pesos per hr.), shady picnic tables, grill pits, volleyball courts and soccer fields plus a few restaurants. Swimming is permitted, but water quality is hardly impeccable. The lake has a large goose population and mosquitos seem to run the show, so bring your insect repellent. (Open daily 8am-7pm; 5 pesos.)

Getting There: Hop on a Camecuaro bus from the station in Zamora (15 min., 6 pesos) and tell the driver you want to go to the lake and not the village. The road to the lake is to your right after you pass a cemetery on your left; it's about a 1km walk from the route to the lake.

GEYSER DE IXTLAN

Near the village of Ixtlan lies an impressive geyser as well as several hot springs perfect for bathing. Unfortunately, the geyser doesn't erupt on a predictable schedule; the best bet to see it in action is to go around 8am. (Tel. (355) 1 63 37. Open daily 7am-8pm; 3 pesos.)

Getting There: Board an Ixtlan bus from the Zamora station (30 min., 7am-8pm, 10 pesos) and tell the bus driver you want to get off at the geyser, the stop is just before the village on the right hand side, next to a Coca-Cola billboard.

SOUTHERN PACIFIC COAST

Because many of the region's indigenous Purépecha lived by the rod and the net, the Aztecs dubbed the lands surrounding Lake Pátzcuaro **Michoacán** (Country of Fishermen). The distinctive Purépecha language (a variant of which is still widely spoken) and the terraced agricultural plots have convinced scholars that they were not originally indigenous to the area but were in fact immigrants from what is today Peru. Purépecha hegemony lasted from around 800, when they first settled Michoacán, to 1522, when the Spanish arrived. Michoacán's red, fertile soil, abundant rain, and mild weather make for bountiful crops, and agriculture swells the state's coffers. The gorgeous beaches and forest-covered mountain ranges serve as prime attractions to wildlife enthusiasts and tourists.

The state of **Guerrero** has been blessed by fortune. During the colonial period, the rich mining town of Taxco kept the state and most of New Spain swimming in silver. More recently, the state's precious commodities have not come from high upon the rocky Sierra de Guerrero, but rather from the rugged shores just past it on the Pacific coast. In the 1950s, Acapulco became the darling of the international resort scene; almost four decades later, wallflower Ixtapa and even quieter Zihuatanejo have managed to take their older sister's role. Today, most of the glitter has subsided, and Guerrero's beautiful colonial towns and Pacific beaches are popular with budget travelers. Oaxaca is fractured into a crazy quilt by the rugged heights of the Sierra Madre del Sur. Despite its intimidating terrain, the land has inspired a violent possessiveness in the many people—Zapotecs, Mixtecs, Aztecs, and Spaniards—who have fought each other over the area. More than 200 indigenous tribes have occupied the valley over the past two millennia. Over one million *oaxaqueños* still speak an *indígena* language as a mother tongue, and more than 20% of the state's population speaks no Spanish whatsoever. This language barrier, and the cultural gap that it symbolizes and

HIGHLIGHTS OF THE SOUTHERN PACIFIC COAST

- Despite 1997's devastating Hurricane Pauline, **Puerto Escondido** (see p. 488) and nearby **Zipolite** (see p. 486) still draw backpackers ready to sun, surf, and smoke on the beach.
- The site of **Monte Alban** (see p. 478) is home to the most important pre-Hispanic ruins in the region and some of the most well preserved in Mexico.
- **Oaxaca** (see p. 461) is a backpacker mecca—some say it's the most attractive city in the country. Its international student population, temperate weather, scenic location, and hot chocolate drive national and international visitors wild.
- **Taxco** (see p. 442) not only offers visitors silver, but also narrow streets, dazzling mountain views, and the beautiful **Catedral de Santa Prisca** (see p. 445).
- Aging, ultra-corny **Acapulco** (see p. 454) may be past its prime, but the **Guerrero coast** (See **Costa Grande** p. 453) north of the city is home to some beautiful beaches, including **Barra de Potosí** (see p. 453).
- Despite over-development and the Western Hemisphere's largest Club Med, Ixtapa and Zihuatanejo still lure travelers to their sunny beaches. Skip **Ixtapa** (see p. 452); **Zihuatanejo** (see p. 451) is where it's at.
- The gorgeous beaches of the stormy **Michoacán coast** (see p. 440) boast powerful waves, privacy, and rugged terrain.
- The quiet mountain jewel of **Pátzcuaro** (see p. 425) and the **nearby area** (see p. 430) are home to an amazing variety of regional handicrafts.

exacerbates, has long caused tensions between the Oaxacan government and its indigenous population. These tensions run through the veins of the enchanting highland colonial city of Oaxaca de Juárez, a perennial tourist favorite for its rich *indígena* culture, superb food, and sublime setting.

MICHOACÁN DE OCAMPO

URUAPAN

Surrounded by red soil, rolling hills, and rows upon rows of avocado trees, Uruapan (ur-Ah-pan; pop. 300,000) sits amid a checkerboard of farmland wrested from the surrounding jungle and mountains. Farmers and their families come to Uruapan to sell their produce and buy bags of fried plantains, wristwatches, and other necessities of modern life. Cool mountain air and plenty of rain keep the city lush and green year-round. While Uruapan is developing into an important center of commerce, the surrounding countryside remains an untainted, naturalist's dream. In town, when residents aren't haggling over prices in the huge *mercado*, they are relaxing with a cup of strong *michoacano* coffee in the city's quality cafes. Tourists come to the Uruapan in droves to explore the nearby waterfall, national park, and Paricutín Volcano.

■ ORIENTATION

Uruapan lies 120km west of Morelia and 320km southeast of Guadalajara. Most sights are within easy walking distance of the *zócalo*, known as **Jardín de los Mártires** on its west side and **Jardín Morelos** on its east end. The statue in the center faces south, looking down **Cupatitzio. Emiliano Carranza** runs into the southwest corner of the square from the west, and continues from the eastern side of the plaza as **Obregón. Venustiano Carranza** runs into the *zócalo*'s north side, and **Manuel Ocaranza** runs one block west of Cupatitzio into the plaza's south side. **Ocampo** runs along its western edge. To reach the *centro* from the **bus station** on **Benito Juárez** in the northeast corner of town, hail a **taxi** (15 pesos) or hop aboard a bus with "Centro" on its windshield—later in the day, you may have to wait at the bus stop on the street in front of the bus station (6am-9pm; 2.50 pesos).

■ PRACTICAL INFORMATION

Buses: Buses leave from Benito Juárez, in the northeast part of town, from the corner of Obregón and 5 de Febrero. Elite (tel. 3 44 50 or 3 44 67) runs cushy first-class service to: **Mazatlán** (12hr., 5 and 7:30pm, 402 pesos); **Mexico City** (6hr., 11:30pm and 12:45am, 193 pesos); **Monterrey** (15hr., 12:30 and 7pm, 492 pesos); and **San Luis Potosí** (8hr., 12:30 and 7pm, 230 pesos). Flecha Amarilla (tel. 4 39 82) runs second-class buses to: **Aguascalientes** (8½hr., 7:30am, 182 pesos); **Guadalajara** (5hr., 6 per day, 113 pesos); **Mexico City** (10hr., 4pm, 165 pesos); **Morelia** (2hr., 6 per day, 50 pesos); **Querétaro** (6hr., 7:10pm, 83 pesos); and **San Luis Potosí** (9hr., 5:10 and 9:30am, 203 pesos). ETN (tel. 4 78 99) and Primera Plus (tel. 4 39 82) offer similar service at usually higher prices. La Línea (tel. 3 18 71) is a good bet for **Guadalajara** (4½-6½hr., 17 per day, 113 pesos).

Tourist Office: Subdirección de Turismo Municipal, East Carranza 44 (tel. 4 30 91). The friendly folks here provide good maps. Open daily 9am-7pm.

Currency Exchange: Bancomer, Carranza 7 (tel. 3 65 22), offers good exchange rates and an **ATM.** Open M-F 8:30am-5:30pm, Sa 10am-2:30pm. A battalion of banks are located a block south of the *zócalo* on Cupatitzio. Competitive exchange rates and ATMs are as common as mosquitoes.

Luggage Storage: At the bus station. 2.50 pesos per 3hr., 5 pesos per day. Open daily 7am-midnight.

GUANAJUATO QUERÉTARO

La Piedad
Vista
Briseñas Hermosa
Lago de Chapala
Ixtlán
San José de Gracia
Sahuayo
Jiquilpan
16
Zamora
Zináparo
27
Cuitzeo
40
15
Carapan
Zacapu
Lago de Cuitzeo
51
Maravatio
Paracho
37
Morelia
Zinapécuaro
Ciudad Guzmán
Peribán
Angahuan
Lago de Pátzcuaro
Quiroga
15
51
Ciudad Hidalgo
JALISCO
Paracutín
Zirahuén
Tzintzuntzan
Tiripetio
Zitácuaro
Paracutín
Uruapan
14
Pátzcuaro
Villa Madero
49
COLIMA
San Juan
Sta. Clara del Cobre
Buenavista
Telpacatepec
Nueva Italia
120
Nocupétaro
Tuzantla
MEXICO
Villa Victoria
120
Apatzingán
La Huacana
Tiquicheo
Coahuayana
Coalcomán
Cuatro Caminos
Aquila
Churumuco
Eréndira
San Juan de Alima
Punta San Telmo
Aguililla
La Vinata
Presa de Infiernillo
51
Tizuapan
Arteaga
37
Infiernillo
Ciudad Altamirano
200
Las Peñas
Lázaro Cárdenas
GUERRERO
N
Caleta de Campos
Playa Azul
OCÉANO PACÍFICO

0   40 miles
0   40 kilometers

Michoacán de Ocampo

Laundry: Autoservicio de Lavandería, Carranza 47 (tel. 4 51 41), at García, four blocks west of the *zócalo*. Wash and dry 3kg for 30 pesos. Open M-Sa 9am-8pm.

Police: (tel. 3 27 33), at Eucaliptos and Naranjo.

Pharmacy: Farmacia Fénix, Carranza 1 (tel. 4 16 40). Open daily 8am-10pm.

Medical Services: The **Red Cross,** Del Lago 1 (tel. 4 03 00), is a block down from the **Hospital Civil,** Calzada Fray Juan de San Miguel 6 (tel. 3 36 17), 7 blocks west of the northern edge of the *zócalo*. Both open 24hr.

Emergency: dial 060.

Internet Access: Logicentro, Juárez 57 (tel. 4 94 94 or 4 77 40). 35 pesos per hr. Open M-Sa 9am-2pm and 5-9pm.

Post Office: Reforma 13 (tel. 3 56 30), 3 blocks south of the *zócalo* on Cupatitzio and left one block. Open M-F 8am-4pm, Sa 9am-1pm. **Postal Code:** 60000.

Telephones: LADATELs line the plaza. Otherwise, make long-distance phone calls or fax from **Computel,** Ocampo 3, on the plaza. Open daily 7am-10pm.

Phone Code: 452.

▌ ACCOMMODATIONS

The place to stay in Uruapan is on or near the *zócalo*, where the ritzy and affordable coexist side-by-side. Straying too far could be hazardous to your health; Uruapan's cheaper hotels, oozing from the eastern edge of the *zócalo*, tend to be sleazy, with tattered bedspreads, filthy bathrooms, prostitution, and a fraternity of jumbo *cucarachas* hosting all night *fiestas*.

Hotel del Parque, Independencia 124 (tel. 4 38 45), 5½ blocks from the plaza, and half a block from the beautiful Parque Nacional. Far and away the best place in Uruapan. Large rooms surrounding an airy patio and squeaky clean bathrooms are popular with backpackers. Singles 80 pesos; doubles 120 pesos; triples 140 pesos.

Hotel Moderno, Portal Santos Degollado 4 (tel 4 02 12), next door to the Hotel Oseguera. A semi-shabby place, but peach-colored rooms with dark wood funiture are OK. Birds, both live and stuffed, keep watch over the lobby TV. Get used to hearing the jingle of the pony ride at the front door again and again. 1 bed 50 pesos; 2 beds 100 pesos.

Hotel Los Tres Caballeros, Constitución 50 (tel. 4 71 70). Go north up Portal Santo Degollado (the eastern border of the *zócalo*), then plunge into the depths of the market for about 2 blocks; the hotel is on the right before you emerge at 16 de Septiembre. Red tile floors and stone stairways lend a subtle charm and the rooms are very clean, but the tiny bathrooms might cramp your style and your legs. Singles 67 pesos; doubles 78 pesos; triples 90 pesos; quads 101 pesos.

Hotel Oseguera, Portal Santos Degollado 2 (tel. 3 98 56), in the *zócalo*. You know where you are? You in da jungle baby! Or so it would seem, with the floor and walls painted every shade of green imaginable and choked with plants; mediocre rooms. Singles 50 pesos; doubles with a balcony 100 pesos.

Hotel Villa de Flores, Carranza 15 (tel. 4 28 00). It ain't the Hilton, but probably the best bet for a reasonably priced upscale hotel. Flores lives up its name with a beautiful flower-dappled courtyard. Singles 185 pesos; doubles 245 pesos; triples 275 pesos.

FOOD

Fulfilling your culinary desires near the *zócalo* is a good bet. The bountiful farmland surrounding Uruapan means that delicious avocado, tomato, and mango dishes are available at down to earth prices. Coffee is a local specialty, and most places serve it up strong and hot.

Mercado de Antojitos, between Constitución and Carranza on the north side of the *zócalo* (look for the sign). An outdoor square where Michoacán specialties can be sampled for a pittance. Dozens of eager chefs vie to cook their personal specialties (such as diced steak) for about 18-25 pesos; even cheaper prices can be found in some of the small restaurants near the *mercado*. Open daily 7am-11pm.

Café Tradicional de Uruapan, Carranza 5B. Follow your nose to the "Tradicional," where locals sit sipping their *café* so slowly that they might lose a race with a second-class Mexican train. Dining here is like sitting inside a cigar box—the cafe's entire surface area is covered in richly stained wood. High prices mean it's probably not the place for a full meal, but enjoy a sandwich (17-24 pesos) along with a wide variety of coffee and ice cream drinks. Open daily 8:30am-10:30pm.

Jugos California, Independencia 9, just off the *zócalo*. Get your health food kicks under artificial palms while imbibing *licuados* (8-12 pesos), sandwiches (10-13 pesos), or fruit, yogurt, and breakfast specials. Open daily 7am-10pm.

Rosticeria Del Buen Sazon, Culver City 28, across from the Parque Nacional has great chicken (20 pesos for a half-bird) and cheap beer (5 pesos). What more do you need? Open daily 11am-5pm.

ENTERTAINMENT AND THE OUTDOORS

Most of the dazzling sights of Uruapan are outside the city rather than inside it. If you're going to be in Uruapan for more than a couple of hours, think about seeing the surrounding landscape.

PARQUE NACIONAL BARRANCA DEL CUPATITZIO. A stunning bit of jungle right on the edge of town, the park boasts waterfalls, dense vegetation, and seemingly endless cool, shaded, cobblestone walkways. It makes for an excellent afternoon walk or picnic, although countless vendors detract from the experience some-

what. The park is found on Culver City at the western end of Independencia. *(Tel. 4 01 97. Open daily 8am-6pm. Admission 4 pesos, children ages 3-10 and over age 70 2 pesos.)*

CASA DE LA CULTURA. Even though it may be tempting to get lost in the jungle, the *casa's* art exhibits, occasional movie screenings, and an archaeological and historical museum on the second floor make the trip worthwhile. Head to García Ortiz 1 just off the north side of the *zócalo*. *(Open daily 10am-2pm and 4-8pm.)*

LA SCALA DISCO. Much of the after-hours scene is set in cafes. The main *discoteca* in Uruapan is just outside of town on the road to Tzaráracua, and a 20-peso cab ride from the *centro*. A young, local crowd dances to U.S. Top 40 and Mexican dance tunes. *(Madrid 12 in Colonia Huerta del Cupatitzio. Located at Madrid 12. Tel. 4 26 09. Cover 10 pesos Tu-Th, 30 pesos F-Sa. Open Tu-Sa 9pm-2am.)*

HASTA LA VISTA, SATAN
At Uruapan's Parque Nacional Barranca del Cupatitzio, you may want to bring along your crucifix for viewing **La Rodilla del Diablo** (The Devil's Knee). Legend has it that the river once dried up, leaving the surrounding lands stark and bare. The village, left without food or water, prayed in desperation. One day, the friar Juan de San Miguel led a procession to the dry river's mouth, carrying an image of the Virgin. The friar halted the procession to sprinkle some holy water on the Virgin's image and on the rocks at the river's mouth. Suddenly, Satan appeared, saw the Virgin, and with a tumultuous shaking of the earth, retreated into the rocks. The flow of water resumed, but one rock still bears the imprint of the knee of the *Príncipe de la Tinieblas* (Prince of Darkness).

NEAR URUAPAN

Uruapan is a convenient place from which to explore the interior of Michoacán. The diverse landscape is home to everything from ill-tempered volcanoes to picture-perfect waterfalls. If you're tired of feigning appreciation for natural things, check out the immensely revered image of Christ that was rescued by the whole village of **San Juan Nuevo** after a volcano. In nearby **Paracho**, a world-famous guitar competition turns into a full-fledged musical blowout for two weeks in August.

PARICUTÍN VOLCANO

A visit to the still-active Paricutín Volcano makes a great daytrip from Uruapan. In 1943, the volcano began erupting. By the time it quit spewing lava eight years later, there was little dust left to settle—the land had been coated in a thick and hardening layer of porous lava. Along the way, entire towns had been consumed and a 700m dark-side-of-the-moon-type mountain had sprung up. The lava covered the entire village of San Juan except for part of the church, which now sticks out of a field of cold, black stone.

At the Angahuán **Centro Turístico** (tel. 452 5 03 83), you can rent **horses** (120 pesos). Plan to get an early start to avoid afternoon thunderstorms, and bring along some warm clothing just in case. The trip is long but worth the time and pesos. Decathlon contenders may consider the six- to eight-hour **walking tours** to the church (3.5km, 50 pesos), or to the volcano (7km, 100 pesos). If you decide to tackle the trails on your own, be sure to always stay on a path with numerous foot (and hoof) prints, as trails are very poorly marked. The Centro Turístico has a small museum in addition to a restaurant. **Cabins** are also available for rent from the tourist center (1-6 people 400 pesos; bunks 70 pesos in a communal cabin).

Getting There: From the *centro*, take a "Ruta Paraiso/Galeana" bus headed for Los Reyes. At the bus stop along the route, you still have a good 3km walk ahead to reach the Centro Turístico on the other side fo the village. Rides to the *centro* are available for 15-20 pesos. **Paraíso Galeana** buses (tel. 4 33 50), headed for Los Reyes, and Angahuán, the closest village to the volcano (50min., every 30min. 5am-8pm, 9 pesos).

SAN JUAN NUEVO PARANGARICUTIRO

Ten kilometers west of Uruapan is San Juan Nuevo, founded after the destruction of the old village by the eruption of the Paricutín Volcano in 1943. Many devotees come to the village for only one reason—to see the **Lord of Miracles,** an image of Christ dating back to the late 16th century. The image is revered for answering countless prayers and performing miracles. When the volcano erupted, San Juan's 2000 inhabitants abandoned the village and began a three-day, 33km pilgrimage carrying their beloved Lord of Miracles. A beautiful rose brick **sanctuary** with pastel tile *capillas* was eventually built to house the image. The interior's white walls and vaulted ceilings are adorned with gold leaf, delicate stained-glass windows, and sparkling chandeliers—altogether an impressive and fitting house for the revered *Señor de los Milagros*. Seemingly not as fitting is the gaudy blue neon sign above the statue that reads "*Si de los Milagros, en ti confío*" (Lord of Miracles, I trust in you). (Open daily 6am-8pm.) The **museum,** Av. 20 de Noviembre, a block past the cathedral down the street to the right, exhibits photos depicting the eruption, as well as before-and-after shots of the village (open M-Sa 9:15am-7pm, Su 9:15-6:30pm; free).

Once you've seen the cathedral and museum, San Juan Nuevo quickly loses appeal. The two main streets, **20 de Noviembre** and **Cárdenas,** which run on either side of the cathedral, play host to several shops and a rather dirty market. The best dining option in San Juan is not to dine in San Juan; most stands are especially unappealing here. If you get stranded in San Juan, the **Hotel Victoria,** Cárdenas 26 (tel. 4 00 10), across from the cathedral, will take care of you with clean, large rooms with TV and some with a view of the cathedral. (Singles 80 pesos; doubles 130 pesos.)

Getting There: Take an **Autotransportes Tancitara** bus to San Juan Nuevo (45min., every 10min. 5:30am-9pm, 4 pesos) from the Central de Autobuses. To get back, wait for the same bus on the corner of Cárdenas and Iturbe two blocks up from the cathedral (45min., every 15 min. until 9:30pm, 4 pesos).

TZARÁRACUA AND TZARARECUITA

The waterfalls at **Tzaráracua** (sah-RA-ra-kwa), 10km from Uruapan, cascade 20m into a series of small pools, surrounded by dense, lush vegetation. The first waterfall, Tzaráracua, is about 1km from the parking lot—walk down the steps to the right or ride a horse down the rocky path to the left (20-40 pesos). At the main waterfall, look but don't swim; there's a dangerous undercurrent. Walk across the water on the bridge or ask a worker to take you over the water in a suspended boxcar (Site open daily 9am-5pm; admission 2 pesos, parking fee 5 pesos).

Tzararecuita, a waterfall with two smaller pools that are perfect for swimming, is another 1.5km beyond the large pool. Feel free to wear only your birthday suit if your heart so desires, but keep an eye on your clothes. The aid of a guide is necessary to find the falls; most children will try to gouge you for 40-60 pesos, but ask around and you may find something cheaper. Although it's not recommended, to get there alone, you can walk up the hill on the left at Tzarácua and continue down on the other side of the river.

Getting There: "Zapatu-Tzaráracua" buses leave from the south side of the *zócalo* at the corner of Carranza and Cupatitzio (every hr. 8am-5pm, 5 pesos). During the week, the schedule is so imprecise that it's possible to be stuck all day; Sundays are a bit more reliable. Taxis cost about 40 pesos.

LOS CHORROS DE VARRAL

While not exactly in Uruapan's backyard, los Chorros de Varral is an area of beautiful waterfalls amidst lush vegetation. The only drawback is that it's about three hours away. From the Central in Uruapan, take a Galeana (tel. 4 51 54) bus to Los Reyes (1¼hr., every hr. 5am-8pm, 26 pesos). Once in Los Reyes, head for the *centro* and grab a "Los Pallilos" *combi* (1hr., every 2hr. 7am-7pm, 6 pesos) on Av. Bravo near the *templo*. From where the *combi* stops, it's about a 4km hike and 1000 steps down to a series of three waterfalls.

PARACHO

Thirty kilometers north of Uruapan, **Paracho** gives aspiring *guitarristas* a chance to strum their hearts out and unleash the *mariachi* within. Carefully crafted six-strings pack just about every store and fantastic bargains are available for all varieties of guitar. For two weeks in August, the town holds an internationally renowned **guitar festival.** Musicians and craftspeople partake in a musical dervish of classical concerts, fireworks, dancing, and guitar-strumming competitions. A smaller, one-day music fest occurs on October 22nd in honor of Santa Ursula. The main street in town is **20 de Noviembre,** which runs by the plaza and the market and is the site of the bus stop. Sights in Paracho are limited to the **Casa de Arte y Cultura** on the corner of the plaza, which displays (who could have guessed) guitars (open sporadically daily 10am-8pm). Hop on a **Galeana** (tel. 4 33 50) bus bound for Zamora via Paracho (45min., every 15min. 4am-8:30pm, 7 pesos) from the Central Camionera.

PÁTZCUARO

Michoacán's earthy jewel, Pátzcuaro (pop. 70,000), is slowly becoming a travelers' favorite. Set high in the mountains, the city is surrounded by rolling hills and forests kept lush by daily showers that extend to the shores of the expansive and polluted Lake Pátzcuaro. The compact and quiet city center is nearly as spectacular as the surrounding landscape—the tolling cathedral bells resonate through cobblestone streets and white stucco colonial-style buildings. The bells can't keep pace with the frequent report of firecrackers, however, which are set off at all hours of the day and night.

This is not even Pátzcuaro's biggest selling point; the town is best known for its crafts. In order to increase economic development, the Spanish Bishop Vasco de Quiroga encouraged residents of each Purépecha village around the lake to specialize in a different craft. Today Pátzcuaro's plazas overflow with stacks of handmade woolen sweaters, meticulously carved wooden toys, and decorative masks.

ORIENTATION

Pátzcuaro lies 56km southwest of Morelia and 62km northeast of Uruapan. To reach the *centro* from the **bus station,** catch a *combi* (7am-9:30pm, 2.50 pesos) or city bus (6:30am-10pm, 2.50 pesos) from the lot to the right leaving the station. A **taxi** costs 12 pesos. The city consists of two distinct sections: the small and easily navigated downtown and a lakefront residential area 2.5km to the north. The downtown centers around Pátzcuaro's two main squares. The smaller **Plaza Bocanegra,** bordered by **Padre Lloreda** to the north, **Dr. Benito Mendoza** to the west, and **Iturbide** to the east, is all bustle and thick crowds; it's also where many of the cheap accommodations and restaurants reside. One block south on Dr. Benito Mendoza is the larger **Plaza Quiroga,** an elegant and quiet plaza with a fountain and well-shaded paths. For shops, pricey meals, and fancy accommodations, this is the place to be. Streets form a rough grid and change names at each plaza. Some addresses on the plazas are not given with the street name, but with the name of the *portal* (arcade). For example, at Plaza Quiroga, Benito Mendoza, which borders the plaza's western side, becomes **Portal Hidalgo.** Summers in Pátzcuaro can be wet and cool, so bring along some rain gear and a light sweater.

PRACTICAL INFORMATION

Buses: Central is off Circunvalación, 8 blocks south of the *centro.* Autobuses de Occidente (tel. 2 00 92) send 'em packing for: **Guadalajara** (5hr., 12:15pm, 90 pesos) and many of the tiny villages around Pátzcuaro. Elite (tel. 2 14 60) heads to: **Nuevo Laredo** (16hr., 3 and 8:30pm, 636 pesos) via **Monterrey** (14hr., 490 pesos); and Tijuana (38hr., 4:40pm, 1155 pesos). Galeana (tel. 2 08 08) rolls to: **Lázaro Cárdenas** (7hr., every hr. 5:30am-9pm, 126 pesos); **Morelia** (1hr., every 10min., 22 pesos); **Uruapan** (1½hr., every 10min., 26 pesos); and the small towns between them. Herradura de Plata (tel. 2 10 45) runs to **Mexico City** (first-class 5hr., 10 per day 7:15am-11pm, 175 pesos; second-class 7hr., 7 per day 7:35am-9:30pm, 160 pesos). Primera Plus (tel. 2 09 70) has cushy service to: **Guadalajara** (5hr., 11:50pm, 100 pesos); **Mexico City** (7hr.; 7 and 10am, 8 and 11:30pm; 160 pesos); **Querétaro** (7hr., 11:30pm, 110 pesos); and **San Luis Potosí** (8hr., 6 and 10:40am, 180 pesos).

Tourist Office: Delegación Regional de Turismo, Plaza Quiroga 50A (tel. 2 12 14). Staff speaks some English and hands out good maps. Open M-F 9am-3pm and 4-7pm, Sa 9am-2pm and 4-7pm, Su 9am-2pm. The **City Tourist Office** (with less information) is on the west side of Plaza Quiroga, in the Presidencia Municipal at Portal Hidalgo 19. Open M-F 9am-3pm and 5-7pm, Sa 10am-7pm, Su 10am-3pm.

Currency Exchange: Banca Serfín, Portal Allende 54 (tel. 2 15 16), on the north side of Plaza Quiroga. Has an **ATM.** Open for exchange M-F 9am-3pm.

Luggage Storage: At bus station, 5 pesos per 1½hr., 10 pesos per day. Open 7am-10pm.

Emergency: Cuerpo de Rescate (tel. 2 02 05). On call 24hr.

Police: (tel. 2 00 04), on the corner of Ibarra and Tangara, 4 blocks from Plaza Quiroga.

Pharmacy: Farmacia del Carmen (tel. 2 26 52), on the corner of Romero and Navarrete. Open 24hr. Open daily 8am-10pm; after hours, knock at the window on Navarrete.

Hospital: Hospital Civil, Romero 10 (tel. 2 02 85), next to San Juan de Dios church.

Post Office: Obregón 13 (tel. 2 01 28), ½ block north of Plaza Bocanegra. Open M-F 8am-4pm, Sa 9am-1pm. **Postal Code:** 61600.

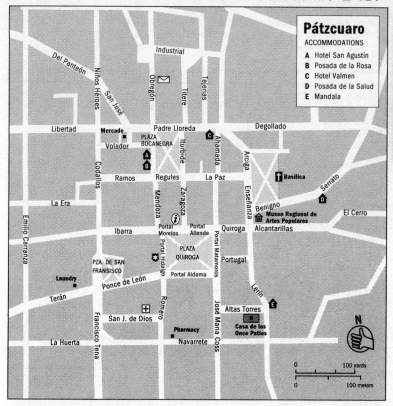

Pátzcuaro

ACCOMMODATIONS

A Hotel San Agustín
B Posada de la Rosa
C Hotel Valmen
D Posada de la Salud
E Mandala

Fax: Informatica Integral, Quiroga 64 in Plaza Quiroga. Open M-F 9:30am-9pm, Sa-Su 9:30am-3pm. Also in the *caseta* in the bus station, and on the north side of Plaza Bocanegra. Open daily 7am-9pm.

Phone Code: 434.

ACCOMMODATIONS

Budget hotels are spread out all over the place, but those in the **Plaza Bocanegra** are right in the middle of things and feature clean and comfy rooms. If you're lucky, you can score a balcony on the plaza and a private bathroom.

Mandala, Lerin 14 (tel. 2 41 76), just past the Casa de los Once Patios. Not the cheapest place in town, but definitely one of the nicest. Beautifully decorated rooms in a friendly environment. Downstairs rooms have shared bath: singles 120 pesos; doubles 240 pesos. Upstairs rooms have private baths and a view of the city: singles 135 pesos; doubles 270 pesos. Includes a great complimentary breakfast.

Posada de la Salud, Serrato 9 (tel. 2 00 58), 3 blocks east of either plaza and a half block past the *basilíca.* A courtyard draped in tropical flowers is surrounded by clean chambers with bathrooms. Singles 110 pesos; doubles 150 pesos; triples 190 pesos.

Hotel San Augustin, Portal Juárez 27B, 3rd fl. (tel. 2 04 42). Dark rooms, some overlooking the plaza have private baths and matching furniture. 60 pesos per person.

Posada de la Rosa, Portal Juárez 29, 2nd fl. (tel. 2 12 76), on the west side of Plaza Bocanegra. Red-tiled rooms have a lone lightbulb hanging from the ceiling over clean hardwood floors and comfortable beds. Singles with communal bath 60 pesos; doubles 70 pesos; triples 80 pesos. Singles with private bath 120 pesos; doubles 150 pesos.

SOUTHERN PACIFIC COAST

Hotel Valmen, Lloreda 34 (tel. 2 11 61), 1 block east of Plaza Bocanegra. Vibrant Aztec tile fills the lime-green courtyards and some of the well-lit rooms have balconies—popular with international travelers. Doors are locked at 10pm sharp. 60 pesos per person.

◖ FOOD

Economical restaurants surround **Plaza Bocanegra** and the accompanying market, while fancier joints cluster in and around the hotels on Plaza Quiroga. *Pescado blanco* (whitefish), *charales* (small fish eaten fried and whole), and *caldo de pescado* (fish soup with various other ingredients) are the specialties of the region—head to an island or near the lake for prices half those in the city itself.

✦ Restaurant Yunuhen, Portal Juárez 27A, (tel. 2 08 94), on the west side of Plaza Bocanegra. This tiny gem, adorned with fascinating murals depicting local history and culture, serves great *comida corrida* for 27 pesos. Open daily 8am-8pm.

Restaurant Posada la Basílica, Arciga 6 (tel. 2 11 08), in front of the *basílica*. A petal-strewn courtyard leads to an elegant, tiled room with colorful tablecloths and windows overlooking the town and nearby lakes. *Pollo en mole* 36 pesos. Open M-W 8am-5pm.

Mandala (see **Accommodations**), has incredibly flavorful vegetarian cuisine that will satisfy even the most ardent of meat lovers. Don't leave Patzcuaro without sampling the fresh ingredients and organically grown vegetables. Huge *menú del día* 34 pesos, and homemade wheat spaghetti (32 pesos). Open every day but Tu, 8:30am-9:30pm.

Restaurant Los Escudos, Portal Hidalgo 73 (tel. 2 12 90), on the west side of Plaza Quiroga, inside the Hotel Los Escudos. The ambience is set by bowtie-clad waiters, attractive wood furniture, and tasteful decor. *Sopa tarasca* 17 pesos and *comida corrida* 35 pesos. Come Saturdays at 8pm to see the *danza de los viejitos,* a dance ridiculing the Spanish. Live organ music daily 3-5pm and 7-10pm. Open daily 7:30am-10pm.

◖ SIGHTS

Along with sights within earshot of the *basílica*, some of the most notable sights around Pátzcuaro are just a short trip from downtown (see **Near Pátzcuaro,** p. 430).

BASÍLICA DE NUESTRA SEÑORA DE LA SALUD. When the Bishop Vasco de Quiroga came to Pátzcuaro, he initiated not only social change but also bold architectural projects. Quiroga conceived the pink-and-gold Basílica, at Lerín and Serrato, as a colossal structure with five naves arranged like the fingers of an extended hand. Each finger was to represent one of Michoacán's cultures and races; the hand's palm was to be the central altar representing the Catholic religion. Today, an enormous glass booth with gilded Corinthian columns and a dome protects the potentially edible statue of the *Virgen de la Salud.* When Vasco de Quiroga asked Tarascan artisans to design an image of the Virgin in 1546, they complied by shaping her out of *tatzingue* paste made from corn cobs and orchid honey, a typical 16th-century statue-making technique. *(Open daily 8am-8pm.)*

PLAZAS. Statues of Pátzcuaro's two most honored citizens stand in the town's principal plazas. The ceremonious, banner-bearing Vasco de Quiroga inhabits **Plaza Quiroga,** a vast and green space. Famous throughout the state of Michoacán, Quiroga encouraged different indigenous peoples to make different crafts. The massive, bare-breasted Gertrudis Bocanegra looks out from the center of **Plaza Gertrudis Bocanegra.** A martyr for Mexican independence, Bocanegra was executed by a Spanish squadron in the Plaza Quiroga in October, 1817. Locals claim that bullet holes still mark the ash tree to which she was tied.

MUSEO REGIONAL DE ARTES POPULARES. Housed within old fort-like walls, and sporting a flower-filled courtyard, the museum displays regional crafts like pottery, copperware, and textiles, as well as an arresting collection of *maque* and *laca* ceramics. *(Enseñanza 20, at Alcanterillas, one block south of the basílica. Tel. 2 10 29. Open Tu-Sa 9am-7pm, Su 9am-3pm. Admission 20 pesos, free on Sunday.)*

TEATRO CALTZONTZÍN. Once part of an Augustine convent, this building on the Plaza Bocanegra became a theater in 1936. Prophecy was uttered upon the theater's erection: one Holy Thursday, the theater will crumble as punishment for the sin of projecting movies in a sacred place. You can take in a drama, musical performance, or movie (probably not on Holy Thursday) in the theater. Look for posters or ask at the adjacent library. The **Biblioteca Gertrudis Bocanegra** is another mural that illustrates the history of the Purépecha civilization from pre-Hispanic times to the 1910 Revolution. *(Open M-F 9am-7pm.)*

SHOPPING

Pátzcuaro's unique handcrafts—hairy Tócuaro masks, elegant Sierran dinnerware, and thick wool textiles—are sold in Plaza Bocanegra's **market** and in the small shops along the passage next to Biblioteca Gertrudis Bocanegra. Bargaining is easier in the market or when you buy more than one item, but don't expect much of a discount on the stunningly handsome wool articles. The thick sweaters, brilliantly colored *saltillos* and *ruanas* (stylized ponchos), rainbow-colored *sarapes*, and dark shawls are Pátzcuaro's specialties. Most shops are open daily from 8am to 8pm. For many of the same items at much cheaper prices, you may want to make the trek to some of the Pátzcuaro's surrounding villages.

Some higher quality and expensive items can be found at **La Casa de los Once Patios,** so named for the 18th-century building's 11 patios, on Lerín near Navarrete. Originally a convent, the complex now houses craft shops and a mural depicting Vasco de Quiroga's accomplishments. The *casa* sells cotton textiles, wooden and copper crafts, and superb musical instruments like guitars (222-1200 pesos), flutes, and *güiros*, at decent prices. (Open daily 10am-2pm and 4-8pm.)

ENTERTAINMENT AND SEASONAL EVENTS

Unless there's an outdoor festival in one of the plazas, nightlife is confined mainly to restaurants and a few bars. At **Charanda's N,** Plaza Vasco de Quiroga 61B, the local chess club meets daily from 6 to 9pm amid wood carvings and potted plants, and live music stirs things up on weekends. (Cover Sa-Su 7pm-Midnight 15 pesos. Open Tu-Su 2pm-1am.) The off-beat **El Viejo Gaucho,** Iturbe 10 (tel. 2 03 68), a colorful Argentine bar and restaurant with art exhibits, features live music—everything from rock and blues to cumbias and *salsas* (cover 15 pesos; music starts at 8pm; open W-Su 6-11pm).

Pátzcuaro parties year-round, but its biggest celebration is without a doubt the spectacular **Noche de Muertos** (Oct. 31-Nov. 2), which holds special importance for the Tarascans. Tourists from around the globe flock to Pátzcuaro and Janitzio to watch candle-lit fishing boats proceed to the tiny island. There, families and neighbors keep a two-night vigil in the haunting graveyard, feasting at the graves of their loved ones. The first night commemorates lost children; the second remembers deceased adults. Soon after Christmas celebrations come to a close, the town is electrified by **Pastorelas,** celebrated on January 6 to commemorate the Adoration of the Magi, and on January 17 to honor St. Anthony of Abad, the patron saint of animals. On both occasions, citizens dress their domestic animals in bizarre costumes, ribbons, and floral crowns. A few months later, Pátzcuaro's **Semana Santa** attracts devotees from all over the Republic. On Holy Thursday, all the churches in town are visited, and on the night of Good Friday, the **Procesión de Imágenes de Cristo** is held, during which images of a crucified Christ are carried around town. The faithful flock from all over the state on Saturday for Pátzcuaro's **Procesión del Silencio,** celebrated elsewhere the day before. On this day, a crowd marches around town mourning Jesus's death in silence, but come Easter Sunday, of course, the real celebration begins. If you aren't around for the bigger festivals and parties, don't fret because most weekends still see bands playing in the plazas and young, attractive people moving to the music.

NEAR PÁTZCUARO

The area around Pátzcuaro is blessed with some of the most diverse landscapes in all of Mexico. Surrounding villages offer beautiful handicrafts, usually at cheaper prices than the cities.

JANITZIO

The tiny island of **Janitzio,** inhabited exclusively by Tarascan *indígenas* whose first language is Purépecha, subsists on its tourist trade. There are basically two directions in Janitzio—up and down. The town's steep main street is lined with stores selling wool goods and hand-carved wooden chess sets and masks. Among the shops, the bulk of which are quite pricey, numerous restaurants offer meals of fresh *pescado blanco* (30 pesos) and *charales* (15 pesos) as well as the aptly named *jarro locos,* a strange concoction of fruit juices, wine, and red seasonings.

Janitzio is best known for the enormous **statue of Morelos** that towers over the island. Inside the statue, a mural traces the principal events in Morelos's life and struggle for independence. Endless steps lead you to the fantastic lookout point right around the height of Morelos' sleeve. As long as you keep walking up you'll reach the statue eventually several paths start right at the ferry docks.

Getting There: First, hop on a "Lago" *combi* or bus (2.50 pesos) at the corner of Portal Regules and Portal Juárez, at Plaza Bocanegra in Pátzcuaro. At the docks, buy a ferry ticket (40min., ferries leave whenever they're full or on the hour, 8am-7pm, 20 pesos round-trip, children under 5 free; and to the smaller and less developed islands of **Yunuen** and **Pacanda,** 24 pesos round-trip). Find out when the last boat leaves the island for Pátzcuaro; Janitzio does not accommodate the stranded.

TZINTZUNTZÁN

The most exciting thing about **Tzintzuntzán** (seen-soon-SAHN; Place of the Hummingbirds) may be saying the name—it is believed to be the phonetic sound of the many **hummingbirds** that flit through the sky. Tzintzuntzán was the last great city of the Tarascan empire. Before his death in the middle of the 15th century, the Purépecha lord Tariácuri divided his empire among his son and two nephews. When the empire was reunited years later, Tzintzuntzán was made the capital. Today, its claims to fame are the delicate, multicolored **ceramics** for sale along Calle Principal.

Yácatas, the ruins of several pre-Hispanic temples, sit on a hill just outside the city. To reach the entrance, walk up the street in front of the market and convent (right where the bus stops). It's a bit of a hike—follow the road all the way around the hill until you reach the small museum/ticket booth. The bases of the structures, all that remain today, are standard rectangular pyramids. The missing parts, however, are what made them unique; each was originally crowned with an unusual elliptical pyramid constructed of shingles and volcanic rock. At the edge of the hill overlooking the lake is a sacrificial block from which victims were hurled; the bones of thousands are said to lie at the base. Another structure was used to stockpile enemy heads. The small museum at the entrance includes some Mesoamerican pottery, jewelry, and a narrative of Tarascan history. (Site open daily 9am-6pm. Admission 17 pesos, free on Sundays and for children under 13.)

Also of interest is the *atrio* and 16th-century Franciscan **convent,** right across from the bus stop in the opposite direction from the ruins. The olive shrubs that now cover the extensive, tree-filled atrium were originally planted under Vasco de Quiroga's instructions over 450 years ago. If you need help finding anything or want more information, head for the **tourist office,** conveniently located on the main street right next to the bus stop. (Convent open daily 10am-8pm.)

Getting There: Tzintzuntzán is perched on the northeastern edge of the Lago de Pátzcuaro, about 15km from Pátzcuaro, on the road to Quiroga and Morelia. Second-class **Galeana** buses (tel. 2 08 08) leave the Pátzcuaro bus station for Tzintzuntzán (30min., every 15min. 6am-7:30pm, 4 pesos) en route to Quiroga. Catch a bus back to Pátzcuaro on the same schedule. The return bus to Pátzcuaro stops near the ferry dock to Janitzio.

SANTA CLARA DEL COBRE

Sixteen kilometers south of Pátzcuaro, Santa Clara truly shines when it comes to crafting copper. Long ago, rich copper mines filled the area, but they were hidden from the Spanish during the Conquest, never to be found again. However, the townspeople's passion for copperwork remains unrivaled. When electricity was brought to the town, blackouts occurred when the artisans hammered the wires into pots and pans. Nearly every store in town sells highly individualized and decorative copper plates, pans, bowls, and bells. Prices here are only slightly better than elsewhere in Mexico, but Santa Clara is unbeatable for quality and variety. For a quick look at some highly imaginative pieces, step into the **Museo del Cobre,** near the plaza. Santa Clara celebrates the **Feria del Cobre** in early August. There is little to see in Santa Clara beyond *artesanías;* budget only a short time for a trip here from Pátzcuaro.

Getting There: Take a Galeana bus from **Lago de Zirahuén** (20min., every 30min. 7am-8pm, 3 pesos), or from **Pátzcuaro,** catch a Galeana or Occidente bus to **Santa Clara** from the main station (every 30min. 6am-8pm, 5 pesos).

LAGO DE ZIRAHUÉN

The Lago de Zirahuén (Where Smoke Rose) makes for a fun trip from Pátzcuaro for those who like the pace of life slow—very slow. You could pull a Rip van Winkle and probably not miss a thing either. Smaller than Lake Pátzcuaro, Zirahuén is bordered by green farmland and gentle sloping hills unobstructed by marshes and islands. To **camp,** hike up one of the ridges that border the lake and set up in any one of the spots overlooking the water. Make sure to bring a tarp and wet-weather gear. If the land is privately owned (usually fenced off), you may have to pay a few pesos; ask before you pitch your tent. A choice spot is the sizable piece of lakefront on the west end of town (left, as you face the lake). The strip, about 15m wide, is covered by grass cut short by grazing horses. The cabañas, a five-minute walk to the right along the dirt road bordering the lake, allow campers to use the bathrooms for 1 peso. Be forewarned; heavy rains from mid-June to early October can turn camping into a soggy experience.

After roughing it in the great outdoors, head to the *lancha* dock for a smooth one-hour ride around the lake (20 pesos in a collective boat; 150 pesos for a private ride, up to 10 people), and then sit down at one of informal lakefront restaurants, where a stack of tortillas, rice, salad, and fresh fish will run you 20 pesos.

Getting There: From Pátzcuaro, catch one of the Zirahuén-bound cabs from Libertad, about three blocks west from the market. Cabs leave daily for Zirahuén at 6, 8am and 6pm (10-50 pesos depending on how many passengers). Taxis returning to Pátzcuaro leave a block inland from the church at "La Posta," by the "Marilu" sign (on approximately the same schedule). A better option is an Occidente bus from the Pátzcuaro bus station (30min., 8 per day 7:15am-6:30pm, 6 pesos).

MORELIA

At 550,000 inhabitants and growing, Morelia is a city caught up in a dizzying whirl of growth and development. Sophisticated department stores and U.S. fast-food joints squeeze into the outskirts of town while colonial houses with imposing stone facades line the main streets. Vendors hawk traditional textiles and wooden crafts alongside bootleg cassettes, sweatsocks, and spare blender parts in the market-saturated *centro.* Nearby stand incongruous relics of Morelia's colonial magnificence in the form of rose-colored stone arcades and grand, white-washed houses. The city is also the center of a proud tradition of Michoacán culture and history, and it has the museums, art exhibits, and performances to prove it. A sizeable student population spices up the cultural scene with theater, dance productions, and concerts. Morelia's varied and vibrant downtown area almost rivals that of Guadalajara's.

✳ ORIENTATION

The streets in Morelia form a large grid, so navigating the city is relatively uncomplicated. That is, except for street signs that must have been meant to read through decoder glasses. Most sights are within walking distance of the *zócalo* and the adjacent cathedral on **Av. Madero,** Morelia's main thoroughfare. North-south streets change name at Madero, while east-west streets change name every other block. Getting downtown from the **bus station** is a quick 10-minute walk, a short cab ride (8 pesos), or a 10-minute bus ride (2.50 pesos). Walk to the left (east) as you exit the building, take the first right onto **Valentín Gómez Farías,** walk three blocks, then take a left on Av. Madero—the *zócalo* is three blocks ahead. The *centro* is the place to head if you're looking for food, lodging, or fun. **Buses** and *combis* serve the city (daily 6am-10pm, 2.50 pesos). Most routes can be picked up on **Nigromante** and **Galeana,** one block west of the *zócalo,* and on **Allende,** south of the *zócalo.* **Taxis** cluster in front of the bus station. Morelia's streets empty out after 10pm, especially on streets parallel to Madero.

🛈 PRACTICAL INFORMATION

TRANSPORTATION

Airport: Aeropuerto Francisco J. Múgica (tel. 13 67 80), on the Carretera Morelia-Cinapécuaro at Km 27. A blue-and-white "Aeropuerto" bus will get you there for 20 pesos. Taxis (tel. 12 22 21) to the airport cost 85 pesos. **Aeromar** (tel. 12 85 45 or 13 05 55). **Mexicana,** Pirindas 435 (tel. 24 38 08 or 24 38 18). Open M-F 9am-6:30pm. **Taesa,** Av. Acueducto 60 (tel. 13 40 50). Open M-F 9am-2pm and 4-7pm, Sa 9am-1pm. All have offices at the airport.

Buses: Leave from the **Central** station (tel. 13 55 89) on Ruiz at Farías. Autobuses de Occidente/La Linea has second-class service to: **Mexico City** (6hr., every 20min., 135 pesos). Elite (tel. 12 24 62) sends buses to: **Acapulco** (second-class 12hr., 5 per day 7am-2:30am, 217 pesos); **Nuevo Laredo** (16hr.; 3, 5, and 9:30pm, 636 pesos), via Monterrey (13hr., 490 pesos); **Reynosa** (16hr., 5pm, 679 pesos), via **San Luis Potosí** (6hr., 177 pesos) and via **Mazatlán** (16hr., 427 pesos). ETN (tel. 13 74 40) has executive service to **Manzanillo** (7¼hr., 10:30pm, 265 pesos) and **Mexico City** (4hr., 24 per day 2am-midnight, 205 pesos). Flecha Amarilla (tel. 13 55 89) goes to: **Colima** (6½hr., 7:40am and noon, 147 pesos); **Guanajuato** (4hr., 4 per day 6:50am-12:50pm, 82 pesos); **Querétaro** (4hr., 12 per day, 75 pesos); and **San Luis Potosí** (7hr., 8 per day 5:10am-4:30pm, 160 pesos). Herradura de Plata (tel. 12 29 88) heads to: **Mexico City** (4½hr., 25 per day 12:30am-11pm, 130-155 pesos). Parhikuni (tel. 13 99 10) sends first-class and *plus* buses to: **Lázaro Cárdenas** (8hr., 9 per day 6:20am-1:30am, 157 pesos); and **Uruapan** (2hr., every 15min. 6am-8pm, 62 pesos). Primera Plus (tel. 13 55 89) runs first-class buses to: **Aguascalientes** (6hr.; 8:50, 9:50, and 10:10am; 137 pesos); **Guadalajara** (10 per day, 107 pesos); **Mexico City** (4½hr., 8 per day, 135 pesos); and **San Luis Potosí** (6hr., 9 per day, 160 pesos). Ruta Paraíso/Galeana (tel. 12 55 05) beats tracks to: **Lázaro Cárdenas** (8hr., every hr. 6:40am-7:50pm, 155 pesos); **Pátzcuaro** (1hr., every 10min. 6am-9pm, 22 pesos); and **Uruapan** (2hr., every 20min. 6am-9pm, 53 pesos). Transportes Fronteras (tel. 12 24 62) serves **Zacatecas** (9hr., 10:30am, 247 pesos).

TOURIST, FINANCIAL AND LOCAL SERVICES

Tourist Office: State Tourist Office, Nigromante 79 (tel. 17 23 71), at Madero Pte., 2 blocks west of the *zócalo.* Staff distributes maps and a monthly list of cultural events. Free city tours 11am. Open M-F 9am-8pm, Sa-Su 9am-7pm.

Currency Exchange: Banks cluster on Av. Madero near the cathedral. **Bancomer,** Madero Ote. 21 (tel. 12 29 90). Open M-F 8am-5:30pm, Sa 9am-2pm; currency exchange M-F 8:30-5pm, Sa 10am-2:30pm. **Banamex,** Madero Ote. 63 (tel. 22 03 30). Open M-F 9am-5pm, Sa 9am-3pm. Has an **ATM.**

Morelia

ACCOMMODATIONS

A Posada Lourdes
B Hotel Colonial
C IMJUDE Hostel
D Mansión Posada Don Vasco
E Hotel Mintzicuri
F Posada de Villa

Laundry: Lavandería Cuautla, Cuautla 152 (tel. 12 48 06), south of Madero. 21 pesos to wash/dry 3kg. Open M-F 9am-2pm and 4-8pm, Sa 9am-1:30pm.

EMERGENCY AND COMMUNICATIONS

Emergency: dial 060.

Police: (tel. 12 00 73 or 12 22 22), on 20 de Noviembre, 1 block northwest of the Fuente de las Tarascas, at the end of the aqueduct. Open 24hr.

Red Cross: Ventura 27 (tel. 14 51 51 or 14 50 25), next to Parque Cuauhtémoc. Some English spoken. Open 24hr.

Pharmacy: Farmacia Fénix, Allende 69 (tel. 12 84 92), behind the *zócalo.* Open M-Sa 9am-10pm.

Hospital: Hospital General Dr. Miguel Silva (tel. 12 94 04), Isidro Huarte and F. de Mogil. Open 24hr.

Post Office: Av. Madero Ote. 369 (tel. 12 05 17), in the Palacio Federal, 5 blocks east of the cathedral. Open M-F 8am-4pm, Sa 9am-1pm. **Postal Code:** 58000.

Fax: Computel, Portal Galeana 157 (tel./fax 13 62 56), on the *zócalo.* Open daily 7am-10pm. Also **Telecomm,** Av. Madero Ote. 371 (tel. 12 03 45), in the Palacio Federal next to the post office. Open M-F 8am-7pm, Sa-Su 8am-1pm.

Internet Access: Telecomm (see above). 25 pesos per hr. Available M-F 8am-2pm.

Phone Code: 43.

ACCOMMODATIONS

Unfortunately, budget hotels that have vacancy are are about as rare as jackrabbits in Morelia. They also tend to fill up quickly, even at unexpected times. Your best bet is to head to the IMJUDE hostel, which isn't very far away.

IMJUDE Villa Juvenil Youth Hostel, Chiapas 180 (tel. 13 31 77), at Oaxaca. A 20min. walk from the *zócalo*. Walk west on Madero Pte., turn left on Cuautla, walk for 6 blocks, then turn right on Oaxaca and continue for 4 blocks to Chiapas or take an *amarilla* (yellow stripe) *combi* from the *centro*. A very happening place. Exceptionally well-maintained dormitories, bathrooms, and red-tiled lobby. Sports facilities and pool. 48 pesos per person. Linen deposit 50 pesos. Open daily 9am-11pm.

Mansión Posada Don Vasco, Vasco de Quiroga 232 (tel. 12 14 84). Spacious rooms come with cable TV, phones, wood furniture, carpeting, and purified water. 1 person 115 pesos; 2 people 138 pesos; 3 people 161 pesos; 4 people 184 pesos. Ask the friendly staff about the availability of fully loaded smaller rooms right off the courtyard (70 pesos).

Hotel Mintzicuri, Vasco de Quiroga 227 (tel. 12 05 90), 2 blocks east and 1½ blocks south of the cathedral. Wrought iron railings overflowing with flowers enclose sparkling clean, cozy, wood-paneled rooms equipped with phones and cable TV. Popular with Mexican tourist families, so come early or call ahead to make sure rooms are available. Singles 110 pesos; doubles 135 pesos; triples 165 pesos.

Hotel Colonial, 20 de Noviembre 15 (tel. 12 18 97), at Morelos Nte. Welcoming courtyard glows a deep yellow. Friendly staff. Rooms have high ceilings, large windows, and private baths; some even have balconies, and all come with *agua purificada*. Singles 100 pesos; doubles 130 pesos without TV, with TV singles 150 pesos, doubles 170 pesos, triples 240 pesos, quads 280 pesos.

Posada de Villa, Padre Lloreda 176 (tel. 12 72 90), 3 blocks south of the Museo de las Artesanías. Gigantic rooms have great views and tasteful decor. Bathrooms are a bit run-down but clean. Singles 90 pesos; doubles 110 pesos; triples 130 pesos. Pastel apartments for 1-2 people 1500 pesos per month.

Posada Lourdes, 340 Del Trabajo, off Morelos Nte. Not the most attractive place from the outside, but rooms are pleasant, clean, and most importantly, cheap. With shared bath singles 45 pesos, doubles 75 pesos; with private bath singles 75 pesos, doubles 95 pesos, triples 120 pesos, quads 150 pesos.

FOOD

Unlike the hotel situation, finding good, cheap food is a breeze in Morelia—almost every thoroughfare has at least one family-run restaurant that dishes out inexpensive *comida corrida* (usually around 15 pesos). The best deals (but not necessarily best quality) cluster around the bus station. Restaurants on the *zócalo* tend to be pricier but are good places for breakfast or a late night snack, since other eateries tend to open late and close early.

Super Cocina la Rosa, Tapía 270, next to the garden. This family-run restaurant draws in droves of customers—try to go at an off time to guarantee a table. Great food (and lots of it) served fresh off the stove daily. *Huevos al gusto* 15 pesos; *comida corrida* 25 pesos. Open daily 8:30am-4:30pm.

Restaurante-Bar La Huacana, Aldama 116 (tel. 12 53 12), at Obeso. A gargantuan oil painting forms the backdrop for the large cafeteria-style dining area. The corner locale is perfect for people-watching. *Comida corrida* 20 pesos. Open M-Sa 11am-7pm.

Restaurante Vegetariano Acuarias, Hidalgo 75, south of the *zócalo*. Good food, but slow service. Set in a blue-tiled courtyard littered with plants, bikes, and an assortment of junk. *Comida corrida* 70 pesos. Breakfast combos 18 pesos. Open daily 8:30am-5pm.

Restaurant Vegetariano, upstairs at Madero 549 Ote. (tel. 13 16 18), across from Sony store. Whole lotta' food for a little prices. Breakfast combos 16-18 pesos, lunch combos 20-22 pesos. Open M-F 10am-5:30pm.

El Tragadero, Hidalgo 63 (tel. 13 00 92). This open-front restaurant affords a great view of the marketplace area. The best part is that the restaurant is open late (for Morelia). *Comida corrida* 28 pesos; *milanesa* 36 pesos; *tortas* 12 pesos. Open M-Sa 7:30am-11pm, Su 7:30am-8pm.

▣ SIGHTS

Packed with museums and cultural centers spanning all aspects of Michoacán's heritage, Morelia is a history buff's dream come true.

MUSEO MICHOACANO. Ecological, archaeological, and anthropological exhibits are displayed on the first floor of this museum, while the second floor features the colonial period, the struggle for freedom, and independent Mexico. The most notable object on display is a huge, anonymous painting completed in 1738, *La Procesión del Traslado de las Monjas de una Universidad a su Convento Nuevo* (The Procession of the Nuns from the University to Their New Convent). A mural around the stairway by Alfredo Zalce will capture your attention—it portrays both the positive and negative aspects of Mexican history, including Spanish colonial imperialism and U.S. capitalist imperialism. Another captivating mural was painted by U.S. citizen Phillip Goldstein. It shows a torture chamber of the Spanish Inquisition surrounded by the Russians and Chinese with a hammer and sycle, hooded members of the Ku Klux Klan, and swastikas, perhaps unremarkable except for the fact that it was painted in 1936. *(Allende 305, 1 block west of the zócalo at Absalo. Tel. 12 04 07. Open Tu-Sa 9am-7pm, Su 9am-2pm. Admission 20 pesos; children under 14, seniors, and Su free.)*

MUSEO DE MORELOS. The former residence of José María Morelos, the parish priest who led the Independence movement after Hidalgo's death, now displays Morelos's religious vestments, military ornaments, and uniforms, as well as other mementos of the surge for independence. *(323 Morelos Sur, 1 block east and 2 blocks south of the cathedral. Tel. 13 26 51. Open daily 9am-7pm. Admission 12 pesos, free for children under 14, seniors, and for all on Sundays.)*

CASA NATAL DE MORELOS. More of a civic building than a museum, the "Birthplace of Morelos" holds glass cases which preserve Morelos's wartime cartography, communiqués, and letters. Also notable are murals by Alfredo Zalce and a shady courtyard watched over by the martyr's bust. *(113 Corregidora, at García Obeso, 1 block south of the cathedral. Tel. 12 27 93. Open M-F 9am-7pm, Sa 9am-1pm. Free.)*

CATHEDRAL. Overlooking the *zócalo*, the massive cathedral has a stunning interior graced by vaulted ceilings, chandeliers, tapestries, and stained-glass windows, as well as a stunning dark wood pipe organ. The church's oldest treasure is the *Señor de la Sacristía*, an image of Christ sculpted by *indígenas* out of dry corn cobs and orchid nectar. In the 16th century, Phillip II of Spain donated a gold crown to top off the masterpiece. *(Open daily 5:30am-8:30pm. Free.)*

CASA DE CULTURA. A gathering place for artists, musicians, and backpackers, the *casa* houses a bookstore, an art gallery, a theater, and a lovely cafe. Dance, voice, theater, guitar, piano, and sculpture classes are offered, and concerts, book presentations, art festivals, and literature workshops are held here (20-30 pesos). This is a great place to find out information on cultural events (tel. 13 12 15 or 13 13 20, ext. 233). The on-premises **Museo de la Máscara** exhibits a small collection of masks from all over the Republic, and the whole complex is in the **Monasterio de los Carmelitas Descalzos.** *(Morelos Nte. 485, four blocks north of Madero. Tel. 12 41 51. Center and museum open M-F 9am-2pm and 5-8pm, Sa-Su and holidays 10am-5pm. Free.)*

CASA DE LAS ARTESANÍAS. This *casa* is a huge crafts museum and retail store, selling colorful macramé *huipiles*, straw airplanes, pottery, carved wood furniture, and guitars. Better prices, however, await in Pátzcuaro. *(Tel. 12 12 48. Humboldt at Fray Bartolome de las Casa. Open M-Sa 10am-3pm and 5-8pm, Su 10am-4:30pm. Free.)*

OTHER SIGHTS. Head to the eastern end of Madero to view the statue of **Las Tarascas,** probably the most recognizable landmark in Morelia. The statue shows three indigenous women making an offering to the heavens. Turn right at the statue and follow Av. Acueducto for about 1km until you reach the **Museo de Arte Contemporano Alfredo Zalce,** which displays a rotating collection of intriguing contemporary art. *(Av. Acueducto 18. Tel. 12 54 04. Open Tu-Su 10am-2pm and 4pm-8pm. Free.)* A bit farther along Av. Acueducto lies the university. Also nearby is the lookout point Santa Maria (ask the tourist office for specific directions). Near the *zócalo* is the **Palacio Gobierno.** Inside, murals by Alfredo Zalce depict the history of Morelia *(Madero 63. Open M-F 8am-10pm).* The **Museo de Arte Colonial** is located a few blocks north at Juárez 240.

🎵 🎭 ENTERTAINMENT AND NIGHTLIFE

Listings of events can be found at the Casa de Cultura and at the tourist office. Bright lights, musical celebrations, and thespian allure draw crowds to the **Teatro Morelos** (tel. 14 62 02), on Av. Camelina at Calzada Ventura Pte, and the **Conservatorio de las Rosas** (tel. 12 74 06), at the corner of Guillermo Prieto and Santiago Tapía. The **Casa Natal de Morelos** shows artsy films and holds cultural events on Fridays at 8pm (films screened Tu-W 5 and 7pm; admission 5 pesos). **Multicinema Morelia** (tel. 12 12 88), on Tapía at Bernal Jiménez, behind the Palacio Clavijero, features Hollywood's latest (open daily 3-10pm; 17 pesos). If you find heavenly bodies more fascinating than scantily clad ones, head for the **Planetario** (tel. 14 24 65), on Ventura Pte. at Ticateme, in the Centro de Convenciones at Calzada (shows Tu-Sa 7pm, Su 6:30pm; 15 pesos). To get there, take the "Ruta Rojo #3" *combi* from Av. Allende/Valladolid, and watch for the *planetario* and convention center on the right.

La Casona del Teatro, Serdán 35 (tel. 17 33 53), at Morelos, one block north of Madero, hosts comic dramas in Spanish (shows Th-Sa 9pm, Su 11am and 7:30pm; admission 30 pesos). The cafe/theater is popular with students and bohemian types who play chess and drink coffee (6 pesos) until showtime (cafe open M-F 9am-9pm, Sa 9am-5pm).

Morelia has a thriving nightclub scene fueled by hordes of local students. Twentysomethings bounce to the latest Spanish and English pop tunes at **XO Club,** Av. Campestre 100. (Tel. 26 07 66. Open bar F. Cover men 90 pesos, women 40 pesos; Sa everyone 40 pesos. Open W-Su 10pm-3am.) You can pay a 15 peso cover for the privilege of drinking 4 peso miniature beers at **Bar Intermedio,** Veracruz, just off Madero Ote. near the post office (open W-Sa 8pm-2am). **Freedom,** Av. Campestre 374 (tel. 15 66 61), hosts local teenage rebels (open daily 1pm-3am). Live *mariachi* Th, rock Fr and Su, at 11pm; M-W, Sa. dance music starts at 9pm (10 peso cover.) For real multi-level, block-rocking club madness, head to either **Akbal** and **Belam** (the cab drivers know where they are). The jungle motifs suit the party animals as they tear up the dance floor and knock back the drinks. Partners dance on the bar, the tables, and every square inch of the terraced dance floor. Beers cost 9 pesos; domestic drinks cost 15 pesos. (Cover 30-40 pesos. Open W-Su 9am-3pm.)

NEAR MORELIA: CIUDAD HIDALGO

Not exactly a tourist hotspot, Ciudad Hidalgo nevertheless offers some worthwhile nearby attractions. The spas of Los Azufres and the Laguna Larga are great outlets for those yearning to enjoy Michoacán's natural beauty. Just don't expect the city to roll out the red carpet for you.

✂ PRACTICAL INFORMATION. Ciudad Hidalgo is a 2hr. bus ride from Morelia. The bus station is on the main street in town, **Morelos,** which run east-west. The *centro* is just a block north from the bus station between **M. Hidalgo** and **Cuauhté-moc,** which run north-south. La Linea/Via 2000 buses depart from Morelos Pte. 9 (tel. 4 09 60) to: **Toluca** (3½hr., 9 per day, 60 pesos); **Mexico City** (4hr., 9 per day, 92 pesos); **Guadalajara** (5½hr., 5 and 11:30pm, 166 pesos); and **Morelia** (2hr., every 20 min. 43 pesos).

✦ ACCOMMODATIONS. Your best bet in Ciudad Hidalgo is the **Hotel Central,** Abasolo 12 (tel. 4 00 55), one block east of the *centro* in the market. Large, clean single rooms with TV and phone go for 90 pesos, doubles 120 pesos, triples 150 pesos, quads 180 pesos. A much less attractive but also less expensive option is the **Hotel San Carlos,** Cuauhtémoc Sur 22, near the bus station. Despite looking like an auto mechanic's garage from the outside, rooms are decent. (Singles 50 pesos; doubles 70 pesos.)

◪ OUTDOOR ACTIVITIES. Stop at the **tourist office** in the Palacio Municipal in the *centro* for more detailed information on nearby attractions (tel. 4 11 79 ex. 18, open M-F 9am-3pm). **Los Azufres,** 23km to the northwest of Morelia, is perfect for a nice, relaxing bath. It'll cost you 20 pesos to enter the site. Nearby, the **Laguna Largas** are a series of manmade lakes or *presos,* perfect for hiking, fishing, or camping. Buses to Los Azufres and Laguna Larga leave daily from the parking lot of M. Hidalgo 40, 1 block south (about 1 hr., 7am and 2pm, 11 pesos). Buses return to Ciudad Hidalgo at 8am and 3pm.

ZITÁCUARO

For the few tourists who venture to Zitácuaro (pop. 200,000) it promises safe, bustling streets, large markets and a population that rises with the sun. The town is close to larger cities such as Toluca and Morelia, yet the forested and mountainous setting make it seem much more remote. Positioned at the top of a hill on the eastern edge of the Sierra Madres Occidentals, it is possible to see a blue mountain soaring over the end of every street in Zitácuaro. Those that enjoy the outdoors can find countless opportunities for camping and hiking in the immediate area, but travelers in the fast lane may not find too much to keep them. Despite the growing population and increasingly urban way of life, tradition has remained as immutable as Zitácuaro's surrounding landscape.

✂ ORIENTATION AND PRACTICAL INFORMATION. Zitácuaro is about 165km west of Mexico City along **Rte. 15.** The winding drive climbs through shaded pine groves to reach almost 2000m above sea level. Since Zitàcuaro is on a hill, it is easy to see down the well-marked streets. The **Plaza Principal** is the geographic center of the city and consists of the **Plaza Cívica de Benito Juárez,** the **Plaza Municipal** and the **Mercado Juárez.** It is bordered by **Lerdo de Tejada** (south), **Dr. Emilio García** (west), **5 de Mayo** (east) and **Av. Miguel Hidalgo** (north). The main avenue of town, **Revolución,** is one block east of 5 de Mayo. North-south streets end in either "Norte" or "Sur" depending on whether they are north or south of Av. Miguel Hidalgo.

On the eastern end of town, **buses** connect Zitácuaro to the rest of the world. From the station at Pueblita Nte. 17 (tel. 37 26 50), at the end of Calle Cuauhtémoc Nte. 2 blocks north of Hidalgo and six blocks east of Revolucíon Nte., Occidental runs buses to: **Mexico City** (every 30min. 5:30-11pm, 66 pesos); **Manzanillo** (3:50-10:25pm, 230 pesos); and **Guadalajara** (8 per day 1:20-11:25pm, 156 pesos). Flecha Amarilla rolls to: **Toluca** (6 per day 2:45-6pm, 40 pesos); and **Morelia** (8 per day 6am-7pm, 55 pesos). Taxis are available to bring you into town (12 pesos; tickets purchased at booth inside). The **tourist office,** Km 4 Carreterra Zitácuaro, (tel. 3 06 75), is quite aways from the *centro,* but the Spanish speaking-only staff provides helpful maps and brochures of eastern Michoacan, Zitácuaro and several nearby parks and small towns. **Banamex**, Lerdo de Tejada 30 (tel. 3 04 07), will exchange currency and has a 24-hour **ATM** (open M-F 9am-5pm, Sa 10am-2pm). Open M-Sa 9am-2pm and 4-8pm. Many **pharmacies** surround the plaza. **Tauro** is at Dr. Emilio García 16 (tel. 3 52 43). **Laundry: Lavendería Roma**, 5 de Mayo Sur 45 (tel. 3 48 91; open daily 8am-6pm). **Public restrooms:** in the *mercado*, (1 peso; open daily 5:30am-8pm). **Emergency:** dial 30021. **Police:** Plaza Municipal (tel. 3 00 21 for 24hr. service), at the north end of the Plaza. **Hospital:** Memorial, Leandro Valle Nte. 10 (tel. 3 11 08), located one block east of Av. Revolucion Nte. **Post office:** Leandro Valle Sur 2 (tel. 1 38 73). **Postal code:** 61500. **Phone code:** 715.

⚐ ACCOMMODATIONS AND FOOD. Large illuminated signs all over **Av. Revolucíon** and the **plaza** area advertise conveniently located although not so cheaply priced hotels and *posadas*. The pesos pay off at the **Hotel Michoacan**, 5 de Mayo Sur 26 (tel. 3 21 59). Pricier but right off the plaza, this peach colored hotel receives guests with scented rooms, TVs, and incredibly comfortable beds. (1 person 100 pesos; 2 people 125 pesos.) Another option is the **Hotel America**, Revolucíon Sur 8 (tel. 3 11 16). This 3-story blue hotel offers parking for guests, private bathrooms, TV, and cheap prices. (1 person 80 pesos; 2 people 110 pesos.)

With locals always on the go, eating options consist mostly of fresh market fruits and vegetables and hot quesadilla and ice cream stands. A few sit down restaurants can be found on Av. Revolucíon. Converse at **Cafe Chips**, Hidalgo Ote. 22 (tel. 3 11 95), a small, friendly cafe just east of Av. Revolucíon. The good food and cheap prices (savory *tortas* 6-8 pesos) satisfy your hunger and your wallet. (Open Tu-Su 8am-10pm.) **Torta la Huerta**, Dr. Emilio García 11 (tel. 3 14 26), behind the *mercado*, serves *tortas* in different styles and *refrescos* (2-4 pesos) that are a great combination with some fresh fruit from the market (open M-Sa 9am-6:30pm).

◉ SIGHTS. Afternoons in Zitácuaro swirl and fade in its **Plaza Cívica de Benito Juárez**, where vendors gather, uniformed school kids play *fútbol* and older *"pensioneros"* try to escape the sun on one of the few shaded benches. The Palacio Municipal watches over the north end of the plaza and holds a stunning mural that tells the story of Zitácuaro's history from the time it was settled by the Mazahuas through independence and the modern day. The small **Jardín de la Constitution,** located on Donaciano Ojeda Sur, just three blocks west of the plaza, provides a **romantic atmosphere** with flowers, fountains, and shady seats for couples looking to get away from the bustle of the plaza.

Most Mexican cities boast a *mirador* where you can reach a view of the city after a few steep steps. Zitácuaro's **Cerrito de la Independencia** is not only a place where people can see all of Zitácuaro but also the miles of lush valleys, forested hills and the spectacular distant blue peaks beyond. To reach the *mirador*, follow Tejada as it crosses Revolucíon Sur and until it reaches Altamiano, then turn right and follow the paved path climbing through the woods. (Open daily 6am-7pm.) Ten kilommeters south of town on the Huetamo Rte., **Presa del Bosque,** provides spectacular views of the countryside from the *mirador.* Just a few local vendors line the main road, but the dirt road off to the right leads to a lake where adventurous souls can swim, camp, fish, and hike. To get there, go to the Tuzuntla taxi stop on Maria Morelos Sur, just south of Zaragoza Pte. Rides to and from Presa del Bosque cost 5 pesos each way. To return, simply flag down one of the numerous passing taxis.

LÁZARO CÁRDENAS

Named after *michoacano* President Lázaro Cárdenas, whose ardent socialist measures included nationalizing oil in 1938, the hot, noisy city of Lázaro Cárdenas (pop. 150,000) is Mexico's most important port on the Pacific. It also houses the largest steel factory in Latin America. The city's size, services, and location make it a likely departure point or pit stop on an exploration of Michoacán's 260km of rugged and beautiful coast, but Cárdenas itself is a filthy pit: get in and get out.

HOLDING COURT The area of eastern Michoacán is not only home to vast coniferous forests and rolling hills peppered with small farming communities, but it is also the site of one of the largest flight phenomenons in nature known to man. Each year, starting in October, over 20 million monarch butterflies traveling at a stateregal 20km per hour migrate from all over the U.S. and Canada and gather in an area just north of Zitácuaro. Some scientists have attributed the mass migration to a behavior dating to the time of the glaciers that caused the butterflies to seek warmer climates, while others insist it is to reach temperatures where reproduction is possible. To visit one of the destinations of the annual convergence, when monarchs cover the trees and the sky for the two months of November and December, take a green bus labeled "Angangueo" from the station in Zitácuaro to El Rosario, the sanctuary. The trees in eastern Michoacan definitely turn orange in the winter, but it sure ain't the leaves.

■ ORIENTATION. Lázaro Cárdenas lies near the border of Michoacán and Guerrero states, 382km southwest of Morelia and 122km northwest of Ixtapa. Most services lie on the town's principal thoroughfare, **Av. Lázaro Cárdenas,** usually near its intersection with **Corregidora.** The main *zócalo*, **Plaza de la Reforma,** is three blocks east of the *avenida's* intersection with Guillermo Prieto. *Combis* and buses run up and down Av. Lázaro Cárdenas and whisk passengers to nearby beaches. **Buses** run out of independent stations on or close to the main drag.

■ PRACTICAL INFORMATION. The **airport** (tel. 2 19 20), named after you-know-who, hosts carriers **Aerosudpacífico** (tel. 7 11 78), **Transporte Aeromar** (tel. 7 10 84), and **Aerolínea Cuahonte** (tel. 2 36 35). Autotransportes Cuauhtémoc and Estrella Blanca, Francisco Villa 65 (tel 2 11 17), four blocks west of Corregidora, send **buses** to: **Acapulco** (6-7hr., 11 per day 11:15am-midnight, 73-91 pesos); and **Tijuana** (45hr., 2:30pm, 988 pesos) via **Mazatlán** (25hr., 476 pesos) and points along the way. Estrella Blanca also provides second-class service to: **Zihuatanejo** (2:30pm, 31 pesos); **Acapulco** (1:15, 2:15, 3:15, and 4:15pm, 95 pesos); and **Tijuana** (2:30pm, 1163 pesos). Autotransportes Galeana, Av. Lázaro Cárdenas 1810 (tel. 2 02 62), provides service to: **Manzanillo** (6hr., 5 per day 4:15-11:30am, 80-93 pesos); **Morelia** (8hr., 13 per day 2am-7pm, 132 pesos) via **Pátzcuaro** (7hr., 126 pesos); and **Uruapan** (6hr., 102 pesos). Estrella de Oro, Corregidora 318 (tel 2 02 75) travels to: **Mexico City** (13hr., 7 and 8pm, 230-290 pesos). La Linea, Av. Lázaro Cárdenas 171 (tel. 7 18 50) runs to: **Colima** (7hr., 8pm, 108 pesos); **Guadalajara** (9hr., 8pm, 202 pesos); and **Mexico City** (14hr., 4 per day 3-11:30pm, 198 pesos). Buses can also be taken from the Galeana bus station to **Manzanillo** (6hr.; 4:30, 5, and 11am; 117 pesos) and **Morelia** (9 per day, 2am-7:30pm, 155 pesos).

Get the maps and info needed to attack the coast from the **Delegación Regional de Turismo,** Nicolás Bravo 475 (tel./fax 2 15 47), one block east of Av. Lázaro Cárdenas and two blocks north of Corregidora, in the big white Hotel Casa Blanca (open M-F. 9am-3pm and 5-7pm, Sa 10am-1pm). **Banamex,** Lázaro Cárdenas 1646 (tel. 2 20 18), exchanges currency and has an **ATM** (open M-F 8:30am-4:30pm, Sa 10am-2pm), as does **BITAL,** Lázaro Cárdenas 1940 (tel. 2 26 33; open M-Sa 8am-7pm). Long-distance international **phone calls** can be made and **faxes** sent from **Caseta Goretti,** Corregidora 79 (tel. 7 31 55; open daily 7am-1am). **Red Cross:** Aldama 327 (tel. 2 05 75; open 24hr.). **Farmacia Paris:** Av. Lázaro Cárdenas 2002 (tel. 2 14 35; some English spoken; open 24hr.). **Hospital General:** (tel. 2 08 21) on Av. Lázaro Cárdenas. **Police:** (tel. 2 18 55) Palacio Municipal, on Av. Lázaro Cárdenas at Av. Río Balsas. **Post office:** Nicolás Bravo 1307 (tel. 2 05 47; open M-F 8am-7pm, Sa 9am-1pm). **Phone code:** 753.

■■ ACCOMMODATIONS AND FOOD. The rent-by-the-hour atmosphere of most budget accommodations in town will make you happy to make your way to the reputable **Hotel Reyna Pio,** Corregidora 79 (tel. 2 06 20), at Lázaro Cárdenas. Clean rooms boast A/C, telephone, mustard-yellow furniture, and 1970s TV sets.

(Singles 100 pesos; doubles 130 pesos.) Fill up that stomach at **El Chile Verde,** Francisco I. Madero 66 (tel. 2 10 85), across from Av. Lázaro Cárdenas. Hot chili peppers dance happily on the walls while waiters serve spicy *enchiladas verdes* (16 pesos) and *comida corrida* (15 pesos) in this casual, open-air cafe. (Open daily 7am-10pm.) The slightly pricier but air-conditioned **El Paraíso,** Lázaro Cárdenas 1862 (tel. 2 32 33), near the Galeana bus station, offers traditional Mexican food amid orange, green, and yellow decor straight out of the 70s. The *sopa de tortilla* (13 pesos) and fish (40 pesos) are both worth a try.

MICHOACÁN COAST

Michoacán's temperamental, wildly beautiful coastline offers solace and tranquility one moment, then suddenly erupts into ripping, turbulent surf. Rte. 200, the solitary coastal route, twists up, down, and around Michoacán's angry terrain. Hills are pushed up against each other; rocks are defaced by crashing white waves spraying against blue skies. Lush tropical vegetation lends a loving touch of green to the state's 260km of virgin beaches. Michoacán's coast should be treated with cautious respect. Powerful waves make the beaches better suited for surfing than swimming, and the currents are strong even in the areas recommended for splashing around in the water. Since there are no lifeguards, exercise great caution. Rte. 200 tends to be deserted and dangerous at night; *Let's Go* does not recommend traveling there after dark.

PLAYA AZUL

Playa Azul (pop. 5000), a small *pueblo* that borders a long stretch of the Pacific 26km west of Lázaro Cárdenas, is renowned for a long stretch of soft, golden sand and majestic rose-golden sunsets. Here, the sea is a temptress—the tide rises high to the shore, tracing the base of a line of *palapa* restaurants, then quickly recedes under crashing waves, good for surfing and boogie-boarding. Swimmers shouldn't stray too deep, as this open stretch of sea has a strong undercurrent. Crowded with Mexican tourists during December and *Semana Santa*, the beach is usually much more quiet during the rest of the year.

◪ ORIENTATION AND PRACTICAL INFORMATION. Far from being a polished tourist town, Playa Azul is typically *michoacano*. Unmarked dirt roads, lined with thatched-roof house and open-air markets are the main thoroughfares, while chickens and tanned locals in bathing suits walk the streets. The village is so small that street names are seldom used (or known) by locals. The **Malecón** borders the beach; it is called **Aquiles Serdán** to the west of the plaza and **Emiliano Zapata** to the east. The other streets bordering the plaza are **Montes de Oca** to the west, and **Filomena Mata** to the east. **Av. Lázaro Cárdenas** runs into Playa Azul from the route, runs perpendicular to the beach, and intersects with **Carranza, Madero,** and **Independencia,** the three main streets parallel to the beach.

Getting There: From Lázaro Cárdenas, take a "Playa Azul" *combi* on Av. Lázaro Cárdenas (45min., every 2min. 5am-9pm, 9 pesos).

Though Playa Azul doesn't have a bank or *casa de cambio*, it does offer most other services. **Market:** Flores Magón, two blocks east of the plaza. **Police:** (tel. 2 18 55 or 2 20 30) across from the PEMEX station. **Farmacia Eva Carmen:** Av. Lázaro Cárdenas at Madero (open daily 8am-9:30pm). **Centro de Salud:** next door to the post office (open 24hr.). **Post office:** (tel. 6 01 09) on Madero at Montes de Oca, just behind Hotel María Teresa (open M-F 8am-3pm). For long-distance **phone calls,** visit the town's **caseta** (tel. 6 01 22) on Independencia (open M-Sa 8am-9pm, Su 8am-1pm). **Phone code:** 753.

▛▟ ACCOMMODATIONS AND FOOD. Bucolic Playa Azul offers several adequate budget hotels from which to choose. Reservations are recommended in August, December, and during *Semana Santa*. **Hotel Costa de Oro,** on Madero three blocks away from Lázaro Cárdenas, is the best deal in town. White stucco walls and an elegantly scalloped bannister lead to clean, comfortable rooms with funky tile floors, fans, and mismatched bedspreads, but no hot water. (Singles 50 pesos; doubles or triples 80 pesos.) **Bungalows de la Curva** (tel. 6 00 68), on Madero at Lázaro Cárdenas, offers a good deal for groups. Bungalows have kitchenettes and basic furniture. A swimming pool is surrounded by a patio with tables for poolside relaxing or dining (2 beds 130 pesos; 4 beds 200 pesos).

Palapa restaurants are so close to the shore that the waves will come up and tickle your toes or even flood your table, but the hammocks swinging between tables remain high and dry. The bubbly owners of **Coco's Pizza** will make you feel right at home and the *camarones al diablo* (shrimp with chile; 30 pesos) are a spicy taste of heaven. (Open daily 8am-9pm.) Inland, **Restaurante Familiar Martita** (tel. 6 01 11), on Flores Magón at Madero, is a cozy family-run restaurant with heavy, carved wooden chairs and fishnets on the walls. The *comida corrida* costs 27 pesos, while breakfast combos go for 20-25 pesos (open daily 7am-midnight.)

PLAYA AZUL TO CALETA DE CAMPOS

Beautiful beaches cover the 43km of coast stretching from Playa Azul to Caleta de Campos. **Las Peñas,** 13km west of Playa Azul, is a beach that is better appreciated from the shore: its surf is terribly turbulent, and its waters are infested with sharks. **El Bejuco,** only 2km farther west, has a sandy cove with tamer waves and fewer rocks. Another 12km west, you'll find **Chuquiapan,** a long stretch of sandy beach with reasonable waves and a shore studded with tall green palms. **La Soledad,** enclosed by rocky formations 4km farther west, is more secluded and cozy, lying at the base of a hill covered with dense vegetation. Its gray sands are strewn with rocks and driftwood and as usual in Michoacán's Pacific coast, rough waters don't make for safe swimming. **Mexcalhuacán,** 2km west, offers a fantastic view from a bluff overlooking a rocky coast and **Caleta de Campos** comes 7km later. **Nexpa,** a sandy beach with powerful waves, is a surfer's heaven 5km west of Caleta. *Palapa* restaurants, known as *enramadas*, line most of the beaches.

Getting There: Buses and *combis* running from Lázaro Cárdenas to Caleta de Campos pass by each of the beaches listed above, except Nexpa (every 30min., 5am-7:30pm; Las Peñas 30min.; Chuquiapan 40min.; La Soledad 45min.). The beaches are a five- to 10-minute walk from the route. To return to Playa Azul or Caleta, you'll have to wave a towel and flag down a *combi*—be sure to confirm when the last one is expected. To get to Nexpa, take a white *combi* from the bus depot at the beginning of Av. Principal in Caleta de Campos (10min., every 40min. 7am-7pm).

CALETA DE CAMPOS

A tiny fishing village 47km west of Playa Azul, Caleta de Campos has a pleasant beach but little else for the fun-loving traveler. The entire town is laid out along its one main street; blink and you'll miss it. But the lack of urban thrills hardly diminishes the green twisted terrain and brilliant blue surf massaging the shore of the area's beautiful beach. A dirt path climbs along the hills to the village above, offering a spectacular view of the coast. Because the water is somewhat sheltered, the surf is calmer than at Playa Azul, and the rolling waves make for good boogie boarding and body surfing. For most of the year, Caleta's two hotels are empty, but they fill up during *Semana Santa* and Christmas.

◪ ORIENTATION AND PRACTICAL INFORMATION. From Lázaro Cárdenas, **Rutas de Transportación Colectiva** (tel. 2 02 62) buses run from the Galeana bus station to **Caleta** (1½hr., every hr. 5:40am-8:10pm, 20 pesos). You can also board a "Caleta" *combi* anywhere along Av. Lázaro Cárdenas (1½hr., every 30min. 5:20-8pm, 20 pesos). To return to Lázaro Cárdenas from Caleta, pick up a bus or *combi* at the stop near the end of Av. Principal (5:30am-8pm). From Playa Azul, get on any bus leaving town, across from the PEMEX gas station (5min., every 10min., 3 pesos). Get off at **Acalpican,** a marked city just a few kilometers north of Playa Azul (be sure to tell the driver where you want to go in advance) and catch a bus labeled "Caleta" at the intersection (every 30min. 5:45am-8:45pm, 17 pesos).

Caleta de Campos has one paved main street, Melchor Ocampo, locally known as **Av. Principal.** The **police, post office** (open M-F 8am-3pm), and **bus stop** are all on Av. Principal. There are few private telephones in town; almost everybody just uses the **caseta** (tel. 6 01 92) located on the right-hand side of Av. Principal as you face away from the church at the far end of the street. Farther up the road is **Farmacia Morelia,** which will sometimes change dollars (open daily 7:30am-9pm). To get to the **Centro de Salud,** turn right on the side street before the paved road runs left and walk three blocks (open 24hr.). **Phone code:** 755.

▐▐ ACCOMMODATIONS AND FOOD. Caleta is home to only two hotels, both of which are nice and affordable. The **Hotel Los Arcos** (tel. (755) 6 01 92 or 6 01 93), next to the church as Av. Principal turns left, has very clean rooms with golden doors, tiled floors and bathrooms and fans. Arch-shaped windows grace each room and provide a spectacular view of the coast. (Singles 90 pesos, with A/C 100 pesos; doubles 120 pesos, with A/C 140 pesos.) It's always Christmas with the red and green bedspreads at **Hotel Yuritzi,** off Av. Principal after the church to the left. Yuritzi has spiffy rooms, fans, and TV. The restaurant downstairs is open only in high season. (Singles 100 pesos, 170 pesos with A/C; doubles 110 pesos, 220 pesos with A/C.) To get to the beach from the hotels, walk to the end of Av. Principal. Pass the church and the Lonchería Bahía, on your right, and follow the dirt road as it bends to the right; the beach lies at the bottom of the hill (a 10-minute walk).

Across the street from Hotel Yuritzi is one of Caleta's only restaurants, **Lonchería Bahía.** The laid-back cafe serves hamburgers (10-15 pesos), *tortas* (13-15 pesos), and fruit drinks (6-8 pesos; open daily 8am-10pm). Also popular is **Enramada Omar,** the third *palapa* restaurant on the sandy cove. It specializes in seafood and serves shrimp any style for 35-40 pesos. (Open daily 7am-9pm).

GUERRERO

TAXCO

Attractive white homes capped with red roofs and framed by a steep green mountain, make Taxco (pop. 150,000) a stunning sight from the road entering town. The hustle and bustle of work and play filling Taxco's streets does not detract from other eye-catchers such as the spectacular Church of Santa Prisca and the glinting wares of silver shops. Cobblestone alleyways coil around *platerías* and churches and the two-way streets are so narrow that people have to flatten themselves along shop walls to let one VW Bug pass. And, of course, beneath all the swarming confusion and old-fashioned beauty are the veins of silver that have shaped Taxco's history. When silver was discovered here in 1524, Taxco became the continent's first mining town with riches enough to lure craftsmen and foreign fortune seekers who eventually helped shape the town's success. Today, tourists buzz through the labyrinthine streets, drawn like bees to the sweet honey of countless jewelry shops.

✦ ORIENTATION

Taxco lies 185km southwest of Mexico City in the state of Guerrero. A hillside position makes its steep winding streets unavoidable. Due to its relatively small size, however, most streets will eventually lead uphill to the *zócalo*, **Plaza Borda,** and the town's centerpiece, the **Catedral de Santa Prisca.** The main artery is **Av. de los Plateros.** From Mexico City, visitors enter Taxco on Plateros through white arches. The road winds past the **Flecha Roja** bus station, becomes **Av. J.F. Kennedy,** and continues to the **Estrella de Oro** bus station before heading out of the city for Acapulco.

Guerrero

To reach the town center from the **Flecha Roja bus station,** turn right out of the station on to Plateros and turn left on **Juan Ruiz de Alarcón,** which continues uphill past some nice hotels. Turn left on Calle Agostin de Tolsa which will take you to the *zócalo.* From the Estrella de Oro station, cross the street and walk up the steep hill known as **Pilita.** When you reach the **Plazuela San Juan,** with a small fountain and a **Bancomer,** veer left and you will come out facing Santa Prisca. Keep in mind that the streets are narrow and uncomfortably steep. A *zócalo combi* will take you to the center from the bus station for 1.50 pesos. Taxis charge 8 pesos.

🚺 PRACTICAL INFORMATION

Buses: From the *zócalo,* head downhill and hang a right on Kennedy to get to **Estrella de Oro** station, Kennedy 126 (tel. 2 06 48), at the southern end of town. First-class service to: **Acapulco** (4hr.; 9:10am, 1, and 3:30pm; 90 pesos); **Cuernavaca** (1¼hr.; 9am, 2, and 4pm; 25 pesos); and **Mexico City** (3hr., 6 per day 7am-6pm, 50-60 pesos). Flecha Roja, Plateros 104 (tel. 2 01 31), about 2km past the city's entrance arches on Platenos sends first-class buses to **Cuernavaca** (1½hr., every hr. 6am-7pm, 25 pesos) and **Mexico City** (2½hr., 8 per day 6am-6pm, 62 pesos). Economic-class to: the **Grutas de Cacahuamilpa** (30min., every hr. 6:30am-3:30pm, 13 pesos); **Mexico City** (3hr., 7 per day 5am-8pm, 50 pesos); and **Toluca** (3hr.; 1, 11:40am, and 2pm; 42 pesos).

Tourist Office: Subsecretaría de Fomento Turístico (tel. 2 22 74), at the entrance to town. "Los Arcos" *combis* end their route in front of the office on the 2nd fl. Open daily 9am-2pm and 5-8pm. English spoken. There is free tourist information in the Flecha Roja station and most hotels on the Plaza Borda offer maps. **Procuraduría del Turista** (tel. 2 22 74 or 2 66 16) offers emergency assistance. Open M-F 9am-7pm.

Currency Exchange: Confía (tel. 2 02 37), on the *zócalo,* has an **ATM.** Open M-F 9am-3pm. **Banco Santander Mexicano,** Cuauhtémoc 4 (tel. 2 35 35 or 2 32 70) off the *zócalo,* changes money until 4:30pm. Open M-F 9am-5pm and Sa 10am-2pm.

Market: Mercado Tetitlán, can be entered on the street to the right of Santa Prisca and weaves downhill around the surrounding alleys. Sells everything from meat to jewelry.

Police: (tel. 2 00 07), on duty 24hr. Some English spoken.

Red Cross: (tel. 2 32 32), on Plateros, next door to the tourist info *caseta.* Open daily 9am-8pm with 24hr. **ambulance service.** Little English spoken.

Pharmacy: Farmacia Guadalupana, Hidalgo 8 (tel. 2 03 95). Open daily 8:30am-10pm.

Hospital: IMSS (tel. 2 03 36), on Plateros. 24hr. emergency service.

Post Office: Plateros 382 (tel. 2 05 01), near the Estrella de Oro station. Open M-F 8am-7pm, Sa 9am-1pm. **Postal Code:** 40200.

Fax: Alarcón 1 (tel. 2 48 85; fax 2 00 01), on the *zócalo*. Open M-F 9am-3pm, Sa 9am-noon.

Internet Access: Azul, Hidalgo 7 (tel. 2 74 03). Minimum 25 pesos for 25min. Additional 1 peso per min. Open daily 8am-10pm.

Telephones: LADATELs found around the main plazas (Plaza Borda and San Juan). **Farmacia Guadalupana,** Hidalgo 8 (tel. 2 03 95), near Plaza San Juan, has a long-distance *caseta*. Open daily 8:30am-10pm.

Phone Code: 762.

ACCOMMODATIONS

Although a good night's sleep does not come cheap in Taxco, almost any accomodation you choose will offer a well-kept, clean room with a classy courtyard, scenic balcony, or even a refreshing swimming pool. Most are also centrally located with silver shops, bars, and artisanry all over the place. Make advance reservations during local holidays and during March, April, and November.

Casa de Huéspedes Arellano, Pajaritos 23 (tel. 2 02 15). From the *zócalo*, walk down the street to the right of the cathedral and descend the stairs through the vendors' stalls; the hotel will be 3 levels down. Live birds and potted plants enliven the dual level entrance of the *casa*, built by the owner's father. A good space for drying laundry and sunbathing; a great place to smoke cigarettes and parlay with Euro-backpackers. Offers extremely clean dorm rooms for up to 6 people (65 pesos per person) or individual rooms with a private bath.

Hotel Los Arcos, Alarcón 4 (tel. 2 18 36), follow Calle Agostin de Tolsa from the north end of the *zócalo* and then turn right on the first street. From its cool shaded courtyard to its extremely large rooftop terrace, this hotel is relaxing yet begging to be explored. Carved wooden furniture in rooms and wrought iron bars on windows make it seem like a medieval manor. Singles 155 pesos; doubles 200 pesos.

Posada de Los Castillo, Alarcón 7 (tel. 2 13 96), across the street from Hotel los Arcos is as exquisite as the pricey silver shop downstairs. All the carved furniture, from the doors to the headboards, was crafted in reassuring earth tones. Even more reassuring are the firm beds with fluffy pillows and clean bathrooms. There is a small but scenic terrace on the fifth floor. Singles 150 pesos; doubles 185 pesos; triples 245 pesos.

Hotel Agua Escondida, Guillermo Spratling 4 (tel. 2 07 26 or 2 07 36), on the Plaza Borda. Although upscale and quite expensive, guests of this stunning hotel wake up to pink sandstone, flowers, and breakfast. Lounge, ping-pong, swimming pool, and video arcade make the hotel worth every peso. Singles 200 pesos; doubles 250 pesos.

FOOD

The narrow cobblestone streets of Taxco lack the push-cart vendors and sidewalk cafes that are so common in other Mexican cities. *Taquerías* and *torterías* are virtually extinct around Plaza Borda, but as you descend into the swarming market areas, their numbers increase. Eating out in Taxco can be quite enjoyable given the numerous restaraunts and bars that offer balconies with lovely views of the populated streets. Watch the sunset slip by while you sip *sangria* or *mescal*.

Restaurante Santa Fé, Hidalgo 2 (tel. 2 11 70), half a block down from Plaza San Juan. Figurines of Mexican *mariachis* brighten up Santa Fé and its satisfying food. Delicious *tortas* (8-10 pesos), tacos (16 pesos), and enchiladas (20 pesos). Open daily 7:30am-10:30pm.

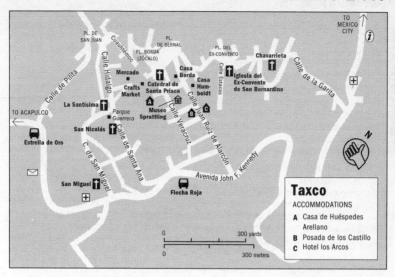

Taxco

ACCOMMODATIONS

A   Casa de Huéspedes
    Arellano
B   Posada de los Castillo
C   Hotel los Arcos

El Rincón del Abuelo, Callejón del Nogal 1 (tel. 2 30 77), at Cuauhtémoc, before Plaza San Juan. The name (Grandpa's Corner) belies the hip sleekness of the cafe. Gringos come in droves for the dance music and healthy entrees especially after 7pm when *tortas* run 14 pesos, *hamburguesas* 25 pesos, and *comida corrida* 35 pesos. Sit upstairs to escape the din of rock music. Open M-Th 8am-midnight, F-Su 8am-3am.

La Concha Nostra, Plaza de San Juan 7 (tel. 2 79 44), 2nd fl. of the Hotel Casa Grande. A bohemian hangout with a stage, old guitars hanging on the walls, live music some Saturday nights and slacker service to match the ambience. While you're waiting for your *quesadillas* (14 pesos), lasagna (26 pesos), or small pizza (15-20 pesos), watch the city's angsty language students blow smoke through their noses and scribble tormented prose in their notebooks. Open daily 8am-midnight; bar open until 2am.

Bora Bora Pizza, Delicias 4 (tel. 2 17 21), on the unmarked street that slopes up to the right from Cuauhtémoc, just off the *zócalo*. Fishing nets and basket lamps dangle from the wooden ceiling. Dimly lit with low tables and stools. Pizzas start at 23 pesos, spaghetti at 20 pesos. Open daily 1pm-midnight.

👁 SIGHTS

EL MERCADO DE ARTESANÍAS. More than 300 shops cater to the busloads of tourists who are drawn to Taxco by the glint of silver. If you're dipping so deep into your pockets that you can feel your knees, head for the artisans market off Veracruz just behind Santa Prisca. Merchants sell silver and peddle pomegranates and painted ashtrays. The silver stands are only open on Saturday, however, so expect it to be busy. *(Open 10am-6pm.)*

CATEDRAL DE SANTA PRISCA. Even more impressive than the silver trinkets that shine from every shop window is the *zócalo's* cathedral, with its beautiful Baroque facade of faded rose stone. Among the designs and figures on the facade, the standouts are the Churrigueresque *interestípite*—decorative inverted columns with a Corinthian flourish at the bottom. The tiled blue dome and intricately carved stonework stands out amongst the white buildings of Taxco. The church is especially beautiful when lit up at night.

CASA BORDA. To the left of the church is a stately 18th-century building that was José de la Borda's home; his family's coat of arms can still be seen beside the entrance. Enter through the bookstore on the *zócalo*. The interior gardens and several floors have been turned into the **Instituto Guerrerense de Cultura.** In addition to a library and dance studio, the center has ample gallery space for rotating exhibitions and photographs of daily life in Mexico. *(Tel. 2 66 17. House and galleries open Tu-Su 10am-8pm.)*

CASA HUMBOLDT. The Casa Humboldt is one of the older colonial homes in town. With its unusual bas-reliefs in Moorish *mudéjar* style, the *casa* served as a rest stop for explorer Alexander Von Humboldt for just one night, and it still bears his name. Nonetheless, this meticulously restored house now holds the collection of the **Museo de Arte Virreinal.** Exhibits provide a look at 18th-century Catholic rituals and dress. *(Tel. 2 55 01. Alarcón 12, down the street past the Hotel Los Arcos. Casa and museo open Tu-Sa 10am-5pm, Su 9am-3pm. Admission 15 pesos, students with ID 5 pesos.)*

EX-CONVENTO DE SAN BERNANDINO. The *ex-convento* was built in 1592 as a Franciscan monastery. Destroyed by a fire two centuries later, the building was reconstructed in Neoclassical style in 1823. The struggle for independence from the Spanish officially ended when the Plan de Iguala was signed within the walls of this *ex-convento* in 1821. Now a school convenes under its roof. *(In the Plaza del Convento; follow Juárez past the city offices. Open daily 8am-1pm and 2-6:30pm. Free.)*

VIEWS OF TAXCO. Perhaps the best sights in town are the **vistas** from surrounding hillsides. One of the more striking views of the city and the surrounding hills can be found from the **Church of Guadalupe.** The Neoclassical church becomes the center of festivities during the celebration of the Virgin in December. From the *zócalo*, take Ojeda, the street to the right of Cuauhtémoc, to Guadalupe, and veer right until you reach the plaza in front of the church. For a more sweeping view, you can take a **teleférico,** or **cable car,** to Hotel Monte Taxco. Take a "Los Arcos" *combi* to the white arches at the entrance of the city (2 pesos). Before passing through the arches, turn left up a hill and bear left into the parking lot. The ride is exhilarating, with waterfalls on one side and the city on the other. *(Tel. 2 14 68. Runs daily 7:40am-7pm. Round-trip 26 pesos, children 14 pesos, hotel guests free.)*

MUSEO GUILLERMO SPRATLING. Named after William Spratling, who helped revamp the city in the 1930s and jumpstart the silver industry with his successful shop, this museum houses his collection of prehistoric indigenous artifacts from the Guerrero area. *(Portfirio A. Delgado 1. Follow the downhill road to the left of the cathedral. the museum is on the left side. Open M-Sa 10am-5pm, Su 9am-3pm. Admission 15 pesos.)*

♫ ENTERTAINMENT AND SEASONAL EVENTS

Taxco's crowded streets somehow accommodate a tsunami of tourists during its two major festivals: the **Feria Nacional de la Plata,** a national contest designed to encourage silver artisanship, during the last week in November and the even more popular **Semana Santa** festivities. On Good Friday, hooded *penitentes* carry logs made out of cactus trunks on their shoulders or subject themselves to flagellation in order to expiate their sins and those of the town, including the ill behavior of tourists. During the annual **Día del Jumil,** on the first Monday of November, Taxco residents make a pilgrimage to the *Huizteco* hill, where they collect insects known as *jumil* to eat live or add, along with chiles, to *salsa*. The 1.5cm-long brown bugs contain more protein per gram than beef.

As the silver shops shut their doors and street vendors pack up their wares, people head to at the **Plaza Borda** in front of the illuminated facade of Santa Prisca. Those still up for dancing after a day of hiking up and down Taxco's relentless hills will have to wait until the weekend. **Windows,** (tel. 2 13 00) in the Hotel Monte Taxco, has the area's hottest dancing. Although accessible only by cable car or taxi, this bar/dance club is beautifully done up in crystal and glass and offers an unparalleled view of the city combined with a ritzy party atmosphere. (Cover 30 pesos; open F-Su 10pm-late.) For a more relaxed evening, move your way to La Concha Nostra in Hotel Casa Grande, Plaza de San Juan 7, for 8-peso beers and great conversation (open daily 8am-2am). Or try **Cine Alarcón,** near Plaza de San Juan. It shows American and "adult-interest" movies for about 20 pesos.

ALL THAT GLITTERS IS NOT...SILVER.

Although unscrupulous sellers and cheating craftspeople occasionally pass off *alpaca* (fool's silver) or *plateados* (silver-plated metals) to unsuspecting tourists, buying silver in Taxco is usually a sure thing. Larger pieces, such as necklaces and bracelets, are consistently striking with their elegant designs or eye-catching combinations of silver and semi-precious metals. Many proprietors speak English and accept U.S. currency, but if you stick with Spanish and talk in pesos while bargaining, you lower the risk of being charged tourist prices. While it's fun to ogle glamorous and expensive silver in the shops around the Plaza Borda, sterling products become cheaper and the employees more amenable to bargaining the farther you go from the *centro*. Bargain at stores with silver workshops by faking out the clerk and heading straight for the artisan. Most shops have two prices: *menudeo* (retail) and *mayoreo* (wholesale), the latter for those profit-oriented people who load their bags with silver in Taxco to resell at lofty prices back home. Remember that only the official ".925" stamp on the object's side guarantees that your shiny new charm is indeed silver; inspect merchandise carefully before purchasing anything.

NEAR TAXCO

GRUTAS DE CACAHUAMILPA

While the mountain scenery around Taxco has a rugged grandeur and some of the most beautiful and natural wonders lie underground in an extensive network of *grutas* (caves). According to lore, the **Grutas de Cacahuamilpa** were once a hideaway for runaway *indígenas*. Twenty huge *salones* (halls) are filled with stalactites, stalagmites, and rock formations in curious shapes, sizes, and colors. The columns and ceilings—some as high as 85m—are the work of the subterranean stream that developed into the **Río San Jerónimo.** *(Caves open daily 10am-5pm. Admission 15 pesos, children 10 pesos.)*

Two-hour tours leave on the hour from the visitors center and afford little opportunity for traipsing about on your own. If your Spanish is good enough, the tour can be hilarious, as the guide points out funny rock shapes and shadows comlete with fabricated anecdotes. You can only enter the caves with a tour guide: the 2km path is slippery and the air is cool and damp.

Getting There: "Grutas" *combis* leave from Taxco's **Flecha Roja** bus station, dropping passengers off at the parking lot for the caves (13 pesos). "Grutas" *combis* also leave the caves every hour to return to Taxco (13 pesos) but often don't show up. Taxis, while always available, cost 80-100 pesos. Flecha Roja buses are supposed to make the trip (30min., every hr. 6:30am-3:30am, 13 pesos), but will drop you off at an intersection a short jaunt from the caves. To get to the parking lot at the caves, take a right, then another right after the curve.

LAS GRANADAS AND IXCATEOPAN

Twenty-six kilometers from Taxco, the ecological reserve of **Las Granadas** is a little more than a hike in the woods. This 5km rock trail curls around mountain tops and dips into the valley, bringing hikers to a stunning natural waterfall. The path is hilly and sunny, so wear comfortable walking shoes and sunblock. To get to the Las Granadas trail, grab a *combi* heading to **Acuitlapan** (40min., every 25min. 7am-8pm). Once there, follow the one road into the tiny town, that is to the left of a Las Granadas sign. As you enter the main square of town and look to the far end where the path starts as a dirt road. The reserve has no set hours and no admission fee and provides a respite from both Volkswagen-clogged streets and silver-pushers. In addition to the flora and fauna, there are stunning natural waterfalls.

Forty-two kilometers from Taxco, the town of **Ixcateopan** is known for both its beauty and its history. The marble and stone streets supply the former, while the

Museo de la Resistencia Indígena provides information on the latter. The remains of Cuauhtémoc, the last Aztec emperor, are said to be kept here in the **Templo de Santa María de la Asunción.** *Combis* leave Taxco from in front of the Seguro Social, on J.F. Kennedy. To get to Ixcateopan, just take the eponymous vehicle (1¼hr., every 30min. 6am-9pm, 13 pesos).

ZIHUATANEJO AND IXTAPA

Six kilometers and a completely different lifestyle separate the side by side beach towns of Zihuatanejo (see-wah-tah-NAY-ho) and Ixtapa (ees-STOP-pah). A combined population of about 80,000 inhabitants thrive almost solely on the tourist trade. With long stretches of sand, endless possible watersports and restaurants that frame the sunsets, both cities have a lot to offer. Though Zihuatanejo and Ixtapa are popular with tourists, it is the night and day difference of the cities that makes a trip here two vacations in one. Ixtapa has been meticulously constructed by Mexican pleasure engineers to cater to moneyed foreign visitors; this glitzy resort has no downtown, no budget accommodations, and a surfeit of fancy restaurants. Meanwhile, Zihuatanejo, only a 15-minute bus ride away, hasn't shaken the grip of the net that marks it as a fishing town. There are budget hotels in its downtown, and they're all a few steps from excellent beaches.

Ironically, the original plan designed the nascent resort paradise around Zihuatanejo Bay, but complications with land rights forced development north to Ixtapa. Although a visit to peaceful Zihuatanejo can be satisfying in and of itself, the glitzy Ixtapa, with its air-conditioned comfort and sophisticated nightlife, adds just the right amount of decadence. Together, the twin towns provide the escape that Mexico's other Pacific beaches hamper with pollution or lack of services.

◨ ORIENTATION

Buses arrive in Zihuatanejo at the **Estrella Blanca** and **Estrella de Oro** stations that are side-by-side on the outskirts of the *centro. Combis* (2.50 pesos) heading to the left as you leave the station or taxis (12 pesos) will bring you to the center of town. Resort-goers usually arrive at the **international airport,** 15km outside of town. Taxis from the airport to Zihuatanejo charge 60-70 pesos.

As seen from the bay, downtown Zihuatanejo extends from the *muelle* (pier) on the left to the canal on the right. **Paseo del Pescador** runs along the waterfront. Seven blocks separate that walkway from **Av. Morelos,** which runs parallel to the water and marks the edge of the town. The two boundary streets perpendicular to the water are **5 de Mayo,** by the pier, and **Benito Juárez,** by the canal.

Ixtapa's main road, **Blvd. Ixtapa,** lies past a phalanx of waterfront luxury hotels on the left and overpriced stores to the right. Buses shuttling between the two cities leave Zihuatanejo from the intersection of Juárez and Morelos, across from the yellow Elektra store; they leave Ixtapa from various stops on the boulevard (15-25min., every 15min. 6am-10pm, 3 pesos from any stop). Cab fare between the two towns runs about 20-25 pesos by day, and 30 pesos at night. **Taxis** in Zihuatanejo can always be found on Juárez, in front of the market.

◧ PRACTICAL INFORMATION: ZIHUATANEJO

TRANSPORTATION

Airport: (tel. 4 20 70). **Aeroméxico,** Álvarez 34 (tel. 4 20 18), on 5 de Mayo, 1 block from the water. Open daily 9am-6:30pm. **Mexicana** (tel. 4 22 08 or 4 22 09), Guerrero at Bravo. Open M-Sa 9am-6:45pm, Su 9am-2pm.

Buses: To reach the bus station from the *centro,* hop on a *combi* labeled "Coacoyul" (7am-8:30pm, 2.50 pesos) across from the market on Juárez. Estrella de Oro (tel. 4 21 75) sends buses to: **Acapulco** (4½hr., 17 per day 5:30am-1am, 51-75 pesos); **Cuernavaca** (8hr., 4 per day 8am-10:10pm, 175 pesos); and **Mexico City** (9hr., 6 per day

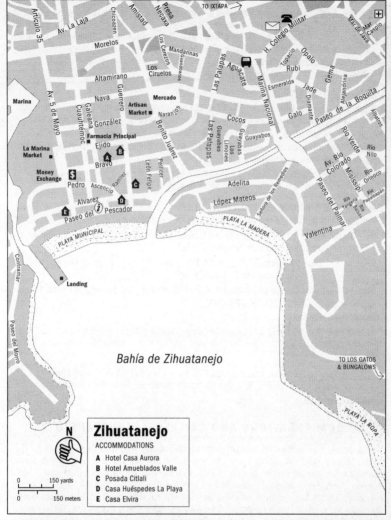

Zihuatanejo

ACCOMMODATIONS

A Hotel Casa Aurora
B Hotel Amueblados Valle
C Posada Citlali
D Casa Huéspedes La Playa
E Casa Elvira

0   150 yards
0   150 meters

Bahía de Zihuatanejo

TO LOS GATOS
& BUNGALOWS

8am-10:10pm, 200-325 pesos). Estrella Blanca (tel. 4 34 77) goes to: **Acapulco** (5½hr., 18 per day 4am-9:30pm, 65 pesos); **Chilpancingo** (6hr., 4 per day 4:20-midnight, 100 pesos); **Cuernavaca** (7½hr., 175 pesos); **Huatulco** (13hr., 7:45pm, 199 pesos); **Iguala** (6½hr., 130 pesos); **Lázaro Cárdenas** (2hr., every hr., 9:13am-11:13pm, 31 pesos); and **Puerto Escondido** (12hr., 167 pesos).

Car Rental: Hertz, Bravo 13 (tel. 4 22 55; fax 4 30 50) rents small VWs US$35 per day with unlimited mileage; US$45 per day in high season. Insurance US$11 per day. Open daily 8am-2pm and 4-8pm. Hertz also has offices in the **airport** (tel. 4 25 90) and in **Ixtapa** (tel. 3 04 44).

TOURIST AND FINANCIAL SERVICES

Tourist Office: Info booth (tel. 4 20 01), on Juan N. Álvarez, to the left of the small town square has maps and basic information. Some English spoken. Open M-F 9am-3pm and 6-8pm, Sa 9am-2pm. **SEFOTUR** (tel. 3 19 67), on Blvd. Ixtapa, across from Hotel Presidente offers a comprehensive *Guía Turística Urbana* to beaches and services. Some English spoken. Open M-F 9am-7pm, Sa 10am-2pm.

Currency Exchange: Banco Santander Mexicano (tel. 4 24 16), Los Mangoes at Juárez with 24hr. **ATM**, and **Banca Serfín** (tel. 4 36 63) with a 24hr. **ATM** at Juárez at Bravo. Both open M-F 9am-5pm, Sa-Su 10am-2pm. **Money Exchange,** Galeana 6 (tel. 4 28 00), has worse rates but no commission. From the beach, walk 1 block on Cuauhté-moc, take a right on Bravo, and make the first right onto Galeana. Offers **fax** and **long-distance** service as well. Open daily 8am-9pm.

LOCAL SERVICES

Bookstore: Byblos, Galeana 2 (tel. 4 38 11) has English magazines, paperback novels, and the handy *Owen's English Language Guide to Ixtapa and Zihuatanejo* (written by a member of Cousteau's team). Open daily 9am-9pm.

Market: The **mercado** on Benito Juárez, 4 blocks from the water, sells fresh produce and has several small countertop eateries.

Laundry: Súper Clean, Gonzalez 11 (tel. 4 23 47), at Galeana. 9 pesos per kg., 27 peso minimum. Same day delivery. Open M-Sa 8am-8pm.

EMERGENCY AND COMMUNICATIONS

Police: (tel. 4 20 40), in the Palacio Municipal in front of Playa Principal.

Red Cross: (tel. 4 20 09) on Av. de las Huertas as you leave Zihuatanejo. 24hr. emergency and ambulance service. No English spoken.

Pharmacy: Farmacia Principal (tel. 4 42 17), Cuauhtémoc at Ejido, 3 blocks from the water. English spoken. Open M-Sa 9am-9pm.

Medical Services: Centro de Salud (tel. 4 20 88), Paseo de la Boquita at Paseo del Palmar. Open M-F 8am-8pm, Sa 8am-3pm.

Emergency: dial 060.

Post Office: (tel. 4 21 92) off Paseo del Palmar. Walking away from the beach, turn right on Morelos, walk a block past the blue wall, and turn right. Open M-F 8am-7pm.

Postal Code: 40880.

Internet Access: Servinet, Cuauhtémoc 128 (tel. 4 43 87), at Gónzalez. 15min. for 15 pesos or 1hr. for 30 pesos, discount for students with ID. Open daily 9am-8pm.

Phone Code: 753.

▮ ACCOMMODATIONS AND CAMPING: ZIHUATANEJO

Zihuatanejo has plenty of budget accommodations within a few blocks of the Playa Municipal. Few places have hot water but the last thing you'll want is a hot shower after baking on the beach all day. Prices rise substantially during the high season (Dec.-Apr.) as do the number of gringos per square foot. If you visit at an off-time, with a large group, or plan to stay several days, you will have excellent leverage for negotiating a discount. The tourist office discourages unofficial camping, partly for safety reasons but if you insist on pitching a tent, **Playa Barra de Potosí** (see p. 453) and **Playa Quieta,** near Club Med in Ixtapa, are the most sensible places to camp.

Casa Elvira, Juan N. Álvarez 8 (tel. 4 26 61), 1 block from the Playa Municipal was the first guest house in Zihuatanejo, and remains a bargain. Recently redone, rooms are cozy, extremely clean, and are nicely decorated with Mexican handicrafts. Bathrooms are colorful and modern. The courtyard is filled with plants, birds, and gregarious family members; step out back and you're on the beach. With strong ceiling fans cooling the rooms it doesn't get more comfortable than this. Singles 100 pesos; doubles 150 pesos. Prices are often negotiable.

Hotel Casa Aurora, Bravo 27 (tcl. 4 30 46), between Guerrero and Galeana. This budget mainstay features a friendly staff, clean, good-sized rooms, and 70s-stlye bedspreads. Rooms upstairs are pricier, but they come with hot water. High season 80-90 pesos per person, with A/C 150 pesos; low season 70 pesos per person, with A/C 100 pesos. Beachside bungalow holds 2 people for 300 pesos; high season 400 pesos.

Hotel Amueblados Valle, Vicente Guerrero 14 (tel. 4 20 84; fax 14 32 20), between Ejido and Bravo. Eight fully-equipped apartments provide guests with a large kitchen/eating area, ceiling fans, balconies, and daily towel service. 1 bedroom (up to 3 people) 180 pesos; 2 bedrooms (up to 5 people) 300 pesos. Prices rise during high season.

Casa de Huéspedes La Playa, Alvarez 6 (tel. 4 22 47), at Guerrero. The best thing about this place is the location. The waves of the Pacific will lull you to sleep as will the soothing light of the moon shining on the sea. Basic and clean, with fans and no hot water. There are no fixed prices but rooms with 2 beds usually cost 100 pesos.

Posada Citlali, Vicente Guerrero 3 (tel. 4 20 43), near Blvd. Álvarez. On the expensive side, but quite charming. Vines dangle lazily in the central courtyard; wooden rockers on the terrace encourage you to do the same. All rooms have overhead fans. Singles 150 pesos; doubles 200 pesos.

◨ FOOD

Like the neighboring hotels, restaurants in Ixtapa are pricey. However, they are spotless and offer an array of authentic-tasting international cuisine. The meal can be a reasonable splurge, especially if you eat at a cafe before they switch to the main menu (around 2pm). For consistent budget eats, restaurants in Zihuatanejo serve freshly caught fish from the bay.

Los Braseros, Ejido 64 (tel. 4 87 36). This exuberant open-air eatery specializes in heavenly stir-fried combinations of meat, veggies, and cheese (31-32 pesos) and a sprinkling of veggie options. Large portions are served with hot tortillas by an attentive staff. Open daily 10am-1am.

La Sirena Gorda (The Fat Mermaid), Paseo del Pescador 20A (tel. 4 26 87), next to the pier. Start your morning off with a stack of hotcakes (20-22 pesos); dine on seafood tacos (22-45 pesos) when the sun goes down. The view of the fishing boats on the water and the painting of fat and jocular mermaids make it all taste that much better. Open Th-Tu 7am-10pm.

Ruben's Hamburgers, Adelita 1 (tel. 4 46 17), on Playa Madera. Follow the Paseo del Pescador to the canal, turn left, and cross the bridge. Walk straight down the street for 2 blocks—it's on the right, up the stairs. A loud, fun, family joint, with a booming jukebox and rolls of paper towels dangling overhead. Get your drinks from the fridge and add up your own check. Delicious *hamburguesas* (20-22 pesos) and sour cream-stuffed baked potatoes (16 pesos). Open daily 6-11pm.

◪ SAND AND SIGHTS

Neither Zihuatanejo's self-conscious charm nor Ixtapa's resorts could ever eclipse the area's natural beauty. In Zihuatanejo, four patches of sand make excellent beaches. They are, clockwise from the municipal pier, **Playa Principal, Playa La Madera, Playa la Ropa,** and **Playa Las Gatas.** Ixtapa overlooks the unbroken stretch of **Playa del Palmar** on the **Bahía del Palmar,** but the prettiest beaches lie beyond Laguna de Ixtapa: **Playa Quieta, Playa Linda,** and, at the bay's west edge, **Isla Ixtapa.**

ZIHUATANEJO

Downtown Zihuatanejo's beach, **Playa Municipal,** in front of the Paseo del Pescador, is more suited to seashell stores and fishing boats than to swimmers. The attractions here are the basketball court, the pier, and the fish unloaded from boats onto the dock. The beach ends at a canal emptying into the bay. A nice cement path traces the boulders separating this beach and **Playa Madera.** About 200m long, this beach used to be a loading place for local hardwood exported from shore and got its name, *madera,* from the Spanish word for wood. Its the hardwood that used to be exported from the shore, but the fine sand and gentle waves bear no trace of its lumberyard past. Good for bodysurfing, the shallow beach hosts a number of restaurants and bungalows.

Zihuatanejo's two best beaches cannot be reached by walking along the bay's shores. Protected from the rough Pacific by the shape of the bay, **Playa La Ropa's** crescent of sumptuous white sand attracts tourists from the hotels on the surrounding cliffs. Because La Ropa is nearly 1km long, it never feels too crowded. Taxis are the easiest way to reach La Ropa (15 pesos). Follow Paseo de la Boquita along the canal to the bridge, cross over, and turn left, passing Playa Madera. The road curves to the right and passes Hotel Casa que Canta. Follow the stone road down to the left to the beach. At the opposite end of the beach, you can reward yourself with a meal at one of the waterfront seafood restaurants.

According to local lore, Purepecha King Calzontzin ordered the construction of a stone wall in **Playa Las Gatas** as protection from the sharks while he bathed. Since then, coral and an abundance of marine life have taken over the stone barricade. The calm, transparent waters welcome **snorkelers** (equipment can be rented for 35 pesos per day). One person **kayaks** can also be rented to explore the bay (all day 160 pesos). Escape the shops and restaurant tables by taking a path (2km) behind the last restaurant to the **Garrobo Lighthouse,** which offers a panoramic view. Since it's well hidden, ask any of the waiters for specific directions to *el faro*. To reach Las Gatas, take a *lancha* from the pier in downtown Zihuatanejo (10min.; every 15min. 9am-4pm, last boat leaves 5pm; round-trip 20 pesos). To walk to Las Gatas from La Ropa over the rocks is possible but not easy. Alternatively you may continue walking on the road that brought you to La Ropa for another 45 minutes and keep to the left as it splits until you reach the beach.

IXTAPA

Well guarded from Blvd. Ixtapa by a line of posh hotels, **Playa de Palmar** is an active, spacious, and beautiful beach. Walk a couple kilometers on the soft yellow sand or stop by a massage hut and have your worries crushed by a Shiatsu master. Without the protection of a bay, the beach is pummeled by sizeable waves, attracting parasailers, scuba divers, and jet skiers. All along the sand next to the swimming pools, people jog and play volleyball and soccer. The beach can be reached from public access paths at its far ends, near the Sheraton hotel or near Carlos 'n' Charlie's. Otherwise, clutch your *Let's Go* confidently, wear your swimsuit proudly, and cut right through the hotel lobbies.

About 6km northwest of downtown lie the virtually undeveloped yet stunning, **Playa Quieta,** and **Playa Linda** beaches. To drive to them from Ixtapa, follow the boulevard northwest beyond most of the hotels and turn right at the sign for Playa Linda. From Zihuatanejo, it is more convenient to use the access road from Rte. 200; go past the exit for Ixtapa in the direction of Puerto Vallarta and take the next left, marked Playa Linda. The road skirts **Laguna de Ixtapa** and hits the beach farther northwest. A taxi to Playa Linda or Playa Quieta costs about 40 pesos from Ixtapa or 60-70 pesos from Zihuatanejo. A "Playa Linda" bus (3 pesos) begins in Zihuatanejo and passes through Ixtapa on its way to Playas Quieta and Linda. Or you can walk along the road for about 4km on the bicycle path. The refreshing clear water and gentle waves of Playa Quieta are perfect for swimming and body boarding. At Playa Linda families sit under blue umbrellas while sipping exotic fruit drinks from the few nearby stands. One or two restaurants also rent horses for 180 pesos per hour for a guided ride (rides leave at 8:30, 9:45, 11am, 3, and 5pm). Buses come every 15 minutes or so to return to Ixtapa (3 pesos) or Zihuatenejo (4 pesos).

Some claim that of all the area's beaches, the most picturesque are those on **Isla Ixtapa,** about 2km off-shore from Playa Quieta. The island is a must for snorkeling enthusiasts. Activity picks up in a few shoreside restaurants by day, but the island's 10 acres remain uninhabited at night. The main beach is **Playa Cuachalalate,** frequented by fishermen and vacationers eager to water-ski. **Playa Varadero** is a small beach with calm waters and *palapa*-covered restaurants. On the ocean side of the island, **Playa Coral** is the least-visited beach of the three. It has no services and is not great for swimming, but the coral makes for excellent scuba diving. To get there, take a boat from the pier at Zihuatanejo (1hr.; boats leave at noon, return at 5pm; 60 pesos round-trip). A cheaper alternative is to take a *microbús* from Zihuatanejo (3 pesos) or from Ixtapa (2.50 pesos) to the pier at Playa Linda and catch a *lancha* (every 15min. 9am-5pm, round-trip 25 pesos).

◪ NIGHTLIFE

Although the beaches of both Ixtapa and Zihuatanejo promise a spectacular day in the sun, the sand, and the waves, the only place to go for nightlife is Ixtapa. **Blvd. Ixtapa,** like most resort strips, is littered with fancy clubs and relaxed bars that rock with the beat of young people having a great time.

IXTAPA

The premier place for dancing is **Christine** (tel. 3 04 56), in front of Hotel Krystal. With its tiered seats, hanging vines, and light show, it is as artificially beautiful as Ixtapa itself. Beer costs 23 pesos, and *bebidas nacionales* go for 27 pesos. (M no cover; Tu and Su 140 pesos for men, 100 pesos for women, open bar for both; Th 60 pesos for men, no cover for women; F-Sa 60 pesos cover for all.) **Carlos 'n' Charlie's** (tel. 3 00 85), at the end of the public access path leading to the end of Playa Palmar next to Hotel Posada Rd., attracts a lot of parched party-goers to its bar and specializes in beachfront dancing (no cover, F-Sa 50-peso drink minimum; open daily 4pm-3am). **Señor Frog's** (tel. 3 22 82) may be a restaurant until midnight, but when the clock strikes twelve, there's no pumpkin to be seen—simply, drunk American dancers climbing on tables to begin the ball. Spiral-designed fans whirl at top speed to keep the party cool along with 23-peso beers. (No cover. Open daily 6pm-3am.)

ZIHUATANEJO

Choices for nightlife in Zihuatanejo are limited. A recent addition to the scene is **D'Latino** (tel. 4 22 30), on the corner of Bravo and Guerrero. This spicy Latin dance club features *salsa* and reggae, with occasional live music. Those in short skirts get down on the dance floor illuminated with black lights as they sip drinks (18-22 pesos) from the fully stacked bar. (Cover M-Th free, F-Su 30 pesos. Open daily 10pm-3am.) If you're in Zihuatanejo at night, dancing is probably not on your mind. Try your hand at singing at **Canta Bar Splash,** a **karaoke** bar on Guerrero between Ejido and Gonzalez. Sip a beer (12 pesos) or a mixed drink (18 pesos) as you croon away into the microphone. (Open daily 6pm-2am.) Drink Corona and watch a *fútbol* match at **Planet Zihua,** a sports bar right next to D'Latino on Guerrero. Pound five beers for 50 pesos.

COSTA GRANDE

The Guerrero coast north of Acapulco is often called the Costa Grande in order to distinguish it from its smaller counterpart (Costa Chica) to the south. Although the stretch from Acapulco to Zihuatanejo/Ixtapa is marked by a dearth of inviting beaches, **Barra de Potosí,** 20km southeast of Zihuatanejo, and **Papanoa,** another 60km farther along Rte. 200, are two hidden treasures ideal for wasting the day away frolicking in the waves.

BARRA DE POTOSÍ

For the traveler whose head is spinning from ruins, cathedrals, and souvenirs, there is no better tonic than a spell at the seemingly infinite stretch of sand known as **Playa Barra de Potosí.** Life here just couldn't get any more *tranquila*. Visitors to this small town consisting of a shallow lagoon, a forest of palm trees and waterfront huts are expected to join in what appears to be a day-long *siesta*. There are 12 or so open air *enramadas* which serve simple seafood dishes at very reasonable prices. While you enjoy the home-cooked food you are more than welcome to relax in one of the many hammocks that swing in the shaded, sandy *enramadas*.

Eat until you're full, walk on the beach, snooze in the shade, it doesn't matter because there is no rush and no limit of surrounding beauty.

Those still unskilled in the art of hammock-snoozing or traveling solo can indulge themselves at **Hotel Barra de Potosí** (tel. 4 82 90 or 4 34 45), an unfinished resort hotel that has nevertheless opened its doors for business. From the *enramadas*, walk away from the lagoon—you can't miss the large white monstrosity. Rooms in the completed portion of the hotel have views of the beach, ceiling fans, washing machines, and kitchens. Not all rooms have the same amenities, but all have access to the beachside swimming pool and restaurant. (4-person rooms with oceanview and kitchen 300 pesos, without kitchen 250 pesos; doubles without either 150 pesos.)

In keeping with the casual spirit, restaurants do not have set menus; rather, they ask you what type of seafood you'd like to eat (expect to spend 20-30 pesos per person). **Enramada Bacanora,** the third restaurant from the right facing the water, offers a very friendly atmosphere and the cheapest prices (open daily 7am-6pm).

If you insist on exerting yourself while in Barra de Potosí (something the locals may not understand), the only option is to hike up the dirt road to the lighthouse that sits atop **Cerro Guamiule** (2000m), the peak near the restaurants that guards the southern entrance to the bay. After a 30-minute walk, you will be rewarded with a view of the bay and its 20km of beaches. After gaping, walk north along the shore of Playa Potosí, the southernmost beach on the bay, to the aptly named **Playa Blanca** (3km). You will pass **Playa Coacoyul** (8km), **Playa Riscaliyo** (19km), and pebbly **Playa Manzanillo** (24km) before reaching another lighthouse (26km) that overlooks the northern edge of the bay. All beaches are free of tourists in the summer months but they fill up with hundreds of domestic visitors during Christmas.

Getting There: From Zihuatanejo, "Petatlán" buses for Potosí leave from a station on Las Palmas, around the corner from Restaurante La Jaiba on Juárez (30min., every 15min. 6am-9pm, 5.50 pesos). Ask to be let off at **Achotes,** an unmarked intersection. A pick-up truck will be waiting (or will be arriving soon) on the side road to collect passengers for the bumpy trip to the *enramadas* (30min., 7 pesos). Trucks return to the intersection from the same spot (every 30min., until 6pm); the bus to Zihuatanejo leaves from the other side of the route.

PAPANOA

Much like Barra de Potosi, **Papanoa** offers small town charm alongside lolling waves. Pigs and roosters scuttle along the road that ends at multiple *enramadas* and the beach. **Cayaqutos,** 2km from town, is a bit more accessible (and therefore more crowded) than **Playa Vincente Guerrero,** 5km from town. And while there's a scarcity of eateries on Cayaquitos, Vincente Guerrero is host to numerous restaurants that will tempt your taste buds with the ever-fresh catch of the day (20-30 pesos; open 7am-6pm).

Getting There: Buses from Acapulco to Zihuatanejo (2½hr., 34 pesos) and back (1½hr., 16 pesos) drop passengers off in Papanoa. In Papanoa, white pick-up trucks carry passengers to and from the beach (until 6pm, 5 pesos). Taxis run to **Cayaqutos** (10 pesos) and to **Vincente Guerrero** (20 pesos). If you plan to leave the beach later than 6pm, arrange for a taxi to pick you up ahead of time.

ACAPULCO

Once upon a time, Acapulco (pop. 2 million) was the stunningly beautiful playground of the rich and famous. Hollywood legends celebrated their silver-screen successes by dancing the Mexican nights away in its chic clubs, and the priviledged few spent their honeymoons hopping between its attractive shores. But time passes and fairy tales fade. Today, Acapulco is a mere shadow of the beautiful, relaxing retreat it once was. Now, the city consists of a crowded beach flanked by side-by-side 14-story hotels and a slum that starts behind them and continues up the hill. This grimmer Acapulco was born when the wealthy stopped vacationing on Acapulco's shores, and hotel jobs could no longer keep pace with the waves

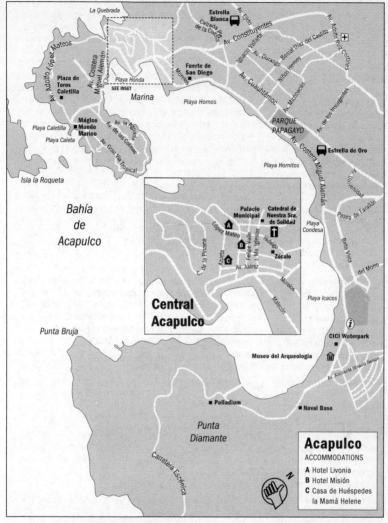

La Quebrada

Estrella
Blanca

Av. Ejido
Av. Constituyentes

Av. Adolfo López Mateos

Calzada Pie
de la Cuesta

Av. Costera
Miguel Alemán

Ignacio Vallarta
Av. Durango

Bernal Diaz del Castillo

Niños Heroes

Av. Michoacán

Av. Adolfo Ruiz cortines

Playa Honda

Fuerte de
San Diego

Moreno

Av. Cuauhtémoc

Plaza de
Toros
Caletilla

SEE INSET

Marina

Playa Hornos

Av. de los Insurgentes

Mágico
Mundo
Marino

Av. la Colinas

Av. de las Colinas

PARQUE
PAPAGAYO

Av. Costera Miguel Alemán

Estrella de Oro

Playa Caletilla

Av. Gran Vía Tropical

Playa Caleta

Av. Universidad

Isla la Roqueta

Playa Hornitos

Paseo de Farallón

Bahía
de
Acapulco

Palacio
Municipal

Catedral de
Nuestra Sra.
de Solidad

Playa
Condesa

Bella Vista

López Mateo

Hidalgo

del Morro

C. de la Pinzona

Azueta

Felipe Valle

J. Ma. Iglesias

Zócalo

Av. Juárez

Moreno

**Central
Acapulco**

Malecon

Playa Icacos

Punta Bruja

CICI Waterpark

Museo del Arqueologia

Av. Almirante Horacio Nelson

Palladium

Naval Base

Punta
Diamante

Carretera Escénica

Acapulco
ACCOMMODATIONS
A Hotel Livonia
B Hotel Misión
C Casa de Huéspedes
la Mamá Helene

N

of immigration drawn seaward from the interior by the prospect of plentiful pesos. Now more than ever, everyone in Acapulco is driven by money—although now, the need to earn it rather than the need to spend it. Relentless vendors and persistent cabbies swarm everywhere, hunting pedestrians like sharks. Peddlers of everything from bubble gum to "free information" run at tourists like eager bulls. But though the high-rise hotels crowding the waterfront have lost the first flush of youth, a roster full of festivals and city beautification projects promise a revamped Acapulco. Perhaps the best time to visit the city is at night when darkness shrouds the grime and allows the streetlamps to evoke Acapulco's fairytale past.

✦ ORIENTATION

Acapulco Bay lies 400km south of Mexico City and 239km southeast of Ixtapa/Zihuatanejo. Rte. 200 feeds into **La Costera (Av. Costera Miguel Alemán)**, the main drag. The traditional downtown area, with the *zócalo* and the cathedral, is in the western part of town right before the bay curves around the marina. **Acapulco Dorado,** full of fast-food chains, malls, and luxury hotels, stretches from **Parque Papagayo** to the naval base. The ultra-chic resorts are found on **Acapulco Diamante,** farther east towards the airport. Most budget accommodations and restaurants lie between the *zócalo* and **La Quebrada,** the famous cliff-diving spot. In southwest Acapulco, a peninsula with **Playas Caleta** and **Caletilla** juts out into the bay.

"Hornos" or "Cici" buses run from Caleta along the Costera all the way to the naval base (3 pesos). "Cine Río-La Base" buses go from the *zócalo* to the base down Av. Cuauhtémoc. To get from the **Estrella de Oro** bus station to the *zócalo* (a 40min. walk), cross the street and flag down any bus heading southwest (3 pesos). A *"zócalo"* bus (3 pesos) will do the trick from the **Estrella Blanca** station. A **taxi** from the *zócalo* to the bus station costs 20 pesos, while one to the airport costs 75 pesos. **Shared taxis** (tel. 62 10 95) can take you to the airport for 45 pesos.

☒ PRACTICAL INFORMATION

TRANSPORTATION

Airport: on Rte. 200, 26km south of the city. Served by **Aerocaribe** (tel. 84 23 42), **Aerolines Internacionales** (tel. 86 56 30), **Aeroméxico** (tel. 66 91 90), **American** (tel. 66 92 27), **Continental** (tel. 66 90 63), **Delta** (tel. 66 94 84), **Mexicana** (tel. 66 91 38), and **Taesa** (tel. 86 56 00).

Buses: Estrella de Oro (tel. 85 87 05), on Cuauhtémoc at Massiu, sends buses to: **Cuernavaca** (4hr., 4 per day 10:40am-8pm, 120-185 pesos); **Mexico City** (5hr., 20 per day 6:45am-1am, 170-250 pesos); **Taxco** (4hr., 5 per day 7am-6:40pm, 110 pesos); and **Zihuatanejo** (4hr., 13 per day 4:50am-4:50pm, 49-70 pesos). **Estrella Blanca,** Av. Ejido 47 (tel. 69 20 29), carts passengers to: **Chilpancingo** (1½hr., every 30min. 3:40am-11:30pm, 34 pesos); **Cuernavaca** (4hr., 9:35am and 2:20pm, 136 pesos); **Mexico City** (5hr., every hr. 6am-6pm, 167 pesos); **Puebla** (7hr., 5 per day 10am-midnight, 199 pesos); and **Querétaro** (9hr., 4:30pm, 264 pesos).

Car Rental: Hertz, Costera 1945 (tel. 85 68 89), past La Gran Plaza on the left. Small VW with insurance 431 pesos per day. Open M-Sa 8am-7pm, Su 9am-5pm.

TOURIST AND FINANCIAL SERVICES

Tourist Offices: SEFOTUR, in the Centro Cultural de Acapulco, a little west of Cici Waterpark on LaCostera. Helpful staff will happily overload you with brochures and maps. Some English spoken. Open M-F 9am-8pm, Sa 9am-2pm. In an **emergency,** contact the **Procuraduría del Turista,** Costera 4455 (tel. 84 45 83 or 84 44 16), in the Centro Internacional in front of CICI waterpark. Open daily 8am-11pm.

Tourist Police: (tel. 80 01 97 or 80 01 74). Officers clad in white wander around the *zócalo*. Office open daily 9am-1am.

Travel Agency: Agencia de Viajes Sol y Luna Excursiones, Costera 170 (tel. 84 51 40), in the Plaza Condes in front of Fiesta Americana. Open M-Sa 9am-9pm.

Consulates: Canada (tel. 84 13 05), Costera at Juan Pérez, in the Continental Hotel. Open daily 10am-2pm. **U.K.** (tel. 84 16 50), in the Hotel Las Brisas. Open M-F 1-3pm and 4-8pm. **U.S.,** Costera 121 #14 (tel. 69 05 56), in the Continental Plaza Hotel. Open M-F 10am-2pm.

Currency Exchange: Banks on Costera have decent rates. All open M-F 9am-3pm. **Casas de cambio** are all along the north side of Costera and are often open until 8pm.

American Express: Costera 1628 (tel. 69 11 00 to 24; fax 69 11 88), on the bottom floor of the shopping center. Open M-Sa 10am-7pm.

LOCAL SERVICES

Bookstore: Sanborn's, Costera 209, 2 blocks from the *zócalo* toward the hotel zone. Selection of English paperbacks. Open daily 7:30am-11pm.

Markets: Mercado, Av. Constituyentes at Hurtado. Open daily 6am-6pm. **Supermarket Comercial Mexicana,** just east of the tourist office. Open daily 8am-10pm.

Laundry: Super Lavandería, José Maria Iglesias 9 (tel. 80 01 46), 1 block from the cathedral. 4kg. for 34 pesos. Open M-Sa 9am-2pm and 3-8pm, Su 10am-3pm.

Internet: Caspro Micro, Horacio Nelson 40-7A (tel. 84 82 54), on the street between Baby'O and Wal-Mart. Sells computer equipment as well.

EMERGENCY AND COMMUNICATIONS

Police: LOCATEL (tel. 85 20 44 or 85 08 62).

Red Cross: (tel. 85 41 01), on Ruiz Cortínez, north of the *zócalo*. Take a "Hospital" bus. 24hr. emergency service. Some English spoken. **Sociedad de Asistencia Médica Turística** (tel. 85 58 00 or 85 59 59) has a 24hr. doctor. English spoken.

Pharmacy: ISSTE Farmacias, Quebrada 1 (tel. 82 34 77), directly behind the cathedral on the *zócalo*. The storefront faces Independencia. Open daily 8am-8pm. **Farmacia Calleta,** Benito Juárez 21 (tel. 82 48 27). Open daily 8am-8:30pm.

Hospital: IMSS, Ruiz Cortínez 128 (tel. 83 38 88), north of the *zócalo* along Madero. Take a "Hospital" bus. 24hr. emergency service. No English spoken.

Emergency: dial 060.

Post Office: Urdareta 1 (tel. 82 20 83), near Wantemóc. Open M-Sa 8am-8pm.

Postal Code: 39300.

Telephones: LADATELs line the Costera. **Caseta Carranza,** Carranza 9, is 2 blocks from the *zócalo* toward the strip. Also has a **fax.** Open daily 8am-10pm.

Phone Code: 74.

▟ ACCOMMODATIONS

Sleeping on the beaches of Acapulco Bay is unsafe. Fortunately, budget accommodations are easier to find here than anywhere else on Mexico's Pacific coast. Although they are a far cry from the pampering, posh hotels the brochures depict, comfortable, conveniently located hotels are quite numerous in Acapulco, especially around the *zócalo*. Be certain to inquire about discounts before paying for a room. However, during *Semana Santa* (Mar.-Apr.), rooms are nearly double the off-season prices, and it's hard to find lodgings without a reservation.

▟ **Casa de Huéspedes Mama Hélène,** Benito Juárez 12 (tel. 82 23 96), at Felipe Valle. French owner holds court over a posse of ping-pong-playing, coffee-drinking, chain-smoking Euro-backpackers as well as some cute, funny pets. No hot water. Singles 90 pesos; doubles 160 pesos.

▟ **Hotel Misión,** Felipe Valle 12 (tel. 82 36 43), at La Paz, 2 blocks left of the *zócalo* as you face the church. The guests chatting over breakfast (15-30 pesos) in the courtyard and the lazy cats sprawled out on the stairway give it a homey feel. Colonial architecture and well-tended plants make staying here as soothing as possible. All rooms have ceiling fans and private baths; some have desks and sofas. 80 pesos per person; in high season 120 pesos.

Hotel Posada Calle Teniente Azuerta 8 (tel. 83 19 30). There's no consistent hot water, but the firm beds and pleasant hospitality of this hotel welcomes those tired from sun, shopping, or *sol*. Flower curtains brighten up the somewhat lockerroom-esque hallways. 70 pesos per person; 2 people 120 pesos.

Hotel Livonia López Mateos 32 (tel. 82 23 29), at Azueta. This cheap hotel with an especially nice staff and powerful ceiling fans will have you resting comfortably, although the bathrooms are not particularly clean. 50 pesos per person.

◯ FOOD

Acapulco's international restaurant scene conspicuously caters to tourists' palates. The many chic restaurants between Playa Condesa and the base are frequented mainly by tourists who don't fret much about money. If you insist on eating on the Costera, try **El Fogón,** across from the Continental Plaza (sandwiches 12-28 pesos; open 24hr.) or **Jovito's,** across from the Fiesta Americana at Playa Condesa (*tacos de mariscos* 25 pesos; open daily 1pm-midnight).

Mariscos Nacho's, Azueta 7 (tel. 82 28 91), at Juárez, 1 block from the Costera. An open-air *marisquería* serving everything from lobster (50 pesos) to *camarones al mojo de ajo* (garlic shrimp; 50 pesos). Nacho's is always bustling with everyone from sun-burned families straggling in from the beach to young hipsters dolled up for a night out. Open daily 8am-10pm.

100% Natural, Costera 248 (tel. 85 13 12 ext. 100), at the corner of Sebastián Vizcaíno, just west of the tourist office. Several other branches line the Costera. Health food restaurant serving hearty sandwiches with sprouts and lettuce (30-35 pesos), fruit salad (19-30 pesos), and chilly, smooth *licuados* (15-20 pesos). Lots of vegetarian options, like soy burgers (24-32 pesos). Open daily 8am-midnight. Other branches open 24hr.

The Fat Farm/La Granja del Pingui, Juárez 10, at La Paz, next door to Mama Hélène. Vege-table soup (8 pesos) is a specialty. Watch TV as you enjoy poultry and meat (20-25 pesos) or fish (28-35 pesos) entrees. Open daily 8am-9pm, high season 7am-11pm.

◉ SAND AND SIGHTS

Unless you've won a game show, the reason you're in Acapulco is to enjoy the beach and booze, and you aren't the only one. Acapulco's beaches aren't quiet and virginal; expect to be harassed by vendors and share the waves with crowds of locals. However, those in the mood for a good dose of unadulterated people-watching will be satisfied. Just don't be surprised if people watch you too.

PENÍNSULA DE LAS PLAYAS. At the westernmost tip of Acapulco Bay, on the seaward side of the peninsula, lie **Playas Caleta** and **Caletilla.** And if you don't mind sharing the water with a couple small fishing boats, the calm water is quite safe for swimming. Hundreds of local families flock to these small beaches, making it hard to find an empty patch of sand anywhere. The narrow causeway that separates the two beaches leads to the island occupied by **Mágico Mundo Marino,** a water park with slides and pools. (Tel. 83 12 15. Open daily 9am-7pm. Admission 30 pesos, under 12, 15 pesos.)

The **Plaza de Toros Caletilla,** Acapulco's main bull ring, sits beyond the abandoned yellow jai alai auditoriums 200m west of Caletilla beach. *Corridas* take place every Sunday at 5pm from December until Easter week, when the best-known *matadores* appear. Buy tickets at the **Centro Kennedy box office** (tel. 85 85 40), Costera at Álvaro Saavedra, or at the bull ring (tel. 83 95 61) after 4:30pm on the day of the fight.

FROM THE COMERCIAL MEXICANA TO PARQUE PAPAGAYO. The stretch of sand along the **Costera,** away from Old Acapulco, is blessed with fewer high-rises and smaller crowds than the beaches at Caleta or farther down the bay. **Playas Tam-arindo, Hornos,** and **Hornitos,** between Las Hamacas Hotel and the Radisson, are called the "afternoon beaches." This is where the fishermen bring in their catches. The waves are moderate, and the sand is ideal for beach sports. An umbrella and 2 chairs are available for 5 pesos. The only drawback is that these beaches are unmistakably urban—only a thin line of palm trees blocks the traffic on Costera.

Those who need a cool, shady break from the relentless sun on the beach venture to **Parque Papagayo,** which sprawls from Costera to Av. Cuauhtémoc. (Tel. 85 24 90. Open daily 6am-8pm.) Entering on Costera by the Gigante supermarket, you'll find a **roller skating rink** (admission 10 pesos, skate rental 2 pesos, inline skates 8 pesos, open daily 4-11pm). The rest of the park has shaded paths for bikes and walkers. There's an aviary in the center surrounded by an artificial lake where you can rent **paddleboats** (10 pesos). Children will find a wading pool, exotic birds from Australia, and a zillion spots for hide and seek.

FROM LA DIANA TO THE NAVAL BASE. A trip to **Playa Condesa,** at the center of the bay, is worth its 2km-plus distance from the *zócalo*. Exercise caution: the waves are strong, and the sea floor drops without warning. The poor swimming conditions don't bother the throngs of sun worshippers who alternately lounge under their blue umbrellas and treat the beach as a runway for their minimal clothing fashion shows. Farther down the bay, between the golf course and naval base, is **Playa Icacos.** As you move toward the base, the waves become gentler.

CICI is a fun-filled **water park.** Let waves toss you down the long, winding water slides, then rush to watch **trained dolphins** perform. To reach the park, follow Costera until you see the orange walls painted with large green waves; otherwise take a "CICI" or "Base" bus. (Tel. 84 80 33. Costera at Cristóbal Colón. Open daily 10am-6pm. Admission 50 pesos. Shows at noon, 2:30, and 5pm.)

PUERTO MARQUÉS. Lacking the prepackaged polish of the strip only a few kilometers away, the beach town of **Puerto Marqués** encompasses an unremarkable ribbon of sand lined wall-to-wall with restaurants so close to the water that the bay's waves lap at diners' feet. The bus ride to this bay is the real attraction, thanks to a magnificent vista from the top of the hill before the descent into town. Buses to Puerto Marqués depart across from Comercial Mexicana supermarket at Playa Hornitos, on the beach side of the street (45min., approximately every 30min. 5:30am-9pm, 3 pesos). As the bus rambles along, the Bahía de Puerto Marqués and the pounding surf of **Playa Revolcadero** come into full view. From Puerto Marqués, it's possible to get to some really nice beaches with even fewer crowds. Catch a "Bonville" bus to get to **Playa Bonville;** it's a big improvement on the crowds and traffic of the downtown beaches.

♫ ENTERTAINMENT AND NIGHTLIFE

In Acapulco, every night is Saturday night: the nightlife busts out all the time, anywhere and everywhere. Most clubs pulsate with activity from 11pm to 5am and charge over 100 pesos for cover, which usually includes open bar. It's always easier and cheaper for women to get in; many clubs offer free admission (and open bar) to women on weeknights. The best clubs cluster in the area around the CICI, on the opposite side of the bay from the *zócalo*.

▨ **Palladium** (tel. 81 03 00), on the Carretera Escénica Las Brisas, is accessible only by taxi (12-15 pesos). It's worth the trip to see this space-age structure perched on a cliff with a truly fabulous view of the downtown lights. This head-and-shoulders-above-the-rest hot spot features a wall of glass; use it to enjoy the panoramic high-tech light and smoke effects and to reflect the runway chic of the clientele. The club reverberates with Mexican and American pop music until midnight when the light descends from the ceiling and the dance party begins. Cover 200 pesos for men, 150 pesos for women, Tu and Th women free until 12:30am. Open bar. Open daily 10:30pm-5am.

Andrómedas (tel. 84 88 15) on Costera, just past Planet Hollywood and the Hard Rock Café is a more accessible venue. Walk up the torch-lit path and enter the castle-like club where scantily-clad women and men in plaid dance to typical disco fare. Cover 200 pesos for men, 150 pesos for women; free for women M, W, F, Su before 12:30am. Open bar. Open daily 10:30pm-5am.

Baby 'O, Costera 22 (tel. 84 74 74). This club is slightly less frenetic and more sophisticated (read: older) than its rambunctious neighbors. No cover M-Th; F-Su cover 100 pesos for men, 50 pesos for women. Drinks 35 pesos. Open 10:30pm-late.

Picante, Privada Piedra Picuda 16, behind Carlos 'n' Charlie's. This spicy gay club is a good alternative to the other high-tech, exclusive discos. The predominantly male clientele of young, lithe bodies writhing to music also enjoy a little late-night racy entertainment. No cover; 2-drink min. Beer 15 pesos. Open daily 10pm-4am.

Nina's, Costera 2909 (tel. 84 24 00), on the beach side near CICI. Features tropical music and a more mature clientele. Cover 120 pesos. Open daily 10pm-5am.

CLIFF DIVERS OF ACAPULCO
It's like nothing you've ever seen nor anything you'll ever want to try. Half naked men hurling themselves off jagged cliffs is not a coming of age ritual for eager young lads but a serious occupation for trained professionals. It is also one of Acapulco's biggest attractions. At **La Quebrada,** cliffs around the northern side of the bay, divers of **clavadistas** perform daily shows where they dive 25 and 35 meters off a less-than-vertical cliff and slip effortlessly into the frothing surf. They make it seem like child's play, but these divers train for years and time each dive so they hit the approaching wave at the perfect moment. Although most spectators congregate at the bottom level, the view is better from the area to the immediate right of the ticket booth. To get to La Quebrada, follow López Mateos, the road on your left side when facing the cathedral's entrance. The walk takes about 15 minutes and ends at the top of a very steep hill. As if the dives weren't enough of a show, all the divers also pray rather theatrically (who can blame them?) at a small shrine before the plunge. After all, it's all part of the everyday business of challenging death and impressing the tourists. Shows at 12:45, 7:30, 8:30, 9:30, and 10:30pm, 15 pesos.

There is a nightlife for non-dancers as well at **Plaza Bahía,** a large shopping mall on Costera past La Gran Plaza on the water side. Speed around a tiny race course at **Go-Karts** (tel. 86 71 47), on the third floor (1-seater 20 pesos for 5min., 2-seater 25 pesos; open daily 10am-11pm). There is **bowling** on the fourth floor at the **Boliche** (tel. 85 09 70; 130 pesos per hr., shoes 7 pesos; open daily 11am-2am) and a snazzy **movie theater** (tel. 86 42 55) on the second floor (tickets 20-25 pesos).

Acapulco's tourist office organizes a variety of festivals designed to lighten the wallets of its tourists. **Festival Acapulco** in May is a celebration of music. In July, Acapulco hosts a **Black Film Festival** in which buff movie stars test their volleyball skills in front of gathering admirers. Men and women from around the globe journey to Acapulco in December to test their cliff diving skills during the **Torneo Internacional de Clavados en La Quebrada.**

NEAR ACAPULCO: PIE DE LA CUESTA

Pie de la Cuesta is known for its truly magnificent sunsets—the lazy light lingers beautifully over the Pacific horizon just before sliding out of view. A single-lane route runs through Acapulco's hills to Pie de la Cuesta, ending at the narrow road that separates the Pacific from the placid waters of **Laguna de Coyuca,** and the hustle and bustle of Acapulco from the serenity of a small beach community.

At Playa Pie de la Cuesta, pleasure-seekers can choose between salt and fresh water. Since the Pacific's rough waves preclude swimming, many head to the lagoon instead, the site of the area's best **water skiing. Sunset** (tel. 60 06 53 or 60 06 54), a ski club, near the air base offers **ski rental** (300 pesos per hr. for up to 3 people; lessons with tours of the lagoon 40 pesos per hr.). Unfortunately, rest and relaxation are all too often interrupted by aggressive *lancha* agents who are more than happy to give tours of the lagoon, for a fee, of course (about 30 pesos per person in a *colectivo* boat). A trip here is worth it, however, as it rewards you with bluer water, cleaner air, and a less crowded beach than Acapulco. **Villa Nirvana** (tel. 60 16 31), a blue-and-white building a few blocks from the bus stop, carves out its own utopia complete with a restaurant, swimming pool, and rooms with fans and private baths (about 120-130 pesos per person; high season 150 pesos). Beyond the pharmacy toward the base is **Acapulco Trailer Park** (tel. 60 00 10), with campgrounds, trailer hook-up sites, bathrooms, ocean views, and a pet raccoon named "Charlie" (50 pesos per night, prices negotiable). If you work up an appetite, take the last road before you reach the base to **Chavelita,** Av. Fuerza Áerea Mexicana Ote. 14 (tel. 48 02 60), with breakfast for 20 pesos, *comida a la cana* for 18 pesos, and beer for 7 pesos (open daily 8am-9pm).

Getting There: Buses leave from Costera, across from the post office in Acapulco. Buses marked "Pie de la Cuesta Playa" go directly to the road along the beach;

those labeled "Pie de la Cuesta Centro" stop on a parallel street in a small marketplace (40min., 3 pesos). From there, turn left down a dirt road; you should be able to see the shimmering ocean in the distance. At the end of the road, turn right to head toward the base. Buses shuttle between the base and the town's *centro* (3 pesos). A *combi* will take you as far as **La Barra,** the enchanted spot where the water from the lagoon flows into the ocean (3.50 pesos). To return to Acapulco, go back to the market and hail a bus in the opposite direction.

OAXACA

OAXACA DE JUÁREZ (OAXACA)

Perched on a giant plateau that gracefully interrupts the Sierra Madre del Sur's descent into the Oaxaca valley, the city of Oaxaca de Juárez (wa-HAH-ka dey WA-rez; pop. 250,000) is a rare beauty. The city's surname was added in honor of native son Benito Juárez, a Oaxacan Zapotec and Mexico's only *indígena* president. It earned its older nickname, "City of Jade," after Hernán Cortés began to build his beloved (but unfinished) estate here in 1535. Cortés's deep green stone buildings have since aged to a dignified yellow, and throughout the streets this style has been lovingly preserved and imitated, giving Oaxaca the feel of a city that lives and breathes its own remarkable history. Especially in the early morning, the city is strikingly beautiful; at first light, the city's tall, green, gracefully aging silhouettes are spectacular.

Oaxaca State

A relatively affluent and cosmopolitan city, Oaxaca has recently become a major destination for tourists of all ages and nationalities who are lured by its prestigious museums, outstanding archaeological sites, and sheer attractiveness. For many visitors, one-month stays at language schools turn into whole summers of immersion, and those who do leave make plans to return to sip rich Oaxacan hot chocolate as soon as they can. In the face of the Teva-wearing crowds, the city manages to retain an air of authenticity rather than dilution. The *zócalo*, lined with sprawling jacaranda trees and outdoor cafes, is one of the most amiable in the Republic. Expect to see all of Mexico represented here: merchants, *indígenas*, and professionals jostle elbows, and restless students tear around on expensive motorcycles or agitate for labor reform. But neither tourism nor politics can do anything to diminish Oaxaca's cultural richness—or colonial allure. Day and night, when streetlights play up and down the stone faces of its magnificent churches, Oaxaca is always a wonder.

⚡ ORIENTATION

Oaxaca de Juárez rests in the Oaxaca Valley, between the towering Sierra Madre del Sur and the Puebla-Oaxaca range, 523km southeast of Mexico City, 435km south of Veracruz, and 526km west of Tuxtla Gutiérrez. Principal access to Oaxaca from the north and east is via **Rte. 190.** While most of Oaxaca's streets form a grid, many change names as they swing by the *zócalo*. It is also common for two or more streets to share the same name, making it wise to specify the neighborhood as well as the street when directing cabbies.

Oaxaca's ground zero is the *zócalo*, a lush, busy city center whose two plazas are bordered by the cathedral, the post office, the *Palacio de Gobierno*, and a variety of cafes and shops. **Av. Hildalgo** runs east-west between the two squares and connects at either end to the congested **Periférico** that circumscribes the city center. Branching off northwards from the *zócalo* is **Calle Valdierso,** which becomes the **Av. Macedonio Acalá,** a tourist hog-heaven. This is the place to go for money-exchange, expensive local crafts, and museums that will help sort out Oaxaca's complex history. Though the *zócalo* and the Acalá are Oaxaca's tourist microcosms, one need not wander far to find lower prices and complete Spanish language immersion.

The area around the **first-class bus station** (on **Calzada Niños de Chapultepec,** 11 blocks north of the *zócalo*) is packed with the town's most popular discotheques. Northeast of the *zócalo* in **Jalatisco** is the tranquil **Parque Juárez** and a pleasant middle class residential area. The **second-class bus station** (7 blocks southwest of the *zócalo*) is located in the **Central de Abastos**, Oaxaca's overwhelming center of trade and market for goods brought from the surrounding villages. South of the *zócalo* and extending to the city outskirts are more congested areas overflowing with delicious roadside fare and some fantastic kitschy bargains. Most parts of the city are easily reachable by foot, and **local buses** rarely cost more than 2 pesos. Don't be scared by the bus system—ask people on the street which one to take and you'll get around town much faster. Service becomes sporadic in the evenings, but reliable **taxis** will zoom the distance for 20-30 pesos.

🔢 PRACTICAL INFORMATION

TRANSPORTATION

Airport: Aeropuerto Juárez (tel. 1 50 40), on Rte. 175, 8km south of the city. **AeroCaribe** (tel. 6 02 29, airport tel. 1 52 47). **Aeroméxico,** Hidalgo 513 (tel. 01 800 021 4000). **Mexicana,** Independencia 102 (tel. 514 72 53), at Fiallo.

To and from the airport: It is possible to hire a private **taxi** from the airport, but it is cheaper and just as easy to share one of the **Transportes Aeropuerto** (tel. 514 43 50) vans with other travelers. Buy a ticket to either the *centro* (15 pesos) or other neighborhoods (36 pesos) at the airport exit. For the same prices, a van will pick you up at your hotel. Arrangements should be made a day in advance by phone or at the office next to the post office on the Plaza Almeda (open M-Sa 9am-2pm and 4-7pm, Su 9am-3pm).

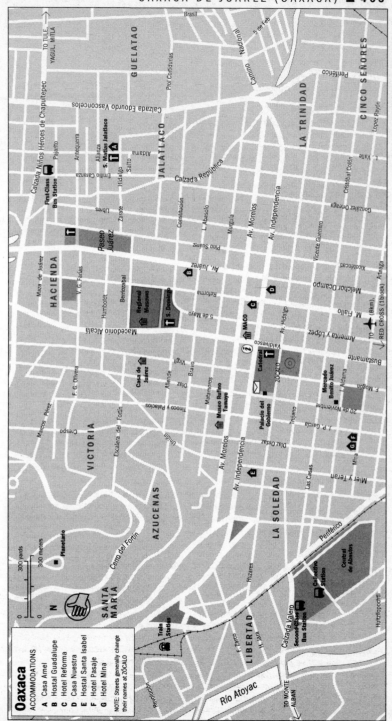

Oaxaca

ACCOMMODATIONS

A Casa Arnel
B Hostal Guadalupe
C Hotel Reforma
D Casa Nuestra
E Hostal Santa Isabel
F Hotel Pasaje
G Hotel Mina

NOTE: Streets generally change their names at ZÓCALO.

N

0 ———— 300 yards
0 ———— 300 meters

■ Planetario

SANTA MARÍA

AZUCENAS

VICTORIA

HACIENDA

GUELATAO

JALATLACO

LA TRINIDAD

CINCO SEÑORES

LA SOLEDAD

LIBERTAD

TO TULE,
YAGUL, MITLA

Brasil

5 de Feb.

Camino Nacional

Prol Cordurias

Calzada Eduardo Vasconcelos

Calzada Niños Héroes de Chapultepec

Anequera
Pajarito

Alianza
Emilio Carranza
Aldama
Satto
Hidalgo

S. Matías Jalatlaco

First-Class
Bus Station

Calzada República

Zárate
Libres
Constitución
L Abasolo
Murguía
Av. Morelos
Av. Independencia

Maza de Juárez

V. G. Farías

Paseo Juárez

Humboldt

Berriozábal

Pino Suárez

Av. Juárez

B

Reforma

5 de Mayo

D

Regional
Museum

S. Domingo

Macedonio Alcalá

MACO

C

Valdivieso

Catedral

i

ZÓCALO

Melchor Ocampo

Xicoténcatl

Vicente Guerrero

González Ortega

Cristóbal Colón

L Valle

López Payón

Periférico

M. Fiallo

TO (8km),
RED CROSS (1block)

Armenta y López

Av. Hidalgo

Bustamante

Arteaga

F.G. Oliveira

Casa de
Juárez

Virgil

Allende
Díaz
Bravo

Tinoco y Palacios

Matamoros

Museo Rufino
Tamayo

Av. Morelos

Unión

Marcos Pérez

Crespo

Escalera del Fortín

Cerro del Fortín

Av. Independencia

Palacio del
Gobierno

20 de Noviembre

Mercado
Benito Juárez

Aldama
F. Mogón

J. P. García

Trujano

Díaz Ordaz

E

Las Casas

Mier y Terán

Miguez

Huzares

Periférico

G F

Mina

Colectivo
Station

Central
de Abastos

Huitzilopochtli

TO MONTE
ALBÁN

Río Atoyac

Calzada Valerio

Second-Class
Bus Station

Train
Station

Revolución

Tejano

Trujano

Zaragoza

Buses: From Oaxaca, it is possible to go almost anywhere in the Republic at any time. The **first-class station** (tel. 515 17 03) is located at Niños Héroes de Chapultepec 1036. From this station, ADO (tel. 5 17 03) runs to: **Mexico City** (6hr., 18 per day, 197 pesos); **Puebla** (4.5 hr., 7 per day, 147 pesos); **Tuxtepec** (6½ hr., 2 per day, 171 pesos); and **Veracruz** (8 hr., 8:30am and 8:30pm, 195 pesos). Cristóbal Colón (tel. 5 12 14) goes to: **Puerto Escondido** (12hr., 9:30am and midnight, 124 pesos); **San Cristóbal** (12hr., 7:30pm, 124 pesos); **Tehuantepec** (4hr., 10 per day, 80 pesos); and **Tuxtla Gutiérrez** (10hr., 2 per day, 174 pesos). Tickets for ADO and Cristóbal Colón are also available at 20 de Noviembre 204. The **second-class station** is just past the Central de Abastos (a big market), across the Periférico from the western end of Trujano. Small regional bus lines, many without signs or ticket windows, provide frequent service to small towns near Oaxaca, usually for under 10 pesos (open daily 9am-2pm and 4-7pm). Estrella del Valle (tel. 4 57 00 or 6 54 29) runs to **Puerto Escondido** (8hr., 8 per day 7am-11pm, 49 pesos).

Car Rental: Budget, 5 de Mayo 315 (tel. 6 44 45). Also at the airport (tel. 1 52 52). VWs cost 400-450 pesos per day, depending on the season. Free mileage. The office in the *centro* is convenient but fares are often lower at the airport (open daily 8am-1pm and 4-7pm). **Hertz** (tel. 6 24 34), on Valdivieso at Hidalgo, across from the American Express office, has similar rates. Slightly cheaper is **Arrendadora Express,** 20 de Noviembre 204A (tel. 6 67 76), which rents **cars, motorcycles, mopeds,** and **bikes.**

TOURIST AND FINANCIAL SERVICES

Tourist Offices: SEDETUR, Independencia 607 (tel. 6 01 23; email info@oaxaca.gob.mx; http://oaxaca.gob.mx/sedetur), across the street from the cathedral, can set you up with maps, brochures and a *cabaña* in one of the *pueblos* outside of the city. English spoken. Open daily 8am-8pm. **CEPROTUR,** also at Independencia 607 (tel./fax 6 72 80) next to SEPROTUR handles grittier problems such as robbery. Open daily 9am-9pm. **Info Booth** at the airport. Also check the *Oaxaca Times* (www.oaxacatimes.com), a monthly English newspaper, for seasonal tourist information.

Consulates: In an emergency, **CEPROTUR** (see above) will obtain consular assistance. **Canada,** Dr. Liceaga 119 #8 (tel. 3 37 77). Open M-F 9am-2pm. **U.K.,** in the same building as the German consulate. **U.S.,** Alcalá 201 #204 (tel. 4 30 54), at Morelos. Hidden under an arched doorway. Open M-F 10am-5pm.

Currency Exchange: Banamex, Hidalgo 821 (tel. 1 6 59 00), at 5 de Mayo, 1 block from the *zócalo* with **ATM** service. Open M-Sa 9am-4pm. **Banco Serfín** (tel. 4 52 26), Independencia 705, across the street from the cathedral also has an **ATM.** Open M-F 9am-5pm. **Cash Express,** Alcalá 201 (tel. 6 22 00), exchanges money at more flexible hours. Open M-Sa 8am-8pm, Su 9am-3pm. Also try **Internacional de Divisas** (tel. 6 33 99), next to the *zócalo* on Alcalá. Open M-Sa 8am-8pm, Su 9am-5pm.

American Express: Valdivieso 2 (tel. 6 65 22 or 6 27 00), at Hidalgo across from the *zócalo*. It also houses a **travel agency** that sells plane tickets and first-class bus tickets to a variety of destinations. English spoken. Open M-F 9am-2pm and 4-8pm; travel agency closes 1 hour earlier.

LOCAL SERVICES

Foreign Bookstores: Librerria Dante Oaxaca, Acalá 403 (tel. 6 03 39) is the sort of place that will always have Frida Kahlo's diary in stock. Filled with glossy photo essays on the region and translations of Carlos Fuentes, this bookstore offers the classiest selection of English-language books in town. Museum bookstores (particularly the one at Monte Alban) are a good bet for quality books on the region. For the other end of the spectrum, **Librería Universitaria** has a small collection of trashy English paperbacks for 10 pesos a piece. Open M-Sa 9:30am-2pm and 4:30pm-8pm.

Libraries: Biblioteca Circulante, Alcalá 305. A haven for displaced U.S. tourists. Everything from the *New Yorker* to *Sports Illustrated*. Open M-F 10am-1pm and 4-7pm, Sa 10am-1pm. **Instituto Welte Para Estudios Oaxaqueños,** 5 de Mayo 412 (tel. 6 54 17). Large collection of English-language books and journals on Oaxacan history and anthropology. Open M-F 10am-2pm. The **Instituto de Artes Gráficos de Oaxaca,** Alcalá 507 (tel. 6 69 80), across from Santo Domingo, has a library as well as changing art exhibits. Open daily 9:30am-9pm. Places of congregation for students, tourists and artists alike, both *Institutos* are situated in old colonial homes and offer courtyard cafes filled with bouganvilla and good conversation.

Cultural Centers: Centro Cultural Ricardo Flores Magon, Acalá 302 (tel. 4 03 95), at Independencia, hosts plays, dance performances, concerts, and gallery openings on a daily basis during peak season. Listings can be found in *Programación Cultural* available at the *centro*. **Instituto Oaxaqueño de las Culturas** (tel. 6 24 83), offers similar programming at the corner of Reforma and Constitución. Listings are in the monthly *Guía Cultura* available free from SEDETUR. **Casa de la Cultura,** González Ortega 403 (tel. 6 24 83), at Colón, has poetry readings and art galleries. Open M-F 9am-8pm, Sa 9am-3pm.

Markets: Oaxaca's **Central de Abastos** is the ultimate shopping experience. Saturday is the market's big day, but vendors offer every type of product every day of the week. A great way to see a less tourist-oriented side of the city is to begin at the *zócalo* and walk 8 blocks west on Trujano to the *Central*. From there, finding the market is easy, though getting out can be more complicated. Open 8am-6pm. **Mercado Benito Juárez,** at the corner of 20 de Noviembre and Aldama, 2 blocks from the *zócalo*, sells crafts, produce, flowers, and clothing. Its annex, **Mercado 20 de Noviembre,** on the next block over, has gastronomic goodies. Both markets open daily 6am-9pm. **Mercado de Artesanías,** at the corner of J.P. García and Zaragoza, offers some artisan wares. Prices and quality are often better in nearby villages where the crafts originate. Open daily 10am-8pm.

Laundromats: Súper Lavandería Hidalgo, J.P. García 200 (tel. 4 11 81), 2 blocks west of the *zócalo*. Open M-Sa 8am-8pm. **Lavandería Clin,** 20 de Noviembre 605B (tel. 6 23 42). Open M-Sa 9am-8pm. Both places wash 3.5kg of clothes for 35 pesos.

EMERGENCY AND COMMUNICATIONS

Emergency: dial 060.

Police: Aldama 108 (tel. 6 27 26 or 6 07 74), south of the *zócalo*, between Miguel Cabrera and Bustamante. Open 24hr.

Red Cross: Armenta y López 700 (tel. 6 48 03 or 6 48 09), between Pardo and Burgoa. Ambulance service. Some English spoken. Open 24hr.

Pharmacies: Farmacia El Fénix, Flores Magón 104 (tel. 6 60 11), next to the *zócalo*. Open M-Sa 7am-10pm, Su 8am-9pm. **Farmacia Héroes de Chapultepec,** Calle Niños Héroes de Chapultapec 1004 (tel. 3 35 24), half a block east of the first-class bus station. Open daily 7am-11pm.

Hospitals: Hospital Civil, Porfirio Díaz 400 (tel. 5 14 22 or 5 32 00), 1.5km north of town. Free medical service. **IMSS,** Chapultepec 621 (tel. 5 20 23), at Reforma. Open 24hr. **Sanatorio Reforma,** Reforma 613 (tel. 6 09 89), at Humboldt. English spoken. Open 24hr.

Post Office: (tel. 6 26 61), in the Plaza Alameda de León. Open M-F 8am-7pm, Sa 9am-1pm. **Postal Code:** 68000.

Fax: Telecomm (tel. 6 49 02), Independencia at 20 de Noviembre, around the corner from the post office. Open M-F 8am-6pm, Sa 9am-4pm.

Internet Access: Though the ever-increasing number of Internet cafes helps keep prices down, one should avoid access providers near the *zócalo*, since their prime location allows them to charge higher rates. For ambience, try **Internet Axis,** 5 de Mayo 412-3 (tel. 4 80 24), in the beautiful Plaza Gonzalo Lucero, down the street from La Iglesia Santo Domingo. Helpful staff and caffeine from **Café Gecko** (located in the same building) make it worth the 30 pesos per hr. rate. **Terra Nostra,** Morelos 600, 2nd fl. (tel. 6 82 92), at Porfirio Díaz offers similar services for 20 pesos per hr. Kill two birds with one stone at **Zelantro,** Porfirio Díaz 208, which offers free internet service with the purchase of a drink from the bar. Open W-Su 9pm-2am.

Telephones: LADATELs are everywhere, with an especially large concentration in front of the post office in the *zócalo*. *Casetas* available at **Computel,** Independencia 601 (tel. 4 80 84), across from the Telecomm office. Open daily 7am-10pm.

Phone Code: 951.

ACCOMMODATIONS AND CAMPING

As Oaxaca attracts more visitors, some old budget standbys have upgraded their rooms in an attempt to lure more upscale tourists. But bargains still await the penny-pinching soul, especially in the busy blocks south of the *zócalo*, which are within easy walking distance of the second-class bus station and all major sights and services. Reservations are a must on *fiesta* weekends, especially during the *Guelaguetza* in July, *Semana Santa* in late March or early April, and during the celebration of *El Día de Los Muertos* in early November.

For longer stays in the city, there are many reasonably priced rooms available for rent. Check the tourist office and the *Oaxaca Times* for listings. **Departmentos del Cuento,** Quintana Roo 107 (tel. 4 22 88), off Berriozabal past La Iglesia Santo Domingo, rents six one- or two-person rooms with kitchen and bath (1500-2000 pesos per month, utilities included). Outside of town in the *Zona Militar*, **Trailer Park Oaxaca,** Violetas 900 (tel. 5 27 96), offers off-the-beaten-path accomodations. Take the "Colonia Reforma" bus from the stop on J.P. García just north of Hidalgo to get there.

NORTHEAST OF EL CENTRO/JALATLACO. Cobblestone streets and a location 20 minutes northeast of the *zócalo* lend Jalatlaco a quiet remove. In the evenings, the nearby **Parque Juárez** fills with dancers practicing *ballet folklorico* and residents out for their nightly *constitutional.*

Casa Arnel, Aldama 404 (tel. 5 28 56, email casa.arnel@spersaoaxaca.com.mex), at Hidalgo. From the *zócalo*, walk 7 blocks pas La Iglesia Santo Domingo in Acalá, turn right on Berriozabal and cross the southern end of Parque Juárez, turning right again on Zarate, which becomes Hidalgo. The hotel is directly across from the Iglesia San Matias Jalatlaco. While Casa Arnel's courtyard jungle has enough mystique to inspire the next García-Márquez novel, the hotel's more practical amenities make it an excellent point of departure for the uninitiated tourist. Bar, Internet access (40 pesos per hr.), a travel agency, spotless rooms, and friendly, helpful staff. Entertainment provided by the social breakfasts and talking parrots in the couryard. Tours of the surrounding areas leave directly from the hotel. Do-it-yourself and full laundry service provided. Singles 90 pesos, 180 with private bath; doubles 180 pesos, 240 with private bath.

Hostal Guadalupe, Juárez 409 (tel. 6 63 65). From the *zócalo*, walk 4 blocks north on Acalá and turn right on Abasalo. Continue for 3 blocks and turn left. The hostel is on Juárez between Abasalo and Constitución. Ideally situated between the buzz of the *zócalo* and the peace of Jalatlaco in an area with an abundance of cheap, tasty food, Hostal Guadalupe may well be Oaxaca's best bargain. Those who don't see the charm in typical budget bathrooms will luxuriate in the communal bath's clean, white splendour and rest easy in the immaculate dorm-style bedrooms. TV, courtyard seating, kitchen-use, and new laundry facilities make this a 40 peso per night steal. Private bedroom with bath 100 pesos.

JUST NORTH OF THE ZÓCALO/EL CENTRO. Old colonial buldings make lovely museums and even lovelier hotels. This part of town not only offers the best architechture, but also the best location for those wishing to stay close to Oaxaca's artifacts and galleries.

Hotel Reforma, Reforma 102 (tel. 6 09 39), between Independencia and Morelos, 4 blocks past the left side of the cathedral. Kick back on rustic, hand-carved wood furniture, and soak in the view of the city. Rooms are usually full; reservations help. Singles 110 pesos; doubles 130 pesos; triples 170 pesos; quads 200 pesos.

Casa Nuestra (hostel), Independencia 906 (tel. 6 96 54) between Armenta y López and Fiallo, 2nd fl. Located 1½ blocks from the *zócalo*, Casa Nuestra is the place for travelers who view life as art. Try your hand at Oaxacan cuisine in the beautifully tiled kitchen under the high, 17th century ceilings. 20 peso per hr. Internet access on the owner's laptop. Shared rooms 75 pesos; private singles 100 pesos; doubles 150 pesos; rooftop hammocks and futons 50 pesos.

SOUTHWEST OF THE ZÓCALO. South of the *zócalo*, there is a plethora of budget hotels; often four or five share the same block, particularly along **Díaz Ordaz.** Because of their proximity to the market and second-class bus terminal, many of these hotels face noisy streets; ask for a room in the back or on an upper level.

Hostal Santa Isabel, Mier y Teran No. 103 (tel. 4 28 65), between Independencia and Hidalgo. Santa Isabel continues to offer some of the cheapest beds in town. Standard dorm-style rooms and serviceable (if not scintillating) bathrooms are supplemented by cheap, 20 peso per hr. Internet access, a bar, and good camaraderie. Key deposit 20 pesos. Beds 40 pesos; private doubles 80 pesos.

Hotel Mina, Mina 304 (tel. 6 49 66), at 20 Noviembre. A favorite among international travelers. The plain rooms feature hard beds, but the communal baths are clean and convenient. Singles 50 pesos; doubles 60 pesos; triples 90 pesos.

Hotel Pasaje, Mina 302 (tel. 6 42 13), 3 blocks south of the *zócalo*. Well-scrubbed, tiled rooms open onto a plant-filled courtyard. Bathrooms are large and clean, but the fluorescent lighting makes everything look a bit withered. Rooms near the street are noisy, but you can smell the chocolate from the nearby sweet shops. Singles 100 pesos; doubles 130 pesos; triples 170 pesos.

FOOD

Fast food may be a last-ditch culinary option in most parts of the world, but in typical Oaxaqueño fashion, even the cheapest, fastest roadside snacks are something of an art. Exotic, delicious, and scandalously inexpensive meals are omnipresent, as are the less chaotic and more costly ones that can be eyed in Oaxaca's many garden courtyards. The only possible limitation on dietetic debauchery in this city is the capacity and strength of the visitor's gut.

Oaxaca has seven versions of **mole,** a rich sauce made of over 30 ingredients including chiles and chocolate. Many restaurants also serve **tlayudas,** large, crisp tortillas topped with just about everything. If you're feeling adventurous, try **botanas oaxaqueñas**—plates full of regional goodies including chile, *quesillo* (boiled string cheese), *chorizo* (sausage), guacamole, and *chapulines* (tiny, cooked grasshoppers doused with chile; they're good, seriously).

Also a must is Oaxaca's cinnamon **chocolate caliente** (hot chocolate). The cafes in the *zócalo* are pricey, but you can find something on the cheaper side south of the *zócalo* on Mina. Another regional specialty is the **tamale,** now found in all parts of the Republic. Made of ground corn wrapped in banana leaves and then baked or boiled, **tamales** come stuffed with beans, chicken, or beef. And there's no better way to wrap up a *comida oaxaqueña* than with a large swig of **mezcal,** the potent cactus-based liquor that is only manufactured in the Oaxaca Valley.

Some of the best and most intriguing fare can be found at the **markets** in various stages of preparation, while more finished dishes can be procured along the amazing line of taco stands on **Guerrero,** just southeast of the *zócalo*.

La Casa de la Abuela, Hidalgo 616, 2nd fl. (tel. 6 35 44), located at the corner of the *zócalo* and Plaza Alameda. La Casa's authentic Oaxacan dishes are an excellent way to get one's culinary bearings before digging into the dimly lit, steaming equivalents offered under market canopies. Savor delicious renditions of Oaxaca's famous *sopa de guias* (squash flower soup) for 20 pesos and *chapulines* (35 pesos) while marveling at the restaurant's postcard quality views of the cathedral and the *zócalo*. Finish the meal with a cup of *té de poelo* (a regional herbal brew) as waiters tell you just how those *chapulines* made it onto your plate. Open daily 1-9pm.

Antojitos Regionales Los Olmos, Morelos 403, at Crespo. For those yet unaccustomed to Oaxaca's big breakfast and diminutive dinner lifestyle, Antojitos is the restaurant you've been searching for. Just when other restaurants are closing their doors for the night, Anojitos fills with locals who gather to socialize and feast on the restaurant's oaxaqueño delicacies. No menus—you can strike up a conversation by asking which dish is best. Whatever they whip up for you, it's guaranteed to be cheap, as the 8 peso *tomate de mole* is the most expensive item on the menu. Open daily 7pm-midnight.

Las Quince Letras, Abasolo 300, (tel. 6 90 16). The Letras' *comida corrida* is so famous that the adjoining street corner has taken on the restaurant's unusual name. Served daily from 2-5pm under the grapefruit tree in the lush garden patio, 35 pesos will buy soup, salad, a main dish, and coffee with desert. The restaurant also offers delicious breakfasts for 22 pesos and dinners when one should be sure to order the *sopa azteca* (20 pesos), a powerful Oaxacan super-stew. Open daily 8am-9pm.

Mariscos Los Jorges, Pino Suárez 806 (tel. 3 43 08), across the street from Parque Juárez, toward the northern end of the park. After their huge, 25 peso, bargain break-fasts (served 8am-1pm), Los Jorges serves delicious Veracruz-style *mariscos* baked in the restaurant's old *indígena* oven. The seafood is excellent both on its own (you can ask to see the fresh fish cuts before ordering) or wrapped up in tacos (30 pesos). Open daily 8am-6:30pm.

Restorán Café Alex, Díaz Ordaz 218 (tel. 4 07 15). An extensive menu that runs the gamut of Mexican cuisine, with English explanations. Garden seating available. Generous break-fasts (starting at 15 pesos), *comida corrida* (27 pesos), and vegetarian specialties (24 pesos) are a cut above the storefront fare outside. Open M-Sa 7am-9pm, Su 7am-noon.

Flor de Loto, Morelos 509 (tel. 4 39 44). Though flourescent lighting and quiet clientele leave this restaurant rather low on ambience, it remains a vegetarian safe-haven in a town of blood-thirsty carnivores. Try veggie soups (13 pesos), *enchiladas de soya* (22 pesos), or the mushroom tacos (30 pesos). Open daily 7am-10pm.

CAFES

Slick, chrome espresso machines seem to have parked in every courtyard of Oaxaca's tourist district, where they pour forth enough delicious brown liquid to please the most hard-core addicts and hook many more. Coffee houses lurk behind almost every door on **5 de Mayo.**

Coffee Beans, 5 de Mayo 46 and 114. Especially wonderful drinks come from the Coffee Bean's freshly ground Oaxacan coffee, while **Café Gecko's** vine-covered colonial courtyard has heavenly appeal. Where there's coffee, there's also art galleries and live music. To find Oaxaca's student and expatriate community, just follow your nose to these venues of mental self-improvement.

SIGHTS

Rather than the last outposts of some long-lost culture, Oaxaca's museums, churches, and historical sights are seemlessly intergrated into the city's daily life. Museum corridors are well trod by tourists and *nativos* alike, and most of the city's old buildings lead a double life: both preserving the past, and serving the state's incredibly active, creative citizens.

CATEDRAL DE OAXACA. Oaxaca's many churches lend themselves to specialization, with each sanctuary serving a unique purpose. The Catedral de Oaxaca (originally constructed in 1535 and reconstructed in 1733 after earthquake damage) dates from a time when the Mexican church and state were one. The building is governmental and imposing, with the structural focus appropriately provided by the ornate bishop's seat—visually driving in the lynch-pin of the church-state hierarchy. These days it is less a place of sanctuary than one of congregation—acting a stage for *zócalo* pagents and the *payasos* (clowns) who rake in laughter and pesos on weekend evenings. *(In the zócalo, across from Palacio de Gobierno. Open daily 7am-8pm.)*

PALACIO DE GOBIERNO. Inside the Palacio, a mural by Arturo García Bustos presents an informative historical collage. Best visited last, the mural acts as a pictoral pop-quiz on the state's history. The wonderful narrative culminates in the center panel where Benito Juárez and his wife Margarita Masa are united under Juárez's oft-repeated phrase, *"El respeto al derecho ajeno es la paz"* ("Respect for the rights of others is peace"). *(In the zócalo. Open 24hr.)*

MUSEO DE ARTE CONTEMPORÁNEO DE OAXACA (MACO). This beautiful colonial building is known as the Casa de Cortés, although historians insist that it was not, in fact, Cortés's estate. Nevertheless, it is an example of vice-regal architecture, a style that was used by the *conquistadores* and their heirs. The museum features both rotating and permanent exhibitions, and shows free movies on its large-screen TV. The impressive permanent collection includes the works of *oaxaqueños* such as Rufino Tamayo, Francisco Toledo, and Rodolfo Morales. The bookstore carries a large number of art books and magazines, and enough postcards to start your own little gallery. *(Tel. 4 71 10. Along the Macadenio Acalá/The Anador Turístico. To the left of the cathedral, a cobbled pedestriam street, the Anador, leads to museums, restaurants, and stores; a block down is the Acalá 202, on the right. Open Su-M and W-Sa 10:30am-8pm; free on Sundays.)*

IGLESIA DE SANTO DOMINGO. The green and gold stones of the Iglesia de Santo Domingo rise up on the right side of the Anador. Higher and mightier than the *catedral*, it is the city's spiritual center as well as its tallest building. Construction on the church began in 1575, and the structure was consecrated in 1611. Since then, the church, one of the best examples of Baroque style in Mexico, has functioned as a place of worship, a museum, and even as military barracks for both sides during the reform wars and the Revolution. the 2m-thick walls have served the church well; it has stood for 400 years, despite Oaxaca's strong earthquakes. The interior is even more spectacular, with waves of gilded stucco that cover the ceiling and walls. The real eye-catcher, though, is the massive gilded altar. Built in 1959 by Oaxacan artists and workers, the altar is one of the most elaborate (and expensive) of its kind. The **Capilla de la Virgen del Rosario,** off to the right as you walk in, also features relatively new altar works. *(3 blocks past MACO, on the Anador Turístico. Open daily 7am-1pm and 4-8pm. Capilla open daily 7am-1pm and 4-8pm.)*

MUSEO REGIONAL DE OAXACA. The ex-convent next door to the Iglesia de Santo Domingo was converted in 1972 into the city's prestigious Museo Regional de Oaxaca, and a year-long renovation has left the 16th century building in better condition than ever. The stellar museum houses a large collection of Mixtec and Zapotec pieces as well as displays on the history of the state of Oaxaca. The collection's prime attraction is the treasure extracted from Tomb 7 in Monte Albán. The exquisite collection of gold, silver, turquoise, bone, and obsidian is one of the best assortments of Zapotec artifacts ever found. *(Tel. 6 29 91. Open Tu-Su 10am-8pm. Admission 25 pesos, Su free.)*

MUSEO DE ARTE PREHISPÁNICO DE MÉXICO RUFINO TAMAYO. The museum shows off the Oaxacan artist's personal collection of pre-Hispanic objects. The figurines, ceramics, and masks that Tamayo collected are meant to be appreciated as works of art rather than artifacts. The result is a wonderful hybrid art gallery and archaelogical museum. *(Morelos 503. Tel. 6 47 50. Between Díaz and Tinoco y Palacios. Open M, W-Sa 10am-2pm and 4-7pm, Su 10am-3pm. Admission 14 pesos.)*

CASA DE BENITO JUÁREZ. Once home to one of Mexico's most famous and beloved presidents, the house was originally owned by Antonio Salanuevo, who became a benefactor to the young Juárez when he moved to Oaxaca from the countryside in 1818. Juárez's subsequent education qualified him to marry the wealthy Margarita Masa and to pursue a career in law and reform-minded politics. The house—living room, bedrooms, kitchen, well, and "bookbinding/weaving shop"—is a replica of a 19th-century, upper-class *oaxaqueño* home. *(One block from Alcalá on the García Vigil 609. Tel. 6 18 60. Open Tu-Sa 10am-7pm, Su 10am-5pm. Admission 17 pesos, free Su.)*

TEATRO MACEDONIO ALCALÁ. The *teatro* is one of the most beautiful buildings in Oaxaca and also an example of the art and architecture fostered by dictator Porfirio Díaz, whose regime (1876-1911) had a taste for French art and intellectual formulas. Díaz's support was instrumental in the theater's construction. On the ceiling, scantily clad Muses float above the giant candelabra. *(5 de Mayo at Independencia, two blocks behind the cathedral. Tel. 6 33 87. Occasionally open for shows M-Sa 8pm, Su 6pm.)*

BASÍLICA OF OUR LADY OF SOLITUDE. A minor but absorbing attraction is the funky museum of religious art located next to the church. The museum houses an astonishing array of objects—ranging from model ships to shell-and-pasta figurines—sent from around the world as gifts to the Virgin, who is said to have appeared here in 1620. *(Independencia 107. Tel. 6 75 66. Three and a half blocks behind the post office. Open M-Sa 10am-2pm and 4-6pm, Su 11am-2pm. Admission 2 pesos.)*

OTHER SIGHTS. For a breathtaking view of the city, head to the **Cerro de Fortín.** The **Escalera de Fortín** begins on **Crespo;** these stairs will take you to the **Planetarium Nundehui** past the Guelaquetza amphitheater. Enjoy a great vista of Oaxaca and the surrounding hills here. The stairs are a favorite destination for fitness fiends, so be prepared to be passed by joggers loping effortlessly uphill. *(Tel. 6 69 84. Planetarium open Th-Su 10am-1pm, 5-8pm. Admission 8 pesos.)* Also worth a visit is the **Centro Fotográfico Alvarez Bravo,** which displays rotating photography exhibits. *(Murguía 302, between Reforma and Juárez. Open Su-M and W-Sa 9:30am-6pm. Free.)*

♫ ENTERTAINMENT

On warm summer nights it's hard to walk around Oaxaca de Juárez without running into entertainment. Street performers on the Acalá, dancers in Parque Juárez, gallery openings north of the *zócalo*, plentiful cinema—both artsy and profane—and live music on every street keep the evenings busy with people of all ages. Some of the cheapest entertainment is to be had on the *zócalo*, where people-watching can be as melodramatic as *telenovelas*. Sit back with the *viejitas* and watch the city's *nietos* toss strange, oblong-shaped balloons into the cathedral spotlights, or join the tableau yourself—soundtrack provided by the *marimba* bands that hammer away under the *portal* (M, W, F-Sa after 7pm). When the streets quiet down around 10 or 11pm, the youth congregate in rocking bars and discotheques that pulsate long into the night. Oaxaca's huge student population keeps a startlingly diverse nightlife thumping year-round.

■ **Zelantro,** Porfirio Díaz 208 at Matamoros, two blocks west of the Acalá. Though the uncategorizable Zelantro offers just about everything—billboards, Internet access, a cushioned room for lounging, and a quieter downstairs restaurant/bar for sensitive, conversational pseudo-intellectuals—its heart is the rooftop dance floor, visible from all parts of the complex. The eclectic musical mix of ska, reggae, *salsa*, and rap works the floor into a groove early on in the night and brews up the air of chill *alegria* that has made the nightclub an "it" club. The clientele are younger twenty-somethings from around the world, dressed down to earth and looking more for sociability than for the altered-state experience provided by the *discotheques*. Beverages range from beer (12 pesos) to *mezcal* (10 pesos) and there is no cover. Though Zelantro tends to get crowded by 11:30 on Thursday through Saturday nights. Restaurant open daily at 11am; nightclub open W-Su 9pm-2am.

K-O's, Gurion 104, right across from the southside of Santo Domingo, continues to be popular among the city's student bourgeoisie and artists, while its proximity to tourist-land helps draw in lots of fresh gringo blood. Trippy William Blake inspired murals and found-object sculptures offer plentiful nooks for conversation etc., lubricated by moderately priced drinks from the crowded bar. No cover. Open Tu-Su 9pm-1am.

La Costumbre, Acalá 501, opposite the entrance of Santo Domingo. The Oaxaqueños filling this ever-popular club have an attitude and style that perfectly matches the bar's neo-baroque decor. A little too tight for dancing, the bar is usually part of a double-billing, coming either before or after an expedition to the discotheques on the north end of town. A good place to find fellow bar hoppers. Open 8pm-2:30am M-Sa.

The discotheques, **Tequila Rock,** Porfirio Díaz 102 (tel. 5 15 00), at Héroes de Chapultepec, and **Snob,** at the intersection of Juárez and Heroés de Chapultepec (both across the street from the first class bus station) are awesome places to dance. Crowded with energetic students in basic clubbing garb (eg. tight black pants), these clubs may be the perfect opportunity for foreign students to blend in. No one will be able to hear your rotten Spanish, and, in the mass of sweaty, gyrating humans, no one will care. Both clubs feature packed and uninhibited dance floors, as well as more removed seating areas for smooching, drinking and other debaucheries. (Cover 30 pesos at both. Open W-Sa. Ask young locals about *días libres*—weeknights when no cover is charged.)

Somewhat older crowds can be found up Porfírio Diaz at **L'Bouche**, (tel 3 81 22). In contrast to the American music played in the discos down the street, this floor moves to slower Mexican tunes and has a less international and more solidly Oaxaqueño clientele. Drinks tend to be 3-5 pesos cheaper than the other clubs, and the cover follows suit at 25 pesos.

Salsa and similar age diversity can be found at **La Candela**, Allende 211, two blocks from Santo Domingo. Whether you are a beginner or an expert, the live band will keep you moving all evening long. (Cover 30 pesos. Restaurant open Tu-Sa noon-5pm; music and dancing 9pm-2am.) For those made geriatric by the previous night's activity, catch an Italian movie at **MACO** or a more recent flick in English with Spanish subtitles at **Plaza Alameda Cinema**, (tel. 6 52 41) at Independencia and Díaz. **Sala Versailles**, M. Ocampo 105 (tel. 6 23 35), three blocks east of the *zócalo*, hosts live shows as well as movies.

✿ FESTIVALS AND SEASONAL EVENTS

On the two Mondays following July 16, representatives from every part of Oaxaca state converge on a hill overlooking the city for the **Guelaguetza**. The event grew out of a tradition of making offerings on the **Cerro del Fortín** (The Hill with the Beautiful View); the days of dancing in the theater on the hill are called *los lunes del cerro* (Hill Mondays). "Guelaguetza" refers to the Zapotec custom of reciprocal gift-giving. During the two gatherings, groups from the seven regions of Oaxaca give audiences a taste of their heritage through dance, music, and dazzling costumes. In between the gatherings, food and handicraft exhibitions, art shows, and concerts take place. Tickets for seats in the front sections are 300 pesos, but seats in the equally large back sections are free and open up a few hours before showtime.

Oaxaca's exquisitely beautiful celebrations for **El Día de los Muertos**, (Nov 1-2) have become a huge tourist draw in recent years. Most travel agencies offer expeditions of the candlelit, marigold filled village graveyards where a communal walk is held on the night of All Souls to welcome home the dead during their brief return from the spirit world. Shops fill with moulded sugar *calareras* (skulls) and dancing skeletons while altars to memorialize the deceased are erected throughout the city.

The night of December 23, Oaxacans celebrate the unique **Noche de los Rábanos** (Night of the Radishes). Masterpieces of historic or biblical themes created with radishes fill the *zócalo*, where judges determine the best. Hundreds of people admire the artistic creations and eat sweet *buñuelos*. Upon finishing the treat, you're supposed to make a wish and throw the ceramic plate down on the ground; if the plate smashes into pieces, your wish will come true.

NEAR OAXACA

The villages surrounding Oaxaca are known both for their artistry and for their ancient Zapotec and Mixtec ruins. As organizations from museums of folk art to the museum-type stores took interest in the imaginative handicrafts made in these villages, many residents left farming work to devote themselves full-time to craft production. Villages often specialize in particular products: **Arrazola** and **San Martín Tilcajate** make wooden animals, **San Bartolo Coyotepec** black clay pottery, **Atzompa** green clay pottery, **Ocotlán** natural clay pottery, **Teotitlán del Valle** wool *sarapes*, and **Villa Díaz Ordaz** and **Santo Tomás Jalietza** textiles and weavings. Likewise, many villages hold *mercados* on specific days to attract visitors: Miahuatlán (Monday), Atzompa (Tuesday), San Pablo Etla (Wednesday), Zaachila (Thursday), Ocotlán (Friday), and Tlacolula (Sunday). All the villages can be reached in under an hour by the **taxi colectivos** that leave from the **Central de Abastos** (5 pesos for nearby towns, 10 for Ocotlán and Miahuatlán). Buses to these towns are cheaper (3-5 pesos) but can also be harder to locate. For an adrenaline rush, rent a bike and transport yourself.

There is a lot to be said for getting out of the hustle and bustle of the city for at least part of the day. The surrounding countryside is lovely, and it's always fun to ride in a bus that has to stop for herds of cows. The **"Tourist Yu'u" program** operated by SEDETUR (tel. 6 01 23) rents out guest houses in the communities of Abasolo, Papalutla, Teotitlán del Valle, Benito Juárez, Tlacolula, Quialana, Tlapazola, Santa Ana del Valle, and Hierve el Agua. Accommodations include four beds, kitchen, and clean bedding; proceeds benefit the community. (Cabin 120 pesos; 1 person 35 pesos; students 25 pesos; campers in the garden 10 pesos.) Additionally, you can try one of the *paseos culturales*, which introduce visitors to the traditional medicinal, agricultural, and artistic practices of 15 villages in the area.

THE RUINS OF MONTE ALBÁN

High above Oaxaca de Juárez, **Monte Albán,** the ancient mecca of the Zapotec "cloud people," now watches over its verdant mountaintop in utter calmess. One of the most important and spectacular pre-Hispanic ruins in Mexico, it is a mistake to leave Oaxaca without seeing it. Mysteriously abandoned by both the Zapotecs and Mixtecs who used it as a sacred capital over 1000 years ago, the site's imposing architecture casts a thought-provoking shadow over the modern capital in the valley below.

Unless you're already an expert on pre-Hispanic civilizations (or you're the type that prefers their ruins unexplained) having a good guide to Monte Albán can really make the visit. Though many travel agencies around the *zócalo* can set you up with hassle-free transportation and excellent guides, it is often cheaper to transport yourself and find a guide once on top of the mountain. The English language guides who hover around the entrance charge a maximum of 150 pesos for a 1½-hour tour, a fee which can be split up to six ways with the friends you brought with you or the other bewildered tourists you found at the site.

Getting There: Autobuses Turisticos buses to Monte Albán leave from the Hotel Rivera del Angel, Mina 518 (tel. 6 53 27), between Mier y Terán and Díaz Ordaz several blocks southwest of the *zócalo*. Monte Albán is only 10km from the *centro*, but the ride throught the city's mountainous outskirsts takes 30 minutes. The normal procedure is to buy a round trip ticket (15 pesos) with the return fixed two hours after arrival at the sight (about the right amount of time for full perusal); if you want to stay longer you can pay an extra 7 or 8 pesos to come back on one of the later buses. During high season (June-Dec), buses from the hotel leave daily every 30 minutes between 8:30am and 4pm. During low season (Jan.-May), buses leave five times per day during the week and six times per day on Sunday. *(Site open daily 8am-5pm. Admission 25 pesos, with video camera 30 pesos. Free Su and holidays.)*

HISTORY. The monolithic, geometrically precise stone structures that constituted the ceremonial center of the city are the culmination of Zapotec efforts to engineer a world that fused the religious, political, and social realms. As Monte Albán grew to become the major Zapotec capital, daily life was carefully constructed to harmonize with supernatural elements: architecture adhered to the orientation of the four cardinal points and the proportions of the 260-day ritual calendar; residences were organized in families of five to 10 people in four-sided houses with open central courtyards. To emphasize the congruence between the household and the tripartite cosmos, families buried their ancestors underneath their houses—corresponding to the level of the underworld. Excavations of burials in Monte Albán have yielded not only dazzling artifacts, but also valuable information on social stratification.

Monte Albán flourished during the Classic Period (300-750), when it shared the spotlight with Teotihuacán and Tikal as a major cultural and ceremonial center of Mesoamerica. This was the greatest of Zapotec capitals—maize was cultivated, water was supplied through complex drainage systems, and the city engaged in extensive exchange networks in Mesoamerica, especially with Teotihuacán (see p. 131). Teotihuacán's influence is visible in Monte Albán's murals and pottery. Artists used representations of divinities to legitimize the kings' power, and many stones share the theme of portraying the sacrifice of defeated enemies.

The history of Monte Albán is divided into five parts, spanning the years from 500 BC until the arrival of the Spaniards in the 16th century. Periods I and II saw the rise of Monte Albán as the Zapotec capital. This time also witnessed a great deal of contact with the Maya culture; the Zapotecs adopted the Maya *juego de pelota* (ballgame) and steep pyramid structure, while the Maya appropriated the Zapotec calendar and writing system. The city reached its peak during the third period, which lasted from 300 to 750.

Almost all of the extant buildings and tombs, as well as several urns and murals of *colanijes* (richly adorned priests), come from this period. Burial arrangements of varying luxuriousness and size show the social divisions of the period: priests, clerks, and laborers lived apart and died apart. For reasons that remain unknown, Monte Albán began to fade around 750. Construction ceased, and control of the Zapotec empire shifted from Monte Albán to other cities such as Zaachila, Yagul, and, later, Mitla. Explanations for the abandonment of the city include drought, overexploitation of resources, and inability of the leaders to maintain stability. The subsequent periods IV and V saw the city taken over by the Mixtec people; this happened to many Zapotec cities. The Mixtecs used Monte Albán as a fortress and a sacred metropolis, taking over the tombs left by the Zapotecs. When **Tomb 7** was discovered in 1932 by Dr. Alfonso Caso, the treasure found within more than quadrupled the number of previously identified gold Mixtec objects. The treasures from Tomb 7 are now on display at the Museo Regional de Oaxaca (see p. 469).

THE RUINS. After passing through the ticketing station just beyond the museum, walk left up the inclined path leading diagonally towards the ruins. You will enter the huge **Main Plaza** at the northwest corner, with the mountain-like **North Platform** on the right, and smaller structures lined up to your left.

Turning left and skirting the east end of the plaza, the first structure on your left is the **ball court.** For it to look like more than a big pile of stones, it is necessary to climb to the top. The game, (a version which is still played in Oaxaca's Zapotec communities), involved four players who used intricate mitts to get the ball into a small niche at the top of their opponent's "T." The sides of the court which now look like bleachers, were once covered by stucco and plaster, and used to bounce the ball off of towards the little goal. This difficult game was used to solve all kinds of conflicts and also a means for ritualistically predicting future events.

Back on the flat Main Plaza, (which is remarkable when one considers that the mountain was originally peaked) and continuing along the west side, look for **The Palace,** which, like the other buildings, is labeled by an informational marker written in Spanish, Zapotec and English. This big pyramid actually served as a home for one of Monte Albán's important dignitaries, and demonstrates that the purpose of these structures was civic and residential as well as religious, setting Monte Albán apart from other pre-Hispanic ruins which served more purly ritualistic or funeral purposes. On top of the pyramid, four main rooms were built around a central patio—another strange convergence of Spanish and Zapotec culture, whose combined influence holds strong in today's architecture.

The building's diagonal from the palace forming the Plaza's south end is the **South Platform,** the site's highest structure. If you climb only one pyramid in Monte Albán, make sure it's this one: the top affords a commanding view of the ruins, the valley, and the mountains beyond. On both sides of the staircase on the plaza level are a number of stelae carved with rain gods and tigers. The stela on the pyramid's right side contains a precise date, but archaeologists lack the point of reference needed to coordinate this date with the modern calendar. The neighboring stela is believed to depict the king of Monte Albán.

Coming back down the stairs of the platform, the first structure you hit is **Building J.** It is formed in the bizarre shape of an arrowhead on a platform and contains a labyrinth of tunnels and passageways. Unlike any other ancient edifice in Mexico, it is asymmetrical and built at a 45° angle to the other structures around the plaza. Its broad, carved slabs suggest that the building is one of the oldest on the site, dating from 100 BC to 200 AD. Many of the glyphs depict an upside-down head below a stylized hill; the glyphs are thought to represent a place and a name. Archaelogists speculate that this image indicates a conquest, the head representing the defeated tribe and the name identifying the region conquered.

The next group of buildings moving north, dominating the center of the plaza are **Buildings G, H, and I**—likely compromising the **principal altar** of Monte Albán. Walking left around these structures to the plaza's west side you will find **The Building of Dancers,** bordered on either side by identical pyramids that were once crowned by one room temples. The haunting reliefs on the center building are known as "dancers" though they most likely depict chieftans conquered by Monte Albán's armies. The more than 400 figures date from the 5th century B.C. and are nearly identical to contemporary Olmec sculptures along the Gulf Coast. Many of the figures show evidence of genital mutilation.

Finish off the Main Plaza by visiting the **North Platform** near the entrance, a structure almost as large as the plaza itself. The mammoth structure contains the largest altar in the site. The path exiting the site passes Monte Albán's fabulous bookstore (filled with books on the region in a variety of languages) and the unreasonably priced cafeteria on the way to **Tomb 104.** Duck underground, look above the entrance, and gaze at the urn. It is covered with a motif which interweaves images of the maize god and rain god. Near the parking lot is the entrance to **Tomb 7,** where the spectacular cache of Mixtec ornaments mentioned above was found. The **museum** at the site's entrance offers a chronological survey of Monte Albán's history and displays sculpted stones from the site's earlier periods. Unfortunately, some of the more spectacular artifacts from the site have been hauled off to museums in Oaxaca and Mexico City.

ATZOMPA, ARRAZOLA, CUILAPAN, AND ZAACHILA

AZTOMPA. A culture and lifestyle different from the sophistication of Oaxaca de Juárez emerges in these small towns, all of which lie near Rte. 131. Atzompa (pop. 11,000) is where that magnificent blend of clay and sprouts, the **Chia Pet®,** was invented. Natural, green-glazed pottery, the town's specialty, can be found here at better prices than in the city. Atzompa's **Casa de Artesanías** is a publicly funded forum that brings together the work of the town's specialized artisans. The selection is good at the Casa, but bargaining is easier with the artisans themselves.

ARRAZOLA. This small, hilly village is the hometown of **Manuel Jiménez,** one of Mexico's most famous artisans. Jiménez is the originator of **alebrijes,** the brightly colored figurines of demons and zoo animals that rank among Mexico's most sought-after handicrafts. While success has made his pieces unaffordable for most (small pieces go for US$170), his workshop is worth visiting. To get there, walk up Arrazola's main road, passing the plaza and turning left at the first intersection. Continue down this perpendicular road past the end of the pavement, following as it turns right. The Jimenéz family home is the gated and only major structure on the right hand side, opposite a corn field. Manuel and his sons Isaías and Angélico who work with him personally meet visitors in their workshop/home, which is decorated with photos and art magazines featuring the family's history. Jimenéz is sage and humorous, and a vocal supporter of Oaxaca's artisan traditions, and artistic innovations. A glimpse of the Jimenéz family's kinetic cedarwood sculptures and the possibility of a conversation with the man himself will make the substantial trek from Rte. 131 well worth the effort. Nearly all the households around the center of town make figurines to supplement their incomes. Pick your way through yards full of goats and chickens to the workshop, or simply follow one of the 10-year-old guides; the owners will happily show you their wares and haggle for a fair price. A medium-sized iguana *alebrije* will cost about 100 pesos.

CUILAPÁN DE GUERRERO. Cuilapán (pop. 11,000) has an isolated but hauntingly lovely 17th-century Dominican monastery, once home to one of the most powerful and wealthy religious orders in Mexico. Although it was never finished, the ruined monastery's stone arcades frame the fields of the surrounding valley and the curves of the hills that embrace it. The highlight of the site— aside from the breathtaking views—is the cell that was once occupied by the Revolutionary hero Vicente Guerrero before his untimely death by a firing squad on the patio outside. Today, all that remains to commemorate the hero is a portrait of him in his cell and a monument where he fell. Built as a retreat for Spanish monks wishing to exile themselves as far as possible from European civilization, a different worldly civilization has grown up around the ex-convent in the last 300 years. The buildings still have an air of contemplative reprieve and the upper floor now serves as a cloister for archaeologists, laboring to recreate the region's complex history in the monk's old stone cells. *(Gates open daily 10am-6pm. Admission 12 pesos, 30 pesos with a videocamera.)*

ZAACHILA. Zaachila (pop. 15,000), the last political capital of the Zapotecs before they fell to the Spanish in 1521, hosts a fascinating market each Thursday. Drop your pesos on preserved bananas and squealing pigs. Under canopies below, a fuchsia and yellow cathedral dominates the middle of town. Behind the church, a street heads uphill to a partially uncovered archaeological site. Until 1962, locals prohibited excavations to prevent outsiders from dissecting their Zapotec heritage. Exploration since has been limited, but two Mixtec tombs with well-preserved architecture and jewelry have been uncovered. The town's gold, turquoise, jade, and bone artifacts (as well as the tourist dollars they would have attracted) have been spirited away to museums in Oaxaca and Mexico City. The eerie tombs—the only decorated ones in Oaxaca—are still worth a visit. Wide-eyed owls (messengers of the Zapotec underworld) stare out from the damp stone walls, while boney, toothy Gods of Death shoot the visitor knowing looks from the dimmer recess of the tomb. *(Open daily 9am-5pm. Admission 12 pesos, Su free.)*

Getting There: Take a *taxi-colectivo* leaving from the parking lot on the side of the Central de Abastos in Oaxaca across from the Inverlat building. Destinations are labeled on the windows and also on signs marking the parking spaces (20min. to Cuilapán, 30min. to Aztompa, Arrazola, or Zaachila; 5 pesos). It's easy to hop from one town to the next; take a *colectivo* back to the main road and flag down another that's headed for your next destination. All four towns are ideally accessible in the course of a day, though your best bet is to start out in Zaachila and hit Cuiliapan, Arrazola, and Atzompa on the way back to Oaxaca de Juárez.

SAN BARTOLO COYOTEPEC AND THE ROAD SOUTH

The drive south from Oaxaca provides more spectacular scenery. Picturesque towns are nestled in the slopes of verdant hills, and, for the eager consumer, there are distinctive crafts and artisanry for sale.

SAN BARTOLO COYOTEPEC. San Bartolo, 12km south of Oaxaca on **Rte. 175,** is the only place in Mexico that creates the ink-black pottery that populates souvenir shops throughout the state. Though the town had been making black pottery (the dark color comes from the local mud) for centuries, it wasn't until 1953 when the diminutive Doña Rosa accidentally discovered that it could be polished that it became an art form. Doña Rosa kept the polishing technique a family secret for 12 years, and then gave it to the town, which has been supported by the craft ever since. Because the polished pottery won't hold water (hint: don't buy the coffee cups), villagers began to cut holes in the vases, making them into luminaires that put a glowing spin on the exquisite patterning typical of Oaxacan crafts. Doña Rosa's son carries on the tradition and gives demonstrations in the Nieto family workshop, several blocks up the town's main street, Benito Juárez, on the west side of Rte. 175. *(Workshop open daily 8:30am-7:30pm.)* Four kilometers farther south, **Santo Tomás Jalietza** has artisans who specialize in weaving on back-strap looms. The town also boasts a 17th-century church dedicated to its patron saint.

OCOTLÁN DE MORELOS. Ocotlán, 33km out of the city, is possibly the most beautiful of the *pueblos* surrounding Oaxaca de Juárez. While many of the region's towns have expanded enough that they blur with one another, as well as the capital, Ocotlán remains a village apart. Above the valley in the foothills of the Sierra Madre del Sur, the town offers a brightly colored and extremely well-used church, a florid *zócalo*, and a huge *mercado*. Less tourist-oriented than other towns, visitors willing to be the market's sole and very conspicuous buyer, will be rewarded with authentic prices for authentic goods. Shop for the *sarapes*, so ubiquitous in town with the women who use them. Afterwards, sit down to a market lunch guaranteed to be fresh and frenetic. The big day is Friday; most of the action takes place between 10am and 5pm. To get to Ocotlán, see the **"Getting There"** p. 49.

OAXACA TO MITLA

The Pan-American Highway (Rte. 190), from Oaxaca east to Mitla, cuts through a valley full of artisanal towns, *mezcal* distilleries, and archaeological sites.

SANTA MARÍA EL TULE. This friendly little town (pop. 7000), just 14km outside the city, houses one of Mexico's great roadside attractions: the **Tule Tree.** The 2000-year-old and 40-meter-tall tree has an astounding circumference of 52m—**largest girth of any tree on earth.** Ask the bus driver to drop you off at El Tule; then ask for *el árbol* (the tree). There is a 2-peso fee to approach the fence closest to the tree, but the glory of this botanical behemoth can be appreciated from anywhere within a 100m radius. The **Dainzú** ruins, 22km from Oaxaca, just off the road branching to **Macuilxochitl,** date from Monte Albán's final pre-Hispanic epoch. A series of magnificently carved figures at the base of the tallest pyramidal monument represent ballplayers in poses similar to the "dancers" at Monte Albán (see p. 478). Two humans and two jaguars, gods of the sport, supervise the contest. Up the hill from the pyramid, another game scene is hewn in the living rock. Bring your walking shoes; the ruins are about 2km away from the main road. (Open daily 10am-6pm. Admission 12 pesos.)

The walls of the church in nearby **San Jerónimo Tlacochahuaya** (pop. 5300), 23km from Oaxaca, illustrate Zapotec decorative techniques as applied to Catholic motifs. (Open daily 7am-noon.) It was built at the end of the 16th century by Dominicans seeking to escape worldly temptations.

TEOTITLÁN DEL VALLE. Twenty eight kilometers from Oaxaca, Teotitlán is the oldest community in the state. The source of extremely beautiful woolen *sarapes* and rugs, Teotitlán is home to 200 to 300 families that earn their livelihood by spinning and weaving. Many allow tourists to visit their workshops and witness the process of natural dye coloring and weaving. Unfortunately, Teotitlán is not as accessible as many of the other stops on the road; it's 4km from where the bus drops you off. There are *colectivo* taxis that run sporadically from the main road to the town. There are a few workshops scattered within walking distance of the main road; owners are happy to demonstrate the spinning process.

Tlacolula de Matamoros (pop. 12,700), 33km from Oaxaca, is one of the largest towns in the area and adds a slightly gritty underside to the rural charm of the region. It hosts a lively market on Sunday mornings—the specialty is the potent liquor **mezcal.** The market is officially open until 6pm, but activity usually starts winding down around 2pm.

YAGUL. Thirty six kilometers from Oaxaca, Yagul was a Zapotec city inhabited from 700 BC to AD 1521. Less impressive archaeologically than Mitla, the rarely-visited Yagul is perhaps more aesthetically striking. A gorgeous 1.5km trek through cornfields and up a hill admirably preps the visitor for the wide, green view that awaits at the top. If you go on a weekday, you'll be able to act out your fantasies of Zapotec kingship with lizards as your only audience members. The city is built into the skirts of a hill overlooking a spectacular mountain-ringed valley. Most of the more famous buildings and tombs are in the **Acrópolis,** the area closest to the parking lot, about 2km north of the route. If you bring some friends, you can start a pick-up ball game in the restored ballcourt, the largest of its kind in the Oaxaca valley. The **Court of the Triple Tomb** is to the left of the ballcourt. Carved with an image that resembles a jaguar, the tomb is in three sections. Stone faces cover the largest section. Beyond the ballcourt rises the **Council Hall;** behind lies the **Palace of the Six Patios,** believed to have been the home of the city's ruler. Heading back to the parking lot, take the trail that climbs uphill to the rocky outcropping to catch a spectacular view of the cactus-covered hills. Look for the small stone bridge; it's behind the tomb on your right as you climb the hill. If you keep going up the rocky path up the hill, you will be rewarded by even more spectacular views and ultimately bathtubs. These two sink-looking bins on the right-hand side of the mountain top are believed to have served as bathtubs for the Zapotecs who inhabited Yagul. There is also a *palapa*-style restaurant before the hill on the way to the ruins where you can quench your thirst or grab a quick bite of *chapulines* (23 pesos) or *mole negro* (39 pesos). *(Open daily 9am-5:30pm. Admission 10 pesos, free Su.)*

Beyond Mitla, **Hierve el Agua** (The Water Boils), 57km from Oaxaca, takes its name from two springs of carbonated water that look like boiling water. The waters are actually not hot and make for refreshing baths.

Getting There: All destinations listed above are accessible via a Mitla-bound bus, which leaves the second-class station in Oaxaca (every 15min. 8am-8pm, 5 pesos to Mitla). Ask the driver to let you off where you want to go. Most people visit these sites on daytrips, but the **tourist office** at Oaxaca (p. 464) can arrange for overnight stays in Teotitlán del Valle, Tlacolula, or Hierve el Agua.

MITLA

Tucked away in a mostly Zapotec-speaking, dusty little village, the archaeological site of Mitla, 44km east of Oaxaca, is smaller and less popular with tourists than the immense Monte Albán. Mitla was built in 800 AD by the Zapotecs; it was later appropriated by the Mixtecs and eventually became the largest and most important of the late Mixtec cities. When the Spaniards arrived in the valley, Mitla was the only ceremonial center of the Mesoamerican Classic period still in use. Ironically, the Catholic archbishop of Oaxaca built his home to echo the horizontal lines of the Zapotec priest's residence in Mitla, thus paying architectural tribute to an ancient indigenous religion virtually exterminated by Catholicism. On the 2km walk through town to the ruins, you may have to weave your way through the herds of goats and cows that occasionally fill the streets. The ticket booth to the archaeological site is on the far side of the red-domed church. To the left of it and behind the church are the three patios known as the **Group of the Church.** One of them has been almost completely buried by the church, and only a few of the original palace walls remain visible. The central patio is on the other side of the church; here, and in the surrounding rooms, you can see pieces of Mixtec decorative paintings glowing red against the stone, supposedly telling Mitla's history. *(Site open daily 8am-5pm. Admission 10 pesos, free Su.)*

More impressive ruins are across the road in the **Group of the Columns.** Perhaps the most striking features of these structures are the intricate geometric designs that decorate both the exterior and the interior. Beyond the entrance are two patios joined at one corner. On the first one, the tombs of the pyramids form a cross; for years, Spaniards thought this proved that the Mixtecs somehow knew the story of Jesus. On the second patio, two temples have tombs that are open to visitors. The tomb in the east temple has large stones covered with mosaic patterns. The roof of the tomb in the north temple rests on a single huge column known as the **Column of Life.** Pilgrims travel here each year to embrace the column; in exchange for the hug, the column tells them how much longer they will live.

On the central plaza back in town, the unexciting **Frissell Museum** contains thousands of figurines from Mitla and other Mixtec sites, all arranged around a courtyard; some descriptions are in English (open daily 9am-5pm; admission 10 pesos).

Getting There: Take a bus from Oaxaca's second-class terminal (45min., every 15min. 8am-8pm, 5 pesos). The bus station is about 2km from the ruins. With your back to the station, walk to your left and turn left at the sign for "Las Ruinas." Make another left onto the main road, and follow it for several blocks through town. Cut through the small *zócalo* on your right, and walk uphill until you get to the church; the ruins will be on your right.

ISTHMUS OF TEHUANTEPEC

East of Oaxaca de Juárez, the North American continent narrows to a slender strip of land just 215km wide known as the Isthmus of Tehuantepec (TEY-wan-teh-PECK). The region, wedged between the Yucatán Peninsula and the highlands of south central Mexico, is home to a thriving Zapotec culture that is primarily matriarchal. The three main cities in the isthmus—**Tehuantepec, Juchitán,** and **Salina Cruz**—serve mainly as stop-over points for tourists to switch buses and refuel. Scorching temperatures ensure that life in the isthmus towns progresses at a lethargic pace.

TEHUANTEPEC

Tehuantepec (pop. 60,000) is the oldest of the isthmus's principal cities. For tourist information, visit the **Casa de la Cultura** (tel. 5 01 14), Callejón Rey Cosijopi (open M-F 9am-2pm and 5-8pm, Sa 9am-2pm). From the **bus station** on the route, Cristóbal Colón (tel. 5 01 08) travels to: **Mexico City** (11hr., 12:40, 5:30 and 9:10pm, 301 pesos); **Oaxaca** (4hr., 6 per day 5:30am-midnight, 88 pesos), and more; buses also go to: nearby **Juchitán** (30min., every hr., 5 pesos): and **Salina Cruz** (20min., every 30min., 4 pesos). To get to town, make an immediate left as you leave the station. Follow this street, which becomes **Av. Héroes,** as it veers to the right and eventually dead-ends. Turn right and walk a few more blocks; make a left on **Hidalgo** and follow it to the *zócalo.* Taxis will take you to the *centro* for 8-10 pesos. **Phone code:** 971.

JUCHITÁN

If grandmothers suddenly ruled the world, it would probably look very much like Juchitán. You have, no doubt, seen the tourist pamphlets of women wearing Elizabethan collars on their head and wonder if that actually happened at one point in Mexico's long, strange history. In this friendly *itsmo* town, it still does, though you'll only see the frilly white during weddings and major holidays. Ordinary days tend to be just as colorful, when the town's huge market fills with *viejitas* wearing traditional dress—a loose fitting, machine embroidered shirt and a long, full floral skirt.

While in most of Oaxaca *artesenías* are made, bought, and sold to tourists, Juchitán's traditional crafts are worn, and the aesthetic seems to be an overwhelmingly important part of life. Flower vendors get the stalls of honor right on the main street of the *zócalo,* and ribbon stores predominate.

While the town's air of authenticity is helped by the virtual absence of tourist traffic, and the stifling heat that embalms it for much of the year, those who catch Juchitán on a breezy day will find plenty to see, and be treated to the wonderful mood the wind blows in.

�PⅠ ORIENTATION AND PRACTICAL INFORMATION. Local buses connect Juchitán with the isthmus towns of **Tehuantepec** (30min.) and **Salina Cruz** (1hr.). Cristóbal Colón (tel. 5 01 08) sends **buses** to: **Mexico City** (11½hr., 5:30, 7:10, and 9pm, 301 pesos); **Oaxaca** (4½hr., 6 per day, 88 pesos); and other destinations. The bus station is on Prolongación 16 de Septiembre. To get to town from the station, follow that street to the right upon leaving the station. It soon splits into **5 de Septiembre** and **16 de Septiembre,** which run parallel and eventually form the sides of the *zócalo. Colectivos* leave frequently on the left hand side of the bus station exit and run to the *centro* (2 pesos).

The **tourist office** (tel. 1 10 01), upstairs in the Palacio Municipal is open M-F 9am-2pm and 6-8pm. Ask for **Rosalinda,** a knowledgeable and English-speaking staff member. **Banamex** (tel. 1 15 48) is located at 5 de Septiembre 12 on the *zócalo* and has a 24hr. **ATM** as well as **currency exchange** (open M-F 9am-2pm). **Police:** (tel. 1 12 35) stationed in the Palacio Municipal. **Post office:** located at Gomez and 16 de Septiembre (open M-F 9am-5pm). **Postal code:** 70000. **Phone code:** 971.

🄵🄵🄲 ACCOMMODATIONS AND FOOD. No visitors means great prices in centrally located hotels, and cheap upgrades into two and three star luxury. **Hotel Modelo,** 2 de Abril 21 (tel. 1 24 51) is a block from the market, and offers spare clean rooms and refreshingly cold shower water. Ask for hot water and they'll look at you like you're nuts. (Singles 60 pesos; doubles 70 pesos.) At **Hotel Don Alex,** 16 de Septiembre 48 (tel. 1 10 64), you can buy A/C to cool off, hot water to warm up, and classy rooms for not too exorbitant prices. (Singles with fans 117 pesos, doubles 175; singles with A/C and TV 165 pesos.) Hotel also offers snazzy restaurant filled with excellent Oaxaqueño art. *Comida del día* 30 pesos. (Open 7am-11pm.)

While the market is a must-eat, **Los Chapulines,** 5 de Septiembre at Morelos, fifteen blocks up from the *zócalo* offers regional cuisine at regional (i.e., low) prices. The A/C will clear your head and help you think rationally before ordering the house specialty, which is, of course, *chapulines* (35 pesos). Cheaper but similarly explosive are the *tacos chapulin* (4 pesos each). Open daily 7am-12pm; sometimes best reached by taxi (5 pesos).

🄶 SIGHTS. It could take a while to see the **market.** When stopping to smell the roses isn't enforced by the heat, it will be by the vendors, who love a good-natured haggle, and whatever gossip you can bring to town. Enquire about the spices, buy lots of flowers, and if you want to take some home with you, try buying some of the festival clothing sold on the second floor of the official market building. Fancier than *ropa ordinario* everyone around you is wearing, these skirts and blouses are made of velvet and ornately embroidered with flowers to emphasize women's powerful connection with nature. While in the market, be sure to try the *topotes*, an interesting variant on the *tostada*, which uses a frisbee-like, airy corn patty as a base in lieu of the ordinary tortilla.

Located at the corner of Dominguéz and Colón, Juchitán's **Casa de Cultura** is well loved, filled with people engaged in various arts workshops and home to a surprisingly wonderful collection of archaeological artifacts found in the region. To get there, walk on Gomez from the *zócalo* towards the Banco Serfín sign, turing right from the bank and passing Parque Chariz on the left—the casa is on the right. (Open daily 9am-2pm and 4-8pm.)

Next door, the church of **San Vincente Ferraro** is also worth a peek. First constructed in 1528, the church has been remodeled various times but still has the air of a 400 year old place of worship. Most of the simple, whitewashed architecture dates from the 17th century.

SALINA CRUZ

Salina Cruz does not have much to offer the tourist aside from the mass of oil refineries that comes into view on the bus ride into town, but its central location makes it a common stop for buses. Cristóbal Colón (tel. 4 14 41) runs **buses** to: **Huatulco** (3hr., 6 per day 12:30am-9:15pm, 51 pesos); **Mexico City** (11½hr., 7:30 and

9:15pm, 341 pesos); **Oaxaca** (5hr., 5 per day, 74 pesos), and elsewhere. The bus station is far from the *zócalo*. To get there, walk right until you hit the main street and then catch one of the blue *microbuses* (1.50 pesos). A taxi will cost about 6 pesos. Estrella Blanca sends second-class buses to **Acapulco** and all stops in between, including **Huatulco** and **Puerto Escondido** (4 per day 6:15am-11pm). The bus station is three blocks to the right of the Cristóbal Colón station on the main street.

BAHÍAS DE HUATULCO

With its wide, palm-lined streets, shiny electric lights, and sprawling resorts, Bahías de Huatulco is a paradise for those who like their vacations packaged, planned, and posh. If everything looks new here, that's because it is: Mexican government officials settled on the area as a prime candidate for resort development in the 1980s and began building from the bottom up in 1986. The recent economic recession seems to have temporarily set back government plans; buildings around Huatulco sit in mid-construction. Still, the entire city has the feel of something like a seaside country club; even the *zócalo* and the supposedly authentic downtown area smack of freshly poured concrete and professional landscaping. Visitors are primarily moneyed Mexicans who save up all year and then seriously spend during their vacation time, assuring astronomical prices for just about everything touched by tourism.

While things would seem dismal for the budget traveler, the way it all pans out can mean gold for those contented to sit on the sand and bask in the sun. With nothing geared towards the backpacker price range or mentality, those traveling cheaply in Huatulco will find themselves alone on the shore watching as yachts of *ricos* pass by on their expensive, all-day tours of the coast. In contrast to the crowded budget lifestyle in the hyped-up ex-pat beach towns further north, the miserly traveler will be able to live a tourist-free existence in Huatulco, sharing meals with the hotel staff in the *barrio* northwest of the *zócalo* and spending long, unmolested hours on the pristine shores of the Bahía's 36 beaches.

◢ ORIENTATION

Huatulco and its *bahías* (bays) occupy 35km of beaches and coves along the southern Oaxaca coast between the Coyula and Copalita rivers, about 295km south of Oaxaca de Juárez. The small downtown area, **La Crucecita**, is in the middle of a string of nine bays, which are, from east to west: Conejos, Tangolunda, Chahué, Santa Cruz, El Orégano, Maguey, Cacaluta, Chachacual, and San Agustín. La Crucecita houses the bus stations and most budget accommodations. The *zócalo*, four blocks from the bus stations on **Gardenia**, is bordered by **Bugambilias** on the other side. **Carrizal**, one more block from the *zócalo*, leads to the bays. **Santa Cruz**, the bay closest to downtown, is the least attractive of the lot. Hotels and an *artesanía* market clutter its main road, **Blvd. Santa Cruz**. From there, the bays of **Chahué, Tangolunda**, and **Conejos** lie to the east. Tangolunda Bay is also known as the **Zona Hotelera** because it houses seven resorts, including **the Western Hemisphere's largest Club Med**. Its main road is **Blvd. Benito Juárez**. From Santa Cruz, the bays to the north are **El Órgano, Maguey, Cacaclutla, Chachacual**, and **San Augustín**.

◢ PRACTICAL INFORMATION

Airplanes: The airport (tel. 1 03 10) is 19km from Santa Cruz. Taxis charge 70 pesos for the 25min. trip; *microbuses* get you within a 200m walk of the terminal for 5 pesos. **Aerocaribe** (tel. 7 12 20) and **Mexicana** (tel. 7 02 43) serve the airport.

Buses: Cristóbal Colón (tel. 7 02 61), Gardenia at the corner of Ocotillo, has first-class service to: **Mexico City** (12½hr., 4:30, 6 and 8:30pm, 357 pesos); **Oaxaca** (7hr., 3:45 and 4:30pm, 134 pesos); **Puebla** (11hr., 4:30 and 6pm, 303 pesos); **Puerto Escondido** (2hr., 3:30, 5, 8am and 5:30pm, 40 pesos); **San Cristóbal** (10hr., 10:45am and

11:30pm, 187 pesos); and **Tuxtla Gutiérrez** (9hr., 10:45am and 11:30pm, 158 pesos). Estrella Blanca (tel. 7 01 02), on Gardenia and Palma Real, sends buses to: **Acapulco** (9hr., 2:15am, 6:15 and 8:15pm, first-class 192 pesos, *ordinario* 143 pesos); **Mexico City** (13½hr., 6pm, 346 pesos); and **Puerto Escondido** (2hr., 2:15am, 6:15 and 8:15pm, 43 pesos). Estrella del Valle (tel. 7 01 93), on Jazmín at the corner of Sabali, provides service to: **Oaxaca** (8hr., 8:45am, 12:45, and 10pm, 68 pesos; *ordinario* 8hr., 8:30 and 12:30pm, 55 pesos).

Car Rental: Pesos (tel. 7 00 70), in the Plaza Open M-F 9am-1pm and 4-7pm.

Tourist Office: SEDETUR (tel. 1 01 76 or 1 01 77), inconveniently located across from the commercial center in Tangolunda on Blvd. Juárez. Open daily 8am-5pm. **Módulo de Información,** Bugambilias 210 (tel. 7 13 09), on the side of the *zócalo* opposite the church is helpful. Open daily 9am-8:30pm during peak seasons.

Currency Exchange: Casa de Cambio Condig, Guamuchil 210 at Bugambilias (tel. 7 12 09) cashes traveler's checks and has a 24hr. **ATM** (open M-Sa 9am-6pm). **Bancrecer,** Bugambilia 1104, exchanges currency. Open M-F 9am-5pm, Sa 10am-2pm. Large hotels also exchange money at slightly less favorable rates.

Market: 3 de Mayo, on Guamacho off the *zócalo* offers an odd combination of regional foods, tourist trinkets, and the standard market produce and meat stands. Open daily 6am-8pm.

Laundry: Lavanderia Abril, Gardenia No. 1403 (tel. 7 17 76) between Pochote and Palo Verde offers same day service for 7 pesos per kg. Open M-Sa 8am-8pm.

Police: At Blvd. Chahué 100 (tel. 7 02 10), in the peach government building about 200m south of the intersection of Guamuchil and Chahué. Some English spoken.

Emergency: dial 060.

Red Cross: Blvd. Chahué 201 (tel. 7 11 88), next door to the post office and police building. Ambulance service. Open 24hr. English spoken.

Pharmacy: Farmacia del Centro (tel. 7 02 32), Bugambilia at Flamboyan. Open daily 8am-10pm.

Hospital: IMSS (tel. 7 02 64), on Blvd. Chahué past the government building. 24hr. service. No English spoken.

Post Office: Blvd. Chahué 100 (tel. 7 05 51), in the peach government building. Open M-F 8am-7pm, Sa 9am-1pm. **Postal Code:** 70989.

Fax: Telecomm (tel. 7 08 94), next to the post office. Also has **telegrams** and **Western Union.** Open M-F 8am-7pm, Sa-Su 9am-1pm.

Internet access: Informática MARE (tel. 7 08 41) located at Guanacaste 203 across from the *mercado* on the 2nd fl. has speedy access but bad prices. 1 peso per min. Open M-F 9am-9pm, Sa 9am-4pm.

Phone Code: 958.

ACCOMMODATIONS AND CAMPING

Camping is a way to escape Huatulco's high-priced hotel scene, but it's allowed only on Cacaluta and Conejos. The other bays are off-limits because they lack security and are hard to reach. Under no circumstances should you try to camp on Santa Cruz or Tangolunda; hotel security will not be kind. If camping isn't your thing, be prepared for slim pickings. All affordable rooms are located in La Crucecita, and even they tend be overpriced, despite the fact that they are near the bus station instead of the ocean. Some families also rent rooms, and those willing to snoop around and negotiate will be rewarded for the effort. Rates rise uniformly by about 50% during the high season (July-Nov.); the listings below indicate low-high season ranges.

Hotel Posada San Agustín (tel. 7 03 68), on Macuil at the corner of Carriza. From the bus station on Gardenia, walk 1 block to the left, turn left on Macuil, and walk for 2 blocks. The futuristic-looking blue and white hotel is probably the cheapest around. Spotlessly clean and bright, and run by a young family, San Agustin has an upbeat, homey air and rooms with fans and balconies. Singles or 1-bed doubles 70 pesos; 2-bed doubles 70-100 pesos.

Posada Lido, Flamboyan 209 (tel. 7 08 10) rents out five eclectically assembled rooms and a shared bath. The family that shares the building and the proximity to the *zócalo* keeps things fun and clamorous. Double beds 100 pesos.

Hotel Benimar, Bugambilias 1404 (tel. 7 04 47), at Pochote, 3 blocks from the bus station on Gardenia. The dusky interior harbors fans, full baths, and the people of the neighborhood who congregate in the lobby to watch TV and swing on the hammock. Singles and doubles 120 pesos; triples 150 pesos.

FOOD

As a resort town, Hualtulco offers cuisine which attempts to break away from the norm, giving visitor's palettes a break from the daily deluge of *tortillas* and *carne*. Usually out of budget price-range, touristy restaurants venturing into the realms of sophisticated Italian pasta and poorly rendered sushi, send their vacationers scattering back to their native cuisine, which they pay hadsome fees for in the restaurants around the *zócalo*. While some places try to capitalize on Oaxacan regional cuisine and others pitch *mariscos*, the best thing to eat in Huatulco is the taco. Uniformly cheap and available around the clock in all its many forms, it is best procured on **Carrizal,** north of the *zócalo*.

Restaurant-Bar La Tropicana (tel. 7 06 61), Guanacastle at Gardenia, across from Hotel Flamboyan. This restaurant may be the exception to the rule that all restaurants on the *zócalo* are overpriced. Sit outdoors and watch folks saunter by or cheer with the crowd that gathers at the restaurant periphery to watch *fútbol* broadcasts. Food is somewhat secondary to location and 24hr. status, but when it eventually comes, it tends to be good. The *filete del pescado* is a very reasonable 35 pesos and the 20 peso sandwhiches are probably the best thing to order. Open 24hr.

Comedor Familiar Arnely II/Restaurant Oaxaqueñito, Guarumbo between Gardenia and Bugambila serves the same dishes as all the other plastic-chair, *comida-tipica* joints in town, but does so with the magic touch that keeps its seats filled. *Tlayudas* (18 pesos), *tostadas* (6 pesos), and tacos (4 for 12-20 pesos) are served in the ex-patio and driveway of the house/restaurant. Open daily from 4pm-1am.

El Fagon, Bugambila, on the left just past the *zócalo*. The restaurant gods also smile down upon El Fogon which tends to pack in an earlier crowd with its cheap tacos and bargain combination plates. Specializing in barbequed chicken, which seems to be a Huatulqueño favorite (20 pesos). Open M-F 3pm-midnight.

SAND, SUN, AND ENTERTAINMENT

Until some kind of efficient public transportation system is installed, Huatulco's nine bays and 36 beaches, spread across 35km, pose a transportation challenge; it's hard to get off the beaten track without shelling out for a taxi or boat. As might be expected in a town designed by the Mexican government to rake in tourist dollars, everything here is carefully arranged to maximize profits, and there is no reason to make the trip to more remote beaches affordable when a huge *lanchista* industry is built around their inaccessibility.

Fortunately, three of the bays (albeit those with big hotels nearby) are accessible by the blue-and-white *microbúses* chartered primarily to get the waiters and maids who live in Crucecita to and from their jobs in Santa Cruz and Tangolunda. Buses pass every half hour form 6am to 6pm and cost 3 pesos. *Colectivos* to these bays are also easy to come by, and leave from the same juncture as the *microbúses* at Guamuchil and Carrizal, a block past the *zócalo*.

Also accessible by foot by the pedestrian walkway branching of Guamuchil to the right 2 blocks from the *zócalo* (15min.). **Bahía Santa Cruz** harbors the *lanchas*, a profusion of *palapa* restaurants, and a huge, overpriced commercial district that sprawls around the *zócalo*. Of its two beaches, **Playa Entrega** is the better, offering good **snorkeling** and less chanch of being squished by a banana boat. A blessing for some and a curse for others, the economic recession suspended the cranes at Chahué in midair, leaving the hotels half finished and the Bahías beach realatively unpopulated. Though construction is starting up again, for the moment, this non-sequitor modern ghost town offers the best nearby beach experience. Also an easy walk from the *crucecita* down Blvd. Chahué the core's two beaches have an easily manageable shorebreak and make for pleasant swimming and quiet sunbathing.

Getting to the other Bahías is not cheap. While taxis will take you to most beaches for under 200 pesos, it is often cheaper to go by *lanchas* leaving from teh **Cooperativa Tangolunda** in Santa Cruz. Prices vary by beach and by the size of the boat, and if you go in the morning, you can probably find people willing to share the ride, making it quite affordable. The *cooperativa* also offers the most economical all-day tour of the bays. The 170 peso ride leaves at 11am and includes stops on **Maguey** and **San Augustín** where you can snorkel with a bilingual guide and get lunch. (Make plans a day in advance. Tel. 7 00 81. Office open daily 8am-6pm.)

Playa Entrega, in Santa Cruz, and **Playa Maguey** are best for snorkeling with warm clear waters and coral reefs making the 40 peso rental fee charged for equipment at the *cooperativa* well worth it. Chahué and Tangolunda have slightly bigger waves and more surf and **Cacaluta** is known for its lush plant life and breezes. In terms of crowds, Entrega, Maguey, San Augustín, and Tongolunda are most popular whereas Cacaluta, **Conejos**, and **El Organo** are your best shots at solitude.

Huatulco's tendency to attract familes of visitors means a fairly low-key nightlife. Folks dance to live bands that play in the *zócalo* every evening except for Tuesday, and get their kicks by riding around on the automobile train which runs tireless loops around Crucecita, blasting Mexican pop favorites. To get to the beach by bus, take the one headed for Tangolunda and ask the driver to stop at Chahué. The sand is a five minute walk across the weedy, lizard *barrio* construction sites.

The third cheaply accessible beach, **Tangolunda,** is also home to the **Zona Hotelera** and the Bahía's swankest resorts. Whilke it's fun to stroll down the long, gorgeous strand and see how the other half lives, the public beach on the eastern side offers beautiful water and is a zone of budget sanctuary. To get htere, ask to be let off the Tangolunda bus at the public beach entrance, oer alternately walk to the right from the hotels when facing the sea. if you want to live it up, you can pay 70 pesos for the day's use of the pools and facilities at the Sheraton, and slightly more at the other resorts.

Though there are plenty of bars and *mezcal* shops in Crucecita, the best ambience is to be found at **Restaurant Bar la Crema** (tel. 7 07 02) at the corner of Guanacaste and Gardenia, on the second floor overlooking the *zócalo*. Though the funky decor and good tunes make the place seem more of an import from Puerto Escondido than a genuine Huatulcan creation, this is probably a good thing. People occasionally dance. (Open nightly 7pm-3am.) Most large hotels also have their own bars, but the only full disco is **Magic Circus** (tel. 7 00 17), on Blvd. Santa Cruz next to the Hotel Marlin (cover Th-Su 60 pesos; open bar Th; open W-Su 10pm-late). Buses stop running at 8pm, so a taxi from La Crucecita (12 pesos) will be necessary both ways.

A NIGHT ON THE TOWN You've spent endless hours conjugating verbs and rolling your "r"s, but you still don't fit in. What you need is something that no seventh grade Spanish teacher could (or would) teach—a brief review of all the slang necessary for a night out on the town. Luckily, *Let's Go* has compiled a list of the basics. Incorporate these into your vocab, and perhaps you'll lose your *gabacho* (gringo) status. The night begins when you meet your friends and greet them, *"¿Qué onda?"* (What's up?). You guys head out *al antro* (to the disco). At the discoteca, grab a *chupe* (drink) or a *chela* (beer) and comment on how *chido* or *padre* (cool) the place is. *Fresas* (snobs) prefer the phrase *de pelos* to denote coolness. Of course, keep your eyes peeled for *papasitos* (studs) and women that are *buenísima* (very fine). Perhaps you'll flirt a bit, *ligar* (to hook up), and—if you are *cachondo* (horny)—maybe you'll *fajar* (to make out/get down) with a fellow discotechie. The next day be sure to review the events of the previous night with your friends, exclaiming *"¡Qué peda la de ayer!"* (I was completely wasted yesterday!).

POCHUTLA

Pochutla serves as the gateway to Puerto Angel and Zipolite; if you're traveling by bus, you'll have to pass through. The lack of services in both beach towns makes Pochutla a good place to stock up on money and expensive pharmecuticals. Most banks, services, and shops—as well as the town's two bus stations— can be found on **Lázaro Cárdenas,** Pochutla's main street. Bus stations and cheaper hotels are located downhill, closer to the entrance to the freeway, while banks and supermarkets are further uphill as the road begins to curve right. The *zócalo*, church, and main outdoor market can all be reached by following Cárdenas uphill, and then turning right on Juárez. **Taxi colectivos** headed towards Puerto Angel, Zipolite and beyond in the downhill portion, across from the Estrella del Valle bus station. To get to faraway places, **Cristóbal Colón** (tel. 3 02 74) on the left hand side of Cardenas as you enter the city, sends buses to: **Huatulco** (1hr., 4 per day 9:15am-9pm, 16 pesos); **Mexico City** (15hr., 2:45 and 7:30pm, 358 pesos); **Oaxaca** (8hr., 4, 5 and 7:30pm, 135 pesos); **Puerto Escondido** (1½hr., 9:30, 10, 11am and 25 pesos); and **Tehuantepec** (4½hr., 9:45am, 7 and 9pm, 73 pesos).

From the bus stations, follow Cárdenas to the left and uphill to get to **Bital** (tel. 4 06 87; open M-F 8am-7pm, Sa 8am-3pm) and **Bancomer** (tel. 4 20 59; open M-F 8:30am-5:30pm, Sa 10am-2pm), both of which have **ATMs.** The **police** station (tel. 24 01 76) is just up the road behind the Estrella del Valle bus station, a block off Cardenás; they handle security issues for the surrounding beaches as well. To get to the **post office,** make a right on Juárez toward the church and the *zócalo;* it's to the left of the church and behind the Palacio Municipal (open M-F 8am-6pm, Sa 9am-1pm). **Postal code:** 70900. **Phone code:** 958.

If the wait for your bus will be a long one, **Hotel El Patio** on Cardenás just up from the Estrella Blanca station on the left is a good place to crash. Though the relaxing hot shower is more likely to be cold, the rooms are clean and well maintained. (Singles 70 pesos, doubles 120 pesos.) Excellent seafood can be found up Cardenás on the right, one block before the *zócalo* at the **Restaurant y Marisqueria Los Angeles,** which serves very cheap *antojitos* (10 pesos) and more costly, but famously good *mariscos* for 35-50 pesos.

PUERTO ÁNGEL

Tucked away between the more glamorous towns of Huatulco and Puerto Escondido, Puerto Angel is a haven for urban escapists. The small fishing town is home to a moderately sized naval base, a few restaurants and hotels, and a scenic cove on the Pacific coast. The town is popular with Europeans, and most visitors are well-traveled, lending Puerto Angel a touch of Bohemian flair. Unfortunately,

Puerto Angel—and Zipolite further down the coast—bore the brunt of Hurricane Pauline's wrath in 1997. Debris, dead palms, and fallen walkways mark her violent passage, and the struggle to rebuild is still in progress, a struggle undertaken without much help from the Mexican government. Still, Puerto Angel merits a visit, especially for those looking to escape the commercialization of Huatulco or the juvenile beach-bum atmosphere of Puerto Escondido.

■ **ORIENTATION.** Puerto Angel is 240km south of Oaxaca de Juárez and 68km east of Puerto Escondido. The *carretera* that connects Pochutla to Zipolite becomes Puerto Angel's main drag as it runs through town, at which point it is first re-named **Av. Principal** as it descends the hillside from Pochulta, and then **Blvd. Virgilio Oribe** once it hits the center. Shortly after it climbs out of town again, a paved sidestreet branches off to the left, and leads to **Playa Panteon,** the town's lounging beach. The "fishing and everything else" beach is **Playa Principal,** which skirts the route. The only significant sidestreet starts out as **Vasconcelos** just up Uribe from the pier, and becomes **Teniente Azuela** as it passes the town's naval station and loops back towards Uribe.

■ **PRACTICAL INFORMATION.** Taxis link Puerto Angel to: **Pochutla** (15min., 10 pesos by *colectivo* and 50 pesos *especial*) and **Zipolite** (25min., 14 pesos by *colectivo* and 70 pesos *especial*) and can be flagged down anywhere along Uribe or Ave. Principal. The *microbús* goes to: **Pochutla** (every 45min. 6am-8pm, 2 pesos), returns to town, and leaves again for **Zipolite** (2 pesos) and **Mazunte** (3 pesos) and will stop for you anywhere along the freeway. Services in Puerto Angel are minimal; most must be begged, borrowed, or imported from nearby Pochutla. While some hotels change money and/or accept dollars, it is the exception rather than the rule—there is no bank in Puerto Angel. **Tourist information,** including a map and a list of budget hotels can be found at the office located in the turquoise building on the right-hand side of Vasconcelos just before it starts to curve. There is a **supermarket,** Super Puerto, on Uribe about 300m after the naval base. **Farmacia Villa Florencia** is attached to the restaurant of the same name on Uribe (open daily 8:30am-9pm). **Emergencies:** dial 060. **Hospital:** the nearest hospital (tel. 4 02 16) is between Puerto Angel and Pochutla. **Centro de Salud** (tel. 4 30 95) offers limited medical services at the top of Vasconcelos to the left on a dirt path (open 24hr.). **Post office:** on Uribe, at the beginning of town (open M-F 10am-3pm). **Postal code:** 70902. **Faxes: Telecomm,** right next door to the post office (open M-F 9am-3pm). There is a long-distance *caseta* at Vasconcelos 3, around the corner from Hotel Soraya that charges astronomical rates for international calls, and offers **Internet access** for the exhorbitant amount of 3.50 pesos per minute (open daily 9am-10pm). **Phone code:** 958.

■ **ACCOMMODATIONS.** A good reason to stay in Puerto Angel is for the opportunity to upgrade from a hammock or grimey *cabaña* to a nicer hotel without stretching the budget. Although prices fluctuate with the tourist tide, Puerto Angel is filled with budget options year-round. The cove is picturesque, and the view from **Hotel Capy** (tel. 34 30 02) is enough to inspire an impressionist revival. Located on the road that connects Playa Panteón to the freeway, the hotel can be reached from the beach, or by turning left at the "Hotel Capy" sign just after Uribe begins its ascent from town. Clean well-maintained rooms have private baths and the common spaces are the real high point. Watch the day turn from light to dark while enjoying the restaurant's *filete de pesca* (30 pesos) or enjoy one of the fruit granola breakfasts (18 pesos) while watching the day turn from dark to light. If it's cloudy, everything will be a dull gray. (One double bed 90 pesos for 1 person, 110 pesos for 2 people; 2 double beds 130 pesos for 2 people and 140 for 3. **Casa de Huéspedes Anahi** (tel. 4 30 89) doesn't have quite the same view, but the rooms are clean, with fans and private baths and the hotel is located just off Uribe near the beach. (Singles 70 pesos, 80 in the high season; doubles 80 pesos, 100 in the high season.) For a real upgrade, those with delicate sensibilities may want to try the clean, secluded, and environmentally-conscious cabins of **La Buena Vista,** in a canyon just up from Panteón. Expensive communal dinners (80 pesos) are usually meatless, and provide a nice touch to the getaway. (2 people 150 pesos; cabins with views and decorated with the proprietor's artwork 350 pesos). Farther up and out, **Cabañas Coco Loco** (tel. 4 30 75) offer great views at good prices. Look for signs leading uphill on the right-hand side of Uribe past the exit for Hotel Capy (Doubles 80 pesos; triples 100 pesos.)

□ FOOD. Much of the fish that fries in Zipolite first saw dry land in Puerto Angel. Located by the basketball court between Playa Principal and Uribe, **Restaurant Maca's** small, open kitchen and colorful blue interior turn out seafood worthy of a large, glossy-paged cookbook. Prices aren't the cheapest, but the freshness of the fish and incredibly tasty dressings make it hard to pass up. (*Filete de pescado* 35-40 pesos); *sopa de mariscos* 50 pesos. Open daily 8am-11pm.) Directly on the main beach, **Restaurant Marisol** keeps fish prices low (25-30 pesos), and serves breakfast for under 10 pesos in a super-informal atmosphere with a view.

◪ SAND AND BEACHES. Though the cove is small, and a little crowded, beaches still have sparklingly water and clean white sand. The **Playa Principal** is right off the road, and closest to the docks and the fishing boats. It offers a little more breathing room than **Playa Panteon**, which is filled with lounge chairs and children splashing in the waveless water. The two beaches are connected by a stone walkway, and encircle a harbor with some excellent snorkeling. Located on Playa Panteon, **Benthos** rents good snorkel gear for 30 pesos (per day), and leads a variety of diving trips. For certified divers, one tank is US$40 and two costs US$60, and night dives are US$50. All trips come with guides and transportation. Uncertified divers can go out for US$70. The office accepts traveler's checks and has a good concept of the best dive spots on the coast.

Beach-wise, the best move to be made is a little bit east to **Playa Estacahuites** (pronounced "a stack o' Wheaties"). Located over the headland from Puerto Angel's Bahía, Estacahuites' two little beaches have pristine, less-visited appeal. Although it can be reached by launch from Puerto Angel (80 pesos) or taxi (starting around 30 pesos), the walk is pleasant and easy. From the Playa Principal, turn right on Uribe and walk uphill out of town going toward Pochetla. The dirt road to Estacahuites branches off to the right, as the road curves uphill, just past the telephone pole numbered E0034. Pass the Abarrots store with the Coca-Cola sign on the right, and follow the main dirt road as it climbs uphill and curves left around a hill. Passing a beached *lancha* on the left and a last Abarrots store on the right, the road plunges steeply down to the beach. Perhaps the cheapest and best place to stay in the area is in the hammocks (20 pesos per night) owned by Felippa Ramirez Cabieras, on Estacahuites just left of the road. She also rents snorkel gear (20 pesos per hour), and will make you food if you get hungry. Snorkeling is good and the beach is *preciosa*, but be careful because emergency services could be hard to come by. The beach is about a 35 min. walk from town.

ZIPOLITE

Zipolite's reputation precedes it. Famous for its fringe atmosphere, locals smile knowingly at the thought of the nude *extranjeros* and the general funky feel the town brings to the coast. The government's distaste for Zipolite's conglomeration of sun-loving, weed-smoking, international backpackers was made painfully obvious in the lack of recovery aid in the aftermath of Hurricane Pauline; however, the beach has largely recovered, and come to flourish again in all its scantily clad, funky splendour.

Although it is a prime stop on the Euro-trail, problems with drug-related crime and the inevitable fall from 60's grace means things aren't as carefree as they once were. Zipolite will continue to be a haven for those who know how to chill as long as the sun shines down on its long, lovely shores.

⁊ ORIENTATION AND PRACTICAL INFORMATION. Just 4 km west of Puerto Angel and close to Pochutla, Zipolite is easily accessible by any of the wheeled vehicles trundling down the poorly-paved coastal road. *Microbúses* run back and forth between Zipolite and Puerto Angel (supposedly every 20min. during daylight hours; 3 pesos), but *piratas* (pickup truck *colectivos*; 2.50 pesos), *colectivos* (5 pesos), *taxis especiales* (20 pesos) seem to pass more frequently. From Pochutla, taxi *colectivos* are 7 pesos during the day, and at night the 25 minute ride will probably have to be made by *taxi especial*, for 70 pesos. In general, transport is in synch with the beach plentiful, easy, and no problem. Just make it clear to the taxi drivers that you won't be overcharged, and they should be fair. Zipolite consists of one long stretch of beach. Get off the bus before the curve right in front of a thick grove of palm trees. Cross the street and walk toward the shining sea. There is a **pharmacy,** small **general store,** and a place that **exchanges money** at pretty poor rates on the road near the entrance from Puerto Angel. For obvious reasons most supplies are cheaper in Pochutla. Zipolite's **police station** is located on a bluff just beyond the beach's east side, and officers patrol frequently. Medical services are best procured in Pochutla or Puerto Angel. In an **emergency** dial 060.

⌐ ACCOMMODATIONS. Lounge around long enough and someone will eventually ask you if you want a *cabaña* for the night. Every *palapa* on the beach has a little village of huts out back, most with relatively clean shared baths. The cheapest *cabañas* go for 50-80 pesos per night and hammocks invariably cost 20 pesos. Whichever you choose, be sure to put valuables in a *caja de seguridad*, a service offered by most *palapas*. Some of the nicer places on the beach are **Tao,** on the western side, which offers clean, safe *cabañas* for 100 pesos; **San Cristóbal** which offers two floors of better-than-average wood and cement rooms for 70 pesos per night (with shared bathrooms). Private baths and a similarly clean atmosphere can be had at **Posada Brisa Mavina,** a blue-and-white establishment farther east down the shore. (100 pesos for 2 beds and private bath.)

⌂ FOOD. Zipolite is all about eating, drinking and then sleeping it off in the sun. Seafood is omnipresent, but the horde of body-concious tree-huggers ensure that vegetarian dishes are easy to find. Food is everywhere, and the best way to pick a restaurant is by the people who happen to be sitting there (most are open daily 8am-10:30pm and charge 35 pesos for their most expensive item). For Italian food, **Nuevo Sol** offers delicious pizzas prepared by the Italian owner.

▟ SAND AND SIGHTS. The only sights in Zipolite are the occasional **sunbathers in the buff,** who do little more than let the rays gleam off their naked curves. You can also watch waves coming in from two directions, creating a series of channels that suck unsuspecting, naked swimmers out to sea. Although ferocious, these channels are not very wide. If you find yourself being pulled away from shore, do not attempt to swim directly toward the beach; rather, swim parallel to the beach until you're clear of the seaward current.

Zipolite is unfortunately plagued by theft, so keep an eye on everything or leave it locked up. A final warning: **scorpions** frequent Zipolite, so either give your cutoffs a good shake before jumping into them or blend in by going about your business in the buff. If you *must* get out and do something, catch a bus to **Playa Mazunte,** which offers some beaches more suited to swimming than Zipolite's, as well as more *palapa* restaurants. **Playa Agustinillo** is on the eastern edge of town, before the Turtle Museum. Playa Mazunte is accessible from the area where the bus stops. Both beaches offer fewer crowds and gentler surf, although there are still significant currents; keep your wits about you. Manzunte's **Museo de la Tortuga** used to hold an impressive collection of turtles from all over the world, but Hurricane Pauline left the building in shambles and sent the turtles back home to the Pacific. It's unknown when the museum will be functioning, but if it's open, this important venue for turtle research and conservation is worth a look.

FARTHER DOWN THE COAST. If the grime of Zipolite gets you down, more unspoiled exploits await down the coast. With the way things are going, **San Augostinillo** will be as developed as Zipolite by the end of the year, but for now, it remains cleaner, less colonized, and under-hyped. The two coves that form the beach harbor have good, fairly manageable surf, which can be harnessed with body boards and fins rented from **Mexico Lyndo** for 30 pesos per hour. A very European scene, with chess boards and folks who share their hammocks with Kafka, awaits under the Augostinillo *palapas*. If you bring your own hammock you can use the facilities at **Palapa** for 10 pesos per night. Redistribute the 10 pesos you saved and spend them on **Restaurante Lupita's** fresh *pescado* (40 pesos). San Augustinillo is easily reached by *colectivo* from Zipolite. A *taxi especial* from Pochutla will cost around 70 pesos.

The next beach to the west just around a headland from San Augustinillo is **Mazunte.** Similarly refreshing in its underpopulation, Mazunte has more in terms of lodgings. The beautiful wooden construction of **Cabañas Ziga** is only matched by the great location on the hill overlooking the beach (1 person 80 pesos; 2 people 100). Hammocks can be rented at **Palapa El Mazunteb** for 20 pesos, and the *cabañas* are an 80-peso-per-night bargain.

MAZUNTE TURTLE MUSEUM, EL MARIPOSERIA, AND LA VENTANILLA

Although the number of people looking out for the environmental health of the Oaxacan coast still seems dangerously small, the interest is growing. An anchor in the education movement is the **Museo de la Tortuga,** which draws large tour buses to Mazunte to view its specialized aquarium of sea turtles. Also a research center, the several tankfuls of animals provide a nice up-close look for those who don't get the chance to see them in the wild. Tours inform guests about the turtle's dependence on Mexico's beaches as a safe place to lay their eggs. Located in Mazunte, the museum can be reached by *colectivos* from Puerto Angel and Zipolite (15min., 15 pesos). (Museum open M-Sa 10am-4:30pm, Su 10m-2:30pm. 20 pesos for adults, 10 pesos for children ages 6-12.)

One and a half kilometers past Mazunte, the **Cooperativa Ventanilla** houses a small colony of families dedicated to the preservation of the wetland wildlife system at the mouth of the river. The group runs hour-long tours in a *lancha* (30 pesos) that goes through the mangrove swamps. The guides point out crocodiles and birds and explain Oaxaca's part in complex migration systems.

The most accessible of the three educational centers, **El Mariposaria,** located on the road between Zipolite and Mazunte, pays a much overdue tribute to the butterflies that appear like confetti throughout Mexico's forests. Located on 8 hectares of land, the visionary Argentinian family organizing the preserve has undertaken the task with supreme care. The tour includes a viewing of the netted butterfly sanctuary, where all the things butterflies do can be observed in minute detail while the multi-lingual staff explains the relationship between the butterflies and the native plants. To get there from Zipolite, walk or take a *colectivo* headed towards Mazunte and get off at the "Mariposario" sign. (Open daily 9:30am-5pm in the high season, and Tu-Su in the low season. Admission 15 pesos.)

PUERTO ESCONDIDO

After passing row after row of trinket stores only to arrive at a beach land-mined with horse droppings and scuzzy *palapas*, new arrivals to Puerto Escondido will probably wonder what all the fuss is about. Although it's clear that everyone goes to this mecca of Mexican beachside pilgrimage, at first, it can be difficult to understand why. And then there's Zicatela. Visible across the cove from town, locals say that it's the third most important surfing beach in the world. Whatever the ranking may be, one needs no engineering degree to see that this comes very close to the perfect wave. Crisply breaking in rapid sets, watching Zicatela's waves crumble is a pastime that transfixes the international crowd of men, women, surfers, kooks, hippies and hipsters swinging in hammocks, nursing drinks on the shore, or simply gathering to gaze at the spectacle of the waves, and the masterful surfers that shoot across their surfaces. If Puerto Escondido's beaches have been sullied by the dark side of toursim, the waves of Zicatela and the vibrant community they attract are redemption, and well worth the pilgramage.

✈ ORIENTATION

Built on a hillside 294km south of Oaxaca on Rte. 175, Puerto Escondido is connected by an airport (3km down Rte. 200, 3 pesos by *minibús*) and numerous bus lines. The city is bisected by **Rte. 200** which divides the uptown grid of streets used by locals from the touristy maze of paths leading downhill to the beach. Bus stations are located uphill in the grid section. To get to beaches and hotels simply walk downhill.

The main tourist corridor, known as **Andador Turistico, Adonquin,** and **Perez Garga** at different sections, loops down from the route, scoops the main beach, and reconnects again at the *crucero*, the intersection of everything. Going farther east from the *crucero* will take you to Zicatela. Locals insist that Puerto Escondido is relatively safe, but recent assaults against tourists serve as a reminder that even the most seemingly secure places can be dangerous. Play it safe by staying in groups and avoiding isolated beaches, even during daylight hours. **Taxis** can be found by the tourist information booth and along the Carretera Costera; they are the safest way of getting around after nightfall.

🛈 PRACTICAL INFORMATION

TRANSPORTATION

Airport: (tel. 2 04 92) can be easily reached by crossing the *crucero* and catching a *mini* marked "Aeropuerto' headed up Av. Oaxaca. At night, resort to a taxi. Airlines include **AeroCaribe** (tel. 2 20 23) and **Mexicana** (tel. 2 00 98 or 2 03 020).

Buses: All of the bus stations are scattered uptown, just past the *crucero*. The parking lot of Estrella Blanca (tel. 582 0427 or 582 0086) can be seen just across the freeway at the curve of Av. Oaxaca. Buses go to: **Acapulco** (7hr.; 7 per day 4:30am-11:30pm; 149 pesos); **Huatulco** via **Pochutla** (1½hr. to Pochutla; 7:30 and 10:30am, 2 and 7pm; Pochutla 27 pesos, Huatulco 43 pesos). Direct to: **Huatulco** (4½hr.; 8, 9:30am, 12:30, 2:30, 4:30 and 6pm; 96 pesos); **Mexico City** (12hr.; 7:30pm and 2am; 304 pesos); and **Zihuatanejo** (11hr.; 8:45pm; 241 pesos). Oaxaca-Istmo (tel. 582 0392) on Ave. Hidalgo just behind the Estrella Blanca station is the cheaper way to get to **Pochutla** (1hr.; 6, 8:30, 11:30am, and 2pm; 15 pesos) and continue on to **Salina Cruz** (60 pesos); and **Oaxaca** (6½hr.; 7:30, 11:15am, 2 and 10:30pm; 70 pesos). Following Hidalgo 3 blocks to the right of Ave. Oaxaca is Estrella de Valle (tel. 582 0050) the best way to get to **Oaxaca** (6½ hr.; 11 per day 7:30am-10:30pm; direct service 70 pesos, 65 pesos for *ordinario*—with stops.) Cristóbal Colón, Calle 1 Nte. 207 (tel. 582 1073) one block past Hidalgo on Ave. Oaxaca and two blocks to the right sends buses to: **Huatulco** (2hr.; 6 per day 8:45am-9:30pm; 40 pesos); **San Cristóbal** (12hr.; 8:45am and 9:30pm; 227 pesos); and **Tuxtla Gutiérrez** (10hr.; 8:45am, and 9:30pm; 198 pesos).

Car Rental: Arrendora Express, Garsga 502 (tel. 582 1355), at Marina Nacional. Car rentals start at 500 pesos per day; bikes 150 pesos per day. Anyone with a credit card and valid driver's license can rent. Open M-Sa 9am-2pm and 4-8pm, Su 9am-2pm.

TOURIST AND FINANCIAL SERVICES

Tourist Office: Módulo de Información Turística (tel. 582 0175), is an amazingly helpful booth located at the beginning of the pedestrian walkway, down Garsga from the *crucero*. Manned by the dedicated and connected Georgina Machorro, advice on everything will be offered in your language or something very close to it. Open daily 9am-1pm and 4-7pm. Main office: (tel. 582 0175).

Currency Exchange: Banamex (tel. 2 03 52), Pérez Gasga on the corner of the Adoquín, exchanges traveler's checks and has an **ATM.** Open M-F 9am-noon. **Bancomer** (tel. 2 04 11), 1 Nte. at 2 Pte., near the bus station, also exchanges cash. Open M-F 8:30am-3pm. **Money Exchange** (tel. 2 05 92), on the Adoquín across from Farmacia Cortés, has bad rates but convenient hours. Open M-Sa 10am-3pm and 6-9pm. Good rates can be had at **Bancrecer,** on Hidalgo between Av. Oaxaca and 1 Pte. Open M-F 9am-5pm, Sa 10am-2pm.

LOCAL SERVICES

Market: Mercado Benito Juárez, 8 Nte. at 3 Pte., 1 block past the post office, all the way up Av. Oaxaca. A fun outdoor market and the place to find good prices. Open daily 7am-6pm, but most lively W and Sa. **Ahorro** (tel. 582 1128) 3 Pte. and 4 Nte. is the big supermarket. Open M-Sa 8am-9pm, Su 8am-4pm.

Laundry: Lavamática del Centro, Pérez Gasga 405, uphill from the pedestrian walkway on the right. 10 pesos per kg. Open M-Sa 8am-8pm, Su 8am-5pm.

EMERGENCY AND COMMUNICATIONS

Emergency: In an extreme emergency, contact Minne Dahlberg (tel. 582 0367), chair of **Friends of Pto. Escondido,** a neighborhood watchdog group of area expats. She will get you in contact with your embassy, the police, or medical help.

Police: (tel. 582 0111 or 582 0155), on the Agencia Municipal on the Carretera Costera, shortly past the *crucero* on the way to the airport. No English spoken.

Red Cross: (tel. 582 0142). Open 24hr.

Pharmacy: Farmacía Moderna (tel. 582 0598), on Gaspa as it curves down from the *crucero.* Open 24hr.

Hospital: IMSS (tel. 2 01 42), 5 de Febrero at Calle 7 Nte. Open 24hr. **Centro de Salud,** Pérez Gasga 409 (tel. 2 00 46), is a small medical clinic open 24hr. for emergencies. No English spoken.

Post Office: (tel. 2 09 59), Calle 7 Nte. at Av. Oaxaca, a 20min. walk uphill from the *crucero* past the bus station. Open M-F 8am-7pm, Sa 9am-1pm. **Postal Code:** 71980.

Internet Access: Un Tigre Azul, in a saffron building on the right, just past the tourist booth and traffic blockade. Service is slow for the 25 pesos per 30min. rate, but at least there is a gallery of work by local artists to stare at while you wait for your email and free coffee from the bar upstairs. Open daily 11am-11pm.

Phone Code: 958.

◤ ACCOMMODATIONS

The beach is not safe for camping, but a multitude of hotels cater to budget travelers, particularly during the off season. During *Semana Santa*, Christmas, and the months of July and August, reservations are an absolute must, and the least expensive places are the rented rooms, trailer parks, and *cabañas* along the beach. There are lots of *cabaña* places across the street from Plaza Zicatela. Price ranges reflect seasonal variation.

IN TOWN

Budget accommodations are best found by walking up from the Adoquin towards the *crucero*. Guests in these places tend to be young Europeans coming from or going to San Cristóbal de las Casas. As you climb, also keep an eye out for the "Se Rentan Cuartos Economicos" sign, which pops up in the grid of streets around the bus stations.

■ **Hotel Mayflower** (tel. 582 03 67), on Andador Libertad. From the bus station, cross the *crucero*, then take a left down a steep hill—the road ends, but stairs descend on the right to the hotel entrance. Clean, brightly tiled rooms with private baths surround a common area complete with hammocks and shelves full of magazines and books written in English, German, and French. An international crowd relaxes at the bar upstairs and the friendly, multilingual owner can provide valuable information about the area. Dorm beds 50 pesos; in the high season 55 pesos.

Cabañas El Estación (tel. 582 2251). From the *crucero*, follow Garsga down as it winds left and look for a sign on the right, across the street from Banamex. Although their *cabañas* are on the shores of a gutter rather than that of the big, blue Pacific, Estación remains truer to the original *cabaña* spirit than any place in town. Each comes with mosquito netting, a hammock and use of clean communal bathrooms, but the reason to stay is the cool people who lounge in the central *palapa*, enjoying the super breakfast that the English-speaking owner throws in with the 60-peso per night bargain. Dinner (35 pesos); hammock accommodations 20 pesos; camping 20 pesos per person.

Los Dos Costas Gasga #302 (tel. 582 0159), in the curve just down from the *crucero*. The best bargain in town is here if you seek a private room and a non-sandy front porch. Though the lobby smells a little suspicious, rooms are clean with private baths. Singles 40 pesos; doubles 80 pesos; triples 120 pesos.

ON ZICATELA

Although crowds of surfers and the spectating hordes complicate Zicatela's prices, it is unquestionable where all the action is. During high season, it's wise to make reservations several weeks in advance.

Hotel Buena Vista (tel. 582 1474) on Calle de Morros, is good for people who have a hard time pulling themselves away from the surf watch. With a most spectacular view of the beach, most of the rooms also come with kitchen so you can fry up your own *huevos*. Clean private bathrooms complete the luxury. Rooms for 2 people range from 100-300 pesos depending on the view. Each additional person 30 pesos.

Cabañas Alden Mavinero, located on the road leading to the Playa Mavinero, whose entrance leads left off the beach just before Zicatela, these prices are among the best. for shared bathrooms, a clean *cabaña* and the good location. Singles 40 pesos in low season, in the high season 70 pesos; doubles 60 and 80 pesos respectively.

PLAYA ZICATELA

Along the beach, 150 pesos in the low season and 180 pesos in the high will buy a decent double in most places. As far as *cabañas* go, **Las Olas** and **Cabañas Acali** both offer very clean, very secure rooms, some with private baths. **Bungalows Zicatela** (tel. 582 0798) has a more laid-back atmosphere and a pool. Although it's getting to be more expensive, **Hotel Acuario** (tel. 582 1027) continues to be a favorite with the surfing crowd. It may be worth the extra pesos to support the hotel's ecological savvy—they've installed a special water purifier that cleans all hotel wastewater and sends it back to sea with minimal environmental damage. While it remains to be seen what sort of crowd **Paco Lolo** (tel. 582 0759) will attract to its hotel rooms, located close to the main restaurants on the beach, the rooms are cheap and prices shouldn't vary much by season (doubles 80 pesos; two beds 110 pesos).

FOOD

When expats don't open hotels to sustain themselves in Puerto Escondido, they open restaurants, usually based on their native cuisine. Italians love the beach, but their lack of tolerance for Mexican coffee and their preference for pasta rather than tortillas has made their share of the restaurant business especially large. It takes up a good portion of Gasga. If you get a hankering for *maiz*, head across the freeway from the *crucero* to **Tagueria Rosa** across from the Estrella Blanca section—it's about as *tipica* as it gets, and refreshingly cheap.

El Cafecito (tel. 582 0516). After the surf, El Cafecito may well be Puerto Escondido's greatest phenomenon. Situated across the street from Zicatela's prime breaders, the outdoor tables are almost always packed with talkative European backpackers, beautiful beach babes, scarfing surfers and hammock vendors. The menu makes everyone happy, offering vegetarian-style Mexican cuisine for under 30 pesos and amazing 15-peso fruit-granola salads for the string bikini set.

SAND AND SIGHTS

Beach, beach, and more beach. The main beach, **Playa Principal,** is just beyond the stores and restaurants that line the Andoquín. This beach, full of *lanchas* and *palapas,* can get awfully crowded. Past Banana's, you'll encounter fishing boats; the stretch of sand from there to the rocks is **Playa Marinero,** great for swimming or sunbathing. Stepping over the rocks will take you to **Playa Zicatela,** one of the world's best surfing beaches. Those dudes bobbing up and down in the water waiting to ride the next killer wave all have several years of experience. Watching them is exhilarating, but do not even think about trying to partake of their "fun"—you risk a fate worse than wiping out. Past Carmen's on the road facing the beach, **Acuario** (tel. 2 10 26) rents **snorkels** (20 pesos) and **scuba gear** (beginning at US$40 for a day's excursion). A few smaller beaches, suitable for snorkeling, lie on the other side of Playa Principal. The distance is short enough to walk, but you can also take a taxi (15 pesos) or a boat. From the tourist booth, walk to the right toward the lighthouse. A staircase will take you over the waves before climbing uphill to a road and an overlook. Follow the road and take the first left; stairs lead to **Playa Manzanillo.** On the other side of a rocky barrier is **Puerto Angelito.** Both tranquil beaches make for good swimming or languid lounging in the shaded hammocks or chairs (10 pesos per day). Even farther removed from civilization is beautiful **Playa Carrizalillo,** offering fewer crowds. It's accessible by boat or taxi from Puerto Angelito, but you can also walk there; head uphill from the beach on Pérez Gasga. When it forks at the Banamex, follow the left-hand side. You will pass a turn-off for Puerto Angelito; continue straight on the dirt road until you come to the Rotary Club basketball courts. Make a left and keep walking downhill. For those rugged adventurers dying to explore secluded beaches, be sure to exercise proper caution. Because of crime, it's best to stick to the established beaches.

NIGHTLIFE

When the sun goes down, sun worshippers turn into bar crawlers, making their way to the many pubs along the strip. In the early evening, every restaurant and bar has a Happy Hour, which oddly enough lasts three or four hours. Two-for-one drinks are one reason why everyone's happy. In addition to alcohol and TV, **Banana's** offers pool and foosball (20 pesos per hr.). Around 10pm, the music starts. **Discoteque Bacocho,** in the Bacocho residential district, is the only full-fledged dance club; you'll have to shower and throw something nice over that thong bikini. Taxis will whisk you over there for 15 pesos. (Cover 25 pesos. Open Sa-Su 10pm-3am.) More informal places line the pedestrian walkway. **El Tubo,** on the Playa Principal, plays reggae, *salsa,* and rock. The bacchanalian crowd spills out onto the beach by the end of the night. (No cover. Open daily 11pm-4am.) **Montezuma's Revenge** and **The Wipeout Bar,** both on the Adoquín, feature live music every night. Keep your ears perked for Santana-esque tunes. (No cover. Music usually runs 10:30pm-1am.)

VERACRUZ

The state of **Veracruz** is one of the hottest, poorest, and most mind-bogglingly diverse in the Republic. Stretching 300km along the Gulf of Mexico, Veracruz encompasses breathtaking beaches, burgeoning cities, and vast spaces filled only by roaming cattle and lush vegetation. Unlike most of Mexico's, its economy is not dependent only on farming. Although many local residents make their livings from tobacco and coffee farming and small-scale cattle ranching, the state's main income comes from oil and fishing. But the state that works hard also parties hard: *veracruzanos*, also known as *jarochos*, are renowned for their delightful senses of humor, their wonderful seafood and coffee, and their Afro-Caribbean inspired music that relies heavily on the *marimba*. The Afro-Caribbean influence dates back to the days when the city of Veracruz was the main slave trading port for the country—it pervades not only the state's music but also its cuisine and ethnic makeup. Local color is supplied by the over-hyped but still vital *curandero* culture. *Curanderos* (medicine men), called *brujos* (witches) by locals, practice a unique mixture of conjuring, devil-invocation, and natural healing.

Mexico's very first light-skinned visitors—Cortés and his ruthless band of *conquistadores*—reached land in Veracruz in 1519 and began the first European trek to the capital from these shores. Today, the state of Veracruz, especially the volcanic hills of La Sierra de los Tuxtlas, remains relatively untouristed; those who come are pleasantly surprised. *Marimba* rhythms and Caribbean colors flow through the steamy port city of Veracruz day and night, and the beautiful mountain city of Xalapa overflows with art and culture.

HIGHLIGHTS OF VERACRUZ

■ **Veracruz** (see p. 508), the state capital, is a sweaty and alluring port city. Spend your days checking out the **Castillo de San Juan de Ulúa** (see p. 512) and your nights dancing to the sounds of *marimba*.

■ The temperate, green, beautiful city of **Xalapa** (see p. 494) is also a cultural center—its **Museo Nacional de Antropología** (see p. 498) is considered the second-best museum in the country.

■ Many movies have been filmed at the unearthly **Cascada de Texolo** (see p. 500). Check out these scenic falls and find out why.

■ Many travelers ditch the beach resorts and instead choose to do their own exploration along the beautiful **Gulf coast** (see p. 518) south of Veracruz.

■ **Papantla** (see p. 504) is not only a clean and friendly town, but also a bastion of Totonac culture—it's the best base from which to explore **El Tajín** (see p. 506), the most impressive ruins in the state.

XALAPA (JALAPA)

Not the kind of capital city willing to stand aside and be bowled over by its bigger, more glam lowland counterpart, Xalapa (hah-LAH-pah) has muscled its way into the state's hot and steamy limelight. A self-declared cultural center, the city has a lot to back up its claim, including an excellent orchestra, burgeoning university, and one of the top archaeological museums in the Americas. With enough coffee, conversation, and art to win over the most erudite sophisticate, the inescapable *marimba*, winding alleys, and plush green countryside earn Xalapa big 10s from judges around the world.

Though respectable citizens spell their town's name (onomatopoeic Nahuátl for "spring in the sand") with an "x," they are still struggling against the more standard Hispanic "j" spelling. The name-game says it all—this is a city that thrives on debate. Though the center bursts with commerce and the clattering of change, work and money are almost always second to coffee-time, when expansive groups of friends fill tables to overcapacity and aggravate waiters in feverent attempts to catch up on their daily conversations. If Xalapa's topography and a predilection for discussion make it difficult to find the shortest distance between two points, visitors will soon find that it doesn't matter, as points in between tend to be as saucy, aromatic, and entertaining as the destination.

■ ORIENTATION

Located at the midpoint of the state, Xalapa is 104km northwest of Veracruz on **Rte. 140,** and 302km directly east of Mexico City. The **train station** is at the extreme northeast edge of the city, a 40-minute walk or 8-peso taxi ride from the *centro.* To get from the **bus station** to the *centro*, catch buses marked "Centro" or "Terminal" (3 pesos); a taxi will cost 12 pesos. There are two bus stations. **CAXA** is the major one for service to distant cities. The **Terminal Excelsior** is a roundabout where you can catch buses to small neighboring towns. Make sure to clarify which bus station you want to go to.

Xalapa, like many other hill towns, can be quite confusing. The downtown area is centered around the **cathedral** and **Palacio de Gobierno. Enríquez,** which runs along **Parque Juárez** and separates the two. Streets that branch from Enríquez toward the park and the Palacio de Gobierno run downhill; streets that split from Enríquez on the cathedral side run uphill to the market and main commercial district. Going away from the park toward the cathedral, Enríquez becomes two streets: **Xalapeños Ilustres** to the left and **Zamora** to the right. In the opposite direction, Enríquez becomes **Av. Camacho.**

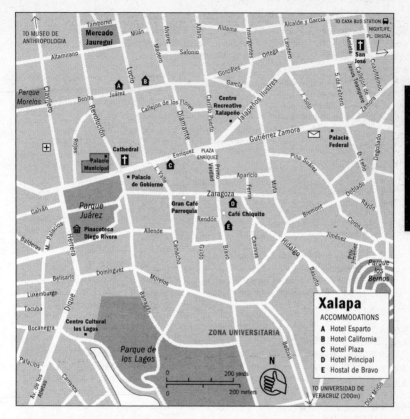

Xalapa

ACCOMMODATIONS

A Hotel Esparto
B Hotel California
C Hotel Plaza
D Hotel Principal
E Hostal de Bravo

TO UNIVERSIDAD DE
VERACRUZ (200m)

🔢 PRACTICAL INFORMATION

TRANSPORTATION

Buses: CAXA, in a state-of-the-art building at 20 de Noviembre 571, east of the city center. The station has long-distance phones, telegraph service, a pharmacy, shopping,
food, and drink. ADO (tel. 18 99 80) travels first-class to: **Catemaco** (5hr., 8 per day,
103 pesos); **Mexico City** (5hr., 22 per day 1am-midnight, 125 pesos); **Papantla** (4hr.,
7 per day, 94 pesos); **Puebla** (3hr., 9 per day, 72 pesos); **San Andrés Tuxtla** (3hr., 11
per day, 99 pesos); **Santiago Tuxtla** (3hr., 10:25am and 7:45pm, 71 pesos); **Tuxtepec** (5hr., 3:35 and 6pm, 77 pesos); and **Veracruz** (2hr., 48 per day 5:30am-
11:30pm, 42 pesos). Slightly slower, slightly cheaper second-class service to almost
identical destinations provided by **Autobuses Unidos (AU).**

TOURIST AND FINANCIAL SERVICES

Tourist Office: (tel. 12 85 00), a kiosk in the bus station, to the far left as you enter the
terminal, is the best source of information. Open daily 8am-10pm. Occasionally there is
a makeshift kiosk run by the Palacio Municipal across from Parque Juárez on Enríquez
that sells handy maps for 5 pesos.

Currency Exchange: Banks with **ATMs** line Enríquez and the surrounding streets. Most will
change money, though better rates can be found at **Centro Cambio Jalapa** (tel. 8 68 60)
or **Casa de Cambio Orisatal,** both located further down the road on Zamora (open M-Sa
9am-3pm and 4-7pm, Su 10am-1pm).

American Express: Carrillo 24 (tel. 17 41 14; fax 12 06 01), 3 blocks from Parque Juárez, past the cathedral off Enríquez. Cashier open M-F 9am-1:30pm and 4-7pm, Sa 10am-1pm. **Viajes Xalapa,** a full-service **travel agency,** with English language assistance, shares the office. Open M-Sa 9am-8pm.

LOCAL SERVICES

Market: Chedraui is a supermarket and pharmacy on the corner of Lucio and Callejón del Flores. Open daily 8am-9pm. The open-air experience of **Mercado Jauregui** starts a block behind the cathedral and sprawls to the Puente Xallitic.

Laundry: Lavandería Salmones, Morelos 13 between Guido and Camacho, downhill from Enríquez. 3kg for 15 pesos, 4 pesos more for 3hr. service. Open M-F 8:30am-8:30pm, Sa 10am-6pm.

Bookstores: Several excellent bookstores are located at the intersection of Xalapeños Illustres and Mata just past the Centro Recreativo. Some sporadically offer English-language books and magazines.

Cultural Centers: Centro Recreativo Xalapa at Xalapeños Illustres 31, where it intersects with Mata and Calle Insurgentes, holds art galleries, cultural information, and classes on everything from *salsa* to political cartooning.

EMERGENCY AND COMMUNICATIONS

Emergency: dial 06.

Police: (tel. 18 18 10 or 18 99 86), helpfully sprinkled throughout the city, on the corner of Arteaga and Aldama and at the Cuartel San José.

Red Cross: Clavijero 13 (tel. 17 34 31 for emergencies or tel. 17 81 58 for administration), a block uphill from Parque Juárez. 24hr. ambulance service.

Pharmacy: Farmacia Semejante, Enriquez 41 (tel. 17 22 20). Open 24hr.

Hospitals: Hospital Civil, Pedro Rendón 1 (tel. 18 44 00), at Bravo. 24hr. emergency care. **IMSS,** Lomas del Estadio (tel. 18 55 55). No English spoken.

Post Office: (tel. 17 20 21), at Zamora and Diego Leño in the Palacio Federal. Open M-F 8am-4pm, Sa 9am-1pm. **Postal Code:** 91001.

Fax: Telecomm, Zamora 70 (tel. 16 21 67), around the corner from the post office. Open M-F 9am-7pm, Sa 9am-5pm, Su 9am-noon.

Internet Access: Cafe Internet Xalapa, Pasaje Enrique Loc 1 (tel./fax 17 51 41; www.cafexalapa.com.mx), located in the indoor mall that runs between Enríquez and Primo Verdad. Though you'll be paying through the nose at 30 pesos per hr., it's probably fast enough to be worth it. The savvy staff is good with both computers and espresso machines (*Café Americano,* 6 pesos). Open M-Sa 9am-9pm, Su 11am-9pm. **Computación Siglo XXI,** (tel. 17 48 12; Lemodmg@Verl.telmex.com), at Diegoleño and Morelos downhill from Enríquez. Offers slower service at much better prices. 18 pesos per hr. Open daily 9am-10pm.

Telephones: LADATELs are outside the Palacio de Gobierno on Enríquez and outside the post office. **Caseta,** Calle Guerro 9, off the southwest corner of Parque Juárez. Open daily 9am-10pm. There are also plenty of phones at the bus station.

Phone Code: 28.

ACCOMMODATIONS

For the penny-pinching traveler, Xalapa is a gold mine. The city is full of comfortable, economical, and convenient accommodations, many of them on **Revolución,** close to the *centro,* the market, and the parks. Not only that, but for 100-150 pesos (the price of budget accommodations in many other cities), you can afford to trade in the budget hotels for the more upscale establishments.

Hotel California, Ortega 11 #1, on the side of a mini-park 1 block off Lucio from Enríquez. What this hotel lacks in luxury it makes up for in price and in its proximity to

Cocina Economica Irma's with 2-peso enchiladas. Rooms are spartan and white, but very clean. One bed 30 pesos, with private bath 45 pesos; 2 beds 40 pesos, with private bath 65 pesos.

Hotel Plaza, Enríquez 4 (tel. 17 33 10; fax 18 27 14). The most central location imaginable, and if you get a room facing Enríquez, you won't forget it—noise is a 24hr. affair. Rooms are nice, though, especially on the 2nd fl., where elegant wooden doors and high ceilings have a better-than-budget feel. All have color TVs and a near-constant *marimba* sound track that drifts up through the shady lobby from the street below. Singles 70 pesos; doubles 90 pesos; triples 100 pesos.

Hotel Esparto, Juárez 6 (17 24 55), 1 block up from Enríquez to the right of the cathedral. A bit pricier but stuffed with beefy amenities—TVs, phones, fans, and tables make up for a lack of ambience, as does the hotel's reasonably priced restaurant (breakfasts for under 15 pesos, open 8am-11pm). Singles 100 pesos; doubles 115 pesos; two beds 135 pesos.

Hotel Principal, Zaragoza 28 (tel. 17 64 00), about 2½ blocks away from the Palacio de Gobierno along Zaragoza. The hotel to match Café Parroquia, Principal is nice, bright, and full of toned-down 70s niftiness. Most of the rooms have TVs, all have phones and the very friendly, very *veracruzano* staff will be happy to help you with laundry service. Singles 90 pesos; doubles 110 pesos; triples 120 pesos.

◖ FOOD

Xalapeño food is cheap, plentiful and always second to *café con leche*, almost a meal in itself. Restaurant owners seem to keep food prices low as a way of encouraging patrons to eat. If you're hungry, you'll be able to eat in the nicer places in the *centro* without doing much financial damage.

CAFES

El Gran Parroquia, Zaragoza 18 (tel. 17 74 01), 1 block downhill from the Plaza de Gobierno. Though the Parroquia began in Veracruz, Xalapa has made it an art. In contrast to its cafeteria-like coastal cousin, the *cafe* is a 70s dream, with tinkling elevator music wafting through the tan, smoky, "recessed lighting" interior—the perfect setting for Bond-style espionage. La Parroquia is patronized by the real dookies, many of whom wear genuine 70s polyester articles and fill the tables with debate discussion and plenty of head-wagging gossip. The ambience is topped off by the justifiably wonderful coffee (9 pesos), succulent pastries, and *antojitos* (18-28 pesos).

Café Chiquito, Zamora 35, directly across from the post office. The kind of place that probably started small, Chiquito has long been luring students and 20-somethings with its cool fountain-courtyard, its cheap eats (all with fresh, handmade tortillas prepared in the courtyard) and its incredible *granitas* (blended, icy coffee drinks topped with a Matterhorn of whipped cream). Just ripe for sappy serialized drama, when not engaged in heart-to-hearts or lovers' quarrels, the 18-30 year-old set mobs tables practicing for the Parroquia-style Big League. Integrating oneself into the web is a bit like hopping in on double dutch—it becomes easier with practice. Main location of 3 cafes located on Bravo, half a block down from Zaragoza. Open daily 8am-11pm.

Calle Carillo Puerto, leading up from Enríquez, is lined with small, pleasant *cafés* with more chill social lives and slightly lower prices. The ambience-free Bola de Oro on Primo Verdad at one end of the Plaza Enríquez also offers good 5-peso cups of coffee. The institution across the street, Café Colón makes its money selling its famous bagged beans, but hot "samplers" of *Café Americano* are worth a sip. More nocturnal scenes, often with music, can be had at Café Calli just down Zaragoza from Parroquia—both stay open into the wee hours and are good places to flirt. Cafes are the inroad into Xalapeño life for foreigners; it's easy to get to know people at Xalapa's coffee houses that have supreme social benefits most other cities don't share.

RESTAURANTS

Restuarant Rosallia, Abosolo 2, across the street from the north end of the market. Fantasize about the Swiss Alps and enjoy passing musicians in the 50 year-old market-side institution. The funny wooden booths and great food attract tired vendors who slake their thirst on cold soft drinks below the restaurant's florid shrine. Super enchiladas (7 pesos for 4); *mole poblano* (10 pesos). Top it off with *café con leche* (3 pesos). Jukebox entertainment abounds when musicians aren't available. Open M-Sa 9am-10pm, Su 9am-2pm.

T-Grill, Xalapeños Ilustres 1. The powerhouse behind this taco emporium is the 2 women who pat *maiz* into fresh tortillas for hours on end. Chat with them about carpal-tunnel syndrome while gorging on the fruits of their labor. Speedy young waiters deliver the goods instantaneously to your table. Five "traditional" tacos filled with *cabeza* and other semi-unsavory animal bits go for 10 pesos; delicious *tacos al pastor* and other taco-related species go for under 20 pesos for an order of 5. Open daily 11am-3pm.

Restaurante La Sopa, Callejón del Diamante 3A (tel. 17 80 69), 2 blocks from the park along Enríquez off one of Xalapa's famous cobblestone alleys. Ultra-hip waiters cater to a similar crowd in this ultra-hip joint, located on—you guessed it—an ultra-hip walkway. Whitewashed arches and red tablecloths are appropriately picturesque. Enjoy the diverse clientele and the amazing *chiles rellenos* (6 pesos) or enchiladas (14 pesos) while tossing back the coffee (of course). A *Veracruzano Huasteco* trio plays on Friday nights while the *Jarrachos* take the stage on Saturday. Open M-Sa 1-6pm and 7:30-11:30pm.

■ SIGHTS

MUSEO DE ANTROPOLOGÍA. This museum is probably the second best museum in all of Mexico, after Mexico City's Museo Nacional de Antropología (see p. 113). But while the Mexico City museum is a monster encompassing cultures from the entire county, Xalapa's museum focuses on just the cultures that inhabited what is today the state of Veracruz. The museum was finished in 1986, and today its shiny marble exhibits feature massive Olmec heads, smiling Totonac figurines, and Huastec skulls and artifacts laid out in chronological order along the rectangular hallway that makes up the main part of the museum. Start your visit at the front, with the oldest and most elusive culture, the Olmecs. Displayed in spectacular marble galleries and outdoor gardens, the museum's 10 Olmec heads are perhaps the most impressive of its 3000 items (for more see **Pre-Hispanic Societies,** p. 7). With the decline of the Olmecs by 400 BC, power shifted north to the Totonac, whose rule stretched from El Tajín through Xalapa. The museum explores the Totonac rise and reign through a large panorama of the huge ceremonial city of El Tajín and through Totonac sculptures and jewels. Finally, the Huastec culture arose and remained powerful until the arrival of the Spanish, whose coming is noted in scrolls at the end of the museum. A fascinating journey through the history of pre-Hispanic Veracruz, the museum is best viewed with the knowledgeable University of Veracruz students who work as guides at the museum. For more information, ask at the ticket booth. The bookstore in the lobby sells an assortment of anthropology books, and there is also a cafeteria. *(To get there, catch a yellow "Tesorería" bus on Enríquez (3 pesos); take a taxi (8 pesos); or walk on Enríquez/Camacho away from the cathedral, then make a left on Av. Xalapa and continue on for several blocks until you see the museum on your left (45min.). Open daily 9am-5pm. Free tours in Spanish given daily at 11:30am (1½ hr.), and English tours can be arranged at any time for 100 pesos. Admission 15 pesos, students 8 pesos. Camera 10 pesos, video camera 40 pesos.)*

PARQUE ECOLÓGICO MACUITÉPETL. If Xalapa is a difficult city to navigate, its probably because every street ends in a park. The green splotches smattered across the hills make it a great city to wander around in. If you ascend a grade, you are almost guaranteed a tree, bench, statue, and view at the top. The biggest, most beautiful park is the Parque Ecológico Macuitépetl, where, with a little trekking, you can enjoy the neat flora and fauna native to the hills around the city. To get there, take a "Mercado-Corona" *colectivo* (3 pesos) from Revolución and Altamirano (1.20 pesos), or hail a taxi (12 pesos). A brick path meanders past liplocked lovers to the summit of an extinct volcano 186m above the city, where a spiral tower offers a view of the city and mountains. *(Park open daily 6am-6pm.)*

UNIVERSITY OF VERACRUZ. Where there are parks, there also tend to be cultural centers. The large, manmade "lakes" of the **Paseo de los Lagos** lap against the hillsides below Enríquez and serve to tranquilize the already verdant University of Veracruz. Not exactly an architectural gem, UV has lots of institutional box-style buildings painted in comely shades of blue and green. Pine trees and Internet access might make it worth a visit, though. A bike path winds around the lakes, passing the campus and a variety of cultural centers. Pop into any one for information on workshops and exhibitions.

PARQUE JUÁREZ. The park serves as Xalapa's surrogate *zócalo*. On the same level as Parque Enríquez, its benches are usually filled with people catching the breeze and taking in the superb vista. Two staircases in the park's platform lead down to a somewhat derelict cultural center, **Agora de la Ciudad,** which harbors a small cafe, galleries, and a screening room where film festivals take place. *(Just up from Herrera from the east end of the Lagos. Center open Tu-Su 8am-9:15pm.)*

CALLEJÓNES. Though Xalapa doesn't exactly tower with colonial majesty, it does take pride in its older **cobblestone alleys,** all of which are associated with gory love stories. **Callejón del Diamante** off Enríquez is named after a diamond which could tell the fidelity of a lover. It was given by a Spaniard to his Mexican wife who lived on the street, and unwisely played hanky-panky with a local while Mr. Spain was across the pond. When he returned, the darkened diamond registered the damage and the Spaniard murdered his wife as punishment. Off Enrique C. Rebsamen is **Callejón de la Calavera,** whose name is related to the not-so-picturesque story of a wife who decapitated her husband in fury over his drunken infidelity. In the story of the **Callejón de Jesus te Ampare,** both lovers are killed by a widower who went mad with jealousy upon seeing the happy couple. "Jesus te ampare" was the only thing the *novia* managed to say to her lover before their demise. Sanctuary from the carnage can be found at **La Iglesia San José,** one of the city's most beautiful churches, which, like the cathedral, dates from the late 18th century.

PINOCATECA DIEGO RIVERA. The city's artistic hightlight is the Pinocateca, a small museum of works by the famous *veracruzano* muralist. The canvasses are an unprecedented treat for those jaded by the "seated flower vendors" that appear on the walls of almost every hotel and restaurant in the country. Containing Rivera's experiments with Impressionism, collage, and Cubism, as well as some quick but exquisite travel sketches, the collection offers fresh and extremely impressive insight into the development of the legendary artist. *(Herrera 5, just below Parque Juárez. Open daily 10am-6pm. Free.)*

LOS MADRES CAPUCHINAS. If you're in the mood to satisfy your sweet tooth while getting a dose of religion, head to the convent of *Los Madres Capuchinas.* The easiest way to get there is to take a cab (7 pesos). Don't let the deserted-looking gate deter you; ring the bell. These nuns have been making exquisite *marzipan* candy/art for over 20 years. Good-sized boxes of delicately colored and delicious fruits, vegetables, and birds go for 25-35 pesos. The store also sells religious art and trinkets. *(20 de Noviembre Ote. 146. Open M-F 9am-6pm.)*

🎵 🎭 ENTERTAINMENT AND NIGHTLIFE

Where there is a university, there is usually nightlife, and a nightlife of two varieties: the public television kind and the music television kind. In Xalapa, both are available year-round and every night of the week.

Fans of the former should check entertainment listings in the local dailies or head down to the **Centro Recreativo** to find out what's happening at the **Teatro del Estado** (tel. 17 31 10). A 10-minute walk up Enríquez and Camacho from Parque Juárez, the *teatro*, at the corner of Ignacio de la Llave, is the home of the super **Orquesta Sinfónica de Xalapa** which performs every Saturday at 8pm. Performances by other university-related and professional groups keep the stage lights warm all week long. Bicker about the bass section afterwards at the Parroquia on Camacho, or in one of the city's other cafes—all of which are usually open and full until midnight. The same street is also the hot spot for the city's usually raging disco fever and free from some of the bourgeois snobbery that runs rampant closer to the university. Crowds tend to be young and uninhibited.

Bistro Café del Herrero, Camacho 8 (tel. 17 02 68), hosts an older, bar-like scene with jam-packed passageways more conducive to pressing rather than dancing. A breath of visual fresh air is provided by the lighted aquariums, home to iguanas whose branch perches bounce to the beat of the U.S.-Mexican rock most nights of the week. They get a break Su and M when the guitar guys play. Open nightly 4pm-4am.

La Bartola, Callejón del Diamante 7, in the cafe district closer to the *centro*. It seems appropriate that an alley named "Diamante" should be home to a ritzy *discoteca*—and ritzy it is. Just after 10pm, the taxis start pulling up to the entrance off Enríquez—unworthy chariots for the princesses who must then float effortlessly across the alley's minefield of cobblestones. TV monitors installed beneath the Plexiglas floor flash incongruous images while a small army of servers scamper between tables (which must be reserved in advance—call 18 77 46 from 5-7pm or email labartola@infosel.net.mx at anytime). Music ranges from pop-fluff to more sophisticated U.S.-Mexican picks. Cover 30 pesos. Open Th-Sa 10pm-5am. Come early or come hot; getting in can be a challenge.

Discoteque La Estación, 20 Noviembre 571 (tel. 17 31 55), just below the first-class bus station. Worth the cover and the trip from the *centro*, La Estación must be reached through a dark, private road that runs through a chirping, whirring Xalapeño jungle. Revelers pulsate in the night with the almost 2000 bodies it takes to fill the station's exquisite wooden dance floor fit for Travolta. A upper floor with balconies overlooking the tropics has live rock music but manages to be a bit more mellow. The clientele is young, but this is the kind of place where anyone willing to get down will fit in. Open W-Sa 9am-2am. Cover Th and Sa 25 pesos; W women free, men 50 pesos; F women free, men pay 70 pesos and get unlimited drinks.

La Mulada, (tel. 12 19 19) across 20 de Noviembre and down Calzada del Tajar. Expensive drinks pay for lots of colorful ambience including a starry ceiling and Goonies-esque barrel-seating. Live plants and a *mariachi* mural give this *discoteca* a distinctly *veracruzano* flair, and the dancing follows suit to a mix of *salsa* and U.S.-Mexican rock. Clientele is young and casual. Open Th-Sa 9pm-3am; Th free bar, men pay 75 pesos.

XCAPE, 20 de Noviembre 641 (tel. 12 50 75), 4 long blocks down 20 de Noviembre to the right of La Estación. Has a more sedentary scene with well dressed patrons clustered around Lilliputian sized tables listening to the live rock provided by a 3-band rotation. From here it will be possible to find even more partying, which usually continues until the steamy, pink Xalapeño dawn. Open Th-Su 9pm-3am; cover 30 pesos.

NEAR XALAPA: XICO AND CASCADA DE TEXOLO

It's hard to believe that **Xico** (SHEE-koh) is located a mere 19km from Xalapa—here, there are almost as many mules on the road as there are automobiles. Xico is known for its cuisine (*mole xiqueño*, a slightly sweeter version of *mole poblano*) and its nine-day festival dedicated to Mary Magdalene, the town's patron saint. The festival begins on July 22 in 1999 and includes bullfights and a running of the bulls.

But if any tourists go to Xico, it's not for the culture or cuisine of the town. Most go for the spectacular **Cascada de Texolo,** located just 3km from the tiny town. The dramatic waterfall crashes into a gorge alive with vivid greenery, the songs of passing birds, and the constant drum of water as it spills into the river below. A restaurant and viewing area are across from the falls. From a bridge leading to the other side of the gorge, several paths yield stunning views of other waterfalls and dense vegetation. If it looks like it could almost be out of a movie, it is. Several American movies, including *Romancing the Stone* with Michael Douglas and *Clear and Present Danger* with Harrison Ford, have used the dramatic falls for key scenes. The falls are also used (somewhat less glamourously) for car and deodorant commercials. In any case, the filming crews have left no trace of their presence. The falls are clear and crisp and relatively free of tourists. The only signs of civilization are the restaurant and the few orange and blue buildings of the electric company that uses the falls to generate power.

The best viewing area is **Restaurante El Mirador.** The restaurant has a charming outdoor seating area and serves up regional specialties (10-15 pesos; open daily 9am-7pm). On the other side of the gorge, two gentle waterfalls are visible. The first appears as soon as you step off the bridge. Down a level by the white picket border, another waterfall plunges from the electricity plant to the river below. Only after returning across the bridge and turning right toward the white fence of the observation deck can you see the water whose rumble you've been hearing so loudly. To truly experience the falls in all their glory, head to the left and go down the cement steps with the orange railings. Go down until you reach a fork in the path (by the *"Peligro"*—"Danger"—signs). The path to the left leads to an electric company building while the path to the right leads to the most spectacular view of *la cascada.* Your persistence will pay off when you reach the base of the falls. The vista is like something out of a fantasy book. Surrounded by the rush of water and playful butterflies, take your time and explore—skip over to the other side of the river to rejoice in the mist generated by the waterfall. Don't forget that the path you came from is the rocky one directly across from the main waterfall.

The rocks are often slippery and deserted, so it is best to exercise extreme caution and to wear appropriate footwear. Also, the walk to the falls is a long and lonely one. Despite the friendliness of the people of Xico, try not to go by yourself and definitely don't try to hike to the falls at night. The insects are also silent and ferocious, so bring plenty of bug repellent.

Getting There: To get to Xico from Xalapa, take the "Terminal" bus from the stop in front of the 3 Hermanos shoe store on Enríquez (not the one on Lucio) and get off at the Excelsior bus roundabout (about 8min., 2.10 pesos). From there, cross the street to blue Excelsior where buses are lined up and take a "Xico" bus (45min., 5.30 pesos).

To reach the falls, alert the bus driver as soon as the blue "Entrada de la Ciudad" sign appears on the right side of the road. The bus will turn right onto a smaller street and let you off. Retrace the steps back to the main street and climb straight up the hill in front of you until you reach a fairly wide dirt T-intersection (about a 5-6 minute climb); head left. Descending the hill, you will reach another fork guarded by a makeshift shrine to the Virgin; bear right after paying respects. The road curves to the right and then downhill to the viewing area and Restaurante El Mirador. If you get lost, ask the (very) occasional passerby for directions to the *cascadas.* To return to Xalapa and develop that film, re-trace your steps, but be aware that the walk will take 40 minutes and is not a smooth one. Taxis sometimes make the trip to the waterfalls, but the ride is also neither smooth nor fast. As you go back downhill from the dirt road, stick to the right of the street to hail one of the blue "Xalapa" buses, which will deposit you back at the Excelsior Terminal. Take a bus marked "Mercado" to head back into town, but make sure it refers to Xalapa and not elsewhere.

TUXPAN (TUXPAM)

The first thing you notice when you step into the heart of Tuxpan (pop. 120,000) is the funky smell, something like seafood, sweat, and sulfur. Although this may sound unappetizing, almost everything about Tuxpan is actually quite palatable. Despite the bustle of the fresh *marisco* markets, couples amble up and down the Río Tuxpan, as the humidity and mellow plaza make for lovely, lethargic lounging. Much like their Olmec, Huastec, and Totonac predecessors, boys stand on the shore flinging their nets repeatedly into the water and fruit vendors traverse the streets near the riverfront selling bananas and mangoes by the bag. If everything seems too loud and crowded elsewhere, fear not—Tuxpan makes for terrifically easy living. For a sandy, salty break, **Playa Azul** is just 12km away. On weekends, the beach overflows with families splashing about.

■ **ORIENTATION.** Tuxpan, 347km northwest of Veracruz, spreads along the northern bank of Río Tuxpan. Activity centers around two foliated plazas. **Blvd. Reyes Heroles** is Tuxpan's main thoroughfare, running along the river. One block north lies **Benito Juárez**, followed, moving north, by **Morelos. Parque Rodríguez Cano** is on the waterfront, just south of the busiest part of town, and **Parque Reforma** is between Juárez and Morelos a few blocks west of Rodríguez Cano. The bridge lies on the east edge of town and streets perpendicular to the bridge and parallel to the water run roughly east-west. Each bus line has its own station; to get to the town center from any one, walk to the river. From the **Estrella Blanca** station, walk toward and past the bridge—from the other stations, walk away from the bridge. To get to the beach, catch a "Playa" bus from the boardwalk by the ferry docks, on the river side of Reyes Heroles (every 10min. 6am-9pm, 7 pesos).

■ **PRACTICAL INFORMATION.** Several bus lines has its own station. ADO, Rodríguez 1 (tel. 4 01 02), three blocks east of Parque Cano down Reyes Heroles, rolls first-class service to: **Mexico City** (5hr., 13 per day, 132 pesos); **Papantla** (1½hr., 8 per day, 28 pesos); **Tampico** (3½hr., every hr., 95 pesos); **Veracruz** (5hr., 12 per day, 124 pesos); and **Xalapa** (5hr., 5 per day, 94 pesos). Estrella Blanca, Turistar, and Futura, at Cuauhtémoc 18 (tel. 4 20 40), two blocks past the bridge and two blocks inland, sends first-class service to: **Matamoros** (12hr., 7 and 9:30pm, 296 pesos); **Mexico City** (6hr., 7 per day, 132 pesos); and **Monterrey** (12hr., 9pm, 326 pesos) as well as second-class service to most nearby destinations. Omnibus, Independencía 30 (tel. 4 11 47), at the bridge, offers first-class service to: **Guadalajara** (15hr., 5 and 9:15pm, 378 pesos); **Mexico City** (6hr., 7 per day, 132 pesos); and **Querétaro** (10hr., 3 per day 5-9pm, 160 pesos).

SIEMPRE FIDEL Mexico has a long tradition of close and friendly relations with Cuba. When Fidel Castro fled the island in the late 1950s, it was in Tuxpan that he organized the revolutionary forces that months later led the country in the fight against Batista's dictatorship. The first hopeful years of the Cuban Revolution are celebrated in the **Casa de la Amistad México-Cuba.** (Photographs of a young, beardless Fidel line the walls, and a colorful mural depicts the valiant leader and his fellow boatsmen disembarking under the watchful gazes of Latin American heroes Benito Juárez, José Martí, and Simón Bolívar. The final room on the tour displays pictures of doctors and farmers, symbolizing Cuba's social progress, as well as a proud look back through the guest book and the diverse crop of visitors expressing support for the Cuban Revolution. To get to the museum, take a blue ferry (1 peso) across the river. Walk right (west) along the sidewalk and continue straight up the dirt road, past the overgrowth to the paved sidewalk, turn left, and enter on the side of the two small, white buildings with the boat out front. *Open daily 9am-2pm and 3-7pm. Admission free, but donations are always welcome.)*

The **tourist office,** Juárez 20 (tel. 4 01 77), on the 2nd fl. of the Palacio Municipal in Parque Rodríguez Cano, provides maps. Enter on the Juárez side—it's a small office across from Hotel Florida. (Open M-F 8am-3pm and 6-8pm.) **Serfin** (tel. 4 09 25), on Juárez between the two parks exchanges traveler's checks and has a 24hr. **ATM** (checks changed M-F 9am-2:30pm; open M-Sa 9am-5pm).

Lavandería Mejico, Reyes Heroles 57 (tel. 4 27 08), three blocks west of the *centro* will wash, dry, and iron your clothes in two hours (7 pesos per kg; open M-Sa 8am-8pm). **Red Cross:** Galeana 40 (tel. 4 01 58), eight blocks west of the *centro* along the river, then four blocks up Galeana, at the mini-bridge. English is spoken. **Emergency:** dial 060. **Police:** Galeana 38 (tel. 4 37 22), next door to the Red Cross, west of the *centro* (open 24 hr.). **Pharmacy: Benavides,** Rodríguez 9 (tel. 4 12 41), at the bridge-side of the market one block in from the river (open daily 7am-10pm). **Post office:** Mina 16 (tel. 4 00 88), from the Parque Reforma, follow Morelos towards the bridge, and then take the second left onto Mina; **MexPost** inside (open M-F 8am-6pm, Sa 9am-1pm). **Postal code:** 92800. **LADATELs** were last spotted in Parque Rodríguez Cano standing still. **Phone code:** 783.

⌐ ACCOMMODATIONS. Budget accommodations in Tuxpan cluster around the two central parks, ensuring a reasonable measure of safety into the evening hours. **Hotel Parroquia,** Escuela Militar 4 (tel. 4 16 30), to the left of the cathedral on Parque Rodríguez Cano, offers rooms with spacious bathrooms, some with TV and balconies overlooking the park and river—all at rock-bottom prices. Full-length mirror, fan, and TV lounge provide all you need. (1 person 86 pesos; 2 people 107 pesos; 3 people 110 pesos; 4 people 150 pesos.) **Hotel El Huasteco,** Morelos 41 (tel. 4 18 59), is half a block east from the northeast corner of Parque Reforma. While claustrophobes may do well to skip the small, windowless rooms, museum lovers should not. Rooms with mosaic walls, skylights and freezing A/C make this feel like the Guggenheim. (Singles 85 pesos; doubles 110-141 pesos.) Those in search of luxury at low rates should head for **Hotel Plaza,** Juárez 39 (tel. 4 07 38 or 4 08 38). Smack dab between Tuxpan's two main plazas, the large rooms come with beautiful wooden furniture and are stocked with phones, TV and A/C. (1 person 200 pesos; 2 people 230 pesos.)

⌂ FOOD. Balancing traditional Mexican decor (simple, elegant wooden furniture and colorful tiles) with modernity (TVs to track *telenovelas* or *fútbol* matches), **El Mejicano,** Morelos 49 (tel. 4 89 04), at the corner of Parque Reforma, serves up tasty regional cuisine. Sample *pescado a la mexicana* (45 pesos) or *antojitos* like *tacos de bistec* (22 pesos). *Licuados* (10 pesos) are made only with fresh, seasonal fruit. (Open daily 6am-1am.) The same owner operates **Cafetería El Mante,** Juárez 8 (tel. 4 57 36), one block west of Rodríguez. Enjoy hotcakes (14 pesos) or *antojitos* (3-19 pesos) amidst a festive atmosphere of red tablecloths, hanging plants, and lots of locals. **Restaurant Don Carlos,** Escuela Amerigo Militar 12, near the Hotel Parroquia (above), is small but very clean. The resident *familia* will whip up delicious dishes of seafood and meat right in front of your face (10-30 pesos). The *comida corrida* is an unbelievable 14 pesos. (Open daily 7am-11pm.)

◙ ⌐ ▣ SIGHTS, SAND, AND ENTERTAINMENT. Tuxpeños are justly proud of their river's relaxed beauty and scenic shores. Palm trees line the boardwalk, and goods are sold up and down the river. Under the bridge, piles of pineapples, bananas, shrimp, and fish can be had for a bare minimum at the huge open-air market which flows out of the indoor market on Calle Rodríguez. Located on the waterfront, **Parque Rodríguez Cano** comes alive every Monday at 5:30pm for the **Ceremonia Cívica,** when government officials make speeches and schoolchildren march in an orderly procession. For those in the mood for a museum trip or interested in delving into Castro's relationship with Mexico, **La Casa de la Amistad Mexico-Cuba,** across the river will enlighten you (see above).

Twelve kilometers from the city center, Tuxpan's **beach** can be crowded and slightly dirty, especially during the high season and hot weekends, but the wide expanse of fine sand stretches far enough for you to stake a claim somewhere down the line under the wild coconut palms. The beach is accessible by the "Playa" bus (every 15min. 6am-10pm, last bus returns to Tuxpan at 8pm; 5 pesos).

There are a number of **bars** in Tuxpan's *centro*, but the town has problems with brawls and rowdy nightowls. Clubs and bars have short lifespans in Tuxpan, and places practically empty during the week are packed during the weekend. The best and safest nightlife in town can be found after the crowds in Plaza Reforma thin out, a few blocks down the river at **Mantarraya** (tel. 4 00 51), Reyes Heroles at Guerrero. The enormous interior is the perfect place to chill and observe the clubbers or to break it down with the young crowd to American pop and techno hits. Live music frequently includes elderly men crooning popular ballads while screaming teens drink and sing along. (Cover 20-40 pesos including 2 drinks. Open Th-Sa 8:30pm-3am.)

PAPANTLA

Papantla (pop. 156,000) is almost picture-perfect. Crawling up the green foothills of the Sierra Madre Oriental, the city looks out onto the magnificent plains of Veracruz. Despite its poverty, the city's white stucco houses have Mediterranean-tiled rooftops, and the white-tiled, always-swept plaza contains Indian stone carvings and wild yellow finches in the trees—even people climbing its steep streets smile between huffs and puffs. Papantla is also one of the few remaining centers of Totonac culture. Conquered by the power-hungry Aztecs around 1450, the Totonac soon took their revenge, helping Cortés crush the Aztec Empire in the 16th century. In modern Papantla, barefoot white-clad *indígenas* share the plaza with tattooed teens. Totonac rituals persist in the flight of the *voladores*, a thrilling acrobatic ceremony once laden with religious meaning, now only performed on weekends for delighted tourists. Papantla makes a good base for exploring **El Tajín**, the awesome ruins of one of the ancient Totonac's major cities, 12km south of the city (see p. 506). So take a deep breath and start up that mile-high street; the view is worth the workout.

◼ **ORIENTATION.** Papantla lies 250km northwest of Veracruz and 21km southeast of Poza Rica along **Rte. 180.** Downtown activity centers around **Parque Téllez,** the central plaza. The white-washed cathedral on Nuñez y Dominguez rises on the plaza's southern side while **Enríquez** borders it on the north. Sloping downhill to the north are **Juárez** (on the east side) and **20 de Noviembre** (on the west side), both perpendicular to Enríquez. **Azueta** starts just west of 20 de Noviembre, also running downhill at a slight angle. **16 de Septiembre** goes up along the right of the cathedral as you face it. To get from the **ADO bus station** to the *centro*, turn left on Juárez out of the station and veer left at the fork. Taxis (8.50 pesos to the *centro*) pass frequently along Juárez. The walk from the station to the *centro* is steep but not long. If you arrive at the **second-class bus station,** turn left outside the station and ascend 20 de Noviembre three blocks to the northwest corner of the plaza.

◼ **PRACTICAL INFORMATION.** Papantla has two **bus stations.** The first-class ADO station, Juárez 207 (tel. 2 02 18), buses to: **Mexico City** (5hr., 9 per day, 116 pesos); **Tuxpan** (1½hr., 4 per day, 28 pesos); **Veracruz** (4hr., 6 per day, 92 pesos); and **Xalapa** (4hr., 8 per day, 74 pesos), but call ahead because buses are often booked before they even arrive in Papantla. The second-class terminal, commonly called Transportes Papantla, 20 de Noviembre 200, heads to the nearby transportation hub of **Poza Rica** (21km northwest of Papantla; 40min., every 20min. 4am-10pm, 6.50 pesos). Pay after boarding. Their ADO station (tel. 2 04 29 or 2 00 85) runs buses to: **Mexico City** (4½hr., every hr., 79 pesos); **Papantla**

(35min., 22 per day, 9 pesos); **Puebla** (5hr., 9 per day, 105 pesos); **Tampico** (4½hr., every hr., 117 pesos); **Tuxpan** (45min., 33 per day, 23 pesos); **Veracruz** (4hr., 17 per day, 102 pesos); and **Xalapa** (5hr., 13 per day, 80 pesos).

The **Chamber of Commerce**, Ramón Castaneda 100 (tel. 2 00 25), sometimes has excellent maps and brochures about Papantla and rudimentary info about El Tajín and the Veracruz state. To get there, follow Lázaro Muñoz (the narrow street running east from the plaza) four blocks downhill and turn right. (Open M-F 9am-5pm, Sa 9am-2pm.) The staff of the **tourist office** (tel. 2 25 35), on 16 de Septiembre across from the side entrance to the cathedral, has maps and tons of information about the Voladores (open M-F 9am-3pm and 6-9pm). A slew of banks on the northern side of the plaza, including **Banamex**, Enríquez 102 (tel. 2 00 01), have 24-hour **ATMs** (open M-F 9am-5pm, Sa 9:30am-2pm; exchanges traveler's checks M-F 9am-2pm). **Clínica IMSS:** (tel. 2 01 94), on 20 de Noviembre at Lázaro Cárdenas, provides emergency medical care. From the ADO station, take a right and walk two blocks to Cárdenas, then turn left; IMSS is half a block up on your right (open 24hr.). **Clínica del Centro Medico:** (tel. 2 00 82), on 16 de Septiembre just down from the tourist office; little to no English spoken (open 24hr.). **Police:** (tel. 2 00 75 or 2 01 50) in the Palacio Municipal (open 24hr.). **Red Cross:** (tel. 2 01 26), on Escobedo off Juárez (some English spoken; open 24hr.). **Farmacia Benavides:** Enríquez 103E (tel. 2 06 36), at the northern end of the plaza (open daily 7:30am-10pm). **Post office:** Azueta 198, 2nd fl. (tel. 2 00 73), with a **MexPost** attached (open M-F 9am-4pm, Sa 9am-noon). **Postal code:** 93400. **Phone code:** 784.

▌ ACCOMMODATIONS. Few lodgings are available in tiny Papantla. A lovely, economical option is to stay at **Hotel Totancapán** (tel. 2 12 24 or 2 12 18), 20 de Noviembre at Olivo, four blocks down from the plaza. Here, hallway murals, crazy colors, funky re-tiling jobs, and large windows make things (unintentionally?) swank and totally cool. Furnishings are simple but complete, and a bedside TV and telephone will put you at ease. Enjoy the most affordable A/C around. (Singles 115 pesos; doubles 140 pesos; triples 160 pesos.) A step up in ritz, **Hotel Tajín**, Núñez y Domínguez 104 (tel. 2 01 21), half a block to the left as you face the cathedral, has a carved stone wall from El Tajín in its lobby. Perched on a hill above the city, the balconies open to panoramic views. Inside the room, amenities include purified water, TV, and phones. Guided horseback tours of the area are available with a week's advance notice (US$30 per hour); call ahead and the staff will help plan tours of the city and surrounding sites (English and some French spoken). Unfortunately, a luxury hotel means luxury prices. (Singles 176 pesos, with A/C 316 pesos; doubles 246 pesos, with A/C 316 pesos; each additional person 50 pesos.)

▐ FOOD. Papantla's few restaurants serve delicacies to tourists looking for regional cuisine. Most eateries stick to beef and pork offerings with just a smattering of seafood. **Restaurant Plaza Pardo** (tel. 2 00 59), on the corner of Enríquez and Juárez, serves up simply out-of-this-world food. Watch wise locals stuff their faces full of soft, delicious *tamales* (5 pesos) and *molotes* (12 pesos), or heavier meat dishes (10-50 pesos). There's a balcony, to boot, that catches a deliciously cool breeze and a superb view of the town: it's an ideal place to watch the *voladores* dance their way to earth. Large, tacky murals and a view of the plaza enliven **Sorrento**, Enríquez 105 (tel. 2 00 67), right next door to Restaurant Plaza Pardo, a popular breakfast hangout. It's no wonder, with these kind of early-morning *menús económicos* (6-14 pesos). Lunchtime *comida corrida* is only 20 pesos, and *antojitos* hover around 10 pesos. (Open daily 7am-11pm.) The town's two markets are situated next to the central plaza: **Mercado Hidalgo,** on 20 de Noviembre off the *zócalo*'s northwest corner, beats **Mercado Juárez,** at Reforma and 16 de Septiembre off the southwest corner of the *zócalo*, hands down.

📷 🎬 **SIGHTS AND ENTERTAINMENT.** Papantla's biggest attractions are the relics of its Totonac heritage. South of the plaza is the **Catedral Señora de la Asunción**, remarkable not so much for its interior, but for the stone mural carved into its northern wall, which measures 50m long and 5m high. Called **Homenaje a la Cultura Totonaca**, the mural was created by Teodoro Cano to honor local Totonac heroes and folklore figures. The plumed serpent Quetzalcóatl is the central focus as its image runs along the full length of the carving. Brimming with history, the mural depicts such wonders as the discovery of corn and eager ballplayers vying for the right of ritualistic death and deification. The mural is truly massive and is the most immediate and impressive structure in Papantla's *centro*.

The cathedral's spacious courtyard commands a view of the *zócalo*. Called the **Plaza de los Voladores**, the courtyard is the site of the ceremony in which *voladores* acrobatically entreat the rain god Tlaloc to water the year's crops. In early June, during the 10-day **Festival of Corpus Christi**, the *voladores* perform as often as three times a day. To get to the festival from the *centro*, take any *pesero* (2.50 pesos) from 16 de Septiembre behind the cathedral and ask for the *feria*, or flag a taxi (15 pesos). During the festival, Papantla itself remains quiet and calm as ever; only a trickle of tourists and small crowds of locals watch the *voladores*. The real action takes place at a fair just outside of town, with artistic expositions, fireworks, traditional dances, and cockfights. Once every 52 years, at the turning of the Totonac century, the festival takes on grandiose proportions.

Papantla's latest effort to enshrine its *voladores* is the **Monumento al Volador**, a gigantic flute-wielding *indígena* statue erected in 1988 atop a hill and visible from all over town. To get to the monument, where you can read explanatory plaques and see all of Papantla, walk up Reforma, the road to the right. Follow the road as it curves left, then make a sharp left before the road starts to slope down and continue uphill. Mountain-climbing picnickers be forewarned: there are no benches and little shade at the monument. There is, however, a small cafe.

NEAR PAPANTLA: EL TAJÍN

The impressive **ruins of El Tajín** only hint at the thriving Totonac civilization that once spread across modern-day northern Veracruz. Named for the Totonac god of thunder, El Tajín served as the political and religious center of the Totonac people. The Totonac people are so named as a Spanish derivative of the Náhuatl *Tutu Nacu*, which means "three hearts" and refers to the three major city centers around which the culture was based; El Tajín is one of these centers. Marked similarities between buildings here and those at Teotihuacán reflect the influence of the Aztec and Maya civilizations. Next to the entrance stands a large

---

LEARNING TO FLY Papantla's *voladores* are renowned for their graceful acrobatics. The performance begins with five elaborately costumed men climbing a stationary pole to a platform at least 28m above the ground. Having consumed courage-enhancing fluids, the *voladores* begin by saluting the four cardinal points: the sun, the wind, the moon, and the earth. Four of the hardy five then wind ropes around the pole, tie them around their waists, and start to "fly"—hanging from the ropes, spinning through the air, and slowly descending to earth. Meanwhile, the fifth man plays a flute and dances on the pole's pin-head. Once off the structure, the *voladores* become *los hombres pájaros* (the bird men). Slowly, they circle the pole 13 times head-down, as the pole turns to lengthen their ropes; this signifies the coming of the rains. Originally, each of the four fliers corresponded to one of the four cardinal directions; positions assumed during descent were related to requests for specific weather conditions. Now, however, the ritual has become more commercial: instead of performing once every 52 years, the *voladores* fly as often as tourists hand over pesos. You can watch the ceremony in Papantla during the festival of Corpus Christi in early June, at El Tajín whenever a crowd of tourists gathers, or in New York or Denmark when the *voladores* go on tour.

pole, the apparatus of the **voladores** (see p. 506). June through August, the *voladores* perform almost hourly; the rest of the year, they descend through the air only on weekends. These daring acrobats—who typically request a 10-peso donation when they are finished—generally perform after a large group has finished touring the ruins. A tiny but useful brochure and map (5 pesos) about El Tajín in English or Spanish can be purchased at the **information desk.** In addition to overpriced plastic carvings, the store adjoining the information desk carries maps and excellent tour guides of Veracruz state, Tuxpan, and Papantla—often better information than is available in the cities themselves.

As you enter the ruins, you will pass the **Museo del Sitio del Tajín.** The museum features original fragments of murals and an eerie, fascinating display filled with sand and ancient skeletons, some with cracked skulls and visible bone injuries—a must-see for the secretly morbid maniac lurking inside you. The meager explanations are in English and Spanish; however, guards will be happy to expand on them, mostly in Spanish.

From the museum, a straight path leads to the ruins. They are not labeled or explained in any way. The best information sources are the blue uniformed "rangers" stationed throughout El Tajín. Totonacs themselves, the rangers may offer to give you an *ad hoc* tour of a certain area; they will eagerly answer any questions, although their English proficiency may be limited. You can also hire a guide from the information desk or tag along with a big tour group.

The **Plaza del Arroyo,** the central rectangular plaza formed by four tiered pyramids, lies just to the left of the gravel road. Each pyramid points toward the northeast at a 20° angle, in a feat of architectural planning maintained in all of the early buildings at this site. The heart of El Tajín is just past the pyramids. Two identical, low-lying, slanted constructions to the left of the observation area form a central ballcourt in which the famous one-on-one game called **pok-ta-pok** (see **Hoop Dreams,** p. 612) was played. Every 52 years, a contest was held between the most valiant ballplayers. The winner gained the honor of being decapitated and sacrificed, putting the modern World Cup to shame. Approximately 17 such courts grace the ruins of Tajín.

Across from the plaza stands an elevated central altar surrounded by two climbable temples. Just left of the altar is a split-level temple that displays a statue of Tajín. This area was known as the **Central Zone** and is notable because of the diverse styles and functions of the buildings. To the northwest stands **La Pirámide de los Nichos,** a fascinating structure with seven levels and a total of 365 niches corresponding to the days of the year. Each niche was once painted in crimson, and blue. The Totonacs kept time in 52-year epochs, during which a single flame was kept continuously burning. At the end of each epoch, the carefully nurtured flame was used to ritually torch many of the settlement's buildings. Each new epoch of rebuilding and regeneration was inaugurated by the lighting of a new flame. Ritual ceremonies are now held annually at the pyramid during the vernal equinox; farmers place seeds in the pyramid's niches and later retrieve them for planting.

Farther north and atop a hill is **Tajín Chico,** accessible either by a series of large stepping stones or an easy-to-ascend staircase off to the west. Whereas Tajín was a public religious and social center, archaeologists hypothesize that Tajín Chico was where the ruling class and political elite actually lived. This is one of the less-excavated areas and is bordered by "no access" signs where more structures may be hidden. However, park officials don't mind if visitors scamper up the higher buildings to get a view of the site and surrounding hills or climb through the tunnel at the back end of the structures. East of Tajín Chico, down the hill and around the curve in the gravel road, is the **Great Xicalcoliuhqui,** a tremendous recreational and religious area that is still being unearthed.

Getting There: El Tajín is accessible via *pesero* from the bus stop in Papantla behind Hotel Tajín on Calle 16 de Septiembre. Buses (every 15min. 5am-8pm, 5.50 pesos) going to Poza Rica pull into Tajín. Ask the man with the clipboard recording the buses for "Tajín", and he'll make sure you get on the right one.

Your bus will first pass through El Chote and stop at the entrance to El Tajín, marked by a stone mural. To return to Papantla, catch a "Papantla" bus just outside the museum (last bus leaves at 5pm, 5.50 pesos), or walk down the access road to the main road and cross the road to the bus stop to catch a *pesero* running back to El Chote (3.50 pesos). From El Chote, you can catch one of the many buses leaving for nearby Papantla (2 pesos). (Ruins open daily. Admission for museum and ruins 25 pesos. Su free with valid student ID.)

VERACRUZ

The oldest port city in the Americas, Veracruz (pop. 327,500) possesses the nearly untranslatable qualities of *sabor*, rich and alluring flavor; and *ambiente*, unique and enchanting atmosphere. Amid a slew of new construction projects, the sounds of *bamba* and *marimba* music play into the warm Gulf nights as tourists and citizens alike sip the city's delicious *café con leche* by day and fall sway to a seductive beat as darkness falls. Since Cortés landed in "La Rica Villa de la Vera Cruz" in 1519, Veracruz has been Mexico's port to the outside world. Pirates long frequented the steamy costal mecca; after colonial contact, the city prospered as the only port in New Spain officially permitted to trade with the mother country. It was here that Juárez proclaimed the laws of the Reforma and here that he staged the reconquest of Mexico from the Hapsburg Emperor Maximilian. Twice the city was occupied by American troops.

Today, Veracuz's streets continue to fill with sailors—as well as tourists—from around the world. Modern Veracruz sprawls along Mexico's Gulf coast, merging with **Boca del Río** (pop. 143,800), the prosperous site of the best beaches, chic discos, and expensive hotels. Touristy beach glitz is undercut by the numerous oil rigs and barges that fill the harbor. A hot, humid urban sprawl dripping with sweat into the night, the twin cities are buffeted by strong winds called *nortes*, a display of nature's force that some people find disagreeable and others spectacular.

■ ORIENTATION

Sprawling along the coast in a series of docks, harbors, and boardwalks, Veracruz is located on the southwest corner of the Gulf of Mexico, 104km south of Xalapa and 424km west of Mexico City. The town's historic *centro*, with its fabulous *zócalo*, fish market, and tree-lined **Plaza de la Republica** (home to the monumental post office and train station) is located at the entry to the main harbor. Streets in the *centro* are laid out in a grid defined by the two harborside walkways—the **Malecon** which runs from the *zócalo* along a dock jutting out into the harbor, and its perpendicular counterpart, **Camacho,** which runs parallel to the coastline, heading south. **Av. Independencia,** the main drag, also runs parallel to the harbor, piercing the heart of the *centro* at the *zócalo* and ending at **Parque Zamora,** a major connection point for inter-city buses.

From Parque Zamora, **Díaz Míron** connects the *centro* to the **Central de Autobuses** to the south, which houses all of the city's major bus lines. To get to the *centro* from the bus station, get on a "Diaz Miron" bus headed north to Parque Zamora (2.50 pesos). Some buses run all the way to the *zócalo*, and others stop at the park, a short seven blocks south of the *zócalo* on Independencia.

Along the south coast, Veracruz merges with the glam suburb **Boca del Rio.** Home to the best discos, the all-night restaurants, and a slightly better coastline, it is easily reached by the "Boca de Rio" buses which leave from **Zaragoza,** one block towards the bay from the *zócalo* (3 pesos). Av. Camacho, the road that connects the two centers, is packed with eateries, hotels, trinket vendors, and typical boardwalk fare. **Buses** become less frequent as the night wears on, and eventually it becomes easier and safer to take taxis back to the *centro*.

VERACRUZ

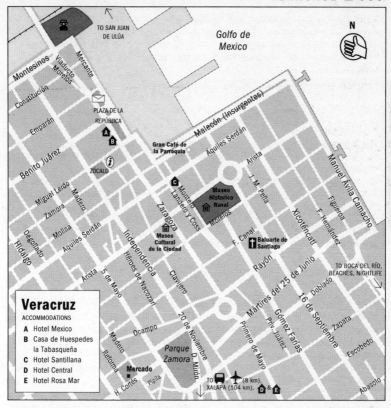

Veracruz

ACCOMMODATIONS

A Hotel Mexico
B Casa de Huespedes
   la Tabasqueña
C Hotel Santillana
D Hotel Central
E Hotel Rosa Mar

🛈 PRACTICAL INFORMATION

TRANSPORTATION

Airport: (tel. 34 37 74) 8km south of downtown Veracruz on Rte. 150. **Aeroméxico** (tel. 35 01 42) and **Mexicana** (tel. 32 22 42, at airport 38 00 08) are both represented by **Viajes Carmi**, Independencia 837 (tel. 31 27 23), north of the *zócalo*. Open M-F 9am-1:30pm and 3:30-7:30pm, Sa 9am-1pm.

Buses: Central de Autobuses, Díaz Mirón 1698. ADO (tel. 37 57 88), with 1st-class service to: **Cancún** (21hr., 2:30 and 10:35pm, 504 pesos); **Catemaco** (3hr., 6 per day, 61 pesos); **Mexico City** (5½hr., 16 per day, 181 pesos); and **Xalapa** (1¾hr., every 30min. 6am-11pm, 43 pesos). Cristóbal Colón (tel. 37 57 88) has 1st-class service direct to **Oaxaca** (6½hr., 11pm, 243 pesos) and **Tuxtla Gutiérrez** (12hr., 7pm, 236 pesos). Cuenca (tel. 34 54 05) sends 2nd-class buses to **Oaxaca** (6hr., 6:30am and 8pm, 121 pesos) and **Tuxtepec** (3hr., every hr. 5am-8pm, 51 pesos). AU (tel. 37 57 32; buses leave from La Fragua, 1 block behind ADO station) offers 2nd-class service to: **Córdoba** (1½hr., 16 per day, all day 6am-12:30am, 47 pesos); **Mexico City** (6hr.; 6am-4pm, 9, 11pm, midnight, and 1am; 110 pesos); **Orizaba** (2½hr., 16 per day 6am-12:30am, 40 pesos); **Puebla** (4½hr.; 2, 8, 10:15am, and 12:30pm; 83 pesos); and **Xalapa** (1¾hr.; every hr. 6am-4pm and 9pm-1am; 38 pesos).

TOURIST AND FINANCIAL SERVICES

Tourist Office: (tel. 32 19 99) on the right side of the Palacio Municipal facing from the *zócalo*. Helpful staff speaks some English and hands out maps and brochures. Open M-Sa 9am-9pm, Su 9am-3pm.

Currency Exchange: There are a slew of banks on the corner of Juárez and Independencia, 1 block from the *zócalo*. **Banamex** (tel. 9 13 80) has 4 24hr. **ATMs.** Open M-F 9am-5pm, Sa 9am-2pm. **Bital** (tel. 32 50 36) also has a 24hr. **ATM.** Open M-Sa 8am-7pm. **Agencia de Divisas Greco** (tel. 32 56 58), on Morelos next to Hotel México offers 24hr. service.

American Express: Camacho 221 (tel. 31 46 36), inside Viajes Olymar, across from Villa del Mar beach. "Villa del Mar" bus stops behind the tourist office on Zaragoza. Open M-F 9am-1:30pm and 4-6:30pm, Sa 9am-noon.

LOCAL SERVICES

Markets: Mercado Hidalgo, on the corner of Cortés and Madero, 1 block from Parque Zamora away from the Gulf, sells fruit, vegetables, *piñatas*, seafood, flowers, meat, you name it. Open daily 8am-6pm.

Supermarket: El Alba (tel. 32 24 24), M. Lerdo between Independencia and Av. 5 de Mayo, 1 block from the *zócalo*. Open M-Sa 9am-2:30pm and 5-9pm.

Laundry: Lavandería Ultra-Clean, Serdán 789 (tel. 32 94 23), between Madero and Av. 5 de Mayo. Same day service, 5 pesos per kg. Open M-Sa 9am-7pm.

EMERGENCY AND COMMUNICATIONS

Emergency: dial 060

Police: (tel. 38 06 64 or 38 06 93) at Sur Zamora.

Red Cross: (tel. 37 55 00) on Díaz Mirón between Orizaba and Pérez Abascal, 1 block south of the Central de Autobuses. No English spoken. Open 24hr. with ambulance.

Pharmacy: Farmacia del Ahorro (tel. 37 35 25) on Paseo del Malecón at Gómez Farías 2 blocks from the *zócalo*. Open daily 7am-midnight.

Hospital: IMSS, Díaz Mirón 61 (tel. 22 19 20). **Sanitario Español,** Av. 16 de Septiembre 955 (tel. 32 00 21), has a good reputation for treating foreigners.

Post Office: Plaza de la República 213 (tel. 32 20 38). Open M-F 8am-8pm, Sa 9am-1pm. **Postal Code:** 91700.

Fax: Telecomm (tel. 32 25 08), on Plaza de la República, next to the post office. Open M-F 8am-7pm, Sa 9am-5pm, Su 9am-noon. **Telegrams** and **Western Union** service too.

Internet Access: Netchatboys, Lerdo 369, between Madero and Av. 5 de Mayo, 1½ blocks from the *zócalo*. 12 pesos per hr. Open M-F 9am-9pm, Sa-Su noon-8pm. **Stationet Internet Café,** Av. 5 de Mayo between Lerdo and Molina. 12 pesos per hr. Open M-F 9am-10:30pm, Sa 10am-10pm, Su 11am-8pm. **Webcafé,** Rayon 579A, is an easy step from Parque Zamora. 12 pesos per hr.; with student ID, 10 pesos. Open M-Sa 9:30am-9pm.

Telephones: LADATELs on the *zócalo* and by the Palacio Municipal and the cathedral.

Phone Code: 29.

■ ACCOMMODATIONS

Veracruz has three peak seasons: *Carnaval* (the weeks before Ash Wednesday), *Semana Santa* (the week before Easter), and summer (July and August). The city is saturated with hotels, but many fill up well in advance during the first two peak periods, and some raise their rates. Rooms with ceiling fans or large windows are not so pricey, but you'll have to pay more for the luxury of rooms with A/C and they're often needed in this steamy city.

NEAR THE CENTRO. Budget hotels cluster on **Aquilés Serdán,** two blocks over from the *zócalo*. The area, full of revelers all night every night, is fun, loud, and relatively safe.

 Hotel México, Morelos 343 (tel. 32 43 60), across the street from the Aduanos building in a superb location. The hotel catches breezes coming off the harbor. The bright, ships-cabin rooms are sure to meet a white glove inspection and include fans and TVs. Singles 90-110 pesos, doubles 130-150 pesos.

Casa de Huespedes La Tabasqueña, Morelos 325. Poorly ventilated rooms could be cleaner, but the fans tend to keep it pretty cool and fend off the mildewy smell. Singles 70 pesos, doubles 140 pesos, triples 190 pesos.

Hotel Santillana, Landero y Cross 208 (tel. 32 31 16), at Dehesa. Rooms with fans, TV, phone, wall-to-wall carpeting, and small bathrooms surround a purple-green courtyard emanating a certain garish charm. Single beds 70 pesos, double beds 170 pesos.

Hotel Central, Díaz Mirón 1612 (tel. 32 22 22), next to the ADO station. When the architects of Tomorrowland were done in Orlando, they designed this modern-looking hotel, complete with a faux-marble lobby. Large rooms and bathrooms have TVs and phones, and some even have balconies. Double bed 150 pesos, with A/C 210 pesos; 2 double beds 200 pesos, with A/C 270 pesos.

Hotel Rosa Mar, La Fragua 1100 (tel. 37 07 47), behind the ADO station. On a forgettable strip of aging storefronts, Rosa valiantly tries to remain a clean, wholesome establishment convenient for catching morning buses. Double beds 140 pesos, with A/C 170 pesos; 2 double beds 170 pesos, with A/C 200 pesos.

FOOD

If the smell of seafood from the docks mixed with the aroma of grinding coffee from the Gran Parroquia compiles 80% of Veracruz's famous *sabor*, the other fraction surely resides in the little restraunts surrounding the fish markets on **Landero y Cross.** With enough kitschy decor to occupy an entire evening's converstaion, these are the places to dig into mountains of fish, shrimp, octopus, and crab hauled out of the Gulf on a daily basis. Steer clear of raw fish dishes but don't leave town without ordering *huachinango a la Veracruzana*—red snapper decked out in olives, capers, onions, and olive oil.

Gran Café de la Parroquia, Gómez Farías 34 (tel. 32 35 84), at Malecón. One of Veracruz's greatest traditions—the entire town always seems to be here and every president since 1810 has joined the diners for the famous *café con leche.* Sit back to people-watch, eavesdrop, and enjoy one yourself. After your glass is half filled with syrupy coffee, clink your spoon against your glass to have it completed with steaming milk (12 pesos). They also serve other great entrees (22-35 pesos). Open daily 6am-1am.

El Cochinito de Oro, Zaragoza 190 (tel. 32 36 77), on the corner of Serdán. A great place to catch both cheap seafood and Veracruzano nightlife—there's a reason El Cochinito has been filled with locals for the last 50 years. The memorabilia scattered over the interior will entertain as you wait for excellent food. *Fillete de pescado,* and fish or shrimp stews all hover around 30 pesos. Open daily 7am-5pm.

Mariscos Tano, Molina 20 (tel. 31 50 50), is a good place for anyone with limited Spanish proficiency. Can't read the menu? Just point to what you want to eat—it'll be stuffed and hanging from the cluttered ceiling. The *mariscos* (shellfish) are great and the photo-history of *Carnaval* on the back wall is museum quality. Open daily 9am-10pm.

Restaurant Familiar Tiburón, Landero y Cross 167 at Serdán. Another civic institution, the interior of "the shark" is a shrine to the veracruzano-Cuban connection. House specialties include anything seafood: *empanadas* (3 for 20 pesos); and *miches al mojo de ajo,* shrimp guaranteed to ward off the evil eye and other *brujas.* Open daily 7am-9pm.

SIGHTS

Veracruz brings new meaning to the term "port of entry." When it wasn't being blasted by bullets or mobbed by mosquitos, the city had to contend with the fierce north wind—both its curse and the reason Veracruz rose to importance as a center for Transatlantic trade. The sightseer's Veracruz is very much like a real-life, large scale "Pirates of the Caribbean," complete with cannon ball scarred fortresses, grand colonial edifices, and long-buried treasure. Be sure to hit the **Castillo de San Juan de Ulúa** and the **Museo Historical Naval**—knowing the gory history makes the nightime *marimba* all the sweeter.

CASTILLO DE SAN JUAN DE ULÚA

Tel: 38 51 51. *Location:* To reach the fort, take a "San Juan de Ulúa" bus (2.10 pesos) in front of the Aduana building in the Plaza de la Repúblic. Taxis should charge around 25 pesos. *Hours:* Tu-Su 9am-4:30pm. *Admission:* 20 pesos, with videocamera 30 pesos; Su free. Guided tours 30 pesos in Spanish and more in English; they are well worth the money.

The Castillo, Veracruz's most important historic site, rests on a fingertip of land that juts into the harbor. Spaniards first arrived at this point on the saint's day of San Juan; "Ulúa" was the greeting the native Totonacs offered the sailors as they disembarked. Construction, using coral as bricks, began in 1582 as part of the system of fortifications built around the Spanish Caribbean to protect the trade fleet and treasure from pirates. In the 400 years that the fort has stood, it has served many purposes, including that of a high-security prison for illustrious and exiled political prisoners—big-name prisoners include Mexican presidents Benito Juárez and Porfirio Díaz. Despite these famous names, San Juan's best-known prisoner was the hero **Chucho el Roto**, a Robin Hoodesque character who stole from the rich and gave to the poor. Chucho's legend has grown to mythic proportions, as he was believed to have escaped from San Juan not once, but thrice.

Enter the site through the arched entrance and head for the last room on the right. As you enter, there are two openings in the wall to the left. The hole closer to the grass leads to some stairs and a dim, dank room that was known as *El Purgatorio* (Purgatory). The other room contains *El Inferno* (Hell), the cell without windows, surrounded by walls 9m thick, where men lost their sense of time and their sanity. Another set of stairs leads to *La Gloria* (Heaven), so named because it was one of the few cells in the Castillo with a window. To maintain your sanity, walk toward the row of 14 arches that hold a small museum. Through the arches, you can take in a panoramic view of the city and of the hungry angelfish nibbling for crackers.

Most of the other rooms in the Castillo are *bodegas*, or storage rooms, but are notable for their stalagmite formations which were 400 years in the making. Also interesting is the yellow house-like building in the center of the courtyard. This **Presidential Palace** served as Porfirio Díaz's home when he was in exile here.

MUSEO HISTÓRICO NAVAL. This museum, and its peppy A/C, is a good place to visit. Packed with entertaining dioramas of man's seafaring history, and an excellent display on Veracruz's naval successes and shortcomings (guaranteed to set you straight on the meaning of all those invasions), the expansive museum navigates Mexico's rich maritime past with military-style precision. On the old grounds of the *Escuela Militar* (Naval School), a short walk from the *zócalo*. (Walk 3 blocks down Independencia and turn left on Arista for 2 blocks; the Naval School is on your right; occupying the entire block bordered by Av. 16 de Septiembre, Arista, Montero, and Morales. Open Tu-Su 9am-5pm. Free.)

BALUARTE DE SANTAIGO. This 17th-century bulwark protected inhabitants from swashbuckling pirates like Sir Francis Drake and it is all that remains of the old city wall that once enclosed the area between the train station and Parque Zamora. The museum inside displays a collection of pre-Hispanic gold ornaments called *Las Joyas del Pescador* since they were rescued from the ocean by a lucky octopus fisherman. (Tel. 31 10 59. On Canal between Av. 16 de Septiembre and Gómez Farías 1 block down from the Naval School. Open Tu-Sa 10am-4:30pm. Admission 14 pesos; Su free.)

MUSEO CULTURAL DE LA CIUDAD. In this museum, paintings, models, dioramas, and Spanish explanations tell the history of the city from pre-Hispanic times to the present. The most interesting attraction is a relic from the building's days as an orphanage. In the back stairwell, a stained-glass window depicts the legend of Talinmasca, an orphan whose transgressions brought thunder, lighting, and the fierce autumn winds called *nortes* to the area. (Zaragoza 397. Down Canal away from the water, and right on Zaragoza. Tel. 31 84 10. Open Tu-Su 9am-4pm. Free.)

CASA DE SALVADOR DÍAZ MIRÓN. A famous *veracruzano* poet, Díaz Mirón occupied the house during the last seven years of his life (from 1921-1928), and the people here say that they have heard his ghost pacing in the upper chambers of the house. Today it serves as a literary center for Veracruz. Recently renovated, the foyer holds a cafe and the rear houses a literary forum. Upstairs you'll find a small museum that replicates what the house looked like while occupied by Mirón. *(Tel. 32 31 31, ext. 146. On Zaragoza, between Morelos and Arista. Open M-Sa 9am-8pm. Free.)*

◖ SAND AND SUNSHINE

The beaches in Veracruz are far from world-class. The general rule is that the farther from the city, the nicer the beach, although it's practically impossible to escape the oil barges and tugboats in the distance. **Playa Villa del Mar** is a fairly pleasant hour-long walk from the *zócalo* along the waterfront on Camache; it is also accessible via one of the frequent "Villa del Mar" or "Boca del Río" buses (3 pesos) that stop on Zaragoza behind the tourist office.

Few people swim at Villa del Mar. Restaurants in huts have set up camp along the boardwalk, and their tables are only meters from the surf, making beachside frolicking almost impossible. However, the restaurant huts and bars create a lively atmosphere and, at night, when Camacho is lit up, the Playa Villa del Mar area is even more festive. The **Acuario de Veracruz** is a popular beachside attraction for local families. This Aquarium is located in the Centro Comercíal Plaza Acuario, a shopping mall on the left when facing the ocean at Villa del Mar. It features fish, sharks, and turtles native to the Gulf. Try to dodge the bird droppings that descend from the toucans flying above your head near the entrance. (Tel. 32 79 84. Open Su-Th 10am-7pm, F-Sa 10am-7:30pm. Admission 20 pesos, children 10 pesos.) Farther on Blvd. Camacho away from downtown Veracruz, luxury homes and pricey resorts hog the waterfront. A peaceful stretch of sand is **Costa de Oro** (Gold Coast), between the orange-pinkish hotels Fiesta Americana and Torremar.

The best beach in the Veracruz area (although that's not saying much) is **Playa Mocambo,** next to the Hotel Torremar, in the neighboring city of Boca del Río. Take a "Boca del Río" bus from Zaragoza and Serdán (30min., 2.10 pesos) and get off at Plaza de Las Americas. From there, cross the street to the Hotel Torremar; the beach is on the other side. At the bottom, veer left to head for the beach or go straight into the **Balneario Mocambo,** which has a clean, Olympic-sized public pool surrounded by artificial palm trees, changing rooms, and a poolside bar-restaurant (Tel. 21 02 88. Open daily 10am-8pm. Admission 18 pesos, children 10 pesos.) Those whose beach experience is defined by attitude rather than turquoise water will find plenty of laid-back lounging in the residential area down the coast from the hotel. The sand is peaceful and the neighborhood barbecues doubling as street restaurants are a great place to meet locals and negotiate cheap, informal lodging. Though the area is very friendly, it is also poor, keep an eye on your bag. The bus back to town can be caught at the nearby open-air market (on the side of the road back to town) or back at the top of Balneario Mocambo's driveway.

♫ ENTERTAINMENT AND SEASONAL EVENTS

In the evening, the hymns of the cathedral spilling out into the *zócalo* yield to the sexy rhythms of *marimbas*. Vendors spread out their wares on the paths, and the bars and restaurants are jam-packed with merry drinkers and traveling *mariachi* bands. On weekend nights some of the world's hottest senior citizens strut to the tropical tunes on the civic dance floor. Apart from spontaneous singing in the *zócalo*, most action takes place along **Av. Camacho,** the stretch of road along the coast that connects Veracruz and Boca del Río. A good landmark for nightlife is the purple high-rise Hotel Lois; just before the violet beacon, Ruiz Cortínes branches off Camacho—a good place to get off the bus.

Café Andrade (tel. 32 82 24), on Blvd. Camacho at the corner of Callejón and Av. 12 de Octubre, across the street from the Plaza Acuario and the Playa Villa del Mar. Beautiful people of all ages flock to the cool outdoor patio and enjoy 8 peso coffee while the cafe sells beans from nearby Coatepec. Open daily 8am-midnight.

Ocean, Ruíz Cortínes 8 (tel. 22 03 55), is the people's nightclub—popular with just about everyone, drawing huge, diverse crowds to its dance floor. Music can be tiresomely typical, but the patrons' upbeat attitudes make up for it. Make table reservations by phone for the night you want to party. Cover 25-30 pesos. Open Th-Sa 10pm-5am.

Master Club Billar, Blvd. Camacho 4 (tel. 37 67 48), is one of the friendliest, safest poolhouses you've ever seen, with TV, music, bar, A/C, and tables for dominoes or cards. Pool 28 pesos per hr. Open daily 1pm-2am.

Carlos 'n' Charlie's, Blvd. Camacho 26 (tel. 22 29 10), has been bestowed on Veracruz by Señor Frog's, the tourist-ridden joint that just keeps on giving. The restaurant regularly fills to the point of immobility—but that's okay, since everyone sits, drinks, and sings along merrily with the *salsa* music. Open Su-Th 9am-midnight, F-Sa 9am-2am.

If dancing to *salsa* music is more your style, mix with the locals and head to **El Palacio de la Salsa,** Calle 12, # 3, four blocks down Camacho from the Cortínes intersection, one block right on Calle Medico Militar and another block left on Calle 12 (cover 20 pesos; open Th-Sa 10pm-6am). A notch above all in style and popularity, is the monolithic stone **Zoo,** (tel. 21 79 35), at Camacho on the corner of Calle Medica Militar. Here, trend setters blow air kisses, scrutinize each other's haute couture, and dance all night. (Cover 30 pesos; Open F-Sa 10pm-6am.) For English-language films, check out **Plaza Cinema,** Arista 708 (tel. 31 37 87), or **Cinema Gemelos Veracruz,** Díaz Mirón 941 (tel. 32 59 70), between Iturbide and Mina (17-20 pesos).

Every December 31 at midnight, *veracruzano* families dress in their Sunday best and fill Blvd. Camacho, looking east to the Gulf to witness the first sunrise of the year. With that auspicious start, a year of celebrations begins. The climax comes early, in late February or early March, just before Ash Wednesday. **Carnaval** literally invades the *zócalo* and usurps the streets with parades, expositions, dance performances, and music. With the requisite ceremonies and parades, a king and queen are crowned. The **Consejo Directivo del Carnaval** (tel. 32 31 31 ext. 149 172) is devoted to organizing the week-and-a-half-long event. During *carnaval* advance reservations are necessary.

NEAR VERACRUZ: ZEMPOALA RUINS

The ruins at **Zempoala** (sometimes spelled **Cempoala**), one of the most impressive archaeological sites in the state, lie 40km north of Veracruz, off Rte. 180. Zempoala was one of the larger southern Totonac cities, part of a federation that covered much of Veracruz in pre-Hispanic times. In 1469, the Aztecs subdued Zempoala and forced the Totonacs to join their federation. Cortés arrived in 1519, attracted to the glitter of the seashells in the stucco used to build the structures (thinking, of course, that they were gold). The Totonacs were happy to lend Cortés soldiers for his campaign against Moctezuma at Tenochtitlán in 1521. *(Open daily 9am-4:30pm; 15 pesos; Su free.)*

Once a city of 30,000 people, the site now consists of stone structures surrounding a grassy field next to present day Zempoala. A museum to your left as you enter displays a small collection of pottery and figurines unearthed here. The structure closest to the entrance is the **Temple of Death.** Continuing to the left, you will see three **pyramids.** Climbing the narrow stairs is forbidden, just like in the old days, when only priests and sacrificial victims were allowed to enter the altars that topped the temples. The pyramid on the left is dedicated to Tlaloc (god of rain), the one on the right to the moon, and the one in the center, decorated with circular stone receptacles for the hearts of people sacrificed in religious offerings, to the sun. Turning to the right, you will encounter the largest structure on the site, the

IF IT'S GOOD ENOUGH FOR IKE... Even if he's sitting at the right cafe, a guy can't claim to really know Veracruz until he's worn the traditional white shirt called a *guayabera*. The name comes from the word *guayaba*, Spanish for "guava." Cuban guava collectors got tired of shimmying up and down the tree countless times, so they designed a shirt with four pockets to expedite the task. From there, the *guayabera* shirt passed to Panama and then Mexico, where Carlos Cab Arrazate added the thin pleats that form vertical stripes connecting the pockets. His grandson continues the family business, **Guayaberas Finas,** Zaragoza 233 (tel. 31 84 27), between Arista and Serdán, in Veracruz city. Everyone who's anyone has bought one of their high-quality, hot-weather shirts—check out Dwight Eisenhower's note of appreciation on the store's wall. Fashion tip: shirts are not meant to be tucked in. *(Open M-F 9:30am-8pm, Sa 9:30am-7pm, Su 10am-4pm.)*

Templo Mayor. When Cortés arrived, the Spaniards erected an altar to the Virgin on top of the temple, literally imposing Catholicism on the Totonacs. In front of the Templo Mayor is the **throne** where the king sat to observe the sacrifices that took place on the platform next to him. The throne also faces the temple known as **Las Chimeneas.** Moving toward the entrance of the site, you will see a fenced-in structure. For the Totonacs, this piece played a central role in the "New Five Ceremony," a five-day fast that took place when a "century" of the ritual calendar ended every 52 years. Every spring Equinox, people still come to the circle to expel negative energy and absorb positive energy.

Getting There: From the 2nd-class bus station on La Fragua, in Veracruz, **Autobuses TRV** sends buses to **Cardel** (45min., 10 pesos), where you can take a bus to Zempoala (15min., 5 pesos). Ask the driver to let you out at **las ruinas,** at the intersection of Av. Prof. José Ruíz and Troncoso Norte. If driving from Veracruz, follow Rte. 180 past Cardel, take the Zempoala city turn-off, and proceed until an obscured "Zona Arqueológica" sign appears on the right (about 1km before town). To get back, stand across the street from where you were dropped off and hail a passing "Cardel" bus (5 pesos). From Cardel, catch a bus to Veracruz (45min.; every 10min. midnight-8pm, every 15min. 8-10pm; 10 pesos).

LA ANTIGUA

If it's difficult to picture Cortés' 16th-century landing in the touristy, trinkety streets of Veracruz, the town of Antigua leaves little to the imagination. Though hardly tourist and trinket-free, the town watches visitors come and go with a complacency akin to that given Cortés, who passed by several times and once (according to local lore) briefly took up residence in the 16th century Andalucian-style home now inhabited by gnarly trees and a reputable *taquería*. It's easy to see why he might have wanted to live here. Located at the mouth of the river system that gave Cortés his "in" to the Aztec empire to the west, the riverside fishing village is refreshingly lush, low-key, and friendly.

■ ORIENTATION AND PRACTICAL INFORMATION. Antigua is most cheaply and easily reached by the 2nd-class buses that leave frequently from the **Central** in Veracruz, around the back of the AV Station (8.50 pesos one way). Usually a stop on the way to some place else, be sure to tell your driver you want to get off at La Antigua and keep a vigilant eye out for your stop, marked by a tollbooth and a small sign. After your *bajada*, cross the road and head up the dirt street on the other side which, after passing lots of idyllic, pastoral scenery, becomes the town's main drag. To get back, walk back down the road and climb on the first form of public transportation headed back to Veracruz. Buses pass frequently from dawn to 9pm. You can also catch a bus from the TRV station in town, but it probably involves more waiting and formality than it's worth. In terms of services, Antigua offers little more than **LADATEL** phones posted around town. Bring essentials with you because you're not going to find them here.

ACCOMMODATIONS AND FOOD. If you feel like sticking around town, nighttime river views and clean, quiet rooms can be had at **Hotel La Malinda,** back down the road from the suspension bridge. (1 person 90 pesos; 2 people 150 pesos). Though just about every household in town will cook you a seafood dinner, La Antigua makes lots of its money through the restaurants. For a touristy scene with a river view and regional dances, **Las Delicias Marinas** have fairly standard prices for good seafood. Shrimp is the specialty, and the famous dishes go for 36-59 pesos. (Open daily 10am-8pm.) Cheaper eats can be found away from the river, back down the road into town.

SIGHTS. Unlabeled streets and the jungle's tendency to interrupt things which are grid-like and orderly makes finding the town's **10th-century buildings** rather like a scavenger hunt. People have different opinions about what the **ruins** on the right as you enter were used for. Overgrown with impressive vines and squid-like trees, the aesthetic effect makes the history a moot point. Crossing the street and taking the perpendicular road branching left of the main road, you'll come to the **Parroquia de Cristo del Buen Viaje** which dates from the mid-17th century, and whose beautifully simple, white interior contains two 16th-century baptismal fonts carved by early *indígena* converts. Passing the *zócalo* and continuing down the street, the famous **Casa de Cortés** is a little back from the road on the left and comes complete with a cannon brought over from Spain by the man himself. A little farther down the street, the monster tree that divides the road holds legendary status as the site where Cortés first donned his arms for his fateful 1519 expedition. Built in 1523, the **Edificio del Cabildo** was the 1st official office of the Spanish government in Mexico. The most beautiful of the buildings is the **Emerito del Rosario.** Finished in 1524, the building features exquisite stations of the cross rendered in Talvera tile. To find these buildings, it's often best to ask locals to point the way.

The best thing to do in La Antigua after watching chickens scuttle in and out of the super-old buildings is to eat the *mariscos* (shellfish) and take a *lancha* ride to see where they come from. After experiencing the novelty of the long **suspension bridge** that spans the Río Antigua, head down towards the deserted beaches at the river's mouth, an hour downstream by *lancha*. If there are enough people, *colectivos* to the *playa* are 25 pesos per person. For 120 pesos, an *especial* will drop you off and pick you up again at a pre-arranged time but it's easier to find *colectivos* for shorter *lancha* tours. Though fishermen repairing their nets and impenetrable vegetation is most of what there is to see, the cooling ride is worth the money.

CATEMACO

In most parts of the world, Catemaco and its surrounding would be covered with rangers, regulations, and well-marked trails. In Mexico, the only people to disturb your pastoral reverie are the *lanchistas*, who stumble over each other for the opportunity to ferry tourists around the town's blue lagoon. *Colectivos* quickly dispel any touristy preconception of the area by whisking visitors to a wilderness of cattle paths and fishing villages that may leave you wondering if you are still on the same planet and in the same millennium as you were when they you left the former *pirata* port. The **Laguna Catemaco** and its islands are often compared to Switzerland, and the intense green of the surrounding foliage does suggest a degree of alpine seclusion. The pulse quickens during *Semana Santa* and the week of the town's patron, Saint Carmen, when hotels fill with gringos and urbanites from the D.F., as they come to enjoy the regional food and to snoop around for the town's much hyped *brujeria* (witchcraft). The carnival atmosphere is entertaining, though, and easily escaped by a trip to the coast or the surrounding hills.

ORIENTATION AND PRACTICAL INFORMATION. Catemaco lies along **Rte. 180** and is a frequent stop for both first- and second-class buses. Streets are poorly marked, but the *basílica* on the *zócalo* is usually visible. From the **Autotransportes**

Los Tuxtlas (second class), turn right and follow the curve of the road, past the "Bienvenidos a Catemaco" arches. Follow a straight path for 10 to 15 minutes until you arrive at the spires of the *basílica*, which awaits at the corner of **Boettinger** and **Madero**. To the left, **Carranza** runs past the Palacio Municipal. Straight ahead, the road becomes **Aldama**. One block downhill to the right is **Playa** and then **Malecón,** which follows the curves of the beach. The **ADO** (first-class) station is on the Malecón, along the waterfront. To get to the church from this station, take a right onto the street and follow it until you reach Hotel Julita several blocks down and then take a right.

First-class ADO **buses** (tel. 3 08 42) leave for: **Mexico City** (9hr., 10pm, 241 pesos); **Puebla** (6hr., 10pm, 187 pesos); **Veracruz** (3hr., six per day 5:30am-6pm, 61 pesos); and **Xalapa** (3hr., 4 per day 6:15am-4pm, 103 pesos). AU (tel. 3 07 77) rolls to: **Mexico City** (9hr., 11:30am and 9pm, 216 pesos); and **Veracruz** (20min., 11:30am and 9:15pm, 54 pesos). Autotransportes Los Tuxtlas rambles to: **San Andrés** all day (20min., every 10min., 4 pesos) as well as most other regional destinations. **Currency exchange: Bancomer** (tel. 3 03 17), across Aldama from the *basílica*. Unfortunately, it operates on a very limited schedule. (Open Tu-Th 9am-1:30pm.) **Market:** on Madero before the *zócalo* (open daily 6am-8pm). **Police:** (tel. 3 00 55) are in the Palacio Municipal on the *zócalo*. **Farmacia Nuestra Señora del Carmen:** (tel. 3 00 91) is at the corner of Carranza and Boettinger (open daily 7am-9pm). **Centro de Salud** (tel. 3 02 47), on Carranza, in a white building with a blue roof, three blocks up from the *zócalo* on the left. Some English is spoken. Open 24hr. **Post office:** on Mantilla, between the lake and Hotel Los Arcos (open M-F 9am-4pm). **Postal code:** 95870. **Internet access: PC Center,** Calle Matamoros 3 (tel. 3 01 70; www.gorsa.net.mx) in a pink building five blocks up from the *zócalo* on the right (open M-Sa 9am-9pm). **LADATELs** line the *zócalo*, and long-distance **casetas** can be found on the right-hand side of the entrance to the Palacio. **Phone code:** 294.

▛▟ ACCOMMODATIONS AND FOOD. Most hotels cluster around the *zócalo* and the waterfront. Hotels fill up during Christmas, *Semana Santa,* and most of July. During these times, prices usually go up by 10-20 pesos. Unfortunately, it is not advisable to camp on the beaches, since crime has been a problem. The **Hotel Julita,** Playa 10 (tel. 3 00 08), one block downhill from the *zócalo* is a great deal, blessed with a kindly owner, an unbeatable location and large rooms with fans, but no hot water. (Singles 50 pesos, doubles 100 pesos). **Hotel Acuario** (tel. 3 04 18), at Boettinger and Carranza, across from the Palacio, provides large, relatively clean rooms with 70s curtains, and some with balconies. (Singles 70 pesos; doubles 110 pesos.)

When choosing a waterfront restaurant, pay attention primarily to the view of the lake, as menus vary little. *Mojarra* and *topote* are two types of fish native to the lagoon, as are *tegogolos,* the famous Catemaco sea snails. *Mojarra* is prepared in a variety of ways, while the bite-sized *topote* is fried up whole and heaped with *tamales.* The best *mojarra* in town can be had at **Los Sauces** (tel. 3 05 48), a modest and modestly priced restaurant on Mocambo at Rayon, three blocks east of Carranza. The restaurant also offers *topotes* (15 pesos), and a nice lakeside view. (Open daily 8am-8:30pm.) One of the most reputable stands near the market is **La Campesina,** on the backside of the *mercado* facing Mocambo. Enjoy fish fillets (20 pesos) and fish with *mole* (15 pesos) on the colorful, communal tables. (Open daily 7am-9pm.) If you're trying to seduce a newfound Huastecan beauty and something classier is in order, head to **La Casona del Recuerdo,** (tel. 3 01 20), across the *zócalo* on Aldama. A haven from the lurking *lanchistas,* there is a terrace out back overlooking a peaceful wooded garden. Somewhat costly, this is probably one of the safer places to try the *tegogolos* for 25 pesos. (Open daily 8am-8pm.)

◪ BEACHES. The rocky beaches of **Laguna Catemaco** don't resemble Cancún, but a dip in the lake can be a refreshing break from the hot Veracruz sun. The water immediately in front of town is not safe for swimming, but a hiking path runs along the edge of the lake—walk down from the *zócalo* to the waterfront and turn left. The trail, bordered by trees knotted with character, will guide you the 1.5km to **Playa Expagoya** and then another 0.5km down the road to the more secluded and sandy **Playa Hermosa**, the first swimmable beach on the trail. The path is not safe at night. It's also possible to swim off a *lancha* in the deeper and sometimes clearer waters in the middle of the lake.

The lake is nearly circular and about 15km across and several small islands dot its smooth surface. The waterfront is lined with long, flat-bottomed, brightly colored *lanchas* equipped with chairs and canopies ready to take you on an hour long trip to the best-known island of the lot, **Isla de Changos.** A group of semi-wild, red-cheeked *changos* (mandrills, a kind of baboon) was brought from Thailand for a scientific experiment by the University of Veracruz in 1979, and the scientists wanted to see if the animals could survive in their new environment. Lo and behold, 18 years later the *changos* are alive, well, and posing for snapshots. Despite strict orders from the scientists not to feed the monkeys, tourists and *lanchistas* cannot seem to withhold chunks of bananas and coconuts from the already **grossly overweight monkeys.** En route to the island, you'll pass a cave-shrine that stands on the spot where Juan Catemasco, a local fisherman, had a vision of the Virgin Mary over a century ago. The town is named for him and his statue and his statue, poised elegantly at the tip of the lagoon, overlooks the calm waters. Negotiate with the *lanchistas* for longer trips, including an exploration of the rivers that feed the lake or a trip to the tropical forests of the nearby national park. The *lanchas* leave from the docking area below the *zócalo*. Go in the morning or on the weekend if you want to share the boat and save money. *(Standard tour of the lake, including the Isla de Changos and the shrine of the Virgin, 180 pesos per boat, 40 pesos per person on a colectivo.)*

ENTERTAINMENT AND SEASONAL EVENTS. Catemaco's **bars** and **discos** are the best in the Tuxtlas area, although that's not saying much. Nightlife only really heats up during the high tourist season—Semana Santa, July, and August. Many bars and clubs shut down or operate irregularly during the off-season. **Chanequa's** (tel. 3 00 42 or 3 00 01), in the Hotel Playa Azul, some distance from Catemaco, caters to the chic crowd that frequents this posh hotel. Walking there at night is difficult and dangerous; a taxi will take you there for 25 pesos. The road along the beach dominates nightlife in Catemaco. Four blocks from the Hotel Julita, one block away from the water on Madero, is **Jahac 45** (tel. 3 08 50), a video bar and disco that sometimes sponsors concerts by bands from the area and is the only club that remains faithfully open during the off-season (cover 30 pesos; open F-Sa after 9pm). Back along Malecon is **Pescado Loco**, which plays a potpourri of music from *salsa* to English pop (cover 20 pesos; open F-Sa 9pm-3am). In addition to *Semana Santa* and Christmas festivities, the town goes crazy on July 16, the day of its Patron Saint Carmen, and on May 30th, the Day of the Fisherman.

PIRATA ADVENTURES

Some say that the only reason to go to Catemaco is for its proximity to secluded beaches on the Gulf Coast. Waves, they will tell you, crash more crisply in the absence of Corona bars and souvenir shops. These beaches are off the beaten track—cattle roam the spaces between fishing villages that have no telephone lines and only the most basic services. The state of Veracruz wants to pave the road to the coast and develop the region for tourism. When this will happen is anyone's guess, but the traveler will visit the area before it does.

Getting to the Gulf Coast near Catemaco is an adventure. Public transportation to the area is limited to **Transportes Rurales's** pick-up trucks, dubbed **piratas** by locals. A four-door vehicle with wooden benches built into its caged-in bed, a *pirata* can carry the entire population of a small town. From Catemaco, *piratas* depart from the eastern edge of town at the entrance to the road. To get there from the *zócalo*, cross Carranza, passing the Palacio Municipal on your left, and walk 6 blocks turning right onto Lerdo. From there, walk 5 more blocks until you pass the last restaurant before foliage takes over the street. Turn left and walk until the intersection of a paved road. From the second-class bus station, a taxi will take you for 7 pesos. Just outside of town the road forks into two main routes: one heads north to **Montepío** on the Gulf Coast and the other goes east, to **Coyame** on the opposite side of Lake Catemaco. Although most people would agree that the windowless, roofless jungle gyms in the back of *piratas* should become a world-class standard of transportation, the system is not for those in a hurry. *Piratas* are scheduled to depart every 50 minutes from 6am to 6pm, but they only do so when enough passengers have gathered to make the trip, making waits of up to two hours not uncommon. Also, rough, unpaved road translates into frequent flat tires, slowing the *piratas* down even more.

THE ROAD TO MONTEPÍO

The first point of interest on the way to Montepío (besides the jaw-dropping views) is **Sontecomapán**, 20km from Catemaco (6 pesos). This is also the end of the paved road. Hold on tight for the points beyond. Sontecomapán is a small town beside an eponymous saltwater lake that empties into the Gulf of Mexico. *Lanchas* are available for excursions on the lake, and farther down the coast. They are expensive, though, at 180 pesos per boat and 30 pesos per person on a *colectivo*. An interesting spot just to the left of the swarms of *lanchas* is the **Pozo de los Enanos** (Pond of the Midgets). This small, fresh-water pond looks right out of a fairy tale, with its crystal-clear water and huge shady trees. In fact, the pond is supposed to be so clear that upon stepping into it, the water creates an optical illusion that makes you appear half your size, thus giving the *pozo* its name. **La Barra** is a fishing community where Laguna Sontecomapán empties into the Gulf of Mexico. To get there, ride a *pirata* 8km beyond Sontecomapán until the road forks. Your *pirata* will normally follow the left fork; you can either negotiate with the driver to take the right fork instead, or you can hop off, take a right, and hike the 5-6km to La Barra yourself. Once there, locals will show you a modicum of hospitality if you introduce yourself politely; a friendly *viajero* will be allowed to camp near someone's home.

The *pirata* route comes closer to the coast near Playa Jicacal and Playa Escondida; ask the driver to let you off (50min., 15 pesos). A half-hour walk through a lush and remote rural area leads to **Playa Jicacal,** a true gem. The long, slightly stony beach is almost completely empty; the only footprints lead to a few modest fisherman's shacks and—inevitably—a *refresco* stand and snack bar. The pink *cabañas* of **Hotel Icacos** (tel. 2 05 56), located right near the entrance to the beach, do little to take away from the natural beauty. Spartan rooms contain two large beds and a fan, but not much else. But hey, who needs hot water when the Gulf of Mexico is just a stone's throw away? (*Cabañas* 100 pesos.) The beach is said to be safe for camping, and hammock-hanging sites may be available. Safety goes hand and hand with good manners, and campers who wish to crash on the beach would do well to ingratiate themselves with the *jicacaleños*.

Instead of turning right to Playa Jicacal, you can walk uphill 30 minutes to the left to get to **Playa Escondida** (Hidden Beach), a beach that lives up to its name. The simple white **Hotel Playa Escondida** (tel. 2 16 14 or 2 20 01 in San Andrés) appears like a mirage. The hotel provides not only access to the small rocky beach below, but also the chance to explore the surrounding jungle. (Singles 100 pesos; doubles 120 pesos.) This beach offers the safest camping in the area, as access is available only through the hotel. Be prepared to pay 25 pesos for this security. Swimming is possible at both beaches, but an undertow and big waves make for less than ideal conditions and access to the beach for non-guests is 5 pesos. Visitors who want a secluded beach without the 30-minute walk through the jungle have the *pirata* drop them off at **Balzapote** (1¾hr., 14 pesos). A handful of houses and a small restaurant-store are all that separates this empty beach from the dirt road.

Further down the road, you can get out at a biological research station owned and operated by the University of Veracruz. Though you never know who you'll find there, the young scientists who are often in residence will generally be happy to show you around, and explain a bit about the surrounding wildlife.

40km and 2hr. from Catemaco, the pirata route ends on the bluff overlooking the beach of **Montepio,** also home to a small town consisting of a handful of buildings, including a little light-blue church whose facade is barely big enough to accommodate the door. Devoted to fishing, the town also serves the tourists who pass up the more spectacular Playa Escondida in favor of the beaches' empty, almost prehistoric appeal. A favorite of the Tuxtlatecos, most visitors are locals who come to cool off for a day or two on the long, narrow beach, and calm channel that separates it from the row of *mojarra*-frying *palapas* and the green hills of the Sierra behind. In a town that needs all the tourist pesos it can get, it is neither safe nor polite to camp on the beach. The cheapest accommodations can be found by asking locals if they rent rooms (*cuartos economicos*) in their homes. Susana Valencia Contreraz, the proprietor of **Loncheria Susi,** (tel. 3 05 03), makes the room rental process a little more formal, but keeps the prices cheap. Rooms come with private bath (singles 40 pesos; doubles 80 pesos). More expensive, but with fans, beachview balconies, and standard hotel service is the new **Hotel Posada San José** (tel. 2 10 10 or 2 20 20 in San Andrés) standing on the bank of the small river leading to the beach. (Singles 150 pesos; doubles 180 pesos.)

The big attraction in Montepío, other than its sunny, steamy shoreline, are the **cascadas** that sweep down verdant foothills just up from the beach. The most surefire means of reaching the falls is with a guide, who wait at the driveway to Posada San José. Most people go by horse, taking the 60 peso guided trip to the **Cascadas Revolucion** located inland, midway down the beach. Excursions to the other *cascadas* can easily be arranged, or you can simply rent the horse and try to find them yourself (20 pesos per hr., 35 pesos with guide). Further afield is **Playa Hermosa,** another 8km down the beach from Montepío. Up a dirt road from the beach, past the handful of the town's buildings, is the **Cascada Cocoliso,** which crashes into a cool, crystalline pool. Turn right after the beer stand and follow the road to its conclusion. If you're too tired to walk back and no *colectivos* seem to be leaving from the town's docks, you can hire a private lancha. Views on the way back are astounding, but they come at a hefty price of 120 pesos.

COYAME

Alternatively, you can take a *pirata* headed for Coyame, 12km from Catemaco, where you can watch the cool waters that are bottled to make the soft drink of the same name bubble up from underground springs. Seven kilometers toward Coyame, the **Proyecto Ecológico Educacional Nanciyaga,** or simply **Nanciyaga** (tel. 3 01 99; 3 pesos in *pirata*), has lured Hollywood producers, beauty queens, and uptight Americans to its cleansing pre-Hispanic therapy. From the road, turn right and walk in front of the "Nanciyaga" sign on a dirt path that leads towards the shore of the lake. For those with money to burn and an aching for new age healing, a couple days at the "ecological" park could be a lot of fun. Guests can stay overnight in candle-lit bungalows and enjoy the Olmec *temazacal* sweat lodge, full-body mud baths, open-air concerts, and boat tours of the lake (220 pesos; full-body mud baths 65 pesos; activities like massages and vegetarian meals require reservations). *Lanchas* or taxis will also take you to Nanciyaga (20 pesos). To return to Catemaco, walk back to the road, cross the street, and flag down any *pirata* headed back to town.

The Coyame area also makes for great hikes, although because of low profit margins, no tourist facilities exist. This means that your hike will be cheap, touristfree, and also a cattle path. One particularly good route begins from the town of **Tebanca,** located near Coyame on the opposite side of the lagoon from Catemaco, a bumpy hour ride by pirata. By following cattle paths and the educated guesses of ranchers, you can explore the **Cerro los Cumbres Bastonal,** a 4½hr. hike. If you start early, it is easy to climb the Bastonal and return in time to catch the last *pirata* back to Catemaco at 6pm.

SAN LORENZO

A pilgrimage best reserved for archaeology buffs, reaching the Olmec artifacts of San Lorenzo is a labor of love. Located in the rolling green hills that cover the southernmost part of the state, the artifacts are the only major attraction in the seemingly endless farmland and jungle. Of the three known ceremonial centers, San Lorenzo is thought to have been the largest and most important, as well as the oldest, flourishing between 1200 and 900 B.C. Though many of the artifacts found during the initial 1947 excavations have been relocated to museums elsewhere, particularly in Xalapa and Mexico City, recent excavations in 1994 have remained in the area, and strengthened the local collection.

The ruins are spread out over two sites: one in the small town of Tenochtitlán and the other a few kilometers southeast in the even smaller town of San Lorenzo. The collection at Tenochtitlán, under a protective shelter near the town's main dirt road, features an assortment of artifacts including one of the famous giant **Olmec stone heads.** Of the 10 heads found at San Lorenzo, this is the only one that has remained at the site.

About 4km farther down the main dirt road and past the microscopic town of San Lorenzo lies the second archaeological zone. Named **Zona Azuzul,** this site is located on the original ceremonial territory occupied by the Olmecs. Two small shelters atop the hill house the modest but remarkably well-preserved collection. The first hut holds four stone statues, two depicting kneeling human forms and the other two depicting jaguar forms. The second hut has another jaguar figure, this one even larger than the first two. These remarkably old statues hint at the origins of the pre-Hispanic obsession with the jaguar, an obsession that began with the Olmecs but later spread to the Maya and other Mesoamerican civilizations. (Site open daily 8am-6pm; free except for a good tip for the site's caretaker.)

NEAR SAN LORENZO: ACAYUCAN

San Lorenzo is best reached through the grimy city of Acayucan, a major transportation hub in the southern part of the state. Though it is very easy to make the trip using the bus station as a base—the *guarda equibaje* will keep your bags and lighten your load. There are plenty of budget accommodations in town, as well as all major facilities. Banks, pharmacies, and food cluster around the *zócalo*, as does the **Hotel San Miguel,** Hidalgo 8 (singles and doubles 50 pesos, with A/C 70 pesos.) The *zócalo* is easily reached by "Centro" buses leaving from the *mercado* (2 pesos). The bus station is on the eastern side of town, near a market and a supermarket. Four bus lines share the bus station. Autobuses Golfo Pacífico Sur (tel. 5 12 46) has service to nearby towns and to: **Acayucan** from **Puebla** (6hr., 151 pesos); **Mexico City** (8hr., 188 pesos); and **Villahermosa** (4hr., 5:45 and 7:35am, 57 pesos). Cristóbal Colón (tel. 5 00 46) provides service to and from: **Tuxtla Gutiérrez** (8hr., 114 pesos); **Veracruz** (5hr., 57 pesos); and other destinations.

Getting There: From the Acayucan *mercado*, go to the line of regional buses and ask for one going to "Texistepec" (sometimes labeled just "Texi") which will bring you to the town's bus depot 4 pesos and 45 minutes. later. This town is still 15 bumpy kilometers from the museum in Tenochtitlán, and 20km from Zona Azuzul. Buses going to Tenochtitlán and Zona Azuzul are usually blue and labeled "Teno" and leave from the same street (45min., every 2hr. 8am-4pm, 7 pesos; to Zona Azuzul 1hr., 10 pesos). To get back from either site you can either wait for the bus, or try catching the *colectivos*, tractors, and other assorted vehicles that pass along the road.

SAN ANDRÉS TUXTLA

Though San Andres Tuxtla doesn't have any particularly glaring attractions, this sensible town of 125,000 is a great place to just be. Lodged between *los dos Tuxtlas*—the lush lakeside resorts of Catemaco and the Olmec artifacts of Santiago, San Andrés is the relatively untouristed anchor that keeps the Sierra de los Tuxtlas peacefully down to earth. A quiet little town, San Andrés serves mainly as a center for the tobacco and cattle industries of the surrounding countryside, and it offers a cache of budget hotels, an entertaining *zócalo* and some nearby natural attractions. As the transportation hub of the region, San Andrés serves as a good base from which to stage repeated daytrips.

■ **ORIENTATION.** Located midway between Catemaco and Santiago Tuxtla on **Rte. 180,** San Andrés is built on and around a volcanic range that hugs the Gulf Coast. The downtown area lies in the slightly raised center of a valley. Both the first and second class bus stations are located on **Juárez,** which branches off of Rte. 180 to the right to become San Andrés' main drag. To get to the center from either station, follow Juárez as it descends a steep hill, crosses a small stream, and gradually ascends to meet the cathedral at the north corner of the *zócalo.* Right before reaching the cathedral, Juárez passes by the **Palacio Municipal** on the right and intersects **Constitución** to the left and **Madero** to the right, in front of the Palacio Municipal. Following Constitución to the left, you will come to the intersection of **Pino Suárez,** where some hotels are located. The walk takes 10 minutes from the bus station; a taxi costs 9 pesos.

■ **PRACTICAL INFORMATION.** Autotransportes Los Tuxtlas (tel. 2 14 62), based in the second-class station, sends **buses** to: **Catemaco** (20min.; every 10min. 4am-10pm, 3 pesos); **Coatzacoalcos** (3½hr., every 10min. 4am-10pm, 43 pesos); **Santiago Tuxtla** (20min., every 10min. 4:30am-9:30pm, 4 pesos); and **Veracruz** (3½hr., every 15min. 2am-10pm, 44 pesos). **ADO** (tel. 2 08 71), at the intersection of Juárez and Rte. 180 (also called Blvd. 5 de Febrero), serves: **Mexico City** (7½hr., 9:45, 10:30, and 11:30pm, 179 pesos; deluxe service 7½hr., 11pm, 280 pesos); **Veracruz** (2½hr., 19 per day 2:10am-9:50pm, 56 pesos); and **Villahermosa** (5hr., 7 per day 7am-3:30pm, 118 pesos). AU (tel. 2 09 84) goes to **Puebla** (6hr., 9:50pm, 164 pesos); **Veracruz** (2½hr., noon and 9:50pm, 34 pesos); and **Xalapa** (4hr., 9:50pm, 88 pesos). Cuenca covers **Tuxtepec** (3hr., 4:30 and 5:30pm, 60 pesos).

The oft-deserted **tourist office** is on the second floor of the Palacio Municipal (Officially open M-F 9am-1pm and 4-6pm, but in all reality, forget about it.) For a map and recommendations, try **Protox Viajes,** across the street from the *mercado.* Exchange money at **Bancomer** (tel. 2 27 92), half a block south of the *zócalo* on Madero (open M-F 8:30am-5pm, Sa 9am-1pm). Or **Serfín** (tel. 2 11 00) at Carranza as it curves to intersect 16 de Septiembre (open M-F 9am-5pm). Both have 24-hour **ATMs. Mercado 5 de Febrero,** spills onto the streets several blocks from the *zócalo.* To get there, walk on Madero, turn right on Carranza and walk uphill. (Open daily 6am-10pm; food stands close at 6pm.) **Laundry: Lava Maac** (tel. 2 09 26), at Hernández and Hernández No. 75, intersection Revolución; 6 pesos per kg. (open M-Sa 8am-8pm). **Police:** (tel. 2 14 99), located on Pasaje Rascón, in the Palacio Municipal; open 24hr. **Red Cross:** Boca Negra 25 (tel. 2 05 00), north of the *zócalo;* open 24hr. **Pharmacy: Farmacia Garysa,** Madero 3 (tel. 2 44 34; fax 2 15 06), in the "Canada" building to the left of the Palacio Municipal; open 24hr. **Hospital Regional** (tel. 2 31 99), at the edge of town, has **ambulance service. Post office:** (tel. 2 01 89) at La Fragua and 20 de Noviembre, one block from the *zócalo* (open M-F 8am-8pm, Sa 9am-noon). **Postal code:** 95701. **Internet access: SAT Internet** (tel. 2 38 05) at the corner of Pino Suárez and Argudín (18 pesos per hr.; open daily 8am-midnight.) **Internepolis** (tel. 2 41 60), three blocks down Pino Suárez, (25 pesos per hr.; open daily 8am-2am). **LADATELs** have made their debut around the *zócalo* and across the street from the Hotel de los Pérez. **Phone code:** 294.

■ **ACCOMMODATIONS AND FOOD.** A large part of San Andrés tremendous appeal comes from the budget accommodations. Two of the best bargains are within spitting distance of each other on Pino Suárez. To get there, walk left from the cathedral and turn right at the orange supermarket, continuing uphill past the movie theater. Visitors of the **Hotel Colonial,** Pino Suárez 7 (tel. 2 05 52), should be

VERACRUZ

forewarned—many who stay here never leave. Mountain view balconies, ceiling fans, and a comfortable lobby full of geckos and good conversation can be had for astounding low prices. (Singles 35-40 pesos; doubles 70 pesos.) **Hotel Figueroa,** Pino Suárez 10 (tel. 2 02 57), is across the street and has almost identical rooms; the only notable differences are that Figueroa has portable fans and reliable hot water. (Singles 35 pesos; doubles 50 pesos.) Those living in the A/C fast lane should upgrade to **Hotel Isabel,** located at Madero 13 (tel. 2 16 17), to the left of the Hotel Parque next to the *zócalo* (singles 145 pesos; doubles 180 pesos).

Several sidewalk cafes on the *zócalo* serve breakfast and coffee and afford a pleasant view of small-town life. Famous for its stash of elegant cakes and pies, **Winni's Restaurant,** located south of the *zócalo* next to the Banamex on Madero, also serves delicious food (*antojitos* 12-17 pesos) to the congregation of locals that gather to chat and smoke around its outdoor tables. (Open daily 8am-midnight.) The older and more affluent lounge at **Restaurant del Parque** (tel. 2 01 98), on the ground floor of the Hotel Parque on the *zócalo* is slightly more expensive (*antojitos* 20 pesos) the classy feel and great coffee are well worth the few extra pesos. (Open daily 7am-midnight). Cheap but filling *comida corrida* is served for 15 pesos to the weary at **El Pequeño Archie,** on Pino Suárez across the street from the movies. An nonstop stream of *telenovelas* is a good balm for lonely travelers, as are the *antojitos* (6-10 pesos; open M-Sa 8am-8pm).

🎦 📺 **SIGHTS AND ENTERTAINMENT.** Even non-smokers will be impressed by the **Fabrica Tabacos San Andrés** (tel. 2 12 00), where Santa Clara cigars are made. From the *zócalo*, walk up Juárez to the ADO terminal and walk around the corner, and continue about 200m down the street past the entrance to the bus parking lot. An open door and the acrid smell of tobacco leaves invites you in. The management welcomes visitors, and if you're polite, someone from the amiable staff will gladly walk you through the entire process, from selecting the leaves to rolling the stogies to putting on the company seal. You can buy some near the entrance: the bottom of the line starts at 105 pesos, while a box of 25 of their finest *puros* goes for upwards of 1000 pesos. Customs regulations may limit the number of cigars you can take back into your country (see p. 39).

The sheer number of video rental stores just about says it all: San Andrés is not exactly a town that parties until dawn. Unless you brought your VCR along, it might be hard to find nighttime entertainment. Most of the action centers on the *zócalo*, where folks in San Andrés gather to meet, gossip, see, and be seen. **Café de la Cathedral,** to the right of the Singer store on the north side of the *zócalo*, used to be a real coffee shop but now functions as one of the most popular bars in San Andrés and begins to fill up around 11pm. On Sunday nights, families bring their children to the square, which becomes a little kiddie carnival with balloons and small electric cars for hire. **Cinemas San Andrés,** on Pino Suárez across from El Pequeño Archie, brings English-language movies to the big screen (15-18 pesos, 3 showtimes daily).

On Independence Day, September 16, giant balloons of colorful paper are flown over the *zócalo*. The town's patron saint is celebrated on November 30 and December 12 is the day of Guadalupe, Mexico's patron virgin. As part of the celebrations, young people playfully hit each other with wooden figures called *mojigangas*.

SANTIAGO TUXTLA

Of the three cities that constitute Los Tuxtlas, Santiago (pop. 50,000) has the least to offer visitors in terms of sights and recreational activities. Its main attraction stems from its close connection to the ancient Olmec ceremonial center of **Tres Zapotes.** Virtually untouristed save the few archaeologists and doctoral students that pass through, Santiago is nevertheless known in the Tuxtlas area for its superstitions and elaborate festivals.

⚐ ORIENTATION AND PRACTICAL INFORMATION. The **ADO bus station**, like everything else in Santiago, is just a few blocks from the *zócalo*. To reach the town center, walk downhill from Rte. 180 where the bus drops you. The first right is **Ayuntamiento,** which leads to the **Palacio Municipal** with its clock tower on the right and the *zócalo* in front of it. From the ADO bus station, walking downhill and then following **Morelos** will bring you to the **Autotransportes Los Tuxtlas** station on the left and **Calle Obregón** on the right. ADO (tel. 7 04 38) sends buses to: **Mexico City** (7hr., 9:20am, 10:45, and 11:30pm, 175 pesos); and **Xalapa** (4½hr., 7:05, 7:50, and 9:20am, 71 pesos). Cuenca sends buses to **Tuxtepec** (4hr., every hr. 4:35am-6:35pm, 34 pesos). Autotransportes Los Tuxtlas buses leave from next to the ADO station for: **Catemaco** (40min., every 10min. 8am-10pm, 7 pesos); and **San Andrés** (20min., 3 pesos). To get to **San Lorenzo** and other surrounding towns take taxi *colectivos* that leave a block from the *zócalo* on the side of the market. For **tourist information, currency exchange,** and **ATMs,** you'll have to go back to San Andrés. Almost all of Santiago's action takes place in the **Mercado Municipal Morelos** which begins on the *zócalo* and continues one block downhill (open daily 5am-8pm). **Police:** (tel. 7 00 92) downstairs in the Palacio Municipal. Open daily 24hr. **Red Cross:** the nearest is in San Andrés; for 24hr. ambulance service, dial 2 05 00. **Super Farmacia Roma:** (tel. 7 09 99), 5 de Mayo just off the *zócalo*. Open daily M-Sa 8:30am to 9pm, Su 8:30am-3pm. **Clínica Doctores Castellanos,** across from the Hotel Castellanos (tel. 7 02 60), provides medical assistance daily from 8am to 8pm. **Post office:** on Juárez across the *zócalo* from the Palacio Municipal (open M-F 9am-5pm). **Postal code:** 95830. **Phone Code:** 294.

▐▐ ACCOMMODATIONS AND FOOD. Built by the Mexican government in the early 80s in an attempt to get Santiago's tourist industry ticking, **Hotel Castellanos** (tel. 7 03 00), on the corner of 5 de Mayo and Commonfort, at the far corner of the *zócalo*, is not only a place to stay but also Santiago's most interesting attraction. The rooms fit together like slices of a pie; each offers A/C, telephones, color TV, and a balcony with a panoramic view. (Singles 207 pesos, with A/C 253; doubles 230 with A/C 275 pesos.) Both less expensive and less stimulating, **Casa de Huéspedes Morelos,** Obregón 15 (tel. 7 04 74), downhill from the bus stations, has basic small rooms with fans and bathrooms (singles 50 pesos; doubles 70-80 pesos; triples 80 pesos).

Grub in Santiago is cheap, and sometimes just that—grub. The area is known for its quirky dishes, however. The finest example can only be had during the rainy season, when small, delicate winged insects seek refuge inside the *zócalo's* streetlamps. In the morning, the bugs are captured, de-winged, and sauteed with *salsa* to make the region's favorite taco filling. This and more normal food can be found in *mercado*, or the restaurant in the Hotel Castellanos (meals 40 pesos) after dark.

▓ SIGHTS AND SEASONAL EVENTS. The **largest Olmec head** ever discovered (45 tons) sits complacently at the far end of Santiago's *zócalo*, shaded from the sun by a large cupola. The head is distinctive not only for its size but also because its eyes are closed. The **Museo Regional Tuxteco,** to the left of the head along the *zócalo*, displays terra-cotta masks of the Totonacs and another Olmec head, along with other artifacts from around the region (open M-Sa 9am-5pm; admission 17 pesos). Celebrations for the **fair** in honor of Santiago, the town's patron saint, take place July 20-29 and include a choreographed fight between Christians and Moors and a *torneo de cintas* in which men dress in medieval gear and ride horses.

NEAR SANTIAGO TUXTLA: TRES ZAPOTES

Half an hour's ride out of Santiago through small tobacco-growing towns and neon green hills is the site of **Tres Zapotes.** One of the three main Olmec ceremonial centers, Tres Zapotes reached its peak between 300 BC and AD 300, but there is evidence that the area was occupied as early as 900 BC. Though the site remains largely unexcavated, what has been found is clustered in the small but fabulously interesting museum in the little town by the same name. Though the written explanations recently installed by INAH help to clarify the inherently baffling artifacts, you might solicit further explanations from the knowledgeable staff. (Open daily 9am-5pm. Admission 10 pesos, free on Sunday.)

The most imposing figure at Tres Zapotes is one of the trademark Olmec stone heads that always seems to carry the label "colossal." The first of the dozen or so Olmec heads to be found, it was discovered in 1862 by a *campesino* who first thought it was an overturned cooking pot. To the left of the head is the **Stela C,** which, together with its more famous upper half (now at the Museo Nacional de Antropología in Mexico City, see p. 113), bears the oldest written date in the Americas—31 B.C., inscribed in late Olmec, or Spi-Olmec glyphs similar to those later used by the Maya. The date is visible on the back of the stela as a bar (representing "5") and two dots, giving a total of seven on the Olmec calendar. **Stela A** lies in the transept to the left. Decorations on the stela include the figure of a man, a serpent coiling upon itself (on the right side), and a man holding an axe (on the left side). **Stela D,** to the right of the head, resembles a tablet. Within the mouth of a jaguar are renderings of three people whose relative heights symbolize their power and importance. The tallest figure, on the far right, is most likely a ruler; the central, skirted figure is perhaps an emissary; the kneeling figure on the left is probably a prisoner of war or someone making an offering. On the left side of the piece, the broad mouth of what is possibly a toad is visible; on the right side a skeletal face is discernible.

Getting There: Exiting the Museo Regional Tuxteco in Santiago, head right and turn right on Zaragoza. Cross the street about a block later and pass through the market and cross the bridge to Morelos, where you can take a *taxi-colectivo* to Tres Zapotes (30min., 8 pesos). You will be let off in the town of Tres Zapotes. From the stop, turn left and walk to the first cross-street. Turn left and walk around the chain-link fence until you see the entrance on your right. Buses marked "Tres Zapotes" also pass through this stop, but while they're cheaper (3 pesos), they're also slower.

CHIAPAS AND TABASCO

For centuries, **Chiapas** has been known for its environmental diversity—its cloud-enveloped heights provide a stark contrast to its basins of dense, lowland rainforest. Chiapas's climate is unique for southern Mexico—the chilly nights and crisp fresh air give the highlands a distinct flavor. Cortés must have had the Sierra de Chiapas in mind when he crumpled a piece of parchment and dropped it on a table to demonstrate what Mexico looked like. In these rugged green mountains, buses career around hairpin turns above deep valleys before hurtling into jungles on rutted roads. One of Mexico's most beautiful cities, San Cristóbal de las Casas, known for its cobblestone streets and surrounding *indígena* villages, rests high amid these peaks.

Throughout the state, you will hear diverse Mayan dialects and find markets and other public places filled with *indígenas*. Indeed, the state is part of the Maya heartland; the Lacandón Rainforest shields the remote ruins of Bonampak and Yaxchilán and is still home to the Lacandón Maya, whose isolation has kept them from both the Spanish Conquest and tourist invasion. Chiapas's *indígenas* remain fiercely traditional—in many communities, schools teach in the local dialect as well as in Spanish, and regional dress, while it varies across communities, is almost always maintained. The EZLN rebellion of 1994 (see p. 17) succeeded in drawing the world's attention to the central Mexican government's lack of attention to the needs and rights of the highland region's poor indigenous villages.

Tabasco, Chiapas's neighbor to the north, is often overlooked in favor of its more glamorous neighbors. But while Tabasco lacks the party attitude of Veracruz and the turquoise beaches of the Yucatán Peninsula, the state has plenty to offer its visitors. Dotted with lakes and swamps, criss-crossed by rivers, and swathed in dense jungle, Tabasco (which literally means "damp earth") is something of a natural beauty. Beaches, most of them untouristed, line its northern side, and the southern and eastern sides are dotted with parks and natural sanctuaries. In the center of it all is the capital city of Villahermosa, struggling to retain its colonial identity in the midst of a modern growth spurt. But perhaps what Tabasco is best known for is its intense heat, humidity, and wetness. The weather behaves like clockwork—be prepared for showers every afternoon during the rainy season (June-Sept.). Happy (and dry) is the well-prepared tourist.

HIGHLIGHTS OF CHIAPAS AND TABASCO

■ The mountaintop city of **San Cristóbal de las Casas** (see p. 541) is the reason many people come to Mexico—inevitably a good visit.

■ The jungle ruins of **Palenque** (see p. 559) are startling. Skip the town and head straight to the gleaming **archaeological site** (see p. 565), set amidst a dense backdrop of beautiful falls, foliage, and wildlife.

■ Be sure not to miss the indigenous villages near **San Cristóbal** (see p. 548), especially the community of **San Juan Chamula** (see p. 549) and its famous **church,** host to a fascinating syncretic religious ritual involving burping.

■ The adjacent archaeological sites of **Yaxchilán** (see p. 564) and **Bonampak** (see p. 567) are worth the jungle trek—they house some of the most well-preserved Maya remnants in the country.

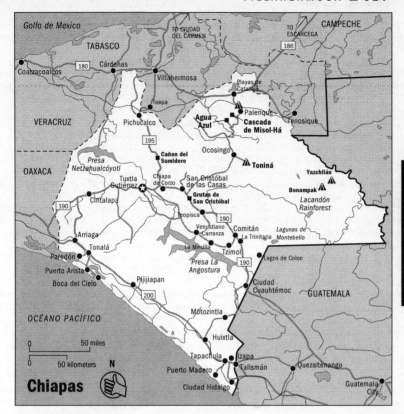

Golfo de Mexico

Chiapas

TABASCO

VILLAHERMOSA

Like the state itself, the capital of Tabasco leads a strange double life. Once a muggy land of teethy fish roasting on smoky fires and endless weedy wetlands, the same damp earth has given rise to ornately decorated pyramids, a menagerie of carved stone, and more recently, a wildly consumeristic metropolis. Villahermosa used to be a sleepy agricultural town, the rich oil reserves found in the state have driven the boom of capitalistic debauchery that keeps Villahermosa's *combis* zipping around at dangerous speeds all hours of the day and night. Fortunately, the old city center offers a more moderate revision of the getting and spending, with enough icy treats to give the visitor an Olmec-sized brain freeze with plenty of benches to sit on while sipping, slurping, and spooning. Villahermosa's rich trove of Olmec and Maya treasures and strategic proximity to Palenque make it a must for those wishing to delve into Mexico's pre-Hispanic mysteries, while the artifacts' matted jungle residences and the chaotic city streets guarantee similar insight into the miracle of refrigeration.

▣ ORIENTATION

Villahermosa is 20km from the border with Chiapas and 298km west of Escárcega. The spine of the downtown area is **Av. 27 de Febrero.** The **Zona Luz,** the city's pedestrian-only downtown area, is bordered by **Av. 5 de Mayo, Zaragoza, Madero,** and 27 de Febrero. **Paseo Tabasco** runs north-south and connects the **Tabasco 2000** complex to the *centro*, intersecting Av. 27 de Febrero in front of the cathedral. *Saetas* **(public buses)** and *combis* (each 3 pesos) run from 6am to 10:30pm. 1st- and 2nd-class **buses** depart from the eastern part of town. An **airport** lies northwest of the city, 14km from the downtown area; taxis shuttle between the airport and the *centro* (40 pesos *especial*, 15 pesos *colectivo*).

To reach downtown from the **1st-class ADO station,** walk 2½ blocks to your right on Mina to Méndez. From there, take a *combi* labeled "Tierra Colorada Centro-Juárez" and get off a few minutes later at **Parque Juárez.** Most hotels are south of the park on either **Madero** or the parallel **Constitución.** Walking from the station to Parque Juárez takes 15 to 20 minutes; upon exiting the terminal, head right down Mina for eight blocks, then turn left onto Av. 27 de Febrero. Eight more blocks take you to the intersection with Madero. To get downtown from the **2nd-class bus terminal,** cross Grijalva on the pedestrian bridge to the left of the station exit, then jump on a bus labeled "Indeco Centro" (3 pesos) and disembark at Parque Juárez on Madero. To make the 25-minute walk from the station, cross the bridge and continue south on Mina for three blocks until you reach the ADO station (see above). A cab ride to the center of town costs about 12 pesos.

▐ PRACTICAL INFORMATION

TRANSPORTATION

Airport: (tel. 56 01 56), on the Villahermosa-Macupana Highway. Most major airlines have offices in Tabasco 2000, including: **Aeroméxico,** Cámara 511, Locale 2 (tel. 12 15 28); **Aviacsa,** Via 3, #120 Locale 10 (tel. 16 57 90); **Aerocaribe,** Via 3, #120, Locale 5 and 6 (tel. 16 50 46); **Mexicana,** Via 3, #120 (tel. 16 31 32).

Buses: The 1st-class terminal is on Mina 297, at Merino, a few blocks east of Juárez. ADO (tel. 12 76 92 or 12 76 27) runs to: **Acayucan** (4hr., 13 per day 1:20am-9:30pm, 85 pesos); **Agua Dulce** (2hr., 6:15am and 6:15pm, 50 pesos); **Balancan** (3hr.; 6:45am, 12:20, 4:25, and 6:10pm; 75 pesos); **Campeche** (5hr., 13 per day, 121 pesos); **Cancún** (11hr., 8 per day 1am-10:10pm, 331 pesos); **Jalapa** (8:40am, 5:05, 7:25, and 10:30pm; 228 pesos); **Mexico City** (11hr., 20 per day, 359 pesos); **Oaxaca** (11hr.; 6, 7, and 9:25pm, 262 pesos); **Palenque** (2hr., 12 per day 3am-7:40pm, 53 pesos); **Puebla** (8hr.; 12:45am, 8:10, 8:40, 9:45, and 11:15pm; 305 pesos); **San Andres Tuxtla** (10 per day, 120 pesos); and **Veracruz** (14 per day, 120 pesos). Servicios Altos offers buses to **Tuxtla Guttierez** (6½hr.; 7:15, 9:30am, 3, 9:10, and 11:45pm; 76 pesos).

Radio Taxi: (tel. 15 82 33 or 15 23 39). On call 24hr.

Car Rental: Renta de Autos Tabasco, Paseo Tabasco 600 (tel. 15 48 30), next to the cathedral. The lowest prices in town for the over-25 set. 466 pesos per day. Open M-Sa 8am-7pm, Su 8am-2pm.

TOURIST AND FINANCIAL SERVICES

Tourist Office: In **Tabasco 2000,** Av. de los Rios 113 (tel. 16 36 33 or 16 28 89), diagonally behind the Palacio Municipal. Sells maps and pamphlets, but these can be procured with much less hassle from the outposts scattered around town. Booths are located at the entrances of **Parque Museo la Venta** (open daily 8am-4pm), the **ADO station** (open daily 9am-3pm and 6-9pm), and the **airport.**

Currency Exchange: Banks are plentiful in the *Zona Luz* and along Paseo Tabasco. **Banamex** (tel. 12 00 11), on Madero at Reforma, has a 24hr. **ATM.** Open for exchange M-F 9am-5pm, Sa 9:30am-2pm. **BITAL** (tel. 10 25 37) has 3 24hr. **ATMs,** at the corner of Lerdo and Juárez. Open M-F 7am-7pm, Sa 7am-5pm.

American Express: Patriotismo 605 (tel. (91) 800 5 00 44). Open M-Sa 9am-6pm.

LOCAL SERVICES

Luggage Storage: At the bus station. Open daily 7am-11pm. (2 pesos per piece per hr.)

Market: Pino Suárez, encompassed by Pino Suárez, Constitución, Hermanos Zozaya, and Grijalva, in the northeast corner of town. Open daily 6am-6pm.

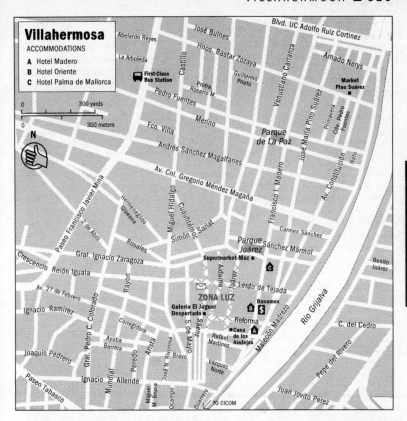

Villahermosa

ACCOMMODATIONS

A Hotel Madero
B Hotel Oriente
C Hotel Palma de Mallorca

First-Class Bus Station

Supermarket: Maz (tel. 14 22 80), on Madero at Zaragoza. Open daily 7am-10pm. Even bigger (*mas gigante*) is **Gigante,** Blvd. Cortines, best reached by *colectivo* (3 pesos).

Laundry: Lavandería Rex, Madero 705, just past Méndez. 30 pesos for 3kg. Open M-F 9am-8pm.

EMERGENCY AND COMMUNICATIONS

Emergency: dial 06.

Police: Aldama 101 (tel. 15 26 33 or 15 26 30), in the *Zona Luz,* is open 24hr. The main office is farther away, on Av. 16 de Septiembre at Periférico (tel. 15 25 17). No English spoken. Open 24hr.

Red Cross: (tel. 15 56 00), on Sandino in Col. 1 de Mayo. Take the "1 de Mayo" bus from Madero. Some English spoken.

Hospitals: IMSS, Sandino 501 (tel. 15 18 45 or 15 16 91). No English spoken.

Pharmacy: Farmacia del Ahorro, in the *Zona Luz* at the corner of Reforma and Aldama, across from the HoJo's. Open 7am-10pm. Also has an **ATM** and **fax** service.

Post Office: Sáenz 131, at Lerdo. Open M-F 8am-4pm, Sa 9am-1pm. **Mexpost,** 27 de Febrero 906, 8 blocks from the *Zona Luz.* **Postal Code:** 86000.

Fax: Telecomm, Lerdo 601 (tel. 14 28 33), at Sáenz around the corner from the post office. Open M-F 8am-7pm, Sa 9am-5pm. **Western Union** and **telegraph** services.

Internet Access: Several providers cluster around Av. 27 de Febrero at Sáenz. **PC Sistems,** Sáenz 230 (tel. 12 21 88) offers service for 12 pesos per hr. Open daily 7am-10pm.

Telephones: LADATELs are abundant all over town.

Phone Code: 93.

ACCOMMODATIONS AND CAMPING

In Villahermosa, cheap means convenient. The closer the hotel is to the *Zona Luz*, the more inexpensive it tends to be. Try the two located side by side on Lerdo for some of the lowest prices in the *zona*. Hotels on Madero are slightly nicer and are also beginning to charge higher rates. **Camping** and **trailer parking** are allowed in **La Choca Park** in Tabasco 2000, but the site lacks facilities.

Hotel Oriente, Madero 425 (tel. 12 01 21). Couch potatoes will appreciate the low prices of TV and the easy access to the VIPS restaurant across the street. Rooms are quiet, clean and equipped with sturdy *ventiladores*. Singles 71 pesos; doubles 132 pesos.

Hotel Santa Lucia, Madero 420 (tel. 12 99 99 ext. 736), has its own cute *pastelería* and an air of classy standardization. The bustle from the *Taqueria la Choza* next door makes the dinky lobby fun, while the labyrinthine upper reaches have recessed lighting and some of the hottest showers around. Make sure to mention the words, *fresco* and *ventana* during check-in, or you could be smothering in one of the stuffier suites. Singles 80 pesos; doubles 110 pesos; triples 150 pesos.

Hotel Palma de Mallorca, Madero 510 (tel. 12 01 44 or 12 01 45), located near the intersection of Zaragoza and Madero. It's all pretty basic, but once you crank up the chiller, you'll notice the difference. Singles with the fan 70 pesos, 133 with the mighty A/C; doubles 153 pesos with A/C.

Hotel Madero, Madero 301 (tel. 12 05 16), near Av. 27 de Febrero. Great central location, but try to get a room that's not on the street. Rooms of varying quality; shop around. Most are clean and equipped with fans and TV. Singles 80 pesos; doubles 150 pesos; triples 170 pesos.

 FOOD

Villahermosa, like the rest of Tabasco, specializes in *mariscos* (seafood) and swamp things. A typical *tabasqueño* dish not for the faint of heart is *pejelagarto* (tortoise sautéed in green sauce and blood and then mixed with pickled armadillo). Another favorite is *peje largato*, a prehistoric-looking fish which is barbecued in its shell-like body and then delivered to your plate, buggy eyes, pointy teeth, and all. If someone offers you *venado* (venison) be informed that wetland deer are rare, and catching them often involves setting the brush on fire and then shooting whatever runs out—a process far too destructive to be palatable. Stick to the *mojarra* (the local fish) flavored with typical ingredients like *chipilín*, *chaya* leaves, and *amashito* chile. The best places to find regional specialties are the roadside restaurants and *palapas* that litter the major tourist routes such as the **Teapa Comalcalco.**

Restaurant Los Tulipanes (tel. 12 92 17 or 12 92 09), in the CICOM complex, specializes in *comida tabasqueña*. Enjoy fresh seafood right on the banks of the Río Grijalva in this sophisticated joint, a local favorite. Unfortunately, it's a tad on the expensive side; seafood dishes start at 65 pesos. Open Sa-Tu noon-9pm, Th-F noon-11pm.

Cocktelería Rock and Roll, Reforma 307 (tel. 12 05 93), right across from the Hotel Miraflores, serves up seafood and local specialties for some of the lowest prices around and provides a swinging, rowdy atmosphere to boot. *Antojitos* around 10 pesos. Open daily 9am-Midnight.

Café Bar Impala, Madero 421 (tel. 12 04 93). A cluttered hole in the wall with superb *tamalitos de chipilín*, *panuchos* (fried tortilla shells stuffed with meat and beans), and tacos (each a mere 3 pesos). Open daily 9am-8pm.

Café la Cabaña, Juárez 303 (tel. 15 32 35) near Av. 27 de Febrero. Villahermosa's fountain of youth, and, as one would expect, a place of congregation for the town's elders. Whether you grab your coffee and run or sit down to bicker around one of the outdoor tables, the superb brew is sure to jumpstart your neurons. Don't miss the frozen *Cappuccino Americano* (7 pesos) or the 13 peso regular cappuccino. Open daily 7am-10pm.

Café el Casino, Juárez 531 (tel. 12 05 10), is an even more hard-core cafe scene decorated with campaign posters and serving only coffee *fuerte* (strong 'n' black) to its *macho* clientele—words like "nonfat," "decaf," and "pasteries" (even in Spanish) will induce blank stares from the Casino's burly baristas.

🔆 SIGHTS

For a city that seems unconcerned with tourism, Villahermosa has a surprising number of fine museums, many of them within walking distance of the downtown area known as the *Zona Luz*. The downtown area is comprised of a series of pedestrian streets lined with specialty *tiendas*, *licuado* stands, gurgling fountains, shaded benches, and more hair salons than should be legal.

PARQUE-MUSEO LA VENTA

*Contact: Tel. 14 16 52. **Location:** To get to La Venta, take the "Tabasco 2000," "Carrisal," "Petrolera," or "Palacio" bus (3 pesos) from Madero in the center to the intersection of Tabasco and Ruiz Cortínez. Walk northeast on Ruíz for 10 min. or cut through the Parque Canabal until you reach the entrance. From the Tabasco 2000 complex, you can reach the museum by following the Paseo Tabasco down to the intersection of Ruíz Cortínez; it is about a 10-15 min. walk, but if you're willing to fork over 12 pesos for a taxi especial, it will spare you a hassle. **Open:** Daily 8am-5pm. **Admission:** 15 pesos **Tours:** Free Spanish tours leave from the park entrance, while English tours can be arranged with independent guides who lurk just beyond the gates. About 150 pesos for 2hr.*

Located in a corner of the city just south of Tabasco 2000, Parque Museo la Venta offers a well conceived contrast to the city's primarily overdone, concrete "attractions." The park features 33 pieces of monumental Olmec sculpure which were lifted from their original location in the jungle of western Veracruz, and re-planted in Villahermosa in 1958 by Carlos Pellicer Camará. Though the well-worn path and chinsy gift shop chip away at the park's intended mystique, there is something to be said for the lush, green backdrop that surrounds the awesome artifacts. The trek begins from a *palapa*-style museum which shelters, in addition to some nifty dioramas recreating the site, an apocalyptic stelae of embracing rulers, one of whom is being ushered away by a skeletal woman, supposedly a foreshadowing of La Venta's demise in 400 B.C.

Along the trails themselves, the oft-reproduced Olmec heads alternate with more complex and puzzling sculptures, many of which depict priests emerging from carts carrying limp children in their arms. Keep and eye out for #10, which, in its unfinished state, has a kind of artistic obliqueness reminiscent of Picasso.

Surrounding the Museo is the **Parque Tomás Garrido Canabal,** which lies on the Laguna de las Ilusiones and surrounds the Parque-Museo La Venta. The main entrance is at the corner of Tabasco and Grijalva. Landscaped alcoves hide benches and fountains. While the *mirador* claims to offer a panoramic view of Villahermosa, all you get in reward for your 40-meter-climb is a good look at a few treetops. You can, however, get a spectacular view of the *lagunas* below.

MUSEO DE HISTORIA DE TABASCO. The best place to begin exploring Villahermosa's sights is at the **Museo de Historia de Tabasco,** at the corner of Juárez and Av. 27 de Febrero in the *Zona Luz*. Located in the famous **Casa de los Azulejos** (House of the Tiles), the museum houses artifacts and pictures detailing the history of the state of Tabasco. The real show-stealer, though, is the tiled house itself. Built between 1889 and 1915 by a wealthy merchant, the bright blue edifice is decorated with Italian and Spanish baroque tiles with a different style adorning each room. Eleven classic sculptures sit atop the roof; the seated female figures are said to be members of the merchant's family. Also note the Egyptian tiles decorating the ledge on the outside walls. *(Open Tu-Sa 9am-8pm, Su 10am-5pm; 5 pesos.)*

CASA MUSEO CARLOS PELLICER. If you're wondering about the man whose name and photo are plastered on every wall in town, head to this small museum focusing on the preservation of Pellicer's family relics (like his nightshirt) displayed with the funiture and decorations of typical, well-to-do *tabesqueño* families in the 19th century. It offers reassuring proof that there was a Villahermosa before Tabasco 2000, and all the detail you could want about this idolized poet and philanthropist. *(Sáenz 203. Tel. 12 01 50. Open Tu-Su 10am-7pm; free.)*

OTHER SIGHTS. Northwest on Paseo Tabasco, away from the city center and Río Grijalva, is **Tabasco 2000,** a complex containing futuristically bland buildings and pedestrian-unfriendly streets that is light years away from the cozy, car-free *Zona Luz.* Take the "Tabasco 2000" bus from the city center and get off by the Liverpool store, right smack in the middle of the complex. The long strip of stucco and concrete buildings includes the city's **Palacio Municipal,** a convention center, several fountains, a shopping mall, and a **planetarium** with **OmniMax** shows dubbed in Spanish. *(Tel. 16 36 41; Shows Tu-F 6 and 7pm, Sa-Su 6, 7, and 8pm; 15 pesos.)*

Carlos Pellicer's name graces yet another museum—the **Museo Regional de Antropología Carlos Pellicer Cámara,** the main attraction at Villahermosa's new **Center for the Investigation of Olmec and Maya Cultures (CICOM).** From the *Zona Luz,* the museum is best reached with a 15-minute walk south along the Río Grijalva. The #1 and "CICOM" buses pass often. The collection focuses mainly on the Olmec and Maya, with a scant selection of artifacts from other cultures. Most of the items and pictures on display are from the nearby archaeological sites of La Venta and Comalcalco. The center also houses a public library, an arts school, a theater, and traveling exhibits. *(Museum open Tu-Su 9am-8pm. Free.)*

Elephants and zebras run free at the ecological reserve known as **Yumká** (Elf Who Tends the Jungle), just 14km from the hustle and bustle of Villahermosa. A multitude of animals from around the world roam the three *tabasqueño* ecosystems: jungle, savannah, and wetlands. A *colectivo especial* is the fastest way to get there (60 pesos). Otherwise, go to the PEMEX station at Ruíz Cortínez in La Colonia; at the corner of Sierra and Cortínez, snag a five-peso bus to the zoo. *(Open daily 9am-5pm. Admission 20 pesos, children 10 pesos.)*

ENTERTAINMENT

Villahermosa presents two basic nightlife options: the discos in the luxury hotels or a myriad of cultural activities. For those wishing to take the mellower road, the **Instituto de Cultura Tabasco** (tel. 12 90 24), on Magallanes in the Edificio Portal del Agua, publishes a monthly calendar of musical, theatrical, and other cultural events; look for it in museums and major hotels. **Cinema Superior** on Madero, one block south of Av. 27 de Febrero, has daily showings of English-language movies at 5 and 7pm (17 pesos). The cafe in the back of **Galería El Jaguar Despertado,** Sáenz 117 (tel. 14 12 44), near Reforma in the *Zona Luz,* sometimes features live classical music or jazz. Even without the tunes, though, fountains, original Mexican art, and the gallery upstairs attract an interesting mix of intellectuals and romantics. A weekly program of cultural events is posted outside the door. (Open M-Sa 9am-9pm, Su 3pm-8pm.) Across the street, **Galería de Arte Tabasco,** Sáenz 122, features a slew of contemporary *tabasqueño* artwork, much of it for sale (open M-F 9am-9pm, Sa 10am-2pm).

NIGHTLIFE

For those itching to hit the discos and nightclubs, head to the *Zona Hotelera* in and around Tabasco 2000. Here, Villahermosa's young and sophisticated get down to the hottest mix of *salsa,* tropical music, and visual stimuli. Taxi drivers are well-acquainted with disco hot spots, and their vehicles are the only efficient means of reaching them.

Disco Etherea (tel. 16 53 73 or 16 53 74), is a local favorite next to the Camino Real Hotel behind the Galerías Tabasco 2000. The sleek purple-and-black club is decorated with groovy Greek letters and yin-yangs and features standard house mixes. Ladies may enter the land of Etherea for free. F open bar. No cover W-Th; F 80 pesos; Sa 40 pesos. Open W-Sa 7pm-3am.

Disco Dasha (tel. 16 21 74 or 16 62 85), in front of the Galerías Tabasco 2000 behind the government buildings. Saturday is "crazy bar." Cover 40-100 pesos for men and 30-60 pesos for women. Th students with ID get in nfree. Open W-Sa 9pm-3am.

Flambouyan (tel. 15 12 34), a sophisticated, elegant bar and club found in the lobby of the five-star Hyatt Hotel featuring live music every night, and rotating bands keep everything fresh. Open daily 9pm-2am.

Rodeo Nocturno Cowboy Palace (tel. 54 00 60), on Carretera Villahermosa-Cárdenas, has something a bit less ordinary. *Música grupera* (country music) has found its home here, among wannabe *vaqueros* in a rodeo setting. Cover 25 pesos. Open F-Sa.

NEAR VILLAHERMOSA

COMALCALCO

Unpublicized and under-touristed, the Maya ruins of Comalcalco are surprisingly spectacular. Uniquely constructed from mounded earth sealed under a cement-like adobe shell, the huge gray pyramids look like thunderclouds that have settled into the jungle, their eroding sides melting into the afternoon storms. Though lots of people stop in Tabasco just long enough to snap a shot with a giant Olmec head before moving on to the Maya cities of the Yucatán, Comalcalco is a wonderful detour. Sure to please those searching for unadulterated quiet time with the ancient pyramids. *(Site open daily 10am-5pm; 20 pesos.)*

One of the best parts of the site is its museum. Just off the parking lot, the cleverly organized display explains nuances of Maya culture, using the many fragments of the stucco facades found at the site for illustration. To see the buildings themselves, follow the main road left from the museum entrance as it passes through an arbor and eventually opens into the main plaza of the city.

With 10 levels, the hulking 25m **pyramid** to the left of the entrance to the site is Comalcalco's best-known landmark. Under an awning on the building's north face squirm carvings of a giant toad and several humans—all that remain of the decorations which once covered the entire surface area of the structure. Farther beyond the pyramid to the right, a road leads up to the **Gran Acropolis,** a huge complex of temples and private residences believed to have housed the city's elite. If you look closely at the dilapidated walls, you'll be able to see the insides of Comalcalco's brickwork and oyster-shell mortar. Among the ruins is the precarious-looking **Palacio,** of which the center support for two vaults remains. Also in the acropolis is what is thought to be a bathtub and cooling system, the necessity of which becomes more obvious after the trek through the jungle. After checking the view, walk back down through the acropolis, keeping an eye out for the different sculptural remnants that have been preserved in protected corners of the structures. Some especially cool reliefs can be found on the eastern side in the small **Tomb of the Nine Knights of Night,** named for the well-dressed figures that line the walls, whose feet are now embellished by shining pesos thrown by visitors.

Getting There: Comalcalco lies 2km outside of a large and chaotic city of the same name, 36km northwest of Villahermosa. Though Comalcalco has a historic church and several budget hotels, it's better to skip the city altogether and make the visit directly from Villahermosa. Taxi *colectivos* to Comalcalco leave frequently from Calle Alberto Reyes at Mina on the other side of the supermarket from the first-class bus station. During the hour-long, 20 peso ride, keep a lookout on the left for the **Church of Cupilco,** whose colorful facade is typical of the small towns in the region, many of which have been settled since pre-hispanic times.

The taxi stops at the edge of Comalcalco's market, facing the *zócalo*. From there, the best way to reach the ruins is by taxi *especial.* Arrange a fee before getting in and try to pay less than 12 pesos. Getting back from the site is easier, especially toward closing time when the bus makes stops at the main gate (3 pesos).

RESERVA DE LA BIOSFERA PATANOS DE CENTLA

Though Tabasco's eco-tourism industry has been slow and cumbersome in its attempts to take flight, the state's predominant feature (after its oil reserves) is its natural beauty. If you're willing to do a little negotiating it's possible to slip through the cracks and see lots of amazing jungle on a very limited budget. One of the best places to do this is the Reserva de la Biosfera, a preserve encompassing 302,000 hectares of the wetlands formed by the huge river systems that wind their way into the state. Set aside by the government in 1992, the land is home to 50,000 people, most of whom live in small fishing villages along the river systems deep inside the preserve. In addition to the Centla's waterfalls, swamps, rivers, and the incredible variety of animals that inhabit them, the preserve is fascinating as a point of conflict between ecological interests and the economic interests of the indigenous peoples who live there. Small turtles sell for 100 pesos in the open market, and the rare venison goes for even more, giving residents a good reason to hunt many of the protected animals. Because the animals are hard to catch in the tangled vegetation, burning the wetlands and catching whatever runs out is both a common "hunting" method, and the bane of the guys who work at the preserves station at **Tres Brazos.**

By writing to ecologica@inforedmx.com.mx or contacting the Subdirector de Recursos Naturales at the Dirección de Ecología, **Sergio Zilli Mánica,** (tel. (93) 15 79 70 or 15 80 20), it is possible to get permission to stay at the Tres Brazos station, visiting the preserve by *lancha* and paying no more than the cost of gas and minimal fees for the food in the station's cheery, little restaurant. The station has two clean, separate dorms for men and women, and a satellite TV that entertains the attendants who keep the place open 24 hours all week. When sending requests, explain that you'd like to stay at the station, see the *patanos* (wetlands) by *lancha*, and don't forget to drop the key word: *ecoturismo*. Requests should work in both English and Spanish. Once you have permission, the office will arrange transportation to the station just south of **Frontera** on the Río Orijalva, about 1½ hours northeast of Villahermosa. Exploring the reserve will take some initiative, but the *lanchistas* and locals will help you out, and the *crocodilos* will insure an exciting time.

LAS GRUTAS COCONÁ

Just a few kilometers from the town of Teapa, south of Villahermosa, **Las Grutas Coconá** were discovered in the late 1800s by two adventurous brothers who were out in the woods hunting. The caves (or *grutas*) contain a path that winds for 500m into the hillside, passing impressive caverns and underground lagoons along the way. Twelve-year-old guides offer their services at the entrance, giving details on rock formations and pointing out where the natural formations resemble something else (the Virgin Mary, the head of a moose, etc.). Once you are inside the cave system, shine your light into the roof—sometimes you can catch bats during their *siestas*. Farther on, you'll enter a breathtaking, acoustically funky, domed cavern replete with mighty stalactites. Beyond, a wooden walkway leads over a pool into a dripping cave. Locals say the pool, although dark, is safe for swimming. On the way back from the final, largest cave, look for a left-hand turn-off where the path diverges below some rocks. Here you can limbo beneath a 1m ledge to reach a secluded emerald pool called *Pozo de los Peces Ciegos* (Pond of the Blind Fish) because the pond is inhabited by tiny, blind...fish. For some real spelunking, you can negotiate with the guides to take you to the unexplored, unnamed *gruta* about 200m away. This *gruta* lacks the wooden path and artificial lights of the first one, so descending into its damp, muddy caverns is truly an adventure. Leave your shoes at the entrance and be prepared to leave caked in dirt. Tours of this *gruta* last anywhere from 1½ to three hours and are not recommended for anyone who is claustrophobic or afraid of the dark. *(Caves open daily 9am-4pm. Admission 20 pesos. Guides cost about 10-15 pesos.)*

Getting There: *Combis* for the *grutas* leave from Calle Bastar on the right-hand side of the church in Teapa (every 30min., 3 pesos). Taxis charge 10-15 pesos. Teapa is one hour from Villahermosa. **Transportes Villahermosa-Teapa buses** go back and forth between the two cities frequently (from Teapa: every hr. 4:45am-7:45pm, 17 pesos) but it is easier to use the red *taxi-colectivos* that gather in front of the bus station in Teapa on Mendez. They leave frequently and as soon as they have five people (45min., approx. every 20min., 20 pesos) and can also be caught in front of the bus station in Villahermosa.

OXOLOTAN

Taking a daytrip to Oxolotan (pop. 2000) is like taking a trip to the middle of nowhere—albeit an exquisitely beautiful middle of nowhere. The town's **Ex-Convento de Santo Domingo** is a good excuse to visit, but the real reason to go is for the bus ride into the mountains, and to kick it in one of the world's sleepiest towns. Amenity-free, staying the night might require a bit of negotiation, but is probably one of the best ways to get into the swing of village life.

By the time the Dominicans finally got around to evangelizing Tabasco in 1550, Oxolotan was an important trade center as the last navigable point for goods brought up the Rio Orijalva. From the town, goods were taken overland to other places in the mountains of Tabasco and Chiapas. By the time the building was finally finished in 1578, though, the town's importance had flagged, and the Dominicans relocated to Tacotalpa, leaving Oxolotan with an impressively grand parish church.

The church has been in use for the last 400 years, and a recent renovation has made the cloister into a typically polished museum. With turqoise doors open to the towering mountains and clouds, the virtually undecorated stone walls and strikingly quiet courtyards have a spare tranquility that permeates the town, whose old *zócalo* is formed by the ex-convento's ex-patio. *(Museum open daily 9am-5pm. Free.)*

Getting There: It's not easy. One bus serves the town, leaving every two hours from Tacotalpa. To get to Tacotalpa, catch one of the *colectivos* (20 pesos) that leave from the Villahermosa station. *Colectivos* stop on Tacotalpa's main drag. To catch the bus to Oxolotan, walk past the market and cross the street to the auditorium, which currently serves as a police station. Wait under the awning for a green-striped bus, which usually leaves every two hours from 9am to 5pm. The town is about 1½ hours into the mountains. Be sure to grab a window seat, because the views are spectacular. Return buses leave every two hours from 8am and the last chance to grab a bus back is at 6pm. If you miss it, you will be stuck. The man who lives in the blue house #256 across from the museum exit does rent rooms, though—and you may be glad you stayed, as the town is welcome respite from Tabasco's wild world and singeing heat.

CHIAPAS

TUXTLA GUTIÉRREZ

An energetic young city, Tuxtla Gutiérrez (pop. 350,000) is the capital of Chiapas and the focal point of commerce and transportation for most of southern Mexico. The city was named for a progressive *chiapaneco* governor who, rather than succumb to imperialist right-wing forces, wrapped himself in the Mexican flag and dramatically leapt to his death from a church spire. In some ways, the city has adopted the indomitable spirit of its namesake. Rather than bow to the pressures of rapid industrialization, Tuxtla has flourished with the help of vibrant citizens, pretty parks, and the vivacious, colorful animals that reside in one of the best zoos in Latin America.

🛬 ORIENTATION

Tuxtla Gutiérrez lies 85km west of San Cristóbal and 293km south of Villahermosa. *Avenidas* run east-west and *calles* north-south. The central axis of the city, upon which the *zócalo* rests, is formed by **Av. Central** (sometimes called **Av. 14 de Septiembre**) and **Calle Central**. Streets are numbered according to their distance from and geographical relation to the central axis. For example, Calle 2 Oriente Sur lies south of Av. Central and two blocks east of Calle Central. Fifteen blocks west of the town center, Calle Central becomes **Blvd. Dr. Belisario Domínguez;** 11 blocks east it turns into **Blvd. Angel Albino Corzo.**

To get to the *centro* from the **ADO/Cristóbal Colón bus station,** walk left on 2 Nte. Pte. (away from the buses) for two blocks. The *zócalo* is two blocks to the left on Av. Central. The **Autotransportes Tuxtla Gutiérrez station** is in a cul-de-sac near Av. 3 Sur and Calle 7 Ote. From the station, turn right and then make another right onto the walled-in alley that doubles as a market. Make the first left onto Av. 2 Sur and continue west to Calle Central—the *zócalo* is two blocks to the right. Travelers from Chiapa de Corzo often disembark at a small station on 3 Ote. between 2 and 3 Sur. Facing the street from the bus stop, head left to Av. Central, then left again for the *zócalo.* Major **bus** lines run west on 2 Sur, east on 1 Sur, north on 11 Ote., and south on 12 Ote. (daily 5am-11pm, 2 pesos). **Combis** (VW van *colectivos*) run frequently through the city (6am-10pm, 3 pesos).

🛈 PRACTICAL INFORMATION

TRANSPORTATION

Airport: Aeropuerto Francisco Sarabia (tel. 5 01 11), 15km southwest of town. **Taxtel** (tel. 5 31 95) runs to the airport and charges 50 pesos; a cheaper option is to grab a cab off the street (12 pesos). **Aerocaribe,** Av. Central Pte. 206 (tel. 2 00 20, at airport tel. 5 15 30). **Aviacsa,** Av. Centra l Pte. 1144 (tel. 2 80 81, at the airport tel. 5 10 11).

Buses: Cristóbal Colón/Maya de Oro, 2 Nte. Pte. 268 (tel. 2 51 22) runs first-class buses to: **Campeche** (12½hr., 3:30pm, 311 pesos); **Cancún** (18hr., 2:30pm, 495 pesos); **Chetumal** (13hr., 2:30pm, 342 pesos); **Escárcega** (9½hr., 12:30pm, 174 pesos); **Huatulco** (9½hr., 10:15am, 158 pesos); **Mérida** (14hr., 3:30pm, 362 pesos); **Mexico City** (15hr., 4 per day, 345 pesos); **Oaxaca** (10hr., 11:30am, 7:15 and 9:15pm, 154 pesos); **Ocosingo** (4hr., 6 per day 5am-midnight, 54 pesos); **Palenque** (6hr., 6 per day 5am-midnight, 92 pesos); **Playa del Carmen** (17hr., 12:30pm, 395 pesos); **Puebla** (13hr., 4 per day, 304 pesos); **Puerto Escondido** (11hr., 9:45am and 10:15pm, 310 pesos); **San Cristóbal** (2hr., every hr. 5am-midnight, 27 pesos); **Tapachula** (6hr., 14 per day 6am-midnight, 138 pesos); **Tonalá** (3½hr., every hr. 6am-11pm, 62 pesos); **Tulum** (16½hr., 12:30pm, 360 pesos); **Veracruz** (12hr., 7:30 and 8:45pm, 310 pesos); and **Villahermosa** (6hr., 4 per day 1-11:45pm, 101 pesos). Autotransportes Tuxtla Gutiérrez, 3 Sur 712 (tel. 2 03 22 and 2 02 88), between 5 and 6 Ote., has less frequent buses to the same destinations at cheaper fares.

Local Transportation: One of the cheapest ways to get to **San Cristóbal** is via **Transporte Colosio** which send *combis* every 10min. from 3am-9pm. To reach Chiapa de Corzo, hop on a **Transportes Chiapa-Tuxtla** *microbús* at the station at 2 Sur and 2 Ote. (25min., every 10min., 8 pesos) or grab one leaving town on Blvd. Corzo.

Car Rental: Tuxtla Rent-A-Car, Blvd. Dr. Dominguez 2510 (tel. 5 13 82), across from the Pepsi-Cola factory. As cheap as they come in the big city; be ready to bargain for lower prices. VW sedan 526 pesos per day. Open daily 7am-7pm.

TOURIST AND FINANCIAL SERVICES

Tourist Office: Dirección Municipal de Turismo (tel. 2 55 11, ext. 214), 2 Nte. Ote. at Calle Central, tucked under the northwest corner of the *zócalo* has a very useful city map and information about surrounding areas. Open M-F 8am-4pm, Sa 8am-1pm.

Currency Exchange: Banamex, 1 Sur Pte. 141 (tel. 2 87 44), at Calle Central. Credit card cash advances and 24hr. **ATM.** Open for exchange M-F 9am-3:30pm.

American Express: (tel. 2 69 98), on Blvd. Dr. Belisario Domínguez, across from the tourist office near Plaza Bonampak, doubles as a **travel agency.** English spoken. Open M-F 9am-2pm and 4-6:30pm, Sa 9am-1pm.

LOCAL SERVICES

Laundry: Lavandería Automática Burbuja, 1 Nte. 413A (tel. 1 05 95), at 3 Pte. 10 pesos per kg. Open M-Sa 8am-8pm, Su 9am-1pm.

Markets: Tuxtla's crazy *mercado* squares off on 1 Pte. between Av. 4 and 5 Sur. A frenzied atmosphere characterizes the whole area filled with food and cheap lodgings.

EMERGENCY AND COMMUNICATIONS

Emergency: dial 06 or call **Policía de Seguridad Pública** (tel. 2 05 30 or 3 78 05).

Police: (tel. 2 11 06), in the Palacio Municipal, at the north end of the *zócalo.* Go left upon entering the building. No English spoken. Open 24hr.

Pharmacy: Farmacia 24 Horas, 1 Sur 716, between 6 and 7 Pte. Open 24hr.

Red Cross: 5 Nte. Pte. 1480 (tel. 2 95 14), on the west side of town. Open 24hr.

Hospital: Sanatorio Rojas, 2 Av. Sur Pte. 1487 (tel. 2 54 14 or 2 54 66). Emergency service 24hr. English spoken.

Post Office: (tel. 2 04 16), on 1 Nte. at 2 Ote., on the northeast corner of the *zócalo* in the corridor to the right of the Palacio Municipal. Open M-F 9am-2pm and 4-6pm, Sa 9am-noon. **Postal Code:** 29000.

Fax: Telcomm (tel. 3 65 47; fax 2 42 96), on 1 Nte. at 2 Ote., next to the post office. Open for **telegrams** and fax M-F 8am-6pm, Sa 9am-1pm.

Internet Access: Cybercafé Net-Hopper, 2 Nte. 427 between 3 and 4 Pte. (tel. 2 01 73) has hip, long-haired staff. 15 pesos per hr. Open daily 9am-9pm. The better option is two blocks down and one block left at **Compucentro** 1 Nte. Pte. 675, (tel. 2 53 53) on the 2nd. fl. Fast service 15 pesos per hr. Open M-F 9am-9pm, Su 10am-2pm.

Phone Code: 961.

▎ ACCOMMODATIONS

Budget accommodations are as they should be in a capital city: affordable, decent, and convenient. The best bargains can be found in the area around the *mercado* where cheap hotels cater to vendors from the surrounding countryside.

▨ **Villas Deportivas Juvenil,** Angel Albino Corzo 1800 (tel. 3 34 05), next to the yellow footbridge over the road. Immaculate, single-sex 4 person rooms have comfortable beds, cooling fans, and spotless communal bathrooms. A favorite with international travelers, the atmosphere is surprisingly tranquil with lots of conversation over the good budget meals and options for pick up games on the basketball courts and soccer fields. From the *centro,* catch a *combi* headed towads Gigante and ask the driver to let you off at INDEJECH. 30 pesos per person. Breakfast, lunch and dinner each 15 pesos.

Hotel Del Pasaje, 5 Sur Pte. (2 15 51), undisputed king of the city's budget hotel market. Located near the *mercado* in the middle of everything, the rooms are in that no-nonsense vein that lends itself to cleanliness and comfort. Singles 60 pesos, doubles 80 pesos; singles with A/C 80 pesos, doubles 90 pesos.

Hotel Don Candido, 5 Sur Ote. 142 (tel. 2 66 06) is pricier, but will please the esthete in you, offering colorful decor and a sunny courtyard of potted plants. Located near the market, this central location is missing the 24-hour in your face noise that can be problematic in the cheaper hotels. Clean rooms have fans, phones and color TVs. Singles 95 pesos; doubles 110 pesos.

Hotel Avenida, Av. Central 244 (tel. 2 08 07), between 1 and 2 Pte., 1½ blocks west of the *zócalo,* is all about location and that fragrant whiff of coffee that lingers around the door. Great for displaced Manhattanites, the main-street location proximity to the best black brew in town and big, clean rooms makes it all worth the price. Singles 100 pesos; doubles 150 pesos.

ⓕ FOOD

Culinary miracles don't happen in Tuxtla, but the city is speckled with inexpensive eateries. Vegetarians should feel right at home in the upsurge of local interest in natural foods. Though *licuados* are nothing new to a town that likes its fruit, the explosion in health food stores means that nutty, grainy, yogurty treats are easy to come by. Carnivores should not fear, though—typically meaty Mexican cuisine still prevails.

 Restaurante Imperial, Calle Central Nte. 263 (tel. 2 06 48), 1 block from the *zócalo* became so popular that the owners opened a sister restaurant across the street. Though the white-washed walls, wood tables and colorful tablecloths make the meal a spiffy affair, the excellent 21 peso *comida corrida,* 17 peso *antojitos,* and 7-13 peso breakfasts are the secret to the imperialism. Open daily 7am-7pm.

Restaurante Vegetariano Nah-Yaxal, 6 Pte. 124 (tel. 3 96 48), north of Av. Central is the leader in the movement to make all of Tuxtla's *pan integral.* Nah has colonized several storefronts around the *centro.* Full blown vegetarian meals go for 27 pesos but the biggest hit is the frozen yogurt which can be mixed with almost every fruit and grain imaginable in the joint around the corner from the pilot store (small 7 pesos). Other location: Central Ote. 649. Open M-Sa 7am-10pm, Su 3-10pm.

La Antigua Fogata, 4 Ote. Sur 115, just off Av. Central. Although the restaurant may look like a tin-roofed shack, they have 24 years of experience behind their scrumptious chicken *al carbón.* Quarter-chicken (25 pesos)—quite a find. Open daily 7:30am-midnight.

👁 SIGHTS

The shady forest foliage of the **Miguel Alvarez del Toro Zoo** offers a refreshing change of scenery from Tuxtla's gritty urban landscape. To get to the zoo, take the "Cerro Hueco" or "Zoológico" bus, which leaves from 1 Ote. between 6 and 7 Sur (every 30min., 2 pesos). The bus traces an indirect and sometimes unbearably slow route to the zoo's front gate. Renowned throughout Latin America, the zoo houses only animals native to Chiapas, including playful monkeys, stealthy jaguars, bright green parrots, and rare quetzals. Many of the enclosed forest's inhabitants roam freely throughout the park. To return to the center, catch the same bus at the zoo's entrance as it goes up the mountain. *(Open Tu-Su 9am-5:30pm; free.)*

The **Conviviencia Infantil** (though many signs still read **"Parque Madero"**) unfurls in the northeast part of town at the intersection of 11 Ote. and 5 Nte. Its focal point is a large and modern theater, the **Teatro de la Ciudad Emilio Rabasa.** Films by Latin American directors and performances of *ballet folklórico* dominate the schedule (check the tourist information center for details). A children's amusement park is on the pleasant *paseo* east of the theater (open Tu-Su 9am-10pm). Past the amusement park is the open-air **Teatro Bonampak,** where free folk dance performances are held (Su 5-8pm). The eastern extremity of Parque Madero is demarcated by a light aircraft next to the open-air theater, upon which several eight-year-old fighter-pilots-in-the-making usually clamber. A broad concourse, lined with fountains and bronze busts of famous Mexicans, leads west of the theater past the **Museo Regional de Chiapas,** which displays the region's archaeological finds (open Tu-Su 9am-4pm; admission 20 pesos, Su free). Farther down the concourse, at the **Jardín Botánico Dr. Faustino Miranda,** you can amble under towering *ceibas* (silk-cotton trees) and admire the colorful grandeur of Chiapanecan flora (open Tu-Su 9am-6pm). Across the concourse is the **Museo Botánico** (open M-F 9am-3pm, Sa 9am-1pm). Back in the center, the air-conditioned **Cinema Vistarama Tuxtla** (tel. 2 18 31), at 1 Sur and 5 Ote., shows mostly American films with Spanish subtitles (admission 15 pesos).

CHIAPA DE CORZO

What Tuxtla Gutierrez lacks in history, colonial architecture, and sights is quickly made up for by Chiapa de Corzo (pop. 90,760) and its spectacular **Canyon del Submerido.** Located 15km and 25 minutes from Tuxtla, the two cities enjoy a simbiotic relationship where Chiapa serves as Tuxtla's main attraction, and Tuxtla reciprocates by taking care of Chiapa's dirty work—allowing the city to remain quaint and scenic. Graced by an unusual 16th-century fountain and church, the town's greatest boon is its proximity to the canyon, carved by the Río Grijalva decending from the highlands. Once unnavigable, the dam built at the edge of the canyon has made it accessible to *lanchas* which leave from Chiapa's dock and zip through the canyon's lush walls, which soar to heights of 1200m above the river. Although usually visited as a daytrip, Chiapa's small town feel and position as a major regional and transportation hub make it an ideal place to kick back and spend the night before heading for the hills.

☑ ORIENTATION AND PRACTICAL INFORMATION. Chiapa de Corzo overlooks the Río Grijalva, 15km east of Tuxtla and 68km west of San Cristóbal. Most sights lie near the *zócalo* **(Plaza Angel Albino Corzo),** which is bounded on the north by 21 de Octubre (the Tuxtla-San Cristóbal Highway), on the east by **La Mexicanidad,** on the south by **Julián Grajales,** and on the west by **5 de Febrero. Boats** leave for **El Sumidero** from the riverbank, two blocks southwest of the *zócalo*, on 5 de Febrero. Because Chiapa is the last stop on Rte. 190 before things get mountainous and the road forks off for San Cristóbal, all buses and *combis* headed north out of Tuxtla make steps to pick up passengers. If you want to find cheap transport, it's generally easier to sit at the edge of the highway at Chiapa and wait for buses to stop than it is to hunt it down in Tuxtla. The highway is easily reached by buses running from the edge of the *zócalo*.

Transportes Chiapa-Tuxtla *microbuses*, heading back to Tuxtla, stop on 21 de Octubre opposite the police station (25min., every 10min., 6 pesos). Contact the **tourist office** in **Tuxtla** for detailed tourist information. **Bancomer** (tel. 6 03 20) is on the eastern side of the *zócalo* with a 24hr. **ATM** (open M-F 8am-3pm, Sa 10am-2pm). **Police station:** (tel. 6 02 26) in the Palacio Municipal, on the northeast side of the *zócalo* (open 24hr.). **Farmacia Esperanza:** (tel. 6 04 54) on 21 de Octubre, one block east of the *zócalo* (open M-Sa 7am-11pm, Su 7am-2pm). **Post office:** Calle Cenullo Aguilar 244, 1½ blocks north of the *zócalo* (open M-F 8am-6pm). **Postal code:** 29160. **Phone code:** 968.

☑ ACCOMMODATIONS AND FOOD. Most people visit Chiapa de Corzo as a daytrip from Tuxtla. However, the **Hotel Los Angeles,** Julián Grajales 2 (tel. 6 00 48), at La Mexicanidad, on the southeast corner of the *zócalo*, makes a good case for staying the night. Tall rooms have wooden bed frames and firm mattresses facing a large, pleasant courtyard. (Singles 80 pesos; doubles 100 pesos; triples 120 pesos; quads 140 pesos.) Since you've come to Chiapa to see the river, you may as well head to the waterfront for mid-range, filling food. Cheaper food can be found at the **market** to the left of the church (open dawn to dusk). **Restaurant Comitán,** to the left as you hit the dock, offers a 25-peso breakfast special, occasional live *marimba* performances, and a view of the river partly obscured by the overgrown banks (open daily 8am-7pm). Back up from the docks at the corner of the *zócalo* at Madero, **Restaurante Los Corredores** looks much more expensive than it is. One of the best places to try *comida típica* in the region, the restaurant offers a beautiful courtyard and a cool, colorful interior. Breakfasts are under 20 pesos and seasonal specialties such as *chiles en nogada* are 25 pesos. Fish fillets with all the fixings are 45 pesos.

☑ SIGHTS. *Chiapañecos* are very proud of their immense **Cañon del Samidero;** the landmark adorns the state seal. A two-hour *lancha* journey begins with humble views of cornfields, but shortly after the Belisario Domínguez bridge, the hills jump to form near-vertical cliffs that rise over 1200m above the water. Protected as a natural park, these steep walls are home to troupes of monkeys, humming-birds, and soaring falcons, while the murky waters harbor crocodiles and turtles. Along the meandering river lies a dripping cave and the park's most famous water-fall, the **Arbol de Navidad.** This spectacular *cascada* plummets from the sky, dash-ing over a series of scalloped rock formations before disintegrating into a fine mist that envelops passing boats. El Sumidero's northernmost extremity is marked by the 200m-high hydroelectric dam **Netzahualcóyotl,** which along with three other dams on the Río Grijalva, provides 25% of Mexico's electricity.

Boats leave as soon as they're full from Chiapa's *embarcadero* (dock) at the end of 5 de Febrero, two blocks from the southwest corner of the *zócalo* (departing daily 7am-4:30pm; 60 pesos per person). Boats can also be taken up the canyon from **Cahuaré,** where the highway to Tuxtla Gutiérrez crosses the river near the Cahuaré Island Resort. The trip down the river is best made during the month of August, at the height of the rainy season, when up to 42 waterfalls can be seen.

Back in Chiapa de Corzo, the *zócalo* contains two colonial structures: a small **clock tower** and a **fountain** shaped like the crown of Queen Isabel of Spain. Often called **La Pila,** this famous Moorish fountain taps underground waterways 5km long and provided the town with fresh drinking water during a 1562 epidemic. Inside the fountain, tile plaques tell the story of Chiapa's colonial-era history. The red-and-white **Catedral de Santo Domingo** sits one block south of the *zócalo* near Río Grijalva. The most famous of the four bells dangling in its tower, Teresa de Jesús, is named after a mystical Spanish saint. (Open daily 6am-2pm and 4-6:30pm.) Alongside the cathedral, a 16th-century ex-convent houses the **Museo de la Laca,** which displays fine examples of Mexican lacquerwork, a handicraft practiced only in Chiapa de Corzo and four other cities (open Tu-Su 10am-4pm; free). You can also join one of the ongoing lacquering lessons during the summer months (check posted schedules in the museum).

During Chiapa's **Fiesta de San Sebastián** (Jan. 16-22), *los parachicos*, men in heavy costumes and stifling masks, dance from dawn to dusk. The fiesta's grand finale is a mock **Combate Naval** between *"españoles"* and *"indios."* More a beauty pageant than a battle, the event features decorated boats, costumed sail-ors, and fireworks.

SEMOJOVEL

As the bus winds closer to Semojovel (pop. 14,000), 3½ hours to the north of Tux-tla Gutíerrez, people hop off and disappear into the dense green curtains that swath the side of the road. The mystery of where they live only straightens itself out by night when the twinkling lights of their remote hillside *pueblos* can be seen against the dark mountains that range around the town.

Cut into the side of one of these mountains, Semojovel serves as a channel through which goods, people, and amber from the highlands first pass on their way to the cities farther south. What there is to see in Semojovel isn't as brilliantly obvious as it might be in the towns around San Cristóbal, but good things come to those who wait, watch, and know how to be pleased by the way the clouds shift over the spectacular panorama.

The main thing to see and do in Semojovel is buy **amber.** When foreigners visit the town, they are instantly mobbed by people carrying baskets of toilet paper and calling out *ambar* and *insectos.* Give them the chance and they will careful unwrap the toilet paper cocoons to reveal shining chunks of the 30-40 thousand year old tree sap, which sometimes entombs pre-historic insects unlucky enough to have been trapped while resting in the primeval forest.

Ⓐ AMBER AND PRACTICAL INFORMATION. Semojovel sits directly above some of the best amber mines in the world, and everybody in town seems to have a foot in the business. Amber suppliers who work with jewelers in San Cristóbal frequently come up and haggle with townspeople, buying both *crudo* (unpolished, uncut chunks) and the jewelry that is carefully shaped out of the brittle material.

While the uninitiated traveler is sure to receive worse bargains than the dirt cheap prices paid by Mexican buyers, the prices will still be far lower than what you'd pay anywhere else in the world. The only official store in town, **Bazar Choj-Choj** (tel. 50 00 47), on 26 de Abril just off the *zócalo*, also charges the highest prices. The jewelry is well-made and is a good pick for anyone uncomfortable with street bartering; it's more fun to plant yourself in the *zócalo* and wait for people to come to you. It can be hard to see the little *insectos*, but if you can find a **loop** (a little magnifying glass) and some good sunlight, you'll be able to see a menagerie of bugs—from little *moscas* (flies) to transparent *mariposas* (butterflies) whose wings have lost their color in the chemical process that turns the sap to amber. Although the mines are just below the town, good luck getting to see them—they are something of a town secret and reputably dangerous.

Semojovel consists of a long main drag, **20 de Noviembre,** which runs across the mountain parallel to the road from Bochil. Most action happens on this street, and on **24 de Febrero,** the parallel street a block down the hill. The two bus companies that connect the town to Tuxtla Gutiérrez are located at the corner of 20 de Noviembre and Ignacio Allende, three blocks south of the *zócalo*. Return buses can be caught at one or the other (3½hr., every hr. 4am-5pm, 23 pesos). From Tuxtla Gutiérrez, buses can be caught from **Transporte Pichuculco** at 5 Ote. at 4 Sur Ote. (4:30, 10am, 1:30, and 5:30pm). It is also possible to get there by *minis*, town-hopping until you arrive. **Pharmacy:** on the *zócalo* opposite the church (open daily 8am-10pm). **Phone code:** 968.

▐▐ ACCOMMODATIONS AND FOOD. Right on the *zócalo*, **Hotel Leon** offers a great location, clean and minimalistic rooms, and a very colorful proprietor. All have fans and private baths and some rooms have half obstructed views of the mountains to the east. (Singles 40 pesos; doubles 50 pesos.) Although the rooms in **Hotel Bugambilias,** Constitución Ote. 5 (tel. 5 03 27), have no views, the balcony is jaw-dropping. You'll pay a little more for the privilege, as well as the TV that comes with. (Singles 85 pesos; doubles 100 pesos.)

Restaurants in Semojovel center around the *zócalo*, with taco stands, a *torta* shop, and a place to buy *licuados*. Located on 20 de Noviembre, half a block past the *zócalo* on the left, a little **patio restaurant** makes what might well be the world's greatest *mole*. The *mercado* located south of the *zócalo* on the left, is a good place to pick up supplies, and to find people from the Maya towns in the hillsides who are doing the same. (Open 8am-1pm.)

SAN CRISTÓBAL DE LAS CASAS

San Cristóbal de Las Casas (pop. 120,000) is nestled in the pine-filled Valley of Hueyzacatlán at an elevation of 2100m. The city derives its popularity from the picturesque and unsullied colonial garden courtyards, red-tile roofs, and narrow streets. The invigorating highland climate is infused by the remarkable diversity of Chiapan culture. Top this combination off with a panorama of lush green mountains enshrouded by spectacular formations of clouds as they tumble down the steep slopes into San Cristóbal's outskirts, and you'll understand why hordes of Mexican and foreign tourists continuously flock here. A large resident contingent of North Americans and northern Europeans rounds out the populace and is primarily responsible for such facets of the city as clothing boutiques, English movies, international cuisine, and heartfelt campaigns to save the Lacandón jungle.

Although San Cristóbal is a much-touristed, aesthetic wonder, its civic life has long been animated by the age-old conflict between *ladinos* and *indígenas*. Founded in 1528 by the invading Spaniards and their Central Mexican allies, San Cristóbal de Las Casas was once the colonial capital of the region—a *ladino* enclave in the midst of Maya territory. Over the years, *ladino* culture has become increasingly dominant in San Cristóbal, and some *indígenas* have adopted Western clothing and manners as their own. For most, however, syncretism has prevailed as Catholicism mixes with shamanistic practices, and most women still wear braids with colorful ribbons and grand *rebozo* scarves. Local merchants travel 20km or more to Sunday markets, dressed in clothing whose patterns haven't altered in centuries, while even the most remote indigenous villages are served by the Coca-Cola truck at least once a week. Step outside the city, and Spanish becomes residents' second language behind the Mayan tongues of Tzeltal and Tzotzil.

> **INSURRECTION.** In the early morning hours of New Year's Day in 1994, Zapatista insurgents caught all of Mexico by surprise by taking hold of parts of the city (for details, see p. 21). As of August 1999, peaceful negotiations between the government and insurgents were still deadlocked, but tourists visiting the sights and neighboring villages of San Cristóbal should not encounter any difficult situations as long as a visa and passport are **always** carried on their person. People who come here with political or human rights intentions, however, could very well face deportation.

✳ ORIENTATION

High in the **Altos de Chiapas,** San Cristóbal lies 83km east of Tuxtla Gutiérrez, 78km northwest of Comitán, and 191km southwest of Palenque. **Route 190,** the Pan-American Highway, cuts east from Tuxtla Gutiérrez, touches the southern edge of San Cristóbal, and then heads southeast to Comitán and Ciudad Cuauhtémoc at the Guatemalan border.

First- and second-class **bus stations** are scattered along the Pan-American Highway. near **Av. Insurgentes.** From the **Cristóbal Colón bus station,** take a right (north) on Insurgentes and walk seven blocks to the *zócalo.* From the other bus stations, walk east on any cross-street and turn left on Insurgentes. Since San Cristóbal is a popular destination for tourists, most of whom travel by bus, book seats as far in advance as possible during Christmas and *Semana Santa.* At all other times, reservations made one day in advance will suffice.

Most of San Cristóbal's clearly labeled streets fall into a neat grid. The *zócalo,* also known as **Plaza 31 de Marzo,** is the city center. The four cardinal directions are indicated by prominent landmarks around town: the church and former convent of **Santo Domingo** are to the north, the gold-trimmed **Templo de Guadalupe** is on the hill to the east, the **Cristóbal Colón first-class bus station** lies to the south, and the **Church of San Cristobalito** resides on the hilltop to the west. Streets change names when crossing imaginary north-south and east-west axes centered at the *zócalo.* Av. Insurgentes connects the town center to the Pan-American Highway, becoming **Av. Utrilla** past the *zócalo.* Municipal buses and *colectivos* criss-cross town with destinations indicated on the window—just wave to catch one (4 pesos). **Taxis** (tel. 8 03 96) line up along the north side of the *zócalo.* Standard fare within town is 12 pesos, while prices to nearby villages are negotiable.

🔃 PRACTICAL INFORMATION

TRANSPORTATION

Buses: The following listings include both **Cristóbal Colón** (tel. 8 02 91) and **Maya de Oro** buses, which both leave from the station on the Pan-American Highway at Insurgentes, 7 blocks south of the *zócalo.* First-class service to: **Campeche** (10hr., 9:30am and 5:30pm, 225-275 pesos); **Cancún** (17hr.; 12:15, 2:30, and 4:30pm; 360-480 pesos); **Chetumal** (12hr.; 12:15, 2:30, and 4:30pm; 250-315 pesos); **Comitán** (1½hr., 12 per day 7am-9:30pm, 45-55 pesos); **Escárcega** (8hr., 12:15 and 2:30pm, 175-185 pesos); the **Guatemalan border** (3hr., 4 per day 12:30am-11:30pm, 90 pesos); **Mérida** (12hr., 9:30am and 5:30pm, 260-280 pesos); **Mexico City** (18hr., 1:50 and 6pm, 395-500 pesos); **Oaxaca** (12hr., 5 and 8pm, 225-300 pesos); **Palenque** (5hr., 10 per day 7:30am-6:30pm, 80-100 pesos); **Puebla** (16hr., 1:50 and

The MCI WorldCom Card.

The easy way to call when traveling worldwide.

The MCI WorldCom Card gives you...

- Access to the US and other countries worldwide.
- Customer Service 24 hours a day
- Operators who speak your language
- Great MCI WorldCom rates and no sign-up fees

For more information or to apply for a Card call:

1-800-955-0925

Outside the U.S., call MCI WorldCom collect (reverse charge) at:

1-712-943-6839

COUNTRY	WORLDPHONE TOLL-FREE ACCESS #
Argentina (CC)	
To call using Telefonica ■	0800-222-6249
To call using Telecom ■	0800-555-1002
Australia (CC) ◆	
To call using AAPT ■	1-800-730-014
To call using OPTUS ■	1-800-551-111
To call using TELSTRA ■	1-800-881-100
Austria (CC) ◆	0800-200-235
Bahamas	1-800-888-8000
Belgium (CC) ◆	0800-10012
Bermuda ÷	1-800-888-8000
Bolivia (CC) ◆	0-800-2222
Brazil (CC)	000-8012
British Virgin Islands ÷	1-800-888-8000
Canada (CC)	1-800-888-8000
Cayman Islands	1-800-888-8000
Chile (CC)	
To call using CTC ■	800-207-300
To call using ENTEL ■	800-360-180
China ✣	108-12
For a Mandarin-speaking Operator	108-17
Colombia (CC) ◆	980-9-16-0001
Collect Access in Spanish	980-9-16-1111
Costa Rica ◆	0800-012-2222
Czech Republic (CC) ◆	00-42-000112
Denmark (CC) ◆	8001-0022
Dominican Republic	
Collect Access	1-800-888-8000
Collect Access in Spanish	1121
Ecuador (CC) ÷	999-170
El Salvador	800-1767

COUNTRY	WORLDPHONE TOLL-FREE ACCESS #
Finland (CC) ◆	08001-102-80
France (CC) ◆	0800-99-0019
French Guiana (CC)	0-800-99-0019
Guatemala (CC) ◆	99-99-189
Germany (CC)	0-800-888-8000
Greece (CC) ◆	00-800-1211
Guam (CC)	1-800-888-8000
Haiti ÷	193
Collect Access in French/Creole	190
Honduras ÷	8000-122
Hong Kong (CC)	800-96-1121
Hungary (CC) ◆	00▼800-01411
India (CC) ÷	000-127
Collect Access	000-126
Ireland (CC) ◆	1-800-55-1001
Israel (CC)	
BEZEQ International	1-800-940-2727
BARAK	1-800-930-2727
Italy (CC) ◆	172-1022
Jamaica ÷	
Collect Access	1-800-888-8000
(From Special Hotels only)	873
(From public phones)	#2
Japan (CC) ◆	To call using KDD ■ 00539-121▶
To call using IDC ■	0066-55-121
To call using JT ■	0044-11-121
Korea (CC)	To call using DACOM ■ 00309-12
To call using ONSE	00369-14
Phone Booths ÷	Press red button, 03, then ●
Military Bases	550-2255
Lebanon	Collect Access 600-MCI (600-624)

COUNTRY	WORLDPHONE TOLL-FREE ACCESS #
Luxembourg (CC)	0800-0112
Malaysia (CC) ◆	1-800-80-0012
To call using Time Telekom	1-800-18-0012
Mexico (CC)	Avantel 01-800-021-8000
Telmex ▲	001-800-674-7000
Collect Access in Spanish	01-800-021-1000
Monaco (CC) ◆	800-90-019
Netherlands (CC) ◆	0800-022-9122
New Zealand (CC)	000-912
Nicaragua (CC)	Collect Access in Spanish 166
(Outside of Managua, dial 02 first)	
Norway (CC) ◆	800-19912
Panama	108
Military Bases	2810-108
Philippines (CC) ◆	To call using PLDT ■ 105-14
To call using PHILCOM	1026-14
To call using Bayantel	1237-14
To call using ETPI	1066-14
Poland (CC) ÷	00-800-111-21-22
Portugal (CC) ÷	800-800-123
Puerto Rico (CC)	1-800-888-8000
Romania (CC) ÷	01-800-1800
Russia (CC) ◆ ÷	
To call using ROSTELCOM ■	747-3322
(For Russian speaking operator)	747-3320
To call using SOVINTEL ■	960-2222
Saudi Arabia (CC) ÷	1-800-11
Singapore	8000-112-112
Slovak Republic	(CC) 00421-00112
South Africa (CC)	0800-99-0011
Spain (CC)	900-99-0014

Worldwide Calling Made Easy

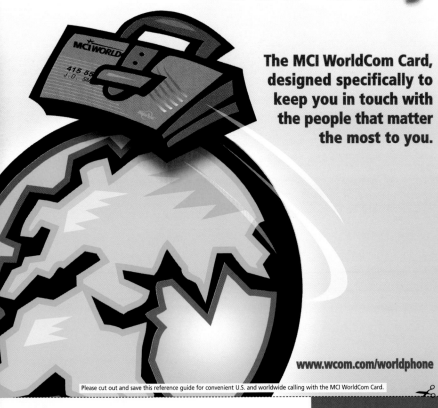

The MCI WorldCom Card, designed specifically to keep you in touch with the people that matter the most to you.

www.wcom.com/worldphone

Please cut out and save this reference guide for convenient U.S. and worldwide calling with the MCI WorldCom Card.

And, it's simple to call home or to other countires.

1. Dial the WorldPhone toll-free access number of the country you're calling from (listed inside).

2. Follow the easy voice instructions or hold for a WorldPhone operator. Enter or give the operator your MCI WorldCom Card number or call collect.

3. Enter or give the WorldPhone operator your home number.

4. Share your adventures with your family!

COUNTRY		WORLDPHONE TOLL-FREE ACCESS #
St. Lucia ÷		1-800-888-8000
Sweden (CC) ◆		020-795-922
Switzerland (CC) ◆		0800-89-0222
Taiwan (CC) ◆		0080-13-4567
Thailand ★		001-999-1-2001
Turkey (CC) ◆		00-8001-1177
United Kingdom	(CC) To call using BT ■	0800-89-0222
	To call using CWC ■	0500-89-0222
United States (CC)		1-800-888-8000
U.S. Virgin Islands (CC)		1-800-888-8000
Vatican City (CC)		172-1022
Venezuela (CC) ÷ ◆		800-1114-0
Vietnam ●		1201-1022

(CC)   Country-to-country calling available to/from most international locations.
÷   Limited availability.
▼   Wait for second dial tone.
▲   When calling from public phones, use phones marked LADATEL.
■   International communications carrier.
★   Not available from public pay phones.
◆   Public phones may require deposit of coin or phone card for dial tone.
●   Local service fee in U.S. currency required to complete call.
▶   Regulation does not permit Intra-Japan calls.
✧   Available from most major cities

MCI WorldCom Worldphone Access Numbers

MCI *WORLDCOM*℠

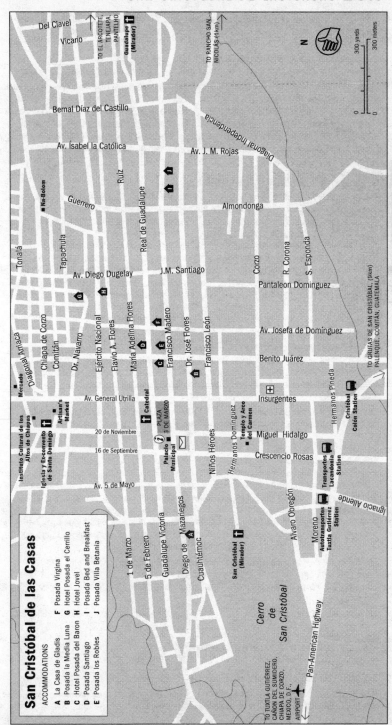

San Cristóbal de las Casas

ACCOMMODATIONS

A La Casa de Gladis
B Posada la Media Luna
C Hotel Posada del Baron
D Posada Santiago
E Posada los Robles
F Posada Virgina
G Hotel Posada el Cerrillo
H Hotel Jovel
I Posada Bed and Breakfast
J Posada Villa Betania

6pm, 370-420 pesos); **Puerto Escondido** (12hr., 7:45am and 6:15pm, 250 pesos); **Tulum** (13hr., 12:15 and 2:30pm, 310-375 pesos); and **Tuxtla Gutiérrez** (2hr., 9 per day 7am-9:15pm, 35-50 pesos).

Car Rental: Budget, Mazariegos 36 (tel. 8 18 71 or 8 31 00), 2 blocks west of the *zócalo*. With prices starting at 370 pesos per day, it's time they changed their name. Open M-Sa 8am-2pm and 4-8pm, Su 8-11am.

Bike Rental: Los Penguinos, Av. 5 de Mayo #10-B (tel. 8 02 02; email pinguinos@hotmail.com), between 5 de Febrero and Guadalupe Victoria. 55 pesos per 5 hr. or 70 pesos per day. English, German, and Spanish tours available through hidden rivers, a mountain bridge, a monastery, and an indigenous village. Open M-Sa 10am-2:30pm and 4-7pm; Su 10am-2:30pm. Tours leave at 8:15am with a 2 person minimum and 1-day advance reservations.

TOURIST AND FINANCIAL SERVICES

Travel Agencies: Viajes Navarra, Real de Guadalupe 15D (tel. 8 11 43), between Belisario Dominguez and Colón, 2 blocks east of the *zócalo* has daytrips to Cañon del Sumidero, Chiapa de Corzo, Lagunas de Montebello, Palenque, and indigenous villages. Open daily 8am-2pm and 4pm-10pm. **Viajes Nichim,** Av. Benito Juárez 4B (tel. 8 35 20; fax 8 39 09) between Flores and Madero, 2 blocks southeast of the *zócalo*. Three-day jungle adventures, horse excursions to nearby villages, and a visit to "Casa de Pascuala and Petrona," home of 2 internationally known weavers, has daytrips to Palenque, Aqual Azul and Misol-Ha and a half-day city tour. Open daily 9am-2pm and 4-9pm. **Viajes Pakal,** Cuauhtémoc 6A (tel. 8 42 93; fax 8 28 19), between Insurgentes and Hidalgo, 1 block south of the *zócalo*. has daytrips to Agua Azul, Grutas de San Cristóbal, Palenque, and nearby villages. Trips to Bonampak, Yaxchilán, and Guatemala can be specially arranged. Open M-F 9am-2pm and 4-8pm, Sa 9am-1pm.

Tourist Office: Main branch located on Hidalgo 1, Loc. A (tel. 8 65 70) ½ block south of the *zócalo*. Open M-Sa 9am-9pm, Su 9am-3pm. The branch office (tel. 8 06 60), at the northwest end of the Palacio Municipal, has even more info. Open M-Sa 9am-8pm, Su 9am-2pm. **Information booth** at the Cristóbal Colón terminal, has maps and brochures. Some English spoken. Open sporadically.

Currency Exchange: Bancomer, Plaza 31 de Marzo 10 (tel. 8 01 37), on the southern side of the *zócalo*. 24hr. **ATM.** Open M-F 9am-5:30pm, Sa 10am-2pm.

LOCAL SERVICES

English Bookstore: La Pared, Hidalgo 2 (tel. 8 63 67), half block south of the *zócalo*, buys, trades, sells, and lends used books. Open M-Sa 10am-2pm and 4-8pm; Su during high season. **Libreria La Quimera**, Real de Guadalupe 24C (tel. 8 59 70, e-mail: lucas@sancristobal.podernet.com.mx), between Belisario Domínguez and Utrila. Anthropology, history, literature, and art books in Spanish. Discounts for students. Open daily 9am-noon, 4pm-8pm. **La Casa de la Luna,** Real de Guadalupe 118 between Guerrero and Isabel la Católica, shows feminist films and has round table discussions and Kundalini Yoga classes. Open M-Sa 10am-2pm and 4-8pm.

Markets: The *mercado* between Utrilla and Domínguez, 7 blocks north of the *zócalo* has the best selection on Saturdays. Open daily 6am-2pm. A huge **artisan's market** forms around the Santo Domingo Church, 5 blocks north of the *zócalo* on Utrilla. Open daily 8am-5pm.

Laundry: Orve, Domínguez 5 (tel. 8 18 02), between Real de Guadalupe and Madero. 28 pesos for 1-3kg, 8 pesos per additional kg. Open M-Sa 8am-8pm.

EMERGENCY AND COMMUNICATIONS

Emergency: dial 060.

Police: (tel. 8 05 54) in the Palacio Municipal, on the west side of the *zócalo*.

Red Cross: Ignacio Allende 57 (tel. 8 07 72), 3 blocks south of the Pan-American Highway. No English spoken. 24hr. emergency service.

Farmacia Regina: (tel. 8 02 41) Mazariegos at Crescencio Rosas. No English spoken. Open 24hr.

Hospital General: Insurgentes 24 (tel. 8 07 70), 4 blocks south of the *zócalo* across from Santa Lucía in Parque Fray Bartolomé. Open 24hr.

Post Office: (tel. 8 07 65) on Cuauhtémoc at Crescencio Rosas, 1 block southwest of the *zócalo*. Open M-F 8am-7pm, Sa 9am-1pm. **MexPost,** in the same office. Open M-F 8am-7pm. **Postal Code:** 29200.

Fax: Mazariegos 29 (tel. 8 42 71), 2½ blocks from the *zócalo*. Open M-F 8am-6pm, Sa 9am-noon.

Internet Access: Tapanco Cybercafe (tel. 8 66 64), 1 de Marzo at Av. 20 de Noviembre is the classiest and most comfortable of all the cybercafes with a 2nd fl. cabin, couches, and a chess table. 12 pesos per 15min. Open daily 8am-11pm. **El Puente,** Real de Guadalupe 55 (tel. 8 37 23), 3 blocks east of the *zócalo*, has more than 300 songs installed in each computer. Listen to your favorite tunes while chatting with friends. 15 pesos per 30min. Open daily 8am-11pm.

Phone Code: 967. When calling in San Cristóbal, add 67 before the 5-digit number.

ACCOMMODATIONS AND CAMPING

Most accomodations lie on **Real de Guadalupe, Madero, Insurgentes,** and **Juárez,** with prices decreasing relative to their distance from the *zócalo*. Camping is only available outside of town (see below). Due to the altitude, the temperature often drops below 10°C (50°F, 283 K), making hot water and blankets indispensable.

La Casa de Gladys, Mazariegos 65, (tel. 8 57 75; email casagladys@latinmail.com), 4 blocks west of the *zócalo*. Murals, hammocks, bamboo curtains, solar and moon tables, and a fountain decorate the colorful courtyard, while well-furnished rooms come with animal throws and firm beds. Kitchen, refrigerator, exceptionally well-decorated private rooms and more sparse *cabañas* (25 pesos per person) as well as communal bathrooms, and board games all make for a pleasant stay. Singles 50 pesos, with bath 70 pesos; doubles and triples, 60 pesos, with bath 80 pesos; dorm beds 35 pesos; camping 25 pesos per person.

Posada Jovel, Paniagua 28 (tel. 8 17 34), 2 blocks east and 2 blocks north of the *zócalo*. Natural lighting illuminates small rooms with colorful *sarape* bedspreads, and multi-level terraces offer a great view of the city and cozy reading areas. Singles 90 pesos, with private bath 120 pesos; doubles 110 pesos, with private bath 140 pesos; triples 130 pesos, with private bath 160 pesos.

Posada Villa Betania, Madero 87 (tel. 8 44 67), 5 blocks east of the *zócalo* has huge, quiet rooms with big, firm beds, and snow white sheets, a table for two, private bath, and fireplace (50 pesos per fire). Clotheslines and a vista on the spacious roof, small gardens, and an intimate kitchen complete the relaxed, familiar atmosphere. Singles 80 pesos; doubles 100 pesos; triples 130 pesos.

Posada Bed and Breakfast, Madero 83 (tel. 8 04 40), 5 blocks east of the *zócalo*. Small, dim rooms open to a brigher, plant-filled lobby and dining area. Tiny, communal bathrooms contrast with the *posada's* rooftop *mirador*. Laundry 10 pesos per kg. Singles 50 pesos, with bath 60 pesos; doubles 90 pesos, with bath 100 pesos; dorm beds 35 pesos.

Posada La Media Lune, Flores, between Insurgentes and Benito Juárez. European art, a swaying hammock, and a picnic table lead to well-decorated rooms with black and white photos and pastel paintings. Over 200 American and French films available. Singles 70 pesos; doubles 90 pesos, both with shared bathrooms.

Rancho San Nicolás (tel. 8 00 57), on the extension of Francisco León, 1km east of town. If no one is around, ring the bell for the *hacienda* across the road. Rooms, camping, and a trailer park in a pastoral setting complete with whispering trees and hot water. **Horse rental** 40 pesos per hr., 80 pesos per day. During high season (mid-July to Aug. and Dec.-Feb.), rooms are often full, so call in advance. RVs 60 pesos; camping 30 pesos; rooms 45 pesos; each additional person 25 pesos.

FOOD

Inexpensive, high quality *comida corrida* joints and bakery shops abound in San Cristóbal. Rev up your afternoon with *sopa de pan* (bread soup) and grainy wheat breads from the Barrio San Ramón. Vegetarian restaurants are as plentiful as *churro* stands. End your meal with exquisite *cerveza dulce* or a cup of Mexico's best coffee.

Restaurante Madre Tierra, Insurgentes 19 (tel. 8 42 97), opposite the Iglesia de San Francisco, 2½ blocks south of the *zócalo.* Everything a *panadería* could be and more. The delicious pastries, healthy breakfasts, and aromatic coffee attract hungry and sweet-toothed souls. Breakfasts are good—and good for you (13-20 pesos). Open daily 8am-9:45pm.

Restaurante Continental, Real de Guadalupe 20 (tel. 8 56 85), in the Plaza of Arte Maya. Gourmet-style appetizers on the house with every meal. *Marimba* music Sa-Su 2-4pm. Breakfast 18-28 pesos; regional and international dishes 28-35 pesos. Open daily 7am-10:30pm.

Cafetería del Centro, Real de Guadalupe 15B (tel. 8 63 68), 2 blocks east of the *zócalo.* *Comida corrida* (soup, entree, rice, bread, *postre,* and coffee) and 23-peso breakfasts fill the tables of this friendly joint. Open daily 7am-9:30pm.

Restaurante París México, Madero 20 (tel. 8 06 95), 2½ blocks east of the *zócalo.* Offers French, Italian, and Mexican fare amidst French, Italian, and Mexican paintings and black and white photos. Extensive *menú del día* comes with a margarita and goes for 35 pesos. Open daily 6am-11pm.

El Gato Gordo, Madero 28 (tel. 8 04 99), between Domínguez and Colón, offers the best priced vegetarian dishes in a hip atmosphere with cartoon drawings on the wall (12-18 pesos). Open F-W 9am-10pm.

La Salsa Verde, 20 de Noviembre 7 and 11, 1 block north of the *zócalo.* It's hard to miss this taco diner with its red and green sign, red lamps, green tablecloths, and pine-covered floor. Tacos 5 pesos each. Open daily 8am-midnight.

Centro Cultural El Puente, Real de Guadalupe 55 (tel. 8 37 23), 3 blocks from the *zócalo.* This cafe/language-school/cinema mixes in local art and jazz as well, all with a distinct leftist flavor. Vegetarians can feast on the cheese, tomato, and avocado omelette (30 pesos). Sandwiches 25 pesos. Open daily 8am-11pm.

CAFES

Café Museo, Flores 10 (tel. 8 78 76), between Utrilla and Domínguez. A coffee museum, botanical garden, and pastry shop all in one, with live music F-Sa 8-10pm. 100% organic coffee 8-20 pesos. Open M-Sa 10am-10pm, Su 4-10pm.

La Selva Café, Crescencio Rosas 9 (tel. 8 72 43), at Cuauhtémoc. Black and white drawings explaining the production of organic coffee, wooden bamboo chairs and stools, and a jungle patio entice coffee sippers and pastry enthusiasts. Organic coffee and tea 8-30 pesos; tiramisu, cheesecake, and ice-cream 5-20 pesos. Proceeds help indigenous coffee producers (same as Café Museo, its sister cafe). Open daily 9am-11pm.

Café Altura, 20 Noviembre 4 (tel. 8 40 38). Blue and gold columns, radiating plants in the day and candle-lit tables in the night exude a romantic aura. Cuban *troba,* Beatles songs, and live poetry add a bohemian flavor in the evening. Open daily 7am-11pm.

SIGHTS

NA-BOLOM

Location: Guerrero 33. In the northeastern section of the city, at the end of Chiapa de Corzo. *Contact: Tel. 8 14 18; fax 8 55 86. Hours: Museum open with guided tours at 11:30am and 4:30pm, in Spanish and English, followed by a 15min. film. Admission: 30 pesos. Museum shop: open daily 10am-2pm and 4-7pm. Library: open M-F 10am-1:30pm. Dinner: at the Blom's, daily 7pm-10pm.*

San Cristóbal's most world-reknown attraction is **Na-Bolom** (House of the Jaguar), a private house that turns into a museum twice daily. Guided tours will lead you through the estate of Frans and Trudy Blom, who worked and studied for many decades among the dwindling communities of the **Lacandón Rainforest** along the Guatemala border. After the death of her husband in 1963, Trudy Blom continued their work, winning acclaim as an ecologist, ethnologist, and photographer before her death in the winter of 1993. Each year volunteers from all over the world carry out the ecological and jungle reforestation projects begun by Mrs. Blom, contribute to the cultural museum and botanical gardens as resident artists, and conduct tours of the Fray Bartolomé de Las Casas Library, and the Bloms' neoclassical *hacienda*. Travelers interested in **volunteering** at Na-Bolom should contact the main office (fax. 8 55 86; email nabolom@sclc.ecosur.mx) at least two months prior to arrival. Positions last three to six months and include meal tickets for Na-Bolom meals. The extensive library's manuscripts concentrate on Maya culture, with numerous periodicals, news clippings, and rare papers dealing with rainforest ecology and the plight of *indígena* refugees. The small, ornate chapel (the building was originally intended as a seminary) now serves as a gallery of colonial *chiapaneco* religious art created by *ladinos* and *indígenas* alike. Other rooms are devoted to archaeological finds from the nearby site of **Moxviquil** (mosh-uee-queel), religious artifacts from the Lacandón Rainforest, and the work of artists in residence. If the museum visit is not enough, stay as a dinner guest at the Bloms' original table set for 33. Just as the table seems never-ending, home-made bread, organic vegetables from Na-Bolom's garden, main course dishes, fruits, and desserts are eternally satisfying at this memorable social and dining experience. (Open daily 7pm-until the food is gone. Meals 77 pesos per person; for reservations call 8 14 18 the morning of or the day prior to your visit). If the two-hour tour and the three-hour dinner is still not enough, stay as a house guest in one of the 15 rooms furnished by Frans and decorated by Trudy, with a fireplace, mini-library, antique bath, and original black and white photos (375 pesos per person; discount for longer stay).

MUSEUM OF MAYA MEDICINE. Also called the Centro de Desarrollo de la Medicina Maya (CEDEMM) on Av. Salomon Gonzalez Blanco 10 a few kilometers north of *El Mercado*. Walk through simulated Maya healing rituals, smell Maya herbs, and listen to shamanic rhythmic prayers in this house and garden of Maya medicine. *(Tel./fax 8 54 38. Open M-F 9am-2pm and 3-6pm, Sa-Su 10am-4pm, Admission 20 pesos. Herbs on sale.)*

ZÓCALO. Since its construction by the Spanish in the 16th century, San Cristóbal's *zócalo* has been the physical and spiritual center of town. The colonial **Palacio Municipal** and the yellow-orange **cathedral,** with its white Corinthian columns and patterned wooden roof, dominate the heart of the city. Consecrated in 1528, the cathedral pews are filled with a bevy of devout followers, and its rafters with a flock of chirping birds. *(Cathedral open daily 7am-7pm.)*

IGLESIA Y EX-CONVENTO DE SANTO DOMINGO. North on Utrilla and beyond the **Iglesia de la Caridad** where La Virgen de la Caridad holds a staff of power, is the Iglesia y Ex-convento de Santo Domingo, whose grounds make up the artisan market. The elaborate stone facade of Santo Domingo houses an inner sanctuary delicately covered in restless gold leaf that sweeps around portraits and over the left nave's exquisite pulpit. *(Santo Domingo church open daily 7am-8pm.)*

SNA JOLOBIL. Tucked into the *ex-convento* is Sna Jolobil , which means "House of Weaving" in Tzeltal. It is a cooperative of 800 weavers from 10 Tzotzil and Tzeltal villages in the *chiapañeco* highlands whose objective is to preserve and revitalize their ancestral weaving techniques. While many of the top-quality, intricately embroidered *huipiles* will cost more than your plane ticket home, Sna Jolobil is a great place to window-shop and view the area's traditional garments. *(Tel./fax 8 26 46. Open M-Sa 9am-2pm and 4-6pm.)* Another cooperative, **J'pas Joloviletic,** is on the opposite side of Santo Domingo *(General Utrilla 43. Tel. 8 28 48. Open M-Sa 9am-2pm and 4-7pm, Su 9am-1pm).*

CENTRO CULTURAL DE LOS ALTOS DE CHIAPAS. Next door to Sna Jolobil, the Centro Cultural houses an excellent multimedia exhibit on the history of San Cristóbal and Chiapas, and a colorful garden.On display are colonial artifacts, photographs, and a collection of Chiapanecan textiles, some of which are hundreds of years old. During the summer, visitors bring along pen-knives to leave their mark on the avocado tree in the courtyard. *(Open Tu-Su 10am-5pm. Admission 30 pesos, Su free. Group tours in Spanish 20 pesos.)*

MERCADO. San Cristóbal's daily morning market overflows with fruit, veggies, and an assortment of cheap goods. There aren't really any *artesanías* on sale though—look to the market around Iglesia de Santo Domingo for souvenirs and jewelry. Try coming on Sunday, when *indígenas* from nearby villages turn out in droves or go to the villages themselves (see **Near San Cristóbal,** below). Utrilla and Real de Guadalupe, the two streets radiating from the northeastern corner of the *zócalo,* are dotted with colorful shops that sell *típico* attire. *(Market open daily 7am-2pm or until the afternoon rain.)*

🎵 ENTERTAINMENT AND SEASONAL EVENTS

While the *zócalo* empties around 11pm, coffeeshops and restaurants host live music into the wee hours. A stroll down Madero or Guadalupe will uncover any number of places to sip a cool *licuado,* kick back and enjoy some Latin strumming. **La Margarita,** on Madero next door to the Hotel Margarita, two blocks east of the *zócalo,* hosts a Flamenco, Rumba, and *Salsa* quintet (music daily 9pm-midnight, with a free "Tequila Boom-Boom"). **La Galería,** Hidalgo 3 (tel. 8 15 47), is a chic courtyard restaurant with live music during the high season (cocktails around 20 pesos; open nightly until 2am). **Café Altura** (see p. 546) serves great coffee, hot poetry, and live music (open nightly, starting at 8pm).

Not to be outdone by the Yucatán, San Cristóbal has its own Ruta Maya—here, the temples are smoke-filled discos with throbbing bodies and flowing taps. Locals and foreigners alike gather at **Cocodrilo** in the *zócalo,* next to **Hotel Santa Clara,** for live music at around 10pm, before heading to Margarita's and La Galería and then on to **Latinos** and **Las Velas,** two discos off the *zócalo* on Madero. Hard-core throbbers twitching for more can drink, dance, and jive at **A-DOVE,** Hidalgo 2 (tel. 8 66 66) with the hip local crowd, a.k.a. *"Las Fresas."* Or chill with the bohemians into the dawn at **Madre Tierra,** Insurgentes 19, across the Iglesia de San Francisco.

For those with aching feet, technophobia, or lack of disco garb, US movies are screened at **Cinemas Santa Clara** (tel. 8 23 45), on 16 de Septiembre between Escuadrón and 28 de Agosto, and **Cinema El Puente** (tel. 8 37 23), on Real de Guadalupe 55, 3 blocks from the *zócalo,* inside **El Centro Cultural El Puente.**

In San Cristóbal and the nearby villages, hardly a week goes by without some kind of religious festival. On Easter Sunday, *Semana Santa* gives way to the week-long **Feria de la Primavera y de la Paz.** Before the riotous revelry gets under way, a local beauty queen is selected to preside over the festivities, which include concerts, dances, bullfights, cockfights, and baseball games. Hotel rooms must be reserved several months in advance. The *fiesta* of the city's patron, San Cristóbal, is celebrated from July 18 to 25 with religious ceremonies and concerts.

NEAR SAN CRISTÓBAL DE LAS CASAS

Sunday morning is the best time to visit the markets of nearby villages. However, because service is always routed through San Cristóbal, visiting more than one village in a single morning is almost impossible. Buses and *combis* leave from the lot one block past the market at Utrilla and Honduras. Destination signs next to the buses are only occasionally accurate; always ask drivers where they're going. Drivers don't leave until the *combi* is completely full, so be prepared to squeeze in and wait.

ROCKETS AND BOMBAS The patron of San Cristóbal de Las Casas is Saint Christopher, formerly the saint for travelers, but desanctified by the Vatican some years ago. His demotion means little to the *Coletos* (a name for San Cristóbal residents derived from the pig-tails worn by Spanish bullfighters) who continue to celebrate the Fiesta of San Cristóbal—July 18 to 15—with energetic enthusiasm.

Among the events of interst is the procession cars, trucks, and *combis* from all over Chiapas that line up and proceed slowly up the road to the top of Cerro San Cristóbal. After each vehicle passes the hilltop chapel with the image of the saint, the driver opens the hood and door on the driver's side so that the engine and controls can be sprinkled with holy water by a Catholic priest. For the chauffeurs of Chiapas, this blessing is essential to keep the vehicle running and avoid accidents for another year on the perilous highland roads.

At high noon on July 24, fireworks are set off that exceed anything you might hear at other times of the year. A former mayor of San Cristóbal once estimated that about 10,000 *cohetes* (sky rockets) are launched on the eve of El Día de San Cristóbal. They are set off in each of the ten *barrios,* as well as off the patios of family homes. *Cohetes* are all manufactured locally and made by pouring gun powder into a hollow bamboo cylinder wrapped with maguey fiber and tied to a long, thin reed. Launching *cohetes* takes skill and expert timing. The *Cohetero* turns the rocket upside down and ignites the bottom of the cylinder with a lighted cigarette. He then turns the rocket right side up and holds it for just the exact length of time for the upward thrust to take hold before it is released. For if he should launch too soon, the *cohete* sets off laterally into the crowd and explodes in the midst of hordes of spectators. If he holds the rocket too long, it will blow up in his hand. One of the most prominent *cohete*-makers in Barrio Santa Lucia was left with only two fingers on his right hand after he miscalculated!

— Evon Z. Vogt, Professor *Emeritus* of Anthropology, Harvard University

Visiting the villages on your own can give you a greater sense of freedom and a lesser sense of being a herd animal, but it can also be like watching a chess game blindfolded without knowing the rules; there's a lot in each *pueblo* that happens behind closed doors. Sometimes joining a tour group is a good idea, especially if the group leader is the energetic and knowledgeable **Mercedes Hernández Gómez.** Something of an expert on local *indígena* culture and a splendid storyteller, Mercedes's five-hour tour includes political, domestic, and spiritual teachings; she takes tourists into a private home, a saint's house, and the *pueblo* church (100 pesos for Chamula and Zinacantán tours). Look for Mercedes and her huge golf umbrella at the *zócalo* every day at 9am. An equally viable option is the intelligent and gregarious **Raúl López** (tel. 8 37 41), a thirty-something local who happily divulges a wealth of information on everything from regional customs to the Zapatista uprising to religion and back again, with refreshing frankness. Raúl and company meet interested travelers on the plaza side of the cathedral. Look for the blue *combis* daily at 9am: the tour covers Chamula and Zinacantán for 90 pesos and the van returns around 2pm).

SAN JUAN CHAMULA

The community of San Juan Chamula, which means "the place of adobe houses" in Tzotzil, (98 villages, 90,000 inhabitants) is the largest and most touristed of the communities around San Cristóbal. Located 10km northwest of San Cristóbal in a lush valley, Chamula's dirt roads, single-story homes, and wandering children are used to visitors. Chamula is known for its colors (black and blue), its *carnaval,* and its shamanic-Catholic church. Visitors come to Chamula to check out the spectacular traditional clothing and to witness a civic and religious structure quite unlike any other in Mexico. Older Chamulan men wear traditional black wool **chuj** (poncho) tied with thick leather belts (black signifying *cargo,* or duty), while the

CHIAPAS AND TABASCO

young men, still unburdened, sport either blue or white *sarapes*. Designs on the sleeves of the tunics indicate the wearer's *paraje* (hamlet). Village officials (elected by a hand-count) and elders drape ribbons over their large sombreros. If you see leaders in their official dress, stifle the urge to snap a shot—the men refuse to be turned into a tourist attraction while they are performing their *cargos*.

Chamulans, who expelled their last Catholic priest in 1867, are famous for their fierce resistance to Mexico's religious and secular authority. Villagers have far more faith in the powers of the village shamans, and Catholic bishops are allowed into the church solely for baptisms. Similarly, the government medical clinic is used only as a last resort, after incantations with eggs, bubbly *refrescos*, and chickens have failed.

Before entering the brightly painted **church** (open daily 5am-7pm), you must obtain a permit (3 pesos) from the tourist office on the *zócalo* and show the permit to the guards outside the church. **Under no circumstances should you take pictures**—the church functions as a hospital, and it is disrespectful to the sick and to the shaman doctor to try to capture a personal ceremony on film. The church's predominant color, green, is meant to recall the ancient Maya practice of praying in caves—hence the pine needles on the floor, the branches, and the flowers. Inside the church, families, candles, and chickens fill the pewless hall as shamans chant petitions to the Catholic saints on a conversational level. Different colored candles signify different prayer requests, and other Maya rituals are aided by ubiquitous soda bottles. The importance of carbonated beverages cannot be overstated; Chamulans believe that **burping** helps to purify the self by expelling evil spirits. Prior to the discovery of fizzy drinks, locals drank gallons of water and *posh* (fermented sugarcane) to achieve the same cathartic effect.

To the left of the church stands a cluster of distinctive, green foliated Maya crosses. The crosses' origin is in the crucifix-shaped *ceiba* , the **tree of life,** featured on the sarcophagus of King Pacal at Palenque. When Fray Bartolomé de Las Casas showed up bearing the Christian cross, he waltzed right into Chamula, where he was believed to be a messenger from the gods. Chamula's small but diverse artisans' **market** is behind the tourist office and the large market on the plaza offers everything from soda to roasted corn.

Private homes usually have brick-mud walls, thatched roofs, and dirt floors, with beds on one end and open fires on the other. No walls divide up the sections, and most homes have sparse furniture. The village has a shire for each saint, which occupies the residence of the current *cargo* holder responsible for that saint—just look for the leaf arches outside signaling the house's holy function. Inside the chapel are ceramic incense bowls, animal-shaped candle-holders, and a leaf curtain separating the holy altar from the seating area, which has little more than a few low benches lining the mud-caked walls and pine needles cushioning the floor. Homes and chapels are generally not open to the public—join Mercedes and her tour for a peek into private Chamulan life (see p. 549).

The best time to visit Chamula is one week before Ash Wednesday, during **Carnaval,** which draws approximately 70,000 *indígenas* and 500 tourists per day. While they coincide with Lent, the festivities have their origins in the ancient Maya ritual concerning the five "lost" days at the end of the 360-day agricultural cycle. Expect to see religious leaders dashing over hot coals in order to purify themselves, as well as men decked out in monkey skins singing and dancing. In addition to Chamula's *carnaval* and the assumption of the *cargo* (Dec. 30-31), the fiestas of **San Sebastián** (Jan. 19-21), **San Mateo** (Sept. 21-22), **San Juan Bautista** (June 22-24) and **Virgen de Fátima** (Aug. 28) warrant a trip to the village.

Getting There: *Combis* to Chamula leave from San Cristóbal on Utrilla one block west and one block north of the market (30min., every 25min. 6am-5pm, 15 pesos). To reach Chamula by car from San Cristóbal, drive west from the *zócalo* on Guadalupe Victoria, and bear right after crossing the small bridge on Diagonal Ramón Larraínzar. At the fork, go right; Chamula is at the end of the 8km stretch of road.

ZINACANTÁN

Eight kilometers from Chamula lies the smaller and colorful community of Zinacantán (pop. 35,000), comprised of a ceremonial center and outlying hamlets, where women fashion ribbons on each braid and men flaunt dazzingly red *chuj*, decorated with colorful stitched flowers and dangling multicolored tassels. During *fiestas*, residents wear high-backed *huaraches* (sandals) in accordance with ancient Maya custom. Many of the women walk about barefoot. This is not an indication of poverty but rather a reflection of the Maya emphasis on the importance of female fertility—they believe that women can draw fertility from the ground.

Somewhat exceptional for a *chiapaneco* village is the fact that Zinacantán has accepted the Catholic clergy. The village's handsome, white-washed **church** dates back to the 16th century and features standard Roman columns and Corinthian arches. Along with the small white convent, it is used both for both Catholic worship, and ritual healing and pre-Conquest forms of worship. You won't find confessionals in the church, though—confession here is a public act, directed at the effigies on the altar. The Catholic priest, independent of the village church, merely busies himself with confirmations, baptisms, and wedding ceremonies. To enter the church you must pay a 10-peso visitor's fee at the tourist booth in front. Tourists who step inside the convent are expected to drop a small donation into the *limosna* box. As with all traditional communities, Zinacantán does not tolerate picture-taking, obvious note-taking, or hat-wearing within its sacred buildings.

Of late, the village's flower industry has flourished, and Zinacantán has gained a considerable economic edge over neighboring San Juan Chamula. Every Sunday morning, town residents inaugurate what they hope will be a profitable weekend by hopping on a taxi to San Cristóbal. Today, many houses in Zinacantán contain stereos, TVs, and gas stoves, although these serve principally as status symbols—many women prefer to cook directly on the ground. The children who bother tourists for pesos or pens will be severely scolded by their parents if caught, unlike the begging kids at San Juan Chamula. If you wander around town long enough, you'll stumble upon a backyard full of women **weaving,** and may well be invited in to browse the selection of clothes and placemats—you won't find souvenirs any more homemade than these.

Zinacantán's festivals include **Fiesta de San Sebastián** (Jan. 19-22), **Semana Santa,** and the **Fiesta de San Lorenzo** (Aug. 18-21).

Getting There: *Combis* to Zinacantán (12 pesos) leave San Cristóbal from the lot near the market (daily 6am-8pm). If driving, follow Guadalupe Victoria west from the *zócalo* and turn right after crossing the bridge on Diagonal Ramón Larraínzar. At the fork, turn left toward the "Bienvenido a Zinacantán" sign.

SAN ANDRÉS LARRAÍNZAR

The site of the Zapatista negotiations during the summers of 1995 and 1996, San Andrés Larraínzar lies 26km northwest of San Cristóbal and 16km from Chamula. Because there are no convenient tours to the village, its 5000 citizens are better disposed toward the outsiders who do make the trip. The village colors are red, black, and white, appearing on most clothing and market items. Mexicans refer to the village as Larraínzar, but local Tzotziles prefer San Andrés. Since many of the villagers are reluctant to carry their produce all the way to San Cristóbal, San Andres's **market** (open F-Su until 1pm) is better stocked than the ones at Chamula or Zinacantán. For a panoramic view of the green valleys and patches of cornfields that surround the city, walk up the hill from the main church to La Iglesia de Guadalupe. **La Fiesta de Carnaval** is the seasonal highlight of this town.

Getting There: Starting at 6am, *combis* (50min., 15 pesos) make several trips to San Andrés from the small terminal behind the San Cristóbal market—continue on the dirt road for about a block; the stop will be on your right. It's best to return before 2pm, soon after the market begins to shut down and before the *combis* stop running. To reach San Andrés by car, take the road northwest from San Cristóbal to Chamula and continue past the village. On a curve some 10km later, a prominent sign announcing "S.A. Larraínzar" points left to a road climbing the steep side of the valley; the village lies approximately 6km beyond the fork.

CHENALHÓ

Chenalhó (pop. 10,000) seems even more remote from San Cristóbal than 32km would suggest. Foreigners are rare entities. In Chenalhó, typical dress for men varies from white or black ponchos worn over pants and bound with heavy belts to short, light, white tunics. Women who have not adopted more current fashions dress uniformly in dark blue *nalgas* (skirts) and white *tocas* (shawls) embroidered with bright orange flowers. A small **store** behind the enclosed market supplies the town with nearly all of its clothing. The **market** spreads out into the plaza in front of the church on Sunday and sells mostly foodstuffs, including *chiche*, a potent drink made from fermented cane. Villagers enthusiastically wave visitors into San Pedro, the church in the town's center, which serves as both a secular and a religious meeting place. Inside, the main aisle often shimmers with the light rising from candles. Chenalhó residents celebrate **Carnaval** and **La Fiesta de San Pedro** (in late June) in style.

Getting There: Autotransportes Fray Bartolomé de Las Casas operates buses to Chenalhó. The bus leaves San Cristóbal from the station on Utrilla north of the market at about 2pm. The bus sometimes does not return until the next day, so make sure you have a ride back to San Cristóbal before you go. Bus trips take two hours. If you get stranded, Chenalhó does have some beds available—just ask to be shown the way. Driving to Chenalhó cuts transit time in half, but the cost to your car's suspension system will be high—the dirt road northwest of Chamula is guaranteed to chatter some teeth.

HUÍTEPEC ECOLOGICAL RESERVE

Often enclosed by clouds, the summits of the mountains of highland Chiapas do not provide unlimited vistas, but rather the chance to ascend into a rare natural setting. The Huítepec Ecological Reserve, situated on the east face of the Huítepec Volcano, offers the chance to explore an **evergreen cloud forest ecosystem,** not found in many other places on the planet. Two trails wind around the park, which is home to some 60 species of birds and 40 other North American avian species during the winter migrations, as well as more than 300 plant species. Those with medicinal properties or religious importance to *indígena* villagers are marked with small signs. The shorter of the two trails makes for a self-led, invigorating 2km hike, rising to a height of 2390m, while the longer 8km hike is headed by a guide. (Open Tu and Th-Su 9am-4pm. Admission 10 pesos. Guided tours of groups of 8 or more 150 pesos.) The owner of Restaurant el Oasis, along with his three dogs, also leads a daily hike from 8am to 3pm to the park, with explanations of flora and fauna along the way (120 pesos).

Getting There: The reserve lies just off the road to San Juan Chamula, 3½km from San Cristóbal, and can be reached by any *combi* headed in that direction; ask the driver to let you off at the "Reserva Huítepec" (15min., every 15min., 5 pesos).

ROMERILLO Y TENEJAPA

El Cementerio de Romerillo, on the way to the small village of **Tenejapa** (pop. 5,000), sits atop **Los Altos de Chiapas** with its 32 tall, blue and green wooden crosses. This indigenous cemetery comes alive during **El Día de los Muertos** with music, *posh*, and all kinds of food. The plank on each mound of dirt is a piece of the relatives' bed or door, and the beaten shoes scattered around are for the spirits to walk and dance on earth. Tenejapa, 28km from San Cristóbal, the nearest and most accessible **Tzeltal** community is surrounded by mountains, canyons, corn fields, cypress and pine trees. Crosses representing the tree of life stand at crossroads, near adobe homes, and in front of **La Iglesia de San Ildefonso**. Saints dressed with indigenous clothing, doves with the sacred heart of Jesus, a crucifix upon the altar, and surrounding candles and incense reflect the intricate syncretism. The women's *huipiles* are also replete with pre-Hispanic symbolism such as the sun, earth, frogs, flowers, and butterflies. The men wear a black poncho tied at the waist with a belt, red and white *calzones*, dark boots, and a purse diagonally around the chest. Religious and community leaders carry a staff of power and a long rosary necklace. Tenejapa's Sunday and Thursday morning *mercados*, **Fiesta de San Alonzo** (Jan. 21), and **Fiesta de Santiago** (July 23) attract crowds from near and far.

Getting There: *Combis* and taxis to Romerillo and Tenejapa leave from San Cristóbal, on Utrilla one block west and one block north of the market (15-20 pesos).

AMATENANGO DEL VALLE

The town of fine pottery is located 37km southeast of San Cristóbal toward Comitán. Women are the sole creators of hand-molded pitchers, vases, pots, doves, and jars. From the backyard of their adobe homes with red-tiled roofs, each piece is baked *a la natural* with firewood, maintaining pre-Hispanic techniques. **La Casa de Julianab** is the most visited cooperative pottery house with an original *temascal* or *baño de vapor* (steam bath). Look for Juliana's sculpture in San Cristóbal, one block east of the Cristóbal Colón bus station.

GRUTAS DE SAN CRISTÓBAL

The Grutas de San Cristóbal lie just off the Pan-American Highway, 12km southeast of San Cristóbal. From the small entrance at the base of a steep wooded hillside, a tall, narrow fissure, incorporating a chain of countless **caves**, leads almost 3km into the heart of the rock. Because of the caves' unusual shape, their floors are not particularly friendly to the feet. Instead, a modern concrete walkway, at times 10m above the boulder-strewn cave floor, navigates 750m into the system. The dimly lit caves harbor a spectacular array of stalactites and columns. Stomping on the boardwalk at certain points generates a rumbling echo throughout the caves. Bring your flashlight and let your imagination run wild uncovering the natural light and shadow formations. (Caves open daily 9am-4:30pm. Admission 12 pesos.)

Getting There: Almost any east-bound *combi* passing across the road from the Iglesia de San Diego in San Cristóbal passes the *grutas* (15min., every 30min., 7 pesos). From the highway, a five-minute walk through the park brings you to the entrance.

COMITÁN

Eighty-four kilometers southeast of San Cristóbal, Comitán (pop. 110,000) is the last major town on the Pan-American Highway before the Guatemalan border (85km away). While rapid growth has transformed Comitán into a maze of tangled streets with occasional steep hills and churches atop, the city is active and its people genial; its verdant multi-terraced *zócalo*, with an arched kiosk, *mariachis*, and *marimba* music on Sunday nights, breeds youthful fun in striking contrast to the lakes and forests. Residents of Comitán enthusiastically welcome the tourists who decide to stay and explore the nearby waterfalls and archaeological sites.

🔀 ORIENTATION AND PRACTICAL INFORMATION. Streets increase numerically in both directions away from the *zócalo* and are named according to the quadrant in which they fall. To reach the *zócalo* from the Cristóbal Colón bus station, cross the **Pan-American Highway** and turn left. After 200m, take the first right onto **Calle 4 Pte. Sur.** Walk five blocks to **Calle Central Benito Juárez**, turn right and then walk five blocks east past the post office to the *zócalo* on **Av. Central**.

Autotransportes Tuxtla Gutiérrez y La Angostura, on the highway between Calles Sur Pte. 1 and 2, has first-class service to: **San Cristóbal** (2hr., 12:30pm, 35 pesos), continuing to **Tuxtla** (3hr., 55 pesos). Nine second-class buses also make the run to: **San Cristóbal** and **Tuxtla** daily (4:50am-6:20pm). You can shorten the walk to the station and **El Centro** by catching a *microbús* on the highway (4 pesos). Cristóbal Colón (tel. 2 09 80), on the Pan-American Highway between Calles Sur Pte. 8 and 4, runs to: **Mexico City** (16hr., 12:10pm-4:30pm, 450-590 pesos); **Ocosingo** (4hr., 4:45pm, 48 pesos); **Palenque** (6hr., 4:45pm, 94); **Puebla** (14hr., 12:10pm-4:30pm, 400-530 pesos); **San Cristóbal** (1½hr., 18 per day, 40-50 pesos); **Tapachula** (6hr., 6 per day 2am-11pm, 90 pesos); **Tuxtla Gutiérrez** (3½hr., 12 per day, 65-78 pesos); and **Villahermosa** (9hr., 4:45pm, 160 pesos). **Taxis** (tel. 2 56 30) cost 25 pesos from the bus station to the *zócalo* and can be found in the *zócalo*.

The **tourist office** (tel. 2 40 47), Plaza Central #6, next to Palacio Municipal, overflows with brochures and maps and a friendly staff (open M-F 9am-3pm and 4-8pm). Guatemalan visas can be obtained from the **Guatemalan Consulate,** Av. 1 Sur Pte. #26 (tel. 2 04 91), at Av. 2 Sur Pte.; a waving blue-and-white flag marks the spot (open M-F 8am-1pm and 2:30-5pm). **Banca Serfín** (tel. 2 12 96 or 2 15 70), at Av. 1 Sur Pte. 1, just off the southwest corner of the *zócalo*, changes U.S. dollars only and has a 24-hour **ATM** (open M-F 9am-3pm). The indoor **market** is on Central Benito Juárez, just before Av. 2 Ote. Sur, one block east of the *zócalo* (open daily dawn-dusk). **Police:** (tel. 2 00 25) on the ground floor of the Palacio Municipal. **Red Cross:** (tel. 2 18 89) on Calle 5 Nte. Pte., 2½ blocks west of the highway. **Farmacia Regina:** Calle 1 Sur Ote. 1 (tel. 2 11 96 or 2 07 54), on the south side of the *zócalo* (open daily 24hr.). **Medical emergencies: Hospital Civil** (tel. 2 01 35 or 2 20 51), on Calle 2 Ote. Sur 13 and Av. 9 Sur Ote. **Post office:** Central Dr. Belisario Domínguez 45 (tel. 2 04 27), 1½ blocks south of the *zócalo* (open M-F 8am-3pm, Sa 9am-1pm). **Postal Code:** 30000. **Internet Access: CCPI Internet,** 1 Av. Pte. Sur #13, between 1 y 2 Calle Sur Pte (email ccpi@comitan.com; 25 pesos per hr.; open M-Sa 9am-2pm and 4pm-8pm). **Café Internet,** Pasaje Morales 12, to the right of the Palacio Municipal (email sinco@comitan.podernet.cm.mx; 30 pesos per hr.; open M-F 9am-2pm and 4-8pm, Sa 9am-2pm).

⌐ ACCOMMODATIONS. Comitán's various new and expensive hotels would likely crowd out the cheaper accommodations if the four best budget accommodations didn't occupy choice spots near the *zócalo*. **Hospedaje Primavera,** Calle Central Benito Juárez #2 (tel. 2 20 41) features shoebox rooms under wooden panels. (Singles 40 pesos; doubles 60 pesos; triples 90 pesos with shared bathrooms.) **Hospedaje Montebello,** Calle 1 Nte. Pte. 10 (tel. 2 35 72), near Av. Central Nte., has pale yellow rooms with red flowers that open to a concrete courtyard (40 pesos per person, with private bath 65 pesos). **Hospedaje Río Escondido,** 1 Av Pte. Sur #3 (tel. 2 01 73), between Calle Central Benito Juárez and 1 Calle Sur Pte., offers a colorful tile courtyard, but with matchbox rooms, you get what you pay for. (Singles 30 pesos; doubles 40 pesos.) **Hospedaje San Francisco,** 1 Av Oriente Norte #13 (tel. 2 01 94), only one block from the *zócalo* on the corner of 1 Calle Nte. is a *hacienda*-style *posada* with red columns and overflowing plants providing comfortable beds, private bathrooms, soap, towels, and toilet paper (rare commodities in Comitán's *posadas*), for an amazing price. (Singles 50 pesos; doubles 80 pesos; triples 70 pesos with shared bathrooms.)

⌐ FOOD. Finding a cheap meal in Comitán is just as easy as downing the delicious *flan*, the universal Mexican *postre*. Several *taquerías*, clustered around the northwest corner of the *zócalo* and on Calle Central Nte., have *comida corrida* for 20 pesos and small tacos for 4 pesos. For bigger and juicier tacos hop into **Taco-Miteco,** Av. Central Norte #5 near El Palacio Municipal. Three tacos for 13 pesos or choose your meal from the photographic menu on the wall stamped with smacking red lips. (Open daily 7am-11pm with TV news in the morning and regional music at night.) For elegant dining at bargain prices, enjoy *Chiapaneco* and international dishes at **Alis,** Calle Central Benito Juárez #21 (tel. 2 12 62) between 1 Av. Pte. Nte., and 2 Av. Pte. Nte. Diego Rivera paintings accent the rustic yellow walls and wooden beam ceiling while you enjoy the three course home-made *menú del*

THINGS THAT GO BUMP IN THE NIGHT

Everything only seems normal in Comitán. Little do visitors know that they are about to enter a zone where the supernatural has not yet lost its grip on the modern age. Ask around discreetly; a good majority of residents will be able to tell you where to find the **Calle de Llorona** (Street of The Weeping One). Many are soundly convinced that you can still hear the shrill cries late at night of a mother who murdered her children in a fit of rage. And that door that just closed behind you? Well, it could have been the wind....or it could have been the mischievous spirit of a playful *huérfano* (orphan children who died before being baptized), often blamed for minor mishaps by locals.

On a more material plane, odd stories circle about, or rather under, Comitán's busy daily life. Several of the city's richest inhabitants came into their wealth not by traditional means (like timber and ranching) but by unearthing buried gold on their property. Less than a century ago, the main currency in more remote towns in Mexico was gold and banks were never really secure from bandits. Consequently, much of Comitán's early wealth wound up underground. Combine these accounts with local stories of even older colonial treasures, and it amounts to buried treasure galore. Skip the expensive hotel. Buy a pick and shovel instead.

día (35 pesos) or *huevos chiapanecos* (scrambled eggs with strips of tortillas and onions, 25 pesos; open daily 8:30am-6pm). For a cultural, musical, and artsy fun time, hang out in Comitán's hotspot, **Café Quiptic,** housed in **La Casa de Cultura** (tel. 2 06 24). Tasty coffee goes for 7 pesos amd enchiladas for 10 pesos. All proceeds directly aid the grassroots organization for farmworkers, **La Sociedad Campesino Magisterial de la Selva.** Or for the cheapest eats mingle with the locals in the **mercado** on Calle Central Benito Juárez, one block east of the *zócalo.* Whole chicken soup with veggies, 10 pesos; *huevos rancheros* or the style of your choice, 10 pesos. (Open M-Sa 6am-6pm, Su 6am-2pm.)

NEAR COMITÁN

TENAM PUENTE

This white stone city, which means "fortification" in Náhuatl, commands two square kilometers of Comitán's valley. This commercial and religious acropolis, with a T-shaped ballcourt, burial palaces, *cruz de la madera* (wooden cross) and tiered pyramid, rises above patios, plazas and wild trees. The site reached its apogee during the classic period. (To reach this beauty located 22km south of Comitán, catch the "Francisco Sarabia" bus from the **Transportes Comitán-La Trinitaria** station on Calle Sur Pte. 1, between Calles Pte. Sur 3 and 4 (30min., M-F 8am and 2pm, 7 pesos) which will drop you off at the access road, a few kilometers from the entrance. If you take a combi, the walk is five kilometers from the entrance. (Site open daily 9am-4pm; admission 5 pesos.)

CHINKULTIC

Check with drivers for the return schedule from Tenam Puente or continue your journey to the next Maya beauty of Chinkultic, 32km from the Comitán-Cuauhtémoc (Pan-American) highway, on the way to Lagunas Montebello. The "Montebello" bus drops you off at the access road, an uphill 2km walk to the entrance. Walk or bike to the entrance (local restaurant owners rent bikes for 20 pesos). Test out the brakes before you fall on the wayside. Follow the sacbe road, traverse the virgin jungle, cross the stone bridge, climb the wooden steps to reach Chinkultic's 7th century pyramid. A grand canyon serves as its backdrop, while a sacred *cenote* admires its grandeur. Sitting atop the acropolis' power structure provides the ideal place for relishing nature and meditating. Chirping birds, lily pads, a cool breeze, and the ripples of **Lago Tepancuapan** are but a few of Chikultic's attributes. Heading back towards the entrance, on the left, lies a quadrangle space for religious sacrifices, scond to those which occured in the sacred *cenote*. Located down the dirt path immediately before exiting, stelae of victorious warriors and ball players guard the ballcourt, resembling a Maya Hall of Fame. *(Site open daily 9am-4pm; 25 pesos.)*

WATERFALLS, LAGOONS AND LAKES

La Cascada de San Cristobalito, also known as **La Cascada de Chiflón** for its whistling sound, and **El Velo de Novia** (the bride's veil) is a 250m waterfall, 45km west of Comitán. To get to Chiflón, take a *combi* to el puente de San Vincente en La Mesilla (not La Mesilla in Guatemala) from the Tuxtla Gutiérrez y La Angostura bus station on the highway (45min., every 30min. 5:45am-4pm, 10 pesos). The journey to the waterfall is a combination hiking, river, and jungle expedition. Fitting through the entrance's barbed wires, wading through the river, grabbing onto tree roots and branches, and clenching your fingers into the mud during the rainy season is only half the adventure. The feeling of victory vibrates within as you set foot on the highest and nearest mount to the waterfall. **Restaurante El Amigo,** the *palapa* on the opposite side of the road, provides hiking guides who are life savers if you're traveling on your own. There are no signs to the waterfalls, making it easy to get lost in a jungle with a few human inhabitants. **El Restaurante** serves fresh fish from the lake, and cooks meat from the ranch for 20 pesos; beer and *botanas* (appetizers) for 10 pesos. Open daily 8am-9pm.

A hop, skip, and a 58km *combi* ride from Comitán lie the pine-covered hills of the **Parque Nacional Lagunas de Montebello** where 68 lakes await exploration in this scenic playground, each sporting distinctive shades of green and blue. The main paths and even the roadside parking provide spectacular views of these natural wonders. Unfortunately, only 16 have trails leading from the main road, and some are notorious for bandit attacks. Be sure to inquire ahead at the Comitán tourist office before undertaking any off-the-beaten-path hikes. Women traveling alone or in small groups should not try to hike the trails, but instead travel in the *combis* to and from the different lakes. *Combis* and buses unload passengers anywhere along the road to **Laguna Bosque Azul** or **Laguna Tziscao** and camping is available at both of these sites. **Alberque Turístico de Tziscao** (tel. 3 13 03) overlooks the trees, mountains, and emerald-blue lake of Tziscao. Bathrooms and showers available for all; large dining and socializing lobby plays *ranchero* music or your own tapes. Home-cooked meals for 15-20 pesos, 6am-10pm; coffee, sodas, beer, chips, and bottled water also available for a few pesos. (Campground 10 pesos per person; outdoor cabins 25 pesos per person; hostel-type rooms 30 pesos per person.) **Rancho El Trapiche,** 800 meters along the windy hiking trail to the right of Laguna Bosque Azul offers two-floor log cabins with large beds (25 pesos per person).

Getting There: From Comitán, the blue "Montebello" bus leaves the station on Av. 2 Pte. Sur, between Calles Sur Pte. 2 and 3 (1hr., every 15min. 5:30am-4:30pm, 12 pesos). The bus swings by the Cristóbal Colón bus station for those who want to head straight to the lakes.

Contrasting with the cool, mineral-colored water of the Montebello lakes are the warm, crystal-clear waters of **Lagos de Colón.** The lakes lie in a valley 39km south of Comitán. Take any bus or *colectivo* headed to Comalapa (40min., every 30min. 7am-5pm, 25 pesos), and ask to be let off at the *crucero* where the 12km road to the Lagos begins, near the small village of **Chamic.** From the intersection take a *colectivo* to the Lagos (15min., 12 pesos); leave early, since these *colectivos* stop running around 4pm, or catch a ride with one of the many local families who relax and barbeque at the lakes during the weekends. This group of 44 lakes intertwine with rushing streams, creating waterfalls. To reach the mouth of the waterfalls, follow the path 100 meters before the lakes into the woods for about 15-20 minutes. Lagos de Colón also houses a pond of baby turtles, mama turtles and papa turtles near its entrance. Unfortunately, the turtles swim amidst soda bottles and beer cans. Another ancient Maya ruin, **Lagartero,** stands 2km from Lagos de Colón.

OCOSINGO

More rural than the bustling *zócalo* first lets on, tourist-free Ocosingo (pop. 27,000) straddles the head of a valley in central Chiapas. As the nearest large settlement to the Lacandón rainforest—the fringes of which harbor the majority of Zapatista rebels, the strategic importance of Ocosingo's location is as obvious as the Mexican *ejército* (military). Ocosingo's residents still bear painful memories of the January 1994 uprising, when a shootout in the market between the army and Zapatista-allied locals claimed dozens of lives. Despite the military backdrop, dusty streets, and ramshackle buildings, Ocosingo is a relatively safe and quiet base from which to explore the nearby ruins of **Toniná** (see below). It's also the home of *quesillo*, huge balls of cheese that are sold from windows and doorways.

◪ ORIENTATION AND PRACTICAL INFORMATION. Ocosingo lies 72km northeast of San Cristóbal de las Casas and 119km south of Palenque. To get to the *zócalo* from either the **Cristóbal Colón bus station** or the **Autotransportes Tuxtla station,** walk uphill two blocks and take a left at the "centro" sign. The *zócalo* is three blocks downhill. The town is laid out in the customary compass grid, but it's small enough that street names can be ignored almost entirely. From the *zócalo*, cardinal directions are marked by the Hotel Central to the north, the Iglesia de San Jacinto to the east, and the Palacio Municipal to the west.

Autotransportes Tuxtla Gutiérrez (tel. 3 01 39), on the highway, offers first-class service to: **Campeche** (7hr., 9pm, 175 pesos); **Cancún** (14hr., 9pm, 305 pesos); **Mérida** (10hr., 9pm, 220 pesos); **Palenque** (2hr., 2am, 60 pesos); and **Villahermosa** (5hr., 4 per day, 100 pesos). Cristóbal Colón (tel. 3 04 31) runs buses to: **Escárcega** (6hr., 11:30am, 2:15pm, and 4:30pm, 145 pesos); **Mexico City** (18hr., 4:15pm, 494 pesos) via **Puebla** (16hr., 4:15pm, 410 pesos); and **Tuxtla Gutiérrez** (3½hr., 5 per day 6:15am-9pm, 95 pesos). **Luggage storage** costs 10 pesos per day. **Banamex** (tel. 3 00 34), in the northwest corner of the *zócalo*, does not change U.S. dollars, but a lengthy procedure (15 minutes of paper-work) will get you cash advances on major credit cards (open M-F 9am-2pm). For any kind of **emergency,** contact the staff at the Palacio Municipal (tel. 3 00 15) or the **police** (tel. 3 05 06), who roost on Calle Central between 1 Pte. and 2 Pte. on Barrio Nuevo (open 24hr.). In case of a **medical emergency,** contact **IMSS** (tel. 3 01 52), 1.2km south of the *zócalo* on 1 Ote. Sur (open 24hr.). **Pharmacy: Cruz Blanca** (tel. 3 02 33), 1 Ote. and 2 Sur, is one block south of the church (open daily 7am-10pm). **Post office:** 2 Sur Ote. 12, one block south of the *zócalo* (open M-F 9am-1pm and 3-6pm, Sa 9am-1pm). **Postal code:** 29950. **Phone code:** 967.

▛▟ ACCOMMODATIONS AND FOOD. Two hotels are a world apart from the seedy, cave-like, slightly cheaper *posadas* found within a couple of blocks of the *zócalo*. **Hotel Central,** Av. Central 1 (tel. 3 00 24), on the north side of the *zócalo*, is an oasis of clean, well-ventilated rooms with comfortable beds and blue spacious bathrooms. Each room comes with bottled water and cable TV. (Singles 120 pesos; doubles 160 pesos; triples 190 pesos.) **Hotel Margarita,** Calle Central Nte. 16 (tel. 3 02 80), half a block north of Hotel Central, is a newly renovated hotel featuring firm beds and spanking new bathrooms (singles 90 pesos; doubles 100 pesos; triples 110 pesos; TV and A/C 20 pesos extra). **Restaurant La Montura,** Av. Central 5 (tel. 3 05 50), in the Hotel Central on the north side of the *zócalo*, is somewhat overpriced, but the outdoor tables under the arcade are the most pleasant in town. Entrees are 40-45 pesos and delicious *tortas* stuffed with *frijoles* and avocado go for 18 pesos. (Open daily 7am-11pm.) **Restaurante Las Cazuelas,** 1 Ote. 127, in the Hotel Agua Azul, serves up tasty food in a tiny log cabin with tree trunk tables. The menu changes at the whim of the chef or the season. All meals cost 15-30 pesos (open daily 8am-9pm).

NEAR OCOSINGO: TONINÁ RUINS

While the **ruins of Toniná** rarely surface on lists of Mexico's can't-miss sights, the tiered-city architecture of the enormous acropolis is certainly hard to find anywhere else. After a brief, conflict-imposed absence, archaeologists and their builders are back at the site, carefully reconstructing the main pyramid. As these ruins don't have the user-friendly plaques present elsewhere, a guide can be very helpful and encouraging to explore the underworld.

The Toniná complex, encompassing 15 acres of ruins, was a religious and administrative capital for the Maya city-state that flourished from 300 to 1000. Structures at Toniná do not share the orthodox symmetry or precise floorplan of Palenque or Chichén Itzá. Many statues have lost pieces to decay and neglect. The governor of Ocosingo took stones from the site to build roads around the turn of the century; because of this, the pyramids will never be fully restored.

The entrance path, which leads across the river east of the ruins and up a small gully, emerges at the **main ballcourt,** with remains of its stone rings and five ground markers. Beyond which lies a **sacrificial altar.** This altar is situated on the first artificially terraced level of the site, the **Temple of War.** The ruins of a smaller ballcourt lie near the steps of the acropolis. Maya calendars and stelae used to decorate the Temple of War, representing the important leaders of three different governments. These extensive glyphs replete with snakes, bats, and jaguars are exposed in the museum at the entrance of the site.

Toniná's chief attraction is a massive **acropolis,** which towers 60m over the plaza. Its seven tiers corresponded to the city's various social strata, from the general populace to the high priests, whose temples are perched on the seventh level. Well-preserved panels and sculptures survive from almost all the levels, but most have been moved to the on-site museum or hauled off to Mexico City. On the first tier the **Palacio of the Underworld** is found in the dark passageways of the labyrinth, with a few **Ik** (god of the wind) windows decorating its facade and inner walls. It is believed that if you travel through the corridors of the labyrinth without manmade light you will gain power from the gods of the underworld. On the second tier, the jaguar deity sits majestically in a lotus position. On the third tier, remnants of **Kulkulcan's** snake emblem curls atop his jagged, butterfly shaped steps. To the right, the thrones of administrative governors still remain in their powerful position. Up this tier, through the patio, and down the narrow stairs to the right is **El Dios del Sol Nocturno** (The God of the Nocturnal Sun), glaring with fiery eyes immediately to the left. A few meters ahead on the far left corner, the earth monster in red fresco is juxtaposed with the underworld, represented by a cross-legged skeleton. Past the fourth tier, the level of governors' bedrooms gives way to the impressive fifth tier's **El Mural de las Cuatro Eras** (The Mural of the Four Eras), on the far right. The underworld twin god is crawling on the bottom right with fire escaping from his mouth and body; crossed bones of death are found in the center along with descending suns. A full-bodied skeleton is grabbing a prisoner's head minutes before killing him. It is said that the engraved profile of the prisoner represents the real prisoner found in the interior of this mural (ask your guide to open the locked gate). At the center of this same level is a royal grave. Here, archaeologists discovered a stone sarcophagus, made of a single piece of limestone, which held a king's body and two unidentified corpses. To the left of the grave is a shrine to Chac, the Maya rain god. The **Altar de Monstruo de la Tierra** is on the right-hand side of the sixth level.

The seventh level of the pyramid was Toniná's religious focal point, and it supports four large pyramids dedicated to a curious mix of cosmic and civic forces. The **Temple of Agriculture,** on the far right of the terrace is decorated with roof combs. This crumbling building contained four private rooms for ranking priests and governors. To the left of the Temple of Agriculture a dark, narrow tunnel leads to a mysterious underworld. To the left rises the **Temple of the Prisoners**. Despite the name, which comes from the reliefs of tied prisoners at the base, archaeologists believe that this mound once housed the king and the royal family. Behind it loom Toniná's two most important temples. The higher **Pyramid of War,** on the right, served as an observatory; from the top of the structure, guards scanned the countryside for foreign heavies. Nearby is the symmetrical **Pyramid of Finances.** From the peak of either pyramid, you can enjoy a brilliant view and a cool breeze. Below the Pyramid of War a statue of **King Zotz-Choj** (the jaguar-bat king), whose giant headdress is adorned with an eagle and serpents, as well as symbols for wind, smoke, and fire was excavated and transferred to the site's museum.

Getting There: The ruins are located 15 bumpy kilometers from Ocosingo (a 20min. drive). By car, follow Calle 1 Ote. south out of town, past the clinic on the right. Bear right past the radio station on the left. Follow the signs for "Toniná ruins". The road to the left of the gate leads to the ruins and museum. Travelers without a car can catch a *colectivo*, a VW bus, from Ocosingo's market (every 20 min., 15 pesos), dole out a steep taxi fare (100 pesos one way), or walk for hours. Approximately 2km before the site, **Rancho Esmeralda** provides cabins (singles 150 pesos; doubles 260 pesos) and horseback riding. *(Site open daily 9am-4pm. Admission 30 pesos, free on Sundays.)*

PALENQUE

You've seen Uxmal. You made it to Chichén Itzá. Still, nothing can prepare you for Palenque, where time-defying temples, palaces, and pyramids gleam like milky diamonds against an emerald backdrop. In all of Mesoamerica, three sites are world-renowned for the degree to which they reflect the beauty, power, and glory of the Maya Classic period. Honduras has Copán, Guatemala has Tikal, and Mexico has Palenque. These impressive ruins straddle a magnificent 300m high *palenque* (natural palisade) in the foothills of the Altos de Chiapas. Dense *selva* (jungle) reaches down to the bases of Palenque's breathtaking pyramids, and the sounds of birds, monkeys, and crushing waterfalls echo off the walls of the grand palace, temples, and numerous courtyards.

On the other hand, the crowded and grimy town of Palenque (pop. 20,000), 8km away, is a memorable for completely different reasons. Nevertheless, it is an important crossroads for travelers arriving from all directions to visit the ruins, sample the water of the famous cascades of Agua Azul and Misol-Ha, make forays into the heart of the Lacandón jungle, and to begin excursions to Maya sites in Guatemala (for information on Tikal, Uaxactún, and El Mirador, see p. 571).

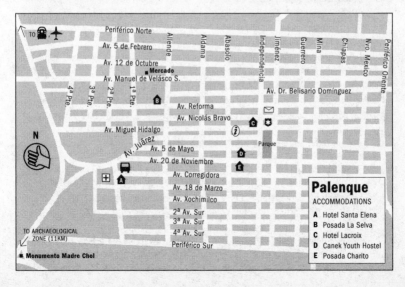

Palenque

ACCOMMODATIONS

A Hotel Santa Elena
B Posada La Selva
C Hotel Lacroix
D Canek Youth Hostel
E Posada Charito

 ORIENTATION

Palenque is in the northeastern corner of Chiapas, 274km from Tuxtla Gutiérrez. Streets running east-west are labeled *avenidas*, while those running north-south are *calles*. **Av. Juárez** runs west, away from the **parque** (town square) toward the ruins and highway. Parallel to Juárez to the south are **Avs. 5 de Mayo** and **20 de Noviembre**. To the north lie **Miguel Hidalgo, Nicolás Bravo, Reforma,** and **Domínguez.** From west to east, the *calles* are **Allende, Aldama, Abasolo, Independencia, Jiménez,** and **Guerrero.** The *parque* is bounded by Hidalgo, 20 de Noviembre, Independencia, and Jiménez. To get to the *parque* from the bus station, walk five blocks uphill (east) on Juárez.

PRACTICAL INFORMATION

Buses: All stations are located 5 blocks west of the *parque* on Juárez. ADO (tel. 5 13 44) runs first-class buses to: **Campeche** (6hr., 8am and 9pm, 160 pesos); **Cancún** (12hr., 8pm, 330 pesos); **Chetumal** (7½hr., 8pm, 195 pesos); **Escárcega** (3hr., 8am, 95 pesos); **Mérida** (8hr., 8am and 9pm, 240 pesos); **Mexico City** (12hr., 6pm and 8pm, 430 pesos); **Oaxaca** (13hr., 5:30pm, 330 pesos); **Playa del Carmen** (11hr., 8pm, 300 pesos); **Puebla** (10½hr., 7pm, 380 pesos); **San Cristóbal** (4 hr., 10am and noon, 85 pesos); and **Villahermosa** (2hr., 12 per day, 65 pesos). Cristóbal Colón heads for: **Campeche** (6hr., 2:10pm, 150 pesos); **Escárcega** (3hr., 2:10, 5:30, and 10:15pm, 87 pesos); **Mérida** (8hr., 2:10pm, 210 pesos); **Ocosingo** (2hr., 9:30am, 6:30pm, 60 pesos); **San Cristóbal** (4½hr., 9:30am and 6:30pm, 95 pesos); and **Tuxtla Gutiérrez** (6hr., 4 per day, 110 pesos). Autobuses de Tuxtla Gutiérrez (tel. 5 12 33) has first- and second-class service and **luggage storage** for 35 pesos a day (½block toward town from ADO station).

Taxis: (tel. 5 10 12). 35 pesos to the ruins; 14 pesos within town.

Tourist Office: In the **Casa de las Artesanías,** at the corner of Juárez and Abasolo. Helpful staff speaks some English and can provide maps of the town and ruins. Open M-Sa 8am-8:30pm, Su 9am-1pm.

Travel Agencies: Na Chan Kan, Av. Hidalgo at Jiménez (tel./fax 5 02 63) on the northeast corner of the *parque* provides good, professional tours to Yaxchilan, Bonampak, Palenque, Misol-Ha, Agua Azul, and Guatemala including a buffet breakfast and home-cooked lunch at excellent prices.

Currency Exchange: Bancomer, Av. Juárez 40 (tel. 5 01 98), 2 blocks west of the *parque* with a 24hr. **ATM.** Open for exchange M-F 9am-3pm. **Banamex,** Av. Juárez 62 (tel. 5 04 90). Open M-F 9am-2pm.

Laundry: Lavandería "Ela," 5 de Mayo at Allende, opposite the Hotel Kashlan. 40 pesos for 3kg. Same-day service. Open M-Sa 8am-9pm, Su 8am-3pm.

Police: (tel. 5 02 49), on Calle Independencia, in the Palacio Municipal. Open 24hr.

Pharmacy: Farmacia Central, Av. Juárez near Independencia. Open daily 7am-11pm.

Medical Services: Centro de Salud y Hospital General (tel. 5 07 33), on Av. Juárez near the bus station, at the western end of town. Open 24hr. No English spoken.

Post Office: Independencia at Bravo, north of the *parque*. Open M-F 8am-3pm, Sa 9am-1pm. **Postal Code:** 29960.

Fax: (tel. 5 03 68) on Hidalgo, 1½ blocks east of the *parque* in the Chaka-max building, next to the post office. Open M-F 9am-3pm, Sa 9am-1pm.

Internet Access: Cibernet (tel. 5 17 10), Calle Independencia between 5 de Mayo and 20 de Noviembre, across from the park. 30 pesos for 30min, 50 pesos per hr. Open daily 9am-9pm.

Telephones: Caseta California, Av. Juárez 4 (tel. 5 11 50 or 5 12 12; fax 5 09 97), half a block from the *parque*. Open daily 8am-3pm and 6-11pm.

Phone Code: 934.

ACCOMMODATIONS AND CAMPING

The town of Palenque has none of the aesthetic appeal of its ruins; this is especially true of its budget accommodations. Budget travelers can either stay in town or sack out at one of the hotels along the highway en route to the ruins. Of the two options, the latter tends to be more expensive, with the exception of **Mayabell Trailer Park and Camping** (tel. 8 06 19), 6km from town and 2km from the ruins, is accessible by *combi* (15 pesos) and allows guests to pitch a tent, string up a hammock, or put down a sleeping bag under a *palapa* for 40 pesos per person (20-peso deposit, 20 pesos for hammock rental). They also have trailer spaces with electricity, water, and decent drainage (30 pesos) and simple car spaces (20 pesos). The few rooms claim terra-cotta honeycomb tiles, plaid bedspreads, standing fans, and private bathrooms. (Singles 115 pesos; doubles 125 pesos; triples 150 pesos; quads 170 pesos; 20 pesos each additional person; 100-peso deposit.)

Posada Charito, Av. 20 de Noviembre 15 (tel. 5 01 21), between Independencia and Abasolo, a half block west from the *parque* has a friendly and familial atmosphere with large rooms, ventilators and private bathrooms. Singles 60 pesos; doubles 70 pesos; triples 80 pesos; 20 pesos per additional person.

Canek Youth Hostel 20 de Noviembre 43 (tel. 5 01 50), is an average hostel with large, rooms, decent bathrooms, and a view of the mountains to the south and fans in each room. Singles 50 pesos for a bed in a 5-person dormitory or 80 pesos for a room with private bath; doubles 90 pesos; triples 120 pesos; quads 140 pesos; 20 pesos per additional person.

Hotel Santa Elena (tel. 5 10 29), on Jorge de la Vega Domínguez, directly behind the ADO bus station. This conveniently located hotel's blue-green tile interior comes with large rooms, fans, and excellent service which make it worth the saggy beds. Ask for less noisy rooms opposite the bus station and show your *Let's Go: Mexico* for a 10% discount. Singles 80 pesos; doubles 100 pesos; triples 120 pesos.

Hotel Lacroix, Hidalgo 10 (tel. 5 00 14), just off the *parque* and next to Na Chan Kan Travel Agency and Restaurant. A large, gaudy Maya mural with Spanish poetry leads the way to cozy, cool, blue rooms with TVs and aquarium blue bathrooms. Singles 110 pesos; doubles 130 pesos; triples 150 pesos.

Posada la Selva, Av. Reforma #69 (tel. 5 06 41), between Allende and 1a Pte., 3½ blocks northeast of the *parque*. *Agua purificada* in the hallway and plants along the entry stairway lead to green and white rooms with sparkling private bathrooms, and if you're lucky, a room with a view of *la selva* (the jungle). Organized tirps to Yaxchilan, Bonampak, Misol-ha, and Agua Azul with in-house agency **Aventura Maya**. Singles 70 pesos; doubles 90 pesos; triples 130 pesos; 20 pesos each additional person.

FOOD

Finding a cheap restaurant in Palenque that serves full meals is like striking gold. For cheap produce, try the **market** on Velasco Suárez, about four blocks northwest of the *parque*. The travel agency on the corner of Av. Hidalgo and Calle Independencia doubles as one of the best bargain joints for eating and hanging out. There is also a surprisingly good restaurant at the ruins.

Restaurante Las Tinajas, 20 de Noviembre 41, at Abasolo. Popularity may have nudged up prices, but the quality local dishes and large, aesthetic servings keep the tourists coming back—for breakfast, lunch, and dinner. Entrees 38 pesos; *licuados* 12 pesos. Open daily 7am-11pm.

Restaurant Maya Palenque (tel. 5 07 81), 20 de Noviembre 38, between Restaurant las Tinajus and Posada Charito, serves healthy and generous yogurt, granola, and fruit platters (18 pesos), mixed salads (14-20 pesos), local dishes (25-40 pesos), and cappuccino. Open daily 6am-11pm.

THE ARCHAEOLOGICAL SITE OF PALENQUE

During the Maya Classic Period (300-900), Palenque was of central importance to the Maya. Though impressive, the **ruins of Palenque** only hint at the former majesty of the city, as only a small fraction of the structures have been excavated from their dense jungle blanket; new discoveries are ongoing.

Palenque owes much of its finery, including its unparalleled stucco bas-relief sculptures, to an early ruler, the club-footed, god-man **King Pacal** (Pak-AL; 615-683). According to inscriptions made at the time of his death, Pacal lived into his fifth *katun* (20-year period) and was then succeeded by his elderly son **Chan-Bahlum.** Chan-Bahlum celebrated his ascension by building a great pyramid-crypt (Temple of the Inscriptions) for his father. After Chan-Bahlum died, Palenque slipped into oblivion; when Cortés arrived in the 16th century, he marched past the abandoned city without noting its existence.

Combis to the site run daily from 5:30am-6pm (15 pesos); catch them off Av. Hidalgo on Allende. Visiting the ruins at night is prohibited and extremely unsafe. Do not take shortcuts to the back entrance of the ruins from the campgrounds or the road—the dense jungle will isolate you from any other tourists who may be nearby. (*Archaeological site open daily 8am-4:45pm; museum located 2km before the site open daily 7am-4pm; crypt open daily 8am-4pm. Admission 35 pesos, free Su.*)

GUIDE TO THE RUINS

On entering the site, a *ceiba* (tree of life) greets you, followed by the tomb of Alberto Ruz, one of Mexico's most famous archaeologists, who was so devoted to restoring Palenque that he insisted on being buried there. To the right rises the steep **Temple of the Inscriptions** with 69 steps representing King Pacal's 69 years of reign. Named for its magnificent tablets, the temple was the burial place of King Pacal and the first substantial burial place discovered in the Americas. After his disappointing discovery of six unimpressive skeletons, Ruz bore into the interior of the crypt. There, he discovered the perfectly preserved, elaborately carved sarcophagus of the king. The figure in the lower center of the tablet is Pacal himself, shown descending into the underworld with the *ceiba* tree directly over him. Ruz and his men had to remove more than 400 tons of rock fill by hand to reach the burial chamber. Visitors must scramble the long way down slippery stone steps in a steep and stuffy tunnel to view the royal crypt. A **hollow duct,** which allowed Pacal's spirit to exit the underworld and communicate with Palenque's priests, is located on the right after the staircase.

A trail leads up the mountainside to the east of the Temple of the Inscriptions. About 100m along this trail, on the right, is the **Temple of the Lion.** Descend the pitch-black stairwell inside the structure, and you'll come upon the site of the ancient well. There, a few faint traces of paint are slowly surrendering to the green slime of the jungle. The trail continues up the hill for 7km before reaching the tiny *indígena* village of Naranjo (approx. 2 hour walk, one-way). Guides can be found for this difficult hike through beautiful terrain. Next to the Temple is a trapezoidal **Palace** complex, consisting of four patios and a four-story tower. This immense complex is replete with religious tributes, such as the relief on the north side depicting the nine gods of the underworld. Other carvings laud the godlike priests and royal families that inhabited its many chambers. The most impressive one is the original coronation of King Pacal at age 12 by his mother on his left. King Pacal sits majestically atop a double-headed jaguar, representing civil and religious leadership. The palace's T-shaped ducts cooled the air and doubled as representations of **Ik,** the god of the breezes. Visitors can clamber down the staircase from the top of the platform to explore the extensive, dimly-lit network of underground passageways with complete remnants of king-size beds and a kitchenette. It is said that the royal family were big-boned and hefty due to their carnivorous feasts (for a comparison, measure up with the Maya sculpted left-leg in one of the outdoor patios). Flat-nosed masks of the rain-god Chac glare across to the north end's stuc-

Palenque Ruins

1 Observatory (El Mirador)
2 Temple of the Foliated Cross
3 Temple of the Cross
4 Temple XIV
5 Temple of the Sun
6 Temples XXI, XXII
7 Temple of the Lion
8 Temple of the Inscriptions
9 Temple XIII
10 Temple of the Skull
11 Temple XI
12 Palace
13 Wall Remains
14 Pelota Ballcourt
15 Temple X
16 Temple of the Count
17 Northern Group
18 Campsite, Queen's Bath
19 Site Museum

CHIAPAS AND TABASCO

coed walls. An exclusively female steam bath and latrines have also been excavated, and eight large sculptures of tortured prisoners will keep you staring.

The path between the palace and the Temple of Inscriptions fords the recently reconstructed aqueduct before leading up to the **Sun Plaza,** another landscaped platform comprised of the **Temple of the Sun,** the **Temple of the Cross,** the **Temple of the Foliated Cross,** and the smaller **Temple 14.** The Temple of the Cross was named for a stucco relief of a cross discovered inside, which inspired a flurry of hopeful religious theories among the *conquistadores.* For the Maya, the cross represents the *ceiba* tree with a snake as its horizontal branch and a bird perched atop it. The outer layer of stucco has worn away, but the inner sanctum protects a large, sculpted tablet and reliefs on either side of the doors.

About to be swallowed again by the jealous jungle, the **Temple of the Foliated Cross** lies across the plaza from the Temple of the Sun. Despite the overgrown path, the inner sanctum contains a carved tablet with tints of red fresco. To the south, through the wall of trees, several unreconstructed temples surround the uncleared **Plaza Maudslay** such as the newly discovered Temples XVII, XX, XXI, and XXII. Downhill from Temple 14 and past the palace lie the vestiges of a **ballcourt.** Palenque is full of small paths leading to unrestored ruins and cascades; bring bug spray and a buddy if you intend to explore on your own.

To the left of the ballcourt is the **Temple of Frederick,** Count of Waldeck, who lived here for three years while studying the ruins in the 1830s. The four other temples that share the platform with the Temple of the Count comprise the **North Group.** After crossing the bridge, waterfall enthusiasts may shower and splash in the **Queen's Bath** (so named for its exclusively female clientele). A second set of falls, **Cascada Montiepa,** is hidden in the jungle, 600m down the road from the ruins. At the right-hand bend, follow the path into the woods. Unfortunately, overgrown banks and shallow water make swimming impractical.

NEAR PALENQUE:
CASCADAS DE AGUA AZUL AND MISOL-HA

Both of these large **cascadas** (waterfalls) have seduced tourists of late, and for good reason. **Agua Azul,** 62km south of Palenque, is a breathtaking spectacle surrounded by luscious vegetarion: the Río Yax-Há jumps down 500 individual falls, then slips into rapids, whirlpools, and calm swimming pools. The rainy season, however, brings the tint of mud down from the highlands into the once-azure falls. There is a tiny beach and swimming area 20 minutes upstream from the falls—if you swim, stay close to the bank and swim with a friend; more than 100 people have met their watery end here (the half-buried crosses with deceased names send clear warning). The falls are best visited as a daytrip. The falls at **Misol-Ha,** higher and less-visited than Agua Azul, are 24km from Palenque and only 2km from the highway crossing. There's a large cataract here, and the swimming area is clean and relatively safe. Bring a flashlight if you want to explore the underground cave behind the falls. There are a few **restaurants** and **food stands** here.

Getting There: The most painless way to visit Agua Azul and Misol-Ha is aboard a **Transportes Chambalu** *combi* (100 pesos round-trip). **Combis** leave daily from the Palenque station at Hidalgo and Allende (9, 10, and 11am) and proceed to Agua Azul, after a 30-minute photo stop at Misol-Ha. Passengers are dropped off by the falls for a three-hour swimming and tanning session. **Buses** between Palenque and Ocosingo or San Cristóbal will also stop at the crossroads for either Agua Azul or Misol-Ha (20 pesos). Since few buses pass after 4pm, you should leave the falls in the early afternoon. *(Admission to each of the falls 8 pesos, 25 pesos per carload.)*

YAXCHILÁN

Rising from the banks of the Usumacinta River, deep within the Lacandón jungle, is a city that neither time nor tourists have touched. Covering eight square kilometers and extending across the river into Guatemala, only a fourth of the site has been fully excavated. Yet the vast number of stelae, lintels, and hieroglyphics have revealed a rich history behind the silent temples. The heavy jungle that still hides many of the structures is far from quiet, though—families of toucans, spiders, and howler monkeys, as well as other wildlife, are more frequent visitors to the ruins than humans. The political trouble of the mid-1990s postponed plans for a museum and a general expansion of tourism at the site, so a journey to Yaxchilán is still like the archaeological expeditions of old. This ancient city is so remote, its carvings so clear, and the enveloping jungle so wild that visitors may later think back and wonder if Yaxchilán was anything but a fascinating dream.

The nearest town to Yaxchilán, **Frontera Corozal,** is 197km southeast of Palenque. The site is a 40-minute *lancha* cruise downstream on the Río Usumacinta, and the strong currents make it a 60 minute trip back. The new road is a smooth ride, and constant patrolling by Mexican security have made it safer. The safest, most practical, and cheapest way to reach the hidden treasures of Yaxchilán is through a travel agency which is insured, connected, and familiar with Mexican security and road block procedures, and has contracted *lancheros* with the best group rate. If you venture off on your own you will not be protected by Mexican security, you will most likely face road block holdups, pay many tolls, and bargain with *lancheros* charging a staggering 900-1300 pesos for a round-trip cruise. On the other hand, prices with Palenque travel agencies range from 450 for one-day trips to 650 pesos for two days. Do not leave your *posada* without your passport and visa due to various army roadblocks. There are travel agencies in Palenque; prices range from 300 pesos for one-day trips to 600 pesos for two days and vary according to demand; prices include meals, boat fare, lodging, and a visit to **Bonampak** (see p. 567). Make sure to get any chores done before leaving—the nearest services of any kind are in Palenque. The handful of permanent residents at the entrance to the site have so recently begun to offer **camping** space that prices have not yet been set. Try the new, self-proclaimed **Centro Ecoturístico Escudo Jaguar** (tel. 5 03 56) in Frontera Corozal offering colorful *cabanas* with firm beds and fans (singles and doubles 250 pesos; triples and quads 350 pesos), as well as a *palapa* with 15 hammock spaces and a common bathroom (70 pesos per hammock) and camping (45 pesos per tent). There is a small restaurant in **Escudo.**

THE ARCHAEOLOGICAL SITE OF YAXCHILÁN

HISTORY. Yaxchilán ("green rocks" in Maya) is famous for its thousands of glyphs, telling an almost-complete story of the city. It had its humble beginnings around 350 as a Maya fishing and farming village along the Usumacinta. Yaxchilán's emblem glyph (a glyph representing a particular polity) began to appear at other places such as **El Cayo, Piedras Negras,** and **Bonampak** after 526, suggesting that it played a role at those sites and may have been a regional capital. Years of bloody conquest and expansion during the reign of Shield-Jaguar (726-742) made Yaxchilán one of the most important cities of the Maya Late Classical Period. Shield-Jaguar's son, **Bird-Jaguar,** took the throne in 752. When questions arose over the validity of his ascension, Bird-Jaguar undertook the greatest construction projects Yaxchilán had ever seen to reinforce his legitimacy. Most of the buildings and stelae in the city date to the period of his rule, and it was during these years that Yaxchilán rose to the peak of its power, through new acropolises, royal intermarriages, and alliances with neighboring regions. Evidence of trade and symbolic influence with cities as far away as Teotihuacán can also be found dating to this period. In 770, a man called Shield-Jaguar II, most likely a son of one of the other wives of Shield-Jaguar I, rose to power and ruled until 808. During his reign, Shield-Jaguar II took several governors of other cities prisoner; one such event is chillingly portrayed on a lintel in Bonampak's **Temple of the Paintings** (see p. 567). By 900, lesser nobles were flouting whatever ruling authority was left and began constructing their houses in the midst of old royal ceremonial centers. Along with many other Maya cities of this time, Yaxchilán was depopulated and eventually abandoned.

GUIDE TO THE RUINS. Yaxchilán is no longer a lost city thanks to the boat cruise along the Usumacinta River and paths into the jungle past unexcavated temples. Visitors enter Yaxchilán through the **Labyrinth,** a maze of pitch-black underground passageways symbolizing the underworld, which have not yet been fully explored. Bring a flashlight to wander the arch halls and admire the original stucco work. At the end of the labyrinth, the front door opens onto the vast **Grand Plaza.** Running west to east, the 500m long and 60m wide plaza was the monumental heart of the city, lined by temples and palaces on both sides. Thankfully, enough structures remain to give a good sense of Yaxchilán's past glory. The first significant structure on the north side of the plaza, to the left of the Labyrinth, is **Building 16.** Three doorways are all that remain of the building, each with carved lintels. The middle one depicts a scene with Bird-Jaguar holding a ceremonial bar dated 743. Further down the Grand Plaza is the **ballcourt,** built for two players during Shield-Jaguar's rule. Five markers were placed in the court, one of which still shows a figure adorned with quetzal and feathers holding a serpent. In between Building 16 and the ballcourt stands a 350 year-old *ceiba* tree of life and to the right lies the remains of a palace.

Continuing east past the palace, visitors arrive at **Stela 1,** which, except for a missing triangular portion, looks as though it was just chiseled. One of Bird-Jaguar's many monuments, it shows the king and his wife undergoing a ritual self-sacrifice. Notice the wife's two self-sacrificed fingers — the middle and ring fingers. Glyphs on the stela give the date of 762, and on either side of the stela are statues representing a jaguar and a crocodile. Still on the north side of the plaza, past Stela 1, stands **Building 6,** also called the **Temple of Chac.** The original stucco still retains some of its colors. A few meters past the Temple, remains of the hierglyphic steps leading to the ancient Maya bridge, connecting Yaxchilán to Guatemala, lie to the left. Lying in a very unmajestic position east of Building 6 is Yaxchilán's most elaborate and important carving—**Stela 11.** Engraved on four of its six sides, this monolith was originally found towering in front of Building 40. After numerous efforts to send it to the Museo Nacional de Antropología in Mexico City, it was unceremoniously dropped here. This key stela depicts the all-important transfer of power from Shield-Jaguar to Bird-Jaguar on the left. On the right, shown with eagle wings on his back, holding a ceremonial scepter, and wearing a sun-god chest plate and a Chac headdress, is the Bird-Jaguar. His emblem glyph is the second from the right along the thin bottom side of the stela. Across from Stela 11 on the south side of the plaza, past some circular altars and another stela dedicated to Bird-Jaguar, is **Building 20.** Next door to the west is **Building 21,** with original stucco on its superior facade and an engraved lintel depicting the birth of Bird-Jaguar; notice his head emanating from the serpent's mouth. Inside Building 21 is a stunning stela of Shield-Jaguar's wife, **Lady Ik-Skul** auto-sacrificing her tongue. The side facing out of the building shows her holding a bowl of self-sacrificial tools under a figure of the rain god Tláloc, an indication of cultural influence from Central Mexican civilizations. A mirror allows visitors to view the other side of the stela, which clearly shows Lady Ik-Skul's passing an obsidian-studded rope through her tongue; glyphs give the date 743. Along the back wall are stucco reliefs that still have some original red, blue, and green colors.

Some minor buildings line the rest of the southern side of the plaza. Before them is a long, steep slope with lintels describing the rise of power of Shield-Jaguar and his first wife, **Lady Fist-Fish,** that climbs past Buildings 25 and 26 on the left, reaching the immense **Building 33** at the top. The best-preserved of Yaxchilán's buildings, it was the result of yet another of Bird-Jaguar's projects and is called the **House of Music.** Legend has it that as storms blow in from the north over Guatemala, the wind creates musical harmonies as it is forced through the many openings of different shapes and sizes of the building's facade. Outside the building is a rare stalactite stela and a sharp stucco work on the lower platform showing a ball game in progress. Inside sits the ominous, decapitated statue of Bird-Jaguar himself. No one knows how, when, or why his head came to rest in the next room, but when archaeologists attempted to replace it, they were stopped by the **Lacandón Maya,** who still regularly hold religious ceremonies at Yaxchilán. One of their central religious beliefs is that the moment the head is rejoined, the end of the world will begin; supernatural jaguars will descend from the heavens and destroy all living beings. Archaeologists have not moved the head. The trail behind and to the right of Building 33 leads to the small **acropolis** composed of Buildings 39, 40, and 41. To reach building 41, cut through the small plaza, and gaze upon its first engraved lintel: Bird-Jaguar is shown grabbing a prisoner's hair before decapitating him. The unimpeded 360° view of the Mexican jungle and Guatemalan highland is well worth the arduous 10-minute hike. It was from here that kings ruled over the lives of approximately 10,000 families. *(Site open daily 8am-4:45pm. Admission 30 pesos, free on Sundays, enthusiastic caretakers will give "free" tours—a tip is expected.)*

THE REAL PEOPLE Travelers visiting the ruins of Yaxchilán or Bonampak may have the fortune to meet a member of an indigenous group. The Lacandón Maya, or **Winik** (Real People) as they call themselves, have succeeded for centuries longer than any other Maya people in maintaining strictly traditional religious practices and beliefs. While the rest intermixed Christianity with their indigenous religions within the first two centuries of Spanish colonialism, the Lacandón accepted no facets of Christianity until the 1950s. At that time, the town of Lacanha Chan Sayab converted to Protestantism; in the 1970s, their neighbors in Mansabak converted to Seventh Day Adventism. Today, the Lacandón in the town of Nahá continue to live entirely outside the influence of Christianity.

Although they are Mexico's only jungle-dwelling people, the Lacandón themselves are not native to the Lacandón jungle; their ancestors emigrated from the Yucatán peninsula in the 13th century. Today, only a few hundred people identify themselves as Lacandón (largely defined by speaking Lacandón Mayan); the settlement near Crucero Bonampak known as **San Javier** is home to a number of Lacandóns. While in Mexico's only rainforest, ask around to find residents who will take you on phenomenal hikes (75-100 pesos) or to one of Na Bolom's **Casas de Cultura** (see p. 546).

NEAR YAXCHILÁN: BONAMPAK

Practically every book, pamphlet, or other published material in the world having to do with Maya archaeology has a reproduction of the murals of **Bonampak.** The murals have single-handedly changed scholars' conceptions of Maya civilization since their discovery in 1946. Maya's religious practices to honor and glorify their gods went above auto-sacrifices. Just to gaze upon these stark murals is more than enough reason to make the short 8km detour from the road to Yaxchilán. The ceremonial center open to the public is much smaller than Yaxchilán's, however, consisting of a near-empty plaza and a hillside that was made into a long, wide series of steps. Since Bonampak does not nearly have the number of engraved glyphs of Yaxchilán, its history is less detailed. *(Site is open daily 8am-5pm. Admission 25 pesos.)*

▣ THE MURALS OF BONAMPAK

The **murals of Bonampak** have certainly aged after 12 centuries and an ill-advised dousing with kerosene by an early restoration team. Yet these one-of-a-kind paintings still have the power to leave visitors gaping in awe. The colors of these murals, painted *al fresco*, are an array of reds, blues, greens, yellows, browns, and various combinations.

Much of what is known about Bonampak pertains to a ruler known as **Chaan Muan II,** who is depicted on grand **Stela 1.** This 6m high slab is the first major sight to greet visitors as they enter the Great Plaza, but it is only carved on its south side, aligned directly with the central floor of the House of Paintings. The uppermost portion is in total disrepair, but enough remains to present the whole figure of the glowering king holding a spear and shield (dated 787) standing atop the gods of corn and the earth monster deity. Two other important stelae are situated close to the plaza on the wide steps: **Stela 2,** on the left and **Stela 3,** a richly attired Chaan Muan II standing over a prisoner. Try to make out the prisoner's bristled beard—facial hair is rarely depicted in Maya art. Stela 2 depicts Chaan Muan II and his mother initiating a political alliance with his wife from Yaxchilan.

The **Temple of Paintings,** or **Building 1,** is a three-room building found just above and to the right of the Great Plaza. Over the three doorways, from left to right, are lintels of **Knotted-Eye Jaguar,** an ancestor of Chaan Muan II; Shield-Jaguar II of Yaxchilán; and Chaan Muan II—all about to execute a groveling prisoner. The two-headed serpent bar is a **staff of rulership**. Inside, the murals of the three rooms combine to form a narrative that reads from left to right. In Chamber 1, the murals depict a procession and the presentation of a heir to the throne, on the right side of the room. Note the musicians and lobster-costumed figure on the lower level to the left. Chamber 2 shows a fierce battle in a forest—over the doorway is a blood-curdling display of tortured prisoners with fingers dripping blood, vainly pleading for mercy from the jaguar-skin robed royalty of Bonampak. The third chamber is a portrait of a victory celebration with more dancers and musicians, as well as of the royal family undergoing more self-sacrificial rituals. Behind and above the Temple of Paintings are a set of buildings numbered four to eight from right to left. Climb up behind Building 4 to get a look at roofless Building 9.

Getting There: Chan-Calan *colectivos* from Palenque make daily stops at **Crucero Bonampak,** which is on the way to Frontera Corozal, 20km northeast. Safety is at risk in *colectivos* since they are not protected by Mexican security, making assaults easier and more frequent. It is advisable to book a one-day tour of Yaxchilán and Bonampak; otherwise it could take up to three days to visit both if traveling on your own.

TONALÁ

Most people don't visit Chiapas for the beaches, but hey, if you've got to go, you've got to go. Tonalá is one of the best, if not the only, major coastal town the state has to offer, and while the beaches nearby don't compare to Oaxaca's golden stretches of sand, **Puerto Arista** and (especially) **Boca del Cielo** are pleasant enough spots to spend a few hours. During *Semana Santa*, Christmas, and weekends in July and August, these seaside stretches fill with Chiapanecan families. During the rest of the year, however, their only guests are the *zancudos blancos*—vicious mosquitos that exploit the holey nature of hammocks. Tonalá proper, though lively, is very hot and humid and offers little in the way of cooling refreshment. Stop for lunch and head for the sand further afield.

■ **ORIENTATION.** Tonalá lies 223km northwest of Tapachula and 172km southwest of Tuxtla Gutiérrez. All **bus stations** are on **Av. Hidalgo,** Tonalá's main street. To get to the *zócalo* from the **Cristóbal Colón** bus station, take a left and head six blocks south. Both the **Autotransportes Tuxtla Gutiérrez** and **Fletes y Pasajes** bus stations are south of the *centro*, so turn right and walk five blocks north. As the coastal highway, Av. Hidalgo runs roughly north-south through town. To the east, **Av. Rayón** parallels Hidalgo, while to the west run **Avs. Matamoros, Juárez,** and **Allende.** Listed from north to south, **Calles Madero, 16 de Septiembre, 5 de Febrero, Independencia,** and **5 de Mayo** run east-west, completing the grid that compose the city center.

◪ **PRACTICAL INFORMATION.** Autotransportes Tuxtla Gutiérrez, Hidalgo 56, five blocks south of the zócalo, has first-class **bus service** to: **Mexico City** (13hr., 5:30pm, 330 pesos) via **Puebla** (11hr., 285 pesos). First-class buses, including Maya de Oro (tel. 3 05 40), leave from the Cristóbal Colón station, six blocks north of the zócalo, for: **Mexico City** (13hr., 8pm, 313 pesos); **Oaxaca** (6½hr., 10pm, 125 pesos); **Puebla** (10hr., 8pm, 269 pesos); **Tapachula** (3hr., every hr. 3am-7pm, 68 pesos); **Tuxtla Gutiérrez** (3hr., every hr. 3am-7:30pm, 65 pesos); and **Villahermosa** (12hr., 10:30pm, 174 pesos). Fletes y Pasajes, Hidalgo 52 (tel. 3 25 94), 50m south of the bridge and three-and-a-half blocks south of the zócalo, sends second-class buses to: **Mexico City** (13hr., 4 per day, 290 pesos); **Puebla** (11hr., 5:45pm, 255 pesos); and **Tapachula** (3hr., 6 per day, 3:30am-6pm, 54 pesos). From the same building, TRF (tel. 3 12 61) has first class service to: **Tapachula** (3hr., 4 per day 6am-5:30pm, 66 pesos); and **Tuxtla Gutiérrez** (3hr., 10 per day, 54 pesos). **Taxis** (tel. 3 06 20) cruise up and down Hidalgo and hang out in the zócalo (40 pesos to Puerto Arista). If you're getting up early, the 24hr. **radio-taxis** (tel. 3 10 41 or 3 26 08), opposite the Colón bus station, will rouse you at your hotel. **Luggage storage** is 5 pesos per day.

The **tourist office** (tel. 3 27 87) is at Hidalgo and 5 de Mayo, two blocks south of the bus station, on the second floor of the Esmeralda building (no city maps; open M-F 9am-3pm and 6-9pm, Sa 10am-1pm). **Banamex,** Hidalgo 137 (tel. 3 0 0 37), at 5 de Febrero, half a block south of the *zócalo*, will **exchange currency** and has a 24hr. **ATM** (open M-F 9am-3pm). **Farmacia la Esperanza,** (tel. 3 00 42) located at Hidalgo Callejon Ote. (open daily 9am-11pm). **Police:** (tel. 3 01 03) on Calle Libertad, two blocks north of Cristóbal Colón and to the right. **Hospital General:** (tel. 3 06 87), Av. 27 de Septiembre at Mina, six blocks south of the *zócalo* and three blocks east before the gas station (open 24hr.). **Red Cross:** (tel. 3 21 21) is on Av. Joaquín Miguel Gutiérrez (open 24hr.). **Clínica de Especialidades:** Hidalgo 127 (tel. 3 12 90), at Independencia south of the *zócalo*, is a hospital and pharmacy; one doctor speaks English (open daily 9am-1pm and 5-7pm; open 24hr.). **Post office:** at Zambrano 27 (tel. 3 06 83), two blocks north and half a block east of the *zócalo* (open M-F 8am-7pm, Sa 9am-1pm). **Postal code:** 30500. **Internet access: ISTANET,** 2 blocks up Hidalgo past the *zócalo* and up the driveway and across from the elementary school. 15 pesos per hr. (Open daily 9am-10pm.) **Phone code:** 966.

◤◳ **ACCOMMODATIONS AND FOOD.** Leaving Tonalá with a good impression of the town often means not spending the night, as lodgings are over-priced and undercleaned. The **Hotel Tonalá** (tel. 3 04 80), a few blocks south of the Cristóbal Colón station, charges high rates for little space in its plain rooms. There is *agua purificada* in the lobby. (Singles 100 pesos; doubles 150 pesos; triples with TV and A/C 150 pesos.) Cheaper accommodations come at a price at **Hotel**

Thomás (tel. 13 00 80), on Hidalgo before the bridge, two blocks south of the *zócalo*. Small, blue rooms are equipped with ceiling fans, and the barely flushing toilets are the best feature of the bathrooms. (Singles 55 pesos; doubles 80 pesos.) **Restaurant Sambors** (tel. 3 06 80), Madero and Hidalgo, on the *zócalo*, has good food, a great *marisco* salad, and an excellent, wide-angle view of the *zócalo*. Enjoy *tortas* for 12 pesos and *licuados* for 9 pesos. (Open daily 8am-1am.) The **Restaurante Nora,** Independencia 10 (tel. 3 02 43), less than a block east of Hidalgo, and a block from the *zócalo*, is a calm refuge from the heat and sun. The congenial owner will make you feel right at home with a tasty three-course *comida corrida*. (30 pesos; open M-Sa 7am-6pm.)

◤ **SAND AND SIGHTS.** Eighteen kilometers southwest of Tonalá, **Puerto Arista** offers 32km of gray, sandy beach and the pounding waves of the Pacific. Hotels tend to be overpriced, particularly during the holidays and in summer. Seafood is plentiful in the beachside *palapas*, and the cheapest accommodations can be found in these places—some of which unofficially offer rooms. A light, clean hotel with sporadic views of the sea, **Hotel Maracaino** located a ways down the beach from the main road, offers singles for 100 pesos and doubles for 150 pesos. To get to Puerto Arista, catch a *combi* leaving from Juárez and 20 de Marzo, two blocks off Hidalgo (45min., 8 pesos). From the same place, *minis* going to **Boca de Cielo,** a beachside estuary, can be caught (1¼hr. from Tonalá). The calm waters have a less-than-pristine feel, and locals will happily rent you hammocks for an absurdly overpriced 50 pesos per night.

TAPACHULA

Tapachula (pop. 350,000), the southernmost town of Chiapas, is alive with sidewalk swapmeets, *cocinas económicas* (cheap food diners), and *marimba* music echoing through the hazy afternoon and into the night. The gold and forest green *zócalo*, the shady palm trees, leafy crowns of trimmed adjoined trees, and the cool fountains provide a haven from Tapachula's loud and dirty, crowded and crass, hot and smelly daily life. During the rainy season, hundreds of Guatemalan immigrants alongside Chiapanecos, crowd under the *zócalo's* canopy of trees, reading newspapers or socializing. For tourists, Tapachula is primarily a point of entry into Guatemala.

■ **ORIENTATION.** Tapachula is 18km from Talismán at the Guatemalan border on Rte. 200 and 303km west of Guatemala City. Tonalá lies 220km to the northwest, along the Pacific coast. *Avenidas* run north-south, and *calles* run east-west. *Calles* north of **Calle Central** are odd-numbered, while those south are even-numbered. Similarly, *avenidas* east of **Av. Central** are odd-numbered, while those west of it have even numbers. Tapachula's *zócalo* is at **3 Calle Pte.** between **6** and **8 Av. Nte.**, northwest of the center. To get to the *zócalo* from the **bus station,** take an immediate left upon exiting onto 17 Av. Ote, walk 1½ blocks and take a left on Av. Central, walk south six blocks. If you take a right on 5 Av. Pte and continue four blocks west, you will arrive at the plaza's northeast corner.

■ **PRACTICAL INFORMATION.** The **airport** is on the road to Puerto Madero, about 17km south of town. It's served by **Aeroméxico,** 2 Av. Nte. 6 (tel. 6 20 50) and **Aviacsa** (tel. 6 31 47 or 6 14 39). Autotransportes Tuxtla Gutiérrez, 11 Calle Ote. 20 (tel. 6 95 13), between 3 and 5 Av. Nte., provides first-class service to: **Mexico City** (18hr., 1pm, 400 pesos); second-class service to **Tuxtla Gutiérrez** (7hr., 11:45pm, 115 pesos). Cristóbal Colón (tel. 6 43 75 or 6 28 80), at 17 Calle Ote. at 3 Av. Nte., sends buses to **Brownsville, TX** (32hr., 10pm, 620 pesos); **Comitán** (6hr., 5 per day, 90 pesos); **Mexico City** (17hr., 5 per day, 560 pesos); **Oaxaca** (12hr., 4:45 and 5:45pm, 275-300 pesos); **Puebla** (16hr., 1:30pm, 2:15, 6:15, and 9:20pm, 440-500 pesos); **Puerto Escondido** (10hr., 11:15pm, 260 pesos); **San Cristóbal** (7hr., 5 per day, 88 pesos); **Tampico** (16hr., 10pm, 425 pesos); **Tonalá** (3hr., 8am, 1, and 4pm, 115 pesos); **Tuxtla Gutiérrez** (7hr., 12 per day 6am-midnight, 150 pesos); **Veracruz** (13hr., 6 and 10pm, 320-370 pesos); and **Villahermosa** (13hr., 11:05am, 6:30pm, 280 pesos). **Fletes y Pasajes,** 3 Av. Norte and 9 Calle Ote., has second-class service to: **Mexico City** (18hr., 3:30pm and 5pm, 385 pesos); and **Oaxaca** (13hr., 12:30 and 6pm, 200 pesos). **Luggage storage** costs 10 pesos per day.

The **tourist office** (tel. 6 14 85 or 6 31 17, ext. 140) is in the Antiguo Palacio Municipal, south of the Iglesia de San Agustín, on the west side of the *zócalo* (open M-F 9am-4pm and 4:30-10pm, Sa-Su 10am-2pm). The **Guatemalan consulate** is on 2 Calle Ote. 33 (tel. 6 12 52), between 7 and 9 Av. Sur. Citizens of the U.S., Canada, and European Union countries don't need a visa. Your passport will get you across the border hassle-free. Citizens from other countries (Switzerland, South Africa, etc.) will need a visa (see p. 35). Make sure to photocopy the first page of your passport and obtain a visa application. Visas take up to eight days to obtain. (Open M-F 9am-3pm.) **Exchange currency** at **Banamex** (tel. 6 29 25), on Av. Central Nte. 9; it has 24-hour **ATM. Police:** (tel. 5 28 51) on 8 Av. Nte. and 3 Calle Pte., in the Palacio Municipal (open 24hr.). **Farmacia 24 Horas:** 8 Av. Nte. 25 (tel. 6 18 11), at 7 Calle Pte. No English is spoken, but they promise free delivery to anywhere within the city daily from 7am to 11pm. **Hospital:** (tel. 8 10 60) on the highway to the airport (open 24hr.). **Internet access: Cybercafe,** Central Ote. #16B between 1 and 3 Nte. (tel. 626 1555, email globalia@tap.com.mx) is a hip coffee shop with computers hidden in the wall. Sip and cyber chat to the beat of Spanish music. 15 pesos per 30min. Open daily 9am-midnight. **Post office:** at 1 Calle Ote. 32 (tel. 6 24 92), between 7 and 9 Av. Nte. (open M-F 8am-6pm, Sa 9am-1pm.) **Postal code:** 30700. **Phone code:** 962.

⌂⌂ ACCOMMODATIONS AND FOOD. Due to the huge influx of Guatemalan refugees, budget accommodations are a dime a dozen in Tapachula, especially near the market. Unfortunately, many hotel rooms are as noisy and dirty as the rest of the city. The two spots listed provide decent accommodations at reasonable prices. **Hotel La Amistad,** 7 Calle Pte. 34 (tel. 6 22 93), between Av. 10 and 10 Nte, has a living room lobby with a multi-leveled ceramic fountain leading to a verdant courtyard and peachy rooms with private clean bathrooms (singles 85 pesos; doubles 110 pesos; triples 150 pesos; quads 195 pesos; quints 230 pesos). **Hospedaje Latino,** 12 Nte (tel. 6 13 41), between 5 y 7 Calle Pte., furnishes a large bed in a square plain room with communal bathrooms (singles 45 pesos; doubles 70 pesos). Lots of cheap taco stands, torta stands, and pastry baskets crowd the streets nearest the *zócalo* (tacos 4 pesos; tortas 8 pesos; corn on the cob 5 pesos; fruit juices 4 pesos). For more cheap eats, head to the **San Juan food market** on 17 Calle Pte., north of the *centro* (open daily 6am-5pm). **Mercado Sebastián Escobar,** 10 Av. Nte. between 5 and 3 Calles Pte., sells produce and baked goods. A variety of aromas exude from the streets of Tapachula due to its rich ethnic mix of German and Chinese immigrants from World War II.

⬛ CROSSING THE BORDER TO GUATEMALA

New policies have made crossing the border easier. For countries that do not need a visa, 30 days in Guatemala is automatically given. If you plan to stay longer, be sure to visit a consulate in Guatemala to ask for more time. Otherwise, be prepared to pay an additional fee when you leave. Mexico charges every tourist 150 pesos upon entering or re-entering, regardless of length of stay. Cross the border early in the day to avoid bureaucratic delay and unofficial closings.

From Tapachula, **Unión y Progreso buses** leave their station on 5 Calle Pte., half a block west of 12 Av. Nte., for Talismán (30min., every 5min., 12 pesos). For those who don't want to spend any time in Tapachula, the bus swings by the Cristóbal Colón bus station on 17 Calle Ote. on its way to the border. Buses from Tapachula drop off passengers at the entrance to the Mexican emigration office. Enter the building and present your **passport** and visa, then follow the crowd across the bridge, where you'll need to pay a toll of approximately 7 pesos. Proceed to a small building on the left to have your passport stamped by Guatemalan authorities; there is a charge of 15 quetzales. A **taxi** from the *zócalo* to Talismán costs 60 pesos. Those crossing the border **on foot** will be besieged by money changers and self-appointed "guides."

The **money changers** on the Guatemalan side of the border generally give better rates for pesos than those on the Mexican side, but your best bet is to avoid small money changers and head for the **Banco de Quetzal,** on the Guatemalan side.

From Talismán, you can take a **bus** to Guatemala City (6 per day, 4am-midnight). Don't travel at night, since this route has recently been plagued by assaults. Should you have to spend the night in Talismán, the **Hotel José Ricardo,** just past the official buildings on the right, offers nice, clean rooms with bathrooms and hot water. The various eateries in Talismán can turn seedy when drunks come out of the woodwork. Women traveling alone should exercise extreme caution. The Tapachulan tourist office recommends that tourists not cross the border at Ciudad Hidalgo, as the bridge there is long and deserted, leaving travelers particularly vulnerable to assault.

GUATEMALA

FLORES AND SANTA ELENA

Surrounded by the tranquil **Lago Petén Itza,** Flores is an island city with a definite emphasis on mellow island life. Flores began life as the Itzá capital of Tayasal, and in 1524, Cortés stopped by just long enough to drop off a sick horse. This must have been quite some horse, for almost a hundred years later the people were found to be worshipping a large idol called **Tzimin Chac** (Thunder Horse). Tayasal was the last city of independent Maya—it withstood the Spanish invasion and didn't fall until 1697. Today, Flores is unhurried, small, and unabashedly geared to tourists; it serves as a welcoming base for visitors to the Petén. Most of the down and dirty business gets done across the causeway in Santa Elena.

⚹ CROSSING THE BORDER INTO MEXICO

There are three established routes from Palenque to **Flores.** In all cases, be sure to clear customs and get your passport stamped on both sides of the border. The longest-standing route is to take a bus to the Guatemalan border post in the town of **El Naranjo** (5hr., 7 per day 5am-2:30pm, Q20). There are a few basic hotels in El Naranjo, but the best idea is to set out early and catch the midday boat to the Mexican border post in **La Palma** (4hr., US$20-25 per person). From there, buses depart for Palenque via **Tenosique**—the last leaves around 5pm, but if you miss it (and you may well), there's camping and a few basic rooms in La Palma.

A faster and sometimes more reliable route is to take the early morning Transportes Pinta bus from Flores to the enjoyable town of **Bethel** (4hr., 5am, Q18). Once there, get your passport stamped by the Guatemalan authorities and catch one of the fairly frequent 30-minute boat rides to **Frontera Corozal** in Mexico. In Corozal (or even Bethel), it's possible to arrange a trip to the ruins at **Yaxchilán.** From Corozal, minibus *colectivos* leave for Palenque until about 2:30pm.

⚹ ORIENTATION

A dusty **causeway** running across the lake separates Flores to the north and Santa Elena to the south. The main street in Flores is **Calle Centroamérico,** a block north of the end of the causeway. Most of the hotels and restaurants can be found along its route around the island. The **Parque Central** is located on top of the hill at the center of town. Santa Elena's main street is **4 Calle,** located three blocks south of the end of the causeway. The **mercado** can be reached from the end of the causeway, three blocks south to 4 Calle, and right for two long blocks. To get to Flores from the bus drop-offs, head east (right as you face the lake) on the main drag until the road signs point you left across the causeway.

▓ PRACTICAL INFORMATION

Buses: First-class buses to **Guatemala City** leave from company offices; buy tickets in advance. Second-class buses depart from Santa Elena's *mercado* from the Fuente del Norte office, and travel to **Guatemala City** (tel. 926-0517; 10-12hr., 12 per day 7:30am-9pm, Q60-130). Transportes Rosita (tel. 926-1245; 12hr., 5:30pm, Q50), and Línea Dorada's deluxe buses (tel. 926-0070; 10hr., 8pm, Q128), half a block down from Fuente del Norte also make the trip. Second-class buses leave the **mercado,** just off 4 Calle for: **Sayaxché** (2hr., 5 per day 5am-3:30pm, Q8); **El Naranjo** (5hr., 7 per day 5am-2:30pm, Q20); **Carmelita** (6hr., 1pm, Q25); **Bethel** (4hr., 5am, Q18); **Melchor de Mencos** and the border with **Belize** (2hr., 10 per day 5am-6pm, Q10), though many of these leave from Transportes Rosita's office on 4 Calle. Transportes Pinita runs to **Tikal** (2hr., 1pm, Q10), and heads on to **Uaxactún** (3hr., 1pm, Q15). For **Cobán,** take a Guate bus as far as El Rancho Junction (about 1hr.).

Minibuses: The most popular way of getting to **Tikal.** Purchase tickets in any hotel or travel agency in Flores or Santa Elena; they'll pick you up at your hotel or at the airport. **San Juan Travel** runs to Tikal (tel. 926-0041; 1¼hr.; every hr. 5am-10am, returns hourly noon-5pm; Q20 one-way, Q30 round-trip). Most minibuses will stop in **El Remate** (30min., Q10-15). San Juan Travel and Mundo Maya/Linea Dorada (tel. 926-0070) go as far as **San Ignacio, Belize** (4hr., US$15 per person), **Belize City** (5hr., US$20 per person), continuing on to **Chetumal, Mexico** (7½hr., US$30-35 per person) for connections to **Cancún, Mexico.**

Airport: 2km east of Santa Elena, accessed by taxi (Q10 per person), public bus (Q1), or foot (15min.). It's easiest to book a flight at an agency in Flores. Aviateca (tel. 926-1238) has the most frequent service to **Guatemala City** (30min.; 7am, 4, 6pm; US$65 one-way, US$89 round-trip). Aerocaribe offers flights to: **Cancún** (1½hr.; M, W, Th, F 4:45pm; US$79); **Palenque** (1hr.; M, W, Th, F 8am; US$79), and **Belize City** (1½hr.; Tu, Th, Sa, Su 8:10am; US$89) via **Chetumal** (1hr.). Flight schedules change often and prices listed above are subject to taxes (10-20%) and a US$20 exit tax. Heading for **Guatemala City** (30min.), Aviateca/Grupo Taca (tel. 926-1238) has 3 flights per day while Tikal Jets (tel. 926-0386) offers 2, and Mayan World (tel. 926-0362) and Rasca (tel. 926-1477) offer 1 each. Aviateca and Tikal Jets use the largest and most comfortable equipment. Tikal charges $68 one-way and from $93 round-trip; Aviateca is a little more. Aviateca/Grupo Taca also flies every day to **Cancún** (1½hr.). **Aerocaribe** (tel. 926-0922) flies to **Cancún** and **Palenque**. Tropic Air heads to **Belize City**.

Taxis: (Tel. 926-0022), in front of nicer hotels in Flores or Santa Elena's market. Run to the airport (Q10 per person), or even Tikal (1-4 people, Q300 round-trip).

Car Rental: San Juan Travel, in Santa Elena next to the causeway. Jeeps US$80 per day, including insurance and unlimited kilometers. **Tabarini** (tel. 302-5900), at the airport.

Tourist Office: INGUAT has offices in Santa Elena's airport and in Flores' *Parque Central.* The airport office (tel. 926-0533) opens when planes arrive; the Flores office (tel. 926-0669) is open M-F 8am-5pm. For more info, especially about treks to out-of-the-way ruins, check out **CINCAP,** the Center of Information, Culture and Handicrafts of Petén (tel. 926-1370), located on the north side of the *parque* in Flores. Open Tu-Sa 9am-1pm and 2-7pm, Su 1-5pm.

Travel Agencies: Nakun (tel. 926-0587), on Av. Barrios off Calle Centróamerico, and **Martsam** (tel. 926-0493), on Calle Centroamérica. Both in Flores.

Currency Exchange: Finding a good exchange rate in Flores is like finding an Enrique Iglesias song without the word *corazón* in it; in other words, it ain't likely. Instead, head to a bank in Santa Elena—there's an abundant supply along 4 Calle. Try **Corpobanco** (M-F 8:30am-7pm, Sa 9am-1pm) or **Banco Industrial** with an **ATM** (M-F 9am-7pm, Sa 10am-2pm).

Laundry: Lavandería Petenchel, on Calle Centroamérica, washes, dries, and folds a load for Q20. Open daily M-Sa 8am-7pm.

Pharmacy: Discotienda Petenitza, on Av. Barrios in Flores, has everything a pharmacy would have, plus a much cooler name. Open M-Sa 8am-9pm.

Post Office: Half a block east of Flores' *parque central*. Open M-F 8:30am-5:30pm, Sa 9am-1pm.

Internet: Tikal Net (tel. 926-0655; email tikalnet@guate.net), on Calle Centroamérica in Flores. Q16 buys 30min. Open daily 8am-noon and 2-8pm. **C@fe.net** (tel. 926-1409), on Av. Barrios in Flores. Q0.50 per min. Open M-F 8am-9pm, Sa-Su 9am-7:30pm.

Telephones: Telgua (tel. 926-1299), 2 blocks south of 4 Calle on the road extending from the causeway into Santa Elena has **fax** service. Open M-F 8am-8pm, Sa 8am-6pm, Su 8am-noon.

ACCOMMODATIONS

Although accommodations in Santa Elena offer the convenience of proximity to the bus station, Flores is generally safer and more enjoyable.

Hospedaje Doña Goya, on the northern side of the island. Flores' best budget accommodation with meticulous, bright, and comfortable rooms with or without bath. Breakfast is served and a rooftop lakeview. Rooms Q25 per person, Q30 with bath.

Posada El Tucan #2 (tel. 926-1467), on the eastern side of the island. Another reasonably priced option. Rooms are about as exciting as an accountant's convention. Singles Q35; doubles Q40; triples Q60.

Hotel Santa Rita (tel. 926-0710), on the west side, near Calle Centroamerico. Run by a friendly family, Santa Rita offers basic, clean rooms with private bath. Rooms on the second floor have lake views. Singles Q45; doubles Q70.

Hotel Posada Santander (tel. 926-0574), in Santa Elena. A hop, skip, and jump from the bus terminal. The overgrown, weed-filled courtyard and cement construction would drive Martha Stewart bonkers, but the rooms (with or without private bath) are clean and safe. Singles Q25, with bath Q40; doubles Q30, with bath Q50.

FOOD

Restaurante El Tucan, on Calle Centroamérica, in the southeast corner of the island. The lakefront terrace makes the generous portions of good seafood and *comida Mexicana* taste even better. *Enchilada suiza* Q32. Open M-Sa 7am-9pm.

La Canoa, on Calle Centroamérica. A good, inexpensive rendition of standard *comedor* food, and then some. Eggs with beans Q10; tacos Q20. Open M-Sa 7am-9pm.

Restaurante Las Puertas, west around the bend from Pizerria Picasso on Calle Centroamérica. A popular place to relax in the evening after a hot day trekking through the ruins. Sandwiches and pastas dominate the menu. Tuna sandwich Q22; spaghetti al pesto Q24. Live performances from time to time. Open daily 7am-midnight.

SIGHTS

If you've got some time to spare in Flores, you might walk 2km south of Santa Elena to the **Actun Can Cave,** which holds 300m of well-illuminated paths as well as several kilometers of unlit paths for the more experienced spelunker (bring your own flashlight). It's also known as **La Cueva de La Serpiente** (Cave of the Snake), but the name reflects legend only. The guard may point out some of the curious formations inside. To get to the cave, follow the continuation of the causeway south; bear left at the fork and then turn right at the sign. (Open daily 8am-5pm. Admission Q7.)

Boatmen will take visitors out for **tours of Lake Petén Itzá**—the typical route includes a *mirador*, a small ruin, a tiny zoo and a stop for a swim. Look for them near the causeway or at the western end of the Calle Centroamérica, near Hotel Santana (Q20 per person); speak with the captain directly rather than with the commissioned agents roaming the streets. If you prefer to do it yourself, you can rent basic **kayaks** along the causeway (1hr. Q10, 2hr. Q15). If a dip in a **pool** sounds inviting, swing by the Yum Kax hotel (non-guests Q10).

EL REMATE

On the eastern shores of Lake Petén Itzá, the relaxed village of El Remate has long been known for its woodcarving, but its location halfway between Flores and Tikal and near the turn-off for the Belizian border, has made it increasingly popular as a base for visiting the entire region. An appealing place in its own right, El Remate also has two nearby attractions: the small archaeological site of **Ixlú** and the wildlife preserve of **Cerro Cahuí**.

To get to El Remate, take a tourist **minibus** headed for Tikal and ask to be dropped in the village (Q15), or hop the Transportes Pinita **bus** departing from the Santa Elena *mercado* (1pm, Q5). A final option is to catch a minibus or public bus heading to the **Belize** border, get off at **El Cruce/Puente Ixlú**, and walk 2km north to El Remate. All Flores-Tikal minibuses pass through El Remate (at least every hr. 5:30-10:30am). The 5:30 service will actually stop at the hotels; later, you'll have to stand on the highway and flag one down. Ticket sellers visit hotels in the evening; you can also buy them any time at La Casa de Don David (see below).

Budget accommodations in El Remate are (for better or worse) more rustic than those in Flores. The town's standout is **La Casa de Don David,** at the junction of the highway and the dirt road veering left along the lake. Owner David Kuhn and his staff provide plenty of tourist information, good cheer, and delicious food (dinner Q28). The rooms, though plain for the price, are comfortable and come with ceiling fan and private bath. (Dorms Q35 per person; singles Q85; doubles Q110.) **Mirador del Duende,** on a hill on the right side of the highway as you enter the village, does indeed have the best view in town. But you'd better hope the owner's claim that the hotel is a "mosquito-free zone" (due to the winds, he says) holds true—the igloo-like bungalows are nothing more than cement shelters with a mattress. Hammock-slingers and campers are welcome, and the restaurant serves inexpensive vegetarian food that apparently has cross-species appeal: meddling monkeys often drop by for a visit. (Camping Q15; bungalows Q30 per person.) **John's Lodge,** on the highway just before the dirt road, offers very basic dorms with mosquito nets, plus a *comedor* and communal bath. The management's friendly and the price is tough to beat. (Q15 per person.)

The **Biotopo Cerro Cahuí,** located about 2km from the highway on the dirt road running along the lakeshore, contains 651 hectares of protected lands, including ponds and wonderfully undisturbed tropical forest. Monkeys, white-tailed deer, and numerous bird species make their home here. Two interconnecting loop trails—4km (2hr.) and 6km (3hr.)—traverse the reserve, just past the first turnaround lies a *mirador* with a wonderful view of the lake. (Open daily 6am-4pm, though visitors may stay later. Admission Q25.) In the little village of **Puente Ixlú (El Cruce),** 2km south of El Remate, stand the largely unrestored **ruins of Ixlú.**

Mario Soto runs a popular sunset **boat trip** to Río Ixlú, home to wildlife and great views (Q40 per person, inquire at Don David's to reserve a place). Ervin Oliveros, who lives in the house behind John's Lodge, offers walking tours to a nearby lake where **crocodiles** are the star attraction (2hr., Q20 per person). Since only Captain Hook wannabes would swim on *that* trip, a better bet for a cooling dip would be the **public beach** across from Mirador del Duende.

TIKAL

One of the most awe-inspiring archaeological sites in the Americas, Tikal attracts visitors from every corner of the globe and seldom disappoints. The Maya ruins, 65km northeast of Flores, encompass more than 3,000 Maya stone constructions. It is little wonder the site was featured in *Star Wars*. With five massive temples rising above the dense jungle, Tikal holds a magical, mythical quality no modern-day movie set (computer-generated or otherwise) could possibly emulate. The buildings themselves are impressive, but the surrounding gloriously untouched tropical forest distinguishes Tikal from all other Maya sites. Nature not only adds to the drama, but sometimes steals the show. Falling fruit signals spider monkeys hidden overhead, remote paths hide parrots, turkeys, iguanas, and wild boars, and lucky early risers may spot a sacred jaguar slinking through the undergrowth.

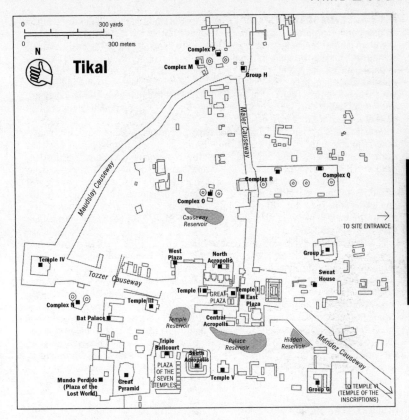

PRACTICAL INFORMATION. Admission tickets may be purchased either along the highway when first entering the National Park (which includes 576 sq. km of forest) or at the ruins themselves (Q50 per person per day; admission purchased at the highway after 3pm is valid for the following day as well).

Buses, airplanes, and many package tours are all scheduled so that you can visit Tikal in a single day. While a day is enough time to see the highlights, a longer visit will allow for a more leisurely exploration and the opportunity to savor the ruins and the jungle as they transform with the changing light.

A few explanatory signs are scattered throughout the ruins, but if you can spare the cash hiring a **tour guide** makes for a more informed visit. Find them in the visitors center and look for name tags that read *Carnet de guía de turismo.* Ask around, especially if you have a specific interest, since levels of specialization vary. (Spanish or English tours available 1-4 people US$40, each additional person US$5; about 4hr.) A more economical option is to purchase a detailed handbook to the ruins. William R. Coe's *Tikal: A Handbook of the Ancient Maya Ruins,* available at the visitors center, is a good choice.

In addition to tour guides, the **visitors center** has a **post office,** souvenir shop, restaurant, and the **Museo Lítico.** This free museum holds a fine collection of stelae from the site, a scale model of Tikal, and photographs of the restoration process. **Museo Tikal,** the park's other museum, sits between the Jungle Lodge and the Jaguar Inn. It features a reconstructed royal tomb, carvings, ceramics, and other artifacts recovered from the ruins. (Admission Q10. Both museums open M-F 9am-5pm, Sa-Su 9am-4pm.)

▐▐█ **ACCOMMODATIONS AND FOOD.** Accommodations at Tikal are limited to one good campground and three expensive hotels. As a result, many budget travelers commute from El Remate or Flores. To **camp,** speak to the cashier at the restaurant inside the visitors center. The campground itself is a vast, grassy expanse across the street. Pitch a tent or sling a hammock under thatched-roof huts (Q35 per person) or try a small wooden cabin with sleeping pad (singles Q40, with sheets and towels Q76; doubles Q80, with sheets and towels Q114). There are communal bathrooms with showers nearby. If you're camping, you can store luggage at the restaurant for free.

Perhaps not surprisingly, Tikal's hotels are overpriced. All three do have restaurants, though, and electricity—but only during certain hours, which means that during the night those fans will make for a lovely yet quite motionless ceiling decoration. The best-looking property is the **Jungle Lodge** (tel. 476-8775), across from the visitors center by the ruins entrance. The lodge offers natural landscaping and attractive bungalows with good beds and fans. The rooms with shared bath are much less appealing but still clean and fan-cooled. Escape the mosquitoes with a dip in the well-kept swimming pool. (Singles US$20, with bath US$48; doubles US$25, with bath US$60.)

The **Tikal Inn** (tel. 926-0065), sits past the Jaguar Inn as you walk from the ruins. Reasonable rooms are bland but pleasant; slightly nicer bungalows are set around an inviting pool. All rooms have a private bath. (Singles US$25, bungalow US$45; doubles US$35, bungalow US$55.) Somewhat less welcoming, the **Jaguar Inn** (tel. 926-0002), offers bungalow rooms with bath (singles US$20; doubles US$32; 4-person dorm US$7 per person).

Café Restaurante del Parque Tikal, in the visitors center, serves fairly reasonable food (fruit plate Q22, spaghetti Q35; open daily 5am-4pm). For the cheapest grub, head to the four *comedores* lining the road from Flores. The best is perhaps **Comedor Imperio Maya,** where portions are huge (*pollo frito* Q30, open daily 6am-9pm).

THE RUINS

HISTORY. The ancient Maya settled Tikal around 700 BC; they were likely attracted by its hilltop location and the abundance of flint for making weapons and tools. The earliest evidence of buildings dates to 500 BC, and by 250 AD—the dawn of the classic period—Tikal had been established as a major population center. At this time, the powerful city of **El Mirador** (65km to the north) went into decline, and Tikal and Uaxactún became the dominant cities of the region. In 378 A.D., Tikal, aided by an alliance with the powerful Teotihuacán of Central Mexico, handily defeated Uaxactún. From then on, Tikal reigned over the Petén and grew in population and splendor. By the sixth century it spanned some 30 square kilometers and supported a population of 100,000 people. The middle of the sixth century, however, saw Tikal's power overshadowed by that of **Caracol** (in Belize's Maya Mountains). For the next 150 years, Tikal seems to have languished. But in 700 AD, the city embarked on a splendid renaissance. Led by the towering **Ah Cacau** (Lord Chocolate), Tikal regained its supremacy in the Petén. Ah Cacau and his successors built most of the temples seen on the Great Plaza today. Around 900 AD, Tikal, along with the entire lowland Maya civilization, mysteriously fell into decline. Theories explaining the downfall include earthquake, deforestation, or a massive popular uprising.

While Postclassic descendants of the original population continued to live and worship at Tikal, they did little of lasting significance other than pillage the ancient tombs. By 1000 AD, the jungle had engulfed the city. Save for a few passing references by Franciscan friars, the modern world did not rediscover Tikal until the Guatemalan government sponsored an expedition led by Modesto Méndez and Ambrosio Tut, who reached the site in 1848.

TOURING THE SITE. One kilometer west of the entrance lies Tikal's geographic and commercial heart, the **Great Plaza.** Towering above the plaza is **Temple I,** the temple of the Jaguar. It was built to hold the tomb of the great ruler Ah Cacau, whose son began construction shortly after his father's death in 721 AD. Today it is Tikal's most recognizable symbol. The 44m-high temple is topped by a three-room structure and a roof comb that was originally painted in bright colors. Unfortunately, it's no longer possible to climb Temple I. You can, however, climb **Temple II** (38m) at the west end of the Great Plaza for views of the plaza.

The amazingly complex **North Acropolis** also stands on the plaza. Built and rebuilt on top of itself, and containing the remains of around 100 structures dating back more than 2000 years, the North Acropolis also contains two huge **stone masks** under thatch roofs. To the south of the Great Plaza is the **Central Acropolis,** a complex of buildings that archaeologists believe were used by the Maya as elite residential areas.

The **West Plaza,** north of Temple II, features a large Late Classic temple. Following the **Tozzer Causeway** north from here you'll reach **Temple III,** still covered in jungle vegetation. Continuing on, **Complex N** is a twin temple design believed to have commemorated the completion of a **Katun,** 20 years in the Maya calendar. At the end of the Tozzer Causeway lies **Temple IV;** at 64m, it's the tallest structure in Tikal. Built in 741 AD, possibly in honor of the ruler Coon Chac, the temple affords a fabulous view from the top.

The **Mundo Perdido** (Lost World), a fairly recent discovery of 38 structures, is capped by the 32m-high **Great Pyramid.** Not much is known about the buildings, but they do appear to be from several historical periods. If you can handle the steep climb, the top of the Great Pyramid boasts one of the park's best views.

Just east is the **Plaza of the Seven Temples.** The visible structures are Late Classic, but the hidden complex dates back at least 2000 years. The central temple has a skull and crossbones inscription, and the north side of the plaza was once the site of a unique triple ballcourt. If you continue to the east of the Plaza of the Seven Temples, you'll pass the unexcavated South Acropolis on the way to **Temple V,** under restoration and currently targeted for completion in 2004. It's worth stopping by to take a look at the striking contrast between the temple's condition before and after restoration.

A 1.2km walk along the **Mendéz Causeway** from the Great Plaza leads to the **Temple of the Inscriptions (Temple VI),** noted for the hieroglyphic text on its 12m roof comb. The text, though badly eroded, is unique to Tikal and provides a date of 766 A.D. **Complexes Q and R,** between the Great Plaza and the entrance, are Late Classic twin pyramids. Complex Q has been well restored and to its left lies a replica of the beautiful **Stela 22,** which portrays Tikal's last known ruler, **Chitam.** The original is now in the visitors center. One kilometer north of the Great Plaza lie **Group H** and **Complex P,** both examples of twin-temples.

While touring the ruins, unusual wildlife may appear from the jungle depths; the animals here are more accustomed to humans and may provide you with some fascinating sightings.

UAXACTÚN

Deep in the tropical forests of El Petén, 23km north of Tikal, hides Uaxactún (wah-shak-TOON), a small, untouristed Petén town that encompasses Maya ruins of the same name. Uaxactún once rivaled Tikal in stature but was resoundly defeated in 378 AD. Tikal retains that edge today, and the ruins here may be a shade disappointing by comparison. Still, the isolation and lack of tourists lend the place its own mystique, and Uaxactún is still one of the best examples of early Maya architecture.

The cheapest way to visit Uaxactún is to take the daily Transportes Pinita **bus** from Flores or Tikal (3hr., 1pm, Q15), and then catch the return bus early the next morning (6am). Some travel agencies in Flores organize daytrips to Uaxactún, and the **Jungle Lodge** at Tikal offers a trip (8am-1pm; US$15 per person, four-person minimum). In the town of Uaxactún, there's a **tourist information** hut on the old airstrip that is occasionally open. If you spend the night here, the good news is you won't have to decide which hotel to pick. The sole option is **Hotel y Campamento El Chiclero** (tel. 726-1095), at the end of the airstrip on the left hand side. Simple, clean rooms offer communal baths and electricity during certain hours. There's also camping and tasty meals are served upon request. (Singles Q42; doubles Q60; camping with hammock Q20 per person, with tent Q30 per person). **Horse rental** (Q20 per hr.) and guided tours to other jungle archaeological sites may be arranged in Uaxactún and El Chiclero is a good source of information. **Comedores** lie along the old airstrip and are a good place to grab a snack.

As you come into town and hit the unused airstrip, **Group E**—the most impressive site—is about a 10-minute walk to your right. Here, three side-by-side temples served as an observatory: viewed from atop a fourth temple, the sun rises behind the south temple on the shortest day of the year and behind the north one on the longest day. Beneath these temples lies **E-VII-Sub,** the oldest existing building in Petén—its foundations probably date back to 2000 BC.

On the other side of the old airstrip, a dirt road beginning at the far end of the field leads to the unexcavated **Group B** and the grander **Group A,** a series of temples and residential compounds. Don't miss the **stelae** scattered about under thatched roofs. Admission to Uaxactún is free, though the road passes through the entrance to Tikal where you'll need to pay Q15 per person (Q50 if you plan to view Tikal that same day).

EL MIRADOR AND OTHER RUINS

Hidden amongst the vast tropical forest north of Tikal are several other Maya sites. They're largely unrestored and uncleared, but it's precisely that rugged mystique—combined with the isolation—that make a memorable visit. Adventurous jungle treks make finding the ruins at least half the fun. The most magnificent and mysterious of these sites is also the most remote: **El Mirador**. Although unrestored, it was once a tremendous city and its scale is at least as great as that of Tikal. Archaeologists believe that the city reached its peak around 2000 years ago, making it the first great city of the Maya world. Overrun by jungle, El Mirador still echoes its former splendor. The 16 square kilometer site features a number of pyramids—including one that, at a staggering 70m, is the **tallest structure anywhere in the Maya world.**

Reaching El Mirador is no easy task; it involves a six-hour bus journey and two tough days on foot and horseback. CINCAP in Flores can set up a five-day tour run through the Ecomaya Spanish School (tel. 926-1363; email ecomaya@guate.net; Q1683 includes food, equipment, and horses). The more economical option is to take the daily bus from Flores to **Carmelita** (6hr., 1pm, Q25). In Carmelita, the jumping-off point for the trek to the ruins, you can arrange for a guide and horse (around US$25 per day), but you must supply your own food and equipment.

Other notable jungle ruins are somewhat easier to get to, though still plenty isolated. **El Zotz,** a large site noted for its huge bat population, is about a 4½-hour walk from Cruce Dos Aguadas (on the Carmelita bus route from Flores) and 30km west of Uaxactún along a sometimes-drivable dirt road. Vehicles or horses may be arranged in Uaxactún. **Río Azul,** an unrestored mini-Tikal, is home to a 47m temple and some impressive tombs. Río Azul is 95km north of Uaxactún, a journey of one day by Jeep (if passable) or four days by horse. Finally, there's **El Perú,** a day's boat trip east of the town of El Naranjo (connected by bus to Flores). This site is noted for its stelae and untamed jungle locale. **Tours** from Flores are run to all of the above ruins; CINCAP is a good first contact. If you plan to strike out on your own, it's essential to first find out the information on these locales from an INGUAT tourist office or another reliable source.

YUCATÁN PENINSULA

Hernández de Córdoba mistakenly ran aground here in 1517; when the freshly disembarked sailors asked the locals where they were, the Maya replied something to the effect of, "We haven't a clue what you're talking about." Unfamiliar with the Mayan language, Córdoba only caught the last few syllables of their reply, "Tectetán," and erroneously dubbed the region Yucatán. This encounter established a paradigm maintained throughout Yucatán history: misunderstanding and continual abuse by outsiders.

Today, the peninsula's culture remains essentially Maya and thrives in the small towns, where the evidence of Western influence arrives in the form of the weekly Coca-Cola truck. Mayan is still the first language of most inhabitants, and indigenous religious traditions persist within the practices of Catholicism instilled in the peninsula almost 500 years ago. Yucatec women still carry bowls of corn flour on their heads and wear embroidered *huipiles* (woven dresses); fishing, farming, and hammock-weaving are all commercial and subsistence essentials for the Mayas of today. But foreign influence fights on: more workers are drawn by the dubious allure of the tourism industry and flood the big cities and resorts to work in gringo-friendly restaurants, make hammocks for tourists, or act as multilingual guides at archaeological sites. The engineering of the pristine pleasure-world of Cancún has brought tourists in by the droves. Developers seized similar areas stretching farther and farther along the Yucatán coast in an effort to emulate Cancún; much of the virgin Caribbean beach land is undergoing Coca-colonization and transformation to McWorld. However, the surging popularity of ecotourism in the past few years has shown dollar-seekers that some kinds of conservation can be lucrative as well.

The peninsula's interstate borders form a "Y" down its center. Yucatán state sits in the crest of the "Y," **Quintana Roo** sees the Caribbean sun rise on the eastern coast, and **Campeche** faces the Gulf Coast to the west. Flat limestone scrubland and tropical forest dotted with *cenotes* (freshwater underground rivers enclosed by naturally forming caves) dominates the landscape. Because of the highly porous limestone subsoil, above-ground rivers do not exist in the Yucatán. Poor soil and the lack of water make farming difficult, so maize remains the staple crop. The prominence of the rain god Chac at most Maya ruins testifies to the eternal importance of the seasonal rains, which fall from May to late summer.

"The Yucatán" refers to the peninsula, not the state, whereas "Yucatán" without the article can refer to either entity. **Yucatán** state's rich history draws thousands of visitors each year, who come to scramble up and down the incomparable Chichén Itzá and other majestic Maya ruins, marvel at old colonial towns, explore the area's many dark caves, and take a dip in the *cenotes*. Quintana Roo's luscious jungle, crystalline coastline, and monumental Maya ruins were idylls beneath the Caribbean sun until the government transformed the area from tropical paradise to tourist factory. Cancún rapidly became the beachhead for what some wryly call "the Second *Conquista*," and the nearby beaches and ruins are following in suit. Although its countryside is dotted with Maya ruins, its coastline is over 200km long, and its colonial history predates Veracruz's, Campeche pulls in fewer visitors than Yucatán to the north or Quintana Roo to the east, perhaps because it lacks a kind of swaggering grandeur—ruins are modest and relatively inaccessible, while the beaches are kept humble by wind and rock.

HIGHLIGHTS OF THE YUCATÁN PENINSULA

■ No visit to the Yucatán is complete without a visit to the Maya ruins of **Chichén Itzá** (see p. 608). You've got to see 'em to believe 'em.

■ Despite its artificiality and the presence of better nearby beaches, visitors from all over the world flock to **Cancún** (see p. 621), Mexico's biggest resort.

■ Some of Mexico's best shopping waits in the bustling city of **Mérida** (see p. 595).

■ Cruise through the **La Ruta Puuc** (**The Puuc Route;** see p. 587): the eclectic assortment of Maya ruins that don't draw Chichén's crowds.

■ Ruins on a beach? The stunning backdrop to the ruins of **Tulum** (see p. 640) is no joke—just look at our cover.

■ The laid-back island of **Isla Mujeres** (see p. 629) draws a hip, international crew of backpackers who come to soak up the sun.

■ Some of the best snorkeling and scuba-diving in the world can be found around the oft-touristed isle of **Cozumel** (see p. 634).

CAMPECHE

CAMPECHE

Once called "Ah Kin Pech"—Mayan for "Place of the Serpents and Ticks"—Campeche (pop. 151,000) is, thankfully, much more hospitable and pleasant than its original name suggests. *Campechanos* today live up to their Spanish baptized name "Campeche" which means friendship and hospitality. When Francisco Hernández de Córdoba arrived, he transliterated the name to Campeche and, by 1540, had begun transforming the small city into a booming trading port. As it grew, Campeche battled buccaneers and pirates, erecting stunning *baluartes* (bulwarks), fortified churches, land and sea gates, and majestic forts, all of which still stand timeless in structure, resembling their original architecture of over 300 years ago. As if to underscore the immutability of the city's spirit, the historic center, with its light, pastel facades, hanging lanterns, and sidewalks raised over the flood-prone cobblestone streets, is an inner sanctum of colonial architecture. With a number of city-sponsored entertainments, beaches, nearby *haciendas* along Ruta Chenes and Ruta Rio Bec, and the biosphere reserves of Calakmul, Campeche is becoming less a stopover and more a destination for appreciating old Spanish beauty and natural wonder.

✦ ORIENTATION

Campeche lies 252km southwest of Mérida and 444km northeast of Villahermosa via **Rte. 180.** All major routes into the city intersect the peripheral highway that encircles it. A smaller road, **Circuito Baluartes,** circumscribes the old city. All main roads converge on the Circuito in the city center. **Avenida Gobernadores** comes in from the Mérida highway northeast of the city, crosses the peripheral highway, and passes the airport, train station, and bus terminals on its way to the Circuito.

To reach *el parque* from the **bus terminals,** catch the "Gobernadores" bus (3 pesos) across the street from the station, and ask the driver to let you off at the **Baluarte de San Francisco.** Turn right into the old city and walk four blocks on **Calle 57** to **Principal.** Front-door hotel escorts by **taxi** from the zócalo cost only 20 pesos, but if you'd rather take the 15min. walk, head left on Gobernadores and veer left again when you reach the Circuito. Three blocks later, turn right on Calle 57 through the stone arch and walk four blocks to the *principal.*

The *centro's* east-west streets have odd numbers that increase to the south. **Calle 8** runs north-south between the *principal* and the western city wall. Parallel to Calle 8 to the east lie Calles 10 to 16. The *principal* lies near the sea, bordered by Calles 8, 10, 55, and 57. To the west, outside the city wall, **Av. 16 de Septiembre**

YUCATÁN PENINSULA

Yucatán Peninsula

and **Av. Ruíz Cortínez** also run parallel to Calle 8. North of the *centro*, Calle 8 becomes **Malecón Miguel Alemán,** running past the Iglesia de San Francisco uphill to Fuerte de San José El Alto. **Av. Resurgimiento,** the coastal board walk south of the city, runs past the *villas deportivas* (youth hostel) and the Fuerte San Miguel on its way to San Lorenzo and Seybaplaya.

A confusing network of **buses** links Campeche's more distant sectors to the old city (3.50 pesos; daily 5am-11pm). The **market,** where Gobernadores becomes the Circuito, serves as the hub for local routes. Buses have no established stops, but they can be flagged down at the **post office** and at **Jardín Botánico** at Calle 51. You'll have to get around the city center on foot, since buses do not run in the historic, colonial center.

🛈 PRACTICAL INFORMATION

TRANSPORTATION

Airport: (tel. 6 31 09) on Porfirio, 13km from the city center. **Aeroméxico** (tel. 6 56 78 or 6 58 78). Taxis to the *centro* from the airport cost 40 pesos.

Buses: From the **second-class station** (tel. 6 28 02), Calle Chile just off Av. Gobernadores. Camioneros de Campeche rolls to: **Dzibalchén** (2hr., 4 per day, 27 pesos); **Escárcega** (2½hr., 6 per day, 34 pesos); **Holpechén** (1hr., 4 per day, 20 pesos); and **Iturbide** (2hr., 4 per day, 50 pesos). Autobuses del Sur speeds to: **Mérida** (2hr., 4 per day, 62 pesos); **Villahermosa** (9hr.,hj 9am, 2pm, 11:55pm, 150 pesos); **Uxmal** (3hr., 4 per day, 50 pesos); and **Muna** (4hr., 4 per day, 60 pesos). The **first-class station** is on Av. Gobernadores #289, 4 blocks north of Circuito Baluarte at Baluarte San Pedro. Autotransportes de Oriente (ADO) rambles to: **Cancún** (7hr., 10 and 11:30pm, 150 pesos); **Chetumal** (7hr., noon, 114 pesos); **Escárcega** (2½hr., 4 per day 10am-8pm, 65 pesos); **Mérida** (2½hr., 12 per day 5:45am-11pm, 70 pesos); **Mexico City** (16hr., 12:45 and 11:45pm, 525 pesos); **Palenque** (5hr., 10:30am, 10pm, and 12 midnight, 155 pesos); **Veracruz** (12hr., 8pm, 370 pesos); and **Villahermosa** (7hr., 12:45pm and 10:30pm, 170 pesos). Cristóbal Colón goes to: **Ocosingo** (8hr., 10pm, 218 pesos); **San Cristóbal** (10hr., 10pm, 210 pesos); and **Tuxtla Gutiérrez** (12hr., 10pm and midnight, 240 pesos). Maya de Oro offers service to **Palenque** (midnight, 165 pesos) and **San Cristóbal** (midnight, 255 pesos).

Taxis: (tel. 6 11 13). Three stands: Calle 8 at 55, to left of the cathedral; Calle 55 at Circuito, near the market; and Gobernadores at Chile, near the bus terminal. Intra-city travel 15-20 pesos, more after dark.

Car Rental: Maya Rent-a-Car (tel. 6 22 33) in Hotel Ramada at Av. Ruiz Cortines #51.

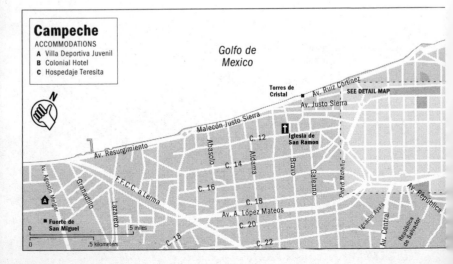

Campeche

ACCOMMODATIONS
A Villa Deportiva Juvenil
B Colonial Hotel
C Hospedaje Teresita

Golfo de Mexico

TOURIST AND FINANCIAL SERVICES

Tourist Office: Calle 55 #3 (tel. 1 39 89 or 1 39 90), next door to the cathedral at the zócalo. A second office located in **Baluarte de Santa Rosa.** Both open M-F 8am-10pm.

Travel Agency: Prof. Augustín Zavala y Lozano, Calle 16 #348 (tel. 6 44 26), gives 4hr. tours of Edzná (9am and 2pm, 160 pesos).

Currency Exchange: Banamex (tel. 6 52 51), at the corner of Calles 53 and 10. Open M-F 9am-5pm, Sa 10am-2pm. 24hr. **ATM.**

American Express: (tel. 1 10 00) Calle 59 between 16 Septiembre and shore. Open M-F 9am-8pm, Sa 9am-1pm.

LOCAL SERVICES

Market: On Circuito Baluartes between Calles 53 and 55. Cheap fruits, vegetables, and meat. Open M-Sa sunrise-sunset, Su until 3pm.

Supermarket: San Francisco de Asis (tel. 6 79 76), in the Pl. Comercial A-Kin-Pech on 16 de Septiembre, behind the post office. Open daily 7am-9:30pm.

Laundry: Lavandería y Tintorería Campeche, Calle 55 #22 (tel. 6 51 42), between Calles 12 and 14. Same-day service 15 pesos per kg. Open M-Sa 8am-4pm.

EMERGENCY AND COMMUNICATIONS

Police: (tel. 6 21 09) on Malecon Justo Sierra, in front of El Balneario Popular.

Red Cross: (tel. 5 24 11), on Av. Las Palmas at the northwest corner of the city wall. Open 24hr.

Pharmacy: Farmacia Gobernadores, next to the ADO station. Open 24hr.

Medical Services: Seguro Social (tel. 6 52 02), on López Mateos south of the city. **Hospital General** (tel. 6 09 20), Av. Central at Circuito Baluartes.

Post Office: (tel. 6 21 34) 16 de Septiembre at Calle 53 in the Palacio Federal. Open M-F 8am-6pm, Sa 9am-12:30pm. **MexPost** (tel. 1 17 30) is located next door (open M-F 9am-6pm, Sa 9am-1pm). **Postal Code:** 24000.

Fax, Telegraphs, and Western Union: (tel. 6 43 90) also in the **Palacio Federal** on the opposite side of MexPost (open M-F 8am-7pm, Sa 9am-12noon).

Internet Access: En Red Cibercafé, Calle 12 #204, behind the acoustic shell. Reach out and email someone while enjoying juke box music, coffee, and pastries. (30 pesos per hr., open M-F 9:30am-11:30pm, Sa 11am-9pm, Su 3pm-9pm).

Telephones: TelMex and **LADATEL** phones throughout the city.

Phone Code: 981.

YUCATÁN PENINSULA

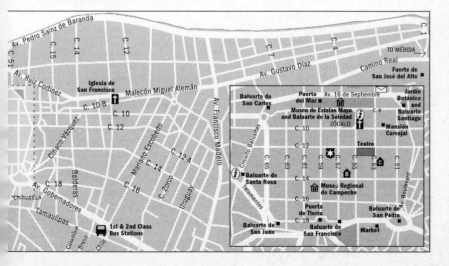

ACCOMMODATIONS

Budget travelers looking for decent accommodations in Campeche may be forced to pay indecent prices. Several good middle-range establishments hover just out of the range of backpackers' pesos, and many of the cheaper places overcharge for what they offer.

Colonial Hotel, Calle 14 #122 (tel. 6 22 22 or 6 26 30), between Calles 55 and 57, 2½ blocks from the zócalo. The retro lime, peach, yellow, and light blue layout saturates the tall ceilings and tiny bathrooms. The agua purificada and 2nd floor terrace will soothe any objections to showering with the sink. Singles 110 pesos; doubles 135 pesos; triples 175 pesos; 35 pesos per additional person; 55 pesos for A/C.

Hospedaje Teresita, Calle 53 #31 (tel. 6 45 34) between Calles 12 and 14. In a residential part of the old city, 3 blocks northeast of *El Parque Principal*. The cheapest place in the *centro*, and for good reason. Large, bare, concrete-walled rooms have fans. Communal outdoor bathrooms lack privacy and light. Singles or doubles 50 pesos, with private bath 60 pesos.

Villa Deportiva Juvenil Campeche (tel. 6 18 02), on Agustín Melgar several blocks east of the water and the coastal highway. From the eastern section of the Circuito Baluartes, take the "Lerma" bus south along the coastal highway to the intersection with Melgar (15 min.), then walk half a block toward the ocean. A black iron gate on the left marks the spot. Single-sex dorm rooms with four bunks and communal bathrooms are often full July-Aug. and Dec.; call to reserve. Bunks 30 pesos plus 30 peso deposit.

FOOD

Campeche has developed some culinary experiences that are just as colorful as its streets. No visitor should leave without sampling *pande cazón* (stacked tortillas filled with baby shark and refried beans and covered with an onion, tomato, and chile sauce). Other local specialties include *pámpano en escabeche* (pompano broiled in olive oil and flavored with onion, garlic, chile, peppers, and a dash of orange juice).

Marganzo, Calle 8 #262 (tel. 1 38 98 or 1 38 99) near Puerta de Mar. Fish your meal from the crystal clear tank underneath the blue and gold archways of Marganzo. The specialty of the house is *El Filere Marganzo*, a traditional family recipe—a fish fillet stuffed with baby shrimp, bacon bits, and great-grandma's special sauce (55 pesos). *Pande Cazón* (35 pesos) is also available. Open daily 7am-10pm.

Restaurant Del Parque, Calle 57 #8 (tel. 6 02 40) at Calle 8. Clean, white, pressed tablecloths and dark red, cushioned chairs make it the height of budget elegance, serving equally tasteful dishes such as *tortas al pastor* (20 pesos) and *pande cazón* (38 pesos). Open daily 7am-10:30pm.

Kiosco "El Principal" (tel. 1 12 11 or 6 22 48) the kiosk in *El Parque Principal*, in the heart of historic Campeche, serves tropical ice-cream with a cookie wafer (20 pesos), club sandwiches (30 pesos), and Campeche beer in a souvenir yard glass. Open Tu-Su 4:30pm-11pm; 9am-11pm during peak season. The only place in town that **rents bikes** (25 pesos per hour).

Nutrivida (tel. 6 12 21), on Calle 12 between 57 and 59. Nutrivida prides itself in serving healthy and oh-so-natural grains, vegetarian burgers (15 pesos), homemade yogurt (10 pesos), low-fat shakes (12 pesos), and decaffeinated coffee with cinnamon (5 pesos) all in a pleasant courtyard. Open M-F 8am-2pm and 5:30-8pm, Sa 8am-2pm.

Cenaduría Portales (tel. 1 14 91), also known as **San Pancho** for its proximity to Iglesia de San Francisco. Take any bus headed north on Malecón Miguel Alemán to the church. Cross the plaza in front of the church and head left to another smaller square. The restaurant huddles beneath the arches straight ahead. An assembly line of highly trained sandwich makers jumps into action at your order and nearly instantly produces not just a sandwich but a work of art for 12-15 pesos. Exceptional *horchata* (sweetened rice water) goes for 8 pesos. Open daily 7pm-midnight. This area is not safe after dark, and the last bus back passes around 10pm.

Restaurant La Parroquia, Calle 55 #8 (tel. 6 80 86) between Calles 10 and 12. A cavernous all-night local eatery with good, cheap food, and TV around the clock. Fat, steaming stacks of hot cakes with honey are 20 pesos. Open daily 24hr.

◉ SIGHTS

Campeche's historical treasures are best seen at night, when spotlights warm up cold stone and the moonlight spills over the ocean. The most convenient way to see Campeche is by "Tranvia," the comfortable **red trolley** that gives a historical tour of the major sights. Catch it in **El Parque Principal** on Calle 10 in front of the kiosk (1hr., M-F 9:30am, 6, and 8pm; Sa-Su 9:30am, 6, 7, and 8pm, 20 pesos). Walking tours of the city leave from the corner of Calles 18 and 59 daily at 4:30pm during July, August, and December (1hr., 18 pesos). Minimum of ten people for both tours. **"El Guapo",** a handsome green trolley gives a guided tour of **Fuerte de San Miguel** (Tu-Su 9am and 5pm) and **Fuerte de San José El Alto** (Tu-Su 10:30am and 6:30pm; both last 1¼hr.; 20 pesos each, does not include admission fee).

FUERTE DE SAN MIGUEL. This fort houses well-documented exhibits describing nearby ruins and displays Maya jewelry, pottery, vessels from Edzná and a jade mask from Calakmul. On the top level, 19 cannons still project protectively over the sea and Campeche to the north with a central watchtower. To reach the fort, take the "Lerma" bus from the eastern end of the Circuito Baluartes, and head south. Ask the bus driver to drop you off at the Castillo stop and then walk up the steep hill on the left until you reach the fork on the road. Take the left turn leading up to the fort. *(Open Tu-Su 8am-1pm, 2pm-7pm. Admission 15 pesos, free Su.)*

FUERTE DE SAN JOSÉ EL ALTO. San Miguel's counterpart to the north is eight kilometers from the *centro*. Built in 1762, San José was amazingly defensible when in use. The path leading to the portcullis winds deliberately so that battering rams could not be used on the gate. The fort's moat was supposedly rife with vicious spikes and the water was obscured with chalk to hide the spikes and surprixe attackers. Today, the ships and armaments have moved inside the fort for an impressive exhibit. The view from San José is kilometers of green shoreline giving way to the urban waterfront. The "Bellavista" or "San José El Alto" bus from the market will drop you halfway up the hill; a five-minute walk will get you to the fort at the top. *(Open Tu-Su 8am-8pm. Admission 8 pesos. Su free.)*

MUSEO DE LAS ESTELAS MAYA. Inside the **Baluarte de la Soledad**, off Calle 8 near Calle 57 behind *El Parque Principal*, the *museo* houses a small collection of well-preserved Maya stelae and reliefs taken from sites in Campeche state. Informative Spanish texts and remaining pictographs elaborate on sculpted figures' occupations. Visitors may also climb the walls of the fort, which is surrounded by a park. A showroom across from the museum occasionally features free exhibitions. *(Museum open M 8am-2pm, Tu-Sa 8am-8pm, Su 8am-6pm. Admission 10 pesos.)*

JARDÍN BOTÁNICO XMUCH'HALTUN. Enclosed by the walls of the Fuerte Santiago at the northwest corner of the city on Calles 8 and 51, the *jardín* makes an inviting stop. Over 250 species of plant thrive in a tiny open-air courtyard shaded by trees and marked by benches, fountains, and frogs. *(Tel. 6 68 29. Open M-F 9am-4pm and 6:30-8:30pm, Sa 9am-1pm and 5-8pm, Su 9am-1pm. Guided tours M-F 9am-3pm.)*

LA PURÍSIMA CONCEPCIÓN. Campeche's cathedral, which used to serve as a second refuge for the Maya and Spanish communities, looms above *El Parque Principal*. Don Francisco de Montejo first ordered the construction of the cathedral in 1540, but builders did not complete the massive structure until 1705. The cathedral's main attraction is its facade. Inside, you'll find the *Santo Entierro* (Holy Burial), a sculpture of Christ in a carved mahogany sarcophagus replete with gold ornaments inside a glass case with silver trim. *(Open daily 7am-noon and 5-8pm. Free.)*

IGLESIA DE SAN FRANCISCO. A little farther from the center of town on Av. Miguel Alemán, this church, built in 1546, marks the place where the first Mesoamerican mass was held and was baptismal site of Hernando Cortes's grandson. The three bells toll for humbleness, obedience, and chastity. Inside, yellow Corinthian arches project toward an ornate altar. *(Open daily 8am-noon and 5-8pm.)* A few blocks south of the *centro*, the **Iglesia de San Román** houses the image of **El Cristo Negro,** greatly venerated by campechanos in Mexico. *(Open daily 6am-noon and 4-8pm. Free.)*

OTHER SIGHTS. Locals usually head south for **sand** and **sunbathing.** The closest stretch of sand is at **Playa Payucán**—great for snorkeling, but rentals are not available. Buses for the beach leave from behind the market (8 pesos). In the southeastern region of Campeche, fauna and ecotourism is alive in Calakmul, the largest biosphere reserve in Mexico covering 1.7 million acres as well as a former Maya ceremonial power house containing over 6,000 ruins. From Campeche go south on 261 towards Escarcega-Chetumal until you reach Rte. 186. Go 95km east on Rte. 186, the town of Conhuas. The entrance is on the right, through a 60 kilometer one-lane road.

▓ ENTERTAINMENT AND SEASONAL EVENTS

Campeche sponsors various outdoor musical, historical, and regional events, including the **Ballet Folklórico** in the Parque Principal. Every Tuesday, Friday, and Saturday night at 8:30pm, an impressive **sound and light show** at Puerta de Tierra, Calles 59 and 18, recounts the dramatic story of *campechanos* staving off foolhardy pirates atop cannons, forts, and ridges. Weather permitting, a *Ballet Folklórico* performance follows the conclusion of the show. (Sound and light show 25 pesos, translated text in English and French is projected onto the wall.). On Saturdays from 7pm-10pm **Sabadito Elegré en La Plaza de la República** features *mariachi* and *danzones.* On Sundays at 8pm, the state band strikes up *campecho* music from the kiosk in the Parque Principal. During high season (July-August and December) more events are scheduled, ask for the *Programa de Actividades* at the tourist information center. **San Román** is Campeche's patron saint, and for three weeks Campechanos celebrate his feast starting September 7.

La Cueva de Las Ranas, near the university on López Mateos, attracts aspiring rock stars and a hip student crowd (open 9pm-3am). The swinging local crowd gets down at **Disco Dragon,** Av. Resurgimiento 87 (tel. 1 18 10). **KY8,** Calle 8 and 59, pumps up the jams across Puerta de Mar every Friday and Saturday from 10pm-3am (cover 50 pesos). **Millenium,** at the end of Av. Resurgimiento attracts the hottest Campeche *salsa* dancers on Friday nights and disco dancers on Saturday night (open 10pm-3am, cover 40 pesos). **Platforma 21,** (tel. 2 61 78), in *Loma Azul* is where *campechanos* groove to a variety of rhymes on two different floors (open F-Sa 10pm-3am, cover 40 pesos).

NEAR CAMPECHE

EDZNÁ

Breathe the Maya air, climb the Maya acropolis, and decipher Maya hieroglyphics at **Edzná** (House of the Grimaces) named for its stucco masks. The **Edificio de Cinco Pisos** (Building of the Five Floors) towers over the surrounding valley atop the monumental **Gran Acrópolis.** Sixty-five stairs, some adorned with hieroglyphics over 1300 years old, lead up to tiers of columns crowned by a five-room temple. During its Maya apogee, the perch atop the monument afforded a view of the network of irrigation canals criss-crossing the valley close to the Río Champotón, 20km to the west. The system of 29 canals, 27 reservoirs, and more than 70 *chultunes* (man-made water cisterns) were built without the use of wheels, metal tools, or domesticated animals. The eastern cardinal side of the Gran Acropolis faces the 15 steep stairs of *Nohoch-Ná* (Large House) resembling a stadium with four large rooms atop its last staircase. As you sit to contemplate the Acropolis facing you, release a yell to hear a grand echo resound throughout the ancient Maya city. Also on display in the entry *palapa* are some of the 19 stelae found at Edzná—one crafted as early as 672, others made during the 10th-century evacuation of the ceremonial center. Along the south side of these two buildings lie the remains of the **Ballcourt** and its western stone ring; the **Small Acropolis**, the oldest building of the site; and the **Temple of Masks** where two three-dimensional stucco masks representing the sunrise and sunset, gaze with sovereign power.

Getting There: One bus makes three daily round-trips from the market in Campeche to Alfredo Bonfil (1½hr., 7, 10, and 11am, 12 pesos), leaving you at the Edzná access road. From there, a sign points the way and gives a distance 1500m too long. To avoid being stranded, be sure to ask the driver when he will return. A water bottle and plenty of insect repellent are a must in Edzna's jungle terrain. *(Site open daily 8am-5pm. Admission 16 pesos, free Su.)*

GRUTAS DE XTACUMBILXUNAAN

The **Grutas de Xtacumbilxunaan** (shta-koom-bill-shu-NAN, "Caves of the Sleeping Beauty") lie 27km from the Yucatán-Campeche border. A guided tour leads down a stone stairway to several deep *cenotes* filled with a *ceiba* staff and rock formations appearing to be a flying eagle, a hanging mop, and a puppy with sad eyes. Hard-core cave lovers toting their own rock climbing equipment can take a two-day journey underground with the guides to visit the seven connected *cenotes* 150m below ground. Bring camping gear and stay in the outdoor *palapa* for free.

Getting There: The *grutas* lie on Rte. 261, 30km north of Hopelchen and 8km south of Bolonchen. Second-class buses drop passengers at the access road (40 pesos). *(Open daily 8am-5pm, 10 pesos. Tours in Spanish only.)*

YUCATÁN

LA RUTA PUUC

La Ruta Puuc is a long stretch between Campeche and Mérida that traverses the Puuc Hills. This area was home to about 25,000 people during the Classic period of Maya civilization (4th-10th centuries). Decimated by diseases introduced by the Spanish, the Maya slowly surrendered most of their cities and ceremonial centers to the jungle. Beginning in the 18th century, the Maya population began a slow recovery. While today's Puuc Maya live in towns under *palapas* scattered along dirt roads, women continue to wear traditional embroidered *huipiles*, and Mayan remains the dominant language.

The easiest way to see the ruins is by renting a car in Mérida (see p. 597). The drive along La Ruta Puuc is one of the most liberating and enjoyable on-the-road experiences—small Maya villages and green jungle line the winding road.

Recently, more and more travel agencies in Mérida and Campeche are offering organized tours through this and other tourist routes such as the **Convent Route** and the **Hacienda Route**. The tourist offices in both cities provide information on arrangements but public transportation is more difficult. Second-class **buses** traverse Rte. 261 frequently, and will stop when requested, but none travel the Sayil-Oxkutzkub road with the exception of the **Autotransportes del Sur** "Ruta Puuc" bus that leaves Mérida at 8am and visits **Kabah, Sayil, Labná,** and **Uxmal,** returning to Mérida at about 4pm. If you don't mind a whirlwind tour through the sites, this bus is an incredible bargain (60 pesos; admission to sites not included). The bus only spends 30 minutes at each site, and leaves promptly; drivers have been known to leave tourists stranded. **Combis** are abundant in the morning and make frequent trips between **Oxkutzkub, Ticul, Santa Elena,** and **Muna** (it is easiest to get a *combi* to Uxmal from Muna), and they will make any trip if paid enough. Unfortunately, with both *combis* and buses, return trips are not always guaranteed. If you can only make it to one or two sights, don't miss Uxmal, and try to see Sayil—they have the best ruins of all.

Most travelers who make the Ruta Puuc more than a daytrip use **Ticul** (see p. 594) as a base or **Santa Elena** (see p. 595), an even more central location that boasts two superb budget dining and sleeping establishments on its outskirts. From either of these places, two to three days should be ample time for exhaustive exploration. Most sites sell *refrescos*, but the only one with accommodations is Uxmal. And at those prices, there ought to be a light-and-sound show for each room.

⏻ PRACTICAL INFORMATION

The Ruta Puuc is a well-marked road that can be driven without purchasing a road map. Simply follow signs to Uman from Mérida, then head toward Muna. From there on, just follow "Ruta Puuc" in Ticul.

Without a car, you'll be faced with relay races. Public transportation in Ticul is not geared toward ruin-happy tourists. While Uxmal and Kabah are fairly accessible if you have luck with *combi* transfers, the lack of traffic on the Sayil-Oxkutzkub road will leave the car-less traveler frustrated and stranded. In general, you should reconcile yourself to changing buses. To reach the ruins around Uxmal, take a Mérida-bound bus from the **Ticul** bus station (tel. 2 01 62), on Calle 24 behind the main church, and get off at Muna (every hr., 10 pesos). *Combis* for Muna leave from **Parque de la Madre**, at Calle 23 between Calle 28 and 30. From Muna, board a southbound bus or *combi* for Uxmal, Kabah, or other sites from the *zócalo* (5 per day, 10 pesos). You can also reach the ruins by catching a *combi* on **Calle 30**, between Calle 25 and 25A, to Santa Elena (about 8 pesos). Change *combis* at Santa Elena for Uxmal, 16km from Mérida, or at Kabah, south of Campeche. *Combis* are most plentiful in the morning. Considering the amount of time it will take to make connections, you might want to reconsider the rush tour bus from Mérida (see p. 596).

To reach the Grutas de Loltún, snag a *combi* to Oxkutzkub at Parque de la Madre; you'll be let off at the intersection of Calles 23 and 26 (15min., 3 pesos). *Combis* and pickup truck *colectivos* leave for Loltún from the lot across from Oxkutzkub's market, "20 de Noviembre." Tell the driver to let you off *en las grutas* (10min., 3 pesos), as everyone else is probably headed for the agricultural cooperative 3km farther down the road. Because the road is more crowded with *combis*, it's easier to reach the Grutas than Uxmal or Kabah. Hitchhikers rarely find rides on any of these roads.

LA RUTA PUUC: THE RUINS

The Ruta Puuc refers to the 254km on Rte. 261 between Campeche and Mérida and the Sayil-Oxkutzkub road which branches off just meters after the Campeche-Yucatán border. Taking this turnoff, **Sayil** is the first archaeological site to materialize (after 5km), followed by **Xlapac** (10km), **Labná** (13km), **Loltún** (25km), **Oxkutz-kub** (45km), and **Ticul** (62km). Alternatively, if the turnoff is not taken, the road winds through **Kabah** (right after the border) and the stunning site of **Uxmal** (23km); 16km from Uxmal lies the junction at **Muna** which leads to the lesser known site of **Oxkintolc** and **Las Grutas de Calcehtok** (26km northeast of Muna).

GRUTAS DE LOLTÚN

Below a dense jungle of mahogany and *ceiba* trees, kilometers of enormous caverns wind through the rock. The ancient Maya first settled this area in order to take advantage of the *grutas'* water and clay. Hundreds of years later, Maya *campesinos* returned to the caves seeking refuge from the Caste War (1847-48). Important caverns include the **Room of Inscriptions,** which dons handprints, and the **Na Cab** (House of the Bees), where you can see the *ka'ob* (grindstones) left by the Maya. Ancient inhabitants broke off the stalactite tips in the **Gallery of Fallen Rocks** to use as weapons, potion for strength and virility, and musical instruments. In the **Gallery of the Five Holtunes** (naturally formed water cisterns as opposed to man-

Yucatán State

N

GOLFO DE MÉXICO

Mar Caribe

Isla Contoy

Isla Holbox

Isla Mujeres

Isla Cozumel

Laguna de Yalahán

Parque Nacional Río Lagartos

Río Lagartos

San Felipe

Parque Nacional San Felipe

Dzilam de Bravo

Chiquilá

Kantunil Kin

Colonia Yucatán

Cancún

Izmal

Puerto Morelas

Playa del Carmen

Cozumel

Akumal

Xel-Ha

Tulum

Kuclcán

Cobá

Parque del Estado de Quintana Roo

Bahía de la Ascención

Punta Allen

Sian Ka'an Biospheric Preserve

Felipe Carillo Puerto

QUINTANA ROO

Xcan

Chemax

El Balam

Valladolid

Tekom

Tepich

Polyuc

Tizimín

Calotmul

Espita

Temozon

Grutas de Balancanché

Chichén Itzá

Yaxuná

Cenotillo

Dzitas

Ichmul

Peto

Santa Rosa

Dziuche

Tzucacab

Sucilá

Lophe

Panabá

San Felipe

Tzilam Gonzalez

Buctzotz

Temax

Tunkas

Kantunil

YUCATÁN

Motul

Izamal

Mayapán

Grutas de Loltún

Tecoh

Ticul

Santa Elena

Labná

Xlapak

Grutas de Xtacumbilxunaan

Hopelchén

CAMPECHE

Edzná

Chentoyi

Tenabó

Calkiní

Becal

Maxcanú

Muna

Uxmal

Kabah

Sayll

Umán

Grutas de Calcehok

Oxkintok

Mérida

Chelem

Progreso

Puerto Teichac

Xcambo

Dzibilchaltún

Hunucma

Sisal

Celestún

Campeche

50 miles

50 kilometers

made **chultunes),** a sculpted jaguar head drips water into cisterns while a huge warrior and eagle glare. The **Cathedral** is a palatial room with cavern vaults that once hosted Maya feasts, assemblies, and religious rites. The shadowy silhouette above the entrance is popularly believed to represent the Virgin of Guadalupe. Several caves contain partially hollow stalactites and columns—strike each one with the heel of your hand and listen to the soft booming sound *("loltún...loltún...")* reverberate throughout the cave system. Archaeologists speculate that the Maya used these formations as a means of underground communication. Remind your guide to point out the creative natural rock formations such as the virile penis, which for the Mayas represented strength, fertility and continuation of life.

Guides will lead English tours, but Spanish ones tend to be more comprehensive; they can also be enticed to lengthen their tours (the caves go on forever) with the promise of a nice, fat tip. As you exit the caves (0.5km from the entrance), you'll stumble on **Restaurant El Huinoc de Loltún,** which prepares a good range of local dishes for about 50 pesos. Get ready to wait—service is slow as molasses, and the restaurant can be packed with people from tour buses.

Getting There: The Grutas de Loltún are 52km east of Uxmal on the Sayil-Oxkutzkub road. To get to Loltún, catch a bus as far as Muna or Ticul, hop in a *combi* headed for Oxkutzkub, then follow signs to the *centro.* Passing the market on your left, walk two blocks, turn right at the sign for Ruta Puuc, then pray for deliverance—Las Grutas are 7km down the road. A pick-up truck in Oxkutzkub's *zócalo* may be willing to make the trip, but it will cost at least 25 pesos. (Entrance to the caves only with tours. Tours daily 9:30, 11am, 12:30, 2, 3, and 4pm. Admission 45 pesos, Su 25 pesos. Restaurant open M-Sa 10am-6pm.)

LABNÁ

Labná's excavated ruins were constructed toward the end of the Late Classic period (700-1000), when the Puuc cities were connected by *sacbe* (paved, elevated white roads). Today, a short reconstructed section of the *sacbe* runs between Labná's two most impressive sights: the palace and the stone arch. To deal with parched conditions, the Maya constructed **chultunes** (stone-carved cisterns), 70 of which are found at Labná. The *chultunes* collected water (up to 8000 gallons in each) and some held the bodies of peasants who couldn't afford to be buried. Only a few of the narrow openings can be seen. Many of Labná's buildings are too far gone to climb, giving rest to the tired and weak-kneed tourist.

Labná's **palace** is on the northern side of the site, to the left as you enter. While the construction of this building occupied the Maya for several centuries, the edifice was never actually completed. Labná's palace is reminiscent of the one at Sayil; they both boast exceptionally ornate second-floor facades. The difference with Labná's palace is in its separate, distinct sections built over seven different patios and two main levels.

Labná is famed for its picturesque stone arch, the **Arch of Labná,** 3m wide and 5m high. Its western facade is intricately decorated in a trellis pattern with two thatchroof Maya huts above its two rooms, while the eastern side is carved in a Grecian style. Archaeologists now believe that the arch previously thought to have been the entrance to another temple served as a ceremonial point of entry for victorious warriors returning from the battlefield.

Beyond the arch, on the base of a pyramid, stands the **observatory,** also known as **El Mirador** (watch tower). Its notable facade rises over the box-like structure and bears tenons, spikes, and dowels that used to support bas-relief sculptures. The top of the observatory affords a view of the entire site; keep your eyes peeled for falcons' nests. Heading back toward the palace, **El Templo de las Columnas** is off the *sacbe* to the right. This "Building of the Columns" is one of the best examples of the Puuc style of 800 to 1000. One of the openings to the *chultunes* that were vital to Labná's 2500 ancient residents can be seen in front of *El Templo.*

Getting There: The final destination on the "Ruta Puuc" bus, **Labná** lies 40km east of Uxmal, 20km before Las Grutas, and 3km beyond Xlapac. Almost no *combis* come and go on this branch of the Ruta Puuc and hitching is reportedly tough. (Site open daily 8am-5pm. Admission 20 pesos, Su free.)

XLAPAC

Xlapac, which means "old wall", lies 3km past Labná, the smallest and often missed ruin on the Ruta Puuc. Gobbling turkeys line the entrance to the one-man ticket counter *palapa*, who carves and sells wooden replicas of Maya iconography. It's vast jungle and chirping birds surround the reddish dirt path leading to *El Palacio*. Even the small palace, integrally Puuc in style, pays homage to Chac with its impressive triple-decker masks of the Maya rain god. South of the palace 300m lies a partially excavated stony structure with remains of fallen columns and carved stones lying on the ground along its perimeter.

SAYIL

The **Palace of Sayil** is an architectural standout among the region's ruins. While time, weather, and the jungle have taken down most of its buildings since its construction between 800 and 1000 AD, the palace is still breathtaking. Between its three terraced levels, the building's 90 rooms exhibit unparalleled ornamental diversity. Walls are carved with rows of slender columns, the second-story frieze depicts the descending serpent-god's body. Elegant second-floor chambers open onto pleasant porticos, each graced by bulging columns. A climb to the top displays a panoramic view of the rolling Puuc hills and a northwest corner aerial view of a large **chultun.**

The *sacbe* leads to **El Mirador,** a lofty temple with once-grandiose columns with large vertical slits underneath the roof-comb top. Left of El Mirador, the path leads deeper into the jungle, where the **Estela del Falo** (Stela of the Phallus) was a tribute to Yum Keep, a Maya god of fertility. A few other temples are barely visible through the dense jungle undergrowth. Before you hop on the road, walk across the street and climb the narrow dirt path to reach **El Templo de las Cabezas** (The Temple of Heads/Masks). Although mask are scarce, the view of Sayil's *palacio* is splendid.

Getting There: Sayil lies 9km past Kabah off Rte. 261 on the Sayil-Oxkutzkub road and 5km past Xlapac. The only public transportation to the site is provided by the **Autotransportes del Sur** "Ruta Puuc" bus (see p. 596). Buses do run, however, from Mérida to Kabah, 10km away on the main highway. Some travelers hitch from Kabah to Sayil. (Site open daily 8am-5pm. Admission 20 pesos, Su free.)

KABAH

Once the second largest city in the northern Yucatán, **Kabah,** which means "Sir of the Strong Hand and Powerful", was built with the blood and sweat of many slaves; their effort has mostly succumbed to the ravages of time, with a few notable exceptions. The striking **Codz Poop Temple** ("rolled up mat" in Mayan), immediately to the right of the entrance, is famous for the elaborate Chac masks, with over 250 Chac noses protruding from its broad facade. Unlike the pure Puuc style characterized by plain columns and a superior decorative frieze, Codz Poop is covered with ornamental stone carvings from top to bottom, resembling the **Chenes style.** Its neighbors to the east, **El Palacio** (a 25m pyramid) and **Las Columnas,** were executed in plainer fashion. The site is thought to have served as a court where justices settled disputes, with gods comprising the jury. Across the street by the parking lot, the short dirt road leads to rubble (right), more rubble (left), and the famous **Kabah Arch** (straight ahead). The arch marks the beginning of the ancient *sacbe* that culminated in a twin arch at Uxmal. The perfect alignment of the archway with the north-south line is testimony to Maya astronomical wisdom.

Getting There: Kabah is bisected by Rte. 261, and lies 23km southeast of its Ruta Puuc cousin, Uxmal. Because of its location on the Campeche-Mérida highway (*vía ruinas*), it can easily be reached by any second-class bus running between Mérida and Campeche. Buses will stop at Kabah only if a passenger notifies the driver beforehand or if the driver sees a person wildly gesticulating on the shoulder of the highway. Things are easier with the "Ruta Puuc" bus (see p. 596). Since almost all the tourists who come to Kabah have cars, those who do not sometimes try to hitch. (Site open daily 8am-5pm. Admission 14 pesos, Su free.)

UXMAL

If you've spent the day visiting all the ruins of the Ruta Puuc in the order in which they have been listed, then you'll be arriving in Uxmal just as the larger crowds are clearing out and as the sun is starting to set, bathing the striking ruins in a flame-yellow light. Meaning "thrice built or occupied," it's not hard to see why Uxmal, once a capital with 25,000 inhabitants, keeps drawing more and more visitors.

◨ ORIENTATION AND PRACTICAL INFORMATION. Autotransportes del Sur (ATS) sends six buses per day from **Mérida** to **Uxmal** (1½hr., 25 pesos), as well as a "Ruta Puuc" bus which visits **Kabah, Labná Sayil, Uxmal,** and **Xlapak** all in one day for just 60 pesos (see p. 596) From **Campeche** you'll have to take the Camioneros de Campeche bus to **Mérida** (3hr., 5 per day, 45 pesos). Ask the driver to stop at the access road to the *ruinas.* To return, grab a passing bus at the *crucero* just outside the entrance to the ruins. The last bus to Mérida and Campeche passes at 8pm. A modern **tourist center** with a small but interesting museum, restaurant, gift shop, photographic supply shop, and bathroom greets you at the entrance to the ruins. The **Kit Bolon Tun auditorium,** also in the tourist center, screens documentaries on the Ruta Puuc and gives 15-minute presentations on Chichén Itzá, Uxmal, and the Yucatán. *(6 shows per day in Spanish and 4 in English, 10:30am-5pm; free. Archeological site open daily 8am-6pm; light and sound show 7pm in winter, 8pm in summer. General admission 90 pesos).*

▣◨ ACCOMMODATIONS AND FOOD. Even the bravest of ruins crumble under the huge prices of Uxmal's lodging and food. Consider staying 30 minutes away in Ticul or Santa Elena, where hotel rooms cost half as much (see p. 594).

◨ THE ARCHAEOLOGICAL SITE OF UXMAL. According to the **Books of Chilam Balam** (see p. 23), a group of Maya historical accounts written in Yucatec Mayan, Yucatán was invaded at the end of the 10th century by Ah Suytok Xiu and his warriors from the Valley of Mexico. Xiu and his successors dominated Uxmal until the city's strength was sapped by civil warfare in the 12th century. Because their priests foretold the coming of white, bearded men, the Xiu did not resist the attacks of Spanish conquistadors on Uxmal. The last Xiu ruler of the city was Ah Suytok Tutul Xiu.

GUIDE TO THE RUINS. The 35m-tall near-pyramid visible upon entering Uxmal is the **Pyramid of the Magician.** As legend goes, the pyramid was built by a dwarf-magician who hatched from a witch's egg and grew to maturity in one year. The legend of the dwarf-magician's birth struck terror into the heart of the governing lord of Uxmal, who, it was prophesized, would be replaced by a man "not born of woman." He challenged the dwarf to a contest of building skills. The dwarf's pyramid, built overnight, easily out-classed the governor's **Great Pyramid,** still visible to the right of the **Governor's Palace.** Grasping at straws, the spiteful ruler complained that the base of the dwarf's pyramid was neither square nor rectangular but oval with massive rounded ends. Having undermined the legitimacy of the dwarf-magician's triumph, the governor proposed that he and his adversary compete to see who could break a *cocoyol* (a small, hard-shelled fruit) on his head. The dwarf-magician, in whose skull a turtle shell had been placed, easily cracked open the *cocoyol.* The governor crushed his own unaltered skull.

Continuing to the west is a large quadrangle—Uxmal's famed **Nunnery.** It was misnamed for the same reason as the one at Chichén Itzá; the Spanish thought its many rooms resembled that of a convent. The four long buildings of this quad were each built on a different level, and each has a distinctive decor. The

northern building is adorned with Chac masks which can be better appreciated standing on the opposite side, underneath the southern facade; the **eastern building** boasts intricate lattice work and Venus symbols; the **southern building** has a series of hut sculptures and the **western building** shows kings and bound prisoners in high relief. The sizeable entryways of the southern building lead to the **ballcourt.** Only one of the glyph-engraved stone signs remains, through which well-padded players tried to knock a hardened rubber ball (see **Hoop Dreams,** p. 612).

Emerging from the ballcourt, head right along a narrow path to the **Cemetery Group,** a small, leafy plaza bounded by a modestly sized pyramid to the north and a temple to the west. Stones that once formed platforms bear haunting reliefs of skulls and crossbones. Returning to the ballcourt, head south to the well-restored **Great Pyramid,** built by the governor in his contest with the dwarf-magician. On top of the pyramid sits the **Macaw Temple,** named for its many engravings of that bird on its facade, inside of which sits a Chac-motif throne. To the west the pyramid looks down on the fretworks of the **Pigeon House.** Behind this structure lie the jungle-shrouded remains of the **Chenes Temple.**

The **House of Turtles** and the **Palace of the Governor** top a man-made escarpment east of the Great Pyramid. The two-story house is on the northwest corner of the escarpment and is adorned along its upper frieze with a series of sculpted three dimensional turtles (turtles symbolized rain and were venerated by the Maya). The larger building is the palace, replete with engravings and arches.

From the Palace of the Governor, try to spot the overgrown, pyramidal **House of the Old Woman,** which lies to the east and can be reached by following the path directly to your left as you emerge from the entrance. About 400m south of the house is the **Temple of the Phalli.** Phallic sculptures hang from the cornices of this ruined building and drained rain from the roof. Experienced guides are available to give more detailed tours of the site (about 65 pesos per person as part of a group).

WHO'S GOT THE TIME?

Archeo-buffs can't help but get chills when viewing a Maya ruin inscribed with the exact date of some vital event. Since before they developed a writing system, the Maya used a sophisticated calender, which could be pictured as fitting together like concentric gears. The basis was a ritual count of 20 days, each of which was given a name and a glyph. A group of 20 days, or *k'in*, was known as a *winal* (month), and a *tun* was a 360-day year. A *k'atun* was a period of 20 years, and it was this division of time that held particularly special meaning, roughly like the Gregorian decade. *Baktuns* were 400 years long, and together, the system could be trakced by what today is called the Maya Long Count. August 25, 1999, for example, would be inscribed as 12.19.6.8.13, with the *baktuns* on the left and the *k'in* number on the right. The original date of the Long Count goes back well before 1000 BC, and the outermost "gear" is set to complete its first full revolution in 2012. This "sacred" calender also corresponded with a "regular" 365-day solar calender, but the 18 months of 20 days left over an unlucky 5-day month called a *wayeb*.

OXKINTOK

Oxkintok lies 42km northwest of Uxmal, on the west end of the rolling Puuc hills. The best way to get to these hidden ruins is by car heading towards the small Maya village of Maxcanú. After following the only sign to the site and asking locals for its exact location you will drive through bushes, trees, and over a hill which is covered by mounds of ruins (300-1050) yet to be excavated. Climb atop the **Ah May Pyramid,** the tallest building of the Maya's ceremonial center and the **Ah Canul Palace** for an awe-inspiring view of the entire site and virgin ruins. Finally, a stroll through the labyrinth's narrow and dark corridors guarantees an eerie adventure. Watch for low ceilings and steep steps.

LAS GRUTAS DE CALCEHTOK

A "not-to-miss" underground Maya cave, **Las Grutas de Calcehtok** is located only 2km northeast of Oxkintok. The cavern is the longest one in all of Yucatán, with four different entries replete with thousands of stalactities and stalagmites, some shaded in red. Rock formations create the profile of Frankenstein with a bird nesting on his head, a llama, and a horse's head. Bits of broken Maya ceramics abound as well as man-made *chultunes*. If you're brave enough, ask the guide to lead you into the Maya ritual and sacrificial terrain; a tip would be greatly appreciated.

TICUL

A bustling provincial town off the Campeche-Mérida highway, **Ticul** (pop. 24,000) is known for its excellent ceramics and cheap, durable shoes. It also enjoys a status as a convenient and inexpensive base from which to explore the Puuc sites of Labná, Kabah, Sayil, Uxmal, and Xlapak as well as the Grutas de Loltún. Aside from obvious differences in size and population, a stay in Ticul is a far cry from one in Mérida. For those with wheels, a number of *cenotes* and colonial buildings await exploration in the nearby towns of **Teabo,** 30km southeast of Ticul, and **Holcá,** 105km to the northeast. **Mayapán,** which lies only 45km to the northeast, was once one of the capitals (along with Chichén Itzá and Uxmal) of an ancient Maya united kingdom. **Maní,** 15km east of Ticul, features a colonial monastery; **Tekax,** 35km to the southeast, a hermitage; and **Tipikal,** an impressive colonial church. Ticul itself is home to an 18th-century church (open 8am-6pm) and pulls out all the stops for the week of its **Tobacco Fair** starting in early April.

🖪 ORIENTATION AND PRACTICAL INFORMATION. Ticul's streets form a grid with the main boulevard, **Calle 23,** which passes east-west through the center. Even-numbered streets run north-south. Most commercial activity transpires between the *zócalo* (at Calle 24) and Calle 30, four blocks to the west and on **Calle 25,** a strip of Maya statuettes pay tribute to their ancient gods.

From Muna, five **buses** run daily to **Campeche** (20 pesos) via **Uxmal** and **Kabah,** from the terminal at the *zócalo*. Hourly buses head north to **Mérida** (10 pesos). The town's pedal-powered **taxis** (*triciclos*) transport passengers for a couple of pesos. **Combis** leave from Parque de la Madre, Calle 23 between Calles 28 and 30, for **Muna** (7 per day, 9 pesos); from Calle 30 between Calles 25 and 25A, for **Santa Elena, Uxmal,** and **Kabah** (10 pesos); and from Calle 25 between Calles 26 and 28, for **Oxkutzkub** (every 15min., 9 pesos).

Bital, Calle 23 #195 (tel. 2 09 79), off the *zócalo*, changes U.S. dollars and traveler's checks (open M-F 9am-2pm, Sa 9am-1pm). **Farmacia San José,** Calle 23 #214J (tel. 2 03 93), is between Calles 28 and 30 (open daily 8am-1pm and 4-10pm; no English spoken). **Dr. Estela Sanabria** can be reached at the same number for 24-hour **medical assistance. Police:** (tel. 2 00 10 or 2 02 10) on Calle 23 at the northeast corner of the *zócalo* (open 24hr.). **Post office:** (tel. 2 00 40) in the Palacio Municipal in the *zócalo* (open M-F 8am-2:30pm). **Postal code:** 97860. **Telegram office:** Calle 21 #192-C (tel. 2 01 46), in the blue-and-white building behind the post office (open M-F 9am-3pm). There is a **LADATEL** across the street from the Hotel Sierra in the *zócalo*. **Phone code:** 997.

🖫 ACCOMMODATIONS AND FOOD. Ticul has several hotels and good restaurants. One option is **Hotel San Miguel** (tel. 2 03 82), on Calle 28, opposite Parque de la Madre and the bargain prices mean you get what you pay for. (Singles 45 pesos; doubles 70 pesos; triples 100 pesos.) **Hotel Sierra Sosa** (tel. 2 00 08) on Calle 24, at the northwest corner of the *zócalo*, has rooms with firm beds, strong fans, *agua purificada*, and TVs loud enough to drown out the sound of hot-rod mopeds outside. (Singles 75 pesos; doubles 90 pesos; triples 115 pesos; add 40 pesos for A/C.)

After a hot day on the Ruta Puuc, Ticul is the place to refuel and rehydrate. **Los Almendros,** Calle 23 #207 (tel. 2 00 21) between Calles 28 and 30, is known worldwide for its *poc-chuc*. The chain of restaurants started here in little ol' Ticul making a delicious, 34 peso *pollo pibil* and *pollo ticuleño*. (Open daily 9am-9pm.) **Restaurant Los Delfines** (tel. 2 04 01), Calle 27, between Calles 28 and 30, serves shrimp dishes, *chile relleno* (45 pesos), and jars of lemonade under an airy *palapa* (open daily 11am-7pm). **Pizzeria la Gondola** (tel. 2 01 12), serves up slimi-slis between sky blue walls and wooden framed mirrors. Free delivery of spaghetti (30 pesos), and pizza (40 pesos; open daily 8am-1pm and 5:30pm-midnight). Ticul's **market** is off Calle 23 between Calles 28 and 30 (open daily 6am-2pm).

SANTA ELENA

This tiny town of 2500 Mayan speaking residents has a park, soda shops, one phone, and an 18th-century church which will soon house original Maya mummies. The town lies 8km north of Kabah and 15km east of Uxmal on the Ruta Puuc. It even has its very own archaeological site of **Multan-Chic**, a small collection of platforms and substructures. The main draws for budget travelers are not actually in the town, but are found along Rte. 261 where it dips 1km south of St. Elena. The **Sacbe Camping-Bungalows** offers weary travelers pristine campgrounds with new shower and toilet facilities, outdoor grills and tables, and even a mosquito-netted thatched hut where the owners serve breakfast and lunch for 25-35 pesos. (Campsites 25 pesos per person; bungalows with hot water, fans, and private bathroom 120 pesos, with common bathroom 85 pesos.) Only 150m north toward Uxmal, on the opposite side of the road, lies the **Hotel/Restaurant El Chac-Mool** (tel. 1 01 91). Large helpings of eggs, tacos, sandwiches (35-40 pesos) and beer (10-12 pesos) are served under a friendly *palapa* roof (open daily 11am-8pm). The owners of the restaurant are the same friendly owners of two large pink-and-white modern rooms adjacent to the dining area with two large comfortable beds and private bathrooms (110 pesos per room).

MÉRIDA

Built atop the ruins of the Maya City, **T'hó,** modern Mérida (pop. 1.5 million) reveals traces of its pre-Hispanic history—the stones of the city's fortress-like cathedral are from the Maya temples from which they were stripped. The Maya called this site "Place of the Fifth Point," to indicate that it was the center of the universe, the spot between the four points of north, south, east, and west. Mérida is now the state's capital and key commercial center. *Jipis* (Panama hats), made from the leaves of the *jipi* palm, come from Becal in the neighboring state of Campeche, hammocks arrive from nearby Tixcocób, and *henequén* is trucked to Mérida from all over Yucatán before being exported as hemp.

Mérida has been a magnet for international tourists since its Spanish colonial days including hundreds of dignitaries and the Pope. Recently *merideños* of Lebanese and Syrian descent have made their home in the city, and a small French community is responsible for the **Paseo Montejo,** Mérida's version of the Champs-Elysées. The Paseo turns into a street of non-stop music and entertainment during **Carnaval.** Jet-setting tourists arrive in Mérida in bulk to spend days shopping and nights whispering sweet nothings in music-filled parks.

Intimate conversations still swirl about the *zócalo*, and every Sunday during *Mérida en Domingo*, Merideños and tourists alike stroll the "White City's" sidewalk cafes, fast-food joints, and colonial mansions.

■ ORIENTATION

Rte. 180 runs from Cancún (319km) and Valladolid (159km) to the east, becoming **Calle 65,** which passes through the busiest part of town, one block south of the *zócalo*. Those approaching on Rte. 180 from Campeche, 153km to the southwest, end up on **Av. Itzáces**, which runs north-south, or on **Calle 81,** which feeds into the north-south **Calle 70.** Av. Itzáces and **Calle 70** intersect **Calle 59,** the best route to the center of town, which runs east to a point one block north of the *zócalo*. **Paseo**

Montejo begins at **Calle 47** two blocks east of **Calle 60,** running north as **Rte. 261.** The *zócalo* fills one city block, bordered by Calle 61 to the north, Calle 62 to the west, Calle 63 to the south, and Calle 60 to the east. To reach the *zócalo* from the **second-class bus terminal,** head east to Calle 62 and walk three blocks; turn left (north) and the *zócalo* is three blocks ahead. Alternatively, take a **taxi** (20-25 pesos), or catch the "Seguro Social" bus (3 pesos), or walk six blocks west on Calle 55 and three blocks south on Calle 60.

Mérida's gridded one-way streets have numbers instead of names. Even-numbered streets run north-south, with numbers increasing to the west; odd-numbered streets run east-west, increasing to the south. Addresses in Mérida are given using an "x" to separate the main street from the cross streets and "y" ("and" in Spanish) to separate the two cross streets if the address falls in the middle of the block. Thus "54 #509 x 61 y 63" reads "Calle 54 #509, between Calles 61 and 63."

Mérida's **camiones (municipal buses)** meander along idiosyncratic routes (daily 6am-midnight, 3 pesos.) Precise information is available at the tourist information office, but the city is small enough so that a bus headed in the right direction will usually drop you off within a few blocks of your desired location; just find a bus stop sign in order to catch a ride. **Taxis** do not roam the streets soliciting riders; it is necessary to phone or to go to one of the *sitios* (stands) along Paseo de Montejo, at the airport, or at the *zócalo.* Expect to pay at least 20-25 pesos for a trip within the *centro.* **Taxi-colectivos** (more commonly known as **combis**), on the other hand, charge only 3 pesos for any destination in the city; **dropoffs** are on a first-come, first-serve basis.

🔒 PRACTICAL INFORMATION

TRANSPORTATION

Airport: 7km southwest on Rte. 180. A taxi charges 50 pesos for the trip downtown. Post office, telegrams, long-distance telephone, and car rental are at the airport. **Aerocaribe,** Paseo Montejo 500B x 45 y 47 (tel. 28 67 90, at airport 46 13 35). **Aeroméxico,** Paseo Montejo 460 x 35 y 37 (tel. 20 12 93, at airport 20 12 60). **Aviateca,** Paseo de Montejo 475 x 37 y 39 (tel. 25 80 59, at airport 46 12 90). **Mexicana,** (tel. 24 66 33), Paseo de Montejo.

Buses: Most bus lines operate out of the main second-class terminal, Unión de Camioneros, Calle 69 #544 x 68 y 70, 3 blocks west and 3 blocks south of the *zócalo.* ADO (tel. 24 83 91) sends buses to: **Cancún** (5hr., 12 per day 5:30am-7pm, 95 pesos); **Chichén Itzá** (2hr.; 8:45, 9:30am and 1pm; 40 pesos); **Chiquilá** (6hr., 11:30pm, 61 pesos); **Playa del Carmen** (6hr., 6 per day 6am-midnight, 120 pesos); and **Valladolid** (3hr., 6 per day 5:30am-midnight, 55 pesos). Autotransportes del Sur (ATS) goes to **Campeche** (3hr.; daily 5, 11am, 8, and10:30pm; 55 pesos) and **Uxmal** (1½hr.; 6, 9am, noon, 2:30, 5:30pm; 20 pesos). ATS provides a special **Ruta Puuc** bus (8am-4pm, 60 pesos, 30min. at each site; admission to sites not included) which visits the archaeological sites of **Labná, Kabah, Sayil, Uxmal, Xlapak** returning around 4pm (see p. 587). Línea Dorada serves **Chetumal** (6hr.; 7:30, 11am, 6, and 11pm; 135 pesos) and **Ticul** (7:30am, 30 pesos). Premier goes to: **Chichén Itzá** (2hr.; 8:45, 9:30am, and 1pm; 32 pesos); **Cobá** (3hr.; 6:30am and 1pm; 72 pesos); **Playa del Carmen** (5hr., 11 per day, 130 pesos); **Tulum** (6hr.; 6, 11am, and 4:30pm; 87 pesos); and **Valladolid** (2hr., 6 per day 5:30am-midnight, 60 pesos). Some buses leave from the **first-class terminal,** called CAME, located around the corner on Calle 70 between Calles 69 and 71. Autobuses de Occidente runs to almost anywhere on the peninsula as well as to: **Cordoba** (17hr., 4 per day, 353 pesos); **Mexico City** (19hr., 4 per day, 460 pesos); **Palenque** (8hr.; 8am, 10 and 11:30pm; 160 pesos); **Puebla** (20hr., 5:30pm, 415 pesos); **Veracruz** (15hr., 10:30am and 9pm, 315 pesos); and **Villahermosa** (9hr.; 7:30, 10am, and 12:05pm; 191 pesos). Expreso goes to **Cancún** (4hr., 12 per day, 95 pesos). The 9:15pm Maya de Oro or Cristóbal bus runs to: **Campeche** (2hr., 60 pesos); **Palenque** (6hr., 155 pesos); **Ocosingo** (8hr., 200 pesos); **San Cristóbal de las Casas** (12hr., 225 pesos); and **Tuxtla Gutiérrez** (16hr., 250 pesos).

Mérida
ACCOMMODATIONS

A Casa Bowen
B Hotel las Monjas
C Hotel Latino
D Hotel Margarita
E Hotel Montejo
F Hotel Trinidad Galería
G Hotel Mucuy
H Hotel Janeiro

Taxis: Found at Palacio Municipal (tel. 23 09 60), on the northwest corner of the *zócalo.* Mercado Municipal (tel. 23 11 35), at Calles 56 and 65, in **Parque de la Maternidad** (tel. 28 53 22) at **Teatro Peón Contreras,** and dozens of other *sitios.* Call **Radio Taxi** (tel. 23 40 46) anytime although it's much cheaper to use the *camiones.*

Car Rental: Mexico Rent-a-Car, Calle 57A (El Callejón del Congreso) Dept. 12 x 58 y 60 or Calle 62 #483A x 57 y 59 (tel. 27 49 16 or 23 36 37). VW Beetles, including insurance, and unlimited *kilometraje* 290 pesos per day (subject to increase during high season). Open M-Sa 8am-12:30pm and 6-8pm, Su 8am-12:30pm. The cheapest car rental in Mérida.

TOURIST AND FINANCIAL SERVICES

Tourist Information: Central Office (tel. 24 92 90), Calles 60 x 57 y 59, in the Teatro Peón Contreras. Distributes *Yucatán Today,* a free guide listing practical info and local events. Additional office at the airport (tel. 46 13 00). Both open daily 8am-9pm.

Travel Agencies: Yucatán Trails, Calle 62 #482 x 57 y 59 (tel. 28 25 82 or 28 59 13; fax 24 19 28; email denis@finred.com.mx). Canadian owner Denis Lafoy is a genial source of info on Mérida and the Yucatán. Arranges cheap Saturday daytrips to Ruta Puuc sites 3 days a week (550 pesos). Open M-F 8am-2pm and 4-7pm, Sa 8am-1pm.

Consulates: U.K., Calle 53 #498 x 58 y 56 (tel. 28 61 52; fax 28 39 62). Open M-F 9am-1pm. **U.S.,** Paseo de Montejo 453 (tel. 25 50 11), at Av. Colón. Bring your passport. Open M-F 8am-1pm.

Currency Exchange: Banamex (tel. 24 10 11), in Casa de Montejo on the *zócalo*. with a 24hr. **ATM.** Open M-F 9am-5pm, Sa 9am-2pm.

American Express: Paseo de Montejo 494 #106 x 43 y 45 (tel. 42 82 00 or 42 82 10). English spoken. Open M-F 9am-2pm and 4-6pm, Sa 9am-1pm. Money exchange desk closes 1hr. earlier.

LOCAL SERVICES

Bookstore: Dante (tel. 24 95 22), Calle 60 x 57, in Teatro Peón Contreras. Guidebooks, maps, and magazines in English, French, and Spanish as well as postcards and CDs. Open M-Sa 8am-9:30pm, Su 10am-6pm.

Laundry: La Fe, Calle 61 #518 x 62 y 64 (tel. 24 45 31), near the *zócalo*. 35 pesos per 3kg. Open M-F 8am-7pm, Sa 8am-5pm.

Market: Four square blocks of covered stalls and street vendors extend south of Calle 65 and east of Calle 58. Open dawn to dusk. **Supermarket: San Francisco de Asís,** Calles 65 x 50 y 52, across from the market in a huge gray building. Open daily 7am-9pm.

EMERGENCY AND COMMUNICATIONS

Police: (tel. 28 25 53 or 28 55 52) on Av. Reforma (Calle 72) x 39 y 41, accessible with the "Reforma" bus. Some English spoken.

Red Cross: Calle 68 #533 x 65 y 67 (tel. 24 98 13). 24hr. emergency and ambulance services (tel. 06). Some English spoken.

Pharmacy: Farmacia Canto, Calle 60 #513 x 63 y 65 (tel. 28 50 27). Open 24hr.

Hospital: Centro Médico de las Américas, Calle 54 #365 (tel. 26 21 11 or 26 26 19), at Calle 33A. 24hr. service, including ambulances. **Clínica de Mérida,** Calle 32 #242 x 27 y 25 (tel. 25 41 00). English spoken in both.

Post Office: (tel. 24 35 90) on Calles 65 x 56 y 56A, 3 blocks from the *zócalo* in the Palacio Federal. Open M-F 7am-7pm, Sa 9am-1pm. Branches at Calle 58 x 49 y 51, at the airport, and at the main bus station. **MexPost** at Calle 58 x 53 y 55. Open M-F 9am-6pm, Sa 9am-1pm.

Postal Code: 97000.

Internet Access: The Instituto Tecnológico de Hotelería, Calle 57 #492 x 56 y 58 (tel. 24 03 87; email itech@finred.com), has a comfortable and social computer lab. 30 pesos per hr. Open M-F 8am-2pm and 4pm-8pm, Sa 9am-2pm. **Cybernet,** Calle 57-A #491 (El Callejon de Congreso); (email voyager@sureste.com), is centrally located with 20 terminals. 10 pesos per 15min., 20 pesos per 30min., 30 pesos per hr. Open M-F 10am-9pm, Sa 10am-3pm.

Fax: (tel. 28 23 69; fax 24 26 19) in the same building as the main post office. Entrance around the corner on Calle 56A. Telegrams as well. Open M-F 8am-7pm.

Telephones: LADATELs are around the *zócalo*. Phone cards sold at a stand in the Palacio del Gobierno on the *zócalo*. Otherwise, you'll be left at the *casetas'* mercy.

Phone Code: 99.

 # ACCOMMODATIONS

Choosing from among Mérida's budget accommodations is like deciding in which bygone era to stay. What were once elaborate, private 19th- and turn of the century mansions are now often affordable hotels. While they may have lost some of the spotless sheen given by armies of servants, many still have their small courtyards, columned porticos, or stained glass.

Casa Bowen, Calle 66 #521B x 65 y 67 (tel. 28 61 09), halfway between the main bus station and the *zócalo*. Grecian columns line the hallway of this backpacker Mecca from the wicker-chaired lobby to the dining room with TV and full bookshelf. The large rooms upstairs have fans and firm beds facing the courtyard. Reservations recommended in Aug. and Dec. Singles 110 pesos; doubles 130 pesos. Rooms with kitchenette and fridge 130 pesos, with A/C 150 pesos; 25 pesos per extra person.

Hotel Montejo, Calle 57 #507 x 62 y 64 (tel. 28 02 77), 2 blocks north and 1 block east of the *zócalo*. Rooms are decorated with large iron-studded wooden doors facing maroon trimmed arches and a lush garden. Inside are wood ceiling beams, wood window porticos, and wooden bathrooms. A 10% discount with *Let's Go Mexico*. Singles 160 pesos; doubles 200 pesos, with A/C 250 pesos; 40 pesos per extra person.

Hotel Trinidad Galería, Calle 60 #456 x 51 (tel. 23 24 63). The winding halls of this creative colonial mansion are filled with works of art, plastic doll altars, and twisted mannequins. All this makes for an interesting stay, no matter which master room you choose. Head past the modern art gallery and the fish-filled fountain to find a masterpiece of a pool. Singles 130 pesos; doubles 140 pesos; triples 170 pesos. Rooms with A/C 180 pesos. Ask for the inexpensive rooms with shared bathrooms (120 pesos).

Hotel Mucuy, Calle 57 #481 x 56 y 58 (tel. 28 51 93), 2 blocks north and 2 blocks east of the *zócalo*. The sunny courtyard and sky blue rooms mask the hotel's central location and elegant glass doors enclose the reading room and piano in the blue-tiled lobby. Singles 130 pesos; doubles 150 pesos; triples 180 pesos.

Hotel Janeiro, Calle 57 #435 x 48 y 50 (tel. 23 36 02). As the name suggests, Hotel Janeiro is a hike from the bus station. There's a shallow pool and garden outside and large plants in the narrow hallways. Singles and doubles with fans 140 pesos, with A/C 170 pesos; 45 pesos per extra person.

Hotel Margarita, Calle 66 #506 x 61 y 63 (tel. 23 72 36) for over forty years Margarita has provided *precios muy economicos* in all of Mérida. A mahogany doorway with bright-colored geometrical tiles leads to cheap but characterless rooms. Singles 70 pesos; doubles 80 pesos; triples 95 pesos.

Hotel la Monjas, Calle 66-A #509 x 63 y 61 (tel. 28 66 32) Spotless white walls with funky green curtains give character to this modern hotel. Singles 95 pesos; doubles 115 pesos; one room with A/C 130 pesos.

FOOD

Mérida's specialties make good use of the fruits and grains that flourish in the Yucatán's hot, humid climate. Try *sopa de lima* (freshly squeezed lime soup with chicken and tortilla bits), *pollo pibil* (chicken with herbs baked in banana leaves), *poc-chuc* (pork steak with onions doused in sour orange juice), *papadzules* (chopped hard-boiled eggs wrapped in corn tortillas served with pumpkin sauce), and the most important dish of the most important meal of the day, *huevos motuleños* (refried beans, fried egg, chopped ham, and cheese on a crispy tortilla garnished with tomato sauce, peas, and fried banana). Given all these options, it's not surprising that there are as many places to eat as there are to shop. Quality varies widely from cook to cook, but some of the best meals in Mérida can be found in the plastic-chair-and-table joints along the *zócalo*. The cheapest food in town awaits at the **market,** particularly on the second floor of the restaurant complex on Calle 56 at Calle 67— *Yucáteco* dishes (10-15 pesos; most stalls open M-Sa 8am-8pm, Su 8am-5pm).

Restaurante Amaro, Calle 59 #507 x 60 y 62 (tel. 28 24 51). Meals are healthy and delicious, offering lean meat and vegetarian options such as *crepes* for 33 pesos. At night, the well-lit courtyard sets the mood along with a refreshing *horchata* (rice milk and almond shake) for 12 pesos; avocado and cheese sandwich 22 pesos; huge, invigorating fruit salads 22 pesos. Meat entrees 35-45 pesos. Open M-Sa 8:30am-11pm.

Restaurante y Café Express (tel. 28 16 91), Calle 60 x 59 y 61, across the street from Parque Hidalgo is one of the oldest dives in the *zócalo* fashioning wooden panels, high ceilings and paintings of Maya temples. Small tables and 2nd floor balcony face the busy street while the service makes the cafe live up to its name. Breakfast and sandwiches are 20 pesos; main entrees 35-50 pesos. Restaurant open daily 7am-11pm.

El Rincón (tel. 24 90 22), Calle 60 x 59 y 61, situated right in Parque Hidalgo. The restaurant for Hotel Caribe has tables indoors as well as in the bustling park. If the staff are in high spirits, they will sing and play the guitar. Serves *sopa de lima* (20 pesos); *arroz con plátanos* (15 pesos), and *pollo pibil* (45 pesos). Open daily 7am-11pm.

Los Almendros and **Los Gran Almendros,** Calle 50 #493 x 57 y 59 (tel. 28 54 59) on Parque Mejorada, and at Calle 57 #468 x 50 y 52 (tel. 23 81 35). The world-famous food has made this a tourist-oriented restaurant, with a picture menu portraying its cuisine better than a thousand words. Typical plates include *poc-chuc* (54 pesos) or *pollo pibil* (35 pesos). Los Almendros open daily 10:30am-11pm with music trio 2-5pm and 7:30-11pm. Less touristy Gran Almendros open daily noon-6pm.

El Louvre, Calle 62 #499-D, on the northwest corner of the *zócalo.* Super breakfast specials, super club sandwiches, super location and super hours make El Louvre more popular than the real thing. Super Specials 20-30 pesos. Open 24hr.

El Tucho, Calle 60 #482 x 55 y 57 (tel. 24 23 23). A festive and upbeat environment, El Tucho, which means "the monkey," wildly entertains families, locals, and tourists. Comedy troupes and regional musicians perform while waiters ferry trays of free *botanas* (hors d'œuvres) from kitchen to table. As long as you keep on drinkin', the food keeps on comin'. Real meals 45 pesos. Open daily 11:30am-9pm.

Café la Habana, Calle 59 #511 x 62 (tel. 28 65 02). Cuba in Mérida sizzles Yucatec dishes with Cuban spices. Daily breakfast and lunch specials for 20-35 pesos amidst black and white poster size photographs. Open 24 hr.

🔘 SIGHTS

In a peninsula of impressive *zócalos*, Mérida's stands alone as a testament to the fascinating history of the Yucatán. Surrounded on all sides by historic palaces and a towering cathedral, the *zócalo* is renowned as the capital's social center. The *zócalo* is busiest on Sundays, when street vendors cram in dozens of stalls; Yucátec folk dancers perform in front of the Palacio Municipal; crowds of people come from all over to enjoy *Mérida en Domingo* as well as the rest of the week.

CATEDRAL DE SAINT IDELFONSO. The 400 year old cathedral has stood watch over Mérida's often convoluted history since 1598, making it the oldest cathedral on the American Continent. The sturdy stone blocks of the cathedral were stolen from the Maya temples of T'hó. Built in the austere *Herrericano* style, the cathedral features rose-colored arched domes and an immense 20m wooden crucified Christ, one of the largest crucifix in the world. *(Open daily 6am-7pm.)*

PALACIO DE GOBIERNO. Built from 1883 to 1892, the *palacio* fuses two architectural styles—Tuscan (main floor) and Dorian (upper floor), situated on the northern edge of the *zócalo.* Inside, gigantic murals narrate the strife-filled history of the Yucatán peninsula. The stairway painting illustrates the Maya belief that their ancestors were made from maize. An image from the *Popol Vuh,* an account of Maya creation written in 16th-century Guatemala, dominates the next layout. *Jarana* performances, the Yucatecan colonial dance, take place under the sheltering balcony of the Palacio Municipal, across the *zócalo* from the cathedral on Monday evenings from 9pm to 10pm. A jail until the 1700s, the building was rebuilt in 1735 with two stories of arches. The Yucatán declared its independence from Spain and joined with Mexico here. *(Palacio open daily 8am-10pm.)*

CASA DE MONTEJO. On the southern side of the *zócalo,* the *Casa* displays a 16th century plateresque portico, constructed in 1549 as the residence of city founder Francisco de Montejo. Built with stones from the Maya temple T'hó, the carved facade follows the Toltec tradition of representing warriors standing on their con-quests' heads. *(Open M-F 9am-5pm.)* **El Museo de la Ciudad,** offers a concise historical background of the "white city" and its colonial structures. *(Calle 58 x 61. Open T-F 10am-2pm and 4-8pm, Sa-Su 10am-2pm. Free.)*

MUSEO REGIONAL DE ANTROPOLOGÍA E HISTORIA. Mérida's most impressive museum, is housed in a magnificent Italian Renaissance-style building called the Palacio Canton on the corner of Paseo Montejo and Calle 43. Most notable of the collections inside are the ancient Maya head-flattening devices for infants, the enamel teeth inserts of jade, a *chac-mool* from Chichen-Itza, and a ballcourt stone ring from Uxmal. The shop behind the ticket counter sells comprehensive English-language guidebooks and postcards. *(Tel. 23 05 57. Museum and shop open Tu-Sa 9am-8pm, Su 8am-2pm. Admission 28 pesos. Su free.)*

MUSEO DE ARTE POPULAR. Located six blocks east of the *zócalo* on Calle 59 x 50, behind the Convento de la Mejorada, the *museo* celebrates the indigenous crafts and artisans of the Yucatán. The small museum shares the building with a school of design, and there is a student lounge where you can rest after the long walk. The displays feature exhibits on modern-day Maya customs and handicrafts. *(Open Tu-Sa 9am-8pm, Su 8am-2pm. Free.)*

CENTENARY PARK AND ZOO. The zoo is at the end of the park and is home to lions, tigers, preening peacocks, flamingos, antelope, Aztec dogs, and jaguars. A miniature train makes regular circuits of the park, but don't expect a quiet ride or a glimpse of many of the dozing creatures. On the corner of Calle 59 and Av. Itzáces (Calle 86). Snag a bus at Calle 65 x 56 (3 pesos) and ask to be let off at "el Centenario," a favorite destination for local schools. *(Park open Tu-Su 9am-6pm. Zoo open Tu-Su 9am-5pm. Both free.)*

MUSEO DE HISTORIA NATURAL. Housed in a 19th-century *hacienda*, this small but ambitious collection chronicles the history of life from the origin of the uni-verse through the emergence of species. Its main entrance is on Calle 59 x 84, one block east of Itzáes, also has a back entrance accessible from the park. *(Open Tu-Su 9am-4pm. Admission 15 pesos. Su free.)*

OTHER SITES. Aging French-style mansions and local and international boutiques line the **Paseo de Montejo;** promenades along the Paseo's brick lay-ered sidewalks culminate in the **Monumento a la Patria.** In faux-Maya style, the stone monument, built from 1945 to 1956, depicts major figures of Mexican his-tory holding rifles and constitutions, alongside jaguars, chac-mools, and snakes. On the other side of the majestic monument, *Ceiba* (the Maya tree of life) stretches above a pool of water enclosed by individual Mexican States' coat of arms. For a tantalizing detour from the Paseo, veer left (southwest) onto **Av. Colón,** a street flanked by closely grouped historic mansions in varying stages of decay.

Mérida takes special pride in the **Teatro Peón Contreras,** on the corner of Calles 60 and 57. The beautiful Italian Renaissance-style building is notable for its marble Rococo interior and for its history; starting in 1624, it served as a university for nearly two centuries. The **Universidad Autónoma de Yucatán,** on Calle 57 x 60 y 62, is a Hispano-Moorish complex built in 1938. The ground floor contains a gallery exhibiting works by local artists and a screening room for a variety of films. *(Galería and video room open M-F 9am-1pm and 4-8pm, Sa 4-9pm, Su 10am-2pm. Free.)*

The many churches, statues, and pocket-sized parks scattered throughout Mérida's *centro* also invite exploration. Among the most noteworthy are the Franciscan **Convento de la Mejorada,** on Calle 59 x 48 y 50; the old **Arco** behind the park; the **Iglesia Santiago,** on Calles 59 x 72, one of the oldest churches in Mexico; and the **Iglesia de San Juan de Dios,** located on Calle 64 x 67 y 71, mark-ing the *centro's* southern limit.

SHOPPING

The fact that Mérida offers the best shopping in the Yucatán is both a boon and a curse. Nowhere is there such a variety of goods, and nowhere are there such nagging vendors and such high-pressure salespeople as in Mérida. If all those pesos you saved by cramming two into a hammock at night, riding dirty second-class buses, and eating stale tacos are starting to weigh you down, then this is the place to find relief. The main **mercado** occupies the block southwest of the Palacio Federal, spreading outward from the corner of Calles 65 and 58. Behind the *palacio*, shops, awnings, and tin-roofed shacks ramble for many blocks both east and west. The only border is the busy Calle 65 to the north, but even there, stands spill onto the other side of the street and around the square across from the Palacio Federal.

The pricier second-floor **artisans' market,** part of a modern building behind and to the right of the Palacio Federal, sells mainly regional clothing: white *huipiles* with colorful embroidery skirting the neckline and hem go for 250-350 pesos, *rebozos* (woven shawls) cost around 220 pesos, and *guayaberas* (Yucatec men's short-sleeve shirts with distinctive vertical columns of double stitching) are between 150 and 250 pesos. Try your hand at bargaining, but don't ruin the experience with excessive haggling. Cheaper goods such as *huaraches* (hand-made leather sandals) are sold on the first floor of the market. Try them and assure a good fit before you buy them. Although jewelry stores line the streets, the best prices are at the smaller *prestas* on the streets, in the market, or at the *zócalo* every Sunday.

🎵 **ENTERTAINMENT**

Mérida's municipal government provides a never-ending series of music and dance events organized by day. Mondays bring **outdoor concerts** with traditional Yucatec dancing and dress (9pm at Palacio Municipal). Tuesdays offer either a 1940s **big-band concert** (9pm at Santiago Park, Calles 59 x 72) or the University's **Ballet Folklórico** (9pm at Teatro Peón Contreras, Calles 60 x 57; 35 pesos). Wednesdays take you through a **musical journey** from the 18th century to the present (8pm at Ermita Park, Calles 66 x 77). Thursdays host **"The Serenade,"** the most historical event in Mérida, with music, poetry, and folklore (9pm at Calles 60 x 55). Saturdays host **Noche Mexicana** on the south side of Paseo de Montejo near Calle 45, a night of *mariachi* national dance performances and arts and crafts (8pm-midnight). Sundays bring **Mérida en Domingo,** when the *zócalo* and surrounding streets are crowded with vendors, strollers, food stalls, and live music (9am-8pm).

When in Mérida, do as *meridéños* do—keep your eyes peeled for announcements of upcoming events glued to walls around the *zócalo* and in the local magazine *Yucatán Today*, section "Mérida, ¿Que Hacer?" The **Teatro Peón Contreras** (tel. 23 73 54) hosts special events and frequent concerts. Just around the corner on the Parque de la Modernidad, an excellent acoustic guitar trio plays mellow tunes at the **Café Peón Contreras** (tel. 24 70 03). The cafe's pricey food can be avoided by enjoying the music for free from one of the park benches (nightly, 8pm-midnight). **Parque Hidalgo** has free **marimba concerts** each night; locals and tourists grab margaritas and some *botanas* (hors d'œuvres) at one of the many outdoor cafes and enjoy the cool evening breeze. **Cinema Fantasio,** at Parque Hidalgo, or **Plaza International,** on Calle 58 x 57 y 59 both offer American movies with Spanish subtitles for 14 pesos. (Evening showings daily around 7 and 9:30pm).

For a less high-brow evening, **drink a beer.** Mérida has many good local beers, such as the distinctive **Montejo León** and the darker **Negra Leon,** both tough to find in other parts of the country. Local establishments give free *botanas* after the purchase of a few beers. Live music and dance abounds at **Pancho's,** Calle 59 #509 x 60 y 62, (tel. 23 09 42; open M-Sa 6pm-3am), or **El Establo,** Calle 60 # 482 A x 55 y 57 (tel. 24 22 89) where young *meridéños* and tourists shoot pool, play table hockey, and dance under sombrero lamp shades (M-Th no cover, F-Su 30 pesos). Another option is **Tulipanes,** Calle 42 #462A x 45 y 47, for a chilling re-enactment of a Maya sacrifice in a sacred *cenote* (show 70 pesos, with dinner 100 pesos). Panchromatic discos with A/C are far from the center; a taxi ride will cost 50 pesos. **Vattya** in Hotel Fiesta Americana, Av. Colón x Calle 60, is where the young and trendy dance (open W-Sa 10pm-2am; cover 40-50 pesos).

NEAR MÉRIDA

DZIBILCHALTÚN

Saying the name is half the fun. Situated 20km north of Mérida en route to the Gulf coast, Dzibilchaltún (dzib-ill-shahl-TOON; Place Where There Is Writing on Stones) sprawls over 60 sq. km of jungle brush. The site flourished as a ceremonial and administrative center from approximately 300 BC until the Conquest. While its influence on Maya culture is of great interest to archaeologists and historians, the excavated site now houses a 300m "ecological path" with nearly 100 different species of birds and labeled plants.

The site also houses **El Museo del Pueblo Maya** which displays carved columns from Dzibilchaltún and Maya ceramics. The museum is the first building to the left of the entrance. The path leading to the museum is lined with an all-star gallery of Maya *stelae* with original sculptures from Chichén-Itzá and Uxmal awaiting to express history. Inside, the precious air-conditioning invites lengthy stays in front of the attractive and informative displays. All lingering questions about the Maya calendar and pantheon will be answered in the first main room, devoted to Maya history and artifacts; the second describes the arrival of the Spanish and the turbulent colonial era, complete with a glass floor that reveals an under-the-sea display.

From the museum, follow the path to **Sacbe No. 1,** the central axis of the site, and turn left. At the end of this road, Dzibilchaltún's showpiece, the fully restored **Temple of the Seven Dolls,** possesses a rare harmony of proportion and style. The seven clay "dolls" discovered in this temple are the same ones on display in the museum. The temple also furnishes further proof of the craftsmanship of the Maya. Shortly after sunrise, a huge shadow mask of the rain god Chac appears as the sun's rays pierce the temple during the spring and autumn equinox.

The other end of Sacbe No. 1 leads to a quadrangle containing a symbol of hundreds of years of history: a Maya temple converted into a chapel for Franciscan missionaries. Just beyond the eastern edge of the quadrangle is the **Cenote Xlacah,** reminiscent of Quintana Roo's oval, freshwater *lagunas*. Xlacah served as a sacrificial well similar to those at Chichén Itzá and as a source of water. Divers have recovered ceremonial artifacts and human bones from the depths of the 44m-deep *cenote*. While the *cenote* is not the most striking of its sort, the water invites a non-sacrificial dip among the water lilies, erect daises, and fishies. A path to the south leads past a handful of smaller structures to the site's exit.

Getting There: Getting to the ruins is a breeze, and the return trip should pose few, if any, problems. Conkal-bound *combis* leave the Parque de San Juan in Mérida as soon as they fill up (about every 30min., 4 pesos). The *combi* will drop you off at the access road to the ruins, a five-minute walk from the entrance. To get back, you'll need to walk back to the Conkal road and wait a short while for one of the many *combis* that run between Mérida and the string of villages past Conkal. Some travelers hitch the 5km to the highway. **Autoprogreso buses** and Mérida-bound *combis* abound on Rte. 261, passing by in both directions every 15 minutes. (Site open daily 8am-5pm. Museum open Tu-Su 8am-4pm. Open at 5:30am during the equinox. Admission 50 pesos, children under 13 and Su free. Parking 7 pesos.)

CELESTÚN

Celestún is an ideal vacation spot on the Gulf with seafood restaurants by the beach, inexpensive waterfront hotels, and pervasive *tranquilidad*. Many come for the warm shallow waters and refreshing breeze, but the main draw is the **Río Celestún Biosphere Reserve,** home to 200 species of birds, including pelicans, cormorants, the occasional stork, and hot pink flamingos. Mexican tourists and biologists flock here in July and August; call your hotel ahead to make sure there's room for you by the Gulf.

⁊ ORIENTATION AND PRACTICAL INFORMATION. Calle 11 in Celestún, on the western shore of the Yucatán, runs into Rte. 281 about 155km from Mérida. Calle 11 passes the *zócalo*, passes **Calle 12** one block later, and hits the **shore** one block after that (as do all odd-numbered streets). Odd numbers increase to the south, while even numbers decrease moving away from the sand and run parallel to the waves. The *zócalo* is bounded by Calles 11, 13, 10, and 8.

Autobuses de Occidente sends **buses** from a small booth at the corner of Calles 8 and 11, at the *zócalo*, to **Mérida** (2hr.; 12 per day 5am-8:30pm; first-class 30 pesos, second-class 20 pesos). **Police:** (tel. 6 20 15) stand guard at the Calle 13 side of the *zócalo*. **Farmacia Don San Luis:** Calle 10 #108 (tel. 6 20 02), between Calles 13 and 15 (open daily from 8am to 11pm). **Health center:** (tel. 6 20 46) on Calle 5 between Calles 8 and 10 (open daily 8am-8pm). **Post office:** on Calle 11 at the *zócalo* and shares a building with the **telegram** service (both open M-F 9am-2pm). Long-distance **phone** calls can be made from **Hotel Gutiérrez**, but be prepared for staggering rates. **Phone code:** 991.

⌨⌧ ACCOMODATIONS AND FOOD. Budget accommodations in Celestún are few but not far between—all are on Calle 12. The **Hotel San Julio,** Calle 12 #93A (tel. 6 20 62), faces a sand patio that opens onto the beach (rooms 100 pesos). **Hotel María del Carmen,** Calle 12 #11 (tel. 6 20 51), has golden rooms with sea views, balconies, and immaculate bathrooms (singles 150 pesos; doubles 200 pesos; triples 240 pesos; 10% student discount). **Hotel Gutiérrez,** Calle 12 #127 (tel. 6 20 41 or 6 20 42), between Calles 13 and 15, lets you fit as many as you like in the stucco rooms with aqua tiles (220 pesos; ask for a room with a view). Restaurants line Calle 12, both on and off the beach, and a few *loncherías* cluster in the *zócalo*. At **Restaurant La Playita,** Calle 12 #99 (tel. 6 20 52), between Calles 9 and 11, sumptuous steaming plates of *jaiba frita* (fried blue crab) with rice and tortillas go for 40 pesos (open daily 8am-8pm). Don't expect to see any pelicans (or much else) from the view at **Pelicano's,** Calle 12 #90 between Calles 9 and 11, but you will get to enjoy gulpfuls of good, cheap seafood such as fried fish (20 pesos) or a heaping plate of crab claws (50 pesos). At **Restaurant Celestún,** Calle 12 #101 (tel. 6 20 32), succulent fish *al mojo de ajo* (with garlic butter; 47 pesos) releases delicious aroma amid larger-and-pinker-than-life painted flamingos plus a beachfront breeze (open daily 10am-7pm).

◪ SIGHTS. Celestún's estuary houses thousands of pink flamingos along its breathtaking Gulf Coast, giving visitors two options. The first heads north to **Isla de Pájaros** (Island of Birds), an avian playground where the name says it all. A stop along the way at a freshwater spring provides welcome relief. The second tour heads south through petrified forests and a river tunnel of intertwined tree branches and vines before winding through the abandoned fishing village of **Real de Salinas.** Both tours can be arranged with *lancheros* at the bridge right before the entrance to the town (1½-2hr. tour 400 pesos). Depending on the tide, a tour will accommodate five to eight people. If you want to combine both tours or explore other areas, fishermen will give tours (3½hr., 550 pesos). Skulk around by the *lanchas* to find a ride and a group to go with, as most guides won't leave with fewer than five people. On Saturday nights, bands from Mérida perform in Celestún's *zócalo*.

MÉRIDA TO CHICHÉN ITZÁ

The route from Mérida to Chichén Itzá harbors small villages that are quintessential Yucatán. Churches are oversized and blackened by time; unexcavated ruins abound; *henequén* is still harvested; and for many inhabitants, Mayan is the primary language. As Rte. 180 heads east from Mérida to Chichén Itzá, it passes the five private *henequén* haciendas of San Pedro, Teya, Ticopó, San Bernardino, and Holactún. Next come the villages of **Tahmek** and **Hoctún** (45km from Mérida). **Iza-**

mal (see p. 606) is only 25km northeast of Hoctún, but buses don't make the detour—catch a direct bus from Mérida (see p. 596).

Back on Rte. 180, you will find **Kantunil** (68km from Mérida). Next is **Holcá, Libre Unión, Yoktzonot,** and finally **Piste.** During squabbles between the territories of Yucatán and Quintana Roo, Libre Unión found itself smack in the middle. The town voted to stick together and become part of the state of Yucatán—thus earning its name, Union of Liberty.

Few travelers hitch or hop buses from one Maya village to another along the busy road between Mérida and Chichén Itzá. Those who choose to hitch should bring water—the waits can be long, and shade is sparse. Second-class bus drivers stop anywhere if requested, but a new fare is charged for each trip, and slow and irregular bus service limits the number of places you can visit in one day. If dusk arrives, be sure to take the next bus to Pisté or Mérida—you don't want to get stranded. If buses are not in sight, there are *palapas* for sleeping in Xocchel and most other towns; ask in the town stores in the *zócalo*. Tourists planning to drive a car through the mesmerizing countryside will have an easier time and just as much of a chance to see small, rural villages, with their characteristic thatched huts, dirt roads, *triciclos*, running chickens, grazing cattle, and Coca-Cola stands.

PROGRESO

Progreso (pop. 40,000) holds the distinction of being the only non-sleepy fishing town on the Yucatán coast. Although the paved streets don't run far in any direction before turning into sand, that hasn't kept the residents from making a small fortune hauling in shrimp, red snapper, octopus, and tuna from the wind-swept waves. A different type of hauling brings in cars and other large goods while *henequén* is exported from Progreso's one long, oversized pier. On the weekends, Progreso's proximity to the capital makes it a popular retreat for *merideños*, many of whom make the 33km jaunt northward to enjoy the clean, sandy beaches of the Gulf Coast, and to add to the town's nightlife. During the week, Progreso reaches a measure of tranquility and is remarkably tourist-free.

🛈 **ORIENTATION AND PRACTICAL INFORMATION.** Calle 19, Progreso's turquoise **Malecón** (coastal avenue), runs east-west along the beach. Odd-numbered roads run parallel to Malecón, increasing to the south. North-south streets have even numbers and increase to the west. Progreso's *zócalo* is bounded by Calles 78, 80, 31, and 33. To reach the *zócalo* from the **bus station** (tel. 5 30 24), Calle 29, between Calles 80 and 82; head east on Calle 29 to the end of the block, turn right, and walk two blocks on Calle 80. To reach the beach, follow Calle 80 in the opposite direction.

Autoprogreso Buses, Calle 62, between Calle 65 and 67, run to Mérida's Autoprogreso station (40min., every 15min. 5am-9:45pm, 10 pesos). *Combis* make a slightly quicker trip for the same price and leave from Calle 31 on the *zócalo*. The bored but helpful staff of the **tourist office,** Calle 80 #176 (tel. 5 01 04), between Calles 37 and 39, provides tourist booklets and maps (open M-F 9am-2pm, Sa 9am-noon; some English spoken). **Banamex,** Calle 80 #126 (tel. 5 08 31), between Calles 27 and 29 (open M-F 9am-5pm with 24hr. **ATM**).

Lavamática Progreso: Calle 74 #150A (tel. 5 05 86), between Calles 29 and 31, provides next-day service (10 pesos per kg; open M-Sa 8am-1:30pm and 4:30-7:30pm). **Supermarket San Francisco de Asís:** at Calle 80 #144 between Calles 29 and 31 (open daily 7am-9pm). **Police station:** (tel. 5 00 26) in the Palacio Municipal on the *zócalo* at Calle 80, between Calles 31 and 33 (open 24hr.). **Farmacia YZA:** (tel. 5 06 84) on Calle 78 at Calle 29 #143 (open 24hr.). **Centro Médico Americano:** (tel. 5 01 18), at Calles 33 and 82 provides emergency medical assistance (open 24hr.; some English spoken). **Post office:** at Calle 31 #150 (tel. 5 05 65), between Calles 78 and 76 just off the *zócalo*, with **telegraph** service (open M-F 7am-7pm). **Postal code:** 97320. **Long-distance phone calls** can be made from the TelMex *casetas* found throughout town. **Phone code:** 993.

⌐ ACCOMMODATIONS. The frequently fluctuating number of vacationing urbanites from the south has made finding budget accommodations as hit or miss as the catch of the day. However, it's hard to go wrong at the **Hotel Miramar,** Calle 27 #124 (tel. 5 05 52), between Calles 74 and 76. The hotel offers spacious, classy rooms with neat bath and skylight or cool, fiberglass Apollo spacecraft rooms with capsule-sized bathrooms. (Moonshot singles 90 pesos, with TV 110 pesos; doubles 130 pesos, with TV 150 pesos; triples 160 pesos). The **Hotel Progreso,** in the center of town, Calle 78 #142 (tel. 5 00 39), near Calle 29, has designer rooms with upside down wine bottles (singles 130 pesos; doubles 140 pesos; with A/C add 40 pesos; extra person 40 pesos). **Hotel Real del Mar,** Av. Malecón #144 (tel. 5 07 98), at Calle 19, is more touristy but right on the beach. Simple but ample rooms come with firm beds, fans, and hammock space. (Singles 120 pesos; doubles 130 pesos; 35 pesos per extra person.)

⌐ FOOD. One fish. Two fish. Red fish. Blue fish. It's all about fish. And it's pretty darn cheap, too. **Pescado Frito** signs are on every corner especially at the beach end of Calle 80. Fish with a view? Try Av. Malecón, the main boulevard along the coast. At **Carabela** (tel. 5 33 07), just east of Calle 72 on Av. Malecón, the handwriting is on the wall; you may sign off too if you finish dishes like the *Super Taco Carabela* (25 pesos) or the *filete empanizado* (35 pesos; F-Sa dancing; open daily 7am-1am). Fish can be observed waddling in from the dock at **Restaurant Los Cocos,** on Malecón between Calles 76 and 78, where a fish served whole and practically still flopping around is ready to be consumed for just 25 pesos (open daily 7am-7pm). At **El Cordobés,** Calle 80 #150 (tel. 5 26 21), right on the *zócalo*, the real treat of *pescado en tikinxic*, a slow-cooked fish specialty with chiles is ready to satisfy the palette for 45 pesos. (Open daily 6am-midnight.)

⌐ SIGHTS. Progreso's kilometers of shallow water, beach boardwalk, and *palapas* attract hordes of visitors in August and remain calm in other months. For an even more placid spot, the beach at **Chelém,** 8km west of town, or the wind-sheltered beach at **Yaculpatén,** just before Chelém are both secluded, quiet areas. *Combis* leave for Chelém every 30 minutes from the parking lot outside Supermarket San Francisco on Calle 80 (8 pesos). If he's not too busy, the custodian of **El Faro** (the lighthouse), at Calle 80 near Calle 25, might let you climb the 120 bright red steps to the top. A step out on the balcony will reveal a view of the ocean and of kilometers of marshy river that give the city its distinctive briny scent. The 2km *muelle* (pier) clings tenuously to the sandy beach, making a great spot to reel in fish in the early morning.

If all that sunbathing and fishing has bored you enough to seek alternate adventures, the largely unexplored Maya site of **Xtambo,** at the end of a 2km access road that intersects with the road to Telchac Puerto 25km east of Progreso, is a fascinating trip. The small area that has just been restored includes two pyramids—one of which supports two large, unidentified stucco masks and offers a panoramic view of the coast—and several smaller structures. There is also the peculiar sight of a functional church built into the side of a pyramid. Many small paths branch out from the site to unexcavated ruins and small villages; the caretaker may be coaxed into acting as a guide. *Combis* headed to Telchac Puerto from Progreso leave the Supermarket San Francisco about every 30 minutes and will drop you off at the access road (15 pesos). *(Site open daily 9am-4pm. Free.)*

IZAMAL

This town (pop. 25,000) is called by several names, which reflects why a visit here is like a physical summary of the past millennia of Yucatán's history. Izamal, or "City of the Hills" in Mayan, is referred to today as the *Ciudad Amarilla* (the Yellow City) because all of its main buildings are painted in colonial yellow with white trim. Yet another name, *La Ciudad de las Tres Culturas* (City of the Three

Cultures), begins to fully describe what there is to be seen and learned in Izamal - a harmonious blend of Maya, Spanish, and Mestizo culture. Word is spreading about this place as enthusiastic residents show off their historical town, pyramids, and natural *cenotes*. The midday and evening tranquility is broken only by the occasional school-produced *ballet folklórico* and the clattering of the *Calesas Victorianas* (horse-drawn carriages) on the broad streets.

◪ ORIENTATION AND PRACTICAL INFORMATION. The road from Hoctún, 24km to the southwest, turns into Calle 31, which runs east-west as do all odd-numbered streets, increasing to the south. This street runs past the **Convent** (on the right going east), passing north-south streets with decreasing even numbers. Calles 28, 31, 32, and 33 frame the town's *zócalo*, municipal palace, and market. The **bus station** is halfway between Calles 31 and 33 on Calle 32, right behind the municipal palace. ADO buses (tel. 4 01 97) leave from the terminal for: **Cancún** (5½hr., 5 per day 5:30am-5pm, 60 pesos); **Mérida** (1½hr., 20 per day 4:45am-7:45pm, 16 pesos); and **Valladolid** (2½hr., 8 per day, 25 pesos). Next door, the Autobuses de Centro del Estado sends a bus to: **Cancún** (5½hr., every 2hr., 46 pesos); **Mérida** (1½hr., every 30min., 11 pesos); and **Valladolid** (2½hr., every 2hr., 17 pesos).

The singularly staffed **tourist office** (tel. 4 00 09), on the corner of Calles 32 and 33, will go out of its way to provide maps, pamphlets, and anything and everything there is to know about the Convent across the street (office open M-Sa 8am-10pm). **Banterers:** on Calle 31 between Calles 26 and 28 changes money (open M-F 9am-5pm). **Police:** directly across from the bus station in the Palacio Municipal (open 24hr.). **Mercado:** on the corner of Calles 30 and 33, offers all sorts of food; it also has **public restrooms. 24hr. Farmacia Itzalam:** (tel. 4 00 32), on the corner of Calles 31 and 32; knock on the door if it looks closed. **IMSS:** (tel. 4 02 41) provides 24-hour **medical attention,** two blocks south and three blocks east of the *zócalo* on the corner of Calles 37 and 24. **Post office:** on Calle 31 between Calles 30 and 32 (open M-F 9am-1:30pm). **Telegram and fax services:** on the corner of Calles 31 and 32 (open M-F 9am-3:30pm). **LADATEL's** can be found outside the bus station and the post office. **Phone code:** 995.

▐▐ ACCOMMODATIONS AND FOOD. In Izamal, the cheapest places to stay are on the *zócalo*, while the nicer and more expensive hotels are farther away. The **Hotel Canto,** on Calle 31 between Calles 30 and 32, has old blue rooms with a ceiling fan for a bargain (singles 60 pesos; doubles 70 pesos; fit 4-5 to a room at no extra charge). The **Hotel Kabul,** next door, nestles right up to the Kabul pyramid and has fans and hammock hooks (singles 70 pesos; doubles 80 pesos).

Don't plan on too much late-night wining and dining in the Yellow City, as most restaurants close in the early evening, but at least a plentiful meal in Izamal won't cost much. **Restaurant Kinich Kakmó,** Calle 27 #299 (tel. 4 04 84), between Calles 28 and 30, serves regional dishes under a plant-ensconced *palapa* for 35-45 pesos and is an excellent conclusion to an exhaustive search of the pyramid 50m away (open M-F 11:30am-6pm; Sa-Su 8am-noon). **Restaurant Portales,** on the corner of Calles 30 and 31A next door to the market, has the best view of the *zócalo* but the cheap, filling meals are more likely to hold your attention (full breakfasts and lunches 18-25 pesos; open Th-Tu 7am-9pm).

▣ SIGHTS. Upon entering the *zócalo* **El Convento de San Antonio de Padua** (Convent of Saint Anthony of Padua) is the most dominating feature of Izamal. This ecclesiastical complex, dedicated to San Antonio, is actually made up of three parts: the **church,** built in 1554; the **convent,** built in 1561; and the immense **atrium,** built in 1618 with 75 arches and second in size only to the Vatican. When entering the church through the atrium after passing a statue of the Pope, several original 16th-century frescoes can be seen on the church's facade; the one dedicated to Santa Barbara is today the most colorful and complete. Inside the Baroque-style church is an ornate altar with a doorway at the top. Izamal's famed statue of the

Immaculate Conception is wheeled out for every Mass. To see the statue and some interesting rooms, head out the left side doors of the church; a flight of stairs to the right will bring you to a room exhibiting pictures and momentos of the Pope's August 1993 visit to Izamal, including the chair he used in the ceremony to officially crown the statue. There is also a showcase of pre-Hispanic artifacts and curious knobs on the wall, used when this room was Izamal's electrical plant. Continue up the stairs to arrive at Mexico's oldest 16th-century *camarin*, where the statue of the Immaculate Conception rests when not in use. Fray Diego de Landa commissioned this statue in 1558 in Guatemala.

There were originally two statues, one of which was sent to Mérida and the other to Izamal. They were called *Las Dos Hermanas*, but in 1829. Izamal's statue was burned in a fire, so Mérida's copy was brought here. It is said, that Izamal's original was saved and taken to the nearby pyramid of **Kinish Kakmó** and every December 8th, at the climax of the town's week-long fiesta, the two switch places in *El Paso de las Dos Hermanas*. Dozens of other legends surround Izamal, more of which can be learned in Izamal's small **museum,** located on the northeast corner of the convent and still inhabited by four monks (note the original sundial above the courtyard). The guides at the foot of the convent will also be more than happy to regale you with stories. The museum details Izamal's three phases of history and has a model of the ancient Maya city as it stood in 500 BC. (Open M-F 9am-3pm. Free.)

It is not until after ascending the **pyramid of Kinich Kakmó** that visitors can appreciate what truly is Izamal's most dominating structure. This massive pyramid, measuring 200m by 180m, is the fifth-tallest and ranks third in volume of all of Yucatán's pyramids, yet even it was outclassed by the **Pap-hol-chac,** the largest pyramid in ancient Izamal, whose remains lie under the convent. Kinich Kakmó (Temple of the Fire Macaw) was built during the Early Classic period from 400 to 600 and is only one of the remaining pyramids that dot Izamal, along with **Kabul, Itzama'Itul, Chal-Tun-Ha,** and **Habuc.** Kinich Kakmó is the most fully restored, though, and offers an awe-inspiring view of Izamal's churches and pyramids as well as the flat Yucatec countryside. (Open daily 8am-5pm.)

CHICHÉN ITZÁ

The faultless architecture and sheer size of the structures of this former Maya capital allow Chichén Itzá (chee-CHEN eet-SAH) to serve as a window to the past on a grand scale. One of Yucatán's premier cultural attractions, the site attracts thousands of visitors hoping to witness and understand the mysteries of this ancient city. Complete with a peculiar mix of Maya and Toltec styles of architecture, the structures inspire endless questions while evoking awed responses to the skill and calculated creativity in the construction of the Maya people. Unfortunately, Chichén becomes a writhing mass of foreign invaders; tour buses bombard the site, and camera-toting travelers take over the ruins, photographing every last *chac-mool*, jaguar, and eagle sculpture.

Despite the hype, the camera crews, and the trash cans, Chichén rightly deserves its status as one of Mexico's most powerful tourist magnets. **El Castillo** is breathtaking from the bottom and harrowing from the top; the **ballcourt** features elaborate carvings and solid rings; the sacred stone *cenote* has yielded enough bones and artifacts to reconstruct the fates of hundreds of human victims; and the observatory attests to a level of astronomical understanding far beyond that of Old World contemporaries. During the equinoxes, March 21 and September 22, busloads of people arrive to watch a serpentine shadow slither down the steps of El Castillo, matching the serpent heads at the base of the stairway. A visit to Chichén might be the pinnacle of any Yucatán experience—and should not be missed.

◪ ORIENTATION AND PRACTICAL INFORMATION. The ruins of Chichén Itzá lie 1.5km from **Rte. 180,** the highway running from Mérida (119km west) through Valladolid (42km east) to Cancún (200km east). As nearly every travel agency in

Mexico pushes a Chichén Itzá package, the ruins tend to get overpopulated around 11am. In order to avoid the stampede, use nearby **Pisté** (2.5km west of the ruins) as a base and get an early start, or visit late in the afternoon and head back to Pisté at nightfall.

Getting to the ruins is easy. If you would rather skip the 20-minute walk from Pisté, catch a taxi (25 pesos) or flag down any eastbound bus (approximately every 30min., 5 pesos). As with all Mexican buses, a vigorous, supplicatory wave to the driver gets you on the road. To get to Chichén Itzá from other towns, see bus listings for Mérida (see p. 582), Cancún (see p. 622), and Valladolid (see p. 615). To head back to Pisté after a day at the ruins, hang out in the bus parking lot until a taxi or bus swings by (every 45min.). Pisté's **bus station** (tel. 1 00 52) is near the Stardust Inn on the eastern side of town. Buses leave to: **Cancún** (1st class 2½hr., 5:30pm, 50 pesos; 2nd class 4hr., 7 per day, 42 pesos); **Mérida** (1st class 1½hr., 3pm, 38 pesos; 2nd class 2hr., 10 per day, 25 pesos); **Playa del Carmen** (5hr., 1 and 3pm, 60 pesos); and **Valladolid** (1hr., 7 per day, 15 pesos). Services at the site are located in the stone edifice at the site's western entrance. Across from the ticket counter is a small **information booth**. The booth often provides free **luggage storage** (open daily 8am-5pm). The Centro Telefónico (tel. 1 00 89) also exchanges **currency**. There are also restrooms, a restaurant, an ice cream parlor, a gift shop (which accepts U.S. dollars), a bookstore with guidebooks, an auditorium showing documentaries about Maya ruins, and a small museum. **Parking** is available right at the site (parking 15 pesos; open daily 8am-9pm).

A single **police** officer sits at a desk in the *comisario* on the eastern side of Pisté's *zócalo*. **Farmacia Isis:** Calle 15 #53, a short way past the *zócalo* toward the ruins (open daily 8am-9pm). **Medical emergencies: Clínica Promesa,** Calle 14 #50 (tel. 6 31 98, ext. 198), in the blue-green building past the *zócalo* and 100m off Rte. 180 (open 24hr.). **Post office:** in a small gray building near the *zócalo* across from Abarrotes "El Alba" (open M-F 9am-3pm). **Caseta:** (tel. 1 01 24) right around the corner from the ticket counter. **Telephones: Centro Telefónico** and **Teléfonos de México** (tel. 1 00 58 or 1 00 59) let you phone home (open daily 9am-9pm). **LADATEL's** can be found along Rte. 180. **Phone code:** 985.

⌐ ACCOMMODATIONS. Even though some luxury hotels have taken a corner of Chichén Itzá, they haven't cornered the market. Plenty of economical lodging awaits in Pisté. All of the places listed below can be found either on or just off Rte. 180, which doubles as the town's main road. At the other end of the spectrum is the **Posada Olalde** (tel. 1 00 86). To find it, take a left off Rte. 180 directly across from the Carrousel Restaurant and continue to walk two blocks down the dirt road. The large, decorated rooms in the main house and the four spotless rooms with *palapa* roofs off the intimate courtyard make the Posada a pleasant stay. During the low season, you can try asking for something *más económico*. (Singles 120 pesos; doubles 160 pesos; triples 210 pesos; 30 pesos per extra person.) Nearby **Hotel El Paso,** Calle 15 #48, offers similar rooms. Bouncy beds make for good jumping games and small windows ensure that no one falls out. (Singles and doubles 100 pesos; 30 pesos per extra person). The attached restaurant offers a well-priced *menú del día* (25 pesos).

⌐ FOOD. Those that are too engrossed with the ruins to think about a meal while on a daytrip to Chichén Itzá are lucky, 'cause few are the options. The air-conditioning at the on-site **restaurant** isn't free; it's paid for through a combination of high prices and small servings (dishes 45-60 pesos with a regional musical and dance performance). Picnickers can save a few pesos by packing a lunch from one of the **small grocers** that line Calle 15 in Pisté. For those determined to save *dinero*, Pisté's main road is lined with small restaurants offering cheap and savory *comida yucateca*. **El Carrousel** (tel. 1 00 78) serves three simple meals a day. Start a long, hot day right with eggs any style (20 pesos) or enchiladas (25 pesos; open daily 7am-10pm). **Restaurant Sayil,** between El Carrousel and the Stardust Inn, has a quiet corner where you can refuel on *pollo pibil* (20 pesos; open daily 7am-10pm). **Restaurant Poxil** (tel. 1 01 16), on the right just past the *zócalo*, is a bigger joint for bigger crowds with bigger dishes of *comida típica* for 40 pesos (open daily 8am-9pm).

THE ARCHAEOLOGICAL SITE OF CHICHÉN ITZÁ

HISTORY. As the Mayan name Chichén Itzá (Mouth of the Well of the Itzás) implies, the area's earliest inhabitants were drawn here by the two nearby freshwater *cenotes* (an underground cavern filled with freshwater). The ritual offerings that were thrown into the three *cenotes*, including pottery, jade, and gold, have provided the basis for archaeologists' theories on the lives of Chichén's previous residents. Later periods in Chichén Itzá's history are illuminated by the **Books of Chilam Balam,** written shortly after initial contact with the Europeans in the 15th century. They describe the construction of many buildings visible today, focusing on the period between 500 and 800, when construction was purely Maya.

For reasons that are still unclear, Chichén lost many of its residents and its political power after reaching its peak from 900 to 1100. There is still much contention on what happened next. A dwindling group of experts adheres to the traditional view (found on most markers) that sometime before 1000, the Toltec tribes of Tula infiltrated the Yucatán and overcame peaceful Maya settlements, bringing with them the cult of the plumed serpent Quetzalcóatl (Kukulcán in Mayan). The more widely accepted view, however, is that Chichén Itzá was a vital crossroads of trade and ideas, and eventually adopted many Toltec practices. Toltec influence is seen in Chichen Itza's symbol, the *chac-mool*, a reclining figure with its head turned sideways holding forth a plate between his hands, awaiting an offering or a sacrifice. In 1461, Chichén Itzá was abandoned by its inhabitants due to a tumultuous war, but religious pilgrimages to the site continued well after Spanish conquest. Today, the relentless flow of tourists ensures that Chichén will never again stand in solitude.

For an even more comprehensive (not to mention air-conditioned) understanding of Chichén and its people, visit the **Centro Cultural Cecijema,** Calle 15 #45 (tel. 1 00 04), in Pisté. The gray building houses a small selection of Maya ceramic replicas as well as attractive rotating exhibits. (Open daily 8am-5pm. Free.)

INFORMATION ABOUT THE RUINS. From the main parking lot and visitors center, the first group of **ruins** is up the gravel path and to the left. A small **museum** in the **visitor's complex** at the entrance to the site recaps the history of Chichén Itzá and displays some sculptures and objects removed from the **Sacred Cenote.** Its **auditorium** screens documentaries about the ruins in Spanish and in English (The entire site of Chichén Itzá open daily 8am-5pm. Admission 50 pesos; Su free. Documentary showtimes vary. Museum and auditorium open daily 8am-5pm. Free.)

Free maps are available at the telephone desk around the corner from the ticket counter. You'll need a guide to decipher some of the symbolism of the ruins or to hear some of the more intriguing, if not totally substantiated, interpretations of the site. Guided tours begin at the entrance. (Spanish, English, or other languages 1½hr., 6-8 people, 300-400 pesos per person depending on the language and duration. Private guides, 2hr., up to 20 people, 400 pesos.)

GUIDE TO THE RUINS. The first sight to meet your eyes is **El Castillo,** Chichén's hallmark (also known as the Pyramid of Kukulcán). This majestic ruin in the shape of a pyramid, built in honor of Kukulcán. It rises in perfect symmetry from the neatly cropped lawn, culminating in a temple supported by pillars in the form of serpents. El Castillo stands as tangible evidence of the astounding astral understanding of the ancient Maya: the 91 steps on each of the four faces, plus the upper platform, total 365 (one for each day of a non-leap year); the 52 panels on the nine terraced levels equal the number of years in a Maya calendar cycle; and each face of the nine terraces is divided by a staircase, yielding 18 sections representing the

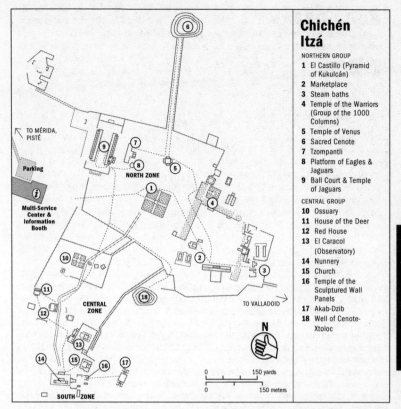

Chichén Itzá

NORTHERN GROUP
1. El Castillo (Pyramid of Kukulcán)
2. Marketplace
3. Steam baths
4. Temple of the Warriors (Group of the 1000 Columns)
5. Temple of Venus
6. Sacred Cenote
7. Tzompantli
8. Platform of Eagles & Jaguars
9. Ball Court & Temple of Jaguars

CENTRAL GROUP
10. Ossuary
11. House of the Deer
12. Red House
13. El Caracol (Observatory)
14. Nunnery
15. Church
16. Temple of the Sculptured Wall Panels
17. Akab-Dzib
18. Well of Cenote-Xtoloc

TO MÉRIDA, PISTÉ

Parking

Multi-Service Center & Information Booth

NORTH ZONE

CENTRAL ZONE

TO VALLADOID

SOUTH ZONE

N

0   150 yards
0   150 meters

YUCATÁN PENINSULA

18 Maya months. Even more impressive is the precise alignment of El Castillo's axes, which, in coordination with the sun and the moon, produce a bi-annual optical illusion. At sunrise during the spring and fall equinoxes, the rounded terraces cast a **serpentine shadow** down the side of the northern staircase. The sculpted serpent head at the bottom of the staircase completes the illusion. A light-and-shadow lunar serpent-god, identical to that of the equinoxes, creeps down the pyramid at the dawn of the full moon following each of the equinoxes. People from all over the world converge on Chichén to see this incredible phenomenon.

Climbing El Castillo is easier than coming down; many tourists descend on their behinds while others hold onto the sturdy rope along the center of the staircase. That sight might elicit a chuckle, but the ambulance parked at El Castillo each day will sober you a bit. Nestled within El Castillo is an early **jaguar temple** that can be entered at the bottom of the north staircase on the western side. (After climbing up steps whose walls sweat as much as you do, you'll be grimacing like the *chac mool* located in the ceremonial chamber. Behind the chamber is a fanged, molding jaguar throne with jade eyes. To the left of the entrance lies the **ballcourt.** The enormous "I"-shaped playing field is bounded by two high, parallel walls with a temple at each end. The **largest ballcourt in Mesoamerica,** it also has an amazing side-to-side echo that repeats seven times in the center. The elaborate game, called **pok-ta-pok,** fascinated the Spanish so much that Cortéz took two entire teams back to Europe in 1528 to perform before the royal court. After that, European ball games replaced their wooden balls with rubber ones. (El Castillo open daily 11am-3pm and 4-5pm. Free.)

HOOP DREAMS The great ballcourts found at Chichén Itzá and other Maya cities once witnessed an impressive game called **pok-ta-pok,** in which two contending teams endeavored to keep a heavy rubber ball (3-5kg) in constant motion by using only their hips, knees, shoulders, and elbows. Players scored by knocking the ball through small stone rings placed high on the court's side walls. The ballgame was much more than a cultural pastime for the Maya; it was symbolic of both a battle between good and evil and a way to keep the celestial bodies in motion (the ball represented the sun; its constant movement through the game symbolized the constant movement of the sun through the heavens). According to the *Popol Vuh* (a 16th-century account of creation by the Quiché Maya), the god of corn (Hun Hunahpu) was decapitated; his head was planted in the ground and became the seed of all corn plants. Magically impregnating a woman by spitting in her pocket, he fathered twin sons, Xbalanque and Hunahpú, who became avid ball players. Infuriated by the noise of the ball bouncing above them, the lords of Xibalba (the underworld) coerced the two into descending to Xilbalba for a ballgame, using the contest as a pretense to kill the brothers. Through their own trickery, however, the twins prevailed, defeating and decapitating the gods—showing the conquest of good over evil. Because of this myth, the Maya believed they were made from corn and continued to play the game in homage to their creators. But pok-ta-pok is not simply a game of skill and diversion: some players were decapitated as offerings to the gods.

A short distance from the ballcourt toward the grassy open area is the **Tzompantli,** Náhuatl for "Platform of the Skulls." When the Spaniards conquered the Aztecs, they were shocked to find ritualized human sacrifice and horrified by the racks in Tenochtitlán designed to display the skulls of the sacrificed. Chichén's Toltec-designed structure served a similar macabre purpose. Today, eerie columns of bas-relief skulls decorate the low platform's walls. Next to the Tzompantli stands the **Platform of Jaguars and Eagles,** named after the *guerreros* (warriors) who were ordered to kidnap prisoners from other tribes for human sacrifices for their gods. To either side of the feathered serpent heads on the balustrades, reliefs of jaguars and eagles vividly clutch human hearts in their claws. To the right of the platform is the **Temple of Venus,** decorated with a feathered serpent holding a human head in its mouth. The temple's reliefs symbolize stars and give information on their motion.

The dirt path leading directly north from El Castillo, over the ancient Maya roadway, links the ceremonial plaza to Chichén Itzá's most important religious center, the **Sacred Cenote,** 300m away. The roughly circular, 60m-wide subterranean pool of water induced vertigo in the sacrificial victims perched on the platform before their 25m plunge into the murky depths. The rain god Chac was believed to dwell beneath the water's surface and would request frequent gifts to grant good rains. Human remains recovered by divers suggest that children and young men were the victims of choice. If they could keep afloat until noon, they were fished out and forced to tell what they had witnessed during the ordeal.

Heading back into the central plaza from the Sacred Cenote, on the left, the **Temple of the Warriors** and the **Group of the Thousand Columns** present an impressive array of elaborately carved columns that at one time supported a roof of some perishable material. On the temple itself (not open to the public), in front of two great feathered serpents and several sculpted animal gods, reclines one of Chichén's best-preserved *chac mools*. The ornamentation of this building has much Toltec influence; a nearly identical structure stands at Tula, the Toltec capital far to the west. The Temple of the Warriors marks the end of Chichén's restored monuments and the beginning of an overgrown area extending to the far southeast of El Castillo. This corner houses the **Temple of the Sculptured Columns,** the back of which hides a couple of beady-eyed masks of Chac. The rest of the quadrangle is comprised of the **Southeastern Colonnade,** the **market** and its courtyard, and the expansive **Western Colonnade.**

A red dirt path on the south side of El Castillo leads to the less photogenic **South Group** of ruins. Beyond the cafeteria and bathrooms, the first pyramid on the right is the **Ossuary,** or **High Priest's Grave.** Its distinctive serpent heads mimic El Castillo. A natural cave extends from within the pyramid 15m into the earth. The human bones and votive offerings found in this cavern are thought to have belonged to an ancient high priest. Past the Ossuary, the road forks, presenting two routes to the second set of ruins in the South Group, often missed by tourists but well worth the visit. The most interesting structure in this group is the **Observatory,** the large circular building on the left-hand side, one of the few circular structures built by the Mayas. This ancient planetarium consists of two rectangular platforms with large, west-facing staircases and two circular towers. Because of the tower's interior spiral staircase (not open to the public), this structure is often called **El Caracol** (The Snail). The slits in the dome of the observatory can be aligned with the important celestial bodies and cardinal directions. El Caracol was built in several stages and layers by Maya builders. Notice the small red handprints on the wall of the building just as you come up the stairs. These were supposedly the hands of the sun god Kinich Ahau. Walking to the left of El Caracol toward the Nunnery at the other end of the clearing, you will pass a tiny, ruined **sauna** and the **Temple of the Sculptured Wall Panels** behind it. Though difficult to decipher, the panels on the exterior walls contain emblems of warriors—jaguars, eagles, and serpents—in three rows.

The largest structure in this part of Chichén is the misnamed **Nunnery,** located on the south side of the quadrangle. Although it was probably a Maya royal palace, its stone rooms reminded Spaniards of a European convent. After several superimpositions and some decay, the building is now almost 20m high on a base 65m long and 35m wide. Above the entrance on the right side of the building, you can still see Maya glyphs. Also on the right side is the **Annex** which predates the rest of the nunnery. Above the doorway facing the small courtyard is a spectacular bas-relief of a seated royal-divine figure. Grab a flashlight and go exploring—many rooms in the nunnery have doorways that lead to dark corridors, home to bats and frogs.

For similar reasons, the elaborate building diagonally across from the nunnery and annex is misnamed the **Church.** Its upper, almost top-heavy walls are encrusted with intricate masks of the hook-nosed Chac. The church is remarkable for its fusion of cultural styles: over the doorway are Maya stone **lintels,** while the use of wood and inclined edges is evidence of Toltec influence. Above the door are representations of the four **bacabs** that hold up the sky at four cardinal points represented by a crab, a turtle, an armadillo, and a snail.

A rocky path runs about 60m east from the nunnery group, past the church to the 18-room **Akab-Dzib** (hidden writing). The oldest parts of this structure are believed to be Chichén's most ancient constructions from the Early Classic Period. The two central rooms date to the 2nd or 3rd century, while the annexes on either side and to the east were added later. Inside the rooms, it is possible, to make out the small, rose-red handprints of Kinich Ahau on the ceiling. The overgrown **Cenote Xtoloc** hides behind the South Group ticket office. To reach it from the office, take the first left 20m into the site. The *cenote* is in the hollow, beyond the small, ruined temple of Xtoloc, dedicated to the eponymous lizard god. There is no path down the steep slope through the undergrowth, and swimming is prohibited because of the dangerous underwater currents. A counterpart to the holy waters of the sacred *cenote*, this pool at one time provided all of Chichén with secular drinking water. Follow **Sacbe No. 5** (road path), which becomes a narrow, winding trail, to get to the back of the observatory.

As if Chichén Itzá couldn't muster enough daytime spectacle, those green panels (whose purpose you've been contemplating all day) pop open for the evening **light and sound show.** The buildings are splashed in red, blue, green, and yellow lights while booming voices detail the history of the site. If you trust your bug repellent, the nighttime stroll from Pisté is quiet and well-lit; otherwise grab a cab for 20 pesos each way. (Spanish version daily 7pm; 17 pesos. English version daily at 9pm; 35 pesos.)

YUCATÁN PENINSULA

CHICHÉN VIEJO

Not many visitors to Chichén Itzá know that another, adjacent site exists, and even fewer bother to visit. Those who do go can enjoy the solitude in which these ruins rise out of the jungle, punctuated by the calls of many birds. Beginning about 1km south of the Nunnery and spreading out southwest of the main site, Chichén Viejo is so named because it was originally thought to be the minor ruins of the first inhabitants of Chichén Itzá. Recent work done at the site, though, suggests that it was probably inhabited around the same time as the rest of the city. Most of the ruins are unrestored, and are scattered throughout the jungle. The **Group of the Initial Series** and the **Phallic Cluster,** the first set of ruins in Chichén Viejo, are easy enough to find on your own. Follow the dirt road (simply marked with arrows) to the right of the Nunnery past the intersection of other dirt paths to a deep well (keep a mental note of the right crossings for the return back home). Shortly beyond the well, a right at the T-junction brings you to the cluster, set in a clearing. Chichén Viejo carries the only dated inscriptions at Chichén Itzá, one of which can be clearly seen on the only remaining lintel of the **Temple of the Initial Series. The Temple of the Four Lintels,** upheld by two columns, features a hieroglyphic inscription corresponding to July 13, 878. The rest of the temple stands in ruin. The main features of the appropriately named Phallic Cluster protrude from the interior walls of the temple, while nine warriors stand watch in the courtyard.

The remaining ruins at Chichén Viejo, reached by taking the path to the right of the **House of the Phalli,** following the rusted cart tracks, and then cutting through the bushes, are best located with the help of a guide. Official guides will charge you almost as much to get to Viejo as they would for a tour of the main site. Unlicensed guides can be very knowledgeable, although few speak English. In the **Principal Group of the Southwest,** glyphs depict the Maya practice of compressing children's foreheads with stone plates—conically shaped heads were considered beautiful, as were crossed eyes and precious stones embedded in the flesh of the face. The Principal Group contains a magnificent **ruined pyramid,** the restored **Temple of the Three Lintels** (dating to 879 AD), and the **Jaguar Temple,** where a handful of columns salute the ancient military order of the Jaguars.

NEAR CHICHÉN ITZÁ

GRUTAS DE BALANCANCHÉN

The inner caves of the **Grutas de Balancanchén** were only re-discovered in 1959 when a local amateur speleologist noticed a passageway blocked with stones. Further exploration opened 300m of caves filled with stalactites carved to resemble leaves on the ceiling and a huge tree-like column, which came to represent the sacred *ceiba* tree, surrounded by dozens of votive vessels with ghoulish masks. Archaeologists have come to believe that the cave was a center for Maya-Toltec worship of the gods Chac, Tlaloc (the Toltec rain god), and Kukulcán (Quetzalcóatl) during the 10th and 11th centuries. For unknown reasons, subterranean worship in Balancanchén stopped at the end of this period, and the offerings of ceramic vessels and stone sculptures rested undisturbed for nine centuries. The impressive **stalactites** and the plethora of **ceramic offerings** definitely merit a visit, but be prepared for an almost incomprehensible Disney-esque tour which dramatizes the cave's history through a series of hidden speakers. A guide, available for questions, paces the group through the chambers along the 1km path. Self-guided tours are not permitted, and you'll need at least two people to start a tour.

Getting There: Located 5km east of Chichén Itzá and 2km past the Dolores Alba Hotel, the caves are easily reached from Chichén or Pisté by hopping on any bus traveling east on Rte. 180 (5 pesos). When you board, be sure to ask the driver to stop there. To get back, catch any westbound bus, but be prepared to wait a while for one. (Tours in Spanish, daily at noon, 2, and 4pm; in English at 9, 11am, 1, and 3pm; and in French at 10am.)

YAXUNÁ

Yaxuná, 30km southeast of Chichén Itzá, is home to the ruins of yet another ancient Maya city. The temple was built by the Maya of Cobá, who were planning to declare war on the people of Chichén. A 100km *sacbe*, the **longest in the peninsula,** linked Yaxuná and Cobá. To keep a close eye on their enemy, the Maya of Cobá aligned their temple with El Castillo.

Getting There: There is no public transportation to Yaxuná, but it's possible to hire a taxi in Pisté (about 150 pesos round-trip; arrange for your driver to wait for you and ask to stop at the *cenotes* and caves between Chichén and Yaxuná). Road conditions are incredibly poor; the trip is only possible during the dry season. The easiest route is to take Rte. 180 to Libre Unión and then left to **Yaxcaba,** a small town with a fascinating history of its own; the Caste War started here in 1847, and the remains of some of those killed lie in the three-towered church, the only one of its kind. The town is 17km down the road from Chichén and 8km from Yaxuná.

VALLADOLID

Valladolid, (pop. 70,000) is the second largest and second oldest city of the Yucatán state after Mérida. The colonial city is paved with cobblestone and studded with French-style love seats, overshadowed by the Franciscan cathedral and ex-convent. Although this city was one of the first Spanish settlements in the Yucatán, Valladolid still preserves a Maya way of life. Mayan dialects may be heard in the food market, between vendors on the street corners, among *indígena* women weaving *huipiles* (white dresses embroidered with colorful flowers across the chest and lower hem) along the *zócalo* and around the city's archaeological sites and natural *cenotes*.

✴ ORIENTATION

Traversed by Rte. 180, Valladolid lies in the heart of the Yucatán state midway between Mérida and Cancún. Even-numbered streets run north-south, increasing westward. Odd-numbered streets run east-west, increasing to the south. The *centro* is bordered by Calles 27, 53, 28, and 60 except for **Cenote X'keken,** in the nearby village of **Dzitnup.** Everything lies within comfortable walking distance from the *zócalo* (circumscribed by Calles 39, 40, 41, and 42). To get to the *zócalo* from the bus station, take a taxi (10 pesos) or walk one block south on Calle 54 to Calle 39. Turn left (east) and follow Calle 39 for six blocks. Or better yet, get off before the bus station at the *zócalo* (look for a big twin-towered cathedral; you can't miss it).

🛈 PRACTICAL INFORMATION

TRANSPORTATION

Buses: Stations on Calle 54 at 37 and Calle 39 at 46. ADO (tel. 6 34 49), on Calle 37 at Calle 54 sends buses to: **Cancún** (2 hr., 7 per day, 58 pesos); **Chichén Itzá** (1hr., 10 per day, 17 pesos); **Mérida** (2½ hr., 9 per day, 50 pesos); **Playa del Carmen** (2½hr., 7 per day, 44 pesos); **Tizimín** (1hr., every hr., 11 pesos); and **Izamal** (1½hr., 2 per day, 26 pesos). To reach **Tinum,** buy a ticket on a Izamal/Mérida-bound bus and ask the driver to drop you off (30min., 8 pesos).

TOURIST AND FINANCIAL SERVICES

Tourist Information: The *ayuntamiento* (city hall, tel. 6 20 63), on the corner of Calles 40 and 41, provides information (open M-Sa 8am-9pm). Historical murals upstairs delineate the Spanish conquest of the Maya (open M-Sa 9am-1pm and 6-9pm).

Currency Exchange: Bancomer (tel. 6 21 50), on the Calle 40 side of the *zócalo* has a 24hr. **ATM** next door. Open M-F 9am-4:30pm, Sa 10am-2pm.

LOCAL SERVICES

Market: The freshest, cheapest fruits and vegetables are in the market 5 blocks northeast of the *zócalo*, bordered by Calles 30, 32, 35, and 37. Get there early for the best picks. Open daily 6am-1pm.

Laundry: Lavandería Teresita (tel. 6 23 93), Calle 33 at 42, self-service 10 pesos for 3kg; full service 7 pesos per kg. Open daily 7am-7pm.

EMERGENCY AND COMMUNICATIONS

Emergency: dial 060.

Police: (tel. 6 21 00) Calle 41, 10 blocks east of the *zócalo*.

Pharmacy: El Descuento (tel. 6 26 44), Calle 42 at 39, on the northwest corner of the *zócalo*, is a 24hr. pharmacy.

Hospital: Hospital S.S.A. (tel. 6 28 83), on Calle 41, 2 blocks west of the *zócalo*, and 5 blocks southwest on Calle 41A.

Post Office: (tel. 6 26 23) on the Calle 40 side of the *zócalo*. Open M-F 9am-2pm. **Postal Code:** 97780.

Internet Access: Internet del Oriente (tel. 6 12 92 or 6 12 95; email orinet@orinet.valladolid.net.mx; www.valladolid.net.mx), 4 blocks west of the *zócalo* in the Super Maz Bazar on Calle 39. 30 pesos for 30min. Open M-F 9am-1pm and 5-9:30pm, Sa-Su 9am-1pm. **Cibercafe and Video Club** (tel. 6 15 25, email bore@chichen.com.mx), 3 blocks west and 1 block north of the *zócalo* on Calle 37 at 46. 15 pesos for 30min. and 20 pesos per hr. Open daily 8:30am-11:30 pm.

Fax: Telecomm (tel. 6 21 70), on the corner of Calles 38 and 39. Open M-F 8am-6pm, Sa-Su 9am-noon.

Phone code: 985.

⌐ ACCOMMODATIONS

The priciest hotels in town are on the *zócalo*. Better bargains are one block west.

Hotel Zací, Calle 44 #191 (tel. 6 21 67), between Calles 37 and 39, can be a vacation from your vacation. Stepping into its courtyard is like finding an oasis, complete with a restaurant fountain and glittering pool. Colonially furnished rooms with royal blue curtains, wooden carved dressers, and cable TV are worth the extra pesos. Singles 140 pesos; doubles 180 pesos; triples 220 pesos; add 40-50 pesos for A/C.

Hotel María Guadalupe, Calle 44 #198 (tel. 6 20 68), between Calles 39 and 41. The colorful bedcovers and new ceiling fans liven up the dark wood furniture. Singles and doubles 80 pesos; triples 100 pesos.

Hotel Mendoza, Calle 39 #204 (tel. 6 20 02), 1½ blocks west of the *zócalo*. The prices haven't changed for the older rooms because neither have the rooms (singles 70 pesos; doubles 90 pesos; triples 110 pesos). Newer, larger suites have better baths and come with cable TV and a fridge. Singles 130 pesos; doubles 150 pesos; triples 180 pesos.

Hotel Lily, Calle 44 #192 (tel. 6 21 63) between Calle 37 and 39, directly across from Hotel Zací. Hostel-like accommodations with shared bathrooms and hammock hooks in every room. Singles 60 pesos; doubles 70 pesos; with private baths 80 pesos.

⌐ FOOD

Valladolid's crossroads location makes it a veritable showcase of Yucatec food. Try the *poc-chuc* (tender slices of pork marinated in a Yucatec sauce, covered with pickled onions), *panuchos* (small tortillas filled with beans and topped with either chicken or pork, and lettuce, tomato, and hot sauce), or *escabeche oriental de pavo* (a hearty turkey soup).

El Bazaar, Calle 39 at 40, is a narrow, *mercado*-like courtyard crowded with several cafes and juice bars right off the *zócalo*. They all serve *comida típica;* the primary deciding factor is which menu to choose from after being bombarded with a handful of "bazaar" waiters. Open daily 6am-midnight.

Restaurante Cenote Zací, (tel. 6 21 07), on Calle 36 between Calles 37 and 39. Set underneath a large *palapa* surrounded by a grove of jungle trees, and atop a *cenote,* this dining experience is bound to be memorable. Excellent Yucatec food (entrees 35-45 pesos) and liquor selection, including Valladolid's *xtabentun,* a delectable concoction of anise and honey (8 pesos). Open daily 8am-6:30pm.

🔲 🎵 SIGHTS AND ENTERTAINMENT

Seekers of *cenotes* and cathedrals are in the right place. Valladolid has two fantastic examples of each. **Cenote Zací** (sah-KEY) is only three blocks east of the *zócalo*, on Calle 36 between Calles 37 and 39. Well-worn stone stairs lead down into a cavernous hollow studded with plunging stalactites, where daredevil divers do their best to imitate those of Acapulco while the weaving bats put on the real show. (Open daily 8am-6pm. Admission 5 pesos, children 2 pesos. Free view from the *palapa* restaurant on the edge.) Though it is farther from the center of town, **Cenote X'kekén** (sh-keh-KEN) is something you definitely shouldn't miss; it is only 6 km from Valladolid. Visit before midday, when a beam of light slices through the circular hole in the roof, reflecting off the dripping stalactites and tree roots, and bathing the room in a soft blue hue; bring a camera, a towel, and swim wear. To get there by car or bike (20min.), take Calle 39 to the highway and ride toward Mérida. Make a left at the sign for Dzitnup and continue to the entrance plaza on your left. Without wheels, take a taxi (20 pesos) or ask the driver of a second-class Mérida bus to drop you off. (Open daily 7am-5pm. Admission 15 pesos, children 7 pesos.)

The most famous church in town is **San Bernardino de Siena,** affiliated with the **Ex-Convento de Sisal,** Calle 41A, four blocks southwest off Calle 46. Built in 1552, the church and convent are the oldest ecclesiastical buildings in the Yucatán. On the altar at the rear of the church is a large image of the Virgin of Guadalupe. Original frescoes are visible behind two side altars. The walk along Calle 41A, **El Paseo de los Frailes** (the street of the friars), is truly a historic one. (Church open M, W-Su 8am-noon and 5-8pm. Admission 10 pesos.) The **Catedral de San Gervasio,** with its colonial-style twin towers, stands protectress over the *zócalo* on Calle 41. It would rival San Bernardino de Siena for the title of oldest church in the state had residents not violated the sacred right to sanctuary. According to legend, two alleged criminals who took sanctuary in the church were discovered and brutally murdered by an angry mob. When the bishop learned of the mob's sinful actions, he closed the church and had it destroyed. It was later rebuilt facing north instead of east, the only church in all of Yucatán to face north. (Open daily 5am-noon and 5-9pm.) For a visual lay-out of all the churches and a history of the Maya culture and religious practices visit the newly built **Museo de San Roque** (tel. 6 20 63), Calle 41 #200, between Calle 40 and 38

El Zaguar is the only late-night *palapa* bar in town. It is located on the corner of Las Cinco Calles, behind a colonial fountain. (Open Tu-Su 7pm-2am. *Cervezas* 15 pesos; margaritas 20 pesos.)

NEAR VALLADOLID: EK BALAM

This newly discovered site of Maya temples, ballcourts, and stelae, occupied from 700-1000 A.D., could soon become a major archaeological attraction in Eastern Yucatán. The unexcavated main temple may place a close second to the Pyramid of Kukulcan in width and height. Today, Ek Balam, meaning "black jaguar" in Mayan, has several structures adorned with impressive rows of long-nosed Chac masks. The ruins are located 20km northwest of Valladolid. Take a taxi to Ek Balam (100 pesos round-trip) from Valladolid; taxi drivers will wait if you ask beforehand and settle the price. (Site open daily 8am-5pm.)

TIZIMÍN

Tizimín (pop. 70,000) occupies a prime location in the middle of one of the finest colonial, archaeological, and nature reserve routes on the peninsula. Both Valladolid to the south and Río Lagarto to the north lie about one hour's drive away on Rte. 295. Along the way are archaeological sites such as Kulubá, Kikil, and Ek Balam, where tourists stumble over sacred Maya ruins faster than archeologists can research them. Taking its cue from Valladolid, Tizimín is capitalizing on its colonial history with the ambitious restoration of many buildings and pastel *portales* (arches) around its beautifully manicured Parque Principal. Tizimín's mornings have the big-city bustle of uniformed schoolchildren rushing to and from class, Tizimileñas on their way to the market, and bikes moving down the narrow streets. Things quiet down in the sultry afternoons, as swinging hammocks in the shade wait for cooling rains.

⚅ ORIENTATION AND PRACTICAL INFORMATION. Even-numbered streets run west-east, decreasing to the east. Odd-numbered streets run north-south, increasing to the south. Almost everything in Tizimín is centered around El Parque Principal which is located between Calles 50 and 52, facing the city's church and El Palacio Municipal. To get there from the main entrance of the bus station on Calle 47, walk west to your right on Calle 47 for two blocks. There will be a bakery on the right, after the first intersection, and a *zapatería* (shoe store) on the left. Turn left on Calle 50 and walk south two blocks towards *La Iglesia de los Tres Santos Reyes*, the large stone church on the left.

Buses leave from the terminal at Calles 46 and 47. **Autobus Noreste** (tel. 3 20 34) has service to: **Kantunil Kin** (1½hr., 4 per day, 25 pesos); **Mérida** (3hr., 6 per day, 45 pesos); **Río Lagartos** (1hr., 3 per day, 15 pesos); **Valladolid** (1hr., 12 per day 4:30am-7pm, 15 pesos); and **Cancún** (3hr., 6 per day, 55 pesos). **Bancomer** (tel. 3 23 81), on the corner of Calle 48 and 51 across Parque Juárez (the small park behind the church), exchanges currency (open M-F 9am-4:30pm, Sa 10am-2pm; 24hr. **ATM**). There is a **LADATEL** on the corner of Calle 50 and 51. The majestic **Lavandería de los Tres Reyes** (tel. 3 38 83), sporting three adorned kings atop its roof, is three blocks south of El Parque Principal on Calle 57 between 52 and 54 (6 pesos for 1kg; open daily 8am-1:30pm and 5-7:30pm). **Police:** located in the Palacio Municipal on the corner of Calles 51 and 52. **Farmacia YZA:** (tel. 3 44 62), on the corner of Calles 51 and 52. Open 24hr. **Hospital General San Carlos:** Calle 46 #461 (tel. 3 21 57), has a 24-hour ambulance service. **Post office:** Calles 52 and 55 (open M-F 8:30am-3pm). **Postal code:** 97700. **Servidnet** has **Internet access** at Calle 52 #368-A (tel. 3 22 85), between Calles 41 and 43 a few blocks north of the only basketball court in the city (30 pesos for 1hr.; open M-Sa 8am-1pm and 5-9pm). **Phone code:** 986.

⌐ ACCOMMODATIONS. Hotel San Jorge, Calle 55 #412 (tel. 3 20 37), is on the southwest corner of *El Parque Principal* sporting a red and blue self-insignia. The hotel prides itself in offering the largest rooms in all of Tizimín with an outdoor pool in the patio and chilled *agua purificada* in the hallway. (Singles and doubles 140 pesos, with A/C 160 pesos.) **Hotel San Carlos,** Calle 54 #407 (tel. 3 20 94), although the farthest from *El Parque*, provides the best comfort with spotless rooms, private bathrooms, and an inviting garden in which to chill and relax (singles 130 pesos, with A/C 140 pesos; doubles 140 pesos, with A/C 160 pesos). **Posada Maria Antonia,** Calle 50 #408 (tel. 3 28 57), sits directly behind the mother statue breastfeeding her baby, on the southern side of the church. The large *POSADA* sign does not reflect its small rooms with two beds, a TV, and a fan. However, this hotel is the cheapest in town and comes with free filtered water. (Singles and doubles 120 pesos; each additional person 125 pesos; add 15 pesos for A/C.)

⌐ FOOD. Fruits, vegetables, and bread abound along Calle 47, providing for a light meal on the S-like "love chairs" of *El Parque Principal*. **El Tío Juan** (tel. 3 32 40), Calle 48 between Calles 47 and 49, prepares the cheapest seafood tacos for

4.50 pesos, the freshest *tortas* (sandwiches) for 4.50 pesos, complete breakfast specials for 18-25 pesos, and the best natural juices for 4 pesos (open M-W and F-Sa 7am-2pm and 6pm-midnight). Willy Canto, the friendly and funny owner of **Restaurante Tres Reyes,** Calle 52 #395 (tel. 3 21 06), has become the culinary and customer-service father of Tizimín. He sponsors house-packing *ranchera fiestas* during the holiday months in the interior *palapa* of the restaurant, which is decorated with colorful paper cuts. Generous meals, big enough for two, are accompanied with a stack of freshly made corn tortillas. (*Pollo con arroz* 35 pesos. Open daily 7:30am-11:30pm.) **Restaurante Portales** (tel. 3 35 05), on the corner of Calles 50 and 51, provides shade under its red awning facing *El Parque*. Eggs are cooked in your selected style for 20 pesos and sandwiches are prepared for 12 pesos. (Open M-Sa 7:30am-1pm, and 6-11pm.)

◙ SIGHTS. Those who make the trip to Tizimín can find out anything they want to know about the region from one man—**Julio Caesar,** the fount of information for the region's famous Maya ruins. Having discovered the archeological site of Kulubá, Caesar can make entering the private ranch on which the site lies much easier. If you can't reach him by phone, try tracking him down at his photography studio. (*Calle 47 #405, between Calles 50 and 52. Tel. 3 38 86. Studio open daily 8am-9pm.*) Both Kulubá and Kikil are within easy reach of Tizimín.

KULUBÁ. Since it's somewhat hard to reach, this site is virtually untouristed and worth visiting. The ruins date from the Late Classical period (AD 800-1000) and are the easternmost point of Puuc architectural influence. The style here resembles the buildings at Chichén Itzá. Although neither building has survived the years intact, the details that remain are impressive. *El Edificio de Las Ues*, a structure about 40m long, 8m high, and 7m wide, is carved with "U"s all along its facade. The original red stucco with which the whole building was once painted can still be seen on the carved portions of the stone. The second partially restored building, the more impressive of the two, features two surprisingly well-preserved pairs of masks of the rain god Chac, as well as other carved ornamentation. (*To get to the ruins, take the Tixcanal-bound bus a half-block from the zócalo and ask the driver to drop you off at Kulubá. Taxis from Tizimín charge 100 pesos for a round-trip jaunt with a wait. Traveling to the site during the rainy season is especially difficult.*)

KIKIL. The tiny town of Kikil (pop. 5000), 5km from Tizimín, has the important remains of the first colonial church and ex-convent of the area, as well as the fresh waters of Nohock Dzonot de Kikil, Mayan for "grand *cenote*," a crystal clear body of water surrounded by a majestic cave-like structure. The church, known to locals as *La Iglesia Kikil*, is just to the right of the highway as you enter Kikil from Tizimín. The church was burned during the Caste War (1847-48) and is now being restored. Legend has it that years ago, some residents of the town threw a stone at a passing Catholic *sacerdote* (priest), who then predicted that the church would be laid to ruin and that Kikil would remain small forever by claiming: "*Este pueblo no progresara jamás!*" Just inside the gate of the little courtyard to your left as you face the church stands an elaborately carved stone baptismal font that rings like a bell when you strike it with your hand. (*Taxis to Kikil cost 80 pesos round-trip with a wait. Alternatively, you can get dropped off by one of the Río Lagartos-bound buses.*)

⚑ SEASONAL EVENTS. Dominating the central square, Tizimín's church was built in 1563 with distinctive castle-like ramparts. Facing the northern side of La Iglesia de los Tres Santos Reyes is the ex-convent, where many of the town's religious processions begin. The most important of these is the **Festival of the Three Kings** (Dec. 30-Jan. 12), when over one million pilgrims and partiers pour into Tizimín from surrounding towns and the countryside. While the parades, dancing, bullfights, and banquets of *comida típica* last for two weeks, the most important day of the festival is January 6, when the pilgrims file through the church to touch the patrons with palm branches. On Sundays around 7:30pm during the academic year, local schools perform **ballet folklóricas,** behind the ex-convent, that are free to the public. In May and June, visitors to Kikil can enjoy the enactment of several traditional Maya ceremonies such as the **Kaash Paach Bi,** spiritual cleansing for the land, and the **Chaa-Chac,** a rain prayer. During the rituals of January and June, the small indigenous town of Kikil participates in a pig head dance ritual, praising and giving thanks to "tsimin," a Maya deity. **Disco Stravaganza,** Calle 44 #321 (tel. 3 28 38), is the place for the not so piouís.

RÍO LAGARTOS

Known affectionately as "*La Ría*," this 53km inlet of ocean water in the northeastern part of the peninsula is much the same today as it was when Hernán Cortés chanced upon it and mistook it for a river. The head of this inlet is commanded by the small fishing village of Río Lagartos (pop. 3500), which is steadily adapting to its role as an ecotourist hotspot and biospheric beauty. "*La ría*" has been declared as one of the most important ecosystem reserves in the world. The 60,000-hectare national park is home to thousands of long-legged pink flamingos, as well as to approximately 300 different bird species, including migratory ones from Canada, Egypt, and other distant places. An exploratory boat ride may lead to an adventure with alligators, jaguars, white-tailed deer, pink and white spoonbills, and hawks.

🚩 **ORIENTATION AND PRACTICAL INFORMATION.** Río Lagartos is easily accessed from Tizimín (48km), Valladolid (100km), and Mérida (210km). The main road, **Calle 10,** runs north-south and ends at the waterfront on the north end. There is neither a post office nor a bank in the village; the town's services are limited to the long-distance **caseta** in the *zócalo*. **Autotransportes de Oriente (ADO)** has frequent buses to Tizimín (1hr., 4 per day, 12 pesos).

🏠 **ACCOMMODATIONS AND FOOD. Posada Leyli,** Calle 14 #104-A (tel. 2 01 06), one block east of the *caseta de teléfonos*, has two rooms overlooking "*la ría*," providing an excellent vista. All rooms are spacious, decorated with pink flamingo walls and sparkling bathroom sinks. (Singles/doubles with shared bathrooms 90 pesos, with private bathroom 100 pesos; room with 2 large beds, private bathroom, and space for 3 hammocks 150 pesos.) **Cabañas Los Dos Hermanos** (tel. 2 00 83), Calle 8, are wooden cabins located near the fresh breeze of the waterfront. Each cabaña has a double bed, fans, and a private bathroom, but no hot water. (80 pesos for a cabin with unlimited people and hooks for hammocks.)

La Económica, Calle 14 near the Navy base, prepares the largest, most succulent fish of "*la ría*," for only 30 pesos (open daily 8am-6pm). **Restaurante Isla Conty** (tel. 2 00 00), Calle 19, provides a varied selection of seafood dishes on the shore as well as complete tourist information and boat tours with the restaurant owner's five *lanchas* (open daily 10am-6pm). **Las Gavotas,** Calle 9 #105, are where the locals hang while enjoying *ceviche* and *sopa de mariscos* (open daily 10am-5pm).

📷 **SIGHTS AND SEASONAL EVENTS.** There are currently three groups of guides offering tours of "*la ría*"—local fishermen, certified ecotourist guides (recognized by their solid dark shirts), and the **"Isla Contoy" tours,** Calle 19 #134 (tel. 2 00 00; email nunez@chichen.com.mx), located in the restaurant. With maps, enthusiasm, and a great love of their *Ría*, the guides will do their best to ensure flamingo sightings and will take you to lesser-known treasures, such as the Maya ruins deep within the park, the colorful salt banks of **Las Coloradas,** and the several waterways hidden under mangrove trees. To see flamingos, early mornings are best, and May through June is their courtship period (from which the flamenco derives) and nesting time. (Prices depend on the season, the number of riders, and the length of the boat tour. The official minimum tariff is 250 pesos per boat.)

Not much happens during the day in this town except a whole lot of fishing: it's not surprising, then, that even less is going on at night. Cool down with some of the local beers, listen to the playful sounds emanating from the *zócalo*, and watch the lighthouse's beacon glance off the rolling waves of the Río. The town fiesta runs from July 20-30, as parades and a circus are put on to honor Santiago Aposto the younger brother of Spain's patron saint.

QUINTANA ROO

CANCÚN

The name Cancún (pop. 400,000) means "snake nest" in Mayan, and it has come to be oddly prophetic—sunburned, scantily clad vacationers bathe in the Caribbean Sea and get down to the beat of nightclub music. Cancún, the island that never sleeps, is Mexico's biggest resort. It was built in the early 1970s by Mexican entrepreneurs striving to match the success of the resort cities of Puerto Vallarta and Acapulco. How did they do it? They input their envisioned climate and setting for a tourist haven into a computer, and presto—Cancún was deemed the ideal spot. The upside-down L-shaped island is bordered on one side by 22km of world-class, white sandy beaches with crystal-clear water and by a mangrove-lined lagoon on the other. It is ideally located on the Caribbean Sea where the temperature seldom dips below 80 degrees. Whether on land or water, cosmopolitan Cancún and its surrounding area have much to offer. Proximity to renowned Maya ruins, biosphere reserves, and impressive coral reefs add to the resort's splendor and attraction. It is no surprise that over two million visitors a year seek out this *gringo* wonderland.

The *Zona Hotelera*, however, is not all that Cancún has to offer. Budget travelers use the international airport as a starting point for trips across the Yucatán Peninsula, and those willing to forego the profit-driven calculation of the hotel zone are often surprised by the bargains that are to be had in downtown Cancún, also referred to as the *centro*. Older, cheaper, and farther from the beaches, downtown Cancún offers a spice of Mexico. A self-guided tour around Av. Tulúm, Av. Yaxchilan, the public markets such as *Mercado 23* and *Mercado 28*, and the *Parque de las Palapas* guarantees a different experience from the tourist strip of the *Zona Hotelera*, all for an affordable price.

◢ ORIENTATION

On the northeastern tip of the Yucatán Peninsula, Cancún lies 285km east of Mérida via Rte. 180 and 382km north of Chetumal and the Belizean border via Rte. 307. Cancún is divided into two areas: downtown (or the *centro*) Cancún, where you'll find more bargains but no beaches, and Isla Cancún (or the *Zona Hotelera*), with fewer bargains but all beach. The main boulevard in downtown Cancún, **Av. Tulum,** runs north-south and parallel to **Av. Yaxchilán** (Yash-chee-LAN), three blocks east. These two streets form a rough parallelogram with **Av. Cobá** and **Uxmal** framing the **Parque de las Palapas** in the center of town. Facing the bus station (south), Av. Tulum is the busy thoroughfare to the left (east) and Av. Uxmal is to the right (west). Downtown, the *centro* lies south of the bus station. On the island, the *Zona Hotelera's* main boulevard is **Paseo Kukulcán,** conveniently marked off in 1km segments.

To reach either section of town from the **airport,** buy a ticket for the shuttle bus *(Colectivos)* **TTC** (100 pesos). Tickets are sold in the baggage claim and buses leave from outside the airport. A private **taxi** (white with green stripes) will charge around 150 pesos for that trip; it'll take at least 60 pesos to go from the beach to downtown, depending on how far into the *Zona Hotelera* you are. Always settle the price before getting into a cab. **Public buses** (5 pesos) marked "Hoteles" run the long stretch between the bus station downtown and the island's tip at Punta Nizuc around the clock. Buses can be caught at any blue sign along Av. Tulum and Paseo

Kukulcán (5 pesos). To get off the bus in the *Zona Hotelera,* push one of the little square red buttons on the ceiling when in sight of your stop—if you don't know where you need to get off, mention the name to the bus driver as you board, with a *por favor.* While many places rent mopeds (useful for exploring the 18km of beaches that stretch from the hostel to Punta Nizuc), buses are much cheaper and just as convenient.

⑦ PRACTICAL INFORMATION

TRANSPORTATION

Airport: (tel. 86 00 28), south of the city on Rte. 307. *Colectivos* 100 pesos, taxis 150 pesos (fixed rates to downtown; buy a ticket at the desk). Airlines include **Aerocaribe** (tel. 84 20 00); **American** (tel. 83 44 60); **Continental** (tel. 86 00 06); **LACSA** (tel. 87 31 01); **Mexicana** (tel. 87 44 44); **Northwest** (tel. 86 00 46); and **United** (tel. 86 00 25).

Buses: (tel. 84 13 78). The **bus station** is located on the corner of Av. Uxmal and Av. Tulum, facing Plaza Caribe. ADO travels to: **Campeche** (6hr., 11:30am and 10:30pm, 170 pesos); **Valladolid** (2hr.; 11am, 1, and 10:30pm; 55 pesos) and **Palenque** (14hr., 3:45 and 5:45 pm, 325 pesos). Premier sends a bus to: **Chichén Itzá** (2½hr., 9am, 50 pesos); **Playa del Carmen** (1 hr., every 15min., 20 pesos); and **Chiquilá** (3hr., 6:15, 8:15am, and 4:30pm; 45 pesos). Save about 25% by hopping on the 2nd class buses that leave from the curbside and go to Mérida, Tulum, and Chetumal.

Ferries: To get to **Isla Mujeres,** take a bus marked "Pto. Juárez" for the 15min. ride to the 2 ferry depots north of town (Punta Sam for car ferries, Puerto Juárez for passenger ferries). Express service *(servicio express)* passenger ferries shuttle across in 20min. (every 30min., 6am-8:30pm, 25 pesos). Normal service (45min., every 2hr. 8am-6pm, 12 pesos) is cheaper than express but takes almost 3 times as long. You can also get to **Cozumel** from Playa del Carmen, south of Cancún—Cozumel is also accessible by bus from the terminal in town (15 pesos).

Taxis: (tel. 88 69 90). The minimum fare within the *Zona* is 25 pesos; a ride into downtown can cost as much as 80 pesos. Within downtown, a taxi ride should run around 20 pesos. Prices are negotiable; be sure to settle the deal before getting in.

Moped Rental: Look for vendors in between Hotel Aquamarine and Hotel Costa Real. Mopeds go for 100 pesos per hour and 500 pesos per day. **Bicycles** and **in-line skates** are also rented, both at 70 pesos per hour or 160 pesos per day. License needed for moped rental; deposits negotiable. Open daily 9:30am-6:30pm.

TOURIST AND FINANCIAL SERVICES

Tourist Offices: Av. Tulum 5 (tel. 87 43 29, ext. 114; email relacionespublicas@cancun.gob.mx), inside the *Ayuntamiento Benito Juárez.* Open M-F 9am-5pm. For national tourist assistance, call toll-free 91 800 9 03 92. **Visitor Office,** located right next door in the little red building at Av. Tulum 26 (tel. 84 65 31), offers similar paraphernalia and help. Open daily 9am-9pm. Ask for Cancún Tips, a free magazine full of useful information and maps in English. Also available at Plaza Caracol (tel. 84 40 44), Av. Tulum 29 in the *Zona Hotelera,* and at the airport.

Consulates: Canada (tel. 83 33 60 or 83 33 61; fax 83 32 32), 3rd fl. of Plaza Caracol at km 8.5. Open M-F 10am-2pm. For emergencies outside of office hours, call the embassy in Mexico City (tel. 91 57 24 79 00). **U.K.** (tel. 81 01 00), in the Hotel Royal Caribbean. Open M-F 8am-6pm. **U.S.** (tel. 83 13 73 or 83 22 96), Plaza Caracol, 3rd fl. at km 8.5. Open M-F 9am-1pm.

Currency Exchange: Bancomer, Av. Tulum 20 (tel. 84 44 00), across from the intersection of Av. Tulum and Calle Claveles. Open M-F 9am-4:30pm, Sa 10am-2pm. The bank also has Visa and MasterCard **ATMs.** Both **Banamex,** Av. Tulum 19 (tel. 84 54 11; open M-F 9am-5pm, Sa 9:30am-2pm), and **Banca Serfín** (tel. 81 48 50), Av. Tulum at Cobá, give cash advances on Visa and MasterCard. They also have Cirrus, Visa, and MasterCard **ATMs** (open M-F 9am-5pm, Sa 10am-2pm).

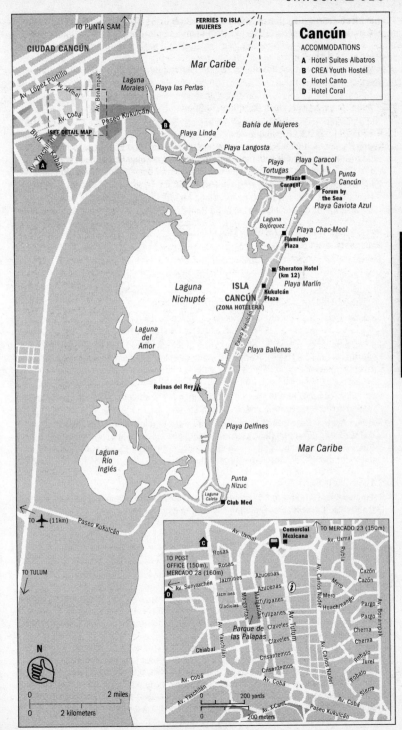

TO PUNTA SAM

CIUDAD CANCÚN

FERRIES TO ISLA MUJERES

Mar Caribe

Cancún
ACCOMMODATIONS
A Hotel Suites Albatros
B CREA Youth Hostel
C Hotel Canto
D Hotel Coral

Av. López Portillo
Av. Uxmal
Av. Bonampak
Laguna Morales
Playa las Perlas
Av. Cobá
Paseo Kukulcán
Blvd. Yaxchilán
Av. Yaxchilán
SEE DETAIL MAP
A

B Playa Linda

Bahía de Mujeres

Playa Langosta

Playa Tortugas
Playa Caracol
Plaza Caracol
Punta Cancún
Forum by the Sea
Playa Gaviota Azul

Laguna Bojórquez
Playa Chac-Mool
Flamingo Plaza

Sheraton Hotel (km 12)
Playa Marlín

Laguna Nichupté

ISLA CANCÚN (ZONA HOTELERA)

Kukulcán Plaza

Laguna del Amor

Paseo Kukulcán

Playa Ballenas

Ruinas del Rey

Playa Delfines

Mar Caribe

Laguna Río Inglés

Punta Nizuc

Laguna Caleta
Club Med

TO ✈ (11km)
Paseo Kukulcán

TO TULUM

N

0   2 miles
0   2 kilometers

YUCATÁN PENINSULA

Detail map:

Av. Uxmal
Comercial Mexicana
TO MERCADO 23 (150m)
Av. Uxmal

C Rosas
TO POST OFFICE (150m), MERCADO 28 (160m)
Rosas
Jazmines
Av. Sunyaxchén
D
Jazmines
Gladiolas
Azucenas
Azucenas
Margaritas
Malaguas
Tulipanes
Tulipanes
Av. Tulum
(i)
Av. Carlos Nader
Rubia
Mero
Mero
Huachinango
Cazón
Cazón
Pargo
Pargo
Av. Bonampak
Cherna

Parque de las Palapas
Claveles
Claveles
Av. Yaxchilán
Chiabal
Crisantemos
Crisantemos
Av. Cobá
Av. Carlos Nader
Cherna
Robalo
Jurel
Robalo
Sierra

Av. Yaxchilán
Av. Cobá
Av. X-Caret
Paseo Kukulcán

200 yards
200 meters

American Express: Av. Tulum 208 (tel. 81 40 00 or 81 40 43), 3 blocks south of Av. Cobá away from the city. Open M-F 9am-6pm, Sa 9am-1pm.

LOCAL SERVICES

Luggage Storage: At the bus station. 10 pesos per 24hr.

English Bookstore: Fama, Av. Tulum 105 (tel. 84 65 86), between Calles Claveles and Tulipanes. Newspapers, magazines, guidebooks, maps, music, beachwear, souvenirs, and U.S. bestsellers. Open daily 8am-10:30pm.

Supermarket: Across the street from the bus station on Av. Tulum is the **Comercial Mexicana** (tel. 84 33 30); you can't miss the big orange-and-white pelican out in front. Department store meets grocery store here with bakery and pharmacy included. Open daily 7am-noon. Smaller but more centrally located is **Super San Francisco** (tel. 84 11 55), Av. Tulum next door to Banamex. Open M-Sa 7:30am-10pm, Su 7am-9pm.

Laundry: Lavandería "Alborada," Av. Náder 5 (tel. 84 15 84), behind the Ayuntamiento Benito Juárez. Self-service 10 pesos. Open M-Sa 9am-8pm. **Tintorería Banderia** (tel. 84 26 69) has dry cleaning. Open M-Sa 9am-8pm.

EMERGENCY AND COMMUNICATIONS

Emergency: dial 060.

Police: (tel. 84 19 13) on Av. Tulum near El Ayuntamiento Benito Juárez.

Red Cross: Av. Yaxchilán 2 (tel. 84 16 16). English spoken. Open 24hr.

Pharmacies: Several along Av. Tulum and Av. Yaxchilán. **Farmacia Paris,** Av. Yaxchilán 32 (tel. 84 01 64), at the intersection with Calle Rosas, is open 24hr.

Medical Assistance: Hospital Americano, Calle Viento 15 (tel. 84 61 33, after-hours 84 63 19), 5 blocks south on Av. Tulum after its intersection with Av. Cobá. For an ambulance, call **Total Assist** (tel. 84 80 82), at Claveles 5 near Av. Tulum. English spoken.

Post Office: (tel. 84 15 24), Av. Xel-Ha at Av. Sunyaxchén. From Av. Tulum, cut through any side street to Av. Yaxchilán and head up Av. Sunyaxchén. The post office is 4 blocks farther. Open M-F 8am-6pm, Sa-Su 9am-12:30pm. **Postal Code:** 77500.

Fax: (tel. 84 15 24) next to the post office. Open M-F 8am-6pm. Telegram service available as well.

Internet Access: Cafe Internet (tel. 87 31 68), at Av. Tulum and Uxmal, next to Comercial Mexicana downtown (22 pesos for 30min.; open M-Sa 9am-8pm). **Sybcom Internet** (tel. 84 68 07), at Av. Náder, behind Comercial Mexicana (12 pesos for 15min., 22 pesos for 30min., 40 pesos for 1hr.; open M-Sa 9am-10pm). **Infonet** (tel. 87 95 16), in Plaza Bonita next to *Mercado 28* (22 pesos for 30min.; open M-Sa 9am-9pm, Su 10am-3:30pm).

Telephones: LADATELs and 50- and 100-peso phone cards make for accessible long-distance calls. **Casetas** throughout the city tend to charge hefty fees.

Phone Code: 98.

▚ ACCOMMODATIONS AND CAMPING

A drive through *La Zona Hotelera* on Paseo Kukulcán is like a highway to the danger zone for your funds. Budget travelers often stay in downtown Cancún or camp at the **CREA Youth Hostel,** at the end of the *Zona Hotelera.* With the exception of CREA, all hotels listed are within a 15-minute walk from Av. Tulum downtown. Prices can fluctuate as much as 25% throughout the year. During high season, phone reservations are a good idea.

Hotel Coral, Sunyaxchén 30 (tel. 84 20 97). Heading west from Av. Yaxchilán, the hotel is 3 blocks down on the left; look for the red-and-white building with a garden inside. The superfast ceiling fans in each room more than make up for the sparse furnishings. The attentive staff keep the bathrooms clean and the *agua purificada* in the halls well-stocked and cold. Check-out 1pm. Singles 130 pesos, with A/C 180 pesos; doubles

180 pesos, with A/C 280 pesos; triples 230 pesos, with A/C 380 pesos. To make reservations, wire payment 10 days in advance.

Suites Albatros, Av. Yaxchilán 154 (tel. 84 22 42), 2 blocks south of Av. Cobá and across the street from the Red Cross. It's easy to forget the extra bit of effort it takes to get here while walking through the shady courtyard and into one of the apartment-like rooms. The classy decor only adds to the full kitchens, large beds, large closets, and A/C. Each of the upstairs rooms has a balcony with laundry lines and sink. Pepe's place is in demand, so reservations are suggested; 3 day advance notice. All rooms are US$25.

CREA Youth Hostel (HI); (tel. 83 13 37), Paseo Kukulcán at km 3. For those who plan to beach or club it, CREA is the closest and cheapest place in *La Zona Hotelera*. Just catch any *Hotelera* bus from the bus station or Av. Tulum and ask to be let off at "CREA." CREA's best asset is its location on the beach. 200 single-sex dorm rooms with 8 bunk-beds apiece. Sheets and pillows provided. No A/C; ask for a room with a working ceiling fan. Use the personal lockers when you leave the room, even to shower. No hot water. Beach volleyball, soccer field, and table-tennis. Locker not included, but place your stuff with hostel security. 50-peso deposit. 15-night max. stay. Check-out 1pm. No curfew. Bunks 77 pesos, or you can pitch a tent on the front lawn for 40 pesos per person.

Hotel Canto (tel. 84 12 67), on Av. Yaxchilán. As you turn off Av. Uxmal onto Av. Yaxchilán, look for the faded pink building 2 blocks down on your right. Besides hot water and A/C, the only benefit Hotel Canto offers is its location in the center of downtown. Singles 200 pesos; doubles 225 pesos; triples 250 pesos.

FOOD

Two simple rules will help the hungry traveler find affordable cuisine for all tastes in Cancún: avoid chain restaurants (in fact, stay away from *La Zona Hotelera* altogether), and steer clear of the roadside booths, which serve meats of dubious origin. For good, inexpensive food, try the many joints between Av. Tulum and Av. Yaxchilán. **Mercado 28,** behind the post office and circumscribed by Av. Xel-Ha, is a unique option for budget fare. Numerous *loncherías* are located in its western courtyard and great deals are found in the center of *El Parque de Las Palapas*. All restaurants listed below are in downtown Cancún.

Acá Los Tacos, Av. Cobá 43 (tel. 84 81 77), near the corner of Av. Yaxchilán, in between Domino's Pizza and Los Chinos. Make your own quesadillas and tacos in this traditional Mexican local dive. If it's your birthday, everything you consume, including drinks, is on the house. Don't forget to leave your mark by signing *El Mural de los Famosos*. Quesadillas and *gringas* 10 pesos; entrees 30-40 pesos. Open daily 6pm-3am.

Café México, Calle Grosella 2 (tel. 84 68 87), on the corner of Av. Sunyaxchen, near Hotel Coral. A place to enjoy home-cooked breakfast, coffee, and desserts next to a *mariachi* silhouette or in the garden patio. Breakfast specials 17-20 pesos; *pan dulce* 5 pesos; coffee 7 pesos. Open M-Sa 7:30-11:30am and 1-4pm.

El Tacolote, Av. Cobá 19 (tel. 87 30 45), 2 blocks east of Av. Yaxchilán toward the *Zona Hotelera*. Look for the sombrero-sporting, taco-gobbling, yellow chicken out front. Delicious grilled chicken and meat with an unlimited stack of tortillas and complimentary nachos and *salsa* start at 25 pesos. Mention *Let's Go* for a complimentary drink of your choice. Open daily 11am-2am.

Restaurante Río Nizuc, Paseo Kukulcán at km 22. Get on the "Hoteles" bus (4 pesos) and ask to be let off at Río Nizuc after passing most of the hotels. Take a left after crossing the bridge down a steep hill, then walk 3min. along a path on the right bank where local fishermen and their children enjoy *El Rio*. Those who make the effort will be rewarded with shady palapas and a beautiful view of the river, jetskiers, and speed boats. Watch the cook prepare enormous servings of fresh, barbequed fish: *tikin xic* (60 pesos). Other entrees 50-60 pesos. Open daily 11am-6pm.

Restaurante Pop, Av. Tulum 25 (tel. 84 19 91), near the corner with Av. Uxmal. Located just about a block from the bus station, the air-conditioned interior and huge helpings provide the perfect recovery from a long bus ride. Any traveler will enjoy starting the day on 3-course breakfasts like *el Yucateco* (35 pesos). Lunch and dinner 30-50 pesos. Open daily 8am-11pm.

⛱ BEACHES

Seeking out unique sights and local culture in Cancún is a little harder than stumbling upon the glimmering, multi-hued ocean, but those who didn't check their brains at the airport will appreciate what the lively inhabitants of this city really have to offer. Even if you stay inland in downtown Cancún, you can take advantage of the well-groomed beaches in front of the luxury hotels in the *Zona Hotelera*. All beaches in Mexico are public property, and travelers often discreetly use hotel restrooms, fresh-water showers, pools, and lounge chairs. If you wisely choose to avoid the resort beach scene, head for the peaceful **Playa Langosta,** west of the CREA, or for the shores south of the **Sheraton Hotel,** some of the safest and the most pleasant in Cancún. Organized beach activities include volleyball, scuba classes, and Mexican-style painting lessons; become a visitor of the hotel for the day to join. Boogie boards can be rented at the small marina on the beach (40 pesos for 2hr.), but Cancún's surf is a whimper to the roar of the rest of the *costa turquesa*. **Playa Chac-Mool,** where waves are about 1m high, is as exciting as it gets. For some free, no-frills encounters with a surprising variety of tropical fish and coral, make your way over near the rocks on the east side of **Playa Tortugas.**

Scuba Cancún (tel. 83 10 11) at km 5, offers diving lessons (US$78), snorkeling (US$26), and other services at comparatively reasonable prices. Certified divers will get the better deals: a one-tank dive with **Mundo Marino** (tel. 83 05 54), at km 5.5, goes for US$50. The dock to the right of the CREA hostel supports a dive shop that offers two hours of snorkeling, equipment included, for about US$30.

🎵🎭 ENTERTAINMENT AND NIGHTLIFE

El Parque de las Palapas, between Avenidas Tulum and Yaxchilán in the very center of town, hosts free regional music and dance performances during the weekends. Admirable foresight or lucky timing could mean enjoying Cancún's celebrated **jazz festival** (mid- to late-May) or the refreshingly native **Caribbean festival** (Nov.) Check with the tourist office for info. For slightly more intense entertainment, death in the afternoon occurs every Wednesday at 3:30pm in the **Plaza de Toros** (tel. 84 83 72; fax 84 82 48), on Av. Bonampak at Av. Sayil. Tickets for the bullfights are available at travel agencies on Av. Tulum for 300 pesos per person (less if you're in a large group; children free) or at the bullring on a bullfight day. Show includes a cockfight and a performance by the **Ballet Folklórico.**

Nightlife in Cancún is all about *fiestas* and nightclubs. **Discos and bars** are both downtown (at the south end of Av. Tulum near Av. Cobá) and in *La Zona Hotelera* at **Forum by the Sea** (km 9 on Paseo Kukulkán). Most establishments open at 9pm and close when the crowds leave, around 5 or 6am. Crowds differ according to time and season—April is for college spring-breakers, June is for high school and college graduates, and late night year-round belongs to the gamut of tourists from all across the world. Dress code for the discos is simple; less is more, and tight is just right. Bikini tops often get women in for free, but use your better judgment for the more laid-back dives. Discos in the *Zona* prefer U.S. dollars.

🎿 **Roots,** Tulipanes 26 (tel. 84 24 37; fax 84 55 47), between Palapas Park and Av. Tulum. Cool Caribbean-colored walls and eclectic artwork with a music motif set the stage for this jazz-n-blues joint. Watch and listen as the best regional musicians play their digs from the bar or the intimate and cushioned listening area, or get a table a little farther back to converse with the mostly European and expat crowd. Live music 3-6 nights a week; shows start around 10pm. F-Sa 30 peso cover (most of the money goes to the local arts association). Open Tu-Su 7pm-2am, menu until 1am.

La Boom (tel. 83 11 52), near the youth hostel (a 10min. walk toward the *Zona*). "Boom your life in La Boom." Two nightclubs, a bar, and a pizzeria under the same roof, Boom offers the least artificial atmosphere to young crowds. Serious dancers groove with lasers and phone booths on stage. Ladies night and open bar vary week to week. Cover US$20.

Dady'O (tel. 83 33 33), at km 9, on Forum by the Sea. Its cave-like entrance makes you feel like you're heading for a disco inferno ("burn, baby, burn"). The cave-scape continues through to a stage and dance floor, surrounded by winding, layered walkways whose crevices sport tables and stools. A cafeteria in the club serves snacks (30 pesos). Laser show nightly at 11:30pm. Numerous wristband-hawking staff members outside will fill you in on the nightly special. Cover US$20. Open daily 10pm-late.

Dady Rock (tel. 83 33 33), next door to Dady'O. Provides the headbanging to complement Dady'O's hip-hopping. Hosts 2 live bands every night and has open bar deals (US$15) several nights per week. Cover US$20. Open daily 6pm-late.

Coco Bongo (tel. 83 50 61), Blvd. Kukulcan km 9.5, Forum By the Sea. Dance and drink to rock, pop, and hip-hop wherever you are. Partiers dance on stage, on the bar, on the tables, and yes, the dance floor. Laser show and the flying mask nightly at 11:30pm. Cover US$10.

Batacha (tel. 83 17 55), km 10.5 in the Hotel Miramar Misión. Live *salsa* and merengue bands underneath refreshing *palapas*. A local favorite. Cover 30 pesos. Open Tu-Su 10pm-4am.

Karamba, Calle Tulipanes just off Av. Tulum, in downtown Cancun. Gay disco with a spacious multi-level floor, pop-art murals, and a colorful variety of dance music to complement the wild lights. Tu-F 2-for-1 beers. Sa cover 25 pesos. Open Tu-Su 10pm-4am.

Backstage, Tulipanes 30 at Av. Tulúm (tel. 87 91 06). Nightly cabaret shows on a Broadway-like theater stage with scarlet curtains makes an evening at Backstage memorable. Three nights no cover, otherwise 30 pesos (drink included). Open Tu-Su 10pm-4am.

ISLA HOLBOX

Isla Holbox (EES-la ohl-BOSH) is a 33km finger-shaped fisherman's island which preserves its sandy streets surrounded by its turquoise crystalline waters and tranquil beaches. It is still a mystery to many foreign tourists, and you'll want it to stay that way. Just off the northeastern tip of the Yucatán Peninsula, it is home to 1600 *holboxeños* and their fishing. The pace of life here is unbelievably peaceful, the beaches and surrounding tiny *islas* inspiring, and the people welcoming. If you think you've never seen such a beautiful sunset, stay another night. **Chiquilá** is the embarkation point for passengers ferrying to Isla Holbox, the hidden treasure of the Yucatán Peninsula.

◪ **ORIENTATION AND PRACTICAL INFORMATION.** Getting to Isla Holbox requires previous planning, but it's well worth it. The easiest way to go is to take the 8:15am **bus** from Cancún (50 pesos), which reaches Chiquilá at 11:30am, and hop on the **lancha** of "Los 9 Hermanos" (boats run every 2hr. 8am-4:30pm; returning to Chiquilá 5am-3:30pm; 25 pesos). There are more options when it comes to returning from Isla Holbox, since both Valladolid-bound and Cancún-bound buses and vans (50 pesos) meet the early boat from the *isla*. Most options mean a 5am ferry ride, though, so be sure to prepare for the mosquitos. Be ready to leap off when the boat strikes the dock, because the buses wait for no one. If the Cancún bus doesn't show, take the Valladolid-Mérida bus to Kantunil Kin; the Cancún bus swings by there at 6:30am. You can always flag down a Valladolid-Cancún bus at Ideal, though waiting in the sun will be torturous. If you miss the last ferry to Holbox, Chiquilá's **Puerta del Sol** (tel. 5 01 21) will welcome you for 100 pesos.

On the Isla, the palm tree median and packed sand of Av. Juárez begins at the dock, runs past **El Parque Benito Juárez,** and ends up on the beach. There is no bank on the island, and locals may not have enough cash on hand to cover your newly planned extended stay. The 24-hour **police** trio may be found sitting on the wooden benches of **La Alcadia Municipal** (tel. 5 20 10), the light blue building on the corner of Juárez and Díaz. The **Centro de Salud,** 200m from the dock, is on the right side of the Juárez in a blue-and-white building which houses a 24-hour doctor. **Fax** and **telegram** service is located on the corner of Juárez and Díaz (tel. 5 20 53; open M-F 9am-3pm). A **public telephone** *caseta* is a half-block east of **Parque Benito Juárez** on Porfirio Díaz (9 pesos for 3min; open daily 8am-9pm).

◤ ACCOMMODATIONS. Posada D'Ingrid (tel. 5 20 70), two blocks from the northwestern corner of Parque Benito Juárez; veer left (see map). Gleaming coral-pink rooms with hot water, sparkling bathrooms, and ceiling fans open up to a *palapa*-roofed patio with lights, speakers, and card tables (doubles 150 pesos; quads 200 pesos). **Posada La Raza** (tel. 5 20 72), Av. Júarez, is located on the west side of Parque Juárez. The husband and wife owners pride themselves in making their *posada* feel like home. A small store, dishes, and refrigerator are available. (Rooms 100 pesos, 150 pesos during high season; discounts for longer stays.) **Posada Los Arcos** (tel. 5 20 43), next door to Posada La Raza, provides rooms with two beds, fans, and breeze from its large courtyard. Los Arcos is the only place in town which rents out bikes at 15 pesos per hour and 60 pesos per day; an excellent way to explore the many kilometers of white sandy beaches. (Singles 100 pesos; doubles 150 pesos.) **Posada Don Joaquin** (tel. 5 20 88), one block northeast of El Parque, on Igualdad, is the third house on the left with a Coca-Cola sign on the upper doorway. Don Joaquin offers the simplest and cheapest rooms of *La Isla*. (Rooms 50 pesos; in high season 80 pesos.) Free **camping** is available on the beach; just ask *el alcade* (the mayor) for a permit. Prices increase in the high season (April during *Semana Santa* and December) by approximately 30-50 pesos.

◖ FOOD. Restaurants in La Isla follow the pace of island life, meandering through time without a fixed schedule. Among them is **Zarabanda** (tel. 5 20 94), one block south of *El Parque* on Palomina. Excellent fish and seafood dishes are prepared under this large *palapa* named after a Caribbean rhythm (30-50 pesos). **Restaurant-Bar Ullamar,** Av. Juárez, directly facing the beach is the place where *Holboxeños* gather to enjoy the seafood specialties of the house (entrees 30-50 pesos). **Restaurant Edelyn** (tel. 5 20 24), C. Palomina, east of *El Parque*, grills large fish for 50 pesos and flips pizza at night on the top floor of its *palapa* log cabin. **La Isla del Colibri** (tel. 5 20 00), Av. Juárez and Díaz, blends natural fruit juices and shakes for 12-20 pesos and slices tropical fruits for a juicy plate of salad (20 pesos with your choice of yogurt and granola). The family at **Conchería El Parque,** on Av. Juárez, one door down from Posada La Raza, cooks up fresh and inexpensive seafood. A chicken or beef dish with a frosty beer will cost about 40 pesos.

◙ ◘ SIGHTS AND ENTERTAINMENT. Shell-lined North Beach is heavenly; for more, head about 8km east from North Beach to Punta Mosquito, where a 25km stretch of virgin beach begins. The main attractions, aside from sunning and sleeping, are the boat trips provided by local fishermen (4hr. cruise 500 pesos; try to get a group together). East of the island is **Isla de Pájaros,** home to nearly 40 species of birds including flamingos and pelicans. Next stop is **Ojo de Agua,** or **Yalahau** by local standards, which is an inlet on the mainland fed by a subterranean freshwater spring. Finally, you'll head across the lagoon that separates Isla Holbox from the mainland (look out for the dolphins) to **Isla Pasión,** at the western end, so named for the couples of birds and *isleños* that relax there during the off-season. During the high season, Isla Holbox caters to daytrippers with its restaurant-bar, live music, and basketball court. To see *holboxeños* at their liveliest, visitors can cruise the brightly lit Parque Juárez at dusk, when old friends and families gather to socialize, enjoy the playground, and watch the basketball games. Head down to the north shore during the night. If conditions are right, you can witness *ardentía*, a rare and completely natural phosphorescent phenomenon. Microorganisms respond to movement in the water by turning bright green; just kick the water or sway it with your hands to see the glow. During high season, **Cariocas Restaurant and Disco,** on Igualdad two blocks off the *zócalo*, is the place to be when the music jams on Friday and Saturday.

ISLA MUJERES

When the Spaniard Francisco Hernández de Córdoba blew into this tiny island (7.5km by 1km, 11km northeast of the coast of Quintana Roo) off-course from Cuba in 1517 looking for slaves to work the Cuban mines, he instead found hundreds of small female statuettes scattered among the beaches. When he named the island *Isla Mujeres* (Island of Women) he did not seem to realize that he had stumbled upon a Maya sanctuary for Ixchel, the Mayan goddess of fertility, the moon, and other virtues. The island was uninhabited until it became a hideout for pirates who, for the 200 years after Córdoba's arrival, marauded the "Spanish Lake."

For years Isla Mujeres was a small fishing village with a culture centered around the sea. In the 1950s it was rediscovered as an ideal vacation spot for Mexicans, shortly followed by Canadians, Australians, Europeans, and Americans. In the 1960s, Isla Mujeres became the hot spot for hippies and backpackers. Today it has become a tourist destination for many and a permanent home for others. Out of 150 residents, only five are originally from Isla Mujeres.

Some present-day inhabitants of the island (pop. 14,500) still fish, but many now sell souvenirs and cater to the daytrippers who arrive each morning from Cancún. It's easy to lose track of time as siestas come and go under the shade of the tree-lined beaches. Here, time just slips away.

✳ ORIENTATION

Just as beach lovers will dream of Isla Mujeres, so will walkers enjoy getting around the island's lively *centro*, although crowds pack the streets from December through April. The town is laid out in a rough grid. Right in front and perpendicular to the dock is **Avenida Rueda Medina,** which runs the length of the island along the coastline, past the lagoon, Playa Paraíso, Playa Lancheros, and the Garrafón Reef. Perpendicular to Medina are the six major east-west streets of the *centro:* Avenidas Mateos, Matamoros, Abasolo, Madero, Morelos, and Nicolás Bravo and Allende, from north to south. Avenidas Juárez, Hidalgo, Guerrero, and Carlos Lazo run parallel to Rueda Medina. Turning left on any of these streets will lead you toward **Playa Norte.** Finally, on the southern tip of the island by El Faro Sur (The Southern Lighthouse) are the remains of a Maya temple, **Ixchel.** A good source of general information is *Islander*, a local publication available at travel agency shops, the ferry dock at Puerto Juárez, and the tourist office on Av. Rueda Medina. Maps are also available on the ferry and in the tourist office. The best way to explore the island for yourself is by renting a moped, a bike, or even a golf cart. The whole trip, with photo and swim stops, won't take more than three hours. Public **buses** go only as far as Playa Lancheros (3 pesos). **Taxis,** on the other hand, roam the length of Isla Mujeres; you should have no problem catching one unless you're mesmerized by the crashing waves along the rocky bluffs on the southern tip until well after dark.

ℹ PRACTICAL INFORMATION

Ferries: To get to the island, catch a boat from **Puerto Juárez,** 2km north of Downtown Cancún and accessible by a "Puerto Juárez" bus (15min., 4.50 pesos) or by taxi (20 pesos) from Downtown Cancún. Normal service boats take much longer but sometimes have live music to pass the time (45min., every 2hr. 5am-6pm, 9 pesos). Express service cruisers leave for the island every 30min. (20min., 6am-9pm, 22 pesos). Arrive early—ferries are notorious for leaving ahead of schedule if they're full. A **car ferry** runs to Mujeres from Punta Sam, 5km north of Puerto Juárez (4 per day; 9 pesos per person, 50 pesos per car).

Taxis: (tel. 7 00 66). Unmistakable bright red cabs line up at the stand directly to the right as you come off the passenger dock. From town to: **Playas Paraíso** (10 pesos); **Lancheros** (10 pesos); **Garrafón** (32 pesos); and the **ruins** (35 pesos).

Moped Rental: Pepe's Moto Rent, Hidalgo 19 (tel./fax 7 00 19), between Matamores and Abasolo amid their dozens of golf carts and mopeds (open daily 8am-6pm; golf carts 100 pesos per hr.; mopeds 50 pesos per hr., 200 pesos per day).

Tourist Office: (tel. 7 03 07) Av. Rueda Medina, first left after exiting the port, on the right-hand side. Open M-F 9am-10pm; Sa-Su 9am-3pm.

Currency Exchange: Bital (tel. 7 00 05), on Rueda Medina to the right when coming off the passenger dock. Open M-Sa 8am-6pm. Also has a 24hr. **ATM** which takes Visa, Mastercard, and Cirrus.

Markets: Súper Betino, Morelos 3 (tel. 7 01 27), on the *zócalo*. Deli and bakery inside. Open daily 7am-11pm. For fruit on the run, try the **fruit stalls** just outside or the mini-market **Isla Mujeres,** on Hidalgo between Abasolo and Madero.

Laundry Service: Lavandería Tim Phó, Av. Juárez 94, at Abasolo. 4kg for 25 pesos; 2hr. turnaround. Open M-Sa 7am-9pm, Su 8am-2pm. **Lavandería Angel,** Av. Juárez local A-3, near the beach. 5 pesos per kg, 4 kg minimum. Slow, but clothes are left spotless.

Police: (tel. 7 00 98) on Hidalgo at Morelos, in the Palacio Municipal. Open 24hr.

Red Cross: dial 7 02 80.

Pharmacy: La Mejor, Madero 18 (tel. 7 01 16), between Hidalgo and Juárez. Open daily 9am-10pm.

Medical Assistance: Centro de Salud, Guerrero 5 (tel. 7 01 17), at Morelos. The white building at the northwest corner of the *zócalo*. Open 24hr. Some doctors speak English, such as **Dr. Antonio E. Salas** (tel. 7 04 77 or beeper 91 98 88 78 68 code 1465), at Hidalgo near Madero. Will make house calls. Open 24hr.

Post Office: (tel. 7 00 85) Guerrero and López Mateos, at the northwest corner of town, 1 block from the Playa Norte. Open M-F 8am-4pm, Sa 9am-1pm. **Postal Code:** 70085.

Fax: Guerrero 13 (tel. 7 02 45), next to the post office. Open M-F 9am-3pm. They also have a **telegram** service and Western Union.

Books: Cosmic Cosas, Av. Matamoros 82 (tel. 7 08 06). Buy, sell, exchange books in all different languages. Open daily 9am-2pm and 4-9pm.

Phone Code: 987.

■ ACCOMMODATIONS AND CAMPING

Prices fluctuate by as much as 100 pesos depending on the season, less so over the length of stay; inquire ahead. All hotels listed below are in town, north of the plaza.

Poc-Na Youth Hostel, Matamoros 15 (tel. 7 00 90), on the North Beach. Whether people are sacking out on a bed (35 pesos; 8-14 to a room), in one of the quiet hammock rooms (35 pesos), or in a tent or hammock in between the patio's trees (50 pesos for 2-person tent), it all comes together under the lazy fans of the *palapa* dining hall. More socializing and less eating goes on here among the largely European crowd. 2 private rooms available (80 pesos). Bring your own hammock, tent, sheets, and lock. Registration closes at 11pm. Check-out 1pm, 17 pesos more to stay later. Cafeteria open 7am-11pm. Reservations recommended during high season.

Hotel Xul-Ha, Hidalgo 23 (tel. 7 00 75), between Matamoros and López Mateos. Sporting large rooms, colorful *tapetes* (Mexican blankets), ceiling fans, and wooden dressers and mirrors, the hotel also offers a color TV, coffee machines, refrigerator, and paperbacks in its lobby. Check-out noon. Singles 200 pesos; doubles 220 pesos; triples 250 pesos; quads 290 pesos. 80 pesos more during peak season. Discounts for longer stays.

Hotel Marcianito, centrally located at Abasolo 10 (tel. 7 01 11), between Juárez and Hidalgo. Pesa, the cocker spaniel, tries to be the first to greet visitors, and the service gets friendlier once you enter the small patio. Well-furnished rooms have ceiling fans and hot water. Singles 140 pesos; add 30 pesos for each additional person; and 70 pesos Dec.-Apr.

Hotel Carmelina, Guerrero 4 (tel. 7 00 06), between Abasolo and Madero. Bright yellow bathrooms liven up the rooms and are well-kept. Singles 150 pesos; doubles 170 pesos; triples 210 pesos. A/C 50 pesos extra.

◖ FOOD

Seafood abounds in Isla Mujeres. Try some *pulpo* (octopus) or *ceviche* (seafood marinated in lime juice, cilantro, and other herbs). Be wary of the restaurants near the plaza as they are a bit pricier and plan ahead since many restaurant owners close between lunch and dinner to enjoy the afternoon life of Isla Mujeres.

Chen Huaye, just off the plaza across from the playground on Av. Bravo. Unlike the wagon wheels in front, the service inside keeps the local dishes rolling. Try the zesty *pescado a la veracruzana* (35 pesos). F-W 9am-11pm.

French Bistro Francais, Matamoros 29, at Hidalgo, has the healthiest menu on the island. No wonder a long line forms around its 10 colorful pillars and banners, representing 10 different cities and countries, during peak season. Yogurt and crepe specials are the popular picks of the morning and grilled seafood, coupled with authentic French flavor, satisfy the bistro's clientele. If this is not enough, the giant red lobster painted on the ceiling, a long stem tulip on each table, and a blown-up map of the Yucatán Peninsula will enchant you into Diana's, Victor's, and Petie's—the Bistro's friendly parrot—artistic restaurant. Open daily 8am-noon and 6-10pm.

Café Cito, Matamoros 42 (tel. 7 04 38), at Juárez. Patrons can pretend they haven't left the beach with the sand and shells under the see-through tabletops of this redecorated cafe. A visit here can replenish both body and soul with freshly made crepes, sandwiches, and orange juice. Open F-W 8am-2pm.

Red Eye Cafe/Ojo Rojo, Av. Hidalgo between Mateos and Matamoros. For a bite to eat on the way to the beach, sample the German-influenced trilingual menu. Enjoy the breeze along the corridor as you delight on sandwiches (20 pesos), breakfast specials (30 pesos), bratwurst or *wiener schnitzel* (30 pesos). Open W-M 6am-3pm.

◗ SIGHTS AND SAND

Many of Isla Mujeres's characteristics, like soft white beaches, crystalline waters, excellent vistas from El Faro Sur, and rocky bluffs, make it a tropical heaven. Starting with the beaches, this opportunity cannot be missed. The most popular and accessible beach is **Playa Norte,** where tourists lounge underneath shady palm trees, splash in its shallow waters, and walk bare-breasted. **Playa Lancheros** and **Playa Paraíso** open up onto Mujeres Bay.

La Isleña travel agency, on Morelos a half block from the dock, offers snorkeling gear (40 pesos) and mopeds (80 pesos per hr.) and organizes trips to nearby **Isla Contoy,** a wildlife sanctuary reef with pelicans, cormorants, and 100 other bird species. The tours include reef snorkeling at **Isla-Che** for one hour. (Tel. 7 05 78. Tour hours are from 8:30am-4pm. Equipment and a fruit breakfast and pescado for lunch included. 350 pesos or US$40. Deposit of at least 50% required the previous day, minimum 6 persons. Agency open daily 7:30am-9:30pm.)

To see and support a group of dedicated individuals helping to save the planet and to have an unforgettable time while doing so, head over to **PESCA,** across the *laguna* from the populated northern half of the island. This biological research station is engaged in a breeding program for three species of sea turtles. Female turtles, captured by PESCA in May, lay their eggs in the safety of the station's beach throughout the summer and are returned to the wild in October. The young are reared for a year before they, too, are released. For 20 pesos, a guide will take you on a stroll through the center to see the giant turtles and their offspring. (Open daily 9am-5pm.)

In the case of the Maya ruins of **Ixchel,** getting there truly makes the trip. The temple was reduced to rubble by Hurricane Gilbert in 1988, yet there is still a partially reconstructed one-room building to be seen as well as an immense panorama of the Yucatán and the Caribbean Sea (located near El Faro Sur).

♫ ENTERTAINMENT

Isla Mujeres's nightlife is commensurate with its small size and laid-back demeanor. **La Palapa,** on Playa Norte to the right of Av. Hidalgo, displays a temporary dance floor on the sand that is garnished in holiday lights and UV artwork. **Bar Buho's** right on shore, off Carlos Lazo, is the popular swing and hammock bar of *La Isla.* Tourists and locals swing from one bar to the next toasting with half-price happy hour bargains during *La Isla*'s sunset. (Beer 15 pesos; margaritas/cocktails 20 pesos. Flexible island hours.)

PLAYA DEL CARMEN

Smack in the middle of Quintana Roo's legendary *Costa Turquesa* (Turquoise Coast), Playa del Carmen (pop. 18,000) is an inviting beach town which serves as a tropical and European crossroads for archaeologically inclined travelers en route to inland temples and pyramids and beach hunters heading for Cozumel and Cancún. Although Playa (as locals call it) used to be a fishing village up until the early 90s, its silky white sand and waters made it a home-grown tourist paradise. The town's sidewalk shops, sunset happy hours, cafes, and people-watching restaurants open onto the sunny pedestrian walkway, where jewelry artists and hammock vendors hawk their wares.

✦ ORIENTATION

Playa is centered around its main transportation centers, the ferry dock and the bus stations. The bus drops you off on the main road, **Av. Juárez,** which runs west from the beach to the Cancún-Chetumal highway 1.5km away. In between the **bus station** and the *zócalo,* perpendicular to Av. Juárez, runs **Av. Quinta** (Fifth Av.) which is one street parallel to the shore and hosts most of the shops and restaurants. East-west *calles* increase by two in either direction; north-south *avenidas* increase by five.

🛈 PRACTICAL INFORMATION

Buses: at the corner of Quinta and Juárez, ADO runs first-class buses to: **Chetumal** (4½hr., 5 per day 7:30am-midnight, 150 pesos); **Coatzacoalcos** (12hr.; 7am, 4:30, and 9pm; 420 pesos); **Córdoba** (22hr., 7am, 577 pesos); **Escárcega** (6hr.; 4:45pm, 220 pesos); **Mexico City** (25hr.; 7am, noon, and 7pm; 610 pesos); **Orizaba** (14hr., noon and 7pm, 595 pesos); **Puebla** (23hr., 6pm, 654 pesos); **San Andrés** (9½hr.; 3:30 and 10pm, 476 pesos); **Veracruz** (12hr.; 3:30 and 10pm, 532 pesos); and **Villahermosa** (12hr., 6 per day noon-9pm, 370 pesos). Cristóbal Colón rolls to: **Ocosingo** (13hr., 4:45pm, 350 pesos); **Palenque** (11hr., 4:45pm, 308 pesos); **San Cristóbal** (15hr., 4:45pm, 372 pesos); and **Tuxtla Gutiérrez** (16hr., 4:45pm, 410 pesos). ATS has second-class service to **Tulum** (1hr.; 10 per day, 28 pesos). Premier goes to **Mérida** (5hr., 10 per day, 185 pesos), via **Ticul** (3½hr., 146 pesos).

Tourist Office: A white and blue booth in the bus station with self-service pamphlets only. Open daily 7am-11pm.

Currency Exchange: Bital (tel. 3 02 72), on Av. Juárez, 1 block west of the *zócalo*, exchanges currency and traveler's checks and has a 24hr. **ATM.** Open M-F 8am-7pm.

Laundry: Maya Laundry (tel. 3 02 61), on Quinta, 1 block north of the plaza, on the right. Wash and dry 15 pesos per kg. Dry cleaning too. Open daily 8am-8pm.

Supermarket: El Súper del Ahorro (tel. 3 03 06), on Juárez, 3½ blocks west of Quinta. Open daily 7am-10pm.

Emergency: dial 060.

Police: (tel. 3 02 91) on Av. Principal, 2 blocks west of the plaza. Open 24hr.

Pharmacy: Farmacia del Carmen (tel. 3 23 30), on Av. Juárez, opposite the bus station. Open 24hr.

Medical Assistance: Centro de Salud (tel. 3 03 14), on the corner of Av. Juárez, across from the post office. Some English spoken. Open 24hr.

Post Office: (tel. 3 03 00) on Av. Juárez, 3 blocks from the plaza. Open M-F 8am-2:30pm, Sa 9am-1pm. **MexPost** in the same building. Open 9am-5pm.

Postal Code: 77710.

Internet Services: Cibernet (tel. 3 21 39) on Quinta and Calle 8 in Plaza Rincón del Sol. 1.50 pesos per min. Open daily 7am-10:30pm. **Cyberia** (tel. 3 21 59; email cyberia@playadel.carmen.com). Calle 4 and Av. 15. 2 pesos per min.; free movie at 7pm, and broadcasts of special events and sports. Inexpensive beer and coffee. Open M-Sa 9am-9pm, Su noon-9pm.

Phone Code: 987.

ACCOMMODATIONS

As Playa's accommodations begin to test the tempting waters of tourist-gouging prices, bargains become more and more scarce. Fortunately, as prices rise, so does quality, but during the high season (Dec. 21-Apr. 15 and July 15-Sept. 15), prices shoot up again. Most establishments lie along either **Quinta** or **Juárez,** close to the beach.

Posada Freud (tel. 3 06 01), on Av. Quinta, 4½ blocks north of the *zócalo.* Palm trees and colorful hammocks seduce passersby to lounge in one of Freud's 11 pastel abodes, each one possessing its own personality and charm. Singles 150-180 pesos; doubles 220-250; triples 350-400; quads 400-450.

Hotel Lilly, the flaming pink building on Av. Juárez, 1 block west of the plaza. Small, cushy beds in clean rooms with fans can be found at the convenient but noisy location near the bus stop. Singles 140 pesos; doubles 170 pesos; triples 200 pesos.

Campamento La Ruina (tel. 3 04 05), on the beach, 200m north of the ferry dock. Popular with Europeans, hostel-style *cabañas rústicas* with ceiling fans and tiny, stiff military beds have communal bathrooms and cooking facilities. Singles and doubles 100 pesos; triples 200 pesos (prices vary with season and room). Hammock-space under the *palapa* 75 pesos, plus 15 pesos for a plastic hammock rental. Pitch a tent in the sand for 45 pesos; 15 pesos per extra camper. Lockers 10 pesos.

CREA Youth Hostel (**HI;** tel. 3 15 08). From the plaza, walk 4 blocks on Juárez, and turn right before Farmacia La Salud. Walk another 4 blocks, passing the big concrete IMSS building; the hostel is 1½ blocks farther on the left. Single-sex dorms with bunk beds. 1 bed 60 pesos with a 50-peso deposit. *Cabañas* with private bathrooms and A/C 200 pesos plus a 100-peso deposit. 10% discount with HI card.

FOOD

It's hard to find a bargain in the glare of Quinta's flashy restaurants, although the occasional all-you-can-eat deal does come along. Cheaper fruit and *torta* experiences are found within the local hang outs along Av. Juárez.

Sabor, 1½ blocks north of the *zócalo* on Quinta. Both locals and tourists enjoy *platillos vegetariano*, coffee and pastry, and healthy breakfast (10-30 pesos) under vines and a bursting tree. Open daily 7am-10:30pm.

Media Luna (tel. 3 05 26), on Av. Quinta, next to Posada Freud. Whether you're relishing one of their healthy breakfasts or simply sipping a frothy *frappuccino helado* sprinkled with cinnamon, you'll want to linger in the padded wooden corners reverberating rhythmic tones. Tasty tropical fruit crepes (40 pesos) and luscious fruit platters topped with granola (25 pesos). Open daily 7:30am-11:30pm.

Tropical (tel. 3 21 11) on Av. Quinta, across Media Luna. Generous portions underneath a shady *palapa*. All natural smoothies 23 pesos; sandwiches 35 pesos; omelette atop whole wheat bread 30 pesos. Open daily 7am-midnight.

Cielito Lindo, on Av. Juárez and Av. 20, 1 block west of the post office. Mermaid, starfish, and fish complement a heavenly sky. *Sopa Azteca*, a thick creamy, cheese, and tomato soup with tortilla chips (25 pesos) is the perfect starter for the *platillos grandes*. Live music daily 10pm-2:30am. *Planta alta* (2nd fl.) open daily 5:30pm-2:30am; *planta baja* open 24hr.

Zas, on Av. Quinta, between Calle 12 and 14. For a classy, jazzy dining experience, savor gourmet food with pizzazz at Zas. Although somewhat hidden and on the upscale side, well worth the one-time splurge. Open daily 7:30am-11:30pm.

◐ SAND, SIGHTS, AND ENTERTAINMENT

Lined with palm trees and fringed by the turquoise waters of the Caribbean, Playa's **beaches** are sandy, white and oh, so relaxing. They are relatively free of seaweed and coral, and covered with scantily clad (if that) sunbathing tourists; the wave that began in Cancún has splashed down to Playa, but fortunately without the officious tourist zoning. If you want an aquatic escape, 120-160 pesos (depending on your bargaining ability) will buy you an hour's worth of **windsurfing.** Windsurfing equipment and other gear can be rented from some of the fancier hotels just south of the pier, or from shacks a few hundred meters north. **Snorkeling** is best off Isla Cozumel; visibility in Playa is murky.

While the pace of life on Playa's European-style 5th Av. is busy with vendors and tourist strollers, locals close shop early. After dark, sun-lovers recuperate from the day's rays swaying in hammocks jiving to guitar-strumming, flute-playing folk music. Come nightfall at **Karen's Grill,** on La Quinta 1½ blocks north of the plaza, waiters start the party by making noise with trays, escorting *muchachas* to the dance floor, and pouring café flambe in a waterfall style, all to the rhythm of *salsa* and merengue (live South American music daily 8-11pm; Happy Hour 7-9pm). For a swingin' time, try the wooden swings underneath the **Blue Parrot Inn Palapa** right on the beach at Calle 12, east of Av. Quinta (open daily noon-1am). Shake and groove to Latin and international dance hits on and about **Capitan Tuix's** wooden ship on the beach, at Calle 4 (open daily 10pm-late). A hankering for Hollywood can be indulged at **Cinema Playa del Carmen,** four blocks west of the *zócalo* and one block north of Av. Principal, has evening showings of U.S. flicks (30 pesos).

ISLA COZUMEL

Cozumel (pop. 75,000) originally drew attention to itself as a key trading center for the Maya and later as a pirate refuge for Sir Francis Drake and Jean Lafitte. In the 50s, Jacques Cousteau called worldwide attention to the natural wonders of the nearby **Palancar Reef,** the second largest worldwide, and the sea life it sustains. It is no surprise that Cozumel is the popular "ecological getaway" for tourists wishing to leave Cancún's confines and explore Mexico (without saying goodbye to luxury, dollars, or sycophantic service). There is more to Cozumel, however, than over-priced dive shops and snorkeling tours; while the red and white diving banner has become the island's unofficial flag, much of the island is undeveloped. Miles upon miles of empty white beach greet the tourist who musters the energy to leave San Miguel de Cozumel the city and explore Cozumel the island. Isolated beachfront cafes and seaside roads offer splendid views of the Caribbean and opportunities to discover the colorful world of the reefs.

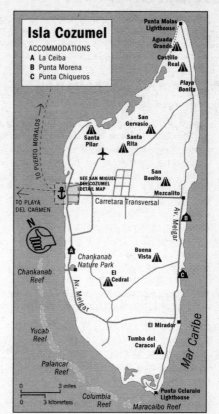

Isla Cozumel

ACCOMMODATIONS
A La Ceiba
B Punta Morena
C Punta Chiqueros

YUCATÁN PENINSULA

■ **ORIENTATION**

The island of Cozumel lies 18km east of the northern Quintana Roo coast and 85km south of Isla Mujeres. The island is most commonly accessed via ferry from **Playa del Carmen** (to the west) or **Puerto Morelos** (to the north). **Ferries** from Puerto Morelos (tel. 2 09 50) transport cars to and from Cozumel twice daily, docking in the island's only town, **San Miguel de Cozumel,** on the west shore (2½hr.; 9am and 1pm; US$50 per car, US$8 per person). Tourist vehicles supposedly have priority, but the **car ferry** is inconvenient and unpredictable. The tourist office recommends securing a spot in line 12 hours in advance. **Ferries** between Playa del Carmen and Cozumel run frequently. Tickets can be bought at the dock in Cozumel and from the booth on Playa's plaza (45min., 12 per day, round-trip 160 pesos). If you are coming from Cancún, an alternative to the bus-ferry ordeal is the 20-minute **air shuttle** operated by Aerocaribe (tel. 2 34 56).

At 53km long and 14km wide, Cozumel is Mexico's largest Caribbean island. Downtown streets are clearly labeled and numbered with stubborn logic. If you don't mind occasionally spine-wrenching road conditions, the rest of the island is easily explored by bike, moped, or safari. Taxis are everywhere.

As you step off the ferry into San Miguel, **Av. Rafael Melgar** runs along the shore, circling the entire island. **Av. Juárez,** a pedestrian walkway for the first two blocks, is directly in front, running perpendicular to the shore and crossing the town. Juárez continues on to cross the island as **Carretera Transversal,** and joins Av. Melgar on the other side. *Calles* run parallel to Juárez and are labeled *Sur* and *Norte* (Nte.) with respect to Juárez. North of Juárez, *calles* increase in even numbers; south of Juárez, they increase in odd numbers. *Avenidas* run north-south, are numbered in multiples of five, and are designated *Norte* or *Sur* with respect to Juárez. **Av. Adolfo Rosada Salas** is between Calles 1 and 3 Sur. Av. Melgar leads south to the main points of interest: the national park at **Laguna Chankanaab** and the popular beach of **Playa Corona** are south of town on the western shore; **Palancar Reef** lies off the island's southwestern tip. The nearly deserted eastern coast is dotted by Maya temples and altars, horseback rentals, camping spots, and a few restaurants and camping spots.

🔁 PRACTICAL INFORMATION

TRANSPORTATION

Airport: (tel. 2 04 85) 2km north of town. **Aerocaribe** (tel. 2 34 56), **Continental** (tel. 2 08 47), and **Mexicana** (tel. 2 29 45) serve Cozumel.

Ferries: Passenger ferries leave for Playa del Carmen every hr. starting at 4am from the dock at the end of Av. Juárez (80 pesos). Arrive early, as ferries sell out several minutes before departure. Buy tickets at the corner of Melgar and the dock. **Car ferries** (tel. 2 08 27) leave from the dock south of the main dock.

Taxis: (tel. 2 02 36 or 2 00 41). From the plaza: 80 pesos to the airport; 110 pesos to Chankanaab; 130 pesos to Punta Morena. Expect to pay more for more people.

Car Rental: LE$$ Pay (tel. 2 47 44 or 2 19 47), on Av. Melgar, about 1km south of town. VW Safaris (US$25 per day), jeeps, and mopeds all available. Discounts for multiple-day rentals. Open daily 8am-8pm. Bring driver's license and major credit card.

Moped Rental: Pretty expensive. Available in the lobby of Hotel Posada Edem (see **Accommodations**) for about 300 pesos.

Bike Rental: Rentadora Cozumel (tel. 2 11 20 or 2 15 03) on Av. 10 at Calle 1 Sur. 110 pesos per day. Return by 6pm. US$25 deposit required. Open daily 8am-8pm.

TOURIST AND FINANCIAL SERVICES

Tourist Office: (tel. 2 09 72), on the 2nd fl. of "Plaza del Sol," the building to the left of Bancomer, on the plaza. Open M-F 9am-2pm.

Consulates: While there are no consulates on Cozumel, Mr. Bryan Wilson (tel. 2 06 54), who works closely with the Mérida U.S. consulate, provides unofficial, free assistance to English-speaking travelers.

Currency Exchange: BanNorte (tel. 2 16 82), right off the dock, exchanges traveler's checks. Bank open M-F 9am-12:30pm. **Bancomer** (tel. 2 05 50), on the plaza, has the same rates but charges a flat fee of US$0.50 per check. Open M-F 9am-4:30pm, Sa 10am-2pm. **BITAL** (tel. 2 01 42), on the plaza, has a 24hr. **ATM.** Open M-F 9am-2:30pm, Sa 10am-1pm.

LOCAL SERVICES

Bookstore: Agencia de Publicaciones Gracia (tel. 2 00 31), on the plaza. Has last week's *Newsweek* for the price of a meal (50 pesos). Open daily 8am-10pm.

Laundry: Margarita, Av. 20 Sur 285 (tel. 2 28 65), near Calle 3 Sur. Self-service 30 pesos per machine for wash and 20 pesos for each drying machine. Open M-Sa 7am-9pm, Su 8:30am-5pm.

EMERGENCY AND COMMUNICATIONS

Emergency: dial 060 or knock on Mr. Wilson's white house at Av. 15 and Calle 13 Sur.

Police: (tel. 2 00 92) on Calle 11 Sur near Rafael Melgar, in the Palacio Municipal. Some English spoken.

Red Cross: (tel. 2 10 58), on Av. 20 Sur at Av. Adolfo Salas. Open 24hr.

Pharmacy: Farmacia Kiosco (tel. 2 24 85), on the *zócalo* near Hotel López. Everything for the sun-happy or sun-sick tourist. Open M-Sa 8am-10pm, Su 9am-10pm.

Medical Services: Cozumel Clinica (tel. 2 32 41) Calle 6 Nte. 132 between Av. 5 y 10 and **Medical Center (CEM),** Av. 20 Nte. 425 (tel. 2 29 19 or 2 14 19), between Calles 10 and 8 Nte. Both have English-speaking doctors. For an **ambulance,** call 2 14 19.

Post Office: (tel. 2 01 06) off Rafael Melgar, just south of Calle 7 Sur along the sea. Open M-F 8am-5pm, Sa 9am-1pm. **Postal Code:** 77600.

San Miguel de Cozumel

ACCOMMODATIONS

A Hotel Flamingo
B Hotel Posada Edem
C Posada Letty

YUCATÁN PENINSULA

Fax: (tel. 2 00 56) next to the post office.

Internet Access: Internet Cozumel (tel. 2 13 17), Local 1, 3 blocks east of the waterfront on Calle 11 Sur. 30 pesos per hr. Open M-F 9am-6:30pm, Sa 10am-2:30pm. **Coffee Net** (tel. 2 63 94), in the Plaza on Av. Juárez. Comfortable chairs in a classy coffee shop. US$6 per 30 min. or US$10 per hr. Open M-Sa 9am-11pm, Su 3-10pm.

Phone Code: 987.

ACCOMMODATIONS AND CAMPING

Hotels in Cozumel are more expensive than in Playa, and extra pesos do not guarantee higher-quality rooms. Peak-season travelers should hunt down a room before noon, and resist being roped into a pricey package deal when stepping off the ferry. Secluded camping spots are at **Punta Morena** and **Punta Chiqueros,** on the island's Caribbean coast. Short-term campers should encounter no problems with the authorities, but for longer stays, consult the tourist office to find out the best camping options.

Hotel Posada Edem, Calle 2 Nte. 124 (tel. 2 11 66), between Av. 10 and 5 Nte, across from the taxi station. Upon docking, go left 1 block, turn right, and walk up 2 blocks. Decent rooms with 2 beds, fans, and *agua purificada* in lobby. Singles 160 pesos; doubles 180 pesos; extra person 50 pesos.

Cabañas Punta Morena, Carretera Transversal km 17. Ideal for those who have their own transportation. Next to a beachfront seafood restaurant, these *cabañas* have the best view around. Rooms lack furniture, but with the mesmerizing seascape, you won't even notice. At night during summer, turtles lay their eggs on the nearby shore. Volleyball court on the beach. Surfboards (200 pesos) and boogie boards (100 pesos) available for rent. All rooms 200 pesos.

Posada Letty (tel. 2 02 57), Calle 1 Sur 272, between Av. 10 and 15. Their business card promises "Cleanliness-Order-Morality." We can only vouch for the first. Big green rooms have big windows with big beds and feel more like a house than a hotel. Singles 200 pesos; doubles 320 pesos; extra person 60 pesos.

Huespedes Punta Allen, Punta Allen 8 (tel. 84 02 25 or 84 10 01), between Uxmal and Yaxchilan. The familial environment with a dining room replete with plants and musical instruments. Includes continental breakfast (toast, orange juice, and coffee). Singles and doubles 250-300 pesos; triples 360-400 pesos.

◐ FOOD AND CAFES

Food in Cozumel tends to be expensive. The key is to avoid places that advertise in English in order to keep extra pesos in your pockets. There are several moderately priced restaurants a few blocks from the *centro*, as well as hidden cafes on side streets. The **market,** on Av. Adolfo Salas between Av. 20 and 25 Sur, offers the standard items: meat, fish, and *frutas*. The small diners outside the market offer generous portions of regional dishes. For a sweet treat, stroll into **Panificadora Cozumel,** on Calle 2 Nte. between Quinta and Melger, where pastries and baked goods will be melting in your mouth for pocket change (open daily 6am-9:30pm).

Casa Denis (tel. 2 00 67), across from the flea market on the *zócalo*. Be a part of *La Familia Denis*, the first traditional restaurant of Cozumel with generational home-cooked recipes, black and white photos of JFK, Jackie Onassis, and Che Guevara fishing with Fidel Castro. If this is not enough, enjoy the breeze and shade of the Mamey tree c. 1880 in the patio. Breakfast (25 pesos); sandwiches (20-30 pesos); *comida regional,* (20-30 pesos). Open daily 7am-11pm.

El Abuelo Gerardo (tel. 2 10 12), on Av. 10, between Juárez and Calle 2 Nte. near the church is a mellow place to grab an ice-cold afternoon beer. *Antojitos* (20-40 pesos), fish fillet (45 pesos), and good breakfasts (25 pesos). Open daily 7:30am-10:30pm.

San Francisco Restaurant, on the southwest coast of the island, km 15. Grab ice-cold and chilled drinks or freshly squeezed tropical drinks with chips, guacamole, and *salsa*. *Antojitos* are 15-37 pesos and a feast of *pescado entero* (whole fish) is cooked in ten different styles—your choice.

Rock-n-Java Caribbean Cafe (tel. 24 40 5), Av. Melgar 602 near LE$$ Pay between Calle 9 and 11 Sur. Healthy breakfast with multi-grain and fruit topped french toast (40 pesos), veggie salads (35 pesos), homemade soups (30 pesos), and flavored coffee (45-25 pesos) are all served on tables with a view of the Caribbean, surrounded by black and white crusty sailor photos. Open Su-F 7am-11pm, Sa 7am-2pm.

The Coffee Bean, Calle 3 Sur, next to Pizza Hut and the shore. Serves succulent, rich, freshly baked homemade desserts such as strawberry cheesecake, pecan pie, apple pie a la mode, and brownie with espresso *helado* and coffee from Chiapas and Veracruz (10-25 pesos). Open M-Sa 7:30am-11pm, Su noon-2pm.

◖ CORAL, SAND, AND SIGHTS

Most visitors to Cozumel have one sight in mind: the beautiful coral reefs around the island. Mopeds and safaris are the best way of getting to an ideal snorkeling spot or discovering a new one. Otherwise, expensive taxis will be the only option.

Heading south out of town on a counter-clockwise circuit of the island, **Hotel La Ceiba** makes a good stop-off point for snorkeling. The hotel has a perfect beach for swimming and a reef and plane wreck offshore waiting to be explored. The **Del Mar Aquatics** dive shop rents out snorkeling gear (US$8 per day) and scuba equipment

(US$45 per day), as well as offering deep-sea fishing, night/day dives, and snorkeling trips (tel. 2 08 44; 200m north of La Ceiba; open daily 7:30am-7:30pm).

Chankanaab National Park, a few more kilometers down the coastal highway, is comprised of a lagoon, friendly dolphins, a botanical garden, museum, restaurant, and a snorkeling area. A stroll through the endemic forest in the botanical garden, past the meter-long, beady-eyed, sunbathing iguanas, brings you to ancient temples. The perfectly oval natural lagoon, once brimming with reef fish, is home to hardy survivors of years of gringo sunscreen attrition. Yet the real attraction is the abundant tropical fish and coral in the Caribbean a few meters away. Matching the capacity crowds on land, the reef teems with eels, anemones, and a cornucopia of colorful fish. The museum focuses on the park's natural resources and houses incredible photographs of the underwater caves in the lagoon. (Open daily 7am-6pm. Admission 120 pesos.)

The best underwater sightseeing in Cozumel is likely to be on the off-shore reefs, accessible by boat. You can rent snorkeling equipment anywhere. The standard rate is US$4-8 per day, plus deposit. Most of the numerous **dive shops** in town are on the waterfront or on Calle 3 Sur, between Av. Melgar and Av. 10. Always consider safety before price; look for shops with **ANOAAT** (Asociación Nacional de Operadores de Actividades Aquaticas Turístico) affiliation. **Blue Bubble Divers** (tel. 2 44 83; www.bluebubble.com), on Av. 5 at Calle 3 Sur, has a friendly, English-speaking staff and a choice of 20 reefs to visit (1½hr. single-tank dive US$45; snorkeling equipment US$6 per day; open daily 7am-9pm). Another option is **Aqua Safari,** Melgar at Calle 5 Sur (single-tank dive US$35; 2hr. snorkeling boat trip US$20; open daily 7am-1pm and 4-6:30pm).

The route along the eastern coast passes many secluded beaches that make for good picnic and camping spots. Always ask before pitching a tent. While the beaches boast magnificent turquoise waters and few tourists, the water is turbulent and somewhat dangerous. Midway along the coast, Carretera Transversal branches west and loops back through the jungle to town.

The ancient Maya sites of **El Cedral** and the **Tumba de Caracol** lie on a bumpy trek to the **Celarain Lighthouse,** on the island's southernmost point. The top of the lighthouse offers a thrilling view of the northern shores of the island. To get to the crumbled stone structures of **San Gervasio,** the only extensively excavated and partially reconstructed Maya ruins on the island, take Juárez out of town. After 8km, a "San Gervasio" sign marks a gravel road branching to the left. Follow the road another 6km. (Open daily 8am-5pm. Admission 40 pesos, Su 20 pesos.) The small, air-conditioned **Museo de la Isla de Cozumel** (tel. 2 14 75 or 2 14 34), on the waterfront between Calles 4 and 6, is filled with photographs, poetry, coral, marine and jungle trivia, and sculptures (open daily 9am-8pm; admission US$5). Check for other cultural events in the **Centro de Convenciones,** between the Plaza del Sol and Bancomer, or in the plaza itself, where locals gather on Sunday nights for that irresistible rumba beat.

◪ NIGHTLIFE

Cozumel's nightlife is targeted toward the spendthrift gringos who jaunt into town from their cruise ships. Boisterous all night long, **Carlos n' Charlie's** (tel. 2 01 91), on Rafael Melgar, one block north of the dock, entertains *norteamericanos* with crazy drinks, slammer contests, and stupid rules of the house (open daily 10am-1am). A mellow, more native crowd enjoys reggae, *salsa*, and merengue at **Joe's Lobster Bar** (tel. 2 32 75), on Av. 10, between Calles 1 and 3 Sur. A live band starts up the action at 10:30pm and the place keeps kicking until 2 or 3am (beers 35 pesos). The full-fledged disco **Neptuno** (tel. 2 15 37), five blocks south of the plaza, has multi-level dance floors bombarded by lasers and throbbing bass (cover 75 pesos; open daily 9pm-early morning). The after party is at **Viva México** (tel. 2 07 99), on Av. Melgar at Juárez, under giant *piñatas*, multi-colored paper cut-outs, and dangling stars overlooking the ocean (beers 25 pesos, cocktails 40 pesos; open daily 10pm-late).

IT'S BETTER WHERE IT'S WETTER The Palancar Reef of Cozumel, the second-largest in the world, continually draws legions of scuba fanatics eager to explore its dramatic underwater formations. While the aesthetics are unmistakable, few visitors realize the biological importance of those majestic coral pillars. Coral is to a reef as topsoil is to a rainforest—without it, the basis of all life disappears. If the coral is destroyed, the entire reef's ecosystem disintegrates. International law prohibits the harvesting of coral, but it does not forbid the purchase or exportation of coral-derived jewelry and crafts. Several shops in Cozumel sell goods made from coral, and, by patronizing these establishments, tourists heighten the demand for coral and adversely affect the splendorous reefs they have come to see. Just don't buy coral.

For action and romance with happy endings and no alcohol, try **Cinema Cozumel,** on Av. Rafael Melgar between Calles 2 and 4, or **Cine Cecillo Borques,** on Juárez between Av. 30 and 35. Borques is cheaper (12 pesos) but more remote.

TULUM

On the edge of the Etaib (Black Bees) jungle, atop a rocky cliff, stands the walled Maya "City of the Dawn." While the ruins do not rival those of Uxmal or Chichen Itzá in terms of scale, many of the buildings are still intact, and their towering location over the breaking waves of the Caribbean is unforgettable. First settled in the 4th century, Tulum was the oldest continuously inhabited city in the New World when the Spanish arrived. Today, sun worshippers of a different kind tramp to the ancient port, complementing their sightseeing with healthy doses of swimming. Unfortunately, Tulum's temples and their natural backdrop, gracing book covers everywhere, are attracting a rising number of daytrippers from Cancún.

◢ ORIENTATION

Located 42km southeast of Cobá, 63km south of Playa del Carmen, and 127km south of Cancún, the ruins are the southernmost link in a chain of tourist attractions on the Caribbean coast of Quintana Roo, and the eastern extreme of the major Maya archaeological sites. Tulum sprawls out over three separate areas: the **crucero** (the crossroads), the beach **cabañas,** and **Pueblo Tulum** (pop. 16,000). Arriving in Tulum from Cancún on Rte. 307, buses first stop at the *crucero*, a few kilometers before town. Here, a couple of restaurants, hotels, and overpriced minimarts huddle together 800m west of the ruins. The access road turns south at the ruins, leading to food and lodging at *cabañas* 2km farther down the road. Pueblo Tulum, 4km south of the *crucero*, also offers travelers a handful of roadside restaurants and services.

Second-class **buses** provide cheap transportation from Tulum to nearby cities and to the sights and beaches that lie to the north on Rte. 307. Some travelers hitchhike from site to site along the highway.

◢ PRACTICAL INFORMATION

Buses: Tulum's bus station is on the eastern side of Rte. 307 right in the middle of the Pueblo. The small waiting room is sandwiched between two currency exchange booths. ADO trucks to: **Córdoba** (12hr., 8am, 396 pesos); **Escárcega** (4hr., 1 and 9pm, 230 pesos); **Mexico City** (22hr., 1pm, 720 pesos); **Veracruz** (12hr., 4:30pm, 582 pesos); and **Villahermosa** (9hr.; 1, 4:30, and 9pm; 370 pesos). Various second-class buses with shifting schedules travel to: **Cancún** (2hr., 2 per day, 75 pesos); **Chetumal** (4hr., 6am and 2:30pm, 90 pesos); **Chichén Itzá** (3½hr., 6am and 2:30pm, 90 pesos); Cobá (30min., 4 per day, 52 pesos); **Escárcega** (8hr., 6am and 2:30pm, 190 pesos); **Mérida** (5hr., 4 per day, 90 pesos); **Ocosingo** (15hr., 4:30 and 5:45pm, 332 pesos); **Palenque** (14hr., 4:30 and 5:45pm, 315 pesos); **Playa del Carmen** (1hr., 10 per day,

56 pesos), **San Cristóbal** (16hr., 4:30 and 5:45pm, 390 pesos); and **Valladolid** (2½hr., 4 per day, 74 pesos).

Taxis: Are available at the crucero, in Pueblo Tulum, along Rte. 307, and at various cabañas. Be prepared to pay more for a taxi than a cabaña.

Tourist Office: There is no tourist office, though a few stands at the ruins can provide sketchy maps.

Currency Exchange: At the *crucero* or next to the bus office in Pueblo Tulum.

Police: (tel. 1 20 55), in the Delegación Municipal, 2 blocks past the post office.

Pharmacy: Súper Farmacia, just past the post office. Open daily 8am-9pm.

Medical Assistance: Dr. Arturo F. Ventre speaks English. Available daily 8am-noon and 6-9pm.

Post Office: a few hundred meters into town on Rte. 307. Open M-F 9am-1pm and 3-6pm. **Postal Code:** 77780. **Phone Code:** 987.

◤ ACCOMMODATIONS AND CAMPING

Tulum offers two lodging options: two- to three-star type hotels, or beachside *cabañas*. The *cabañas* cannot be beat for price and location, just a short walk to the ancient Maya civilization upon a cliff. An endless stream of *cabañas* line the beachfront, where you can chill with mellow international travelers, listen to local singers, and perfect your tan. Bring mosquito netting and repellent, because those bugs are the big nasty.

Cabañas Santa Fe, just off the paved road, 1km south of the ruins. Follow the signs to Don Armando's and turn left. If you don't mind the perpetual sand, you can shack up here with backpackers from all over the world. Several sticks 'n' *palapa* combos to choose from: bare *cabaña* with sand floor and small hammock 40 pesos; 1-bed *cabaña* with cement floor 140 pesos; 2-bed *cabaña* 200 pesos; hammock rental 40 pesos per night. During high season, be prepared to stand in line early in the morning to sign up for a room; no reservations allowed.

Don Armando Cabañas (tel. 4 76 72 or 1 13 54), on the access road 1km south of the ruins, is a humble paradise with a volleyball court. The *cabañas* are generally solid and secure, and the communal facilities are more than outhouses. *Cabaña* with 1 bed and 1 hammock 120 pesos, with 2 beds 150 pesos; 2 double beds 250 pesos. Deposit 50 pesos. Camp or hang a hammock for 30 pesos per person.

◤ FOOD

Although the points of interest in Tulum tend to be rather spread out, a hearty and inexpensive bite of *típico* food is never too far away. Both the *pueblo* and the *crucero* have satisfying restaurants as well as *mini-súpers;* the former are slightly cheaper and provide sustenance for daytrips.

La Chica Poblana, in Pueblo Tulum is the place to savor delicious family cooking; *comida corrida* (28 pesos) and tasty *huevos moluteños* (20 pesos) in the *pueblo.* 15 pesos gets you the day's entree with beans and tortillas. Open daily 8am-midnight.

Restaurante El Crucero, in Hotel El Crucero. Comfortable and shady interior provides respite from Maya sun. Breakfast (fruit salad, orange juice, toast, and coffee) for 30 pesos. Open daily 7am-9pm.

Restaurante Santa Fe, at the campground on the beach. Reggae tunes, *salsa* rhythms, and local guitarists, are the perfect complement to the fresh fish (40-60 pesos), and *cabaña*-made, wholesome breakfasts (30-40 pesos). 2-for-1 Happy Hour during high season. Restaurant and bar open daily 7am-11pm.

◉ SIGHTS

Tulum has a rare and exquisite combination of temples and beaches. Stoic watch-towers, set alight by every sunrise, overlook crystal-clear waters.

THE RUINS

While a sharp increase in tourists necessitated the cordoning off of most of **Tulum's** historic buildings, the architecture and murals can still be admired from a short distance away. Tulum lies a brisk 10-minute walk east of Rte. 307 from the *crucero*. For the Homeresque, the amusement-like park train (15 pesos) covers the distance in slightly less time. Admission tickets are sold at a booth to the left of the parking lot. (Open daily 8am-6pm. Admission 40 pesos; Su free. Guided tours available.)

The first thing visitors see in Tulum is the impressive **dry-laid wall** surrounding the city center's three landlocked sides. The wall, made of small rocks wedged together, was originally 3.6m thick and 3m high. It shielded the city from the aggression of neighboring Maya city-states and prevented all but the 150 or so priests and governors of Tulum from entering the city for most of the year. After Tulum's defeat at the hands of the Spanish in 1544, the wall fended off English, Dutch, and French pirates and, in 1847, gave Mayas refuge from government forces during the Caste War. Representations of the Maya Descending God cover the western walls and are illuminated every evening by the rays of the setting sun.

Just inside and to the left of the entrance lies a grave and the remains of platforms that once supported huts. Behind these platforms are the **House of the Halach Uinik** (the House of the Ruler), characterized by a traditional Maya four-column entrance; the **Palacio,** the largest residential building in Tulum; and the **Temple of the Paintings,** a stellar example of Postclassic Maya architecture. Well-preserved 600-year-old murals inside the temple depict deities intertwined with serpents, fruits, flowers, and corn offerings. Masks of **Itzamná,** the Maya Creator, occupy the northwest and southwest corners of the building.

El Castillo, the most prominent structure in Tulum, looms to the east, over the rocky seaside cliff. Serving as a pyramid and temple, it commands a view of the entire walled city with a double-headed, feathered serpent sprawled across the facade and a diving god in the center. It also served as a lighthouse, allowing returning fishermen to find the only gap in the barrier reef just off-shore. Its walls, like those of many buildings in Tulum, slope outward, but its doorposts slope inward. The castle's architectural and structural eccentricities are due to its numerous rebuildings.

In front of the temple is the **sacrificial stone** where the Maya held battle ceremonies. Once the stars had been consulted and a propitious day determined, a warrior-prisoner was selected for sacrifice. At the climax of the celebration, attendants painted the warrior's body blue—a sacred color of the Maya—and the chief priest cut his heart out and poured the blood over the idols in the temple. The body was given to the soldiers below, who were thought to acquire the strength to overcome their enemies through cannibalism.

To the southwest of El Castillo on the same plaza is the **Temple of the Initial Series.** Named after a stela found here, the temple bears a date that corresponded to the beginning of the Maya religious calendar in the year 761. The **Temple of the Descending God,** with a fading relief of a feathered, armed deity diving from the sky, stands on the opposite side of the plaza. Perched on its own precipice on the northeast side of the beach, the **Temple of the Winds** was acoustically designed to act as a storm-warning system. Sure enough, before Hurricane Gilbert struck the site in 1988, the temple's airways dutifully whistled their alarm.

THE BEACH

Swimming, splashing, and tanning on the beach are popular ways to end a hot day in Tulum, and nude bathing is no longer a rare phenomenon. Off-shore, waves crash over Tulum's **barrier reef,** the largest in the Americas; it runs the full length of the Yucatán peninsula, including Belize. Although the water is not as clear as at Xel-Ha or Akumal (see below), the fish are just as plentiful. To enjoy them, rent **scuba and snorkeling equipment** from the **dive shop** (tel. 1 20 96) at Cabañas Santa Fe (60 pesos per day for snorkeling; open daily 8am-3:30pm). The 500m swim to the reef is often a struggle against a north-south current (see p. 644). The shop plans trips to the reef and a nearby *cenote.* Another option is to snorkel or dive in Cenote Dos Ojos (you must be an experienced diver).

To escape the beaches, waves, and salty water, bike are available from Cabañas Santa Fe (50 pesos per hr.) to visit one of the *cenotes* in the woods near Pueblo Tulum. Look for a small patch of gravel, large enough for two cars, on the right side of the road as you head toward Chetumal. Follow a rugged path to the serene **Cenote Escondido** or the smaller **Cenote Cristal** 100m farther down the road.

NEAR TULUM

SIAN KA'AN BIOSPHERE RESERVE. Seven kilometers south of Tulum on the coast road lies the 1.5-million-acre **Sian Ka'an Biosphere Reserve.** Sanctuary to over 345 species of bird as well as every endangered cat species of southern Mexico, the reserve also guards a wide range of wetland, marine habitats, and coral reefs as well as 27 Maya sites. Entrance is free but limited, and *lancha* tours are given exclusively by Sian Ka'an biologists. For more info, contact **Amigos de Sian Ka'an** in Cancún, Av. Cobá 5 (tel. 98 84 95 83; email sian@cancun.rce.com.mx), in Plaza América.

XEL-HA AND AKUMAL. Xel-Ha' (SHELL-ha) "Where the water is born" is famous for its natural aquarium, almost 2m deep, amidst jungle, caves, and coves. Visitors splash around all day in the *caleta* (inlet) nearby and admire parrot fishes and meter-long barracudas toward the rope that marks the open sea. For relative peace during busy times, cross the inlet and explore the underwater caves or stay dry and visit the sea turtle camp, where a ritual altar was discovered. Use caution and don't go duck-diving under overhangs on your own. The steep 250-peso entrance fee to the caves includes visits to two *cenotes*, a natural river, underground sea caves, and a hammock siesta. You still have to pay for snorkel equipment rental, available near the inlet for 80 more pesos. (Open daily 8am-5pm. Admission 250 pesos.) Try arriving before noon, when busloads of tourists from the resorts overrun the place. Lockers (10 pesos plus a 5-peso deposit) and towels (15 pesos plus a 50-peso deposit) are available at the shower area.

Xel-Ha also maintains a small archaeological site on the highway, 100m south of the entrance to the inlet. **El Templo de Los Pájaros** and **El Palacio,** small Classic and Postclassic ruins, were only recently opened to the public. The former (the ruin farthest into the jungle) overlooks a peaceful, shady *cenote* where swimming and jumping off a rope swing is permitted. The jungle at Xel-Ha is rife with mosquitoes, so bring insect repellent.

A few kilometers north of Xel-Ha toward Playa del Carmen lies the bay of **Akumal,** "place of the turtles" in Mayan. Green and Hawksbill turtles crawl up on the beach from June to August. An older, wealthier crowd is drawn to its older, wealthier underwater activities. The **Akumal Dive Shop** (tel. 987 4 12 59) rents snorkeling equipment (US$6 per day), organizes snorkeling and scuba trips (US$30 per person; US$35 per 1-tank dive; dive shop open daily 8am-1pm and 2-5pm).

Getting There: Xel-Ha lies 15km north of Tulum; Akumal is 10km farther north. Get on any northbound bus and ask to be let off at either site (5 pesos). Taxis charge exorbitant rates. Hitchhiking here is tough because the traffic is fast and the wait can be unnerving. Getting back to Tulum at the end of the day, when buses begin to come less and less frequently, can be challenging. Vigorously wave down a bus on its way to Tulum or Cancún. Locals will usually be able to tell you when the next one is due to pass.

CENOTE DOS OJOS. Cenote Dos Ojos, 1km south of Xel-Ha', is the **longest and most extensive underwater cavern in the world,** stretching for 33,855m. It was originally a dry cave system with limestone formations in shades of amber as well as calcic stalactites, stalagmites, and natural wind-etchings. The whole system was flooded long ago, preserving the caves in their new underwater condition. Snorkelers and divers find a haven in "the place of hidden waters", along with tetras, mollies, and swordfish. You must be an experienced certified open water diver with extensive experience, including night dives, to venture into Dos Ojos.

The trip begins with a bumpy 20-minute ride in an open truck. Monstrous bugs whiz by as you zip through the dense jungle. A complete underwater circuit of the caves, at a depth of 10m, takes about 45 minutes. Meanwhile, snorkelers can explore the larger of the two cave entrances. For divers and snorkelers alike, this is a unique opportunity to explore a spectacular unspoiled cave system that has only been explored since 1993. The dive costs US$80 (plus US$25 equipment rental). Snorkelers pay US$45. Three trips depart daily from **Dos Ojos Dive Center** (tel. 98 76 09 87), several hundred meters south of the park entrance, usually leaving at 9, 11am, and 1pm. Trips also leave from the **Cabañas Santa Fe** (see p. 641).

COBÁ

Deep within the Yucatán jungle, and guarded by shallow lakes, Cobá receives less attention than her big sisters, Chichén Itzá and Tulum. The government has poured less money into the site, leaving an estimated 6500 buildings unexcavated. The site's isolation only heightens the impressiveness of its towering **Nohoch Múl,** the tallest Maya structure (42m) in the northern Yucatán. The town of Cobá itself, unfortunately, consists of only a bus stop, a few restaurants and shops, and a photocopy machine.

To get to the **ruins of Cobá,** walk south on the main street in town as far as the T-junction at the lake. Here, take a left onto the Av. Voz Suave (Soft Voice); the ruins are a five-minute walk down the road. Regardless of when you arrive at the site, bring a water bottle and wear a hat. And unless you feel like being sacrificed to the mosquito, bring plenty of repellent as well. (Ruins open daily 8am-5pm. Admission 30 pesos, Su free.)

GUIDE TO THE RUINS

Once through the gate, the site's four main attractions are laid out before you in a "Y"-shaped formation, with the entrance and the ruins in Groupo Cobá at the base of the "Y." Past the entrance, and after an immediate right, looms the impressive **Temple of the Churches,** built over seven 52-year periods, each one associated with a new chief priest. Only the front face of the temple has been excavated, revealing a corbel-vaulted passageway that you can explore. Rising out of the jungle to the northeast are the gray steps of the ruins' centerpiece, **El Castillo.** In front of the structure is a stone sacrificial table, upon which animal offerings were made to Chac, the rain god. The stela depicts Chac; another nearby features a kneeling Maya. Follow a second passageway farther south to the **Plaza del Templo,** where assemblies were once held. The red plant dye still visible on the walls of the passageway dates from the 5th century. A mortar here hints at the staple food of the ancient (and contemporary) Maya—maize. Return to the main path for a look at the **ballcourt** with its intact stone arches.

A 1km walk up the "trunk" of the "Y" takes you to the other sites. Follow the right branch for another kilometer to reach a collection of eight stelae in the **Grupo Macanxoc.** On the way, a well-engineered Maya *sacbe* awaits your walk. This particular road is 20m wide and raised 4m from the jungle floor. The ornate stone slabs of the Grupo Macanxoc were erected as memorials above the tombs of Maya royals. Especially impressive and well preserved is the first, the **Retrato del Rey.** The king is shown standing on the heads of two slaves, bow and arrow in hand, wearing a *quetzal*-feather headdress.

Continue north to the left-hand branch of the "Y." After 200m, follow an unmarked trail on the right to the three stelae of **Chumuc Múl.** The first stela depicts a kneeling Maya ballplayer. Sure enough, this is the tomb of a victorious captain. You can make out the *chicle* ball in the upper-left-hand corner. The second stela depicts a princess, while the third portrays a *sacerdote* (priest). His seal is stamped on top of the slab, along with a jaguar's head, a common Maya symbol of worship. Two hundred meters farther up this branch of the "Y," you'll run into **Sacbe No. 1.** This thoroughfare ran from Chichén Itzá, 101km to the west; runners were posted every 5km so messages could be sent between settlements via a series of quick dashes. During the city's height (900-1200), Cobá is believed to have been the major crossroads in a commercial region of 17 cities. Images of the honeybee god around the site are a reminder of this ancient economic hub—the Maya used honey (along with salt, coconuts, and jade) as a medium of exchange.

The tour climaxes with the breathtaking sight of the **Nohoch Múl,** the tallest Maya structure in the Yucatán with 127 steps. The pyramid's nine levels, where Maya priests once led processions, display carvings of the "diving god" similar to the ones in Tulum. Atop the top level, enjoy the view of Lake Cobá, Lake Macanxoc, and the rest of the ancient Maya commercial and religious city.

CHETUMAL

Residents of Quintana Roo are very proud of Chetumal (pop. 200,000), the relatively new capital of the youngest state in Mexico, which straddles the border with Belize. Although Chetumal (pop. 200,000), was founded in 1898 to intercept shipments of arms to Maya insurgents and to prevent illegal timber harvesting, it was leveled in 1955 after a hurricane. The complete reconstruction explains the wide avenues, modern architecture, and waterfront boulevard. The city is also home to an extensive shopping district and a world-class museum.

✦ ORIENTATION

Tucked into the Yucatán's southeastern corner, Chetumal is just north of the Río Hondo, the natural border between Mexico and Belize. There are three principal approaches to the city: on Rte. 186 from Escárcega (273km), along the Caribbean coast from Cancún (379km), and from Mérida via Valladolid (458km). The **bus terminal** at Av. Insurgentes and Av. Belice is Chetumal's ground transportation hub.

Take a taxi (12 pesos) into town, or walk 4km through shadeless streets. Chetumal's thriving shopping district lines **Av. de los Héroes,** starting at **Av. Efraín Aguilar** at the city's market and extending 1km south to the bay. This compact commercial area encompasses a handful of Chetumal's hotels and restaurants. At the southern terminus of Héroes lies **Blvd. Bahía,** a wide avenue flanked by statues, small plazas, and playgrounds that follows the bay for several kilometers. From here you can see part of Belize, the long, distant spit of land off to the right as you face the sea.

🛈 PRACTICAL INFORMATION

Airport: (tel. 2 35 25), 5km south of the city on Aguilar. **Aerocaribe** and **Mexicana,** Héroes 123 (tel. 3 01 13 or 2 63 36), at Plaza Baroudi. **Aviacsa** (tel. 2 76 76), Lázaro Cárdenas at 5 de Mayo.

Buses: (tel. 2 98 77) on Insurgentes at Belice. ADO (tel. 2 51 10) offers first-class service to: **Campeche** (7hr., noon, 190 pesos); **Cancún** (5hr., 7 per day 12:30-11pm, 170 pesos); **Escárcega** (4hr., 6 per day 9am-9pm, 110 pesos); **Mexico City** (22hr., 4:30 and 9pm, 600 pesos); **Palenque** (8½hr., 11pm, 245 pesos); **Playa del Carmen** (4hr., 7 per day 12:30-11pm, 145 pesos); **Veracruz** (15hr., 6:30pm, 400 pesos); **Villahermosa** (9hr., 5 per day 9am-9pm, 220 pesos); and **Tulum** (4hr., 7 per day, 108 pesos). Cristóbal Colón trucks to: **Ocosingo** (9hr., 9:15pm, 178 pesos); **San Cristóbal** (10hr., 8:15 and 9:15pm, 270-310 pesos); and **Tuxtla Gutiérrez** (12hr., 9:15pm, 310 pesos).

YUCATÁN PENINSULA

Batty's Bus heads south to **Belize City** (3hr., 3 per day, 90 pesos). TRP goes to **Tulum** (4hr., 11:45pm, 96 pesos).

Tourist Office: Information booth (tel. 2 50 73) on Calderitas across from the market. Open M-Sa 9am-1pm and 6-8pm. Maps of the city and the mini magazine *Costa Maya* also available in local travel agencies.

Currency Exchange: Bancomer (tel. 2 53 00), on Juárez at Obregón, has good rates, short lines, and a 24hr. **ATM.** Open M-F 9am-4:30pm, Sa 10am-2pm.

Consulates: Belize Obregón 226 (tel. 2 01 00), west of Juárez, next to Bancomer. To enter Belize for 30 days, all that is needed for U.S., Canadian, and EU citizens is a valid passport and a bus ticket. Open M-F 9am-2pm and 5-8pm, Sa 9am-2pm. **Guatemala,** Chapultepec 354 (tel. 2 30 45), at Cecilio Chi. Again, U.S., Canadian, and EU citizens don't need a visa. For those who do, the process is quick and almost painless (US$15, see p. 35). Open M-F 10am-2pm.

Market: Altamarino Market, also known as **El Mercado Viejo** at Aguilar and Héroes. Vendors peddle everything from souvenir t-shirts to what's-this-for to a damned-if-I-know. Open daily 6am-6pm. **Súper San Francisco de Asis,** next to the bus station.

Police: (tel. 2 15 00) on Insurgentes at Belice, next to the bus station. Open 24hr. **Tourist Safety Line:** (tel. 91 800 90 392).

Red Cross: (tel. 2 05 71) on Chapultepec at Independencia, 2 blocks west of Héroes, in the back of Hospital Civil Morelos. Open 24hr.

Pharmacy: Farmacia Canto, Av. Héroes 99 (tel. 2 04 83), conveniently located at the northern end of the market. Open M-Sa 7am-11pm, Su 7am-5pm.

Hospital: Hospital General, Quintana Roo 399 (tel. 2 19 32), at Juan José Sordio.

Post Office: Plutarco Elías Calles 2A (tel. 2 25 78), 1 block east of the *mercado*. Open M-F 8am-7pm, Sa 9am-1pm. **Postal Code:** 77000.

Internet Access: Astronet, Hérones 125, Local 21 Plaza Baroudi 2nd fl. (tel. 2 95 81, email aflores@astro.net.mx). Across from Hotel Los Cocos, only 2 computers are at your fingertips for a hefty price. 30 pesos per 30 min., 50 pesos per hr. Open M-F 9am-2pm and 5-10pm, Sa 9am-2pm. **Ecosur,** Obregón 157 (tel. 2 39 60; email sondereg@ecosur.com.mx), at 16 de Septiembre, houses a few more terminals for a slightly lower price. 20 pesos per 30 min. Open M-Sa 9am-2pm and 5-8pm.

Phone Code: 983.

ACCOMMODATIONS

Chetumal's budget accommodations are far from fancy, but they do score points for location. All are within easy walking distance of the *mercado*. A scenic **trailer park** in Calderitas, 9km northeast of Chetumal, offers electricity, water hookups, and clean bathrooms (vehicles 60 pesos; tent or hammock space 30 pesos per person; big bungalows with kitchen 90 pesos for 1-2 people).

Hotel María Dolores, Obregón 206 (tel. 2 05 08), half a block west of Héroes. Look for the Donald Duck image pointing the way to aqua-colored rooms with strong fans and private bathrooms. *Agua purificada* in lobby. U.S. dollars accepted. Singles 105 pesos; doubles 112 pesos; triples 125 pesos.

CREA Youth Hostel (Villa Juvenil Chetumal) (HI; tel. 2 34 65), on Heroica Escuela Naval at Calzada Veracruz, at the eastern end of Obregón adjacent to **El Teatro Constituyentes.** For once, a youth hostel within manageable walking distance, with large communal bathrooms and rows of sinks. Reception open daily 7am-midnight; arrange with night guard to return later. *Agua purificada* in lobby. Small but clean single-sex rooms with 2 bunk beds each. Bed with sheets, pillows, and locker 40 pesos. Fills July-Aug.; call to reserve.

Hotel Brasilia, Aguilar 157 (tel. 2 09 64), at Héroes, across from the market. Rooms are hit-or-miss; all are clean but some are cramped—ask to see one first. Friendly management will store backpacks. Singles 100 pesos; doubles 120 pesos; triples 145 pesos; quads 170 pesos; add 20 pesos for TV and A/C.

☕ FOOD

Chetumal offers a spicy blend of Mexican and Belizean dishes, as well as several cafes. For cheap eats, try the cafe/restaurants at the end of Héroes, on 22 de Enero near the bay, or *las loncherías* (small diners) at the market on Héroes and Aguilar, or the eateries on Obregón, west of Héroes.

Restaurante Pantoja, Gandhi 181 (tel. 2 39 57), past Hotel Ucum, just north of the market. An extremely popular family restaurant, and with good reason: *la comida casera* (homemade food) is *muy rica* and piping hot. Enchiladas (22 pesos) are *riquísimas*. Thirst quenching lemonades (8 pesos). Open M-Sa 7am-9pm.

El Taquito, Plutarco Elías Calles 220, near Juárez, 1 block west of Héroes. Get your hands dirty with the locals as you savor *antojito* after *antojito*. Tacos and quesadillas 7 pesos. Open M-Sa 9am-4pm and 7pm-midnight.

La Mansion Colonial, Blvd. Bahía 8 (tel. 2 26 54), across from the Lázaro Cárdenas Monument at the south end of Calzada Veracruz, offers a romantic rustic setting overlooking *La Bahía de Chetumal.* Enjoy gourmet Mexican fare, an all-you-can-eat salad bar (32 pesos), vegetarian dishes, and wholesome breakfast deals (20-28 pesos) amidst columns and semi-low arches. Friday evenings schmooze with wine, cheese, and live music. Open Su-Th 7am-midnight, F-Sa 7am-2am.

Espresso Cafe, Calle 22 de Enero 141 (tel. 2 18 66 or 2 18 97), at the southern tip of Hidalgo near *la bahía.* Sip Chiapas, Veracruz, or Colombian coffee while indulging on homemade desserts and admiring erotic art and golden apple trees. Open daily 8am-12:30pm and 7pm-12:30am.

⚓ SIGHTS, SAND, AND SHIPS

People come from far and wide to visit **El Mercado.** If you think having your name written on a grain of rice is hip, you'll love this market. At the northern end of the market is the **Museo de la Cultura Maya,** on Héroes between Ghandi and Colón. This high-tech, interactive modern museum is heralded as one of the best in the world devoted to Maya culture. As visitors journey through the Maya's three-leveled cosmos—the earth, the underworld, and the heavens—one witnesses full-scale stelae with glyphic text, sculptures, underground see-through models of the famous Maya temples, Bonampak's ceremonial lintels in brilliant colors, and representations of the Maya calendar and numerical system. (Museum open Tu-Th 9am-7pm, F-Sa 9am-8pm, Su 9am-7pm; gift shop open daily 9am-4pm. Cinemuseo Sa-Su 6pm. Admission 30 pesos, Su free.)

The nearest beach is the *balneario* at **Calderitas,** a 15-minute bus ride from Chetumal. Buses leave from Av. Colón, between Héroes and Belice (every 30min. 5am-10pm, 8 pesos). Although the water is turbid and the shores rocky, the beach packs crowds in during summer and school holidays. Much nicer, both for atmosphere and for swimming, are the *cenotes* near the town of **Bacalar,** 36km away. *Combis* leave from the corner of Hidalgo and Primo de Verdad in front of the public library (30min., every 25min., 15 pesos). The route passes **Laguna Milagros** and **Cenote Azul** before reaching Bacalar. Quieter than the Bacalar, both have bathing areas, dressing rooms, and lakeside restaurants. The huge dining room by Cenote Azul, though expensive, is right on the water.

Past the Fuerte de San Felipe in Bacalar lie the docks of the **Laguna de Siete Colores,** named for the seven hues reflected in its depths. The fresh water is warm, clear, devoid of plant or animal life, and carpeted by powdery limestone, making it excellent for swimming. Nearby are bathrooms, dressing rooms, fruit vendors, expensive dockside restaurants, and a campground.

Much farther afield from Chetumal, the small seaside town of **Xcalac** (254km, 3hr.), the southernmost center of population on the spit of land extending south from the Sian Ka'an Biosphere Reserve, provides mellow bungalows, restaurants, snorkeling, and boat rentals. Nearby off the coast lies the enticing **Banco Chinchorro, the second largest shipwreck site in the world,** making for a deep-sea treasure-hunting dive. **Buses** (45-65 pesos) to Xcalac and the closer, **Mahahval** (154km from Chetumal) depart daily at 7am from Av. 16 de Septiembre at Gandhi, 20m from the Restaurante Pantoja.

NEAR CHETUMAL: KOHUNLICH

Kohunlich, the ancient Maya ceremonial center of the early Classic period famous for its stucco masks of the Maya sun god, is also a garden of palm trees replete with wild flowers. Its name originates from the English term **Cohune Ridge**, a tropical palm with copious foliage. More than 200 unexcavated Petén- and Río Bec-style architectural structures await excavation within the depths of the jungle. The 5th-century masks of Kohunlich, with hints of red hue, ascend along the sides of the temple by the same name. The 2-3m tall masks vividly portray the revered power of the Maya sun god **Kinich Ahau** through features such as thick eyebrows and lips, sharp eyes, and balls of amber hanging from the nose. Climbing the temple's 30-plus steep steps ensures an elevated blood pressure, a panoramic view of its surrounding lush vegetation, and **Plaza of the Stelae**—one of Quintana Roo's largest ceremonial centers. To the east of the plaza stands the **acropolis**, the largest building, with 8m vaults, and the half-demolished rooms of the **residential complex** and the **palace**. To the south of the plaza a ballcourt lies stripped of stone arcs and markers. The farthest excavated structure is the Building of the 27 Steps which served as a residence for the Maya elites between AD 600-1200. Niches of all sizes line the walls, used to store incense canisters or home furnishings.

Getting There: Kohunlich lies 67km west of Chetumal on Rte. 186. Hop on any *combi*, from Av. 16 de Septiembre and Primo Verdad in Chetumal heading toward Francisco Villa or Nicolás Bravo (1hr., every hr., 25 pesos). Ask to be let off at the *crucero* of Kohunlich. The entrance is 9km down a bumpy dirt road. Options are few: hitch, walk, or crawl to beat the heat or impersonate a tortoise.

APPENDIX

INTERNATIONAL TELEPHONE CODES

Once you are in Mexico, getting lines to foreign countries can be difficult. Many public phones don't access international lines. Dial 09 for an English-speaking international long-distance operator. You then need to dial the international calling code (a few listed below) of the country you are trying to reach before dialing the phone number. If you speak Spanish fluently and can't reach the international operator, dial 07 for the national operator, who will connect you (sometimes even a local operator can help). The term for a collect call is a *llamada por cobrar* or *llamada con cobro revertido*. Calling from hotels is usually faster. For specifics, refer to p. 42.

TELEPHONE CODES			
Australia	61	South Africa	27
Ireland	353	U.K.	44
New Zealand	64	U.S./ Canada	1

WEIGHTS AND MEASUREMENTS

Mexico, like the rest of the Napoleonic world, uses the metric system. Check out the inside back cover for handy conversions.

MEASUREMENT CONVERSIONS

1 inch (in.) = 25.4 millimeters (mm)	1 millimeter (mm) = 0.039 in.
1 foot (ft.) = 0.30 m	1 meter (m) = 3.28 ft.
1 yard (yd.) = 0.914m	1 meter (m) = 1.09 yd.
1 mile = 1.61km	1 kilometer (km) = 0.62 mi.
1 ounce (oz.) = 28.35g	1 gram (g) = 0.035 oz.
1 pound (lb.) = 0.454kg	1 kilogram (kg) = 2.202 lb.
1 fluid ounce (fl. oz.) = 29.57ml	1 milliliter (ml) = 0.034 fl. oz.
1 gallon (gal.) = 3.785L	1 liter (L) = 0.264 gal.
1 acre (ac.) = 0.405ha	1 hectare (ha) = 2.47 ac.
1 square mile (sq. mi.) = 2.59km^2	1 square kilometer (km^2) = 0.386 sq. mi.

LANGUAGE AND PRONUNCIATION

Pronunciation in Spanish is straightforward. Vowels are each pronounced only one way: a ("ah" in father); e ("eh" in ethical); i ("ee" in eat); o ("oh" in oat); u ("oo" in boot); y, by itself, is pronounced like the Spanish i. Most consonants are pronounced the same as in English. Important exceptions are: j, pronounced like the English "h" in "hello"; ll, pronounced like the English "y" in "yes"; ñ, pronounced like the "gn" in "cognac"; rr, the trilled "r"; h is always silent; x has a bewildering variety of pronunciations: sometimes it sounds like the "h" in "hello," sometimes like the "cz" in "czar." Stress in Spanish words falls on the second to last syllable, except for words ending in "r," "l" and "z," in which it falls on the last syllable. All exceptions to these rules require a written accent on the stressed syllable. The Spanish language also has masculine and feminine nouns and gives a gender to all adjectives that end in "o." When describing a man, the adjective ends with an o: *él es un tonto* (he is a fool). When describing a woman, it ends with an a: *ella es una tonta* (she is a fool).

PHRASEBOOK

See the inside back cover for a quick, condensed list of useful phrases.

ENGLISH	SPANISH	ENGLISH	SPANISH
		The Bare Minimum	
Church	Iglesia	I would like...	Quisiera.../Me gustaría
Closed	Cerrado	In Spanish, how do you say...?	¿Cómo se dice... en español?
Could you speak more slowly, please?	¿Podría hablar más despacio, por favor?	Man	Hombre
Could you tell me...?	¿Podría decirme...?	Mr./Mrs./Miss	Señor/Señora/Señorita
Do you speak English?	¿Habla inglés?	My name is...	Me llamo...
Excuse me	Con permiso/Perdón	No	No
(Very) Expensive	(Muy) Caro	Open	Abierto
Good morning!	¡Buenos días!	Please	Por favor
Good afternoon!	¡Buenos tardes!	Thank you very much!	¡Muchas gracias!
Good evening/night!	¡Buenas noches!	What?	¿Qué?
Goodbye!	¡Adiós! or ¡Hasta luego!	What did you say?	¿Qué dijo?/¿Mande?
Hello	Hola Bueno (phone)	What is your name?	¿Como se llama? (form.) ¿Como te llamas? (inf.)
How are you?	¿Cómo está ? (formal) ¿Cómo estás? (informal)	What time is it?	¿Qué hora es?
How do you say...?	¿Cómo se dice...?	When?	¿Cuándo?
I'm fine, thanks	Estoy bien, gracias	When does it open?	¿A qué hora abré?
I'm sorry	Lo siento/Perdón	Where is the bathroom?	¿Dónde está el baño?
I don't know	No sé	Woman	Mujer
I don't speak Spanish	No hablo español	Yes	Sí
I don't understand	No entiendo	You're welcome!	¡De nada!
		Crossing the Border	
Age	Edad	Customs	Aduana
Backpack	Mochila	Border	Frontera
Baggage	Equipaje	Passport	Pasaporte

ENGLISH	SPANISH	ENGLISH	SPANISH
		Getting Around	
Airplane	Avión	Road	Camino
Airport	Aeropuerto	Round-trip	Ida y vuelta
Arrivals & Departures	Llegadas y salidas	Second class	Segunda clase
Avenue	Avenida	South	Sur
Bus	Autobús/Camión	Stop!	¡Alto!
Bus depot	Estación de Autobuses/Central Camionera	Straight ahead	(Siempre) Derecho
Bus stop	Parada	Street	Calle
Caution!	¡Atención!/¡Cuidado!	Subway	Metro
Daily	Diario/diariamente	Taxi depot	Sitio
Danger!	¡Peligro!	Ticket	Boleto
Driver	Chofer	Ticket window	Taquilla
East	Este or Oriente (Ote.)	Toll	Cuota
Every half hour	Cada media hora	Train	Ferrocarril/Tren
Every hour	Cada hora	West	Oeste or Poniente (Pte.)
First class	Primera clase	All the way to the end	Al fondo
(To) get aboard	Subir	Does this bus go to...?	¿Se va este autobús a...?
(To) get off	Bajar	How long does it take?	¿Cuánto tarda?
Highway	Autopista/Carretera	How much is a ticket to...?	¿Cuánto cuesta un boleto a....?
Hitchhike	Pedir aventón	I lost my baggage.	Perdí mi equipaje.
Map	Mapa	I want a ticket to...	Quiero un boleto a...
North	Norte	To the left/right	A la izquierda/derecha
One-way	Ida	What bus line goes to...?	¿Qué linea tiene servicio a...?
(I'm going) On foot	(Me voy) A pie	What time does the bus leave to...?	¿A qué hora sale el camión a...?
Passenger	Pasajero	Will you give me a ride to...?	¿Me da un aventón a...?
Reserved seat	Asiento reservado	Where is ... Street?	¿Dónde está la calle...?
Reservation	Reservación	Where is the road to...?	¿Dónde está el camino a...?
		Accommodations	
Air conditioning	Aire acondicionado	Manager	Gerente
Bath or Bathroom	Baño/Servicio/W.C.	Motel	Motel

ENGLISH	SPANISH	ENGLISH	SPANISH
Bed/Double bed	Cama/Cama matrimonial	Pillow	Almohada
Blanket	Cobija	Private Bathroom	Baño privado
Boarding house/ Guest house	Casa de huéspedes	Room	Cuarto/Recámara/ Habitación
Cold/Hot water	Agua fría/caliente	Sheets	Sábanas
Dining room	Comedor	Shower	Regadera/Ducha
Fan	Ventilador/Abanica	Swimming pool	Alberga/Piscina
Hotel	Hotel	Do you have a room for two people?	¿Tiene un cuarto para dos personas?
Inn	Posada	Do you have any rooms available?	¿Tiene cuartos libres?
Key	Llave	Do you know of a cheap hotel...?	¿Sabe de algún hotel barato?

		Eating and Drinking		
Apple	Manzana	Meal	Comida
Beer	Cerveza/Chela/ Cheve	Meat	Carne
Bakery	Panadería	Menu	Menú/Carta
Bottle	Botella	Milk	Leche
Bread/Sweet bread	Pan/Pan dulce	Napkin	Servilleta
Breakfast	Desayuno	Orange	Naranja
Coffee	Café	Purified water	Agua purificada
Dessert	Postre	Rice	Arroz
Dinner	Cena	Salt	Sal
Drink	Bebida	Seltzer Water	Agua mineral (con gas)
Eggs	Huevos	Snack	Antojito/Botana
Fixed menu	Comida corrida	Soda	Refresco
Fish	Pescado	Spoon	Cuchara
French fries	Papas Fritas	Spring Water	Agua mineral (sin gas)
Fork	Tenedor	Steak	Bistec
Glass	Vaso	Strawberry	Fresa
Ice cream	Helado	Supermarket	Supermercado
Juice	Jugo	Tea	Té
Knife	Cuchillo	Vegetarian	Vegetariano
Lime	Limón	Wine	Vino
Liquor	Licor	I am hungry	Tengo hambre
Lunch	Almuerzo/Comida	Check, please	La cuenta, por favor

		Bank, Post Office, and Telephone		
Address	Dirección	Money	Dinero
Air mail	Correo aereo/Por avión	Number	Número

ENGLISH	SPANISH	ENGLISH	SPANISH
Bank	Banco	Operator	Operador
A call	Una llamada	Package	Paquete
To call	Llamar	Postcard	Postal/Tarjeta postal
To cash	Cambiar	Post office	Oficina de correos
Certified	Certificado	Signature	Firma
Change	Cambio	Stamp	Estampilla
Check	Cheque	Telephone	Teléfono
Collect	Por cobrar	Traveler's check	Cheque de viajero
Dollar	Dólar	Weight	Peso
Envelope	Sobre	Do you accept traveler's checks?	¿Acepta cheques de viajero?
Letter	Carta	I would like to call...	Quería llamar...
Long distance	Larga distancia	The number is...	El número es...

Health and Medicine

ENGLISH	SPANISH	ENGLISH	SPANISH
Allergy	Alergia	It itches	Me pica
Antibiotic	Antibiótico	Medicine	Medicina
Aspirin	Aspirina	Pain	Dolor
Bandage	Venda	Pill	Pastilla
Birth control pills	Anticonceptivos	Prescription	Receta
Blood	Sangre	Shot	Inyección
English	Spanish	English	Spanish
Burn	Quemadura/Quemada	Sick	Enfermo/Enferma
Condom	Condón/Preservativo	Stomachache	Dolor de estómago
Cough	Tos	Sunburn	Quemadura de sol
Dentist	Dentista	Toothache	Dolor de muelas
Doctor	Doctor/Médico	I need aspirin.	Necesito aspirina
Drugstore	Farmacia	Where is there a doctor?	¿Dónde hay un médico?
Fever	Fiebre	I am sick.	Estoy enfermo(a)
Flu	Gripe	I have a headache	Me duele la cabeza
Hospital	Hospital	I have a cough/a cold	Tengo tos/gripe
Headache	Dolor de cabeza	Help!	¡Ayuda! or ¡Socorro!

Days and Numbers

ENGLISH	SPANISH	ENGLISH	SPANISH
Sunday	Domingo	Today	Hoy
Monday	Lunes	Tomorrow	Mañana
Tuesday	Martes	Day after tomorrow	Pasado mañana

APPENDIX

ENGLISH	SPANISH	ENGLISH	SPANISH
Wednesday	Miércoles	Yesterday	Ayer
Thursday	Jueves	Day before yesterday	Antes de ayer/ Anteayer
Friday	Viernes	Week	Semana
Saturday	Sábado	Weekend	Fin de semana
0	cero	21	veintiuno
1	uno	22	veintidos
2	dos	30	treinta
3	tres	40	cuarenta
4	cuatro	50	cincuenta
5	cinco	60	sesenta
6	seis	70	setenta
7	siete	80	ochenta
8	ocho	90	noventa
9	nueve	100	cien
10	diez	101	ciento uno
11	once	200	doscientos
12	doce	300	trescientos
13	trece	400	cuatrocientos
14	catorce	500	quinientos
15	quince	600	seiscientos
16	dieciseis	700	setecientos
17	diecisiete	800	ochocientos
18	dieciocho	900	novecientos
19	diecinueve	1000	mil
20	veinte	1 million	un millón

GLOSSARY OF TERMS

agua (purificada): water (purified)
ajo: garlic
amigo: friend
andador: pedestrian walkway
antiguo: old
antojitos: appetizers
arroz: rice
artesanía: artisanry
avenida: avenue
bahía: bay
balneario: spa; bathing place
bandidos: bandits
baños: bathrooms
barra libre: open bar
barrancas: canyons

batido: milkshake
basílica: basilica (type of church)
bodega: winery
botanas: appetizers
buena suerte: good luck
buen provecho: bon appetit
calle: street
callejón: little street; alley
cascadas: waterfalls
cama: bed
camarones: shrimp
camión: bus
campesino: farmer
cantina: saloon-type bar (mostly-male clientele)

capilla: chapel
casa: house
casa de cambio: currency exchange booth
caseta: phone stall
castillo: castle
catedral: cathedral
cenote: freshwater sinkhole
centro: center (of town)
cerro: hill
cerveza: beer
ciudad: city
colectivo: shared taxi
colonia: neighborhood
combi: small local bus
comida: food
comida corrida: fixed menu
consulado: consulate
correo: mail
costa: coast
crucero: crossroads
cuarto: room
cuevas: caves
cucaracha: cockroach
de paso: bus that picks up passengers by roadsides
diablo: devil
dinero: money
Dios: God
dulces: sweets
embarcadero: dock
extranjero: foreigner
farmacia: pharmacy
faro: lighthouse
fiesta: party; holiday
fonda: inn
frijoles: beans
frutas: fruits
fútbol: soccer
gabacho: gringo, whitey
glorieta: traffic circle
gobierno: government
gratis: free
gringo: whitey
grutas: caves
güera: blond
iglesia: church
indígena: indigenous person
isla: island
jardín: garden
lago: lake
laguna: lagoon
lancha: a launch (boat)
lavandería: laundromat
libre: free
licuado: milkshake
limosna: alms
lonchería: li'l lunch place
maquiladora: a large, foreign-owned factory
malecón: promenade
mar: ocean; sea
mariscos: seafood

menú del día: pre-set meal
mercado: market (often outdoor)
microbús: minibus
mirador: viewpoint
monte: mountain/peak
mucho/muy: a lot
museo: museum
norte (Nte.): north
nuevo: new
oriente (Ote.): east
palacio: palace
palapa: palm-thatched beach bungalow
panadería: bread shop
parque: park
paseo: promenade
pescado: fish
pesero: local bus
pico: peak
pirámides: pyramids
plátano: banana
playa: beach
pollo: chicken
poniente (Pte.): west
posada: inn
postre: sweet; dessert
poza: well; pool
primera clase: first-class
pueblo: village; community
queso: cheese
refrescos: refreshments
río: river
ruinas: ruins
sacbe (Mayan): upraised, paved road
sacerdote: priest
sala: waiting room
salida: exit
salúd: health
sarape: woven, colored shawl
segunda clase: second- class
selva: jungle
servicio de lujo: luxury service
simpático: friendly/nice
sol: sun
sopa: soup
stela: upright stone monument
supermercado: supermarket
sur: south
taquería: li'l taco stand
tejano: Texan
telenovela: soap opera
templo: church; temple
tienda: store
típico: typical, traditional
torta: sandwich
turismo: tourism
turista: tourist; diarrhea
tranquilo: peaceful
vaquero: cowboy
valle: valley
zócalo: central square
zona: zone; region

APPENDIX

DISTANCES (KM) AND TRAVEL TIMES (BY BUS)

	Acap-	Chihua-	Cancún	El Paso	Guadala-	La Paz	Maza-	Mérida	Mexico	Monter-	Oaxaca	Puebla	San Cris-	San Luis	Tijuana	Veracruz
Acapulco		2440	1938	2815	1028	4917	1429	1779	415	1402	700	544	1036	828	3228	847
Chihuahua	24hr.		3262	375	1552	3237	1031	2945	1496	834	2154	1625	2785	1195	1548	1841
Cancún	33hr.	47hr.		3637	2442	6499	2963	319	1766	2506	1693	1895	902	2267	4810	1421
El Paso	29hr.	5hr.	54hr.		1549	3009	1406	3320	1871	1209	2529	2000	3127	1569	1320	2216
Guadala-	15hr.	17hr.	45hr.	25hr.		4159	521	2125	676	885	1222	805	1853	348	2340	1021
La Paz	60hr.	46hr.	96hr.	41hr.	60hr.		3508	6180	4733	4071	5279	4862	5883	4283	1689	5050
Mazatlán	21hr.	15½hr.	53hr.	25hr.	8hr.	50hr.		2646	1197	940	1743	1326	2374	799	1819	1542
Mérida	29hr.	42hr.	4hr.	47hr.	40½hr.	92hr.	40hr.		1449	2189	1374	1791	743	799	4491	1104
Mexico	6hr.	20hr.	26hr.	25hr.	10hr.	68hr.	18hr.	22hr.		950	546	129	1177	413	3044	345
Monterrey	18hr.	12hr.	38hr.	17hr.	11hr.	60hr.	17hr.	32hr.	12hr.		1533	1116	1918	537	2382	1085
Oaxaca	9hr.	29hr.	29hr.	34hr.	17hr.	77hr.	27hr.	24½hr.	9hr.	21hr.		417	631	959	3590	450
Puebla	7hr.	22hr.	24hr.	27hr.	12hr.	71hr.	20hr.	20hr.	2hr.	14hr.	4hr.		1048	542	3285	303
San Cris-	16hr.	39hr.	17hr.	44hr.	28hr.	88hr.	19hr.	12½hr.	18hr.	30hr.	12hr.	16hr.		1590	4193	833
San Luis	10hr.	14hr.	31hr.	18hr.	6hr.	60hr.	12hr.	27hr.	5hr.	7hr.	20hr.	16hr.	23hr.		2743	846
Tijuana	46hr.	22hr.	72hr.	17hr.	36hr.	24hr.	26hr.	66hr.	44hr.	36hr.	53hr.	46hr.	62hr.	36hr.		3361
Veracruz	13hr.	28hr.	21hr.	33hr.	17hr.	76hr.	26hr.	13hr.	8hr.	17hr.	8hr.	4½hr.	13hr.	13hr.	52hr.	

INDEX

INDEX

READER QUESTIONNAIRE

Let's Go

Name: _____

Address: _____

City: _____ State: _____ Country: _____

ZIP/Postal Code: _____ E-mail: _____ How old are you? ____

And you're...?   in high school   in college   in graduate school
employed   retired   between jobs

Which book(s) have you used? _____

Where have you gone with Let's Go? _____

Have you traveled extensively before?   yes   no

Had you used Let's Go before?   yes   no   **Would you use it again?**   yes   no

How did you hear about Let's Go? friend   store clerk   television
review   bookstore display
ad/promotion   internet   other: _____

Why did you choose Let's Go? reputation   budget focus   annual updating
wit & incision   price   other: _____

Which guides have you used? Fodor's   Footprint Handbooks   Frommer's $-a-day
Lonely Planet   Moon Guides   Rick Steve's
Rough Guides   UpClose   other: _____

Which guide do you prefer? Why? _____

Please rank the following in your Let's Go guide: (1=needs improvement, 5=perfect)

packaging/cover 1 2 3 4 5	food	1 2 3 4 5	maps	1 2 3 4 5
cultural introduction 1 2 3 4 5	sights	1 2 3 4 5	directions	1 2 3 4 5
"Essentials" 1 2 3 4 5	entertainment	1 2 3 4 5	writing style	1 2 3 4 5
practical info 1 2 3 4 5	gay/lesbian info	1 2 3 4 5	budget resources 1 2 3 4 5
accommodations 1 2 3 4 5	up-to-date info	1 2 3 4 5	other: _____ 1 2 3 4 5

How long was your trip?   one week   two wks.   three wks.   a month   2+ months

Why did you go? sightseeing   adventure travel   study abroad   other: _____

What was your average daily budget, not including flights? _____

Do you buy a separate map when you visit a foreign city?   yes   no

Have you used a Let's Go Map Guide?   yes   no   **If you have, which one?** _____

Would you recommend them to others?   yes   no

Have you visited Let's Go's website?   yes   no

What would you like to see included on Let's Go's website? _____

What percentage of your trip planning did you do on the web? _____

What kind of Let's Go guide would you like to see? recreation (e.g., skiing)   phrasebook
spring break   adventure/trekking   first-time travel info   Europe altas

Which of the following destinations would you like to see Let's Go cover?
Argentina   Brazil   Canada   Caribbean   Chile   Costa Rica   Cuba
Morocco   Nepal   Russia   Scandinavia   Southwest USA   other: _____

Where did you buy your guidebook?   independent bookstore   college bookstore
travel store   Internet   chain bookstore   gift   other: _____

Please fill this out and return it to **Let's Go, St. Martin's Press,** 175 Fifth Ave., New York, NY 10010-7848. All respondents will receive a free subscription to **The Yellowjacket**, the Let's Go Newsletter. You can find a more extensive version of this survey on the web at http://www.letsgo.com.

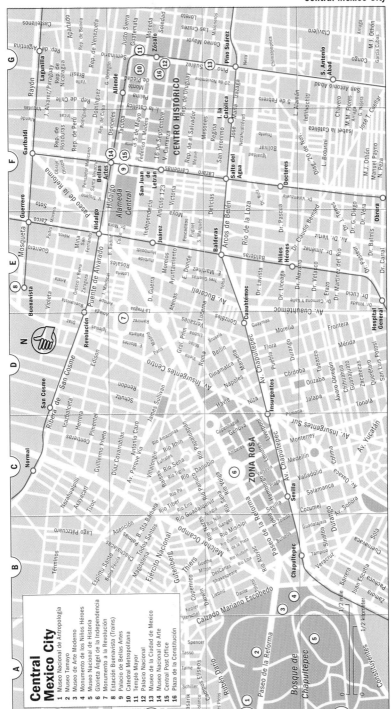

Central Mexico City

1 Museo Nacional de Antropología
2 Museo Tamayo
3 Museo de Arte Moderno
4 Monumento de los Niños Héroes
5 Museo Nacional de Historia
6 Glorieta Ángel de la Independencia
7 Monumento a la Revolución
8 Estación Buenavista (Trains)
9 Palacio de Bellas Artes
10 Catedral Metropolitana
11 Templo Mayor
12 Palacio Nacional
13 Museo de la Ciudad de Mexico
14 Museo Nacional de Arte
15 Central Post Office
16 Plaza de la Constitución

Mexico City Metro

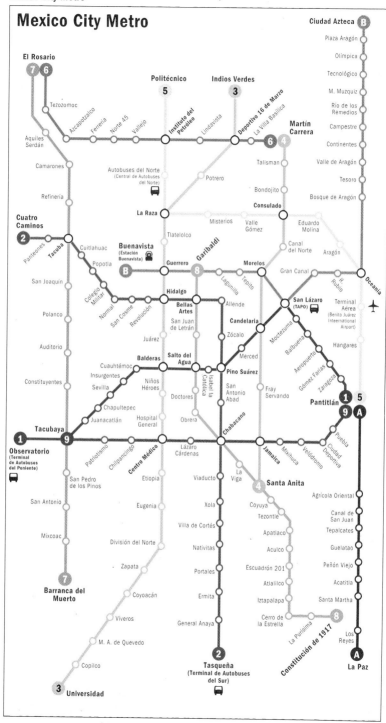